National Intelligencer Newspaper Abstracts 1867

Joan M. Dixon

HERITAGE BOOKS
2009

HERITAGE BOOKS
AN IMPRINT OF HERITAGE BOOKS, INC.

Books, CDs, and more—Worldwide

For our listing of thousands of titles see our website at
www.HeritageBooks.com

Published 2009 by
HERITAGE BOOKS, INC.
Publishing Division
100 Railroad Ave. #104
Westminster, Maryland 21157

Copyright © 2009 Joan M. Dixon

All rights reserved. No part of this book may be reproduced or transmitted in any form or by any means, electronic or mechanical, including photocopying, recording or by any information storage and retrieval system without written permission from the author, except for the inclusion of brief quotations in a review.

International Standard Book Numbers
Paperbound: 978-0-7884-4789-1
Clothbound: 978-0-7884-8105-5

NATIONAL INTELLIGENCER NEWSPAPER
WASHINGTON, D C
1867

TABLE OF CONTENTS

Daily National Intelligencer, Washington, D C, 1867: pg 1

Alexandria, Va, Museum: 385-387
Amnesty: 402; 403-406
Annapolis, Md Gaz: 467
Appointment of Cadets to the Military Academy: 223
Appropiations-1st Session of 39th Congress: 7; 8
Army Bulletin: see index pg 548
Army Officers: 107-108
Atlantic Cable: 529

Baseball: 396
Beginnings of Washington City: 438-442

Capitol Police Force-Washington: 138
Catholic Miracle: 49; 436
Chesapeake & Ohio Canal Presidents: 363
Christ Church, Georgetown: 365
Christmas Tree: 537
Church of the Ascension-David Burns estate: 447
Circuit Court: see index pg 559
Cissy is cured by a Miracle: 436
Coal Mine Explosion-Virginia: 151
Colored High School-Washington: 44
Columbian College Law School graduates: 457

Commencements:	Academy of the Visitation: 281-282
	Dolbear Commercial College, New Orleans: 151
	Georgetown College: 285-286
	Georgetown College-Med Dept: 85
	Gonzaga College: 283
	Rock Hill College, Howard Co, Md: 275

Condemnation proceedings for the Washington & Point of Rocks R R: 534
Confirmations & Rejections: see index pg 560
Criminal Court: see index pg 562

i

Death of Ex-Govn'r John Albion Andrew, of Mass: 469
Death of Prof Alex'r Dallas Bache: 74
Death of Samuel C Bartlett: 163
Death of Rear Admr Chas H Bell: 234
Death of Wm A Bradley: 368
Death of Lt Col Isaac K Casey: 96
Death of John Coburn: 367
Death of M'me Sophie Despau, nee Carriere: 417-418
Death of Samuel Drury: 132; 252
Death of Mr Edwin Green: 370
Death of Jas F Haliday: 509
Death of Fitz Greene Halleck, poet: 492
Death of Mr Johnson Hellen: 30; 31; 33; 37
Death of Hon Philip Johnson: 47; 54
Death of Edw Wm Johnston: 514
Death of Dr Wm Jones: 270
Death of Dr David Livingstone, African Explorer: 124
Death of Hon Henry S Magraw: 51
Death of Gen Thos Francis Meagher: 291
Death of Col Theodore O'Hara: 252
Death of Rear Admr Geo Pearson: 279
Death of Col John Patterson Pepper: 81
Death of Hon Geo Read Riddle: 137
Death of Rear Admr Cadwalader Ringgold: 181
Death of Mrs Teresa Bagiola Sickles: 61
Death of Col Marcellus Steedman: 59
Death of Richard C Washington: 224
Death of Wm Washington: 274
Death of Hon Jas M Wayne: 286
Death of Nat P Willis, poet: 32
Deaths at the residence of Mrs Al Hebron: 360
Douglass, Hon Stephen A-estate: 412; 432

Equity Court: see index pg 568
Estate of Abraham Lincoln, late President of the U S: 444-445
Excommunication: 499

Fairfax, Va: 321-322
Fire at the Central Hotel, Washington: 101
Fire in Georgetown: 342
First Colored Convention-Texas: 10
Funeral of Mr Chas F Browne: 132; 233
Funeral of Col Jas E Harrison: 472
Funeral of Mr Ferdinand Muhlinghaus: 101; 105

Georgetown Corp Ofcrs: 14; 69
German Lutheran Church, Gtwn: 543
Glenwood Cemetery, Washington: see index pg 574
Golden Wedding: Mr & Mrs Jos Hettig: 411
Golden Wedding: the Pleasants: 99
Grace Church Parish, Montgomery Co, Md: 430

Howard University: 376
Howe, Elias-sewing machine: 425

Income of the Royal Family of England: 355
Income of various Men and Women: 66; 191; 238; 253; 411; 463

Jefferson Davis released on bail of $100,000: 204
Jennings Estate: 373-374
John H Surratt capture & trial: see index Surratt pg 614
Julian Gardiner will: 186
Jurors-Washington: 40; 79; 165; 166; 183; 239; 250-251; 464; 481; 493

Kalorama, or Rock Hill: 340-342
Locomotive in America: 392; 421

Maj Gen Chas Griffin & son-yellow fever: 540
Major Generals according to rank: 520
Massacre of 2nd Cavalry: 24
Men of the Times in England: 184-185
Merrill, S M-story of: 276; 284
Metropolitan Police: 36; 476; 510
Midshipmen: 259
Miss Clara Barton-roll of missing men: 12
Mrs Lincoln's finances: 253; 422-423
Murder: Henry Johnson kills Thos Smoot: 262-263
Murder of Hugh Sproull: 125
Murder of Geo Trussel by Mollie Trussell: 59

National Cemeteries: 129-130
Navy Bulletin: see index pg 596
New York tenement house fire: 526

Oak Hill Cemetery: see index pg 597
Officers of the steamer Swatara: 55; 74; 76
Old Citizens-Washington: 398
Oldest Inhabitants-Washington: see index pg 597
Oldest Wooden House: 435

Patent Laws: 541
Patents granted to Washingtonians: 63
Pay of the Regular Army: 125
Police Officers who have died: 221
Postmasters: see index pg 601
Providence Society-Washington: 527
Public Schools-Medals & Premiums: 309

Quartermasters-U S Army: 83

R R Accident-Buffalo: 524-525
R R Accident-Cincinnati: 11; 335; 465; 497
Ramble about Town-Washington: 268-269
Re-interment of Booth, Surratt, Payne, Alzerold, Herold, & Wirz: 424
Reminiscences-Washington: 528

St Matthew's Church: 400
St Paul's Episcopal Church, Washington: 476
Senate nominations & appointments: 34; 41-42
Sisters of Charity: see index pg 610
Steamer Santiago de Cuba disaster: 220
Steamship Andalusia disaster: 103
Steamship City of Bath disaster: 73
Smothered to death: 95

Three Iron-clads: 505
Triple Funeral: 372

War Dept Claims Commission: see index pg 619
Washington Property sold for Taxes: 156-158
West Point Graduates: 264-265
Whereabouts of Ex-Confederate Generals: 520

Index: pg 547

          Dedicated to:
                    Our third grandchild:
                    Christopher Thomas Bednarik
                    Born: Jan 9, 1989
                    Annapolis, Anne Arundel Co, Md

PREFACE
Daily National Intelligencer Newspaper Abstracts
1867
Joan M Dixon

The National Intelligencer & Washington Advertiser is hereafter the Daily National Intelligencer. It was the first newspaper printed in Washington, D C; Samuel H Smith, the originator. The same was transferred to Jos Gales, jr on Aug 31, 1810; on Nov 1, 1812, the paper was under the firm of Jos Gales, sr, & Wm W Seaton. The Library of Congress has microfilm of the paper from the first issue of Oct 31, 1800 thru Jan 8, 1870, the final paper. The Evening Star Newspaper of Jan 10, 1870 reports: The Intelligencer is discontinued: the proprietor, Mr Alex Delmar, says that having lost several thousand dollars, & being in poor health, he has resolved to discontinue its publication.

Included in the abstracts are advertisements; appointments by the President; Hse o/Rep petitions; passed Acts; legal notices; marriages; deaths; mscl notices; social events; military promotions; court cases; deaths by accident; & maritime information-officers-crews. Items or events which might be a clue as to the location, age or relationship of an individual are copied.

No attempt has been made to correct the spelling. Due to the length of some articles, it was necessary to present only the highlights of same. Chancery and Equity records are copied as written.

The index contains <u>all</u> surnames and *tracts of lands/places*. **Maritime vessels** are found under barge, boat, brig, frig, schn'r, ship, sloop, steamboat, tugboat, yacht or vessel.

ABBREVIATIONS:
AA CO	ANNE ARUNDEL COUNTY
CMDER	COMMANDER
CMDOR	COMMODOR
ELIZ	ELIZABETH
ELIZA	ELIZA
MONTG CO	MONTGOMERY COUNTY
PG CO	PRINCE GEORGE'S CO
WASH, D C	WASHINGTON, DISTRICT OF COLUMBIA

BOOKS IN THE NATIONAL INTELLIGENCER NEWSPAPER SERIES: 1800-1805/1806-1810/1811-1813/1814-1817/1818-1820/1821-1823/1824-1826/1827-1829/1830-1831/1832-1833/1834-1835/1836-1837/1838-1839/1840/1841/1842/1843/1844/1845/1846/1847/1848/1849/1850/1851/1852/1853/1854/1855/1856/1857/1858/1859/1860/1866/1867/1868/1869-Jan 8, 1870. SPECIAL: CIVIL WAR 2 VOLS, 1861-1865

DAILY NATIONAL INTELLIGENCER NEWSPAPER
WASHINGTON, D C
1867

TUE JAN 1, 1867
Reception day at the Executive Mansion will begin at 11 o'clock with the members of the Cabinet, Foreign Ministers, Judges of the Supreme Court, Senators & Representatives in Congress, Judges of the Supreme Court of D C, & of the Court of Claims; at 11:30 A M, ofcrs of the army, under the escort of the Sec of War, & of the navy & marine corps, under that of the Sec of the Navy, will be received. The public reception will commence at 12 M, & continue until 2 P M. Visitors will enter by the main door of the Mansion, & pass out by the stile erected at one of the north windows. Mrs Patterson & Mrs Stover, daughters of the Pres, will assist him in the reception. All the members of the Cabinet will receive at their residences from 12 to 3 P M, except Sec Seward & Welles, whose mansions will be closed, on account of recent domestic afflictions. Gen Grant will also receive at his residence. The Mayor of the city will receive his friends at the City Hall.

Police affairs. 1-The detectives have ferreted out & locked up for further examination Alex'r Ferris, Edw Hathaway, & Martin, alias Reddy Walsh, as professional burglars, charged with opening the safe of F M Magruder, about a week ago. 2-Albert Green was arrested on Sat for wasting Potomac water & fined $5. 3-Henry A Doyle, A B Jackson, & Jas Robinson were arrested on a charge of gambling: each fined $10. 4-J W Bailey, restaurant keeper, was arrested for keeping open after hours: fined $20. 5-Jos & Arthur Toliver were sent to the work-house in default of security for good behavior. 6-Frank Haley was arrested as a suspicious character, & sent to the work-house. 7-Edw Davis & Richd West were arrested on the same charge: fined $3.

Criminal Court-Judge Fisher. 1-Martha Volany was found guilty of stealing a table-cloth: sentenced to 5 weeks in jail. 2-Robt Hainey, indicted for keeping a bawdy-house, a *nolle pros*, was entered. 3-John Mardis, indicted for an assault & battery, submitted his case, & received a nominal sentence. 4-John Ross, indicted for an assault & battery with intent to kill Claibourne Madison, was convicted. Motion made for a new trial. 5-Geo W Barnes, found guilty of petty larceny: received a nominal sentence. 6-Zachariah Thomas, Thos Fogarty, & Patrick Brannan, indicted for the larceny of a blanket, watch, etc, from Jas Dolan, a *nolle pros* was entered.

Three persons in one family, named Bruner, died in Cincinnati on Monday, & two other members are still quite sick, from eating diseased pork.

Died: on Dec 31, Mrs Mary Ann Dick, of heart disease, in her 63rd year. Her funeral will be on Wed at 2 o'clock, from 750 N J ave south.

Navy Bulletin, Dec 24. Appointment Revoked: Mate Geo H Russell, of the ship **Memphis**. 2-Honorably Discharged: Acting Ensign Walter A DeWitt, from Feb 14, 1866. 3-Detached: Acting Ensign Wm A Stannard, from duty at League Island, & placed on sick leave.

Postmaster Gen Randall has made the following changes since Dec 26, 1866:
Md: Winfield, Carroll Co, J W Dennis, vice E R Pickett, removed.
Ark: Marion, Crittenden Co, G W Burrers, vice J Butler, resigned.
Indiana: Oakland City, Gibson Co, J Mayhew, vice W L Laster; North Madison, Jefferson Co, Mrs H Smith, vice J Roberts; Heller's Corners, Allen Co, I Heller, vice J Goshen, removed; Jasonville, Greene Co, A J Morgan, vice W C Price, resigned; Enterprise, Spencer Co, J W Jones, vice W Stevenson, resigned; Westville, Laporte Co, A Allen, vice C S Steinberg, resigned; Blue Grass, Fulton Co, I Ball, vice J Matthison, resigned; Calao, Laporte Co, C Hills, vice W Masters, resigned.

On Sunday the team attached to the carriage of Gen Augur took fright & run away, & threw the driver, Peter Coorin, from his seat, injuring him seriously. He was conveyed by ambulance to Providence Hospital. He died yesterday morning.

Miss Jenkins, daughter of Thos Jenkins, residing near Eastern Branch Bridge, has received quite unexpectedly, through the hands of John F Ellis, 306 Pa ave, one of Chickering & Sons' magnificently finished full grand action piano. She had invested one dollar in a chance at the fair & she held the lucky number.

Dissolution of the copartnership under the name of Ramsburg & Ebert, this day, by mutual consent. –Jacob Ramsburg, Wm Ebert, Gtwn, D C
+
New copartnership formed under the firm of Jacob Ramsburg & Sons; manufacture of Buckskins, Buckskin Gloves, Sheepskins, Grinding of Sumac, Wool Pulling & dealing in Domestic Wool. –Jacob Ramsburg, V E Ramsburg, C S Ramsburg

Supreme Court of D C, 80 Equity, Docket 7. Riggs et al vs Thos Smith's heirs et al. Wm R Woodward, trustee, reported he has sold at private sale lot 39 in square 182, in Wash City, to John & Chas H Shorter, for the sum of $393.92, & they have complied with the terms of sale. –A B Olin, Justice -R J Meigs, clerk

We have this day disposed of our stock in trade to Messrs Creighton M Wheeler & Theodore F Browning, of Wash City. –E Wheeler & Son-[Hardware, & Bldg Materials]

WED JAN 2, 1867
Balt, Jan 1. Judge B D Magruder, of Annapolis, was brought before U S Com'r Brooks this morning on an indictment against him for a violation of the civil rights bill. The first indictment for refusing to receive negro testimony, the second is for selling colored persons into slavery as a punishment for crime. The Judge gave bail in the sum of $2,000, to answer the charges before the U S Court at the spring term.

Died: on Dec 29, in Martinsburg, Va, Dr Reuben Summers, aged 65 years.

Dept of the Interior, U S Patent Ofc, Wash, Dec 28, 1866. Ptn of Wm Wickersham, of Boston, Mass, praying for the extension of a patent granted to him on Apr 19, 1853, for an improvement in Sewing Machines, for 7 years from the expiration of said patent, which takes place on Apr 19, 1867. –T C Theaker, Com'r of Patents

War Dept Claims Commission: claims filed during Dec, 1866.
Jas M Ashley for value of 2 saddles & 2 bridles. J H H Woodward, atty.
Thos A Elliott for rent. Geo S Thompson, atty.
Lucinda Trimble for damage to property: no atty.
Richerson, Carroll, & C M Fleetwood: payment of vouchers. Geo S Thompson, atty.
John W Tunnell for hay & straw. Do.
Richerson & Carroll for corn. Do.
E A Otis for services as an atty. No atty.
R J Stringfellow for rent. Striblen & Simpson, attys.
Milton Jackson for damage to property. Do.
Wm Richardson for value of a mule. Do.
P H Foley, Avery & Co, B Toledana, M Pugh, Geo Jackson, C M Gillis, & heirs of J B Brown, for goods seized by the Gov't. John Jolliffe, atty.
A J Martin for rent of bldg. No atty.
F McNerhany for property taken by the U S. No atty.
C D Outten for services as Gov't detective. No atty.
C W Vinson for reward for recovery of stolen public funds. No atty.
John Aiken for damages for loss of cattle, etc. No atty.
Henry Queen for quartermaster's stores. Owen & Wilson attys.
J H Maddox for tobacco taken as captured by the U S authorities. J S Black & Lewis E Parsons, attys.
Jos Segar for rent. No atty.
Alfred Cooke for services at York, Pa. No atty.
Geo M Branner-military fees: transportation of cotton. Watterson & Crawford, attys.
Arthur Bland for value of a horse. H W Hawes, atty.
John Brown for value of a horse. W A K Cone, atty.
Henry A Ealer for cotton taken my military forces. R J Atkinson, notary.
Chas Ridgeley for value of horses. No atty.
A F Numa Broa for rent. August Barg, atty.
Mrs Minerva Morris for cotton taken by U S authorities. R A Florey, atty.
John Lockwood for balance claimed due on contract for wood. Enoch Totten, atty.
Francis C Zollar for damages to property. Do.
Louis Gilbaux for ordnance stores. No atty.
J W Page for money advanced & services rendered. No atty.
Francis Simmons for pay as a scout. Tucker & Sells, attys.
J D S Keen for expenses in the Provost Marshal's Dept. Morrow & Hay, attys.
Andrew Low for quartermster's & subsistence stores taken for use of the army. Chipman, Hosmer & Co, attys.
Paschal McFullar-cotton seized at Pittsburg Landing, Tenn. Stewart, Riddle & Co, attys.

J L Cain, A A Kyle, A Kennedy, J W C Hazen, & Corran & Deckerson, for cotton taken by the U S. No attys.
Jas H Garter, [guardian] for use of property & timber. Tucker & Sells, attys.
C L Gorton or Chas Wheeler for money paid as commutation, etc. No atty.
John Wilson for compensation for arrest & detention. State Dept for the British Minister.
Martin Howard for corn taken for military purposes. Do.
Hugh Sturdy, E L Morse, & Myron A Wood for secret service. W O Watts, atty.
Saml C White for rent. No atty.
Vincent Dockery, Wm H Rexvost, Stewart Rexvost, & Elias Smith for services. Tucker & Sells, atty.
J J Martin for supplies taken by Gen Greierson. Thos S Durant, atty.
Geo H Walker for rent of land. No atty.
Delos B Carrol for property taken by U S ofcrs. A S Cox & Co, attys.
Moses Maples for subsistence stores. H H Hawes, atty.
Larkin H Davis for pay for corn. W H Hawes, atty.
John W Young for return of money & jewelry. McPhail & Raphun, attys.
Jas G Browne for bricks taken by the military authorities. Owen & Wilson, attys.
Mrs Oliver Garner for pay for corn. Tucker & Sells, attys.
J W Mathias, administrator of Jacob H La Rue, for timber. H M Carr, atty.
Mrs Sallie Webster for rent. John D McPherson, atty.
Capt John Reid for pay for services. Chipman, Hosmer & Co, attys.
Henry Sheets for shoeing horses. Hon Wm H Koontz, atty.
Wm F Clark for services as assist provost marshal. Jay Cooke & Co, assignees.
Mrs Mary Jane Stinson for rent of Park Hotel, New Orleans. Alex'r T Steele, atty.
Maurice Roche for liquors, etc, taken by provost guard. No atty.
Richd H Chamberlaine & Geo B Davids-use of Atlantic Iron Works. A B Magruder, atty.
Rebecca A Curd for quartermaster's stores. H M Carr, atty.
C L Lancaster for damage to farm & use of horses. Busteed & Co, attys.
Leonard B Johnson for timber. Jas C Wetmore, atty.
Albert Peacock for services as guide & scout. No atty.
R S Scruggs for medicines & medical instruments. Tuck & Sells, attys.
John E Ziegler, Philip Roser, & Chas Glatfelter for property taken by the army. Do.
Mary S Wilson for destruction of property. No atty.
R W Holman for stock of goods lost. Wm H Boyce, atty.
Benj Fahenstock for subsisting a rebel prisoner. Todd & Squire, attys.
H W Applegate for services as a detective. No atty.
S Fernankez for rent of store. T E Lloyd, atty.
Jeremiah McCraith for damage to property. No atty.
Thos H Simmington for balance of pay for services. W H Hills, atty.
Mary Sullivan for commissary stores. A S Cox & Co, attys.
Mary Quigley, do. Do.
Dr Saml S Puckett for destruction of property. Do.
Isaac Walker for rent of bldg in St Louis, Mo. Browning & Ewing, attys.
Ann C Carroll & Mariah C Fitshugh, excs: increase of rent for lots. Ira N Burnett, atty

M B Baer for money alleged to have been taken by U S soldiers. H Graw, atty.
F W Posthoff for supplies taken by the army. John D McPherson, atty.
Wm Blissner for sutlers' goods seized by provost marshal. No atty.
Peter Pulman for rent. Gilbert S Miner, atty.
David Smith for two Binninghurst & Requabatteries. No atty.
J D Bright for occupation of property by military authorities. J J Bright, atty.
Benj H Atkinson for wood taken by the army. Tucker & Sells, attys.
Louis Noel Dubus for value of a mule. August Barg, atty.
Edw W Sanders for destruction of property, use of saw mills, etc. No atty.
Wm Irwin, jr, for property destroyed by U S troops. No atty.
Andrew Peacock for mules & horses alleged to have been seized by U S authorities. The British Minister, through the State Dept.
J J Caldwell for balance due him for sugar & molasses on books of Sequestration Commission. No atty.
J Kinney for services. Chipman, Hosmer & Co, attys.
A C Graham for 2 certificates turned over with funds seized as belonging to Provost Marshal Robinson. No atty.
Statement of the action had on claims during the present month:
Rejected: H R Bonneral; Marcus Walker; Richd Berry; Henry Polkinhorn, jr; A Austeile; C T Venniegerholz; Isaac Burton; John L & Wm Usrey; Michl Ryan; Jas H Gibbons; Michl O'Day; David Young, Michl Kreis, A Dolphy, M Lynch, & Geo J Strubblefield; Thos L Pleasants; B Maas; J Lacaze & Co; Manora Sayre; Wm Barnes; Wm Lowe; John
M Tracy; Ayres, Taylor & Co; Chas C Walcott, [Warden of the Ohio State Penitentiary;] John Kennarty; Geo Lott; Peter Paul; Mrs Eliza A Clark; Wm Sagar; Wm T Brown; Benj J Grubb; Jas A Stewart; Aldridge James; Jas H Gaskins; Geo Hamilton; Mrs Maria W D Orme; Edw Swann; & E C Dewey.
Allowed in part: Wm J Minor; John Wells & Sons; & J R Maddox-2nd claim.
Allowed: Jas T Mason; Gustave Caynot; Montgomery Hunt; S B Monhouse; Fritz Johnson; Wm A Huff; John Holloran; John B Griffin; & Asop Buck.
Returned to the claimant: Clayborne Laderson; Mrs Eliz A Belt; John W Hall; J M Conner; Robt W Carter; Peter Gilliam; Henry G Jones; John R Siler; Lloyd Mitchell; Wm H Stevens; Jas M Salter; John Parsons; B B Burroughs; Duncan Graham; Seaborne Skinner; John Bigham; Isaac Fisher; Jas Jett; Caleb S Hallowell; & Wm Burley; -De Witt Clinton, Brvt Lt Col, Recorder

THU JAN 3, 1867
Mrs Pageot, wife of the former French Minister to this Gov't, died on Nov 18 last, of pneumonia, in the south of France. Her venerable father's death preceded hers only a few days.

Regular meeting of the Oldest Inhabitants of the Dist of Columbia was held yesterday: John S Williams, vice president in the chair; A McDonald Davis, sec. The members present very kindly contributed for the relief of Mr Saml Welles, who is still very sick. Mr J C Brent proposed that members should pay a fee of $1 upon initiation, & thereafter $1 a year. Aquilla K Arnold was proposed as a member of the association.

On Tuesday, a man whose name was found on his person, Myhen St Clair, was found in the canal, by Mr Danl Sweeney, who with others got him out & carried him to Sweeney's house, & administered to his relief. He was taken to the asylum for further treatment, but he expired Tuesday night. It is thought that he is a discharged soldier, & that he got into the canal accidentally.

Criminal Court-Judge Fisher. 1-Jos Taylor pleaded guilty to larceny & was sentenced to 1 year in the penitentiary. 2-Wm Anderson was convicted of larceny of chickens, & sentenced to 15 days in jail. 3-The motion of a new trial in the case of Petesto Carlo & Henry Ivil, convicted of robbery on Dec 11th, was denied, & they were sentenced to 3 years each in the Albany penitentiary. 4-Mary Glasco, convicted in 2 cases of larceny, was sentenced to 1 year in the Albany penitentiary for each offence. 5-Ellen Noland, alias Ellen Ale, was convicted of keeping a disorderly house. 6-Eliz Jones, was found guilty for keeping a bawdy house, & sentenced to 15 days in jail.

Brvt & Assist Surgeon Thos G Mackenzie, U S A, died on Tues last at the Kalorama Hospital after an illness of but 4 days. His complaint was congestion of the lungs. His body was forwarded to Balt yesterday where it will be interred.

Lt Gen Sherman published a general order announcing the death of Brvt Col Boswell M Sawyer, of his body staff, which occurred at St Louis on Dec 26. Col Sawyer commenced his military career as a private in the 1st Wisc infty; rose from grade to grade, during the Vicksburg campaign, & became adj general of the 15th corps. He then filled the same post in the Army of the Tenn, & lastly to the Military Division of the Mississippi, until the war was over & the regular army organized, when he received the commission of capt of the 25th infty, the post he held at the time of his death.

Newark, N J, Jan 2. Reward for Murderer. The Govn'r offers a reward of $5,000 for the apprehension of the burglars who shot Mrs Aaron Ward, jr, in her room, in this city, on Dec 31, 1866. [Feb 22nd newspaper: Thompson, the negro burglar, who some weeks since, shot Mrs Aaron Ward, of Newark, N J, has been sentenced to 30 years in the State prison.]

Trustee's sale, by decree of the Circuit Court for PG Co, [Md] in Equity, passed in the case of Mary A Markwood & Rebecca Duvall vs John D Beall & others: public sale on Jan 24, the real estate of which Stephen Onions, late of said county, died seized & possessed, containing about 350 acres. It adjoins the lands of Perry W Browning, & the late John F Carter, about 3 miles from Bladensburg. Title indisputable. –N C Stephen, trustee

The mysterious disappearance of Mr Lewis Fox, of Rochester, N Y, causes great anxiety to his friends, who entertain the idea that he had either committed suicide or been foully dealt with.

Appropriations made during the first session of the 39th Congress:
Payment of the rewards offered by the Pres of the U S & ofcrs of the War Dept in Apr & May, 1865, for the capture of the assassins of the late Pres, Abraham Lincoln, & the Sec of State, Hon Wm H Seward:
For the capture of Payne: $5,000.
For the capture of Atzerott: $25,000.
For the capture of Booth & Herold: $70,000.
Act for the relief of Mrs Mary Lincoln, widow of the late Pres of the U S: $25,000.
Act for the relief of Jas G Clarke: $6,483.96.
Act for the relief of Chas F Anderson: $7,500.
Act for the relief of Thos F Wilson, late U S Consul at Bahia, Brazil: $1,500.
Act for the relief of R L B Clarke: $1,500.
Act for the relief of Francis A Gibbons: $563.19.
Act for the relief of the heirs of Lt Joshua D Todd, late of the U S navy, deceased: indefinite.

The mysterious disappearance of Mr Lewis Fox, of Rochester, N Y, causes great anxiety to his friends, who entertain the idea that he had either committed suicide or been foully dealt with.

Chancery sale of house & lot on south B st, near N J ave, Capitol Hill; by decree of the Supreme Court of D C, in Equity No 806, Iardella vs Iardella, pronounced Dec 6, 1866: sale on Jan 17 next, of part of lot 11 in square 690, with a good 3 story brick dwlg. -Jas E Williams, John N Oliver, trustees -Green & Williams, aucts

Supreme Court of D C: in Equity, No 716, Docket 8. Wm H Terrett et al vs Wm W Terrett et al. Wm F Mattingly, trustee, reported that on Nov 19, 1866, he sold the real estate in the proceedings at public auction to Michl Green, for $6,060, that said Michl Green assigned all his interest to Bryan Green, & that said Bryan Green has complied with the terms of sale. –A R Olin -R J Meigs, clerk

FRI JAN 4, 1867
Indian outrage in Western Texas: the Kiowas killed a Mr Box & captured his wife, three daughters, one of them a young child, & an infant. The infant died from injuries received in a fall of the mother from the mule which she was riding. The Noconee Comanches captured Mrs Sarah Jane Luster, killing Mrs Bab, with whom she lived & carrying off Mrs Bab's two children, Rodolphus & Baintha, aged 14 & 11 years. Mrs Luster escaped upon a fast horse, but after riding all night & a day found herself again a prisoner among the Kiowas. She again fled with these Indians, who treated her with comparative kindness, & reached the white settlements on the Santa Fe road, where she is now. The goods intended for Satanta & other Kiowa chiefs, who took part in the capture of the Box family have been withheld.

The Avenue House, 7th & C sts, was sold on Wed by Green & Williams, aucts, to Mr Jesse B Wilson, for $80,900.

Postmaster General changes since Dec 31, 1866:
Delaware: Millsborough, Sussex Co, J H Benton, vice D Burton, failed to bond.
Ark: Madison, St Francis Co, W D Bordin, vice J H Pearce, resigned.
Ohio: North Ridgeville, Lorain Co, Henry Linden, vice J P Brown, resigned; Rodney, Gallia Co, V Soles, vice J M Saunders, resigned.

Mr Perkins, an employe in the dyeing establishment of Mr Drew, between 9th & 10th sts, on Pa ave, was knocked down yesterday & killed by a runaway horse while crossing the street. The horse was ridden by a negro at the time of the runaway, & he was thrown upon the pavement & severely injured. Mr Perkins was between 50 & 60 years of age.

Appropriations made during the first session of the 39th Congress: Act for relief of:
1-J Judson Barclay: $3,000.
2-Wm G Lee: $28,428.50.
3-Henry Horne [in coin] $400.
4-Wm Cook: $200.
5-Liston H Pearce: $510.
6-Thos W Stevens: $1,025.50.
7-Alois Klous/Klaus: $32.
8-Jas P Johnson: $202.50.
9-Mrs Eleanor C Ransom: $400.
10-Sgt McKimon: $58.45.
11-Col DeAhna for military services: indefinite.
12-Col Lewis F Fix: indefinite.
13-Fontaine T Fox, jr: indefinite.
14-Miss Clara Barton-reimburse: $15,000.
15-Owners of the British vessel **Magiecienne**: $8,645.
16-Owners of the bark **Maria Henry**: $12,000.
17-A T Spencer & Gurdon S Hubbard: indefinite.
18-Purchase of the library of Jas L Petigru, of S C: $5,000.
19-Caroline A Randall, widow of Chas B Randall: $175.
20-Relief of Eliz Woodward & Geo Chorpenning, of Pa, for destruction of property by Indians between Salt Lake & Calif prior to Jul 1, 1852: $28,175.
21-Mrs Mary Philps for expenditures made by her in raising & equipping troops for the U S in the late rebellion: $20,000.
22-To Geo Chorpenning for property destroyed by Indians between Salt Lake & Calif prior to Apr 1, 1856: $26,370.

Criminal Court-Judge Fisher: 1-Henry Clay Deane was admitted an atty & counsellor of the Supreme Court-D C. 2-Chas Parker was convicted of larceny & sentenced to two weeks in jail. 3-Henry Osbury was found guilty of presenting forged claims for pensions at the N Y State agency ofc. 4-Mich Gleason, charged with burglary: not guilty. 5-Dennis Barrett, David Fitzgerald, & Henry Howe were found guilty of the charge of trespass.

Police matters: 1-Henry H Middleton was arrested for selling liquor in quantities less than a pint without a license: fined $20. 2-J G Adams & J B Oldcott were arrested for violating the water regulations: each fined $5.58.

Mrd: Jan 2, at St Luke's Church, at Portland, Me, by Rev Dr Burgess, Mr John F Wilson, of Wash City, to Miss Clara D Dyer, daughter of Alfred Dyer, of Westbrook, Me.

Orphans Court of Wash Co, D C. Letters of administration on the personal estate of Riter Tridy, late of Wash, D C, deceased. –August Schroeder, adm

Wm Eichbaum, city treasurer of Pittsburgh, died on Sunday, aged 81 years. He was postmaster of the city before Jackson's Presidency.

An old gentleman & his wife, named Vandeventer, living near Florida station, on the Hannibal & St Joseph railroad, were murdered in cold blood last Wed night. It is supposed the crime was committed for money.

Dr J C S Monkur, well known as one of the most successful practitioners of East Balt, died at his residence on Broadway yesterday. He was born on Jan 1, 1800, & had just attained his 66th year. He was one of the early graduates of the Univ of Md & for some time filled the professor's chair in Wash Med College. –Balt Sun, 3rd.

St Anna's Hall, a Select School for Young Ladies, near Brookeville, Montg Co, Md. Apply to Rev O Hutton, A M, Rector.

SAT JAN 5, 1867
Navy Bulletin for Dec 27 & 28, 1866. Ordered: Passed Assist Paymaster R B Rodney, to duty at the Naval Academy; Acting Ensign Geo W Beverly, to the ship **Peoria**; Mate Geo W Pratt, to the receiving ship **Vermont**; Paymaster Chas S Perley, to temporary duty as inspector in charge of provisions & clothing at the Norfolk navy yard. Detached: Acting Master Jas H Simpson, from the command of the ship **Relief**, & placed upon waiting orders; Mate A T Jennings, from the **Relief**, & granted leave of absence; Acting Ensigns A A Very, C K Waite, Henry Taylor, & E G Blanchard, from the **Relief**, & placed on waiting orders; Acting Master G Mitchell, from the **Peoria**, & was ordered to the ship **Pawnee**; Acting Assist Paymaster J Q Barton, from the **Relief**, & ordered to settle his accounts; Mate John C Howard, from the receiving ship **Vermont**, & ordered to the **Peoria**; Acting Assist Surgeon Passmore Treadwell, from the **Relief**, & granted leave of absence; Boatswain Zachariah Whitmarsh & Carpenter Josiah D Pinner, from the **Peoria**, & placed on waiting orders; Paymaster Gilbert E Thornton, from duty as inspector of provisions & clothing at Norfolk navy yard, & ordered to settle his accounts. Resigned: Midshipman E R Culver, of the Naval Academy.

Mrd: on Dec 25, at Boscawen, N H, by Rev Milton L Severance, J R Eastman, Prof of Mathematics, U S Navy, to Miss Mary J Ambrose, of Boscawen.

The first colored convention in Texas-at Bastrop. Procession formed at the residence of Mrs Fulleylove; Dr Richd G Parker, an excellent colored man, who has travelled extensively in Europe & the U S, addressed the audience. He advised them to leave politics alone, & to till the soil The Lt Govn'r of the State of Texas, Hon G W Jones, made some very intelligent remarks. A memorial & address to the freedmen in Texas was read by Jeremiah J Hamilton, chief marshal of the day, & secretary of the Central Cmte.

Chas H Utermehle, age 30 years, a man in the flush of life, one born in our midst, & honorably associated with the public affairs of Wash, has suddenly departed this life. Mr Utermehle died at his residence yesterday after a brief but painful illness, contracted by a cold on Christmas day, & terminating in pleuro-pneumonia. In the Criminal Court yesterday afternoon Dist Atty Carrington announced his death. He leaves a wife & one child. His funeral will take place this afternoon at his late residence, 359 6th st. [Jan 7th newspaper: Rev Mr Pinckney, D D, of the Church of the Ascension, officiated, reading the burial service of the Episcopal Church, after which the remains were interred in the ***Congressional Cemetery***. The pall bearers were: Messrs A T Bradley, E Carusi, R H Laskey, J F Ennis, & W F Mattingly, of the Washington bar, & Edw Kolb, Julius Ross, & Conrad Eber, of the Schutzen Corps.]

Police Affairs: 1-John Mortimer was arrested for carrying weapons & was fined $20, & sent to the workhouse in default of payment. 2-A Strauss & John Loliger were arrested for wasting Potomac water: each fined $5 & costs. 3-Patrick Deely was arrested by Ofcr W H Evans, for selling liquor in quantities less than a pint without a license: fined $20.90. 4-Moses Daniels was arrested for larceny of a shoulder of meat, & also for assault & battery on C Lanckton, the owner. The assault was dismissed & the prisoner was committed to jail for larceny. 5-Louisa Sanford, John T Rudd, John D Bickly, & Lewis Rothchild, were arrested for violating the snow law: each fined $2.58.

N Y, Jan 4. Loss of the schnr **E M Dyer**, bound to Gtwn, S C, from Richmond, state that A Bryant, C H Bryant, & J H Sweeney, seamen, were washed overboard & drowned. Capt Jeremiah Harding & Geo Nickinson, seaman, died after being taken off the schnr. The others aboard were saved by the British brig **Meg**. It is stated that the brig **Jenny Morton**, of Balt, refused assistance to the **Dyer**.

Criminal Court-Judge Fisher. 1-John Moulton was indicted for the forgery of certain papers, with a view of obtaining a pension. It was shown that the prisoner was entitled to a pension as claimed by him. He was acquitted, & discharged. 2-Henry Eggers, alias Henry Taylor, was convicted of larceny, & sentenced to 1 years in the Albany penitentiary.

Died: on Jan 3, Col Alfred Russell, in his 62nd year. His funeral will take place from his late residence, 10th & K sts, on Jan 5 at 1 o'clock.

Died: on Jan 2, in New Castle, Dela, Saml Adams Danforth, son of the late Rev Joshua N Danforth, of Alexandria, Va.

Chancery sale of improved property on 20th st, between E & F sts: by decree of the Supreme Court of D C, in Equity 656, in which Thos Cogan is cmplnt, & Jane McManus et al, are dfndnts: trustee will sell, on Jan 15, part of lot 5 in square 122. –Eugene Carusi, trustee -Jas C McGuire & Co, aucts [Mar 23rd newspaper: Sale postponed until Mar 21, 1867.]

MON JAN 7, 1867

Military Items. Geo D Hill, formerly capt 1st Michigan cavalry, has passed the examining board & commissioned a 1st lt in the 42nd U S infty, Veteran Reserve Corps. Brvt Capt W H Bisbee, 1st lt 18th U S infty, is announced as aide-de-camp to Maj Gen Cooke, commanding the dept of the Platte. Leaves of absence for 3 months has been granted to Surgeon John Vansant.

The shoeshop of Jas Okers, 214 F st, was forcibly entered yesterday & robbed of leather & shoe findings to the value of about $70.

New Orleans, Jan 5. Mr Pervis Spears was murdered on Sunday in Warren Co, Miss, by a band of negroes, & his house burned after being sacked. Two negroes were arrested.

Examining Surgeons: The Com'r of Pensions has made the following additional appointments of examining surgeons of pensioners: Dr I W Beckwith, Jefferson, Ind; Dr Jas C Whitebill, St Louis, Mo, & Dr John Hawkins, Petersburg, Ind.

Navy Bulletin for Dec 29. Ordered: Acting Ensign Jos M Simms, to the ship **Ascutney**. Appointments Revoked: Acting 2nd Assist Engineer Enos Hosier, Dec 15; Mate H A Rogers. Detached: Acting 2nd Assist Engineer Geo Cowle, from the ship **Estrella** to the ship **Tallapoosa**; Acting 2nd Assist Engineer S K Carter, from the **Tallapoosa**, & ordered to the ship **Estrella**.

Orphans Court-Judge Purcell. 1-An account of the personal estate of Wm Douglas, deceased, was submitted to the court on Sat by his admx, Sophia E Douglas. 2-The first account of John S Paxton, guardian of Mary & Catharine, orphans of Josiah Baum, deceased, was submitted & settled. 3-Francis E Boyle gave bonds in the sum of $1,000, & was appointed guardian to the orphans of Thos & Mary Dreyer, deceased.

Sandusky, Jan 5. A train on the Cincinnati, Dayton, & Lake Erie railroad was thrown from the track today by a broken rail, near Green Springs. Killed were Mrs Jas Edmonson & Mrs Dennis, of York, Ohio; Henry Starr, of Dayton, & a boy named Phillips. Among the injured were Miss Hughes, of Tiffin, Ohio, collar bone broken, & J Palmer, road master, very badly hurt. [Jan 8th newspaper: Mrs Demoss & a boy named Starr were killed.]

Mr Robt Broom, who has been from early life an attache of the Supreme Court, died suddenly on Sat from disease of the heart.
+
Died: on Jan 5, Robt Hewitt Broom, 2nd son of the late Col Chas Broom, of the Marine Corps. His funeral today, at 12 M, from the residence of Miss Smith, Pa ave & 4½ st.

Died: on Dec 30, at Hoosick Falls, N Y, Mrs Sally Parsons, widow of Seth Parsons, aged 79 years.

Sale by order of the Orphans Court of Wash, D C, of the personal effects of Riter Tridy, deceased, at auction, on Jan 10th, at the late residence of the deceased, on 8th st, between G & I sts south, opposite the Garrison, & the household & kitchen furniture. -August Schroeder, adm -Green & Williams, aucts

Miss Clara Barton has issued Roll No 5 of the missing men of the Union armies, & invites information in regard to them, to be addressed to her in this city. The following names appear in this list:

Dist of Col:
David R Lane, co D, 1st cavalry

Md:
Arnold, Francis M, co D, 7th infty.
Bacar, Jos, Co _, 9th infty.
Cox, Anderson, Co A, 2nd infty.
Donald, Geo W, bugler, co F, 3rd cavalry
Farrow, Jas, co I, 7th infty.

Bidlow, Albion L, co H, 1st cavalry
Williams, Guilford, co E, 2nd infty

King, Hiram, co C, 7th infty.
Shanes, Danl S, co I, 1st cavalry
Stottenmeyer, Geo L, co I, 3rd infty,
P H B
Welles, Geo G, co G, 8th infty

On Dec 29, the residence of the Jesuit fathers & the church adjoining, at St Thomas, near Port Tobacco, Md, was entirely destroyed by fire. In attempting to save the organ in the gallery of the church, it fell to the floor & broke in pieces. These bldgs were probably among the oldest in that section of Md.

N Y, Jan 6. Rev Moses Cummings, a prominent clergyman of the denomination- Bible Christians, & for many years editor of the Christian Herald, died in this city today.

Isaac Coney, a well known citizen of Boston, died at Brattleboro on Thu, aged 65.

A son of Mr Geo Lovett, of Fitchburg, Mass, 7 years of age, was drowned by breaking through the ice, while skating, on Wed.

TUE JAN 8, 1867
Gen C H S Williams, a prominent lawyer of San Francisco, committed suicide on Jan 3 by blowing out his brains with a Derringer pistol. The act was supposed to have been done while laboring under a temporary fit of insanity, brought about by long sickness.

Navy Bulletin for Dec 31. Resigned: Acting Ensign Wm B Mix, of the ship **Peoria**. Ordered: Surgeon P S Naler, to temporary duty at the Naval Hospital at Norfolk, Va. Detached: Acting Ensign N D Campbell from the ship **Memphis**, & ordered to the **Peoria**; Acting Volunteer Lt Geo R Durand, from the ship **Penobscot**, & ordered to the ship **Osceola**; Acting Volunteer Lt L G Varrals, from the **Osceola**, & ordered to the **Penobscot**.

Dr J Rufus Tryon, Assist Chief of the Bureau of Medicine & Surgery of the Navy Dept, has been promoted to the grade of passed assist surgeon U S navy, to rank from Dec 21, 1866.

Postmaster General changes made since Jan 2, 1867:
Md: Patuxent, Anne Arundel Co, H C Chaney, vice D D Woodward, resigned.
Ky: Mount Savage, Carter Co, H D Rucker, vice W H Jacobs, declined.
Pa: Wurtemburg, Lawrence Co, H E Staffer, vice J W Hyde, resigned.
Va: Woodstock, Shenandoah Co, A Heller, vice S F Coulton, resigned.

Died: Jan 6, Juliet Grayson, wife of E B Grayson. Her funeral will be on Jan 9 at 2 o'clock, from her late residence, 472 M st, between 12th & 13th sts.

Died: Jan 5, Sophia Tucker, aged 9 years, daughter of Simpson P & Lizzie T Moses.

By deed of trust dated Jan 20, 1863, recorded in Liber N C T No 1, folios 28 etc, of the land records of Wash Co, D C, I shall sell, at public auction, on Jan 21, of the tract of land, being part of **Aaron**, & part of Lots 1 & 8 in Dundas' subdivision, with improvements thereon. –Amaziah Underhill, trustee -Green & Williams, aucts

WED JAN 9, 1867
Died: on Jan 4, at New Castle, Dela, Mrs Maria Johns, widow of Hon Kensey Johns, late Chancellor of the State of Delaware, in her 74th year.

Chas Eames, recognized in his specialty, the admiralty jurisprudence, as one of the most accomplished members of that exalted bar, was stricken down with apoplexy in the midst of a forensic effort before the Supreme Court yesterday, & lies in a precarious condition.

Mr E R Parker, colored, is announced as an independent candidate for Mayor of Alleghany City, Pa.

Orphans Court-Judge Purcell. 1-Yesterday the will of the late Prather Lee, of Gtwn, was filed & fully proven. 2-Letters of administration were issued to Geo Lautner on the estate of Henry Nettle; bond, $1,000. 3-Catharine Hines was appointed guardian to the orphan of David Hines; bond, $2,000. 4-Mrs Mary Fleming renounced her right to administer on the estate of John Fleming, dec'd, & letters of administration were issued to Patrick Fleming; bond, $1,600. 5-The second & final accounts of the admx w a of Hamilton J Smith, deceased; of guardian of orphan of Thos Corcoran;

of second & supplemental of executor of Thos Lumpkin; & seventh income account of exc of John B Kibbey, were approved & passed. 6-In the case of Woolley vs Whitall, the court decided that the case had to be properly presented & fairly tried & that the motion for a rehearing could not be justly granted. The will, therefore, of Martha R Woolley is set aside, & as the executor appointed has acted in good faith, the Court ordered that the expenses attending the suit should be paid out of the property claimed by the deceased.

Police Affairs: 1-Chas Collins & Augustus Simms, under several charges of larceny, were committed to jail. 2-Edw Hathaway & Martin Welsh committed to jail for court, charged with robbing the safe of F M Magruder & Co, about 2 weeks since.

Gtwn Affairs: Corporation Ofcrs:
C M Matthews, Recorder
Wm Laird, clerk
J D Robinson, Flour Inspector
C F Shekell, Tax Collector
J H Reynolds, Market Master
Wm Simms, inspector of lumber
W H Craig, Weigher of Hay

D O'Leary, Wood Corder
M V Buckey, Trustee of the Poor
E G Brown, Harbor Master
Saml P Trepler, Chinmey Sweep
H W Brewer, Surveyor
Henry Addiston, Street Com'r
M V Buckey, Police Magistrate

Judges of Election:
J F Birch
G W Strand
J T Gatewood
W H Birch
C H Demar
W H Craig
Geo Rhodes

Wm Magee
Jas A Donnelly
E G Brown
Jacob Ramsburg
C A Offutt

Isaac Birch, Corp Messenger. Guardians of Gtwn Schools: A C Hyde, T A Newman; J H Wilson. For Small Pox Physicians: Dr A Peters & Dr D McCormick

John Van Horn, a prominent citizen of Chicago, shot his wife through the head on Sunday, because she interfered to prevent his whipping one of their children. He then attempted to blow his own brains out, but was prevented. Both parties are still alive, & the man has been held in $5,000 bail

Criminal Court-Judge Fisher. 1-Mary Turner found guilty of larceny. 2-John Hollohan, indicted for larceny, sentenced to 3 days in the common jail. 3-Lewis Gardon, guilty of larceny. 4-Thos McCormick & his wife, jointly indicted for keeping a bawdy-house. McCormick was not present, & the counsel for Mrs McCormick asked the Court to instruct the jury that as she is the wife of Thos McCormick, she was not responsible, & the jury returned a verdict of not guilty.

On Dec 20, six men entered the house of J W P Doyle, Hill Co, Texas, killed him & his son, Rufus, & then robbed the house of $1,400 in coin, some currency, & 9 drafts for $1,000 each.

Clerical promotions in the Treasury Dept: Third Auditor's Ofc: J H Benedick, W F Crane, Augustus Ward, Geo G Cox, C E Blanchard, D W Batchelder, Priestly Young, E M Dawson, jr, J S Phillips, C S Wheeler, N C Dodge, & W H Walton, from first to second class. W H Gaines, M Eastwood, G P Hopkins, Wm Thompson, & T R Jones, from second to third class. John Trimble, third to fourth class; G F Johnson, $1,000 to first class. Bureau of Statistics: Jas Ryan, J E Smith, Harvey Fowler, & S L Loomis, second to third class. Francis Lowndes, from third to fourth class. Ofc Com'r of Customs: A L Munson, from third to fourth class.
Ofc Solicitor of the Treasury: W E Bendy, from first to second class.
Ofc Treasurer of the U S: J P Wood, from first to second class.
Ofc Register of the Treasury: C H Smith, from second to third class.
Sec's Ofc: W H Foard, from first to second. Fred Chase, from third to fourth class.

Navy Bulletin for Jan 2, 1867. Detached: Acting Master John McGowan, jr, from the ship **Monongahela**, & placed on waiting orders; Lt Cmder Henry B Ramsey, Master Francis Morris, & Ensign Isaac Hazlett, from the **Monongahela**, & placed on waiting orders. Ordered: Acting Master John V Cook & Acting Ensign Louis Kenney, to duty at League Island, Pa. Honorably Discharged: Acting Master Geo W Hyde & Acting Ensign J E N Graham.

Mr Wm A Janes, a route agent on the Balt & Ohio railroad, was arrested at Wheeling, Va, on Sat, on suspicion of robbing the mail.

Dept of Interior, U S Patent Ofc, Wash, Jan 3, 1867. Ptn of Christopher Duckworth, of Mount Carmel, Conn, praying for extension of a patent granted to him on Jun 28, 1853, for an improvement in Shuttle Box Motion in Looms, for 7 years from the expiration of said patent, which takes place on Jun 28, 1867.
-T C Theaker, Com'r of Patents

Trustee's sale, by decree of the Circuit Court for PG Co, in equity, passed in a cause wherein Geo Forbes is cmplnt, & Jas I Bowie & Catharine Bowie are dfndnts, the undersigned, as trustee, will sell at public sale, at Croom P O, near the premises, [on Dec 20 next,] postponded until Jan 20th, 1867, all that part or portion of the real estate of the late Robt W Bowie, called **Mattaponi**, which was assigned & laid off to Catherine Bowie as & for her dower, containing 300 acres, more or less, & being the same land the reversion in fee of which was purchased by Jas I Bowie of Caleb C Magruder & Wm H Tuck, trustee, & is more particularly described in a deed of the reversionary interest of the same from Wm H Tuck & C C Magruder, trustees, to Jas I Bowie, bearing the date of May 31, 1856. This farm adjoins the lands of C C Magruder, Dr John T Eversfield, & others. There is a large & commodious Brick Mansion with all necessary out-bldgs for a first class farm. No member of the family desires to become the purchaser of this property. Full competition is invited, as the sale will be peremptory. –Danl Clark, trustee

THU JAN 10, 1867
The ladies of Sec McCulloch's family will receive as usual on Wednesdays.

The N Y papers record the death, at Pau, France, on Dec 13, of Geo Sullivan, late of that city, in his 83rd year. He was a son of Govn'r Jas Sullivan, of Mass, & a nephew of Gen John Sullivan, of the Revolutionary army. He was a graduate of Harvard Univ, & married the eldest daughter of Govn'r Thos L Withrop, of Boston, a lady of great personal beauty, inherited from her mother, the lovely Eliz Temple, daughter of Sir John Temple, & grand-daughter of Gov'r Bowdoin. Mr Sullivan removed to N Y about 40 years ago, & engaged in the practice of the law. He spent several winters here during the administration of Mr Monroe. Mrs Sullivan preceded her husband to the tomb by a few months, having died at Pau last summer. Mr Sullivan leaves one son, a distinguished member of the bar of N Y, Geo R J Bowdoin, who assumed the name he now bears in accordance with the will of his illustrious ancestor, Gov Bowdoin, on attaining his majority. Mr Bowdoin is a graduate of West Point, & married a grand-daughter of Alex'r Hamilton.

Willie P Henley, grandson of Mr J T Evans, of Wash City, who accidentally shot himself with a pistol in the hand on Christmas day, died last night from lockjaw, produced by the wound. Up to Sunday the wound was considered in a favorable condition, but lockjaw supervened during the evening, since which time he was in constant agony.

A newsboy of Toronto, Henry Martin, whose father was killed at Bull Run, has fallen heir to $200,000 through the death of an uncle, who accumulated a large fortune in Texas, & saved. He joined the Confederate army, & was killed at Shiloh. Detectives had been searching for young Martin for the last 3 months. Having found him, he went to Rochester, N Y, on Sat, where his mother is residing.

Mr John W Morgan, a citizen of Richmond, died suddenly on Tuesday.

Circuit Court-Judge Wylie. 1-John Hart & Wm Brown, indicted for larceny, a nolle pros, was entered. 2-Jas Coleman, indicted for the larceny of a gun, was convicted & sentenced to 1 year in the penitentiary. 3-Wm Jones, indicted for an assault & battery; Geo Williams, alias Wm Jones, for larceny, a nolle pros was entered. 4-Emanuel Warner, indicted for larceny, plead guilty, & was sentenced to the Albany penitentiary for one year. 5-Mary E Brown, indicted for keeping a bawdy-house, was found not guilty.

Brvt Brig Gen F A Stratton, lately of the volunteer service, to be constructing engineer of the Navy Yard in this city, in place of Wm Dennison, detached.

Mrd: on Jan 8, at the residence of Reuben Clark, by Rev Fr O A Sears, Clinton M Sears to Miss Mary E Forteney, all of Wash City.

Died: on Jan 9, Margaret Eslin, wife of Jas Eslin, in her 68th year. Her funeral will take place from her late residence, north of Columbian College, this evening at 1 o'clock P M.

Memphis Bulletin, Jan 6. On Friday on board the steamer **T L McGill**, enroute to the city, an old man, A G Wilson, from Champaign Co, came on board carrying a double barrelled shot-gun in his hand. After a while Wilson sat down to watch a card game. During the game a young man named Henry Brown was addressed by the party as reb. In the morning Mr Brown & Mr Langford, who was from Atlanta, Ga, were standing together, when Mr Wilson raised his gun & shot & killed Mr Langford. Mr Brown saw the muzzle of the gun pointed at him, & quickly stepped back, thus saving his life. Wilson was in a frenzy and there was great difficulty in disarming him. Wilson was arrested & placed in the hands of the sheriff.

Dept of the Interior, U S Patent Ofc, Wash, Jan 5, 1867. Ptn of Thos J Sloan, of N Y, praying for the extension of a patent granted to him on Apr 26, 1853, for an improvement in Machine for Pointing & Threading Screw Blanks, for 7 years from the expiration of said patent, which takes place on Apr 26, 1867.
-T C Theaker, Com'r of Patents

Col Jas Merrick died at his residence, near Long Marsh, on Monday last. He was attacked with congestive chills a few days before his death, from the effect of which he never recovered. Col Merrick was one of our most highly respected & wealthy citizens, of genial disposition. –Centreville [Md] Citizen

On Thu, Mr Wildo, a German, living near Milwaukie, Wisc, was seriously injured by being thrown from his vehicle by his horse taking fright. Mr David Racke, another German, succeeded in capturing the horse, & driving back the animal again became frightened, throwing Mr Racke out of the vehicle, & instantly killing him.

FRI JAN 11, 1867
Postmaster Randall made the following changes in postmasters since Jan 6:
Maine: Webb's Mills, Cumberland Co, E Brown, vice R M Webb, deceased.
Conn: New Milford, Litchfield Co, W B Allen, vice G D Copley, resigned.
Va: Taylorsville, Hanover Co, J Serritt, vice J D Lane, resigned; Cedar Bluff, Tazewell Co, Miss R A Prather, vice J Norton, resigned; Smithfield, Isle of Wight Co, Mrs T Lapping, vice W S Rud, resigned; Newport News, Warwick Co, P Davis, vice A N Fretz, resigned; Jetersville, Amelia Co, L C Angel, vice Mrs M Atwood, can't take the oath. Minn: Hokah, Houston Co, J T Foster, vice D S Clements, declined. Wisc: Richland City, Richland Co, W Carl, vice Mrs H M Baugham, deceased.

Navy Bulletin, Jan 3 & 4. Deserted: Mate Thos Newton, from the ship **Paul Jones**, Nov 27, 1866. Ordered: Acting Ensign Jas B Russell, to the ship **Memphis**. Honorably Discharged: Acting Ensign Eugene P Palmer, from Dec 31.

The Com'r of Pensions yesterday appointed Dr Michl Lahmer, of Oregon, Mo; Dr T M Gould, of Raymond, N H; Dr Jos P Root, of Wyandotte, Kansas; & Dr Henry M Avery, of Morristown, N J, examining surgeons of pensioners.

Mrd: on Jan 9, at 253 12th st, by Rev Dr Hall, Mr Wm M Constable, of Wash City, to Miss Sarah A T Wills, of Petersburg, Va. [Petersburg papers please copy.]

Mrd: on Jan 10, at Trinity Parish, John Henry Hommon Elis to Mrs Mary Emma Webster, of Fairfax Co, Va.

Died: on Dec 27, 1866, at Omaha City, Neb, at the residence of her son-in-law, John T Holtzman, Mrs Eliz Wells, widow of Richd Wells, formerly of Gtwn, D C, aged 76 years.

Died: Sat last, at his residence, in Queen Anne District, in Md, Wm Clark, aged 66 years.

Charleston, S C, Jan 10. A sailor of the British brig **Carmen**, named Jas Salvo, was killed while the vessel was loading, this morning.

Orphans Court of Wash Co, D C. Letters of administration on the personal estate of John Flemming, late of Wash City, D C, deceased. –P Flemming

SAT JAN 12, 1867
Mr & Mrs Howard Paul, admirable artistes are to sing today before the President & the household at the Executive Mansion.

Equity Court-Judge Wylie, Jan 11, 1867. 1-Mary E Brooker vs Benj C Brooker; #755. Decree, divorce from the bonds of matrimony. 2-Sarah McNeir vs Wm McNeir. #724. Decree, divorce from bed & board, the cmplnt to have the custody of the children. 3-Ellen Starr vs J T Williams. #727. Decree, substituting Jno F Callan trustee instead of S S Williams, deceased.

Died: on Jan 11, Mary Ann, wife of Geo C Scheffer. Her funeral is tomorrow at 2 P M, from St John's Church. [N Y Herald & Tribune please copy.]

Obit-died: on Dec 29, at the residence of her parents, in Port Tobacco, Md, Eliza C, eldest child of Wm & Mary Boswell, in her 18th year. Returning but a few months since, on the completion of her scholastic education, to the scene of her childhood, she gently passed away.

House of Reps: Jan 11: 1-Cmte of the Whole: bills that were passed-relief of: Timothy Leydon; of Johnson A Dawson, of Mount Sterling, Ky; of Edw Blanchard; of Henry Rudd, of Henry Co, Iowa; of Norman J Hall; of Hiram Paulding, rear admiral U S Navy. 2-Bills referred to the Cmte of the Whole: bills for the relief of Jas Hooper, of Balt, Md; & of E J Curley. 3: Cmte of Claims: bill for the relief of Margaret Ann Laurie; & ptn of I W Nye: laid on the table.

The funeral of Lt Henry H Wilson, son of Senator Wilson, took place at his father's residence, in Natick, on Wednesday afternoon. The services were conducted by Rev C M Tyler, & the remains were buried in the family lot.

Mr Jas O'Brien, a saddler & harness maker of Balt, died suddenly, of congestion of the brain, while witnessing the performance at the Holliday Street Theatre on Wednesday.

Orphans Court of Wash Co, D C, Jan 12, 1867. In the case of Wm J Hickey & Cecelia P Hickey, adms of Wm Hickey, deceased, the administrators & Court have appointed Jan 31 next, for the final settlement of the personal estate of the said deceased, of the assets in hand. -Jas R O'Beirne, Reg/o wills

MON JAN 14, 1867
Navy Bulletin, Jan 5. Detached: Mate Fred'k V Voelekers, from the receiving ship **Vermont**, & ordered to the ship **Memphis**. Appointment revoked: Mate Thos Wilson, of the ship **Connemaugh**.

Capt Saml Samuels gets $5,000 for bringing in the yacht **Henrietta** first in the yacht race.

Gen Fullerton resigned from the army & returned to the practice of the law at St Louis.

Gen John S Preston has returned from Europe to his home in Columbia, S C.

Orphans Court-Judge Purcell. 1-The second account of J Bayard H Smith, exc of the estate of Anna M Thornton, deceased, was approved & passed. 2-The first & final account of Mary Camelia Cook, admx with the will annexed of Abaham Cook, deceased, was approved & passed. 3-The first & final account of Rebecca S Parker, admx with the will annexed of Henry Parker, deceased, was approved & passed. 4-The first & final account of Louisa K Leach, admx of the estate of Jas B Leach, deceased, was approved, passed, & distribution ordered to be made among the heirs. 5-The first & final account of Henry Whitall, exc of the last will & testament of Martha R Woolley, deceased, was approved & passed. 6-Letters of administration on the estate of Leana Harris were issued to Melinda Davis; bond $600. 7-Letters of administration on the claim against the Gov't of John C Archibald, deceased, late of Lawrence, Kansas, were issued to Jas H Holmes; bond $600. 8-Letters of administration on the estate of Chas H Utermehle, deceased, were issued to Naomi Utermehle & Eugene Carusi; bond $10,000. 9-Letters of guardianship were issued to Chas B La Porte, appointing him guardian to the minor child of John & Hannah Walter; bond $700.

Miss Kate Hofmeister, residing in Boonville, Mo, a few nights since, while waltzing at a ball, suddenly threw up her hands & fell to the floor, & expired in a few moments.

Equity Court-Judge Wylie. 1-Mary E Brooker vs Benj C Brooker: ptn for divorce, setting forth that they were married Jan 5, 1864,in Phil, her maiden name being Myers, & charging that the respondent made no provision for her support; that he has committed adultery; that in July last, after repeated threats to take her life, he came to her house with the avowed purpose of taking away her furniture, & assaulted & cruelly beat her. Decree granting a divorce a vinculo matrimonii, & allowing complnt to assume the name she bore before marriage. 2-Sarah McNeir vs Wm McNeir: ptn for divorce, setting forth that the parties were married in 1857, [the maiden name of the cmplnt being Hefferman,] & that there are 2 children by said marriage. It charges that during the marriage he has been habitually drunk, has frequently abused her, & finally, in 1861, deserted her. Decree granting a divorce a mensa et thoro, & giving cmplnt the guardianship of the children & the control of the property, & the respondent to pay the costs of the suit. 3-Ellen Starr vs J Tucker Williams: decree substituting John F Callan as trustee in place of S S Williams, deceased. 4-Zephaniah Jones vs Horace Stringfellow et al. Order approving Mrs Matilda Hamilton as guardian ad litem to infants. 5-Ed P Gilbert vs Jas L Barbour et al. Order approving Mrs Matilda Hamilton as guardian ad litem to infants.

Mr John E Owens, the comedian, is nightly delighting large audiences at the Broadway Theatre, N Y.

Miss Nellie Dean, of Chicago, figures on a Pittsburgh skating pond as a professional performer, & gets $200 a week & her expenses.

An insane man, Manuel Urah, who had escaped from his keeper, near Sparta, Wisc, was recently shot in the woods by a Mr Amey, who mistook him for a deer.

The Confederate Gen A P Stewart has settled in Memphis & is teaching school with his brother, Prof J D Stewart.

Chas Dickens has begun public readings of "Barbox Brothers" & the "Boy at Mugby,' in the city of Leeds. The London journals report that "Mugby Junction" has had a sale of 250,000 copies.

Miss Jennie Cameron, daughter of Gen Simon Cameron, was recently married at Harrisburg to Wayne McVeigh, a talented lawyer of Chester.

Boston, Jan 12. Letters received in New Bedford announce the death of Capt Philip Howland, of the bark **Martha & Susan**, of that port, Nov 11, near Pitcairn's Island, where he was buried.

Mrs Lincoln was presented with a medal on Monday last, in Chicago, by a gentleman from France, on behalf of 30,000 French people, in token of their respect for the memory of Abraham Lincoln.

Died: on Dec 11, near San Antonio, Texas, Fenton M Fewell, son of Jesse Fewell, late of Prince Wm Co, Va.

Died: on Jan 4, at Manchester, Mo, Mary, wife of Joel Cruttenden, formerly of Gtwn, D C, in her 82nd year.

Died: on Jan 11, in Wash City, Theodore Putnam, son of Rev Lewellyn & Sarah Putnam Pratt, aged 4 years.

Died: on Jan 13, Wm M Steuart, aged 29 years. His funeral is on Tuesday at 1 P M, from 402 E st.

Cincinnati, Jan 12. A young lady, Christine Kett, was murdered at Dayton, Ohio, yesterday. She was found lying in the kitchen of her house with her head terribly shattered by a pistol ball. No clue to the murderer.

Supreme Court of D C, Equity No 716. Wm H Terrett et al vs Wm W Terrett et al. Trustee's account & distribution on Jan 19, my ofc, at 2 PM. –Walter S Cox, auditor

Supreme Court of D C; Equity No 52-Docket 7. Zephaniah Jones vs Horace Stringfellow et al. A Thos Bradley & Wm Y Fendall, trustees, reported that they sold, on Jan 2, the real estate in the bill mentioned, with improvements & appurtenances, for $80,900 to Jesse B Wilson, who had complied with the terms of sale. –R J Meigs, clerk

Supreme Court of D C, Equity No 1,637. Emma Smoot vs Wm H C Mockabee et al. The above cause is referred to me to state the indebtedness of Wm Mockabee, deceased, to Saml C Smoot, deceased, & other creditors, & the account of Am__oa Green, adm of said Wm Mockabee. Parties interested to meet at my ofc on Jan 19. –Walter S Cox, auditor

Supreme Court of D C; Equity No 761. Saml C Smoot et al vs John M Turly et al. Trustee's account & distribution of the fund on Jan 19, at my ofc, at 2 o'clock. –Walter S Cox, auditor

Orphans Court of Wash Co, D C, Jan 8, 1866. In the case of Catharine A Talburtt, admx of Geo H Talburtt, the administratrix & Court have appointed Jan 31 next, for the final settlement of the personal estate of the said deceased, of the assets in hand. -Jas R O'Beirne, Reg/o wills

Orphans Court of Wash Co, D C, Jan 12, 1867. In the case of Edwin C Morgan, adm of Wm Walker, deceased, the administrator & Court have appointed Feb 8 next, for the final settlement of the personal estate of the said deceased, of the assets in hand. -Jas R O'Beirne, Reg/o wills

Orphans Court of Wash Co, D C, Jan 12, 1867. In the case of John H Semmes, adm of Rose M Harle, deceased, the administrator & Court have appointed Feb 7 next, for the final settlement of the personal estate of the said deceased, of the assets in hand. -Jas R O'Beirne, Reg/o wills

Orphans Court of Wash Co, D C, Jan 12, 1867. In the case of Richd T Morsell, adm of Ann E Beall, deceased, the administrator & Court have appointed Feb 7 next, for the final settlement of the personal estate of the said deceased, of the assets in hand. -Jas R O'Beirne, Reg/o wills

TUE JAN 15, 1867
Topeka, Kansas, Jan 11. Jos Bogy, a brother of the Com'r of Indian Affairs, is holding councils with the various Indian tribes in Kansas relative to their removal to the Indian Territory. It is expected that no tribal organization will exist in this State in one year from now.

Naval: Capt N Collins, commanding the U S steamer **Sacramento**, reports the arrival of that vessel at Funchal, Maderia, on Dec 9.

Changes made by the Postmaster General Randall since Jan 11, 1867.
West Va: Wick, Tyler Co, W Morris, vice J Bullman, deceased.
Tenn: Olivers, Anderson Co, A M Griffith, vice W C Griffith, resigned; Boyd's Creek, Sevier Co, S Anderson, vice S Felke, resigned; McMillan, Knox Co, B R Strong, vice J C Strong, can't take the oath.
Texas: Jacksonville, Cherokee Co, D C Owen, vice A J Lowell, resigned; San Loandro, Calif: Alameda Co, R C Nabb, vice H Keeney, deceased; Percadero, Santa Cruz Co, J Garrettson, vice C Kinney, resigned.

Phil, Jan 14. The boiler in Z Patton's steam plaster mill exploded this afternoon, killing A Alford instantly. Jas Duffy & Mr Gallacher, foreman, severely injured. Wm Sherman, of N Y, who was passing at the time on the sidewalk, was injured by flying bricks.

Equity Court, Justice Olin & Wylie presiding, Jan 14, 1867. 1-John Thompson vs Lewis A Bell et al: No 809, Dec 8. Order reference to auditor. 2-Geo C Humes et al vs John G Clark et al. No 770, Doc 8. Order substituting Elbert G Emack trustee instead of M St C Clarke. 3-Alex'r Ray vs Murray et al. No 844. Order Substituting W R Woodward trustee instead of J C C Hamilton, deceased. 4-Albert J Carew vs Chas H Dant et al. No 767. Order substituting P B Stilson trustee instead of Jas Dull. 5-John Thompson et al vs Lewis A Bell et al. No 809. Order appointing E P Cross guardian ad litem for Lillie D Ray & Lucy Conner. 6-Julia A Van Ness vs Barney Barry. No 651, doc 7. Order appointing Wm H Philip trustee to sell. 7-Robt J Walker vs Trustees of Bank of Metropolis. Order overruling motion to dissolve injunction. 8-Lynch vs Carpenter et al. Order for injunction.

Navy Bulletin: Ordered. Passed Assist Paymaster Danforth P Wright, to the ship **Huron**; Acting Ensign B O Low & Mate J S O'Brien, to the ship **Marblehead**.

Criminal Court-Judge Fisher, Jan 14, 1867. 1-Henry Smith, Peter Robinson, & Andrew Powers were tried for a riot at the house of Mrs Murray, across the Eastern Branch, & found not guilty. 2-Henry Smith, indicted for an assault & battery, was found guilty of assault. He was also indicted for the larceny of a pistol & turkey, convicted of the larceny of the latter. 3-Noah Brooks, indicted for an assault & resisting an ofcr, was convicted & sentenced to 12 days in jail. In a case of an assault against the same party a nolle pros was entered.

Mrd: on Jan 14, Gen Frank Wheaton, U S A, to Maria B Miller.

Accident on the Va & Tenn railraod on Sunday night, along New River Bluff, when the sleeping car was thrown down an embankment. Those injured were Col J S Sidney, of Galveston, Texas, shoulder dislocated; Maj Gouldman, Galveston, head, right arm & hand injured; S W Bullock, N Y, face severely cut; Mr Little, **Fort Wayne**, Ind, back injured; Mr Packman, Tenn, shoulder & eye bruised; Mr Watson, of Phil, hand slightly hurt; Mr Miller, conductor of the sleeping car. badly hurt internally.

Died: on Jan 13, John M, child of Stephen M & Margaret T Curran, in his 6th year. His funeral will take place this morning at 11 o'clock, from the residence of his parents, 568 M st, between 7th & 8th sts.

Died: on Jan 13, Wm M Steuart, aged 29 years. His funeral is today at 1 o'clock, from 402 E st.

Miss Laura Keene, the actress, is on a visit to Mobile, having been obliged to give up her engagements in the North on account of ill health.

Orphans Court of Wash Co, D C. Letters of administration on the personal estate of Chas H Utermehle, late of Wash City, D C, deceased. –Naomi Utermehle, Eugene Carusi

WED JAN 16, 1867
Navy Bulletin, Jan 7. Appointment Revoked. Acting 3rd Assist Engineer Philip Lettig.

Brvt Brig Gen T J Rodman has been ordered by Maj Gen Dyer, chief of ordnance, to proceed to **Fortress Monroe** arsenal to examine & test the "Mann gun," & a 15 inch carriage altered by Brvt Col Baylor.

Equity Court-Justice Olin presiding, Jan 15, 1867.
1-Francis Sweeny vs Jacob E Lyon et al. No 839. Order granting injunction.

Criminal Court-Judge Wylie, Jan 15, 1867. The case of Francis Harrison, indicted for the murder of Sarah Harrison, his wife, on Oct 3, was taken up. The parties resided on 19th st, between L & M, & after the death of the deceased an inquest was held, at which time it was testified that the accused frequently beat her with a heavy stick, & the physician, [Dr G N Hopkins] testifying that death was caused by the blows, the jury rendered a verdict of manslaughter.

Orphans Court of Wash Co, D C, Jan 15, 1867. In the case of Edw C Dyer, adm w a of Eliza Cassin, deceased, the administrator & Court have appointed Feb 9 next, for the final settlement of the personal estate of the said deceased, of the assets in hand. -Jas R O'Beirne, Reg/o wills

Fort Laramie, Jan 14. The following are the names of the members of the 2nd cavalry killed in the recent massacre at *Fort Phil Kearney*:
2nd Lt Horatio S Bingham, killed Dec 6, 1866.
Killed on Dec 21st, 1866:

Sgt Jas Baker
Cpl Jas Kelley
Bugler Adolph Metzgar
Saddler John McCarthy
Pvt Thomas Anderson
Pvt Thos Brogden
Pvt Wm S Bugbee
Pvt Wm L Conroy
Pvt Chas Cuddy
Pvt Patrick Clancey
Pvt H S Denning
Pvt Hugh Duran

Pvt Robt Daniels
Pvt Anderson M Fitzgerald
Pvt Nathl Furman
Pvt John Gitter
Pvt Danl Green
Pvt Chas Gampfel
Pvt Ferd Homer
Pvt Park Jones
Pvt Geo W Nugent
Pvt Frank Payne
Pvt Jas Ryan
Pvt Oliver Williams

Mrd: on Jan 10, by Rev Mr Longnecker, of Balt, Edwin Stuart, of Phil, to Miss Kate Clay, daughter of Wm T Dove, of Montrose, Montg Co, Md, formerly of Wash City.

Died: on Jan 14, Thos Greeves, aged 19 years. His funeral will be from the residence of his grandmother, Mrs S A Greeves, 357 9th st, on Jan 16, at 2 P M.

Madame Parepa is about to become the wife of Carl Ross, the violinist. We record the fact with pleasure & wish all happiness to the union of so much talent.
–N Y Weekly Review

Orphans Court of Wash Co, D C, Jan 15, 1867. In the case of Christopher Ingle, adm of Mary C Ingle, deceased, the administrator & Court have appointed Feb 8 next, for the final settlement of the personal estate of the said deceased, of the assets in hand. -Jas R O'Beirne, Reg/o wills

THU JAN 17, 1867

Capt John S Paxton, brevet lt colonel & commissary of subsistence U S volunteers, has been honorably mustered out of the service by order of the Sec of War.

Equity Court-Justice Wylie presiding, Jan 16, 1867. 1-Mary Jan Selby vs John W Selby. No 820. Decree & order pro confesso vs dfndnt, appointing Benj G Lovejoy executor. 2-R J Walker vs Covington Smith, exc of R Smith. No 749. Order overruling exceptions to dfndnt's answer. 3-R J Walker vs Chas Hill et al. No 748. Order overruling exceptions to dfndnt's answer.

Criminal Court-Judge Olin presiding, Jan 16, 1867. 1-In the case of Jas H C Wilson, indicted for assault & battery, nolle prosequi was entered. 2-Timothy Land & Jas McKenney, indicted for assault & battery; their recognizances were forfeited; also, case of Wm Burke; also, case of John Clark; also, case of Jos Goodrick; also, case of Henry Wilford; also, case of David R Smith; also, case of John Riddle. 3-Jas Franklin, indicted for larceny, recognizance forfeited. 4-Tiney Carrol, indicted for larceny; a nolle prosequi was entered. 5-Mary Turner, convicted of larceny, sentenced to imprisonment one day in jail. 6-Wm Auffert & Jas Johnson, implicated with Jeremiah Haggerty for forging soldiers' discharge papers & final accounts. Case not closed.

Alex Smith, the poet, is dangerously ill.

Manchester, N H, dated Jan 14. Last evening, in this city, Mr Hatch, formerly a saloon-keeper, some time since became enamored of Mrs Batchelder, residing on Mount Pleasant st, & whose husband is living in Boston. The hopelessness of his guilty passions seems to have unsettled his reason. Mrs Batchelder & Mrs Davidson were in a room together, when Mr Hatch came in, fired a shot at Mrs Batchelder, which did no injury. The two ladies fled from the room. Mr Hatch shot himself through the lungs. The wound is a mortal one. The doctors who attended Hatch state he has been insane for some time past.

Yesterday a lady named Mrs Leonard, at 50 Jefferson st, was seriously & probably fatally burned by her clothes taking fire from a stove. She had just moved into the house & was putting carpet down when her clothes caught fire. Dr McCormack was called, & rendered all the assistance he could, but it is thought she will not recover. [Jan 18th newspaper: Mrs Leonard is not expected to recover; this brings much sadness in the neighborhood where the lady resided with her family.] [Jan 19th newspaper: Mrs Leonard died Thursday afternoon.]

Mrd: on Jan 8, at **Sherwood Forest**, the residence of the bride's parents, by Rev Henry Wall, John Tayloe,jr, son of Col John Tayloe, of King Geo, to Jane E Fitzhugh, daughter of Henry Fitzhugh, of Stafford, Va.

Died: on Jan 4, at Manchester, Mo, Mary, wife of Joel Cruttenden, formerly an old resident of Gtwn, D C, in her 82nd year.

Murder on *Fell's Point*, Balt, last evening, at a cooper shop, 33 S C st, Wm Wallsmith, aged 23, was killed by Jos Garrison. An altercation ensued between them, & Garrison inflicted a most horrible wound, partially servering Wallsmith's head from his body, causing instant death. –Balt Commercial, 15th.

Adolphus Schwartz, one of the passengers by the steamer **Bremen**, which arrived at N Y on Tuesday from Bremen, was arrested by order of U S Marshal Murray, on a charge of forgery, committed in Vienna, the sum involved being 160,000 florins, amounting to $100,000 of our currency.

Caleb Stowell, a well-known & respected citizen, & leading builder, of Boston, died on Saturday, aged 74 years.

Hon Wilkins Updike, for half a century one of the leading public men of Rhode Island, died on Monday at his residence in South Kingston, aged 82 years.

FRI JAN 18, 1867
Postmaster Gen Randall made these changes in postmasters since Jan 12, 1867.
Md: Norbeck, Montg Co, N C Flank, vice J N Bennett, resigned; Unity, Montg Co, SW Davis, vice N M Hobbs, resigned.
Va: Talcott, Charlotte Co, J F Ford, vice T W Smith, resigned; Red bank, Halifax Co, W Cleburne, vice W Reese, can't take the oath.
N Y: Olcott, Niagara Co, Mrs L Armstrong, vice T Armstrong, deceased.
Mich; Benton Harbor, Berrin Co, H C Martin, vice C Hubbard, deceased.
Iowa: Bloomfield, Davis Co, J Boyer, vice S W Sayles, non-resident of the postal district.

Criminal Court-Judge Olin presiding. 1-Wm Offutt & Jas Johnson, implicated with Jeremiah Hagerty for forgery of discharge papers, were convicted, & Offutt & Johnson were each sentenced to 2 years in the Albany county jail. 2-Emanuel Hoffman, indicted for arson, the Dist Atty entered a nolle prosequi. 3-The case of Sanford Conover, for perjury, will be brought up on Jan 28th.

Navy Bulletin, Jan 9, 10, & 11. Dropped: 2nd Assist Engineer Edw W Koehe.
Ordered: Lt Cmder Jas Stilwell, to the ship **Susquehanna**; Capt John Guest, to duty at the Portsmouth N H Navy Yard; paymaster Chas W Abbot, to the **Susquehanna**.

Police Matters. 1-Rebecca Harris, for disorderly conduct in church: fined $5. 2-John Kaiser was arrested for keeping a dog without a license: fined $10.

Mrs Cockburn, the mother of the Solicitor Gen of Canada, was burned to death on Wednesday in Cobourg, C W, her clothes catching fire while she was standing in front of a grate.

John Fielder, a German, found lying on 10th st, on Monday night, nearly frozen, & who was sent to the asylum, died on Wednesday. He leaves & wife & 2 children residing on 9th ave, N Y.

Mrd: on Jan 17, at St Matthew's Church, by Rev Fr McNally, Wm John Miller to Miss Frances M, daughter of Andrew J Joyce, all of Wash City, D C.

SAT JAN 19, 1867
Mr Thos B Cuming, one of the oldest & most esteemed merchants of N Y, died on Tuesday, in his 78th year.

Boston, Jan 18. Cmdor G S Blake, a member of the Light-house Board, aged 62 years, was lost yesterday in the snow storm, & has not yet been heard from. He served 47 years in the navy. [Jan 21st newspaper: Cmdor Blake who was supposed to have perished in the snow, has returned home. He took refuge in a hut near his house.]

Tragedy at Valparaiso, Ind. On Tuesday, on the Pittsburgh & *Fort Wayne* road, Chauncey Page, a jeweller, some time since, separated from his wife because of troubles, & she went into a family of an old man as a servant. Page went to the house, quarreled, threw his wife on the floor, beat & kicked her in a terrible manner, & left her for dead. H then took a poker from the fireplace, attacked his wife's mother & killed her, set the house on fire & fled to the woods. The only person who escaped from the house was a young girl, who was terribly mangled & is not expected to recover.

Yesterday dense smoke was seen issuing from the western end of the conservatory adjoining the *Executive Mansion*, & one of the guards on duty there discharged his musket, thus giving an alarm, which was taken up by others. An effort was made to turn in an alarm from N Y ave & 15th st, but the apparatus of the large bells was out of order, on account of the cold weather; it was then turned in by Sgt Walker at Willard's Hotel. The conservatory of the Mansion was formerly on the east side of the bldg, but during the administration of Pres Buchanan it was torn down, & the new one erected on the west side over the row of one story bldgs, used for the storage of wood & coal, the roof of which was of copper. The fire was first discovered immediately over the boiler, & it is thought to have originated from a defective flue. The loss will probably reach $30,000. Many of the plants were very rare & cannot be replaced. Mr Kerichar, the chief gardner, succeeded in getting a number of the plants out before they were reached by the flames. Mr Wm Slade, the steward at the Mansion properly provided the firemen by furnishing suitable refreshments.

Wash Board of Trade. John H Semmes was re-elected Pres; John T Mitchell first & Saml Bacon second Vice Presidents.

MON JAN 21, 1867

M Belloe, historical painter, & since 1830 the superintendent of the Imperial School of Designs in Paris, died recently, aged 86 years.

Navy Bulletin, Jan 11 & 12. Ordered: Mate Anthony F Jennings to the ship **Monongahela**; 3rd Assist Engineer Albert Engard, to the ship **Marblehead**. Honorably Discharged: Acting Ensign R C Dawes. Detached: 3rd Assist Engineer Chas F Nagle, from the **Marblehead**, & ordered to examination; Lt Cmder Wm Gibson, from the command of the ship **Tahoma**, on the reporting of his relief, & ordered North for his examination; Lt Cmder Bancroft Gherardi, from duty at the Naval Rendezvous, Phil, Pa, & ordered to command the **Tahoma**.
Appointment Revoked: Acting Ensign L H White.

Police Affairs. 1-Hugh Fitzsimmons, a barkeeper, for violating the law by selling liquor without a license was fined $20. He became enraged against the cmplnt, & proceeded to take the amount out of his back, when he was again arrested for assault & battery. He was held to bail to answer at court. 2-Chas Carter, a negro laborer, was arrested for disorderly conduct on the streets: fined $5, in default of which he was committed for 30 days. 3-Darby Cohen, tavern-keeper, was arrested for selling liquor without a license: fined $20.90. 4-Chas Hertmiller, Chas Hagerman, John Shul, Wm Gallant, & Carol Hoffman, were arrested for neglecting to clean the snow from their pavements: fined Hertmiller $5, & the others $2 each.

Orphans Court-Judge Purcell. 1-Yesterday the caveat to the will of the late Jos Follansbee was withdrawn, & the will being proved by two witnesses, [the third being out of the country,] was admitted to probate for personalty, & letters of administration were issued to Saml A Peugh, who gave bond in $3,000. 2-An exemplified copy of the will of the late Walter Herrons, of Norfolk, Va, was filed. 3-Mrs Naomi Utermehle was appointed guardian to orphan of the late C H Utermehle; bond, $7,000. 4-The first individual accounts & the first general account of the guardian of the orphans of Danl Brown, as also the first & final account of the administrator of Danl Brown; the first & final account of the administrator of Geo Johnson; the second & supplemental account of the administrator de bonis non of the late Cmdor C W Morgan, with an account of the personal estate, were proved & passed by the court.

Alexandria: the charges preferred against Mr Jas F Walsh, the Superintendent of the Night Watch, by Mayor Latham, of gross neglect of duty, the most flagrant violations of law, & malfessance in ofc, have been sustained. Jas F Walsh is dismissed as Superintendent of the Night Watch.

Aunt Milly, a colored woman, formery belonging to Capt Jas M Harris, residing near Rockfish Gap, Nelson Co, died at the residence of that gentleman on Jan 7th, in the 136th year of her age. She was born in 1731, in the beginning of the reign of George II. She was a cotemporary of Pope, Swift, & Bolingbroke, though probably she never heard of them. –Charlottesville Chronicle

Mrd: on Jan 16, at the First Baptist Church, by Rev A D Gillette, D D, Mr J W Vanderpoel, of N Y, to Bessie, daughter of the late Jas B Clarke, of Wash City. No cards.

Died: on Jan 19, in Wash City, after a lingering illness, Thos H Donaldson, in his 72nd year. His funeral will be from the residence of his son, Jas Donaldson, 358 18th st, on Jan 21, at 2 o'clock P M.

Died: on Jan 20, Clinton Beall, aged 2 years & 9 months, son of Richd H & Virginia B Willet. His funeral will be on Jan 22 at 2 o'clock, from the residence of his parents, 473 13th st west.

Memphis, Jan 20. The steamer **Platte Valley** has not gone to pieces, & some baggage is saved by cutting through the deck. Nothing further is known in reference to those lost, as they were chiefly from the North, & all books are lost.
+
Among the lost on the steamer **Platte Valley** was Judge McBride, of Monroe Co, Missouri.

Hon Saml Chilton, of Fauquier Co, Va, died at his residence in Warrenton on Monday last, after a protracted illness, in the 63rd year of his age. He was an able lawyer & a good counsellor.

The real estate of the late Col John F Carter, of Wash City, in this county, was sold by N C Stephens, trustee in equity, on Jan 15 as follows: **Melrose tract**, 199 acres, bought by Messrs Geo W Cochran, John W Boteler, & Geo E Kennedy, for $8,500; small tract of 12 acres purchased by Mr Perry W Browning for $102; undivided interest of Col Carter in a tract of 225 acres purchased by Mr Chas W Boteler for $1,250. –Prince Georgian

Orphans Court of Wash Co, D C, Jan 19, 1867. In the case of Eben L Childs, exc of Rebecca Winn, deceased, the executor & Court have appointed Feb 9th next, for the final settlement of the personal estate of the said deceased, of the assets in hand. -Jas R O'Beirne, Reg/o wills

TUE JAN 22, 1867
The Postmaster General has made the following changes since Jan 17, 1867:
Louisiana: Jackson, East Feliciana parish, Miss S McKenna, vice A McKenna, deceased; Lloyd's Bridge, Rapides parish, G H Sales, vice H A Frisbie, resigned.
N J: Phillipsburg, Warren Co, C Sitgraves, vice L M Teel, removed.

Brvt Brig Gen H C Gillem, colonel 24th U S Infty, assigned to the command of the Military District of Mississippi.

The Fourth Auditor on Saturday issued a certificate to Geo M Colvocoressis for $19,101, being his share of prize money for the capture of the blockade-runner Stephen Hart.

A bust of Lord Macaulay has, with the permission of the Dean & Chapter, been placed in Westminster Abbey by his sister, Lady Trevelyan. It rests upon a handsome bracket, designed by Mr Scott, in the immediate neighborhood of the grave & of Addison's statue, in Poet's Corner.

Navy Bulletin, Jan 4. Placed on Sick Leave of Absence: Acting Ensign Abraham A Very. Detached: Cmdor Thos Turner, from duty in connection with iron-clads at League Island, Pa, & placed on waiting orders; Cmder John Irwin & Lt Cmder Edw Y McCauley, from duty at League Island, Pa, in connection with iron-clads, & placed on waiting orders. Midshipmen A H Carter, J N Hemphill, Louis N Hawsel, Edw Woodman, Benj S Richards, & Wm J Moore, from the ship **Osceola**, & ordered to the ship **Monongahela**. Ordered: Cmder Geo W Raymond & Lt Cmder Edw W Henry, to duty at League Island, Pa, in connection with iron-clads; Cmdor O S Glisson, to command the naval station at League Island, Pa; Acting Ensign Henry Taylor, to the ship **Vermont**; Acting Volunteer Lt Geo W Rodgers, Acting Masters John C Marony & Chas Ackley, & Acting Ensigns John H Chapman & F H Waite, to duty at League Island, Pa, in connection with iron-clads.

Died: on Jun 21, at his residence, in Wash City, Johnson Hellen, in his 66th year. His funeral will take place from 432 D st on Jan 24, at 11 o'clock A M.
+
Mr Johnson Hellen, a lawyer, long & favorably known to nearly every resident of Wash, died yesterday after a short illness. Surrounded by wealth, & enjoying an enviable reputation, he has been summoned to the spirit land in the full maturity of life. [Jan 23rd newspaper: Mr Hellen was a native of Wash City, & in early life studied law, & was admitted to practise in Montg Co Court, but returned to Wash City, where his family resided; married & settled here. He was admitted to the bar of the Circuit Court of the District on May 14, 1826, on motion of Mr Swann, the U S Atty at that time. He was one of the oldest inhabitants of our city, & one of the oldest surviving members of the bar of the late Circuit Court. His tall, spare, & striking figure & expressive face bid strangers to inquire who he was.]

Died: Jan 20, Josephine, daughter of John & Catharine Brannan, aged 1 year, 3 months & 5 days.

Died: on Jan 20, in Gtwn, D C, Eleanor, wife of Saml Cropley. Her funeral is this afternoon at 3 o'clock.

Died: on Jan 21, at her residence, in Wash City, Mrs Ellen M Elwood, in her 54th year. Her funeral is on Jan 23 at 2 o'clock P M. [Star]

Having determined to retire from business, we offer our beautiful assortment of Jewelry & Fancy Goods at First Cost. –A M Townshend & Co, Jewellers, 516 7th st, Wash.

Ex-Govn'r Miller, of Minnesota, has removed his residence to Phil.

Arthur B Masoner, formerly lt & regimental quartermaster of the 7th Ky cavalry, committed suicide at the Spencer House, in Cincinnati, on Thu, by taking morphine.

New Orleans, Jan 21. The remains of Gen Albert Sidney Johnston will be taken to Austin, Texas, on Wednesday, for final burial.

Personal. Capt Edw Hays, from Brooklyn, N Y, will find a letter for him at Welcker's Restaurant, 424 15th st, between N Y ave & H st.

Supreme Court of D C; Equity No 665, Docket 7. Galt vs O'Brien. Wm Y Fendall, trustee, reported that he sold the leasehold estate in part of lot 26 in square 513 for $1,150, to Michl Hoover, who has complied with the terms of sale. –R J Meigs, clk

Orphans Court of Wash Co, D C, Jan 19, 1867. In the case of Harriet B Coolidge, excx of Richd H Coolidge, deceased, the executrix & Court have appointed Feb 23 next, for the final settlement of the personal estate of the said deceased, of the assets in hand. -Jas R O'Beirne, Reg/o wills

Hon E D Holbrook, of Idaho, & ex-Govn'r Cummings, of Idaho, had a personal difficulty yesterday at Willard's Hotel, the principal damage being the breaking of several glass globes of the gas chandelier under which the affair took place.

WED JAN 23, 1867
Orphans Court-Judge Purcell. 1-Yesterday letters of administration with the will annexed were issued to John D McPherson on the estate of the late Timothy Winn; bond, $8,000. 2-The first & final account of the administrator of P E Brinsmade, & the first account of the guardian of the orphan of Nelson C Driver, were approved & passed. 3-The death of the late Johnson Hellen, a member of the bar, was announced by M Thompson, & after some appropriate remarks by the Judge, in respect to his memory the Court adjourned.

Criminal Court-Judge Fisher. The Dist Atty has entered a ***nolle pros*** in each of the following cases: R Hawlett, indicted for perjury; Geo Boston, for larceny; Elias Robinson & Chas Blue, for burglary; Geo Rawlings, convicted of an assault & battery in 2 cases; Jos R Wooster, indicted for an assault with intent to produce abortion; Geo Smith, convicted of larceny; Saml Surbury & Augustus L Willis, indicted for libel; Jas Coleman, assault & battery; Richd Lucas alias Sonny Lucas, larceny; same party with Mathew Robinson, larceny.

Gtwn: the stable of Mr Chas Mix, on Valley st, was entered on Monday night, & 2 valuable carriage horses were stolen therefrom.

Police Affairs: 1-Thos H Matthews, for larceny of a hat, was committed to jail for court; 2-Ann Geary, for petty larceny, sent to jail for court. 3-Herman Smith, selling liquor on Sunday: fined $20. 4-S Benzinger, for creating a nuisance by depositing a cart load of slaughter house offal in the canal at the foot of 9th st: fined $5. 5-Jas Henry, colored, by way of mitigating the severity of the weather, helped himself to about 2 cords of Mr Geo T Raub's wood, for which offence he will be warmed at the expense of the District until his case is tried in court.

Nat P Willis, the poet & essayist, died on Sunday last, his 60th birthday, at *Idlewild*, his residence, on the Hudson river, where he has for some years lived in retirement, the victim of consumption, which was the cause of his death. [Jan 24th newspaper: Nathl P Willis was born in Portland, Me, Jan 20, 1807; his father & grandfather were publishers, the latter having been an apprentice in the ofc with Benj Franklin, & a member of the famous Boston Tea Party. His father was one of the founders of the Boston Recorder, the first firmly established religious newspaper in the country. Nathl the third [both father & grandfather bore the name Nathl] received the rudiments of education at the Boston Latin School & the Phillips Academy at Andover, & graduated from Yale College at age 20 years. In England, in 1835 he married Mary Leighton Stace, daughter of Commissary Gen Stace, in command of the Royal Arsenal at Woolwich. In 1837 he returned & purchased a retreat on the Susquehanna river, near Oswego, N Y, which he christened *Glen Mary*, after his wife. It was there in 1839, that his daughter Imogene was born. After the death of his wife, he returned to Europe. In 1845, in N Y, he married Cornelia, the only daughter of Hon Jos Grinnell, of New Bedford, Mass, by whom he had a son & 2 daughters. Not long after his second marriage he selected *Idlewild* as his home.]

Alexandria: The little daughter of Mr Lewis Brill, who was so severely burned last week at Mr Harmon's, we regret to learn, is lying in a critical condition, & not expected to recover.

Toronto, Jan 22. Thos Carney, convicted of Fenianism, has been sentenced to be hung on Mar 15. Geo J Matthews has been discharged.

Franklin, Ky, Jan 20. The jury have returned a verdict of murder in the first degree against W P King & Abe Owen. The remaining 10 prisoners will be tried for robbery in the recent railroad affair.

Mrd: on Jan 22, by Rev Fr Walter, Mr Andrew T Owens, of Oxford, Miss, to Miss Sallie A Davis, of Wash City. No cards.

Died: on Jan 21, in Gtwn, Miss Lizzie E Faxon, aged 20 years & 10 months, daughter of Chas Faxon.

Died: on Jan 2, at St Anthony, Minn, Rev W A Smallwood, D D, aged 62 years.

Died: on Jan 21, at his residence in Wash City, Johnson Hellen, in his 66th year. His funeral will take place from 432 D st, on Jan 24, at 11 o'clock A M.

THU JAN 24, 1867
Navy Bulletin for Jan 15 & 16. Appointment Revoked: Acting Ensign F J Locke. Ordered: Paymaster Arthur Burtis, jr, to the ship **St Louis**, League Island, Pa; Lt Cmder V J Cromwell, to the Naval Academy. Detached: Passed Assist Paymaster Geo H Griffing, from duty in connection with iron-clads at League Island, Pa, & ordered to settle his accounts.

Criminal Court-Judge Fisher. 1-In the cases of David Moore, Jos P Gloetzback, Peter Sweitzer, & Fred'k Stahl, indicted for a nuisance, a *nolle pros* was entered. 2-Kate Simmons, convicted of keeping a disorderly house-sentenced to jail for 30 days.

Alexandria Gaz: Capt E E Mulliner, of the steamer **E C Knight**, died suddenly on Sunday last. He was caught by ice some 3 weeks ago in Quantico Creek, & had been lying there in company with the U S gunboat **Ascutney**, & the schnr **J S Havens**, ever since. Accompanied by Mr Sharp, the chief engineer of the steamer, & Capt Alfred Lewis, of the **J S Havens**, they started in a small boat, upon which skates had been placed, for this city. The severe snow storm of Sunday compelled them to put back, when the boat was struck against a cake of ice, was upset, & the back of Capt Mulliner's head struck against the projecting piece of ice, his skull was fractured, & he died that evening. The capt's body, encased in a box, was brought to this city yesterday, over the road from Quantico, taken in charge by Capt Jos Denty, the former cmder of the **E C Knight**, at whose house it was laid out & prepared for interment, & will be forwarded by express at once to where he resided, Freeport, Long Island. The brother of the deceased, who accompanied the body to this city, expresses his warmest thanks to the ofcrs & crew of the **Ascutney**.

I have this day succeeded my father, Wm Tucker, in the Merchant Tailoring Business, 426 Pa ave, between 4½ 6th sts. –Wm E Tucker, Jan 21, 1867, Wash City.

Alex'r Smith, poet, author of the "Life Drama," "City Poems," Alfred Hagart's Household," & other books, died on Jan 5, near Edinburgh. He was still young, just entered his 37th year. -N Y Post

Despatch from New Orleans, published in the N Y papers on Monday, stated that Mrs Horton, widow of Rev Mr Horton, who was killed in the July riots in that city, had been endeavoring for some time past to bring a suit against the city but had been unsuccessful. All the prominent lawyers of that city have declined to aid her.

Senate nominations confirmed: Edw Uhl, of N Y, Consul of the U S at Guatemala.
Wm W Averill, of N Y, consul gen'l of U S for British North American Provinces.
Geo F Kettell, of N Y, consul of the U S for Rhenish Bavaria.
Andrew J Stevens, of Iowa, consul for the U S at Windsor, Canada.
Madison E Hollister, of Ill, consul for the U S at Buenos Ayres.
Leroy Tuttle, assist treasurer of the U S at Wash, D C.
Jas A Hall, collector of customs at Waldoborough, Maine.
Thos McElrath, appraiser of merchandise, port of N Y.
Thos H Ridgate, 3rd lt in revenue-cutter service, vice Thos R Marshal, resigned.
F A Barnard, of N Y, to be com'r for th U S to the Paris Exposition.
Robt S Chilton, com'r of emigration.
Jas S Nelson, com'r of the Gen Land Ofc.
Stephen J Dalles, of Ill, to be principal clerk of surveys in Gen Land Ofc.
Saml M Black, register of land ofc, Legrand, Oregon.
Danl Chaplin, receiver of public moneys at Legrand, Oregon.
Danl Sigler, of Ind, register of land ofc, Natchitoches, La.
Edw D Thompson, register of land ofc, Santa Fe, New Mexico.
Edw A Allen, receiver of public moneys at Omaha, Neb.
Augustus L Chetain, assessor of internal revenue for the district of Utah.
Wm Breeden, assessor of internal revenue, New Mexico.
John S McFarland, assessor of internal revenue, 2nd district of Ky.
J Crochett Sayres, assessor of internal revenue, 6th district of Ky.
Benj Gratz, assessor of internal revenue, 7th district of Ky.
Thos J Carlisle, assessor of internal revenue, 3rd district of Tenn.
Wm S King, assessor of internal revenue, 3rd district of Mass.
Senate nominations rejected:
Thos J Stables, collector of customs, Belfast, Maine.
John M Davis, collector of customs, Genesee, N Y.
John Hanscom, collector of customs, Saco, Maine.
N Martin Custis, collector of customs, Oswegatchie, N Y.
John Atchinson, collector of customs, Port Huron, Mich.
W F Johnston, collector of customs, Phil.
Jos R Flanigan, naval ofcr, Phil.
E S Cocherell, collector of internal revenue, 8th district of Ky.
H S Blanton, collector of internal revenue, 7th district of Tenn.
Geo J Stealley, assessor internal revenue, 1st dist of West Va.
Thos V Shallcross, collector internal revenue, 1st dist of West Va.
Leroy Cofrau, collector of internal revenue, 9th district of Ky.
John M Duke, collector of internal revenue, 9th district of Ky.
John Bigler, assessor internal revenue, 4th district, Calif.
Asa Falkner, collector internal revenue, 3rd district, Tenn.
Solon Chase, assessor internal revenue, 1st district, Maine.
John C Sanborn, assessor internal revenue, 6th district, Mass.
John P Kilgore, appraiser of merchandise, Phil.
W B Randolph, capt, revenue cutter service.

It was reported in Concord, N H, last night, & it is very probably true, that David Parker, the well-known leader of the Canterbury Shakers, died yesterday. He had been sick from erysipelas for some days. –Boston Journal, Tuesday.

New Orleans, Jan 23. The remains of Gen Albert Sidney Johnston were placed on board the Galveston steamer this afternoon for removal to Texas. Among the Confederate generals present were Gens Beauregard, Barry & Hood. The services were impressive.

Franklin, Ky, Jan 23. Wm P King & Abe Owen, the train robbers, who subsequently killed Harvey King, one of the band, have been sentenced to be hanged on Mar 22. The remaining 10 prisoners charged with robbing the train were granted continuances until June.

Portland, Maine, Jan 23. Mr & Mrs A W Clark, of this place, & 4 of their boarders, Mr & Mrs Henry Kingsbury, Mr & Mrs Jas Dyer, came near losing their lives last night by poison. Mrs Kingsbury & Mr Dyer are still in critical situations. The attending physician pronounced the poison arsenic. How it was adminsitered is a mystery.

Chicago, Jan 23. The jury in the Stewart divorce case, wherein Emily J Stewart sought divorce from her husband, Rev Hart L Stewart, on the ground of adultery, brought in a verdict of not guilty, this afternoon. The case has been before the Superior Court of this city for the last 12 days, & the jury was out 18 hours.

Died: on Jan 19, at Cambridge City, Ind, Mrs Rettie S H Underwood, aged 20 years, 10 months & 10 days, wife of John I Underwood. Also, Rettie Gilberta Underwood, infant daughter of John I & Rettie S H Underwood. The mother died, as she had lived, a true Christian. Her end was perfect peace.

FRI JAN 25, 1867
Miss Laura Harris has arrived in Paris, & will soon make her appearance at the Athene.

Postmaster Randall made the following changes in postmasters since Jan 2, 1867:
<u>Ky</u>: Morehead, Rowan Co, G W Bocock, vice J Hargis, removed; Smileytown, Spencer Co, J Hougland, vice M Wakefield, resigned.
<u>West Va</u>: Sisterville, A S Thistle, vice C V McCoy, resigned.
<u>Ark</u>: Smithville, Lawrence Co, E Thornburgh, vice W J Moore; Indian Bay, Monroe Co, C C Clark, vice T J Key, resigned.
<u>Texas</u>: Livingston, Polk Co, Mrs Mary Kirgan, vice A Kirgan, deceased; Bagdad, Williamson Co, J D Mason, vice Mrs E Heenaz.
<u>Nevada</u>: La Platte City, Churchill Co, M W Hoyt, vice J E Pierce, resigned.

Died: Jan 24, in Salem, Mass, at the residence of his daughter, Mr John McKim, in his 78th year. His funeral will take place in Wash City, of which notice will be given.

The following appointments of members of the Metropolitan Police were made yesterday by the Metropolitan Police Board:

John A Swindle	S Tucker	L Jacobs
M H Greene	D W Jarboe	C P Hickman
E D Reed	R W Taylor	F W Langley
H C Volkman	Wm E Skelley	J J Gorman
Chas W Sebastian	Wm G Bird	Thos Marden
John A Haney	Chas Leach	John F Guy
Wm Cunningham	J W Richardson	C V McDermot
Thos Hamilton	Benj Fairchild	Andrew J Barnes
Jas Monroe	Thos Auldridge	Thos Cavanaugh
Jos Hampshire	Benj Ross	H T Eaton
A G Columbus	D Lynch	B F Peters
C W Proctor	B C Berry	

A special despatch from Annapolis from the Balt American, dated yesterday, says: "It is rumored here this morning that Surratt, the conspirator for the assassination of President Lincoln, is at the Naval School, where he is said to have arrived during the past night.

Police Affairs: 1-Peter Schneider, a repentant thief, who stole a gold watch & chain from his employer, returned the articles, & was turned over to the police & held for trial at court. 2-Geo E Ward, a gallant tar, was arrested for assault & battery, & committed to jail for court. 3-Leonard Huyck, the banker, has been committed to jail for court, in default of bail, for grand larceny of U S bonds amounting to $13,000. 4-Edw Wolf was fined $20 for violation of the liquor law. 5-Thos Morrow, a restaurant keeper, was arrested for passing & having in his possession a quantity of counterfeit fractional currency. Morrow was held to bail for court. 6-The cases against Henry Hemsler, Henry Martin, & Addison Hemsley, arrested on a similar charge, were dismissed.

N Y World. Gold medal presented to Edwin Booth Jan 22, at Winter Garden, inscribed:
TO EDWIN BOOTH
IN COMMEMORATION OF THE
UNPREDEDENTED RUN OF HAMLET
AS ENACTED BY HIM IN NEW YORK CITY
FOR ONE HUNDRED NIGHTS

Madam De Teschenberg, wife of the principal editor of the Vienna Gazette, had just supped gaily at the ball the other evening, & was about to depart, when, a waltz striking up, she told her husband she would just waltz three turns before going. But after the first round she requested her partner to stop, & almost immediately expired. She was an exceedingly fine woman & in the prime of life. –Foreign paper

Mr Wm Scott, an extraman connected with the Metropolitan Truck Co, was seriously injured on Wed while proceeding to the fire. He dismounted while the truck was going up Capitol Hill, slipped, falling under the wheels of the truck. He was taken to his home, where he was properly cared for.

Quenby. If this should meet the eye of Jos or Saml Quenby, sons of the late Francis Quenby, of Houghton Conquest, Bedfordshire, or any persons acquainted with them, they are requested to communicate to Mr E Quenby, Kempston, Bedford.

Despatch from Lewiston, Maine, date Jan 21: awful tragedy in Auburn, Maine, during the past week. Two old ladies, named Mrs Kingsley & Mrs Clark, 60 & 70 years of age, were found murdered in their own house, about 2 miles from town, at a place called Young's Corner. The murderer's motive was rape. A man named Johnson has been arrested on suspicion, & is now in Auburn jail. [Jan 26th newspaper: Lewiston Journal of Monday: shocking tragedy in West Auburn, Maine, last week, in which the victims were Mrs Susannah Kennedy, a widow aged about 64 years, & Miss Polly Caswell, a maiden lady, aged about 37 years, who resided together alone in a cottage. Both had been murdered; a most horrible scene.] [Feb 15th newspaper: Mrs Kinsley's was the scene of the murders, at West Auburn. The negro hit Mrs Kinsley over the head with a chair, demanding money; she said it was with her daughter in Lewiston; Polly Caswell was struck from behind with an axe, & then struck her with a chair, killing her. Mrs Kinsley was then stabbed in the neck, giving a mortal wound. The murderers did not find any money. The negro asserts that when he entered the house he had not the least idea that murder was contemplated, but when the work was commenced he says he did his part. It is not known if Verill was the second person; he had been arrested,] [Feb 18th newspaper: Clifton Harris, colored, & Luther J Verrill, white, were arraigned Feb 14 in Lewiston, Maine, charged with being the murderers of Mrs Kinsley & Miss Caswell on Jan 17. Harris plead guilty, & the latter not guilty. Both were remanded to Auburn jail for trial in this county on the 4th Tues of April next.]

The funeral of the late Johnson Hellen took place from his residence, 5th & D sts, yesterday: services conducted by Rev B A Maguire, Pres of Gtwn College; Jos H Bradley, sr, John Carroll Brent, Gen Thos Ewing, Wm B Webb, & Wm Gunten being the pall-bearers. The cottege was a very long one, & proceeded to **Mount Olivet Cemetery**, where the remains were placed in the vault.

Died: Jan 24, in Salem, Mass, at the residence of his daughter, Mr John McKim, in his 78th year. His funeral will take place in Wash City, of which notice will be given.

SAT JAN 26, 1867
Died: on Jan 24, in Gtwn, D C, after a long & painful illness, Mrs Jane H Dement, consort of the late Richd Dement, of Wash, D C, in her 72nd year. Her funeral will be from the residence of her son, Wm H Compton, Congress & Stoddard sts, Gtwn, D C, tomorrow, Sunday, the 27th, at 2 o'clock P M.

Died: on Nov 16, at Camp Grant, Richmond, of apoplexy, Mr Ebenezer P Piggott, in his 40th year, eldest son of the late Mason A & Ann R Piggott, of Wash City.

Died: on Jan 21, Mary Mildred, infant daughter of J Fendall & Edwardana Cain, aged 1 year & 8 months.

Navy Bulletin for Jan 18. 1-Resigned: Mate Geo H Appleton. 2-Ordered: Passed Assist Surgeon Edw M Stier, to duty at the Naval rendezvous at Boston, Mass.

An engine, with 20 employes on board, was thrown from the track of the Long Island railroad, near Jamaica, on Wed, one man, Jas McLaughlin, being instantly killed, & the engineer was mangled, perhaps fatally.

Mr Richd B Mullikin, residing in the *Forest*, after lying ill with pneumonia for some time, expired on Sunday, Jan 20. His wife, who had been also prostrated with the same disease, died 2 days afterwards. They had been married for many years, had lived as examples of conjugal life, & leave a large family of children to mourn so severe a loss. Mr Mullikin was long one of our county commissioners, & discharged his duties with great acceptability. He was very popular & highly respected.
–Prince Georgian

Rouse's Point, N Y, Jan 25. Collision between the express & mail trains on the Ogdensburg & Lake Champlain railroad occurred this morning. The engineer, Wm Davis, of the Western mail train was killed; Benj Pecor, fireman on the express train, had his ankle crushed. Passengers injured: Mrs Thos P Cantwell, seriously in the face & head; Mrs Mary Joseph, of West Alburg, Vt, seriously cut in the head; Edw Missile, of Stottesville, C E, seriously injured in the leg. Several others, including Geo Barnum & Mayor Forrest, were more or less bruised.

Balt, Jan 25. A young man 19 years of age, Wm Hixley, was shot & fatally wounded by a policeman tonight. He had failed to halt when ordered.

Rochester, Jan 25. Rev Joel Lindsley, the man who whipped his 3 year old child to death, last Jun, in Selby, Orlens Co, is now undergoing a trial for manslaughter at Albion. Great excitement over the trial. [Jan 28th newspaper: Rev Lindsley has been found guilty of manslaughter in the 2nd degree.]

Liszt has quitted his residence in the Monte-Mario, Rome, where he lived up to now, & gone to the monks of Santa Francesco Romano, whose cloister is in the middle of the ruins of the old Forum.

The Baroness Deslandes, connected with the great banking firm of Oppenheim & Co, of Cologne, threw herself from a window of her house there on Dec 26, on hearing of the sudden illness of a child she had left in France. She died from her injuries on Dec 31st, aged 24 years.

Dept of the Interior, U S Patent Ofc, Wash, Jan 21, 1867. Ptn of Alfred J Watts, of Brooklyn, N Y, praying for the extension of a patent granted to him on Apr 26, 1853, for an improvement in Processes for Preparing Gold, for 7 years from the expiration of said patent, which takes place on Apr 26, 1867. -T C Theaker, Com'r of Patents

Orphans Court of Wash Co, D C. Letters of administration on the personal estate of Prather Lee, late of Wash Co, D C, deceased. –Eliz Lee, admx c t a

MON JAN 28, 1867
Navy Bulletin. Ordered, Jan 19. Gunner Thos Robinson, to ordnance duty at St Helena. Honorably Discharged, Jan 19. Acting Volunteer Lt & Pilot Martin Freeman, to take effect Jan 20; Acting Ensign Geo W Prindle, Jan 13.

Police Affairs: 1-Thos Peace: violating a Corp law by selling goods by samples, fined $20. 2-Robt Jones & Geo Williams: grand larceny, committed to jail for court. 3-Isaac Johnson, colored, on charge of petit larceny, committed to jail for court.

Mr S S Hoover, of Wash City, purchased of Mrs L A Tarleton 30 acres of land, about 2½ miles from Wash City, on the Bladensburg road, for $11,000. The place has on it a handsome residence with the necessary outhouses. Green & Williams, aucts, sold a tract of land in Wash Co called *Aaron*, & part of lots 1 & 8, in Dundas' subdivision, with improvements, to Rezin Aswold, for $8,000; & lot 12 in square 788, on south A st, between 3rd & 4th sts, at 11 cents per foot, to Catharine A Shawner.

Orphans Court-Judge Purcell. 1-On Sat, the will of the late Johnson Hellen was filed & partially proven. He nominates his son-in-law, G Fant, his friend, John B Blake, & sons Clifton, Clarence, & Frank Hellen, executors & trustees of the personal estate; Dr Blake & Mr Fant guardians to his sons Chas, Eugene, & Jos Hellen, & bequeaths his improved property, with the exception of his present residence, to the executors, the proceeds of which he directs to go to the children which he names, giving a specified sum to each, & among other annuities provides for one of $500 to Eliza Goddard, a colored woman. 2-Letters of administration were issued to Michl Connor, on the estate of Catherine Noonon; bond, $100. Sophia C Snyder was appointed guardian to the orphans of John M Snyder; bond, $20,000. 3-The 3rd general account of the guardian to the orphans of John Crome, & the 3rd & final account of the same, & the first & final account of the executrix of Valentine Blanchard, were approved & passed.

On Friday last Ofcr Gordon, of the 6th Ward, arrest Sgt Wm C Walter, of the Marine Corps, charged with killing Pvt Jas Streeks, on Jan 23. The marines were getting a supply of ice for the barracks from the river. Pvt Streeks was placed under arrest for some cause, & in an altercation, Sgt Walter, being in charge of the squad, struck Streeks with an ice-hook, which caused his death. Walter is held until further investigations have been made.

Dept of the Interior, U S Patent Ofc, Wash, Jan 23, 1867. Ptn of Jas S Taylor, of Danbury, Conn, praying for the extension of a patent granted to him Jay 3, 1853, for an improvement in Machines for Shrinking Hat Bodies, for 7 years from the expiration of said patent, which takes place on May 3, 1867.
-T C Theaker, Com'r of Patents

Jurors drawn on Friday to consitute the petit jury of the Circuit Court to be held on the first Tuesday in Feb:

B F Thorn	Jas Anderson	D E Irving
Warren Lowe	Geo H Grant	Chas Homiller
J H Sherwood	R H Willet	Jos Betzwell
Silas H Moore	M W Galt	Chas H Lloyd
Jos Redfern	Jas A Crane	Saml C Wroe
T W Miller	Jos Venable	Henry C Bergling
Thos Goodrich	David McClellan	W W Bean
H Clay Stewart	Francis Columbus	Thos Dewdney
Edw Hawley	John Saul	

Dept of the Interior, U S Patent Ofc, Wash, Jan 25, 1867. Ptn of Rollin White, formerly of Springfield, Mass, but now of Lowell, Mass, for the extension of a patent granted to him on Apr 3, 1855, & reissued to him in 3 divisions on Oct 27, 1863, for an improvement in Repeating Firearms, for 7 years from the expiration of said patent, which takes place on Apr 3, 1869. -T C Theaker, Com'r of Patents

House of Reps: 1-Cmte on Foreign Affaris: bill for the relief of Geo W Fish, consul at Ningpo: passed. Same cmte: joint resolution to pay to Townsend Harris, of N Y, formerly consul general at Japan, $1,645.83, for diplomatic services, etc, between Oct, 1856, & Jan, 1858: passed. Same cmte: joint resolution for the allowance to Jas Keenan, late U S consul at Hong Kong, exchange upon his balances: passed. Same cmte: bill for the payment of $2,354.24, to Henry P Blanchard, for services as marshal at Canton, China: passed. 2-Cmte on Invalid Pensions: bill for the relief of Sol P Smith, 115th N Y volunteers. Bill for the relief of Reuben Clough: laid on the table. Bill for the relief of the minor children of Jacob M Henshaw, deceased: passed. Bill for the relief of Peter Anderson: laid on the table. Bill for the relief of Barbara Fry: passed. Bill granting pension to Jane Clemens, of D C: passed. Bill giving increased pension to John J Soban: passed. Bill granting pension to Hiram Hedrick, of Peoria, Ill: passed. Bill for the relief of Lemuel Wooster; relief of John Morean, of Machias, N Y; & of the minor children of Solomon Long: all passed.

Col Thos Means, confined in prison for assaulting citizens & abusing his wife, was, on Jan 2nd, taken from the custody of the sheriff, & hung in the court-room till dead, by a party of 15 or 20 men in disguise, at Fernando de Taos, New Mexico.

Eliz Cady Stanton, Chas Lenox Redmond, Louisa Jacobs & Susan B Anthony are stumping N Y State in favor of universal **suffrage**, including ***woman suffrage***.

Appointments confirmed & rejected by the Senate.
On Sat the following nominations were confirmed:
Hugh J Anderson, Auditor Treasury for the Post Ofce Dept.
Chambers McKibbin, Assist Treasurer, U S Mint, Phil.
Archibald L Snowden, Chief Coiner of the Mint, Phil.
Noah L Jefferies, com'r to ascertain the amount of money expended in West Va.

Surveyors of Customs:
Henry W Gladding, Warren & Barrington, Rhode Island.
Wm L Ashmore, Burlington, N J.
Richd R Bolling, Louisville, Ky.

Postmaster: Frank Clendennin Madison, Whitesideley, Ill.

Collectors of Internal Revenue:
John A Hunter, 12th Dist Ohio.
Stephen J McGroaty, 2nd Dist Ohio.
Nathl S Howe, 6th Dist Mass.
Henry A Grant, 1st Dist Conn.

Assessors of Internal Revenue:
Geo B Arnold, 13th Dist Ohio.
Wm M Fitzhugh, 7th Dist Va.
Austin Savage, Idaho.
W C Binney, 5th Dist Mass.

Rejections: The Senate rejected the following:
Wm Millward, Director of the Mint, Phil.
John McGinnis, of Ill, U S Minister to Stockholm.

Assist Assessors of Internal Revenue:
Joshua W Warner, 6th Dist, Ohio.
Thos Miller, 7th Dist, Ohio.
Wm E Schofield, 8th Dist, Ohio.
Frank Baker, 9th Dist, Ohio.
Basil C Brown, 14th Dist, Ohio.
Matthew D Freer, 26th Dist, N Y.
Wm Quail, 24th Dist, Pa.
Basset Langdon, 1st Dist, Ohio.
Andrew S Holladay, __ Dist, Nebraska.
Thos Halley, 21st Dist, N Y.
Owen D Downey, 2nd Dist, West Va.
Luther Stephenson, 2nd Dist, Mass.
H R Coggshell, 5th Dist, Pa.
J F Hubbard, 19th Dist, N Y.

Collectors of Internal Revenue:
Wm Welleseley, 23rd Dist, N Y.
Morgan L Harris, 8th Dist, N Y.
Julius A Pean, 6th Dist, Ohio.
John R Finn, 14th Dist, Ohio.
Geo W Thatcher, __ Dist, Idaho.
John T Tanner, 3rd Dist, Ala.

H W Fish, 21st Dist, N Y.
Chas S Cary, 31st Dist, N Y.
Thos W Egan, 9th Dist, N Y.
David H Abell, 25th Dist, N Y.
Geo M Beebe, Nevada.
Calvin E Pratt, 3rd Dist, N Y.
Geo W Barry, 5th Dist, Maine.
E W Pierce, 1st Dist, Mass.
Church Howe, 8th Dist, Mass.
Nathl C James, 5th Dist, Pa
Collector of Customs:
M H Beaumont, Perth Amboy, N J.

Supreme Court of D C. #640. H E Gross & wife vs Rosina Steiner et al. Auditor to state the trustee's accounts & the rent account of Rosina Steiner & the shares of the parties interest in the fund, at his ofc on Feb 21, at 12 o'clock.
–Walter S Cox, auditor

Govn'r Swann has granted a futher reprieve, until Mar 1, to Wm Jones, the colored man in jail at Marlboro, under sentence of death, for committing rape.

Jessie McDermott, Guardian of Geo R McDermott, Chas F McDermott, Frank P McDermott, & Jessie H McDermott, having reported to the court that, inpursuance of its decree ratified & approved by the Supreme Court of D C, she sold the interest of her said wards in the following property in Wash City: strip of ground adjacent to the dwlg house built on lot 20 in square 105, which was owned by the late Wm McDermott, save & except the four feet adjacent to & east of said dwlg, with a depth equal to the depth of said lot 20, at public auction, for the sum of $1 per square foot, to John G Clark, & the purchaser has complied with the terms of sale.
–Wm F Purcell, Judge of the Orphans Court. –Jas R O'Beirne, Reg/o Wills

TUE JAN 29, 1867
Chambers session, Court in Equity, before Justice Olin. 1-McIntyre vs Rodier. No 762, Docket 8. Order of court for trustee to show cause why he shall not pay F Shafer $100. 2-Grass et al vs Steiner et al. No 640. Order appointing E Carnes trustee, instead of C H Utermehle, deceased.

Orphans Court of Wash Co, D C, Jan 22, 1867. In the case of John Lang, administrator c t a of Eleanor R Lang, deceased, the administrator c t a & Court have appointed Feb 16, 1867, for the final settlement of the personal estate of the said deceased, of the assets in hand. -Jas R O'Beirne, Reg/o wills

Orphans Court of Wash Co, D C. Letters of administration on the personal estate of Catharine Noonan, late of Wash, D C, deceased. –Michl Conner, adm

Mrd: on Jan 24, at the residence of John Bowie, Anne Arundel Co, Md, by Rev Dr Pinckney, Chas W B Harris, of Brooklyn, N Y, to Amelia G Bowie, of Md.

Mrd: on Jan 12, at London, at the residence of his Excellency Manuel Carvallo, Chilian Minister at Brussels, London, & Paris, Senor Jose D Merino Benavente, of Chili, to Miss Henriqueta Carvallo, 3rd daughter of the Minister & grand-daughter of Jas H Causten, of Wash City.

Died: on Jan 27, at the residence of Wm M Belt, 487 H st, Edw C Dyer, in his 47th year. His funeral will be at St Patrick's Church, on Jan 30, at 9½ o'clock A M. [Jan 31st newspaper: the late Mr Ed C Dyer, well known & respected merchant, was buried at *Mt Olivet Cemetery*, yesterday.]

The funeral of Mr John McKim, of Wash City, will be this afternoon at 2 o'clock, at Christ Church, [Episcopal,] on G st south, near the Navy Yard.

Died: on Jan 26, at his home, in Newark, Dela, Mr A B Waller, aged 66 years, long a resident of Wash City, where he was well known & highly esteemed. At the time of his decease he was a valued & efficient general agent of the Post Ofce Dept. A devoted family & large circle of friends mourn his loss.

Died: on Jan 25, Mrs Jane C, wife of John H Batham, aged 50 years.

Mrs H C Butts, Teacher of Vocal Music. Residence: 452 12th st, between G & H sts, Wash. [Ad]

Estwick Evans, a native of N H, died on Nov 20, 1866, in N Y, but his remains were brought to Washington. Rev Dr Pinckney, to whom he was much attached, pronounced a just tribute to his memory, as a man of great ability & virtue, who walked in the light of the Divine Word & died in the communion of the Catholic Church. –R R G

Home School, under the care of Miss Eliza C Adam, has opened in Alexandria, Va. The number of Boarders is limited to 8, & no day scholars received. References: Judge Wylie, & Mrs R F Buel, Wash; Rev Dr Packard, Fairfax Theological Seminary; Col Geo W Brent, & Rev J T Leftwich, Alexandria. Miss Eliza C Adam, Washington & Prince sts, Alexandria, Va.

WED JAN 30, 1867
Jos Southard, one of the conductors on the Orange & Alexandria railroad freight train, in coupling the cars at Orange Court House on Friday, had his hand badly injured.

Mr Orlando G Henderson, on Sat last, while on King st, accidently shot himself in the calf of the leg with a pistol. No serious injury is anticipated from the wound.

The colored High School in Washington contains 48 single desks, fashioned after the Boston school furniture; Miss Lord has her school under the most complete control. Intermediate Dept Highest Division: Miss L Wright, Clinton, Mass; 44 scholars. Intermediate-2nd Division: Miss Kate G Crane, Worcester, Mass; 46 scholars. Intermediate-3rd Division: Miss E A Hubbard, Utica, N Y, 44 scholars. Primary Dept-Highest Division: Miss Martha C Hart, Clinton, Mass; 55 scholar. Primary-2nd Division: Miss Sophie P Parsons, Utica, N Y; 38 scholars. Primary-3rd Divison: Miss H E Hamil, Hartford, Conn. Primary-4th Division: Miss Rebecca H Elwell, Hartford, Conn. The above comprise the 8 schools, four below & four above, in the large house. Miss A S Simmons, Essex, Mass, has a primary school in one of the small schoolhouses in which some 40 small children were learning the alphabet.

The value of the estate of the late Edw Mott Robinson, of New Bedford, Mass, is sworn at four and a half millions.

Police Affairs: 1-S S Adams, hailing from the rural districts, was arrested yesterday for huckstering without a license & fined $5. 2-King Hutchinson, a negro butcher, for an assault & battery upon Benj Price, gave bail for his appearance in court. 3-Sadie Hutchinson, charged by her employer, Wm Sullivan, with petit larceny, was held to bail for court. 4-Hansel Harris, arrested for the larceny of an overcoat, the properyt of Geo Paine, colored, was held for examination. The coat was stolen at the John Wesley Chapel during the religious service on Jan 20. 5-Orphan boy Thos Conlan was found wandering about in the cold on Monday night, & Lt Johnson, of the Second Precinct, took charge of the little fellow, who had strayed away from his grandparents. He was restored to his protectors yesterday morning. 6-Jas Digny & Jos Boyd were each fined $1.58 for violating the hack law, by running without a number. Augustus Barton & Chas Bruce, for the same offence, each fined $1.

New Orleans, Jan 29. The State Senate adjourned on account of the death of A A Abney.

Phil, Jan 29. Admiral Tegethoff, the hero of the great naval battle of Lis_a, visited the U S navy yard in this city today, & was received with field honors. He afterwards visited the fleet of monitors at League Island.

San Francisco, Jan 28. Calif leprosy in the Sandwich Islands. The leprosy prevailed to a fearful extend in the island of Waulauki. Thos F Wilson had taken charge of the consulate, as there was no consul in the place.

Balt, Jan 29. 1-Mrs McTavish, daughter of Chas Carroll of Carrollton, was buried from the Cathedral today. The funeral was largely attended. 2-Mr Richd P Bayley, State printer, died last evening. 3-Mr Danl Ruttle, one of the oldest printers in the country, died today.

Orphans Court of Wash Co, D C. Letters testamentary on the personal estate of Thos Johnson, late of Wash, D C, deceased. –Edmund Keefe, Thos McGrath, excs

Dept of the Interior, U S Patent Ofc, Wash, Jan 23, 1867. Ptn of John Tree, of Lowell, Mass, praying for the extension of a patent granted to him May 10, 1853, for an improvement in Knitting Looms, for 7 years from the expiration of said patent, which takes place on May 10, 1867. -T C Theaker, Com'r of Patents

Supreme Court of D C; Equity No 562. Zephaniah Jones vs Stringfellow & others. The above cause has been referred to me to state & report the trustees' account, & to ascertain & report what other creditors of Ann R Dermott, besides the cmplnt, are entitled to be paid out of the fund arising from the sale reported by the trustees. Parties interested are to appear before me at my ofc, Feb 9 next.
—Walter S Cox, auditor

Dept of the Interior, U S Patent Ofc, Wash, Jan 23, 1867. Ptn of John Tree, of Lowell, Mass, praying for the extension of a patent granted to him May 10, 1853, for an improvement in Warp Net Fabrics, for 7 years from the expiration of said patent, which takes place on May 10, 1867. -T C Theaker, Com'r of Patents

Orphans Court of Wash Co, D C. Letters of administration on the personal estate of Ann Roberts, late of Wash City, D C, deceased. —Wm E Roberts

Navy Bulletin. Ordered. Third Assist Engineer F Lovaire, to the ship **Michigan**. Resigned: Midshipman E C Turner, of the Naval Academy. Detached: Capt Robt N Stemble from the command of the ship **Canandaigua**, & placed on waiting orders; Mate Thos Cinelar, from the ship **Potomac**, & granted leave of absence. On Leave for Discharge: Acting Engineer Olin A Thompson.

Mr Ebenezer Wesman, 70 years of age, a soldier of the war of 1812, died suddenly at his residence, in Charlestown, Mass, on Sat, of heart disease. He was an esteemed citizen, & for the last 40 years a well-known iron manufacturer.

Hon Saml A Brown, a prominent lawyer, died at Lowell, Mass, on Sunday.

Orphans Court-Judge Purcell. 1-Yesterday the will of Thos Johnson bequeathing his estate to his son & daughter was filed & fully proven. Letters testamentary were issued on the estate to Edw McKeefe & Thos McGrath; bond, $800. 2-Letters of administration on the estate of Ann Roberts were issued to W E Roberts; bond, $1,200.

THU JAN 31, 1867
Mr A Kamara, superintendent of the Empire Woollen Works, in Brooklyn, committed suicide on Mon night by hanging himself from a beam in the upper story of his factory. Depression of spirits on account of business affairs is supposed to be the cause of the deed.

Navy Bulletin. Appointed: Oliver W Griffiths, of the ship **Saranac**, a carpenter. Resigned: Assist Surgeon Fred'k Krecker. Honorably Discharged: Acting Assist Paymaster Edw D Hayden from Feb 2, 1867; Mate Arthur B Arey.
Detached: Paymaster Robt Pettit, from duty as president of the examining board at Phil, & placed on waiting orders; Paymaster Jas D Murray, from duty as a member of the examing board at Phil, & ordered to resume his duties on the ship **Constellation**; Paymaster Jas Fulton & Passed Assist Paymaster Wm W Woodhull, from duty as members of the examining board at Phil, & placed on waiting orders; Acting Volunteer Lt F F Baury, from the Naval Hospital at N Y, & granted sick leave of absence.

On Sat last Mr John S Garland left his home on G st, between 19th & 20th sts, since which time nothing has been heard from him. He is a small, spareman, about 5 feet 5 inches high, & had on a brown, officer's overcoat, when last seen.

A man named Fred'k Guscetti was arrested in NY C, a few days ago, for fraud upon the Pension Ofc. He was formerly a member of the 47th N Y volunteers, & applied for a pension, under the name of Rollinger. It was ascertained that he was receiving a pension under the name of Guscetti, & had received over $500 pay under the name of Rollinger. He was committed for trial. Rollinger was a companion of the accused in the regt, but died in the Andersonville prison.

We record the death of Chas Augustus Davis, [of the old & well known firm of Davis & Brooks,] who died Sunday, somewhat suddenly, of Bright's disease of the kidneys. The orginal attack being pneumonia. He was widley known to the general public as a raconteur, a story teller of rare ability & absconding novelty. Mr Davis, at the ripe age of 72, is now gathered to his fathers, leaving behind many pleasant recollections. [He was the original N Y Jack Downing, not the Portland, Me, original, for he yet lives.] -N Y Express

Mrs Jane M *Sweet, of Kennebunk, Maine, has been indicted for the murder of her husband, Dr Nathl Sweet, last fall, by poisoning him with strychnine. She says that she only put it in his whiskey to cure his love for liquor, & that she accidentally gave him an overdose. [Feb 15th newspaper: The trial of Mrs Jane M *Swett, of Kennebunk, Maine, for homicide in causing the death of her husband by administering to him morphice, was concluded at Saco on Tuesday, Mrs Swett being convicted of manslaughter. On Sep 22 last Mrs Swett went out to the barn at an early hour & placed a teaspoonful of morphine about 10 grains, in weight, into a bottle of whiskey which her husband had hid in the hay.
*Two spellings of the last name: Sweet/Swett.

Police Affairs: 1-Jas Bateman was fined $20 for selling liquor without a license.
2-John Richards, charged with grand larceny, was locked up for examination.
3-Martha S Tidings was fined $3 for disorderly conduct in the colored Baptist Church in the 7th Ward.

Mrd: on Jan 30, at the Church of the Epiphany, Wash, D C, by Rev J V Lewis, Henry Francis Lyster, M D, of Detroit, Mich, to Winifred Lee, daughter of the late Capt Thos L Brent, U S A.

Mrd: on Jan 29, by Rev Geo L Mackenheimer, Robt C Jones, of Montg Co, Md, to Geo S, youngest daughter of the officiating minister.

Died: on Jan 29, in Wash City, Benjamin Pickarell, in his 85th year.

New Orleans, Jan 30. J J Bryant, a well known keeper of a taro bank in this city, was shot & killed at the St Charles Hotel tonight by John Fred'k Tate, a well known Texan lawyer. The difficulty originated in consequence of a forged check being passed upon Bryant by a third party.

Geo C Williams, committed for theft at Manchester, N H, on Thursday, killed himself by jumping from the corridor of the jail to the basement.

Irvin A Denson, formerly master-at-arms on the U S gunboat **Cayuga**, committed suicide by shooting himself through the head, on Sunday, in Brooklyn.

Two large boilers at the Delaware rolling mill, on Phillipsburgh, N J, exploded on Jan 21, killing Geo Richards, the first heater, & injuring 6 other employes.

FRI FEB 1, 1867
Hon Philip Johnson, Rep in Congress from the 11th District of Pa, died suddenly, at 8 o'clock P M yesterday, at his rooms, on H st, between 9th & 10th sts, in Wash City. Mr Johnson was in his seat on Friday last, although then complaining of feeble health. His indisposition assumed a more aggravated character but he was not thought by his medical attendant to be dangerously ill until last evening, when his illness suddenly increased, & terminated in his death, which is contributed to congestion of the liver. Mr Johnson was 49 years old on Jan 17th; a native of N J, but in 1839, removed to Northampton Co, Pa; his education was received at Lafayette College, after which he spent 2 years in the South, teaching school. Upon his return from the South he studied law, & was admitted to practise in 1848. Mrs Johnson was with him during his illness, & at the time of his death. His remains are to be taken to Easton, Pa, for interment. [Feb 15th newspaper: The remains of the late Hon Philip Johnson, will be removed this morning from the vault in the ***Congressional Cemetery***, to his late home at Easton, Pa for interment. The remains will be accompanied by Hon Saml McLean, of Montana, & Hon Mr Holbrook, of Idaho; Mr Ordway, sgt-at-arms of the House; Jas L Mingle, & D H Neiman, a cmte of citizens from Easton & other friends & relatives of the deceased.]

Gtwn Affairs: 1-Mr Chas S English, one of the police com'rs, fell on the ice yesterday & hurt himself so much that he was unable to attend to the duties of his ofc. 2-Thos McGuire also fell & broke his leg.

Police Items: 1-Catharine Gibbons was arrested for stealing a pair of pants from J Grady: she was sent to jail for court. 2-L S McDaniel was arrested on Wed for burglariously entering the White House, on N J ave, between B & C sts, kept by Mr McCausley, & stealing an amount of money from a man named Marshall Sproeger, a stranger in the city McDaniel admitted the robbery & said he only took $29. He was committed to jail for Court. 3-L Vanderhyden, a peddler of meerschaum pipes, was arrested for peddling without a license: fined $20.

Navy Bulletin, Jan 23. Honorably Discharged: Acting Chief Engineer Jas B Fulton, Jan 15; & Jos B Starr, Jan 24. Acting 2nd Assist Engineer Richd Nash, from Jul 15, 1865; Acting 3rd Assist Engineer Wm H Allen, Jan 10, 1867. Resigned: Midshipmen Edw F Welles, of the Navy Academy; Acting 3rd Assist Engineer John M Young, of the ship **Paul Jones**.

Albert Sidney Johnston, cmder of the rebel forces in the Mississippi dept fell at the battle of Shiloh. He was probably the best soldier in the Confederate army, & was an accomplished scholar, & a thorough gentleman. [Gen Grant made notice of his death, & an armistice was maintained during his funeral ceremonies.] Recently his remains were exumed & taken to Galveston, Texas, where great preparations were made for interring them with public obsequies, yesterday. But Gen Griffith, the Federal commandant at that post, interfered. He ordered that there should be on the occasion no ringing of bells, no public or private demonstrations of any organized association & that all persons who participated should appear as member of the family or friends of the deceased. These conditions were refused, & during the day the remains lay in state, while the principal business throughout the city were closed & draped in mourning. Such displays have often been tolerated by victors of the vanquished. –Albany Journal, [Rep] [Johnston was a Kentuckian; a great soldier; had endeared himself to the Texans by resigning his commission in the U S service, in 1834, & entering that of the Republic, having been the Adj Gen & senior Brig Gen of its army, then its Sec of War, &, before returning to the regular army, the colonel of its first regt raised for our war against Mexico, & lastly, it champion in the attempt at secession. Rochester [N Y] Union]

Dr Stephen Duncan, formerly of Natchez, Miss, died at his residence in Wash Square, N Y, on Wed, from an attack of paralysis, at the ripe age of 80 years. He was before the war the richest planter on the Mississippi, & the war swept away, of course, all his slave property, as well as all his other investments South, except the bare land. Mr Duncan was beloved by all who knew him, & he leaves not, we think, an enemy behind.

Galveston, Jan 31. B S Osborne, late capt of the Mexican gunboat **Brave**, has been dismissed from the service on the charge of misappropriating money & desertion. Osborne is well known in N Y. He served some time in Eldridge st for giving information on to the enemy during the rebellion.

Thos J Seliott, formerly from Va, a clerk at the Nashville railroad depot, was killed there on Sat by being accidentally run over by a locomotive.

A Canadian Roman **Catholic Miracle**. A document has been published by authority of the Roman Catholic Bishop of Quebec, giving the particulars of a miraculous cure effected lat New Years' day by the Immaculate Virgin Mary, & the authenticity of which is certified by Dr Lachanine, a graduate of the Lavel Univ. The scene of the miracle was the <u>Jesus Mary Convent</u>, at Point Levi, opposite Quebec. In Nov 1862, a nun of that institution, Sister Mary F Thomas, after an attack of pleurisy, went into a consumptive decline. Last May hemorrhage of the lungs commenced. In the month of Dec she had to take to her bed, being unable to dress herself. The symptoms became worse, & her confessor began to administer the last consolations of religion. At this stage the superior of the convent told her to pray for a cure. She did so, addressing herself to the Immaculate Mary. The other nuns did the same, & all were inspired with a firm faith that New Year's day would witness a cure. On Dec 31st candles were kept burning all day before the image of Mary. At six o'clock on New Year's morning she arose, after a refreshing sleep, perfectly cured. When the doctor came she opened the door to him, & he, on seeing her, was thunderstruck, & believed he was dreaming. He now certifies that on Dec 31st she was in the last stage of pulmonary consumption, & that on Jan 1st she was instantly cured, & that the cure is a miracle.

Edmund Hawks, one of the oldest residents of Oswego, N Y, died in that city on Monday.

Mrs D J Whiting committed suicide by hanging herself in the cellar of her residence, 145 Chelsea st, East Boston, on Monday.

A negro man, Thos W Jones, was shot & killed on Tuesday, by a white soldier, John Brennam, on duty at the Libby Prison, Richmond. There were about 20 negroes assembled at 19th & Cary sts, & the sentinels have orders to prevent any such assemblages, & Brennan being on duty at the time ordered them to disperse. The negroes refused, & Brennam, on their refusal, fired, the ball passing through the body & left arm of Jones, who died shortly after. Brennam will be examined by a military commission.

A large fire occurred at Hagerstown, Md, on Sunday night, burning the Eagle Hotel, kept by Mr Saml Shaw, who lost nearly all his furniture & is not insured. The following additional places were destroyed: Hagerstown Mail ofc-fully insured; clothing stores of J D Swartz, & Fell, Heimer & Bro, goods nearly all saved; & the drug store of J H Snively & Co, whose goods were partly saved. The loss of bldgs will fall on Messrs Wm Heyser & Geo Fechtig, both of whom are insured.

Mr Wm P Baum, an old & respected citizen of Pittsburgh, Pa, is dead.

John Bolan, employe of the Dwight Manufacturing Co, at Chicopee, Mass, whose arm was caught in the machinery & torn off a few days since, died on Sunday. Amputation was performed by dislocating the arm at the shoulder, but too late to save his life.

Supreme Court of D C, in Equity No 794. Jno P Murphy, guardian to Kate Neary, against Catharine Neary & Ann T Neary, heirs at law of the late Thos Neary, deceased. Statement of the trustee's account & distribution of funds, on Feb 7, at my ofc, 38 La ave, Wash. -E Carusi, special auditor

SAT FEB 2. 1867
The Senate on Soldiers. 1-N Martin Curtis, appointed Collector of the Customs, Dist of Oswegatchie, N Y, Aug 3, 1866, was rejected by the Senate Jan 22, 1867. Gen Curtis, in Apr, 1861, raised a company of volunteers, & on May 15 following was mustered into service as capt in the 16th N Y volunteers, & continued in service until Jan 15, 1866, when he was mustered out as brig general & brevet major general, to which position he was promoted upon his own merits, for gallant & meritorious services. In the attack upon *Fort Fisher* Gen Curtis was wounded, losing one eye. 2-John Atkinson, appointed Collector of Customs, District of Port Huron, Mich, Aug 3, 1866, & rejected by the Senate Jan 22, 1867. Lt Col Atkinson entered the army as 2nd lt 22nd Mich volunteers; promoted to capt & major of that regt, & to lt colonel of the 3rd Mich volunteers; took part in the campaigns against Gen Bragg from Cincinnati & Louisville to Chattanooga; under Gen Sherman at Atlanta; under Gen Thomas in defence of Nashville & Murfreesboro, & the last campaign in East Tenn; went to Texas, & was mustered out in Feb, 1866. 3-M H Beaumont nominated for Collector of the Customs, Dist of Perth Amboy, N J, & rejected by the Senate Jan 26, 1867. Col Beaumont entered the army in 1861; promoted 6 times during his term of service, which ended in Jul, 1865, when he was mustered out as colonel of the 1st N J cavalry. He was seriously wounded & permanently disabled in the action at Hatcher's Run, Va, Feb 6, 1865. His regt was in 69 general engagements, battles & skirmishes. 4-Thos W Egan, appointed Collector of Internal Revenue, 9th Dist of N Y, Aug 28, 1866, & rejected by the Senate Jan 26, 1867. Gen Egan entered the service Jul 1, 1861, as lt colonel 40th N Y volunteers, promoted to colonel Jan, 1863, & to brig general Sep, 1864; participated in the battles of Yorktown, Wmsburg, Fair Oaks, Glendale, Malvern Hill, second bull Run, Chantilly, Fredericksburg, Chancellorsville, Gettysburg, Mine Run, Wilkderness, Po River, Spottsylvania, North Anna, Polopotony, Coal Harbor, Petersburg, Strawberry Plains, Deep Bottom, & Boydton Roadd. He was wounded Jun 16, 1864, storming the enemy's works near Avery house, Va. Recommended for promotion for gallant conduct by Pres Lincoln, & Gen Grant has recommended him as an ofcr whose military record was of the first order. He left the service as a brvt major general Jan 15, 1866. 5-E W Pierce, appointed Collector of Internal Revenue, 1st Dist of Mass, Aug 3, 1866, & rejected by the Senate Jan 26, 1867. Col Pierce entered the service at the breaking out of the rebellion as colonel of the 29th Mass volunteers, lost his right arm in the battles before Richmond, & was honorably discharged in Nov, 1864. 6-Church Howe, appointed Collector of Internal Revenue for the 8th Dist of Mass, Aug 27, 1866,

& rejected by the Senate Jan 26, 1867. Capt Howe entered the service in 1861, in the old 6th Mass volunteers, & afterwards served as major & aide-de-camp to Gen Sedgwick. 7-Wm W Mosley, appointed Collector of Internal Revenue for the 23rd Dist of N Y, Oct 1, 1866, & rejected by the Senate Jan 26, 1867. He entered the service in the 149th N Y volunteers & was discharged May, 1863. He then served on the staff of Gen Slocum as confidential aid; was brevetted for meritorious services in Sherman's march to the sea, & for gallant conduct at the battle of Bentonville. 8-Luther D Stephenson, appointed Assessor of Internal Revenue, 2nd Dist of Mass, Nov 9, 1866, & rejected by the Senate Jan 26, 1867. He entered the service as capt of Co A, 32nd Mass volunteers, in Oct, 1861; promoted to major Aug, 1862, & to lt colonel in Dec, 1862; served with credit, receiving wounds at Gettysburg, Pa. He resigned Jun 28, 1864. 9-Wm E Schofield, appointed Assessor of Internal Revenue for the 8th Dist of Ohio, Aug 24, 1866, & rejected by the Senate Jan 26, 1867. He entered the service on the breaking out of the rebellion as capt 82nd Ohio volunteers; participated in the battles of Chancellorsville & Gettysburg; was provost marshal of the 20th corps during the Atlanta campaign. 10-Calvin E Pratt, appointed Collector of Internal Revenue, 3rd Dist of N Y, Aug 11, 1866, & rejected by the Senate, Jan 26, 1867. He entered the service in May, 1861, as colonel 31st N Y volunteers; was promoted to brig general Sep, 1862, & resigned as such in Apr, 1863. 11-Bassett Langdon, appointed Assessor of Internal Revenue for the 1st Dist of Ohio, Aug 2, 1866, rejected by the Senate Jan 26, 1867; entered the service as major 1st Ohio volunteers in 1861; served with distinction in the battles of Shiloh, Stone River, Liberty Gap; Chattanooga, & Chicka mauga; was severely wounded at Lookout Mountain, & was mustered out with his regt in 1864. 12-Julius A Penn, appointed Collector of the Internal Revenue, 6th Dist of Ohio, Sep 3, 1866, & rejected by the Senate Jan 26, 1867; entered the service at the breaking out of the war in co E, 22nd Ohio volunteers; was elected capt; subsequently promoted to major; served with distinction & gallantry& bears the marks of wound received in battle; was honorably discharged at the expiration of his term of service, having received injuries which prevented him from remaining longer in the service. [Since the above was in type we learn that Maj Gen Couch, appointed collector of the port of Boston, has been also rejected by the Senate. We have not his military record at hand, but it is familiar to the country.]

Hon Henry S Magraw, at present a member of the Md State Legislature, was seized suddenly on Tuesday last, with apoplexy, the disease that terminated in his death yesterday. Mr Magraw was born at West Nottingham, Port Deposit, Md, on Dec 17, 1815; educated at the academy there; studied law in Lancaster, Pa, admitted to the bar; was married & removed to Pittsburgh, where he engaged in the practice of his profession, & was eminently successful. In 1852 he went to Calif; on his return was elected State Treasurer of Pa; after this he purchased his father's estate in West Nottingham, Md, & removed to that place with his family. The body will be taken to his late residence in Md this morning, attended by a large number of friends & relatives.

Norristown, Pa, Feb 1. B F Hancock, father of Gen Hancock, died this morning, aged 67 years. The deceased was collector of internal revenue for the 6th Dist of Pa. Gen Hancock has arrived at home from the West.

Died: on Feb 1, of heart disease, Capt Edmund Barry, aged 48 years. His funeral will take place from the residence of his mother, 584 N J ave, Capitol Hill, on Sunday at 3 o'clock P M. [Balt & Richmond papers please copy.]

Died: Jan 31, 1867, at his residence, in Gtwn, Jos N Fearson, in his 72nd year of his age. His funeral will take place from his residence, 17 Congress st, Feb 3 at 2 P M.
+
Mr J N Fearson was one of our oldest citizens, well known & highly esteemed, having occupied various positions of trust & profit.

Mrd: on Jan 31, at St Aloyisus Church, by Rev Danl Lynch, S J, Valentine H Cuming, son of the late Wm Cuming, to Mary Louisa McLean, daughter of the late Wm McLean, of Chestertown, Md, & grand-daughter of Elias Marsh, of Wash City. [Md papers please copy.]

Navy Bulletin, Jan 25. <u>Orders Revoked</u>: Capt Chas W Pickering, to the command of one of the vessels in the European squadron. The revocation of the appointment of Mate Edwin D Richardson, dated Nov 28, 1865, & an honorable discharge has been granted him from that date. <u>Honorably Discharged</u>. Acting Assist Paymaster Josiah H Benton, from Sep 25, 1865. <u>Ordered</u>: 2nd Assist Engineer Geo R Holt, to duty at the Naval Academy; Acting 3rd Assist Engineer Russell A Wade, to temporary duty on board the ship **Chattanooga**. <u>Detached</u>: Capt Jas H Strong, from inspection duty at the N Y NavyYard, & ordered to the command of the ship **Canandaigua**.

The following nominations have been sent to the Senate: Hyland R Hulburd, to be Comptroller of the Currency; Col Wm G Moore, to be secretary to the Pres; & Mr Justus Steinberger, to the paymaster in the regular army, with the rank of major.

Hospital Steward Ernest Merz, U S A, has been relieved from duty in the Dept of the South, & ordered to duty in the Dept of Ark. Pvt Edw L Nix, 36th infty, has been appointed hospital steward in the regular army, & ordered to duty in the Dept of the Platte.

Balt, Feb 1. Judge Ezekiel Chambers, of Kent Co, died at his residence in Charleston on Wed, Jan 30. He was one of the most eminent & distinguished men of the State.

<u>War Dept Claim Commission, Wash, D C, Jan 31, 1867. Statement of claims filed during the month of Jan, 1867.</u>

Benj Thornton	Mrs E L Colemen
Wylby Woodbridge	T C McKee
M B Leonard	Mary Ann Johnson

Robt Adger
Thos Garvey
Jas G Brown
R T Hunt
John A Stevenson
Maj G Chapin
A F Gamtreaix
Mrs Wm F Gilliam
Mrs Mary Boyle
Jean Marie Laurie
Saml McGaughey
John H Tucker
Mrs F Chesley
John D Miller
Natalie Biraghe
Walter F Herrick
Ambrose Morrison
John Mitchell
Matthew Allison
John G Gelstrip
H H Neilson
Mrs E F Carter
J C Van Wickle

Mrs Margaret Myers
John M Powell
Saml D Finckle
L M Long
G H Bayne-heirs
Jos R Shannon
D M Murtenbaugh
C F Urguhart
Mrs Francis Abells
Henry Alley
Francis Foster
Mrs M A Peters
Mrs Teresa Warner
C P Goodyear
Wm Broadders
Fred'k Andress
Easton Sanders
Mrs Elibabeth Landholt
E M Marshall & Horace Hewitt
A C Hunt & H R Hunt
D W Bligh & J S Gallagher
John T Cox & W S Newbury

Action had on claims during the present month:
Claim allowed:
Angelo Miazzo, agent
Jules Courche
M C Brickley
Mrs Julianne Hobble
Julius Fauk
Thornton Aldman
Mrs Julia H Addison

Wm A Orman
John H King
C W Vinson
Adam King
J W Page
J D Skeen

Claim rejected:
Wm Richardson
F McNerhany
Henry Queen
Chas Ridgeley
John Lockwood
Francis C Zellar
Thos Kehoe
Thos Neal
Amherst W Stone
Robt A Phillips
Thos Keddy
Jas E Price & Co

John B Dearing
Mrs Nancy Lear
Allan Pearce
John B Sweet
Cochrane & Tileston
M Oglesby
Fendal Carpenter
Thos C Case
Wm Faux or E C Drew
Jas Keeney [or Jas Keenan]
Mrs Julia A Armistead
Wm H Rogers

Returned to Claimant:
Fred'k Schroag
Claim allowed in part:
J & J Prom & Co
Cornelius Halpine

A W Hurlbut

E A Otis

MON FEB 4, 1867
The funeral of Alfred Kiger, a well known colored hackman, but late a messenger in the Patent Ofc, took place from the 15th st Presbyterian Church yesterday. The remains were followed to the grave by a large number of friends, & were escorted by Eureka Lodge No 5, F & A M, [colored,] of which the deceased was a past ofcr. The Mosart Band, [colored,] headed the funeral procession.

Real estate sale: Two story frame house & lot on 9th st, between P & Q, being part of lot 3 in square 397, to John W Lewis, for $1,900. A farm of 1,500 acres, in Chas Co, Md, for B D Spalding, for $20,000. Four story brick house & lot on 8th st, between I & K, to John W Dwyer, for $6,000. Brick house & lot on R st, between 8th & 9th, lot 14 x 90, to Mrs Fitzgerald, for $900. Lot 12 in square 247, Mass ave & 14th st, containing 29,400 square feet, to John O Evans, for $22,500. Two story frame house on 7th st, lot 21 x 242, to Mrs Herridon, for $1,800.

Orphans Court-Judge Purcell. 1-Sat the will of the late Eleanor Baden, bequeathing her property to her son, Wm Wallace Baden, whom she nominates as executor, was filed & partially proven. 2-Letters of administration were issued to Martha C Jordan on the estate of Cornelius Noonan; bond, $300. Also, to Eliza Von Kamecke, on the estate of Theodore Von Kamecke; bond, $3,600. Also, letters of guardianship to the same; bond, $2,000. 3-The first & final accounts of the administrator of Jas Shea, 6th general of the guardian to the orphans of Joshua Gibson, first individual of guardian to Robt Gibson, & 4th individual of guardian to Martha Gibson were approved & passed.

The Com'r of Pensions on Sat made the following appointments of examining surgeons for pensioners: Dr E V Bell, Terre Haute, Ind; Dr John R Smith, Kertsville, Mo; & Dr Ira Russell, Winchendon, Mass.

The funeral ceremonies of the late Hon Philip Johnson, M C, from Pa, took place in the hall of the House of Reps yesterday. The remains were removed from the late residence of the deceased, 454 H st, attended by the pall-bearers, Hon Myer Strouse, of Pa; Hon John Hogan, of Mo; Hon N F Dixon, of R I; Hon R P Spalding, of Ohio; Hon L S Trimble, of Ky; Hon J M Humphrey, of N Y; Hon Lewis W Ross, of Ill; Hon N G Taylor, of Tenn. Mr Lemuel Williams was the undertaker. The procession proceeded to the ***Congressional Cemetery***, where the remains were deposited for future interment.

Trustee's sale of valuable vineyard, near the Nat'l Race Course & Insane Asylum, by deed of trust dated May 2, 1865, duly recorded: sale of 7¾ acres, being part of ***Kosciuszko Place***. –Fred W Jones, trustee -Cooper & Latimer, aucts

Navy Bulletin, Jan 26. Passed: Assist Paymaster A W Bacon, to be passed assist paymaster from Aug 1, 1866; Assist Paymaster A Clarence, to be passed assist paymaster from Nov 7, 1866; Assist Paymaster Rufus S McConnell, to be passed assist paymaster from Nov 27, 1866.

Orphans Court of Wash Co, D C, Feb 2, 1867. In the case of John H Semmes, adm of Louisa Collins, deceased, the administrator & Court have appointed Feb 26, 1867, for the final settlement of the personal estate of the said deceased, of the assets in hand. -Jas R O'Beirne, Reg/o wills

Died: on Feb 1, in Wash City, Hon Henry S Magraw, of Md. His funeral will be from his late residence, West Nottingham, Cecil Co, Md, on Feb 5 at 10 o'clock.

Died: on Feb 3, at the residence of his brother, Singleton Goldin, of consumption, in his 46th year. His funeral will take place from 427 Mass ave, at 4 o'clock, on Feb 5.

Died: on Feb 3, after a short illness, Fannie, youngest daughter of John B & Mary H Peyton, aged 10 years, 4 months & 26 days. Her funeral will take place from her grandmother's residence, No 5 Indiana ave, on Tue morning at 11 o'clock.

Died: on Feb 2, Capt John P R Crawford, of Richmond, Va. His funeral will take place from the Southern Methodist Church, 9th & M sts.

Bishop Williams has ordered a monument to the memory of Benedict Jos Fenwick, late Bishop of Boston, & founder of Holy Cross College, in Worcester. The monument is to be erected at the grave of the Bishop, in the College grounds.

TUE FEB 5, 1867
Yesterday D V Burr foreman of the grand jury, presented to the clerk of the Criminal Court an indictment against John H Surratt. Accompanying the indictment is a presentment charging John Wilkes Booth with the murder of Abraham Lincoln, & John H Surratt, David E Herold, Lewis Payne, & Geo A Atzerodt for being present, aiding & abetting, on or about Apr 14, 1865. Their indictment proper charged that John H Surratt, or or about Apr 14, 1865, did murder Abraham Lincoln. The second count charges that John H Surratt & John Wilkes Booth did murder Abraham Lincoln. The Third count charges with the murder of Abraham Lincoln, John H Surratt, Lewis Payne, John Wilkes Booth, David E Herold, Geo A Astzerodt, & Mrs M E Surratt. The fourth count charges that John Wilkes Booth, John H Surratt, David E Herold, Geo A Atzerodt, Lewis Payne, & Mary E Surratt did conspire & confederate together to kill & murder Abraham Lincoln. It was rumored yesterday evening that the steamer **Swatara**, with Surratt on board, was lying at the mouth of the Potomac, awaiting a break up in the ice to come direct to the Navy Yard.

A negro man named Robt Carter, employed about the post ofce of Lynchburg, Va, has been arrested on a charge of robbing the mail.

Dissolution of the copartnership between N C McKnew & S P Bell, under the name of McKnew & Bell, this day, by mutual consent. –N C McKnew, Saml P Bell [The business will be cont'd at the old stand, 405 Pa ave by N C McKnew. –Feb 4]

Groceries, mules, & wagon at auction, on Feb 8, at the store of Messrs H S Taylor & Co, 360 7th st, near I st; sale of the entire stock of groceries. –W L Wall & Co, aucts

Postmaster Genr'l made the following changes of postmasters during week ending Feb 2:
Louisiana: New Carthage, Madison Co, C S Jeffries, vice P A Lawnard, failed to bond.
Florida: Gainsville, Alachua Co, W Porter, vice J M Richardson, resigned.
Vt: East Middleburg, Addison Co, J P Champlin, vice Mrs A Needham, resigned; Franklin, Franklin Co, Jas Randall, vice L S French, resigned.
Mass: Russell, Hampden Co, G D Parks, vice H Parks, resigned; Scotland, Plymouth Co, Miss H K Chipman, vice G Chipman, deceased.
West Va: Adaline, Marshall Co, J W Richmond, vice J Ermsley, failed to bond.
Missouri: Spring Hill, Livingston Co, E W Lingh, vice W Anderson, not bonded; King City, Gentry Co, E Bonnell, vice P Ball, insane.
New Mexico: Bernalillo, J McCastillo, vice E Perea, resigned.

Army Bulletin, Jan 31, & Feb 1.
1st Lt Saml R Schenck, 41st infty, has permission to delay starting to his regt until Mar 5.
Lt Chas L Robe, 29th U S infty, is relieved from duty in connection with recruiting at Norfolk, Va.
Brvt Maj C B Penrose, commissary of subsistence, is granted 30 days leave of absence on surgeon's certificate of disability.
2nd Lt Louis H Rucks, 9th cavalry, is granted 21 days delay in reporting to his regt.
Brvt Lt Col Chas Bartlett, 30th U S infty, has had leave extended him until the physicians deem it safe for him to join his regt.
2nd Lt Wm Harper, 6th cavalry, has 15 days delay, in reporting to his regt granted him.
2nd Lt H B Quimby, 39th infty, has permission to delay starting to his regt until Feb 2.
1st Lt Henry C Ward has had his leave extended for 10 days.

Died: on Feb 4, suddenly, Mrs Henrietta H Brown, wife of Rev B Peyton Brown, aged 29 years. Her funeral will take place from the Foundry M E Church, 14th & G sts, on Feb 6, at 11 o'clock. She will be buried at Annapolis Junction the same afternoon, at 3 o'clock.

Navy Bulletin, Jan 28. Retired: Carpenter Guert Ganesvoort.

Orphans Court of Wash Co, D C, Feb 2, 1867. In the case of John C Riley, adm of Augustine N Y Howle, deceased, the administrator & Court have appointed Feb 26 next, for the final settlement of the personal estate of the said deceased, of the assets in hand. -Jas R O'Beirne, Reg/o wills

J S Beck & J P Barrineau, who were arrested by order of the military on account of the death of the negroes in the burning of the Kingstree, [S C,] jail, have been released from Castle Pinkney, where they were confined. The release was made upon the requisition of T B Logan, Dist Judge, for the transfer of the prisoners to the civil authorities.

L A Benoist, a prominent & wealthy banker of St Louis, died at Havana a few days since. He had gone there for the benefit of his health.

WED FEB 6, 1867
Navy Bulletin, Jan 29. Honorably Discharged: Mate Edw Kearns, from Jan 28. Detached: Cmder John J Cromwell, from the ship **Miantonomah**, & ordered to return home; Cmder Francis A Roe, from command of the ship **Madawaska**, & ordered to the ship **Tacony**; Paymaster Wm G Marcy, from the **Madawaska**, & ordered to settle his accounts; Acting Masters Wm T Breck, Jas Birtwirtle, Acting Ensigns August Adler, A F Bachford, Chas G Rogers, Mates W S Baldwin, Geo E Flander, Edw Culbert, & N V Walker, from the **Madawaska**, & ordered to the ship **Yantic**. Passed Assist Surgeon J B Ackley, 1st Assist Engineers Wm Ross, Jas M Clark, Chas H Greenleaf, John Formance, C A Magee, Henry Snyder, 3rd Assist Engineer Robt Crawford, & Boatswain Isaac T Choate, from the **Madawaska**, & placed on waiting orders; 1st Assist Engineer Geo P Hunt, from the **Madawaska**, & granted leave of absence; 1st Assist Engineer Geo W Melville, from special duty at Boston, & ordered to the **Tacony**; 2nd Assist Engineer Jas A Chasmar, from special duty at Boston in connection with the ship **Franklin**, & placed on waiting orders; Acting Master Geo D Newcomb, from the ship **Sabine**, & ordered to the **Tacony**; Acting 2nd Assist Engineer Thos D Crosby, from the ship **Pi_guin**, & ordered to the **Tacony**.
Resigned: 2nd Assist Engineer W A Driggs & W J Reid, of the **Madawaska**.

Army Bulletin: Brvt Maj Gen Griffin, commanding the Military District of Texas, issued order No 5, Jan 28, 1867: The Gen takes this method of complimenting Capt John A Wilcox, 4th U S cavalry, & men under his command, for conspicuous good conduct in a recent encounter with a hostile band of Indians encamped on Mud creek, 20 or 30 miles from *Fort Clarke*, towards El Paso.

Fire damaged the bakery of Mr J G Schoef, on O st, between 12th & 13th sts, yesterday; it also partially destroyed Mr Schoef's house.

Mr Geo C Houston, late of Wash City, & a native of Concord, N H, died at that place on Jan 30, age about 26 years.

Orphans Court-Judge Purcell-Feb 5. 1-The will of the late Eleanor Baden was further proven & admitted to probate as regards personalty. Letters of administration with the will annexed were issued to Thos E Baden; bond, $2,000. 2-Letters of administration were issued to John N Trook, on the estate of Thompson Jarvis; bond, $1,000. 3-John Geo Bright was appointed guardian to the orphans of Mina Utermehle; bond, $2,000. 4-The first & final account of the administrator of Harriet Wilkes was approved & passed. 5-The will of the late Jos N Fearson, of Gtwn; bequesting his estate to his widow, with the exception of the tavern known as Conrad's Tavern, in Tennallytown, to his niece, Mrs Barrett, was filed, fully proven, & admitted to probate. The estate is valued at about $122,000.

Edw Paxton was arrested on Monday by Sgt Skippon, on the charge of stealing a carriage from Mrs Sophia Ailer. The accused was the foreman of the stables attached to Dorsey's Hotel, & Mrs Ailer's carriage had been left in the stable at livery. Paxton took the carriage & entered it for sale in the name of Wm James at Messrs Brown & Co's bazaar. The carriage was sold for $120, & Paxton pocketed the proceeds. He is held for further examination before Justice Thompson.

Jas Callaghan, age 14 years, missed his footing, or became dizzy, & fell into the water. He was carried down the Potomac river some 60 yards, when he was rescued by a man in a little skiff. The noble rescuer was Jerry Raub, a waterman.

Port Deposit, Feb 5. The remains of Hon Henry S Magraw were buried this morning in the graveyard belonging to the Presbyterian Church to which his father had been pastor for more than 30 years. Dr Magraw represented Cecil Co in the present House of Delegates.

Richmond, Feb 5. Edw H Wayland, the Erie railroad clerk who absconded from Jersey City with $15,000, was arrested here tonight.

Died: on Feb 5, in Gtwn, Mrs Annie V Taylor, wife of Rev A A E Taylor. The funeral services will be held in the West St Chapel, corner of West & Congress sts, Gtwn, on Thursday, at 3 o'clock.

Died: on Feb 4, at the rectory of Rock Creek parish, Upton R Buck aged 49 years. His funeral will take place at the church on Feb 6, at 2 o'clock.

Gen Jos L Amee, formerly chief of police of Boston, & quartermaster in Gen Sheridan's command, died Monday, at Boston, aged 67 years.

Fenian prisoners: Col Robt Lynch, Rev John McMahon, Mr Haven, John Quinn, Thos School, Danl Whalen, & Mr Hayden, were quietly sent from Toronto to Kingston Penitentiary, on Sat, by railway. All except Fr McMahon, were ironed, sufficiently to prevent an attempt at escape. F H Welthan, the last Fenian prisoner, against whom no bill was found, was discharged on Saturday.

THU FEB 7, 1867

Mr W H Carlin, the accommodating & popular conductor of the passenger train on the Loudoun & Hampshire railroad, was caught between 2 cars this evening, while coupling them at Herndon station, & seriously injured.

Yesterday, in the Equity Court, Judge Olin, presiding, a decree was issued divorcing Saml Wood Wyvill from the bonds of matrimony with Laura V H Wyvill, on the ground of adultery.

One of the bravest, best, most popular, most honorable, most amiable citizens of Lexington District-of all South Carolina-was Col Marcellus Steedman, leader for some time during the late war of the 6th S C volunteers. Since the close of the war he had been living on his farm on Edisto, engaged at the same time in merchandise. His dwlg & store where under the same roof. On Feb 8, he walked out into his piazza, & as he turned to go in was shot by some persons unseen. As he fell, he cried out. His wife rushed forth, dragged him in & bolted the door. He survived but 3 hours. The wretched & bereaved woman, with her 2 little children, spent the whole night alone with the corpse, fearing to give the alarm. After the shot, Col Steedman recognized the voices of 2 negro men, formerly slaves of his father. This, with their names, he disclosed to his wife before he died. The two monsters were arrested in Aiken the following day, & made full confession. They had no grudge against Steedman, but killed him for his money & to rob the store. They intended also to murder the lady & children, but their hearts failed them. Col Steedman was only about 30 years of age.
–Edgefield [S C] Advertiser

Died: on Feb 6, in Boston, Caroline De Frondat, daughter of S Masi, of Wash City. Her funeral will take place from St Patrick's Church, on Feb 8, at 2 o'clock.

Miss Mollie Trussell, of Cosgriff, who was sentenced to the penitentiary, at Joliet, for one year for killing Geo Trussell, her paramour, at Chicago, last summer, has been pardoned by Govn'r Oglesby, after a confinement of about 1 month within the walls of that institution. The Chicago Tribune states that during the whole time of her short incarceration there the rules of the prison were violated in her case by allowing her to wear her own clothes, to occupy a private room, to receive many visitors, & to fare sumptuously. [Feb 11th newspaper: Miss Mollie Trussell, who was recently pardoned, determined before her release to forsake all her former associates, abandon entirely her former mode of life, & retire to the seclusion of a convent, & she adheres to her determination.]

Mrd: on Jan 31, by Rev Mr Olds, Mr F W Weber, member of the Marine Band, to Miss Mary Muligan, of Balt.

Mrd: on Feb 5, at the Church of the Epiphany, by Rev Dr C H Hall, Albert Aston, U S Navy, to Rose M, daughter of R C Washington, of the Post Ofc Dept. No cards.

Mrd: on Feb 5, at the residence of the bride's father, Dr Grafton Tyler, by Rev W W Williams, Granville F Hyde to Miss Susan Tyler, all of Gtwn. [Marlboro & Balt papers please copy.]

Orphans Court of Wash Co, D C. Julia H Addison, guardian to her minor son, Chas Morris Addison, having reported to the court that in pursuance of its decree ratified & approved by the Supreme Court of D C, that she sold the interest of her said ward in the following property, in Wash City: lot 3 in square 184, to Gen Richd D Cutts, & that instead of complying with the terms of sale, he has paid the whole purchase money in cash, with interest for 6 & 12 months, in all amounting to $1,348.30.
–Wm F Purcell, Judge of the Orphans Court of D C. –Jas R O'Beirne, Reg/o Wills

Gen Logan is going to build a residence in Chicago.

Capt Wm E Beale, a well-know citizen of Balt, died on Tuesday, aged 55 years. He was a native of Alexandria, Va, but went to Balt at an early age, & as a carpenter & builder succeeded in amassing quite a handsome property.

Mr John E Owens, the comedian, closed an engagement at Louisville on Saturday.

General Custer was at St Louis on Saturday.

FRI FEB 8, 1867
Court of Equity-Judge Olin. 1-Murray vs Mattingly; No 849. Decree substituting Saml T Lewis trustee, in place of W J Stone, jr, deceased. 2-Dorsey & wife vs T B Florence; No 257. Order on dfndnts' solicitor to return papers into court.

Navy Bulletin, Jan 31. 1-Ordered: 2nd Assist Engineer Wm A Winda_, Carpenter Davis Robinett, & Gunner Wm Wilson, to duty at the naval station, League Island; 2nd Assist Engineer John Van Hovenburg, to duty on the ship **Monongahela**.
2-Detached: 2nd Assist Engineer C W Breaker, from the **Monongahela**, & granted sick leave of absence. 3-Deserted: Mate E V B Smith, from the ship **De Soto**, on Dec 8, 1866.

Senate: 1-Bill to incorporate the Metropolitan Gas-light Co of D C, naming John R Elvans, Geo Savage, D P Holloway, Wm Bebb, P H Allback, T B Brown, A Watson, M Loomis, T H Phillips, Wm A Cook, H A Pierce, & Geo Burgess as corporators, with a capital of not less than $500,000 nor more than $1,000,000, & authorizes the construction of gas works for the lighting of the cities of Washington & Gtwn: referred to the Cmte on the District of Columbia.

Chancery sale of valuable property on E st north between 10th & 11th sts; by decree passed by the Supreme Court of D C, in cause No 651 Equity, docket 7, wherein Julia A Van Ness is cmplnt, & Barney Barry is dfndnt; public auction on Feb 26, on the premises, the west half from front to rear of lot 12 in square 348, with improvements thereon. –Wm H Philip, trustee -Green & Williams, aucts

Mrs Teresa Bagiola Sickles, wife of Maj Gen Danl E Sickles, died in N Y on Tuesday, of disease of the heart. [Feb 12th newspaper: The funeral of Mrs Sickles took place from St Joseph's Church, 6th ave, yesterday; pall-bearers: Maj Gen Gordon Granger, Brig Gen H E Tremain, Dr John M Carnochan, Senor Fabri Co_ta, Edw Vermilye, Maj Gen A Pleasonton, Brvt Gen Chas K Graham, Jas T Brady, Wm H Field, & John King. Upon the coffin was a silver place with the inscription: TERESA B SICKLES, AGED 31 YEARS. DIED FEBRUARY 5, 1867. The afflicted husband, accompanied by his young daughter, his parents, now advanced in years, & Mr & Mrs Bagiola, the parents of the deceased lady, occupied seats near the alter. The mortuary mass was offered by the pastor of the church, Rev Fr Farrell, assisted by Frs Boyce & Parsons. The funeral cortege proceeded to the *Catholic Cemetery*, in Second ave, where the remains were temporarily depostied, to be removed eventually for permanent interment elsewhere. Gen Sickles will leave for Charleston next week, with his daughter. –N Y Herald, Sunday]

Chancery sale of valuable property on E st north between 10th & 11th sts; by decree passed by the Supreme Court of D C, in cause No 651 Equity, docket 7, wherein Julia A Van Ness is cmplnt, & Barney Barry is dfndnt; public auction on Feb 26, on the premises, the west half from front to rear of lot 12 in square 348, with improvements thereon. –Wm H Philip, trustee -Green & Williams, aucts

Mrd: on Feb 5, at the residence of the bride's mother, by Rev Robt Leachman, T S Jones, of Montgomery Co, Md, to Bettie, 3rd daughter of the late Wm T & Mariana Summers, of Fairfax Co, Va.

Supreme Court of D C; No 832 Equity; Eliz Cross, petitioner, vs Israel P Cross, dfndnt. The petitioner states that the parties to this suit were married in Washington City, on Nov 1, 1860; that the petitioner has one male child, Thos Cross, about 4 years of age, & that the dfndnt has been guilty of adultery in said city during their said marriage, & the petition prays that a diver e a vinculo matrimonii from the bonds of the said marriage may be granted to the petitioner, & that she may have the guardianship & custody of her said child. The dfndnt is a non-resident of said District. He is to appear in this court in person or by solicitor on or before Mar 25th next, & answer the petition. –A B Olin -R J Meigs, clerk

SAT FEB 9, 1867
Gen Jos J Bartlett has been nominated minister resident at Stockholm, vice McGinnis, rejected.

Binghamton, N Y, Feb 8. Jas Ryan, of Onondega Co, was arrested here last evening on the arrival of the Syracuse train, for the murder of his stepfather, Jerry Denham, & lodged in jail. This morning, on going to his cell, he was found dead, having hung himself with his suspenders.

Mr Wm Baker, an old citizen of Balt, died on Monday, aged 57 years.

Navy Bulletin, Feb 1. 1-Ordered: Acting Masters C C Bunker, Jas B Wood, & Acting 1st Assist Engineer Thos McCausland, to sail from N Y for Panama on Feb 11 for duty on the ship **Saginaw**; Chaplain Jules D Benglass, to the Navy Yard at Mare Island, Calif. 2-Resigned: Acting Ensign Mortimer B Wheeler.
3-Detached: Lt Cmder Louis Kempff, Assist Surgeon Wm Commons, 1st Assist Engineer Wm G Buchler, 2nd Assist Engineers D W Frafley, Thos La Blanc, Acting Master H K Lapham, Acting Ensigns R B Crapo, W B Arrants, J Potts, W J Herring, Mates Danl Ward, Chas J Murphy, R W Collins, Acting 3rd Assist Engineers Wm H Wingate & August Abjoison, from the ship **Suwanee**, & ordered to return home; Chaplain Nathl Frost, from the Mare Island [Calif] Navy Yard, on the reporting of his relief, & placed on waiting orders; Lt Cmders Geo W Wood, G W Harwell, Lt Frank Wildes, Master Chas C Clark, Passed Assist Surgeon Louis Zengen, & Victor M Osborne, from the ship **Vanderbilt**, & ordered to the **Suwanee**; Chief Engineer E Lawton, 1st Assist Engineers Jas Renshaw, R H Gunnell, 2nd Assist Engineers Edw Gay, John Lowe, & Acting 3rd Assist Engineer Warner B Bayley, from the ship **Madawaska**, & placed on waiting orders; Lt Cmder Chas L Franklin, Paymaster J C Folfree, Boatswain J Cooklan, & Carpenter F H Bishop, from the **Vanderbilt**, & ordered home; Passed Assist Surgeon Wm H Johnson, Acting 2nd Assist Engineers Peter Anderson, A L Gilmore, Acting 3rd Assist Engineer R F Baker, & Gunner Cornelius Dugan, from the **Vanderbilt**, & ordered to the **Saranac**; Mate F H Wing, 2nd Assist Engineer, E M Breese, Acting 1st Assist Engineer John Loyd, & Acting 2nd Assist Engineer Geo H Moore, from the **Saginaw**, & ordered to return home; Assist Surgeon David Mack, jr, Gunner Geo Fause, 2nd Assist Engineers F L Vanderalice & Geo F Sawyer, from the **Saranac**, & ordered home; Acting 2nd Assist Engineer G H Whittemore, Acting 3rd Assist Engineers Edw T Peake & A L Grow, from the **Vanderbilt**, & ordered to the **Saginaw**. Retired: Capt Chas W Pickering.
Order Revoked: Acting Ensign E G Blanchard, to the ship **Tacony**, & he is granted leave of absence.

Mrs G H W Runge, committed suicide at Wilmington, N C, on Monday last; cause, insanity.

A new county, called ***Robertson Co***, has been established in Ky. It is carved out of parts of Mason, Bracken, & Harrison Counties. The county seat is to be Mount Olivet.

Equity Court-Justice Olin; Feb 8, 1867. 1-Andrew Stallings vs Benj Smith et al. No 788. Decree appointing Fred'k W Jones trustee to sell real estate. 2-In Re. Jas G Ellis. De lunatico inquirendo. No 612. 3-Order: Rule on Thos Lewis to answer for contempt of court.

Died: on Feb 7, Ann Agnes, wife of John McDermott, aged 38 years. Her funeral will take place from the residence of her husband, 67 La ave, on Feb 10 at 1:30 o'clock P M. [Herald.]

Died: on Feb 8, at the residence of her son-in-law, 328 8th st, Mrs Mary J Fisher, widow of the late Adam F Fisher, of Balt, Md. Her remains will be taken to Balt on Feb 10 for interment.

Henry Lee, a prominent citizen of Boston, died on Wed, aged 85 years. He received the electoral vote of S C for Vice Presidence at the re-election of Andrew Jackson in 1823.

MON FEB 11, 1867

Navy Bulletin, Feb 3. Detached: Lt Cmder Jas G Maxwell, from the N Y Navy Yard, & ordered to the ship **Yantic**; Acting Ensign Fred'k Elliott, from the ship **Jamestown** on the reporting of Acting Volunteer Lt King, & ordered East; Acting Ensign Chas S Kelley, from the ship **Wyoming** from Sep 8 last, & granted leave of absence. Ordered: Lt Cmder Ed E Potter, to duty at the Naval rendezvous at Boston; 1st Assist Engineer John H Hunt, 2nd Assist Engineers Jas H Chasmar & Chas H Greenleaf, to the ship **Suwanee**.

Judge Pliny Merrick, who died at Boston on Friday, left $10,000 to his native town of Brookfield, Mass, for the establishment of a public library, & an equal amount to the Children's Friend Society at Worcester. His whole estate is valued at $158,000.

Army Bulletin: Capt & Assist Quartermaster J H Morgan, Military Storekeeper of the Ordnance Dept, is granted 60 days leave; 2nd Lt Edw Hallard, 22nd infty, is granted 90 days leave; 2nd Lt E W Stone, 21st infty, is ordered to join his company in the Dept of the Potomac; 1st Lt Reuben C King is granted 60 days delay in reporting to his regt from Jan 12; Capt Chas Newbold, the order relieving him from duty in the Military District of New Mexico, is suspended until early spring; Col H G Gibson is granted 7 days delay while enroute to join his battery of the 3rd heavy artl; Brvt Col J Hayden 15th infty, is ordered to the Adj Gen to submit an improved company desk of his invention for adaptation to army use, & on the completion of his duty to return to his station; 2nd Lt E Clark, 16th infty, is granted 30 days delay in joining his regt at Savannah, Ga.

Lt Gen Sherman has been in N Y for a number of days, stopping at the residence of his niece, on 9th st. It is stated that he will leave today for the West.

The Senate has rejected the nomination of Wm Wales, editor of the Balt Commercial, as Surveyor of the Port of Balt. Mr Wales was appointed a few months ago in place of Edington Fulton, of the Balt American, removed.

Balt, Feb 10. A heavy northwest storm of wind set in on Sat night. A boat capsized in the harbor, & 6 persons are supposed to be drowned. Second Despatch. Jas Young, Joshua Davis, & Wm Cadell, ferrymen; Thos Holt & Mr Mazon, passengers, are parties supposed lost on the capsized ferry boat.

Orphans Court-Judge Purcell. 1-The will of John McCue, deceased, was filed & fully proven. The will of Jos Mansfield, deceased, was filed for probate. The will of Eleanor Baden, deceased, was admitted to probate & record & letters of administration w a granted to Thos E Baden; bond, $2,000. 2-Letters of administration on the estate of John P R Crawford, deceased, were granted to Evan Hughes; bond, $1,000. 3-E C Morgan was appointed guardian to Wm P Wilkes; bond, $2,000. 4-The first & final accounts of Richd T Morsell, adm of Anne Beall, deceased; Geo W Johnson, adm of Geo Johnson, deceased, & Abraham Blakely, exc of Eliz Miles, deceased; also, the first general account of Virginia Whittlesey, guardian to the orphans of Comfort S Whittlesey, deceased, & also her first & final individual account as guardian to Robt H Whittlesey, were approved & passed.

Louisville, Feb 9. Hon Henry Grider, whose death was announced in the House today, was a soldier in the war of 1812, under Gen Shelby. He served several years in both houses of the Ky Legislature, & was for 9 years a member of the National House of Reps.

J D Barrow, a well-known banker of this city, died on Sat of pulmonary consumption. He has been long & favorably known in this community as an honorable & upright man.

Wm D Astor, of N Y, has recently given $50,000 to the Astor Library, which was founded by his father, John Jacob Astor.

S G Woolfold, of Ky, travelling in Tenn, was robbed by highwaymen near Memphis, & left in the road with both legs broken. He was known to have about $1,000 with him before the robbery.

Orphans Court of Wash Co, D C; Feb 9, 1867. In the case of Horatio R Maryman, exc of Zachariah Hazel, deceased, the executor & Court have appointed Mar 5 next, for the final settlement of the personal estate of the said deceased, of the assets in hand. -Jas R O'Beirne, Reg/o wills

Mr Jas Hughes, the cashier & book-keeper of R B Smith & Co, *coal dealers, left Cincinnati in his buggy Thur, heading to his residence, 3½ miles from the city. He was attacked & shot through the head & instantly killed. The horse took fright & ran away, the corpse still clinging to the vehicle, & the murderers failed in their designed robbery. The murderers escaped. Mr Hughes was 69 years old, & leaves a family. [Appears to be *coal. Letter was missing.

TUE FEB 12, 1867
Com'r Barrett, of the Pension Bureau, yesterday made the following appointments of examining surgeons of pensioners: Dr Lewis Davenport, Detroit, Mich; Dr Wm Collins, Madison, Ind; Dr D Little, Logan, Ohio; & Dr Jacob Y Cantwell, Decatur, Ala.

Mrs Julia Jones, wife of Mr Jones, jeweller, on Bacchus st, between Calliope & Liston Walk, New Orleans, committed suicide on Tues last by shooting herself through the heart with a pistol. It appears that the sister of the deceased was married at her house on the Monday previous to the suicide, & the thought that she was to be deprived of her society is supposed to have induced her to put an end to her existence.

The Cmte on Public Bldgs & Grounds have under consideration the propriety of purchasing the property left by the late Mr Isherwood, situated in contiguity to the northeastern part of Wash City. This estate is composed of 100 acres of land. It has been offered to the Com'r of Public Bldgs for $75,000, & we understand he strongly recommends its purchase. The farm is already occupied by army depots.

Mr G N Carlton was placed under arrest at N Y on Friday, to answer a charge of embezzling upwards of half a million of dollars from the Gov't while acting as deputy collector or treasury agent at Memphis, Tenn.

Criminal Court-Judge Fisher. 1-Yesterday the jury in the case of Sanford Conover, alias Chas A Dunham indicted for perjury, returned a verdict of guilty. 2-John Bell, was convicted of larceny & sentenced to the Albany Penitentiary for 1 year. 3-Danl Wayne, indicted for larceny, was convicted. 4-Jas Franklin was found guilty of larceny, & sentenced to 1 year in the Penitentiary.

Govn'r Geary on Sat issued a warrant for the execution of Alex'r B Wiley, of Luzerne Co, on Mar 15. Wiley was convicted for the murder of Aleck McElwee in May last.

M Victor Cousin, left his library, worth $50,000, to the Sorbonne, with a fund for its maintenance.

Rev Dr Nathl Hewitt, so well known as one of the ablest temperance advocates 30 or 40 years ago, died on Feb 3, at his residence in Bridgeport, Conn, in his 80th year.

Mrd: on Feb 11, at the Seaton House, by Rev R J Keeling, D D, Mr Mordecai Plumer, of PG Co, Md, to Miss Adeline Pratt, of Balt. [Balt & Marlborough papers please copy.]

Mrd: on Feb 7, at Brattleboro, Vt, by Rev Fr Frothingham, Lt Col A T Dunton, of Montpelier, Vt, to Mrs Mary B Farr, daughter of Rev Addison Brown, of Brattleboro.

Died: on Feb 9, at his late residence, n e corner of 11th & F sts, J D Barrow. The funeral services will take place at Wesley Chapel at 3 P M, on Feb 12th, & the remains will be taken to **Glenwood Cemetery**.

For rent: the residence of the late Wm Redin, 76 Gay st, Gtwn, adjoining the property of Dr Grafton Tyler, & immediately opposite that of Judge Dunlop. This property will not be rented to be used as a boarding house. Apply on the premises.

Orphans Court of Wash Co, D C, Feb 9, 1867. In the case of Mary E Fisk, excx of Chas B Fisk, deceased, the executrix & Court have appointed Mar 5 next, for the final settlement of the personal estate of the said deceased, of the assets in hand.
-Jas R O'Beirne, Reg/o wills

WED FEB 13, 1867
Navy Bulletin, Feb 4. 1-Detached: Chief Engineer Mortimer Kellogg, from duty at Bridgewater Forge, Mass, & ordered to duty on board the ship **Patos**; Acting Ensign Hugh Jones, from the Naval Hospital at Chelsea, Mass, & granted leave of absence; Mate Geo E Simmons, from the ship **Ino**, & granted leave of absence. 2-Resigned: Acting Master Gardner Cottrell, of the ship **Frolic**. 3-Honorably Discharged: Acting Volunteer Lt Chas Norton, from Feb 3. 4-Ordered: 3rd Assist Engineer Fred'k Schober, to duty at the naval station at League Island, Pa.

Orphans Court-Judge Purcell. 1-The will of Richd Henry Lee was filed & fully proven. 2-The will of Martha Hauntman was filed. 3-The will of Edw C Dyer was filed & fully proven. 4-The first account of J Bayard H Smith, exc of Ann C Smith, deceased, was proved & passed.

Army Bulletin: 1-1st Lt John A Winebrener, Ord Dept, is granted 3 months leave of absence, to take effect from the date of being relieved from duty at Scott Foundry, Reading, Pa. 2-Brvt Maj John H Knight, 30th U S infty, is granted an extension of 4 months of the time given him to delay joining his company. 3-Brvt Maj August Thieman, capt 33rd U S infty, has been sentenced by court-martial to be suspended from rank & pay proper for the period of 3 calendar months, & to be reprimanded in orders by the Maj Gen commanding the Dept of the east. The offence of Maj Thieman was absence without leave. 4-The recruiting station established in the Military Division of the Pacific by Maj Gen Halleck for the 8th U S cavalry has been discontinued.

Capt Stephen Ward, of Kennebunk, well known as one of the largest ship builders in Maine, fell dead at the Boston Depot, in Portland, last Tuesday; supposedly a case of heart disease. He was about 55 years of age.

Leutze, the painter, is recovering from an attack of erysipelas.

It is stated that Edwin Booth's share of the income at the Winter Garden Theatre, N Y, amounts to $500 per night.

The Providence Post claims that Miss Amalia Hauck, of Maretzek's opera troupe, was born in that city, & lived there until she was 6 years old.

Criminal Court-Judge Fisher. 1-Wm Duncan, indicted for larceny; the recognizance, $200, was forfeited. 2-Susan Blackwell, indicted for larceny; recognizance, $200, was forfeited. 3-Gideon Hoover & Thos Burwell, indicted for assault & battery; recognizance, $1,000, forfeited. 4-John Rosette, indicted for assault & battery; recognizance forfeited. 5-Hugh Fitzsimmons, indicted for assault & battery on a woman, was acquitted. 6-Albert Miller, for an assault & battery on John Williams with a hatchet, was fined $50, & committed to the charge of the Marshal until paid. 7-Margaret Colbank, alias Margaret Copeland, indicted for larceny, pleaded guilty, & was sentenced to imprisonment in the jail for half an hour. 8-Wm Scott, indicted for receiving stolen property, was found guilty.

Col Lynch, the Fenian prisoner, is a fireman in the foundry at the Kingston Penitentiary, & Rev Mr McMahon does duty as a puddler.

Died: on Feb 9, at Forestville, PG Co, Md, of pneumonia, Lilly C, infant daughter of Dr H Waring & Lavinia T Brent.

Mrd: on Feb 12, by Rev Dr White, J Swinton Baynard, of S C, to Jenny, daughter of Jas Riordan, of Wash City.

Dissolution of the partnership existing between Robt J Walker, E P Stanton, & Duncan S Walker, by mutual consent. The undersigned have entered into a partnership under the name of Robt J Walker & Son. They will Practice in the Supreme Court of the U S, the courts of D C, & several Depts of the Gov't. Ofc 217 F st, near 15th st. –R J Walker, Duncan S Walker

Public auction on Mar 4, the beautiful farm on which Gen Schoeff resides, 9 miles from Wash, & 3/4ths of a mile from Scaggs' Switch Station, in PG Co, Md. The farm contains 150¼ acres; a spacious dwlg house, containing 15 rooms & porch, & numerous out-houses. The stock, farming utensils, etc can be purchased at a fair valuation by the purchaser of the Farm. -Green & Williams, aucts

Orphans Court of Wash Co, D C. Letters testamentary on the personal estate of Jos N Fearson, late of Gtwn, D C, deceased. –Mary Ann Fearson, admx

THU FEB 14, 1867
Navy Bulletin, Feb 5 & 6. 1-Ordered: Acting Chief Engr J Q A Ziegler, to the ship **Monongahela**; Acting Ensign Thos G Watson, to duty at the naval station at Mound City, Ill; Acting Ensign Oscar W Farenholt, to duty on board the receiving ship **New Hampshire**. 2-Resigned: Acting Master Geo D Newcomb & Midshipman Wm E Harmon. 3-Placed on the Retired List: Lt Cmder Wm C West. 4-Detached: Chief Engr Wm H Rutherford, from the **Monongahela**, & granted sick leave of absence. 4-Appointment Revoked: Acting Ensign Edw W Halcro, of the receiving ship **New Hampshire**.

Wm Cleever was held in $500 for his appearance at court, on the charge of committing an assault & battery on Mary Ann *Reeve, a girl of 14 years. [Mar 26th newspaper: W C Cleaver was indicted for the murder & horrible outrage upon the little girl Mary Ann *Rives, [on Feb 10th last;] who subsequently died.] *Two spellings of Reeve/Rives. Also, 2 spellings of Cleever/Cleaver.]

Assist Quartermaster M A Wainwright, on duty at Chattanooga, Tenn, forwards to the U S Treasury $50, which he has received from C C Guilford, an ex-employe of the Quartermaster's dept, who states that he wronged the Govn't of that amount, & having changed his course of life, desires to make reparation.

Criminal Court-Judge Fisher. 1-Albert Miller, convicted of assault & battery, fined $50. 2-Martha Ann Smith, indicted for larceny, a *nolle pros* was entered. 3-Geo Washington & Henry Bones, were convicted for larceny; in two other cases a *nolle pros* was entered. 4-Henry Campbell, indicted for larceny, plead guilty.

Mrd: on Feb 13, at Trinity Church, by Rev Dr Keeling, Theodore Oscar Chestney to Kate Piercy Murphey. No cards. [Balt, Richmond, & Norfolk papers please copy.]

Mrd: on Feb 12, at Foundry Church, by Rev Mr Tudor, Wm J Lewis to Miss Annie M P Haslup, all of Wash City. No cards.

Died: on Feb 13, at the residence of her daughter, Mrs A J Brown, Mrs Mary Harrington. Her funeral will be on Fri next at 3 o'clock P M, from the First Baptist Church, on 13th st.

Mrd: on Feb 12, by Rev Fr *McAnaly, Jos Allen, of Ill, to Miss Margaret Catharine, eldest daughter of Wm Forsyth, of Wash City.
+
Fashionable Wedding. Yesterday at 10 o'clock, at the residence of the bride's father, between Jos Allen, of Ill, & Miss Margaret Catharine Forsyth, the eldest daughter of our highly respected Surveyor of Wash City, Wm Forsyth. The Rev Fr John *McAnally, of St Matthew's Church, & the large company present, offered their congratulations to the happy pair, wishing them every happiness in their new sphere of life. [*Two spellings of the name McAnaly/McAnally.]

Dept of the Interior, U S Patent Ofc, Wash, Feb 8, 1867. Ptn of Lauren Ward, adm of the estate of Richd Ward, deceased, of Naugtucket, Conn, praying for the extension of a patent granted to Lauren Ward, as adm, on Jun 28, 1853, for an improvement in Machines for Turning Irregular Forms for 7 years from the expiration of said patent, which takes place on Jun 28, 1867.
 -T C Theaker, Com'r of Patents

Mrs Jefferson Davis was in Norfolk on Saturday.

FRI FEB 15, 1867

In the death of Capt Wood, of N Y, who was lost from the yacht **Fleetwing** in the great ocean race, a singular presentiment of his wife has been fulfilled. Over the date of Dec 15, 1866, she wrote her mother: "My husband sailed for Europe on the yacht **Fleetwing**, the 11th, & I am completely prostrated with grief & anxiety, feeling that he will never return. You will think this childish, but to me it is reality."

Painters' Union: meeting last evening at German Hall, on 11th st. Delegates elected to the Workingmen's Convention: Wm Beron, Donald McCathran, & Mr Mulligan.

A new *Executive Mansion*: one recommendation was *Eckington*, as a residence for the President. At that sweet retreat, within easy riding distance of the city, might be established a comfortable, convenient, & spacious mansion.
+
I cannot but express my surprise that the beautiful domicil of the former editor of the Nat'l Intelligencer, [the late Mr Gales,] should not have been taken as the summer residence of some of our wealthy inhabitants. The roomy portico of the house, large & commodious, commands a view of the surrounding country & portions of the city. Dr Bradley, who had charge of the house & grounds under the Gov't, speaks of the whole as a beautiful & healthy residence. Feb 4, 1867.

Army Bulletin. Brvt Capt J R McGinness is ordered to resume his duties in the Ordnance Ofc. Brvt Capt Geo D Ramsay, jr, has been granted 25 days leave of absence. Brvt Brig Gen R H K Whitely is authorized to proceed to N Y Arsenal on public business & return. Brvt Col D H Buel is authorized to proceed to Manchester, N H, on public business & return. Brvt Col S V Benet is authorized to proceed to the Watervliet Arsenal on public business & return. Brvt Brig Gen Wm Maynadier & Brvt Col T G Baylor have been detained as members of a board of ofcrs to meet in Wash City for the purpose of determining the calibre, the number of each calibre, & the proportion of rifled guns which will be required for the armament of fortifications. Capt M Y Wylie, military storekeeper, is granted 3 months leave of absence. Capt J M Todd is granted 3 months leave of absence. Brvt Lt Col J McAllister is granted 30 days leave of absence.

Gtwn: Francis Wheatley elected Pres; J Carter Marbury, sec. Vote for Mayor, which resulted in the nomination of H Addison, the present incumbent, by the following vote: For H Addison, 12; J C Hieston, 3; Jas Goddard 3; R R Crawford, 2. The following gentlemen were nominated for the Common Council:

John M Stake	Geo Waters	Esau Pickrel
E B Barrett	F W Joes	Wm H Bohrer
J B Davidson	J J Kane	David Edes
Wm Clabaugh	Jas Goddard	

Navy Bulletin, Feb 7. Resigned: Midshipman A Y Comstock.
Ordered: Chief Engineer Eldridge Lawlor, to duty at Bridgewater, Mass.

Died: on Feb 13, John McGarvey, in the 47th years of his age, a native of the county of Donegal, Ireland, but for the last 22 years has been a resident of Wash, D C. His funeral will take place from his late residence, 27th & K sts, on Friday at 2 P M.

The President has withdrawn the nomination of Hon Geo Bancroft to be collector of the port of Boston.

<u>Criminal Court</u>-Justice Fisher. 1-Thos Rye, alias Thos Ryan, indicted for an assault & battery with intent to kill John E Ayers. Both were clerks in the employ of the Gov't, & on New Year's night visited "Booker's Division," where the difficulty occurred. Both were intoxicated at the time. Rye/Ryan was found guilty of assault & battery, not intent to kill, & sentenced to 2 months in the county jail & fined $150. 2-Susan Blackwell, indicted for larceny, the Dist Atty entered a ***nolle pros***. 3-Benj F Beveridge, for an assault & battery on Uriah H Painter, at the Capitol in Jul last, the court sentenced him to pay a fine of $150, & committed him to the care of the Marshal until paid. 4-Wm Nelson pleaded guilty to the charge of larceny, & was sentenced to 3 days imprisonment. 5-Andrew Bombury was sentenced to 3 months imprisonment in the county jail on the charge of assault & battery on Wm Crow.

In N Y, Mrs Mary Groetsch, a German woman, 54 years of age, committed suicide by swallowing a quantity of arsenic, she had previously purchased to kill rats with. Mrs Groetsch spent every cent she had on lottery tickets; her husband said she must stop or they must separate; they occupied separate rooms; Mrs Groestsch became despondent.

The President has withdrawn the nomination of Hon Geo Bancroft to be collector of the port of Boston.

Capt Henry E Rainals, lately in charge of the Freedman's Bureau, Dist of Meridian, Miss, died in this city yesterday afternoon. He entered the army as capt in the 1st Long Island regt, & was severely wounded at the battle of Fair Oaks. Having joined his regt before his wound healed he contracted chronic diarrhoea, from which he never recovered, & which was the cause of his death. He had just been commissioned to a lieutenancy in the regular army.

Mrd: on Feb 12, at the Church of the Immaculate Conception, by Rev P F McCarthy, Enoch Clay Moreland, of Wash Co, D C, to Miss Mary E Clarke, of Wash City.

A man named Nichols murdered his wife & two children in Brookfield, Mo, on Monday night & then killed himself. [Feb 23rd newspaper: Mrs Nichols was the second wife of Mr Nichols, & she had two children when they married, & he had two daughters. Quarrels over his will not leaving anything to her children resulted in his shooting his wife & her children, & then himself.]

Died: on Feb 14, Elijah Edmonston, member of the Board of Aldermen. His funeral will take place on Feb 17 at 3 o'clock, from his late residence, 536 H st. [Star.]

Pickens Court House, S C, Feb 9, 1867. *Fort Hill*, the house of the late Hon John C Calhoun, will be sold, at this place, on Mar 4 next, on a credit of 8 months.
–Robt A Thompson, C E P D

SAT FEB 16, 1867
Elijah Edmonston died on Thursday. Dr Eliot had given up all hopes of his recovery 10 days ago. At the time of his death, Mr Edmonston was in his 57th year; he leaves a family of a wife & 5 children. The funeral will take place from the residence of the deceased, 536 H st, at 4th st, at 3 o'clock tomorrow.

Court in Equity-Justice Olin. 1-Blake vs Wood et al. No 871. Order appointing John B Blake guardian *ad litem* to infants. 2-Murphy vs Neary. No 796. Order final ratification of trustee sale & for conveyance. 3-Cassin vs Bozzle et al. No 751. Order setting aside *pro confesso* vs Eliz Bozzle, & requiring personal service. 4-Frazier vs Crome. No 700. Order final ratification.

Criminal Court-Justice Fisher. 1-Nelson Lindsey, larceny: 1 year in the Albany Penitentiary. 2-Patrick Fitzgerald, assault & battery on Thos Reagan: 6 months in jail.
3-Hillary Green acquitted on the charge of larceny. Geo Smith acquitted on the same charge. 4-Hugh J Friel was convicted of assault & battery on Hugh Fitzsimmons.
5-Geo Coster, Albert Foster, & Conway Johnson, were convicted of stealing a coat from Frank Glover. 6-Michl Cleary, indicted for larceny a *nolle prosequi* was entered.

Supreme Court of D C; Equity No 736. Robt F Mason & Marianne C Mason, vs Wm Virginia Mason. Parties interested in the account of the trustee & distribution of the fund, to appear at my ofc on Feb 21st. –Walter S Cox, auditor

$250,000 waiting an owner. The heir found in Chicago. In 1863 a rich widow, daughter of Dr B F Patterson, came from Mobile & remained for some time in one of our principal hotels; she did not sympathize with the rebellion; converted her money & was possessed of $60,000; her only companion was her little girl. After the war she went to Mobile, found her father missing, & no doubt dead, his estates were ruined; came to Wash City for awhile; met a Mr D___, [blank as copied,] son of a well known rebel gunmaker at Richmond. They removed to the oil regions, but were unsuccessful. Her husband went to the frontier to try to repair his fortunes, while the wife returned to Chicago, with enough to sustain her for a week. She found that in her father's right she was heir to the great estate that was, as yet, was unclaimed. Her work at the sewing machine & his labors as a locksmith were gladly abandoned.
–Chicago Republican

Supreme Court of D C; Equity No 671. H Sidney Everett et al vs Helen C Everett, Edw Everett, & Louisa Everett. Parties interested in the account of the trustee & distribution of the fund, to appear at my ofc on Feb 23rd. –Walter S Cox, auditor

Orphans Court of Wash Co, D C. Letters of administration on the personal estate of John Snyder, late of Wash Co, D C, deceased. –Chas E Sherman, adm

Death of Dr Russell's wife-in an English paper. On Jan 24, at the Parsonage, Henley-in-Arden, Warwicks, died Mary, the wife of Wm Howard Russell, LL D, the well known special correspondent of the Times. The deceased was 2nd daughter of Mr Peter Burrowes, of Kilpatrack, County Dublin, & was married to Mr Russell in 1846. During the height of the Crimean war, she went out to the East to her husand, & was by accident present at the battle of Tehernaya, where she rendered assistance to the wounded Russians. During Mr Russell's absence in India in 1858 she had a serious illness, from which she never completely recovered; and, after the death of her last son, [born Nov 14, 1860,] she sank gradually to her rest.

St Louis, Feb 14. Shocking railroad accident on the Hannibal & St Joseph railroad last night about 30 miles east of St Joseph, when a wheel under the baggage car broke, the ties on the bridge raked off, & 2 cars were thrown into the creek. C F Wentworth, of Chicago, was killed, & 14 or 15 others injured.

San Francisco, Feb 14. Robt Dinsmore, treasurer of Sutter Co, absconded on Feb 10, being a defaulter in $12,000.

Cincinnati, Feb 15. Hausen Bumgarden was hung at Marietta today, for the murder of John T Eabarke, in Sept last.

It is said that **Prior Park**, near Bath, England, which was orginally built by Ralph Allen, [Fielding's Squire Allworthy,] & the place where Pope wrote the "Essay on Man," is about to be purchased by the Catholics, probably for a college.

MON FEB 18, 1867
Henry St Marie, the witness by whose evidence the identity of Surratt, the alleged accomplice of Booth, Atzerodt, & Paine, was determined, arrived at this port yesterday in the steamer **St Laureate**, & went direct to Washington by the evening train. He is a French Canadian; he states that when teaching in Md he made the acquaintance of Surratt & Weichman, the chief witness at the conspiracy trial. St Marie went to Europe & entered the Papal Guard as a zouave. Shortly after he entered the service. While at a festival, St Marie met Surratt, who approached & asked him if he was not an American. He replied that he was. You remind me of an American named Surratt; are you he? Oh no, replied Surratt. All the better for you, said St Marie. Subsequently, when excited with wine, Surratt confessed that he was the man of whom St Marie spoke, & at times talked about the Canadian roads, & the assassination plot. –N Y Times, 16th

Army Bulletin. Leave of absence for 20 days has been granted to Brvt Maj Gearay R Ihre, paymaster, from Mar 22. Thirty days leave of absence is granted to Capt Richd Robbins, 11th infty, who, at the expiration of that period, is ordered to join his regt. 2nd Lt Edw Donovan, 41st U S infty, is granted 30 days leave of absence.

Tragedy at Dekalb, N Y, on Feb 8, when an old man, Thos Hand, was found dead in the cellar of his house, where he had been thrown after being murdered, by an axe to the head. Mr Hand was a bachelor & lived along. John Kennedy & Isadore Levine have been arrested on suspicion of being the murderers.

Concord, N H. Thos W Brickett, of Pembroke, committed suicide on Friday by hanging himself.

Savannah, Feb 15. The steamship **City of Bath**, of the Boston & Savannah line, which left Boston on Feb 5 for this port, was burned at sea off Cape Hatteras. Mr Apthrop & Mrs Souble, passengers, are among the missing. Survivors: Chas Davis, Patrick Donovan, Jeremiah O'Brien, & Frank Toby. Passengers supposed to be lost: Capt Coney; Mead, 1st mate; Bacon, 2nd mate; A Colder, chief engineer; Jno Wiggin, engineer; Chas A Clark; Talbot, steward; Moses Taylor, steward; Banks, quartermaster; John Ryan, fireman; Chas Potter, cook; a 2nd cook-name unknown; 3 coal passers-John Hamilton, Wm Flyman, & one name unknown; two sailors, names unknown.

Portland, Feb 16. Belle Boyd, the Confederate spy came a passenger in the ship **Moravian** yesterday.

Maj H C Ransom, of Hartford, Conn, on Thu, while laboring under a temporary fit of insanity, threw himself from a window of his residence, falling 15 or 20 feet, crushing his skull & causing instant death.

Died: on Feb 17, Geo W Cudlipp, in his 25th year. His funeral will take place from his late residence, 454 8th st, on Feb 19 at 2 P M.

Died: on Feb 16, after a short but painful illness, Charles Lovejoy, infant son of Charles B & Regina A M Hough. His funeral is this morning at 11 o'clock A M, from the residence, 282 9th st, between M & N sts.

Died: on Feb 17, George H, son of the late Orris S Paine, in his 32nd year. His funeral will take place from the residence of his mother, at 251 I st, Feb 19, at 3 o'clock P M.

The house of H G Dur, at Milton, Mass, was entered on Thu last, during the absence of the family, & a trunk was carried off, containing $10,000 in U S bonds.

Portland, Feb 14. This afternoon Henry Kernan, a seaman on board the bark **Mary E Libby**, was stabbed to the heart by Chas Johnson, a runner in Mrs Robt Douglass' boarding-house. The murderer was arrested.

Bailiff sale of one frame Blacksmith & Paint shop, on Feb 19, on N Y ave, between 6th & 7th sts, by writ of distress, issued against Fred'k Gogelein. –Geo T Gibbons, Jos F Kelley, Bailiffs.

Orphans Court of Wash Co, D C, Feb 12, 1867. In the case of Jas S Harvey, exc of Rachel Harrison, deceased, the executor & Court have appointed Mar 19 next, for the final settlement of the personal estate of the said deceased, of the assets in hand. -Jas R O'Beirne, Reg/o wills

Orphans Court of Wash Co, D C. Letters testamentary on the personal estate of Edw C Dyer, late of Wash, D C, deceased. –Thos J Fisher, S S Boadman, excs

TUE FEB 19, 1867
Prof Alex'r Dallas Bache, Superintendent of the Coast Survey, died on Feb 17, at Newport, R I, in his 67th year. He was born at Phil, in Apr, 1806; graduated at the Military Academy in 1825; remained there one year as assist professor resigned from the Corps of Engineers, he filled, at intervals, until 1843, an important chair in the Univ of Pa; withing the same period he was, during 5 years, president of Girard College. Prof Bache was appointed, in Dec 1843, to the vacant post of Superintendent of the Coast Survey. The Coast Guard will be draped in black & closed on the day of the funeral. -Hugh McCulloch, Sec of the Treasury

Navy Bulletin, Feb 9 & 11. Ordered: Sailmaker Wm N Maull, to the ship **Monongahela**; Lt Cmder Wm P McCann, to the Naval Rendezvous, Phil, Pa; Lt Cmder Saml Maguire, to command of the ship **Mahaska**. Order Revoked: Midshipman Henry C Wismer, to the ship **Tacony**, & he is granted sick leave of absence. Placed on the Retired List: Cmder A D Hurrell. Honorably Discharged: Acting Volunteer Lt Jas E Wheeler. Placed on Waiting Orders: Acting 1st Assist Engineer Danl L King. Detached: Lt Cmder John A Howell, from the ship **De Soto**, to take effect May 1, 1867, & granted leave of absence; 2nd Assist Engineer Wm E Sibley, from special duty at N Y, & ordered to the ship **Susquehanna**; 2nd Assist Engineer John F Bingham, from the ship **Pawnee**, & granted sick leave of absence; Surgeon Delevan Bloodgood, from the ship **Vermont**, & ordered to duty on the ship **Jamestown**; 2nd Assist Engineer Wm H **De Hart**, from the **Susquehanna**, & ordered to the **Pawnee**.

Brvt Maj Gen Butterfield is ordered to furnish a funeral escort from the command at **Fort Columbus**, N Y harbor, to accompany the remains of the late Brvt Maj J F Calhoun, assist surgeon, U S A, to Rahway, N J, where he is to be interred.

In equity before Judge Olin, Feb 16, 1867: Mary Buckley vs Wm Buckley; ptn for divorce a *vinculo matrimonii*, upon the ground of adultery. Ordered that the dfndnt pay the petitioner $40 per month, *pendente lite*, & also $50 for her counsel fees.

The U S steamer **Swatara**, Cmder W W Jeffries, having on board John H Surratt, arrived at the navy yard at 5 o'clock yesterday. None of the crew or any person on board has been allowed to come on shore, except Cmder Jeffries, who delivered his despatches to the Admiral commanding the navy yard, & then immediately returned on board.

Orphans Court-Judge Purcell. 1-On Sat the will of the late Edw C Dyer was admitted to probate, & letters testamentary were granted to Thos J Fisher & Sylvester B Boarman, the execs, each giving bond in $100,000. Mr Boarman was appointed guardian to the children, giving bond in $6,000. 2-Henry Reynolds renounced his right to administer on the estate of his deceased brother, Jos Reynolds, late of Miss, & letters of administration were granted to Edw Simms, who gave bond in $6,000. 3-Letters testamentary on the estate of the late John McKim were issued to Alex'r H Rice & John W McKim, who gave bond in $2,000. 4-Marion B Judah was appointed guardian to the orphans of H M Judah, late of the U S army. Bond, $3,000. 5-The first accounts of the guardians to the orphans of Comfort S Whittlesey; the fourth of the guardian to the orphans of Owen Murray; & fifth of guardian to the orphans of Silas H Hill, were each approved & passed.

Died: on Feb 17, Mrs Mary R Nourse, widow of Col M Nourse, in her 88th year. Her funeral will be from her late residence, 461 13th st, between E & F sts, on Feb 19 at 11 o'clock A M.

Died: on Feb 18, suddenly, at his residence, in Alexandria, Va, Geo D Fowle, brother-in-law of Dr Wm P Johnston, in his 46th year.

Died: on Feb 18, of pneumonia, Mary, infant child of Wm W & Mary E Laskey, aged 5 months & 4 days. Her funeral will take place from the residence of her parents, 543 Md ave, on Feb 20, at 3 o'clock P M.

Rev Henry Ward Beecher's novel is called the "Call of the Clergyman." He receives $25,000 for writing it.

Lord Ernest Vane Tempest has been sent to prison in London for 3 months for an assault.

Richmond, Feb 18. Lt J S Newburg, 12th infty, committed suicide this morning at the Ballard House by taking laudanum…He was under arrest at the time.

Orphans Court of Wash Co, D C. Letters of administration on the personal estate of Jos Reynolds, late of Harrison Co, Miss, deceased. –Edw Simms

U S Marshal's sale: in virtue of 2 warrants of sale issued by the Supreme Cout of D C, I will sell at public sale, for cash, at the foot of 9th st wharf, on the Potomac river, on Feb 25, the barge **H F Tracy**, her furniture, tackle, etc, in favor of Geo H Landon, No 177, & Nelson Osborn, No 178, Admiralty. D S Gooding, U S Marshal, D C.

WED FEB 20, 1867
It is understood that ex-Govn'r Thos H Ford & Col Sol Hinckle have been retained as counsel in the case of John H Surratt, on the charge of murder.

The steamer **Swatara**, from Alexandria, Egypt, is a third rate screw steamer, carrying 10 guns. Her list of ofcrs: Cmder, Wm N Jeffries; lt cmders, Jas O Kane, Henry F Picking; surgeon, John C Spear; paymaster, G F Barton; engineer, Henry L Synder.

Clerical promotions in the Treasury. J K P Gleason, A L Guerney, & C H Evans, from 1st to 2nd class, in the Bureau of Statistics, & John Lynch, from 3rd to 4th class, in the 6th Auditor's ofc.

Navy Bulletin, Feb 12. Resigned: Chief Engineer B E Chassing. Detached: Acting Ensign Henry Taylor, from the ship **Vermont**, & granted leave of absence. Ordered: Acting Assist Surgeon McDrennan, to duty at the naval rendezvous, Phil. Appointment Revoked: Acting 3rd Assist Engineer John Deturbe, of Gettysburg.

Orphans Court-Judge Purcell. 1-Yesterday the will of the late Margaret Mackel was fully proven. The testatrix leaves $1,000 for the sole use of Lizzie Wagner, & directs that of the balance of her property one-half shall be divided between Margaret Ulle, Edw Ulle, Michl Mackel, & Lizzie, & the other half between her two brothers. Wm Grupe is named as exc, & letters testamentary were issued to him; bond $4,000. 2-Letters testamentary were issued to Adeline Lee, on the estate of Richd Henry Lee; bond $2,000. 3-Jane McDermott was appointed guardian to the orphans of Thos Hughes; bond $500; & Johana Kieffer to the orphans of Philip Kieffer; bond $500. 4-First & final account of the administrator of M St Clair Clarke was approved & passed.

The following named prisoners, convicted at the present term of the Criminal Court here, were, on Monday, sent to the Albany Penitentiary, to serve out their terms of sentence: Thos Shepherd, John Bell, Jas Franklin, Henry Campbell, Nelson Lindsey, Jeremiah Johnson, Edw Smith, Matthew Connelly, Arthur Grigsby, & Robt Bundy, convicted of larceny, sentenced to one year each; Chas Collins & Augustus Simms, 18 months each; Clinton Smith, Henry Boves, & Geo Washington, 2 years each; Francis Harrison, convicted of manslaughter, sentenced to 5 years.

Yesterday the funeral of Mr Geo H Paine, the topographer of the Water Board, took place, & the Corp ofcs were closed, & the ofcrs generally attended his funeral.

Lawrence, Mass, Feb 19. The inquest in the case of Ingalls Damon, an old man whose remains were found in the ruins of his barn, which was burned on Wed, was concluded on Sat, & resulted in the arrest of Edw P Hunman, husband of Damon's daughter, on suspicion of having caused the death of the old man.

Yesterday Wm Cleaver was arrested on the charge of committing a horrible outrage on the person of Mary Ann Reeves, a little girl of 13 years of age. She died on Monday from the effects. Cleaver is in custody at headquarters & will be committed to jail for court on the charge of murder.

Mrd: on Feb 19, by Rev T R Howlett, Wm H Whitley, M D, of N J, to Alice, eldest daughter of Wm Wurdemann, of Wash City.

For sale *Oakland*, one of the finest estates in Chas Co, Md, containing 1,000 acres of land; improved by first-class new brickdwlg & outhouses of every description, 3 tenant houses, 6 tobacco barns, & mill in perfect order. –V D Stockbridge & Co, Real Estate Brokers, 7th & F sts.

Orphans Court of Wash Co, D C. Letters testamentary on the personal estate of Richd Henry Lee, late of Wash, D C, deceased. –Adaline Lee, excx

THU FEB 21, 1867
Navy Bulletin, Feb 13. Detached: Cmder Chas H Cushman, from the command of the ship **Mahaska**, on the reporting of relief, & placed on waiting orders; Passed Assist Paymaster W W Woodhull, from special duty at Phil, & ordered to the ship **Yantic**; Mates G E Plander, Edw Culbert, & N B Walker, from the **Yantic** & placed on waiting orders. Honorably Discharged: Acting Assist Paymaster Tracy Coit, from Apr 15, 1866. Order Revoked: Acting 1st Assist Engineer M S Thornbohn, to the ship **Saranac**, & he is ordered to the ship **Mohican**. Discharged: Acting 3rd Assist Engineer F W Moore, jr.

Criminal Court-Judge Fisher. 1-Yesterday, Jos Bryant, convicted of manslaughter in causing the death of Wm E Burnside, was sentenced to 2 years in the Albany Penitentiary. The Court remarked that there were mitigating circumstances, & imposed the lowest number of years on this account. 2-Wm Walters, sgt of the Marine Corps, was arraigned on the charge of manslaughter in causing the death of Pvt J S *Streets, of the same corps. The parties were on their way to the river, on Jan 25 last, when some difficulty insued in the squad when under the charge of the sgt, at which time he struck the deceased over the head with an ice hook. The case was continued until today. [Feb 22nd newspaper: Wm Walters hit Streets during a struggle to get hold of the ice hook. Streets had been acting in a mutinous way. Deceased had given some words to Walters.] [Feb 23rd newspaper: Wm Walters, indicted for manslaughter of Jas *Streeks, the jury returned a verdict of not guilty. [*Two spellings of the name Streets/Streeks.

The Com'r of Pensions yesterday made the following appointments of examining surgeons of pensioners: Dr J C Rutherford, Newport, Vt; Dr W R Tompkins, Gallatin, Tenn; Dr John W Cook, Nantucket, Mass; Dr Jas Davidson, Marion, Ill; Dr John E Eddy, Alleghany, N Y; Dr A B Wilson, Ashford, N Y, & Dr Thos J King, Machias, N Y.

Indianapolis Journal: Yesterday attention was attracted to the liquor shop of a German, Andrew Nolte, by smoke rising from it. He had long been an intemperate man, & recently his wife left him & applied for a divorce because of his confirmed drunkenness. He was found lying dead behind his counter, his clothes still burning.

John H Surratt is looked for with interest by the public, we state that the prisoner is comfortably fixed in his apartments at the jail; & as he complains that he has had but little room for exercise, Warden Brown has decided to allow him the privilege of exercising at certain hours of the day in the main corridor of the 2nd floor of the jail. He will have no communication with the other prisoners. Warden Brown has allowed him the privilege of smoking & Surratt appears to enjoy himself hugely in puffing his pipe. He inquired about his sister in an adjoining county in Md. He guessed she was at her grandmother's. Our reporter informed that Miss Surratt has been engaged as a tutoress in the family of a gentleman residing near Surrattsville. She is expected to arrive in Washington City in a day or two.

On Tuesday Lena Bruner, alias Dittrich, was arrested on the charge of larceny of clothes from various parties. She was confined in the Central Guard-house, & yesterday she went with Ofcr Beatty to search her house. While there the woman drank a two-ounce bottle of prussic acid; medical aid was called. She may possibly recover.

Mrd: on Jan 22, at **Hern Cliffs**, the residence of the bride's father, by Rev Chauncey Colton, Rudolph A King, of Wash City, to Bettie W Moore, daughter of Wm P Moore, jr, of Northampton Co, Va.

Died: on Feb 18, in Brooklyn, Harry Purcey, infant son of Kingman F & C Grace Page, recently of Wash City, aged 6 months & 20 days. Of such is the kingdom of Heaven.

Suicide of a brother of Gen Rousseau, of Ky. Edmund P Rousseau, a brother of Hon Lovell H Rousseau, committed suicide by shooting himself. The tragedy occurred at the residence of the deceased, on Walnut st, beyond 18th st, on Wed. He used a pocket pistol. His age was about 45, & he was a brick-mason by trade, & most honorably connected. He was the younger brother, we believe, of Gen & Richd Rousseau. He leaves a wife & 4 children. Mrs Rousseau was on a visit to her friends in Memphis where she was informed by telegraph of his suicide.
–Louisville Journal, Friday

On Monday Lt S Newlin, of the 21st U S Infty, was found dead in his room at the Ballard House in Richmond. A broken laudanum bottle was found in the yard just below his window. We hear he was from Phil, & was of a highly respectable family. He was a young man of good appearance, about 22 or 23 years of age. He had been stationed at City Point, & was to have been tried on Tuesday by court-martial for being engaged in a dueling affair.

FRI FEB 22, 1867
Navy Bulletin, Feb 14. Detached: Surgeon M Duvall, from the ship **Jamestown**, & placed on sick leave of absence. Placed on Waiting Orders: Acting Master Wm M Howarth. Ordered: 1st Assist Engineer Robt Potts, & 2nd Assist Engineers Nelson Roes & John Lowe, to special duty on board the ship **Richmond**.

Jurors for the Mar Term of the Criminal Court:

Richd Harrison	John W Morgan	Amon Woodward, jr
Jesse B Wilson	Chas A Upperman	Saml Gregg
Benj Swain	L T Cartwright	J C Fearson
S M Golden	Jas Dobbyn	L A Stone
Jas Coleman	Alex'r Rutherford	Geo Courtney
John H Howlett	Geo H Tulley	Geo E Kennedy
Robt Clarkson	D M Ball	Wm B Downing
J C Barry	W C Bamberger	

Petit Jurors:

Andrew Jackson	Isaac Hertzberg	Geo P Kidwell
Geo Seitz	Jas T Ferry	Henry Hogg
Henry Somborn	Patrick Quirk	Henry H Haliday
Emanuel Gordon	J Aigler	Jacob Newrath
Geo Barr	C Hager	B T Swart
Alfred Wright	Thos Gaddis	Owen O'Hare
John P Hilton	E M Chapin	Mathew Pabst
Hillary Smith	Jos Keleher	John Webster
W C Bestor	F F Vernon	

Mr B L Jackson, merchant grocer of Wash City, & Miss Eliza Canby, of Montg Co, Md, were married yesterday, at 10 o'clock, by Rev W Pinkney, at the Episcopal Church of the Ascension, on H st, between 9th & 10 sts. Miss Canby was attended by her sister. There was a large congregation. The wedding party left for the North in the 11:15 train.

A late letter from Paris says: the venerable Lord Brougham, now verging on his 90th year, passes from the stage. Few men have left more numerous or more substantial memorials of fame. He has now gone of his own accord into history.

Milwaukie, Feb 20. Boiler explosion at Wisc Paper Co's mill this evening: killed were Isaac Hill, engineer, & his wife; Denis Short, foreman, & a Mrs Jordan.

Independence Belge: Fearful catastrophe has brought desolation upon the family of M Simon Oppenheim, one of the heads of the great banking firm of Solomon Oppenheim & Co, of Cologne. His daughter, M'me the Baroness Deslandes, who married one of the youngest of the sub-prefects of the French Empire, had come to spend the Christmas holidays in Cologne with her family, leaving her two young children, whom she did not wish to expose to the inclemency of the weather, behind her in France. On Dec 26, she received a letter from her governess informing her that her little daughter had been coughing for some hours, but that the doctor said it was of no consequence. She went to her chamber on the second story, & in a moment of frenzy, & threw herself out of the window. Her husband & sister-in-law had been looking for her, & found her chamber window open. She died on Dec 31, at age 24.

Phil. Geo Ellar was arrested on Apr 16 last, charged with the commission of a gross outrage upon the person of a little girl named Louisa Leis, the daughter of Thos Leis, living at 850 Orchard st; Ellar lived at 870. Leis & his wife & daughter were in daily attendance in the court, for a week past. On Thursday, as Ellar entered the court house, Leis arose from his seat, the gleam of a revolver was seen as the polished barrel was levelled at the prisoner, a quick report followed, &, with a single agonizing "Oh!" Ellar fell. A scene of confusion followed. Judge Ludlow was on the bench; ladies fainted; the wife of Ellar was in the court & presented a piteous spectacle. Ellar's body was placed in a coffin. -Phil North American, Thu

Dept of the Interior, U S Patent Ofc, Wash, Feb 16, 1867. Ptn of Geo N Reed & Pescisal Tuttle, adms of the estates of Jos H Tuttle, deceased, of Geneva, N Y, praying for the extension of a patent granted to the said Jos H Tuttle Jun 21, 1853, for an improvement in Saws, for 7 years from the expiration of said patent, which takes place on Jun 21, 1867. -T C Theaker, Com'r of Patents

SAT FEB 23, 1867
Criminal Court-Judge Fisher. 1-John H Brooks, charged with bastardy, the appeal was dismissed. 2-Henry Osbury, convicted of presenting false claims, was sentenced to 18 months in the penitentiary; Taylor Collins, for larceny, one year; John Ross, assault & battery with intent to kill, 2 years; Lewis Gordon, larceny, 1 year; Isaac Washington, false pretences, 1 year.

Died: yesterday, of consumption, Thos D Larner, aged 39 years. His funeral will take place this Saturday at 3 o'clock, from the residence of his uncle, Thos Donoho, 366 D st, near 9th st.

Providence, Feb 22. Pres Johnson has commuted to imprisonment for life the sentence of Robt Crow, who was to have been hanged next Friday, for the crime of murder on the high sea.

Association of Oldest Inhabitants held a meeting at City Hall yesterday. Col Peter G Washington presided, assisted by Col J S Williams & Mr J F Callan. W W Corcoran appeared in the meeting, & was invited to a seat on the platform. Mr Jos H Bradley read an ode written Feb 22, 1827, by Richd Wright, a citizen of Wash. Prof Donald MacLeod read selections from Washington's farewell address. Col J C Pickett & J Carroll Brent read orations. Dr John B Blake presented to the association several relics of the olden time: papers of the meeting of the first court of the District, Jun 22, 1801; list of attys & ofcrs, all of whom are dead, the late Gen Walter Jones being the last survivor, & also a list of the members of the Union Fire Co, previous to 1813, but two of whom, Chauncy Bestor & Seth Hyatt survive. New members were proposed & elected: Lewis, Nathl, & Saml Carusi, W H Standford, W M Ellis, Alex'r Boreland, Jas Anderson, Sept Tustin, H B Walker, & Solomon Hubbard. The deaths of Jos N Fearson, John Meem, & Elijah Edmonston, members of the association, were announced.

Miss Anna Surratt visited her brother, John H Surratt, yesterday, & had a long interview with him. Both exhibited great emotion.

Martin Hoyberger bought a small frame house of 4 rooms, on 5th st, between N & O, for the sum of $825, cash, yesterday.

Naval Intelligence: Lt Cmder Fleming announces the sudden death of S M Kellogg, Fleet Surgeon of the South Atlantic Squadron, & Acting Passed Assist Surgeon T K Chandler, the latter from yellow fever.

Navy Bulletin. Placed of Leave of Absence for Discharge: Acting Ensign Cephas K Waite. Ordered: Lt Cmder Edw Y McCauley, to duty as fleet capt & chief of staff of the North Atlantic Squadron.

Last night Wm Snobel, a German shoemaker, who had been for some time on hostile terms with Jacob & Eliz Henry, & their son, all of whom dwelt in the same tenement house with himself, assaulted the three of them. Snobel stabbed Jacob Henry to the heart, then inflicted severe wounds on his wife & son. Jacob died instantly; Mrs Snobel it is feared will not survive. The murderer was taken into custody by the 20th Precinct police. -N Y Herald

TUE FEB 26, 1867
Navy Bulletin, Feb 18. Honorably Discharged: Acting Master F P B Sands, Acting Assist Paymaster Arthur Sibley, from Sep 21, 1865. Resignation Revoked: Acting Assist Surgeon O A River, dated Jun 19th, & he is placed on leave of absence. Resigned: Midshipman Chas E Starr. Order Revoked: Sailmaker Wm N Waull, to the ship **Monongahela**, & he is placed on waiting orders.

Died: on Feb 25, at the residence of his father, in Montg Co, Md, of inflammation of the lungs, Dorsey Clagett, youngest son of Smith & Mary Ann Thompson, aged 3 years & 12 months. He will be buried at Rock Creek Church on Feb 27 at 12 M.

Died: on Feb 24, after a long & painful illness, Col John Patterson Pepper, in his 72nd year. The funeral of Col Pepper will take place from his late residence, 408 Pa ave, today at half past 2 o'clock P M. [Phil papers please copy.] [Feb 27th newspaper: The remains were taken to the *Congressional Cemetery*, where they were deposited in the vault for future interment.]

Estate of Jos Veazie, late of Providence, R I. Municipal Court of the City of Providence, Feb 12, 1867. The ptn of Amos M Warner, adm of the estate of Jos Veazie, late of Providence, deceased, intestate, praying that this court will pass an order for distributing the personal estate of said deceased, in his hands, & among the heirs of said deceased. Meeting on Jul 9 next, at the Municipal Court Room for consideration. –Levi Saulsbury, clerk

Rev Michl McCarron, Archdeacon of the Catholic Diocese of N Y, died in that city on Saturday.

Charleston, S C, Feb 25. Hon Isaac E Holmes, formerly a member of Congress from Charleston, died today.

Indianapolis, Feb 21. Alex'r Pape, a laborer of this city, died last night of hydrophobia, having been bitten about 10 weeks since.

Household & kitchen furniture at auction on Mar 4, at the residence of the late Wm Redin, 76 Gay st, between Congress & Wash sts, Gtwn. –Thos Dowling, auct

Dept of the Interior, U S Patent Ofc, Wash, Feb 21, 1867. Ptn of Alex'r J Walker, of N Y, N Y, praying for the extension of a patent granted to him May 24, 1853, for an improvement in Spirit Lamps, for 7 years from the expiration of said patent, which takes place on May 24, 1867. -T C Theaker, Com'r of Patents

Col Wm G Moore was on Sat confirmed by the Senate as paymaster in the army. Col Moore is a son of Capt W W Moore, president of the Common Council.

Dr Railly J Clark died at Glen's Falls on Wed last, in his 90th year. It is stated that he drew up the consititution of the first regularly organized temperance society in the U S, at the town of Mareau, Saratoga Co, in 1808.

Murder of Union soldiers. Proof in the record establishes that Cpl Corbit & Pvts Emery Smith & Mason Brown, of co A, 1st btln of Maine volunteers, were wilfully & deliberately murdered at Brown's Ferry, on the Savannah river, in S C, on Oct 8, 1865, The report does not prove beyond a reasonable doubt, the guilt of the dfndnts, J C Keys, F G Stowers, Robt Keys, & Elisha Byrum. They were arrested by military authorities. They were sentenced to imprisonment for life. The prisoners were removed from the Dry Tortugas to **Fort Delaware**. –Hon Edmund Cooper, Cmte to inquire into the murder of the Union soldiers in S C.

WED FEB 27, 1867
Died: on Feb 26, suddenly, Mrs Amelia Wallingsford, in her 88th year. Her funeral will be from the residence of her son-in-law, Isaac W Ross, Wed, at 2:30 P M.

Dublin, Feb 26. Capt McCafferty, formerly of the U S army, & recently a leading member of the Fenian organization in America, & companion of Head Cortre Stephens, was arrested in this city on suspicion of having been concerned in the recent outbreak at Killarney.

Nelson Ebertson, convicted in the Circuit Court of Alexandria Co of assault & battery with intent to kill, & sentenced to 12 months in the county jail, on Friday last, was pardoned by the Govn'r.

Phil, Feb 26. Despatch from Newmarket, Middlesex Co N J: Mrs Dr Lester Wallace *Correll was murdered about 12 o'clock last night. The murder was committed by 2 men, & the house was robbed. [*Aug 16th newspaper: Correll is spelled Coriell] [Aug 29th newspaper: Bridget Durgan, who murdered Mrs Coriell, some time since, will be hung on Friday next, at New Brunswick, N J; she confesses she alone murdered Mrs Coriell, not for robbery, but to supplant her mistress in the affections of her husband. Mary Gilroy, confined in the same jail on suspicion that she was accessory to the murder, knew nothing of the murder.]

THU FEB 28, 1867
Orphans Court-Judge Purcell. 1-Letters of administration on the estate of Thos Ewall, deceased, were issued to Wm F Purcell; bond $15,000. 2-The first & final account of John Riley, administrator of A N Y Howle, deceased, & the first & final account of John H Semmes, administrator of Louisa Collins, deceased, were filed. 3-Letters testamentary on the estate of Jos W Fearson, deceased, were issued to Mary Ann Fearson. 4-The will of Chas Stoske was filed & partially proven.

Mrd: on Feb 21, at Grace Church, N Y, by Rev A G Mercer, D D, Col D A Fell to Caroline P, daughter of B H Cheever, of Wash.

The Pres has nominated the following Quartermasters, U S A:
To be Colonels: Maj Robt Allen, Maj J L Donaldson, Maj D H Rucker.
To be Lt Cols: Maj R Ingalls, Maj J C McFerran, Capt R Tyler, Capt J A Ekin.
To be Assist Quartermasters, with rank of Capt: Amos S Kimball, S B Lauffert, D W Porter, E J Strong, Jas T Hoyt, Gilbert C Smith, John C V Furey.
With rank of Major: John G Chandler, Wm Myers, R N Batchelder, C G Sawtelle, J J Dana, Jas A Potter, M I Ludington.
With rank of Col: D H Vinton, Osborn Cross, Rufus Ingalls, E B Babbitt, R E Clary.
With rank of Lt Col: M S Miller, A Montgomery, S Van Vliet, L A Easton, R W Kirkham.
To rank as Major: H C Ranson, J M Moore, A J Perry, Tredwell Moore, A R Eddy, J D Bingham, H C Hodges.
To rank as Capt: N S Constable, W A Wainwright, Thos B Hunt, E B Kirk.
To rank as Lt Col: S B Holabaird, C H Tompkins.
To be Assist Paymaster Gen, with rank of Colonel: Danl McClure.
To be Deputy Paymaster Generals, with rank of Lt Col: C H Fry, N W Brown.
To be Paymasters: E D Judd, J C Dewey, H O Brigham, Chas H Halsey, Wm Smith, B Mayer, J L Hodge, R D Clark, C M Terrell, J W Nichols, H B Reese, V C Hanna, J H Nelson, T H Stanton, D M Adams, C J Sprague, W R Gibson, J W Smith, P P G Hall, C W Wingard, E J P Canby, W B Rochester, G W Candee, J E Burbank, N Vedder, J S Walker, G Pomeroy, W H Johnston, P M McGrath, E H Brooke.
To be Medical Storekeepers: Geo Wright, G T Beall, A V Cherbonnier.
To be Chief Medical Purveyor, with rank of Lt Col: R S Satterlee.
To be Assist Medical Purveyors, with rank of Lt Col: Dr C McDougall, Dr E Habadil, Dr R Murray, Dr C Sutherland.
To be Surgeons: Dr C Wagner, Dr J P Wright, Dr C C Gray, Dr W C Spencer.

Died: on Feb 27, at the residence of his son-in-law, Saml J Randall, Gtwn, D C, Aaron Ward, of Sing Sing, Westchester Co, N Y. [Mar 5th newspaper: The funeral services over the remains of the late Gen Aaron Ward took place on Sunday in St Paul's Episcopal Church at Sing Sing, N Y.]

Chancery sale of valuable real estate s e corner of 13th st west & K st north at auction, by order of resale, at the risk & cost of the defaulting purchaser, dated Feb 10, 1867, passed in a cause pending in the Supreme Court of D C, in which Adelaide J Brown is cmplnt & Thos B Brown & others are dfndnts: No 254 Equity, Docket 7. Public auction Mar 24 of lots 14 thru 17 in square 285, Wash City, with improvements. –Jos H Bradley, jr, trustee. –Cooper & Latimer, aucts

Executor's sale of one four seat carriage & set of double harness, one fine diamond set; enamelled chase hunting case watch; etc, at public auction, on Mar 2, by order of the Orphans Court of D C., belonging to the personal effects of the late Edw C Dyer, deceased. Terms cash. -Green & Williams, aucts

Orphans Court of Wash Co, D C, Feb 26, 1867. In the case of Chas W Boteler & John W Boteler, adms of Chas W Boteler, sr,deceased, the administrators & Court have appointed Mar 23 next, for the final settlement of the personal estate of the said deceased, of the assets in hand. -Jas R O'Beirne, Reg/o wills

FRI MAR 1, 1867
Navy Bulletin, Feb 21. Placed on Leave for Discharge: Acting Ensign Jas Softly. Honorably Discharged: Acting Ensign M M Wheeler, from Feb 2: Acting Assist Paymaster Wm H Byron, from Dec 4, 1865.

Yesterday Patrick Goldin, a blind man, & his wife got on car #10 of the Wash & Gtwn railroad, & had but six cents with which to pay their fare. The conductor having arrived at the bridge over Rock creek went to collect his fair, & Patrick, not having enough, was ordered out. In getting off the platform he struck his foot against one of the side pieces which guard the track, & fell against the rail with force sufficient to throw him over, & he was precipitated about 40 feet to the ground. He was taken to his home on Bridge st, in Gtwn, where Dr Pelins is attending him. He was seriously injured.

On Wed Thos McIntyre, a well known Corp employee, was set up by Wm Scott, a pressman at the Treasury Dept. Scott invited him to go with him to Gockler's saloon, 4th & K sts; McIntyre said he would go in with him, but did not want to drink. On entering the saloon, Bub Gettings, a step-brother of Scott's, walked in & deliberately drew a pistol & fired. Fortunately he missed his aim, but he then struck McIntyre on the head. McIntyre is seriously ill & unable to leave his bed. Yesterday Scott gave himself up to the police. The origin of the affair is said to be some family ill-feeling.

Commencement of the Medical Dept of Gtwn College will be held on Tuesday next, at Wall's New Opera House, when the following gentlemen will graduate & receive their diplomas as M D's:

Wm C Tilden, Vt-valedictorian
Walter O Alexander, D C
John Frazier Boughter, Pa
Saml Brook, Mass
Geo W Blake, Md
Benj B Babcock, Pa
Patrick H Brennan, Pa
Rufus Choate, D C
Thos Conant, Mass
Saml W Caldwell, Pa
J Nelson Clark, Pa
Richardo D DeL'French, N Y
Andrew I Buntoon, N H
Robertson Howard, D C
Franklin T Howe, Mass
Wm Hale, N Y
Albion B Jamison, Pa
Wm B Lyon, Pa
Danl S Lamb, Pa
Granville Malcom, Pa
Valentine McNalley, Conn

Chas E McChesney, N J
Willan J L Nicodemus, Md
Fred'k Wooster Owen, N Y
Jos T O'Connor, Pa
Albert A Pierce, Mo
Lewis E Rauterberg, D C
Benj R Raines, Mo
Chas Roys, D C
Algernon Marble Squire, N H
Harlen S Smith, N Y
Chas W Sonnenschmidt, D C
John E Smith, D C
Thos H Trott, D C
Granville S Thompson, N Y
Chas M Tree, D C
John W Van Arnum, Wis
David C Waters, N Y
J Harry Wright, N Y
John L Wolfe, Pa

Died: on Feb 25, at Vernon, Windham Co, Vt, Ebenezer Howe, an old & highly respected man, after a long & painful illness, having filled many high ofcs during his time, for years a State Senator.

Louisville, Feb 28. Wm Barton, whilst firing at Capt Britton, formerly of the Confederate States army, accidentally shot Brig Gen Ely Murray, U S army, in the leg. The affair occurred at a law school, where all three are students.

Mrs Geo E Pugh, wife of Senator Pugh, of Ohio, died in Cincinnati, a day or two, in her 35th year of her age. Mr Pugh [nee Teresa Chalfant] was famous in Washington for her beauty & accomplishments.

Among the few brevet pormotions after death recently confirmed by the Senate was that of 1st Lt Bayard Wilkeson, son of Saml Wilkeson, killed at age 19, at the battle of Gettysburg, in command of battery G, 4th regular artl, promoted to be capt for gallantry in the battle of the Deserted House, & to be major for gallantry at Fredericksburg, & lt colonel for gallantry at Gettysburg. Mr Saml Wilkeson was the Gettysburg correspondent of the N Y Tribune, & many will recollect the anguished cry with which his letter commenced-"Describe a battle! When the central figure is the mangled body of an only son, killed in command of a battery placed where no battery ought to have been!"

Died: on Feb 14, at Hoosick Falls, N Y, Mrs Wealthy D Adams, in her 69th year.

Decorated China. We are receiving per ship **John Bright**, from Liverpool, a very handsome assortment of rich decorated Toilet Sets; also, decorated French China Dinner Sets. –Webb & Beveridge, Odd Fellows' Hall, 7th st.

Chancery sale of valuable real estate s e corner of 13th st west & K st north, at auction; by order of resale, at the risk & cost of the defaulting purchaser, dated Feb 10, 1867, passed in a cause pending in the Supreme Court of D C, in which Adelaide J Brown is cmplnt, & Thos B Brown & others dfndnts, No 254 Equity, Docket 7; sale, on the premises, on Mar 25, lots 14 thru 17 in square 285, Wash City, with improvements. –Jos H Bradley, jr, trustee -Cooper & Latimer, aucts

Proposals for hardware for the Treasury Extension. Treasury Dept, Ofc of Supervising Architect, Feb 28, 1867. A B Mullett, Supervising Architect.

SAT MAR 2. 1867

Gen Aaron Ward, long known & much esteemed in social & political circles, departed this life on Feb 27, at the residence of his son-in-law, Hon Saml J Randall, in Gtwn, after a brief illness. He was distinguished as a gallant young ofcr in the ward of 1812; devoted himself to the practice of the law, & in 1825 was elected from the Westchester district as a Rep in Congress; was re-elected & served several terms in Congress till 1843-44.

Alexandria. Last night, Mr Jas H Simpson, residing over his bakery, on Fairfax st, near King, was awakened by the suffocating effects of smoke, which filled his bedroom, & was found to issue from the cellar of the adjoining house, occupied by Mr Edgar Speiden as a family grocery store. Powder was stored there & Capt Walsh, of the night watch, & young Mr Taylor Arnold, having learned its location, plunged through the smoke bringing two kegs out. The fire was the work of an incendiary.

T D DeBow, editor of DeBow's Review, died on Feb 27, at Elizabeth, N J; was born in Charleston, S C, in 1820; widely known as a statistician & a strong advocate of the slave-labor system. He was at one time Superintendent of the U S Census.

On Monday, locomotive 229, belonging to the N Y Central Railroad, exploded her boiler, while standing on the track, below the Broadway crossing in Albany. About one-third of the boiler passed through the roof John Tracey's distillery on Colonie st. Henry Ford, engineer, nose broken & other injuries, & will probably recover; Mich Quinn, fireman, arm broken, scalded, but not fatally injured; Conrad Julius, foreman of a tin shop at West Albany, injured slightly; Capt Carroll & Ofcrs Kreachler, White, & Bulger, of the police force, were slightly hurt. Alex'r Carvin was scalded, but not dangerously.

War Dept Claims Commission. Wash, D C, Feb 28, 1867. The following claims have been filed with the Commission during the present month:
Claim of schnr **Amytis**, for her destruction while in service of the U S.
M L Rood & A H Hager, for ordnance stores.
Sanford Robinson, services in Engineers' Dept.
Stephen Kruse, for property taken by U S troops.
Saml Haycroft, for lumber taken by U S troops.
A C & R G Lee, for destruction of property by U S authorities.
Chas Spencer, for ordnance boat furnished Gov't.
Jas H Holmes, for services in carrying despatches.
Thos Higginbotham, for lead furnished St Louis Arsenal.
O P Mason, for services as provost marshal of Nebraska
Warren & Moore, destruction of property at Nashville, Tenn
Sue Murphy, destruction of property at Decatur, Ala
Geo W Grahame, for value of stores lost with steamer **Tigress**.
Jas G Cady, for services in Provost Marshal Dept.
Wm Gray, for rent of property in Manchsester, Va.
Margaret Edes, for rent of property in Wash, D C.
Robt M Richards, for property destroyed.
C C Bliss, for rent of property at Little Rock, Ark.
John Pearce, for horses seized by U S troops
Wilkins W Wagoner, for supplies furnished
Bird Douglas, for pasturing public animals.
Thos B Poindexter, heirs of, for value of horse Panic.
Elihu S Marshall, for property destroyed.
Gibbs & Besse, for sutlers' goods taken by the rebels in Louisiana.
Andrew Seitz, for timber used for fortifications.
Mrss S V Muller, for lumber used for fortifications.
A P Weller & Levi W Gritten, for horses stolen by Indians.
Richd Merryman, for horses stolen by Indians.
H J Ruddington, for rent of & damages to property.
A T Mauphin, for printing press & materials taken by U S authorities.
Jas J Bowen, for property taken near Vienna, Va.
Mrs Eliza B Hurdesty, heirs of, for moneys seized from banks of New Orleans.
A B Ayres, for lumber used for fortifications.
Taliaferro & Grant, for transportation of stores in New Mexico.
J T Stockbridge, for rent of *Meridian Hill*.
E E Clark, for property taken from his plantation near Helena, Ark.
John L Crise, for value of horse taken for use of army.
Butler H Bisby, expenses in recovering pine logs.
M M Yeakle, for value of mule taken by U S Troops.
R V Montague, for cotton used in fortifications.
J Millinger, for hotel used for barrabcks at Nashville, Tenn.
W W Cones, for proceeds of sale of cotton by Quartermaster's Dept.
Jas E O'Farrell, for cotton seized at Mobile, Ala.
A C & A G Hills, for type & printing materianls taken at New Orleans, La.

Crescuiss Cordobla, for services as spy & guide in New Mexico.
Benj Corder, for services as teamster in New Mexico.
Jose Maria Condert, for rent of surgeons quarters in New Mexico.
Jose Baca, for use of horse in New Mexico.
Juan Jose Goruile, for services as teamster in New Mexico.
Antonio Frugillo, for services in Quartermaster's Dept, New Mexico.
Pablo Pino, for transportation of wagons, etc; & for use of mules, in New Mexico.
Saml Cross, for hauling logs near Victoria Station.
Lewis F Cosby, for value of logs used for block houses.
Alex'r Copeland, for extra duty service as blacksmith.
Chas H Lane, for rent of house & lot in Wash, D C.
David L Finch, for value of trees cut from his premises.
Geo A Hanson, adm of Thos Lawson, for compliance with contract made by Gov't as to rent of property
John H Bush, for wood taken from his premises.
D K Abeel, for value of horse & equipment.
Chas C Hudson, for medical supplies furnished the army at Wilmington, N C.
Franz Dummerth, for value of mule taken by U S troops.
Bernheimer Brothers, for clothing.
Geo P Evans, for printing circulars, etc, at Richmond, Va.
W G Clarke, for rent of property in St Louis, Mo.
Mrs M L Russell, for medical & hospital stores.
Claim of steamer **Fancy Brandies**, for reimbursement of ransom.
Dixon Colley, for goods seized in Colordo Territory.
S & H Sayles, for kerseys furnished the U S Gov't.
John A Williams, for use of steamer **Calahaula**.
John L Kidwell, for rent of property in Wash, D C.
Joshua Hill, for cotton taken from his ware-house in Ark.
Martha L Russell, for subsistence stores for use of army.
David Hill, Jerry Nuns, Sanford Kennel, Geo Jackson, Edmund Alford, David Frazier, John James, Henry Clay, Coleman Sparks, & Litcher Gentry, for services at *Camp Nelson*, Ky.

N Y, Mar 1. Geo Wagner was executed at the Tombs at 9 o'clock today for the murder of his wife.

Death penalty abolished in Illinois. Springfield, Ill, Feb 28. A bill virtually abolishing captial punishment has passed both houses of the Legislature.

N Y, Mar 1. Amos J Williamson, editor of the Sunday Dispatch, & chairman of the Republican Union Central Cmte, died yesterday at New Orleans.

Phil, Mar 1. Thos V Scott was found dead in 7th st this morning. His death is supposed to have been caused by a blow from a slungshot. He was a musician & had been playing at a party. His violin was lying broken beside him. No clue to the perpretrator.

Charleston, Mar 1. The negro Horace Greeley was executed this morning for the murder of Mr R Barnwell Rhett. Before death, he made a confession of his guilt, which he had heretofore stubbornly denied. But a few persons were present at the execution.

Final action had upon claims during the persent month.
Allowed:
John Brown
Hugh Sturdy & others
Vincent Dockery
John H Wardwell & Co
Moses Mids
Wylly Woodbridge
J B Raverdy & others
C L Gorton
Henry Sheets
G A Lilliendahl
L B Johnson
Mrs Sally Webster
Mrs Ann C Carroll & another

John Wilson
Danl Smith
W S Newberry
Maj Gordon Chapin, 14th U S infty
Caleb Hanford
Durlop, Moncure & co
D F Bligh & another
Benj Fahnstock
Walter F Herrick
Rebecca A Curd
A C Hunt & another
G Gildenstrip

Rejected:
Jas Tongue
Hargous & Co
John F Javens
John Aiken
Columbus Reid
Louis Paul Cayen
L L Ferriere
Jas G Brown
John Reid
Mary Jane Stinson
Maurice Roch
John M Powell
R W Holman
Saml M Puckett
L H Davis

Moses Maples
Peter Pulman
Mary Ann Johnson
John A Stevenson
A F Gautreaux
Saml C White
John H Tucker
Mrs Mary Quigly
A J Martin
Mrs E F Carter
Matthew Allison
Mrs Mary Sullivan
John W Alver
C J Van Wickle

The Chicago papers of Saturday contain a lengthy communication from Rev Hart L Stewart, withdrawing from further contest of the divorce suit, on account of a lack of means to defend it.

Mrd: on Feb 21, at Grace Church, N Y, by Rev A G Mercer, D D, Col D A Pell to Caroline P, daughter of B H Cheever, of Wash.

Mrd: on Feb 20, at St Peter's Church, Brooklyn, N Y, by Rev Mr Paddock, Mr Richd G Olcott, of Wash City, to Miss M Louise Keeler, of Brooklyn.

Mrd: on Feb 28, at the residence of the bride's parents, by Rev Fr Lynch, S J, Dr Carlos Carvallo, 2nd son of his Excellency Senor Don Manuel Carvallo, Envoy Extraordinary & Minister Plenipotentiary of Chili to Great Britain, to Mary Emma, 2nd daughter of Buckner Bayliss, of Wash City. [N Y papers please copy.]

Died: on Mar 1, in Wash City, Mrs Ann Eliz Burch, relict of the late Jos A Burch, in her 76th year. Her funeral will take place on Mar 2 at 3 o'clock, from the residence of her son, C J Burch, 388 H st, between 13th & 14th sts.

Died: yesterday, Mary Isabella, wife of Jos F Hodgson, Intendant of the Wash Asylum, in her 36th year. Her funeral will take place on Monday morning, at 9 o'clock precisely from the Asylum. Carriages will be in waiting at 410 7th st, Harvey's, undertaker, & at the Wallach School-house.
+
Mrs Joseph F Hodgson, matron of the Wash Asylum, died yesterday, after a protracted illness, of consumption. She was noted for her gentleness of disposition & kindness of heart. The inmates of the asylum all mourn her loss, but the saddest mourners are the bereaved husband & 4 orphan children. [Mar 4th newspaper: The remains of Mrs Hodgson will be taken to St Patrick's Church, where requiem mass will be offered at 11 o'clock.]

Chancery sale of improved property on 20th st west, between E & F sts; by decree of the Supreme Court of D C, passed in cause No 656, Equity, in which Thos Cogan is cmplnt, & Jane McManus et al are dfndnts: sale on Mar 21, in front of the premises, part of lot 5 in square 122. [Improvements not noted.] -Eugene Carusi, trustee -Cooper & Latimer, aucts [late clerks with Jas C McGuire & Co, aucts.]

Steinway Pianos for sale: Grand, Square, & Upright Cabinet Pianos. At the World's Fair, in London, Steinway & Sons received the endorsement of superiority of their Pianos over all makers of the world. –W G Metzerott & Co, 318 Pa ave, sole agent [Ad]

Geo Wilner, Paperhanger & Upholsterer, importer & dealer in French & American paperhangings & upholstery goods. 454 9th st west, between D & E sts. [Ad]

MON MAR 4, 1867
Martin W Bates, aged 19 years, was hanged at Burlingame, Kansas, on Feb 20, for the murder of Abel Palley.

Mrd: on Feb 26, at the residence of the bride's parents, Perth Amboy, N J, by Rev Smith Pyne, D D, Mr Philip Van Rensselaer Van Wyck, of N Y, to Salvadora, daughter of the late John T McLaughlin, U S N.

Died: on Mar 2, in Harrisburg, Pa, Mary Ross, wife of Rev B B Leacock, & only daughter of the late Dr E W Roberts.

Died: on Sunday, in Wash City, at the residence of her brother, Admiral Shubrick, Mrs Decima C Heyward, widow of the late Jas H Heywood, of South Carolina.

On Sat Ofcr Guy found the dead body of a man lying on the pavement on K st, near Pa ave. He had been shot in the head & a knife was nearby. He was about 30 years of age & on his coat was the name of A D Titsworth & Co, Chicago, Ill. Money was found on him, so that it is evident he was not killed for the purposes of robbery. If not identified, the body will be buried today, at the expense of the city, in Potter's Field.

Ofcrs in this District who have been confirmed by the Senate Friday: E M Chapin, & Wm Martin, as Justices of the Peace for Wash Co. Col Jas R O'Beirne, as Reg o/Wills for Wash Co. [Col O'Beirne is well known to our citzens as formerly provost marshal & late a deputy marshal of this District.] Edw C Eddie, as Register of Deeds for this District, vice R M Hall, removed.

To those wanting Farms in Va: 200 tracts of superior Valley Land, 160 acres each, in Piedmont district; price $3 per acre. Title perfect. Warranty deeds given.
-T B Wigfall, Hillsville Post Ofc, Carroll Co, Va.

Real estate sales: west half of lot 12 in square 348, with improvements, to Julia A Van Ness, for $2,050; part of lot 13 in square 876, on 8th st, between A & B sts, to Enoch Tottin, for $800; part of lot 1 in square 76, on 20th st, near K, improved with two frame houses, to H Ross, for $1,015 for each house.

On Monday Mr H Hobart Smith was admitted an atty & counsellor at law of the Supreme Court of D C.

Orphans Court of Wash Co, D C. Letters of administration on the personal estate of Cyprian A Morton, late of Wash Co, D C, deceased. –Jas Goszler, adm, d b n

TUE MAR 5, 1867
Confirmations & Rejections:
Confirmations:
Superintendent of Indian Affairs: Theodore T Dwight, for Nevada.
Collector of Customs: Thos Russell, for Boston & Charlestown, Mass.
Com'r of Paris Exposition: Abram S Hewitt, of N Y.
Appraiser of Merchandise: Chas M Harley, of Phil, Pa.
Consul: Felix Agnus, of Md, at Londonderry.
Assessors of Internal Revenue: J L Englehart, 7th Dist of Pa; A C Morrill, 2nd Dist of Maine.
Collectors Internal Revenue: Robt McLaren, 2nd Dist of Minn; John J Randall, 2nd Dist of Minn.
Registers of Land Ofc: Jas R McClure, Junction City, Kansas; Edmund Browning, Indianapolis, Ind.

Receivers of Public Moneys: Wm Boaz, Indianapolis, Ind; Cyrus Aldrich, St Cloud, Minn; Lucas K Stannard, Taylor's Falls, Minn.

Justices of the Peace: Zach B Brooke, John S Hollingshead, T J Gardner.

Postmasters:

John Crawford, Crawfordsville, Ind
Robt R Bush, Elkhart, Ind
Ezra Read, Terre Haute, Ind
Cyrus P Morford, Attica, Ind
John M Wilson, New Albany, Ind
M D Tackett, Greensburg, Ind
Edw W Truman, Kokomo, Ind
John Hendricks, Shelbyville, Ind
Wm Schoenemoun, Mich City, Ind
Jas H Tetter, Peru, Ind
Azariah T Whittlesey, Evansville, Ind
Jas Vaughn, Lawrenceburg, Ind
E A Jones, Richmond, Ind
Isaac Baker, Princeton, N J
Henry A Greene, Jersey City, N J
Wm B Robinson, Salem, N J
Darius Wells, Paterson, N J
Jos B Oliver, Rahway, N J
Wm H Streeter, Houghton, Mich
Mrs Harriet L Guigan, Schuylkill, Pa
Jas H McClelland, Alleghany, Pa
Clinton Cullom, Meadville, Pa
Wm R Brown, Napa City, Calif
Jas Gibson, Va City, Montana
John Potter, Helena, Ark
Wm Morgan, Danville, Ill
Chas M Blair, **Fort Scott**, Kansas
Wm S Webb, Junction City, Kansas
Robt A Gilmore, Chicago, Ill
Harmon Seymour, Boonesboro, Iowa
J W Chubbuck, Gold Hill, Nevada
Byron B Bacon, Columbia, Calif

Rejections:

Justices of the Peace for the Dist of Columbia: Wm R Bradford, David R Smith, W W Tucker, Donald McCathran, O E P Hazard, H C McCoy, Geo Forrest, M P Callan, Jas Lynch, Thos D Hodgkin, & E R Barrett.

Pension Agent: Ezekiel K Cox, Columbus, Ohio.

Surveyor General: Wm B Thornbury, of Nevada, for Surveyor General of Nevada.

U S Atty: Chas C Whittlesey, for Eastern Dist of Missouri.

Indian Agents: Henry W Martin, Fond du Lac agency.

Postmasters:

Wm H H Taylor, Hamilton, Ohio
Chas H Sage, Circleville, Ohio
Jas Hagle, Xenia, Ohio
Jacob R Hubbell, Dayton, Ohio
Jefferson Palm, Warren, Ohio
Lamuel McKee, Troy, Ohio
Matthew C Hale, Sidney, Ohio
Danl Lupton, Salem, Ohio
Wm M Mifford, Mount Vernon, Ohio
Isaac A Bryant, Bucyrus, Ohio
Robt Flint, Fond du Lac, Wisc
Edw Hicks, Green Bay, Wisc
Thos J Ruger, Janesville, Wisc
John J Craven, Newark, N J
T C Moore, Camden, N J
Albert H Stanborough, Morristown, N J
Henry C Kelsey, Newton, N J
Henry Bertram, Watertown, Wisc
Michl Dunn, **Fort Leavenworth**, Kansas
Wm H Hoyt, Burlington, Vt
Norman Seymour, Mt Morris, N Y
John E Page, Marshalltown, Iowa
Ellianan Smith, Towanda, N Y
Jas McKean, Mercer, Pa
Saml J Harris, Columbus, Ind
Andrew G Wood, Warsaw, Ind
Chas C Hill, Princton, Ind
Gideon Blair, Plymouth, Ind
Edwin S Organ, La Porte, Ind
J J Nash, Kendallville, Ind

Saml M Graham, Delphi, Ind
C L Shrewsury, Madison, Ind
J B Marshall, Valparaiso, Ind
Walter Barber, Susquehanna Depot, Pa
Chas H Taylor, Grand Rapids, Mich
F W Anthony, Jackson, Mich
Foster Pratt, Kalamazoo, Mich

Wm J Edwards, Niles, Mich
Jas Munroe, Marshall, Mich
Wm Haslet, Dowagiac, Mich
Edw Van Demosk, Bottlebuck, Mich
Chas W Fonda, Three Rivers, Mich
Solomon E Bliss, East Saginaw, Mich

On Sat night the residence of John Ginnochio, an Italian grocer of Richmond, Va, was robbed of $1,200 in currency, several hundred dollars in gold, & a number of valuable articles of jewelry, the value of the stolen property amounting to about $5,000.

Queen Victoria is again to appear as the leader of the London fashions. On Feb 27 she is to hold a drawing-room in which she will for the first time leave off mourning, & the foreign ministers have received instructions to congratulate her Majesty on her re-appearance in the state ceremonies.

Supreme Court of D C; No 560 Equity; docket 7. John H Ingle et al vs Eliza B Ingle et al. John C Keanedy/Kennedy & Wm B Webb, trustees, reported they sold lot 25 in Reservation B, to Fred'k W Plugge, for $13,700; lot 30 in Reservation B, to Thos E Young, for $11,900; lot 18 in Reservation C, to S C Magruder, for $1,016.73; lot 1 in square 971, to Thos Young, for $1,500; & east half of lot 3 in Reservation 11, to John H Ingle, for $1,000; & the purchasers have complied with terms of sale.
–A B Olin, Justice -R J Meigs, clerk

Dissolution of copartnership between Chas Parmer & Jas T Walker, Merchant Tailors, doing business at 481 7th st, this day dissolved, Mar 5, by mutual consent. The business will hereafter be carried on by Jas T Walker, at 484 7th st.
–Chas Parmer, Jas T Walker

Orphans Court: 1-On Sat the wills of Johnson Hellen, Chas Stocke, Enols Rozal, & John McGarvey, deceased, were fully proven. The will of John P Pepper was filed for probate. The will of Elijah Edmonston was filed & partially proven. 2-Letters of administration d b n were granted to Jas Goszler on the personal estate of Cyprian A Morton, deceased; bond $1,500. To Asbury Lloyd, on the personal estates of T P McManus, deceased, & John Fetherstone; bond $400 each. To Benj Wood, on the personal estate of Austin Woodland; bond $500. 3-The first general & first individual accounts of Catharine A Talbert, deceased; the first & final account of Morris Adler, administrator w a of Mary Ann Clark, deceased; the first general & individual accounts of Morris Adler, guardian to Wm V Mason, & the balance & distribution account of the personal estate of Louisa Collins, deceased, by John H Semmes, administrator, were approved & passed.

Mrd: on Feb 27, in N Y C, by Rev Dr Parker, of Amherst, Richd Tylden Auchmuty to Ellen, daughter of the late Augustus Schermerhor.

Court of Appeals of Md; Oct Term, 1866. Annapolis, Mar 4, 1867. Bruscup, administrator, vs Jas Taylor & wife. Appeal from the Orphans Court for Balt City. Bowie, Chief Justice, delivered the opinion of the court. Ordered, that all proceedings in the Orphans Court of Balt City in this cause be suspended & stayed until the appeal of said Jas & Margaret Taylor from the orders & decrees heretofore passed in said cause, to wit: on Oct 20th, 1866, & on Feb 4, 1867, be heard & determined

Patrick H Myers, chief clerk of the Nat'l Hotel at Louisville, Ky, drowned himself on Sunday, while laboring under temporary aberration of mind.

About 7 o'clock yesterday morning, Stephen Fletcher, aged about 15 years, was killed on board the schnr **Sarah Jay**, at Balt, by a negro boy, Wm H H Peters.

John S Hollingshead & Zach B Brooke were confirmed by the Senate as Justices of the Peace in & for Wash Co, D C. Among the rejections, we are sorry to state, is that of W W Tucker, a well known gentleman to our citizens, having been for many years the principal police reporter for the Evening Star; long experienced in police matters.

On Wed, Mr Geo Brown, of the firm of L C & G Brown, dry-goods dealers, Jersey City, suddenly fell dead, from disease of the heart, while conversing with a friend in relation to his approaching marriage, which was to have taken place on Thursday afternoon. The sudden announcement of his death to the lady to whom the deceased was engaged had the effect to destroy her reason.

WED MAR 6, 1867
Army Bulletin. Brvt Lt Col Thos Wilson, commissary of subsistence, ordered to Winchester, Va, on inspection duty; 2nd Lt John C Gilmore, 30th U S infty, is granted permission to await orders pending the Senate's action on his appointment as capt of the 38th U S infty; Brvt Lt Col R M Hall, 1st U S artl, is granted 30 days delay in joining his regt; Capt Henry W Patterson has been relieved from special duty & is ordered to join his company at **Fort Wayne**, Mich, with 30 days delay granted him if he desires it.

Henry B Tyler, formerly a major in the Marine Corps, who, during the war, served in the Confederate army, has, through Messrs Brent & Merrick, commenced a suit against John D Defrees for the possession of the west half of lot 6 in square 445. The property was libelled by the court during the war, & under the confiscation act the life interest of the plntf was sold to the dfndnt. This, we believe, is the first suit of the kind instituted here.

A negro cut the throat of Mrs Vincent with a razor at Opelika, Ala, last week, & was pursued by the citizens. When overtaken he defied his pursuers & was shot.

The Com'r of Pensions yesterday made the following appointments of examining surgeons: Dr Henry S De Ford, Ottawa, Kansas; Dr Wm F McLean, Evansburg, Pa; Dr Geo W Cooper, Garnet, Kansas; Dr Rollin E Warner, Port Henry, N Y; Dr Safford E Hale, Elizabethtown, N Y; & Dr W O McLevel, Shelbyville, Missouri.

Orphans Court-Judge Purcell, Mar 5, 1867. 1-The will of John McGarvey, deceased, was admitted to probate & record, & letters testamentary issued to Michl F Moran; bond $6,000. 2-The will of Ennola Rozel, deceased, was admitted to probate & record, & letters testamentary issued to Margaret Rozel; bond $1,000. 3-The will & codicils of John P Pepper, deceased, were partially proven. 4-Letters of administration on the personal estate of Wm Ebert, deceased, were granted to Eliz Ebert; bond $1,000. She was appointed guardian of the children of Wm Ebert; bond $600. 5-The 2nd account of Julia H Addison, guardian to Chas M Addison, was approved & passed.

By a rule of the Albany penitentiary, the following prisoners confined there, & convicted in the Criminal Court of this Dist, have received commutation for good behavior, & the warrants have accordingly been issued by the Pres: Wm W Bowie, John Johnson, Wm Samuels, Wm Woods, Chas H Tyler, Jonas Day, Wm White, Mary Cady, John Henry, Jas Taylor, Harry Wise, Archey Vickens, Chas Williams, Horace Brent, Henry Hillary, Geo W Allen, John H Lawler, Taver Larose, & Eliz Brown.

A little daughter of Alfred Woodruff, of Greenfield, Mich, was bitten some time since by a rabid dog. A few days ago she was attacked by hydrophobia, suffering terrible agonies, which continued till after consultation was had with physicians, who decided, that as the sufferer could not possibly survive, considerations of humanity demanded that the sufferings be ended by some means, in accordance with which, during a severe paroxysm, the child was smothered to death.

Prof John H Alexander died of typhoid fever, at age 54 years, in this city, on Sat last. He was a member of most of the scientific associations of the country. Prof Alexander was a leading layman of the Protestant Episcopal Church. His funeral took place yesterday from St Luke's Church, on Carey st, near Lexington.
-Balt Commercial, Tues.

Junius Brutus Booth kept a protrait of Washington in his drawing room. No visitor was permitted to stand in the presence of the picture with covered head. For 30 years he held the first position on the American stage. All forms of religion & all temples of devotion were sacred to him & in passing a church he never failed to bare his head; he worshipped at many shrines; admired the Koran; in synagogues he was known as a Jew, because he conversed with the rabbis & learned doctors, & joined their worship in the Hebraic tongue; he read the Talmud, & strictly observed many of its laws. Several fathers of the Roman Catholic Church recount pleasant hours spent with him in theological discourse, & aver that he was of their persuasion, by his knowledge of the mysteries of their faith.

Died: on Mar 5, in Wash City, at the residence of his parents, Lt Col Isaac K Casey, son of Hon Jos Casey, Chief Justice of the Court of Claims, in his 24th year. Born in Pa, on Jan 17, 1844, Col Casey was, during his youth, educated at home until he was prepared to enter upon his higher academic studies at Princeton, in the College of N J, where he remained more than 2 years, when, on leaving, he soon afterwards entered the army, in response to the summons which, in 1861, caused so many others to fly to arms in defence of the country. He volunteered at first as a private soldier, but was afterwards appointed a lt of cavalry by Govn'r Curtin, & subsequently, by Pres Lincoln, an aide-de-camp, with the rank of capt. He served in the army more than 4 years; participated in the second battle of Bull Run, battles of South Mountain, Antietam, & Fredericksburg, on the occasion of Burnside's attack, in which last named encounter he was slightly wounded. Twice brevetted for gallant & meritorious services, he left the army in 1866, with the rank of lt colonel. He was suddenly arrested by that insidious disease, consumption, which struck him down in the full flush of manly vigor. His funeral services will be held today at 4 o'clock, at the residence of his parents, 388 C st, whence on the following day his remains will be conveyed to Harrisburg, for interment.

Mr Saml F Tourtelotte, a well known & respected citizen of Worcester, committed suicide on Monday by shooting himself with a pistol. No cause can be assigned for the act, though he has of late been depressed in spirits. He was about 60 years of age.

In Beverly, N J, on Sunday afternoon, while Rev John Nichols, pastor of the Universalist Church, was preaching his farewell discourse to that society, he was attacked with paralysis, & had to be conveyed to his home, where he died at 11 o'clock in the evening.

Merchant Tailors have entered into copartnership: Geo T Keen, formerly of 509 9th st, & S W Gilbert. Fashionable clothing: 320 E st, between 13th & 14th sts.

The partnership existing between Walter Harper & John T Mitchell, under the firm of Harper & Mitchell, is this day dissolved by mutual consent. The business will hereafter be conducted by J T Mitchell. –Walter Harper, John T Mitchell, Mar 6.

Orphans Court of Wash Co, D C, Mar 5, 1867. In the case of John P Hurley, adm of Jeremiah Hurley, deceased, the administrator & Court have appointed Mar 30th next, for the final settlement of the personal estate of the said deceased, of the assets in hand. -Jas R O'Beirne, Reg/o wills

Mrd: on Mar 4, by Rev J N Coombs, Chas E Hunt, of N Y C, to Miss Sidney T Johnson, of Wash.

Mrd: on Mar 4, by Rev Fr McNally, Jos C Squires, of Phil, to Miss Mary Ella, daughter of Wm Brown, of Wash City.

THU MAR 7, 1867
Court of Equity-Judge Olin. 1-*In re* Mary Burch, lunatic. Order appointing cmte to take charge of her property. 2-Henry B Goodyear et al vs A O Daily. Josiah Bacon vs A L Daily. Josiah Bacon vs Thos O Hills. Henry B Goodyear vs Thos O Hills. Nos 825 to 1828. These were cases brought before the court in pursuance to the decree of the Circuit Court granting a temporary injunction, prohibiting the parties from using vulcanized rubber in dentistry. The court granted a final injunction. This decision makes it necessary for dentists using vulcanite to take out a license from the owners of the patents. 3-Dyer et al vs Dyer et al; #795. Order appointing commission to take infants' answer. 4-King & Co vs Cornwell; #3,417. Judgment by default, & judgment confirmed.

Navy Bulletin, Feb 21. Resigned: Acting Ensign F C Warner, of the ship **Lenapee**. Ordered: Chief Engineer Wm H Rutherford, to special duty on the ship **Richmond**. Detached: Lt Cmder Edw C Grafton, from the command of the ship **Gettysburg**, & placed on waiting orders; Lt Cmder John H Rowland, Midshipmen Robt M Berry, David H Stewart, Theodore S Williams, Saml F Clarkson, Ransome B Peck, Thos C Terrall, Acting Volunteer Lt H W Grinnell, Acting Ensign John C Lord, John F Churchill, A F H West, Chas L Beckshaft, Acting Passed Assist Surgeon Geo L Simpson, 1st Assist Engineers Albion, Buchanan, Boyce, Wilson, & Acting 3rd Assist Engineer Geo Holton, from the **Gettysbrug**, & placed on waiting orders; Assist Paymaster Henry T Shelding, from the **Gettysburg**, & ordered to settle their accounts.

Geo B Jones, a colored man, was elected one of the constables of Blackstone, Mass, on Monday.

Hon Clark B Cochrane, ex-member of Congress from N Y, died at Albany on Tuesday.

Criminal Court-Justice Fisher: 1-Lucinda Briscoe, charged with larceny; Wm A Warton, same charge, & Jas A Mason, same charge, the recognizances were forfeited. 2-Augustus R Nixon & Augustus Hapler, charged with assault & battery, a *nolle prosequi* was entered. 3-The Marshall returned the following to serve as jurors: A M Campbell, Jas M F Gibson, Jas J Barrett, Columbus C Thomas, & M R Coombs.

Wm M King & Wm H Anderson were arrested for stealing two valuable horses from the stable of Mr A H Marks, 398 G st, on Feb 26. The horses were discovered at a sale stable on 9th st Monday. King & Anderson were locked up at headquarters for examination. King is one of the most expert horse-thieves out of the penitentiary. A year since he escaped from Elkton jail, confined for stealing 5 horses.

Boston, Mar 6. J S Clements, recently the head of the dry-goods firm of Clements, Tasker & Co, committed suicide this morning by taking laudanum. He had previously exhibited signs of insanity.

Hartford Times, Wed. On Thur of last week Mr Chas C McRae, a florist, living on Hawthorn st, purchased at Dr White's drug store a bottle of dandelion bitters for an appetizer & tonic. The bitters were made & Mr & Mrs McRae took a tablespoonful the next morning, & their 6 years old daughter, only swallowed a little bit, disliking it. Mr McRae went to work, but on the way his eyesight began to fail him & he sank in a state of partial insensibility. Mrs McRae & her daughter became ill but by vomiting they had some relief. A nursing baby also suffered in the same way, taking the poison in the mother's milk. The medicine was found to be a preparation of belladonna, the poisonous extract of the dandelion plant. Mrs McRae & the children have recovered. Mr McRae's condition is a little better & recovery is nearly certain. Jeremiah Sullivan, age 16, had been sent to purchase the dandelion extract by Dr White.

Balt, Mar 6. Despatch was received here today, & read in the Southern Methodist Conference, announcing the death of Bishop Soule, of Nashville, at the age of 84. He was the senior Bishop of the Methodist Church in the U S. [Mar 9th newspaper: Rev Joshua Soule, D D, died in Nashville, Tenn, yesterday. He was born in Bristol, Maine, on Aug 1, 1781; he was licensed to preach in 1798; ordained elder in 1802; was appointed presiding elder of the Maine dist in 1804. –Balt Sun]

Mrd: on Mar 5, at the residence of the bride's parents, by Rev Fr Rochefort, Geo A Bentley, of Winchester, Va, to Georgie A Plant, of Wash City. No cards.

Mrd: on Mar 5, at the Church of St John, by Rev J V Lewis, W R Russell, M D, to Pauline, youngest daughter of the late Louis Augustus Fleury, Wash. No cards.

Mrd: on Mar 5, in Wash City, at the Church of the Epiphany, by Rev C H Hall, D D, Dr Jas Lawrence Turner, of N Y C, to Margaret Molineux Woodbury, eldest daughter of the late Elisha Woodbury, formerly of N H.

Died: on Mar 5, of consumption, after a lingering illness of 6 months. Robert Stevens, eldest son of Robt W & Ann E Middleton, of Wash City. His funeral is this afternoon at 3½ o'clock, from his father's residence, 342 9th st.

Hon Jackson Hadley, an old & prominent citizen of Milwaukie, died on Sunday.

Supreme Court of D C. In Re Jas G Ellis, 612 Equity, Docket 7. John T Lenman & Valentine Harbaugh, trustees, report that they sold real estate in said cause for the sum of $11,300, & the terms of sale have been complied with. –A B Olin, Justice -R J Meigs, clerk -Wm F Mattingly, Solicitor for Cmplnts.

Dept of the Interior, U S Patent Ofc, Wash, Mar 2, 1867. Ptn of Wm S Hyde, of Townsend, Ohio, praying for the extension of a patent granted to him Jun 21, 1852, for an improvement in Cultivator Ploughs, for 7 years from the expiration of said patent, which takes place on Jun 21, 1876. -T C Theaker, Com'r of Patents

FRI MAR 8, 1867

A despatch received in Petersburg, Va, on Monday, announced the arrival of Rev Geo T Williams at Annapolis, Md, in a condition of hopeless insanity. The Petersburg Index says that this result has been apprehended by his friends for some time, but, they have determined not to enter the plea of insanity at his trial in N Y on the charge of picking a lady's pocket in a Broadway stage, but to rest the case, as before, solely on its merits.

The Com'r of Pensions made the following appointments of examining surgeons: Dr Jos W Hastings, Warner, Mass; Dr G H Arnold, Woodbury, Conn; & Dr W D McLeod, Shelbyville, Missouri.

For Rent: Handsome country seat near Balt, Md, with or without furniture. The owner having leased his Farm & wishing to go abroad, offers that valuable residence, **Sudbrook**, adjoining the village of Pikesville; the house is a new & substantial one, 55 x 65 feet, 3 stories high, built of stone with an air space between the outer walls & the brick lining; with numerous out-houses. –Thos Hill, agent for J Howard McHenry, corner of Fayette & St Paul sts, Balt, Md.

Army Bulletin. 1-Brvt Col M M Blunt, 7th U S infty, is granted 6 months leave of absence. 2-Brvt Capt E H Liscum, 30th U S infty, is granted 30 days leave of absence. 3-2nd Lt R E Lamder, 7th U S infty, is granted 30 days delay in joining his regt. 4-Capt Edwin Pollock, 9th U S infty, has had his leave of absence extended two months. 5-1st Lt T M K Smith is relieved from duty in the recruiting service & ordered to join his regt in the Dept of the Gulf. 6-Brvt Col W E Merrill, corps of engineers, is relieved from court-martial duty. 7-1st Lt R C Clermont, 4th U S cavalry, is granted 20 days delay in joining his regt. 8-Brvt Maj E De W Breneman, assist surgeon, is relieved from duty at the headquarters of the army & ordered to report in person to the commanding general & medical director of the Dept of Missouri for assignment to duty, this order to take effect Apr 6. 9-Privates Alfred Vincent, Danl D Peabody, Fred'k Patterson, Geo G Darling, & Cpl Alex'r Frainas have been appointed hospital stewards of the army by the Sec of War, & assigned to duty in the several military depts respectively.

The golden wedding of Mr & Mrs B F Pleasants was celebrated Monday at their residence, 13th & F sts, amid a large gathering of the family & their more intimate friends. There were present 4 children, 15 grandchildren, & 2 great grandchildren, with one son & 3 daughters-in-law, & the fact was disclosed that but two deaths have occurred in the entire 50 years of the family history. The great-grandparents are 72 & 68 years of age, respectively, & were born in the State of Ky, but have been for many years residents of Wash City. Col Pleasants is at present, & has been for the last 31 years, chief clerk of the Solicitor's ofc of the Treasury. Among the invited guests were Hon Edw Jordan, Solicitor of the Treasury, with his wife; Hon H A Risley, Assist Solicitor of the Treasury; Judge Olin & lady, Assist atty Gen Ashton & lady; Geo S Gideon, Cmdor Powell, of the navy; & Richd Cutts.

Criminal Court-Justice Fisher. 1-John Angerman was found guilty of assault & battery: fined $33. 2-Jos Henry, convicted of larceny, sentenced to 5 days in the county jail. 3-Solomon Herman, alias Jew Sol, guilty of larceny. 4-Marshal Tait, acquitted of the charge of larceny.

Died: on Mar 6, after a long illness, Mr Hillery C Spalding. His funeral will take place from St Patrick's Church on Sat morning at 10 o'clock. His relatives & friends are respectfully requested to attend. [Mr is correct.]

Valuable real estate near Pa ave at auction; on Mar 22, on the premises. We will sell the south 24 feet 9 inches of lot 26 in square 254, improved by a well built 3 story brick dwlg, containing 14 rooms, with gas throughout. Also, adjoining the above, we will sell the north 24 feet 6 inches of lot 27 in square 254, unimproved. Both lots have a depth of 105 feet 10½ inches to a 30 foot paved alley in the rear. This real estate belonged to the late Col M Nourse, & is situated on the west side of 13th st, between E & F sts north, & near Pa ave. –Wm & Jos E Nourse, excs of Michl Nourse. -Cooper & Latimer, aucts

SAT MAR 9, 1867

Rev Henry Ward Beecher & family will join the Brooklyn excursion to Paris & the Holy Land, under the management of C C Duncan.

On Tuesday last, Fred'k Guscetti, alias Jacque Roellinger, & Chas T Drennan, alias Wm Mulligan, were convicted in the U S Dist Court, at N Y, of causing fraudulent claims for pension to be transmitted to the Pension Ofc under the name of Roellinger, a soldier who died at Andersonville. Guscetti obtained some $900 from the Paymaster General's Ofc, for which offence he would have been tried in D C, if not convicted in N Y.

Navy Bulletin, Feb 29. Honorably Discharged: Acting Volunteer Lt Alfred Weston, from Mar 27. 2-Detached: Acting Ensign Oscar W Farenholt, from the ship **New Hampshire**, & order to the ship **Ohio**; Acting Ensign John Lernail, from the ship **Newbern**, & ordered to the ship **New Hampshire**; 3rd Assist Engineer S P Budd, from the ship **Saranac**, & ordered home. 3-Resigned: Midshipmen S W Dourman, Kingsland Weare, A A Crane, F B Sweet, J B Pratt, J S Jarnagin, Dick Van Horn, & J W Perkins, of the Naval Academy; Mate Geo E Plander.

Army bulletin. Capt T J Eckerson, assist quartermaster U S volunteers, ordered to report to Maj Gen McDowell, at San Francisco, for examination; Brvt Brig Gen R E Clary, assist quartermaster, is ordered to relieve Brvt Maj J W McKim in his duties at Boston, Mass; Brvt Brig Gen S B Holabird, Deputy Quartermaster Gen, is ordered to report to the commanding general of the Dept of the Dakota for assignment to duty as chief quartermaster of the Dept.

Sec of the Treasury yesterday appointed John Jay Knox, Deputy Comptroller of the Currency, vice H Hulburd, appointed comptroller; to enter his duties immediately.

Fire at 8 o'clock at the Central Hotel, 6th & Pa ave, & in a short time was in ruins. The falling walls of the Central had the effect to break through the rear walls of the bldg occupied by Peter Emrich as a lager beer saloon, & also the brick bldg back of the hotel. The falling walls of Emrich's house buried in the ruins a number of persons, some were dead, before assistance could be rendered. F Muhlinghaus, aged 41, agent Germania Fire Ins Co, terribly bruised, lived about an hour after being taken from the ruins. John **Ihrig, barkeeper at Emrich's, dead when taken from the ruins. Mr B Ostermayer, baker on F st, between 12th & 13th sts, leg badly mashed. Lep Turpin & Capt Harry Browning, slightly bruised. Up to an early hour this morning, the body of Peter Emirch, proprietor of the house, & a woman engaged as a cook in the saloon, had not been taken from the ruins. The basement floor was occupied by Jos Van Arden as a saloon & restaurant; the 1st floor was occupied by Lulley & Sons as an auction & commission house; the bldg was owned by Thos Gelston, of Balt, who during the war kept the hotel. The scene when the body of Mr Muhlinghaus was brought out was very affecting; his wife, upon seeing the dead body of her husband, burst forth with agonizing shrieks. The little daughters of Mr Emrick were crying bitterly. Dark rumors were afloat that the fire was caused by an incendiary. Maj Richards ordered Ofcr Wesley Thompson to arrest Alonzo & John *Lulley; who were locked up for an examination on the charge of arson. [Mar 11th newspaper: The bodies of Ihriz & Emrich were taken in charge by Mr Anthony Buckley, undertaker, & the body of Lully was taken by his friends. Mr B Ostermayer, baker, died from his injuries on Sat. The funeral of Mr Muhlinghaus will take place tomorrow at 2 o'clock, from his residence on Mass ave. That of Chas *Lully took place yesterday from his late residence on Missouri ave. The funeral ceremonies of Mr Emrich will take place today at 2 PM. The funeral of John **Ihriz will take place at the same time.] [Two spellings of *Lulley/Lully; **Ihrig/Ihriz.]

The Episcopal Lutheran Synod of Md, after deliberate & patient investigation, has withdrawn its license to preach the Gospel from Wm A Fry, at present serving St John's Luthern Church, [German] on 4½ st. Reason: unministerial conduct, & his contemplated defiance of the authority & discipline of this Synod, of which he has been a licentiate.

The African explorer, Dr Livingston, is reported by the cable to have been killed by the Caffres. He was born in Glasgow, Scotland, in 1815; in 1856 he reached England & published an account of his travels. The attempt in which he is said to have lost his life was undertaken with a view to explore a route from Southern Africa northward by the interior. –Phil North American

Mr Saml V Noyes, who for some time past had charge of the money-order ofc at the City Post Ofc, as well as performed the duties of the sec of the Board of Aldermen of Wash City, on Thursday, received notice that his services would no longer be required at the Post Ofc. Our reporter was unable to learn the cause of his dismissal.

Nominations confirmed by the Senate yesterday:
Postmasters:
J M Hedrick, Ottumwa, Wisc
Willard McKinstry, Fredonia, N Y
Matthias A Pike, Saratoga Springs, N Y
Chas Stebbins, Owego, N Y
B P Cilley, Manchester, N H
Clarke Dunham, Burlington, Iowa
Geo W F Vernon, Fred'k, Md
Alfred Bowen, Shelburne Falls, Mass
Wm Poole, Niagara Falls, N Y
J F Monk, Watertown, Wisc

Collectors of Internal Revenue:
David Howe, 5th Dist, Maine
W Budington, 13th Dist, N Y
Chas Kennedy, 31st Dist, N Y
Jesse S Leyford, 2nd Dist, Maine
Thos Moonlight, Dist of Kansas
Gillet V Stevenson, 4th Dist, Ind
W W Wilson, 4th Dist, Ohio
Jas Armstrong, 2nd Dist, Iowa

Assessors of Internal Revenue:
Eben F Stone, 5th Dist, Mass
Nathl Wales, 2nd Dist, Mass
Chas A Harrington, 19th Dist, Ohio
Geo Neason, 2nd Dist, Iowa
Jos G Bowman, 1st Dist, Ind
Elias Nigto, 11th Dist, Ohio
Geo J Bergen, 5th Dist, Ill
Wm B Elliott, 3rd Dist, Pa

Collector of Customs: Wm Hobson, Saco, Maine.
Consul: Henry B Ryder, at Clemente, Saxony.

Nominations rejected by the Senate yesterday:
Postmasters:
Henry V Colt, Genesee, N Y
Edw R Pratt, Daville, N Y
M S Wood, Oncida, N Y
Hiram W Dixon, Hudson, N Y
Jas S Murray, Waverly, N Y
Patrick McGuire, Cold Stream, N Y
Franklin Carter, Lima, N Y
Chas A Weisbrod, Oshkosh, Wisc
Thos L Smith, Dover, N H
Warren Barnhart, Independence, Iowa

Assessors Internal Revenue:
Jacob Zeigler, 23rd Dist, Pa
John M Matthews, 4th Dist, Ohio

Collectors Internal Revenue:
Thos Johnston, 23rd Dist, Pa
John Barthlon, 4th Dist, Md

Naval Ofcr: Geo H Kingsbury, Boston & Charlestown, Mass.

MON MAR 11, 1867
Army Bulletin. Maj Isaac Lynde is placed on the retired list, & ordered to report to the Commanding General of the Dept of Dakota for court-martial duty; Brvt Maj John S Turnbull, 3rd U S artl, has had his leave of absence extended 7 days; 1st Lt O M Mitchell, 17th U S infty, leave of absence extended 30 days, on surgeons' certificate of disability; Brvt Capt A H D Williams, 5th U S cavalry, is granted 30 days leave of absence; Brvt Brig Gen Wm H Penrose, capt 3rd U S infry, is relieved from duty as Acting Judge Advocate of the Dept of the Missouri, & is succeeded by Capt Robt Chandler, 13th U S infty, who is assigned to that duty temporarily.

Mrd: on Feb 14, at the residence of the bride's parents, by Rev C W Miller, J Warren Johnson, formerly of Loudoun Co, Va, to Jennie Keene, of Wood Co, West Va.

Navy Bulletin, Mar 2. Detached: Surgeon Chas Eversfield, from duty at the N Y navy yard on Apr 1, & placed on waiting orders. Resigned: Midshipmen W R Cist & J C Richberg, of the Naval Academy. Ordered: Surgeon Geo Peck, to duty at the N Y navy yard on Apr 1.

Capt West's report on the burning of the steamship **Andalusia** off Cape Hatteras. We left N Y on Sat, Mar 2; on Sat & Sun the wind was strong with heavy sea; on Sunday evening I head the cry of Fire! Coming out of the engine room; I saw the lights of the ship **Manhattan** coming toward us; boats from the Manhattan picked up some from the Andalusia; much praise to the chief ofcr of the **Manhattan**, Mr McCrea. Passengers missing: W J Pease, of N Y, & 3 gentlemen names not known. Lost or Missing: Edw North, purser; Frank Dougherty, seaman; Antoine Martin, seaman; Jacob Lockman, N Y pilot; Mich Griffen, porter; Jas Mcmullen, 3rd engineer; Hugh Farmer, stoker; Patrick Herman, fireman. Saved,35; missing 12.

The Com'r of Pensions had made the following appointments of examining surgeons of pensioners: Dr H K Neff, Huntingdon, Pa; Dr R B Watson, Lock Haven, Pa; & Dr Geo L Owen, Bainbridge, Ill.

Orphans Court-Judge Purcell. 1-The will & codicils thereto of John Pepper, deceased, were admitted to probate & record for personalty, & letters of testamentary were issued to Henrietta P Pepper & Wm P Hicks; bond $15,000. 2-The will of Elijah Edmonson, deceased, was fully proved & admitted to probate & record, & letters testamentary were issued to Mary Edmonston; bond, $5,000. 3-The will of Henry Edwin Rainals, deceased, was filed, fully proven, & admitted to probate & record, & letters testamentary were issued to John C Kendrup; bond $1,000. 4-Henrietta P Pepper was appointed guardian to John Geo Lee, orphan of Alex'r Lee, deceased; bond $6,000. 5-The first & final account of John Fagan, administrator of Patrick McNeil, was approved & passed.

Mrd: on Feb 14, in the Catholic Church, at Berne, Switzerland, by Monseigneur Band, Court Louis Joannini, Ceva of St Michel, Counsellor of Legation to his Italian Majesty, to Mary, daughter of Geo Harrington, American Minister, near the Swiss Confederation.

Died: on Mar 10, at his residence, in Wash City, Mr Geo Washington Young, in his 71st year. [Mar 12th newspaper: His funeral will take place this morning, Tues, at 10 o'clock, at St Patrick's Church.]

Died: on Mar 8, Peter Emrich, in the conflagration at Merchants' Hotel. He was born in Blebelheim, Germany, aged 43 years, 9 months & 12 days. He leaves a wife & 7 children to mourn his loss. His funeral will take place today, Monday, at 3 P M, from Masonic Hall, 9th & D sts. [N Y & Phil papers please copy.]

Died: on Mar 10, Mrs R Ricketts. Her funeral services will take place at the Foundry Church, G & !4th sts, this afternoon, at 3 o'clock.

Died: on Mar 10, Mrs Ellen Hogan, wife of John C Hogan, & 2nd daughter of Jas B Davis, in her 23rd year. Her funeral will be on Mar 12, Tuesday, at 2 o'clock, from 721 3rd st, at M st, East Washington.

Obit-died: on Mar 2, at Winnsboro, S C, Mrs Minnie Boyce Du Bose, in her 22nd year, after a protracted illness, attended at times with the most intense suffering. Never did life close upon a lovlier character. One grave incloses her remains & those of her infant daughter.

The funeral of John P Ihriz, killed at the late fire at Central Hotel, will take place this afternoon, at 2 o'clock, from the Lichau House, Louisiana Ave, near 6th st.

Dept of the Interior, U S Patent Ofc, Wash, Mar 4, 1867. Ptn of Jas Rees & Robt Crichton, excs of Henry Carter, deceased, & Jas Rees, of Pittsburgh, Pa, praying for the extension of a patent granted to Henry Carter & Jas Rees, Nov 22, 1863, antedated Jun 3, 1853, for an improvement in Nut Machines, for 7 years from the expiration of said patent, which takes place on Jun 3, 1867. -T C Theaker, Com'r of Patents

TUE MAR 12, 1867
The Senate yesterday acted upon the following nominations:
Confirmations: Paymaster: Saml A Pierce
Consuls: Chas Stewart, of Pa, at Copenhagen; Enoch J Smithers, of Delaware, at Smyrna.
Marshal Consular Court: A W Boleinius, of Pa, at Bangkok, Siam.
Collector Internal Revenue: Alonzo J Pope, 4th Dist, Iowa; Wm J Landrum, 8th Dist, Ky; Jas Buffington, 1st Dist, Mass.
Assessor Internal Revenue: Wm C Kueffner, 12th Dist, Ill.
Register Land Ofc: Jas H Kidd, Ionia, Mich.
Receiver Public Money: Osmond S Tower, Ionia, Mich.
Postmasters:
Luke H Roberts, Alfred, Maine
Jonathan A Hill, Auburn, Maine
Geo Naylor, Pekin, Ill
David C Ambler, Charleston, Ill
Chas R Tyler, Green Bay, Wisc
Chas Reach, Valparaiso, Ind
O H P Bailey, Plymouth, Ind
John W Munday, Laporte, Ind
Abram Wright, Red Wing, Minn
Cyrus Aldrich, Minneapolis, Minn
Pension Agents:
Henry Boynton, Augusta, Maine
Alex'r H Adams, Lexington, Ky
Jno J Bloomfield, Springfield, Ill

Ellen Sanderson, Springfield, Ohio
Solomon O Kingsbury, Grand Rapids, Mich
Christian Smith, Warren, Pa
Mrs Martha A Gordon, Contreville, Pa
R E Bowen, Millbury, Mass
John J Jacques, Waterbury, Conn
Cowley Townsend, Salem, Ohio
Harriet E Drury, Troy, Ohio

David Cross, Concord, N H
Edw C Reddington, St Johnsbury, Vt

Rejected:
U S Atty: Geo B Kellogg, Eastern Dist of Missouri.
Pension Agent: Milton H Butler, Detroit, Mich.
Consul: Thos Kirkpatrick, at Panama.
Postmasters:
John Wiseman, Wash, Iowa Albert R Barlow, Conostata, N Y
Wm H McClure, Cedar Falls, N Y Wm B Sipes, Phil, Pa
J P Evans, Waterloo, Iowa Wm L Hursey, Clarksburg, West Va
Andrew J Scott, Elkton, Md H C Conolly, Rock Island, Ill
Assessors of Internal Revenue:
John R Reid, 1st Dist of N Y Edw M Phelps, 5th Dist of Iowa
Jas Kolquin, 2nd Dist of Ind

Criminal Court-Judge Fisher. 1-Melville Kurtz found not guilty of larceny in two cases. 2-Solomon Hennan, indicted for larceny, a *nolle prosequi* was entered. 3-Jas A Mason found not guilty of larceny. 4-Leonard Drudge & Saml Strogger, indicted for larceny, a *nolle prosequi* was entered. 5-Thos Armstrong & Wm Cole were found guilty of stealing 450 pounds of iron, valued at $450. 6-Chas Hill was found guilty of an assault & battery with intent to kill Peter Brooks.

John H Surratt: no positive day had yet been set for the trial, although it is supposed that it will take place about Mar 18th or 20th. The prisoner is at the jail, enjoying excellent health, & spends the most of this time in reading. His sister visits him almost every day, & his brother Isaac has had several interviews with him during the past week.

The funeral of Mr Ferdinand Muhlinghaus took place from his residence, 477 Mass ave, between 6th & 7th sts, & was attended by the German Schutzen Corps & the Arion Singing Club, as well as large numbers of ladies & gentlemen, friends of the deceased. The mohogany coffin was furnished by Mr C Fries, undertaker. The remains were borne to **Prospect Hill Cemetery**, [adjoining **Glenwood**,] where they were interred, the Arions Singing Club chanted a solemn dirge over the grave. The funeral expenses of John Ihriz were defrayed by voluntary contributions; the coffin was of polished black walnut; the pall-bearers were: Messrs Asbury Lloyd, Capt H R Howlett, Capt Browning, Wm Turpin, P Reagan, & John Renear. The funeral procession joined the funeral procession of Mr Emrich, & moved to **Oak Hill Cemetery**, where the remains were interred. The remains of Mr Emrich had been laid in State in the hall of the Masonic Association 9th & D sts, & for hours before the funeral the hall was crowded with persons anxious to look upon the face of one so well known to the community as was Mr Emrich. Capt J Tyler Powell was marshal for the occasion, & the pall-bearers were: Messrs Julius Ross, H Will, J C Bailey, Nicholas Acker, Mr Johannsen, & Lewis Kettler.

Mrd: on Mar 7, by Rev Dr Sunderland, Marcellus, son of the late Dr Gamaliel Bailey to Emelyn Webster, daughter of Prof Chas G Page, all of Wash City.

Real estate sold: Mrs Rachel S Solomon purchased the **Ratcliff property**, 354 K st, **Franklin Row**, for $14,000 cash. Mrs Virginia E Norwood bought a small brick house & lot, on 13th st, Island, between C & D sts, for $1,025. Mr Henry Fisher purchased lot 83 in square 207, on 14th st, 20 x 40, at fifty cents per square foot.

Gtwn: last week the large 3 story brick dwlg on 3rd st, near Frederick, the property of Mr Henry King, was purchased by Mr E B Barrett, for Mrs Jos N Fearson, for $10,500, at private sale.

Died: on Mar 8, at his father's residence, 62 Congress st, Gtwn, Venerando Goodnow Pulizzi, aged 4 years, 7 months & 15 days, eldest child of Venerando & Irene Pulizzi. All knew & loved "little Goodie" for, though young in years, his heart & his intellect were developed in an extrordinary degree. –C P H

Richmond, Mar 10. Edw W Taylor, a prominent citizen of Petersburg, was drowned there today while endeavoring to cross the Appomatox. The new railroad bridge there has been washed away.

Army Bulletin. Brvt Lt D J Hancock, 7th U S infty, is granted 30 days leave of absence; 2nd Lt Henry H Abell is granted 30 days delay in joining his regt. Brvt Capt Saml Canby has had his leave of absence extended until Apr 30.

Wm Baker, one of the oldest & most respected merchants of Balt, died on Sunday, in his 86th year.

Master Richd Coker, the boy soprano, is about to return to Europe. He gave a concert in Phil last night.

Orphans Court of Wash Co, D C. Letters testamentary on the personal estate of John P Pepper, late of Wash, D C, deceased. –Henrietta Piercy Pepper, Wm P Hicks, excs

Dept of the Interior, U S Patent Ofc, Wash, Mar 4, 1867. Ptn of Hamilton L Smith, of Gambier, Ohio, praying for the extension of a patent granted to him Jun 7, 1853, for an improvement in Paper Files for 7 years from the expiration of said patent, which takes place on Jun 7, 1867. -T C Theaker, Com'r of Patents

N Y, Mar 11. Dr Edw Ruggle, the artist, died at his residence, in Brooklyn, last night.

Nat'l Bank of Commerce, of Gtwn, D C. –J G Hammer, Cashier [Ad]

WED MAR 13, 1867
The funeral of Mr B Ostermayer was yesterday from his late residence, on F st, between 12th & 13th sts. The remains were interred in **Prospect Hill Cemetery**.

Orphans Court-Judge Purcell, Mar 12, 1867. 1-The will of Mary Ann Maria Dives was fully proven. 2-Jas Penky was appointed administrator on the personal estate of Gazaway Patterson, deceased; bond $300. 3-Letters of administration on the personal estate of Thaddeus Morrice, deceased, were granted unto Marcellus Morrice; bond $6,000. 4-Geo F Atkins was appointed guardian of John Green, orphan of Wm Green; bond $500.

Criminal Court-Judge Fisher, Mar 12, 1867. 1-Dennis Mackall, under the age of 16, was found guilty of larceny. 2-John Mackall, indicted for receiving stolen goods, was found not guilty. 3-Martin Welch, impleaded with Edw Hathaway for burglary, & was found not guilty.

Confirmation of Army Ofcrs on Monday:
Capt Saml S Carroll, 10th regt U S infty, to be lt colonel of the 21st regt U S infty, Jan 22, 1867, to fill an original vacancy.
Capt Alex'r McD McCook, 3rd regt U S infty, to be lt colonel of the 26th regt U S infty, Feb 5, 1867, to fill an original vacancy.
Capt Jos A Mower, 3rd regt U S infty, to be colonel of the 39th regt U S infty, Jul 28, 1866, to fill an original vacancy.
Col John R Lewis, 1st regt Veteran Reserve Corps, to be major of the 44th regt U S infty, Jan 22, 1867, to fill an original vacancy.
Additional Paymaster Geo E Glenn, U S volunteers, to be paymaster, Jan 17, 1867, to fill an original vacancy.
Maj Chas P Kingsbury, to be lt colonel in the Ord Dept, Dec 22, 1866, vice Wainwright, deceased.
Capt John Hamilton, 3rd artl, to be major of the 1st regt of artl, Aug 13, 1866, to fill an original vacancy.
Capt John C Tidball, to be major of the 2nd regt of artl, Feb 5, 1867, to fill an original vacancy.
Capt Horatio G Gibson, to be major of the 3rd regt of artl, Feb 5, 1867, to fill an original vacancy.
Capt Chas H Moran, to be major of the 4th regt of artl, Feb 5, 1867, to fill an original vacancy.
Surgeons:
Assist Surgeon Jos H Bill, to be surgeon, Jul 28, 1866, vice Crane, appointed assist surgeon general.
Assist Surgeon de Witt C Peters, to be surgeon, Jul 28, 1866, vice Satterlee, appointed chief medical purveyor.
Assist Surgeon Chas H Alden, to be surgeon, Jul 28, 1866, vice McDougall, appointed assist medical purveyor.
Assist Surgeon John Vansant, to be surgeon, Jul 28, 1866, vice Murray, appointed assist medical purveyor.
Assist Surgeon Chas C Byrne, to be surgeon, Jul 28, 1866, vice Sutherland, appointed assist medical purveyor.
Assist Surgeon Francis L Town, to be surgeon, Oct 20, 1866, vice Tripler, deceased.

Corps of Engineers:
Maj John D Kurtz, to be lt colonel, Aug 8, 1866, vice Humphreys, appointed chief of engineers.
Capt Godfrey Weitzel, to be major, Aug 6, 1866, vice Kurtz, promoted.
1st Lt Asa H Holgate, to be capt, Jul 28, 1866, vice J H Wilson, appointed lt colonel of the 35th infty.
1st Lt Garret J Lydecker, to be capt, Aug 8, 1866, vice Weitzel, promoted.

Died: on Mar 11, William M, 2nd son of John & the late Catharine Wilson, in his 24th year, after a long & painful illness, which he suffered with Christian fortitude. His funeral will take place from the residence of his mother-in-law, Mrs C Riggles, 406 16th st, betwee I & K sts, on Thursday at 2 o'clock.

Died: on Mar 6, at Tennallytown, D C, Mrs Rebecca W Miller, wife of E P Miller, & daughter of the late Dr Saml J Cramer, of Jefferson Co, Va, aged 47 years.

Mrd: on Tuesday, by Rev Dr Holmead, rector of Grace Church, at the residence of the bride's father, W J Bodell, of Pa, to Anna, daughter of Mr Arthur Yeatman, of this place. No cards.

Retirement of Senor Tassara: Yesterday, Senor Tassara, who had been for 10 years the representative at Washington for the Gov't of Spain, took formal leave of the President. His retirement will be deeply regreted.

Confirmations & rejections by the Senate yesterday:
Confirmations:
Consuls: G H C Salter, Hankow, China; Henry J Cuniffe, Paso del Norte, Mexico; Orville Allen, of Mich, at Trinidad Island.
U S Attys: A D Griswold, Western Dist of Mich; Richd Williams, Dist of Oregon; Wingate Hayes, Dist of Rhode Island.
Assessors of Internal Revenue: Clifford S Phillips, 2nd Dist, Pa; B F M Hurley, 4th Dist, Md; Wm H Wheeler, 22nd Dist, N Y; Jas B Weaver, 1st Dist, Iowa; Henry Harden, 2nd Dist, Wisc; Smith S Wilkinson, 3rd Dist, Wisc.
Collectors of Internal Revenue: Kent Jarvis, 17th Dist, Ohio; Wm O Collins, 6th Dist, Ohio; Wm B Allen, 2nd Dist, Ill; Chas M Hammond, 6th Dist, Ill; Henry M Lewis, 2nd Dist, Wisc; Geo W Fish, 6th Dist, Mich.
Indian Agent: Wm F M Arny, for Indians of New Mexico.
Pension Agent: Jos P Wiggins, Indianapolis, Ind.
Postmasters: Geo B Raymond, Elgin, Ill; Francis Foster, Kansas City, Mo; Levi Darbee, Wmsburg, N Y.
Surveyor of Customs: Benj H Smith, Gloucester, Mass.
Collectors of Customs: John H Beidler, Dists of Montana & Idaho; Theodore F Crawford, Dist of Delaware; David B Owen, Cape Vincent, N Y.
Register of Land Ofc: Henry C Ripley, East Saginaw, Mich.
Receivers of Public Moneys: Thos Laylor, East Saginaw, Mich; Joel Huntoon, Topeka, Kansas.

Rejections:
Minister to Austria: Hon Edgar Cowan, of Pa.
Com'r of Indian Affairs: Lewis V Bogy, Missouri.
Surveyor of Customs: Sheridan C Hunt, St Louis; Jos Severns, Phil.
Supervising Inspector of Steamboats: Jos Cragg, for 3rd Dist.
Naval Ofcr: John Quincy Adams, Dist of Boston & Charlestown, Mass; Sydenham E Ancona, Phil, Pa.
Consul: John Farrell, of Md, to Naples.
Assessors Internal Revenue: Benj Pyatt, 10th Dist, Ill; G Thomson Gridley, 3rd Dist, Mich; Jacob Cooke, 1st Dist, Mich; O D Harris, 2nd Dist, Missouri; Jeremiah Hoffman, 10th Dist, Pa; Martin S Eichelberger, 15th Dist, Pa; Wm Steers, 9th Dist, Ill.
Collectors Internal Revenue: Robt Crane, 9th Dist, Pa; Peter A Keller, 15th Dist, Pa; John B Hopper, 1st Dist, Md; Nathl A Elliott, 18th Dist, Pa; Thos H Byrd, 2nd Dist, Missouri; Thos W Eagan, 9th Dist, N Y.
Postmasters: Wm W Taylor, Concord, N H; Wm Gramm, Kanawha, West Va.

St Louis, Mar 12. Mrs Lucretia Pope, mother of Maj Gen Pope, died here today.

THU MAR 14, 1867
Mr Jas Wortham, of Tenn, was yesterday nominated by the Pres to the Southern Superintendency of Indian Affairs, in place of Hon Wm Byers, of Arkansas, rejected by the Senate.

Mr R G Barnwell, associate editor of DeBow's Review, contradicts the statement that Mr J D B DeBow is dead, & says it was Franklin DeBow, brother of the editor, who died in N Y a few days since. –Exchange. [The above statement has been since denied by the New Orleans Crescent, which says that Mr J D B DeBow is dead.]

Navy Bulletin, Mar 6. Ordered: Mate Edw Culbert, to the ship **Swatara**.
Detached: Acting Ensign Abraham H Berry, from duty with the hydrographic ofc, & granted leave of absence; Mate Edw K Green, from duty on board the ship **Ohio**, & granted leave of absence. Resigned: Midshipman J T C Hoffman, of the Naval Academy.

The Com'r of Pensions has appointed Dr Jas A Armstrong, of Camden, N J; & Dr Emanuel Haun, of Council Bluffs, Iowa, examining surgeons of pensioners.

Army Bulletin. Capt Saml Munson, 9th U S infty, 6 months leave to be given when the Commissary General of the Military Division off the Pacific deems his services can be spared. Capt Geo E Atwood, 27th U S infty, ordered to join his regt. Brvt Capt Chas S Nowland, 30 days leave is granted. Brvt Maj Gen R B Ayres, lt colonel 28th infty, delays in joining his regt, excused until further ordered.

Hon Wm C Bradley died at his residence in Westminster, Vt, on Mar 3, at age 85 years. He was the son of Gen Stephen R Bradley, & was born in Westminster, Mar 23, 1782; studied law & was admitted to the bar in Windham Co, in 1802.

Equity Court-Justice Olin, Mar 8, 1867. Willard P Tisdell & Sarah F Tisdell, his wife, vs Mary Stone & Wm F Stone. The bill was filed in Jan, 1866, & shows that the said Sarah F Tisdell & W F Stone are the children & the only children & heirs at law of Woodford Stone, & that the said Mary Stone is the widow of the said Woodford Stone, & states that Woodford Stone died intestate & seized, of certain real estate, described in the bill, in Wash City, & prays a sale of the same & distribution of the proceeds amongst the parties to the suit, according to their respective rights. The dfndnts, in their answer denied the death of Woodford Stone. So far as they were informed, all the facts in regard to his alleged death are as follows, to wit: Woodford Stone sailed from the port of Balt on or about Feb 13, 1864, upon the schnr **Alert**, for Port Royal, S C, with a cargo of merchandise, upon which there was an insurance, & neither he nor schnr, nor any person on board, has ever since been heard of or from, & the presumption is that all were lost at sea. The insurance ofc, it is understood, have paid the insurance, thereby admitting the loss; & since the filing of her answer, in which she denied the death, Mary Stone, the widow, has obtained from the Orphans Court letters of administration upon the estate of her said husband thereby admitting his death, & the case has been referred to the Auditor of the court to take testimony, & ascertain & report to the court whether or not Woodford Stone is dead, & of what real estate he died seized. M Thompson, solicitor for cmplnts; Bradley & Bradley for dfndnts.

Wm Quirk & Fred'k King, employed in the rolling mill at East Tanuton, Mass, were instantly killed on Monday by being caught in the gearing.

Hon Wm C Bradley died at his residence in Westminster, Vt, on Mar 3, at age 85 years. He was the son of Gen Stephen R Bradley, & was born in Westminster, Mar 23, 1782; studied law & was admitted to the bar in Windham Co, in 1802.

Confirmed by the Senate yesterday: Postmasters: Jas C Parrott, Keokuk, Iowa; Jas A Walter, Kalamazoo, Mich.
Com'r at Paris Exhibition: Paran Stevens, of N J.
Rejections:
Postmaster: Geo R Shane, Ellicott's Mills, Md.
Assessor of Internal Revenue: John Norris, 30th Dist of N Y.
Collector of Internal Revenue: Jas B Strong, 30th Dist of N Y.

Phil, Mar 12. Govn'r Geary today signed the death warrant of Albert Teufel, convicted of the murder of Capt Jas Wirle, at Bristol, Pa, in Nov last. He will be executed on Apr 18, at Doylestown, Pa.

Dept of the Interior, U S Patent Ofc, Wash, Mar 7, 1867. Ptn of Ralph J Falconer, of Wash, D C, praying for the extension of a patent granted to him Jun 7, 1853, for an improvement in Hose Coupling, for 7 years from the expiration of said patent, which takes place on Jun 7, 1867. -T C Theaker, Com'r of Patents

Sister Mary Vincent, aged about 40 years, & for a considerable period attached to the St Vincent Orphan Asylum, on Fayette st, Balt, died on Tuesday night.

Orphans Court of Wash Co, D C, Mar 12, 1867. In the case of Alfred Ray, exc of Eliz Butler, deceased, the executor & Court have appointed Apr 6, next, for the final settlement of the personal estate of the said deceased, of the assets in hand.
-Jas R O'Beirne, Reg/o wills

FRI MAR 15, 1867
Circuit Court, Mar 14, 1867. Geo U Utermehle vs Nat'l & Metropolitan Bank. This was a motion in the case to quash the writ of replevin, & for the return of the property. The property in controversy, consisting of $35,000 of Gov't & Wash City bonds, was specially deposited in the said bank by the late Chas H Utermehle, & is now claimed by said Geo W Utermehle as his property, he alleging that the said property was entrusted by him to the said C H Utermehle for safe keeping. It is contended by the administrators of the late Chas H Utermehle, on the other hand, that the bonds & the property of Chas H Utermehle, hence the motion to quash the writ & return of property. The motion was heard yesterday, & the court reserves his decision until today.

Col Levi C Turner, so long & so favorably kown as Judge Advocate of the War Dept, & formerly a judge in N Y State, died at his residence, in Wash City, on Wed. His disease was apoplexy. At the time of his death he was in his 61st year. His funeral will take place tomorrow afternoon, from the Church of the Epiphany on G st. [Mar 19th newspaper: Judge Turner was born in Sullivan Co, N H. He leaves a widow, a daughter, Mrs Randolph, & a son.]

Bridget Durgan, the servant girl, has confessed to the murder of Mrs Dr Coriell, at Newmarket, N J.

Despatch from Hudson, N Y, dated Mar 11th: Murder at Germantown, last Sat, the victim was the wife of John Welch, an itinerant Irish laborer, of vagrant habits. Her body was found by the roadside & Welch has been arrested as the murderer. The murdered woman has a brother, John Ross, employed at the Brooklyn Navy Yard, & 3 sisters in N Y C.

On Sat last on the East Pa railroad, near Temple Station, two young ladies, Miss Kauffman & Miss Groff, started for the railroad, intending to go to Reading. They missed the train & proceeded down the railroad toward the city. They heard a train coming, when Miss Kauffman's right foot was caught in the cow trap; Miss Groff tried to release her. Miss Kauffman was shockingly mangled, both her legs horribly mutilated, & Miss Groff was struck on the head & breast. Miss Kauffman died about noon. Miss Groff is still living, but hopes are scarcely entertained of her recovery.

The Hon Jos A Wright, the U S Minister to Prussia, it is announced by letters from Berlin, is lying seriously ill in that city. His affection is dropsy, & his recovery is doubtful.

The Senate yesterday confirmed the following nominations:
Confirmations:
Postmasters:
Thos J Ruger, Janesville, Wisc
Fred'k S Lovell, Kenosha, Wisc
Sylvester B Allis, Cold Spring, N Y
Jos G Palen, Hudson, N Y
Elbert A James, Chattanooga, Tenn
Wm Polleys, Waverly, N Y.
Collectors Internal Revenue: Franklin Travis, 7th Dist, Tenn; Jos Ramsay, 4th Dist, Tenn; Peter A Wilkinson, 3rd Dist, Tenn; Robt Little, 3rd Dist, Ill.
Assessors Internal Revenue: Jas H Hart, 4th Dist, Ohio; Danl E Nevin, 23rd Dist, Pa;.
Consuls: G H Heap, of Pa, at Tunis, vice Ames Perry, resigned; Benj Le Fevre, of Ohio, at Batavia, Java.
Com'r of Education: Henry Barnard, of Conn.
Rejections:
Postmasters: Isaac H Hildebrand, Huntingdon, Pa; J H Reeve, Newburgh, N Y; Jeremiah Askley, Geneseo, Ill; Chas E Glass, Carlinville, Ill; A W Rowley, Susquehanna Depot, Pa; H M Wead, Peoria, Ill; Chas Case, Waukegan, Ill; Geo Isenstein, Clarksville, Tenn; & J J Lash, Kendallville, Indiana.
Naval Ofcr: L P Ashmead, Phil.
Collectors of Internal Revenue: Wm P Moore, 3rd Dist, Mo; Wm C Webb, 6th Dist, Tenn; Edw F Ward, 5th Dist, Mo; Jas W Black, 6th Dist, Mo.
Assessors of Internal Revenue: Jas V Kelso, 2nd Dist, Ind; John H Thomas, 7th Dist, Ohio.
U S Marshals: Geo H Gordon, Dist of Mass; Norman S Andrews, Eastern Dist of Mich; Jas Henry, Western Dist of Mich.
U S Atty: Geo W Maguire, Eastern Dist of Mo.

SAT MAR 16, 1867
The Portland Press nominates Senator Fessenden, of Maine, for President in 1868.

Yesterday, an elderly colored woman, Betsy Neal, residing in Marble alley, while sitting on a bed, fell back & instantly died; supposed that the cause was heart disease.

Died: on Mar 7, Mrs Frances Stewart, widow of the late Walter Stewart, in her 76th year.

Died: on Thu, Miss Mary A Magee, aged 60 years. Her funeral is this morning at 11 o'clock, from the residence of A E Perry, F, between 6th & 7th sts.

Died: on Mar 15, John A Meldon, of Ohio, aged 22 years. His funeral will take place from the residence of his father-in-law, Andrew Duffy, 117 south C st, on Mar 17, at 3 o'clock. [Cincinnati, Lancaster, & Chillicothe papers please copy.]

Wash City Ordinance: Act for the relief of Wm Booth: to pay him $125, full indemnity & complete satisfaction for the loss of his horse by reason of the defective condition of the gutter at N J ave & K st north. Approved, Mar 13, 1867.

Patents granted to Washingtonians. 62,544: Judson F Jones, of Wash, D C. I claim the combination of the switch lever, F, cog-wheel, E, cogged bar, D, with incline, d, gravitationg & locking bar, K, removable key, J, & trigger, L, operating as described & represented. 62,589: Adjustable Runner to be Attached to Chairs, etc. Alex'r Adamson, Wash, D C. I claim the construction of the adjustable metallic runners, in combination with the sockets & brace rod, to be attached to a chair of small carriage for the purpose herein set forth. 62,707: Mary Van Vranken, Wash, D C. I claim a perforated stand attached to the bottom of a kettle or boiler & adapted to be used upon an ordinary gas-burner, substantially as & for the purpose specified.

Wash City Ordinance: Act for the relief of Wm Booth: to pay him $125, full indemnity & complete satisfaction for the loss of his horse by reason of the defective condition of the gutter at N J ave & K st north. Approved, Mar 13, 1867.

King & Dickey's powder mill, 3 miles from Xenia, Ohio, exploded on Monday: two men, Jasper Luck & Ira McManagan, were instantly killed. McManagan had been a soldier, & while in the army had a finger shot off of one hand; by this his remains were recognized.

A little girl, 4 year & 7 months old, Sarah Jane Kennedy, was shot dead by Eliza Ammon, at Guttenberg, yesterday. The mother testified that she was dressing the child when Eliza Ammon was sweeping the floor. Ammon laid the broom down & picked up a loaded gun, cocked it at my child, pulled the trigger, & shot her in the head. The jury found that Sarah Jane Kennedy came to her death through carelessness. Ammon resided at Guttenberg, was about 28 years old, & was born at West Hobokan, & did washing for a living. She was committed to the county jail to await the action of the grand jury. -Newark [N J] Advertiser

The partnership existing between Donnelly & Offutt, having ceased by mutual consent, they will offer at public auction, on Mar 18, at 188 Bridge st, Gtwn, all their Groceries, Wines & Liquors, etc. –Thos Dowling, auct

Albert D Richardson, a well known newspaper correspondent, was shot in Amity st, N Y, on Wed, & severely wounded, by Mr Danl McFarland, a lawyer. Jealousy is alleged to be the cause of the act.

By deed of trust from Ferdinand E Hassler & wife, & Grafton D Hanson, trustee, dated Jun 30, 1855, recorded in Liber J A S, No 101 folios 469, of the land records of Wash Co, D C, as surviving trustee, I will sell, at public auction, on Apr 1, 1867, the west 31 feet by the depth of the lot, No 4, in reservation No 11; fronts on B st north, between 2nd & 3rd sts, with a 2 story brick dwlg house.
–Henry C Simms, surviving trustee -Cooper & Latimer, aucts

MON MAR 18, 1867

Sale of real estate: Mary L Walker bought a 2 story frame house & lot on 8th st west, between S & T sts north, for $785; a 2 story frame house & lot on H st north, between 6th & 7th sts east, was sold to Jas Edwards, for $760.

Hiram Woodruff, the celebrated horse trainer, died yesterday, at his residence on Long Island, of an attack of congestion of the lungs, added to a liver complaint. Mr Woodruff was born in Bucks Co, Pa, on Feb 22, 1817; his father & uncle were well known turf-men. When a lad he removed to Phil, & in that city & Balt first appeared as a jockey. On his removal to N Y he was sought after by owners of horses, who desired to secure his services for the racing seasons. On Feb 22 last he celebrated his 50th birthday with his friends, although he was then ailing. Although successful, he was never a wealthy man. -N Y Herald of Saturday

Orphans Court-Judge Purcell, Mar 16, 1867. 1-An account of the personal estate of Rachel Harrison, deceased, was settled today by her executor, Jas S Harvey. 2-The fourth & final account of Rosa O'Brien, guardian to Jos Atkins, orphan of Saml Atkins, was settled. 3-Letters of administration upon the personal estate of Peter Emrich, deceased, were issued today to Maria Emrich, upon a bond of $10,000. Maria Emrich was appointed as guardian to Henry P, Eliza, Henrietta, Clara, George, & Alphonso Emrich, orphans of Peter Emrich, deceased.

Balt, Mar 17. Enoch B Hutton, a member of the Md House of Delegates, died suddenly at the City Hotel, Annapolis, this afternoon.

Died: on Mar 16, in Wash City, Chas Eames, in his 55th year. His funeral will take place from his late residence, 356 H st, on Mar 19, at 12 o'clock. [Mar 19th newspaper: Hon Chas Eames was a native of New Braintree, Worcester, Mass; a graduate of Harvard College; & held for a considerable time a prominent position in the Navy Dept.]

Died: on Mar 17, after an illness of 12 hours, William, son of Alex'r & Mary Rutherford, aged 23 years. His funeral will be on Mar 18 at 3 o'clock P M, from the residence of his parents, 307 E st, between 13 & 13½ sts.

Marshall, Mich, Mar 13th. Mrs J F Thompson has been for a long time sick & confined to her bed; her housework was done by Emma Morey, a daughter of one of the neighbors, a girl 16 or 17 years old. Mrs Thompson suspected Emma of poisoning her. The girl admitted she sprinkled poison, arsenic, in her food 5 separate times. She is a dull, ignorant girl, with no very clear perceptions of right & wrong.

Gen Jos Markle died on Friday at Pittsburgh, aged 92 years. He was a prominent Old Line Whig, & was defeated for the Governorship of Pa in 1842 by Shunk. He was a soldier in the whiskey war in 1798, & in the war of 1812.

Saml Bornport, of East Des Moines, Iowa, a few days since whipped his little nephew of 6 years nearly to death with a black snake whip. He had been arrested, & his trial is now in progress.

Orphans Court of Wash Co, D C. Letters of administration on the personal estate of Peter Emrich, late of Wash City, D C, deceased. –Maria C Emrich, admx

TUE MAR 19, 1867
Gen W P Benton, collector of internal revenue at New Orleans, died a few days since.

A despatch from Memphis says S H Rowland, night clerk at the Worsham House, received news on Sat, from England, of having fallen heir to an estate of 8 millions of dollars.

Navy Bulletin, Mar 11. Detached: Cmder David B Ridgely, from the command of the ship **Lancaster**, & placed on waiting orders; Lt Cmders Wm B Cushing, Fred'k Pearson, W R Bridgman, A S Baker, Lt Wm W Hendrickson, Acting Ensign Wm H Webb, Surgeon F E Potter, Passed Assist Surgeon John D Murphy, Chief Engineer B B H Wharton, acting 1st Assist Engineer Chas H Crank, 2nd Assist Engineer Chas Irich, Acting 2nd Assist Engineer Benj W Fowler, 3rd Assist Engineer Francis P Hallowell, Acting 3rd Assist Engineer Chas D Southall, Boatswain J B F Langton, Carpenter Wm D Foy, Sailmaker Stephen Seaman, & Gunner S D Hines, from the **Lancaster**, & placed on waiting orders; Cmder A S Baldwin, from duty as lighthouse inspector, & placed on waiting orders; Paymaster Edw Foster, from the **Lancaster**, & ordered to settle his accounts.
Ordered: Passed Assist Surgeon J B Ackley, to the ship **Constellation**.
Honoraby Discharged: Acting Ensign F A S Bacon, from Mar 10th.

Confirmations yesterday by the Senate of the following:
Registers of Land Ofc: Michl Field, St Croix, Wisc; Gilbert E Porter, Eau Claire, Wisc; Geo A Metzgar, La Crosse, Wisc; Henry W Briggs, Visalia, Calif; Vespasian Smith, Bayfield, Wisc; W G Stewart, Sioux City, Iowa; Chas B Richards, **Fort Dodge**, Iowa; Jones H Baker, Booneville, Missouri; Stephen H Alban, Stevens Point, Wisc. Receivers of Public Money: Almonson Eaton, Stevens Point, Wisc; Wm R Smith, Sioux City, Iowa; Saml S Burton, La Crosse, Wisc; Henry Clay Williams, Eau Claire, Wisc; Asaph Whittlesey, Bayfield, Wisc; Chas G Bockius, Marysville, Calif; Jas Rowe, Chillicothe, Ohio; Henry C Burbank, St Cloud, Minn; Wm H Pratt, Humboldt, Calif; Chas Pomeroy, **Fort Dodge**, Iowa.
Surveyor of Customs: John Knowlton, Portsmouth, N H.
Assessors of Internal Revenue: Jacob S Bugh, 5th Dist, Wisc; Geo B Bingham, 1st Dist, Wisc; Wm Mutchler, 11th Dist, Pa; Benj Acton, 1st Dist, N J.
U S Atty: John W Noble, Eastern Dist, Mo.
Medical Purveyor: Surgeon Chas Sutherland.
Paymaster U S Army: Jas R Mears
Maj General by Brvt: Brvt Brig Gen John H Gleeson.

Postmasters:
Jos Whitten, Columbus, Ind
John C Hannum, Delphi, Ind
Christopher F Coffin, Madison, Ind
Geo M Rynd, Lockport, Ill
Fred'k W Swift, Detroit, Mich
Wm J Post, Elmira, N Y
Philip Lawrence, Mineral Point, Wisc
David McBride, Sparta, Wisc
Alonzo Leech, Joliet, Ill
R H Lee, Camden, N J
Peter Pursell, Wilkesbarre, Pa
John F Congor, Newton, N J
Joshua R Smith, Meridian, Miss
C J Rawling, Wheeling, West Va
Jas M Boreman, Parkersburg, West Va
Mrs Frances E Lathrop, Columbia, Mo
S J Burnett, Warrensburg, Mo
Henry H Bingham, Phil, Pa

Supervising Inspector of Steamboats: John Devinning, 7th Dist.
Collectors of Customs: Jas H Kelly, Genesee, N Y; Wm B Peters, Frenchman's Bay, Maine
Collector of Internal Revenue: Albert Head, 6th Dist, Iowa
Indian Agent: Lewis M Baca, for New Mexico; E S Stover, for Kansas agency; Albert Wiley, Sacs & Foxes

Rejections:
Postmasters:
Chas Slingluff, Norristown, Pa
Wm W Rives, Paris, Ill
Mich Reap, Pittston, Pa
Fred'k Schrader, Scranton, Pa
David Pendergast, Carbondale, Pa
Fitz H Stevens, St Jos, Mich
Geo H Hall, St Jos, Mo
Jas A Patterson, Jefferson, Ind
S H Roberts, Brooklyn, N Y

Pension Agents: Fred'k J Knapp, New Orleans, La; Rufus Campion, Macon City, Mo
Indian Agents: Robt S Moore, for Pawnees, in Nebraska; Thos B Ward, for Omaha agency
Quartermaster: Jas M Moore
Medical Purveyor: Eugene A Abadie

Lt Col J C Audenried, A D C, is granted 6 months leave of absence, with permission to go beyond the sea.

Aaron Burr Stinemetz, of Martinsburg, Va, was arrested on the charge of having forged the name of the President, David Canby, & Secretary, Jos T Hoke, of the Board of Supervisors of Berkeley Co, Va, to bonds of the county, issued in payment of volunteers during the late rebellion. He was originally from Chicago, Ill, where his family resides, but has been living in Martinsburg for 3 years past.

On Sat 3 ruffians entered the bar-room of Mr Bachmeyer's hotel, near Newark, N J, & committed a murderous assault on the proprietor & his son, Julius, a young man. Both were shot. Young Bachmeyer discharged a loaded gun at one of the assailants. He was removed from the place by his companions, & the 3 have thus far escaped arrest.

Cincinnati, Mar 12. The steamer **Mercury**, at Arkansas Cut Off, on Mar 13, struck a snag & sunk. Ninety-five passengers were lost. She had a cargo of 1,400 bales of cotton, besides a large assorted freight for Mississippi & Cairo.

Died: after a long & painful illess, John L Corcoran, in his 42nd year. His funeral will be from his late residence, 66 Pa ave, between 21st & 22nd sts, on Mar 19 at 3 o'clock P M. [Death date not given.]

Died: on Mar 18, Mary Frances, infant daughter of Thos R & Rose E Byrnes, aged 2 months & 27 days. Her funeral will be from the residence of her parents, 545 Mass ave, this afternoon at 3 o'clock P M.

Died: on Mar 14, in Wash City, Walter Robert, infant son of Dr Bedford & Mary E Brown, of North Carolina, aged 3 months & 28 days.

Phil, Mar 18. 1-B W Faley, for 16 years mayor of Covington, Ky, died on Sat. 2-Saml Washington, late of Culpeper, Va, & a descendant of the Washington family, died at Delphi, Ohio, this morning, aged 81 years.

WED MAR 20, 1867
Lt Col J C Audenried, A D C, is granted 6 months leave of absence, with permission to go beyond the sea.

Orphans Court-Judge Purcell. 1-The will & codicils thereto of Geo W Young were partially proven. The will of Thos Donoho, deceased, was filed & fully proven. 2-Letters of administration on the personal estate of Alfred Russell, deceased, were granted to Mary E Russell; bond $2,000. 3-The 6th general & 6th individual accounts of Caroline C Acker, guardian to the orphans of Jacob Acker, deceased, & the 3rd general & 3rd individual of Jas B Munro, guardian to the orphans of Geo A Munro, were approved & passed.

Court in Equity-Justice Olin. Alice Biggs vs Wm Biggs; decreeof divorce, with the privilege of resuming her maiden name, & to have the custody of the two children.

Hon Z Chandler, U S Senator from Mich, bought the beautiful residence built by the late Mr Fowle, of Alexandria, on H st, between 14th & 15th sts, for $33,000 cash. The mansion is one of the most elegant & spacious in the District.

A frame house & lot on 4th st, between K & L sts, was sold to Chas Pearson, for $1,325. Part of lot 4 in square 526, on K st, near 4th west, was sold to Danl Wiber, at 30 cents per square foot.

Alexandria. The grocery store of Mr H W Loomis, corner of King & Columbus sts, was burglariously entered last night, & robbed of a large amount of property.

Confirmations & rejections by the Senate yesterday:
Confirmations:
Postmasters:

Allen P Richardson, Jefferson City, Mo
Geo H Swift, Cuba, N Y
Albert G Clark, Toledo, Ohio
Richd Beabam, Ann Arbor, Mich
Wm Snyder, Franklin, Ind
Saml D Trull, Cohoes, N Y
W W Lander, Salem, Mass
John N Runyan, Warsaw, Ind
Norman H Pratt, Kenowee, Ill
Wm L Seaton, Jackson, Mich
Perry Jaslyn, East Saginaw, Mich
Orson F Parker, Paw Paw, Mich
Wm H Campbell, Dowagiac, Mich
Calvin Hood, Sturgis, Mich
Harvey Palmer, Niles, Mich
Saml S Lacey, Marshall, Mich
Albert Rannay, Three Rivers, Mich
E Bowen Crandall, Cazenovia, N Y
W S Green, Salem, Ill
Wm Kearns, Molina, Ill
Chas H Russell, Appleton, Wisc
W C Lemert, Bucyrus, Ohio
D G Williams, Dubuque, Iowa
Wm Standeford, Shelbyville, Ky
Wesley H Stack, Paducah, Ky
Jas M Moore, Columbus, Ky
Jas Howard, Mt Sterling, Ky
Thos J Bidwell, Chico, Calif
David T Moneypennyy, Maryfordville, Ky
David L Payne, **Fort Leavenworth**, Kansas

Consuls: Geo Gerard, at Maracaibo; Henry H Wells, at Naples; Chas Creamer, at Revenna; C A Perkins, at Stockholm

Assessors of Internal Revenue: Mark Flanigan, 1st Dist, Mich; Jas S Robinson, 5th Dist, Ohio; John T Hogue, 7th Dist, Ohio; Elisha F Rogers, 6th Dist, Ohio; J H Veazie, 2nd Dist, La; Mack J Leaming, 5th Dist, Mo; Benj F Robinson, 4th Dist, N J; Robt B Hathorn, 5th Dist, N J.

Register Land Ofc: Ephraim C Holmes, Deaver City, Colo

Receiver Public Money: G C Havens, Stockton, Calif

Collectors of Internal Revenue: Bloys B Wilson, 5th Dist, Ohio; Leonard F Ross, 9th Dist, Ill; Jas Craig, 6th Dist, Mo; Geo H Green, 2nd Dist, Mo; Henry C Witter, 23rd Dist, Pa; Hilburn McClure, 18th Dist, Pa; David Caldwell, 17th Dist, Pa; Geo Sanderson, 9th Dist, Pa.

Assayer of Branch Mint: Isaac N Jones, Charlotte, N C

U S Marshal: Saml H Jones, Western Dist, Tenn; Jos Seal, Dist of Delaware

Surveyor of Customs: Josiah T Brown, Quincy, Ill; Oliver B Dorrance, Portland, Maine

Naval Ofcr: Francis A Osborne, Boston & Charlestown, Mass

Ministers Resident: Jos J Bartlett, at Stockholm; Peter J Sullivan, at Bogota

Collectors of Customs: Richd W King, Pamlico, N C; John J Randolph, St Mary's, Ga; Robt R Congdon, Gtwn, S C; Danl C McIntyre, Corpus Christi, Texas; Jos Parker, Albemarle, N C; Alanson Hinman, Oregon

Rejections:
Postmasters:

Danl L Bush, Sidney, Ohio
Thos J Anderson, Newark, Ohio
Reason B Spink, Wooster, Ohio
Wm C Moorhead, Zanesville, Ohio
A R Van Cleaf, Circleville, Ohio
Achilles Scatterday, Gallipolis, Ohio

Wm H Woodward, Hillsboro, Ohio
Robt Thompson, Mount Vernon, Ohio
Elliot N Hollingsworth, Albion, Mich
Abbot H Edwards, St Chas, Mo
Richd B Owen, Springfield, Mo
Geo W Shields, Hannibal, Mo
J J Thomas, Newport, Ky
N Seymore, Mount Morris, N Y

Assessor of Internal Revenue: Geo W Haynie, 11th Dist, Ill
Surveyor of Customs: Edw Hammond, Balt, Md
Receiver of Public Money: Sarell R Jamison, Brownsville, Nebraska

St Louis, Mar 18. A Cairo despatch says the crew & passengers rescued from the steamer **Mercury**, recently sunk in the Arkansas river, have arrived at that point. Many are badly frozen from standing in the water, the only shallow place they could occupy being 4 feet deep. Capt Dickinson reports that the crew of the steamer **George D Palmer** plundered the wreck of the **Mercury**, & after these saved from the wreck had been transferred to the **Palmer** their luggage was rifled, & even the underclothes of the ladies & the boots & shirts of men were stolen. Capt Dickson charges the carpenter of the **Palmer** with being the head of the robbers, & implicates his capt & other ofcrs in the transaction.

The hotel thief, Hugh Donnelly, was arrested at the Owen House for robbery, but discharged yesterday on a writ of habeas corpus, the prosecution failing to prove the man the one who committed the act, yet it was patent to all that he was the thief.

Notice: If the descendants of Clement Wood, [son of Margaret & Carey Wood,] who came to this country in 1785, at 15 years of age, will communicate with the subscriber, they will hear of something important. Address Andrew B Booth, Baton Rouge, La.

Orphans Court of Wash Co, D C. Letters testamentary on the personal estate of Matilda S Holmead, late of Wash, D C, deceased. –C A James

Orphans Court of Wash Co, D C. Letters of administration on the personal estate of Alfred Russell, late of Wash City, D C, deceased. –Mary E Russell

Dept of the Interior, U S Patent Ofc, Wash, Giles F Filley, of St Louis, Mo, praying for the extension of a patent granted to him Jun 14, 1853, for an improvement in Cooking Stoves, for 7 years from the expiration of said patent, which takes place on Jun 14, 1867. -T C Theaker, Com'r of Patents

THU MAR 21, 1867
On Tuesday, while workmen were employed in pulling down the wall of the ten-pin alley, on the premises of Maj Williams, N J ave & H st, the wall fell suddenly, & Mr Thos Sutton, sr, & his son, Thos, & Fred'k Slusher were caught by the falling structure. Mr Sutton, sr, was seriously injured, & his son & Slusher slightly.

Col Wm C Wood, chief of the detectives of the Treasury Dept, arrested a noted counterfeiter, Chas Ulrich by name. Plates for printing notes were also captured.

Yesterday Jno Colbert, a very respectable old colored man, was found dead in a shanty on E st, between 17th & 18th sts. He was a private watchman for unoccupied houses in that vicinity. He was afflicted with asthma; no foul play suspected. His body was given to the family of deceased for burial.

Balt, Mar 20. Jas Tarr, a merchant of Hillsboro, Caroline Co, Md, was found in bed on Sat, with his throat cut. He was known to have a large amount of money in his possession. There is no clue to the murderer.

John McDermott & Bros, Coach-Makers & Carriage Dealers, 455 Pa ave, near 3rd. [Ad]

The Old-Established Firm of S Goldstein & Co, licensed pawnbrokers, 34 4½ st west. Goods bought for cash & sold at private sale.

Confirmations & Rejections by the Senate yesterday:
Confirmations:
Postmasters:
A Bencine, Salisbury, N C
Chas A Frazier, Charlotte, N C
Mary J Richardson, Albany, Ga
Asahel R Smith, Rome, Ga
Willis C Goodwin, Americus, Ga
Fred Borhuler, Cedar Falls, Iowa
Horace Barrow, Waterloo, Iowa
Geo W Taylor, Winchester, Va
Dillard M Young, Marietta, Ga
Henry J Webb, Montrose, Pa
Edw J Sullivan, Harrisonburgh, Va
Henry Massie, Charlottesville, Va
Robt Campbell, Lexington, Va
Jas M Allen, Greenville, S C
T R Verdier, Beaufort, S C
Jos C Simonds, Greensboro, Ala
J J Pitmas, Huntsville, Ala
Jane Yarrington, Enfaula, Ala
Jacob Henry, Decatur, Ala
Wm E Huilan, Milledgeville, Ga
A T Maupin, Staunton, Va
Consul: Alex'r Jourdan, of Pa, at San Juan, Porto Rico
John H Cartter, to be Associate Justice Supreme Court of Arizona
Saml H Torrey, to be U S Atty for the Dist of Louisiana
Sylvanus T Nye, to be Register of the Land Ofc at Stockton, Calif.
3rd Assist Engineer Robt W Milligan, to be 2nd Assist Engineer
Assessors of Internal Revenue: Bassett Langdon, 1st Dist of Ohio; Anthony Reckless, 2nd Dist of N J.
Rejections:
Postmaster: Adolphus E Jones, Cincinnati, Ohio
Surveyor General: Wm B Thornbury, for Nevada
Assessors of Internal Revenue: Jos G Booey, 6th Dist of Tenn; Judson S Farrar, 5th Dist of Mich.
Collector of Internal Revenue: Noah D Taylor, 5th Dist of N J
Surveyors of Customs: Thos W Stevens, Albany, N Y; John P Murphy, St Louis, Mo

Died: on Mar 19, at the residence of Miss Nichols, in Gtwn, between West & Stoddard sts, Robt S Patterson. His funeral is this evening at 3½ o'clock.

San Francisco, Mar 20. Terrible explosion occurred in the harbor of Hong Kong on Jan 17. The hulk **Zephyr**, used as a store for powder, blew up. She was totally destroyed. The Bremen schnr **Shemsis** was damaged, & about 40 persons killed.

Capt H B Hendershott [retired] is relieved from duty on the recruiting service. Maj Henry D Wharton, [retired] is ordered to Gen Butterfield for assignment to duty on the recruiting service at Balt. The following ofcrs are ordered to be mustered out of service: Capt John L Woods, brevet major, assist quartermaster U S volunteers; Col Jas Curry, Subsistence Dept, & commissary of subsistence U S volunteers; Surgeon Elisha Griswold, U S volunteers, & Assist Surgeon Henry M Lilly, U S volunteers.

Navy Bulletin, Mar 13. Detached: Mate F A Dran, from iron-clad duty at New Orleans, La, & granted leave of absence. Ordered: Mate N B Walker, to the ship **Alleghany**.

Clerical promotions in the Treasury Dept during the month ending Mar 15, *1866.
1st Comptroller's Ofc: B W Warner, first to second class
Internal Revenue Bureau: E R Hutchinson, second to third class
Second Auditor: Josiah Humphrey, first to second class
Fourth Auditor: Lewis Carpenter, first to second class
Fifth Auditor: G M Crowe, H M Lawrence, E B Rheem, W Woodburn, Geo A Digges, C M Heaton, W Carter, W Bratton, J Trzeciak, J W Burnham, first to second class; C D F Kearson & R B Detrick, second to third class.
Sixth Auditor: Alfred Wallace, first to second class; M C Munson, J C Wheeler, J O Wilson, third to fourth class.
Secretary's Ofc, loan branch: H H McIntyre; J M Dwyer, first to second class.

Rev B R Hanley, author of "Nellie Gray," & other favorite songs, died in Chicago on Saturday.

Col L W Noyes, a prominent citizen of Nashua, N H, died on Monday.

On Mar 12, Mr Jas W Armington shot & killed, in the vicinity of Bristersburg, Va, a gray eagle measuring 6 feet 9 inches from tip to tip of its wings, & its main talon was 2 inches in length.

Charlotte Hall School, St Mary's Co, Md, have appointed, for 1867, N F D Browne, Principal; W T Briscoe, Vice Principal; E T Briscoe, Assist Teacher. The students are drilled daily in U S Military Exercise, under the care of Capt J G Barber, an efficient & experienced instructor. –Gen Walter Mitchell, Pres of the Board of Trustees

Gtwn: Dr Robt Patterson, a well know & esteemed citizen of Gtwn, died Tuesday, at the residence of Col J McH Hollingsworth. His funeral will take place tomorrow evening at half-past three o'clock at **Oak Hill Cemetery**.

FRI MAR 22, 1867

Tammany Hall was sold in N Y on Wed to Chas A Dana, formerly Assist Sec of War, for $175,000. The intention of Mr Dana & his friends is said to be to turn the Hall into an ofc from which to issue the new morning Radical paper of which we have heard so much. It is said it will appear on May 1.

The House of Reps yesterday passed joint resolution to change the name of Morris Judkiewicz, of the Dist of Columbia, to that of Morris Judd.

What's in a name. Among the colored voters registered in the First Ward is Ananias Wm Jas Andrew Jackson Jones.

Navy Bulletin, Mar 14. Detached: Paymaster Geo F Cutter, from duty as inspector in charge of provisions & clothing at the Boston Navy Yard, on Apr 1 next, & placed on waiting orders; Lt Robt B Reill, from the ship **Potomac**, & placed on waiting orders; Acting Volunteer Lt Ezra Leonard, from the ship **Glasgow**, & ordered North; Acting Volunteer Lt W D Urann & Acting Ensign Arthur O Leary, from the ship **Buckthorne**, & ordered North; Acting Volunteer Lt D C Kells, Acting Ensigns E H Miller & E Wingate, from the ship **Tallapoosa**, & ordered North; Acting Master W H Mayer, from the ship **Estrella**, & ordered North; Acting Ensigns W J Dumont & E E Strong, from the ship **Paul Jones**, & ordered North; Acting Ensign Emile J Eafer, from the ship **Daffodil**, when she is sold, & ordered North.
Ordered: Paymaster Gilbert E Thornton, to duty as Naval Storekeeper at the Naval Academy, Apr 1 next; Paymaster John B Rittenhouse, to duty as inspector in charge of provisions & clothing at the Boston Navy Yard, on Apr 1 next.

Army Bulletin: 1-Brvt Maj Gen J M Schofield, formerly Assist Com'r of freedman's affairs for the State of Va, & recently appointed cmder of the First Military Dist of the South, has, at his own request, been relieved from duty as Assist Com'r, & is succeeded by Brig Gen Orlando Brown, colonel 24th U S colored troops.
2-The Pres has accepted the resignation of Assist Surgeon E De W Breneman, [brevet major,] U S army, to take effect Apr 1 next.

The **pay of officers** of the regular army on its present peace footing is as follows:

Gen Grant, $18,120	Brig Gen Rosecrans, $5,517
Lt Gen Sherman, $14,814	Colonels, $4,500
Maj Fen Halleck, $7,717	Lt Cols, $3,994
Maj Gen Meade, $7,717	Majors, 3,765
Maj Gen Sheridan, $7,717	Capts, $3,049
Maj Gen Thomas, $7,717	1st lts, $2 713
Brig Gen McDowell, $5,517	2nd lts, $2,653

Robt G Brammell writes the following note to the N Y World: In your issue of this morning I see it asked "If Prof De Bow is dead?" I answer that he died at Elizabeth, N J, just 3 weeks ago.

Wilkesbarre, Pa, Mar 21. Alex'r B Wiley was hung here today for the murder of Mrs McElwee in May last. On the scaffold he declared that he did not intentionally kill her.

Confirmations & Rejections by the Senate yesterday.
Confirmations.
Consuls:
Chas Milne, of N J, at Cobijah, Bellvis   Geo Gerard, Pa, at Cape Town
D R Boice, of N J, at Hamilton, Canada West
W Hudson Lawrence, of N J, at Moscow
G M Prevost, of Pa, at Zacatecas
Collectors of Internal Revenue: Arthur P Gorman, 5th Dist, Md; Jacob Weart, 5th Dist, N J; John B Headley, 4th Dist, N J
Postmasters: Anthony W Street, Salt Lake City, Utah; Ferdinand Switz, Pilot Knob, Mo; Lewis F Klosterman, Cape Girardeau, Mo
U S Marshal: J N Patterson, Dist of N H
Collector of Customs: Nelson G Isbell, Dist of Mich
Rejections:
Surveyor of Customs: Henry W Tracy, Phil, Pa; Robt Cathcart, Balt, Md
Assessors of Internal Revenue: F M Williams, 12th Dist, Pa; John S M'Kiernan, 19th Dist, Pa
Naval Ofcr: Arthur D Markley, Phil, Pa

SAT MAR 23, 1867
Ex-Senator Foster has been nominated by the Pres as Minister to Austria.

Navy Bulletin, Mar 15. Detached: Lt Cmder Jos P Fyffe, from the Boston Navy Yard, & placed on waiting orders. Ordered: Acting Ensign C H Beckshaffe, to the ship **Potomac**; Acting Ensign A F H West, to the ship **Sabine**; Mate Fred'k Miller, to the ship **Constitution**; Mate Robt Robinson, to the ship **Santee**; Assist Surgeon Augustus T Peck, to duty at the Naval Hospital & station at Pensacola, Fla. Resigned: Mate Wm H Yeaton, of the ship **Vandalia**. Placed on the Retired List: 2nd Assist Engineer David Hardee.

Army Bulletin. 2nd Lt Geo A Ebbets has, upon his own application, been transferred from the 17th to 26th U S infty, to date from Nov 23, 1866. Capt D A Ward, 39th U S infty, has been relieved from duty on the recruiting service. Brvt Maj H R Gillman, assist surgeon, is relieved from duty in the Dept of Dakota & is ordered to report to Retiring Board. 1st Lt A B Bonnaffon, 35th U S infty, is granted 30 days delay in joining his regt. Capt Chas Newbold, 19th U S infty, is granted 30 days delay in joining his regt. Brvt Brig Gen Rufus Saxton is authorized to delay reporting to the commanding ofcr & chief quartermaster of the Dept of the Missouri until further orders.

Dr John R Muller, of Balt, died on Thur from typhus fever, after a short illness.

John Owenby, Sheriff of Adair Co, Mo, who absconded with $2,000 of the State money a short time ago, was recently arrested at Little Rock, Ark, & brought back.

Consulate of the U S A, Island of Zanibar, Dec 9, 1866. Dr David Livingstone, the celebrated African explorer, left here on Mar 9 last for the exploration of the river Rovauma, & that region between the great lakes of Central Africa, of which, as yet, but little is known. The sad intelligence was received here on the 5th instant by the arrival of several native members of the expedition, from whom but little of importance could be elicited save the fact of Dr Livingstone's death.
+
From Mataka to Alake was an 8 day march; on crossing a wide water in Canves, they followed the border of the lake for several days & thus struck inland. They were suddenly attacked in a bush country, by a band of Mavite. Dr Livingstone killed the most forward of the attacking party, but was surrounded & cut down by one blow of a battle-ax, which cut half through his neck. Almost all those who stood near Dr Livingstone were killed, although they seem to have done considerable with their rifles. This happened about 6 weeks ago, or about Oct 25. Only one of the survivors saw Dr Livingstone fall, but they buried his body when the Mavite had gone.
–Edw D Ropes,
+
U S Consul [To Hon W H Seward, Sec of State.] [Jun 4th newspaper: Letter dated Johanna, Feb 23: The only witness states that they were traveling over a large plain, the Doctor & 9 Africans were ahead; suddenly he heard the Africans cry out "Mavela, Mavela." He ran on & saw a number of men rushing on the Doctor & the Africans. Three made for the Doctor, who shot two, but was cut down himself by the third. At dusk they returned to the spot where Dr Livingstone was attacked & found his body, the bodies of the two Mavelas whom he shot, also the bodies of four of the Africans. They buried the Doctor, & then set off as fast as they could go on their return to the coast, escaping two or three times from bands of Mavelas, reached Knilos, on the coast. The <u>Mavelas</u> are killing the unfortunate negroes, who have neither courage nor the means of defending themselves.]

The lady whose death under suspicious circumstances was announced on Wed, at the Irving House, in N Y, proves on investigation not to have been the wife of Lt Col Kimball, who was killed by Col Corcoran, but of another ofcr of the same name, who was killed on the Texas border during the Mexican war. The death has caused considerable excitement.

Balt, Mar 22. Isaac Roby, aged 70 years, residing in Allegany Co, Md, was brutally murdered in his own house on Sunday last. No one was near the house at the time, except his son, & another son's wife. The son has been arrested on suspicion of having committed the deed.

Troy, Mar 22. Hiram Coone, who was convicted of the murder of Mrs Larker, in the town of Petersburg, in Oct last, was executed today at the jail in this city. He made a statement denying his guilt.

Horrible murder in Noblestown, Pa, on Mar 18: three men went to the house of Hugh Sproull, a wealthy farmer & demanded his money; he refused them, & told them he knew them. One of them then seized Miss Sproull, an aged sister of Mr Sproull, carried her upstairs & bound her to the bed with ropes; the other two attacked Mr Sproull & beat him with a pair of tongs, & inflicted on him stabs that must have proved fatal in themselves. They threw a quilt over the corpse & robbed the house, getting over $100. Miss Sproull remained as the murderers left her until the next evening, before the crime was discovered & she released. There is a clue to the murderers, & they are being tracked. Mr Sproull was a bachelor, 60 years old.

Bonham [Texas] News: The time-honored venerable mansion of the lamented Gen Saml Houston is being torn down to be replaced by brick & mortar. This old house has been respected for one-quarter of a century on account of its traditional history.

A civil suit at Hastings, Miss, against Thos Eagan, who killed a soldier in Dakota Co, in 1864, has resulted in a verdict of $1,846 damages to the widow of the murdered man. Eagan had previously been tried for murder & acquitted.

Sale of personal property, by deed of trust dated Aug 17, 1865, executed to me by Isaac C Bryant, & recorded in Liber R M H, No 2, folio 481, of the Chattel Records for Wash Co, D C: I will sell two scows, at Galt's Wharf, foot of 17th st & Canal, on Apr 4, to satisfy the lien thereon. –John E Norris, trustee -Crown & Walker, aucts

MON MAR 25, 1867
The pay of army ofcrs: Amount per annum received in each grade after deducting the income tax: [The N Y Tribune, lately copied in the newspapers, gives a very exaggerated statement of the amount of salary received by Army Ofcrs.]

General: $16,465.10	Major: $2,493.15
Lt Gen: $13,919.10	Capt, cavalry: $1,909.15
Maj Gen: $7,956.85	Capt, foot: $1,738.15
Brig Gen: $5,513.50	1st Lt, cavalry: $1,538.93
Colonel: $3,068.20	1st Lt, foot; $1,400.90
Lt Col: $2,734.70	

This includes the additional pay voted by the 39th Congress, which last for two years from Jul 1, 1866.

Mr Horace Greeley was in Wash City on Saturday.

Edw Franklin, seaman on the steamship **Australian**, was drowned outside of N Y harbor on Friday, by being washed overboard during the gale then prevailing. Capt Benj F Horton, a Hell-Gate pilot, was also drowned on the same day, while attempting to land at City Island in a yawl-the latter upsetting.

Orphans Court-Judge Purcell, Mar 23, 1867. 1-The will of Bernard Ostermayer, one of the victims of the late disastrous fire at the Central Hotel, bequeathing all his property to his wife, during the term of her life, was filed & fully proven. 2-The will of Mary E Nourse, deceased, was also filed & fully proven. 3-The will of Chas Eames, deceased, was filed & fully proven. 4-Letters testamentary on the personal estate of Bernard Ostermayer, deceased, were granted to Catharine Ostermayer; bond $2,000. 5-The first & final account of Horatio R Maryman, executor of Zachariah Hazel, deceased, & the first & final account of John Chandler, adm w a of Hamilton J Smith, deceased, were approved & passed.

The funeral of the late H O Whitemore took place yesterday from his residence on the Island. The remains were taken to Alexandria & interred in the Methodist cemetery in that city. The Eastern Lodge I O O F & the Osage Tribe of Red Men accompanied the remains to Alexandria.

John H Surratt-in jail. Sleeps soundly, eats heartily, reads the newspapers, smokes his pipe, & if the weather permits, is allowed to walk, under guard, in the jail yard. The people in Lower Md provide him with not only the substantials, but the delicacies of life. He will be tried when the Dist Atty is ready.

On Friday Mr Littlehales, about 40 years of age, well known in the locality as a quiet, peaceable man, was murdered near his residence at the colliery, Glen Carbon, Schuylkill Co, Pa. He was Superintendent of the Glen Carbon Coal Co.

Wm S Roberts, a son of Marshall O Roberts, died in N Y on Thursday, aged 26 years.

The remains of the murderer Wiley, hung at Wilkesbarre, Pa, on Thu, were on Sat taken up to satisfy some persons who doubted his being dead.

Died: on Mar 22nd, at New Castle, Dela, Mrs Hannah Couper, relict of the late Dr Jas Couper, sr, in her 89th year. Her funeral will take place from her late residence, on Mar 26, at 11 o'clock A M.

Died: on Mar 23, Mary M, daughter of Clarence B & Laura E Baker, aged 3 years & 2 months. Her funeral will take place from 269 I st, between 17th & 18th sts, on Mar 25, at 3 P M.

TUE MAR 26, 1867
Supreme Court of D C; Equity 856. Wm B Todd et al vs Julia Hallinan, Eliz Pursell, Wm Pursell, Mary Condon, Philip Condon. Report of debts due by Thos Halinan [or Halloran] at the time of his death, the value of his real & personal estate & evidence tending to show to whom said real estate had descended, & who are entitled as heirs & next of kin: to appear at my ofc on Mar 30. –Walter S Cox, auditor

Criminal Court-Judge Wylie, Mar 25, 1867. 1-Wm Brown, alias Saml Collins, was found guilty of an assault & bettery with intent to kill Jesse Given, & sentenced to 1 year in the Albany penitentiary. 2-Jas Grady & John Richards, indicted for larceny; recognizance forfeited. 3-Jenny Carter, Jas Jackson, & Abraham Wallace were found guilty of larceny, & sentenced to 6 months in the county jail. 4-Alex'r Washington, indicted for larceny; Geo Washington, same offence; Wm Jones et al for robbery in 3 cases, & for assault with intent to kill, the Dist atty entered a *nolle prosequi*.

Army Bulletin. Capt Jas A Bates, 43rd infty, is granted 4 months leave of absence, with permission to go beyond the sea. Capt Dudley Chase, leave extended 60 days. 2nd Lt R J Armstrong, 1st infty, 30 days delay in joining regt. 2nd Lt D W Lockroad, corps of engineers ordered to duty at Willett's Point, N Y harbor. 2nd lt L A Nesmith, 12th infty, 30 days delay in joining his regt. Capt Thos Barnard, assist quartermaster U S volunteers, ordered to cemeterial duty in the Dept of the Gulf. Brvt Maj W H Bartholomew, 34th infty, leave extended 30 days. The following changes in ofcrs' stations are ordered by the Sec of War:
Brvt Lt Col Lawrence Kipp, 3rd artl, to Hilton Head, S C.
Brvt Maj Frank J Smith, 4th artl, to **Fort Whipple**, Va.
1st Lt Jas B Hazeltine, 4th artl, to Battery Rodgers, Va
1st Lt H H C Dunweady, 4th artl, to **Fort Washington**, Md.
1st Lt Robt Craig, 4th artl, to **Fort McHenry**, Md.
1st Lt Geo W Sheldon, 4th artl, to **Fort Wayne**, Mich.
1st Lt Chas S Smith, 4th artl, to **Fort Delaware**, Dela.
Brvt Maj H S Gansevoort, 5th artl, to Pensacola Harbor, Fla.
Brvt Maj Gen H W Benham, corps of engineers, to **Fort Warren**, Boston harbor.
Brvt Lt Col C E Blunt, corps of engineers, to Oswego, N Y
Capt J N Tardy, corps of engineers, to Wash, D C.
Capt S M Mansfield, corps of engineers, to Willetts Point, N Y harbor.
Brvt Lt Col Franklin Harwood & Brvt Capt G J Sydecker, corps of engineers, as assistants to Brvt Brig Gen T J Oram, at Buffalo, N Y.
Brvt Capt D P Heap, corps of engineers, as assist to Maj J B Wheeler, at Milwaukie, Wisc.
Brvt Lt Col Chas McCormick, surgeon, is relieved from duty as member of the board to retire disabled ofcrs, convened by special order No 5, Jan 4, 1867, & Brvt Col R Murray, assist medical purveyor, is detailed in his place.

Lt Cmder Chas C Fleming, commanding the U S steamer **Penobscot**, under date of St Thomas, West Indies, Feb 23rd, reports the death of 3 of the crew of that vessel from yellow fever: Bernard Smith, 2nd class fireman; Edw Tommy, landsman, & Thos Sullivan, 2nd class fireman. There is no epidemic on board the vessel.

Hartford, Mar 25. Mr A A Clark, formerly one of the proprietors of the Hartford Courant, died in this city this afternoon at age 47 years.

Supreme Court of D C; Equity 856. Wm B Todd et al vs Julia Hallinan, Eliz Pursell, Wm Pursell, Mary Condon, Philip Condon. Report of debts due by Thos Halinan [or Halloran] at the time of his death, the value of his real & personal estate & evidence tending to show to whom said real estate had descended, & who are entitled as heirs & next of kin: to appear at my ofc on Mar 30. –Walter S Cox, auditor

WED MAR 27, 1867
Hon Henry Butler, of Warwick, R I, died suddenly on Monday in that town. He was a Democratic candidate for Congress, but withdrew from the canvass last week.

Orphans Court-Judge Purcell, Mar 26, 1867. 1-The will of Chas Eames, deceased, was admitted to probate & record, & letters testamentary issued to Fanny Eames; bond $5,000. 2-The will of Thos Donoho, deceased, was admitted to probate & record, & letters testamentary issued to Andrew P McKenny; bond $3,000. 3-Caroline S Risque gave an additional bond in the sum of $5,000 as guardian to the minor children of Ferdinand W Risque, deceased. 4-The fourth account of Madaline V Dahlgren, guardian to Vinton A & Romaine M Goddard, the orphan children of Danl C Goddard, deceased, was approved. 5-The will of the late Johnson Hellen was admitted to probate & record, & letters testamentary issued to John B Blake; bond $60,000.

Criminal Court-Judge Wylie, Mar 26, 1867. 1-Alex'r Adams guilty of assault upon his wife, & sentenced to 3 months in the County Jail. 2-Geo Smackum, for an assault upon his wife, Jane Smackum, was sentenced to 3 months in the County Jail. 3-Wm Carrol & Jas Parks, for larceny of $56.50 from Michl Heil, sentenced to 3 years in the Albany Penitentiary. 4-Jas Boyd, alias A F Boyd, indicted for larceny. Verdict not guilty. 5-In the case of Lebin Coleman, indicted for larceny, a *nolle prosequi* was entered.

Portland, Me, Mar 25. Geo Rolfe, an inoffensive man, aged 35 years, was murdered on Sunday in the Williams House, in Falmouth, by Ebenezer Williams, aged 21 years, who shot him through the heart with a rifle & then cut off his head with an axe. Williams is an imbecile, under guardianship, but being supposed harmless, was allowed to occupy the house, with Rolfe, who was a pauper, as his servant. Williams went to the house of his guardian & stated gleefully what he had done. The body was found laid out for burial, & the head in a pail of water. [Mar 29th newspaper: Williams guardian was his uncle, John Williams. Although he had once raised his gun at his uncle he was not regarded as dangerous. Eben Williams was worth about $25,000. The insanity of the murderer is herditary, his father having committed suicide while laboring under the same disease.]

Mr B F De Bow, brother of the editor of De Bow's Review, whose death we chronicled some weeks ago, died at Elizabeth, N J, on Monday morning.

Pottsville, Mar 2. On Sat, 4 Irishmen broke into the house of Henry Rapp, a farmer living near Kingtown, in this county to rob. A neighbor, Jacob Johnson, went to his assistance, when one of the robbers shot him dead & wounded Rapp.

Mrd: in Wash, D C, by the rector, Rev R J Keeling, D D, Wm G Eadie, M D, of N Y, to Miss Emma C Jacobson, of Mobile, Ala. [No marriage death given-current item.]

Confirmations & rejections by the Senate yesterday:
Confirmations:
Maj Gen by Brevet-Thos A Smith, late brig gen, mortally wounded at Farmville, Va.
Brig Gen by Brevet-Louis R Francine, late colonel of volunteers, mortally wounded at Gettysburg, Pa; Lewis Zahn, late colonel 3rd Ohio cavalry.
Colonels by Brevet-Brvt Lt Col Chas J Mills, killed at Petersburg, Va; Brvt Lt Col Philip Kearney, late major N J volunteers, mortally wounded at Gettysburg, Pa.
Lt Colonels by Brevet-Geo W Todd, late major 91st Pa volunteers, killed at Fredericksburg, Va; Brvt Maj Wm H Chester, late capt 73rd N Y volunteers, killed at Gettysburg, Pa; Brvt Maj Francis M Bache, late capt 16th U S infty.
Majors by Breve-Selah J Reeve, late capt 63rd N Y volunteers; Brvt Capt Jas C Noon, killed at Fredericksburg, Va; John H Dickerson, late capt & assist quartermaster.
Capts by Brevet-Jas W Allen, late 1st lt 10th Ill; Manning Livingston, late 1st lt by brevet 3rd U S artl.
1st Lts by Brevet-Chas H Carroll, late 2nd lt 5th U S artl; Manning Livingston, late 2nd lt 3rd U S artl.
2nd Lts, U S Army-Nathl Wolf, late 1st lt 28th Ky volunteers, in 34th U S infty; Henry E Scott, late private 22nd N Y cavalry, in 6th U S cavalry; John W Hines, late 1st lt Tenn volunteers, in 10th U S infty; Geo H Palmer, late capt 83rd N Y volunteers, in 27th U S infty; Geo T Cook, of Ill, in 6th U S infty.
Capt, U S Army-G F Robinson, late major 14th Missouri cavalry, in 10th U S cavalry.
Register of the Land Ofc-Wm S Winfield, at Ironton, Missouri.
Receivers of Public Money-Jos Reed, at Ironton, Missouri; John E Phelps, at Springfield, Missouri.
Consul-Geo W Grandey, of Vt, at San Juan del Sur.
Rejections:
Postmasters: Wm Oram, Hyde Park, Pa; T P Metler, Rolls, Missouri.
Collector of Internal Revenue: Abraham H Reynolds, 12th Dist, Pa.
Receiver of Public Moneys: Caleb B Clements, at Denver, Colorado.
Register of the Land Ofc: Saml Kneeland, at Springfield, Missouri.

Our Nat'l Cemeteries: the cemeteries completed, with the number of soldiers interred therein, are as follows:
Yorktown, Va: 2,180
Seven Pines, Va: 1,356
Glendale, Va: 1,197
Cold Harbor, Va: 1,930
City Point, Va: 5,463
Fort Harrison, Va: 813

Cemeteries to be completed after the winter, with the number of bodies to be interred therein:
Poplar Grove, Va: 5,007
Winchester, Va: 4,189
Danville, Va: 1,216
Richmond, Va: 3,052
Antietam, Md: 2,743
Fredericksburg, Va: 13,174

For sale or rent-160 acres of land, 7 miles from Wash, on the Balt & Wash turnpike road: a portion of *Riversdale*, the farm of the late Chas B Calvert, containing 1,400 acres. Also, one small cottage, with outbldgs, & lot of 12 acres, at Ellaville, finely situated. Apply to Geo H Calvert, jr, Hyattsville P O, PG Co, Md.

THU MAR 28, 1867
Patents issued to Washingtonians. 1-Two patents for fetters or hopples for horses, to Robt N Eagle. 2-To David M Lawrence, for a metal clasp for barrel-hoops. 3-To John W Martin, for improved gate. 4-To Emmett Quin, for improved steam-guage. 5-To Hiram Beadle, for automatic boiler-feeder. 6-To H H Etter, for burning fluid. Mr Etter claims for his patent the ingredients when mixed in the porportions specified, for the purpose of producing a safe & brilliant light.

On Monday last the Journeymen Paperhangers Association elected the following ofcrs: John W Hayes, pres; John G Culverwell, vice pres; John W Falconer, recording sec; W W Lower, financial sec; John Coon, treasurer.

Confirmations & rejections by the Senate yesterday.
Confirmations:
Com'r of Indian Affairs: Hon Nathl G Taylor, of Tenn.
Collector of Internal Revenue: Thos Jones, jr, 18th Dist, Ohio.
Indian Agent: Jas Worthen, of Tenn, Southern Superintendency.
U S Marshal: Norman S Andrews, Eastern Dist of Mich.
Rejections:
U S Atty: S L Warren, Western Dist of Tenn.

Change of orders: Brvt Maj Frank G Smith, 4th U S artl, has been ordered to *Fort Whipple*, in the county, & 1st Lt Jas B Hazleton, 4th U S artl, to Battery Rodgers.

Cooper & Latimer, aucts, sold yesterday, part of lot 28 in square 254, with a 3 story brick dwlg thereon, to Wm Thompson, for $11,000; also, part of lot 27 in square 254, adjoining above to John Alexander, for $1.65 per square foot. The above property belonged to the estate of the late Michl Nourse, & is on west side of 13th st west, between E & F sts north.

Elegant residence for sale: the House formerly occupied by the late Wm Noyes, & at present occupied by Gen Davis. The main bldg is situated on the corner of West & Green sts, Gtwn, D C; is 4 stories high, & contains 8 spacious rooms. There is also attached a handsome back bldg containing 5 rooms, embracing kitchen, dining, bath, & sleeping apts. -A M Noyes, Intelligencer Ofc

Court of Equity-Justice Olin, Mar 27, 1867. 1-Spurrier vs Heiskell: No 872: Order appointing John W Gaither, John W Hardy, & Wm Clark a commission to appoint guardian ad litem. 2-Shugrue vs Fogarty: No 77: Order *nisi*, confirming trustee's sale. 3-Miller et al vs Ellin et al: No 811: Decree appointing John B Turton trustee to sell, etc.

Mrs W G Bean, who lives near Ernst Station, Ohio, went on Sunday to the residence of her father, on Pleasant Hill, taking with her two of her 4 children, a blind girl of 3 years & an infant of 8 months. In the kitchen of her father's house there is a cistern with a trap-door, & into this the blind child accidentally fell. The mother, in delirium, fell head first with the infant in her arms, into the cistern. When the people of the house reached the scene the mother & her two children were dead.

Supreme Court of D C: No 777-Equity Docket 8. Catherine Shugrue et al vs Danl Fogarty. The trustee reported he sold the south part of lot 4 in square 526, with improvements, to Chas Pearson, for $1,325, & the purchaser has complied with the terms of sale. –A B Olin, Justice -R J Meigs, clerk

Dept of the Interior, U S Patent Ofc, Wash, Mar 18, 1867. Ptn of Sherburne C Blodgett, of Bridgeboro, N J, praying for the extension of a patent granted to him Jan 3, 1854, ante-dated Jul 3, 1853, for an improvement in Hemming & Cording Umbrella Covers, for 7 years from the expiration of said patent, which takes place on Jul 3, 1867. -T C Theaker, Com'r of Patents

Navy Bulletin, Mar 20. Detached: Paymaster A H Gilman, from duty as paymaster at Portsmouth, N H, on Apr 1 next, & ordered to continue to act as paymaster & inspector in charge of provisions & clothing at the navy yard at that place; Acting Ensign Jas McVey, from duty at Mound City, Ill, & placed on waiting orders; Mate Geo H Borven, from the ship **Tallapoosa**, & granted leave of absence.
Ordered: Paymaster S N Carpenter, to duty as paymaster at Portsmouth, N H, on Apr 1 next; Acting Ensign Wm F Hodgkinson, to the ship **Peoria**.
Honorably Discharged: Acting Assist Paymaster Wm Ives, from Jan 3, 1866.

FRI MAR 29, 1867
Close-out sale of Donnelly & Offutt, 188 Bridge st, Gtwn, on Mar 29, consisting of Wines, Liquors, Sugars, Teas, Wooden Ware, Tobacco. Fixtures, Measures, Scales, etc. Also, a fine Family Carriage & excellent Mare, Harness, etc. –Thos Dowling, auct

The Roman Catholics are erecting a fine bldg for a school-house on E st south, between 3rd & 4th sts east. It is being built by subscriptions from Fr Boyle's church on Capitol Hill, & will cost about $15,000. The dimensions are 45 x 115 feet; to be completed by May 1.

Died: on Mar 7, at *Cedar Mount*, Montg Co, Md, after a painful illness, Mrs Sarah K, beloved wife of John H Kidwell.

Died: on Mar 28, Mary, wife of Saml Drury, in her 73rd year. Her funeral will take place Sat next at 9 o'clock, from St Matthew's Church.

Board of Police. 1-Application of John Loeliger & Chas Peterson for a liquor license was rejected. 2-Pvt Peter A Becker, charged with gross neglect of duty: dismissed the force. 3-Pvt Thos Shea, charged with leaving his beat, & conduct unbecoming an ofcr, was sentenced to be dismissed the force, with the loss of all pay & allowances from Mar 1st. 4-Pvt R A Radcliff, charged with violating the rules, & conduct unbecoming an ofcr: dismissed the force. 5-Pvt Danl Lynch, charged with neglect of duty, was fined $10. 6-Pvt Robt Padgett, for neglect of duty, fined $20. 7-Pvt Geo W Cross, for neglect of duty, was sentenced to be reprimanded.

Alexandria Affairs. 1-In the **United States cemetery**, located at the southwestern limits of this city, there are 3,601 graves. 2-The Demosthenean Society of St John's Academy has elected the following ofcrs to serve until Oct 1, viz: Henry McQuade, pres; Julian Higdon & Richd Collins, vice presidents; Jos H Dunn, sec; Willie L Allen & Geo W Dearborn, jr, assist secretaries; J Marriott Hill, treasurer. 3-The sacrament of Confirmation is to be administered in St Mary's Church, in this city, on the first Sunday of April, by the Rt Rev Bishop of Richmond. 4-Corp ofcrs elected for the ensuing year at a meeting of the City Councils: John L Smith was chosen capt of the night watch; W D Corse, treasurer; & Geo W Dearborn, harbor master. Sixteen night watchmen were also chosen. 5-Rev John B Emig, of Gonzaga College, Wash, preaches in St Mary's Church every Wed evening at 7 o'clock. Every Friday evening at the same hour the devotion called "The Way of the Cross" takes place.

Dayton, Mar 28. Saml Tate, jr, a well known floor merchant of this place, was waylaid last evening at the bridge near the mill, & shot & robbed. It is thought he cannot recover. There is no clue to the murderers.

The funeral of Chas F Browne took place on Mar 9, at **Kensal Green Cemetery**, London, attended by about 2,000 persons, including Americans, members of the Savage Club. Ladies closed around the mouth of the tomb, & showered beautiful flowers upon the coffin. The plate was inscribed: Charles F Brown, Aged 33 years. Known to the world as Artemus Ward. The will of the deceased gives $500 each to two children of Mr Higinston, his agent. To his mother he leaves a life interest in the whole of his real estate, valued at least $25,000, & at her death it passes into the hands of Horace Greeley, as trustee, for the purpose of founding an asylum for decayed printers. The rest of his personalty is devoted to the object of providing for the education of Geo Stevens, an intelligent youth of 14 years, who has been his constant attendant & companion for the last 2 years. The will provides for his apprenticeship for 2 years in a printing ofc, & then his removal to college for the perfecting of his education. He wished Geo to go first into the printing ofc, "that he might ascertain how little he knew, & how important it was to learn."

Navy Bulletin, Mar 21. Honorably Discharged: Mate C J Andrews
Discharged: Acting Master Jas M Williams, of the ship **Peoria**.

On Fri last, Mr Parsons, a wounded soldier of the war, & late postmaster at Niagara Falls, was arraigned before the U S Court at Utica & pleaded guilty to an indictment for opening letters. In consideration of his services to the country, he was let off with the lenient fine of $150.

Criminal Court-Judge Wylie, Mar 28, 1867. 1-John Robinson was convicted of larceny & sentenced to 6 days in jail. The same party was convicted on a second similar charge, & sentenced to an additional 6 months in jail. 2-Emanuel Cox, was convicted of larceny, & sentenced to 6 months in jail.

Court of Equity-Justice Olin, Mar 28, 1867. 1-In re Jas D Marr, a lunatic: No 896: order granting commission *de lunatice inquirendo*. 2-Shanks vs Hitz et al. No 891. Order reference to Auditor to state account of rents, profits of real estate of Michl Shanks, deceased. 3-Driggs vs Driggs. No 710. Order granting dfndnt $50 monthly alimony pending the suit, & to dfndnt's solicitor fee of $50. 4-Royel or Rile vs Royel or Rile. No 897. Order to file petition.

Circuit Court-Chief Justice Cartier, Mar 28, 1867. 1-Schonborn vs Class: verdict for plntf for $54.50, with interest from Dec 15, 1855. 2-O B Ingalls vs A D Moore & M C Conover. No 275. Verdict for plntf for $175. 3-Eliza Trunnell vs Wm D Trunnell. No 3,508. Motion granted for plntf to file bill of particualrs. 4-Allison Nailor vs Violet A Williams, admx of W H Williams. No 439. Case on trial.

Army Bulletin. Capt Edwin Pollock, 9th infty, ordered to report to Gen Butterfield for duty in the recruiting service. Capt C J Wilson, 16th infty, is granted 20 days delay in joining his regt at Macon, Ga. 2nd Lt A K Bush, 2nd artl, is granted 25 days delay in joining his regt at *Fort Point*, Calif. Brvt Col E G Marshall, 5th infty, is ordered to join his regt. Brvt Lt Col C G Bartlett, 30th infty, is ordered to join his regt in the Dept of the Platte. Capt J F Rodgers, military storekeeper, is assigned to duty at St Louis, Mo. Capt N D A Sawyer, military storekeeper, is assigned to duty in the Military Division of the Pacific. Capt H Sieber, military storekeeper, is assigned to duty at *Fort Union*, New Mexico. 2nd Lt Chas Hay, 36th infty, is granted 15 days delay, at the expiration of which he is directed to proceed to *Fort Kearney*, Nebraska. Leave of absence for 6 months has been granted Brvt Col J Simpson, with permission to go beyond the sea. 2nd Lt Thos H Rich, 32nd infty, is granted 15 days delay in joining his regt at Tuscon, Arizona Territory.

Robt L Walpole, a prominent lawyer & Democratic politician, died at Indianapolis on Tuesday.

Rev Arthur Burtis, D D, Prof of Greek in Miami Univ, Oxford, Ohio, died on Friday.

John A Allderick, a Republican member of the Delawware Legislature, late Mayor of Wilmington, & a prominent lawyer, died at his residence in Newcastle yesterday.

Hon Fred'k Stone, while on his way to the Nat'l Capital, was, we learn, taken quite sick of the scarlet fever at the residence of Col John W Jenkins, where he now remains. We are glad to state that he has now nearly recovered. Port Tobacco Times

Confirmations & rejections by the Senate yesterday:
Confirmations:
U S Attys: D T Corbin, Dist of S C; Wm Dorsheimer, Northern Dist of N Y; Franklin J Dickinson, Northern Dist of Ohio.
U S Marshal: Casper E Yost, Dist of Nebraska.
Collector of Customs: E K Foster, jr, St Augustine, Fla.
Registers of Land Ofc: John Keely, at Roseburg, Oregon; Jos Keyes, at Menasha, Wisc.
Collectors of Internal Revenue: Silas D Gifford, 10th Dist, N Y; M Fisk, 3rd Dist, Louisiana; Benj C Gunn, 5th Dist, Mich; Geo O Erskine, 1st Dist, Wisc; Bernard Swartz, 2nd Dist, Mo; John Crane, 5th Dist, N C; John F Weldman, 11th Dist, Ind.
Naval Storekeepers: H C Keene, Boston; Edw Hooker, N Y; Dominick Lynch, Phil; S J Wailes, Wash; Chas A Morse, Mare Island, Calif.
Secretary: Jas Tufts, for Montana.
Consul: Jas R Low, of Calif, for Tehuantepec.
Assessors Internal Revenue: Jonathan Biggs, 11th Dist, Ill; John H Fox, 2nd Dist, Mo; G Thompson Gredley, 3rd Dist, Mich; Levi Bacon, jr, 5th Dist, Mich; Quincy D Whitman, 6th Dist, Ill.
U S Surveyor General: Phineas W Hitchcock, Dist of Nebraska.
Receiver of Public Money: Stewart Goodrell, Des Moines, Iowa.
Pension Agents: David F Burton, Dover, Dela; Jas M Rice, Quincy, Ill; Jas D Thompson, Des Moines, Iowa; Henry Barnes, Detroit, Mich.
Postmasters:

Hiram M Goodspeed, Ligonier, Ind
Henry C Marsh, Muncie, Ind
Moses T Willard, Concord N H
Geo P Woodbury, Milford, Mass
Erwin Heath, Oshkosh, Wisc
Hugh McKelvy, Alleghany, Pa
Sallie Kit Keyser, Gonzales, Texas
Edw E Downey, Brownsville, Texas
Jacob C Garrigus, Lacon, Ill
J B Lowry, Daville, West Va
John B Maher, Old Point Comfort, Va
Jos S Miner, Bridgeton, N J
Jas A Pinney, Idaho City, Idaho
Leroy S Dyer, Salem, Oregon
T B Robb, Savannah, Ga
David A Allen, Brenham, Texas
Noah W Harris, Waco, Texas
Donald Campbell, Jefferson, Texas
Jas R Stanbery, Newark, Ohio

John J Douglass, Waynesville, Ohio
Maria S Hood, Mt Vernon, Ohio
Wm H Harper, Lima, Ohio
Noyes P Chapman, Canastola, NY
John W Stebbins, Rochester, N Y
Thos S Dawes, Saugerties, N Y
Wm Glenny, Ithica, N Y
Allen C Livingston, Fulton, N Y
Alonzo Snow, **Port Deposit**, Md
Mrs Bettie Lackey, Jefferson City, Mo
John R Slack, Decorah, Iowa
Jas M Shurtz, Marshalltown, Iowa
Henry J Brown, Anderson, Ind
Chas M Theeman, Indianola, Texas
Wm B Comrie, Johnston, N Y
Henry W Gustine, St Jos, Mich
Phineas Grover, Albion, Mich
Albert M Patterson, Crestline, Ohio
Jas Freeman, Corry, Pa

Chandler Ford, Battle Creek, Mich
Whitney Jones, Lansing, Mich
Saml H Clark, Irredina, N Y
John C Smith, Canajoharie, N Y
Hamlet B Adams, Coldwater, Mich
Chas E Grover, Gloucester, Mass
Elmore Y Smith, Galion, Ohio

Zelotis Perrin, Clyde, Ohio
Jas L Mickey, Fostoria, Ohio
Dinah Crew, Carlinville, Ill
Hamilton Norton, Pole, Ill
Allen F Miller, Galva, Ill
Jas G Wright, Napierville, Ill
Margaret Walker, Sidney, Ohio
W S Newton, Gallipolis, Ohio

Rejections:
Minister to Austria: Frank P Blair, of Mo
Secretary: H P Bennett, for Colorado
Consuls: E C Ledyard, at Saltillo; Frank G Noyes, at Panama.
Naval Ofcr: Henry W Slocum, N Y
Surveyors of Customs: John Maguire, St Louis, Mo; Chas J Norris, Llewellynsburg, Md
Pension Agents: B F Stone, Macon City, Mo; John Frederick, Albany, N Y
Naval Storekeepers: Andrew Stimson, Kittery, Maine; Jas D Brady, Norfolk, Va
Assessors of Internal Revenue: Walter Carlin, 10th Dist, Ill; Ralph B Little, 12th Dist, Pa; Freeman N Horn, 4th Dist, Wisc; Lewis D Irwin, 9th Dist, Ill; Isaac Coles, 1st Dist, N Y; Jos J O'Donohoe, 3rd Dist, N Y.
Collectors of Internal Revenue: David K Oyster, 3rd Dist, Mo; Allen P Richardson, 5th Dist, Mo; Chas H Richmond, 3rd Dist, Mich; Wm A Morton, 9th Dist, Pa; Wm S Maynard, 2nd Dist, Mich.
Collectors of Customs: David R Austin, District of Miami, Ohio; Benj Lankford, Eastern Dist of Md
Naval Civil Engineers: B F Chandler, Portsmouth, N H; Alfred Young, Phil, Pa; Wm R Singleton, Norfolk, Va
Postmasters:
Irving Littelle, Macon City, Mo
H M Pedon, Shelbyville, Ill
B F McCormick, Waverly, Iowa
Wm C Hershberger, **Fort Madison**, Iowa
Moses Osmon, Fairburg, Ill
John F Johnson, Seymour, Ind
Washington Stark, Aurora, Ind
Fielding B Roberts, Carrollton, Ill
Henry V Sullivan, Quincy, Ill
John B Wolf, Clinton, Ill
Lucien B Pillsbury, Farmington, Maine
Walter Drew, Waukegon, Ill
Andrew C Russell, Danville, Pa

W D Williams, Rock Island, Ill
Allen McKean, Towanda, Pa
Richd Baylis, St Johns, Mich
Edwin Saunders, Saginaw, Mich
Robt H Lindsey, Boise City, Idaho
Wilson S Culbertson, Alliance, Ohio
C O Arnold, Wellsville, Ohio
Thos S Bardwell, Marion, Iowa
Saml D Clay, Gardiner, Maine
Geo S Whitney, Mt Morris, N Y
Abram Lavier, Dansville, N Y
Edw S Nash, Lima, N Y
Lemuel D Ferguson, Clarksburg, West Va

Hats for the Spring. B H Stinemetz, Hatter, 234 Pa ave, near 13th st, Wash City. [Ad]

Supreme Court of D C, Mar 26, 1867. No 895 in Equity. Wm H Wood, Francis M Scala, et al, cmplnts, vs Geo W Wood, Geo Devers, & Wm F Scala, dfndnts. On motion of cmplnts by M Thompson, their solicitor it is ordered that the dfndnts Geo W Wood & Geo Devers, each cause his appearance to be entered herein, on or before the first rule day occuring 40 days after this day; otherwise the cause will be proceeded with as in case of default; Provided a copy of this order be published in the Nat'l Intell once a week until the said sale day. By order of the Court, R J Meigs, clerk

Dept of the Interior, U S Patent Ofc, Wash, Mar 20, 1867. On the ptn of Geo Sharp, of Phil, Pa, praying for the extension of a patent granted to him Jan 5, 18<u>64</u>, for an improvement in Design for Spoon Handles, for 7 years from the expiration of said patent, which takes place on Jul 5,1867. -T C Theaker, Com'r of Patents

SAT MAR 30, 1867
Confirmations & rejections by the Senate yesterday.
Confirmations:
Assessor of Internal Revenue: Richardson L Wright, 5th Dist of Ill
Collectors of Internal Revenue: Jos Barnsley, 5th Dist of Pa; Wm Kellogg, 5th Dist of Ill
Surveyor Gen: A P R Safford, of Nevada
1st Lt U S Infty: John H Coster
Rejections:
Postmasters: Chas Faxon, Clarksville, Pa; Carlton B Davis, Milton, Pa

London, Mar 29. It is announced that King George, of Greece, is soon to marry a niece of Queen Victoria.

Cleveland, Mar 28. The house of Mr Heckel, with 5 of his children, was burned last night at Suffield Centre, Ohio.

Court in Equity-Justice Olin: Mar 29, 1867. 1-Keyworth vs Towers. No 847. Order appointing Mrs E P Towers guardian ad litem to Wm P Towers. 2-Linthicum vs Jones. No 249. Order ratification of trustee's sale of Jun 28, 1865, *nisi*.

Circuit Court-Chief Justice Cartter, Mar 29, 1867. 1-Smithson vs Stanton. No 2,724. This is the case brought to recover damages for false imprisonment during the war. Judge Hughes, for the plntf, filed a motion for oyer, inspection, & copies of records, etc. Dfndnt, through Mr Fendall, asked & obtained leave to withdraw the plea of the general issue. The case stand now upon the special pleas, setting forth the copies of the letters written by Smithson, aiding & abetting the rebellion, & the circumstances which led to the arrest of the plntf. 2-B F Morsell, vs Henry W Hamilton. No 422. Referred to John C Kennedy, & continued.

Died: Mar 29, Ferdinand Machie, infant son of A S & Mary Eliz Cox. His funeral will be from their residence, 349 10th st, between L & M sts, on Sunday at 3 P M.

Criminal Court-Judge Wylie. 1-Yesterday Robt Richardson, alias Bob Rocks, was found guilty for the larceny of a watch, & was recommended to the mercy of the Court. He was sentenced to 6 months in jail. 2-Geo H McCauly, was convicted for larceny & sentenced to jail for 6 months. 4-Moulton Fullerton, indicted for an assault & battery on Mrs Mary Sigston, was tried, but the jury failed to agree on a verdict.

Wanted-Everyone to know that I am now selling at my New Store, 502 7th st, under Odd Fellows' Hall, the same style of goods as I sold formerly on the avenue, under the late firm of Burns & Wilson, at fair prices. Try me. –G B Wilson

There is at present on exhibition at the jewelry establishment of Brown & Spaulding, 566 & 570 Broadway, an elegant specimen of American workmanship. This is a cane made from the tree underneath which Gen Grant received from the Confederate Gen Pemberton the surrender of Vicksburg, Jul 3, 1863. The handle, of solid gold, is inscribed: "Presented to Hon E B Washburne, of Illinois, by Brevet Major J A Rawlings, chief of staff to General Grant." Three more canes, of a similar design, made from the same wood, are now being made for Generals Babcock, Parker, & Fletcher, who, it will be remembered, compose a part also of Grant's military family. The entire thing is unique & in good taste, & reflects credit upon Messrs Brown & Spaulding, who originated the design & executed the work. –Journal of Commerce

No 249-Equity 7. Linthicum et al vs Mary Jones et al. The trustee reported he has sold lot 15 in Peters' square, in Gtwn, to Mary Jones, for the sum of $3,100; lot 16 in same square to Chas A Bucker & John Marbury, jr, for the sum of $2,357.28, & lot 17 in the same square, to L Thos Davis, for the sum of $1,581; & that the purchasers have complied with the terms of sale. –A B Olin, Justice -R J Meigs, clerk

MON APR 1, 1867
The death of Hon Geo Read Riddle. An affection of the lungs precipitated his death. The dread messenger came suddenly & unexpectedly. Geo Read Riddle, Senator from Delaware, was born in Newcastle, Dela, in 1817, & graduated at Delaware College; originally an engineer, he was employed on various canals & railroads in his own State & Md, but studied law, & was in 1848 admitted to the bar; served as the deputy atty until 1850, when he was elected to the 32nd Congress, & re-elected to the 33rd. In 1864 he was elected to the U S Senate; a Democrat, he has long been recognized as a leading man of his party in the State. A descendant of Geo Read, of Revolutionary memory, he was justly proud of an ancestor whose political principles he ever sought to maintain & illustrate. [No death date given-current item.]

Jas Clay Potts, age 20 years, employed by the Southern Express Co as messenger on the Mobile & Ohio railroad, absconded from West Point, Miss, Mar 16, taking with him a pouch containing upward of $20,000. The company offers a reward of $2,500 for his arrest.

Mr Matthews, the stepfather of Speaker Colfax, who has been dangerously ill at the residence of Mr Colfax, on 4½ st, was much better last evening, & is now considered out of danger.

Mary Lynch, a servant employed in the family of Nathan Lazarus, at Hartford, Conn, has been arrested on suspicion of having poisoned his 4 children. The children are yet suffering, & the recovery of 3 of them is still a matter of doubt.

Army Bulletin. Maj M H Kidd, 10th cavalry, & 2nd Lt J L Churchill, 24th infty, are granted 30 days leave. 1st Lt David Fairly, 7th cavalry; 1st Lt R M Taylor, 12th, & 2nd Lt John K Sullivan, 37th infty, are granted 30 days delay in joining their regts. 1st Lt Geo M Fleming & Brvt Brig Gen B S Roberts, major 3rd cavalry, are granted an extension of their leave of absence, the latter 3 months & the former 10 days. 2nd Lt Henry H Kuhn, 42nd infty, is granted 10 days delay in joining his regt. Brvt Lt Col R M Hall, 1st artl, has the permission to delay joining his regt extended 30 days. 1st Lt W B Kennedy, 10th cavalry, is granted 30 days delay in joining his regt. Brvt Maj August Thieman, 33rd infty, is ordered before the retiring board. 2nd Lt L W Barnhart, 4th cavalry, is ordered to report in person to the Adj Gen at Washington. Brvt Lt Col N B Harron, surgeon, is assigned to duty in the depts of Ga, Ala, & Fla, as Medical Director. Brvt Majors W F Randolph & W H Stone, & 1st Lt Paul Riemer, 5th artl; Brvt Maj Gen A McD McCook, 26th infty; Capt Richd Robbins, 39th infty; Capt John C Gilmore, 38th infty; Brvt Maj John H Butler, 42nd infty; Capt Kenelm Robbins, 43rd infty, & Capt D W Burk, 45th infty, are relieved from their duties & ordered to join their regts.

Navy Bulletin, Mar 22. Detached: Sailmaker Geo Thomas, from the ship **Savannah**, & placed on waiting orders. Ordered: 3rd Assist Engineer E T Phillippi, to the ship **Peoria**. Sailmaker Robt L Tatem, to the **Savannah**. Resigned: 2nd Assist Engineer Webster Lane, of the **Peoria**. Honorably Discharged: Acting Assist Paymaster M T Trumpbour, to date from Sep 7, 1865.

Mr Geo Y Brown, Sgt-at Arms of the Senate, & Col N G Craway, Sgt-at-Arms of the House of Reps have made the following appointments to the new Capitol police force, which those ofcrs were authorized to create: John W Westfall & Col John Coughlin have been appointed lts of the force. The privates already appointed are: from Maine, Amasa K Walker; N H, Col John Coughlin; Vt, Stephen W Baxter; N Y, John W Westfall; Ohio, W W Cromer; Kansas, Chas G Prentice; Nevada, Wm E Burton; N J, John Giberson; Mass, Capt Stephen A Boyden; Minn, Thos Mullen; Mich, Wm E Creary; Oregon, H R Kincaid; Ill, E T Bowers; Md, Chas Poffenberger; Ind, Col John Lindley. Superintendent of the crypt, John Bridges. No appointments from States that have yet to hold their elections have been made, & further applications from other States are still under advisement. A handsome uniform is to be selected, & the force is to be clothed & armed as rapidly as possible. A new force will assemble at the guard-room of the Capitol this morning at 11 o'clock, to be mustered, pledged, & sworn in. A very large proportion of the selections thus far made are the heroes of many well fought battles.

Our fellow citizen, Dr John K Walsh, [son of Dr Jos Walsh, of the Navy Yard,] has been appointed an A A surgeon U S army. He leaves today for the South, having been assigned to duty in that section of the country.

Orphans Court-Judge Purcell, Mar 30, 1867. 1-The will of Mary R Nourse, deceased, was admitted to probate & record, & letters testamentary issued to Jos E & Wm Nourse; bond $3,000. 2-Letters of administration on the personal estate of John Ford Muhlinghaus, deceased, one of the victims of the late fire on the avenue, were granted to Catherine Muhlinghaus; bond,$1,000. 3-Julia V Ragan gave a renewed bond as guardian to the orphans of Danl Ragan, deceased, in the sum of $2,500. 4-The second & final account of Chas H Utermehle, by Eugene Carusi & Naomi Utermehle, adms of said deceased, & the fourth general & fourth individual accounts of Marcia A Johnston, guardian to the orphans of John R Johnston, deceased, were approved & passed.

Court in Equity-Justice Olin, Mar 30, 1867. 1-Thos Y Conley et ux vs Geo Skaggs et al. No 771. Order appointing Emily Fuller guardian *ad litem* for Edw F Fuller, Mary Fuller, & Minnie Fuller. 2-*In re* John Hitz, executor. No 899. Order referring case to Auditor, to inquire into the circumstances of the case & report. 3-Eliz Cross vs Israel P Cross. No 832. Order to take testimony.

Court in General term-Justices Olin, Fisher, & Wylie, Mar 30, 1867. 1-Thos J Durant, of New Orleans, & Nathl Carusi, jr, of Wash, were admitted to the bar. 2-In the case of Caroline M Willard vs Jos C Willard, the appeal was dismissed. 3-Philp P Stilson was appointed U S Com'r for D C.

Circuit Court-Chief Justice Cartter, Mar 30, 1867. Allison Nailor vs Violet A Williams, admx of W H Williams. This is an action to recover an amount of money growing out of a claim assigned by the dfndnt to the plntf many years ago, against the State of Louisiana, for slaves taken from the dfndnt while taking the same through New Orleans to the Texas market for sale. Verdict for the dfndnt.

Balt, Mar 31. The funeral of Rev Chas W Chase, colored Presbyterian preacher, took place today with the largest demonstation of the kind ever witnessed here. There were 100 carriages in the procession, & the colored population enmasse on the streets.

Died: on Sat last, after a long illness, Kate, 2nd daughter of Col L A Whiteley, in her 14th year. Her funeral is this morning at 11 o'clock, from the residence of Dr R F Hunt, 519 12th st.

Died: on Mar 30, Mary Paine, eldest daughter of Henry C & Margaret C Fillebrown, aged 10 years & 1 day. Her funeral is today at 4 o'clock P M, from the residence of her grandmother, 251 I st.

Ezekeil Husted, a turner at Prince's melodeon factory, in Buffalo, NY, accidentally shot himself with a pistol on Sat, causing instant death.

Chas D Tuller, the late cashier of the Hartford Bank, on trial for alleged abstraction of bonds amounting to $20,000, was found guilty on Friday. His sentence was deferred to await a decision on the application of his counsel for a new trial.

Confirmations & rejections by the Senate on Saturday.
Collectors of Internal Revenue: Gen Jas B Steedman, of Ohio, 1st Dist of Louisiana; Henry A Guernsey, to the 18th Dist of Pa.
Assessors of Internal Revenue: John W Frazier, to the 1st Dist of Pa; Calvin W McLane, to the 10th Dist of Ill.
Postmasters: Wm Cromwell, at Bloomington, Ill; Saml G Smith, Peru, Ill; Leroy S Brown, Natchez, Miss; Henrietta Davies, Columbus, Miss; Louisa Cameron, Tallahassee, Fla; Geo Phillips, Key West, Fla.
Register of Land Ofc: Nathl S Goss, at Humboldt, Kansas.
Receiver of Public Money: David B Emmert, of Humboldt, Kansas.
To be Colonel U S Infty: Capt Ranold S McKenzie, of Corps of Engineers.
To be Capt U S Infty: Jacob H Smith.
Collector of Customs: Patrick S Slevia, Dist of Miami, Ohio.
Surveyor of Customs: Jesse M Harrison, Dubuque, Iowa
Appraiser of Merchandise: Lander Valentine, Portland, Maine.
The Senate rejected the following nominations:
Paymaster U S Army: Wm H Johnston, late paymaster of volunteers.
Brig Gen by Brevet: Brvt Col Jas B Fry.
Register of Land Ofc: Abram S Wadsworth, at Traverse City, Mich.
Collectors of Internal Revenue: Chas W Baker, 8th Dist of N Y; Thos McGrath, 4th Dist of Pa.
U S Marshal: Ansel D Wass, Dist of Mass.

D L Wells & Co, Auctioneers, corner 6th st & Louisiana ave. [Ad]

Chancery sale of valuable improved & unimproved property in Gtwn & Wash; by decree of the Supreme Court of D C, passed on Feb 5, 1867, in cause No 604, Docket 7, Felf vs Dowling et al; public auction on Apr 11next, at the premises, parts of lot 9 in Holmead's Addition, & part of lot 181, Beall's addition to Gtwn, the same fronting on Bridge st, between Montgomery & Green sts, & facing the end of Pa ave as extended into Gtwn. The property will be sold in 3 parcels, viz: the 3 story brick house with the lot which is 20 feet by 120 feet deep; & the 2 story frame houses west of the brick house, separately, with lots respectively attached to the same. On Apr 12, 1867, at the premises, we will sell the subdivision lots known as lots B & C in Sweeny's subdivision of lot 4 in square 579, in Wash City; each having a front of 22 feet 5 inches on 2nd st west, between south C & south D sts, & a depth of 105 feet to an alley in the rears. The titles are perfect.
-F W Jones, Chas M Matthews, trustees -Thos Dowling, auct

Dept of the Interior, U S Patent Ofc, Wash, Mar 25, 1867. Ptn of Edmund Munson, of Utica, N Y, praying for the extension of a patent granted to him Jul 19, 1853, for an improvement in Eyes for Mill Stones, for 7 years from the expiration of said patent, which takes place on Jul 19, 1867. -T C Theaker, Com'r of Patents

Orphans Court of Wash Co, D C, Mar 30, 1867. In the case of Sarah C West, admx of Clement L West, deceased, the administratrix & Court have appointed Apr 23, next, for the final settlement of the personal estate of the said deceased, of the assets in hand. -Jas R O'Beirne, Reg/o wills

Orphans Court of Wash Co, D C. Letters of administration on the personal estate of Jno Ferd Muhlinghaus, late of Wash City, D C, deceased. –Dervoliun Muhlinghaux, admx

TUE APR 2, 1867
Detroit Advertiser of Mar 23. Accident on Friday on the Great Western railway, near Woodstock, killed John Farrell, the conductor, who was the sole occupant of the conductor's car at the time. He lingered about 3 hours in intense agony until death relieved him of his sufferings. He lived at London, & leaves a wife & family there. Mr Rogers, the baggage master, was literally roasted alive. The baggage cars with all their contents were burned.

A gentleman from the South purchased 180 acres of land in Vansville district, on the route of the Potomac railroad, for the sum of $3,500. It was owned by Dr W W Duvall, of this county. -Marlborough [Md] Prince Georgian

Promotions in the clerical force of the Treasury. 1-First Comptroller's Ofc: Merritt Brown, first to second class. 2-Treasurer's Ofc: Geo Wood, third to fourth class.

Navy Bulletin, Mar 25. Detached: 2nd Assist Engineer Myron H Knapp, from the ship **Wachusett**, & granted sick leave of absence from Oct 25th last; Carpenter Wm H Jenkins, from duty at the N Y Navy Yard, on Apr 15 next, & placed on waiting orders.
Order Revoked: The order dismissing Mate Fred'k K Dumont, dated Jul 17, 1863, has been revoked, & his resignation accepted from that date.
Ordered: Carpenter Wm D Foy, to duty at the N Y Navy Yard, on Apr 15 next.

On Sat last Judge Smalley, of the U S Dist Court of N Y, sentenced Fred'k Guscetti, alias Jacques Roellinger, to 7 years imprisonment at hard labor for fraud upon the Pension Ofc.
Chas T Drennon, for fraud, was sentenced to 6 months in the county jail.

Splendid marble quarry in Buckingham Co, Va, on the James river, for sale. Correspond with me, Philip A Darneille, Norwood, Nelson Co, Va.

Fortress Monroe, Mar 29. The sloop **R L Simonson** belonging to Hampton, Va, sunk in the York river during the recent gales, & all on board perished: Wm Hedick, of Phil; Chas Cleaveland, of N Y; J C Wood, of Norfolk; & a colored man from Hampton. Hedrick & Cleaveland had both been pilots in the service of the Gov't during the war.

Presbury et al vs Haw et al; No 532, in Equity. By decree of the Supreme Court of D C, passed in the above cause on Mar 2, 1867, I shall sell, on the premises, on Apr 25 next, lots 58, 60, 61, 63, 64 thru 74, being the lots owned by the late Jesse B Haw, deceased, in Haw's subdivision of part of *Mount Pleasant farm*. –John F Ennis, trustee -Green & Williams, aucts

War Dept Claims Commission, Wash, D C, Mar 30, 1867. The following claims have been filed with the Commission during the present month:
Claim of David R Godwin for cotton seized in Louisiana.
Wm Jones for property destroyed in Va.
J W Butler for services as a detective.
Mr Soule for property taken in Ga.
Wm D Bennett, A S Larabee, & Thos Britton, for services in Minn.
L R Smooth for 2 locomotive engines.
Jas C Strong, for back pay as an ofcr in the U S army.
A J Mackay for corn delivered in Texas.
J D Ryan & Co for printing, etc.
Thos Antisell, M D, for damage to his property.
Jas Lindsley for sand taken by the U S authorities.
Mrs Jane Taylor for destruction of property.
Presly R Peyton for gold taken by U S ofcrs.
Wilson G Harwood for cotton taken in Tenn.
J L Hatton for rent of property.
J R Keller for services as fireman.
Chas Holt for services as bridge builder.
Thos Thornton for value of mule, saddle, & bridle.
John H Hays for boats, etc, taken by U S forces.
Wm Towers for loss of horses & damage to hack.
Jos Markham for property taken by U S forces.
Reece Hughes, for property taken by U S Gov't.
Wm Hughes, heirs of, for work on hospital grounds.
J C & H C Burbank & Co for damage to property.
Francis W Guy for services as pilot.
Wm J Morris for services as scout.
Mrs E B Male & Gorham, Dennis & Co for rent of property.
G Haggis for damages to property.
Andrea Doid for difference in price of corn.
Solomon Lowry for cotton taken in Ga.
Geo May for timber used in fortification.
Francis J Lippitt for commutation of fuel & quarters.

John Zumstein for sutler's good taken by U S troops.
Wm H Bailey for services as clerk.
Abel Gilbert for balance due on contract for grain.
A H Markland for property destroyed in Ky.
Wm Bailey for machinery seized by U S authorities.
Cyrus Firdley for services as teamster.
John F Rhodes for liquors taken by provost marshal.
Wm H Jones for hospital supplies. Earl D Barden for lumber & use of mill.
Wm H Bailey for compensation for capturing rebel mail.
Simpson Brothers for lumber taken by U S authorities.
John Lamb for pay while held as deserter. Wm Only for services as carpenter.
Benj S Shryock for wood furnished in Missouri.
Fred'k Hock for use of wagon & team.
Jos B Dalamara for damage of property in West Va.
J W Stevenson for wood furnished the Gov't.
Wm Dillon for use of the steamboat **Morning Light.**

Final action had upon claims during the present month:

Rejected:

Mrs M A Peters	Heirs of W H Bayne	John Ford
Jacob Hirsch	S Fernandez	Wm H Irwin
Jos Segar	Chamberlain & Davids	Rhodes & Badgely
H O Eater	Mrs Olive Garner	Wm Low
A F Numa Brow	Jas G Browne	Mrs F Chesley
Mrs Minerva Morris	L H Davis	J D Miller
Andrew Lowe	Moses Maples	Natale Biraghi
J H Carter	H H Martin	Mrs E L Cleman
Martin Howard	J E O'Farrell	Edw Sanders
Jos Block	E M Marshall	Jean M Laurio
D M Murtersbaugh	Horace Hewitt	Mrs Mary Boyle
Chas C Hudson	W W Cones	John H Tucker
Wm Jones	Joshua Hill	Edw King
Mr Soule	Mrs E W Turner	Jacob Augustine
T Antisell, M D	John H McKee	J C Van Wickle
J Markham	Jules Penodin	O N Cutler
E E Clark	Robt Gray	L N Dubas
R V Montague	Mrs Mary J Holland	Ignatius Z
Miss Sue Murphy	Eugene Bourcey	Chutkowski
C C Bliss	Jos de Fillippi	Mrs M Irwin
John Pearce	F Segura	S S Cresconi
M M Yeakel	Mrs Philomene Segur	Mrs L E Segur
J J Bowen	Mrs Josephine Gasselin	Dr Jas Syme
Withenburg & Doyle	Mrs Azaline Fay	Mrs C A Grove
A J Ruddington	Jules Couche	Zeringue & Hymel
L L Ferriere	John T Armstrong	Mrs Flora A Darling
C F Urguhart	Antoine Caire	

-De Witt Clinton, Brvt Lt Col, Recorder

WED APR 3, 1867

Orphans Court-Judge Purcell, Apr 2, 1867. 1-The will & codicile thereto of Geo W Young, deceased, were admitted to probate & record, & letters testamentary issued to Henrietta E Young; bond $10,000. 2-Letters of administration on the personal estate of John L Corcoran, deceased, were granted to Ursula Corcoran; bond $3,000. 3-John B Turton was appointed guardian to the orphans of Benj Ellin; bond $20,000. 4-The third general & third individual accounts of Jas Kelleher, guardian to the orphans of Wm Bush, were approved & passed.

Court of Equity-Justice Olin, Apr 2, 1867. Benning vs Benning et al. No 792. Order appointing Evan Hughes *ad litem* to Lucy & Martha Benning.

Criminal Court-Judge Wylie, Apr 2, 1867. 1-Wm Carroll & Jas Parks, convicted of larceny, each sentenced to 3 years in the Albany penitentiary. 2-Solomon Herman, convicted of larceny, was sentenced to 2 years in the Albany penitentiary.

Army Bulletin. 1-Delay in joining their regts have been granted to: Lt D G Risley, 42nd infty, 10 days, in reporting for duty to Maj Gen O O Howard; Lt Jos F Hill, 6th cavalry, 15 days; Capt John B V Wiele, 10th cavalry, 30 days; 2nd Lt Geo W Evans, 32nd infty, 15 days; 2nd Lt D T Stiles, 26th infty, 30 days; 2nd Lt Sylvester Soper, 40th infty, 30 days; Capt E Trotter, 45th infty, 30 days; 2nd Lt W H Bower, 45th infty, 15 days; 2nd Lt E T Duggan, 18th infty, 15 days; 1st Lt L H Warren, 39th infty, 30 days; 2nd Lt J M Bell, 7th cavalry, 45 days. 2-The delay granted Lt Bol R H Bowerman, 31st infty, is extended till Apr 15. 3-Brvt Col H G Gibson, 3rd artl, is ordered to report to the commanding general of the Dept of the East for assignment to a post. 4-Brvt Brig Gen J C Tidball, major 2nd artl, ordered to report to the commanding general of the Dept of the East for assignment to a post. 5-Maj A P Morrow, 9th cavalry, & Capt R McClerment, 41st infty, are relieved from their present duties & ordered to join their regts. 6-Brvt Majors Ely McClellan, S A Starrow, & W D Woolverton, assist surgeons U S army, are ordered to report to Brig Gen Brown, president of the Army Medical Examining Board, to be examined for promotion. 7-1st lt R C Churchill, 4th artl, ordered to join company K, of that regt, at **Fort Delaware**.

Criminal Court-Judge Fisher. 1-Alonzo Perry guilty of larceny of a coat valued at $10. 2-Benj Simpson guilty of larceny: sentenced to 2 months in the county jail. 3-Henry Harris, convicted of larceny of property valued at $43, was sentenced to 1 year in the Albany penitentiary.

Senate yesterday rejected the nomination of J C G Kennedy, to be Com'r of Agriculture.

Mr Wm R Hill, one of the oldest druggists in Richmond, Va, died on Sat.

On Tuesday last a lot on the north side of B st, between 2nd & 3rd sts, improved by a 2 story brick dwlg, was sold to W F Cudlip for $6,000.

The following prisoners convicted of various offences, will be forwarded to Albany to serve out their sentences:

Solomon Herman, larceny, 2 years
A W Lee, larceny, 3 years
Wm Connel, larceny, 3 years
Jas Parks, larceny, 3 years
Wm Brown, alias Sam Collins, larceny, 1 year
Wm Royston, alias Joshua Reed, larceny, 3 years
Wm Davis, Larceny, 3 years
Wm Broadus, robbery, 5 years
Henry Harris, larceny, 1 year

Brownstown, Ind, Apr 1. On Sat night Brooks & Tally were hung by the mob, for the murderer of an old lady who lived near Clear Springs, Jackson Co, Ind, some months ago. Their intent was robbery. Tally's last request was that his body might be given into the hands of his wife, who lived at Richview, Ill.

Mrd: on Apr 1, at the residence of the bride's mother, by Rev Fr Lynch, S J, John K Walsh, A A Surg, U S army, to Miss Helen L Ivey, all of Wash, D C.

Orphans Court of Wash Co, D C. Letters of administration on the personal estate of Mary R Nourse, late of Wash, D C, deceased. –Wm Nourse, J E Nourse, excs

Orphans Court of Wash Co, D C. Letters testamentary on the personal estate of Johnson Hellen, late of Wash, D C, deceased. –Jno B Blake, exc

Dept of the Interior, U S Patent Ofc, Wash, Mar 27, 1867. Ptn of Wm Mann, of Phil, Pa, for the extension of a patent granted to him Jan 11, 1853, ante-dated Jul 11, 1852, for an improvement in Manufacturing Copying Paper, for 7 years from the expiration of this application, which took place on Jul 11, 1866, this application having been authorized by act of Congress. -T C Theaker, Com'r of Patents

H Koppel, Merchant Tailor, 15th st, opposite the Treasury Dept-superior imported spring goods, reasonable rates, best materials. [Ad]

THU APR 4, 1867
Hon A J Preaux, a member of the Louisiana Legislature, died suddenly on Thursday last, of disease of the heart.

Criminal Court-Judge Fisher, Apr 3, 1867. 1-Susan Beckley, not guilty of larceny. Order to restore property. 2-Andrew Manning, for assault & battery, a *nolle prosequi* was entered. 3-Robt Fisher, Geo Washington, Thos Talberts, & Jas Henry, were indicted for burglariously entering the store of John S Hayden, & were convicted of larceny, but not of burglary. 4-Kate Ford was convicted of keeping a bawdy house.

Died: on Apr 3, Richd Randall, in his 70th year. His funeral will be on Apr 4, from the residence of his brother, Geo A W Randall, 12th & D sts, at half-past 3 P M. [New Orleans papers please copy.]

The trustees of the Foundry M E Church having by law of Congress been empowered to sell their *graveyard* on 14th st, near the boundary, have made arrangements for its disposal to Messrs Riley & Brother, of Wash City, for the sum of $18,700. Before the sale is made the trustees will see that the remains of all persons buried there, & which have not been removed by their friends, are removed to **Glenwood Cemetery**.

Died: on Apr 2, Benedict C Milburn, of Alexandria, Va, in his 63rd year. His funeral will take place from his late residence, 89 South Pitt st, Alexandria, Va, today at 2½ o'clock P M. [Balt & St Mary's, Md, papers please copy.]

Harrisburg, Apr 3. Govn'r Geary issued the warrant today for the execution on May 5 of Robt Fogler, of Wash Co, for the murder of Robt W Densmore on Dec 7, 1866.

All dfndnt's right, title, claim, & interest in & to lots 8 & 9 in square 255, in Wash City, D C, seized & levied upon as the property of Allison Nailer, will be sold to satisfy execution No 2,883, Supreme Court, D C, in favor of Edw M Grinder. -D S Gooding, U S Marshal, D C

Dept of the Interior, U S Patent Ofc, Wash, Mar 28, 1867. Ptn of Benj Irving, of N Y, N Y, praying for the extension of a patent granted to him Aug 30, 1853, for an improvement in Steam Boilers, for seven years from the expiration of said patent, which takes place on Aug 30, 1867. -T C Theaker, Com'r of Patents

FRI APR 5, 1867
Ex-Govn'r of Md, has been confirmed by the Senate as Collector of Customs at the port of Balt, Md.

John F Bridget opened yesterday his new & handsome carriage repository on the avenue, between 4½ & 6th sts.

Court in Equity-Justice Olin, Apr 4, 1867. 1-H Sidney Everett vs Helen C Everett. No 617. Order ratifying & confirmning sale of property. 2-Eliz Cross vs Israel P Cross. No 832. Decree of divorce granted, & the plntf released from all obligations thereof, & to have the custody of her child. 3-Catherine Rile vs Michl Rile. No 897. Order granting the plntf alimony to the amount of $7 per week. 4-Louisa Hardy vs Henry J Hardy. No 880. Order to take testimony. 5-Lettie H Smith vs Jas C Smith. No 852. Order to take testimony.

Phil, Apr 4. 1-Saml C Morton, late Pres of the Board of Trade & of the American Fire Ins Co, of Phil, & a prominent merchant, died last evening. 2-Dr Caspar Wistar, a well-known & highly-esteemed physician of Phil, died this morning.

Mr B C Milburn, an old & highly esteemed citizen of Alexandria, died last night, at his late residence on Pitt st, after a painful illness of some 6 weeks.

Association of Oldest Inhabitants regular meeting was held on Wed; Col P G Washington, President; Mr J Carroll Brent reported that 1,000 copies of the address of Col J C Pickett, delivered on Feb 22, had been printed for distribution. A cmte, consisting of Messrs Lewis Johnson, Maj Chauncey Bestor, & John Waters, was appointed to inquire into increasing the revenue of this association. The chair announced the death of Mr Geo W Young, an old & well known citizen. Col Washington, Mr Chauncey Bestor, Mr Lewis Johnson, Dr John B Blake, Mr Fielder Dorsett, Mr John F Callan, & others, spoke of the life & virtues of the deceased. The following were nominated for membership, & duly elected: Messrs Marshall Brown, Cmdor Junius J Boyle, John Cranch, Jas Charles, Valentine Harbaugh, Jonathan Forrest, & John King. Mr J Carroll Brent presented a drawing for the archives of the association, given to him by Mr C B Baker, of the First Episcopal Congregation Church, [Christ Church] Washington. It was orginally a tobacco house on Dr Carroll's farm, on N J ave, about 3 squares below the Capital. A small school room was attached at the west end, where the rector, Rev Andrew T McCormick, taught for some years previous to 1805. The drawing is a hasty sketch made with a pen by Thos Underwood, one of the pupils of 1803-4, on the inside of the cover of an old Latin grammar. The bldg was occupied by the congregation until 1807, when they occupied a bldg near the Navy Yard.

Criminal Court-Judge Fisher, Apr 4, 1867. 1-Peter McKenney indicted for breaking into the house of Michl Boyland. The jury was unable to agree upon a verdict. 2-Harrison Wilkinson, indicted for larceny. In this case a ***nolle prosequi*** was entered. 3-Wm Peters found not guilty for an assault & battery on Patrick Donoghan. 4-Annie Merwin, convicted of keeping a bawdy-house, was fined 75 cents & cost, making a total of $20.

At Warsaw, Ind, about 6 weeks ago, one Lawrence Hart took from the poorhouse a boy 4 years old, named Winfield Hines. Three weeks afterward the child was missing. It's mother made inquiry as to what had become of it, & was told that it had been given away to a man living in Ohio. A search was made; Hart fled; & the boy's mangled body was found in an old well. Hart's wife testified that her husband's treatment of the boy was brutal & cruel in the extreme. The county com'rs have offered a reward of $500 for the apprehension of Hart.
+
A Hart, who murdered his adopted son, a little child of 4 years of age, near Warsaw, Ind, on Feb 24 last, was arrested today at Independence, near Mount Vernon, Ohio. Hart was discovered at his sister's in Independence.

Mrd: on Apr 3, at Poughkeepsie, by Rev P K Cady, Theo O Ebaugh, of Wash, D C, to Anna, youngest daughter of Paul H Lalouette, of N Y C.

Died: on Apr 3, Emma Waters, infant daughter of Capt Wm H & Virginia A Nalley, aged 18 months. Her funeral will be on Friday at 3 o'clock P M, at 592 H st.

Valuable private residence in Gtwn, D C, at auction on Apr 24, that desirable residence of the late Wm Redin; fronts 100 feet on Gay st, between Wash & Congress sts; the house is large & substantially built, containing 16 rooms, with fine cellars; gas & water throughout; in excellent order. Immediate possession given. -Thos Dowling, auct

Supreme Court of D C, in Equity No 651, Docket 7. Julia A Van Ness vs Barney Berry. The trustee reported he sold the property described in the proceedings to Julia A Van Ness, the creditor; that she has credited the purchase money upon the notes held by her. -A B Olin, Justice -R J Meigs, clerk

Orphans Court of Wash Co, D C, Apr 2, 1857. In the case of Chas S Wallach, exc of Parrott A Prindle, deceased, the executor & Court have appointed Apr 27 next, for the final settlement of the personal estate of the said deceased, of the assets in hand. -Jas R O'Beirne, Reg/o wills

Orphans Court of Wash Co, D C, Apr 2, 1867. In the case of Jos Gawlor, adm of Michl G Stapleton, late of U S A, deceased, the administrator & Court have appointed Apr 27 next, for the final settlement of the personal estate of the said deceased, of the assets in hand. -Jas R O'Beirne, Reg/o wills

Mr B M Brown, 84 years old, & a resident of Dayton, Ohio, for the last 30 years, is undergoing the process of voluntary starvation. According to the Journal, of that city, he & his family assert that he has taken no food since Feb 28. He feels no pain & asserts that he has no appetite. He is reduced to a skeleton, & expects death.

Richmond, Apr 4. Geo W Randolph, formerly Confederate Sec of War, died yesterday.

SAT APT 6, 1867
Gen Meredith, of Indiana, who was on yesterday rejected for Surveyor General of Montana by the Senate, received a telegram that his son, Capt & Brvt Maj David M Meredith, stationed at Montgomery, Ala, was dead. Capt Meredith entered the service at the breaking out of the rebellion, & was dangerously wounded at the battle of Chickamanuga. He was about 25 years of age. Gen Meredith left for his home in Indiana on the train last evening. –M C

Criminal Court-Judge Fisher, Apr 5, 1867. Kate Ford, convicted of keeping a bawdy-house, was fine $1.

Hon Lovell H Rousseau, of Ky, was yesterday confirmed by the Senate as brig general of the army. In view of the great service & influence Gen Rousseau had in the war of the rebellion, confirmation was anticipated.

The brick dwlg & lot, the residence of the late Jas Vansant, on Pitt st, was sold to C W Wattles for $3,509.

Confirmations & rejections by the Senate yesterday. Confirmed: Alex'r Asboth, of Miss, as Minister Resident to the Republic of Uraguay. Also, the following Consuls: Francis P Knight, at Wen Chwang, China; E Sturmsfels, of N Y, at Maracaibo; Julius Morius, of Mich, at Coblentz; Thos R King, of Rhode Island, at Belfast. J A Johnson, of Rhode Island, Consul General at Beirout. Thos Kibly Smith, of Ohio, at Panama. The Senate rejected the nomination of Hon Jas W Nesmith, ex-Senator from Oregon, to be Envoy Extraordinary & Minister Plenipotentiary to Austria; & also rejected S J Wailes, to be naval storekeeper at Wash D C. Col Wailes was a gallant soldier of Md during the rebellion.

Army Bulletin: Brvt Brig Gen M D Hardin, major 43rd infty, is granted one year leave of absence, from Jun 1, with permission to go beyond the sea. Capt Theodore Schwan, 10th infty, is granted 6 months leave of absence, with permission to go beyond the sea. Brvt Col Chas Ewing, 22nd infty, is granted leave of absence until Jun 30, 1867; 2nd Lt W F Halleck, 27th infty, is granted 2 months leave of absence. The leave of absence granted Brvt Maj Gen A Pleasanton is further extended 6 months. Brvt Maj S C Greene, 24th infty, is ordered to report to Gen Pope. Brvt Maj Gen G W Getty, colonel 37th infty, is ordered to report to Lt Gen Sherman. Brvt Lt Col F W Schaurte, 2nd cavalry, is ordered to join his company at *Fort Laramie*. Capt V Van Anterp, military storekeeper, is assigned to duty at San Antonio, Texas. 1st Lt J C De Grers, 9th cavalry, is ordered to report to Gen Sheridan. 1st Lt W A Cameron, 5th artl, is assigned to company B. 1st Lt Edw Hunter, 12th infty, is ordered to report to Gen Sherman for assignment to duty with Gen Getty.

Circuit Court-Chief Justice Cartter, Apr 5, 1867. Douglass vs Douglass. No 1,150. Case still on trial. This is a suit brought to recover certain hot-house plants, camelias, etc, alleged to belong to the plntf as a portion of the estate of John Douglass.

Richmond Whig. Hon Geo W Randolph, the grandson of Thos Jefferson, a little under 50 years of age, died at home, recently. He has been in declining health for several years, & last fall, after 2 or 3 years in Europe in the vain quest of health, returned home, as he expressed it, to die. He held a commission in the navy; adopted the profession of law; was a leading member of the Convention of 1861; a strong advocate of secession; among the first in the field as major of the howitzer btln from this city; whose first gun was fired by him at Bethel; after being promoted to brigadier, he was invited by Pres Davis to the position of Sec of War, of which he discharged in a most satisfactory manner. [Death date not given-current item.]

Died: on Apr 5, in Wash City, Col Wm R Bradford, late of Ky. His funeral will take place on Sunday at 3 o'clock, from his late residence, 572 N J ave.

Died: on Apr 5, Sarah E, wife of John J Byrnes, in her 24th year. Her funeral will be on Sunday at 3 o'clock P M, from Mass ave, between 2nd & 3rd sts.

Died: Apr 4, after a short illness of typhoid pneumonia, Mrs Catherine Ivey. Her funeral is this morning at 9½ o'clock A M, from her late residence, 552 7th st, Navy Yard.

Leavenworth, Kansas, Apr 5. Ex-Brig Gen Jos Bailey, sheriff of Vernon Co, Mo, was brutally murdered while discharging the duties of his ofc, by 2 brothers, Lewis H & Perry Pixley, on Mar 26. The citizens have subscribed $3,000 reward for the apprehension of the murderers. [Apr 11th newspaper: the murder of Gen Bailey was for the purpose of obtaining money, & the murderers succeeded to get over $1,000; Perry Pixley is about 24 years old; Lewis Pixley is 25. They are supposed to be in Kansas, or on the Western Missouri border. The victim of this cruel outrage, Gen Bailey, was the engineer, who, by his skill & resources, saved the entire gunboat fleet of Cmdor Porter at the time of the disastrous Banks expedition up the Red River in 1864, as well as the immense fleet of transports which accompanied them in that campaign. His deeds have lately been placed before the public eye by Mr J S C Abbott, in his "Heroic Deed of Heroic Men," in which Gen Bailey is placed as one of the principal heroes of the war, & with justice.]

Dept of the Interior, U S Patent Ofc, Wash, Mar 16, 1867. Ptn of Richd A Tilghman, of Phil, Pa, praying for the extension of a patent granted to him Oct 3, 1854, ante-dated Jan 9, 1854, for an improvement in Process for Purifying Fatty Bodies, for 7 years from the expiration of said patent, which takes place Jan 9, 1868.
-T C Theaker, Com'r of Patents

MON APR 8, 1867
Richd Batchelder, a railway conductor, was knocked from the top of a freight train, between Lawrence & Salen, on Friday, & instantly killed.

Mr Tilman Gregory, a very wealthy planter, residing near Augusta, Ark, fell into an altercation over a game of cards with Dr Dameron, in the course of which, both being intoxicated, both shot each other dead.

Walter Forrester, an old man 67 years of age, & a gardner by occupation, met a sudden death on Sat. He was in the shoe shop of Mr O'Brien, in Uniontown, across the Navy Yard Bridge, & a child was playing with an old revolver. Mr Webster, supposing the pistol to be unloaded, struck the gun with the shoemaker's hammer. It exploded, the charge killing Mr Forrester almost instantly. Mr Webster was exonerated from all intention to commit manslaughter.

Died: on Apr 6, Mr Andrew Small, a native of Dendee, Farforshire, Scotland, but for the last 37 years a resident of Wash City, in his 73rd year. His funeral will take place from his late residence, 650 L st, on Apr 8, at 2 o'clock P M.

Died: on Apr 7, Saml Stinemetz, in his 41st year. His funeral will take place on Tuesday, at 3 o'clock, from his late residence, 479 E st, near 4th.

Coal mine explosion at the coal pits at Clover Hill, Chesterfield Co, Va, on Wed last. Names of white men killed: Thos Layton, wife & 6 children; Patrick Donahoe, 2 children; Jas Lockett, wife & 4 children; Wm Thomas, wife & 5 children; Beverly Amonet, wife & 3 children; Joe Confry, wife & 1 child; John Alasko, wife & 3 children; Jas Alasko, wife & 1 child; John Weale, wife & 5 children; Peter Logan, wife; Geo Moore, wife & 6 children; Jim Harper, wife; Nat Roberts, wife; Albert Isaacs, wife & 3 children; H McGruder, wife & 3 children; Wm B Robertson, wife & 5 children; Geo Puckett, Tom Puckett, Jim Puckett, not married, but have one sister; Geo Taylor, mother & 2 sisters; Saml Fowler, 6 children; Nich Hackett, father & mother, aged & infirm; Robt Bowman, wife & 3 children; Wm Goode, wife & 3 children; Wm Cosley, wife & 3 children; Wm A Cole, Thos Cosley, John T Kerner. Eighty one women & children are utterly destitute. Names of the negroes killed: Carter Cox, Beverly Anderson, Giles Patterson, Gus Cox, Dick Hobson, Andrew Branch, Henry Finny, John Arits, Washington Hunt, Wm Simms, Asa Coleman, Edmund Jones, Simon Stokes, John Owens, Randal Jackson, Wm Thweatt, Price Jackson, Chas Jefferson, Dr Faulkes, Redd Jefferson, Wyley Gibbs, Ellett Trent, Edmund Johnson, Jos Turpin, Phil Bossieau, Henry Bossieau, Aaron Wood, Elijah McTyre, Jim Selden, Danish Langford, Robt Belman, Frank Wiles, Albert Jones, Dick Mann, Danl Osborn, Henry Owens, Henry Howard, Jordan Gates, Wm Kirby.

Oswego, N Y, Apr 5. The schnr **Lydia Ann**, which left Charlotte on Apr 1, for Port Hope, when off Charlotte, Thos Vance, the mate was lost overboard. His son, Arthur, took the yawl to rescue his father, but got adrift in the trough of the sea & could not get back to the vessel. It is feared that he is also lost.

Executor's sale of 2 story frame house & lot at auction, on Apr 18, on the premises, the south half of lot 6 in square 8_9, having 25 feet front on 4th st, between B & C sts, with the well built house, belonging to the estate of the late Thos Donohoe, deceased. -A P McKenna, exc -Green & Williams, aucts

The 35th anniversary of the Dolbear Commercial College was celebrated at Lyceum Hall, in New Orleans, on Feb 25. The degree of Master of Accounts was conferred upon the following named graduates:

Geo A Jones, Ala	T R Beall, Miss
Arthur Claiborne, La	W H Day, La
F S Mallery, Ala	W F Green, Miss
P J Flanegan, La	C J Bier, La
A C Luckie, Ala	R H Lacy, Texas
J E Decuir, La	J T Marsh, La
Henry Miller, La	G C Swift, Ala
G E Thurmond, Miss	John Taylor, La
Henry Sarran, La	J J Yerby, Texas
John C Pickens, Miss	J C Pullen, La
J E Guyol, La	Richd Cross, Miss
Wm F Seffert, Texas	J H Phillips, La
J F Weckerling, La	G Ottomeyer, Ark

L B Hollingsworth, La
L Bogan, La
V Lemantia, Italy
H B Mistrot, La
Emile A Louis, Paris

H Paland, La
H A Despommier, La
B F Sides, Ala
Jas Opry, La
Mark Kahn, La

TUE APR 9, 1867
Valuable property on 14th st west near Ohio ave at auction; on Apr 16, part of lot 3 in square 257, a well built 2 story & attic frame house having a fine front, running back to a good alley, being the residence of the late Grafton Powell, deceased. Also, 2 handsome bldg lots adjoining. -Green & Williams, aucts

Deaths of well-known citizens. 1-On Saturday Mr Andrew Small, a well known citizen, died at his residence on L st north. Mr Small was a Scot by birth, but had resided here for a long series of years & had amassed quite a fortune. He leaves property estimated at about $250,000, & it is said that in his will he leaves the bulk of it to benevolent & religious associations. 2-Mr Saml Stinemetz, who for several years past has carried on the hat & shoe business on 7th st, died at his residence on E st, near 4th, this morning. His funeral is this afternoon, & will be attended by Columbia Lodge, I O O F, of which he has for many years been a member. 3-On Friday last Col Wm R Bradford, formerly of Ky, died at his residence on N J ave. He was formerly a clerk in the Patent Ofc, & had previously served as an ofcr in the Mexican war, but of late years had been acting as a conveyancer & for a short time as magistrate. He will be recollected by our citizens, as the capt of the volunteer company known as the Walker Sharpshooters.

Within the past 8 months a beautiful ***National Cemetery*** has been erected in the vicinity of Yorktown, & contains the remains of 2,181 Union soldiers, who fell during McClellan's memorable struggle on the Peninsula. The bodies here interred were obtained only by the greatest exertion, with limited means of conveyance, from the different battle & skirmish fields at Lee's Mills, Grafton Church, Warwick Court House, Wmsburg, Bickerton, White House Landing, Cumberland, West Point, Brick House Point, King Wm Court House, Enoch's Church, Crump's Cross Roads, Hanover Court House, Young's Mills, Ship Point, Upper Grafton Church, & Mechanicsville. Some 600 bodies were taken from the ***National Cemetery*** at Yorktown & reinterred. Pa, N Y, & Mass regts have the largest number buried here, but many other of the Eastern, & also Western regts, are now & then seen engraved on the head-boards.

Died: on Apr 8, of disease of the brain, Chas Thoma, in his 19th year. His funeral will take place from the residence of Mr John Ruppert's farm, near 7th st, beyond the first toll-gate, on Wed next, at 8 o'clock A M.

Died: on Apr 7, Saml Stinemetz, in his 41st year. His funeral will take place on Tuesday, at 3 o'clock, from his late residence, 479 E st, near 4th.

Court in Equity-Justice Olin, Apr 8, 1867. 1-Adams vs Smith et al. No 840. Order appointing J R Barr guardian *ad litem* to Rebecca Coltman. 2-Ragan vs Ragan et al. No 743. Order proconfesso against Thos Ragan, & appointing John L Yates guardian *ad litem*.

Valuable farm near the city at public auction, on May 1: Farm known as the *Abercrombie Farm*, on the map of 1860, containing 89 acres of land, in Wash Co, about 1 mile from the Bladensburg Toll-Gate, & adjoining the lands of Dr Palmer, Gen Hickey, & W W Corcoran. This place is improved by a new brick house, & all necessary out-bldgs. –V D Stockbridge & Co, 7th & G sts. -Green & Williams, aucts

Circuit Court-Chief Justice Cartter, Apr 8, 1867. 1-Johanna Brown vs Michl Moriarity. No 3,616. Judgment by default. 2-Wm Douglass, adm of John Douglass, vs Henry Douglass. No 1,150. This is a suit of replevin brought by Wm Douglass, adm of the estate of John Douglass, sr, to try the right of property of John Douglass, sr, in which certain camelia plants, called japonicas, which have been in the possession of Henry Douglass since 1847. The plntf claims that they are the remnant of their father's old collection, while the dfndnt claims that he has since 1840 to the present time, collected them by purchases, gift, & propagation. The number in dispute is 176, valued at $10,000. This is the 3rd trial of the case; two previous were unable to agree. The arguments were concluded yesterday.

Marshals sale on Apr 29, of dfndnts right, title, claim & interest in lot 28 of square 398, with improvements, in Wash City, seized & levied upon as the property of Wm M Brown, & will be sold to satisfy judicials 53 to Oct term, 1859, in favor of Benj F Morsell. –D S Gooding, U S Marshal, D C

Books & Stationery. American & Foreign Publications for sale. McConnell & Herberts, Book & Periodical Depot, 458 7th st, opposite Post Ofc, Wash, D C. [Ad]

Carter Place offered at private sale; much admired site on the Heights of Gtwn, D C, a long time the residence of the late Col John Carter, & after his death occupied in succession by the Ministers of England & France. It fronts 726 feet on Road st, 4_0 on Stoddard st, & 704 on Wash st, & contains upwards of 9 acres of land. –John Marbury, Gtwn

WED APR 10, 1867
The Pres issued his warrant of pardon to Z _ Vance, late Govn'r of N C. The pardon was issued on the recommendation of Senators Wilson, Johnson, Ross, Ferry, Yates, Reps Stevens, Mr Horace Greeley, & a large number of others.

The body of a man found drowned in the Potomac yesterday was identified to be that of Lewis Morris. He is supposed to have been in the water since Feb 26, as at that time he went to the river to catch drift-wood, & was never heard from until his body was found floating in the water.

Mr John D Hammack, well known as the proprietor of Hammack's restaurant, died in Wash City yesterday. He has been in ill-health for some time, & his death was therefore not unexpected.
+
Died: on Apr 9, John D Hammack, in his 39th year. His funeral will take place on Apr 11 at 1 o'clock, from his late residence, 202 Pa ave, corner of 15th st. [Apr 13th newspaper: The funeral of the late John D Hammack was very largely attended; services were conducted by Rev Dr Samson; the funeral proceeded to the **Congressional Cemetery**, where the remains were interred with the appropriate services of the Order of the Odd Fellows, of which he was a member.]

Buffalo, Apr 9. The popular actress, Sallie St Clair, wife of Chas M Barras, died here this afternoon.

Hon David F Caldwell died at Salisbury, N C, on Thursday.

Mrs Harriet Beecher Stowe has been travelling through the extreme South.

Meyran Sanford, clerk in the ofc of the Pa Central railroad, committed suicide at Chicago, on Saturday, by taking laudanum.

Geo Slocum, a banker of Detroit, was killed on Thur, by the accidental discharge of his gun, while on a gunning expedition in the river Rouge, near Detroit. He was highly respected.

J P Davis, proprietor of the American House at Fox Lake, Wisc, committed suicide on Mon by taking morphine, leaving a wife & a large family. No cause is assigned for the commission of the act.

Miss Celina Eller, the young lady at Beck's Station, near Indianapolis, who was recently taken with hydrophobia in its worst form, is rapidly recovering under a treatment of bromide of potassium, & hopes are entertained of her speedy & perfect cure.

<u>Court in Equity</u>-Mr Justice Olin, Apr 9, 1867. 1-Dyer vs Dyer. No 795. Order appointing T B Dyer guardian *ad litem* to Jennie C Dyer.

<u>Circuit Court</u>-Chief Justice Cartter, Apr 9, 1867. Douglass vs Douglass. Verdict for plntf, with the exception of 9 camelia japonicas.

Dept of the Interior, U S Patent Ofc, Wash, Apr 3, 1867. Ptn of Wm E Ward, of Port Chester, N Y, praying for the extension of a patent granted to him Dec 28, 1852, for an improved method of Heading Screw Blanks, rivets, etc, for seven years from the expiration of said patent, which takes place on Dec 28, 1866.
-T C Theaker, Com'r of Patents

Army Bulletin. Brvt Lt Col R E A Crofton, 16th infty, leave of absence extended 10 days. Maj Chas A Morgan, 4th artl, relieved from recruiting service, & assigned to the command of *Fort Delaware*, Dela. Capt P S Michie, corps of engineers, is ordered to report to the Superintendent of the West Point Military Academy for assignment. Capt W J Twinning, corps of engineers, is transferred from the Dept of the East to the Dept of Dakota. 1st Lt R W Petrikin, corps of engineers, is ordered to the Dept of the Platte. Brvt Lt Col J D Stubbs, assist quartermaster U S volunteers, has been relieved from duty as chief quartermaster & disbursing ofcr in N C, & is succeeded in that position by Brvt Maj R O Tyler, to whom Col Stubbs is directed to report for duty as post & depot quartermaster at Charleston, S C. Surgeon DeWitt C Peters is relieved from duty in the Dept of Wash, & is ordered to repair to St Louis, Mo, & report to the medical director of the Dept of Mo to accompany a detachment of recruits ordered to New Mexico. Leave of absence for 30 days on surgeon's certificate of disability is granted Capt Henry Johnson, medical storekeeper.

On Mon last, Hiram Lee, living about 4 miles from Westport, Mo, was killed by the discharge of a double-barrelled gun through the window of the room in which he was sitting. The murderer is supposed to be one of his neighbors with whom he had an old quarrel.

Navy Bulletin. Detached: Acting Boatswain Wm D Allen, from special duty at the Wash NavyYard, & placed on waiting orders. Honorably Discharged: Acting Ensign Jas M Jackson. Ordered: Boatswain Edw B Bell, to special duty as foreman of laborers at the Wash Navy Yard.

Orphans Court-Judge Purcell, Apr 9, 1867. 1-The will of Andrew Small, deceased, was filed & fully proven. After directing that his remains shall be interred in the burial place on his farm, near Darnestown, Md, & a monument to cost from $500 to $1,000 to be erected over his grave, the deceased bequeathes his farm of 430 aces, with stock, house, & furniture, & $5,000 in money, to his nephew, John Small, & legacies of $1,000 each to a number of his nephews & grand nephews & nieces, & $35,000 to the Melville & Darnestown Presbyterian Church. The will is dated Aug 29, 1866, & nominates his friends S Humphrey, J A Ruff, & J B Monroe, excs. 2-The will of Mary Ann Magee, deceased, was filed & partially proven. 3-The will of Thos Mason, deceased, was admitted to probate & record. 4-Letters of administration of the personal estate of Robt S Patterson, deceased, was granted to Edgar Patterson. Bond, $50,000. 5-Letters of administration on the personal estate of Wm H Thompson, deceased, were granted to Isabella K Thompson. Bond $1,000. 6-Ursula Corcoran was appointed guardian to the orphans of John L Corcoran, deceased. 7-The first & final account of Alfred Rhey, exc of Eliz Butler, deceased; the first & final account of Margaret Ann Dukes, admx of Levin Dukes, deceased, balance in distribution account of the personal estate of said deceased to legal heirs; also, the first general & first individual accounts of Margaret Ann Dukes, guardian to the orphans of Levin Dukes, deceased, were approved & passed.

Criminal Court-Judge Fisher, Apr 9, 1867. 1-Beverly Mortimore found not guilty of larceny. 2-Chas Hopkins found guilty of assault & battery, with intent to kill Danl R Hudson. 3-Louisa Clarke was found guilty of stealing $80 from Hannah Constine.

Kaufman's portrait of Gen Sherman sitting by his camp fire is said to have been sold for $3,000.

Register's Ofc, Apr 9, 1867. The following property was sold for taxes May 9, 1865, & if not redeemed at this ofc, with the interest & cost of advertisement, prior to May 9, 1867, Corp deeds will issued to the purchasers, in accordance with existing laws.

Ames, Andrew J
Adams, Alex'r
Ashford, Craven
Alexander, Columbus
Austin, Seth C
Ackley, Thos
Austin, Wm
Bayliss, Buckner
Bevan, C F & W F
Bomford & Decatur
Ball, Dabney
Burd, Eburn
Burd, E & J H
Buckey, Geo
Bonford, Geo
Balmain, H W
Behren, J H & W Heron
Beuhler, J F
Brasnahan, Michl
Basse, Martin
Byrne, Moriah
Brady, N, in trust
Bauman, Paul
Briscoe, R G
Boarman, Richd A
Boarman, Ralph
Bowen, Sayles J
Brereton, Saml
Black, Saml
Baugert, Sebastian
Brown, Wm, in trust
Benter, Wm F
Cazenove, A C
Cox, Cornelius
Cleary, D M

Carroll, D of D'n
Chapman, Eliz
Chancellor, E M
Costigan, Ellen
Coltos, Edwi
Clarke, G D
Cox, J E
Combs, J J
Clark, J S
Costigan, John
Cromwell, Jos W
Coombs, J J, & J Welsh
Colineau, L G
Carter, Lavinia
Chandler, M & W S
Connor, Michl
Crutchett, Jas
Coyle, M & others
Cuvilier, M J
Callan, N
Carter, R W
Casey, Stephen
Cain, Thos
Cox, W S, trustee
Dixon, Geo O
Dove, Geo M
Deibstich, Herman
Douglass, Hy
Dodge, H H, et al, in trust
Donelan, Jas B
Delaney, John
Davis, Jas H
Devling, John S
Downey, Michl
Dove, Marmaduke

De Voss, P J
Dennison, R A
Downs, Solomon
Down, Thos C, & J Miles
Dewees, Wm
Dougherty, Wm
Ely, Alfred
Edson, Augustus
English, H F, & C S
Ellis, Robt
Flannagan, Ann
Farrell, B
Falconer, Elisha
Felson, Henry
Fisher, H, & Thos Gunton
Fearson, Jos N
Ford, J T
Fling, Jas W
Fitzgerald, Jas
Freidenwall, Jonas
Forrest, Mary
Fraser, jr, Jas
Foley, P, in trust
Frazier, Wm
Gladmon, A B
Gibson, Eliza
Graham, G M, in trust
Gray, J S
Goheens, John F
Gardner, Jacob B
Gadsby, John
Gunnell, Wm H
Hay, Alex'r
Harvey, C H
Holohan, Christopher
Hanson, G D, in trust
Henning, G F
Hay, Henry
Harkness, J C
Harkins, John
Howard, J F
Hall, John
Hastings, J A
Hunter, Louisa
Hough, O R
Henry, Robt

Higgins, S A
Harris, T D K
Hoffman, Theresa
Herbert, W J
Howell, W P & J W Morsell
Ingle, C
Jillard, Geo E
Jewell, J G
Jones, M T
Johnson, Sophia
Jenkins, Thaddeus
James, Wm
King, Cora
Kingman, E
Kirk, Geo E, in trust
Klopfer, H A
Keaney, Jas
Kelly, Miles
Lindins, Danl
Lloyd, Eliz
Little, Frank
Lewis H H
Larman, Hy
Larned, Jas
Loeliger, John
Lambell, K H
Lyddan, Michl
Lenox, Peter
Lewis, S L
Lewis, Saunders
Lawson, Thos
Law, Thos
Lamon, Ward H
Lenox, Walter
Middleton, Arthur
Mulligan, A E
Miller, Andre
Manquette, Antonie
McAlliser, Chas
Myers, H, & F McGhan
Miller, jr, C
Major, D G
Middleton, E J, trust
Mace, F & S A Busey
Mohun, F
Markell, G H

Matingly, Geo
McKnight, G B
Maryman, H R
Maryman, H R, trustee
Matthews, H C & J H Coffin
Marbury, John, in trust
Mitchell, J F
Maguire, Jas
Mackall, L
McKenzie, Lewis
Moses, S D
Mitchell, T A
Maxcy, Virgil
Nash, Henry
Naylor, H, in trust for E J Beale
Osbourne, E, & children
Obold, F S, in trust
Osman, Jos
O'Dwyer, jr, John, in trust
O'Neale, Rhoda
O'Connor, Thos
Parker, A R
Parker, G & T
Peters, Henry
Peake, John
Pella, John
Page, K F
Prout, Mary
Prather, O J
Peter, Robt
Phillips, Saml
Peugh, S A
Platt, S H
Pumphrey, Thos, et al
Philip, W H & W B Todd
Rich, David
Roberts, E, & others
Riggs, Geo W
Rowland, Jas W
Robertson, J W
Rawlings M G
Riley, P C

Rider, Thos
Reading, Wm
Shepherd, A R
Slater, Eliz
Stewart, Geo
Smithson, Geo
Stinchcomb, J H
Stone, J H
Smith, Jas
Shelton, Jos
Smith, Jas M
Sumers, Jas H
Smith, Margaret
Snyder, Nicholas
Simmons, Washington
Theikuhl, A & F
Taylor, Geo
Thompson, J E
Thompson, John
Thompson, M
Terrett, W H
Tilghman, W H
Todd, Wm B
Vanbibber, A
Van Patten, C H
Van Wyck, P C
Wiltberger, C H
Wilkins, D
Watson, E A
Wunder, H S
Wilson, J R
Withers, John
Wilson, J S
White, M R et al
Wood M A E
Wharton, R S
Williams, S B
Whitmore, Wm
Wilson, Wm
Yeabower, C, et al
Young J
Young, M

Orphans Court of Wash Co, D C. Letters of administration on the personal estate of Robt S Patterson, late of Wash, D C, deceased. –Edgar Patterson, adm

By deed of trust to me from Henry De Mariel & wife, dated Mar 15, 1866, recorded in Liber R M H, No 10, page 414, land records for Wash Co, D C, I shall sell, on the premises, by public auction, on May 10th: part of a tract called ***Long Meadows***, bounded on the south by the land of Henry Douglass, on the north by the lands of Alex'r B Abercrombie; on the west by the lands of Wm W Corcoran & John A Bertroff, containing 96 acres, more or less. Also, all of another adjoining part of ***Long Meadows***. –Henry O Hood, trustee -Green & Williams, aucts

THU APR 11, 1867
Wm Goodwin, nominated as Collector of Customs at Phil, was rejected by the Senate yesterday.

In the Senate in the confirmation of Maj Gen Rousseau as brig gen in the regular army, upon a motion to confirm the nomination yesterday there was a tie vote.

Criminal Court-Mr Justice Wylie. 1-Chas Howard pleaded guilty to stealing 6 billard balls, value of $30, & was sentenced to jail for 6 months. 2-Mary Buckley received a nominal sentence, having been convicted of keeping a bawdy-house. 3-Maria Payne, for same offence, a like sentence. 4-John Hughes was sentenced to the Albany Penitentiary for stealing 26 gold rings, valued at $166, the property of S B Simons. [Length of time not given.] 5-Alex'r Gordon was convicted of larceny. 6-John Craft was convicted of an assault & battery on Thos E Dant, & fined $20 & costs, & committed to jail until paid. 7-Jas H Mangum was arraigned on the charge of passing counterfeit currency notes. 12 witnesses testified of his good character. The prosecution introduced 9 witnesses to prove the intent of the prisoner in passing the notes, of which a large number were found on his person. Mr Mangun has lived for 25 years in the vicinity of Wash, is a farmer, & owns several acres of cultivated land near the city. The witnesses testified to his uniform good character as an honest, industrious, & peaceable man. He has a wife & 5 children. He was arrested at the 7th st market, & about $16 in fifty cent notes were found in his possession. The case will be concluded today.

Court in Equity-Mr Justice Olin, Apr 10, 1867. 1-Blake vs Wood. No 871. Decree appointing Dr John B Blake trustee, instead of Christopher Andrews, deceased.

Transmitted over the wires of the police telegraph to all stations last night:
Capt C W Keyes, who resides at 609 I st, near 4th, left his home yesterday at 6 P M, & has not been seen or heard of since. He is about 5 feet 9 inches high, brown hair cut short, full red face, gray eyes, chin whiskers & moustache, & wears a wooden leg below the knee. This fact that Capt Keyes is a man of steady, sober habits, makes his disappearance yet more alarming to his friends.

The grand jury has ignored the indictment against Dr Aarn W Miller, charging him with manslaughter in causing the death of Lilla Hollingsworth, on Dec 23 last, by an alleged error in a prescription he had prepared for her.

Foreign papers record the recent death of Admiral Sir Phipps Hornby, G C B, Rear Admiral of the United Kingdon, at age 81 years. The deceased admiral entered the navy in May, 1797.

Balt, Apr 10. The Gorsuch brothers, charged with the murder of Knight Templar Jas Welsh, of Wash, on Nov 20 last, were brought out on a writ of habeas corpus before Judge Crain, of the Court of Appeals, & were remanded for the action of the grand jury.

By deed of trust from Thos McGrath & wife, dated May 7, 1858, recorded in Liber J A S, No 154, in folios 161 thru 153, land records of Wash Co, D C, I will sell, at public auction, on Apr 30, part of lot 6 in square 866, at 6th & Mass ave, with all the privileges & appurtenances to the same belonging. –B B French, trustee -Green & Williams, aucts

Orphans Court of Wash Co, D C, Apr 9, 1867. In the case of Bertha Lehne, excx of Henry Lehne, deceased, the executrix & Court have appointed May 4 next, for the final settlement of the personal estate of the said deceased, of the assets in hand. -Jas R O'Beirne, Reg/o wills

Chancery sale by decree of the Supreme Court of D C, in the cause of Barnes & al vs Barnes & al. No 881, equity, dated Mar 26, 1867. Public auction on the premises on May 2, lot 21 in square 514, with 3 frame houses, fronting on M st. On May 3, lots 7, 8, 10 thru 12 , & part of lot 9, in square 838; lots 7 & 12 improved by two 2 story frame houses, fronting on 5th & 6th sts. Also, lot 26 in square 724, with two frame houses, fronting on 2nd st, between D & C sts. On May 6, part of lot 1 in square 797, on Va ave, with 2 brick houses. On May 7, on the premises, 6½ st west, between D & E sts, 6 frame houses on parts of lots 39 thru 42 in square 465. –Walter S Cox, trustee -Cooper & Latimer, aucts

$5 reward for return of lost Bull, without horns. Return to Chas Ebel, 529 9th st, or giving information of its whereabouts.

FRI APR 12, 1867
Mr Edw Mattingly, a member of the Oldest Inhabitants Association, & who has been a resident of Wash for upwards of 60 years, died at his residence near the Navy Yard on Wed, in his 88th year. Mr Mattingly had been an invalid for sometime previous to his death.

An interesting boy, aged 10 years, the only son of our fellow-citizen Hubert Schutter, was accidentally killed at <u>Rock Hill College</u>, Ellicott's Mills, Md, yesterday morning, by a baseball-bat in the hands of a fellow student
+
Died: on Apr 11, suddenly, at <u>Rock Hill College</u>, Ellicott's Mills, Md, John Henry Schutter, only son of Hubert & Hester Ann Schutter, aged 10 years. His funeral will be from the residence of his father, 426 9th st, between G & H, on Apr 13 at 3 P M.

Jas R O'Beirne, Reg/o wills, announces May 4, as the day of final settlement of the estate of Henry Lehne.

$50 reward for the Hobbs estate will be paid by the heirs for such information as will lead to its exact situation. It is supposed to be in some part of Md. The family names are Jewel, James, Thomas, Job, & Silas, who died about 40 years ago, & the heirs were advertised for about 10 years ago, but do not know where the records of it are. Address M E F Pollock, Atty for the heirs, St Louis, Mo.

Maison De France, 279 Pa ave, between 10th & 11th sts, French Confectionary & Restarurant. –N Demongeot, proprietor

W H Clagett & H B Sweeny, Real Estate Brokers & Auctioneers. [Ad]

Circuit Court-Chief Justice Cartter, Apr 11, 1867. 1-Herman Koppel vs Geo Seitz. No 3,575. Judgment for plntf for $100.80, with interest from Apr 14, 1866. 2-Davis et al vs Lansdale et al. No 253. This is the case sent down by the Orphans Court to test the sanity of the testator in devising her personal property. Mrs Jemima Conner bequeathed certain property to dfndnt, Mrs Eliza Hunter. It is charged by the plntf that she was *non compus mentis* at the time, & the object of the suit is to test the validity of the will, & whether she was of sound mind, & whether undue liberty was exerted upon her at the time.

Court of Equity-Mr Justice Olin, Apr 11, 1867. 1-Laforge vs Laforge. Decree *amensa et thora*. Custody of the child of the petitioner.

Criminal Court-Mr Justice Wylie. 1-Jas H Mangum was found guilty of passing counterfeit money, & was recommended to the mercy of the court. In two other cases the Dist Atty entered a *nolle prosequi*. 2-John Russell, convicted of keeping a bawdy house, was fined $50 & costs, & committed to jail until the fine & costs are paid. 3-Arthur Chase, convicted of larceny, was sentenced to 11 months in the county jail. 4-Alex'r Gordon, convicted of larceny, was sentenced to 2 years in jail. 5-John Steward, indicted for bigamy, was found guilty. The accused married a slave woman near Fredericksburg, & during the war he came to this city, where he married a second time. 6-Wm Gibbs, convicted of larceny, received a nominal sentence.

Com'rs sale of valuable bldg lot fronting on G st north, between 2nd & 3rd sts, at auction, on Apr 29, by decree of the Supreme Court of D C, dated Jun 15, 1866, in the cause of Foote et al vs Philips, No 668 Equity: sale on the premises of lot ___ [blank as copied] in square 564, a handsome bldg lot. –Thos Lewis, Job W Angus, Jos Hodgson, John L Garner, Wm Dixson, Com'rs -Green & Williams, aucts

SAT APR 13, 1867
Chas D Nowton, collector of the port of Buffalo, died on Thursday, after a brief illness.

A telegraph on Wed brought the sad intelligence that Mrs Maria Greene, in attempting to get upon a train at Columbus, Ohio, was almost instantly killed. Mrs Greene was the wife of Maj S C Greene, for several years in the Commissary Dept here, under Gen Beckwith & Col Bell, & at present serving upon the staff of Gen Pope. Mrs Greene was on her way from Louisville to Buffalo, where her family reside. During her residence in this city her charming manners & estimable qualities won for her the affections of a host of warm & devoted friends, who will sencerely lament her untimely death.

Mr Alfred Mellon, the eminent London musical conductor & composer, is dead. [No death date given-current item.]

Mrd: on Apr 9, in Petersburg, Va, at the residence of the bride's father, by Rev John Collins McCabe, D D, rector of St Luke's Church, Bladensburg, Md, W Gordon McCabe, only son of the officiating clergyman, to Jennie, daughter of Edmund Osborne.

Died: on Wed, Edw Mattingly, in his 88th year. His funeral will take place from his late residence, 76 3rd st east, between M & N south, this afternoon at 2 o'clock. Carriages will be in waiting at Harvey & Co's, [undertakers, 410 7th st,] at 1 o'clock, for the Association of Oldest Inhabitants, who are earnestly requested to attend.

Real Estate. 1-Jos Herron purchased a 2 story frame house & lot on 11th st, near Md ave, on the Island, for $1,190. The lot is 16 feet front by 99 feet 10½ inches deep.

Large stock of sugars, coffees, teas, tobacco, rice, flour, etc at auction, on Apr 17, at the Grocery Store of E F Queen, on K st, between 7th & 8th sts. Also, on the same day, on the premises, the 2 story brick house, having a fine store room, known as Queen Hall, on leased ground rent, to run nearly 9 years at very low rent.
-Green & Williams, aucts

The Gen Post Ofc is lighted by carburetted hydrogen gas manufactured in the basement. Yesterday an explosion occurred in that portion of the basement which is under the west wing of the bldg in the 3rd room from the n w corner. Mr Jas A Kennedy, superintendent of the City Post Ofc, Mr H H Doubleday, & Mr L B Moses, clerks in the City Post Ofc, were badly injured by the explosion. Mr Kennedy was taken to his residence on F st, between 6th & 7th sts. Mr Doubleday to his residence on 7th st, between L & M sts. Mr Moses was taken to the residence of Postmaster Bowen, as Mrs Moses, his mother, being very ill at his residence, it was feared that it would cause her death to learn of the accident. They were all burned about the face, head, hands & arms. Mr Moses was terribly burned also about the body, & it is thought he cannot live. [Since the above, we learn that Mr Moses died last night.] [Apr 20th newspaper: Mr Kennedy is still alive, but in a very critical condition, & but slight hopes of his recovery. Mr Moses, who lost his life in the calamity, was robbed of his watch & $60 in money prior to his removal from the scene of the calamity.]

Phil, Apr 12. C W Bullock, inventor of the celebrated Bullock printing press, died today. A few days ago he had his leg crushed by some machinery, & gradually sank after amputation had been performed. He was 56 years of age.

Saml C Bartlett, of Salisbury, N H, died on Sunday last, aged 87 years. He was a native of, & we believe all his life dwelt in Salisbury, remaining in the business of a dealer in the usual merchandise of a country store up to near the close of life. He was of a family well known for the strength of their understanding & solidity of character. Ishabod, of Portsmouth, & James, of Dover, were lawyers; Levi, a Boston merchant, died a few years since, & Daniel, also of Boston, & a merchant, is still residing there. [To those should be added Dr Peter Bartlett, who died in Peoria, Ill. Eds Int.] Five sons survive the deceased: Prof Saml C, of Chicago Theological Seminary; Jos, a clergyman in Maine; Amos P, of Peoria, Ill; Judge Wm H, of this city, & Levi, of Salisbury. The illness of Mr Bartlett was brief, & of that inflammatory character induced by the extremely wet & chilly atmosphere of the last 40 days, which has carried off many people. Aged as was Mr Bartlett, he was by no means in retirement, & will be missed by his fellow-citizens.
-Concord [N H] Statesman
+
The celebrated Bartlett family of N H were contemporaries with Danl & Ezekiel Webster, & were born in the town of Salisbury, where also the Boston lawyer, Richd Fletcher, of "word for word, letter for letter, & comma for comma" memory in Congress, once practised the legal profession. The Greenes of Boston were born in the adjoining town of Boscawen, next to which was Hopkinton, the native place of the once famous London banker, Timothy Wiggin. Ishabod Bartlett as a member of Congress for a short period, when quite young, fearlessly antagonized, in the House, Henry Clay on a personal issue, when the latter was "soaring in all his pride of power & place." But Mr Bartlett's great powers were given to an almost uninterrupted practice of the law, for 3 decades, & ending practically somewhat before the period when Gen Franklin Pierce received the Presidential nomination, an event which was one of great gratification to the former. At the Stafford bar were Jas Bell, a very able lawyer, brother of Saml D Bell & Dr Luther V Bell, the former a late judge of the Superior Court of the State. There were also at the same bar John P Hale & Danl M Christie, the latter an eminent lawyer. Ichabod Bartlett & Geo Sullivan were the leading counsel of the Merrimack bar, in connection for a short time with Ezekiel Webster who fell dead while addressing the jury. At the Hillsborough bar Mr Bartlett had to contend with the Athertons, father & son; also the two brothers Farley, who were solid men indeed in their profession. Jas U Parker was equally distinguished.

MON APR 15, 1867
Navy Bulletin, Apr 6. Ordered. Passed Assist Paymaster Saml S Wood, jr, to the ship **Relief**; Acting Master J M Williams, to duty in the Gulf squadron. Detached. Mate Chas T Remmonds, from the ship **Tallapoosa**, & granted leave for discharge.

Court in Equity-Mr Justice Olin, Apr 12, 1867. 1-John McGuire et al vs Wm R Woodward et al. No 909. Order vesting title in trustees of First Colored Baptist Church in Gtwn, & appointing Wm R Woodward guardian ad litem to the orphan children of Wm J Stone. 2-Martha E Barnes vs Wm T Barnes. Decree granting divorce from the bonds of matrimony. Apr 13, 1867. 3-Chinn vs Chinn. No 860. Order appointing guardian *ad litem* to infants, & also granting amendment to bill. 4-Cassin vs Bozzle. No 751. Decree *pro confesso* against Isabella Bozzle.

Orphans Court-Judge Purcell, Apr 13, 1867. 1-The will of Andrew Small, deceased, was admitted to probate & record, & letters testamentary issued to John A Ruff; bond $200,000. 2-The will of Anton Bauer, deceased, was fully proven & admitted to probate & record. 3-The wills of John C Frepell, John D Hammack, & Gabriel Barnhill, deceased, were filed & partially proven. 4-The will of John Blosser, deceased, heretofore filed, partially proven, & admitted to probate & record for personalty, was fully proven. 5-The will of Saml Stinemetz, deceased, was filed, fully proven, & admitted to probate & record, & letters testamentary issued to Mary E Stinemetz & Benj H Stinemetz; bond $20,000. 6-Maria C Emrich was appointed guardian to the orphans of Peter Emrich, deceased; bond $6,000. 7-Letters of administration on the personal estate of Hillary C Spalding, deceased, were granted to Jas Fullerton; bond $400. 8-The third general account of Lydia Ann Hoover, guardian to the orphans of Saml Hoover, deceased, & the second & final individual account of said guardian, with Thos Z Hoover, were approved & passed.

The funeral of Mr F Kroeger, who was one of our most prominent German citizens, took place yesterday from the late residence of the deceased, 7th & G sts. The remains were interred in *Prospect Hill Cemetery*; services were conducted by Rev Dr Finckel.

The funeral of Mr Moses, a victim of the explosion at the Post Ofc, took place yesterday from the residence of Mr S JBowen, on H st.

Maj Geo L Stearns, of Medford, Mass, died in N Y a few days since.

The wife of ex-Govn'r Cummings, of Ga, died at Springfield, Mass, on Friday.

A physician of Goshen, 30 miles from Cincinnati, named Hanker, 60 years old, committed suicide on Thursday because his children opposed his marrying again. He bequeathed his watch & carriage to the widow he had intended to lead to the altar, & requested that he be buried in his proposed bridal garb

John Bartlett, a deaf mute, 75 years of age, was instantly killed on Thursday by being run over by a train of cars, near Woonsocket, R I.

Orphans Court of Wash Co, D C. Letters of administration on the personal estate of Hillary C Spalding, late of Wash, D C, deceased. –Jas Fullerton, adm

Messrs Geo A Trenholm, ex-Sec of the Confederate treasury, his son, Wm C Trenholm, T D Watner, & Jas Welsman, all members of the Charleston firm of Frazer, Trenholm & Co, & John B Lafitte, their agent during the war at Nassau, were personally served on Sat, by a deputy sgt-at-arms from Washington, with a summons to appear before the Judiciary Cmte in this city on May 10 next, in relation to the business of blockade-running & the assets of the firm remaining at the close of the war.

Valuable first class residence or business sites on the n e corner of 9th & D sts west, at public auction, [the late residence of Hudson Taylor.] The lot having a front of 100 feet on 9th st, improved by a double 3 story brick house, with a 2 story back bldg. -Cooper & Latimer, aucts

Orphans Court of Wash Co, D C. Letters testamentary on the personal estate of Andrew Small, late of Wash City, D C, deceased. –John A Ruff, exc

Orphans Court of Wash Co, D C. Letters testamentary on the personal estate of Saml Stinemetz, late of Wash City, D C, deceased. –Mary E Stinemetz, Benj H Stinemetz, excs

Orphans Court of Wash Co, D C, Apr 13, 1867. In the case of Thos H Troll, adm of Thos P Troll, deceased, the administrator & Court have appointed May 7 next, for the final settlement of the personal estate of the said deceased, of the assets in hand. -Jas R O'Beirne, Reg/o wills

Balt, Apr 14. 1-Dr W H Dalrymple, a well known physician of this city, died yesterday of typhoid fever, contracted while in the discharge of his professional duties. 2-Mr Timothy Keely one of the oldest citizens of Balt, died on Sat, at the residence of his son-in-law, Chas M Dougherty. Mr Keely more than half a century commenced business here.

TUE APR 16, 1867
Criminal Court yesterday: trial of Wm E Cleaver for the murder of Mary Ann Reeves, in Feb last. Jurors: Fairfax V Vernon, Geo F Kidwell, Jedediah Gittings, Hillary Smith, Jacob Aigler, Thos Gaddis, Isaac Herzberg, Rudolph Richards, Geo B Fillebrown, & Jacob Scheifley, leaving 2 more to be sworn in today. Jurors challenged as to having formed an opinion or opposed to capital punishment: Wm H Barnes, Matthew Pabst, Emanuel Gordon, Geo Seitz, Jas J Barrett, Owen O'Hare, Jas W Gibson, Thos Carden, John T Lewis, Chas T Bell, & Wm J McCollum. The following were challenged by the prosecution: Robt H Graham, Cornelius Boyle, John H Brewer, & Jas Keleher; & the following by the defence: Christopher Hager, Patrick Quirk, Columbus C Thomas, Michl R Coombes, Jacob Newrath, Armstead M Caldwell, John T Headley, Geo Klotz, Madison Gassaway, J T C Clark, H B Rochat, Michl Conner, & Jas Casparis.

Mrs Shepherd, a milliner, shot Mr A Lederman on Friday at la Crosse, Wisc, for slander. The wound of Mr Lederman is not considered fatal.

Advertisements: 1-J W Kraft has succeeded G E Kennedy in the ownership of the famous grocery store near Odd Fellows Hall. 2-Jas Fullerton announces that he is administrator of the personal estate of Hillary C Spalding. 3-John A Ruff announces that he has letters testamentary upon the personal estate of Andrew Small. 4-J R O'Beirne, Reg/o wills gives notice that May 7 is the date of the final settlement of the estate of Thos P Trott.

Mr John G Myers, of Portland, Maine, a railroad contractor, was found dead in his bed, at Lovejoys Hotel, N Y, on Sunday. It is alleged he had been beaten & severely injured in a restaurant on Broadway.

At Junction City, Kansas, on Apr 8, Wm Moore, while seated at the breakfast table with his wife & children, drew a revolver & shot his wife dead. In about 2 hours after, he obtained a pillow, laid his wife's head upon it, laid down on the floor beside her, deliberately shot himself through the head, & died in a few minutes. Moore had for several years threatened to enact this terrible tragedy.

Last Sunday, two little girls at Franklin, Ohio, one the daughter of Mr Fred McCutchon, & the other of Mr Lewis Cottle, were playing together in Mr Peter Dickey's lumber yard, &, it is supposed, in attempting to climb up a pile of lumber, pulled it over on them, crushing them beneath its weight. When found life was extinct in both, one having its neck broken, & its back in 3 places, & the other was smothered.

The firm of C Woodward & Son is hereby dissolved by mutual consent.
-C Woodward, L S Woodward. C Woodward has disposed of his entire interest in the firm to his son, L S Woodward, who will carry on the Hardware, Stove, & House-furnishing business at the old stand, Woodward Block, 318 D st, between 10th & 11th sts.

WED APR 17, 1867
Dr Wm J Smith, of Lawrenceburg, Pa, was arrested at Pittsburgh, on Sat, for passing counterfeit money; about $80 worth was found on his person.

Trial of Wm E Cleaver for the murder of Mary Ann Reeves: two more jurors were accepted: John M Stake & Thos M Phillips. Mrs Sarah Reeves, the mother of Mary Ann Reeves, said the child enjoyed good health, although somewhat delicate. Francis Reside, sworn. Have known the prisoner for 10 years; he is a married man, & know him to have been a married man about 2 years; he has no children, & is a man of muscular development. Mary Roberts [colored] sworn. I knew the prisoner & Mary Ann Reeves. I cautioned the girl against having anything to do with him; he freqently followed her.

N Y, Apr 16. Gottfield Naibel, a musician, murdered his wife, by cutting her throat, at his residence in James st today. He has not been arrested yet.

Died: on Apr 15, at Wilmington, Dela, Elsie S, only daughter of Ann E & the late E F Starr, in her 21st year.

Died: on Apr 6, at Watson's Landing, Westmoreland Co, Va, of consumption, Jane Medora, wife of Saml P Carusi, & daughter of the late Warren D Watson.

Died: on Apr 15, without a struggle, at the residence of her father, Julia A White, in her 20th year, after a long & painful illness, the wife of Saml S White, & daughter of Hon Wm F & Mary F C Purcell. Her funeral will take place from Wesley Chapel, on Apr 18, at 3:30 o'clock P M. [Phil papers please copy.]

I offer for sale my Farm, 4 miles from Wash City, terms moderate. Apply to Jos B Bryan, 345 Pa ave, Wash, or to John Hyatt, at Hyattsville depot, Wash railroad. -Geo W Taylor, jr

Adms sale of household & kitchen furniture at auction on Apr 19, at 447 Mass ave, between 6th & 7th sts, being the estate of Mr Ferdinand Muhlinghaus.
–H Colman & Co, aucts. –B C Brooker, Salesman

Household & kitchen furniture at auction on Apr 24, at the residence of T Remick, 126 Bridge st, Gtwn. -Thos Dowling, auct

Dept of the Interior, U S Patent Ofc, Wash, Apr 8, 1867. Ptn of Isaac Brown, of Cecilton, Md, praying for the extension of a patent granted to him Jul 19, 185_, for an improvement in mode of driving saws, for seven years from the expiration of said patent, which takes place on Jul 19, 1867. -T C Theaker, Com'r of Patents

Land Warrants Wanted: Wm Hurley & Co, Exchange Brokers, 408 Pa ave. [Ad]

THU APR 18, 1867
Rev David D Field, D D, died at Stockbridge, Mass, on Monday, in his 86th year. He was for more than 60 years a preacher. Since the death of his wife, 5 or 6 years ago, his health has been slowly declining. He leaves six sons, three of whom live in this city-David Dudley Field, Cyrus W Field, & Rev Henry M Field, editor of the Evangelist. Another son is Stephen J Field, one of the judges of the Supreme Court of the U S; still another was for some years president of the Senate of Mass.
–N Y Post

Trial of Wm E Cleaver: Lt Eckloff: Henrietta Wells kept the house; she is the same Anna Wells. Geo M Miller, of the detective police force was sworn: prisoner admitted he had improper connections with Mary Ann Reeves several times. Leonard Reeves, father of the deceased, was sworn: Cleaver admitted he had intercourse with her, but that it was nothing uncommon with her.

At Omoo, Wisc, on Apr 8, Mrs Furman, who had been separated from her husband for about 2 years, administered a dose of strychnine to her little daughter, aged about 2 years, in some milk, & after the child died, she took a dose of the poison, & died soon after.

Rt Rev John Timon, Roman Catholic Bishop of that city, died at his residence last night, of erysipelas. He was a native of this country, & consecrated Bishop on Oct 17, 1847. He was the first Bishop of the Diocese of Buffalo. His body will be laid in state at the residence until after Holy Week, & then be removed to the Cathedral on Monday, & buried on Tuesday. -N Y Tribune

Henry Bowen, a venerable citizen of Providence, R I, died on Tues. He was Sec of State of R I for 30 years, 1819 to 1849, &, previously, for 2 years was Atty Gen.

The remains of J Paget, French Minister in this city during the Jackson administration, are about to be removed from Nashville to France. He married Miss Lewis, a Tennessee belle, & died at Nashville in 1864.

Col Chas Farnsworth was drowned at Savannah, Ga, on Monday evening, together with a man named Wilder, who was with him in a sailboat. Col Farnsworth was born in Hartford, Conn.

Balt, Apr 17. Archbishop M J Spalding, of the Diocese of Balt, is lying dangerously ill of inflammation of the bowels, at the archiepiscopal residence in this city. It is feared that the disease will prove fatal.

The last of the Penns. Granville John Penn, the great grandson of Wm Penn, the Proprietary of Pa, died in London on Mar 29. Mr Penn was the eldest surviving son of Granville Penn, of Stoke Pogis, who was the eldest son of Thos Penn, one of the joint Proprietaries of Pa. Thos Penn was the eldest son of Wm Penn, by his second wife, Hannah Callowhill. The only surviving descendant of the founder of the Commonwealth of Pa who bears the name of Penn is an unmarried brother of the late Granville John Penn, who was also a bachelor, so that the name will soon be extinct. There are several descendants of the founder, however, of other names, among whom may be mentioned Lord Northland, Lady Gonun, & the Penn Gaskill family, of Phil.

Divorce cases in the Supreme Court of D C: Wm Beckett vs Frances S Beckett; Louisa Hardy vs Henry J Hardy.

<u>Court in Equity</u>-Mr Justice Olin, Apr 17, 1867. Fowler vs Dennis. Order appointing Wm P Laselle guardian *ad litem* to the children of Mr Dennis.

FRI APR 19, 1867
Ex-Govn'r Gilmore, of N H, died at Concord on Wed, after a lingering & painful illness, aged 55 years. He was Pres of the N H Senate in 1859, & Govn'r of the State during 1863 & 1864.

The Senate confirmed the following nominations yesterday:
John Van Lear, Assessor Internal Revenue, 4th Dist of Md.
Jos W Cake, Collector of Customs at Phil.
The Senate rejected the following nominations yesterday:
John R Finley, Surveyor of Customs at Phil.
C J Biddle, Naval Ofcr at Phil.
Thos M Yeatman, Postmaster at Cincinnati.

Ads: 1-Mrs Emma Bryant desires to rent a large house. 2-J W Kraft, 508 7th st, has everything on hand in the grocery line.

Trial of Wm E Cleaver: John Grinder sworn: knew the deceased some 18 years, knew her place of residence; her general reputation was that she was a prostitute. Geo Walker testified that the deceased did not sustain a good character for chasity. Mrs Geo Walker, wife of the proceeding witness, could not say anything good about her; she drank, swore, ran in the streets, & kept company with men & boys.

Died: on Apr 2, at his residence, in Autauga Co, Ala, Dr John Wood, a native of Chas Co, Md, in his 64th year. He left his native State in 1829 & settled in Ala, & pursued the occupation of a cotton planter. In the death of this estimable man Alabama has lost a valuable citizen, the poor a friend, & his family a devoted father. –J

The remains of the late Henry D Cooper are in the vault at **Glenwood Cemetery**, & will be interred on Apr 20, 1867, at 4 o'clock P M. The relatives & friends of the family wishing to attend will please take notice.

Mr J W Townsend, aged about 36 years, chief clerk of the general freight agent of the Balt & Ohio railroad at Camden Station, was killed yesterday by falling from a train at the Relay House, on Wash Branch. It appears he had on Tues removed his family, consisting of his wife & 4 children, together with his furniture, from the City to Relay, where he intended to reside. He was much esteemed & spoken of as a fine gentleman. –Balt Sun, 17th

Govn'r –Elect Jas E English pays taxes at New Haven, Ct, on an estate of $255,000.

Dept of the Interior, U S Patent Ofc, Wash, Apr 10, 1867. Ptn of Thos D Burrall, of Geneva, N Y, praying for the extension of a patent granted to him Dec 6, 1845, extended for 7 years Dec 6, 1859, & reissued on Oct 10, 1865, for an improvement in Corn Shellers, for seven years from the expiration of said patent, which takes place on Dec 6, 1867. -T C Theaker, Com'r of Patents

N Y, Apr 18. Prof Livingston was shot this morning at 17 Jefferson st. He was employed as a lecturer at Barnum's Museum. Cady, the man who fired the fatal shot, asserts that he acted in self-defence, Livingston having made an attempt on his life. An inquest will be held.

Plymouth, Me, Apr 18. Henry Hunt was washed off the bowsprit of the schnr **Willis Lincoln**, & a boat containing a man named Geo Land was launched to save him, but it upset & both men were lost.

Chancery sale of 2 fine bldg lots fronting on 7th st west, between north H & Pres Place, at auction, by decree of the late Circuit Court of this Dist, dated Oct 26, 1859, passed in the cause of Augusta McBlair & others vs Wm Gadsby & others, No 1,415 Equity, & of decree of the Supreme Court of the Dist, substituting me for the original trustee: auction on May 11, of lots 28 & 29 in square 167. —Walter S Cox, trustee -Green & Williams, aucts

SAT APR 20, 1867
Balt, Apr 19. We are happy to announce that the Most Rev Archbishop Spalding is improving.

Confirmations by the Senate yesterday: Gen F J Herron, Marshal of Louisiana; S J Wailes, Naval Storekeeper at Wash; & John Partridge, Postmaster at Elkton, Md.

Trial of Wm E Cleaver: Jas Keleher was sworn: the bldg occupied by Eddie Wells, in Marble Alley, where the offence was committed was owned by him. John Stant, sworn: knew the deceased about 8 years, & well acquainted with others who knew her. Richd Doherty sworn: knew the deceased; she did not sustain a good character for chasity. John Evans sworn: knew the deceased 5 or 6 years; did not have a good opinion of her character for chastity. Robt Campbell sworn: knew the deceased; character was bad. Same for Wm Campbell-sworn. [Apr 22nd newspaper: The jury returned a verdict of guilty of manslaughter. The counsel for the accused have entered a motion for a new trial.]

On Thu, while one of Fowler's ice wagons was passing along Md ave, the horse became frightened at a passing train of cars & ran off, throwing the driver, Fred'k Hager, from his seat, & breaking his leg near the ankle. He was conveyed to his home, on H st, near 7th.

Thos P Cahill, age 13 years, while coming out of the Boyleston School yard, at Boston, on Wed, was struck in the temple by a portion of the fence, which a violent gust of wind blew down, & was instantly killed.

Mrd: on Apr 18, at Annapolis, Md, by Rev S V Leech, Julian Brewer to Susan, daughter of the late Walter McNier, of Annapolis, Md.

Ex-Govn'r Gilmore, of N H, died at Concord on Wed, after a lingering & painful illness, aged 55 years. He was Pres of the N H Senate in 1859, & Govn'r of the State during 1863 & 1864.

Exec's sale of improved & unimproved property fronting on East Capitol st, between 4th & 5th sts, at auction, on May 14, parts of lots 7 & 8 in square 817, improved by a good 2 story & attic brick house, with back bldg, with a bakery; also a good bldg lot adjoining, belonging to the estate of the late Margaret Mackel, deceased.
–Wm Groupe, exc -Green & Williams, aucts

Died: on Thu, Eliz Rousseau, wife of Chas Rousseau, aged 27 years. Her funeral will take place this afternoon at 4 o'clock, from her residence on B st, Capitol Hill.

MON APR 22, 1867
Thos Jefferson Weaver, one of the most eminent citizens of Cincinnati, died within the last few days. He was the son of David Weaver, who removed from Balt, Md, at an early day, & become one of the pioneers of the Queen City. He was a brother, husband, father, friend, of noble character & an honest man.

Orphans Court-Judge Purcell. 1-The will of Gabriel Barnhill, deceased, was admitted to probate & record for personalty. 2-The will of John D Hammtrack, deceased, was finally proven & admitted to probate & record, & letters testamentary issued to Thos Miller; bond $6,000. 3-An exemplified copy of the will of John W Brown, deceased, from the ofc of Register of Wills for PG Co, Md, was filed & ordered to be placed on record. 4-Letters of administration on the personal estate of Theodore August Wm Groese, deceased, was granted to Geo Willner; bond $6,000. 5-Letters of administration on the personal estate of Fred'k H Kroeger, deceased, were granted to Margaret A Kroeger; bond $2,000. 6-The first account of Robt W Fenwick, guardian to Kate Ball, orphan of W N Ball, deceased; the fourth account of Susan Whitney, guardian to Ann E Whitney, orphan of C S Whitney, deceased; the fifth general act of Thos Cogan, guardian to orphans of Owen Murray, deceased; & the first & final account of said Cogan, as guardian to John Francis Murray, were approved & passed.

Ads. 1-E A Maedel, U S Coast Survey Ofc, desires to rent two rooms in a quiet family. 2-F X Dooley, on Capitol Hill, has on hand all the popular patent medicines.

Messrs Cooper & Latimer, aucts, will sell at public auction, this afternoon, that very desirable property late the residence of Hudson Taylor, on n e corner of 9th & D sts.

Died: on Apr 20, Jas I Richey, in his 25th year. His funeral will be from the residence of his father, H Richey, 509 H st, this afternoon, at 4 o'clock.

H L Vervalin, an old & well-known merchant of Buffalo, N Y, died on Saturday.

Benj Hogan, charged with shooting some men in Babylon, in the Pa oil regions, last summer, was arrested at Saratoga, N Y, on Fri. A large reward was offered for his arrest.

Alfred H Foxcroft, late bookkeeper for the firm of Geo H Francis & Co, merchants, 24 Warren st, N Y, it is reported embezzled $20,000 in U S bonds from his employers; $10,000 of these, with $1,200 in money, were recovered. No arrest was made.

At Mount Morris, Pa, on Sunday, Martin Cane got up about midnight, procured an axe, returned to his bed & beat out the brains of his wife. He then went into the yard & hung himself by his suspenders to a tree. The woman was alive when discovered by the neighbors, but died in a short time.

Orphans Court of Wash Co, D C. Letters testamentary on the personal estate of John D Hammack, late of Wash City, D C, deceased. –Thos Miller, exc

Orphans Court of Wash Co, D C. Letters of administration on the personal estate of Theodore August Wm Groese, late of Wash, D C, deceased. –Geo Willner, adm

Dept of the Interior, U S Patent Ofc, Wash, Apr 5, 1867. Ptn of Simon M Elder, adm of the estate of John A Elder, deceased, of Portland, Maine, praying for the extension of a patent granted to said John A Elder, Jul 26, 1853, for an improvement in Curving the Backs of Books for seven years from the expiration of said patent, which takes place on Jul 26, 1867. -T C Theaker, Com'r of Patents

TUE APR 23, 1867
Dr Benj B Coit, the pioneer physician of San Francisco, dropped dead in the street on Thursday. The cause was heart disease.

W O Cruse, an old citizen of Huntsville, Ala, died on Tues, from a burn received from the bursting of a lamp. He was 74 years old, a native of Md, & served in the war of 1812. He was at the battle of Bladensburg.

Mrs Parkhurst, wife of Jos Parkhurst, of Agency City, Iowa, on Apr 16 threw herself into the Des Moines river, & was drowned. She had for some time been insane.

Mr Chas Kane, a stage-manager of the American Theatre, at Balt, was accidentally shot a few evenings since by a ball from a Derringer pistol, in the hands of Mr Chas King, the doorkeeper. The ball penetrated the leg, between the knee & thigh, but, although painful, the wound is by no means considered dangerous.

Ads. 1-John F Ellis advertises parlor organs & melodeons for sale or rent. 2-Wm Ballantyne, at his store, 498 7th st, has a variety of books for sale. 3-Mr Wm Stewart is now keeping the Everett House, where board can be obtained at $9 per week.

Pres Johnson yesterday issued pardons to the following persons, who are now fulfilling their sentences for crime in the Albany penitentiary: Chas Smith, pardoned by reason of his age & infirmities on recommendation of the jury that convicted him; John Burman, pardon recommended by Dist Atty Carrington, Mayor Wallach, & others; Emma Cole, recommended by Judge Fisher & Dist Atty Carrington; Jas Carroll, recommended by Hon Roscoe Conkling & the Mayor of Utica, N Y, & others; & Wm Smith, recommended by Judge Fisher & the jury that convicted him. In all of the above cases the time for which the prisoners were sentenced has nearly expired.

Rear Admiral H H Bell, Cmder A J Drake, & Lt Cmder Treviell Abbot have been placed on the retired list, by order of the Sec of the Navy.

Court in Equity-Mr Justice Olin, Apr 22, 1867. Wood vs Wood et al. No 895. Order appointing A Devers guardian ad litem to infants.

WED APR 24, 1867
Mrd: on Apr 23, at *Tudor Place*, Gtwn, D C, by Rev W W Williams, Armistead Peter, M D, to Martha Curtis, daughter of the late Cmdor Beverly Kennon.

Died: on Apr 23, suddenly, at Woodland, PG Co, Md, Covington Hill, daughter of Wm B & Catharine B Hill.

Deserted: Mates E N Parker & Robt Mowison, U S navy, are reported to have deserted the naval service.

Martin Cameron, a bookkeeper, was found dead in a cistern in Memphis on Apr 16. He had been deranged from the effects of sickness, & no doubt is entertained that he committed suicide.

Criminal Court-Mr Justice Fisher, Apr 23, 1867. 1-Alfred Snowden was convicted of petty larceny & sentenced to 60 days in the county jail. 2-Lloyd Diggs, was found guilty of the charge of larceny. 3-Frank Kenny, indicted for an assault with intent to kill Edw Hines, was found not guilty.

Augusta, Apr 23. Last night Jerry Reid & a man named Meister had an altercation. Reid fired at Meister, shooting W Meintzer, who interposed to prevent the difficulty. A brother of Meintzer's then shot Reid. Both parties are dead. The affair is much regretted by the community.

Mobile, Apr 23. Mrs Van Hazen, the wife of a merchant of this city, died instantly after taking medicine. The druggist placed prussic, instead of tartaric acid, in the prescription.

N Y, Apr 23. The *Old Bowery Theatre* was sold today for $106,000.

Supreme Court of D C, Equity No 806, Docket 8. Iardella et al vs Iardella et al. The trustees reported that on Dec 24, 1866, they sold part of lot 11 in square 690, with improvements, to Geo F Gulick, for $6,750; & on Jan 17, 1867, sold another part of said lot & improvments to Josephine B Hicks, for $1,900; both have complied with the terms of sale. –A B Olin, Justice -R J Meigs, clerk

Dept of the Interior, U S Patent Ofc, Wash, Apr 18, 1867. Ptn of Geo T Parry, of Phil, Pa, praying for the extension of a patent granted to him Aug 2, 1853, for an improvement in Anti-friction Boxes, for seven years from the expiration of said patent, which takes place on Aug 2, 1867. -T C Theaker, Com'r of Patents

Dept of the Interior, U S Patent Ofc, Wash, Apr 8, 1867. Ptn of Wm Butterfield, of Boston, Mass, praying for the extension of a patent granted to him Jul 4, 1854, for an improvement in Sewing Machines, for seven years from the expiration of said patent, which takes place on Nov 24, 1857. -T C Theaker, Com'r of Patents

Dept of the Interior, U S Patent Ofc, Wash, Apr 17, 1867. Ptn of Nathl Gear, of Marietta, Ohio, praying for the extension of a patent granted to him Nov 8, 1853, for an improvement in Machine for Turning or Cutting, Irregular Forms, for seven years from the expiration of said patent, which takes place on Nov 8, 1867.
-T C Theaker, Com'r of Patents

THU APR 25, 1867
Criminal Court-Mr Justice Fisher, Apr 24, 1867. 1-Fred'k Buckner was acquitted of larceny. 2-Alfred Glenn was convicted of larceny, & sentenced to jail. 3-Anna Faulkner, convicted of the same offence, was sentenced to 2 months in jail. 4-Annie Lutz, who was also indicted with the last above named, was acquitted.

Geo W McKenney, late of Waverly, but formerly known to hosts of people in the country, while at the Nat'l Hotel, was suddenly deceased, from a sudden attack, arising mainly from an affection of the heart. He was the soul of humor & kind feeling. His funeral will take place at St Peter's Church, on Friday, at 2 o'clock P M.

Ads. 1-Matthew Gault & Wm Williams have formed a copartnership in the slate & roofing business. Orders may be left with Jones & Collins, on 9th st. 2-W Wilkinson offers for sale his comfortable & cozy residence, with spacious grounds, at the corner of R & 15th sts. 3-Chas O Brown & Co, of Gtwn, have purchased from T T Page his drug & apothecary store, 19th & Pa ave. They are to have a soda fountain & fancy goods.

From papers found in the pocket of the man found drowned yesterday, it appears he was a soldier named Wm Dixon. The deceased was buried at the expense of the county.

Mrd: on Apr 23, at **Grassland**, D C, by Rev F A Ciampi, S J, Edmund P Zane, of Balt, to Maria Louisa, daughter of the late Hamilton Loughborough.

Died: on Apr 23, in Wash City, in his 78th year, Chas Keenan, for many years a resident of Wash as an ofcr of the Gas Co, & formerly of Balt, Md, of which place he was a defender in 1814. His funeral will be at St Patrick's Church, F st, 9 o'clock A M, today.

Yesterday, at Christ Church, in this city, Bishop Vail, of Kansas, was united in holy wedlock to Ellen, daughter of the late assist Bishop Bowman, of this diocese. The nuptial ceremony was performed by Bishop Clarkson, of Nebraska, an early & dear friend both of the bridegroom & of the late father of the bride, who made the long journey expressly for the purpose. –Phil Gaz, Tuesday

Memphis, Apr 24. Fatal affray in Memphis; a row occurred in a saloon on Wash st last night. Policeman John Cloridge was killed; a fireman, John Cosgrove, had been arrested on suspicion of being the murderer.

Hon R N Saunders, of N C, died at his residence in this city, yesterday, after a protacted illness, at age 76 years. He was born in Caswell Co in Mar, 1791; in early manhood he removed to Tenn, where he studied law under Hon Hugh Lawson White, & was licensed to practice in 1812; he then returned to N C. –Raleigh Sentinel, 22nd

Gen Sheridan has appointed Mr T C Thomas, a colored broker, one of the registers of voters in New Orleans.

Mrs Mary A Green, better known to theatre goers as Mrs Mary A Marshall, died in Boston on Saturday, from cancer in the stomach.

Caleb Cheeshapteamuck, an Indian, graduated at Harvard College in 1865, & died in Charlestown the next year, aged 20-the only Indian who ever received a degree at Harvard.

Mr C H Bennett, the well-known English draughtsman on wood, is dead. His illustrations of "Pilgrims Progress" are known in this country. He was in his 38th year.

Supreme Court of D C, 711 Equity, docket 8. Robt McDuell & wife vs Lydia Lake et al. [Geo Durance & Eliza R his wife; John Curack & Virginia M F his wife; John Baker; Jas Bennett & Jane his wife; Thos Baker, Bernard Caston & Magdalena his wife; Margaret Shortly, Geo Shortly, Julia A Shortly, Wm Shortly, John Shortly, Martha J Shortly, Thos Baker, & Rachel J Baker] On motion of the plntf, by Fendall & Ashford, their solicitors, it is ordered that the dfndnts cause their appearance here on the first rule day occurring 40 days after this day; otherwise the cause will be proceeded with as in case of default. –A B Olin –R J Meigs, clerk [Apr 25, 1867.]

FRI APR 26, 1867
Ads. 1-Mr Louis Weiser has a suitable establishment at Metzerott's bldg for teaching drawing & painting. 2-Jas M Towers, on 7th st, offers for sale his cigar & tobacco store. The lease is for 3 years, & the position very central.

Farm of 350 acres, Orange Co, Va, was sold to Wm Latham, Pen Yan, N Y, for $9,380.

Criminal Court-Mr Justice Fisher, Apr 25, 1867. 1-Benj F Isherwood was acquitted of maintaining a nuisance. [Unkept lot which he did not own, as thought.] 2-Jos Duncan was acquitted of larceny. 3-Fred'k Demlin was acquitted of the charge of receiving stolen goods. 4-Sentences were passed upon the following prisoners: Sanford Conover, perjury, 10 years in the Albany penitentiary; Wm Cole, larceny, 1 day in jail; Chas Hill, assault & battery with intent to kill, 2 years in the penitentiary. 5-Robt Fisher, Geo Washington, & Thos Talbot, for larceny, 18 months in the penitentiary. 6-Alonzo Perry, larceny, one year in the penitentiary. 7-Chas Hopkins, assault & battery with intent to kill, 2 years in the penitentiary. 8-Warden Brown expects to leave for Albany in the early part of next week with reinforcements.

A grand wedding took place in Balt on Tuesday, Mr Prince, a wealthy gentleman of N Y, married Miss Morris, grand-daughter of Hon Reverdy Johnson.

Izador Aileinger, a well known citizen of Cleveland, Ohio, was found murdered in his store on Tuesday; robbed of $300 in money. No clue to the murderers has been obtained.

A horrible murder at Cambria, Columbia Co, Wisc, last Thu. Mr Bartlett, 60 years of age, killed his wife with a hatchet, & attempted the life of his son.

Phil, Apr 25. This afternoon Mrs Magilton, aged about 62, was found murdered at her residence, in Shippen st, at 13th st. Her throat was cut with a razor & 7 contused wounds appeared on the head, inflicted with a hammer, which had been left beside her. Geo Winnemore was taken in custody on suspicion of having murdered Mrs Magilton. Winnemore had tea with the old couple on the previous evening; they were friends. Nothing was missing from the house. The deceased was the mother of Col Magilton. The early return of the husband may have prevented him from plundering the house. Winnemore was a soldier in the late war, & was in debt to the tavern keeper where he boarded. He also was anxious to obtain money to emigrate to Montana. [Jun 17th newspaper: Geo Winnemore, convicted of the murder of Mrs Magilton, in Phil, was on Sat sentenced to be hung. He protested his innocence, & said he would have laid down his life to protect her. He denied that the razor found in her house belonged to him.]

Jas Moore died from intemperance on Wednesday, in the county jail, where he had been taken on Tuesday. The body was laid out decently by the police.

The large farm lying north of the Insane Asylum, & back of Uniontown, 375 acres, was sold to John R Elvans, for $52,000 cash down.

Mrd: on Apr 25, by Rev Mr Lewis, of St John's Church, Chas G Kerr to Ella, youngest daughter of Hon Reverdy Johnson.

Died: on Apr 24, of typhoid fever, Jennie Champlin Knight, aged 4 years, eldest child of Octavius & Mary E Knight. Her funeral will be from the residence of her parents, 406 F st, near 7th, at 3 o'clock P M, on Apr 27.

Valuable business property on Pa ave between 4½ & 6th sts, at public sale, on May 6, on the premises, occupied for the last 10 years by Geo W Cochran, as a cigar store; improved by a 3 story front & back bldg. -Cooper & Latimer, aucts

Dept of the Interior, U S Patent Ofc, Wash, Saml Darling, of Bangor, Maine, praying for the extension of a patent granted to him Aug 30, 1853, for an improvement in Apparatus for Grinding & Shaping Metals, for seven years from the expiration of said patent, which takes place on Aug 30, 1867. -T C Theaker, Com'r of Patents

Metropolitan Patent Steam Bakery, 347 Cst, between 4½ & 6th sts. -Tho Havenner

SAT APR 27, 1867
Ads: 1-Mrs A G Gaston, on 8th st, importer of fine millinery, announces her opening day of those commodities, with straw hats & bonnets. 2-P Androit, French tailor & professor of cutting issues a card of interest to the trade.

Green & Williams, aucts, sold at auction, yesterday: a 3 story brick house on 13th st, Island, between B & C sts, to Christian Rupert, for $2,250; lot 13 in subdivision 893, with 2 story frame house, for $900 to W Dekstadt; 3 story brick house on K st, between 3rd & 4th sts, to Mr John Bresnahan, for $2,530. -Cooper & Latimer, aucts, sold yesterday, on the premises, near *Good Hope*, adjoining the farm of Dr Lieberman, 5 acres & 24 perches to Thos Geary, for $132 per acre; also, 5 acres & 2 roods of the same tract, to Dr H N Wadsworth, $115 per acre.

Mr Francis Reeside has been appointed master bricklayer of the Treasury extension, by Capt A B Mullet, the engineer in charge. Mr Reeside is a well-known resident of the 7th Ward, & being a first class mechanic, he will no doubt make a good boss.

Died: on Apr 11, at the residence of her mother, near Laurel Hill, Richmond Co, N C, Miss Eliz McLaurin, aged 20 years & 10 months. [Canadian papers please copy.]

Household & kitchen furniture at auction on May 2, at the residence of Rev Dr Keeling, [late rector of Trinity Church,] on 3rd st, between C & Pa ave.
-Green & Williams, aucts

Supreme Court of D C, Apr 26, 1867. No 2,854. Louis Curts, plntf, vs Sandy Skinner, dfndnt. On motion of the plntf, by Mr R S Davis, his atty, it is ordered that the dfndnt cause his appearance to be entered here on or before the first rule day occurring 40 days after this day; otherwise the cause will be proceeded with as in case of default. –Geo P Fisher, Justice S C D C -R J Meigs, clerk

MON APR 29, 1867
Ads. 1-Mr H Cassidy, 436 9th st, has 12 acres of fine rye for sale. 2-Mr L F Clark, 248 Pa ave, is selling window shades at reduced prices.

The funeral of Mr Albert Brewer, late a member of the Metropolitan Police force, took place yesterday, from his late residence, 3rd & Mass ave. The remains were interred in the *Congressional Cemetery* with the ceremonies of the Odd Fellows orders, of which he was a member.

Mis Madeline Henriques, a popular actress in N Y, made her last appearance on the stage at Wallach's Theatre on Friday. She is about to be married to Mr Jennings, the correspondent of the London Times in this country.

The Balt American says: W R McCullough, eldest son of Hon Hiram McCullough, died suddenly a short time since at St Domingo. He was engaged in business there, & fell victim to the malarious fever in that climate.

Died: on Apr 28, Mrs Sarah Wright, wife of Lewis Wright, in her 60th year. Her funeral is on Apr 20 at 3 o'clock, from her late residence, 623 Md ave, between 12th & 13th sts, Island.

Died: on Apr 27, at the residence of his brother, in Wash City, Henry Ott, of Harrisonburg, Va, in his 58th year. [Richmond papers please copy.]

Dept of the Interior, U S Patent Ofc, Wash, Apr 22, 1867. Ptn of Julius Herriet, of N Y, N Y, praying for extension of a patent granted to him Aug 2, 1853, for an improvement in Elastic Type for printing on irregular forms, for 7 years from the expiration of said patent, which takes place on Aug 2, 1867.
-T C Theaker, Com'r of Patents

Executor's sale of leases of Hammack's Restaurant, furniture, china, glassware, oil paintings, French-plate mirrors, etc, on May 9 & 10, at the residence of the late John D Hammack. –Dr Thos Miller, exc -Cooper & Latimer, aucts

TUE APR 30, 1867
Criminal Court-Mr Justice Fisher, Apr 29, 1867. 1-John Rosette, indicted for assault & battery, & Thos Morrow, for passing counterfeit money; cases continued. 2-Eliza Sommers was fined & paid $200 for keeping a bawdy house. 3-Leonard S McDaniel, alias Lawrence S McDaniel, indicted for larceny; the recognizance was forfeited.

Died: on Apr 29, at Campbell Hospital, Richd Busteed, jr. His funeral will take place from St Patrick's Church, 10th & F sts, at 10 o'clock Wed morning.

Large stock of groceries at auction on May 1, at the Grocery Store of Strafford Evans, on 9th st, between M & N sts. -Green & Williams, aucts

Dept of the Interior, U S Patent Ofc, Wash, Apr 12, 1867. Ptn of Richd Montgomery, of N Y, N Y, praying for the extension of a patent granted to him Jul 12, 1857, for an improvement in Sheet Metal Beams, for seven years from the expiration of said patent, which takes place on Jul 12, 1867.
-T C Theaker, Com'r of Patents

Dept of the Interior, U S Patent Ofc, Wash, Enoch Hidden, of N Y, N Y, praying for the extension of a patent granted to him Jun 21, 1853, reissued Sep 8, 1863, & again reissued Mar 15, 1864, for an improvement in Side Lights for Ships, for seven years from the expiration of said patent, which takes place on Jun 21, 1867.
-T C Theaker, Com'r of Patents

WED MAY 1, 1867
It is reported that Mr T B Brown is to be suspended from his position as warden of the jail of this District, on the charge that he interfered in the registration of the 4th Ward by securing the registration of the names of the parties who had once been rejected for cause by the commissioners. Mr Brown & his friends deny the charges. In the performance of his official duties he has ever been faithful & efficient, & has possessed, to an unusual degree, the confidence of the Judges of the Supreme Court of D C.

Orphans Court-Apr 30, 1867. 1-John Ferguson was appointed guardian to Belle Ferguson Lee & Lamon H Lee, orphans of Harvey & Mary F Lee, late of Sacramento, Calif; bond $1,000. 2-Helen Stern was appointed guardian to the orphans of Jos Stern, deceased; bond $4,000. 3-The second & supplemental of Chas S English, Sarah Frances Budd, [late English,] Robt P Dodge, & Walter S Cox, excs of David English, deceased; the first & final account of Jas Goszler, adm of Wm J Goszler, deceased, & the distribution account of said deceased to his legal heirs, were approved & passed.

Cincinnati, Apr 30. Geo Goltz, Saml Case, & Alex'r Aulgar were hung in this city today, for the murder of Jas Hughes in Feb last.

Criminal Court-Mr Justice Fisher, Apr 29, 1867. 1-Richd Bennett & Jas F Davis were convicted of the charge of assault & resisting Ofcr G C Harris, & each fined $5. On the indictment of assault, a verdict of not guilty. 2-Fred'k Chatain & Eliza Chatain were acquitted on the charge of larceny. 3-Nathl Hines, committed to jail on a charge of forgery, was released, the grand jury failing to present an indictment. 4-The trial of John H Surratt will commence on May 27.

Mrd: on Apr 24, at St Aloysius Church, by Rev Fr Stonestreet, Juan A Pizzini, of Richmond, Va, to Miss Cecilia P Hickey, eldest daughter of the late Gen W Hickey, of Wash City.

Died: on Apr 30, suddenly, Jas McColgan, jr, youngest son of Jas & Mary McColgan, in his 24th year. His funeral will be from the residence of his parents, 251 Pa ave, between 12th & 13th sts, tomorrow at 2 o'clock P M. The remains will be taken to Balt for interment.

Died: on Apr 25, Mrs Mary E, wife of Dr Saml B Fisher, of Warrenton, Va.

Mr Leutze is in Wash City, quietly painting a full-length portrait of Mrs Fred'k Seward. He has just finished a very bold & striking portrait of Miss Seward.

Wm Simmes, a farmer of Wirt Co, West Va, hung himself in his barn on Saturday.

In Chicago, on Thu, Stephen W Tomlinson was seen going to his boarding house to dress for his marriage with Miss Emma Knowles, which was appointed for that afternoon; but he did not reach the house, & has not been seen since.

Trustee's sale of small tract of unimproved land near 7th st turnpike; by decree of the Supreme Court of D C, passed in cause No 818, Equity, Summy vs Dickinson et al, substituting me as trustee, I shall, on May 22, sell at public auction, lot B, No 5, of the subdivision of that part of **Bell's Plains**, **Tamar's Outlet**, & **Indolence**, known as **Padworth**, conveyed by B O Tayloe et al to Wm Little, containing 4 acres, 1 rood & 25 perches, more or less. It adjoins the lands of Messrs Gleeson, Summy, & Heine. -W Y Fendall, trustee -Green & Williams, aucts

THU MAY 2, 1867
Ads: 1-Mrs Geo W Ward, near Winchester, Va, will take a few families for board in that healthful region. 2-Albert Colby wants agents to sell the book just published entitled the "Life of Christ." Apply at 207, opposite Willard's.

John Durham, a shoemaker, was instantly killed a day or two since at Getchell's Corner, Me, by a base-ball player. Durham, with a knife in his hand, was watching a game, when one of the players ran against him accidentally, driving the knife into his heart.

Indianapolis, Ind, May 1. John S Johns was murdered at Gosport, last night. He was found at his ofc with his head knocked in; & $200 belonging to the telegraph & railroad companies missing. There is no clue to the murderers.

Lynching in Jessamine Co, Ky, on Apr 24. A negro boy of 18 shot through the head & instantly killed a white boy of similar age, Richd Crowl. The murderer had an accomplice, & both were arrested & lodged in jail at Nicholasville. On Sat a mob entered the jail, took out the two prisoners, & hung them on a tree.

St Louis, Apr 30. An Omaha despatch says the report telegraphed from Leavenworth to the N Y Herald, on Apr 21, that Gen Augur was about a mile west of *Fort Phil Kearney*, with 6,000 troops, & that 11,000 Indians were encamped between *Fort Kearney* & *Fort Smith*, waiting for the grass to commence hostilities, & Gen Hancock's expedition being in distress, is pronounced an unmitigated hoax at Gen Augur's heaquarters. A *Fort Laramie* despatch of the 20th says the Indians had surrounded Horse Shoe Station, & that fighting was now going on. A telegraph supply train was attacked on Apr 21, 70 miles west of *Fort Laramie*, & all the stock driven off & all the provisions destroyed. No more work can be done on the telegraph line without an escort.

Mrd: on May 1, 1867, by Rev Dr Chas H Hall, of Epiphany Church, Chas W Hite, of Madison, Ind, to Miss Jessie C Courtenay, of New Orleans, La.

Rear Admiral Cadwalader Ringgold, U S Navy, died on Apr 29, at the residence of Mr Vernes, 33 Union Square, & was in every respect sudden & unexpected. Shortly after arising he was seized with an apoplectic fit, & soon expired. He was a native of Md, in which State he was born in 1802; on Mar 4, 1823, he entered the navy, & on May 17, 1828, was promoted to the rank of lt; on Jul 16, 1849, he was commissioned as a commander; on Jul 16, 1862, he was promoted to the rank of commodore, & continued in active service until Dec, 1864, when he was placed on the retired list. A few weeks ago he was promoted to the rank of rear admiral, & ordered on duty to succeed the late Rear Admiral Gregory as superintendent of iron-clads with headquarters in this city. The late Rear Admiral was 44 years, one month, & 25 days in the naval service, during which time 20 years & 11 months were spent at sea. At the time of his death he was in his 65th year. His remains will be conveyed to his native State of Md for interment. -N Y Herald, Apr 30th
+
N Y, May 1. The funeral of Rear Admiral Ringgold took place today. A detachment of marines followed the remains to the *Trinity Church Cemetery*.

War Dept Claims Commission, Wash, D C, Apr 30, 1867. Statement of claims received by the Commission for the month of Apr, 1867.
Claim of John A Middleton, & others, for rent of & damage to farm in D C.
Campbell Phelan & Wallace Davis for commutation of quarters & fuel.
Harrison H Cook, for pay for grazing cattle near Petersburg.
Andrew Szabo, for property destroyed at Bayou Sara, La.
Elias Sheads; Jas Thompson; & Frank Swisher, for hospital supplies.
A B Harford, for rent of property at Memphis, Tenn.
Mrs Jos Gales, for restoration of fencing on her property.
Martin Gridley, for rent of & damage to property in Shelby Co, Tenn.
Wm Weigart, for rent of property in St Louis, Mo.
Robt Waggenstein, for subsistence stores furnished Gov't.
C N Gary, for the value of a horse taken by the U S authorities.
M W Walton, for funds & horse taken from him in Va.
R L Patterson, for forage & cattle taken from him in Va.

E E Simpson, for return of moneys taken from Bank of Louisiana.
C W Alexander; Henry Diven; & Hugh Sturdy, for srvcs in executing special orders.
Wm Robinson, for services as guide & scout.
Wm Vinson, for lumber & rent of house.
W T Berry, for property taken in the erection of a fort at Nashville, Tenn.
S B Corbett, for corn, etc, furnished the Quartermaster's Dept.
Henry S Bulkley, for remuneration for detention of train.
C O Beens, for nails & shovels furnished the U S Gov't.
D V Colclazar, for damages to property near *Fort Stevens*.
Geo A Lamb, for services as scout.
Nathl M Simonds, for articles furnished at *Camp Douglas*.
Geo Knapp & Co, & McKee, Fishback & Co, for advertising at St Louis.
Henry Hollingsworth, for indemnity for losses sustained as a purchasing agent for the Gov't.
E A Smith, for mules delivered to the Gov't.
Peck & Brocten, for services of team.
Putnan & Denslow, for services of team.
O P Wiggins, for services as guide.
T J Bayant, for services of team.
M H Knapp, for bridles & leather.
F J Curtis, for one saddle.
S C Stoneburner, for services as chief clerk.
Bela S Buell, for one horse, saddle & briddle.
J H Gaskill, for one saddle & bridle.
E B Smith, for one saddle.
Dr Jas B Hinkle, for medicine, etc, furnished to U S prisoners.
S A Wilkins, for damages to his farm near *Fort Stevens*.
Jesse E Peyton, for reimbursement of amount recovered against him for occupying farm as a cavalry camp.
Pierre Klaine, for property taken by U S troops in Arkansas.
Jas F Bailey, for services in capturing rebel mail carrier.
John G Holloway, for rent of land near Columbus, Ohio.
Final action had on claims during the present month:

Allowed:

Wm J Mino	J W Page	Jas H Holmes
Leonard Pierce	Benj Fahenstock	Margaret Edes
J W Pomfrey	Isaac Walker	John Bruce
Petr Swartzwalder	Thos Garvey	W W Withenberry
Geo A Smallwood	L D Finckel	Easton Sanders
Thos A Elliott	A H Hagar	

Rejected:

Seabright & Furman	A C Graham	C Emmerick
Caroline P Walker	Saml McGaughey	Luther R Smoot
Benj H Atkinson	Stephen Kruse	Geo P Evans
Wm Irwin	John H Bush	

-De Witt Clinton, Brvt Lt Col, Recorder

In Limestone Co, Texas, some days ago, two twin children, brother & sister, named Dunbar, 4 years old, strayed from their home into the woods. After searching for them for 3 days, they were found, about 2 miles from home, locked in each other's arms, dead.

FRI MAY 3, 1867
Mr Spofford, the Librarian of the Congressional Library, has completed the arrangement of the Smithsonian & Peter Force collections, which swell the number of volumes to 170,000. Mr Lucius M Boltwood, who was for a number of years librarian of Amherst College, has been appointed Assist Librarian.

Jurors to serve in the May term of the Circuit Court-Wash:

Jos Bryan	Danl Black	E Ubhoff
John E Cox	D R Kelley	Horatio N Easby
Chas Ball	E B Barrett	Benj Prosise
Geo Turnburke	Thos A Richards	Chas Wilson
Geo A Springman	Wm Cammack	Robt Cohen
Nicholas Mills	J F Sanner	John H Russell
Wm F Given	P Shoemaker	A M Appler
J P Klengle	John E Kendall	F A Lutz
John W Tucker	Frank McGham	

Hon Benj Eggleston, of Cincinnati, was married in N Y C on Sat to Miss Mary E Davis, of Cincinnati.

Personal: 1-John C Cox, chief clerk of the Interior Dept, is quite sick & unable to be at his ofc. 2-Dr F S Walsh, an old & much esteemed citizen, for many years past president of the Board of Trustees of Public Schools, will leave the city next week for Europe, where he will be absent about 3 months. Dr Walsh will visit his parents in Ireland, after which he will go to the Paris Exposition. 3-Capt Alex Roberts who during the war served with distinction as an ofcr of the 38th N Y volunteers, leaves this morning for Texas, having been appointed a special inspector of customs at Brazos de Santiago. Capt Roberts is one of the 12 mounted inspectors recently appointed by the Sec of the Treasury for the purpose of preventing smuggling on the Mexican boundary.

Association of Oldest Inhabitants: monthly meeting held Wed, Mr Wm A Bradley presiding, & Mr J C Brent, sec. Messrs Geo B Smith, John Gordon, & Cmdor Jas M Watson, of the U S navy, were elected members. Mr John F Callan spoke of the late Edw Mattingly, one of the oldest members of the association, lately deceased. Mr J Carroll Brent has provided a new photograph album of exquisite beauty & immense capacity, in which to set the photograph likenesses of the members.

Cooper & Latimer, aucts, sold yesterday 3 small frame houses on M st north, between 4th & 5th sts west-one to J Geo Naylor for $1,560; one to Geo C B Mitchell for $1,640; & one to A Lewis for $1,490.

Judge Fisher yesterday overruled the motion for a new trial in the case of Wm E Cleaver, convicted of manslaughter, & sentenced him to 5 years in the Albany penitentiary. Jos Ward, convicted of attempt at arson, was sentened to 2 years in the Albany penitentiary.

Yesterday, as the workmen were engaged in driving piles for reconstruction of the wharf belonging to the heirs of the late J N Fearson, one of the handles of the hoisting apparatus broke, & the other reversing suddenly, struck a laborer, Saml King, on the back of the head, inflicting a very severe wound. Dr Magruder attended him & he was conveyed to his home in Alexandria. It was feared that the wound would prove fatal.

There are now in the jail here the following persons, who have been sentenced to confinement in the Albany Penitentiary for terms stated: Wm E Cleaver, manslaughter, 5 years; John Hughes, larceny, 3 years; Solomon Smith, larceny, 2 years; Martha Smith, larceny, 2 years; Robt Fisher, burlgary, 18 months; Chas Hill, assault & battery with intent to kill, 2 years; Sanford Conover, alias Chas A Dunham, perjury, 10 years; Jos Ward, attempt at arson, 2 years; & Chas Hopkins, assault & battery, with intent to kill, 2 years. These persons will be taken to Albany the beginning of the week.

Men of the Times in England. The Duke of Cambridge. Geo Wm Fred'k Chas, Duke of Cambridge, is Cmder-in-Chief of the British army. He is son of the late Duke of Cambridge, grandson of George III, & of course first cousin of Queen Victoria. In 1771, when the Duke of Cumberland, brother of George III, married Mrs Horton, an act was passed by Parliament prohibiting the descendants of George II from contracting marriage, if under 25, without consent of the Sovereign-if over 25, without consent of Parliament. This act, still unrepealed, is the key to the secret memoirs of the royal family of England from that day till now. The lives of that brood of nine sons & six daughters, issued of George III & Queen Charlotte, if ever written, will furnish a chapter in the Chronique Scandaleuse unsurpassed in interest by the private memoris of Louis XV, or the history of the Dukes of Orleans. When the Pricess Charlotte died, in 1817, not one of the seven sons then living had any legitimate children. The Prince of Wales separated from his wife, whom he had received in a fit of drunkenness & discarded on awakening to sobriety, & had returned to Mrs Fitzherbert. The Duke of Cumberland, King of Hanover, a country detached from the English dynasty by salique-law when Victoria ascended the throne, was not then father of his blind son, who has just now lost his crown. The Duke of Clarence was allied by morganatic marriage to Mrs Jordan, whose oldest son, as Earl of Munser, became Govn'r Gen of India, & whose descendants, under the name of Fitzclarence, still hold high official positions under Gov't. The Duke of York, who, though guilty of every crime forbidden by the decalogue, & whose death made bankrupt a thousand tradesmen, yet received the honor of the most conspicious monument in London, which was selling commissions in the army to satisfy the demand of his imperious paramour, Mrs Clarke. The Dukes of Kent, Sussex, & the rest were only less notorious in crime & shame. The decease of Princess Charlotte, heiress apparent to the throne, awakened the debauchees from their indifference. The hope of issue from the King was dead. Not a descendant from George III, in the male line of the third generation, was living. Urged on by the clamors of the people, who dreaded another German Sovereign, & tempted by the offers of Parliamentary grants, five of the sons of George III, the youngest of whom was past 40 years, obtained Princesses of foreign birth in marriage, the only issue of all which was a daughter, Victoria, to the Duke of Kent, & a son & daughter, George & Mary, to the Duke of Cambridge. The former is the subject of our sketch. His Royal Highness the present Cmder-in-Chief of the British army was born in 1819. Like his father & grandfather, he is a stout, well-built man of middle height, heavy in movement, cold in address, ungracious in manner, with that singular charistic shared by the Queen & inherited for 150 years in the family, of protuberant eyes, flush to the face. Though he has enjoyed every advantage, & risen through every grade of service, he is scarcely up to mediocrity in mental abilities. In no nation but England, & no century but the 19th, would he reach or retain his present position. He does not possess the first element of a cmder-in-chief. Not only is he slow in apprehension, sluggish in thought, phlegmatic in temperament, & infirm in purpose, but he also inherits that liability to insantiy which is the curse of his race. Whilst free from the vices that made the names of his royal uncles a disgrace to England, he also, debarred from marriage without the consent of Parliament, long since formed a left-handed alliance, & has around him a family of legally unrecognized sons & daughters. No charge of unfaithfulness has ever been brought against him.

Hamilton [Canada] Times: on Wed, at Mr Hadden's mill, near Kilbride, in the township of Nelson, Lucy Higgins, a young woman, residing in Mr Hadden's family, visited the mill & while there her hoopskirt caught on a circular saw going at full speed, & she was drawn upon the dangerous piece of machinery, & died within half an hour after the accident.

Harrisburg, May 2. Govn'r Geary has signed the death-warrant of Gottlieb Williams, fixing the execution for Jun 4. Williams killed an old lady, named Miller, last fall.

Mrs Danl Kent, of East Wallingford, Vt, left her house to go to her husband, who was boiling maple sap in the woods. She lost her way & was found dead from exhaustion within 20 rods of home.

Richmond Despatch: The Govn'r yesterday appointed John Oliver, a mulatto man of this city, a notary public for the city of Richmond & county of Henrico. Oliver is the first negro notary public ever appointed in Va. He is a man of respectability & intelligence.

Among the passengers who sailed from N Y on the ship **Scotia** on Wed were Geo Peabody, Gen Preston, of S C; John G Saxe, Lester Wallack & family, Manager Wheatley, & John W Borney. Hon C Cole, & Cmdor Watson, U S navy, sailed on the ship **Ocean Queen** for Aspinwall.

The Gardiner will declared void. Trial for the week past in the Circuit Court of Richmond Co, determined by the verdict of the jury to the effect that Juliana Gardiner, at the time of executing & publishing the instrument dated Oct 4, 1864, as her last will & testament, was not of sound & disposing mind, memory, & understanding; that it was procured by fraud & undue influence; that she did not devise her real estate to the persons upon the condition & to the effect declared & expressed therein; & that therefore the said Juliana Gardiner died intestate as to her real estate, making no disposition of it whatever. The counsel for Mrs Tyler, Mr Wm M Evarts, moved for a new trial. This was denied. Mrs Juliana Gardiner was the widow of Cmdor Gardiner, who was killed by the explosion on board the steamer **Princeton**, in 1844. Their daughter, Miss Julia Gardiner, married Pres Tyler on Jun 26th following. At the breaking out of the rebellion political differences of opinion gave rise to bitter animosity; Mrs Tyler & her mother sympathizing with the rebels, & her brother, Mr David Gardiner, the plntf in this suit, supporting the Union cause. He had for years had the management of his mother's estate; but the settlement of Mrs Tyler & her children at the homestead was followed by troubles which compelled him to remove his family to another home. Mrs Gardiner required him to surrender the agency of her estate early in 1864, & on the 4th day of the subsequent Oct, about 4 hours before her death, signed a will leaving her property, about $180,000, to Mrs Tyler for the term of her natural life, or till the Gov't of the U S should reimburse Mrs Tyler for the losses consequent upon the war in the property left to her by her husband, the former President. The Surrogate of Richmond Co, refused to admit this will to probate, on the ground of undue influence exercised on the mind of the testatrix; & Mrs Tyler appealed the case to the general term of the Supreme Court of the Second Judicial District. The Surrogate's decision was overruled. Mr Gardiner carried the case to the Court of Appeals, where the original ruling of the Surrogate was sustained. He then instituted the present suit for the partition of the property under the statute, precisely as though his mother had died intestate. Mrs Tyler set up the will of Oct, 1864, in defence, & the verdict of the jury has resulted adverse to her expectations. –N Y Post

Court of Equity-Mr Justice Olin. Madison vs Madison: No 765: decree of divorce.

The consecration of the first Episcopal Bishop of Montana, Rt Rev E Sylvester Tuttle, took place on Wed, at Trinity Chapel, at N Y.

A new yacht, for Mr Pierre Lorillard, was launched at N Y yesterday. It is said to be the largest yacht ever built in America. She goes to the French regatta.

SAT MAY 4, 1867
Mrd: on Apr 18, at Winchester, Va, by Rev Norvall Wilson, Wm W B Gallaher, jr editor of the Va Free Press, Charlestown, to Miss Belle Wilson, daughter of the officiating clergyman.

Died: on May 2, in Gtwn, D C, Mrs Mary Ann Fearson, widow of the late Jos N Fearson, in her 63rd year. Her funeral will take place on May 6, at 8½ A M, from her late residence, & from Trinity [Roman Catholic] Church at 9 A M.

Indianapolis, May 3. The money stolen from the railroad ofc at Gosport & the clothes of the murderer, Willis McMinaway, were found buried under an ash hopper in McMinaway's yard. McMinaway is a citizen of Gosport, & had been assisting Johns, the murdered man, in loading freight & collecting freight bills. His wife says he did not come home until midnight & left at 5 in the morning for Quincy. Second despatch. Willis McMinaway was committed for trial. Excitement is still very great, & it was with difficulty that lynching was prevented.

Columbus, Ohio, May 3. The Moulders' Union at Ironton is on strike. Some of the moulders went to work, but the strikers ran them out of town, & in the row one of the strikers, Chas Severon, was killed.

Pittsburgh, May 3. Last night girl named Mollie Griffin, commited suicide, at a house of ill-fame, by taking poison. Remorse & the desertion of her friends drove her to the act.

Fortress Monroe, May 3. Mrs Jefferson Davis left her for Washington last eveninng for the purpose of conferring with Pres Johnson upon her husband's release.

Absecom, N J, May 3. This morning Jas Yeats, of Bikersville, N J, killed his little grandchild, aged 8 years, with a hatchet, & then went to his own house & hung himself. [May 7th newspaper: Friday morning Mr Jas Yates, of Bickersville, N J, killed his little grandchild, aged 8 years, with a hatchet, & then went to his own house & hung himself in a room.]

On Tuesday, near Dundas, Minn, a farmer, Alfred Hoyt, killed his neighbor, Josiah Stanford, with an axe. Hoyt then proceeded to the house & attempted to murder Mrs Stanford, but she evaded him until her two sons rescued her & seized the murderer. Hoyt says he is glad he killed the old man, & is only sorry that he did not kill the old woman. A quarrel respecting cattle running at large was the cause.

Wash, D C, May 2, 1867. Notice is hereby given that certificate of tax sale for lot sub 17, in square 197, sold May 9, 1865, has been lost or mislaid, & that application will be made to the Collector for a copy of the same. –Susan Tenney

Dept of the Interior, U S Patent Ofc, Wash, Apr 30, 1867. Ptn of Wm Miller, of Pensacola, Fla, adm of the estate of Jos R Miller, late of Jersey City, N J, deceased, praying for the extension of a patent granted to said Jos R Miller Aug 2, 1853, for an improvement in Submarine Tunnels, for seven years from the expiration of said patent, which takes place on Aug 2, 1867. -T C Theaker, Com'r of Patents

The undersigned would sell his books, stationery, & retail trade for $8,000. They are worth more. The business is never large-always solid. Store, fixtures, cellar, & wareroom at a moderate rent. –Franck Taylor, Bookseller

MON MAY 6, 1867

Marine Corps. Brvt Lt Col Hayward has been detached from the command of the Marine Guard at the Wash Navy Yard, & ordered to the command of the guard on Admiral Farragut's flagship. 2-The case of Maj W Y Field, formerly commanding the guard at the Wash Navy Yard, who was tried & found guilty of drunkenness by a court-martial in Phil, has been reviewed by the Pres, who orders a new trial.

Mr C M Fay, real estate agent, sold a house & lot on Pa ave, between 6th & 7th sts, to Mr T E G Pettengill, for $2,700.

Ads: 1-Mr Jas S Clayton, successor to Wm Grosse, is the proprietor of the new brand cigar, "The Rose." Everything in the tobacco line can be found at his store. 2-J W Colley give notice that he has sold his stock of dry goods to Messrs Carter, Yates & Wiswall, & desires persons indebted to him to call & settle.

Jas Fishback, who has been for a long time in charge of the State War Claims Division of the Third Auditor's ofc, tendered his resignation in that ofc as clerk on Sat, to accept the assessorship of internal revenue for the 10th Dist of Ill, to which he has been appointed & confirmed.

Gtwn: Thos Dowling, auctioneer, has sold the following property: frame house & lot, on Beall st, between Montg & Monroe sts, to Robt White, for $1,000; a 3 story brick store & dwlg on Bridge st, between Jefferson & Congress sts, to B F Moxley, for $5,000; the residence of the late Wm Redin, on Gay st, between Congress & Wash sts, to Wm King, for $15,500; two lots, each fronting 30 feet on Gay st, between Wash & Green sts, to Richd Cruit, jr, for $22.50 per front foot.

Died: on May 1, Dr Wm B Vinson, of Seneca, Montg Co, Md, in his 69th year, after a brief illness. The deceased entered the family of Dr John B Davidge, of Balt, & under the auspices & instructions of that distinguished gentleman pursued his studies & collegiate course & received his medical diploma. Soon thereafter he took up his residence near the place of his birth, where he died among relatives & friends, much esteemed.

Died: on May 5, Emma Frances, daughter of the late Andrew & Eliza Coyle. Her funeral services will be held at the N Y ave Church, [Rev Fr Gurley, pastor,] on May 7 at 4 o'clock P M.

U S Marshal's sale: on May 11, one brown horse, one light wagon, & one set harness-the goods & chattels of John T Russell, & will be sold to satisfy execution No 9,362, in favor of Thos Fahey. –D S Gooding, U S Marshal, D C
-W L Wall & Co, aucts

U S Marshal's sale of a valuable farm in Wash Co, D C, on May 27 next, in front of the Court House door in said District, for cash, part of a tract called *Woodly*, containing 33 acres, 3 roods & 18 perches of land, more or less, with all & singular improvements thereon. Also, I will sell the whole of square 720; lot 8 in square 683, & lots 9 & 10 in square 685, in Wash City, with improvements thereon. Seized & levied upon as the property of Robt J Walker, & will be sold to satisfy execution No 3,300, in favor of Columbus Alexander. -David S Gooding, U S Marshal

Lumber, Lumber, C B Church & Co, corner of Md ave & 11th st. [Ad]

U S Marshal's sale on May 27, lot 19 in square 285, fronting 26 feet 4 inches on K st, south side, by 142 feet 6 inches deep, in Wash City, with improvements thereon, seized & levied upon as the property of Jos B Stewart, & will be sold to satisfy executions 2,192 & 2,145, in favor of the State Bank of Minnesota. -David S Gooding, U S Marshal

Trustee's sale of valuable real estate in St Mary's Co, Md. By decree of the Circuit of St Mary's Co, sitting as a court of equity in the case of Johns Hopkins & others vs Thos W Gough & others, the undersigned, trustee, will expose to public sale, at the Court-house door in the village of Leonardtown, St Mary's Co, Md, on Jun 4, all the real estate belonging to the said Thos W Gough, in said county, & levied on by the Sheriff of St Mary's Co, in virtue of sundry executions against the said Thos W Gough, & consisting of the following tracts of parcels of lands: 1-The real estate on which the *Clifton Factory* is located, contains 350 acres, more or less. 2-Very valuable farm, *Belvidere*, containing about 400 acres of land. 3-Valuable tract or parcel of land adjoining *Belvidere*, & is supposed to contain 1,400 acres, more or less. 4-Valuable real estate known as *Gough's Wharf*, on Britton's bay, contains 330 acres, & the land nearly adjoining it about 100 acres. Will be sold separately on in conjunction, to suit a purchaser. –Peter W Crain, B G Harris, trustees

Mourning Dress Goods Depot-Jos J May & Co, 308 Pa ave, between 9th & 10th. [Ad]

Wanted-Every Lady to know that she can buy French Whalebone Corsets at $1.50. Hoop Skirts & Corsets made to order, & warranted to fit; also altered & repaired at Chas Baum's, 49 Louisiana ave, between 6th & 7th sts.

TUE MAY 7, 1867
On May 1st the shoe-shop of John T Lucas, colored, on 12th st, was robbed of boots & shoes to the value of $30 or more. Two notorious colored thieves, Geo Smith, alias Bute, & Jos Johnson, alias Major, were arrested & committed to court. A pair of the boots stolen was found upon one of them.

On Wed night a planter named Smith Wilson, residing near Memphis, while talking to his wife, was shot dead by some one who fired at him through the window.

Trial of John H Rogers, late paying teller of the Mechanics' Bank of Balt, was commenced at Balt yesterday. Chas Callender, an examiner of national banks, stated that he had discovered false entries in the books of the bank to the amount of $317,000. Rogers was employed in the bank for 28 years. Saml M Wentz, indicted for the same offence, plead guilty, but sentence in this case was deferred until a verdict is rendered in Rogers' case. [May 11th newspaper: May 10-the jury in the case of John H Rogers, rendered a verdict of guilty on the 4th count of the indictment, namely making a false entry on the paying teller's book, with intent to defraud, but recommended him to the mercy of the court.]

Ads: 1-Mr Thos Lucas, 22nd & K sts, offers for sale a lady's saddle-horse. 2-Mrs M N Abbey has removed her bath rooms to 312 F st, near 11th st.

Court of Equity-Mr Justice Olin, May 6, 1867. 1-Eckells et al vs Barrett et al. Order appointing a guardian ad litem for Louisa J Barrett. 2-Wood et al vs Wood et al. Order appointing a guardian ad litem for Wm F Scala.

Mrd: on May 2, by Rev C C Meador, at the residence of the bride, Mr Gustavus A Brandt, of N C, to Miss Sarah L Barnard, of Wash City. No cards.

Mrd: on Apr 30, at Lexington, the residence of L T Williamson, by Rev Mr Foley, J Henley Smith to Mary Rebecca, daughter of the late Alex'r Young.

Died: on May 5, Emma Frances, daughter of the late Andrew & Eliza Coyle. Her funeral services will be held at the N Y Church, [Rev Dr Gurley, pastor,] on May 7 at 4 o'clock P M.

Chancery sale of valuable & handsomely improved property on 5th st, near F; by decree of the Supreme Court of D C, in which Robt J Brent, use of First Nat'l Bank of Wash, is cmplnt, & Eliz Brown is dfndnt, said cause being No 719 Equity: public auction on Jun 1st next, lots 11 & 12 in square 488. –W Y Fendall, trustee -Cooper & Latimer, aucts

WED MAY 8, 1867
Orphans Court-Judge Purcell. 1-Yesterday the will of the late Mary Ann Fearson, widow of the late Jos N Fearson, bequeathing her estate to Mary Julia Barrett, wife of E B Barrett, with a codicil bequeathing a house & lot on High st to Mrs Eliz Darnes; $1,000 to Trinity [Catholic] Church; house & lot on South st to Ella Sabina Fearson, & 3 houses on South st to the sons of Saml & Evanna Fearson, was filed & fully proven. 2-Letters testamentary were issued to A K Browne on the estate of Richd Busteed, jr; bond $1,000; & of administration c t a on the estate of the late Gen Bender to Eugene Carusi; bond $6,000. 3-The first & final accounts of the administrator of Thos P Trott; of guardian to orphan of Geo Poe, deceased; & fifth & final account of guardian to orphan of John A Donohoo, were approved & passed.

Michl Farrell, a tailor, was murdered in N Y on Monday by another tailor, named Sullivan. Jealousy is supposed to have been the motive to the commission of the act.

A daughter of Sheriff Dissoway, of Bethlehem, Pa, aged about 10 years old, a few weeks ago, while at school, complained of pain in her eyes, & asked permission to go home. Before she reached her home, only 500 yards from the school, she was totally blind. All efforts to restore her sight have proved a failure.

John Q Thompson was arrested last evening by Ofcr Tucker on the charge of committing an assault & battery upon Mr Edw Kent, one of the barkeepers at the Metropolitan Hotel. Thompson had already tarried too long over his wine elsewhere, & asked Mr Thompson to trust him for 2 drinks. He refused to do so, & this excited the ire & indignation of Thompson, who then assaulted Mr Kent. Thompson was locked up for a few hours & then released on bail.

Mrd: on May 7, in the Foundry [M E] Church, by Rev J B Meek, Owen B Bestor to Miss Hattie A Cromwell, all of Wash. [Balt Sun please copy.]

The Chicago papers are publishing the income tax lists. The highest income returned is that of Cyrus H McCormick, $169,760; next, that of Peter Schuttler, $111,625. These are the only ones exceeding $100,000. J D Cole, jr, J L McCormick, & H T Dickey, return incomes from $50,000 to $60,000; L Z Suiter, F H Gardner, P F W Peck, & Lyman Bair, from $60,000 to $70,000; Geo Armooer/Amocer, B P Hutchinson, Welsey Munger, from $70,000 to $80,000.

Executor's sale of valuable property, consisting of brick & frame houses & lots in Gtwn & Wash, belonging to the estate of the late Dr Benj S Bohrer. Sale on May 27 next, of part of lot 47 on south side of Bridge st, improved by a 2 story brick store & dwlg-house occupied by Mr J S E Thorn. Part of lots 6 thru 8, south side of Bridge st, near the bridge, improved by a small frame house, occupied by Saml Muncaster. Part of lots 180 & 181, on north side of Bridge st, improved by a 2 story brick house, rented to Mr Hughes. Part of lots 1 & 12, south side of Bridge st, improved by a 2 story brick house, rented to Mrs Dowling. Parts of lots 13 & 14 on east side of High st, improved by a 2 story brick house, rented to Mr John Kaiser. Part of lots 20 thru 22, on north side of the canal, east of Congress st wharf, occupied by Mr Von _asen. Part of lot 213 on the east side of Fred'k st, improved by a 2 story frame house, rented to B R Bohrer. Lots of parts of lots 262 thru 164, & 300, on Heights of Gtwn, containing some 17 acres of land, from which is now taken the celebrated yellow sand for Gov't & other moulding purposes, probably the most commanding site in the District, named **Mount Alto**. Lot 4 in square 13, in Wash, improved by a 2 story brick house, occupied by Mr John Hoover. Lot 1 in square 27, on Pa ave, near the Circle, improved by a double 2 story frame house, rented to Mr John K Watt. Inquire of the executor, or of Mr C F Shekell, in Gtwn, D C.
–Geo A Bohrer, exc -Thos Dowling, auct

Maj Gen Hooker, who is still in poor health, has been granted leave of absence from Jun 1st, with permission to go abroad.

Orphans Court of Wash Co, D C. Letters testamentary on the personal estate of Richd Busteed, jr, late of Wash City, D C, deceased. –Andrew K Brown, exc

A tailor, Frank Holtkamp, 45 years of age, committed suicide at Cincinnati, on Monday, be cutting his head half off with a razor. Desertion by his wife was the cause.

Lt Floyd W Nunn, a storekeeper at Summerville, Noxubee Co, Miss, was murdered on the night of Apr 12th, while in bed. Two brothers named Fitzgerald were arrested, confessed the crime, & were hung by a mob. Some $1,200 out of $1,500 stolen at the time of the murder was recovered. [May 9th newspaper: Fitzgerald, aged 17, was arrested in Lexington, Miss, charged with 5 murders: killed a negro in De Soto Co, in this state; a white man in Tenn; a freedman on his father's premises since the surrender, assassinated Mr John W Shilcutt on Feb 26 last, at the residence of Col Richd Cooper, in this county, & his crimes culminated in the murder of Mr Nunn, of Summerville, on the 12th, & captured on the 18th.]

THU MAY 9, 1867
Henry Steele, jr, a notary public, has been convicted in N Y of making false certificate, upon which money was illegally paid to a pensioner's atty.

A bill in chancery has been filed in Chicago in behalf of the heirs of the late Hon Stephen A Douglas, to compel an account & settlement on the part of the atty who undertook the settlement of the estate, but who, it appears, under the garb of reverence for the memory of the great Douglas & friendship for his family, has been plundering the heirs & converting the proceeds of the estate to his own use.

Mrd: on May 8, by Rev Dr Gray, at E St Baptist Church, Mr Arthur M Muzzy to Miss Rosa May Andrews, both of N Y. [N Y papers please copy.

Obit-died: on Apr 23, at Woodland, PG Co, Md, Covie, beloved daughter of Wm B & Catharine B Hill, & grand-daughter of the late Richd Smith, of Wash City.

St Louis, May 8. Hon Saml Marshall, Congressman from the 11th District, died at his residence in McLeansboro a few days ago.

Louisville, May 8. Hon Elijah Hise, just elected to Congress from the 3rd Dist, committed suicide this afternoon by blowing his brains out with a pistol. He left a note saying, in the present state of the country, his advanced age precluded his doing this country any good, & he sought relief in death. [May 15th newspaper: In his note dated Apr 21, 1867: There is a codicil to my will in my coat-pocket, since placed in the hands of my wife. –E Hise]

Balt, May 8. Mrs Burnet, residing at 21 Elliot st, was burned to death today by an explosion of camphene in an indiscreet attempt to light a fire in a cooking stove.

Executor's sale of valuable improved real estate belonging to the estate of the late Andrew Small, deceased, at auction, on May 15 next,: lot A of ***Zephaniah Jones subdivision*** of said square, on Mass ave, between 10th & 11th sts, improved by a 3 story brick bldg, numbered 363. Also, lots 18 & 19 in ***Windsor & Ford's subdivision*** of lots 9 & 10 in square 397, on 8th st, improved by two 2 story brick bldgs, numbered 139 & 141. Also, lot 14 in square 397, on 8th st, with a two story brick bldg, numbered 131. On May 18: lots 16 & 17 in square 451, on N Y ave, improved by a 3 story frame house, encumbered by a lease, which expires Sep 1868, numbered 286. Also, part of lot 2 in square 515, on L st, improved by a 3 story brick house, numbered 650. On May 20: lot 4 in square 381, improved by a 2 story brick bldg. Part of lot 4 in square 387, on La ave, with a 2 story frame bldg, numbered 87. Part of lot 5 in square 381, on La ave. This lot is now renting for $100 per annum. –J A Ruff, exc -Fitch & Fox, real estate brokers -Green & Williams, aucts

FRI MAY 10, 1867
Ads: 1-The residence of Dr J C Benzinger, at Catonsville, 6 miles from Balt, is offered for sale. 2-A farm of 285 acres, adjoining Hon F P Blair's ***Silver Spring*** farm, is offered for sale.

Hammack's Restaurant, leases, furniture & fixtures, as a whole, was sold yesterday ato L S Wells, for the sum of $8,200.

Cooper & Latimer, aucts, sold at auction, yesterday, part of lot 1 in square 797, fronting 52 feet on Va ave, & running back to I st, improved by 2 brick houses, to John Shanahan, for $2,290.

A young man, Jerome Baner, while hunting in Irondequoit Bay, near Rochester, N Y, was killed by the accidental discharge of his gun.

Mrs Bennett, who was burned to death in Balt on Wed, while attempting to ignite a fire by pouring camphene on the stove, leaves 4 children to mourn her loss.

Mr T Sandford, for many years one of the editors of the Mobile Register, died on Apr 30.

Fortress Monroe, May 9. Ex-Pres Pierce arrived here this morning. His arrival is important, as it is connected with the trial of Jeff Davis.

Jos H Shaffield's French Confectionery, 216 Pa ave, between 12th & 13th sts. Parties, fairs, weddings, etc, furnished at the shortest notice, & on the most reasonable terms.

SAT MAY 11, 1867
Rochester, N Y, May 10. The body of Lewis Fox, the billiard-player, who mysteriously disappeared in Dec last, was found this morning floating in the river at Charlotte, 7 miles from this city.

Hartford, Conn, May 10. Chas F Pond, president of the Hartford & New Haven railroad, died at his residence in this city this evening, of paralysis.

Phil, May 10. Geo W Winnemore was today convicted of murder in the first-degree. He killed Mrs Magilton a few days ago.

Chancery sale of desirable bldg lots near the Observatory; by decree of the Supreme Court of D C, dated May 8, 1867, in chancery cause No 771, Thos Y Couley & wife vs Geo B Skaggs et al: public sale, on May 27 next, of lots 8, 11, & 12, in square 61. -R T Morsell, trustee -Cooper & Latimer, aucts

Mrd: on May 9, at Grace Church, Plainfield, N J, by Rev S C Thrall, French F Mix, of Gtwn, D C, to Maria S, only daughter of Maria & the late Edw Roche, formerly of N Y C.

Mrd: on May 9, by Rev Jabez Fox, Dr Thos F Moses, of Springdale, Ohio, to Hannah Appleton, only daughter of John Cranch, of Wash City.

Died: on May 10, Mrs Annie J Ketcham, in her 31st year. Her funeral will be on Sunday at 2 o'clock P M, from her late residence, 314 8th st, between L & M sts.

Died: on May 10, in his 47th year, Thos Fitzgerald Campbell, of N Y C, & late of the Ofc of Commissary General of Prisoners in Wash, D C. The remains will be taken to N Y for interment. [N Y C papers please copy.]

Died: on May 7, at Bellevue, near Warrenton, Va, Eliz, widow of the late Maj Mann Page Lomax, U S Army.

MON MAY 13, 1867
Mr John F Deal, an old resident of Phil, was killed near Camden, N J, on Thursday. He was, with several friends, waiting at the Fish House for the train, & being confused by the arrival of two trains failed to get off the track in time. He was struck by the locomotive & instantly killed.

Died: on May 9, of consumption, Geo Munro, a native of Rosshire, Scotland, but for the last 10 years a resident of Wash City, in his 45th year of his age. His funeral will be on May 13 at 3 o'clock P M, from the residence of his aunt, 322 Mass ave.

Orphans Court of Wash Co, D C. Letters testamentary on the personal estate of Mary Ann Fearson, late of Wash City, D C, deceased. –Mary Julia Barrett, excx

List of soldiers nominated during the 39th & 40th Congresses for postmasters by the Pres, subsequently rejected by the Senate, with a synopsis of the testimonials in their behalf.

Farmington, Maine. S Clifford Belcher, nominated by the Pres Apr 2, 1867, rejected by the Senate Apr 3, 1867. He is a young man of unblemished character, fine abilities, served his country as capt in the 16th regt Maine volunteers, & received a severe wound in the head.

Auburn, Maine: Benj F Beals, nominated Feb 19, 1867; rejected Mar 2, 1867. He served in the army until he lost an arm in the Red river campaign under Gen Banks. At the time of his nomination he was serving as chief clerk in the ofc, & if appointed meant to retain the services of Mr Burrill, a comrade-in-arms, whose health is permanently disabled.

Newburyport, Mass. Dennis Condry, nominated May 11, 1866; rejected Jul 13, 1866. He tendered his services to the Sec of the Navy Apr 11, 1861, & was appointed to the command of the gunboat **Ashland**; though wounded, he remained in the service until the close of the rebellion.

Brooklyn, N Y. Saml H Roberts, nominated as postmaster by the Pres on Mar 2, 1867; rejected by the Senate on Mar 18, 1867. He served with distinction during the war, & attained the rank of brvt major general for numerous important services in the field & before the enemy. By Gen Grant he was highly commended for gallantry on the battle field, & for valuable service rendered in breaking up the contraband trade between Richmond & Fredericksburg, & for the assistance afforded Gen Sheridan during his memorable raid upon the James River Canal. Gen Roberts was subsequently [on Apr 20, 1867] re-nominated for postmaster, & confirmed by the Senate on the same day.

Canastota, N Y. Albert R Barlow nominated on Mar 8, 1867; rejected on Mar 11, 1867. As a soldier, his performances for more than 2 years on the battle field had been a most conspicuous kind, & he did not leave the army until a serious wound made it absolutely necessary.

Cuba, N Y. Cyrus P Shepard, nominated Apr 5, 1867; rejected Apr 8, 1867. He entered the army as a private, & at the end of 4 years was honorably discharged, having, in the meantime, been promoted to the rank of captain.

Newburgh, N Y. J Henry Reeve, nominated Feb 23, 1867, rejected Mar 2, 1867. He was again nominated on Apr 17, 1867, & rejected by the Senate Apr 18, 1867. On Apr 19, 1861, Mr Reeve was enrolled as a private in the 3rd regt N Y infty, & remained until the close of the war. In the assault upon *Fort Fisher*, where he lost a limb, in Jan, 1865, his bravery was especially noticeable, & for this & other gallant services he was made major by brevet by the Sec of War in Oct of the same year.

Jos Lomas, nominated Apr 15, 1867; rejected Apr 16, 1867. As a soldier he was courageous & faithful, & the loss of a leg testifies to his devotion to the Union. He was recomended by a large number of the citizens of Newburgh.

Camden, N J. Timothy C Moore, nominated Mar 2, 1867; rejected on the same day. He enlisted as a private in the 4th regt of N J volunteers, on Apr 20, 1861, & when discharged from the service was colonel of the 34th regt of volunteers from the same State. On May 8, 1866, he was made brevet brig gen for gallant & meritorious conduct.

Newark, N J. John J Craven, nominated Mar 2, 1867; rejected on the same day. He served in the army with distinction & was honorably discharged.

Coatesville, Pa. Eliz P Humphreys, nominated Feb 15, 1867; rejected Mar 1, 1867. Mrs Humphreys was a lady of deserving character, & with a large family, dependent upon her for support, her husband having been killed in a railroad accident. Her ptn for the ofc was endorsed by the citizens of Coatesville, & one of her sons served with credit in the army for 2 years.

Wmport, Pa. Jacob Sallade, nominated on Feb 19, 1867; rejected on Mar 1, 1867. Col Sallade is a man of energy; his services as paymaster of volunteers were of great value to the Union.

Towanda, Pa. Jas Wilburn, nominated Apr 4, 1867; rejected Apr 5, 1867. Mr Wilburn was a solider during the late war & behaved bravely on many occasions.

Tamaqua, Pa. John Sheifly, nominated Jul 23, 1866; rejected Jun 27, 1866. Capt Sheifly served in the army with great credit to himself.

Plumer, Pa. Robt Taggart, nominated Apr 15, 1867; rejected on the same day. A capt in rank during his term of service, he was subsequently brevetted major for gallant & meritorious conduct on the battle-field.

Phil, Pa. Wm B Sipes, nominated Mar 8, 1867; rejected on Mar 11, 1867. Gen Sipes urged by his former associates of the 7th Pa volunteer cavalry, which he commanded during the war, for the position of postmaster.

Newcastle, Pa. Edw O'Brien, nominated Feb 15, 1867; rejected on Mar 4, 1867. Re-nominated on Apr 17, 1867, rejected on Apr 18, 1867. Col O'Brien gave evidence of his soldier like qualities during the Mexican war, & was leader of the forlorn hope at the battle of Chepultepec; at the late war he again volunteered, & gained fresh laurels by his brilliant charges at Fredericksburg & Chancellorsville; wounded severely, disabled.

Milton, Pa. Carlton B Davis, nominated Feb 15, 1867; rejected on Mar 2, 1867. Re-nominated on Mar 21, 1867; rejected on Mar 23, 1867. While in the army, & close to the war, he was always efficient & courageous.

Mercer, Pa. Jas S McKean, nominated Mar 2, 1867; rejected on the same day. His conduct while in the army was most satisfactory in every particular.

Hyde Park, Pa. Augustus Davis. Nominated on Feb 15, 1867; rejected on Mar 2, 1867.
Dr Davis, as surgeon during the war of the 125th regt of Pa volunteers, was of the most honorable character.

Danville, Pa. Saml S Gulick, nominated on Feb 15, 1867; rejected on Mar 1, 1867. His conduct during 2½ years of service in the army secured for him the approbation of his associates & superiors.

Balt, Md. Wm H Purnell, nominated Feb 14, 1866; rejected May 24, 1866. Col Purnell raised for the field soon after the first battle of Bull Run what was known as the Purnell Legion, a regt 1,200 strong, & commanded it for 6 months. He was perhaps the earliest public advocate of emancipation in Md, & chairman of the first free State convention held in Md.

Elkton, Md. Andrew Biddle, nominated Apr 5, 1867; rejected Apr 8, 1867. His career in the army, as a soldier, was a highly honorable one.

Kanawha Court House, Kanawha Co, West Va. Wm Gramm, nominated on Mar 8, 1867; rejected on Mar 12, 1867. Mr Gramm rose from rank of 2nd lt to major of his regt, the 7th West Va cavalry; was prisoner of war for nearly a year, & for 8 months of that time at hard labor in the Richmond penitentiary as a hostage for a guerilla capt.

Clarksburg, Harrison Co, West Va. Wm L Hursey, nominated Mar 8, 1867; rejected Mar 28, 1867. Mr Hursey was a lt in the West Va volunteers.

Cincinnati, Ohio. Wm N H Taylor, nominated Mar 2, 1867; rejected on the same day. Renominated on Apr 15; rejected on Apr 16. Mr Taylor, at his own expense, raised the 5th Ohio cavalry, & served gallantly at its head for 32 years, at the expiration of which time he was compelled by ill health to relinquish the military service.

Cincinnati, Ohio. Col Adolphus E Jones, nominated on Mar 12; rejected on Mar 20. Renominated on Apr 5; rejected on Apr 6. Col Jones served as provost marshal of the First & acting porvost marshal of the Second, Third, & Fourth Ohio Dists, with the approbation of the War Dept, & the satisfaction of the people residing within the sphere of his duties.

Cincinnati, Ohio. Col Hunter Brooke, nominated on Apr 11; rejected on Apr 12. Col Brooke enlisted as a private soldier in Apr, 1861, & by his bravery in the battles of Mill Springs, Shiloh, Murfreesboro, Chickamauga, Missionary Ridge, the 1st & 2nd Nashville campaigns, was promoted through the grades to lt colonel, with which rank he served in 1865 & 1866 as Provost Marshal Gen & Judge Advocate Gen of the Dept of Alabama, & was mustered out in Sep of the latter year, after an honorable & continuous service of over 5 years.

Circleville, Ohio. Col Harley H Sage, nominated Mar 2, 1867; rejected on the same day. Col Sage entered the military service as a private in Co B, 13th Ohio volunteer infty, in Apr, 1861, & was commissioned a 2nd lt on May 29, 1861, serving with his regt until Sep 6, 1861, when compelled by private business at home to retire. This transacted, he again entered the ranks on Oct 8, 1861, from which he was promoted to a captaincy on Dec 20, 1861. For bravery at the battle of Corinth he was on Oct 4, 1862, promoted to the majority of his regt, & served until May, 1863, when by a death in his family he was against constrained to resign his commission. On the call for 100 days men, he again took the field at the head of the 155th Ohio Nat'l Guard. Upon his muster out at the expiration of this regt's term of enlistment, he was appointed colonel of the 179th Ohio infty, with which he continued until the close of the war.

Troy, Ohio. Saml McKee, nominated to & rejected on Mar 2, 1867. He served his country faithfull in the war for the Union.

Bucyrus, Ohio. Isaac Z Bryant, nominated to & rejected on Mar 2, 1867. During the first 3 months of the war Mr Bryant lost an arm, & was thus incapacitated from further service in the army.

Toledo, Ohio. Gen Henry S Commger, nominated on Mar 25, 1867; rejected on Apr 2, 1867. Served with credit to himself & fidelity to his country during the late war.

Toledo, Ohio. Gen John W Fuller, nominated on Apr 2, 1867; rejected Apr 5, 1867. Gen Fuller entered the U S military service as colonel of the 27th Ohio, & taking part in all the campaigns in the West, was appointed brig gen for gallantry at Corinth; &

for similar bravery, while commanding a division in Gen Dodge's corps, & was brevetted major general Jul 22, 1864. Hon [late Maj Gen] G M Dodge; & Hon R P Spalding, testify to his excellent character.

Wooster, Ohio. Lt Reason B Spink, nominated on Mar 18, 1867; rejected on Mar 19, 1867. After the firing upon *Fort Sumter*, he enlisted in the 4th Ohio volunteer infty, & remained until within 6 months of the expiration of his 3 years term of service, when he was forced by sickness to resign the commission of lt his gallantry had secured for him. Capt Lemuel Jeffreys, nominated on Apr 12, 1867; rejected Apr 15, 1867. He entered the military service in Apr, 1861, as a private in Co E, 4th Ohio regt, & served as such until the battle of Antietam, when, from disabilites received & gallantry displayed, he was promoted by Pres Lincoln to a captaincy in the Veteran Reserve Corps, which latter position, from increasing ill health, he relinquished in May, 1866.

Hillsborough, Ohio. Wm H Woodson, nominated Mar 2; rejected Mar 19, 1867. He served for 18 months as quartermaster to Col Collins' cavalry, at or near *Fort Laramie*.

Van Wert, Ohio. Waldo T Davis, nominated on Apr 1 1867; rejected on Apr 5, 1867. Renominated Apr 18, 1867; rejected on Apr 19, 1867. Mr Davis entered the military service as a private, & was promoted through successive grades to capt in the 64th volunteer infty.

Van Wert, Ohio. Norman K Brown, nominated Apr 12, 1867; rejected Apr 13, 1867. He enlisted as a private early in 1861, & was honorably discharged after 4 months service. On the organization of the 64th Ohio volunteer infty he again enlisted as a private in that regt; remained to the close of the war; promoted to be it lt colonel. He left a lucrative business to serve his country; returned at its close disabled & without means of support.

Kalamazoo, Mich. Dr Foster Pratt, nominated & rejected on Mar 2, 1867. Dr Pratt entered the army in 1861 as a surgeon of the 13th Mich infty, & remained with his regt in the field until the close of the war.

Niles, Mich. Wm J Edwards, nominated & rejected on Mar 2, 1867. Enlisted as a private in the 6th Mich infty in Aug, 1861, promoted for good conduct throught the intervening grades to a captaincy; honorably mustered out in the fall of 1865 with his regt.

Battle Creek, Mich. Edw Van Demark, nominated & rejected on Mar 2, 1867. He enlisted as private in Merrill's Horse, in the fall of 1861, & served with credit to himself for his entire 3 years' enlistment.

Three Rivers, Mich. Chas W Fonda, nominated & rejected on Mar 2, 1867. Mr Fonda served in the army as adjutant of the 19th Mich infty, & his record as a soldier is irreproachable.

St John's, Mich. Lt Richd Baylis, nominated on Aug 20, 1866; rejected on Mar 28, 1867. Lt Baylis served with distinction in the army, & was honorably mustered out for wounds received in battle. He served for a time upon the staff of Maj Gen Geo A Custer, meeting with that ofcr's entire approbation.

Ann Arbor, Mich. Richd Beahan, appointed on Mar 15; rejected on Mar 19, 1867. Capt Beahan raised & gallantly commanded a company in the 14th Mich infty during the late war. His devotion to his country was manifested in various battles.

Saginaw, Mich. Capt Edw Saunders, nominated on Mar 21,1867; rejected on Mar 28, 1867. Capt Saunders served faithfully in the army until the close of the war as a captain in the 29th Mich infty. His reputation as a soldier is unblemished.

Owasso, Mich. Wm K Tillotson, appointed on Sep 3, 1866; rejected on Apr 5, 1867. Mr Tillotson entered the military service in 1861, & remained until the close of the war; was honorably mustered out as a 1st lt in the 5th Mich infty. His disabled left hand, incurred in the service of his county, & incapacitating him from active labor, attests his devotion to the flag.

Donaquiac, Mich. Wm Hazlett, nominated & rejected on Mar 2, 1867. He entered the military service as 2nd lt of Co M, 1st Mich cavalry; honorably mustered out after 3 years.

Delphi, Ind. Saml M Graham, nominated on Jul 23, 1866; not acted upon. Again nominated & rejected on Mar 2, 1867. He served a 3 year term of enlistment in the 2nd Indiana cavalry.

Warsaw, Ind. Andrew G Wood, appointed by the Pres on Nov 2, 1866; nominated & rejected by the Senate on Mar 2, 1867. Capt Wood entered the army as a private; receiving promotions for gallant & meritorious services, was mustered out as capt.

Aurora, Ind. Wash Stark, nominated on Mar 26; rejected on Mar 28, 1867. He was renominated for the position, on account of having served through the war.

Aurora, Ind. John L Giegoldt, nominated on Apr 9, 1867; rejected Apr 10, 1867. Capt Giegoldt received an honorable discharge, after honorable service, holding the rank of capt in the German regt of Indiana volunteers.

Bloomington, Ind. Wm D Voss, nominated Mar 2, 1867; not acted upon by the 39th Congress; was again nominated Apr 5, 1867, to the 40th Congress; rejected Apr 6, 1867. Mr Voss is a wounded soldier, incapacitated from labor, & is also represented by prominent citizens to be of unblemished moral character & excellent acquirements.

Jeffersonville, Ind. Jas N Patterson, appointed Oct 31, 1866; rejected Mar 18, 1867. Mr Patterson entered the service as 1st lt in Rousseau's regt, & served gallantly until loss of health obliged him to resign.

Muncie, Ind. Wm A McClellan, nominated on Mar 2, 1867; rejected by the Senate. Capt McClellan was a gallant & meritorious soldier, whose fortunes were identical with the glorious 84th Indiana infty.

Waulkgan, Ill. Chas Case, nominated on Mar 12, 1867; rejected on Mar 14, 1867. He served faithfully in the army, during the late war, & possessed all the qualities requisite for the discharge of the duties of the ofc.

Waulkgan, Ill. Walter Drew, nominated on Mar 18, 1867; rejected on Mar 28, 1867. He was a volunteer in the 96th regt Ill infty, & served on many battle fields, losing an arm on one occasion. His is liberally educated, & bears a most excellent character.

Waulkgan, Ill. Walter A Hastings, nominated on Apr 5, 1867; rejected on Apr 8, 1867. Capt Hastings was an ofcr in the 96th regt ill volunteers, & served for more than 3 years in the field; suffered a severe wound in one of the engagements in which he fought.

Waulkgan, Ill. Burtis B Stone, nominated on Apr 11, 1867; rejected on Apr 12, 1867. Lt Stone served in the army throughout the whole war, & the record made by him was such as any soldier might envy. His character is above reproach, & his competency was not doubted.

Woodstock, Ill. Orson H Crandell, nominated on Apr 1, 1867; rejected Apr 8, 1867. Dr Crandall served 4 years in the army during the late war as surgeon of the 21st Mo volunteers, & acquired a very high reputation in that capacity.

Fairburg, Ill. Moss Osman, nominated on Mar 16, 1867; rejected by the Senate. Maj Osman gave up most flattering business propects in order to do service in defence of his country. He was capt of Co A in the 104th Ill infty; brevetted major for gallant conduct before the enemy.

Waulkgan, Ill. Fielding B Roberts, nominated on Mar 15, 1867; rejeccted on Mar 28, 1867. Mr Roberts entered the army as private in the 61st Ill infty & served to the close of the war. He was wounded twice; 3 months a prisoner at Andersonville; his health is now much impaired, & his family is large.

Waulkgan, Ill. Jerome B Nulton, nominated on Apr 2, 1867; rejected on Apr 6, 1867. Col Nulton served to the close of the war as colonel of the 61st Ill infty. As a soldier he was active, vigilant & brave.

Carlinsville, Ill. Chas E Glass, nominated on Mar 8, 1867; rejected on Mar 14, 1867. Mr Glass served 3 years in the army as a private soldier; distinguished himself particularly at the battle of Pittsburg Landing; health is now much impaired, the result of disease contracted while in the service.

Charleston, Ill. Wm Jeffries, nominated on Feb 15, 1867; rejected on Mar 2, 1867. Lt Jeffries entered the service as a private in the 63rd Ill infty, & was promoted to a lieutenancy before the close of the war. He fough gallantly in many battles, & accompanied Gen Sherman in his march from Atlanta to N C.

Pekin, Ill. Edw L Williams, nominated Feb 15, 1867; rejected Mar 1, 1867. Capt Williams first entered the service on Apr 17, 1861, as private in the 8th regt Ill infty; remained in the army 3 years; was promoted to capt for meritorious conduct; at the last call for volunteers he was made capt of a company in the 146th Ill infty; was in active service in that capacity until the regt was mustered out at the close of the war; his health was much damaged by the hardships he underwent in the field.

Canton, Ill. Aarom Amsler, nominated Jan 29, 1867; rejected Feb 23, 1867. Lt Amsley was an ofcr of the 103rd Ill infty; served in the 15th army corps, Army of the Tenn, for a long period; was with Gen Sherman in all his campaigns; many ofcrs vear testimony to his high moral character, & efficient manner he discharged every duty.

Canton, Ill. Theo W Thornton, nominated on Apr 1, 1867; rejected by the Senate. He made for himself a most enviable record during the war, & was recommended for this ofc under the belief that few possessed greater capacity for the discharge of its duties to the satisfaction of the community.

Clinton, Ill. John B Wolf, nominated on Feb 15, 1867; no action taken; renominated on Mar 25, 1867; rejected Mar 28, 1867. He served during the war in the 107th regt Ill infty, & acquitted himself on all occasions in the most soldierly manner; well educated, very popular; of most upright principles.

Elgin, Ill. Jonathan Kimball, nominated on Feb 12, 1867; rejected on Feb 23, 1867. Lt Col Kimball entered the army as a private in the 7th Ill infty, the first regt raised in that State after the commencement of the war. He was in continuous service until Apr, 1866, when he was honorably mustered out as lt colonel of the 58th Ill infty.

Genesco, Ill. Jeremiah Ackley, nominated on Mar 9, 1867; rejected on Mar 14, 1867. Maj Ackley spent 3½ years in the army, entering it as a private, & discharged with the rank of major. He was wounded 3 times, & once so severely that its effects will be painfully felt through life.

Havanna, Ill. David Sollenberger, nominated on Mar 26, 1867; rejected by the Senate. Capt Sollenberger served most honorably for 3 years in the 2nd regt Ill cavalry.

Kewana, Ill. Orville D Bassett, nominated on Feb 12, 1867; rejected on Mar 2, 1867. Mr Bassett was a member of the 42nd regt Ill infty & was distinguished for his bravery during the war. His health was impaired by long & arduous service.

Lacon, Ill. Stephen W Cummins, nominated on Feb 12, 1867; rejected on Feb 23, 1867. Mr Cummins entered the army as a private in the 11th Ill infty, Co B, in Jul, 1861, & served faithfully in various parts of the South for 4 years. He was at one time dangerously wounded both in the arm & hip, & is now somewhat crippled. His father, now an aged man, was a soldier during the war of 1812, & fought at New Orleans under Gen Jackson. Both father & son are now somewhat in dependent circumstances; & this appointment could not have been given to a person more capable or deserving.

Lockport, Ill. Harvey S Weeks, nominated on Feb 12, 1867; rejected on Feb 23, 1867. The capacity & general fitness of Mr Weeks for this appointment were unquestioned. He served gallantly during the war as a member of the Chicago Mercantile Battery, & at the end of 3 years was honorably discharged.

Quincy, Ill. Wm R Lockwood, nominated on Feb 12, 1867; rejected on Feb 23, 1867. Col Lockwood served ably during the war as principal ofcr of the 33rd regt Ill volunteers.

Quincy, Ill. Henry V Sullivan, nominated on Mar 2, 1867; rejected on Mar 25, 1867. Maj Sullivan's services in the army were of a most valuable character.

Rock Island, Ill. Jas F Copp, nominated on Feb 12, 1867; rejected on Feb 24, 1867. Capt Copp entered the service as orderly sgt of the 89th Ill infty; badly wounded at Stone River; recovered in season to participate in Gen Sherman's march from Chattanooga to Atlanta, & fought gallantly in almost every battle of that campaign; distinguished himself in the battle of Nashville, & when mustered out had reached the rank of captain.

Rock Island, Ill. Henry C Connelly, nominated on Mar 8, 1867; rejected on Mar 11, 1867. Maj Connelly was an ofcr of the 14th Ill cavalry; was one of those mainly instrumental in capturing the famous raider, John Morgan. His character as a lawyer & citizen is above reproach.

Rock Island, Ill. Wm D Williams, nominated Mar 15, 1867; rejected on Mar 28, 1867. Very few ofcrs served in the late war with better claims for distinction than Col Williams; ofcr of the 89th regt Ill infty; he displayed from Stone river to Nashville all the qualities which make men loved & respected. His associates of the 4th army corps, Army of the Cumberland, have born willing testimony to his many gallant deeds.

Champaign, Ill. Joshua Dickerson, nominated on Feb 12, 1867; rejected on Feb 23, 1867; renominated on Apr 20; rejected again by the Senate. Mr Dickerson enlisted in the army during the summer of 1861; was honorably discharged as orderly sgt of Co C, 38th Ill infty, at the expiration of 4 years' continuous service.

Jerseyville, Ill. Jos H Buffington, nominated on Feb 12, 1867; rejected on Feb 20, 1867. Mr Buffington, with 2 of his sons, served in the Union army during the rebellion.

Jerseyville, Ill. Mr Clark C Buffington, nominated on Apr 5, 1867; rejected on Apr 8, 1867. Mr C C Buffington served in the Union army; was renominated on Apr 20 following; rejected on the same day.

Jerseyville, Ill. Jas S Daniels, nominated on Apr 11, 1867; rejected by the Senate. Mr Daniels was likewise a Union soldier.

Paris, Ill. Wm S Cook, nominated on Feb 12, 1867; rejected by the Senate. A most honorable career of 3 years in the army during the late war caused Mr Cook to be very generally recommended by his fellow citizens for this appointment.

Shelbyville, Ill. H M Pedon, nominated by Mar 21, 1867; rejected on Mar 28, 1867. Capt Pedon served through the war with merit, as an ofcr of the 14th Ill infty.

Litchfield, Ill. B M Burnett, nominated on Apr 5, 1867; rejected on Apr 8, 1867. He enlisted in the army in Jun, 1861, & was honorably discharged after 4 years of arduous & continuous service.

Litchfield, Ill. Danl McLennan, nominated on Arp 17, 1867; rejected on the same day. He was formerly a capt in the 32nd Ill infty.

Litchfield, Ill. Robt N Peyden, nominated on Apr ; rejected on Apr 20.

Sparta, Wisc. Saml Hoyt, nominated on Feb 15, 1867; rejected on Mar 1, 1867. Mr Hoyt enlisted in the beginning of the war; served 3 years in the 1st Wisc battery in the most faithful manner.

Oshkosh, Wisc. Chas W Felker, nominated on Feb 12, 1867; rejected on Feb 21, 1867. Capt Felker acquitted himself most honorably while serving in the army.

Fond du Lac, Wisc. Edw S Bragg, nominated on Feb 1, 1867; rejected on Feb 23, 1867. Sacrificing a lucrative professional business, his ardor led him to accept a captaincy in the 6th Wisc infty on May 5, 1861; served for a long period in the Iron Brigade of the Army of the Potomac; was promoted until he attained the full rank of brig gen, & remained in the army until the close of the war.

Janesville, Wisc. Wm Ruger, nominated on Feb 1, 1867; rejected on Feb 25, 1867. Capt Ruger was one of a family of 4 brothers, all of whom hastened to the field in the early part of the war, one of whom, [Thos H Ruger,] reached the rank of brevet major general before its close. Capt Ruger entered the service as adjutant of the 13th Wisc infty, & was most actively engaged throughout the West & Southwest until a very severe wound [which caused him to be left on the field,] received at New Hope Church, during the Atlanta campaign, compelled his retirement from the army.

Columbus, Wisc. Chas L Derring, nominated on Mar 14, 1867; nomination was not acted on by the Senate. Lt Derring's service in the army was of long duration & of the most gratifying character, both to himself & friends.

Columbus, Wisc. Harvey K Dodge, nominated on Feb 12, 1867; rejected on Feb 25, 1867. Lt Dodge enlisted in the 1st Wisc infty in the early part of the war, & served for a long period in the Army of the Cumberland, on all occasions performing his duties with zeal, energy & bravery.

Red Wing, Minn. W W DeKay, appointed on Aug 21, 1866; rejected on Mar 2, 1867. Capt DeKay served 3 years in the army.

Cedar Falls, Iowa. W H McClure, appointed on Aug 20, 1866; rejected on Mar 14, 1867. Lt McClure at the breaking out of the rebellion abandoned a large & lucrative business. He was severely wounded at Pea Ridge, Arkansas, from which he has never recovered.

Fort Madison, Iowa. W C Hershberge, appointed on Nov 6, 1866; rejected on Mar 28, 1867. Lt Hershberge enlisted in the army Jan 23, 1862; re-enlisted as a veteran Feb 25, 1864; promoted to 2nd lt Jan 4, 1865; honorably discharged Aug 2, 1865.

Independence, Iowa. Warren Barnhart, appointed on Oct 5, 1866; rejected on Mar 8, 1867. Mr Barnhart served his country honorably during the late war.

Marshalltown, Iowa. John E Page, appointed on Sep 19, 1867; rejected on Mar 2, 1867. Capt Page was for more than 3½ years a soldier & prisoner of war, & was severely wounded.

Washington, Iowa. H W Anderson, nominated on Mar 18, 1867; rejected on Apr 5, 1867. Mr Anderson served as a private soldier in the 19th Iowa infty.

St Joseph, Mo. Geo H Hall, appointed on Nov 17, 1866; rejected Mar 18, 1867. Gen Hall was a brave & faithful soldier through the late unhappy struggle in our country.

Harrisburg, May 12. Some time ago two brothers name Look, from Lancaster, Pa, were brutally murdered near Vicksburg, where they were opening a plantation. The Govn'r of Pa offered a reward for the murderers; today he received a despatch from Gen Gillem at Vicksburg, announcing the capture of two brothers named C L & A R Broome, who are the alleged murderers.

Orphans Court of Wash Co, D C. Letters testamentary on the personal estate of Mary Ann Fearson, late of Wash City, D C, deceased. –Mary Julia Barrett, excx

Dept of the Interior, U S Patent Ofc, Wash, May 10, 1867. Ptn of Jas C Cooke, of Middleton, Conn, praying for the extension of a patent granted to him Jul 27, 1852, & reissued Apr 7, 1863, for an improvement in forming Button Backs & Connecting the Eyes thereto, for seven years from the expiration of said patent, which takes place on Jul 27, 1866. -T C Theaker, Com'r of Patents

On Wed Wm H Seymour, residing in Hampshire, Kane Co, Ohio, shot Wm H Seymour, his son, dead. The son was given to violent bursts of passion, in which condition he would abuse his father in most violent terms. He had seized his father & undertook to put him out of the house, when the father seized a gun & discharged its contents into his bowels. He died almost immediately.

Administrix's sale of Coal Ofc, scales, etc, by order of the Orphans Court of D C.; sale on May 15, at the foot of 6th st & the canal; belonging to the late Woodford Stone. –Mary A Stone, admx -Cooper & Latimer, aucts

N Y, May 11. The steamer **Arizona** brings Panama advices to the 4th. Cmder Leonard Paulding, of the steamer **Wateree**, died of dysentery on Apr 29. Deceased was a son of Admiral Paulding, & leaves a wife & 3 children. [May 18th newspaper: He was a native of N Y C, & had been 27 years in the navy, during which time he had been less than 2 years unemployed; his health had been rapidly failing for some months prior to his decease; on Apr 25 he was seized with acute dysentery; his burial took place on the 30th; he was buried in the naval cemetery on the island of Flamenco, an island uninhabited save by the dead. He was widely known in Gtwn.]

TUE MAY 14, 1867

A despatch received in this city from a member of Mr G E H Day's family, dated St Louis, bring intelligence that Judge Day died on his way to his former home in St Anthony, Minn. Mr Day's health has been failing for a number of months. His family, in deference to his wishes, left this city with him on Tuesday, Apr 30th on their way to St Anthony, although it was believed by many of his friends that he would not reach Minnesota alive.

A cable despatch of May 11 announces the death of Jos A Wright, U S Minister to Prussia; he was a native of Pa; when a young man emigrated to Indiana; elected to Congress from Indiana in 1843; elected Govn'r of Indiana in 1849 until 1857; was in 1857 appointed by Pres Buchanan the Minister to Prussia, which position he held until the accession of Mr Lincoln to the Presidency. He returned to this country in 1861, & acting with the War Democrats, was in 1862 elected U S Senator from Indiana, serving one session. In 1863 Pres Lincoln appointed him U S Com'r to the Hamburg Exhibition. He was appointed Minister to Prussia a second time, by Pres Johnson, in 1865, & continued to fill that position up to the time of his death.

Yesterday a soldier, Jerome Gary, formerly a member of Co G, 44th N Y infty, was drowned by bathing in Rock Creek. He was an inmate of Kalorama Hospital. His body was recovered, & his friends in N Y were notified of the sad calamity.

Richmond, Va, May 13. Jefferson Davis released on bail of $100,000, for his appearance at the Circuit Court of the U S for the District of Va, to be held at Richmond, Va, on the fourth Monday of Nov next. Acknowledged this thirteenth day of May, 1867. The names of the sureties were severally called, & they repaired to the clerk's desk & signed the paper:

Jefferson Davis
Horace Greeley, N Y
Augustus Schell, N Y
Aristides Welch, Phil
David K Jackman, Phil
W H McFarland, Richmond
Richd Barton Haxall, Richmond
Isaac Davenport, Richmond
Abraham Warwick, Richmond

Gusavus A Myers, Richmond
Jas Lyons, Richmond
Wm W Crump, Richmmond
John A Meredith, Richmond
Wm H Lyons, Richmond
John Minor Botts, Va
Thos W Doswell, Va
Jas Thomas, jr, Richmond

The name of Horace F Clark, of N Y, was added, as he having sent a note for that purpose. When the name of John Minor Botts was called it was hissed. Mr Chandler said the requisite number had been obtained, with the exception of two or three only. The Court: The Marshall will discharge the prisoner. The Marshal did so, when deafening applause followed. Mr Davis stood up closely pressed on all sides. Old friends heartily congratulated him, while a number of strangers were introduced. Mr Davis was greeted with cheers as he left the court room; both by those who followed & the crowds on the streets.
+
Richmond, May 13. Jefferson Davis, on his release, telegraphed his brother, Jos C Davis, in Miss, the fact, & informed him he would write from N Y. Mr Davis & wife visited the grave of their son at a late hour this evening at ***Hollywood Cemetery***. The first names signed to the bail bond after that of Jefferson Davis are, Horace Greeley, Augustus Schell, of N Y, & John Minor Botts. It is stated that the grand jury has indicted John C Breckinridge, Judge H W Thomas, of Fairfax, & four others for treason. Jefferson Davis & family went on board the ship **Niagara** tonight at 10 o'clock. She sails for N Y tomorrow morning. He goes thence to Canada.

Berlin, May 13. The funeral of the late American Minister, Gov Wright, took place today, & was attended by all the American residents & visitors here, & by a large number of citizens of Berlin.

Mrs Henry Mohwinkle & her 3 children had a terrible fall from the 3rd story of a tenement house, in Cincinnati, on Wed. In the rear of the structure for drying clothes, is a bridge that connects with the house. While all were on the bridge it gave way. The two oldest children sustained fractures of the skull & will not survive; the mother was badly bruised, & baby was uninjured.

Saml H Wentz was sentenced on Sat to 6 years imprisonment in the city jail at Balt, he having previously plead guilty to the charge of embezzlement & misapplication of the funds of the Nat'l Mechanics' Bank.

Hickman [Ky] Courier. Miss Mary Godsy, living nearby, has been asleep for 12 years. At age 12, after an ague fit, she went to sleep, & has been in a state of coma most of the time since. She wakes at intervals for the purpose of yawning, but soon sinks into a slumber again. She has grown considerably, & preserves her beauty & flesh.

For sale: I offer my valuable mill property, on Rock Creek, adjoining the cities of Wash & Gtwn; the house is large & commodious; attached is a miller's house, stabling, etc. Apply at 55 Water st. –Evan Lyons, Gtwn

WED MAY 15, 1867
Sir Hypolite La Fontaine, Bart, the last baronet of royal patent in Canada, died at his residence, in Montreal, on Friday.

Orphans Court-Judge Purcell. 1-An exemplified copy of the will of Matilda E Van Ness, deceased, from the Surrogate's Court, N Y, was filed & ordered to be admitted to probate & record. 2-The will of Ellen Toner was partially proven. 3-The will of Jos S Mansfield, deceased, was admitted to probate & record, & letters testamentary issued to Saml A H McKim; bond $10,000. 4-The will of Wm Barbour, deceased, was admitted to probate & record & personalty, & letters testamentary issued to D Rittenhouse Shuman; bond $1,000. 5-Letters of administration on the personal estate of Sarah Patterson, deceased, were granted to Jas Penkey; bond $500. 6-The first account of Saml W Owen, guardian to his infant children, the first account of W E Morcoe, guardian to Mary V, Wm E, Florence E, & D Walker Howard, infant heirs of Martha E Howard, deceased, & the first & final account of Saml W Owen, guardian to Mary E Owen [now Edwards] were approved & passed.

Mr John B Sayres for several years past superintendent of the Wash & Gtwn railroad, has resigned his position.

Died: on May 13, at his residence near Laytonsville, Montg Co, Md, Benj Bohrer, in his 63rd year. His funeral will be this evening, May 15, from the chapel in *Oak Hill Cemetery*. [No time is given.]

Died: on May 5, in PG Co, Md, Eliz Sibley, in her 81st year, & John T Sibley, in his 49th year. [Marlboro Gazette copy.]

Died: on May 14, Richd Barry, in his 63rd year. His funeral will take place from his late residence, 28 Missouri ave, between 4½ & 6th sts, at 10 o'clock Thu morning, & proceed to St Peter's Church, Capitol Hill, where the funeral services will be performed.

Trustee's sale of valuable improved property & water power, near Gtwn, D C, at auction on Jun 6th, 1867; by deed of trust from John S Berry & Co, to the subscriber, made Feb 23, 1856, recorded amongst the land records of D C, in Liber J A S No 111, folio 303: that portion of the old Foundry property, lying west of Gtwn [excepting the section including the two stone mills assigned to D L Shoemaker & Brother, by articles recorded in Liber J A S No 147, folio 306, & the extreme eastern angle conveyed by John Corcoran, by deed recorded in Liber J A S, No 203, folio 35.] On the property to be sold is a very valuable Distillery & fixtures, now in successful operation. -Hugh Caperton, trustee -Thos Dowling, auct

Valuable Fairfax land for sale; by decree of the County Court of Fairfax Co, rendered in the case of Jackson vs Jackson, I will sell, on Jun 17, 1867, at the Fairfax Court House, the valuable Hotel, at Dranesville, formerly kept by Geo W Jackson. –Jas T Jackson, Com'r of Sale

Orphans Court of Wash Co, D C. Letters testamentary on the personal estate of Wm Barbour, late of Wash, D C, deceased. –D Ritt Sherman, exc

Louisville, May 14. The remains of the late Bishop Saville, of the Roman Catholic Church, who died at Bardstown, Ky, on Sat, reached here today & were escorted to the Cathedral by about 8,000 people. The remains will be in state at the Cathedral.

Fortress Monroe, May 14. The steamer **Niagara** arrived at Norfolk this afternoon, with Mr Davis & family & Miss Powell among the passengers. She sailed tonight for N Y. Mr Davis visited the fortress this afternoon.

San Francisco, May 12. The wife of Gov McCormick died suddenly at Prescott on Apr 30th.

Trustee's sale of valuable real estate in St Mary's Co, Md; by decree of the Circuit Court for St Mary's Co, dated May 13, 1867, at the Court-house door, in Leonardtown, St Mary's Co, on Jun 6: a tract of land known as ***Deep Falls***, containing 498 acres, more or less; dwlg house is large, well built, & commodious; numerous out-bldgs. Also, tract of land known as ***Wicomico Fields***, a part of the estate of the late Gov Jas Thomas, known as ***Motley Hall***, containing 289 acres, more or less; bldg improvements consist of a new Tenant's House, & necessary farm bldgs. –D S Briscoe, F Stone, trustees

THU MAY 16, 1867
Under our obituary head is an announcement of the death of Mrs McNerhany, wife of Francis McNerhany, of Wash City. For near 2 years his household has been one of affliction, sickness, & death. Mother, children, & other dear relatives have yielded to the dread destroyer. Several young children are left without that instruction which is indispensable to the formation of the youthful character. Alone he takes up the duty of father & protector.
+
Died: on May 15, aged 35 years, Margaret, beloved wife of Francis McNewhany. Her funeral will take place from her late residence, 460 I st, between 6th & 7th sts, on May 17, at 9½ o'clock A M, & proceed to St Peter's Church, Capitol Hill, where services will be performed at 10 A M.

Died: on May 14, Richd Barry, in his 63rd year. His funeral will take place from his late residence, 28 Missouri ave, between 4½ & 6th sts, at 10 o'clock Thu, & proceed to St Peter's Church, Captiol Hill, where the funeral services will be performed.
+
Obit: Mr Richd Barry departed this life after an illness of some weeks' duration. This gentleman has filled with honor offices of importance & distinction in our midst, where he has for many years enjoyed the esteem & confidence of all who have known him. For many years he was the secretary of the Board of Common Council of Wash City. He also held Gov't positions of importance.

Died: Wed, Georgie, only son of Joana F & Geo T Bright, U S N. His funeral will take place this afternoon, at 4 o'clock, from the residence of Mrs Bright, 294 B st.

The following persons were killed by the explosion of the steamer **Lansing**, running between Rock Island, Ill, & Port Byron, on Tues: Geo White, pilot; Wm Wassign, cook; Jas Tracy, fireman; W H Noble, of Burlington, & W H Beebe, of Colara. H Curtis, of Dubuque, is missing & supposed to be drowned.

On Monday Marshall F Harris, of Wethersfield, Conn, while on his way from New Haven to N Y, was robbed of $5,000 in bank notes, along with some articles of wearing apparel, by a man named Francis H Lyons, with whom he became acquainted on the steamer **Elm City**, & who, by invitation, shared Mr Harris stateroom with him. The thief has been arrested.

A Cuban, named Garrette, was burned to death at Steubenville, Ohio, on Tuesday. His linen coat, which he was wearing, took fire from a gas jet.

Yesterday Geo W Burch, alias Wm Mortimer, was arrested & committed to stand trial for the robbery of Jabez Jay's boot store, on May 1, & the shooting of Pvt Jos Williams, of the 3rd Ward Police, on last Christmas morning.

Mobile, May 15. During the melee last night Tabril Alsen was killed; Saml Britton, [colored,] was killed; Thos Taylor, D H Howard, David Parsons, of police, were wounded; L B Sebury & Goldsmith I Gouch, both colored, were wounded. All is perfectly quiet today. It is reported that Dr Nicholson & Pierre Mitchell have since died.

Wheeling, Va, May 15. Folger, who murdered Dinsmore in Dec last, was executed at Wash, Pa, this afternoon. He reaffirmed his former confession of the complicity of young Montgomery, son of Hon W Montgomery, who was tried at the last session of the Circuit Court & cleared. Folger's confession produced a profound sensation in the community.

Mrd: on May 14, by Rev Mr Ames, O M Loomis, of Pitsburgh, Pa, to Ann N Welsh, daughter of M M Welsh, of Wash City.

Dissolution of the copartnership existing between A J Radcliffe & W H Tenney, by mutual consent, having expired by limitation. –A J Radcliffe, W H Tenney
+
W H Tenney has resumed the business at his old stand, 125 Bridge st, corner of High; having had 30 years experience in the Grocery Business.

Dept of the Interior, U S Patent Ofc, Wash, May 10, 1867. Ptn of Thos Crossley, of Bridgeport, Conn, praying for the extension of a patent granted to him Aug 16, 1853, for an improvement in Printed Carpets, for seven years from the expiration of said patent, which takes place on Aug 16, 1867. -T C Theaker, Com'r of Patents

Orphans Court of Wash Co, D C, May 11, 1867. In the case of Wm H Frear, adm of Chas B Wilder, deceased, the administrator & Court have appointed Jun 4th next, for the final settlement of the personal estate of the said deceased, of the assets in hand. -Jas R O'Beirne, Reg/o wills

For sale: some fine farms near Wash City, several on the line of the railroad now being made from this city to the Point of Rocks. –F Mace, 517 7th st.

FRI MAY 17, 1867

Cmdor Danl B Ridgely has been assigned to duty as a member of the Board of Visitors to the Naval Academy, & Acting Volunteer Lt Cmder H H Garrenge to the command of the U S steamer **Guard**.

Hon Isaac Newton, Com'r of Agriculture, left this city yesterday for Pa, where he goes to recuperate his health. John W Stokes, formerly Chief Clerk of the Dept, has been recalled to that position, & is now acting Com'r during Mr Newton's absence.

Phil, May 16. Thos Leis, who was yesterday acquitted of the murder of Geo Eiler in the Criminal Court room last Feb, on the ground of insanity, was brought before the court this morning upon a application for his discharge, he now being perfectly same. The prisoner was discharged.

By telegram it is learned that the French steamer **Pereire** arrived safely at Brent on May 14, from N Y, which port she left on May 4. Archbishop Spalding, Prof N R Smith, & other prominent citizens of Balt took passage by this steamer. –Balt Sun

Rochester Democrat of Sat. Two boys, Frank Vance & Jas Callahan, were on the river at Charlotte, picking up drift wood, when they saw the body of a dead man. The boys towed it to shore. It was identified as the body of Louis Fox, the celebrated billiard player, whose mysterious disappearance on Dec 4 last created much excitement. Mrs C A Kellogg is the last person known to have conversed with him. There is no reason why Mr Fox should have committed suicide, as his family relations were satisfactory & his pecuniary circumstances were good. Mr Fox had an insurance of $2,000 upon his life, which his heirs have never been able to collect, owing to the impossibility of furnishing proof of his death.

Very valuable & desirable residence in Gtwn, D C, at auction: on May 22, in front of the premises, I will see the residence of the late M de Bodisco, Russian Minister. This property fronts 70 feet on 2nd st, between Frederick & Market sts, entending back 194 feet. The house is large & substantially built, containing 14 rooms, besides good basement & attic rooms, with fine dry cellar, with wash-house, smoke-house, etc, convenient & in good order. Possession on Jun 17 next. -Thos Dowling, auct

Greenbrier White Sulphur Springs will be opened on Jun 1, 1867.
–Geo L Peyton & Co

Phil, May 16. A man named Jas Schafer, today, cut his wife's throat with a razor & then cut his own. His wife may recover, but he cannot. The parties reside in the extreme southern part of the city.

N Y, May 16. Abraham McFarland, for over 20 years connected with the Commercial Advertiser, died this evening.

$200 reward for recovery of a pair of dark bay Horses & conviction of the thief. –Jno B Clagett, Brightwood Post Ofc, D C

SAT MAY 18, 1867
Hon Geo Bancroft, of N Y, appointed by the Pres, Envoy Extraordinary & Minister Plenipotentiary of the U S at Berlin, vice Jas A Wright, deceased.

Phil Ledger, May 17. Yesterday a young man, Jas Poyner, a teamster by occupation, who resided with his grandmother, Mrs Maria Shaffer, 633 Wharton st, made an attempt to murder his cousin, Miss Maria O Craft, by cutting her throat, after which he drew the razor across his own throat, inflicting a serious wound. Poyner & Miss Crawford had been brought up by the grandmother, & he is said to have proposed marriage, which she would not listen to on account of their near relationship. She is about 16 & Poyner was 26. The grandfather of Poyner & Miss Curtis, Jas Shaffer, is a well known teamster of the lower part of the city. At a late hour last evening Poyner was still alive in the Pennsylvania Hospital.

Powell Griscom was accidentally killed last night at Texas, Balt Co, by falling from a wood train of cars under the wheels, which passed over his body. He was instantly killed. Mr Griscom resided at Texas, & was the proprietor of a stone quarry there, employing a large number of persons. –Balt American

Thos Dowling, auct, sold a 2 story brick house on 4th st, between Market & Frederick sts, to Mr Jacob Staub, for $300.

Alexandria Gaz of yesterday. Several of our male schools had their usual May excursions in to the country yesterday, one of them under the charge of Capt Wm E Baker. While he was with some boys exploring an excavation made by soldiers during the late war, termed The Wild Man's Cave, some of the smaller boys strayed to the Alexandria canal to bathe, & one, Jas Arthur Carlin, eldest son of Mr Wm H Carlin, conductor on the Alexandria, Loudoun, & Hampshire railroad, was drowned. Young Carlin was a bright boy, aged about 14 years. No blame can be attached to Capt Baker in the matter, as the boys had been expressly forbidden by him to go into the water at all.

Detroit, Mich, May 17. Horrible murder last night in East Saginaw; Edw R King, a shoemaker, stabbed a blacksmith, John Seely, with a knife several times, causing immediate death. The murderer escaped.

Buffalo, May 16. This afternoon the roof of the Buffalo Union Puddling Mills, 90 x 200 feet, fell in, burying 100 workmen in the debris. Killed were Chas B Milligan, Geo Pierce, Fred'k Foster, & Jas Murphey. Milligan was a native of Phil, aged 28 years, unmarried, & the foreman. His remains will be taken to Phil for burial. [May 20th newspaper: Fred'k Foster was a young lad who had just commenced work at the mills. Geo Pierce, foreman of the slaters, died shortly after reaching his residence. Injured: Ellis Hanson, August Chur, Adam Robbe, Jefferson Stephenson, Barney Kinney, Richd Peer, J F Tattoo, Dennis O'Leary, Michl Keating, & Chas Durgan.]

The draggers who have been searching for the body of Julia Forrest, who is supposed to have drowned herself on Tues night last, have been unsuccessful in their efforts.

Died: on May 16, at his residence 450 12th st, Archibald McNeill, in his 78th year. His funeral will take place tomorrow, Sunday, at 2 o'clock P M.

Boston, May 17. A young woman, Alice C Abbott, has been arrested on the charge of causing the death of her stepfather, Washington Pickering, by poison.

Mr J McCrummill, Grand Master of the Grand Unite [colored] Order of Odd Fellows, died on May 12, at his home in Phil.

S B Hempstead, postmaster at Adel, Iowa, was arrested on Monday for robbing the mail. A detective mailed a decoy to his ofc containing money. The marked money was found in the postmaster's possession.

Public sale of valuable real estate in Culpeper Co, Va; by decree of the Circuit Court of Culpeper Co, in the suit of Miller, etc, vs Miller, etc, & Barbour etc, vs Barbour: sale on Jun 8, of a tract of land in said county known as the *Fleetwood Estate*, near Brandy Station, containing about 1,500 acres. –J Y Menefee, J C Gibson, Com'rs

MON MAY 20, 1867
Orphans Court-Judge Purcell, May 17, 1867. 1-The last will & testament of Chas Keenan, of Wash City, D C, deceased, was partially proven. He appointed therein his wife, Eliz Keenan, as his executrix. 2-The last will & testament of Mary Ann Magee, of Wash, D C, deceased, was admitted to probate & record. She nominates therein Augustus E Perry as her executor, & letters of administration were granted to the same; bond $6,000. 3-The last will & testament of Ellen Toner, of Wash, D C, deceased, was partially proven. She appoints therein her sister, Eliza Heinson, as her executrix. 4-The first & final account of Robt White, adm of Wm Hardy, deceased; the fourth account of Harriet Donohoo, guardian to Francis C Donohoo, orphan of John A Donohoo, deceased, the first account of Jas Tyler, guardian to Jas W Tyler orphan of Dr Allen Tyler, deceased, & the fifth account of John Shanahan, guardian to Catharine Temocley & John Scanlon, orphans of the Thos Scanlon, deceased, were approved & passed. 5-Wm Queen was appointed guardian to Chas Posey, minor heir of Richmond Posey, deceased; bond $1,000.

The Exchange Hotel in Richmond was robbed of diamonds to the value of $800; a young man named Thos W Russell was arrested & locked up at police headquarters; he is from St Louis, & belongs to a fraternity distinctively known as hotel thieves.

Obit-died: Meeting of the Third Auditor's Ofc, held to announce the death of their friend & associate, Archibald McNeill. –A M Gangewher, chairman
-A L Hazelton, sec

Hon Wm A Graham, of North Carolina, has been pardoned by the President.

A despatch from St Paul, Minn, announces that Moses A Hawks, who killed his wife to get the insurance on her life, has been indicted for murder in the first degree. The lady was a young bride, & was killed by the discharge of a pistol which her husband was cleaning.

Furnished house to let. The undersigned, whose family will spend the summer North, desires to let the House he now occupies, on 4th st, for 3 months from Jun 10th. It will not be rented as a boarding house. –D E Somes, 476 7th st, opposite the Post Ofc.

Orphans Court of Wash Co, D C. Letters testamentary on the personal estate of Mary Ann Magee, late of Wash City, D C, deceased. –Augustus E Perry, exc

TUE MAY 21, 1867

The following promotions have been made in the Treasury Dept: Wm H Armstrong, O F Dana, John T Crone, & A H Sawyer, from first to second class; C W Eldridge & J H Mott, from second to third class; G B Heywood & C C Adams, from third to fourth class clerkships in the Internal Revenue Bureau. C C Walden, from first to second class in the Second Comptroller's Ofc; S E Gough, from first to second class in the ofc of the Com'r of Customs; W F Clark, from second to third class in the secretary's ofc; T A Gilmore, E S Jones, F E Garnet, A H Parke, & C H Townsend, from first to second class in the loan branch in the Secretary's ofc. S Yorke At Lee, librabian at the Treasury Dept, has been promoted from third to fourth class clerkship.

Mrs Haslett, wife of Mr Thos Haslett, of Westport, Jackson Co, Mo, committed suicide on May 2 by shooting herself through the heart with her husband's pistol. She had been laboring under mental depression caused by an imaginary fear that herself & family would come to want. She leaves a husband & 4 children.

Coroner Woodward yesterday held an inquest at the residence of Mr T E W Feinour, 573 H st, on the body of Mr Lewis R Hopkins, who died at 11 o'clock Sunday night. Hopkins, age 23 years; purchased laudanum to the value of $1, at the drugstore of Mr E M Sears, on 11th st; he took about an ounce & a half; he died that night. The deceased was a coach-maker by trade, respectably connected, honest & sober.

On Sunday, Thos T Thompson, colored, died in a stable in the alley between C & C sts & 12th & 13th sts. He died from natural causes, & being a pauper, his remains were interred at the expense of the Corporation.

Orphans Court of Wash Co, D C, May 18, 1867. In the case of Sarah S Dougherty, excx of Lydia S English, deceased, the executrix & Court have appointed Jun 22 next, for the final settlement of the personal estate of the said deceased, of the assets in hand. -Jas R O'Beirne, Reg/o wills

N Y. May 20. In a club-room in Knox's bldg, Broadway & Fulton st, an ex-army ofcr, Frank B Fisher, committed suicide by shooting himself through the head.

Mrs Susan Green, wife of Jas W Green, a stone-cutter, who resides on Church st, Oregon Hill, two weeks ago gave birth to twins. Since then her physician, Dr Orlando Fairfax, has regarded her as partially deranged & cautioned the family to see that she had no opportunity to go out. Her husband has been very attentive & from exhaustion he fell asleep. She got up & went outside. A search disclosed her body in a well in the yard. Mrs Green was about 40 yearsof age, & leaves 8 children, including the infant twins, who are still alive & cared for. She also leaves a married daughter. –Richmong Whig, 17th

Died: on May 19, Lewis R Hopkins, son of the late Philip & Ann Maria Hopkins, formerly of Annapolis, Md, but for the last 25 years a resident of Wash City, aged 29 years. His funeral will take place from his late residence, 573 H st, between 4th & 5th sts, this afternoon at 4 o'clock.

Died: May 19, Eliza Eugenia, the beloved wife of Leroy C Bishop, in her 23rd year. Her funeral will be from her late residence, 512 12th st, near Pa ave, today at 4 P M.

Died: in Wash City, on the *29th instant, after a short & painful illness, Matthew E Duvall, of PG Co, Md, in his 49th year. His remainswill be taken to Page's Chapel on Wed, May 22nd inst, for interment. [*The date: 29th instant, copied as written.]

Died: on May 20, Miss Prudence Aiken, after an illness of several months, aged 72 years. Her funeral is this afternoon at 3 o'clock, from the residence of W N Rowe, 351 C st, between 4½ & 6th sts.

Application has been made to the Mayor of Wash for a deed to be issued to the undersigned, for all of lot 19 in Reservation 11, by virtue of a bond of conveyance from the Com'rs of Low Grounds, executed on or about Apr 3, 1826, to David A Hall, assignee of O B Brown, assignee of F May & T Sewall, who, at public sale made by said Com'rs on said day, were the purchasers of said Lot, the title to which by subsequent conveyance, has become vested in the undersinged, & the said bond properly belongs to her, but has been lost or mislaid to that it cannot be found. –Mary B Dayton Attest: C H Wiltberger, Sec Com'rs Low Grounds.

Supreme Court of D C, in Equity No 532. Presburg et al vs Jesse B Haw's administration & heirs. The above cause is referred to me to audit the account of the trustee & the claims of creditors; same to appear in my ofc, May 25.
—Walter S Cox, auditor

Elegant residence for sale; the house formerly occupied by the late Wm Noyes, & at present in the occupancy of Gen Davis; the main bldg is situated on the corner of West & Green sts, Gtwn, D C; is 4 stories high, contains 8 spacious rooms; & a back bldg of 5 rooms is attached. —Wm M Bryant, Real Estate Broker, 495 7th st.

Household & kitchen furniture at auction on May 24, at the residence of Wm Wilkinson, north K st, corner of 15th st. -Green & Williams, aucts

WED MAY 22, 1867
The solid men of Washington, together with the amount of their incomes, as appears from the returns made to the Collector of the Internal Revenue:

CmdorJ H Aulick, $7,872
Jas Alden, $2,384
C B Baker, $3,032
W D Baldwin, $3,260
Sarah H Coleman, $61,754
Dr Geo Clymer, $2,089
W W Corcoran, $35,353
John H Clarke, $3,421
Cornelia A Dikeman, $8,888
Dr D R Hagner, $2,820
W S Huntington, $13,091
S Phillips Lee, $3,450
Saml V Niles, $5,877
L F Pourtales, $2,128
B Ogle Tayloe, $6,377
John F Webb, $4,135
Capt H A Wise, $2,169
John Alexander, $6,7980
R J Atkinson, $5,911
D J Bishop, $2,437
N W Burchell, $3,225
Mary J Blair, $3,305
Mrs F Blanchard, $10,188
R A Crawford, $7,200
Catharine Cruit, $2,036
H A Chadwick, $21,890
John Chapman, &9,987
W W Danenhower, $3,453
Jas W Denver, $16,693
Mrs Jane Farnham, $2,687

M W Galt, $9,870
Dr W P Johnson, $16, 153
A T Keickhoeffer, $11,117
John T Lenman, $8,812
J H Lathrope, $6,920
Thos A McLaughlin, $3,062
Danl McFarland, $2,706
John McLellan, $7,758
Allison Nailor, $4,132
R W Pearson, $2,743
Geo H Plant, $12,702
G A W Randall, $2,795
H C Swain, $2,836
Thos A Stevens, $2,538
Jas J Shedd, $4,079
A B Stoughton, $7,092
Thos M Shepherd, $2,757
Wm E Spalding, $2,000
Jos Travers, $6,357
Michl Talty, $3,429
Geo H Wakefield, $7,743
Harvey M Waterson, $7,200
Caleb C Willard, $17,056
Jos F Brown, $4,200
John A Baker, $4,080
Wilson E Brown, $3,902
H S Davis, $3,910
Henry D Cooke, $69,659
Jos B Bryan, $2,681
Saml Bacon, $4,030

John W Boteler, $4,063
Jos H Bradley, $7,261
Wm H Clagett, $4,919
P M Dubant, $2,687
Jas Y Davis, $10,593
W D Davidge, $8,505
John F Ellis, $2,261
M G Emery, $7,897
Jas Bryan, $3,481
W A Bradley, $8,176
John R Elvans, $3,099
Peregrine W Browning, $3,058
Marshall Brown, $20,015
Wm Bates, $3,408
Fitzhugh Coyle, $3,195
Geo W Cochran, $7,969
Thos J Durant, $7,344
J E Clarke, $7,193
Thos Ewing, jr, $5,712
C B Church, $4,403
Jerome Callahan, $2,230
R B Donaldson, $3,068
Alex H Draper, $5,500

S Fowler, $6,701
Robt G Fenwick, $7,351
Wm Galt, $8,777
Geo F Gulick, $4,944
Lewis Johnson, $4,070
D W Middleton, $7,661
Dr S A H McKim, $4,183
Geo W Goodall, $4,179
Wm Gunton, $10,159
Wm Orme, $6,363
John Purdy, $5,758
Gen U S Grant, $4,798
W B Kibbey, $9,763
F A Lutz, $7,561
John R Murray, $6,354
Gustave Lansburg, $13,335
Jas C McGuire, $9,092
A R Potts, $6,184
John H Semmes, $9,897
A R Shepherd, $20,244
W B Todd, $15,488
Wm H Tayloe, $35,995

The residence of Mr G Washington Young, at *Giesboro Point*, is offered for rent.

Antoine Joseph Jobert de Lamballe, the celebrated French surgeon, died in Paris about May 1st.

The trial of Ebon E Leach at Coldwater, Mich, for the murder of his wife & a lawyer of that town, Geo Brown, on Dec 3, 1866, has been closed by a verdict of guilty, & the prisoner has been sentenced to hard labor for life in the penitentiary. Mrs Leach was a milliner at Coldwater; her husband was jealous of the attentions of Mr Brown to her. He killed them both as they were walking together.

Last Sunday Chas B Almond, a noble intelligent boy, about 12 years old, son of Mr B Almond, of this city, in company with Mr Draper Short, were leading mules to water. Chas was leading the gentler of the two with a coil of rope being held around his hand. For some reason the mule became frightened by Mr Fred Krouse's buggy, & the mule started to run, dragging the poor boy behind him. The mule finally stopped & the boy was picked up in a most terrible plight. He was taken to his mother's residence & all efforts to resuscitate him were unavailing. He died about 2 hours later. About 2 years ago, a little son of Mr Noah Berry, the adjoining neighbor of Mrs Almond, was thrown from a horse at the identical spot & died soon after. –Platte City Reveille, May 10

Double Murder. Port Colborne, C W, May 21. On Sat night Menno Graybill shot his brother-in-law, John Wallace, through the heart, & then was shot himself by his own brother, Saml Graybill.

The body of Julia Forrest, alias Mrs Julia Heintz, whose husband, it is said resides or did reside in Fred'k City, Md, was found this morning clothed only with a chemise, shoes & stockings, floating under the Long Wharf, foot of Duke st, by Ferdinand Davis. She was Mr John Hart's housekeeper. The body was taken to Mr Hart's residence, where it was coffined, & buried this evening. –Alex Gaz, 20th

Supreme Court of D C; 688-Equity, Docket 7. Stephen J Cook et al vs Jas F Cook, et al. Ordered that the sale made & reported by John C Norris, trustee, be ratified & confirmed. -A B Olin -R J Meigs, clerk [No details of the sale were given.]

Supreme Court of D C; 881-Equity, Docket 8. Jas T Barnes et al vs Martha E Barnes et al. The trustee reported he sold part of lot 21 in square 514, to John Bresnahan, for $1,560; other part of same lot to Dudley A Denison, for $1,640; The central part of said lot to Archibald Lewis, for $1,490; lot 27 in the subdivision of original lots 7 thru 12 in square 838, to R E Olmstead, for $1,375; lots 16 thru 19 of same subdivision, to same purchaser, for $1,391.20; lot 20 of the same, to Martha E Barnes, for $1,250; lot 21 of same, to Wm C G Bosse, for $291.40; lot 22 of same, to Jane S Davis, $291.40; lots 23 thru 25 in same, to S C Clarke, for $990.60; lot 26 of same, to Jas T Barnes, for $800; lot in square 797, on Va ave, to John Shanahan, for $2,290; & 6 houses on parts of lot 40 thru 42 in square 465, to Martha E Barnes, for $4,425; & the purchasers have complied with the terms of sale. –A B Olin, Justice -R J Meigs, clerk

Dept of the Interior, U S Patent Ofc, Wash, May 17, 1867. Ptn of Chas Watt, of Putney, England, & Hugh Burgess, of Royer's Ford, Pa, praying for the extension of a patent granted to them Jul 18, 1854 & ante-dated Aug 19, 1853, reissued Apr 5, 1863, for an improvement in Process of Treating Wool & other vegetable substances in the Manufacture of Paper Pulp, for seven years from the expiration of said patent, which takes place on Aug 19, 1867. -T C Theaker, Com'r of Patents

Supreme Court of D C. Collier C Frayser, Margaret Frayser, Geo Berg, Henrietta Berg, & John Crome, vs Emmz E C Crome. The above cause is referred to me to state the trustee's account & distribution of the fund; appear at my ofc on May 25. -Walter S Cox, auditor

Dept of the Interior, U S Patent Ofc, Wash, May 16, 1867. Ptn of Henry Ritchie, of Newark, N Y, praying for the extension of a patent granted to him Aug 23, 1853, for an improvement in Padlock, for seven years from the expiration of said patent, which takes place on Aug 23, 1867. -T C Theaker, Com'r of Patents

Died: Apr 30th last, at Ferrol, Spain, Lucas Cordero, in his 31st year, son-in-law of Geo L Berdan, of Wash City. [Louisville, Ky, & Jacksonville, Ill, papers copy.]

THU MAY 23, 1867
Additional list of: Solid men of Washington, together with the amount of their incomes, as appears from the returns made to the Collector of the Internal Revenue::

Walter W Burdette, $3,588
M W Beveridge, $3,928
C C Buckey, $2,221
Geo Baum, $2,472
Alex'r T Britton, $2,226
T N Barnes, $2,074
Philip T Barry, $4,495
R Buckly, $2,208
Chas A Blavens, $3,320
Wm Ballantyne, $2,137
Mrs Susan M Burche, $2,842
Marshall Brown, $20,015
John A Baker, $6,580
Wilson E Brown, $3,922
John W Boteler, $4,063
H S Benson, $14,625
Jas L Barbour, $9,777
Wm H Baldwin, $2,000
Edw Baldwin, $2,000
Wm Bates, $3,408
David W Brown, $2,970
Wm B Boggs, $3,468
M V B Bogan, $2,763
Jos H Bradley, $7,261
Fred Bates, $3,408
W C Bestor, $2,982
Mrs Frances Blanchard, $10,188
Henry Baldwin, $2,414
J W Baker, $9,515
Jas W Barker, $2,908
H Birch, $2,266
Davl Breed, $4,157
Thos Blagden, $10,912
S P Brown, $3,935
Robt Cohen, $2,156
Cm Campbell, $2,765
Eliz Cropley, $2,146
Geo W Cropley, $2,483
Germond Crandall, $2,079
Walter S Cox $4,943
John E Cox, $2,249
J J Coombs, $4,130
Chas F Cummins, $2,346

Wm McL Cripps, $3,180
C Cammack, jr, $2,000
Wm D Colt, $2,321
Benj Carlton, $2,396
S D Castleman, guardian, $2,779
Benj Darby, $2,304
John Dickson, $4,310
Edw Dunn, $2,708
Jas B Dodson, $#,000
Richd Delafield, $4,870
W L Dawson, $4,232
Gen Justice Dimmick, $5,324
Wm Dixon, $3,074
Wm Dixon, $9,074
Wm Eagan, $2,053
Rudolph Eichhorn, $3,652
Chas L Elliott, $6,400
Chas Edmonston, $3,888
W B Entwisle, $2,754
Danl S Evans, $2,403
J O Evans, $7,730
A Eberly, $2,650
Dr J Eliot, $2,768
John Furguson, $3,220
Jas E Fitch, $4,428
Jos Fugitt, $2,548
Margaret C Freeman, $63,622
Margaret Freeman, $61,579
Mary Ann Fearson, $5,798
Peter Fegan, $2,596
Bladen Forrest, $2,614
Chas Ford, $3,114
Dr Chas M Ford, $2,700
Georgiana L Force, $2,264
T J D Fuller, $3,067
Wm Fletcher, $2,178
L A Gobright, $2,366
Wm H Godey, $4,899
H J Gray, $2,226
H Gasch, $2,093
Sarah H Greeves, $5,681
Robt H Graham, $2,081
F W Giesking, $2,152

J Grinder, $2,762
A Gillette, $2,282
Michl Green, $5,469
A Green, $3,915
Edwin Green, $4,783
P H Hooe, $2,822
Isaac Heiberger, $3,400
E D Hartley, $2,652
Robt A Hooe, $2,507
Wm E Howard, $2,865
Isaac Herzberg, $3,846
Chas Herzberg, $2,475
T M Hanson, $4,162
S H Howell, $2,228
Geo C Henning, $2,665
Bernard Hayes, $3,500
Geo Hill, jr, $3,000
J A Hamilton, $3,955
Flodoardo Howard, $4,999
J C Harkness, $3,741
T M Harvey, $2,104
Dr J C Hall, $4,677
Benedict Hutchins, $2,956
A Hyde, $3,071
Wm Helmick, $3,557
W H Harrover, $2,093
Walter Harper, $6,336
U D Hilton, $2,162
Johnson Hellen-estate, $4,705
Thos L Hume, $4,448
Mrs S Ireland, $7,086
A J Joyce, $3,635
B L Jackson, $2,304
W B Jackson, $2,313
Dr W P Johnston, $16,153
C B Jewell, $4,019
A F Kimmell, $1,082
J E Kennedy, $4,676
August Koch, $3,605
J C Kendell, $4,390
Horatio King, $5,004
W B Kibby, $8,765
H L King, $4,415
Wm King, $4,361
Moses Kelly, $4,586
Endecotte King-guardian, $2,949

J L Kidwell, $2,199
Dr H Lindsley, $4,050
Dr H Lindsley-guardian, $3,292
C H Lieberman, $2,601
J E Libby, $2,774
P W Lowe, $2,338
Jos Libbey, jr, $3,154
Dr W C Lawrence, $6,652
C H Lane, $2,177
E M Linthicum, $10,304
Max Lansburgh, $2,135
John W Lewis, $4,401
Thos Lewis, $4,261
John Little, $2,558
Louisa Libbey-admx, $4,710
John Lane, $4,200
Geo Lowery, $5,246
Rev J V Lewis, $2,059
JW M Moses, $2,545
A L Merriman, $2,006
John More, $4,315
Chas Mades, $2,000
J R Murry, $6,354
B Miller, $8,234
B F Moxley, $2,884
Dr L Mackall, $2,277
Dr H Magurder, $2,785
John Marbury, jr, $2,177
J C McKelden, $4,500
John Markriter, $4,580
J W Morsell, $2,615
W D C Murdock, $2,952
Wm Marbury, $2,384
Dr J E Morgan, $2,308
Thos Miller, $4,447
W H Morrison, $3,203
John Marbury, jr, $2,000
Richd B Mohun, $9,288
Francis Mohun, $8,799
D W Mohun, $2,291
S A H Marks, $2,210
Thos McGill, $3,712
Frank McGham, $2,831
Henry D Mears, $4,704
Geo Mattingly, $8,053
Wm S Mitchell, $6,934

H Moran, $2,042
Rodney Mason, $3,157
John Marbury, $4,763
J H McDaniel, $2,722
J J May, $5,451
R T Merrick, $2,730
John McLelland, $7,759
W G Metzerott, $10,909
Saml Norment, $11,132
T A Newman, $2,876
J G Naylor, $8,470
Mrs S Otterback, $5,406
Jos Prather, $2,210
G W Phillips, $4,051
C F Peck, $4,000
Anthony Pollak, $2,331
Henry Polkinhorn, $2,930
Thos Parker, $4,161
E A Patterson-adm, $3,199
Esau Pickrell, $3,603
Nicholas Phelan, $3,126
Alex Provost, $14,998
W G Palmer, $2,653
Mrs Ann Pickrell, $3,848
Jas Pilling, $2,588
Thos J S Perry, $6,404
A H Pickrell, $3,046
A E Perry, $6,423
W H Phillips, $7,119
Franklin Philp, $5,063
Bushrod Robinson, $3,127
B W Reed, $2,763
Dr Joshua Riley, $4,140
Christ Ruppert, $2,725
Isaac Rosenthal, $1,097
Thos A Richards, $4,243
Franklin Rives, $7,648
Jefferson Rives, $8,210
G W Riggs-trustee, $12,290
Saml Redfern, $3,614
G W Riggs, $58,058
C F E Richardson, $4,336
Alfred Richards, $3,994
W R Riley, $3,433
Henry K Randall, $4,221
W W Rapley, $2,050

Alex Ray, $24,056
A Ross Ray, $3,400
Albert Ray, $3,700
H Semken, $3,194
Saml Simmons, $3,365
J W Shaw, $3,000
J H Shreves, $3,098
Mrs E D E N Southworth, $4,700
Admiral J S Smith, $2,156
H Clay Stewart, $2,098
Walter Stewart, $2,254
Wm Stickney, $2,086
Mrs Eliz J Stone, $4,849
Mrs Mary Stone-excx, $2,182
Edw Simms, $3,008
Edw S Swann, $2,247
J J Sullivan, $2,328
John Saul, $6,966
A S Solomons, $9,062
Dr S C Smoot-estate, $2,329
Lloyd Simpson, $3,452
E M Stanton, $3,460
Jas H Simpson, $5,964
J Towles, $2,874
Franck Taylor, $7,504
Owen Thorn, $5,724
Saml Tilston, $2,412
P Thyson, $4,178
J S Topham, $3,407
M Thompson, $2,163
G W Utermehle, $11,820
P W Verplanck, $2,486
J Van Riswick, $3,034
W Wall, $9,658
J L Welch, $16,142
P H Welch, $2,621
U Ward, $3,607
M D Wyvill, $2,364
Capt Henry A Wise, $2,100
Chas Wheatley, $2,241
Saml E Wheatley, $2,244
F Wheatley, $8,093
J G Worthington, $6,979
Edw P Welch, $6,285
Theodore Wheeler, $6,641
Jesse B Wilson, $3,499

N Wadsworth, $2,390
Col Edw Wright, $7,066
Hon Richd Wallach, $2,449
W H Ward, $4,900
U Ward, $3,607
Wm Wurdeman, $2,208
J Q Willson, $5,767
J C Willard, $22,017
Caleb C Willard, $17,056

E G Wheeler, $4,482
W H West, $2,434
J M Witherow, $3,712
W B Williams, $2,875
C Woodward, $2,170
G Waters, $3,827
Patrick White, $3,291
Mark Young, $3,000

M L Prosise has just erected a beautiful 3 story pressed brick front house, designed for store & dwlg, on the east side of 10th st, between D & E sts; carpenter, Mr C Woods, was the contractor; Mr J McCollum, bricklayer; Mr Geo Patten, plasterer; & Holland & Kelley, painters.

Montreal, May 21, 1867. Jefferson Davis arrived here this morning, accompained by 3 or 4 gentlemen, & looking very well. His reception was very quiet. He drove at once in a covered carriage to Mrs Howell's house. His arrival was not generally known for some hours.

Indian war-attack on the Mowry Mines [silver-mining works,] in Arizona: Oscar Buckalew, nephew of Senator Buckalew, of Pa, is among the wounded. 1,700 attacked the mines, but were driven off, leaving 5 dead.

Trustee's sale of very valuable improved property on 21st & H sts, at auction; by decree of the Supreme Court of D C, passed in chancery cause No 595, Francis M Jarboe against Junius J Boyle et al, dfndnts, on Mar 22, 1867; sale on Jun 27 next, of original lots 19 & 20 in square 79, in Wash City, with a large 3 story brick house, with large backbldg, 12 rooms, water & gas, & a brick stable in the rear. –Saml L Phillips, trustee -W L Wall & Co, aucts

Atlantic City, May 22. This morning the steamer **Santiago de Cuba**, Capt Behn, went ashore about 100 yards from the beach; bound to N Y, with 400 souls on board; the passengers were all landed safely, excepting five, & two of the crew, who were drowned by the upsetting of a lifeboat. The baggage is all on shore. Lost: Mrs Eunice Salone Gross, Miss Sarah McAver, Mrs Mary Watkins, Mrs Marcella Rickers, Martin McNulty, John Smith, & Mary Louisa Gross. Two of the bodies of the drowned persons, John Smith & Mary L Gross, have not yet been recovered.

Household & kitchen furniture at auction on May 31, 1867, at the residence of F Stinzing, on 7th st, between M & N sts. -Green & Williams, aucts

Watertown, N Y, May 22. Last night the steamer **Wisconsin** was burned, 3 miles from Cape Vincent, & from 25 to 30 lives lost. The boat was run shore on Grenadier Island, above Cape Vincent, & all the passengers who obeyed the capt's orders & remained on board were saved.

Public sale: by decree passed by the Orphans Court of Montg Co, Md: sale on the premises, all the real estate of the late Enos Gone, deceased; a tract of land of 70 acres, on the public road leading from Rockville to *Mitchell's Cross Roads*, with a comfortable dwlg-house, barn, stabling, & all necessary out-bldgs.
–Julia A Gone, trustee

Executors public auction of household & kitchen furniture, by order of the Orphans Court of Wash Co, D C. Executor's of the last will & testament of John P Pepper, deceased, late of Wash Co, auction on May 27, 408 Pa ave, between 4½ & 6th sts.
-Henrietta P Pepper, Wm P Hicks, excs -Cooper & Latimer, aucts

Dept of the Interior, U S Patent Ofc, Wash, May 17, 1867. Ptn of Arshal H McKinley, of Higginport, Ohio, praying for the extension of a patent granted to him Aug 16, 1853, for an improvement in Socket for Auger Handles & Braces, for seven years from the expiration of said patent, which takes place on Aug 16, 1767.
-T C Theaker, Com'r of Patents

FRI MAY 24, 1867
C W Thorn calls attention to his wholesale bonnet & ribbon store, 487 8th st. [Ad]

Mr McNerhany's residence, containing 9 rooms, near the Navy Yard; for rent.

Board of Police Com'rs: Lt Cornelius Noonan assigned to duty by the Maj & Superintendent as day inspector of the force, having immediate command & supervision of the sanitary police company, & that Lt John F Kelley be assigned to duty as night inspector of the force, having immediate command & supervision of the detective corps. Wallace Lloyd was appointed a regular patrolman, vice Chas P Reese, ineligible. The cmplnts against Privates A M Sprague & H E Marks were dismissed. Jesse W Kitchen & Silas S Chamberlain were appointed additional patrolmen; the applications of Anthony Rodier & Henry Chatain for liquor licenses were approved. The application of Benj Corley for license was rejected. Police ofcrs who have died while serving on the force since its organization:

Thos Shakespeare, Aug, 1862
John E S Hilton, Aug, 1862
John Leach, jr, Dec, 1862
Ezekial Simpson, Dec, 1862
Chas Macdonald, Aug, 1863
Benj F Morris, Jan, 1864
Chas Cook, Mar, 1864
Wm B Thomas, Dec, 1864
Geo R Renneker, Feb, 1865
Remegius Burch, Mar, 1865
Randal Colburn, Aug, 1865
Alex'r Clements, Feb, 1866
Geo B Lipscomb, Apr, 1866
Albert Brewer, Apr, 1867

We are indebted to John F Ellis, music dealer, 310 Pa ave, for a copy of his latest song, "Brown Eyes." Words by Will A Coulter, U S A; music by Fr Kley, of Wash City.

N Y, May 23. An awful tragedy occurred lately in the court room at Matanzas: a man, Santiago Manzanet, shot his own wife & mother during the progress of a suit for alimony. He was secured. Mr Manzanet has a literary reputation.

Springfield, Mass, May 23. Simon Peck, of Griswoldville, on Wed, murdered Elmira Cheney, who was living in his house, to protect Mrs Peck from the passion of her husband. He struck her with a heavy club, & then assaulted his wife, until she was senseless. Peck was then brought down by a stone thrown by his son, 11 years old, who witnessed the affair. Peck was committed to the Greenfield jail. He is a man of violent temper, & it is thought was insane at the time of committing the deed.

Died: on May 18, in N Y C, in his 74th year, after a short illness, Elbridge Gerry, eldest son of the late Elbridge Gerry, signer of the Declaration of Independence.

I offer for sale the Farm I recently occupied, called **Rockburn**, near Good Hope, containing 65 acres, with a comfortable dwlg house of 10 rooms, & all necessary out-bldgs. There are 4 good bldg lots, three of five acres each, & one of ten acres. Apply to T M Hanson, Intelligencer Bldg, room No 9. –A Addison

Edmund J Underhill, of Washington, in Dutchess Co, N Y, shot himself in the town of Stanford on Wednesday.

Joel Lindsey, who whipped his son to death, has been released from the Auburn jail on bail, in order that he may stand a new trial, an order for which has been obtained by his counsel.

Trustee's sale: by decree of the Circuit Court of Chas Co; court of Equity, public sale, at the Court-house door, in Port Tobacco, on Jun 18, all the real estate of which the late Chas W Barnes died seized, consisting of a Farm, in said county, containing about 120 acres, more or less; near the farms of Col Jenkins & Mr Carrington; improved by a new & excellent dwlg house. Also, the house & lot in Port Tobacco, now occupied by Mr Jenkins, & also the one now occupied by Mr Covell. All in good repair. Possession given on Jan 1, 1868. –F Stone, trustee

Jas McCann, a porter in the employ of Farwell & Co, in Chicago, stepped upon a dummy to descend from the 5th floor of a warehouse, on Monday, when the machinery gave way, & he fell with such force as to kill him instantly.

Mr Thos Nowland, of Charlevoix, Mich, was chopping wood, & his wife & daughter, aged 18 months, were standing near. The child, unperceived by either parent, crawled to the log on which the father was chopping, &, getting beneath the ax, received the descending blow on the head, killing it instantly.

MAY 25, 1867
About 11 o'clock Thu night Mr Jesse Sisson, an aged citizen of the 7th Ward, walked over the bank at K st south & 7th st, & fell 20 to 25 feet, severely bruising the head & hips, but, we believe, breaking no bones.

Appointment of Cadets at large to the Military Academy, 1867.
Wm Boerum Wetmore, N Y   Rufus M Williams, Tenn
John B Weller, jr, Calif   Jacob Rebhun, Mich
Chas C Morrison, Ohio   Wm J McDonald, D C
Vinton A Goddard, D C   Fred'k Kege, sgt 1st artl
Bainbridge Reynolds, son of Gen J J Reynolds, U S Army
Thos Corbin Davenport, son of Cmder Davenport, U S N

Cooper & Latimer, aucts, sales of real estate yesterday. Part of lots 16 & 17 in square 451, on N Y ave, between 6th & 7th sts, with a 3 story frame dwlg, to Anthony Best, for $1,485; pat of lot 2 in square 515, on L st, between 4th & 5th sts, improved by 3 story brick house, to Mary Lawson, for $2,630; part of lot 4 in square 515, on La ave, with a 2 story frame house, to Anthony Buchley, for $6,050.

Capt Wm McConihe, 2nd N Y volunteers, has been brevetted major by Govn'r Fenton, of N Y, for gallant & meritorious conduct during the late war, particularly at the battle of Chancellorsville, where he was wounded in the right lung by a minie ball.

A case is now in the Equity Docket of the Supreme Court of the District for the purpose of having a distribution of the reward of $20,000 for the capture of Booth offered by the Corporation. This suit was brought by Messrs Stewart & Riddle, in Nov last, for Gen L C Baker, Lt Col E J Conger, & L B Baker, E P Doherty, J R O'Beirne, Clarvoe, McDevitt, & others.

Mrd: on May 20, at Charleston, Kanawha Co, West Va, by Rev Jos R Wheeler, of Alexandria, Va, Mr Richd J Ryon, of Wash, D C, to Miss Anna Isabella Summers, of Charleston, W Va.

Mrd: on May 23, at the residence of the bride's father, **Mount Beverly**, PG Co, Md, by Rev J Martin, Lt John Hunter, 10th infty U S A, to Miss Lizzie, eldest daughter of Jos Beasley.

Mrd: on May 23, in Wash City, at the Israel Bethel Church, by Rev Dr Hunter, John Pinkney to Miss Georgiana Ingram, all of Wash City. No cards.

Mrd: on May 9, at the residence of the Danish Consul, by Rev Dr Finckel, Mr Waldemar E Bends, formerly of Denmark, to Miss Anna M Clausen.

Died: on May 24, Andrew J McCalla, eldest son of Gen John M McCalla. His funeral will take place from 9 Indiana ave, Sat, at 11 o'clock.

Died: on May 24, at his residence, in Wash City, Richd C Washington, of the Post Ofc Dept. Notice of the funeral will appear in the Sunday paper.
+
Mr Richd C Washington died yesterday, in his 64th year. He was a direct descendant of Lawrence Washington, the elder brother of the father of Geo Washington, & was born in Westmoreland Co, Va. He had been a resident of Wash City for many years, & occupied at the time of his death the position of chief clerk in the appointment ofc of the Post Ofc Dept, & has been connected with this dept for over 20 years. He was, at the time of his death, one of the vestry of the Church of the Epiphany. His funeral will probably take place on Sunday from this church.

London, May 24. Sir Archibald Allison, the historian, is dead.

Toronto, May 23. Geo Albert Mason, the Southern spy, suspected of being connected with the plot to assassinate Pres Lincoln, left here by train for N Y, accompanied by an American detective, under a safe conduct from Sec Seward, to give evidence against John H Surratt, & also in a robbery in which he took part when with Mosby's guerillas.

Mobile, May 21. John M Parkman, defaulting president of the First Nat'l Bank of Selma, confined in the Cahawba jail, escaped yesterday & plunged in the river, & was drowned.

Excellent & handsome household & kitchen furniture, pianoforte, china, damask curtains, carpets, etc, at auction on May 29, at the residence of Edw Jordan, Solicitor of the Treasury, 478 12th st near M st. -Cooper & Latimer, aucts

Richmond, May 24. A boat upset in the James river this morning, drowning Richd P Mundin, a stage carpenter at the theatre in this city, & Geo Bray.

Orphans Court of Wash Co, D C. Letters of administration c t a on the personal estate of Geo Bender, late of Wash City, deceased. –Eugene Carusi

Brvt Maj Gen M C Meigs, Quartermaster General, U S Army, has been granted 6 months leave of absence, on account of sickness, with permission to go to Europe.

MON MAY 27, 1867
The funeral of the late Richd C Washington took place yesterday afternoon, at the Church of the Epiphany, & was attended by a large concourse of the citizens of Washington. Rev Dr Hall, the rector of the church, conducted the services, which were according to the solemn burial rites of the Episcopal Church. Dr Hall also spoke of the character of the deceased in a feeling manner, & at the conculsion of the services the remains were taken to *Oak Hill Cemetery* for interment. The pall-bearers were Gen St John B L Skinner, Mr Jas Marr, Dr Lacey, Mr Gurley, & Dr Macdonald, of the Post Ofc Dept; Mr Geo C Whiting, of the Interior Dept; Gen Maynadier, & Col L E Middleton.

Orphans Court-Judge Purcell, May 25, 1867. 1-The will of Martha Hauptman, of Wash, D C, was admitted to probate. She appoints Edw Sevame as her exc. 2-The will of Wm S Corson, of Wash, D C, was filed & partially proven; he appointed his wife, Annie J Corson, & Jas Molan, as his excs. 3-The will of Prudence S Aiken, of Wash, D C, deceased, was proven & admitted to probate & record. She appoints Mr L A Gobright as her sole executor. 4-The will of Ellen Toner was admitted to probate & record. 5-Letters of administration were granted to Eliza Barron upon the estate of Richd Barron, deceased; bond $20,000. Also, to Jas B Munroe upon the estate of Geo Munroe, deceased; bond $1,000; & to Mr L A Gobright upon the personal estate of P S Aiken, deceased; bond $1,200. 6-The first individual account of Sophie E Douglas, guardian to Henry C Douglas, orphan of Wm Douglas, deceased & the first general of the same, guardian to the same, were approved & passed. 7-Clemetina Downs was appointed guardian to Mary E Downs, orphan of Jas Downs, late of Wash, D C; bond $1,000. 8-The return of sale by Dr Miller, exc of J D Hammack, deceased, of the effects of said Hammack under an order of the Orphans Court of Wash Co, D C, exceeded $8,000. Judge Purcell was petitoned by several attys representing the creditors to order a private sale of said property or allow some purchaser to take it at the appraised value, which was about $5,000. This the Judge refused, stating that all judicial sales should be at public auction, to the highest bidder, according to the law. It will now be perceived that by this order of the Judge the estate has gained over $3,000.

The Bodisco property on Second st, was sold at auction on Wed, by Thos Dowling, auct, to A H Herr, the present occupant of the house for $9,500. The stable & adjoining land in rear of the house was afterwards put up at auction, &, though not advertised to be sold, $3,300 was offered & refused.

Hon D S Gooding, marshal of the District, has been unexpectedly called to Greenfield, Ind, by the sudden & serious illness of his father-in-law. Mr Gooding & his family left for Indiana last evening.

Died: on Sat, Eliza Malone, in her 42nd year, wife of Lawrence Malonne. Her funeral will be from her residence, between 2nd & 3rd sts, & E & F sts, on Mon at 3 o'clock.

Died: on May 14, at Uniontown, Pa, Wm Stone, aged 74 years & 10 months. Mr Stone was born in Westmoreland Co, Va, in 1792, & was an Old Line Whig, & for many years a subscriber to the Nat'l Intelligencer. He served through the war of 1812; moved from Loudoun Co, Va, to Uniontown, Pa, in 1832, where he lived until he died.

Died: on May 26, in Gtwn, Miss Jane Reynolds, after a short but painful illness. Her funeral will be Monday, 5 P M, from the residence of Wm H Simms, 43 Fred'k st.

Died: on May 25, at the residence of her father, C C Hyatt, Hyattsville, Mary E Middleton, wife of Reuben Middleton, aged 42 years. Her funeral is today at 12:30.

Died: on May 23, at Hoosick Falls, N Y, Betsey A Wood, wife of Walter Wood, aged 46 years.

Wm H Schenig has been arrested & committed for court to answer the charge of robbing his brother, Geo R Schenig, of valuable articles of wearing apparel, jewelry, etc, of amount sufficient to give him a residence of several years in the penitentiary if proven against him. Schenig had already served considerable time in a cell.

Fort Monroe, May 26. Mich McCarty, the bugler of the **Fortress Monroe** garrison, was killed last night by a man named Clark, keeping a store at Mill Creek. Clark was arrested by the military; & placed in Hampton jail, to be tried by the civil authorities.

Excellent pianoforte, French plate mirrors, household & kitchen furniture at auction on Jun 3, at the residence of Mrs Jas Dull, 248 F st, between 13th & 14th sts. -Cooper & Latimer, aucts

Savannah, May 26. Mr J E Hoyes, proprietor of the Republican, who was fined & imprisoned for libel in March last, was yesterday released by pardon of Govn'r Jenkins.

Geo Brumbaker, whose wife & daughter died of cholera in Louisville last summer, brought suit against the city, claiming $25,000 damages. He alleges that epidemic in the part of the city in which he lived was caused by the overflow which was brought about by the street not being properly graded to allow the water to run off.

Mr Jas H Poindexter, an old citizen of Richmond, died on Thursday last.

A prisoner in the penitentiary at Rochester, N Y, Ambrose Dean, committed suicide on Sat by hanging himself by his neck to his cell-door with a strap.

Orphans Court of Wash Co, D C. Letters testamentary on the personal estate of Prudence S Aiken, late of Wash City, D C, deceased. –Lawrence A Gobright, exc

Notice to all whom it may concern, that, on Dec 22, 1866, I bought a piece of land from Christian Abel, for which I gave him my notes for $800. Three notes, making the amount-one for $200, payable twelve months after day; another note payable two years after date, for $300; & one other note, payable three years after date, for $300; which said notes were obtained by false representation, the land for which the said notes were given said Abel having no legal title to it, & I hereby forewarn all persons from buying or negotiating said notes, as I do not intend to pay the same or any part thereof. -John Hess

TUE MAY 28, 1867
Mrs Jane Parris can accommodate permanent & transient boarders at her house, 256 south 8th st, n w corner Spruce st, Phil, Pa. [Ad]

Yesterday the gable end of the well-known residence of the Brereton family, 7th & F sts, split from the roof to the foundation, caused by the excavation for the new 4 story marble front bldg proposed to be erected by Higgins & Berry on the adjoining lot, which excavation extends below the foundation of the Brereton house. A general scamper of occupants occurred inside; the granite sills of the 7th st front of the house gave way & fell, portions of the north gable end, where the bricklayers & laborers had been at work, also fell. The bldg is badly damaged throughout, & will have to come down. Fortunately no one was hurt.

J Hubley Ashton, who, for some time, has so creditably filled the ofc of Assist Atty Gen of the U S, retires on Jun 1st. John M Binckley succeeds him.

Died: on May 27, Martha, wife of Henry King, aged 47 years. Her funeral will be from her late residence, 48 3rd st, Gtwn, D C, on Wed at 5 o'clock P M. [Balt papers please copy.]

Died: on May 21, in her 87th year, at the residence of her son, Dr Chas McLean, of Balt Co, Md, Mrs Eliza McLean, relict of the late Cornelius McLean, of Wash City.

Miss Madeline Henriquez, who recently retired from the stage at Wallach's Theatre, N Y, was married on Sat to Mr Louis Jennings, the American correspondent of the London Times.

Mr Jas Fields, an old & respected citizen of Balt, died on Sat, aged 76 years. He belonged to one of the oldest families in Md, his grandfather having been one of the original settlers in St Mary's Co who came over from England with Lord Baltimore.

Geo W Lee, of Chicago, who was assaulted & robbed in his room on Wed, is considered out of danger.

Mrs Sadler, nurse of the hospital at Libby Prison, in Richmond, on Sat, by mistake, took corrosive sublimate for calomel, & despite efforts to save her, she died on Saturday.

The trial of John H Surratt, indicted for murder, & for entering into a conspiracy to murder the late Pres Lincoln, was fixed for yesterday, in the Criminal Court of this District, Judge Fisher presiding. At 10 o'clock the court was formally opened by the crier, Mr Wm A Mulloy, the counsel for the defence, Messrs R T Merrick, J H Bradley, sr, & J H Bradley, jr, being present. The counsel for the prosecution, Hon E C Carrington, Dist Atty; Nathl Wilson, Assist Dist Atty; A G Riddle, & Judge Edwards Pierrepont, of N Y appeared & took their seats. The prisoner was brought in; he looked pale & careworn; he was visited in the jail yesterday by his brother & sister; the brother, Isaac Surratt, was brought here from Texas, & is a witness on behalf of the prisoner. John H Surratt wears a heavy moustache & goatee; he shaved all his face except his chin & upper lip yesterday for the first time since his imprisonment.

Dept of the Interior, U S Patent Ofc, Wash, May 22, 1867. Ptn of Danl Noyes, of Abington, Mass, praying for the extension of a patent granted to him Oct 25, 1853, for an improvement in Machine Hammers, for seven years from the expiration of said patent, which takes place on Oct 25, 1867. –T C Theaker, Com'r of Patents

Guardian's sale of valuable unimproved real estate at auction; by order of the Orphans Court of D C; sale on Jun 6 next, of square known as square south of square 439, fronting on 7th & 8th sts. –Ann E West, guardian -Green & Williams, aucts

Household & kitchen furniture at auction on Jun 4, at house-38 G st, between 21st & 22nd sts, formerly the residence of Gen Jas A Brown. -Green & Williams, aucts

WED MAY 29, 1867
The Pres yesterday appointed Mr John Hay, formerly private secretary to Pres Lincoln, Charge d'Affaires at Vienna, Austria, to fill vacancy caused by resignation of Mr Motley.

Miss Fannie P Hatch, the public school teacher whose alleged cruel whipping of a pupil at Springfield, Mass, has been a source of great excitement, was on Monday, arraigned on a charge of assault & battery, & held in $200 bail to answer.

In the Appointment Division, at the Post Ofc Dept, Mr Jas H Marr has been promoted to be the chief clerk, at $2,000 per annum, vice Richd C Washington, deceased; Hugh Nesbit is promoted from 2nd to 3rd class, vice Mr Marr, $1,600 salary; Isaac Morris, jr, is promoted from 1st to 2nd class, $1,400 a year; vice Nesbit, & Frank E Forbett has been appointed to a 1st class clerkship to fill the vacancy, vice Morris.

Died: on May 28, in Wash City, Danl Webster Phelps, 5th son of the late Hon S S Phelps, of Vt. His funeral will take place at Mrs Peters, 1st st east, below B st, on May 30 at 11 o'clock A M.

U S Marshal's sale of parcel of ground, the east half of lot 117, in ***Threlkeld's addition*** to Gtwn, on Third st, improved by a 2 story frame dwlg house, seized & levied upon as the property of Michl Moriarty, & will be sold to satisfy fieri facias No 3,616, in favor of Joanna Brown. –David S Gooding, U S Marshal D C

Supreme Court of D C, No 939 Equity. Jas S Wilson et alia vs Thos Anderson, Romania Anderson, & Wm H Wilson. The subpoena issued to compel the dfndnt's appearance having been returned into the Clerk's ofc by the Marshal May 27, 1867, endorsed <u>Not Found</u>, it is, on motion of the cmplnt, May 28, 1867, ordered by the court that the dfndnts cause their appearance to be entered in this suit on or before the first Tuesday of July next, otherwise the bill will be taken for confessed.
–A B Olin, Justice -R J Meigs, clerk

Died: on May 28, at his residence, 641 L st, W W Jeffries, of N Y C. [N Y C papers please copy.]

Orphans Court of Wash Co, D C, May 28, 1867. In the case of Wm O Nixon, exc of Alfred V Scott, deceased, the executor & Court have appointed Jun 22 next, for the final settlement of the personal estate of the said deceased, of the assets in hand.
-Jas R O'Beirne, Reg/o wills

Oak Hill Cemetery. The annual meeting of the stockholders owning 350 square feet or more will be held at the Chapel, in the Cemetery, on Monday, Jun 3, at 5 o'clock P M, for the election of a board of managers for the ensuing year.
–J W Deeble, secretary

THU MAY 30, 1867
Mrs Kate Lawrie, who resides near the Navy Yard, paid a visit to some friends on Mass ave on Monday. She seated herself on entering the house, was in a very cheerful humor, & conversed with much spirit & animation. Suddenly she leaned backward in her chair, closed her eyes, & appeared to have fainted. Mr Davison's family bathed her temples with water, but she did not come to; the physician attended her, but the patient was no more. Disease of the heart was probably the cause of her sudden demise. Mrs Lawrie was about 28 years old, & has left a husband & 2 children to mourn her loss, her youngest child being but 3 months old.

Mrd: on May 28, at the residence of the bride's father, by Rev Fr Hitzelburger, Mr J Robt Shaw to Miss Eliza Jane, daughter of John T & Mary A Cassell, all of Wash, D C. No cards.

Died: on May 29, Fred'k A Burch, in his 41st year. His funeral will take place from the Thirteenth St Baptist Church on May 31, at 3 o"lock.

Died: on May 28, at his residence, 641 L st, Mr Wm W Jeffries, late of N Y C. His funeral will take place from his late residence this morning at 10 o'clock.

Hon Albert Smith, brother of Admiral Joseph Smith, U S Navy, died in Boston yesterday. Mr Smith was born in Hanover, Plymouth Co, Mass, Jan 3, 1793; graduated at Brown Univ in 1813; admitted to the bar; in 1817 he removed to Maine; in 1820 he was sent to the Gen Court of Mass; was for a number of years postmaster in Maine; was a Rep in Congress from 1839 to 1841; & in 1842 was appointed the U S com'r to settle the northeastern boundary under the Ashburton treaty. Business was completed in 1847.

Montgomery, Ala, May 28. The U S Dist Court, Judge Busteed, presiding, convened here today. Geo W Gayle, who was indicted for alleged complicity in the assassination of Pres Lincoln, presented a full pardon from the Pres of the U S, & the indictment was dismissed on payment of costs. The disposition of the case meets with general approval.

FRI MAY 31, 1867
Attempt at suicide. Yesterday Capt Ruth, a clerk in the Ofc of Indian Affairs, attempted to commit suicide by shooting himself with a pistol, at his residence, 169 G st south, between 4½ & 6th sts. The pistol was one of Moore's patent, & two of the shots took effect in the forehead, one flattening upon the skull, which was extricated; the other could not be found. He has been troubled with an idea that he would become insane, though no positive evidence of insanity had previously been developed by him. He is over 50 years of age, & has a family in good circumstances.

Alexandria, Va, May 30. The engine Rapidan, of the Orange & Alexandria railroad, exploded this evening at Fairfax station, killing Engineer Lynch & Fireman Roso.

Fortress Monroe, May 30. This morning Norfolk was thrown into intense excitement by the falling of 2 brick tenements, on Market Square, & both occupied. All the victims have been recovered excepting a lady named Mrs Cheshire, who was last seen endeavoring to rescue her child. She was horribly mutilated, & must have died instantly.

Poughkeepsie, May 29. Jas H Jackson, a prominent lawyer, was dangerously wounded last night by a ball from a revolver fired by his son, who is insane. The son has been placed in jail.

Erie, Pa, May 29. Rev Julius Seymour was arrested here yesterday for embezzling $15,000 worth of revenue stamps. He was formerly a clerk in the Internal Revenue Ofc.

Supreme Court of D C; No 589 Equity. Wm P Lisdell & wife vs Mary Stone & Wm T Stone. The above cause is referred to me to take testimony & report whether Woolford Stone is, & of what real estate he died seized. Meet at my ofc on Jun 5, at 12 o'clock M. -Walter S Cox, auditor

Supreme Court of D C; No 804 Equity. Augustus Brown vs Wm Beake, Thos Brown, John Fowler, Jefferson Roberts, & others. The above cause is referred to me to take testimony & report whether it will be for the interest of the infants & other parties to sell the premises mentioned in the bill. Meet at my ofc on Jun 5, at 12 o'clock M. -Walter S Cox, auditor

Mrd: on May 30, by Rev Dr Pinkney, Brvt Maj J Hartwell Butler, U S A, to Ida De Mariatigue Fatio, daughter of the late Capt Lewis C Fatio.

Died: on May 30, after a short but severe illness, John B, son of Michl & Rose S Green, aged 2 years. His funeral will be from the residence of his parents, 13th & L sts, at 10 o'clock, Sat, Jun 1.

Died: on May 25, at LaS___r, Minn, John Gordon. [Troy N Y, & San Francisco, Cal, papers please copy.]

SAT JUN 1, 1867
Green & Williams, aucts, real estate sales during the week just closed: part of lot 14 in square 589, with a frame house fronting on First st, between C & D sts, to Hannah Roche, for $800. Lot 6 in square 866, with improvements, to Saml Cook, for $2,850, fronting at the corner of 6th st & Mass ave. House & lot fronting on Chestnut st, between 14th & 15th sts, to Patrick Holloran, for $800. Lot 6 in square 412, 22x 90 feet, fronting on F st, between 8th & 9th sts, Island, to E F Zell, at 22 cents per foot.

Wm Linkins, at his provision store on 20th st, between G & H sts, sells beef at from 15 to 25 cents per pound, mutton 12½ to 20 cents, & other meats at reduced priced.

Davis & Scanlon will open their new billiard saloon at 369 D st, near 7th, this evening.

Mr Chas H Ashton, a clerk in the Treasury Dept, residing on 8th st, above L, was taken with a severe hemorrhage Thursday, & died yesterday. He was a member of Metropolis Lodge of Odd Fellows.

Mrd: on May 25, by Rev R Ridder Meade, at *Carleton*, the seat of the bride's father, Albemarle Co, Va, Richd Hall, of Ellangowan Terrace, Montreal, Canada, to Emma Estelle, daughter of Hon Alex'r Rives, Judge of the Supreme Court of Va.

Died: on May 30, after a short but severe illness, John B, son of Michl & Rose S Green, aged 2 years. His funeral will be from the residence of his parents, 13th & L sts, at 10 o'clock, on Jun 1.

Wilmington, Del, May 31. The trial of Jos W Pratt, for the murder of J Pusey Smith, in this city in Apr last, was concluded at Newcastle yesterday with a verdict of not guilty, on account of insanity. Adultery between the deceased & Pratt's wife was part of the defence. Wayne McVeigh, of West Chester, was one of the prisoner's counsel. The result is generally satisfactory.

Trustee's sale of valuable unimproved real estate; by decree of the Supreme Court of D C, passed in a chancery cause, Mary E Cayner et al, against Edw A Maynett et al, dfndnts, on May 30, 1867: public auction on Jun 11, of the east half of lot 17 in square or Revervation C, in Wash City. Also, lot 17 in W B Todd's & W H Gunnells subdivision of square 465 in Wash City. –Richd R Crawford, trustee -Cooper & Latimer, aucts

New Brunswick, N J, May 31. The trial of Bridget Dergan, for the murder of Mrs Coriell, of Newmarket, closed today. The jury was out 20 minutes, & rendered a verdict of guilty of murder in the first degree.

Trustee's sale of valuable property consisting of real estate, wharves, water rights, & privileges, together with warehouse & machinery therein; by deed of trust dated Oct 16, 1866, by Thos P Morgan & wife & Geo Rhinehart & wife, in my favor as trustee, to secure the payment of a promissory note for $25,000, dated Oct 16, 1866, & payable to the order of Wm Clark, together with the interest to grow due thereon & which said mortgage is recorded in Liber R M H No 22, folio 15, of the land records for Wash City; & whereas default has been made in the payment due on said note, according to the terms set forth & in said deed of trust, now in pursuance of said trust, I will sell upon the premises, at public auction, on Jun 10th: part of lots 2 & 3 in square 9; property is known as the Morgan & Rhinehart Bone Factory, Wharves, etc, at the foot of G st. -Jas P Gregory, trustee -Cooper & Latimer, aucts

By deed of trust to me from Mary Ann Thecker, dated Dec 13, 1865, & recorded in Liber A M H No 12, folios 22 thru 25, of the land records for Wash Co, D C, I will sell, on Jul 1, in Gtwn, part of lot 72, in old Gtwn, beginning on the south side of Cherry alley, at N W corner of Cecil alley, & running thence with Cherry alley west about 44 feet 6 inches, to a west corner of lot 76, etc, with 2 brick tenements standing thereon. –W H Tenney, trustee -Thos Dowling, auct

MON JUN 3, 1867
Sat evening, while a boy named Chas Marders was engaged with others in removing some barrels from a wagon preparatory to building a bonfire, he fell from the wagon & broke his shoulder-bone. He was carried home where medical attention was summoned.

On Sat morning, as several of the students of the Nat'l Deaf Mute College, in Wash City, were bathing in the Eastern Branch of the Potomac, near the foot of P ave, two of their number, Mrs Jas Cross, of Alleghany City, Pa, & Mr Malachi Hallowell, of Hudsonville, Ill, were drowned. Both were exceellent swimmers, & it is probable that their drowning was caused by sudden cramps. Mr Cross was a printer, & a member of the Typographical Union, & spent his holidays working in the Nat'l Intelligencer ofc. He was of a kind & gentle disposition that endeared him much to his fellow typos.

Orphans Court-Judge Purcell, Jun 1, 1867. 1-The will of the late Christopher Yeabower was admitted to probate & record, & letters testamentary were issued to Louisa Yeabower; bond $5,000. 2-The will of the late Matthew E Duvall was filed. 3-Letters of administration on the estate of Anne Patton were issued to Catherine Patton; bond $300. 4-L A Gobright qualified as executor of the will of Prudence Aiken, giving bond in $1,200. 5-Jane Walker declined to become guardian to her daughter, Alice Walker, & at her request Geo Seaton was appointed guardian; bond $500. 6-The first & final account of the administrator of Jas H Moore, & account of personal estate & second account of guardian to orphan of Danl Ragan, were approved & passed.

On Friday a pleasure fishing boat capsized off Fisher's Island, near New London, Conn, & sunk in 15 minutes. A boy named Rogers went down with the boat. Capt Jas Fish swan ashore in a rough sea, after a hard struggle of 2 hours in the water. He was completely exhausted when he reached shore. Capt Strang Holt, Capt Coddington Fish, & Carl Beckwith were lost. All were prominent citizens of New London.

Leavenworth, Jun 1. On May 27, 3 deserters from the 38th infty, at **Fort Hays**, went to the house of P J Peterson, on the Smoky Hill route. Finding Mrs Peterson, aged 50 years, alone, they dragged her into the cellar & outraged her person in a horrible manner. On May 30th they were captured; they confessed their guilt, & a mob went to the jail & killed them. Their bodies were thrown into the river. Mrs Peterson is not expected to survive.

On Sat night a child in the house of Mrs Catharine Royal, on 9th st, accidentally set fire to a bed, but the fire was extinguished before the arrival of the engines. On the dept's return from this alarm they went another fire at a frame slaughter house on 16th st, between N & O, belonging to Mr Hazel. The bldg was destroyed; loss about $800.

Died: yesterday, Sunday, Wm R Wilson, aged 35 years. His funeral will take place on Tuesday, at 10 o'clock, from the residence of his father, John D Wilson, 155 F st, between 19th & 20th sts.

Died: on Jun 1, J Ford, aged 2 years & 1 month, son of Wm B & Annie R Redgrave. His funeral is this afternoon at 3 o'clock, from 417 H st.

Died: on Jun 1, in Wash City, Jas Cross, of Alleghany City, Pa, aged 25 years. His funeral is Jun 3, at 3 P M, in the chapel of the Nat'l Deaf Mute College.
+
Died: on Jun 1, in Wash City, Malachi Hollowell, of Hutsonville, Ill, aged 18 years. His funeral is Jun 3, at 3 P M, in the chapel of the Nat'l Deaf Mute College.

The remains of Chas F Browne, better known as Artemus Ward, reached N Y on Friday by steamer from Europe, & will be conveyed to Maine for interment.

Orphans Court of Wash Co, D C. Letters testamentary on the personal estate of Christopher Yeabower, late of Wash Co, D C, deceased. –Louisa Yeabower, excx

Orphans Court of Wash Co, D C, Jun 1, 1867. In the case of John A Baker, exc of Thos Baker, deceased, the executor & Court have appointed Jun 29th next, for the final settlement of the personal estate of the said deceased, of the assets in hand. -Jas R O'Beirne, Reg/o wills

War Dept Claims Commission, Wash, D C, May 31, 1867. List of claims received by the commision during the month of May, 1867.
Claim of L B Johnson, for lumber taken & used by the Gov't.
John Olando, for services of schnr **Julia Smith**.
John J Lusich, for restoration of sloop **Union**.
Jas H Cross, for return of moneys taken by provost marshal
J H Wilkinson, for extra compensation as commissary for prisoners of war.
Philip Pendleton, for rent of property.
Martin Kenofsky, for money taken from him while under arrest.
David Fultz, for horses & provisions taken by U S troops.
Theodore Lichtenheim, for wood furnished U S Gov't.
Joel E Parr, for damage to property by U S troops.
Walter J Pace, for property destroyed by U S troops.
Adeline Shirley, for damage to property.
J W Meeks,jr, for moneys advanced to pay extra duty service.
Chas B Gardner, for bricks used by U S troops.
John Bulfinch & others, for services & repairs to brig **Ocean Belle**.
J C Jones, for services of schnr **Messenger**.
Jas G Anderson, for services as provost marshal
Elijah Williams, for services at *Fort Smith*, Ark.
W J Tucker, for services at *Fort Smith*, Ark.
E Ennam, for services & hire of teams at *Fort Smith*, Ark.
Jas Turner, for services & hire of teams at *Fort Smith*, Ark
J M Provine, for rent & damage to property.
De Witt Clinton, Brvt Lt Col, Recorder

TUE JUN 4, 1867
Rear Admiral Chas H Bell, commandant of the N Y navy yard, under date of Jun 1, transmits to the Navy Dept the painful intelligence of the death of Capt John P Bankhead, U S Navy, which occurred at Acton, mouth of the Red Sea, on Apr 27 last. Admiral Bell states that Capt Bankhead left the ship **Wyoming** at Yokohama, Japan, on Mar 1, being obliged to give up the command of that vessel on account of ill health. After touching at Hong Kong, China, on Mar 11, he proceeded to Suez, & died on board the steamer **Simta**. The intelligence of his death was brought by his steward, who was with him at the time, & who arrived in N Y on May 31, from Southampton, England. Capt Bankhead was a native of S C, & a son of Gen Jas Bankhead, U S Army. He was born on Aug 3, 1821, & was in his 46th year at the time of his death; had performed 21 years 7 months continuous sea service; entered the navy as midshipman on Aug 10, 1838; was warranted passed midshipman May 20, 1844; promoted to a master May 8, 1850; to a lt Apr 7, 1852; to a cmder Jul 16, 1862; to a capt Jul 26, 1866. During the war he served on board the U S steamer **Susquehanna**, & was at different times in command of the U S steamer **Pembina**, steamer **Florida**, steamer **Otsego**, & the iron clad **Monitor**. The latter vessel was lost while under his command.

The trial of Rev Joel Lindsey, indicted for whipping his child to death, was concluded at Albion, N Y, on Sat. The jury failed to agree, standing 10 for acquittal & 2 for conviction, & they were discharged. The prisoner then plead guilty of manslaughter in the 4th degree, & was sentenced by the court to pay a fine of $200.

Toronto, C W, Jun 3. Jefferson Davis arrived here today to attend the wedding of one of his countrymen, which takes place at St John's Cathedral tomorrow.

Nashville, Jun 3. The impeachment trial of Judge Frazier concluded; verdict-guilty of charges preferred. The verdict removes him from office, & disqualifies him fron holding any office hereafter.

Boston, Jun 3. Lucina M Sargeant, a well-known author, died at West Roxbury yesterday, aged 81 years.

Mrd: on May 30, by Rev Dr Moncure, E P Nalle to Millie S, daughter of Augustus Wallace, of Stafford Co, Va.

Mrd: on May 30, by Rev Dr Pinknay, Brvt Maj J Hartwell Butler to Ida De Mariategue Fatio, daughter of the late Capt Louis C F Fatio.

Died: Jun 3, Clinton M Sears, aged 27 years. His funeral will take place on Wed at 4:30 P M, from the residence of his brother, Chas A Sears, 310 F st, between 11th & 12th sts. [Balt & Richmond papers please copy.]

For sale: the Loudoun Bookstore, Leesburg, Va, desiring to retire from the business, I offer for sale the Stock & Fixtures. Possession given immediately. Address Rev H R Smith, Leesburg, Va.

Large stock of Gentlemen's Clothing at auction, on Jun 5, at 242 north side of Pa ave, between 12th & 13th sts, the branch store of Mr A Straus, who is compelled to remove by Jul 1st. -Cooper & Latimer, aucts

Dept of the Interior, U S Patent Ofc, Wash, May 29, 1867. Ptn of John Krauser, of Tylersburg, Pa, praying for the extension of a patent granted to him Aug 30, 1853, & reissued Oct 11, 1861/64, for an improvement in Cider Mills, for seven years from the expiration of said patent, which takes place on Aug 30, 1867.
-T C Theaker, Com'r of Patents

Orphans Court of Wash Co, D C, Jun 1, 1867. In the case of Chas M Matthew, exc of Geo E Curtis, deceased, the executor & Court have appointed Jun 29th next, for the final settlement of the personal estate of the said deceased, of the assets in hand.
-Jas R O'Beirne, Reg/o wills

Supreme Court of D C, Equity: Stephen J Cook et al vs Jas F Cook et al. All parties interested in the trustee's account & distribution of funds, to appear before me on Jun 8. –Walter S Cox, auditor

WED JUN 5, 1867
Yesterday of prisoners confined in the jail here, succeeded in breaking out of the jail bldg. Two were recaptured. Those who escaped are Wm F King, an alleged nororious horse-thief; John Mortimer, alias Burch, charged with burglary & robbery, Wambold, a notorious confidence operator. Francis Caton was caught by one of the guards. John Wilson was caught at the corner of 5th & I sts. [Jun 7th newspaper: Three of the prisoners were recaptured yesterday: King, Mortimer, & Smith, alias Johnson, the most notorious of the characters that escaped.]

Geo Haver & Mrs E H Stubbs, from Michigan, were drowned in Lake Minnehaha, in Minn, on Monday, while attempting to cross the lake.

Real Estate: 1-C S Mattoon purchased a 3 story brick house & lot on N J ave, between B & C sts, for $4,000 cash. 2-Henry Douglass bought two 2 story brick house & lots on 8th st, between C & D sts, for $1,600 cash. 3-B F Gilbert bought a frame house & lot, corner of F & 10th sts, for $6,000. 4-Mrs Jane Thompson bought lot 12 in square 247, 75 x 104 feet on Mass ave, between 13th & 14th sts, for $9,013. 5-Part of square 623 for the <u>Sisters of Visitation</u> for $30,000. [No other information.]

Yesterday the body of Margaret Deitz, alias Parks, alias Patis, was discovered hanging in the upper story of a house at N Y & 3rd st. She was quite dead. She had been living with a man named Dilks or Deitz, who from a letter found on her person, is believed to have a wife & family in Phil. She has 2 children, one in Calif & the other in Balt. Dilks abandoned her a short time since, leaving her in a destitute condition.

At the meeting of Metropolitan Division, No 19, Sons of Temperance, last night, Mr Geo Maher tendered his resignation as W P of the Division. Mr J H Thompson, W A, was elected W P. Mr Jas Lynch, Treasurer, was elected W A & Mr C Denham was elected Treasurer.

On Monday, while Mr Alex'r Shilling was in the restaurant on E st, & standing near the bar, some one coming in pushed against him & his legs caught in the iron rod in front of the bar, & his right leg was broken, & his left leg seriously injured. He was conveyed to his home on 11th st, near E, & attended by Dr Lieberman.

Toronto, C E, Jun 4. A fashionable wedding took place today at St John's Cathedral. Wm Hyde, editor of the St Louis Republcan, was married to Miss Benson, a Southern lady, who has been residing here for some time. Mr Davis, J M Mason, Gen Jubal Early, Col Dorsey, & other Southern celebrities were present. When Mr Davis was recognized, he was loudly cheered.

Memphis, Jun 4. Wm M Rogers, a policeman was brutally murdered by Tom Prewith this morning. Prewith was drunk, & approached Rogers, ordering him to get down on his knees & ask for mercy. On his refusing, Prewith placed a pistol at his throat & fired, the ball coming out at the back of his head, killing him instantly. The murderer is in jail.

Phil, Jun 4. The execution of Gottleib Williams, for the murder of Mrs Miller in Sep last, took place in Moyamensing Prison at 11:30 A M today. Williams made no confession, & Rev Mr Allen stated in his behalf that he acknowledged the first murder laid to his charge, knowing nothing of the crime for which he was to die.

Mrd: on Jun 4, by Rev Byron Sunderland, Jas Wright Clarke, of Ohio, to Miss Frances Marian Nailor, youngest daughter of Allison Nailor, of Wash City. No cards.

Died: on Jun 4, at his residence, in Wash City, Simon Flynn, aged 47 years. His funeral will take place from St Patrick's Church on Jun 6 at 10 A M.

Died: on Jun 4, in his 61st year, John Hood, formerly of Phil, but for the last 30 years a resident of Wash City. His funeral will be from his late residence, 185 B st, corner of 9th, [Island,] on Jun 6 at 4 P M.

Robt Ottarson died in Springfield, Pa, last week. He had been insane for 30 years, but recovered his senses on his death bed, & conversed intelligently of occurrences that transpired the day & week prior to his insanity, making inquiries about his oxen, the work on the farm, & old neighbors who had been dead for years. The intervening space was a perfect blank in his memory.

The Charlottesville Chronicle announces the death of Franklin Minor, who died very suddenly on Wed last, at his residence at Ridgway, 4 miles from Charlottesville. Mr Minor was widely known through the State as a literary & scientific gentleman, as well as a practical farmer.

Chancery sale, by decree of the Supreme Court of D C, cause 856, wherein Wm B Todd et al are cmplnts, & Julia Hallinan et al are dfndnts: sale on Jun 19 next, of lot 14 in square 563, in Wash City, with a two story frame dwlg thereon.
–A Thos Bradley, trustee -Cooper & Latimer, aucts

Supreme Court of D C, No 1,006 Equity Docket 5. Jas Adams et al vs John P Ingle et al. Jas Adams & John H Ingle, surviving trustees, sold the real estate in said cause, lots 14 thru 19 in square 728, to Geo T Brown, for $20,000, & the purchaser has complied with the terms of sale. –A B Olin, Justice -R J Meigs, clerk

THU JUN 6, 1867
Since the publication of the list of income returns at the internal revenue ofc the following have been received:

Thos Berry, $9,984
Richd Barry's estate, $3,624
J W Bulkley, $2,236
J F Brown, $3,935
John C Clayton, $2,434
E C Carrington, $4,664
E R Clark, $2,536
J W Carlisle, $21,279
Edw Hall's estate: $4,871
Prof Jos Henry, $3,825
D P Holloway, $4,091
Z Jones, $3,189
Jos F Kelley, $2,490
Thos Lewis, $4,261
P Laurance, $13,006
Benj Laurance, $13,006
Miss Emma Lindsley, $2,702
John Little, $2,558
W B Moses, $1,545
John T Mitchell, $2,669
Dr J F May, $2,766
Jas Pilling, $2,588
Wm Ruggles, $2,135
W M Shuster, $7,044
J W Simms, $2,677
Elias Travers, $2,828
John W Thompson, $1,840
Z Tobriner, $3,323
W B Williams, $2,875
Adeline Whelan, $2,059
Mrs Ellen T Woodhull, $4,602
W B Webb, $4,948
Wm Wilson, $5,657
A Zeverly, $2,280

Mrd: on Jun 4, at Harrisburg, Pa, by Rev B B Leacock, Alex'r Ray, of Wash City, D C, to Miss Susan, daughter of the late Judge Bucher.

Died: on Tue, Thos Goodall, aged 73 years. His funeral will take place this afternoon at 2 o'clock, from his late residence, 659 N J ave.

Died: on Jun 5, Mary Bovall, wife of J Edw Jones, of Bristol township, Bucks Co, Pa, formerly of Phil. [Phil, N Y, & Charleston, S C papers, please copy.]

On Tuesday a man, Chas Ames, was hit & badly wounded by a stone thrown by another man, Fred'k Reiter. Reiter has been arrested & admitted he threw the stone, but alleged that Ames was intoxicated, & attempted to drive his wagon over his [Reiter's] little son.

Albany, N Y, Jun 4. Hon L Harris Hiscock, a member of the Constitutional Convention, has just been shot dead at Stanwix Hall, by a man who talks deliberately of the deed & says he can justify it. The man who shot Hiscock is Gen Cole, a lumber dealer of Syracuse, N Y. Gen Cole remarked that Hiscock had been his best friend, but that while absent in the army, [where he achieved the rank of general of cavalry] Hiscock had dishonored his wife, &, added Gen Cole, I have the evidence in my pocket. Gen Cole quietly awaited the arrival of the police, & was taken to prison. [Jun 26th newspaper: N Y, Jun 25. The grand jury at Albany yesterday found a true bill against Gen Cole, charging him with murder in the first degree in the killing of Mr Hiscock.]

Hartford, Conn, Jun 5. Rev Joel Haines, D D, for nearly 50 years pastor of the First Congregational Church in this city, died at Gilead today, aged 78.

Balt, Jun 5. Saml Clifford, who has been on trial for the past 2 days in the Criminal Court of this city for the murder of W H Pereigoy some 8 or 10 months ago, the jury rendered a verdict of guilty of manslaughter.

Dept of the Interior, U S Patent Ofc, Wash, May 31, 1867. Ptn of Oliver P Drake, of Boston, Mass, praying for the extension of a patent granted to him Aug 30, 1853, & reissued Nov 15, 1864, for an improvement in Apparatus for Combining Hydro-Carbon Vapor with Air, for seven years from the expiration of said patent, which takes place on Aug 30, 1867. -T C Theaker, Com'r of Patents

Chancery sale, by decree of the Supreme Court of D C, passed Apr 20, 1867, in cause 712, Jos L Shoemaker against Mary Shoemaker et al; public auction of that desirable country residence known as ***Clover Hill***, belonging to the estate of the late David Shoemaker, on the new road, 1 mile west from Gtwn, containing about 17½ acres, with fine dwlg house, barn, stabling, & all necessary out-bldgs. Also, we will sell part of lot 163 in Beatty & Hawkins addition to Gtwn, fronting 32 feet on 3rd st, with a well built 2 story brick dwlg, containing 9 rooms. –F W Jones, Edw J Shoemaker, trustees -Thos Dowling, auct

FRI JUN 7, 1867
Ads: 1-Mr John H Semmes offers for rent a desirable residence near Md & Va aves. 2-Mr J G Matlock has found a new leather carriage lap apron. 3-The steam-propeller will be sold at Annapolis on Jun 11th.

Jurors for the June Term of the Criminal Court-Wash. Grand Jury:

John Gaynor	August Ockert	Geo L Sheriff
Jas R D Morrison	Geo E Jillard	Leonidas Coyle
J J McQuillan	Bernard Hayes	John J Berrett
Jas Fraser	B F Gray	V Willett
Wm H Carico	Jedediah Giddings	F H Findley
Benj E Gittings	Allen Dorsey	Wesley Ballenger
Job McCristal	Thos F Galt	Robt Peak
Wm W Birth	Harrisson Fowler	

Petit Jury:

Peter E Little	Poulus Thyson	Randolph Eichhorn
Timothy D Daley	Wm S Thompson	Francis B Lord
Reuben Bacon	Danl Lightfoot	Danl Collins
Andra Gullard	John E Hilton	John Robinson
C F Cummings	Francis W Bivin	E Humphreyville
Edw Reynolds	Thos Boyne	John Cook
Peter Hepburn	Jonas Glick	John McGrann
Resin Arnold	J F Berkly	Benj Owens
T A Newman	Wm J Gallant	

Board of Police Com'rs-Jun 6, 1867. 1-The resignation of E G Handy, as police magistrate was received & accepted, & W W Tucker was appointed police magistrate in his stead. Mr Tucker has been acting in that capacity for some time. 2-Ofcr S S Lester, charged with neglect of duty, was fined $10 & reprimanded. 3-Ofce Chas W Sebastian, charged with gross neglect of duty was dismissed the force. 4-Wm L Dulaney was appointed an additional patrolman, to do duty at the Centre Market, for 90 days. 5-The application of Benj Cole for liquor license was approved. Motion for an injunction to restrain Adams Express Co from selling a frame bldg on B st north, between 2nd & 3rd sts. The owners [the Lumpkin heirs & Mr Going,] of the lot upon which the bldg is erected had never given their consent to its erection, but that the express company had take squatter possession. Justice Olin declined to issue an injunction & to make the same perpetual, for the reason the owners of the lot had never given consent to the erection of the bldg it belonged to them, & the company could give no valid title. If, however, the company persisted in the sale, & the bldg was removed, the owners of the lot would have proper cause for bringing a suit at law to recover the value of the bldg.

The <u>Wash Schutzen Corps</u> held its annual meeting at Seventh-st Park on Wed, & elected the following ofcrs for the ensuing year: Pres, Chas Kloman; Vice Pres, Fred'k Hugle; 1st Shooting-master, Mr Henzo; Treasurer, John Augerman; Sec, Mr Storch; Corr Sec, Mr Kandler; Ensigns, L Emmert for American flag, Mr Exanters for the German flag, & Henry Hull for the flag of the association; Cmte of Arrangements, Messrs Blount, Kellian, Voigt, Helmuth, & Beler.

Thos J Durant, who was appointed by Gen Sheridan Govn'r in place of Wells, peremptorily declines the appointment. [Mr Benj F Flanders is hereby appointed in his stead. By command of Maj Gen P H Sheridan; Geo L Hartsuff, Assist Adj Gen.]

Rt Hon Lord Monck will sail, with his family, from England for Canada on May 13th. The English Gov't has overlooked his action in the Lamiraude extradition difficulty, & promised him the Governor-Generalship of the new dominion for just so long as he chooses to hold it.

Phil, Jun 6. This evening the steam boiler in the manufacturing establishment of Ward & Geis, sash & cabinet makers, near 10th & Chestnut sts, exploded, demolishing the whole bldg, 5 stories high & over 150 feet deep. The bodies of the dead are so mutilated that they cannot be recognized. Rescued alive, but greatly injured: F W Jenkins, engineer; John Germain, fireman; Jos Todd, Geo Clark, & John Cushack. [Jun 8th newspaper: Seventeen bodies have been taken from the ruins, including the body of Mr Greasey, the proprietor. Adam Stewart, who was buried in the ruins, was protected by the beams forming a bridge over him, & dug his own way out, almost uninjured, after being buried alive almost 12 hours.]

<u>Mountain House</u>, Capon Springs, Hampshire Co, Va. This popular Watering Place is now open for the reception of visitors. –Saml M Mullin, proprietor

Supreme Court of D C, Jun 5, 1867; No 966 Equity. Luanna Dewees, petitioner, vs Alex'r W Dewees, dfndnt. This case is for divorce. On motion of the petitioner, by M Thompson, her solicitor, it is ordered that the dfndnt cause his appearance to be entered herein on or before Jul 20, 1867; otherwise the cause will be proceeded with as in case of default. –A B Olin, Justice -R J Meigs, clerk

SAT JUN 8, 1867
Court in Equity-Mr Justice Olin, Jun 7, 1867. 1-John Keyworth et al vs Eliza P Towers; order appointing John N Olliver trustee to sell. 2-Geo E Mattingly vs Jas H Darrow; order granting injunction. 3-Wilson vs Terrett et al. Decree appointing W F Mattingly trustee to convey. 4-Thompson et al vs Bell et al. Decree appointing John Thompson trustee to convey.

It is reported that Mr Ferdinand McCloud, of Lake City, Fla, who is temporarily sojourning at the Nat'l Hotel in Wash City, had disappeared from his room. His friends are much concerned about him, as he was known to be in possession of a large amount of money. Diligent search was made for him yesterday by his friends & some members of the police force.

Mrd: on Jun 6, at St Aloysius Church, by Rev B F Wiget, Mr Christian Eckloff to Miss Mary A Conner, both of Wash City.

Mrd: on Jun 5, at Devonshire Pl, Phil, by Rev C H Hall, of Wash City, Brvt Maj Gen J G Parke, U S A, to Ellan Palmer, daughter of the late Geo Blight.

Mrd: on Jun 6, at the Church of the Ascension, by Rev Wm Pinckney, D D, Lt Chas Humphreys, U S A, to Katie, youngest daughter of John Gass, formerly of N H.

Household & kitchen furniture at auction on Thursday next, at the residence of Francis McNerhany, on I st south, between 6th & 7th sts. -Green & Williams, aucts

An appeal by Benj F Butler from a decree of the Surrogate directing the appellant to make a further return as executor of the assets in Mass, Louisiana, & Calif,of his brother, Andrew J Butler, deceased, came up in the Supreme Court at N Y on Thu. In the inventory filed by Benj F Butler on Aug 23, 1865, it appears that the assets were $76,391.04, whereas it had been admitted that the estate was worth $200,000, & the assets of the testator in the above named States were not included in the appraisement. Decision reserved.

U S Marshal's sale; by 4 writs of fieri facias issued from the Clerk's Ofc of the Supreme Court of D C: public sale on Jun 18 next, of the frame bldg formerly occupied as the Nat'l Express & Transportation Co, near the canal wharf, between 9th & 10th sts, seized & levied upon as the property of said company, to be sold to satisfy executions in favor of No 3,646 in favor of Theodore O Chestney; No 3,647 in favor of Lawrence R Thomas; No 3,648 in favor of McC Y Barry; No 3,649 in favor of Arthur H Anderson. –D S Gooding, U S Marshal, D C

Guardian's sale, by order of Orphans Court of D C, dated May 21, 1867; public sale on Jun 24, the south 49 feet 3 inches front of lot 10 in square 402, running back with that width 79 feet. Also, lot 10 in square 514; & lot 5 in square 584. -Virginia Hollingsworth, Guardian of Margaretta B Dougherty. -Cooper & Latimer, aucts

Supreme Court of D C, May 29, 1867. 931 Equity Docket 8. Danl Robertson vs Margaret Robertson. The subpoena having been issued on May 3, 1867, & placed in the hands of the Marshal for service was returned by him on May 17 "not found." An order of publication is therefore prayed by cmplnt against said dfndnt to appear & answer his bill of cmplnt for divorce; otherwise that the same be taken for confessed. –A B Olin, Justice -R J Meigs, clerk

Supreme Court of D C, Jun 7, 1867; Equity, No 971. Wm Gereocke vs Anna Gereocke. It is ordered that the dfndnt cause her appearance to be entered herein on or before the first day occurring 40 days after this day; otherwise the cause will be proceeded with as in case of default. –R J Meigs, clerk

Richmond, Va, Jun 6. Edw A Pollard has entered a suit against Wm James, revenue collector for property in Washington sold by confiscation & purchased by James.

Trustee's sale of valuable improved property, by deed of trust from John Crowley & wife & Thos Coleman & wife to the subscriber, dated Mar 22, 1866, recorded in Liber R M H folios 491, land records of Wash Co, D C: public auction on Jul 1 next, lots 32, 35 thru 37, in square 498, in Wash City, with two 4 story brick dwlg houses, supplied with gas & water, & one large brick bldg used as a bottling establishment. –A Thos Bradley, trustees -Cooper & Latimer, aucts

MON JUN 10, 1867
A new evening paper, to be called the **Evening Express**, will appear today.

The Maison Doree property, in N Y, has been leased for ten years, at $26,000 per annum, for a retail dry goods store.

Nicholas Keller jumped from a train near *Fort Wayne*, Ind, on Thu, & fractured his skull so that he died the next day.

Lewis Warrington, the son of Mr Lewis Warrington, of Wash City, & a grandson of the late Cmdor Warrington, has been appointed to a 2nd lieutenancy in the cavalry service. When the war opened, though then a mere boy, less than 14 years of age, he sought service as a soldier, & was in military employment till the rebellion closed. He greatly distinguished himself for his horsemanship, & for his promptitude & efficiency in every duty, attracted the attention, in an especial manner, of Maj Gen Augur & other leading ofcrs of this dept. It is through these influences with the commendation of Gen Grant, that his appointment has been made.

Gen Cole, who shot Hiscock, a member of the Constitutional Convention of N Y, has been fully committed for murder.

Orphans Court-Judge Purcell. 1-On Sat, the will of the late Matthew E Duvall was fully proven & admitted to probate, & record & letters testamentary issued to Wm P Brook; bond $4,000. 2-The will of the late John C Frizzell was fully proven & admitted to probate & record. 3-The will of Archibald McNeil was fully proven & admitted to probate. 4-Two wills of Eliz Morrison were filed, one of which was fully proven as regards personality, & the other partially proven. 5-Letters of administration de bonis non on the estate of the late John Snyder were issued to Chas E Sherman; bond $2,000. 6-The second acount of the guardian of orphan of Thos Neary was approved & passed. 7-Messrs W D Davidge, J H Johnson, & Mr Clark, of Md, filed a caveat to the will of the late Mary Ann Fearson, in the names of Robt L McPherson, of Gtwn, & S T McPherson, of Balt, & also the Taylor heirs, of Balt, on the ground that the deceased, at the time of executing the alleged will, was not of sound & disposing memory, & because improper & undue influence by Mrs Julia A Barrett, to whom the bulk of the estate, valued at about $168,000, is bequeathed, was exercised. It is understood that ex-Govn'r Pratt is engaged in this case.

Hiram Thomas, a man 70 years old, living in Bracken Co, Ky, has been sentenced to be hung in August for murdering his wife.

Mrd: on Jun 4, at the Thirteenth-street Baptist Church, by Rev Geo W Samson, Jas H Barker, of Phil, Pa, to Eliz B Reynolds, of Wash City.

Died: on Jun 7, Mrs Mary F Abercrombie, aged 72 years, widow of the late Jas Abercrombie, of Balt. Her funeral will take place from the residence of her son-in-law, Jos Saxton, 602 N J ave, Capitol Hill, on Jun 12 at 11 o'clock. [Balt, Phil, N Y, Boston, & Memphis papers please copy.]

Died: on Jun 7, in N Y, Mrs Ellen L Dale, widow of the late Dr Geo M Dale, aged 33 years. Her funeral will be on Monday at 3 o'clock P M, from the residence of her brother, Dr W Evans, 537½ H st.

Obit-died: on May 28, Lewis S Semmes, aged 22 years. [Poem followed, signed L A P.] Port Tobacco Times please copy.

Dept of the Interior, U S Patent Ofc, Wash, Jun 3, 1867. Ptn of Stepehen Morse, of Springfield, Mass, praying for the extension of a patent granted to him Sep 6, 1853, for an improvement in Iron Car Brakes, for seven years from the expiration of said patent, which takes place on Sep 6, 1867. -T C Theaker, Com'r of Patents

Healing Springs, Bath Co, Va: delightful watering place is now open for the reception of visitors, with accommodations for 300 persons. –John L Kubank, agent

Farms for sale-valuable country seats: ***Blue Plains***, 450 acres, subdivided; fronting the river, between Giesboro & Alexandria Ferry. A farm of 150 acres in Montg Co, Md, near Chain Bridge; on the Conduit road, thoroughly improved, commands picturesque views of the Little Falls of the Potomac. –Maury & Ingle, Real Estate & Ins Brokers, 373 D st, near 7th, Wash.

TUE JUN 11, 1867
Ads. 1-Lt Sinon, at the Arsenal, offers for sale a fine buggy. 2-I F Mudd, under Germania Hall, on D st, near 9th, makes boys' suits of every style.

York, Pa, Jun 10. On Sunday night Mr & Mrs Alfred King, residing at 30 East 19th st, retired to their sleeping apartments, & as they did not make their appearance today, a servant went to the apartment, & discovered the husband & wife both lying dead on the bed. A pistol was found on the bed, three chambers of which had been discharged. The supposition is that King first shot his wife, having previously given her chloroform, & then killed himself.

The Court was formally opened on the Surratt trial yesterday by the crier, Mr Wm A Mulloy, attys for the defence, Mr Merrick & the Messrs Bradley, being present. Judge Fisher entered the court room at 9:30 A M. The Dist Atty & Mr Pierpont, counsel for the prosecution, subsequently entered the room. The prisoner was brought into the court by Marshall Gooding. He was handcuffed, clean shaven, except a moustache & goatee, & wears his hair hanging long about his neck. He was dressed in a dark suit. After being in the court a few moments the handcuffs were taken off. His face is very pale, & he wears a careworn, troubled look. By 11 o'clock the court room was literally crowded. In the Supreme Court of the District of Columbia. The U S vs John H Surratt. Indictment-murder.

Chancery sale of valuable improved business property & dwlg house, by decree of the Supreme Court of D C, passed on Jun 7, 1867, cause No 847, wherein Keyworth et al are cmplnts, & Towers et al are dfndnts, the trustee will sell, on Jul 2, part of lot 12 in square 490, [near the property of John Spicer;] also, on Jul 3, a dwlg house & lot on K st, between 8th & 9th sts-Mount Vernon Place, being part of lot 2 in square 402. -John N Oliver, trustee -Green & Williams, aucts

Supreme Court of D C, in Equity, No 815. John P Von Essen vs Benj Fawcett, Marion Fawcett, & the unknown heirs of Martha Clagett. The object of the bill is to procure a sale of a lot & house in Gtwn, adjoining the post ofc, on Congress st, formerly owned by Andrew Hough, for division among parties in interest. It states that the dfndnts named above claim some interest in the property, which claim it charges to be unfounded, & that they are non-residents. On motion of the cmplnt, by W S Cox, his solicitor, it is ordered that the dfndnts above named cause their appearance to be entered herein on or before the first rule day occurring 40 days after this day, otherwise the cause will be proceeded with as in case of default. –A B Olin, Justice -R J Meigs, clerk [*Two spellings of Fawcett/Faucett.]

Dept of the Interior, U S Patent Ofc, Wash, May 31, 1867. Ptn of Bernard Hughes, of Rochester, N Y, praying for the extension of a patent granted to him May 16, 1854, for an improvement in Trip Hammer, for seven years from the expiration of said patent, which takes place on May 16, 1867. -T C Theaker, Com'r of Patents

WED JUN 12, 1867
Among the recent appointments to the army are Capt Geo Aarme, 10th U S Cavalry, & B F Grafton, U S infty.

A special order was issued yesterday mustering out of service Capt Geo W Cushing, [brvt major,] assist quartermaster, U S volunteers, & Surgeon Robt Reyburn, Brvt Lt Colonel, U S volunteers, to date from Jun 3, 1867; also, the order dated Aug, 1865, honorably mustering out of service Capt Geo T Castle, [brvt major,] commissary of subsistence, U S volunteers, is amended to take effect Aug 29, 1865. The above ofcrs are mustered under provisions of General Order, 79, 1865, for the discharge from service all ofcrs unemployed, or whose services are no longer needed. The resignations of the following ofcrs have also by the above-named special order been accepted: Capt Wm P Robeson, 7th U S cavalry, Jun 8, 1867; 2nd Lt Benj K Davidson, 30th U S infty, Jun 8, 1867.

Wm E Shoomaker, 322 E st, has been appointed sole agent for D C for all the celebrated brands of Rhine wines.

Died: on Jun 6, at Weston, Platte Co, Mo, Martha Ann, wife of Chas A Perry, formerly of Montg Co, Md.

Obit-died: on Jun 11, in Wash City, in his 72nd year, Jas Rhodes, a native of St Mary's Co, Md, but for the last 60 years a resident of Wash City. Mr Rhodes was one of our oldest & most respectable citizens. In all the relations of husband, father, relative, friend, & citizen he illustrated the noble & generous qualities which mark the true Christian gentleman. His funeral will take place from his late residence, 648 8th st, at 10 o'clock on Jun 14, & proceed to St Peter's Church, where service will commence at 10½ o'clock.

The golden wedding of Rt Rev Geo Upfold, D D, the Episcopal bishop of the diocese of Indiana, was commemorated at Indianapolis, on Jun 8. The Bishop received many gifts, amounting to about $1,100, & other remembrances amounting to fully $600 more.

N Y, Jun 11. Revolution in Peru. A passenger in the steamship **Arizona**, from Aspinwall, reports the death of Mr Prevost, U S Consul at Guayaquil.

Orphans Court of Wash Co, D C, Jun 11, 1867. In the case of Jas Fitzpatrick, exc of Dominick Conroy, deceased, the executor & Court have appointed Jul 2 next, for the final settlement of the personal estate of the said deceased, of the assets in hand.
-Jas R O'Beirne, Reg/o wills

The Liverpool papers announce the recent death of Mr Wm F Brough, well known in this country as an actor & dramatic agent. He died at Liverpool, a few days after his arrival from N Y; he was an Englishman by birth, & made his first appearance at the Worthing Theatre, Sussex, in 1819, as a bass singer. Only a few weeks ago the deceased started for his native country, accompainied by his wife, [& the Webb sisters,] & while on the voyage was taken ill with rheumatism, a disease which had troubled him considerably for several years. He was in his 70th year at the time of his death. He was an uncle of the popular Liverpool comedian, Mr Lionel Brough, & also of the well-known burlesque writer, Mr Wm Brough.

The copartnership existing between Theodore Gassaway & H C Howard, is this day dissolved by mutual consent. H C Howard will sign for the late firm in settlement.

Marshal's sale, on Jun 20, on the premises, one large frame slaughter house & fence, on the fork of the Little Falls road & Foxhall's lane, above Gtwn in Wash Co, D C, seized & levied upon as the property of John Bateman & will be sold to satisfy execution in favor of Chas A Buckey & John Marbury vs John Batemen & Thos N Johnson, No 2,217. –D S Gooding, U S Marshal, D C –Thos Dowling, auct

Orphans Court of Wash Co, D C. Letters testamentary on the personal estate of Eliz Monson, late of Wash, D C, deceased. –A Lindenkohl, exc

THU JUN 13, 1867
Annual Commencement of the Columbian College Law School last evening, at the National Theatre. Names of the graudates:

H W Barry	Geo F Graham	C N Richards
H D Beam	M Edwin Hall	Chas Roller
Chas H Buxton	H C Harmon	Thos S Samson
Chas L Catlin	H C Herr	Will F Scott
Fred'k Chase	G B Holden	Albert N Seip
A P Childs	W A Hunt	Frank A Spencer
A W Chilton	E P Jacobson	Wm E Spencer
Henry V Cole	J G Kimbell	Winfield S Strawn
J W Corey	R G Kirkpatrick	A K Tingle
C Eaton Creacy	Young Lanktree	Wm D Todd
Theo E Davis	H K Leaver	Edw Tompkins, jr
Wm H Day	J M Mason	M Trimble
Wm S Dodge	Jas S McCrellis	John B Waifel
Wm H Doolittle	M C McCullough	Woodbury Wheeler
Benj Eglin	C G McLeran	J N Whitney
Edgar T Ensign	J Fred Meyers	H A Wilder
Reginald Fendell	N B Milliken	John C Wilson
E E Forsyth	S A Moulthrop	W L Wilson
H R French	John L Murphy	Jos Woodruff
E M Gibson	J McC Perkins	
J Mason Goszler	H R Pollard	

Lynchburg News of Monday. John Kay, has been sentenced to 8 years in the penitentiary for forging the name of Mr W B Moses, of this city, to a draft for $2,100, & obtaining the money for the same of the First Nat'l Bank in this city.

Mr John C Maydell, cigar maker, living at 165 north Paca st, was killed in Balt on Monday. He took passage upon a car of the Catonsville railroad that left the station at 10 o'clock, & when arriving opposite **Mount Olivet Cemetery** he attempted to jump from the car while in motion, & he fell & was run over, being maimed in a shocking manner. After lingering in great pain for an hour he expired.

Mrd: on Jun 11, in Wash City, at the house of the bride's father, by Rev Wm Rhoberts, D D, of N Y, assisted by Rev Dr Gurley, Wm H Rhoberts, of N Y C, to Miss Sarah E McLean. [N Y papers please copy.]

Died: on Jun 12, John Williams Rawlins, son of Maj Gen John A & Emma Rawlins, aged 10 months. His funeral will take place on Jun 14 at 5 o'clock, from the residence of Gen Rawlins, 78 Gay st, Gtwn.

Gen Sherman, with the concurrence of Sec Stanton, has agreed to allow Govn't Hunt, of Colorado, to equip 500 volunteers for Indian service.

Mrs Eliz Walker committed suicide in N Y, on Sat, by taking Paris green.

Phil, Jun 12. Yesterday while John Clepner, a blacksmith was beating his wife, Fred Ditmer, a son of Ditmer, the well-known brewer, interfered to save the woman, when Clepner stabbed him, inflicting a wound which, it is thought, will prove fatal. Clepner has been arrested.

John Wells, of Greencastle, Ind, attempted suicide last Tuesday, by throwing himself before a train on the railroad. He was stuck on the head & his skull badly fractured, but he was still alive at last accounts.

A **chalice**, belonging to St Michael's Church, in Charleston, which was stolen during the burning of Columbia, where it was deposited for safe keeping during the siege of the former city, has been recovered from one of the pawn shops of N Y C.

Trustee's sale of 112 acres of land, with the improvements, near Beltsville, adjoining Carroll's Factory, in Montg Co, Md, at auction on Jul 3 next, I shall sell **Mizpah**, with improvements, consisting of a two story dwlg house, barn, & other out-houses. -J W Barnaclo, trustee -Green & Williams, aucts

For rent, that delightful residence lately occupied by Col J M Nichols, near St Aloyisus Church & the residence of Gen U S Grant, Gen Williams, & Mayor Wallach, containing 15 rooms, with all modern improvements. Apply to Rev B F Wiget, at 530 I st, or to Harvey Clarke, & Given, coal ofc, 475 10th st, between D & E sts.

Supreme Court of D C, Jun 12, 1867. 961 Equity-Docket 8. Catharine Dodson vs Jacob Dodson. The petition in this cause is for a divorce. It is ordered that the dfndnt appear on or before Jul 26 next, otherwise the cause will be proceeded with as in case of default. —A B Olin, Justice -R J Meigs, clerk

FRI JUN 14, 1867
The Pres has been appointed Alex'r Bliss to be Sec of Legation at Berlin. Saml Strong has been appointed Revenue Inspector for the Dist of Columbia.

Receivers sale of pianos, maple & rosewood veneering, scales, iron plates, & screws for pianos, etc, by order passed by the Supreme Court, D C, on Jun 1, No 86, in a cause pending wherein Andrew F Dessan is cmplnt & Henry Kaiser is dfnfnt: public auction on Jun 14, on the premises, 451 10th st. —A Thos Bradley, Receiver -Nagle & Co, aucts

Ads. 1-N Demongeot, dealer in human hair & perfumery, has removed his store from 10th & D sts to 279 Pa ave, between 10th & 11th. 2-Mr C Gautier, 252 Pa ave, has on hand a very large sotck of summer wines, which he offers at reduced priced.

New Orleans, Jun 13. The Picayune: the El Comercio, of Matamoras, of the 7th from, gives the following extract from a letter of the 2nd from Monterey: Gen Miramon has died of a fever which attacked him after he was wounded at Queretaro. Castillo, Majia, & several others have been shot.

Thos A Mitchell, of Wash City, firm of Mitchell & Son, has recently sold, in N Y, 30,750 acres of land in Botetourt Co, Va, [part of the original Barclay tract,] at $1.75 per acre; purchasers A I Baum, A Richardson, G A Wheelock, Wood, & others.

Thos Dowling, auct, has sold a lot on the south side of Second st, adjoining the Bodisco property, fronting 70 feet on Second st, with a depth of 150 feet, to W P Sanger, for $37 per front foot.

New Orleans, Jun 3, 1867. Letter of Judge Abell to the Pres: I am an old man, & will venture to say that if the laws are permitted to be trampled upon, all the ofcs, under one pretext or another, will fall into the hands of extreme men; they will want no new constitution; the peope will have power to make none, or, if permitted, it will be rejected, the object of the act of Congress defeated, & the people tantalized. Since writing the above, Govn'r Wells has been removed, & Mr Thos J Durant appointed in his stead.

John Gaynor, 36 Market Space, Gtwn, D C: I am distilling a Superior Whiskey, equal to any known in the market. I have an experienced French distiller, to reproduce from fruits in foreign countries, such as Cherry Wine & Brandy, French Brandy, & Holland Gin.

Richmond, Jun 13. J J Philips was arrested, charged with the murder of Mary J Pitts, of Caroline Co. The dead body was found near Richmond some months ago.

Trial of John H Surratt yesterday: The Judge ordered the talesmen ordered yesterday to be called, as follows: Wm B Todd; Geo Mattingly-this gentleman sent a letter to the Court, in which he states, that while willing to serve his country, he is exempt on 2 grounds-he is engaged in carrying the U S mails, & is over 65 years of age-he was excused. Wm H Tenney; Wm P Dole; Andrew J Joyce-this gentleman sent a note to the Judge from Dr Thos Miller, saying that Mr Joyce's child is dangerously ill, & his presence is necessary at home. No objection was interposed. Mr Joyce was excused. Franck Taylor asked to be excused on the ground of business interests requiring his attention elsewhere, & which would materially suffer should he be compelled to serve as a juror. Judge Fisher excused Mr Taylor. John R Elvans; D P Holloway, former Com'r of Patents-he said he was not competent to serve as a juror, not being a citizen of the District, but having his residence in Indiana. It was true he had been transacting business here for the last 6 years, but intended to return to Indiana. He was not even a taxpayer. The court excused him. Thos Blagden; Riley A Shinn; Richd M Hall-this gentleman said his business would suffer were he compelled to serve as a juror, & the interests of many others suffer. There was no one in his ofc who could transact business in his absence. The court replied that on such excuses, nine out of ten would be relieved from service. Thos J S Perry; Franklin Philp-sent a letter saying he was obliged to leave the city on business. Mr Carrington thought this was not sufficient & asked that process be issued to compel his attendance. Geo H Plant sent a note saying he was unwell, & for this reason asked to be excused. Mr Carrington said Mr Plant should appear in person, if he could. Reuben B Clark; John Van Riswick; S P Brown-exhibited a certificate from a physician, stating his health would be impaired by confinement as a juror. He was excused. Z D Gilman; Jos A Brown; Z C Robbins; Cornelius Wendell; Valentine Harbaugh-this gentleman was excused on a certificate from a physician stating that he was under medical treatment, & that 2 members of his family are sick. Jos Gerhardt asked to be excused, owing to exposure in the war, & disease, he could not hear well, being a litle deaf in one ear. The Judge said they would manage that the gentleman should hear. Horatio N Easby; Thos Berry; Wm W Moore-this gentleman asked to be excused on the ground that he was unwell, & besides the public interests would suffer, as he was connected in an official capacity with the Metropolitan Railroad Co. The Court refused to excuse Mr Moore. J H Crane-listed; no remarks. Mr Elvans asked to be excused on the ground of previous service as a juror; but the reasons assigned were not deemed sufficient by the Court. Wm P Dole, formerly Com'r of Indian Affairs, sent a not asking to be excused, for the reason that he is not a citizen, etc. The Court ordered an attachment to be issued for Mr Dole. The Marshal reported that Wm P Dole could not be found, & that Franklin Philp had left Washington to take passage for Europe. The clerk called the names of the additional talesmen as follows: Robt Ball, Henry M Knight, John F Ellis, Terrence Drury, Wm M Shuster, & Saml Fowler. The two last named did not respond to their names, & measures were taken to compel their attendance. Mr Fowler was brought into court, when the Judge said: Mr Fowler, you were attached to appear here at 1 o'clock. Mr

Fowler replied: I meant no disrespect. I intended to come in time. Attachments were out for Messrs Dole & Plant. Bailiffs were sent out to summon additional talesmen. J Russell Barr & Wm H Morrison were added to the list, the requisite number was procured in the person of Jedediah Gittings. Jurors selected: Wm B Todd, John R Elvans, Thos Bladgen, R M Hall, Thos J S Perry, Wm M Shuster, Z D Gilman, Horatio N Easby, Thos Berry, Robt Ball, Saml Fowler, & J R Barr [age 55.] These gentlemen were requested to stand up & be sworn. Mr Blagden said he could not be sworn as a juror, having expressed an opinion. The Court. Mr Blagden, they think you such a gentleman that you would make an honest verdict. Mr Perry said that he had formed an opinion, & was against capital punishment. Mr Gilman said: I am, too. Messrs Fowler, Shuster, Easby, & Gilman, severally said that they, too, had made up this minds & formed opinions. Todd, Blagden, Shinn, Hall, Berry, Clark & Elvans were told by the Court to stand aside.

New Orleans, May 18, 1867. Maj Gen P H Sheridan, Commanding 5th Military Dist. Sir: A copy of the following order was delivered to me at 2 o'clock 18 minutes P M of the day of its date: Headquarters 5th Military Dist, New Orleans, La, Mar 27, 1867. General Orders No 5. Andrew S Herron, Atty Gen, State of Louisiana; John T Monroe, Mayor, city of New Orleans, & Edmund Abell, Judge First District Court, City of New Orleans, are hereby removed from their respective ofcs, from 12 M today, & the following appointments made, to take effect from the same date, viz: B L Lynch, to be Atty Gen, State of Louisiana; Edw Heath, to be Mayor city of New Orleans, & W W Howe, to be Judge 1st Dist Court, city of New Orleans. Each person removed will turn over all books, papers, records, etc, pertaining to his ofc to the one appointed thereto & the authority of the latter will be duly respected & enforced. By command of Maj Gen P H Sheridan. Geo L Hartsuff, Assist Adj Gen. Geo Lee, 1st Lt 21st U S Infty, Acting Assist Adj Gen.

North Platte, Nebraska, Jun 7, 1867. To Geo W McClellan, Second Assist Postmaster General: C M Davis, special agent of the Post Ofc Dept, killed by the Indians day before yesterday, an American Ranche; also, two drivers. –Geo K Otis [American Ranche is the locality of the alleged murders on Jun 5. Information from Montano gives report that Bosman was killed.]

SAT JUN 15, 1867
Drowned, in Bronx river, Westchester Co, N Y, on Jun 5, Claude Saxton, only son of Dr Gustave Q & Clara Virginia Pope, of this city.

<u>Trial of John H Surratt-Jun 14. The names of talesmen ordered yesterday were then called. The following offered no excuses, viz:</u>

Thos Lewis	Geo A Bohrer	Fred'k Bates
Matthew G Emery	C C Snyder	Moses T Parker
Wm H Harrover	U H Ridenour	Nicholas Acker
John McDermott	Geo J Seufferle	John T Mitchell
Geo T McGlue	Thos E Lloyd	Wm Ballantyne
Jas McGrann	W W Burdette	Wm Flynn

Patrick Fleming	W B Williams	Geo L Sheriff
Jas Y Davis	Norman B Smith	Saml Bacon
John A Markriter	Peter Hepburn	Wm Bryan
Columbus Alexander	Wm J Redstake	Amos Hunt
Wm H Baldwin	Wm McLain	Lot Flannery
John W Simms	Jas Maguire	Isaac W Ross
John T Given	Wm H Barbour	

Thos Young was excused on account of his being an invalid. Jas Kelley said he was in Gov't employ, & he was accordingly excused. Wm Orme was excused, his physician certifying that he was physically incapable of sitting on a jury in a protracted case. Wm Helmick offered as an excuse that he had conscientious scruples upon the subject of capital punishment. Decided to be a question for Judge Fisher to pass upon. Douglas Moore & Geo Crandall were excused upon physician's certificate of illness. Jenkin Thomas presented a certificate from Dr Magruder, certifying that he was subject to attacks of inflammator rheumatism, & asked to be excused. Mr Carrington suggested that any man was liable to attacks of illness. Judge Wylie declined to excuse Mr Thomas. When the name of Mr B H Stinemetz was called, Judge Wylie said he had a note stating that Mr Stinementz was ill, & he would therefore be excused for today. Jos L Pearson said he was not a taxpayer, & asked to be excused. He said owned no real estate, but paid school taxes. Judge Wylie thought Mr Pearson was a competent juror. C H Lane, Francis Lamb, Wm H Tenney, & John Grinder, were excused by reason of physical disablity. Geo F Gulick said he had no excuse to offer except that his father-in-law died last night. Judge Wylie said that the court would not sit today, & probably not tomorrow, & he would excuse Mr Gulick now. Poulus Thyson was excused for reasons satisfactory to the Court. Mr A B Stoughton said he would not offer his personal business as an excuse, but he hoped to be excused as business entrusted to him by clients would suffer. He was not excused. Jas S Tophan was excused on account of the serious illness of a child, who is supposed to be in a dying condition. J J May was returned by the Marshal *non est*. Jas C Kennedy said he was not a resident here. He paid taxes on property, but claimed his citizenship in N Y & voted there. Judge Wylie said it was a question of domicil, & he excused Mr Kennedy. John Wilson said he had no excuse to offer on account of illness in his family. They were all well, but there was no one but himself to attend to his business, & that would suffer if he were on the jury. He had not been able to see his physician this morning, or he might have obtained a certificate for himself. Judge Wylie said that, in consideration of the present condition of Mr Wilson, he would await a certificate from his physician. P W Browing claimed to be a resident & voter in Md, & was excused. Geo W Riggs was excused on account of important business which could not be neglected. Geo Gillard has been previously summoned as a member of the grand jury for the ensuing term of the court, & was accordingly excused. John Alexander was returned as in N Y, but he would be summoned upon his return to this city.

Died: on Jun 16, Rudolph, infant son of Jas S & Ann M M Topham, aged 4 months & 19 days. His funeral will be from the residence of the parents, 180 4th st, on Sunday, Jun 16, at 3 o'clock P M.

Saml Drury, one of the oldest citizens, & who has for many years been esteemed for his noble qualities of mind & heart, died at his residence, 133 I st, on Thursday night. Mr Drury, had for 30 years, filled the position of police magistrate, & was for many years a prominent member of the Levy Court. It is but a short time since the death of his wife, & he had been unable, on account of ill health, since her burial, to attend to any business.
+
Died: Jun 13, Saml Drury, in his 79th year. His funeral will be from his residence, 133 I st, between 22nd & 23rd sts,*this evening, Jun 15, at 9 o'clock A M. [*Copied as written.] [Jun 17th newspaper: The funeral of the late Saml Drury took place on Sat from St Matthew's Church; the remains were placed in the hearse, & the cortege proceeded to **Mount Olivet Cemetery**, where they were placed in the public vault beside the remains of his late wife. The following gentlement were pall-bearers: Wm Wilson, Chas Sioussa, Thos Evans, Geo Kidwell, Wm Brown, & Henry Rochat.]

Died: on Jun 16, Rudolph, infant son of Jas S & Ann M M Topham, aged 4 months & 19 days. His funeral will be from the residence of the parents, 180 4th st, on Sunday, Jun 16, at 3 o'clock P M.

Police Affairs. 1-John H Brooks, alias Grant, arrested for an assault with intent to kill Ann H Grant, was committed to jail for court by Justice Walter. 2-Jas Alston was committed to jail for court of stealing a mule from Jas Selden last Dec. Alston confessed his guilt, & stated that he exchanged the animal with a man named Sexton for a cow. 3-Bruce Dent, a colored man, was arrested for cruelly beating his wife & committed to jail for court. A younger member of the family encouraged the father to resist the ofcr when he attempted to take Dent into custody, & was fined $5 for his share in the transaction.

Col Theodore O'Hara, of Ky, died on Friday last, in Barbour Co, Ala, where, since the close of the late war, he had been residing, engaged in the cotton business with a relative. He was an ofcr of the old army, & served with great gallantry & distinction in the war with Mexico. He gave the aid of his sword to Gen Lopez in the ineffectual effort to republicanize Cuba, & was for a time associated with Gen Walker in the Nicaragua expedition. At the commencement of the rebellion he joined the Southern army, & served first upon the staff of Gen Albert Sidney Johnson, & afterward upon that of Gen Bragg. The first-named General he received in his arms after the fatal wound which terminated his life at the battle of Shiloh. He wrote "The Burial of our Dead," on the occasion of the reinterment of the remains of the members of the Ky regt who fell in Mexico. This piece has recently had the singular compliment paid it of having selected from it, as an inscription for a monument recently erected in Boston to the Union dead, the following lines:
"On Fame's eternal camping ground
Their ailent tents are spread,
And memory guards with solemn round
The bivouac of the dead." -Columbus [Ga] Sun, 9th.

Balt, Jun 14. J Brooke, ice, butter, & cheese merchant of this city, was discovered this morning on the roadside with 2 pistol-shots, in his head, his horse & buggy near him. It was first supposed to be a case of highway robbery, but now believed to be an attempt at suicide. He was removed to the Infirmary, & is still alive.

John Clark, the venerable president of the Citizens Nat'l Bank of Balt, died on Thursday, at the age of 80 years.

The household effects of Mrs Lincoln, wife of the President, are to be sold at public auction, at Springfield. The furniture is valued at $14,000. Mrs Lincoln's income is stated to be only $2,000.

Mr Duvall Ridgely, son of F L Ridgely, president of the Union Ins Co & Board of Underwriters, committed suicide at St Louis, on Wednesday, by taking strychnine. For the past year he was assistant general ticket agent of the Iron Mountain railroad, at St Louis, but was a few days since discharged for intemperance, which caused him to put an end to his life.

The widow of the late Rev Dr Joel Hawes, of Hartford, Conn, died on Tuesday, aged 76 years. Her husband, who was the oldest minister in Conn, died last Wednesday, at the age of 78 years.

MON JUN 17, 1867
Orphans Court-Judge Purcell. 1-Saturday the will of the late Emma Frances Coyle was filed & partially proven. After the payment of her just debts, she bequeathes the balance of her property to her sisters, Mary Elnora & Laura Virginia Coyle, whom she nominates as excecutors. The last-named filed an anunciation. 2-The will of the late Simon Flynn was filed & fully proven. He bequeathes his estate to his wife, Mary Flynn, whom he nominates as executrix, with full power to lease or sell for the benefit of the children. 3-The will of the late Lewis Patten, bequeathing his estate to his wife, &, at her death, to the children of his daughter, at Culpeper, Va, & nominating Rev W E Walker, of N J, was filed & partially proven. 4-The will of the late Clinton M Sears was filed, fully proven, & admitted to probate, & letters testamentary were issued to Wm Leslie Sears; bond $6,000. He bequeathes the stock & fixtures of his store to his brother above-named, in trust, the proceeds to be divided, one-half to the brother, & the remainder between his wife & mothers. His real estate is left to his wife & sister as tenants in common. 5-Ellen Sweeny was appointed guardian to the orphans of Bernard Farrell; bond $500. 6-The following accounts were approved & passed: First & final of administrations, w a, of Basil Patterson, & account of personal estate of same; first of administratrix of J P Laylor; second & supplemental account of Forest Queen, executor of the will of Sarah F Hughes, & balance & distribution of same.

Died: on Jun 15, in Wash City, Mrs Emelya Webster, wife of Maj Marcellus Bailey, & daughter of Prof Chas G & Mrs P W Page. Her funeral services will be today at 3 o'clock P M, at Rev Dr Sunderland's Church, on 4½ st.

Trial of John H Surratt, Sat. Jurors: Norman B Smith was excused by reason of physical disability. Matthew G Emery was excused on account of the illness of his wife, a physician certifying that her removal to another air was absolutely necessary, & also that Mr Emery was not in good health. Wm H Harrover said he would rather not sit upon a jury like this. He had not formed an opinion, & had no conscientious scruples upon the subject of capital punishment; but he produced a physician's certificate, & was excused. Danl Breed, had formed an opinion, & had come fully to a conclusion in the case. Declared to be incompetent. John R Elvans had formed an opinion from the evidence given at the trial of the conspirators; but, so far as he could analyze his own mind, he did not believe the opinion he had formed would prevent the rendition of an impartial veridct. He had no conscientious scruples upon the subject of capital punishment, & was declared a competent juror, but was challenged by the prisoner's counsel. Thos Blagden had formed an opinion, & was so biased that he found that he could not decide impartially. He was excused. John Van Riswick had not formed an opinion. Jos F Brown had formed an opinion, & believed his mind was so biased that it would be difficult for him to decide impartiality. He would be afraid to trust himself. He was declared incompetent. Thos Berry had formed an opinion from reading an acount of the trial of the conspirators, & from the account of the arrest of Surratt. His bias was not strong enough to prevent his rendering an impartial verdict; had no scruples regarding capital punishment; he was declared a competent juror, & was sworn. John H Crane had formed an opinion, but did not think it so biased his mind as to make him partial; he was opposed to capital punishment, but would render a veridict in accordance with the law & facts; declared competent, & challenged by the prosecution. Wm Helmick had formed an opinion & was against captial punishment; he was excused. Moses Parker, Geo T McGlue each had formed an opinion; challenged by the prisoner. Geo A Bohrer would like to hear the names of the other conspirators read. Judge Wylie said it had no bearing on the case. Mr Bohrer was declared competent, & was sworn. C C Schnieder had formed an opinion, but his mind was not so biased: accepted & sworn. Upton H Ridenour had formed an opinion; his bias was so strong that he would fear to sit upon the jury-excused. Isaac Ross had formed an opinion; challenged by the prisoner. Geo S Seufferle had formed an opinion; challenged by the prisoner. Thos E Lloyd had formed an opinion; was declared incompetent. W W Burdett & Fred'k Bates had each formed an opinion; strongly opposed to captial punishment: declared incompetent. Nicholas Acker had formed an opinion, but was not opposed to captial punishment. He said he was partly American & partly German; he was born in Germany, but lived long here. He was declared a competent juror, & was excused upon producing a physicians certificate of disability. John L Kidwell was excused upon producing a certificate of 3 physicians that his attendance at his drug store was absolutely necessary to the public health. John T Mitchel had formed an opinion, feared it might be a life-long regret with him to be placed on the jury; he was excused. Jenkin Thomas was excused upon physician's certificate that he was subject to rheumatism, & was now suffering from it. Jos L Pearson & Wm Ballantyne each had formed an opinion; were challenged by the defence. Wm Flinn was excused on account of having a sick child at home. Patrick Fleming had formed an opinion: challenged by the prosecution. Jas

Y Davis, Wm McLean, & Columbus Alexander, were accepted & sworn. John Markriter was excused upon a physician's certificate of disability. John W Simmons had scruples about capital punishment; declared incompetent. John T Given was declared competent, but the bailiff could not find him. Washington B Williams, Augustus B Stoughton, Peter Hepburn, & W J Redstrake were declared incompetent. Jas Maguire had formed an opinion, but was not opposed to capital punishment; declared a competent juror. Mr Maguire said he would like to be excused. He was of the same religious faith as the prisoner, & had seen it stated that the prosecution did not want Catholics on the jury. Judge Wylie said that did not incapacitate him, or have any effect upon his right to serve. He thought Mr Maguire competent. Challenged by the prosecution. Saml Bacon was excused on account of illness. Wm J Murtagh was excused on account of being a public ofcr. Amos Hunt had formed an opinion; not opposed to capital punishment; challenged by the defence. John Wilson, Wm H Barbour, Geo L Sheriff, John Alexander, Wm Bryan, Lot Flannery, Patrick White, John Ray, C M Sioussa, Benj Summy, Jos G Waters, & Thos E Clarke, all declared incompetent. Geo Clendennin had charge of **Glenwood Cemetery**; he was excused. Jacob Ramsburg, no scruples regarding capital punishment; challenged by the defence. Wm M Galt had formed an opinion, but was not biased; challenged by the defence. N C McKnew was challenged by the defence. Lemuel Towers was excused on the ground of physical disability, as was also Geo T Langley. The jury is composed as follows:

Wm B Todd	Thos Berry	Wm McLean
J R Barr	C C Schneider	B F Morsell
Robt Ball	Jas Y Davis	Benj E Gittings
Geo A Bohrer	Columbus Alexander	Wm W Birth

Ads. 1-Geo H Plant, N Y ave & 15th st, will sell, at low prices, a large stock of hand-made bricks. 2-Chas C Callan offers his drug store, with fixtures, for sale.

St Louis, Jun 15. Ofcr of the Union Pacific railroad was killed by the Indians: L A Hill, division engineer on the Union Pacific railroad was killed on Jun 12, about 40 miles north of Laporte, & Mr Archer, inspector of the road, was severely wounded. Mr Hill's body was perforated with 19 arrows & 5 pistol-balls, & he was scalped. Gen Custer is expected to strike the Cheyennes that were stampeded last Monday by Gen Hancock.

On Sat Rebecca Marshall, about 7 years old, was run over by a wagon at 7th & Pa ave. Her head was severely cut, & it was thought that one of the wheels had passed over her body. She was conveyed to the Seaton House & attended by Dr Shelby, of Balt.

Died: on Jun 15, in Wash City, Mrs Emelya Webster, wife of Maj Marcellus Bailey, & daughter of Prof Chas G & Mrs P W Page. Her funeral services will be today at 3 o'clock P M, at Rev Dr Sunderland's Church, on 4½ st.

Francis Whitman, of Lonsdale, Wisc, on Tues, in jumping from his carriage to the ground, struck a revolver, which was in his pocket, against the wheeling, causing it to explode, the ball entered his left side, near the heart, & he expired soon after.

Mobile Tribune, Jun 4. Saml Lyons, junior member of the firm of Jas Tait & Co, sent his wife & family away from the city several months since, & it is safe to presume that his absconding was premeditated. He left the city himself on Monday last, & it is stated he carried away about $50,000. The exact extent of Mr Tait's loss is not yet ascertained.

P T Barnum has bought a $100,000 house on Fifth avenue.

Adm's sale of lease, good will, furniture & fixtures of a valuable restaurant on Pa ave, near 6th st; by order of the Orphans Court of D C: public auction on Jun 19, on the premises, the Restaurant formerly kept by Peter Emrich. –M C Emrich, admx -Green & Williams, aucts

TUE JUN 18, 1867

Trial of John H Surratt-Jun 17. Mr Nathl Wilson, Assist District Atty addressed the jury: The prosecution will prove that the prisoner at the bar was present aiding & abetting the murder, & that a few moments before the shot was fired he was present in front of the theatre in consulation with Booth. It was a premeditated plot. The jury will hear how he boasted how he had shot down unarmed Union soldiers, while they were escaping from rebel prisons. It was he who left at Surrattsville the arms which Booth took possession of in his flight, & one of which was taken from him after his death. Two hours before the fatal shot was fired he purchased disguises, which the assassins were to use in their flight. He fled to Europe & there he expressed a wish that he could return & serve Andrew Johnson as Abraham Lincoln had been served. In England he found no sympathy. He hid himself in the Papal army, & enlisted as a private soldier, but was recognized & discovered by the companion of his youth. We had, it is said, no treaty of extradition with Rome, but so horrible was the crime, & so notorious was his name, that the Pope & Cardinal Antonelli surrendered him. He escaped again by leaping from a precipe, a leap which would have been impossible to any one, except one who fully realized his guilty, & knew his life was worthless. He fled to Egypt & was pursued by the law, & from Alexandria his face was turned homeward to the land he had polluted with murder. He is here now for trial. <u>Witnesses called</u>: Surgeon Gen Barnes was called to attend the President professionally on Apr 14, 1865, at the house of Mr Peterson, on 10th st, & remained with him until he died. The Pres lived until tweny minutes past seven on the morning of Apr 15. He did not speak at all. Dr Stone, Ford, Lieberman, & others were present. Jas M Wright sworn, chief clerk in the Bureau of Military Justice; he had a package that had the ball, & he had the pistol. Wm T Kent sworn: was at **Ford's Theatre** on the night of the assassination; he picked up the pistol, in the box which had been occupied by the Pres. Lt Col Henry N Rathburn, of Albany sworn: he accompanied Pres Lincoln, Mrs Lincoln, Miss Harris to the theatre on Apr 14; heard them play Hail to the Chief, & the President received three cheers;

in the 3rd act he heard the report of a pistol; seized a man who wrestled himself from his grasp & received a deep wound between the arm & shoulder. The man then sprang toward the front of the box & over it. Col Jos B Stewart sworn; he was at ***Ford's Theatre*** on Apr 14; sat in front of the orchestra; he heard the man say *Sic Semper Tyrannis*; outside the witness told John Wilkes Booth to stop, witness was so near the horse that the first two or three strides splashed the mud in his face. Mr John D Pettit sworn; he occupied a room at 339 F st, below 10th; could hear the actors in the play; heard whistling in the alley & saw a horse, but could see nothing else. Jas P Ferguson sworn: was at ***Ford's Theatre*** on Apr 14; witness kept a restaurant near the theatre. Henry Ford told him if he wanted to see Gen Grant he should secure a seat that day. Witness secured a seat near the private box to be occupied by the President. He saw Booth that day talking to Jas Maddox, an employe at the theatre. Jos Dye was called; recruiting sgt in the U S army, now stationed in Phil; in Apr, 1865, he belonged to Battery C, P artl, stationed at ***Camp Barry***; the same being about 2 miles from the theatre; witness identified Surratt as being with Booth that night outside of the theatre.

Nicholas H Owings had been appointed Register & Jas Lutterill, Receiver of Public Moneys at Fair Play, Colorado Territory.

Hon Geo Bancroft & family, Miss Maggie Mitchell, Mr A T Stewart, A Buistat, the artist, sailed for Europe on Saturday.

Augusta, Ga, Jun 17. A white man named W S Flynn, a storekeeper on Albany Gulf road, was murdered by two freedmen, his head & face being chopped with an axe, & his house burned. The murderers were arrested by colored men. The culprits were saved from lynching with great difficulty.

Mrd: on Jun 16, by Rev Dr Finkel, John Buchler, of Wash, to Mary Warmbold, of Balt.

Died: on Jun 16, at Brooklyn, N Y, Brvt Col Robt O Abbott, surgeon U S army.

Died: on Jun 5, at Phil, Dr Wm Shippen, in his 76th year of his age.

Lynchburg, Jun 17. R H Glass, editor of the Republican, was shot in the street today by the sons of E Booker, in consequence of an article reflecting on their father. The shot took effect in the eye, the ball lodging in the head. Mr Glass is comfortable, but the issue is as yet uncertain.

Orphans Court of Wash Co, D C. Letters testamentary on the personal estate of Clinton M Sears, late of Wash, D C, deceased. –Wm Leslie Sears, exc

WED JUN 19, 1867
Mrd: on Jun 18, at Trinity Church, Gtwn, by Rev Fr McGuire, J Hatley Norton to Mrs Louisa R Leach, of Rosedale, D C.

Yesterday the first & second floors of the warehouse of Mr Benj Darby, flour merchant, on Water st, near High st, Gtwn, fell through with a tremendous crash. Mr Wm France was killed; he fell into the cellar & was buried beneath the corn for some 4 hours before his body could be found. He was about 27 years old & was waiting for the rain to cease. His body was taken to the shop of Mr John F Burch, undertaker, where it was embalmed, & today will be sent to his father, who resides near the Relay House, Balt Co, Md. Mr Benj Darby escaped injury by jumping out of the window. Mr Zeph English, whose business is in the same street, was precipitated into the cellar, & nearly suffocated, but was rescued after 2 hours.

Trial of John H Surratt-Jun 18. Susan Ann Jackson-sworn; maiden name was Susan Mahoney; was married 2 weeks after Mr Lincoln's assassination; was living at Mrs Surratt's house on H st; witness saw Surratt in the dining room, after that, talking to his mother. Witness was examined by Capt Orffutt the Monday after the assassination. Witness Sgt Jos M Dye was 23 years old from Wash Co, Pa, where he resided before the war, going to school, & working at his trade as a printer. He told his father about the night of the assassination. Jas Sangston-sworn: in 1865, & is yet, book-keeper at the St Lawrence Hall, a hotel in Montreal Canada: the name of John Harrison, registered on the books; the name was in Surratt's handwriting. David C Reed was called; living in Washington about 30 years; had known the prisoner since he was quite a boy; Reed was in Washington on the day of the murder of the President.

The Gazette de France announces that the medical attendants have declared that Empress Charlotte will never recover her reason. It is the opinion of the physicians that her nervous system has received a shock which must soon result in her death.

Orphans Court-Judge Purcell. 1-The last will of Simeon Flynn, deceased, was fully proven, & admitted to probate & record, & letters testamentary granted to Mary Flynn, excx; bond $8,000. 2-The fifth account of Andrew Jackson, guardian to the orphans of Susan & John A Jackson, deceased, was filed & passed by ordered of the Court. 3-The first & final account of Jas W Gibson, guardian to Susan Gibson, orphan of Joshua Gibson, deceased, was filed, approved, & passed. 4-The first & final account of the same as guardian to Margaret Ann Gibson, orphan of Joshua Gibson, deceased, which was approved & passed. 5-The will & codicil of the late Jas Rhodes was filed & proven. 6-The will of John C Frissell, deceased, was filed & proven, & admitted to probate. Letters testamentary issued to John Frissell; bond $400.

Waldemar Bodisco, Sec of the Russian Legation, who left here a short time ago for St Petersburg, to convey to his Gov't the ratified Russian-American treaty, arrived at N Y on Monday, in the steamer **Pereire**.

Memphis, Jun 17. Moses H Reese, formerly leader of the 8th Iowa battery, was shot & mortally wounded in his bed this morning by a brewer named Rogers, who was arrested & lodged in jail.

Trustee's sale of valuable Farm in Fairfax Co, Va; by deed of trust from John Flynn & wife, dated Nov 5, 1859, recorded in Liber B No 1, folio 333, et seq, of the land records of said county executed by the said John Flynn & wife to secure 3 certain promissory notes for $666.66 2/3 each, payable in two, three, & four years respectively, with interest from Nov 5, 1859, in favor of & payable to Alex'r Aldrich, & default having been made in the payment of said notes & the subscriber having been requested in writing by the assigns of said Alex'r Aldrich, will sell at public sale on Jul 11 next, all that tract of land called **Keene tract**, on the upper side of the Occoquan Bay, in the Parish of Truro, Fairfax Co, Md, containing 63 acres, more or less. –Chas S Wallach, trustee -Green & Williams, aucts

The following recently graduated midshipmen have been detached from the Naval Academy & ordered to the under-mentioned vessels:

To the ship **Quinnebaug**:

Robt E *Cavmody	John F Sullivan	Fred'k W Greenleaf
Edw A McClellan	Walton Goodwin	Frank W Nichols.

To the ship **Minnesota**:

Jas M Grimes	Richd Rush	Chas W Christopher
Geo H Church	Wm H Jaques	Edwin C Pendleton
John Pillsbury	Edw W Henricks	Fred'k A Howes
John P Merrill	Chas Belknap	Geo J Mitchell
Andrew P Dunlap	Wm S McGunnegle	Albert R Conden
Edwin D Tausig	Edw R Wood	Park Benjamin
Erasmus Dennison	Edw W Remey	Uriel Sebree
Wilham S Cowles	Geo S Daval	Fred'k G Hyde
Allen G Paul	Henry C Hunter	Henry B Mansfield
Alfred Cravens	Fernando P Gilmore	Edw W Bridge
Hamilton Perkins	Jonathan M Wainwright	Jacob W Miller
Conway H Arnold	John O B Bleecker	Albert Ross
Edw W Sturdy	Wm D Nicholson	Clifford H West
C Logan	Eugene H C Leutze	Jos G Eaton
Horace E Jones	Jas M Miller	Wm Little
Patrick Cunningham	Fred'k N Wise	

To the ship **Franklin**:

Benj H Tilley	Fred'k Collins	Lewis D Webster
Jos L Stickney	Harry Knox	Sidney A Simons
Wm B H Frailey	Cornelius R Meeker	
Wm M Paul	Chas P Shaw	

[*Copied as written.]

Indian troubles; despatch from Omaha, Neb, dated Jun 9, fight between some passengers & 20 Indians, within 5 miles of **Fort Monroe**, & a son of Gen Davis was wounded. Davis is now lying in the hospital at Sedgewick, with gunshot wound, not at all dangerous. Davis fought until he was wounded. He is a nice gentleman, & a brave little fellow.

For sale: the dwlg, goodwill, & fixtures of a first-class Bakery, at 8 South Fairfax st, Alexandria, Va. Apply on the premises for particulars. –Jas H Simpson

The undersigned will sell at private sale the farm now in his occupancy, located between Rockville, Montg Co, Md, & Gtwn, D C; contains 196 acres. It will be shown by Mr Wm Hagar, who resides upon it. Title is perfect. Apply to Granville F Hyde, 63 Water st; Grafton Tyler, Wash & Gay sts, Gtwn.

Monterey Springs, The Home Place, is now ready to receive boarders. H Yingling, proprietor; address either Hagerstown of Fountain Dale Post Ofc, Adams Co, Pa.

Orphans Court of Wash Co, D C, Jun 18, 1867. In the case of Sarah Willett, admx c t a of Marinus Willett, deceased, the administratrix & Court have appointed Jul 13 next, for the final settlement of the personal estate of the said deceased, of the assets in hand. -Jas R O'Beirne, Reg/o wills

Orphans Court of Wash Co, D C, Jun 18, 1867. In the case of John J Bogue, adm of Henry C Willstorff, deceased, the administrator & Court have appointed Jul 13 next, for the final settlement of the personal estate of the said deceased, of the assets in hand. -Jas R O'Beirne, Reg/o wills

THU JUN 20, 1867
Trial of John H Surratt-Jun 19. Mr Carroll Hobart-sworn: is conductor of a train on the Vt Central railroad; prisoner looked like the man he let ride to Milton, who was with another man. Chas H Blinn sworn: is a clerk in the Weldon House at St Albans, Vt; two men came into the depot & left, found a handkerchief near where they had been; it had the name J H Surratt. Mr Scipiano Grillo was called; was living near the Navy Yard in 1865; kept a restaurant in *Ford's Theatre*; knew J W Booth by sight, knew David Herold & Atzerodt. Saw the three of them on Apr 14, 1865, at different times. Robt H Cooper-sworn: witness is not now in the army; was discharged in Jun, 1865; was in the volunteer service, from Beaver, Pa; I live there now; entered the army in 1862; was in Capt Thompson's Independent Pa battery; in Apr, 1865, was stationed at *Camp Barry*, a line sgt; on the day of the assassination, I came into town with Sgt Dye; we sat down on a platform in front of the *Ford's Theatre*; saw the President's carriage. Proceedings were interrupted by the witness being taken with a slight cataleptic fit, to which he was subject. We went to the oyster-saloon & a man came in & told us the President had been shot. We started back to camp.

The following persons were pardoned by the Pres: Jas Coleman, sentenced to the penitentiary at Albany about 6 months since for larceny; Jas H Mangum, convicted of passing counterfeit money, sentenced to the penitentiary; Jas H Jackson, convicted of assault & battery, & sentenced to 6 months in jail; Chas Howard, convicted of larceny, & sentenced to 6 months in jail. Mr T B Brown, warden of the jail was yesterday officially notified of the fact. Steps were at once taken to have them released from durance.

August Mueler offers for sale his property near Kalorama Heights; also, several lots adjoining.

Died: on Jun 19, in Wash City, Hon Isaac Newton, in his 68th year. His remains will be taken to Phil for interment. His friends are invited to accompany the remains to the Balt Depot on Jun 21 at 2 P M, from the residence of his son, Isaac Newton, jr, corner of 11th st & Md ave.

Died: on Jun 18, Catharine A Hall, 3rd daughter of the late Ignatius & Eliz Hall, formerly of Wash City. Afflicted with a dropsy that baffled the skill of the most emiment physicians, she bore her sufferings with a fortitude unsurpased.

On Friday last, John Grace, a former member of the 17th Va regt, was struck on the head with a gun by a colored man, named Arington, & died from the resulting injuries on the following Sunday night.

Brvt Col Robt O Abbott, surgeon U S A, died at Brooklyn on Jun 16. He had been on sick-leave absence for several months past, & was greatly prostrated by a long illness. The immediate cause of his death was a carbuncle on the shoulder. Newark Daily Adv

Hiram Powers, who has now lived in Italy nearly 30 years, is talking of coming home.

Balt, Jun 19. In the case of Geo Bennett, who was tried in the Criminal Court for the murder of Harman Plumper, the jury rendered a verdict of guilty of murder in the second degree.

N Y, Jun 19. Wm T Skidmore, who assassinated W B Charr with an air-gun, & whose trial had been progressing in King's Co Court, Brooklyn, was this morning found dead in his cell.

Valuable tract of land containing about 32 acres on the Bladensburg Pike at public sale: on Jun 29, on the premises; adjoins the farms of Allen Dodge, John C Rives, & J W Morsell, belonging to the estateof the late John Veech, & is being sold to enable the heirs to close up the estate. -Cooper & Latimer, aucts

FRI JUN 21, 1867
The President, we understand, has appointed Arthur McArthur, of Wisc, to be Com'r to the Paris Exposition; also, Edw S Davis, to be Receiver of Public Moneys, & J Works, to be Register of the Land Ofc at Austin, Nevada.

Trustee's sale of valuable Farm property in Wash Co, D C, near Tennallytown, at public auction on Jul 24, with improvements, on the premises; all that parcel of land, being the tract called *Friendship*, containing about 50 acres, more or less.
–C E Rittenhouse, trustee -Thos Dowling, auct

Trial of John H Surratt-Jun 20. Edw L Smith-sworn: since 1860 had resided about a mile from Surrattsville; knew the prisoner very well; stayed at his home in Jan or Feb, 1865. John Lee-sworn: now lives in Miss between Meridian & Vicksburg; previously lived in Wash; had been a sgt of Co E, 95th N Y volunteers; ordered to Washington in 1862 for duty as detective on Col Baker's force; had seen John H Surratt at the bar. Saml A Rainey-sworn: have lived in Washington 20 years, & traded in horses & kept a livery stable; in 1861 kept horses at 6th & C sts; on Jan 1, 1865, took a stable on 6th st, below Pa ave, with Dr Wm E Cleaver, & from Jan 1 to Jun 1, we were partners; knew John H Surratt & have seen him at the stable several times. Wm E Cleaver-sworn: same information as above; has known Surratt 11 or 12 years; he addressed me as "Doc," & I addressed him as John; Booth & Surratt often came together to the stable. This time Surratt took a seat in the ofc, waiting for the rain to stop, & told me he was going to kill Lincoln, the old scoundrel, as he had ruined Maryland & the whole South, & he would kill him himself; Surratt showed his pistol. Booth came in at 8 o'clock & Surratt chided him for being so late. Mr Brooks Stabler-sworn: had charge of J C Howard's livery stable, on G st, in 1865; he knew Booth Atzerodt, & Surratt.

Henry Johnson, a butcher, about 44 years old, whose place of business & residence is in Gtwn, learning that his wife had a habit of stopping at a house on 6th st, for some time past, suspecting an improper intimacy on her part with Mr Thos Smoot, who was formerly in his employ, watched the premises yesterday. He went inside & found Smoot & his wife together, Smoot lying in the bed, & his wife sitting on the edge of the bed holding Smoot's hand. Johnson deliberately fired 3 pistol shots at Smoot, two of which took effect in his head, & death ensued about 20 minutes after. He left the house & delivered himself up to Ofcr Thos Smeed, & also handed him the revolver. Mr Aholiab Sawyer, the gentleman who occupies the house, testified that Mr Johnson, alias Smoot, & Mrs Johnson had been occupying a room in his house for 5 or 6 months, & that he had always regarded them as man & wife, & understood that they had been married about 2 years. Mr Millard, a boarder, thought they were man & wife. Miss Jane E Dorsey testified that she is a niece of Mrs Sawyer, & knew the deceased & Mrs Johnson. They had been living in the house about 5 months & were regarded as man & wife. She heard only two shots fired. Molly Ann Day, a colored woman, employed as a servant in the house; no evidence of any importance was elicited. Mrs Rebecca Sawyer testified that her husband, Mr Aholiab Sawyer, had been employed in the folding-room at the Capitol, but had been out of employment for some time, & that she had been keeping boarders; her niece, Miss Jane D Dorsey boarded with her, & was formerly employed at the Treasury. Mrs Johnson said that she & Mr Smoot were legally married about 2 years since on Capitol Hill, but did not remember the name of the priest. She was asked why she did not live with her mother, & was informed that her mother did not like her husband. Mr Smoot, our reporter was informed, was 36 years of age, & his wife & 5 children reside in Alexandria. He served as a sgt during the rebellion in the 17th Va infty, Confederate army. His brother arrived here last evening. Mrs Johnson left the house as soon as Smoot was shot, & has not since been heard from. She is reported to be a large woman, with coarse features, large nose, & black hair. She has 3 children, a daughter married, who is a widow, & 2 boys aged 9 & 11 years. Henry Johnson is a mild, pleasant-looking man, with sandy complexion & light blue eyes. [Jun 22nd newspaper: Mr Johnson was visited by his two sons, who brought him breakfast. They stated that their mother was at home in Gtwn, & had returned Thursday night. The body of Smoot was taken to Alexandria yesterday & conveyed to the residence of his wife, at Wilkes & Pitt sts, & will be buried today at 9 o'clock. Whatever blame is to be attached to the fearful act of her husband she believes should rest upon her.]

Mrd: on Jun 19, at the residence of the bride's parents, by Rev Chas H Fulmer, Mr Chas C Ivey to Miss Georgie Curran, all of Wash City.

Geo W Nichols, alias Cavanagh, Tom Burns, alias Sneak, & Wm Elrod were arrested yesterday while making an attempt to break open & rob the clothing store of Mr Saml Fuld, 22nd & Pa ave.

Rev Thornton A Mills, D D, secretary of education for the ministry in the Presbyterian Church, fell dead in the ferry house at Hoboken on Wednesday afternoon.

Ex-policeman Wm T Skidmore cut his throat in his cell at the King's Co jail, Brooklyn. He was discovered this morning. Skidmore shot & killed Mr Wm B Carr with an air gun, on May 21, & was about to be tried for the murder. The act was discovered by Harmon King, who was confined in the same cell with him on the charge of shooting a man in Wmsburg. He must have died almost instantly.

I am authorized by Mr Chas Dodge to sell his very desirable property in Montg Co, Md, about one mile above Cabin John Bridge, on the Potomac Aqueduct. The residence [which is very complete,] with about 230 acres of land, will be offered as a whole or subdivided. Public auction on Jun 26. -Thos Dowling, auct, 174 Bridge st, Gtwn.

SAT JUN 22, 1867
Trial of John H Surratt-Jun 21. Jas W Pumphrey-sworn: keeps a livery stable at 244 C st; knew John Wilkes Booth; Booth came in for a horse; Surratt came up & said he knew Mr Booth, & that he would take good care of the horse; Surratt also said he would see the horse paid; this was about 6 weeks before the assassination. On Apr 14, at 12 o'clock, Booth came & engaged a horse. I gave him a bay mare & English saddle & bridle, & I have not seen them since. John Fletcher-sworn: I reside at Nailor's livery stable, near 13th st; on Apr 14, 1865, I saw Atzerodt & Herold at Nailor's stable, but they were not together. John J Toffey-sworn: I reside at Hudson City, N Y; on Apr 14, 1865, I was in the Veteran Reserve Corps, & commanded a company at Lincoln Hospital. That night one of the guards captured a horse, saddle & bridle; the horse was sweating very much. I had heard of the assassination, & took the horse to Gen Augur's headquarters & gave him up; the horse was identified- it having but one eye. Miss Honora Fitzpatrick-sworn: I met John W Booth at Mrs

Surratt's, 541 H st; I was boarding there; saw Lewis Payne at Mrs Surratt's. Geo F Chapin-sworn: I lived at Stockbridge, Vt, & am a farmer. Lived there since Feb, 1866. In Apr, 1865, was in Burlington when Mr Chas Blinn gave me a handkerchief marked John H Surratt. I gave it to Mr Geo Grinnet one of Baker's detectives. I was a detective at the time, but not one of Mr Baker's. [Mr Blinn mentioned his mother had gone to his brother's funeral.] Benj W Vanderpoel-sworn: I live in N Y C, & have lived there all my life. I knew John Wilkes Booth; he used to visit the Lone Star Club; saw him there with Surratt 2 or 3 times.

West Point graduates. The position is, that the cadets who take a high rank in the Academy are almost always the only members of their class who show solid abilities in active life, either as military men or in any other calling demanding mind in which they may engage. Among the names in the Engineer Corps, we recall those of Maj Generals Barnard, Tower, Wright, Newton, Humphreys, Smith, Foster, Gillmore, Parke, Warren, Weitzel, Wilson, Meade, Pope, Reynolds; & in the cavalry: Maj Generals Ward, Palmer, Pleasanton, Merrit, Granger, Emory, & Stanley. Many of the best scholars are by request assigned to the Adj General's, Quartermaster, & Ordnance Depts. Two or three instances only in the whole history of West Point in which a cadet who, graduating much below the middle of his class, has subsequently commanded much attention for his force & weight of character. Gen Canby graduated the 30th in his class of 31; & Gen Sheridan the 34th in a class of 52. Names of the most distinguished generals in the recent war that are found in the West Point catalogues. The following, which we furnish, with the year of graduation & the number indicating the class rank in each case:

1822 Gen Mansfield, 2
1826 Albert Sidney Johnston, 8
1827 N B Buford, 6; Leonidas Polk, 8; G J Rains, 13
1828 R C Tilghman, 2
1829 Robt E Lee, 2
1830 John B Magruder, 15
1831 Jacob Ammen, 12; A A Humphreys, 13; W H Emory, 14
1832 B S Ewell, 3; Philip St Geo Cocke, 6; Erasmus D Keyes, 10
1833 J K Barnard, 2; G W Cullum, 3; Rufus King, 4
1835 Geo Morrell, 1; Geo W Meade, 19
1836 Danville Leadbetter, 3; M C Meigs, 5; D P Woodbury, 6
1837 H W Benham, 1; Braxton Bragg, 5; Jubal A Early, 18
1838 G T Beauregard, 2; Irvin McDowell, 23
1839 Isaac J Stevens, 1; H W Halleck, 2; J B Ricketts, 16; E O C Ord, 17
1840 W T Sherman, 6; G H Thomas, 12; Wm Hays, 18
1841 Gen T B Tower, 1; H G Wright, 2; Amiel W Whipple, 5; Nathl Lyon, 11
1842 John Newton, 2; G W Rains, 3; J D Kurtz, 4; Wm S Rosecrans, 5; Gustavus W Smith, 8; Mansfield Lovell, 9
1843 Wm B French, 1; U S Grant, 21
1844 A Pleasanton, 7; S B Buckner, 11; W S Hancock, 18
1845 Wm F Smith, 4; Thos J Ward, 5; Thos J Rhett, 6; C P Stone, 7; Fitz John Porter, 8

1846 Geo B McClellan, 2; Chas E Blunt, 3; John G Foster, 4; Jesse L Reno, 8; D N Couch, 13; Thos J Jackson, [Stonewall,] 17
1846 Orlando B Wilcox, 8; A P Hill, 15; A _ Burnside, 18; Chas Griffin, 23
1847 Q A Gillmore, 1; John G Parke, 1; Absalom Baird, 9; Rufus Saxton, 18
1848 G K Warren, 2; W T Magruder, 11
1849 A C Gillem, 11
1850 Henry W Slocum, 7
1851 Jas B McPherson, 1; John M Schofield, 6
1852 G W Custis Lee, 1; Oliver O Howard, 4; John Pegram, 10; J E B Stuart, 13
1853 G Weitzel, 2
1857 John C Palfrey, 1; Geo C Strong, 5; J L Kirby Smith, 6
Of the general ofcrs of the army at the present time Generals Sherman, Halleck, Meade, Thomas, Rosecran, Pope, Scofield, Howard, & *Terry stood high; Generals Grant, McDowell, Cooke, Hooker, & Ord stood about the middle; while Generals Hancock, Sheridan, & Canby stook low in their respective classes. [Jun 24th newspaper-correction: Gen Alfred Terry is a distinguished graduate of Yale, not West Point. In enumerating the able Union Generals which the South, through West Point, gave to the war, we failed to remember Maj Gen Ormsby McKnight Mitchell, of Ky, who graduated No 15, in 1829, in a class of 46.]

J K Bridge, Grand Sec of the Order of the Sons of Temperance of this Dist, was united in the holy bonds of wedlock to Miss Lillian A Hazzard, a well-known lady visitor of the Order. The ceremony was performed on Tuesday at the Indian Queen Hotel, in Phil.

Supreme Court of D C, Jun 20, 1867. 818 Equity, Docket 8. Summy vs Dickinson et al. Will Y Fendall, trustee, reported he sold lot B, No 4, for $1,454.06 to Geo W Mitchell, & he has complied with the terms of sale. –R J Meigs, clerk

Board of Police Com'rs. The complaints against Ofcrs F A A A Evans, B Fairchild, & N C Ray were dismissed. Ofcr Wm E Dunn, for neglect of duty, was ordered to be reprimanded. Ofcr John C Mansfield was fined $50, & Ofcr Peter W Fowler $10, for neglect of duty. Edw L Lambrie was appointed a patrolman of the regular force, for duty in Gtwn, vice Chas W Sebastian. The following appointments of additional patrolmen were made, for duty at the places indicated, viz: Wm Wilson, at the Treasury Dept; Jas A Dodd, at Centre Market; John J Hill, at Northern Market; E G Townsend, at Kendall Green & Campbell Hospital; Henry Norris, on Pa ave, between 12th & 14th sts, & F L Payne, on Pa ave, between 9th & 10th sts. The applications of Jas Guild & Chas Zailner, for liquor licenses, were rejected.

A little boy aged about 10 years old, son of Mr Barron, builder, was drowned while fishing at the 7th st wharf. He was sitting on the wharf, & losing his balance, fell in, & was drowned before assistance could be obtained. The body was recovered & taken to the home of his parents.

MON JUN 24, 1867
Mills, the Franconia murderer, escaped from the jail at Haverhill, N H, on Friday, but was subsequently caught. He dug out a stone 5 feet long & 2 feet wide between the cells, & raised up a door 7 inches, & crawled under it to the spaceway. He ran about three-quarters of a mile, & finding that he was pursued, sat down & gave himself up.

Spelling contest on Sat. Geo M Davis, of the 4th Dist Male Grammar School, spelling 49 of 50 difficult words correctly, won the first prize, a handsome writing case; Chas Lewis, of 1st Dist, was second, having missed only 2 words.

Executor's sale of valuable improved property belonging to the estate of the late Andrew Small at auction, on Jul 1: part of lot 4 in square 104, being the east 28 feet front by 166 feet 5 inches deep, on the north side of E st, between 20th & 21st sts, improved by a 2 story front & rear brick bldg, numbered 171. –J A Ruff, exc -Green & Williams, aucts

Orphans Court-Judge Purcell, Jun 22, 1867. 1-The last will & testament of John Strobell was proven & admitted to probate. 2-The last will & testament of Emma Frances Coyle was proven & admitted to probate. 3-Jacob A Walter, Geo Savage, & Wm Galt, bonded as guardians to Genevieve & Lizzie Golden, orphans of the late Geo & Annie Golden. 4-Mrs Amy B McNeill was admitted & bonded as executrix of Archibald McNeill, deceased.

Savannah Republic, Jun 17. On Friday night last, two colored men, Joe Williams & Green Jackson, entered the little country store of Mr W S Flynn, about 3 miles from Station 7½ on the Albany & Gulf railroad; Jackson struck Flynn with a hatchet, cutting his skull almost in two; they then chopped him up, & set the store on fire. Both were arrested on Saturday.

Orphans Court of Wash Co, D C. Letters testamentary on the personal estate of Archibold McNeill, late of Wash City, D C, deceased. –Amy B McNeill, excx

Orphans Court of Wash Co, D C, Jun 22, 1867. In the case of Thos H Lane, adm of Andrew J O'Bannon, deceased, the administrator & Court have appointed Jul 13 next, for the final settlement of the personal estate of the said deceased, of the assets in hand. -Jas R O'Beirne, Reg/o wills

Capt Fitz, formerly of the firm of Donahoe, Ralston & Co, bankers, died at San Francisco, Jun 6. In a clause in his will he bequeaths $20,000 to the Sec of the Treasury, the interest to be applied in cancelling the national debt.

Mr John W Price, of Edgefield Dist, S C, aged about 25 years, was brutally murdered, Wed last, on the Washington road, 6 miles from the city, by a band of armed negroes, 7 or 8 in number. Claiborne Lockhart, a colored man-servant, who accompanied him, was the only witness. Mr Price was robbed of about $450. –Augusta [Ga] Consitutionalist, 14th.]

Trial of John H Surratt, Jun 22, 1867. Wm H Bell, colored-sworn: he is a servant of Sec Seward's, & was there on Apr 14, 1865. Hon Fred'k W Seward-sworn: I am Assist Sec of State; reside at Madison Pl, on 15th st, & did reside there in Apr, 1865; Gen Augur's headquarters was just below my residence. I was in my room, which adjoins that of my father, in the 3rd story; the house fronts *Lafayette Square*; my father's room was in the front part of the house, & my room adjoined his; in my father's room was my sister, who has since died, & a soldier named Robinson; I was in my own room, & my wife was there also; my mother was in her room back of that of my father; [witness described the wounds his father had received by being thrown from a carriage-his right arm broken.] On Apr 14 I heard someone come upstairs; he was a stout man & said he had medicine to deliver from Dr Verdi; he persisted; I told him to go away; I turned around & saw the man with a navy revolver in his hand; the man attacked me, & in the scuffle we fell into my father's room, remembering nothing distinctly, except two persons picking up my father, who was bloody. Mrs Fred'k Seward-sworn: she saw a man grappling with her husband; Miss Seward, my sister-in-law, asked me not to allow them to carry her father off; I saw Col Seward come upstairs when Paine went out; he had a gash across his forehead. Col Augustus Seward-sworn: testified that he was in bed the night of the assassination, & was awakened by the screams of my sister. Jas L Maddox-sworn: I was property-man at **Ford's Theatre** on Apr 14, 1865; I heard the report of a pistol; was standing on the left side, near the Pres; box; I saw John W Booth; I saw him in front of the theatre in the afternoon of Apr 14, on horseback. John V Pyles-sworn: resides in PG Co, Md, was a justice of the peace there, knew John H Surratt; witness had left home & was working at his mother's; Mr Surratt came to me to sign papers, as a justice of the peace; he seemed to be urgent to do the business, & we proposed to go over to my brother's, & while walking along Surratt said he wanted to go away & avoid the draft; he said he wanted money to make his mother secure.

Wilmington, Jun 23. The mail train going West on the Manchester & Wilmington railroad broke through the trestle work near Peacock Station last night, & J H Harrelson, overseer of the hands, & a section-master named Byrd were killed.

Mrd: on Jun 19, Memphis, Tenn, at St Peter's Catholic Church, by Rev Fr Lilly, Col John W Dawson, formerly of Wash City, to Miss Kate C Mageveny, daughter of Eugene Mageveny, of Memphis.

Died: on Sat, in Alexandria, Va, Maj Robt Brookett, in his 75th year. His funeral will be on Jun 25 at 10 o'clock, from his late residence on Wash st. [Star please copy.]

TUE JUN 25, 1867
In N Y yesterday John Schmidt, a German, aged 65 years, attempted to kill his former mistress, Eliz Kauker. Schmidt then cut his own throat, & died soon afterwards.

Excellent household & kitchen furniture at auction on Jun 28, at the residence of Wm H Rohrer, 115 Gay st, between Congress & High sts. -Thos Dowling, auct

Trial of John H Surratt, Jun 24, 1867. John Greenawalt-sworn: in 1864-66 kept the Pennsylvania House, on C st; Atzerodt boarded at the house, & Booth came there to visit him; prisoner came frequently to visit. John M Lloyd-sworn: have lived here since Oct, 1865; previously lived at Surrattsville, & kept a tavern there; moved to Surrattsville in 1864 till Oct 1865; occupied the house of Mrs Mary E Surratt, & was engaged in farming. Have seen Herold & Atzerodt, both at my house.

Springfield, Mass, Jun 23. A widow named Maria Gilmore, who lived alone, took a single-blade knife, cut a gash in her abdomen, & tore her bowels from her body. Strange as it may seem she lived an hour & a half, & during that time she was attended by the priest, & made her will, bequeathing a considerable property. The cause of the suicide is supposed to have been insanity. Mrs Gilmore was 65 years of age.

U S Marshal's sale: on Jul 11 next, of lots 20 & 21, in Old Gtwn, fronting 23 feet 6 inches on the west side of Potomac st, improved by a 2 story frame bldg, in Gtwn, D C, siezed as the property of David Trunnell, & will be sold to satisfy execution 3,508, in favor of Eliz A Trunnell. –D S Gooding, U S Marshal, D C

Orphans Court of Wash Co, D C, Jun 22, 1867. In the case of Saml Fowler, adm of Mary M Dufief, deceased, the administrator & Court have appointed Jul 13 next, for the final settlement of the personal estate of the said deceased, of the assets in hand. -Jas R O'Beirne, Reg/o wills

A ramble about town: The equestrial statue of Jackson was inaugurated Jan 8, 1853, whe whole cost to the Gov't, including the pedestal & iron railing, being $28,500. *Lafayette Square*, the site selected by Pres Fillmore for its location, is one of the most beautiful enclosures in Wash City. Clark Mills was employed to execute the statue. The equestrian statue of Washington was inaugurated on the anniversary of Washington's birthday, Feb 22, 1860. ***Western Holmead's Burial Grounds*** is located at 20th & Boundary sts, in the N W section of Wash City; it was one of the earlier, if not the original & earliest burial place of the city; there have been but a very few memorials raised here in the last 20 years; the bodies should all be removed, as those of the *Foundry cemetery* have just been removed. Most of the monuments were erected 40 or 50 years ago. The most elaborate had the name of Lenthall in German text upon the entrance; upon the eastern slope of the roof is inscribed: "John Lenthall, Builder, who died on 19th September, 1808, aged 46 years: On the western slope is the following: "He was an industrious and upright citizen, a lover of justice, and zealous in the discharge of his duty. When living he was esteemed for his usefulness, and in death lamented by those who knew the value of talents and integrity in his profession." On the same monument is the following: "In memory of Jane, wife of John Lenthall, and daugther of Robert King, born at Pickering Yorkshire, England, and departed this life in Washington, Aug 9, 1852." Near this memorial is a heavy sandstone slab to the memory of Robt King, who died in 1821, & another to Nicholas King, who died in 1812, & to his wife Margaretta, who died in 1821. These memorials are enclosed in the same lot, with granite posts

& iron chains. John Lenthall, chief of the Bureau of Construction & Repair of the Navy Dept, is his son, & the mother of Dr Stone's mother was his daughter. A handsome marble shaft perpetuates the memory of Jas L Cathcart, who died in 1865, at the age of 80 years, & of his wife, Jane Backer Cathcart, who died in 1846. She was the daughter, it is recorded, of John Woodsides, a Revolutionary soldier, which will be recorded upon the tombstones of another generation of the sons & daughters of those who fought for the Union in the great American rebellion. We copied the names of Margaret Tweedy, who died in 1823, & of Eliz, who died in 1831; Mrs Eliza W Hutton, wife of Jas Hutton, & daughter of Jas Cathcart; Jas Daugherty, a native of Ireland, who died in 1826, aged 58 years; Danl Somerville, Robt Underwood, & Jas Rease, all dying in 1812; Jas Birth, who died in 1844, & Anne, his wife, who died in 1854; Janet, the wife of Jas Birth, who died in 1818; also, that of their son, who died in the same year; Jas Larned, of Wash, D C, son of Hon Simon Larned, of Pittsfield, Mass, who died in 1849, & his wife, Anne Jane, who died in 1837; Huldah Wilson, wife of Wm W Wilson died in 1837, aged 47 years; Richd Freeman, who died in 1815; Jane Summers Cooke, wife of Peter W Cooke, who died in 1818; marble headstone to the memory of John Reed. Lorenzo Dow, a native of Coventry, Conn, became at age 19 years, against the wishes of his parents, an itinerant Methodist preacher-for 40 years he was known everywhere; his wife, Peggy Dow, whom he married in 1804, accompanied him fearlessly. Sandstone slab: "To the memory of Lorenzo Dow, who was born in Connecticut, Oct 18, 1777; died Feb 2, 1834, aged 56." *Foundry Burial Ground* exists no longer; the remains have all been transferred. One monument only, the remains from beneath which were long ago removed, remaining to be removed: to the memory of Rev Danl Southall, minister of the Methodist Episcopal Church in the State of N C; born of religious parentge, in Amelia Co, in 1768, became a minister of the Va & N C Conference in 1789, was located in 1799, & died in 1830. Upon the square opposite & south of this was formerly located *St Matthew's Burying Ground*, which was some years ago vacated, as this has now been. *Colored Cemetery*, adjoining the *Foundry Burial Ground*, is exceedingly wet & inappropriate, & has but a few bodies deposited there. *St Peter's Burial grounds*; this old cemetery has received no interments for some years; measures are being taken to transfer all remains in these grounds to *Mount Olivet Cemetery*. Fr Boyle is waiting to secure the necessary authority from Congress. One of the marble memorials is peculiar: Gentle Christian, pray for the soul of Ann Peabody, who died in her eighty-second year, the 7th of July, 1843. As a child, wife, mother, or friend, she was always affectionate, sincere, most faithful and true. Blessed Mary, Immaculate Mother of God, intercede for her! This family is said to be distantly allied with that of the illustrious philanthropist whose name they bear.

Fortress Monroe, Jun 21. The U S steamer **Winooski** arrived at Hampton Roads today, with 40 cases of yellow fever on board. Jos Cooper, a seaman, died after exhibiting unmistakable symptoms of the black vomit, & was buried at sea, May 13.

Died: on Jun 23, after a short illness, Mrs Jane Lepreux, aged 69 years. Her funeral will be from the residence of her son, Pa av & 12th st, on Tuesday at 3 o'clock P M.

Annual Academic Exibition of Columbian College, last night; Mr Otis T Mason, long & honorably known as the head of this dept. Those who received the honors of the year, together with those admitted upon the advanced course: admitted to the freshman class: G W Brown, S E Atkinson, Chs E Fraser, L T Bremmerman, F Havener, S M Larrison, John H Reeves, T H Paramour, R H Harkness, R W Diggs, W R Havener, W & H Brown, & A F Curtis. Admitted to the scientific course- French & Jas M Lugenbeel, E C Santos, Wm Holmead, Frank Summy, A B Buff, V Blanchard, & V H Olmstead. Punctuality & deportment: S E Atkinson, L F Bremmerman, C E Fraser, F Lugenbeel, J H Bremmerman, C C Clark, W P Floyd, C L Johnson, Chas Kloman, G W Lane, C Banders, H S Beech, G Folkner, & G W Palmer. Best scholar of the first class-gold medal: L E Atkinson, L T Bremmerman, & R H Hockness. Prizes in second class: J E Bangs & Jos H Bremmerman. Third class, prizes awarded to H L Beech & G W Palmer.

Yesterday, Jas Westcott, who was arrested on Sat, charged with keeping a house on Pa ave for gambling purposes, was fined $20 & costs.

WED JUN 26, 1867
Trial of John H Surratt, Jun 25, 1867. John M Garrett-sworn: resides in Caroline Co, Va; lived there in Apr, 1865, at same place where I live now; knew Wilkes Booth; saw him at my fathers' house 2 days, I think, before he was killed there; he was brought there by men named Jett & Riggles; I saw Booth when he rode to the house. Lucien B Baker-sworn: now resides in Lansing, Mich; in 1865 was employed by Gen Baker as a detective; I had been quartermaster of the 1st Dist of Columbia cavalry; I am one of the party who went in pursuit of Booth after the assassination. Lyman S Sprague-sworn: in 1865 I was a clerk at the Kirkhouse House in this city; saw the name of Geo A Atzerodt, Chas Co, occupying room 126, on a page torn from the register. Saml K Chester-sworn: am an actor & resided in N Y in 1865; was acquainted with Wilkes Booth.

Dr Wm Jones died last evening, in his 78th year. He was born in Montg Co, Md, but was for just half a century a resident of Wash City. Here he has reared a respected family, & has been a prominent member of society. In latter years he has been at times seriously attacked by rush of blood to the head, & two or three years since he was partially paralyzed. He served in the District militia, & was surgeon in the war of 1812. After the army he formed a partnership in the practice of his profession with Dr Blake the elder. He was Postmaster of the city in the time of Gen Jackson, & also during the term of Mr Buchanan. [Dec 25th newspaper: Dr Jones was married Dec 21, 1821, to Sarah L Corcoran, a daughter of the late Thos Corcoran, sr, of Gtwn. She departed this life Sep 24, 1843, after a long illness, during which he was most constant & devoted in his attentions to her.]

Died: on Jun 24, Saml Tilston, aged 40 years. His remains will be taken to **Greenwood Cemetery**, Brooklyn, N Y, for interment, on the 4½ o'clock P M train of Jun 26. His friends are invited to accompany his remains to the Balt depot, from 173 B st south, Island, at 2:50 P M.

Col C T Campbell, special agent of the Indian Bureau, has just returned from the Upper Missouri, & reports to the Com'r of Indian Affairs that a considerable body of hostile Indians, consisting of Sioux, Blackfeet, & Crows, had assembled at the Head Waters of Hart river, about 150 miles west of New *Fort Sully*. Murders are frequent. The hostile bands are said to be well provided with arms, ammunition, horses, & mules.

Died: on Jun 25, Hyman Barron, infant son of Geo R & Maria A Hall. His funeral will be from the residence of his parents, 11th & Mass ave, today at 5 o'clock.

Died: on Jun 24, at Unity, Montg Co, Md, Mrs Nancy Colgate, relict of the late Wm Parker, of Wash City, in her 85th year. [Fred'k Md papers please copy.]

Balt, Jun 25. This evening, on Balt st, Columbus Fornshall, a restaurant keeper on West Balt st, was shot by Frank Hart, a printer engaged in the Gazette ofc. The cause of the alleged difficulty was the slander of Fornshall's wife by Hart, who boarded in the house of Fornshall. Fornshall accused Hart of slander which the latter denied, when Fornshall knocked him down. Hart drew a pistol & shot his assailant, killing him almost instantly.

Trustee's sale of valuable unimproved real estate at auction, on Jul 3, by the last will & testament of the late John Hellen: sale of lot 7 in square 161, fronting 61 feet 9 inches on Conn ave, between L & M sts. To be sold on Jul 2: lots 13 & 14 in square 449, on 7th st; lot A in Johnson Hellen's subdivision of lots 13, 14, etc, in square 568, fronting on 3rd st; & lot 16 in square 568, fronting on F st. –John B Blake, H G Fant, Clifton Hellen, Frank C Hellen, trustees. -Cooper & Latimer, aucts

Executor's sale of an excellent horse, buggy, harness, saddle, & bridle, at auction; by order of the Orphans Court of D C; execs will sell the estate of the late Saml Stinemetz, deceased, at public auction, at J G Matlock's Livery Stable, on G st, between 6th & 7th sts. –Mary E Stinemetz, B H Stinemetz, excs -Cooper & Latimer, aucts

THU JUN 27, 1867
44th Commencement of Columbian College; awards presented to: A B Duvall, Jos H France, jr; John T Beckley; Lee Chiswell. Orations by: Sidney W Handy, of Md; John T Beckley, of Md; John H France, jr, of D C; W Veirs Bouie, of Md; Lingan B Allen, of Va; John LeConte, of Ga [excused] Jos T Clarke, of D C; Andrew B Duvall, of D C; John Pollard, of Va; John H Wright, of Va.

Trustee's sale of valuable bldg lots in the first ward; by deed of trust from Saml Duvall & wife, dated Oct 1, 1866, recorded in Liber R M H, No 25, folio 442, of the land records of Wash Co, D C: public auction on Jul 8, of lots 7 & 8 in square 183. –Eugene Carusi, trustee -Cooper & Latimer, aucts

Trustee's sale of improved property on 20th st, between E & F sts; by decree of the Supreme Court of D C, passed in chancery No 636; Thos Cogan vs Jane McManus et all; public auction on Jul 8, of part of lot 5 in square 122, with a frame dwlg. -Eugene Carusi, trustee -Cooper & Latimer, aucts

Leavenworth, Kansas, Jun 25. A passenger from Denver City gives the particulars of the attack on 2 coaches, by 100 Indians, on Jun 15. It was a running fight, continued for an hour & a half. Geo W Brownell, of Galena, Ill, aged 60 years, was killed; H Blake, of Phil, was wounded in the shoulder. S J Harrison, of Boston, escaped uninjured. Two soldiers & one driver were also killed. The Indians were eventually repulsed.

Trial of John H Surratt-Jun 26, 1867. Col Henry W Smith-sworn: am a ofcr of the U S army, stationed at Vicksburg, on duty with the Freedman's Bureau; was in Wash at the time of the assassination; commanded the party that arrested Mrs Surratt; arrested her on Monday, Apr 17, & arrested Payne at the same time; I was ordered by Gen Augur to arrest Mrs Surratt; she was at her house, 541 H st, in the parlor talking to Miss Annie Surratt, Miss Jenkins, & Miss Honora Fitzpatrick. I saw a colored woman in the house named Susan Ann Jackson. Chas Dawson-sworn: he was a clerk at the Nat'l Hotel in 1865; when Booth left, Apr 14, 1865, he left a trunk & valise behind him, which were placed in the baggage-room of the hotel. Col Richd C Morgan-sworn: in Apr, 1865, was in the service of the War Dept, & on the night of Apr 17 was sent to the Surratt house, & went there with Col Smith. I saw Mrs Surratt, Miss Jenkins, & Miss Fitzpatrick; also a colored woman in the basement; she was tall & rather black. Mrs Mary B Benson-sworn: now resides in Canada; was in N Y in Nov, 1864; my little daughter was with me; saw two men, one called the other Johnson, riding in the car & heard some of their conversation; when they left my daughter picked up a letter & handed it to me, thinking it was mine. The letter was not sealed & revealed a plan to assassinate. I took it to the Hoffman House & read it to Gen Scott, & at his direction I took it to Gen Dix. Henry R McDonough-sworn: in 1864 I was cashier of Adams Express Co in Wash City; John Surratt was employed by the company from Dec 30, 1864, to Jan 13, 1865; he was paid for 2 days service, & he never came back. He was to be paid at the rate of $50 per month.

Orphans Court of Wash Co, D C, Jun 25, 1867. In the case of Simeon Matlock, adm of Chas B H Matlock, deceased, the administrator & Court have appointed Jul 20th next, for the final settlement of the personal estate of the said deceased, of the assets in hand. -Jas R O'Beirne, Reg/o wills

Yesterday Geo W Hooks was brought before Judge Wylie on a writ of habeas corpus, upon application of H C Gooding, prisoner's counsel, to have the prisoner discharged from custody. Hooks was arrested here about 3 weeks ago on a charge of stealing $10,000 from Paymaster Hixon, at Charleston, S C, on Mar 1st last. The prisoner served in the Union army & lost an arm, & for some time previous to the robbery was employed as a night-watchman at the Planters Hotel in Charleston, S C. On Mar 1 he left for his home in Willimantic, Conn.

FRI JUN 28, 1867
Receiver's sale of the furniture & fixtures of an eating house & dining saloon, by decree of the Supreme Court of D C, passed in cause 985, equity, Flaesch vs Flaesch; public auction on Jul 1, 1867, on the premises, 428 E st, near 8th st, known as the "Dining Saloon & Eating House." -John J Johnson, Rcvr -J T Coldwell & Co, aucts

Wilkesbarre, Pa, Jun 27. Chas Denison, a member of Congress from the 12th Dist, died this morning. His funeral will take place on Sunday afternoon.

Trial of John H Surratt, Jun 27, 1865. Wm R Conger-sworn: resides at St Albans, Vt; native place, always lived there; Tue & Wed after the assassination I was keeping a saloon near the depot at St Albans-I think I saw the prisoner there. I tried to have him arrested; I came across Albert Sawles, cashier of the Nat'l Bank, we followed him, saw Edw A Sawles, a lawyer, his brother, but we did not arrest the man. Mrs E W McClermont-sworn: can't fix the day it occurred, but it was 3 or 4 days after I heard of the Pres' assassination, I was on the lookout; my saloon was near the depot. I was looking for Booth. Edw A Sawles examined: resides at St Albans, Vt; same details as given above by his brother Albert Sawles. Lewis J Weichmann sworn: resides at Phil; first met Surratt at St Chas College, Ellicotts Mills, Md, in Sep, 1859; in 1862, latter part, I accepted a position as teacher in St Matthew's Institute, on 19th st, between G & H & continued there for about a year & 10 days; in the middle of Jan, 1863. I for the first time met Surratt since we left collge; I visited his home at Surrattsville in Mar, 1863, & there met his mother & his sister Annie. The father was not then living. At one time I was introduced to David E Herold. Weichman's appearance upon the stand created quite a sensation; he fixed his eyes upon the prisoner & looked at him steadily; the testimony was given slowly, & with the utmost deliberation.

Ads. 1-W G Metzerott & Co have just received a large assortment of Steinway's pianos & Masson & Hamlin's cabinet organs. 2-Mr Thos Coyle publishes a card in regard to the lease of sand-banks in the Howard Univ property. 3-John F Ellis calls attention to his large stock of pianos, parlor organs, & melodeons.

Spelling Contest: names of the successful competitors: Amanda Sailor, Emma Swallow, Kate Brown, Lues Goodrich, who correctly spelled 96 out of 100 words correctly, & on Saturday will again met at the school-house where the contest will continue.

Danl Shannon purchased part of lot 11 in square 396, on 9th st, between O P sts, improved by a 2 story frame house, containing 6 rooms, for $1,545.

St Stanislaus Female Academy-the first annual commencement took place yesterday morning; Rt Rev Bishop Whelan, of Wheeling, W Va, conferred academic honors upon Miss Mary E Eckloff, who delivered the closing address.

Trustee's sale of valuable real estate in Chas Co, Md, by decree of the Circuit Court for Chas Co, Md, sitting as a court of Equity; public sale in front of the Court-house door, in Port Tobacco, Md, on Jul 23rd next, the real estate of which the late Raphael H Boarman died seized & possessed, in said county: ***Boarman's Meadows & Boarman's Rest***, containing about 400 acres, more or less-this farm lies on Zachia Swamp & is improved by a large Brick Mansion & all necessary out-bldgs, & is a productive farm. Also, a Farm called ***Part of Calvert's Hope***, adjoining ***Boarman's Meadows***, containing 200 acres, more or less, with necessary improvements.
–F Stone, R H Edelin, trustees

U S Marshal's sale: on Jul 3, at H G Lorch's Billiard Room, on E st, between 7th & 8th sts, the goods & chattels of said billiard room, seized & levied upon as the property of H G Lorch, & will be sold to satisfy execution 3,573, in favor of Theodore Sheckels & Wm B Downing. –D S Gooding, U S Marshal, D C

Died: on Jun 26, at Saltsburg, Va, Sarah L, beloved wife of T N McConnell. Her funeral will be from the residence of her father, 482 Pa ave, today at 3 o'clock P M.

Obit-died: on Jun 21, near Brentsville, Prince Wm Co, Va, after an illness of some 2 or 3 months, Wm Washington, aged 74 years, son of Bailey Washington, of Stafford Co, Va, & brother of Col Wm Washington, deceased, of the Revolution, & third cousin of Gen Geo Washington, the Father of his country. His brother, Col Henry Washington, of D C, survives. He was noted in early life for versatility of talents, at which time he studied medicine; afterwards entering the regular army as an ofcr in the war of 1812, in which he served with honor & distinction, & at the close of the war, was honorably discharged. After the war he engaged in private pursuits. He has descended to the tomb without a stain upon his name, & without an enemy, with a firm reliance upon the Redeemer of the World. [Charleston, S C, Tallahassee, Fla, & Warrenton, Va, papers please copy.]

SAT JUN 29, 1867
Dept of State: Hon H E Pack, U S Resident Minister & Consul General of Hayti, died of fever on Jun 9.

Trial of John H Surratt, Jun 28, 1867. Lewis J Weichman was recalled for the continuation of his examination by Mr Pierreport. The night of the assassination he was at Mrs Surratt's house when an ofcr came in looking for Booth & John H Surratt. He showed me a piece of cravat with blood on it, & said, it is the Pres' blood; J Wilkes Booth had murdered Abraham Lincoln, & John H Surratt has assassinated the Sec of State.

Died: on Jun 28, of consumption, Margaret, wife of Wm H Dempsey, & daughter of John Tretler, in her *26th year. Her funeral will take place from her late residence, 418 6th st, between F & G sts, on Sunday at 3 o'clock P M. [*The first letter of the age is partially missing-possibility that it is a 2.]

The funeral of Dr Wm Jones took place yesterday from his late residence, 403 C st, near 3rd, & was attended by the members of the Medical Society of D C & also members of the Oldest Inhabitants Association & the Washington Monument Society. The services at the house were conducted by Rev Thos Addison, of Trinity Church, Gtwn. The cortege then proceeded to **Oak Hill Cemetery**, Gtwn, where the interment took place. The following gentlemen acted as pall-bearers: Col Peter G Washington, John A Smith, Philip R Fendall, Gen R C Weightman, Edw Simms, Chas Forrest, Maj Thos L Smith, & Lewis Johnson. The members of the Medical Society accompanied the remains to the cemetery.

Ads. 1-Mr J W Colley asks those indebted to him to call & settle. 2-The steamer **Hi Livingston** will leave 7th st wharf every Friday morning for the mouth of the Potomac & Cone river.

Commencement at <u>Rock Hill College</u>, Ellicott City, Howard Co, Md, on Thursday. Boys from D C who received awards: Hugh Caperton, Parke G Young, J Jerome McManus, Edwin B Frank, W C Claubaugh, Thos W Drane, Robt B Mosher, Theodore N Handy, Chas A Stewart, Eugene McCarthy & Wm H Collins. Medals were awarded to: John W Renehan, Carroll Manor, Md; Jos N Vasquez, Ecuador, So America. [Jul 1st newspaper: we accidentally omitted the name of John L Eliot, a son of Dr Eliot of Wash City, who was awarded a medal.]

Died: on Jun 24, Charles R, aged 4 months, infant son of Richd D & Annie M Cornick, formerly of Princess Ann Co, Va. [Norfolk & Richmond papers please copy.]

Died: on Jun 25, suddenly, in Balt, Richd C Potts, formerly of the U S navy.

Died: on Jun 16, at Spring Hill, near Mobile, Ala, Mrs Camilla Donaldson, wife of Saml C Donaldson, formerly of Balt, & daughter of Cornelia Livingston & the late Chas Cortland Hazard, of Mobile.

Died: on Jun 14, Francis B Whiting, aged 83 years, an honored citizen of Va, & in early life an officer of the U S navy.

Died: on Jun 28, Allan More, infant son of Dr John N & Helen H McCalla. His funeral will take place from 404 C st, on Jun 30th, at 6 o'clock P M.

Albany, N Y, Jun 27. On Tuesday last, in the village of Onenta, Otsego Co, Victor Beach, a son of the late Saml B Beach, murdered his mother by shooting her. He then shot himself, but will recover.

Cincinnati, Jun 27. The steamer **W F Curtis** was burned to the water's edge at Marietta, Ohio, this A M. No lives were lost.

Hon Geo R Davis, one of the oldest & most respected citizens of Troy, N Y, died on Tuesday.

Rev S M Merrill, formerly of North Adams, Mass, about whom a newpaper paragraph was recently published, charging him with eloping with a young lady, fell out of fishing boat in the Saranac river, at Plattsburg, on Wednesday, & was drowned. [Jul 6th newspaper: The body of Rev S M Merrill, of Troy, who was drowned a few days ago, has been found, which puts to rest the rumors that he was not dead.] [Jul 12th newspaper: Rev Merrill is reported to be alive. A letter received by Mrs Merrill from a friend in Detroit, reports that he was seen there on Jul 5.] [Aug 13th newspaper: Trial of Rev Mr Merrill for ministerial misconduct took place in Plattsburgh last week. He confessed to the principal charges against him, with one exception, & was suspended from the ministry until the next meeting of the Troy Conference, to be held in Albany, in Apr, 1868.]

Rev J L M Curry, formerly a member of the U S Congress, & subsequently of the Confederate Congress, from Ala, but now an eminent Baptist clergyman, was married in Richmond, Va, on Tues, to Miss Mary W Thomas, daughter of Jas Thomas, of that city.

Orphans Court of Wash Co, D C, Jun 25, 1867. In the case of Sarah J M Gales, admx w a, of Jos Gales, deceased, the administratrix w a & Court have appointed Jun 20 next, for the final settlement of the personal estate of the said deceased, of the assets in hand. -Jas R O'Beirne, Reg/o wills

Thos Dowling, auct, sold yesterday a lot, improved by a 2 story brick dwlg, on s e corner of Bridge & Market sts, to John Sioussa, for $5,275; also, parts of lots 20 & 21, fronting on the west side of Potomac st, running back 82 feet, with 2 story frame dwlg, to John W Gross, for $1,025.

N Y correspondent says: in the Superior Court, on Wed, in the everlasting case of Forrest vs Forrest, Judge Barbour directed that an order be entered directing the payment of alimony to plntf, the effect of which is to compel Mr Forrest to pay the lady alimoy from the time the divorce was granted, many years ago. It is believed that the courts & the public have now heard the last of this litigation.

N Y, Jun 27. Chas A Brockaway has been convicted of counterfeiting U S fractional currency.

MON JUL 1, 1867
Trial of John H Surratt, Jun 29, 1867. Louis J Weichman was cross examined. Judge Fisher said he felt very unwell today, & had a high fever.

John McIntosh, a lawyer, shot & killed Geo Hemm, recorder of Jackson Co, Kansas, on Wed, at the county seat.

Sgt Maj Dunn, of the Marine Corps, is having erected on G st, between 8th & 9th sts, a large 3 story frame residence, 11 rooms, fitted up with all modern improvements; when finished will cost about $6,000. Mr Dan H Mead is having erected on 6th st east, between D & E sts, a 2 story frame bldg with 8 rooms & kitchen. Dr J H Thompson, of the Columbia Lying Hospital, is having a large frame residence, 40 x 50 feet, with French roof, erected on Mass ave, between 13th & 14th sts, which will cost about $12,000. J H Darrow, is erecting for Mrs Rebecca Edmonston, two fine 3 story press-brick front houses, on I st, at 9th. Gen O O Howard's residence, near the site of the University, will be a beautiful bldg, & will cost about $14,000. It is to be built of the American bldg block, & Mr T Harvey has the contract.

Fort Wallace, Kansas, Jun 22, via Salina, Kansas, Jun 27. This post was attacked yesterday by about 400 Indians. The garrison, consisting of 40 men, belonged to the 3rd infty & 7th cavalry, under command of Lt Hale. Sgt Dummel & Pvt Bacon, of the 7th cavalry, & Pvts Wooldroff & McNally, of the 3rd infty, were killed. John Haney & Geo Gaffney, of the 7th cavalry, & Jos Winehouse & Patrick McCarty, of the 3rd infty, were mortally wounded. The Indians lost 20 of their number. Another attack is imminent.

London Times. The Archduchess Matilda, the intended mother of the future kings of Italy, the daughter of the conqueror of Custozza, & grand-daughter of the hero Aspern & Essling, a princess, in her 19th year, died on Thur last, of a lucifer match. She inadvertently trod on one which was lying on the floor as she leant out a window talking to one of her relatives; her summer dress was in a blaze before she was aware of it, & she sank to the ground in an agony of pain, from which only death released her. Humbert, Prince of Piedmont, heir to the throne of Italy, must look elsewhere for a bride.

Died: on Jun 26, at Port Jefferson, Mrs A W Owen, of Wash City.

Died: on Jun 30, Fannie, infant daughter of John S & Fannie Blackford, aged 9 months. Her funeral is this afternoon at 5 o'clock, from 33 First st, Gtwn, D C.

Dissolution of the partnership under the name of Klein & Helmus this day by mutual consent. Wm Helmus will continue the Restaurant in house 569 7th st, in rear of Tharp's Cigar Store, between D & E sts. –H W Klein, Wm Helmus

The death of the last descendant of Zwinglus, the famous Swiss reformer, is chronicled in the Swiss papers. He died at Dittikon, at age 60, leaving behind many relics that had belonged to his illustrious ancestor.

Orphans Court of Wash Co, D C. Letters testamentary on the personal estate of Jane Lepreux, late of Wash City, D C, deceased. –Augustus Lepreux, exc

Orphans Court of Wash Co, D C, Jun 29, 1867. In the case of Jas M Smith & John W DeKrafft, administrators w a of Nicholas B Van Zandt, dec'd, the administrators & Court have appointed Jul 23 next, for the final settlement of the personal estate of the said deceased, of the assets in hand. -Jas R O'Beirne, Reg/o wills

TUE JUL 2, 1867
Trial of John H Surratt, Jul 1, 1867. Lewis J Weichman was recalled. Dr Lewis Jos Archibald McMillan-sworn: I am a surgeon, out of the service now; two years ago I was in the service of the Montreal Queen Steamship Co, & from Apr to Oct, 1865, I was surgeon of the steamer **Peruvian**. Left Quebec for Liverpool on Sep 16, 1865, we arrived about a week later at Londonderry, Ireland, I know the prisoner at the bar; he crossed the ocean with me to Londonderry on that voyage. I never suspected who the person was.

The late Emperor Maxmillian Ferdinand of Mexico was the son of Archduke Francis Charles of Austria & Princess Sophia of Bavaria. He was born on Jul 6, 1832; in 1846 he entered the Austrian navy; on Jul 27, 1859, he married the unfortuante Maria Carlotta, a daughter of the late King Leopold I of the Belgians. He was appointed Admiral & Cmder-in-Chief of the Austrian navy in 1859, & retained this position until his acceptance of the Mexican crown. [Jul 3rd newspaper: New Orleans, Jul 2. The trial of Maximillian, Majia, & Miramon ended on the 14th, & they were sentenced to the executed on Jun 16. Juarez suspended the execution 3 days, & they were shot at 11 A M on the 19th ult. It is reported that Maximilian was shot in the face, & the Mexican generals in the back as traitors.]

Mr Anthony Addison, of PG Co, Md, in attempting to aid the driver of his mowing machine to manage a refractory mule, a few days since, was suddenly caught by one of the angular knives, & had his left leg so nearly severed, that amputation was deemed necessary. The operation was successfully performed by Dr John H Bayne, assisted by Dr Coombs, of Wash City.

Admiral Farragut. Mrs Farragut & Mrs Capt Pennock had engaged passage in the ship **Fulton**, on Jul 6. On Wed Pres Johnson wrote Mrs Farragut, not merely authorizing her to go, but saying he would be pleased if she would accompany the Admiral in his flagship **Franklin**-that the regulations of the service did not sanction it, but that all rules & regulations were suspended in the present case. The compliment was gratefully accepted by Mrs Farragut, & Sec Welles tendered a passage to Mrs Pennock. The Admiral & both ladies left his residence yesterday, to steam down to the lower bay, whence the flagship put to sea. –N Y Times, Sat

Capt Luther Redfield died at Monroe, Ohio, a few days ago, aged 87. He was a soldier in the war of 1812. On the morning of his death, he arose & dressed as usual. Sitting in his chair he at once complained of pain & faintness, & without a struggle, he died.

Mrd: on Jun 27, at the residence of the bride's father, in PG Co, Md, by Rev Dr McCabe, Mr Jas Seymour Cowan, of Balt Co, Md, to Miss Ellen Clay, daughter of Jas M Wright, Chief Clerk of the Bureau of Military Justice. No cards.

Serious affray near *Fort Whipple* on Sunday at a dance given by some colored people, at a tavern. Rioters defied the soldiers & the order was given to fire, which resulted in seriously wounding a man named Geo Mahony & killing one Griffin Burke, a resident of Gtwn, whose body was turned over to his friends for burial. The remainder of the party surrendered. Burke came to his death by a minnie ball fired by some person unknown.

Lewiston, Me, Jul 1. The Washburne Homestead, in Livermore, was totally destroyed by fire on Sat. The house had been fitted up in fine style by Govn'r Washburne, Congressman E B Washburne, & C C Washburne, who were accustomed every summer to make a pilgrimage to their birthplace.

Portsmouth, N H, Jun 1. Rear Admiral Geo Pearson, U S N, died here today, aged 68. [Jul 3rd newspaper: The deceased was born in 1799; was a native of N H; was appointed to the navy as one of the quoto from Mass, & on Mar 11, 1815, was commissioned as a midshipmen; remained serving on board of the ship **Independence**, until Jan 13, 1825, when he was promoted to the rank of lt; on Sep 8, 1841, he was promoted to the rank of Cmder, & on Sep 14, 1855, was commissioned as Capt, until 1865, when placed on the retired list, & yet further promoted to rank of Cmdor, his commission dated Jul 16, 1862; in 1865 Cmdor Pearson was placed in command of the Pacific squadron, untiil 1866, when he returned home. He leaves a widow & one daughter. –N Y Herald]

Richmond, Jul 1. The remains of Gen A P Hill were brought to the city today & interred in *Holywood Cemetery*.

Intending to devote myself exclusively to the manufacture of Furniture, I have disposed of all my stock in trade belonging to the Undertaking Business, to Anthony Buchly, my former apprentice, who can be found at all times at his place of business: 303 Pa ave, between 9th & 10th sts. –Saml Kirby

Trustee's sale of valuable unimproved real estate at auction; by the last will & testament of Johnson Hellen; public auction on Jul 5 of part of lot 2 in square 185, on I st, between 16th & 17th sts, adjoining the residence of Geo W Riggs. On Jul 6: part of lot 4 in square 489, on 6th st; & lot 2 in square 521, on 4th st. –John B Blake, H G Fant, Clifton Hellen, Wm F Hellen, C C Hellen, trustees -Cooper & Latimer, aucts

Died: on Jul 1, Charles, youngest son of H L & C V Chapin, aged 11 months. His funeral will take place from the residence of his parents, 529 13th st, Island, Jul 2, at 10½ o'clock.

Guardian's sale of bldg lots on 8th st, between K & L sts, & n e corner of 5th & L st, at auction, by order of the Orphans Court of D C., dated May 21, 1867; public auction on Jul 9 next, part of lot 10 in square 402. Also, lot 10 in square 514; & lot 5 in square 484. –Virginia Hollingsworth, Guardian of Margaretta B Doughty -Cooper & Latimer, aucts

War Dept Claims Commission, Wash, D C, Jun 29, 1867. List of claims received by the Commission during the month of Jun, 1867.
Claim of Mary Ann Pierce, one of the legatees of the will of Mrs Eliza Hurdi_ty.
John G White, for destruction of barge **Col E E Kendricks**.
Preston *Armyx, for tobacco taken in Tenn. [*Copied as written]
A A Mitchell, for services in the 14th army corps.
H G Ludlow, for haversacks furnished the Gov't.
Joshua Caldwell, for services in capturing steamer **Laurel Hill**.
Malcolm Cameron, for services in capturing steamer **Laurel Hill**.
John Glenn, for services as blacksmith.
L C White, for quinine taken in 1864.
S B Davidson, for brandy & quinine taken in 1862.
Jas Woods, for kettles taken at Nashville, Tenn.
Baker & Fulsom, for services of brig **Edwin N Filler**
Sebastian Grober, for lumber, etc.
A L Stamps, for services rendered & stores furnished the Quartermaster's Dept.
J C White, for rent & damages to property at Wmsport, Md.
Wm H Gregerson, exc of the estate of Geo Gregerson, deceased, & John Lightner, for compensation for the use of Lightner's patent for axle boxes.
-De Witt Clinton, Brvt Lt Col, Recorder

WED JUL 3, 1867
N Y, Jul 2. This morning an ofcr of the 23rd Precinct of police arrested Thos Kealy on the charge of being the person who murdered Col O'Brien in 2nd ave during the riots of Jul, 1863. The ofcrs claim to have strong evidence in their possession.

Admiral Wilkes, U S Navy, has 1,500 acres of land at High Shoals, N C, carries on extensive iron works, employs 150 laborers, & has established a school for freedmen, of which his wife & daughters are the teachers. They have 150 pupils.

Died: on Jul 2, at Alexandria, Va, Geo Thornton Baldwin, youngest son of Almon & the late Matilda S Baldwin. His funeral is this afternoon, at his late residence, 106 Luke st.

Died: on Jul 2, Alexias, youngest child of Alex'r R & Mary G Shepherd. The funeral will be from 358 10th st, this evening, at 5 o'clock, P M.

Mrd: on Jul 2, at the residence of the bride's father, by Rev Dr Pinkney, Mr Wm P Titcomb, of Maine, to Alice, 2nd daughter of C E Upperman, of Wash City. No cards.

Supreme Court of D C, Jul 2, 1867. Catharine Homann vs Dewald Homann. On motion of the plntf by Mr Schmidt, his counsel, it is ordered that the dfndnt cause his appearance to be entered on or before the first rule day ocurring forty days after this day, otherwise the cause will be proceeded with as in case of defaut. –L Schmidt -R J Meigs, Clerk

Trial of John H Surratt, Jul 2, 1867. Capt Wm M Wemershkirch-sworn: was in the army in 1865 as an ofcr; on Apr 17, was at Mrs Surratt's house; Maj H W Smith & 2 detectives, Samson & Rosch were with me; I saw Mrs Surratt on that occasion, & afterwards saw her at the Arsenal during the trial of the conspirators. At the Arsenal I also saw a man whose name was Payne or Powell. Henry Benj St Marie-sworn: in 1866, in Apr, was in the Papal states, at Valetra; about 40 miles from Rome; was a soldier of the Papal army, in the 9th company. They were called the Papal Zouaves. I saw the prisoner there & I knew him. I asked the prisoner how he got out of Washington, & he told me he left the night of the assassination or the next morning, & said he was so disguised that no one could recognize him as an American, & that he was disguised as an Englishman, with a scarf over his shoulder.

Annual Distribution of Premiums at the Academy of the Visitation yesterday. Fr Stonestreet, of St Aloysius Church, addressed the graduating class; Pres Johnson addressed the class with much feeling. Students who received premiums.

Mary Dulaney, Va
Florida Walker, Fla
Maggie Lewin, Md
Lucy Garrett, Texas
Mary Walsh, Wash, D C
A Corkery, Richmond- Va
Julia O'Neil, Gtwn
Angelo Monteiro- Richmond, Va
Mary Weaver, Gtwn
Emma Kidwell, Gtwn- D C
Saida Bird, Ga
Mary J Bailey, Texas
Cora Reed, Ark
Belle Bocock, Va
Hallie Early, Va
Mamie Reilly, Dela
Mamie Fisk
M Lilly, Pa
Bertha Honore, Ill
Mary Newcomer, Md
Mary Conrad
Josephine Dickson, Mo
Hattie Postlewait
Annie Morgan

Fanny Dulany
Effie Nicholson
Louise Smith
Lizzie Williams, Tenn
Cora Brown, D C
Louisa Myrick, Ga
Mary Myrick, Ga
Mary McCay, Md
Alice Osborne, Phil, Pa
Ellen Murphy, Ala
Annie Lee, Md
Fannie Hansberger, Va
Mary Murphy, N Y
Annie French, D C
Josephine Dowell, Va
Lucy *Mhoon, Tenn
Lizzie Williams, Tenn
Va Hill, La
Amy Graham, La
Ida Mapp, Ga
Luy Garrett, Texas
Fannie Howe, D C
Mary Ellen Brown, D C
Mary Wittenaur, D C
Annie Barnes, D C

Mary Carr, D C
Mary Armour, D C
Fannie Abell, Md
Lena Johnson, La
Jenny Walters, Md
Sallie Martin, Md
Clara Carlton, Md
Lillie Bowie, Md
Alice Poore, Mass
Alice Dixon, Va
Martha Smith, Md
Maggie Boucher, D C
Maggie Brown, D C
Virginia Offutt, D C
Christina Mackall, D C
Laura Griffin
Ida Dearing
Lilly Sims
Ellen Murphy
Mattie Walker
Christina Mackall
Lizzie Butler, D C
Valeria Hubbard, D C
[*Mhoon-copied as written.]

Kate Finley, D C
Cora Boucher, D C
Lulie Essex, D C
Belle Shermer, Pa
Rosa Sims
Ella Fowler
Minnie Crawford
Mary Walsh
Irene Forrest
Jennie Caperton
Mary Mosher
Lizzie Lilly
Madaline Augustine
Annie Price
Nannie Laub
Bessie Everts
Rachel Godey
Amy Graham
Dettie Beninghaus
Calle Mundy
Millie McKay
Ada Mapp

Admiral Radford yesterday appointed C W Oakely, gate-keeper & general detective at the Wash Navy Yard. He was formerly a clerk in the Commandant's dept.

The eloquence of Mrs Stanton & Miss Anthony had very little effect on the suffrage cmte of the N Y State Convention. –Boston Post

Orphans Court-Judge Purcell. 1-Yesterday the Goldin case, which has attracted considerable attention in this community for the past 2 or 3 days was taken up. Rev Jacob Walter, pastor of St Patrick's Church appeared in answer to the citation, bringing with him Genevieve & Eliz Goldin, the children, whose guardianship is contended for. Mr John F Ennis appeared for Rev Mr Walter, & Mr Ingle for Eliz Goldin. The petition was read by the latter, the response by the former. The petition of Eliz Goldin sets forth that her brother, Geo Goldin, late of Wash, died on Apr 10, 1865, leaving 3 children, Geo Goldin, Genevieve Goldin, & Eliz Goldin; that for some time previous to his death he committed said children to her care; that ever since his death, as well as before that time, she has maintained & educated them with all the care, affection, & tenderness of a mother, & is still ready & willing to do so. She further sets forth that on Jun 22, 1867, one Jacob A Walter called at Mrs Sessford's house, where she had placed them, &, without the knowledge or consent of the petitioner took away the said children, & that they are now confined, as she is informed & believe, in the orphan asylum, at 16th & G sts, in Wash City. She is also informed that on the same day the said Jacob A Walter procured from the Orphans Court letters of guardianship of the said children, & that said letters were issued under a misapprehension. In conclusion, she prayed that the said letters of administration might be revokded. The answer of the Rev Jacob A Walter denies that the children were taken from Mrs Sessford by him & confined in the orphan asylum, & states that his only object in assuming the guardianship was to provide them with a home & a good moral & religious education, they being penniless orphans. After hearing the evidence in the case, the Judge stated that he would render his decision on Saturday next. 2-The first & final account of David A Burr, guardian to the orphans of Jos Owens, & the third account of Jas Fitzpatrick, exc of Dominick Conroy, were passed & proved.

The annual commencement of Gonzaga College, formerly known under the name of Washington Seminary, took place last evening at Gonzaga Hall, in the presence of the parents & friends of the pupils. Prologue: Thos Harvey, John Drew; Hymn, Wm Harlan; Poem, Wm Douglas; Discourse, John Brady; Poem, Chas O'Leary; Discourse, Wm W Boarman; Poem, John F Cox. [Editor's note: we regret that our space will not permit of an enumeration of all those who received their well deserved rewards of merit.]

THU JUL 4, 1867

Trial of John H Surratt, Jul 3, 1867. Chas H M Wood, colored, sworn: barber by business & has been here since 1862; in Apr, 1865, worked at the shop of Booker & Stewart, on E st, under Jos Hall's; I now have a barber shop under the Ebbitt House; I knew Booth before the assassination; have cut his hair & shaved him-knew him well. Chas Ramsell-sworn; lives in Boston, Mass; was in the war in company D, 3rd Mass heavy artl; came here in May, 1864, remained till Sep, 1864; on the day of the assassination I came here from *Fort Bunker Hill*; thought he had seen the prisoner the next day. Frank M Keason-sworn: clerk in Gen Land Ofc; resided here 6 years; came from Indiana; in 1865 resided at 10th & F sts, near that theatre; saw the Pres' carriage drive up the day of the assassination. Theodore Benj Rhodes-sworn: lived on Capitol Hill, Wash City; been living here since 1862; works at repairing clocks & watches; on the day of the assassination; went to see the stage about 12 o'clock. Wm S Thompson-sworn: he is a druggist at 15th & N Y ave; in business there since 1859; Herold was a clerk with witness either in 1862 or 1863. Wm Norton-sworn: lives at Charlotte Hall, St Mary's Co, Md; came here in 1861; came here as a witness 2 weeks ago last Monday; in Apr, 1865, lived in T B, Md; saw none of the conspirators at the time; saw some arms brought there by David Herold-2 guns, 2 carbines, a pistol, a knife, & ammunition; also, a rope & a wrench, & a horse & buggy.

Supreme Court of D C, Jul 2, 1867. Edw F Queen et al, cmplnts, vs Henry P Queen & wife, dfndnts. Dfndnts to appear on or before the first rule day occurring 40 days after this day, otherwise cause will be proceeded with as in case of default.
–R J Meigs, clerk

Supreme Court of D C, Equity 936; Docket 81. Jas P Ferguson, plntf, vs Martha E Ferguson, dfndnt. The object of this suit is to obtain a decree against the dfndnt for a divorce from the bonds of matrimony on the charge of adultery, contained in the bill of cmplnt, placed in the hands of the Marshal of D C, returned "not to be found." Dfndnt to appear on or before the first rule day, 40 days after this date, otherwise the cause will be proceeded with as in case of default. –R J Meigs, clerk

Celebration today; picnic & grand display of fireworks at Analostan Island. Oldest Inhabitants: Dr Blake will read the Declaration of Independence; oration will be delivered by Col Peter G Washington; Prof Jacobs will perform on the trapeze; Prof Cock's band has been engaged. Cmte of arrangements for the day: Messrs G A Bohrer, Wm B Todd, & Robt Ball. [Jul 6th newspaper: July 4th: Dr Blake announced the death of Jas Rhodes, late member of the association. Nominated & elected as members: J L Elliot, Walter T Brooke, E Kingman, John Brannan, R B Owens, & John Van Riswick. Edw Simms Vice Pres, vice Dr Jones, deceased.]

Queer case of drowning. Troy papers on Friday: Rev S M Merrill, pastor of the Methodist Church at Plattsburg, was drowned in the Saranac river. It appears that Merrill had secured an insurance on his life, in an accident insurance company, for the sum of $6,000. This was to expire on Thursday noon. On Wed he drew $200 on his salary, & towards evening took 2 of his own boys, & another boy of the village of Plattsburg, & went out fishing in the Saranac river. When it became dark, & while pulling in the boat anchor, he suddenly went overboard. The boys pushed the boat after him, but he told them to never mind him, he was well enough. He disappeared in the darkness. He may be drowned, but the case makes it appear very doubtful. It is much more likely that he has gone to parts unknown to his neighbors & interesting family.

Mrd: on Jun 30, in Wash City, by Rev Dr Gurley, Mr Henry B Bennett to Mrs Mary L Selee, both formerly of Massachusetts.

Mrs Codwise, 284 G st, between 13th & 14th sts, has a few unoccupied rooms, where a neat, comfortable home may be found, with best quality table-board.

Valuable residence in Gtwn at auction, on Jul 15, known as the **Shaaf property**; lot fronts 117 feet 5 inches on First st, between High & Potomac sts, with a depth of 150 feet, with the privilege of a wide alley, from Potomac st; with a brick dwlg house, containing 13 rooms, kitchen, & cellar; large brick stable, carriage-house, etc. -Thos Dowling, auct

Elmwood, French & English Home School for Young Ladies, near Laurel, Md, reopens on Sep 20th, with a limited number of pupils. –Mrs Burr, Laurel Post ofc, PG Co, Md.

Prof H Masson, of the Post Ofc Dept, & daughter, & Mrs Gen Jeffries, start today, Jul 4, for Paris & a tour through Europe.

SAT JUL 6, 1867

Trial of John H Surratt, Jul 5, 1867. Andrew Kaldenbach-sworn: lives in Wash; know where Surratsville is; known Mr John M Lloyd; was there in 1865, found firearms in Lloyd's house; I found the arms in Apr, 1865, in a partition between the plastering. On the night I found the arms a detective was there searching, & I found the carbine. The detective was Geo Cottingham. Hon A B Oline-sworn: was in the city on the night of the assassination; went in company with Senator & Miss Harris the next day to examine the premises; it was represented that the Pres had been shot through the door. Walter H Coleman-sworn: resides in Wash; head of division of the ofc of the Sec of Treasury; been in that ofc since 1864; knew Mr Geo W Cushing. I think I saw the prisoner with Booth. Geo W Cushing-sworn: [hard of hearing;] is clerk at the Treasury; been there since 1861; on Apr 14, 1865, took a walk up the avenue with Mr Coleman; saw Booth on horseback. Geo S Kountz-sworn: is general agent of the Balt & Ohio railroad; lived here since 1862; witness' family detained from reaching this city the next morning. Guards were placed on the cars & the platforms. Thos Lincoln-sworn: is son of the late President; was with father at City Point in Mar, 1865; while there a man came up twice to see the Pres, but was not permitted; witness stated that the prisoner looked very much like that person.

Annual commencement of Gtwn College on Wed; this is the oldest Catholic university in the U S, its origin dates back as far as 1785, when several gentlemen under the leadership of Rev John Carroll, afterwards first Archbishop of Balt, formed the design of establishing an academy at Gtwn, Potomac river, Md. The first bldg was erected in 1789, the year the town was incorporated. In 1792 the schools were opened, & in 1798 the institution was designated as The College of Gtwn, Potomac river, state of Md. In 1815 Congress raised it to the rank of a university, & under this act of incorporation the first class graduated in 1817. As the valedictory address was concluding, Pres Johnson, accompanied by Mrs Patterson, Col O'Beirne, & the Pres' little son, entered the hall, the College band playing "Hail to the Chief." Degree of Master of Arts was conferred on: Edw S Riley, A B, Pa; Henry M Brent, A B, N Y; Francis X Ward, A B, Md; Edwin McCahill, A B, N Y; Noble S Hoffar, A B, Dist of Col; Julius S Soper, A B, Dist of Col. Honorary degree of Master of Arts was conferred on: Jas B Pye, Texas; Jas C Normile, Kansas; John B Dimitry, Louisiana; Chas P Demitry, Louisiana; Jos M Toner, M D, Dist of Col. The degree of Bachelor of Arts was conferred on the graduationg class: Saml H Anderson, Md; Robt M Douglas, Ill; Bladen Forrest, Dist of Col; Geo H Fox, N Y; Chas C Homer, Md; Arthur Lee, Md. Statement of honors for good scholarship & good conduct for the year presented to: Chas C Homer, Md; Robt M Douglas, Ill; Chas C Homer, Md; Saml Anderson, Md; Geo H Fox, N Y; Bladen Forrest, D C; Arthur Lee, Md; Wm A Hammond, Md; Francis J Kieckhoefer, D C; D Clinton Lyles, Md; N Calvin Collier, Ga; Jas V Coleman, N Y; Henry A Seyfert, Pa; Wm F Rudolph, Mo; Matthew Wilson, D C; Wm F Rudolph, Mo; Stephen R Mallory, Gla; Algernon C Chalmers, Va; Sands W Forman, Calif; Jas McV Mackall, D C; Eugene D F Brady, Dela; Henry Walters, Md; Stephen R Mallory, Fla; Geo F Munce, Pa; Martin T Dickson, Mo; Edw Key, Md; John T Hedrick, D C; Thos A Kelly, Pa; Alfred N Williams, Va; W Lewis Menger, Texas; Dennis Sheridan, Md; Seaton G Bailey; Wm

L Menger; G Gordon Posey, Thos Badeaux; Dennis Sheridan, Henry P Luckett; Francis Scales; Thos H Stack, Va; Wm L Brenner, Ga; Francis A Cunningham, Pa; Arthur E Elliot, S C; Robt J Murray, D C; Wm W Hill, Md; Devereaux Doyle; Wm Brenner; Alfred Elliot; Peabody Morse; Wm Hall; Henry Rogers; Jas Collins; Brenton Boggs; Richd R McMahon, Va; Chas L Gordon, D C; Thos L Repplier, Pa; John V Camalier, Md; Chas Ray, La; Geo A Camalier, Md; John R Ross, Md; John B Northrop, Va; Jas C Acheson, Va; Jos F Talbot, Md; Luis de Puebla, Mexico; Chas S Abell, Md; Chas M Caughy, Md; Edw H Corkery, Va; W Reynolds Cowardin, Va; Geo F Munce, Pa; Richd L Dickson, Mo; W Maffitt Turner, Mo; Jos E Washington, Tenn; Jos O'Farrell, D C; Wm L Brenner, Ga; Dennis O'Connor, Ga; Chas A Repplier, Pa; Richd R McMahon, Va; Raphael Provosty, La; Webster Weast, Md; Francis M Neal, Md; Oliver Provosty, La; Henry H Burton, Calif; Saml H Scales, Wisc; Saml H Scales, Wisc; Robt V Simms, D C; Massillon H Marsteller, Va; Theodore Johnson, Ark; Benj Lewis, La; Edw G A Adams, Md; Nicholas J Cruger, Ga; Bernard Offutt, D C; Vincent A Hubbard, D C; Henry J Elley, Miss; Geo D Lyles, Md; Robt J Murray, D C; W Elliott Johnstone, S C; Stephen R Mallory, Fla; Jas M Mackall, D C; Chas E Rodney, Mo; Chas T Goodman, Va; Maurice N Langhorne, Va; Henry Walters, Md; Jas T Duffy, D C; Francis Wassmer, Va; Chas C Lancaster, Md; Marion J Crownrich, La; Wm W Watson, Mich; Jas H O'Neill, Va; John J O'Neill, Pa; Chas A Ball, D C; John Waddey; Jos L Bragassa, Va; Mark H White, Texas; Wm D Smith, La; R Woodley Hayden, Md; Wm T Williams, D C; Andrew J Byrne, Va; Jos M Semmes, Tenn; Richd J McGrann, Pa; Talemachus A Badeaux, La; A Francis Johnson, Tenn; Robt M Durney, Md; Benj Lewis, La; John H Braceland, Pa; Clarence W Hoyt, Idaho; Henry J Elley, Miss; Giles E Power, Va; Hs V Coleman, N Y; Jose E Lanas, Peru; Matthew Wilson, D C; Alfred N Williams, Va; Marion Crownrich, La; Jas W Collins, D C; John A Herron, D C; Wm Larman, D C; Wm Lazenby, D C; Geo F Stump, D C; Geo W Talburtt, D C; Wm B Browne, D C; Gabriel Bustamente, Mexico; M Jos Tuohy, D C. [Some names are repeated due to class, division, additonal awards, premiums, etc.]

Hon Jas M Wayne, of the U S Supreme Court, died at his residence yesterday. He had been ill of typhoid fever for about 2 weeks, & his death was apprehended from the commencement of the attack. We learn that his wife & daughter, Mrs Cyler, Dr Cyler, his son-in-law, & two grand-sons were with him at his last moments. He was in his 77th year; born in Savannah, Ga, in 1790. He entered <u>Nassau Hall</u>, now Princeton College, where he counted among his fellow-students some of the leading men of the present day. He then studied law, but his father having died a few months afterwards, he left for the North; returned & commenced the practice of his professon. His funeral will take place on Sunday at 5 o'clock P M, from his residence on I st, between 13th & 14th sts. [Jul 8th newspaper: The services for Justice Wayne were conducted by Rev J V Lewis, rector of St John's Church; at the conclusion the remains were taken to **Oak Hill Cemetery**, & were placed for the present in the family vault, the intention being to send the body to Georgia next winter for burial at the native place of the deceased. The pall bearers were Admiral Shubrick, Hon Caleb Cushing, Gen Dyer, Gen Rickets, Senators Poland & Trumbull, Jas Carlisle, & W W Corcoran.]

The exercises on Wed at the Washington <u>Academy of the Visitation</u>, corner of G & 10th sts, took place in the parlor of the academy. Not having the accomodations, the scholars attending are those who reside with their parents & friends; but the sisters intend not long hence to build an academy which will accommodate both day & resident scholars. Honors of the Senior Circle were awarded to: Christina Callan, Anna Callan, Julia McKelden, Marianne Polkinhorn, Mary E Jones, & Ella McGrann. Second honors to: Anna Scott, Phebe Elliot, Anna Handy, Anna Klink, America Henning, Mary Saul, Genevieve Cleary, Kate Shyne, Anna Bartholow, Kate Harkness, & Delia Handy. Mscl Awards to: Fannie Flint, Fannie Wilson, Mary E White, Mary Saul, Jane Ryan, Kate E Harkness; Maggie Newton, Anna Bartholow, Helena Gorlinski, Victoria Le Compte, Mary Walsh, Esther Simpson, Anna Lauck, Ella Farquhar, Jeannie Evans, Julia Greer, Mary F Schneider, Bertha Chilton, Mabel Bartholow, Amalia Bastianelli, Fannie Joyce, Mary Jones, Anna McCullough, Caroline Goff, Anna Adamson, Mary J Boyle, Elberta Bennett, Virginia Shankland, Mary Clark, Ellen Ryan, Fannie Kuhl, Lulie Newton, Clara Postelwait, Florence Cook, Missouri Ricketts, Elvie Fletcher, Hattie Mattingly, Rosalie Spignul, Bertha Chilton, Josephine Cleary, Ella Farrar, [for being the smallest girl in the school] E Birnie, M Noyes, B Torney, L Blount, & F Stoops.

Died: on Jun 31, suddenly, of cholera, at **Fort Harker**, Kansas, Wm Edw Armes, aged 18 years, son of Mr J Armes, of Wash City. This young man left this city a few weeks since to accompany his brother, Capt Geo A Armes, to join his regt, about to proceed against the Indians.

Died: on Jul 5, Saml DeVaughan, in his 68th year. His funeral will be from his late residence, 403 E st, between 9th & 10th sts, on Jul 7 at 3 o'clock. [Jul 8th newspaper: At the conclusion of the funeral, the remains were taken tothe **Congressional Burial Ground** for interment. The pall-bearers were Messrs Milburn, Smith, Brown, Cate, Boswell, Nutze, Humes, & Edwards.]

MON JUL 8, 1867
Trial of John H Surratt, Jul 6, 1867. Mr J H Bradley, jr, opened the case for the defence, & said the time had at last arrived, in this case when the prisoner could say something in support of his own innocence, & when not only his own guiltlessness may be shown but the pure fame of his departed mother may be vindicated.

W T Metzerott, S Stone, T Stone, Mrs Berger & daughter, & Mrs Bowman & daughter, of Wash City, were among the passengers who left N Y, for Europe, Wed, per steamer **City of New York**.

The telegraph has announced the death of Lazarus W Powell, ex-Govn'r of Henderson Co, where he was born on Oct 6, 1812, was in his 56th year of his age; graduated at St Joseph's College, Bardstown, in 1833; studied law at Transylvania Univ; admitted to the bar in 1835. In private life he was an excellent gentleman, perhaps a little eccentric, but still kindly, benevolent & sociable.
[No death date given-current item.]

Zack Smith, a young freedman, has applied to the Sec of War for a cadetship at West Point from the First Congressional District of South Carolina.

G Fred Maddox, of St Mary's Co, Md, a member of the State Senate, has been appointed on the staff of Govn't Swann, with the rank of colonel.

Orphans Court. 1-The ptn of Eliz Golding, for revocation of the letters of guardianship granted to Rev Jacob A Walter over the children of the late Geo & Annie Golding, was decided. Judge Purcell remarked that it was the duty of the Court, under the peculiar circumstances of this case, to exercise its best descretion. It seemed that the petitioner had set forth that the guardianship had been ordered under a misapprehension; that one of the reasons set forth for revocation was that petitioner did not desire these children to be educated as Catholics, yet she had placed them in a Catholic institution to be educated, which was inconsistent with the declaration referred to. The Court held that it was its duty to see that a guardian be appointed of good character & known respectability, & stated that, in the opinion of the Court, the order appointing Mr Walter had been properly made, & after a thorough investigation of all the facts in the petition, & the answer, he could but refuse to revoke the appointment. This case has attracted the attention & excited quite a degree of interest in the minds of a certain class of this community.
2-The 6th account of the guardian of Anna B Spedden was presented & approved.
3-The 3rd & final account of the guardian of Chas B Littleton was approved.
4-Jos R Cassin was appointed guardian to Roberta Dyer, orphan of Robt W & Mary Eliza Dyer; bond $10,000. 5-The court then took up the contested will of Mary Ann Fearson, in which the alleged heirs at law attempt to upset the will on the ground that the deceased was of unsound mind. The case was argued by counsel up to the time of the adjournment of the court.

Savannah, Ga, Jul 7. E J Westmoreland, British Consul at Brunswick, Ga, was killed at that place by Capt Martin on Jul 5. Deceased had been married only 4 hours. Martin was arrested & brought to this city. Great mystery exists regarding the affair.

Mrd: at the Church of the Epiphany, Wash, D C, by Rev Chas Hall, D D, Augustus J Albert, jr, of Balt, Md, to Julia, daughter of the late J W Doughty, of St Louis, Mo. [No marriage date given-current item.] [Richmond, Petersburg, & St Louis papers please copy.]

Died: on Jul 6, Mrs Anastatia Burke, aged 68 years, a native of the county Limerick, Ireland, & for the last 16 years a resident of Wash. Her funeral wil take place this evening at 3½ o'clock, from the residence of her son, 58 Ohio ave.

Died: on Jul 7, Mrs Caroline Parker, wife of Thos Parker, of Wash City. Her funeral will take place on Jul 9 at 10 o'clock A M, from St Aloysius Church.

David Reed had both arms blown off by the premature explosion of a cannon at Terra Haute on Thursday.

Mark Schriven, of Petersburg, Monroe Co, Mich, was struck by lightning on Wednesday morning, & killed.

Chicago has had a fashionable wedding. Eugene W Jerome, of N Y, a nephew of *the* Jerome, was married on Monday to Miss Paulina Von Schneidan, daughter of a deceased Swedish nobleman, who was at one time Consul of Sweden at Chicago.

Rev B F Morris committed suicide by hanging, in the cellar of his house in Springfield, Ohio, last Friday. He was lately a clerk in the State dept, in this city, & was 50 years old. Formerly he preached in Lebanon, Ohio; Rising Sun, Indiana; & other places.

Jas T Sanger, a prominent citizen of Chicago, died on Wed. He was well known throughout the entire Northwest, having for a long time been largely engaged in public improvements. The firm with which he was connected built at a cost of $12,000,000, over 450 miles of our railroads, the Calif Central railorad, & the Illinois penitentiary, at Joliet.

Jos Williams, a colored man, murderer of John Reddick, another colored man, was hung on Friday at New Brunswick, N J. Instead of a drop through a trap, the condemned was suddenly hoisted from the ground about 2 feet by means of a pulley & a heavy weight.

Trustee's sale of valuable Patuxent Lands in St Mary's Co, by decree of Circuit Court for St Mary's Co, dated Jun 17, 1867, the undersigned trustee, will offer at public sale at the Court-house door, Leonardtown, on Aug 6 next, the following property: **Scotch Neck**, containing 352 acres, more or less; **Burdett's Neck**, 152 acres, more or less. **Scotch Neck** has a comfortable frame dwlg, meat house, stable, & barns. –Jas S Downs, trustee

Dept of the Interior, U S Patent Ofc, Wash, Jun 28, 1867. Ptn of Harvey Lull, of Hoboken, N J, praying for extension of a patent granted to him Jan 31, 1854, & antedated Jan 2nd, 184, for an improvement in Shutter Hinges for seven years from the expiration of said patent, which takes place on Jan 2, 1868.
-T C Theaker, Com'r of Patents

Dept of the Interior, U S Patent Ofc, Wash, Jun 29, 1867. Ptn of Ephraim L Pratt, of Boston, Mass, praying for the extension of a patent granted to him Oct 4, 1853, for an improvement in Machines for paring apples, for seven years from the expiration of said patent, which takes place on Oct 4, 1867. -T C Theaker, Com'r of Patents

Farm, portable steam saw & grist mill, lumber, posts, etc, at auction, on Jul 17, on the premises, the fine Farm, on which Geo Page, resides, in PG Co, Md, near the **Long Old Fields**, adjoining the farm of Mr Rowzee, on the Marlboro road; contains 126 acres; conveniently arranged dwlg house with 10 rooms, barn, wagon shed, ice-house, & other outbldgs. The farm will be sold first. -Green & Williams, aucts

Norfolk Day Book of Wed. On last Friday, 3 black men went to the house of Reeves Foscue, in Jones Co, N C, & shut the whole family up in the outhouse on the premises; they then robbed the house of all its contents. When the family thought to relieve themselves from confinement, the scoundrels set upon them, & committed some of the most cruel murders ever recorded. The first victims were Mr Foscue & wife, who were murdered before their children's eyes. They next seized Mrs Whitty, a daughter of Mr Foscue, & her child, an infant of 4 or 5 months, killing the infant first & then the mother. Miss Foscue caught up another child & started to run, when she was fired upon, & they were both wounded. She continued to run & when she reached a neighbor's house, 2½ miles distant, the child was found to be dead. The sheriff of Craven left Newbern with a posse on Tuesday to find & arrest the murderers of the Foscue family.

Yesterday lightning struck the brick barn of Mr Jos Young, whose residence is near *Sheridan's Point*, on the Potomac, & was destroyed, with it contents. The bldg was erected by Gen Washington, & was located on a portion of the original *Mount Vernon* estate. –Alexandria Gaz, Sat

TUE JUL 9, 1867
Ex-Govn'r John A King, of N Y, on Jul 4th, whilst delivering an oration at Jamaica, Long Island, was seized with a sudden illness & fainted. Being conveyed from the stand to his home, his entire left side was found to be paralyzed, from the effects of which he died on Sunday afternoon.

Trial of John H Surratt, Jul 8, 1867. Theodore Benj Rhodes was recalled: on Apr 14, the outside door of the theatre was open; he went upstairs & entered the box; was in the box when the chair was brought up. Mr John T Ford was called: now resides in Balt; in 1865 was the proprietor of *Ford's Theatre* in Wash City; it was built under my direction & supervision; diagram of the theatre was explained to the jury. Mr Henry Clay Ford-sworn: resides in Balt; in 1865 was treasurer of *Ford's Theatre*, & myself & brother Jas R Ford, had management of the theatre in absence of J T Ford; saw Booth at 11 o'clock on the day of assassination; he came to the theatre from F st; got a letter from the ofc, & commenced reading it; few minutes before that I received information that the Pres was coming that night; don't remember any one informing Booth of the fact. Mr Raybold, whose duty it was, was ordered to prepare the box. I afterwards prepared the box myself. At that time Edw Spangler was on the stage fixing the scene. Jas J Gifford recalled: was at the theatre on Apr 14; built the theatre; stated that there was but one door to Boxes 7 & 8, & no other exit or entrance. C V Hess-sworn: resides in 5th st, Phil; in 1865 was connected with the company performing at *Ford's Theatre*; assigned a song after the American Cousin that night; it was to be performed for the Pres. L J Carland-sworn: resides in Boston; was costumer at *Ford's Theatre* in 1865; saw Booth in front of the theatre several times during the day; was in the paint gallery when Peanut John came after Spangler to take a partition down.

For sale: Landon Female Seminary & Farm attached: in Fred'k Co, Md, embraces 158 acres of land; adjoining the village of Urbana, Fred'k Co, Md. Seminary is large & commodious, having been arranged for a first-class boarding school. The Farm House is in good condition, it being & other out houses good & mostly new. Apply to Saml Hinks, Urbana, Fred'k, Md.

Supreme Court of D C, Equity 1006. Jas Adams, Jos Ingle & others, vs John P Ingle, John A Bailey & others. The above cause is referred to me to state the account of the trustees & the distributive shares of the parties interested in the sale made by them of the Old Capitol property. Stockholders of the Old Capitol property, & others interested, are to appear before me on Jul 13, at my ofc, at 11 A M.
–Walter S Cox, auditor

Miss Caroline Richings, the well known cantatrice, fell down stairs at her summer residence, near West Chester, Pa, on Thursday, & seriously injured herself in the side & head. Her life was at first despaired of, but she is now rapidly recovering.

Virginia City, Montana Territory, Jul 5, 1867. Gen Thos Francis Meagher, Secretary & acting Govn'r of this Territory, fell from the deck of the steamer **Thompson**, at **Fort Benton**, on the evening of the 1st instant, & was drowned. He had been absent for the last fortnight on public business, & had succeeded in procuring arms for the troops engaged in the defence of the Territory, & transacting other military business demanded by our present exigency. His death is greatly lamented. Gen Meagher was born in Waterford, Ireland, on Aug 3, 1823, & was 44 years of age. He took a prominent part in Irish politics as one of the leaders of the Young Ireland party, & after being convicted on the charge of treason, was sentenced to death. This sentence was commuted to banishment for life to Van Dieman's Land. Thence he escaped, obtained passaged by a sailing vessel, & arrived in this port in May, 1852, where he was received with much enthusiasm. He raised a company for the 69th regt in 1861 & accompanied it to the field. Early in the war he was assigned to the command of the Irish Brigade, & shared its fortunes in nearly all the campaigns of the Army of the Potomac. He was wounded at the battle of Fredericksburg, but speedily recovered & resumed his command. He was recently appointed Secretary of Montana, & as acting Govn'r had declared himself in favor of a vigorous & energetic prosecution of a war against the Indians. [Aug 16th newspaper: High Mass of Requiem was offered in the Church of St Francis Xavier, for the repose of the soul of the late Gen Meagher, on Aug 16th. Seated in the principal pews were Col Kavanagh, Col Jas Kelly, Gen Burke, Capt Doran, Capt Brennan, Capt Lyon, Capt Stacom, Lt Collins, Lt Powers, Lt Kerr, Adj Hargous, Capt Dempsey, Lt Col Quinlan, Maj Hagerty, John Hennessy, Mr Fitzpatrick. The requiem mass was sung by Rev Mr Lory, assisted by Fr Hudson as deacon, & Fr Thierry as sub-deacon, & Rev Mr Belencour as master of ceremonies. Rev Fr Loyzance & Fr Moylan, president of St John's College, Fordham, were present in the sanctuary. The choir was composed of the following artists: Soprano, Madame Dessane, Madame Paulick; Alto, Madame Veter, Madame Verner; Tenor, Mr Grosschell, Mr Singzan; Basso, Mr H Schurcardi, Mr A Schurcardi. –N Y Express, 14th.]

Ads. 1-Jas Crutchett offers for rent the bldgs known as the Soldiers' Rest. 2-The attention of our readers is called to the card of Walter H S Taylor, agent & atty.

The undersigned will sell at private sale the farm now in his occupancy, located between Rockville, Montg Co, Md, & Gtwn, D C; contains 196 acres. It will be shown by Mr Wm Hagan, who resides upon it. Title is perfect. Terms made known on application to Granville F Hyde, 63 Water st, or to Dr Grafton Tyler, Wash & Gay sts, Gtwn.

Trustee's sale, by decree passed by the Supreme Court of D C, in chancery No 812, wherein Wm A Ward et al are cmplnts & Henry A Clark et al are dfndnts: public auction on Jul 24, of part of lot D, W B Todd's subdivision of lot 1, in square 352, on Md ave, between 10th & 11th sts, improved with a 4 story brick dwlg. –Wm F Mattingly, trustee -Green & Williams, aucts

WED JUL 10, 1867
Trial of John H Surratt, Jul 9, 1867. J R Eastman-sworn: professor at the Nat'l Observatory; on Apr 14, 1865 the moon rose at 2 minutes past 10; at 11 o'clock no stars except those of the first magnitude could be seen even with a glass. Jas R Ford-sworn: resides in Balt; was connected with *Ford's Theatre* in 1865; in April, 1865, was business manager; my brother was in Richmond; I knew John W Booth; had known him 10 years. On the evening of the assassination I went to Balt with Mrs Ford's sister, & returned at 10:25. I rode up on an F st car from the depot, & arrived at the theatre at 10:40. The assassination had then occurred. Wm Dickson-sworn: am chief engineer of the Govn't Fire dept here, & was so in 1865; on Apr 14, at 9 o'clock or after, an alarm of fire was struck, & I rode out H st, finding it was a bonfire, I returned by H st. Mr A Kiesecker-sworn: in 1865 I resides at 6th & H sts, & reside there yet, at 541 H st; in 1865 my house fronted on 6th st, & since then I have changed the front to H st. I went to bed at 11 o'clock, & did not hear of the assassination till next morning. Jas Lamb-sworn: am a scenic artist & was engaged in my profession at *Ford's Theatre* in 1865; I am English by birth, & have lived in this country 28 years; I took no part in the late struggle. Lt Chas M Skippen-sworn: witness is a lt of police; in 1865 was sgt of police; there was an eating saloon in the square, kept by Gilbert. Wm A Boss-sworn: resides at 489 14th st; knows John Lee; never heard his reputation for truth & veracity questioned until after he testified at this trial. Lee told witness that he did not know John H Surratt. S W Owen-sworn: resides at 212 Pa ave; resided in Wash City 30 years; knows John Lee. Joshua Lloyd-sworn: lived on Captiol Hill; was detective at the depot, under Col O'Bierne, during the war; knows John Lee. Chas Kimball-sworn: lives in Wash; has lived here all his life; has been a constable 15 years; knows John Lee. Col Jas R O'Beirne-sworn: resides in this city; is Reg of Wills; during the war was an ofcr in the army, till Jan, 1865; was provost marshal of the District, & had charge of the enrolment here from Jan, 1865, about 6 months; knows John Lee. Saml K Brown-sworn: resides at 2nd & Pa ave; was connected with Col O'Beirn in the provost marshal's ofc; knew Lee; his reputation for truth & veracity was bad.

Ad. Wm H Jones, pump-maker, will be found on 12th st, near E st.

Fire yesterday consumed a row of frame dwlgs, one being a small frame dwlg occupied by Mrs Louden, on 18th st, between K & L sts. The houses in the block adjoining her residence were owned by Geo Pleufger & J Schaffer. The loss is about $3,000, which is partly covered by insurance.

Yesterday a large force of laborers, under charge of Mr Peter McNamara, commenced work of cutting down the bank at the foot of 9th st, & the work will be steadily pushed forward until the street is cut through to the river. It is expected to have the grading & gravelling completed in 10 weeks.

Mr Constantine Bodisco, an attache of the Russian Legation, & son of the lamented Russian Minister, was married yesterday evening, at the Church of the Epiphany, to Miss Charlotte Burton, of Gtwn. There was a very large & fashionable audience to witness the interesting spectacle. The fashion, the youth, & the beauty of both Washington & Gtwn thronged with extraordinary elegance to the occasion.

Orphans Court-Judge Purcell-Jul 9, 1867. 1-Letters of adm were granted Wm Albert King on the personal estate of Thos Holloran. 2-The last will & testament of the late Saml Davis, formerly of Phil, was received & filed. 3-The sworn statement of Adelaide J Brown, admx of the estate of O B Brown, that all claims & legacies have been satisfied, was received & recorded. 4-Margaret Heiss bonded as guardian of the orphan children of the late John Nipfla/Nipfia. 5-The account of Margaret Smidley, [now Parker,] guardian to the orphan children of the late Antoine Smidley, was received & filed. 6-A decree was passed ordering Mina Uhlman, guardian of the orphans of the late C J Uhlman, to sell, at public auction, lot 18 of <u>Todd's subdivision,</u> of square 668, for the support & maintenance of said orphan children. 7-Letters of adm were granted to Chas T Iardella on the estate of Dorcas Galvin, deceased; bond $5,000. 8-The last will & testament of the late Dr S De Vaughan was presented by Mr Richd I Ryan, in the presence of Mr John De Vaughan & Saml Bayfield. It was admitted & proven. Dr Alex'r McDonald Davis is named by the deceased sole executor & administrator of the will & estate. The value of personal & real estate is variousy estimated at from $200,000 to $300,000. All the personal property is willed to deceased's sister, Susan Bayfield; to the same a life-estate in a quantity of real estate, which reverts, after her death, to her 3 chidren, Mary Rebecca Bayfield, Catharine Sophia Harrison, & Martha Ann Mitchell; also, to these 3 nieces, a quantity of real estate. To his mother certain life annuities, rents, etc, & to his brother, John De Vaughan, & his brother-in-law, Saml Bayfield, each a quantity of real estate. The amount bequeathed to each is not yet known. The will is not yet admitted to probate. 9-The argument in the Fearson will case was resumed. For petitioners, Messrs Davidge, Clarke, & Johnson; for respondents, Messrs Dunlop, Cox, & Jones. This is a case involving over $200,000, the deceased being one of the wealthy landholders of Gtwn & surrounding country. After argument the case was continued, & the court adjourned.

Washington Zouaves meeting on Monday; gentlemen elected ofcrs for the ensuing year: Capt, J Tyler Powell; 1st Lt, J H Miller; 2nd Lt, N E Bates; Quartermaster Sgt, H H Carew; Orderly Sgt, Lewis J Prue; Surgeon, Dr John E Smith.

Mr John Gillespie, a market man, was waylaid yesterday while on his way to Wash City, by a party of men, & robbed of a small amount of money & his horse. The robbery took place on the Columbian College road, about 3 miles from the city.

Died: on Jun 4, at the Pare of *Manes, near Paris, France, Henrietta, daughter of Gen Hugh & Henrietta Ewing, aged 9 months. [*Manes read Ma nes.]

Memphis, Tenn, Jul 9. Warren A Pettit, alias Wilson, formerly of Schuylerville, N Y, & late an attache of Everett's Theatre, was shot through the heart by his mistress, Lottie Sherwood, this morning, & instantly killed. The woman has been arrested.

The prettiest walk in Washington is the walk from 7th st canal bidge to Henning's One-Price Clothing store, at Md ave. Those who have never seen it will be gratified at the prospect on the way & at the end.

Trustee's sale of valuable property, by deed of trust from Marcellus Marceron & others, dated Apr 4, 1867, recorded in Liber E C E, No 1, folio 461, of the land records for Wash Co, D C: public auction on Jul 17 of part of lot 5 in square 1,000, with a small tenement, corner of south N & 11th sts east. –John J Johnson, trustee -Cooper & Latimer, aucts

Orphans Court of Wash Co, D C. Letters of administration on the personal estate of Thos Halloran, late of Wash Co, D C, deceased. –W Albert King, adm

THU JUL 11, 1867
Chas Fred'k Anderson, an eminent architect, died on his farm, in PG Co, Md, of dropsy, on Jul 9, aged about 70 years. The wings of the Capitol are modelled substantially after designs furnished by him under an act of the Senate inviting plans for the enlargement of the Capitol in 1850. The 39th Congress appropriated $7,500, which sum was paid to him some year & a half ago, since which time he had been residing where he died. His home has been in this city the most of the time since 1850.

Mrd: on Jul 10, in Wash City, by Rev Geo Mackenheimer, J M Alden, U S N, to Lottie E Bowie, 2nd daughter of the late G W Bowie.

Died: on Jul 10, Miss Rosetta Maria Sweeney, aged 18 years, niece & adopted daughter of Mr & Mrs Anthony Best. Her funeral will be from the residence, 500 11th st, at 9 A M, Sat.

The House of Rep appears to be determined to persist in the unparalleled outrage of excluding from their seats the members of Congress elect from Ky. Some of these gentlemen are excluded, & a sovereign State denied representation in the Nat'l Councils, solely upon the simple assertion of Hon John A Logan, of Ill, that he had heard that at some time or other they were charged with disloyalty to the Govn't.

+

State of Ill, Gallatin Co: Wm M Davis, of Equality, in the county & State aforesaid, being sworn, says that on May 25, 1861, I left Williamson Co, under Capt D Brooks, for the army of the Confederate States, & did join that army, & was badly wounded at the battle of Shiloh; & I futher state that I went to that army by & under the advice & influence of John A Logan & his brother-in-law, H B Cunningham, who told me that Logan would join us in 2 or 3 months, or in a short period of time. –W M Davis, subscribed & sworn on Oct 2, 1866, before me, R D Pearce, J P.

+

The following exposition is from the Chicago Times. The Dickey alluded to by Mrs Logan was the opponents of Gen Logan for Congress: When Logan spoke at Carbondale last week, his mother & sisters were present. In the course of his speech he denied that he had ever given any one money to enter the rebel service; whereupon, his sister, Mrs Blanchard, remarked,"That's a lie, John; you gave money to my husband to go into the rebel army" A little later Logan denied that he ever was in favor of the rebels, to which his mother replied,"That's a lie, John. Hurrah for Dickey!"

Mr R M Hall closed the sale of the farm of Z Williams, oppostie the Insane Asylum Grounds-148 acres-at $19,732. Purchased by Alex R Shephard & Dr Nichols, Superintendent of the Insane Asylum.

Trial of John H Surratt, Jul 10, 1867. Thos J Raybold-sworn: lives at 61 North Howard st, Balt; was at ***Ford's Theatre*** on Apr 14, 1865; had charge of the front of the theatre; was also in charge of boxes; saw Mr Jas R Ford give a ticket for the Pres' family that night to a messenger. Dr Wm O Baldwin-sworn: was a medical ofcr during the war, U S army; knew John Lee, who was a detective at the provost marshal's; Lee's reputation was bad among the people around the ofc. John H Wise-sworn: knew John Lee; had never heard his reputation for truth & veracity questioned. V B Manson-sworn: he is a clerk in the War Dept; knows John Lee; his reputation as a man of truth is bad; would not believe his oath in a case of life & death. Witness is a clerk in the same dept with Mr Calvert, who testified yesterday. Lemuel L Orme-sworn: lived in PG Co; am a farmer & trader; knows John T Tibbetts; his reputation is very bad for truth & veracity; known him from a boy. Wm J Watson-sworn: resides in PG Co, Md; knows John T Tibbetts; his father is witness' nearest neighbor; has always lived in that vicinity; witness is not his uncle; he heard that witness' grandmother & Tibbetts' great grandmother were cousins, but don't know anything about that. Tibbetts never told witness that Mrs Surratt told him she would give $1,000 to any one who would kill Lincoln. B J Naylor-sworn: lived in PG Co, near Mr Watson. Witness is a farmer; knows John T Tibbetts. Tibbetts' character is bad in the neighborhood. Geo E Orme-sworn: lives in Aquasco District,

PG Co, Md; has lived there nearly all his life; John T Tibbetts was raised near there; his character for truth is bad. Francis A Ward-sworn: resides in PG Co, Md; knows John T Tibbets; his reputation for truth & veracity bad; would not like to credit him under oath. He was slightly acquainted with Dr Mudd. Bernard Henze-sworn: resides in this city; keeps Metropolitan Hall; kept it in Apr, 1865; was in Phil on Apr 14, 1865; left his hall in charge of his brother, Mr Nachman, & Police Ofcr Voss. Martin Henze-sworn: resides in Phil; was at the Metropolitan Hall in Apr, 1865; witness kept neutral during the war. Geo Nachman-sworn: is a musician; a German, from the Rhine; was at the Metropolitan Hall in 1865, & in Apr was the leader of the orchestra there. Augustus Voss-sworn: is a police ofcr; in Apr, 1865, was in charge of the lower portion of the 2nd Ward; was employed by Mr Henze to keep order in the Hall. Thos Garey-sworn: lives in D st, between 1st & 2nd sts; has lived in Wash 18 years; keeps a livery stable; knows Wm E Cleaver; his reputation for truth is bad. Wm Horner-sworn: lived in Wash; lived here 47 years; knows Cleaver ever since he came to Wash; his reputation as to truth is very bad. Jas W Pumphrey-sworn: lives in this city; is an Englishman; knows Cleaver; general reputation is bad. John C Cook-sworn: lives in Wash; had lived here since '43; knows Wm E Cleaver; reputation is very bad. John Rainey-sworn: lives in this city; knows Cleaver; his character is very bad. Henry Middleton-sworn: lived in this city; has lived here 18 years; knows Cleaver & his characer is very bad. John Holoran-sworn: has been employed in this city in various occupations; now keeps a small gorcery on F st; has no license to sell liquor. Jas Foy-sworn: has lived in this city 36 or 37 years; knows Cleaver, whose reputation is pretty bad.

Information received of the death of Hon Allen A Hall, U S Minister to Bolivia, at La Paz, the capital of that Gov't, May 28, 1867. He emigrated to Tenn from N C, his native State; commenced his profession as a lawyer at Nashville; turned his attention to the press, & for 30 years was connected with the leading newspapers of Nashville; In 1841 he withdrew from editorial charges to accept the position of charge d'affaires to Venezuela, tendered to him by Pres Harrison, which he filled during the Administration of Pres Tyler; returned to Nashville in 1845, he took charge of the Nashville Whig; in 1840 accepted the position of Register of the Treasury-appointed by Pres Taylor; was then appointed Assist Sec of the Treasury, under Hon Wm P Meredith; later, in 1863, he was appointed Minister to Brazil by Pres Lincoln.

Died: on Jul 6, of cholera infantum, John Edward, infant son of Jas E & E Augusta Williams, aged 8 months & 27 days. [Fred'k, Md papers please copy.]

Died: on Jul 10, in Wash, of typhoid fever, Frederick G, youngest son of S H & Sarah F Kauffmann, aged 5 years, 4 months & 18 days. His body will be taken to Ohio for burial.

From the Plains. Indian depredations are reported on the Platte river. Lt Kidder, of the 2nd cavalry, with 10 men & a guide, who left **Fort Sedgwick** on Jun 29, with despatches to Gen Custer, has not been heard from, & fears are entertained for their safety.

Boston, Jul 10. 1-Danl DeShon, formerly a leading merchant of this city, died last night at his residence in Waltham. 2-Wm Darr, a resident of this city, was robbed last night, on a horse-car, of $1,500 dollars in seven-thirty bonds, & $500 in greenbacks.

For rent or sale: the ofc of the late Wm Redin, on Gay st, Gtwwn, suitable for a lawyer or physician. Also, a brick stable & carriage-house on Dunbarton st, in the rear. -Wm King, on the premises.

FRI JUL 12, 1867
Saml Elliott Coues, for many years president of the American Peace Society, died in Portsmouth, N H, on Jul 3, at the age of 70 years. He resided for several years in Wash, whence he removed above a year since to Portsmouth.

Trial of John H Surratt, Jul 11, 1867. Jackson Pumphrey-sworn: has lived in Wash 53 years; is a carpenter & builder; knows Wm E Cleaver; has known him for 20 years; he has a bad reputation for truth. Twelve years ago my brother told me that no confidence was to be placed in Cleaver's word. I had 3 sons & advised them to go in the Union army, & they did so. Talmadge J Lambert-sworn: resides on H st, between 21st & 22nd sts; is clerk in Paymaster Gen's ofce, since 1863; the house is east of Mrs Surratt's. Mrs Frederika R Lambert-sworn: lives in Wash; in 1865 lived on H st, between 4th & 5th; was there on the night of the assassination; heard a voice shouting, "The President is shot." I raised the window & asked 2 soldiers passing by, & they said that the President was shot & Wilkes Booth had shot him. Margaret Williams [colored]-sworn: I heard a voice say the Pres had been shot. I live with Mrs Lambert, & lived with her when the Pres was killed. John T Holloran-sworn: in 1865 I lived at Mrs Surratt's, in H st, I went to board there in Feb, 1865; besides myself & family, Lewis J Weichman, Miss Dean, & Miss Fitzpatrick boarded there. Miss Jenkins stopped there about a week ago. One day I met Atzerodt. John A W Clarvoe-sworn: is a detective in the Metropolitan Police, was at Mrs Surratt's on the night of Apr 14, 1865, about 2:30 in the morning, with partner, McDevitt; went to capture Booth, & to arrest John H Surratt. Mrs Eliza Holohan-sworn: wife of John T Holohan; boarded at Mrs Surratt's from Feb 17 to Apr 17, 1865; mingled socially in the family; met them at all times. Eliza Hawkins, late Eliza Simms, sometimes called Rachel, colored-sworn: witness knows Susan Mohoney, now Susan Jackson, who lived at Mr Surratt's in Apr, 1865. Susan said John Surratt looked like his sister, Anna. Witness was much attached to the family; lived with them 6 years. Last time witness saw Susan was last fall. Never had any difference with her. Witness was married to a man named Tom Seavers, who went away when the colored people went away; witness would rather stay & take care of her children than to go away with him & suffer.

Died: on Jul 11, after a long & painful illness, Malinder Mulloy, wife of Thos J Mulloy, aged 48 years. Her funeral will be from her late residence, on Mass ave, between 6th & 7th sts, on Sat at 4 o'clock. She leaves a husband & 6 children to mourn her loss.

Died: Jul 11, in Gtwn, Lucy S, infant dght of Wm S & Mary A Matthews, aged 10 mos. Her funeral is at 6 P M from the residence of her parents, 8th & High sts, Gtwn.

Trustee's sale, by decree passed by the Supreme Court of D C, in chancery, cause No 429, wherein Catherine Dyer is cmplnt, & Edw O Dyer, [deceased] et al are dfndnts: public auction on Jul 25, of lot 7 in square 315, on 12th st, with the bldgs thereon. -Wm L Dunlop, trustee -Cooper & Latimer, aucts

Accidents: 1-Mr J A Hunter, employed at the Treasury Dept, was severly hurt on Wed, by being struck in the hand with a sledge-hammer. The blow severed one of his thumbs & cut the palms of his hands, inflicting painful injuries. 2-A colored boy, Festus Lee, in the employ of Christopher Massi, was run over yesterday on 9th st, & died almost instantly.

Supreme Court of D C, in Equity 168-docket 7. Fendall Marbury, adm of Wm Lyles, deceased, vs John Douglass et al. On motion of the cmplnt by Messrs Fendall & Fendall, his solicitors, it is ordered that the dfndnts, Thos J Fisher & Wm H Smith, appear on or before the first rule day occurring 40 days after this day; otherwise the cause will be proceeded with as in case of default. –R J Meigs, clerk

Dept of Interior, U S Patent Ofc, Wash, Jul 8, 1867. Ptn of Joshua Gibbs, of Canton, Ohio, praying for extension of a patent granted him Oct 4, 1853, for an improvement in Machine for Grinding Plow Castings, for seven years from the expiration of said patent, which takes place on Oct 4, 1867. -T C Theaker, Com'r of Patents

Trustee's sale of property on 4½ st; by decree passed by the Supreme Court of D C, in chancery cause No 592, wherein Richd H Clarke et al are cmplnts, & Rice W Payne et al, are dfndnts: public auction, Jul 29, of part of lot 12 in square A, in Wash City; improved with a 2 story brick house. –Wm F Mattingly, trustee -Cooper & Latimer, aucts

SAT JUL 13, 1867
Trial of John H Surratt, Jul 12, 1867. Detective J A W Clarvoe recalled: on Apr 15 arrived at the house of Mrs Surratt, McDevitt & myself were to enter the house. Rapped at the door, & a young man in shirtsleeves, barefooted, & hatless, opened the door. He gave his name as Lewis J Weichman. I rapped at Mrs Surratt's door, asked her where John was, & she said she did not know. Jas A McDevitt-sworn: on Apr 14, 1865, he took steps to arrest the murderers of the President. Went to Mrs Surratt's with Clarvoe. Frank H Atkinson-sworn: resides in Elmira, N Y; is an alderman there; is bookkeeper for Stewart & Offert; witness was there in 1865. Jos Carroll-sworn: lives in Elmira, N Y; lived there in Apr, 1865; was cutter in Stewart & Offert's store about the time of the assassination. Lt Chas M Skippen-sworn: was at Mrs Surratt's house on the night in question with ofcrs McDevitt & Clarvoe. Dr E Wyvill: resides in PG Co, Md; knew Mrs Surratt; never drove two horses or any kind of horses home from Mrs Surratt's house in the country; was never at her house in his life.

Mrs Stephen W Routh, a daughter of Gen John A Quitman, of Miss, died in Louisville on Monday night, of consumption.

Charleston, S C, Jul 12. Information received that the steamboat **P E Belt** had been capsized by a squall in Waccamow river, on Jul 5, & 7 persons drowned, including Capt Garrison, L W Daggett, a lady, & 4 negroes.

Court of Appeals of Md, Apr Term, 1867: Annapolis, Jul 12 1867. 1-Geo Smith exc of John Hoye, & others, vs Jeremiah Townshend & others. Appeal from the Circuit court for Allegany Co. Cause remanded for further proceedings, without affirming or reversing. 2-Peter E Nutzy & others vs Mary Green. Appeal from the Orphans Court of Fred'k Co. Order affirmed, with costs to the appellee.

Louisville, Jul 12. Two manufactories were destroyed by fire at Evansville, Ind, on Wed. Michl McGinnis, a workman, was burned to death; three other men were badly burned.

Episcopal High School for Boys, 3 miles west of Alexandria, Va; the 28th session begins on Sep 25, 1867. Address the Rector, Rev Wm F Gardner, Theological Seminary Post Ofc, Fairfax Co, Va.

Orphans Court of Wash Co, D C, Jul 9, 1867. In the case of Mina Uhlman, admx of Chas J Uhlman, deceased, the administratrix & Court have appointed Aug 3 next, for the final settlement of the personal estate of the said deceased, of the assets in hand. -Jas R O'Beirne, Reg/o wills

A horrible crime occurred in Harrison Co, Ind, on Monday last. A man named Kemper, his wife, 2 daughters, & 3 sons murdered a man named John Babey, by hurling stones at him. The murder was brought on by a lawsuit, which resulted adversely to Kemper. Kemper, his wife, & one son, were arrested.

MON JUL 15, 1867
Died: on Jul 13, of consumption, Douglass Tolson, in his 42nd year. His funeral will be from his late residence, on N Capitol st, between G & H sts, on Jul 15, at 10 A M.

Died: on Sat, at the residence of her sister, Mrs Mary A Bannerman, Miss Eliz Foster, aged 61 years & 3 months. Her funeral will take palce from the late residence of the deceased, 13th & E sts, this morning at 11 o'clock.

Died: on Sat, in Staunton, Va, of typhoid fever, Alex H H Stuart, jr, son of Hon A H H Stuart, aged 21 years.

Died: on Jul 13, Andrew Johnson, infant child of Andrew & Rebecca M Jackson, aged 18 days.

Orphans Court-Judge Purcell-Saturday. 1-The accounts of Sarah Willet, admx of Maurice Willet, dec'eased; Catharine Banman/Bauman, excx of Paul Banman/Bauman, deceased; Mary E Sipes, guardian of Sarah C Sipes, orphan of Henry M Sipes, deceased; Jos H Fletcher, guardian of John J Kidwell, orphan of J J Kidwell, deceased; & of Wm O Nixon, guardian of W O Nixon Scott, orphan of Alfred V Scott, were received. 2-The last will & testament of Anastasia Burke was received & filed. 3-Adelaide J Brown, admx of the estate of Obadiah S Brown, deceased, made sworn return that all claims against said estate, as far as presented or known, had been satisfactorily settled. 4-The ptn of Edw S Thompson, husband of Harriet D Thompson, was received. It prays that the administrators of the estate of Wm Richards, deceased, father of Mrs Thompson, be made to make a settlement of the estate. The Court ordered that the administrators be cited to appear in court next Sat. 5-Letters of guardianship were issued to Mr M A Bassett, guardian of the orphan children of Sidney D Bassett. The sureties were H Clay Wood & Jas R O'Beirne. 6-The Court announced that it was not yet prepared to render a decision in the Fearson will case.

Mr J C Marks has withdrawn from the firm of Marks, Eckels & Co. The plumbing & gas-fitting business will be conducted by the remaining members of the firm.

Trial of John H Surratt, Jul 13, 1867. Jos Carroll was recalled; told Knapp he saw Surratt on the 13th or 14th. Jos H Bradley, sr,-sworn: Mr Failing delivered this book to witness two or three weeks ago, & it has not been out of witness' possession since till today, & had not been altered in any manner. Miss Olivia Jenkins-sworn: in Apr, 1865, resided at Mrs Surratt's, on H st; I know Mr Weichman, Miss Surratt, John Surratt, & Miss Fitzpatrick; remember the day the Pres was assassinated. David Barry-sworn: resides in PG Co; am now an ofcr of the Md Constitutional Convention; during the late war I lived in Va for 2 years; returned to PG Co in 1862; was never in the army myself; had 2 sons in the Confederate army; I live a mile & a half from Surrattsville; was there on Mar 25, 1865; saw John Surratt there then. Bennett F Gwynn-sworn: lived in PG Co, Md, about a mile from Surratsville; knew Mrs Surratt; saw her at Surrattsville on Apr 14, 1865. J Z Jenkins-sworn: witness is a brother of Mrs Surratt; witness is not in the habit of coming to town frequently. Bernard J Early-sworn: knew Michl O'Laughlin; witness saw him the morning of Good Friday, the day the Pres was murdered. Edw A Murphy-sworn: witness lives in Wash; is a plumber by trade; knew O'Laughlin. Wm Failing-sworn: is a little deaf; living in Canandaigua, N Y; keeps the Webster House; the book before witness is the register of that hotel. Frank O Chamberlain-sworn: lives in Canandaigua; keeps the Webster House; purchased the hotel from Failing. Jos H Bradley, jr-sworn: went to Canandaigua, arrived there on Mar 16, 1867; went to the Webster House; found the name of John Harrison registered there.

Died: on Jul 14, Jas Riordan, aged 80 years, a native of Cork Co, Ireland, & for nearly 50 years a resident of Wash City. His funeral will be on Jul 16 at 9 o'clock A M, from his late residence, on 15th st, to St Matthew's Church.

Orphans Court of Wash Co, D C. Letters testamentary on the personal estate of Chas Eames, late of Wash, D C, deceased. –Fanny Eames, excx

Orphans Court of Wash Co, D C. Letters of administration on the personal estate of John Finster, late of Wash, D C, deceased. –Geo Juenemann, adm

Orphans Court of Wash Co, D C, Jul 13, 1867. In the case of Emily Fuller & John E Fuller, adms of Edw H Fuller, deceased, the administrators & Court have appointed Aug 6 next, for the final settlement of the personal estate of the said deceased, of the assets in hand. -Jas R O'Beirne, Reg/o wills

Chas F Meister, a watchmaker, who had a store under Barnum's Hotel, in St Louis, went on board the steamer **Mississippi** on Tuesday, took off his coat & vest, plunged into the river & was drowned. He was in prosperous circumstances, but his mind had been deranged for time past by dwelling upon the idea of constructing some marvelous sort of clock which should immortalize his name.

TUE JUL 16, 1867
Trial of John H Surratt, Jul 15, 1867. David C Robinson-sworn: lives in Elmira, N Y; was at the Brainard Hotel in 1865; made diligent search for the register of that hotel of 1865, but is unable to find it. August Bachus-sworn: in Apr, 1865, witness kept the Winter Garden concert saloon; on Good Friday there was no music or dancing before 8 o'clock P M. Mrs Annie Bachus-sworn: witness lived at 318 D st in Apr, 1865, at Winter Garden. Jos N DuBarry-sworn: resides in Harrisburg, Pa; is general superintendent of the Northern central railorad; has been some 5 years; in Apr, 1865, was at Harrisburg, Pa.

Col Henry R Rathbone was married at Albany on Thursday last, Jul 11, to Miss Clara Harris, the accomplished daughter of Hon Ira Harris, & sailed for Europe in the ship **Ville de Paris** on Saturday.

Mr Andrew Zimmerman was found by Ofc Mullins, of the 6th Precinct, on Monday, lying on a sidewalk on his beat, suffering from the effect of a pistol shot, the wound being caused by the accidental discharge of his own pistol. He was taken to the station-house, where Dr Keasbey dressed the wound & he was then removed to his residence.

The house of Mr Phillip Wallach, 380 C st, was entered yuesterday, & after ransacking the premises, the burglars departed-they were warded off by an unwelcome alarm.

Mrd: on Jul 15, by Rev Fr Gubitosi, S J, Richd M Dawes, of Wash City, to Miss Josephine Amici, youngest daughter of Henry Johnson, of Langley, Va. No cards.

The last fight at *Fort Wallace*-the fort was attacked by 400 savages-7 men killed. Engagement with the Indians on Jun 24. Chas Clark, the bugler, fell, pierced by 5 arrows. Sgt Fred'k Williams with his little force held out nobly until his horse was killed, & one by one the soldiers fell. For two hours Capt Barnitz waited with his thinned squadron for another advance of the Indians, but they prudently held back. Nathan Frail was shot with 4 bullets & 3 arrows, his scalp was torn off; Frank Rahme was riddled with balls & arrows; Jas Douglas was shot through the body with an arrow, & his left arm hacked to pieces. He was a Scotchman, a brave fellow. Welsh was killed, but a search failed to discover his remains. Sgt Williams lay dead beside his horse. Horse & rider were stripped bare of trappings & clothes. Cpl Jas K Ludlow was shot through the body with an arrow, & his recovery is not even possible.

The Senate yesterday confirmed & rejected the following nominations:
Confirmed:
Minister: Geo Bancroft, at Berlin, Prussia.
Sec of Legation: John Hay, of Ill, at Vienna; Alex'r Bliss, of N Y, at Berlin.
Assist Surgeons: Lewis S Pitcher, of Mich; J Albert Howke, of Pa; Ed C Thatcher, of Pa.
Capt: Cmder F K Murray.
Cmders: Lt Cmders Wm Gibson & E W Henry.
1st Assist Engineers: 2nd Assist Engineers D Hardee, R B Potts, J D Toppin, & 3rd Assist B Kavanaugh.
2nd Assist Engineers: 3rd Assist Engineers G W Beard, C Uber, F A Ashton, E Stiles, & Henry C Christopher.
Postmasters: Mrs Hattie C Fay, Rochester, Minn; John Fronz, Port Royal, S C; Danl Kellogg, jr, Brattleboro, Vt; Saml Saviers, Tecumseh, Mich; Edwin R Brink, Wilmington, N C; Selah Bosworth, Marietta, Ohio; Helen Surgens, Warren, R I.
Surveyor of Customs: Thos Jernegon, Mich City, Ind.
Assessor Internal Rev: H O Herrick, 3rd Dist, S C.
Assist Treasurer: John S Walker, New Orleans, La.
Consul: Eugene Schuyler, of N Y, at Moscow.
Coll of Customs: Wm Silvey, Newark, N J; John B Dillingham, Michimackinac, Mich.
U S Army: Inspectors General, with rank of Lt Col: Maj Wilson H Davis, Maj Jas Totten, Maj Roger Jones.
Navy Dept: Chief of Ordnance Bureau, Henry A Wise.
Capts: Cmder Thos H Patterson, Cmder Edw L Nichols.
Cmders: Lt Cmders Philip C Johnson, John Waltars, S L Reese, Bancroft Guerwardi, Henry Wilson, A E R Benham, Josson S Skeritt.
1st Lt Marine Corps: 2nd Lt Wm S Muse.
Surgeons: Passed Assist Surgeons Louis Zenzon, John H Clark.
Rejected: Postmasters: Saml Neil, Van Wert, Ohio; Elijah T Smith, Owassie, Mich; Chas E Collins, Mt Vernon, Iowa.
U S Consul: Orrin J Rose, of Ill, at Toronto.

Died: on Jul 14, Florant M Meline, chief of the Division of Accounts in the ofc of the Treasurer of the U S. His funeral services will be held at St Matthew's Church, 15th & H sts, on Jul 16, at 10 o'clock A M. [Cincinnati & Phil papers please copy.]

Died: on Jul 15, in Wash City, in his 65th year, Uriah Forrest, of Rockville, Montg Co, Md. His funeral is this afternoon at 4 o'clock, from the residence of his brother, 208 I st.

Died: on Jul 15, William Furguson, infant son of Wm P & Eliz A Westwood, aged 5 months & 10 days. His funeral will be from Capt Price's, Ga ave, between 3rd & 4th sts, on Tuesday, at 4 o'clock.

N Y, Jul 15. Bishop Scott, of Oregon, is dead.

Richmond, Jul 17. Adolph Wolff, a well known merchant, who closed business recently & went South, was brought back today from Alabama, charged with obtaining goods on fruadulent pretences from parties here. He had also dealt largely in Balt, N Y, & Cincinnati. [Jul 17 newspaper: Adolph Wolff: the charge of obtaining goods on false pretences, has been discharged here, but has been sent to Balt, on a requisition from the Govn'r of Md.]

WED JUL 17, 1867
Trial of John H Surratt, Jul 16, 1867. Mr Frank O Chamberlain recalled: took possession of the Webster House in Apr, 1865; register was in daily use there until Dec 41, 1865. David H Bates, recalled: register of Webster House exhibited; witness recognizes the name, John Harrison, here as in Surratt's handwriting. J B Tinsley-sworn: in Apr, 1865, I was employed at the Spotswood Hotel, in Richmond; he presents the register of the hotel; I believe the register of Harry Sherman, on Mar 29, 1865, to have been written by John H Surratt. Henry Hall Brogden-sworn: In Mar & Apr, 1865, I was employed in Richmond; on Mar 29, 1865 I saw the prisoner there; I knew who he was, & he passed under the name of Harry Boerman. Jas J Gifford recalled: witnes was in Carroll prison with Weichman. John Matthews sworn: was in this city in Apr, 1865, playing at ***Ford's Theatre***; saw Booth on Apr 14; he was on horseback. Stephen F Cameron sworn: was in the Confederate service during the war; went to Europe in company with Dr McMillen, in the steamer **Nova Scotia** from Quebec; Dr McM stated that Surratt told him he was in Elmira on Apr 14, 1865, & only learned there for the first time that the President had been assassinated. Witness know S J A J Cresswell, late Senator. Knew Jas M McCulloch, then in Elkton, Md; was in business in Cecil Co, Md, for a time; afterwards became an Episcopal minister; was admitted to deacon's orders by Bishop Whittingham; studied in the Theological seminary in N Y C; was educated in Md & N Y; went South in 1861; became a Roman Catholic by conviction. Witness' early religious education was conducted by a Catholic aunt. Witness attended an Episcopal church at 11 years. Witness' father was Protestant.

Mr Wm Talbert was arrested yesterday by Ofcr Jones, of the 7th Precinct, on the charge of selling goods by sample in Wash City. He was fined $20, but promised to pay the amount, provided he was dismissed on paying the required license.

Orphans Court-Judge Purcell, Jul 16, 1867. 1-Benj H Chewes was appointed guardian to his son Benj H Chewes, jr; bond $500. 2-John T Kelley was appointed guardian to the orphans of Lewis Dukes, late of Gtwn, D C, deceased; bond $6,000. 3-The first & final account of the adm of Mary M Dufief, deceased; the first & final account of the adm of Alfred M Partello, deceased; the first account of the adm of Thos Milstead, deceased, by Chas H Lloyd, adm; & the 2nd general & 2nd individual account of the adm of Saml Horner, deceased, were approved & passed. 4-The Fearson will case was called up; by the will now in litigation all the property was bequeathed to her niece Mrs Barrett, of Gtwn; the estate involves over $160,000. Mr Robt L McPherson, of Gtwn; Saml T McPherson, of Balt; Geo W Taylor, Henrietta Taylor, & John Shaw, of PG Co, Md, all relatives of the deceased, had petitioned the court that the will be set aside. The case has been on trial for some months past. Many of the interested parties were in court, together with the attys on either side. Judge Purcell, in reviewing the case, said: The case has been well argued, & the will was prepared by an able & eminent jurist, Judge Dunlap. The witnesses to the will were highly respectable witnesses-that is one thing & the course of the will is another. The Judge then cited several legal references for his authority in maintaining that the proper course had not been taken. The will had been probated without the legal notices having been served to one of more of the heirs of petitioners, who resided within the jurisdiction of the court, [at Gtwn.,] & the law directly provides that such notices shall be served upon all heirs within such jurisdiction, unless such heirs sleep upon their rights. In less that 30 days after the will was probated, the petitioners filed their petition, in which they aver that they had received no legal notice, & the answer of the respondent or legatee admitted that no such notice had been served. The probate of the will was therefore set aside. Judge Purcell further remarked that the revocation of the probate carried with it the appointment of the executor. This decision will necessitate the appointment of a receiver. Mr Jones, one of the counsel for Mrs Barrett, appealed from the decision made above, & the case will go to the Supreme Court.

Ad. Mr John Mills, 504 Pa ave, has reduced the price of boots to $12.00.

Nominations confirmed or rejected by the Senate yesterday:
Confirmed: Saml Blachford, Judge U S Dist Court for the Southern Dist of N Y, vice Saml R Betts, resigned. Wm B Sheriff, postmaster, Paris, Ill, vice Wm W Rives, rejected. E M McAllister, postmaster at Champaign, Ill, vice Joshua Dickenson, rejected. Louis D Palmer, postmaster at Litchfield, Ill, vice J S Young, rejected.
Rejected: Jas R Booth, to be U S Dist Atty, Dist of Delaware. Wm H Gilman, postmaster, Belvidere, Ill. Hon Henry J Raymond for the Austrian mission was virtually rejected by the Senate on Monday.

Mr Chas C Harris was introduced to the Pres by the Sec of State, & delivered his credentials as Envoy Extraordinary & Minister Plenipotentiary of his Majesty the King of the Hawaiian Islands.

The cornerstone of Christ Church, in Gtwn, was laid yesterday without ceremony. The aricles, consistingof the plate & coins taken from the old cornerstone; proceedings of the Episcopal Convention held in Md in 1866; a list of names of the pastor & vestryman choir, organist, architects, & builder; specimens of U S currency, nickel & gold coins, revenue & postage stamps; copies of the Natl' Intelligencer, Evening Union, Chronicle, & Evening Express, were placed in a box made of zinc, & deposited in the large stone forming the corner.

Late robberies. Monday the stable of Mr Jacob Viehmeyer, 14th & C sts, was robbed of over $30 worth of harness. Mr Fushgart, keeper of a jewelry store on Pa ave, yesterday reported that his store had been robbed of 17 gold & silver wtaches, valued at about $1,200. Twelve of these watches had been left for repairs by various parties.

Yesterday Jos Richter was accidentally shot in a house on 12th st, near C st, by a woman named Mollie Johnson. The man was taken to the Central Guard house, & his wounds were dressed.

Fire yesterday in a small wooden bldg on M st, between 6th & 7th sts, owned by Mr Geo Mattingly, loss about $300.

Mrd: on Jul 16th, at St John's Church, by Rev Dr Lewis, Redford W Walker to Phoebe A, youngest daughter of Wm A Elliott, all of Wash, D C.

Died: on Jun 13, at **Ford Dodge,** Kansas, from wounds received from the hands of the Indians, while in the discharge of his duty in the 7th U S cavalry, Jos V Wise, in his 23rd year, of Gtwn, D C.

Died: on Jul 12, at **Southampton**, the residence of her son, Dr Jas Waring, in St Mary's Co, after a long & painful illness, Mrs Kitty Waring, widow of the late Edw G Waring,of **Waring's Grove**, PG Co, Md, in her 80th year. [Upper Marlboro, Md; Richmond & Alexandria Va; Galveston, Houston, & Liberty Texas papers please copy.]

Two girls murder their stepmother in Tenn: Mrs Hicks & her two stepdaughters, Mary & Kezie, had for some time lived unpleasantly together. They forcibly conveyed their unfortunate victim, Mrs Hicks, to the smoke-house near by, & commenced a series of tortures; they first attempted to strangle their victim to death, but failed; they poured melted lead into the ear of their helpless victim, & then struck her on the head with an axe. They left her and then went to church. Mrs Hicks revived enough to tell the neighbors who found her, what had happened. She has since died of her injuries. The murderers are still at large.

We regret to announce the death of the child of Maj A C Richards, Superintendent of the Metropolitan Police.

THU JUL 18, 1867
Trial of John H Surratt, Jul 17, 1867. Jas L Maddox recalled for the defence: witness was in Carroll prison with Weichman; went with Weichman to Winder's Bldg, where an examination was had. Question: Did you hear an ofcr tell Weichman that if he did not testify to more than he had already told he would hang him? Mr Carrington: I object; your honor has already ruled it out. J A W Clarvoe recalled: was in Canada in 1865. John T Ford recalled: witness was in Carroll prison with Weichman; was there 39½ days; witness told him he was mistaken as to the time "Pescara" was performed.

Ad. 1-All persons are warned against negotiating a note drawn by S M Burche, in favor of America G Pedrick, for $350. 2-Thos Russell & Co, successors to E C Dyer & Co, have just received an extensive stock of summer wines.

Trustee's sale, by decree of the Circuit Court for PG Co, sitting in Equity, public sale, on Aug 1 next, all the real estate, about 40 acres, of which the late Benj Piles died seized & possessed; this land adjoins the farm of John E Berry, & others, in Spalding's Dist, PG Co, & is the same property upon which Saml Godfrey now resides; improved by a commodious dwlg, stable, & other out-bldgs.
–C C Magruder, trustee

Trustee's sale of valuable property in Gtwn, D C; by deed of trust from Hezekiah Miller, dated Dec 27, 1866, one of the land records of Wash Co, D C; public sale on Jul 27, of the west 42 feet 2½ inches of lot 7, in Beall's addition to said Gtwn.
–Geo Magruder, trustee -J B Wheeler & Co, aucts

Mrd: on Jun 26, at St Paul's English Lutheran Church, by Rev J G Butler, Mr A Geib, of N Y, to Miss Maria E Speir, of Wash, D C.

Mrd: on Jul 15, at the residence of the bride's father, by Rev Dr Holmead, Milton B Miller, of Pittsburgh, Pa, to Hattie, daughter of Jas S Magee, of Wash City.

Died: on Jul 17, Mrs Hannah C Triplett, in her 63rd year. Her funeral wil be from the residence of her husband, Thos J Triplett, 252 7th st, between M & N sts, at 3 o'clock P M, on Jul 18.

Died: on Jul 17, after a brief illness of one week, of congestion of the lungs, Geo W Keating, aged 57 years. His funeral will be on Jul 19 at 4 o'clock P M, from his late residence, near **Glenwood Cemetery**. May he rest in peace. [Alexandria, Va, papers please copy.]

Died: on Jul 13, at **Mount Pleasant,** PG Co, Md, the residence of Mrs Sarah C Waring, Mrs Mattie C Clagett, wife of Henry W Clagett, & daughter of Col John D Bowling, in the 24th year of her age.

Died: Mrs Sarah, wife of Thos Simms, of the city of Gloucester, England. She was born in Worcester, England, Jul, 1777; died in Tallahassee, Jul 6, 1867. Admired & loved by all who ever became acquainted with her, & she has had from her trial of life, & Christian virtue, associations with the heavenly world for more than 40 years. –Jas Crutchett

Died: on Jul 17, in Wash City, suddenly, at his residence, Alford A Sloan, aged 48 years, formerly of Burlington, N J.

Died: on Jul 17, in Gtwn, John C, son of Jos & Catharine Weaver, aged 2 months & 17 days. His funeral will take place Thursday afternoon, at 4 o'clock, from his parents' residence, 350 High st, Gtwn.

Trustee's sale of valuable real estate in Gtwn, D C, by deed of trust, from John Clements & wife, dated Aug 11, 1842, recorded among the land records of D C, in Liber W B No 92, folio 506; public auction on Aug 1, of lot 67 in Threlkeld's addition to Gtwn & District aforesaid, fronting on the east side of Fayette st, improved with a brick dwlg & other bldgs. –Ed M Linthicum, trustee
-Thos Dowling, auct

FRI JUL 19, 1867
Trial of John H Surratt, Jul 18, 1867. Rev J A Walter-sworn: knew Mrs Surratt, & was her spiritual adviser; was present at Mrs Surratt's execution. John J Reeves-sworn: resides in Montreal, Canada, a tailor by occupation. I know the prisoner; made a <u>Garabaldi coat</u> for him in 1865. The Garabaldi is a plaited garment, plaited back & front. It has plain wristbands; buttons close up to the throat. I saw Surratt at my store between 11th & 18th of Apr. He left his measure on Apr 8th & 9th. Sarsfield B Nagle-sworn: resides at Montreal, & am an advocate; resided there since 1859. I know St Marie resided in Montreal 1859, 1860, 1861. I was educated at St Mary's Jesuit College, & knew Dr McMillan there. Knew McMillan when he was going to the Univ, & also when he resided at Lennoxville. Louis W Sicotte-sworn: [Maj O'Beirne sworn as interpreter.] Mr Carrington objected to this man testifying through an interpreter. Court decided the witness should first try to speak in English. Sicotte-I reside in Montreal, Canada; am an advocate by profession; is now employedin the Crown Law Dept; have resided in Montreal since 1858. I was in Lapiere last winter-it is St Marie's native place. Dr Ludjer La Belle-sworn: I live in Montreal; I am an advocate; am city counseller for 4 years; I knew St Marine since 8 years; I was not his friend or intimate associate, but had many opportunities to see him. Jos DeTilley-sworn: [examined through Maj O'Beirne,] resides in West Shefferd, Canada; is a farmer; has resided there 7 years; knew Dr McMillen.

Court in equity-Chief Justice Cartter. 1-Louisa Hardy, vs Henry J Hardy. Decree of divorce, the plntf to have charge of the children. 2-Keyworth et al vs Maury. Order appointing Mahlon Ashford guardian ad litem. 3-Geo F Emmons vs John H Clarke. Order directing the dfndnt to pay the plntf $1,513.30, with interest.

Mr Fred'k Foot was seriously injured yesterday when thrown from his cart; they were pronounced not to be dangerous, & he was taken to his home on the Island.

Rambles about town. One of the smaller proprietors of the territory upon which Wash City is located was a Dutch man, by the name of Funks; his land was that section of the city bordering on the Potomac, back to the neighborhood of G st north, & embraced, perhaps, between 19th & 24th st. Funk, having some of the townsite ideas in his head, laid out a city, & named it after his native place, Hamburg. He built a wharf, some of the remnants may be seen at the foot of 22nd st west. When the canal was built the old wharf was mostly cleaned out. He sold out early, & went into Md, near Hagerstown, where he planted another hamlet, which also took his own unsavory name. The spot he reserved for a church is the site upon which the German Lutheran Church, [Rev Mr Finekel,] pastor, now stands, 20th & G sts. Funk's house, built of brick brought from Holland, was in ruins in 1800. The old Glasshouse was near Funkstown wharf. Besides that, some half a dozen brickhouses were erected there for the use of the operators of the glass establishment. The owners were Andrew & Geo Way, who came here in 1800 with the Gov't, as printers. Dr Nathl Jewett succeeded them in the business, who after some years relinquished the establishemnt to Mr Cornelius McLane. About 1835 Cmdor Rogers became the owner, when Mr Lewis Johnson & Col Truman Cross leased the premises & embarked in the business. Their glass was of the most admirable quality. In 1838 they were compelled to shut down due to the flood of cheap glass which came into the country from the pauper labor of Europe. Col Cross was the first victim of the Mexican war. Entering the army in 1814, an ensign of the 42nd infty, he had risen to assist quartermaster general, with the rank of colonel, in 1838, & was assigned to duty with Gen Taylor in 1846. A few days after our army arrived at Matamoras, Col Cross was missed from camp. A party was sent out in search, & his body was found where a Mexican coming into camp had informed them the body of an American had been discovered. In riding out for his usual exercise he had been captured by a band of notorious rancheros, & after being robbed, was shot. His remains were buried in front of the eastern curtains of **Fort Brown**; the funeral took place on Apr 24. Col Cross was a native of PG Co, Md, & a handsome obelisk marks the spot to which his remains have been transferred in the **Congressional Burial Grounds**. When the estate of Cmdor Rogers was settled, the glass-works, standing idle some years, were purchased by Mr Chas L Coltman, & the property now belongs to his heirs. Some year or two before the war, the works were converted into a lampblack factory, but is soon fell through. Upon one end of the structure the sign, Wilson's Lampblack & Patent Roofing factory, shows what was the last attempt.

Distribution of medals & premiums to the pupils of the 3rd Dist public schools, yesterday, at the East Wash Methodist Church, on 4th st. Rev G V Leach offered prayer; medals were awarded to C P G Scott; Mary E McNantz; John Mellis, Jesse Brown, Lizzie Stomberger; Benj Poole, Ida Wilkerson, Geo Britt, Julia Tucker, Walter Walsh, Ella Conner, Richd C McAuly, Laura Collinsworth, Minnie Ruff, Loa Walker, Clara Oswill, Isaac Jacobs, Kate Andrews, Geo W Dulin, Rosa Steile, Willie Mahew, Jos Williams, Thos Kilafoyle, Inez Goodrich.

Hon Linton Stephens, of Ga, the half brother of Hon A H Stephens, was recently married to Miss Mary W, daughter of E H Slater, M D, of Boston. The marriage ceremonies were performed at the Episcopal Residence in Richmond, Va, by Rev Fr Bapst, S J. Mr Stephens is a conspicuous lawyer in his native State, & between the two brothers, who are the only surviving members of the family, there has existed throughout their lives a most uncommon tenderness of attachment. They reside together on a splendid estate, of which the parental homestead forms a part, & upon which all the colored people who were formerly attached to the estate as slaves still remain as freedmen.

C C Woodman committed suicide at the Hoffman House, in N Y, on Tuesday, by shooting himself with a pistol.

Died: on Jul 18, Saml Redfern, in his 73rd year, a native of Derbyshire, England, the past 47 years a resident of Wash City. His funeral will take place from his late residence, 252 H st, between 18th & 19th sts, at 3 o'clock, Sunday.
[Balt Sun please copy.]

Obit-died: in the 15th year of his age, after a long & painful illness, Marion Albert, 5th son of Dr Jos & Eliz Walsh. His funeral is this morning, the 19th, at 10 o'clock, from his parents' residence, 493 E st south. Friends of the family are invited without further notice. Obsequies at St Peter's Church, Capitol Hill, at 10½ o'clock. Ally was, indeed, a gifted lad; idolized by his parents; but alas, in the midst of his studies at <u>Gonzaga College,</u> of which he was a model pupil. Death sped his fatal arrow.
–A Friend [Death date not given.]

SAT JUL 20, 1867
Trial of John H Surratt, Jul 19, 1867. Mr Bradley, sr, said that of the witnesses waited for yesterday, the principal one was Fr Boucher, who had left for this place on Tuesday, & had not yet arrived. Mr Richd Sutton-sworn: had a very large experience in examining & comparing handwriting. [Papers exhibited.] Witness did not think the Toney letter, addressed to Atzerodt, was in the same handwriting as the letter written to Weichman by Atzerodt. Did not think Booth's telegrams & the Selby letter were in the same handwriting. Witness did not think the Sebly letter was written in a natural hand.

Mr J A Whipple, of Boston, has the largest establishment, & is one of the most successful photographers in the U S. –Springfield Republican

The Senate yesterday confirmed the following nominations:
Benj Thompson, of Minn, agent for the Sissiton & Wapiton bands of Santee Sioux Indians in Dakota Territoty.
Henry P Deane to be Surveyor of the Customs for the Dist of Portland & Falmouth, Maine.
To be Registers of Land Ofcs: John Cleghorn, of Iowa, at Sioux City, Iowa; Edw L Davis, of Nevada, at Austin, Nevada.
Receiver of Public Moneys: Jefferson J Works, of Nevada, at Austin, Nevada.
Danl D Hitchcock, of the Cherokee Nation, to be Pension Agent at **Fort Gibson**, Cherokee Nation.
Frank Cowan, of Pa, to be Sec of the Pres to sign patents for lands sold, or granted, under the authority of the U S.
M V Buckey, to be Justice of the peace for Wash Co, D C.
The following nominations were rejected-as Deputy Postmaster:
Howard Bledscoe, at Boize City, Idaho.
Andrew J Baker, at Seymour, Jackson Co, Ind
Jas King, at Greensburg, Ind
Tilgham H Gentry, at Bloomington, Ind
Willis B Goodwin, at Jeffersonville, Ind.

Chancery sale of valuable real estate at auction; no 976-Equity; Johanna E Rupert & John Rupert, cmplnts, vs Bernard Grier & Louisa Thoma, dfndnts. Decree of this Court passed on Jul 16, 1867, sale on Aug 8 next, of lots 1 thru 5 & lot 17, in subdivision of lots numbered 1 thru 5 & lot 24, in square 620, & parts of lots 22 & 23 in same square. Also, lot 11 in square 673, with improvements, which are on part of lot 22, with a large 3 story, basement, & attic brick house, containing 13 rooms; the lot fronts 70 feet on M st, & 136 feet deep; on lot 23 is a large 2 story frame house, with basement; lot fronts 137 feet & 3 inches on North Capitol st, with a depth of 70 feet; lot 24 has 3 two story frame houses, with basements, fronting on Pierce st; lot 11, in square 673, has 2 frame bldgs. -Bernard Grier, exc & trustee -Green & Williams, aucts

Supreme Court of D C, Jul 18, 1867; No 786 in Equity-docket 8. Johnston vs Johnson et al. Wm J Miller, trustee, reported he had sold part of lot 4 in square 786, for .48 per square foot, to Rose Anna St Clair, who has complied with the terms of sale, & the aggregate amount of sale being $1,408.20. –R J Meigs, clerk

MON JUL 22, 1867
Dept of the Interior, U S Patent Ofc, Wash, Jul 13, 1867. Ptn of Norman Millington, of Shaftsbury, Vt, for himself & S M George excx, with Abraham R Gardner & Leland J Mattison, excs of the estate of Dennis J George, deceased, praying for the extension of a patent granted to said Millington & George on Oct 18, 185_, for an improvement in Machines for Figuring Carpenters' Squares for seven years from the expiration of said patent, which takes place on Oct 18, 1867.
-T C Theaker, Com'r of Patents

Wm H Huestis was on Sat, confirmed to be the warden of the Wash City jail, thus deposing Mr T B Brown, the present warden.

Trial of John H Surratt, Jul 20, 1867. Dr Augustus Bissell-sworn: resides at 218 West 22nd st, N Y. Was in Elmira Apr 14, 1865; was at Brainard House there, & saw the prisoner at the bar there on that day. I was on crutches. Surratt asked me if I had been to war, & I gave him no satisfaction. Isaac H Surratt-sworn: testified that his brother, the prisoner at the bar, is 23 years of age; he was born Apr 13, 1844. John J Reeves was recalled: witness now had his books in court, & can tell the date Surratt was at his shop in Montreal, & measured for a Garibaldi coat; it was on Apr 7, 1865. John C Bartlett-sworn: lived in Wash; was driving stage for John Thompson to T B in Jan, Feb, Mar, & Apr, 1865; made round trips every day; during the month of Apr there were no pickets beyond Good Hope. On Apr 14 went to T B but there were no pickets beyond the bridge.

The Senate on Wed confirmed & rejected the following nominations:
Confirmed:
John Matherland, Tenn, Minister to Bolivia
U S Consuls:
Benj Tripp, jr, Mass, Santiago, Cape de Verde Islands
Stephen Higginson, jr, Mass, Batavia
J McLeod Murphy, Tabasco
Rufus Meade, Vt, San Juan del Sur
Elisha Lee, Conn, Guayaquil
A Lacombe, Puerto Cabello
M J Gonzales, Martinique
Com'r under treaty with Venezuela: David M Talmadge
Collector of Internal Rev: Oscar J Averill, 27th Dist of N Y
Assessor of Internal Rev: Henry L Bryant, 9th Dist of Ill
Associate Justice of Supreme Court: Perry E Brocchus, New Mexico
Collector of Customs: Denard Rumley, Wilmington, N C
Receivers of Public Moneys: Richd Hurley, Lewiston, Idaho Territory; Jas Torrans, Washington, Ark
Registers of Land Ofcs:
Stephen S Fenn, Lewiston, Idaho Territory
Nicholas H Owing, Fair Play, Colorado Territory
David C Tuttle, Washington, Ark
U S Marshal: Austin J Mattingly, at consular court of Bankok, Siam
Jail Warden: Wm H Huestis, Wash, D C
Postmasters:
Michl Dunn, **Fort Leavenworth**, Kansas
Edmund Billinger, Gonzales, Texas
Saml B Morgan, West Meridan, Conn
Alpheus M Beebe, Owasso, Mich
Medical Purveyor, U S A: Surgeon J H Baxter, with rank of lt colonel

1st Lts-Revenue Cutter service: J Fred'k Schultz, Robt H Woods, Chas B Barlowe, Fred'k W Sparrell, Chas H Dixon, Geo M Hunter
2nd Lts-Revenue Cutter service: Wm A Willis, Jas Moore, Wm W Cornell, Wm E Chester, Geo E Hansell, D Francis Tozcer
3rd Lts-Revenue Cutter service: Jas McVeah, Geo Gerard, Saml A Brooks, Thos E Ashmead, Winslow B Barnes, Chas H Read, Wm Carlton, jr, Lemuel C Cowan, Jas F Otis, Geo R Babeman, Thos S Smythe, Geo Williams, Horatio D Smith, J E M Graham, Robt Barslow, John Walker, F A Murray
Rejected:
U S Ministers: John A McClernand, of Ill, to Mexico
E C Loomis, of Mich, to Republic of Hayti
Secretaries of Legation: Mareus Otterburg, of Mexico
Ward H Lamon, Consul General to Havana
Consol: T Scott Stewart, of Pa, at Osaca, Japan
Assessor Internal Rev: Davis S Hammond, 10th Dist of Pa
Jos P Santmyer, 1st Dist of Ohio
Register of Land Ofc: Leonard B Ayers, Maysville, Calif
Receivers of Public Moneys:
Hugh T Waddell, Natchitoches, La
Alex'r L Field, New Orleans, La
Thos Holliday, Irentor, Mo
H A B Johnson, Booneville, Mo
U S Atty: John B Pennington, Delaware
Inspectors Gen, with rank of lt colonel:
Maj Nelson H Davis; Maj Jas Totten; Maj Roger Jones

Died: on Jul 17, at the rectory of St Luke's Church, Bladensburg, Md, in her 43rd year, Mrs Maria V McCabe, beloved wife of Rev John Collins McCabe, D D, & daughter of the late Capt Wm Noyes, of Gtwn, D C. Her mortal remains sleep in **Greenmount Cemetery**, Balt, Md.

Died: on Jul 21, Adam Gaddis, sr, aged 76 years. His funeral will be from his late residence, Ga ave & 10th st, on Jul 23 at 4 o'clock.

Orphans Court of Wash Co, D C. Letters testamentary on the personal estate of Jas M Wayne, late of Wash City, D C, deceased. –Mary J Wayne, Henry C Wayne, Jno W Cuyler, excs

Orphans Court of Wash Co, D C, Jul 20, 1867. In the case of Emma Derrick, admx of Alex H Derrick, deceased, the administratrix & Court have appointed Aug 17 next, for the final settlement of the personal estate of the said deceased, of the assets in hand. -Jas R O'Beirne, Reg/o wills

London, Jul 4, 1867. Jennings Estate. All persons interested are invited to attend at Mr Brutton's ofc, 28 King Wm st, Strand, on Tuesday, Jul 16, at 12 o'clock. Valuable information can be had.

Dept of the Interior, U S Patent Ofc, Wash, Jul 13, 1867. Ptn of David M Smith, of Springfield, Vt, praying for the extension of a patent granted to him Oct 25, 1852, for an improvement in Spring Clamp for clothes lines, for seven years from the expiration of said patent, which takes place on Oct 25, 1867. -T C Theaker, Com'r of Patents

TUES JUL 23, 1867
Trial of John H Surratt, Jul 22, 1867. Rev Chas Boucher-sworn: resides in parish of St Hiliare, Canada; am rector of that parish; in 1865, resided in the parish of St Liboire; I recognize the prisoner at the bar; I saw him in Apr, 1865, at St Liboire; about Apr 22, 1865; he was with Mr Jos Dutilley, who brought him to my place; the prisoner remained at my house about 3 months, then he went to Montreal, & later to Europe. Mr Geo W Strayer-sworn: in Apr, 1865, I was an engineer on the Northern Central railway; am still im the employ of the railroad as engineer. Jos C Rogers-sworn: in Apr, 1865, I was a conductor on the Northern Central rairoad. Z B Glines-sworn: I was charged with the duty of collecting fare at the ferry at Wmsport; it was a rope ferry; Drohan, the ferryman, was there every day. Maurice Drohan-sworn: in Apr, 1865, I ran the ferry at Wmsport. Chas J Hepburn-sworn: he was trainmaster on Apr 13, 1865, on the Phil & Erie railroad. Geo W Hambright-sworn: in Apr, 1865, was conductor on N C railway, between Sunbury & Balt. Major A C Richards, Superintendent of Police-sworn: I know Mr Hollohan; had a conversation with him & others in N Y, after they returned from Canada.

Fort Phil Kearney, Dakota, Jul 21. Eighteen hundred Crow Indians have visited me. The council was highly satisfactory-their friendship undoubted. The warriors are anxious to join the expedition against the Sioux & Cheyennes, who are still killing our people in this country. –J F Kinney, Special Indian Agent

Mr Robt Toombs, of Ga, has not been pardoned by the Pres, as stated in some of the papers.

Gen Saml Chandler, a volunteer in the war of 1812, died at his residence, in Lexington, Mass, on Saturday.

Gen Grant has ordered the arrest of Brvt Maj Gen S W Crawford, for disobedience of orders in having failed to report to his regt at Louisville, as required by speical orders from the headquarters of the army.

Supreme Court of D C; Equity No 249. E M Linthicum et al vs Mary Jones, Chas S Jones et al. Parties in the cause, & creditors of Richd Jones, deceased, are to appear at my ofc, Jul 27, regarding trustee's account, & claims upon the fund.
–Walter S Cox, auditor

Died: on Jul 21, Adam Gaddis, sr, aged 76 years. His funeral will be from his late residence, Ga ave & 10th st, on Jul 23 at 4 o'clock P M.

Fort Wallace, Kansas, Jul 15, via *Fort Riley*, Jul 21. Custer's command arrived at *Fort Wallace* on Jul 12th & 13th, & found the bodies of Lt Kidder & 10 men of M Troop 2nd cavalry. Lt Kidder left *Fort Sedgwick* on Jun 29, with despatches from Sherman to Custer. The bodies were so mutilated as to be unrecognizable. Gen Custer left *Fort Wallace* with an escort of 70 picked men, under Capt Hamilton, & came through to *Fort Hayes*, 156 miles, in 55 hours, losing 3 men, killed near Downer. The Indians swarm along the route, & are bolder & more determined than ever before. Two stages were probably captured near Castle Rock, as just after leaving there between 200 to 300 Indians were seen. The troops will hold the forts & the route, but for the time being the stage lines must discontinue operations.

St Louis, Jul 22. A telegram from Gen A J Smith, dated *Fort Harker*, Jul 20, to Gen Sherman, states that reliable information has been received that Bishop Larney & party, recently reported to have been attacked near *Fort Larned*, & 8 men killed, & the women taken captives, passed *Fort Dodge* 55 miles west of *Fort Larned*, in company with a large train, on Jul 16. The reported massacre must, therefore, be false.

The partnership under the style of Littlefield & Clagett, for the publication of the "Death Bed Scene of Lincoln," has this day been dissolved by mutual consent. –J H Littlefield, Dorsy Clagett [Dorsy Clagett will continue the publication of the Picture, at 396 D st, between 6th & 7th sts, having purchased the copyright from the above firm.]

WED JUL 24, 1867
The Springfield Republican says Miss Houghten, of North Adams, who was lately mixed up in the Rev S M Merrill scandal, has written the gentleman, since his pretended drowning at Plattsburg, telling him that it is now his duty to leave his family & share his fortunes with her, even if they have to go to the ends of the earth.

Trial of John H Surratt, Jul 23, 1867. Ezra B Westfall-sworn: in Apr, 1865, he was train-master on Phil & Erie railroad. Dr Lewis J A McMillen recalled: I have had a quarrel with Rev Mr Boucher. Mr Boucher owed me money & I wrote to him, but he never answered me. Dr John Erskine-sworn: is a physician at Waterloo, C E; knows Dr McMillen; his character was perfectly good. Mr Ernest Racicot-sworn: resides at Sweedsburg, C E; am an advocate at the bar there; have known Dr McMillen for 15 years. Mr Levi A Perkins-sworn: resides in Township of Potter, C E; is clerk of the Comrs' Court & Court of Justice. Dr Jos W Guppy-sworn: in 1865 was assist superintendent Erie [N Y] railway. Almiron Field-sworn: resides at Elmira, N Y, lived there 2 years since May 1; in Apr, 1865, was at Elmira, negotiating for the purchase of the furniture of the Brainard House, & I purchased it. Chas H Blinn recalled: on Apr 17, 1865, I picked up a pocket-handkerchief. [Mr John T Hollohan called in.] That is not the man who dropped the handkerchief-not the slightest resemblance. Lewis T Weichman recalled: I know John T Hollohan. Jos Wells-sworn: resides at Elkton, Md; I knew a man named Stephen F Cameron, who resided there in 1861, & professed to be sort of a minister; his reputation was not good. Jas S Crawford-sworn: resides in Elkton, Mc; am clerk to the County Com'rs; knew Cameron. Jas T McCulloch-sworn: lived in Elkton; have known S F Cameron many years prior to 1861. John Torbert-sworn: resides in Elkton; was born there, & left in 1859; knows S F Cameron, his wife & family. He was considered a half crazy man. Jos L Mahan-sworn: resides in Elkton, Md; knew Cameron; his general reputation for truth was bad. John V Reardon-sworn: resides in Elkton, knows S F Cameron & his family. I am a coachmaker. Frank Titus-sworn: resides at Elkton; went there since 1855; know S F Cameron-reputation very bad. Michl McNamara-sworn: resides on Capitol Hill, Wash; knew a man who is a witness here, named John T Tippett. He enlisted in my company, co B, 1st D C cavalry. His general reputation for truth & veracity was good. John H Clark-sworn: resides in Wash & has resided here since mustered out of service; knew Tippett; I was for a while It of his company; Tippett's reputation was good. Lafayette C Baker commanded that regt, but was never with it. It was commanded by Lt Col Conger in the field. John E Lowe-sworn: resides in Wash, on 5th st, between N & O sts; resided here 6 years next Oct; am a tailor; know John T Tippett; have known him 18 years; has a good reputation. John A Campbell-sworn: knew John T Tippett; knew him in the regt. John W Kelley-sworn: Resides at Wash, 12th & Md ave; am employed in the Monument Grounds; Tippett is employed at the Monument Grounds as a blacksmith; always heard him well spoken of. Jas Gibson-sworn: resides in Third Ward of Wash; keeps a restaurant; has know Tippett for 11 months. Robt F Martin-sworn: lived in Uniontown, D C, across the Eastern branch; has known John T Tippett 15 years; lived near him in PG Co, Md; never heard his character questioned except since I saw about the trial in the papers. Danl Garner-sworn: lived in PG Co, Md; has known Tippett since he was a child; lived within 4 miles of his father's; never heard his character questioned. Reuben S Ives-sworn: resides in PG Co, Md; knew John T Tippett; never heard his character questioned. John L Kelley-sworn: lived here since 1862; knew Tippett. I am foreman of the U S horshoeing shop, & have hired Tippett as a horseshoer; his reputation was very good. Edmunk Rockett-sworn: is 76 years of age; lives in PG Co, Md; knew Tippett & his family well. John bore one of the best characters of any young man in the county. Have lived in PG Co 50 years, was not born there. Wm Lloyd-sworn: have known Tippetts 3 months. Jos J Colclazer-sworn: has known Tippett since Jan; worked in the same shop with him, & he bears an excellent character. John Ogden-sworn: resides in Wash, has so for 5 years; known Tippett since Jan 1; of good character. Eugene Bowen-sworn: lives at Monument Lot; am a mounted messenger for Col Bell; have known Tippett for 8 months; would not doubt Tippett's word.

Yesterday Mr Carl Keiffer was seriously injured at Mr Chas Kotz's restaurant while unloading some lager beer kegs. One of them slipped & fell upon his hand, crushing one of his fingers so badly that it had to be amputated. The operation was performed by Dr Brentman.

Real estate sale yesterday: a farm called **Long Meadows**, containing 96 acres, on the Eastern Branch, near Bladensburg, was sold to Pete F Hornig, for $8,850.

Orphans Court-Judge Purcell, Jul 23, 1867. 1-The last will & testament of Jas Riordan, of Wash City, D C, deceased, was fully proven, & letters testamentary issued to Martha Riordan; bond $6,000. He bequeaths his residence to his wife, Martha Riordan; also his 2 lots in Alexandria, his 2 negro women, & all the personal estate & bonded stocks in his possession to her & her assigns forever. 2-Chas H Don was appointed guardian to Henry R S Snoud, orphan of Simpson R Snoud, deceased; bond $2,000. 3-Helen Reed presents a petition to the court to cite A K Browne to show cause why he should not pay to her a certain sum of money, now on deposit, pertaining to the estate of Col Richd Bustee, jr. 4-The first & final account of Wm G Moore, exc of Virginia B Baldwin, deceased; the first & final account of Wm *Emmett, guardian to the orphan of Henry & Louisa *Emmitt, deceased; the second & final & general & individual accounts of Margaret Ann Duker, [now Collison,] guardian to the orphan of Levin Duker, & an account of the personal estate of Virginia B Baldwin, deceased, by Wm G Moore, exc, were approved & passed. 5-The last will & testament of Philip Wetzal, deceased, was filed & approved. 6-The will of the late Saml Tilston was filed & fully proven, & letters testamentary issued to Abraham Wyckoff; bond $80,000. [*Two spellings of Emmett/Emmitt.]

Springfield, Mass, Jul 23. Ashiwara, one of the Japanese students at Monson, committed suicide, by hanging, on Sunday. Mental depression, amounting to almost insanity, was the cause of the act. [Jul 27, 1867: Ashiwara was suffering from a chronic disease, which had for many months afflicted him; there was little or no hope of relief. He was about 30 years old, & left a wife at his home in Yokohama. –Springfield Republican]

St Louis, Jul 23. John W Matthews, the agent of the U S Express Co at Weston, Mo, absconded last week with from eight to ten thousand dollars belonging to the company. Matthews was a member of the firm of Matthews & Co, grocers, which made an assignment about a month ago.

Miss Azoa Phelps got on a reaper, in Hudson, Mich, to take a ride on Jul 17. The horses ran away; she was thrown upon the knives, had one hand cut off, & was shockingly mangles. Her injuries are supposed to be fatal.

Orphans Court of Wash Co, D C. Letters testamentary on the personal estate of Jas Riordan, late of Wash City, D C, deceased. –Martha Riordan, excx

Died: on Jul 20, at Rock Island, Ill, Rev Hervey H Hayes, formerly chaplain in the U S navy, aged 71 years. His funeral will be from his late residence, 467 6th st, on Thursday, at 2 o'clock P M.

THU JUL 25, 1867
Savannah, Jul 24. W C Wylly, one of our most respected citizens, & a veteran of the war of 1812, died last night.

Orphans Court of Wash Co, D C. Letters testamentary on the personal estate of Saml Tilston, late of Wash Co, D C, deceased. –Abraham Wyckoff, exc

Trial of John H Surratt, Jul 24, 1867. Francis C Speight-sworn: lives in N Y C, & is capt of 29th Metropolitan Police. Patrick D Kilduff-sworn: lives at 918 Broadway, N Y; lived there since 1858. Col Jos B Stewart recalled: on the night of the murder I followed Booth out of the theatre. Maj A C Richards, Superintendent of Police, recalled: Weichman was not arrested to my knowledge on the day after Apr 14. Michl Mitchell-sworn: resides at Waterloo; knows Dr McMillen & his good character. Edmund Frechett-sworn: resides at Montreal; has known St Marie for many years; good reputation. Alexis Burnet-sworn: resides in Montreal, & is a lawyer. Francis Reeside-sworn: lives at 610 7th st, Wash; is a brick-layer; has known Wm E Cleaver for 10 to 12 years. Chas Kimball recalled; lives in 7th Ward, Wash; lived here all my life; has known Wm E Cleaver, never heard his reputation questioned. Robt Pywell-sworn: lives in D st, Wash, since 1843; known Cleaver for 15 or 16 years; never heard his reputation questioned. J W Coomes-sworn: had lived in Wash all his life; is a detective of Metropolitan Police; have known Cleaver for 7 or 8 years; his reputation is good. Jas Kelleher-sworn: am a livery-stable keeper; have known W E Cleaver 15 or 16 years; his reputation for truth & veracity is very bad at present. Mrs Sarah R Kimball-sworn: lived at 12th st, Wash, since 1864; had a colored woman, Susan Jackson, in her employ for 2 years; her reputation is good, as far as I know. Mrs Kezia Wheeler-sworn: resides at 12th & G sts, for 3 months; lived in Wash City 3 years; knows Susan Jackson; she in the employ of my sister, Mrs Kimball, & I resided in her family. Jackson had a good reputation. Miss Katie Kimball-sworn: resided at 12th & G sts, Wash, knew Jackson about 2 years; good reputation. Saml Jackson, colored-sworn: Susan Jackson is my wife; we were married about a fortnight after the Pres was killed. Alphonso Donn-sworn: lived at 8th & D sts; is doorkeeper at the *Executive Mansion*; employed there 4 years; prior to that was a Metropolitan policeman; has known John Lee, for 3 or 4 years. Geo W Theaker-sworn: resides in Gtwn, D C, & was born & raised there; keeps a restaurant; has known John Lee 3 years. John Keefe-sworn: lives on Capitol Hill; keeps store on 6th st; knew Wm Cleaver for 2 or 3 years. Geo F Waldo-sworn: resides at Waverly, N Y; lived there 20 years; has know Dr Bissell part of 8 years. Vincent M Coryell-sworn: resides in Waverly, N Y; lived there 18 years; knew Dr Bissell. He ia a Methodist clergyman on the superanuated list. C T Bliss-sworn: resides at Waverly, N Y; is a physician; formed Dr Bissell's acquaintance about 3 years. Jas J Reeve-sworn: is a hardware merchant in Waverly, N Y, knows Dr Bissell. Geo R Howard-sworn: lived at Elkton, Md; during the war was a Union man, & raised a regt for the war in 1862, & commanded it until his health compelled him to resign. I knew Stephen F Cameron in Elkton; never heard his character questioned. Danl Bratton-sworn: resides in Elkton, Md, has for 27 ot 28 years; knew Cameron; would not hestitate to believe him under oath. Eli Cosgrove-sworn: resides within 15 miles of Elkton; had a slight acquaintance with Cameron. John Partridge-sworn: resides in Elkton, Md, since 1837; knew Cameron; would believe him under oath. R G Reese-sworn: resides in Elkton 20 years; knew Cameron; would believe him under oath. Wm J Purnell-sworn: resided at Elkton 17 years; last 4 or 5 in the army. I enlisted as a private, & was discharged a captain; am now in the U S mail service; knew Cameron; would believe him under oath. Thos Drennen-sworn: resides within 1 mile of Elkton; prior to 1861 lived in Elkton; knew Cameron; went to parties with him; would believe him under oath. John R Hogg-sworn: had lived in Cecil Co, Md, 45 years; knew Cameron; would believe him under oath. Prof Harkenss-sworn: am employed at the Nat'l Observatory; on Apr 14th I was making observations of the stars. Hon Hiram McCullough-sworn: lived at Elkton; knew Cameron; would believe him under oath. Dr Chas Ellis-sworn; resides in Elkton; was a surgeon in the U S army in the war; learned Cameron's reputation for truth & veracity was very good. I associated with him & his friends. Jas R Brown-sworn: ia a magistrate in Elkton; knows Cameron; would not hestitate to believe him under oath. Aaron G Tate-sworn: resides at Eklton; knows Cameron; would believe him under oath. Jos P Cantwell-sworn: resides at Eklton; knows Cameron; would believe him under oath. I was an out & out Union man during the war. David Scott-sworn: lived in Elkton since 1851; knew Cameron; would believe him under oath. John N Miller-sworn: I was a Union man in the war, & support Pres Johnson; knew Cameron; would believe him under oath. Jas B Groome-sworn: resides in Elkton; knew Cameron; do. Saml B Ford-sworn: resides in Elkton; knew Cameron; do. Reuben B Ford-sworn: resides in Elkton; knew Cameron; his reputation for truth & veracity was good. Perry Litzenberg-sworn: resides in Elkton; knew Cameron; associated in same society; character for truth never doubted.

Died: on Jul 24, at *Cliffburne*, Wash, D C, Charles Henry, infant son of Gen Charles M & Augusta R Tompkins. His funeral will take place from the Church of the Epiphany on Jul 25 at 5 o'clock P M.

Died: on Jul 24, at Wash, after a lingering & painful illness, Mrs Rachel Cartwrights, in her 67th year. Her funeral will be from the residence of her sister, Mrs E Herbert, 542 H st, between 6th & 7th sts, on Thursday at 5 o'clock. [Md papers copy.]

Died: on Jul 23, at *Poplar Springs*, Howard Co, Md, Wm Winston, son of Capt Frank & Alice S Monroe, aged _1months & 18 days. [The space before the 1 is blank followed by months.]

Savannah, Jul 24. W C Wylly, one of our most respected citizens, & a veteran of the war of 1812, died last night.

Orphans Court of Wash Co, D C. Letters testamentary on the personal estate of Saml Tilston, late of Wash Co, D C, deceased. –Abraham Wyckoff, exc

Supreme Court of D C, in Equity No 397-docket 8. David Porter Heap et al vs Gwynne Harris Heap et al. Wm B Webb, trustee, reported he has sold the real estate in the proceedings therein: lot 38 in square 369, to J R C Oldham, trustee for Everett, who has complied with the terms of sale. –R J Meigs, clerk [Purchase price not given.]

FRI JUL 26, 1867
Trial of John H Surratt, Jul 25, 1867. Artemus Stevens-sworn: resides in Lennoxville, Canada; resided there all his life; is a farmer; knew Dr McMillen. Chas F Wetmore-sworn: resides at 18 Clinton Pl, N Y C; knew Dr Bissell. Recalled: Prof Harkness; Jos N Dubarry; & Geo S Koontz; Geo W McMahon-sworn: has lived in N Y C; had a saloon with Dr Bissell at 1,160 Broadway. Francis X Archansbault-sworn; resides in Montreal; is a lawyer. T J Logan-sworn; on Apr 14 the night was remarkably clear. C A Tinker-sworn: was telegrapher in this city in 1865. Morrell Mareau-sworn: is a telegraph operator; in 1865 was in the ofce of the American Co here. John George-sworn: was baggage master between Wash & N Y, on Apr 15, 1865. Wm Roberts-sworn: was in Elmira in Jun, 1866; saw Mr Jos Carroll, a tailor, there. John W Browning: sworn: is a clerk in the ofc of Comissary General of Provisions. Mrs M A Fithian [formerly Sherman]-sworn: lives at 10th & C sts; first husband, Mr Sherman, was an alderman of Phil. I knew John Lee's reputation while he was an ofcr under my husband; his character for veracity was good. John E Hatfield-sworn: lives at 339 10th st; lived in Phil a number of years; knew John Lee in Phil; reputation good. Wm Parker-sworn: lived in Wash, at 7th & T sts; is a clerk in the Treasury Dept; knew John Lee; good reputation. Wm T Parker-sworn: resides in Phil; kept a restaurant at 6th & Chestnut sts; knew John Lee in Phil; good reputation.

Lemuel G Perry, a student of Brown Univ, died last week of an abscess brought on by excessive exercise at the time of the Univ match game of baseball, between the students of Harvard & Brown some 2 weeks since.

Suicide. Ellen Beavers, aged between 16 & 17 years, the daughter of Wm Beavers, formerly of Wash City, but now a resident of PG Co, Md, threw herself into the Potomac yesterday, from the steamer **Thomas Collyer**, on her way from Wash City. It is stated that she had received chatisement from her father a week ago, & had left her home, & gone to her sister's in Washington, but, having apparently made up her mind to return to PG, & to live there with her brother-in-law, Mr Jas E Spencer, was on her way back, accompanied by him, when she deliberately took her own life. The friends of her family were dragging the river for her body this morning. –Alexandria Gaz of yesterday. [Jul 27th newspaper: The body of Ellen Beavers was caught this morning by Mr John Williams, who was dragging for it. It was conveyed to the house of Mr Geo Beavers, the girl's brother, near Wolfe st. A jury composed of T A Stoutenburgh, the Coroner, & Washington Fisher, Jas Nickens, Geo Seaton, Harrison Blackburn, Robt Williams, & Geo Seaton, jr, colored, & T J Edelin, A D Warfield, Eli Pettey, Orlando Wood, Jas Owens, & Jos Hopkins, white, held an inquest upon it. Messrs Geo Beavers & Jas Spencer, the brother & brother-in-law of the deceased, protested against colored men holding an inquest upon the body of their sister. The protest was only an obstruction; the inquest proceeded. Mr Richd Rudd was summoned as a juror, but refused to serve when he discovered that he was to be associated with colored men. –Alexandria Gaz of yesterday]

Died: on Jul 25, John H D'Bille, a native of Bremen, in his 63rd year. He entered the service of the U S in 1828, & served in the 1st regt of artl; was in the Black Hawk campaign under Gen Scott in 1832; & during the Florida war was under Gen Jesup, in 1836; in 1839 he collated at Wash Arsenal, & was appointed hospital steward which position he retained until 1850; he was then employed as a clerk at the Arsenal, & served the Gov't faithfully till a few weeks of his death. His funeral will be place from his late residence, I st, between 4½ & 6th sts, Island, today, at 2 P M.

Died: on Jul 23, at Flintstone, Allegany Co, Md, Clement, aged 21 months & 17 days, son of John Clement & Cornelia Fill, of Wash, D C. [Express, Sunday Herald, & Evening Star copy, & send bill to Nat'l Intelligencer.]

Portland, Me, Jul 25. A special despatch to the Star says that Rev R G Chase & wife, Miss Hample, Miss Tazelwell, & L Harmon, of Phil; & S F Clark & wife, of Farmington, Mass, & Capt C Robinson, of Tremont, were all capsized in a boat & drowned in Bar harbor, off Desert Island, yesterday.

John P Appleby, a young man engaged as a letter-carrier in the Balt post ofc, was arrested on Tuesday charged with purloining letters from the office.

August Belmont is making extensive improvements in his recently purchased estate, near Babylon, Long Island. He proposes to have a race course & several fish-ponds.

Dept of the Interior, U S Patent Ofc, Wash, Jul 18, 1867. Ptn of Harry Whitaker, of Buffalo, N Y, praying for extension of a patent granted to him Oct 18, 18__, for an improvement of High Pressure Engines to Screw Propellers, for seven years from the expiration of said patent; takes place Oct 18, 1867. -T C Theaker, Com'r of Patents

SAT JUL 27, 1867
Trial of John H Surratt, Jul 26, 1867. Alvia Jarvis-sworn: resides in Waverly, N Y- been there 23 years; was a justice of the peace there; knew Dr Bissell; would believe him under oath. G P Pannell-sworn: resides near Waverly, N Y; lived there some 30 odd years; knew Dr Augustus Bissell; would believe him under oath. Nelson F Penny-sworn: resides at Waverly, about 6 years last Apr; knew Dr Bissell; would believe him under oath. Dr C M Noble-sworn: is a practicing physician of Waverly, N Y; resides there 14 years; first knew Dr Bissell 7 years ago; I would believe him under oath. G B Eldred-sworn: resides at Montrose, Pa; lived there 30 years; knewn Dr Bissell, while living at Montrose; 5 or 6 years ago he had a bad reputation for truth & veracity. Gordon Z Dimock-sworn; ia a physician of Montrose, Pa; knows Dr Bissell-reputation very bad. C Cushman sworn; lived in Montrose, Pa, been there 43 years; Dr Bissell's reputation very bad. D J W Cobb-sworn: physician of Montrose, Pa; while Dr Bissell lived there his reputation was bad for truth & veractiy. A D Butterfield-sworn: resides at Montrose; knew Dr Bissell in Bradford Co, Pa, township of Pike; Bissell had a bad reputation there. Geo Greene-sworn: lived at Waverly, N Y, been constable of the town for the last 3 years; knows Dr Bissell, whose reputation for truth is bad.

Fairfax city [Va] was founded in 1748, the year in which Washington turned 16 years old, & set off with Geo Fairfax on his first surveying expedition. Geo Fairfax was the eldest son of Wm Fairfax, of Belvoir, whose daughter Washington's eldest brother, Lawrence, had married. Lord Thos Fairfax had this same year returned from England, to take up here his permanent residence. He had inherited from his aunt, the wife of Lord Culpeper, the immense domain known as the **Northern Neck of Va**, & Washington & young Fairfax started out to explore the region for him. Lord Fairfax was an eccentric, but very generous & hospitable. He had been educated at Oxford Univ, & bred in the best English society. He was passionately fond of the chase, & after some years at Belvoir, he went over the Blue Ridge, built a home in the wilderness, about 13 miles from Winchester, calling it **Greenway Court**. He lived & died in a small story-&-a-half house, & had some 150 negro servants living in log huts about him in the woods. When he heard of the surrender of Cornwallis, it is said that he called his favorite servant, saying:"Come, Joe, carry me to bed, for it is high time for me to die." He died in 1782 at 94 yrs of age; his estate, according to Parliamentary record, 5,280,000 acres, the largest in America at the Revolution-was confiscated. The estate had come down to him from Thos Lord Culpeper, his grandfather, to whom it had been granted by Chas II in 1681, on a rent of L6. 13s. 4d. Lord Fairfax was buried at Winchester, under the communion table of the Episcopal Church, the ground upon which it stood having been given by him for the construction of the church. This old stone church was torn down many years ago, & the remains of Lord Fairfax buried under the new church, & in it a marble slab placed to his memory. He was jilted, it is said, in early life, & seeking asylum here, was never married. Geo Wm Fairfax, who went on the surveying tour with Washington, had been educated in England, & was 18 years older than Washington. His father, the owner of **Belvoir**, adjoining **Mount Vernon**, was lt of the county of Fairfax, Collector of the Customs of South Potomac, & president of the King's Council of Va. At his death, in 1757, Geo succeeded to his estate, & resided at **Belvoir**, having married a daughter of Col Carey, of Hampton. He was a member of the King's Council. In 1773 he went to England to attend to some property that had fallen to him in Yorkshire, & the revolutionary strife opening, he never returned. During the war he was conspicuous for his kindness to American prisoners in England, & died at Bath in 1787, aged 63 years. A portion of his estate in Va was confiscated. Washington was named executor of his will, by which, as he had no children, he bequeathed his estate to the second son, Fernando, of his only surviving brother. Bryan Fairfax, 3rd son of Col Wm, married a daughter of Wilson Carey, & his residence in Fairfax Co was known as **Tarleston Hall**. He was near the age of Washington, & they were warm friends to the last. In 1791, on the death of his uncle Robt, in England, 7th Lord Fairfax, he suceeded as the 8th & last Baron in the line, though he never assumed the title. He was an Episcopal clergyman in his later years, & presided over Christ's Church, Alexandria. He inherited **Belvoir** from his father, & died at **Mount Eagle**, near Cameron, in 1802, aged 75 years. The last descendant of the family bearing a family name in this country, Dr Fairfax, of Fairfax Court-House, died during the rebellion. In 1778 Washington was surprised by a visit of Mr Fairfax at **Valley Forge**. He had determined to go to England, & remain till the war was over, as his situation among his old associates, who were nearly all rebels, was uncomfortable. Washington received him with warm kindness, & gave him a passport to N Y. But when he arrived there his heart failed him at the thought of separation from his family, & he returned to Alexandria again, visiting Washington, on his return, at his camp. It is a familiar history that Washington's first military expedtion was as a lt colonel of a regt of 6 companies-300 soldiers-against the French & Indians on Wills Creek, or Cumberland river, as it was afterwards named. He left Alexandria with 2 companies, 150 men, in Mar, 1754, & Col Fry, with the other companies were conveyed up the Potomac with the artillery. Washington refused the command of the regt. He was then but 22 years old. Washington's first achievement in a public capacity was with the Ohio country, to conciliate the Indians in 1753, when 21 years old. Alexandria: The old stone mansion, which is still standing, was built of sand stone imported from England & upon the key-stone of the arch above the front entrance were carved J S C 1752; J S Carlile, 1752. It is still to be seen today. It is from this bldg that the Mansion House Hotel took its name; the main structure was built for the use of the old Bank of Alexandria, which exploded in the time of the general crash in Gen Jackson's day. It was used for a post ofc, & finally sold by the U S authorities to Jas Greene, who still owns it, in 1848. Mr Greene afterwards added to the premises by purchasing the stone mansion & lot adjoining, & connecting the two structures by an immense intervening bldg for hotel purposes; furnished in a most superb manner, every foot of the floors & staircases being covered with carpet. In the early months of the war he was notified on a Saturday to clear his house & give it up for hospital purposes on the succeeding Monday. The hospital moved in as they were still removing furniture to a warehouse. At the close of the war the Mansion House was returned to Mr Greene, & it is again in excellent condition.

Equity Court-Jul 26. 1-A decree was made divorcing Luanna Dewees from the bond of matrimony with Alex'r Dewees, giving her the custody & guardianship of her two children. 2-Saml Hooper agt G A Bassatt et al; order appointing B G Lovejoy guardian *ad litem*.

Columbia, S C, Jul 26. A lad named Houchey, a newsboy on the S C railroad, was killed by the train running over him near Bambury this morning.

Charge of Bigamy. Nathl S Morgan, late a cmder in the U S navy, was arrested-the charge was that of bigamy, in marrying in this city, on Jul 10, Miss Martha Wroe, [daughter of a well known resident of Wash, Saml Wroe,] he having at that time a wife residing in Hartford, Conn, to whom he was married in 1857. It appeared that Morgan had been alternately residing in Wash & Conn, living in each place with one or the other of his wives. He suddenly disappeared; the detectives discovered him engaged as a clerk for Mr Walter Godey, of Gtwn, under the assumed name of Watson. He was held to bail for $1,500 for his appearance at the next term of the Criminal Court of this District. Justice Chas Walter entered as bail for the prisoner, & he was discharged from custody.

Indianapolis, Jul 26. Hon David McKee, an ex-member of Congress, & postmaster at Lafayette, Ind, shot himself dead at his home this morning.

Nomination of Gen Grant for President. N Y correspondent of the Phil Ledger, writing on Wed: Do not underrate the improtance of the formal nomination of Gen Grant by the Union Republican General Cmte last evening. Mr Delafield Smith was chief engineer of the business; he is the U S District Atty. He was among the pasengers who went down to Long Branch, N J in this afternoon's boat.

Mrd: on Jul 25, by Rev Dr Hill, Wm H Wiggins, of N Y C, to Jennie E Parish, of Wash, D C. No cards.

L B Heitman purchased lot 11 in square 55, with a new two story frame house upon it, situated on I st, between 22nd & 23rd sts, for $2,150.

Judicial sale of a valuable farm in Culpeper Co, Va; by decree of the Circuit Court of said county, pronounced on Jun 5, 1867, in the case of Smoet vs Brandt's administrator: public auction on Sep 2 next, of that beautiful farm called *Brandywine*, formerly owned by Danl F Slaughter, & by him sold to Dr Logan Brandt, containing 336¾ acres, more or less. This farm adjoins the lands of Rev Philip Slaughter, Wm Major, Mrs Catherine Crittenden, & others, & lies at the foot of *Slaughter's Mountain*. –Henry Shackelford, John W Bell, Jas W Green, com'rs

Dept of the Interior, U S Patent Ofc, Wash, Jul 23, 1867. Ptn of Saml Pratt, of Hammonton, N J, praying for the extension of a patent granted to him Oct 25, 185_, for an improvement in Screw Nails, for seven years from the expiration of said patent, which takes place on Oct 25, 1867. -T C Theaker, Com'r of Patents

MON JUL 29, 1867
Trial of John H Surratt, Jul 27, 1867. Summing up of the evidence! Mr Carrington spoke on Sat for 3 hours, & his address to the jury today will occupy the entire day. Counsel for defence will follow, & Mr Pierrepont will close the argument. The arguments will probably consume all of this week.

The sad news of the death of Henry Dunlap, of this city, by drowning, whilst bathing at Cape May yesterday, reached his parents at an early hour of the day by telegraph. He was between 17 & 18 years old, son of Chas Dunlap, who for many years kept a grocery store at Howard & Lexington sts. Young Dunlap had graudated from High School but a few weeks ago, & was enjoying his first bath about daylight, when he was carried out by the undertow. The body was recovered at 4:30 P M, & placed in charge of Messrs J T Peirson & D P West, of Balt, & should arrive here this morning. –Balt Sun, 24th

A S Rockwell, a jeweler, a native of N J, & lately residing in Memphis, fell from a 3rd story window in Billings' Bldg, St Louis, on Tuesday night, & was killed.

Sir Walter Scott. The original manuscripts of Sir Walter Scott's poems & several of his novels & other prose works, are to be sold at auction, by order of the executors of the late Mr Robt Cadell, of Edinburgh. The manuscripts are in perfect state of preservation, & uniformly bound in Russia, with uncut edges.

Appointments of Pastors of the Catholic Church. On Sunday next the following changes will take place: Rev John McNally, assist pastor at St Matthew's Church, has been assigned to the charge of St Stephen's Church, now being erected. Rev Desiderius De Wulf has been appointed assist at St Matthews [Rev C J White, D D, is the pastor.] Rev Felix Berotti, assist pastor of St Peter's, on Capitol Hill, has been appointed pastor of the church for the colored people. This edifice is dedicated to the memory of Blessed Martin de Parras. Rev Jeremiah Henricks is to be Fr Boyle's assist, in place of Fr Berotti. Rev Henry Spryt has been appointed pastor of the Missions connected with Elkridge Landing.

Orphans Court-Judge Purcell, Jul 27, 1867. 1-An exemplified copy of the will of the late W W Taylor, of Balt, was exhibited & admitted to probate. 2-The will of the late J Letitia Speake, of Wash City, D C, deceased, was filed for probate. She appointed therein, as her executor, Erasmus Y Middleton. 3-Abraham Wycoff was qualified as executor of Saml Tiltson, late of Wash, D C, deceased; bond $80,000. 4-Letters testamentary were issued to Sarah Keating, on the estate of Geo W Keating, late of Wash, D C, deceased; bond $4,000; to Nathl B Myers, on the personsl estate of Martha M Myers, deceased; bond $300; to Jos Gaylor upon the personal estate of Jas Cronan, deceased; bond $400. 5-The first & final accounts of the administrator of R G Campbell, deceased; the first & final account of the administrator of R H Marlock, deceased; & the second account of the guardian of the orphans of John Henry Buchannan, deceased, were approved & passed. 6-The answer of H E Brown, executor of the estate of Richd Bustee, to the ptn of Helen R Reed, was presented & read. By order of the Court the demurrer was overruled & the said executor required to answer. 7-*In re* Mary Ann Fearson. In answer to the motion heretofore made an administrator *pendente lite* or letters *ad *coltizendona*, was filed, & arrangements commenced by consel pro & con. [*Possible spelling-letters very light.]

Waldo F Davis, late postmaster at Van West, Ohio, was held to bail on Friday in the U S Dist Court in Cleveland, on the charge of embezzling money from letters. Bail was not forthcoming, & Davis was committed to prison.

Sgt John Lynch, of Cincinnati, a member of the Fenian army under Gen O'Neill, which invaded Canada in Jun, 1866, died at the hospital of the <u>Sisters of Charity</u> in Buffalo, on Sat, of a gunshot wound received at the battle of Ridgway.

The N Y Tribune says: John Slidell is at present living near Paris, as well as his son-in-law, Erlanger, the Hebrew Banker. Although he is most anxious to pass his last days in America, he has latterly given up all hope of ever again seeing his native land.

Cassville [Mo] Republican of Jul 17. On Jul 4, an 8 year old daughter of Mr Martin, of Barry Co, deliberately shot & killed a brother of 4 years. She said she killed him because he pulled her flowers, & declared if the other children pulled any more of them, she would shoot them too. A physician intimated the girl was insane.

Exec's sale of large stock of groceries at public auction, by order passed by the Orphans Court of Wash Co, D C. The undersigned, exc of the last will & testament of Saml Tilston, deceased, late of said county, will sell the same on the premises 399 Pa ave. The store was recently occupied by Saml Tilston, successor of Wyckoff & Dennison. –Abraham Wyckoff, exc -J B Wheeler & Co, aucts

Executrix's sale of a valuable Farm containing 106 acres, more & less, 1½ miles from Washington, at auction. Sale of *Locust Grove* on the *Fenwick Farm*, containing 106 acres of fine gardening land; with 3 dwlg houses, one of which is a large room, & conveniently arranged bldg; stabling, barn, & other necessary out-bldgs. This property fronts on the back road leading from Washington to Bladensburg, also on the railroad, from which is a road to the turnpike by *Mt Olivet Cemetery*. One of the tenements, with a small portion of land is rented for $350 per year. Title indisputable. –M E Smith, excx -John A Smith, agent -Green & Williams, aucts

Property at auction on I st, between 5th & 7th, on Aug 5: parts of lots 15 & 16 in square 43; improved by 4 brick houses on the rear of the lots, 2 story, tin roofs, & a good French house on the front of one of the lots. Title indisputable. –E M Chapin, Agent heirs W Werden, deceased. -Green & Williams, aucts

Jacob Weill, a young man, drowned yesterday while bathing in Lyon's mill-dam, near Gtwn. Is it supposed he was taken with a cramp. His body was delivered to his relatives. Weill was about 18, & for some time past employed in the shoe store of Mr H Somers, Bridge st, Gtwn.

Died: on Jul 28, David H Stick, aged 34 years. His funeral will be from his late residence, 676 L st, between 2nd & 3rd sts, this afternoon at 4 o'clock P M.

Died: on Jul 27, Jane E Clarke, infant daughter of Worthington & Mary J Dorsey, aged 5 months & 28 days. Her funeral will take place from the residence of her parents, on Dunbarton, between Congress & Washington sts, Gtwn, today at 5 P M.

TUE JUL 30, 1867
Deaths of well known citizens. 1-Mr E C Morgan, well & favorably known as an able practitioner at the bar of the Dist courts, died at his residence, 3rd & D sts. For some time past he has been lingering, & suffering great pain, & his death was not unexpected. His funeral is this afternoon at 4:30 P M. 2-Mr Eburn Bird, an old & well known citizen of the 7th Ward, died suddenly on Sunday of hemorrhage. He was walking about on the previous day in apparent usual health. He held the position of Corporation Lumber Inspector at the time of his death.

Equity Court-Chief Justice Cartter. 1-Frances Hawkins vs John L Hawkins. The order directs that the bill for divorce be dismissed at the cost of petitioner, & that the injunction heretofore granted against the dfndnt be dissolved. 2-Dorsey et al vs Florence. In this case a formal decree was entered, embodying, substantially, the judgment of the court as rendered in this case. It directs the payment by Mr Florence to the plntfs of the purchase money [$3,000] of the half-interest in a house at the corner of Pa ave & 17th st. This concludes this branch of the suit. The case of Towers vs Williams et al, relating to an incumbrance on the property, is still in court, not adjudicated.

Died: on Jul 29, Edwin C Morgan. His funeral will be from his late residence, corner of 3rd & D sts, this afternoon at 4:30 P M. [Jul 31st newspaper: E C Morgan; the remains were conveyed to the *Congressional Cemetery*; pall-bearers: Jos H Bradley, sr; Jas W Carlisle, Dr John B Blake, John J Johnson, Jas R Roach, John E Norris, John Van Riswick, & E J Middleton.]

Died: on Jul 29, Alice Victoria, only child of Thos & Wanda Williams, aged 7 months & 7 days.

Mr Geo Papendic, a broker of Boston, has died from a cut received from the bursting of a glass bottle, from which he was drawing a cork.

Supreme Court of D C; Equity 947-docket 8. Henry Cryer vs Cornelia Cryer. The bill of cmplnt charges adultery in the dfndnt, & prays for a decree to dissolve the bonds of matrimonty between the parties; subpoena issued on May 20, 1867, passed into the hands of the Marshal of D C, & was returned *non est*. Dfndnt to appear & answer the bill on or before the first Tuesday in Sep, 1867; otherwise the said bill to be taken for confessed. -R J Meigs, clerk

Bishop Rosecrans, of Cincinnati, it is said, is to be the successor of the late Bishop Timon, of Buffalo.

A very fat green turtle will be served, without abstraction of any of his luscious parts, today, at Hamlin's, on 6th st, Wash.

Richmond, Va, Jul 29. Govn'r Pierpont was this morning assaulted, at the *Executive Mansion*, by Mrs Driscoll, who was immediately arrested by the police. The assault was made because the Govn'r pardoned a man who was convicted of killing her son. The Govn'r was not injured.

WED JUL 31, 1867
Among the passengers who sailed on Sat for Europe in the French packet **Europe**: Mrs H D Cooke, Miss Kate M Cooke, Master Jay Cooke, Master H D Cooke, & Pitt Cooke, of Phil; Mrs Geo Jones & daughter, of N Y; & C Bodisco, of the Russian Legation.

Chancery sale; by virtue of a decree of the Supreme Court of D C, in chancery No 856, wherein Wm B Todd et al are cmplnts, & Julia Hallinan et al are dfndnts: public auction on Aug 21 next, of lot 14 in square 563, in Wash City, with a two story frame dwlg. -A Thoms Bradley, trustee -Cooper & Latimer, aucts

Orphans Court-Judge Purcell, Jul 30, 1867. 1-The will & codicil of John Rhodes, of Wash, D C, deceased, was admitted to probate & record, & letters testamentary issued to Eliz Ann Rhodes; bond $2,000. 2-The will of J Letitia Speaks, of Wash City, D C, was fully proven & admitted to probate & record, letters testamentary were issued to Michl E Bright; bond $2,000. 3-Jacob L Darwart was qualified as administrator to the personal estate of Cornelia Martin, deceased; bond $3,500. 4-John F Meline, jr, was qualified as administrator to the personal estate of Florant M Meline, deceased; bond $4,000. 5-Martha E Barnes was appointed guardian to the orphans of Jas Barnes, late of Wash, D C, deceased; bond $9,000. 6-The first & final account of Henry Seith, guardian to Augusta Seith, [now Chapman,] & the first individual account of Martha E Barnes, guardian to Jos Barnes, orphan of Jas Barnes, were approved & passed. 7-The Court postponed the hearing of the argument in the petition to appoint a receiver for the Fearson estate, owing to the illness of Walter S Cox, one of the attys for the legatees. 8-In repetition of Kate M Glazebrook against Mary E Langley, guardian to Richd M Glazebrook. This cause coming on to be heard, both parties being present, & witnesses examined on both sides. The court is of the opinion that injustice was done Mrs Kate M Glazebrook by certain ex parte affidavits heretofore filed, & the Court is further of the opinion that the said Kate M Glazebrook did not abandon the said minor child or her late husband, Thos J Glazebrook, deceased; & ordered that the said petition be entered of record. 9-Mr Fendall announced to the court the death, on yesterday, of Mr E C Morgan. After which the Court adjourned.

Court of Equity: the bill of Frances Hawkins vs John L Hawkins for divorce, on the ground of adultery, was dismissed.

Died: on Jul 30, Gertrude H, youngest daughter of the late Wm & Emily Dalton, in her 18th year. Her funeral will be from the M st Methodist Church, this afternoon, at 4 o'clock P M.

Died: on Jul 30, of bilious dysentery, Anna Maria, 2nd daughter of Mary J & the late John T Killmon. Her funeral will be from the residence of her mother, 2nd & D sts, on Thursday at 10 A M.

Marshal's sale on Aug 10 next, of one piano & cover, seized & levied upon as the goods & chattels of Francis Sweeny, & will be sold to satisfy said returno, & fieri facias, for cash, in favor of David S Gooding. –D S Gooding, U S Marshal, D C -W L Wall & Co, aucts

Marshal's public sale of schnr **Eagle**; for cash, Aug 5, at foot of 11st st, on the Potomac river, Wash City, D C. Danl Jackson is plntf. –David S Gooding, U S Marshal, D C

St Anna's Hall, a school for Young Ladies, near Brooksville, Montg Co, Md, will reopen on Sep 16th. –Rev O Hutton, A M, Rector.

Orphans Court of Wash Co, D C. Letters testamentary on the personal estate of Jas Rhodes, late of Wash City, D C, deceased. –Eliz Ann Rhodes, M E Knight, excs

Balt, Jul 30. This morning Geo Hanna, aged about 35, residing at 84 Centre Market Space, stabbed his wife in the breast with a huge butcher knife, & then drew the knife across his own throat, from which he died almost instantly. The woman is supposed to be mortally wounded. The cause is domestic infelicity.

THU AUG 1, 1867
Court of Equity, Chief Justice Cartter. 1-Myers vs Myers et al. Order appointing Jane C Myers guardian *ad litem*. 2-Green et al vs Harris. Decree appointing F W Jones trustee to sell.

Geo A Drescher was arrested yesterday, charged with assaulting Gotlieb Solp with intent to kill. The affair took place in the bakery of Mrs Vought, on H st, between 12th & 13th sts. On Jul 12, 1865, Solp received a serious blow across the head from an axe-handle, it is alleged, in the hands of Drescher; the latter made his escape from this city, but had temerity to return against after 2 years' absence. He was committed to jail, in default of $2,000 bail, to await the action of the grand jury in his case.

The copartnership existing between J H Barker & S Brinthall, is this day dissolved by limitation. Mr J H Barker is authorized to collect all the outstanding accounts of the late firm of Barker & Brinthall, I st, between 9th & 10th sts. –J H Barker, S Brinthall

Mrd: on Jul 29, at the Church of the Epiphany, by Rev Dr Hall, Brvt Lt Col Asa B Casey, U S A, to Miss Laura M Colby, of Wash City.

FRI AUG 2, 1867
A brilliant wedding took place yesterday at *Ingleside*, the residence of Gen Hiram Walbridge. The step-daughter of the Gen, Mrs Helen Simpson was united in matrimony to Dr J Phillips, Rev Dr D P Gurley officiating. Among the distinguished guests present, with many ladies, were Chief Justice Chase, Gen Spinner, Dist Atty Carrington, Henry D Cooke, Wm S Huntington, Joshua Pierce, [who gave away the bride,] & Surgeons Bradley, Middleton, & Carvalho, & others of the U S army. Gen & Mrs Walbridge gracefully dispensed their usual abundant hospitality.

Mr Jas F Essex, of Gtwn, died yesterday at his late residence in that city. Mr Essex was a wealthy & much esteemed resident; he was about 67 years of age, & a worthy member of Potomac Lodge.
+
Died: on Aug 1, Jas F Essex, sr, in his 67th year. His funeral will be from his late residence, 14 High st, Gtwn, D C, on Aug 4 at 3 o'clock P M. [Aug 5th newspaper: The funeral ceremonies of the late Jas T Essex, took place yesterday; religious services conducted by Rev Mr Shermer, of the Methodist Episcopal Church; pallbearers: Messrs J Hieston, Morris Adler, Wm H Wheatley, Wm E Beall, Saml Cropley, & Jenken Thomas. The body was interred at **Oak Hill Cemetery**, & was followed to the grave by a large & imposing funeral procession. At the grave the Masonic ceremonies for the burial of the dead were rendered in the usual solemn & impressive manner.]

Died: on Aug 1, after a week's illness, of hemorrhage of the bowels. Richd Harrison, late of Thorn, Yorkshire, England, aged 75 years, 2 months & 12 days. His funeral will be on Aug 4 at 3 o'clock P M, from McKendree Church, on Mass ave, between 9th & 10th sts. His late residence was 294 8th st, near M st north.

War Dept Claims Commission; Wash, D C, Jul 31, 1867. Statement of claims filed with the Com'r for the month of Jul, 1867.
Claim of Jas Crux, & of John H Garges, for destruction of property at Anandale, Va.
W H Fitzpatrick; Jonathan Mitchell; Wm S Reynolds; Jacob Barnhart; Henry Diggs; Isaac Jaraman; John Massingill; S O Whitten; Wm Allen; Sylvester Cooper; Chas Francis; Valentine Keel; & Wm Robbins, for services as scouts.
W D Higgins, for loss of horse & equipments.
Anthony Jourdan, for sutler's stores.
Thos H Potter, for services as secret police.
Haines & Campbell, for printing orders, etc, by the Petersburg [Va] Express.
Thos Powell, for rent of bldgs near Knoxville, Tenn.
John E Hayes, for advertising in the Savannah Republican.
Mrs Charlotte Roden, for compensation for services.
Wm Cameron & Co, for advertising in the Nashville Union.
Manderson & Keyser, for damages in the erection of **Fort Marshall**, Balt, Md.
-De Witt Clinton, Brvt Lt Col, Recorder

Public sale of valuable property, by decree of the Circuit Court of PG Co, [Md] in Equity; sale on Aug 19 next, a portion of the real estate belonging to the late Dr Archibald S Magruder, containing about 85 acres-about 1 mile south of Bladensburg, with a new & commodious cottage, kitchen, & all necessary out-bldgs, including a barn. Dr T L C Magruder, of Bladensburg, will show the property.
–C C Magruder, jr, trustee

Prof Chas Anthon, an eminent classical scholar, died in N Y on Monday, in his 70th year. Some of his works have become standard books in colleges & schools.

On Wed the widow of the late John P Wait committed suicide at Melrose, Mass, by drowning. She took with her to the pond her daughter, 12 years old, who is of weak intellect, who says her mother took off her shoes & stockings, & told her to carry them to a store & leave them, & then deliberately walked into the pond. The child did as she was told. The woman was about 50 years of age, in destitute circumstances, & had been in the habit of using a large quantity of opium.

SAT AUG 3, 1867
W J Bullock, a one-armed Confederate soldier, is teaching a colored school in Brookhaven, Miss.

Asa Keeler, postmaster of a village of Wyoming Co, Pa, recently deceased, was appointed by Pres Monroe. He was the oldest acting postmaster in the U S.

Wm Richardson, son of Capt Richardson, of the barge **Delhimes**, was drowned on Thursday at *Fort Washington*. He was sitting on the edge of the stake boat, & losing his balance, fell backward into the river. His body has not yet been found.

On Thu the son of Chas Miller, butcher, residing in 10th st, was kicked in the face by a horse belonging to Mr Arnold. It is doubtful whether the lad recovers from the injury, the physicians being of the opinion that the skull is fractured & the spinal column dislocated.

List of ofcrs at the jail: Warden, W H Huestis; Deputy Warden, A B Cate; guards, John Bell, Benton Russ, Joah Noyes, Isaac W Ross, Amon Duvall, Robt Strong, Robt Waters, & Jas Coleman. M T E Chandler, John T Cronin, & John Shaw, former ofcrs, resigned their positions. Mr Huestis returned from Albany on Wed having turned Sanford Conover over to the keeper of the penitentiary for a residence at that place for 10 years.

At Lafayette, Ind, on Thu, Hon Danl Mace, ex-Congressman, & present Postmaster, committed suicide by shooting himself with a pistol. Deceased was stricken with paralysis while in this city, a year ago, & never entirely recovered. He was a great sufferer, & has contemplated self destruction for some time. Mr Mace was a native of Ross Co, Ohio, where the first years of his life were spent. He was admitted to the bar & removed to Indiana. In 1855, his time having expired, the deceased retired to private life, in which he ever remained.

Duel between Littleton Wells, about 22, & Sanford B Roberts, about 24, about a mile from the Welby Post Ofc, Ky, on Jul 21, 1867, left Wells dead, & Roberts sinking rapidly; & cannot possibly live more than an hour. The duel was over the hand of a young lady of the neighborhood. Wells leaves a widowed mother & 2 sisters to mourn his loss. Roberts leaves no family.

The undersigned, this day, have formed a copartnership, under the style of H F Davis & Co, for the transaction of a Wholesale Grocery & Provision Business at 399 Pa ave, the storehouse formerly occupied by the late Mr Saml Tilston.
–H F Davis, B Edw J Eils

MON AUG 5, 1867

Mr Robt Radcliffe, from Nanjemoy, St Chas Co, Md, was run over by car No 8 of the Metropolitan horse railroad last evening near N J & D st, & his left arm was found badly fractured at the elbow joint; he was removed to the American House, & consultation was held to decide whether an operation would be performed.

Application made for new certificate of land warrant No 56, 366, for 80 acres in the name of Marvin Morgan, granted Apr 10, 1854, the same alleged to be lost or destroyed. –Jos H Barrett, Com'r

On Sat Mr Henry B Bowen recovered the body of Capt Enoch F Ruth, who left his residence on Friday, & was traced to the 6th st wharf, where his hat was found. Saturday morning the body was seen floating astern the tugboat **Fisher**. Jury rendered a verdict that the deceased came to his death by suicide from drowning, while laboring under insanity. Capt Ruth was Chief Clerk of the Finance Division, Indian Ofc, Dept of the Interior, & was about 50 years of age. He was a son-in-law of Hon Alex'r Dimitry, formerly translator of the State Dept, & leaves a widow & several children. In June last he attempted suicide by shooting himself in the head with a pistol; the wound was not serious. Arrangement are being made for his interment.

Orphans Court, Aug 3, 1867. 1-John De Vaughn filed his objections to the probate of the will of the late Saml De Vaughn, giving as his reasons that the proper probate is not the last will of the deceased, & was revoked, cancelled, & annulled; that it was procured by undue influence & fraud, & was not properly executed. 2-The Fearson will case was taken up, the question being on the appointment of a collector to take charge of the estate during the pendency of the appeal taking from the revocation of the letters, & Mr Cox, for the legatee, argued against the appointment of the collector. Messrs Davidge & J H Johnson appear for the contestants of the will. 3-The last will & testament of J Andrew Fisher, of Wash, D C, deceased, was filed & partially proven. He constitutes & appoints therein his wife Margaret Fisher, as his excx. 4-The will of J Philip Wetzel, of Wash, D C, deceased, was filed & fully proven, & letters testatmentary granted to Mary Wetzel; bond $5,000. 5-The fourth & supplementary account of the exc of Susan H Swahan, deceased, & the first & final account of the guardian of Augusta Seitz [now Chapman] were approved & passed. 6-Wallace St C Redman was qualified as adm on the personal estate of John W Burke, deceased; bond $3,000. 7-Wm Y Fendall was qaulified as adm of personal estate of Edwin C Morgan, deceased; bond $1,500. 8-Mary Wetzel was appointed guardian to the orphans of Philip Wetzel, deceased; bond $1,000.

As we go to press, we regret to hear of the death Col E E Camp, U S army, who died last evening, at the residence of his father-in-law, J P Keller.

John E Norris, atty for Miss Jennie Perry, has entered suit in the Circuit Court of this District, against Mr Thos Hoover for breach of promise of marriage. The damages have been laid at $3,000.

Fr W H Holman, the oldest methodist minister in Ky, died at Centreville, Ind, on Friday, aged 77 years.

Mr Saml Beadlee died at Boston on Thursday, in his 80th year.

The foundry of Chas Kilgour, in Cincinnati, was destroyed by fire on Saturday morning. The loss : $20,000.

Died: on Aug 4, Mrs Eliz A Beall, wife of the late Horatio Beall, & daughter of the late Samson Simms. Her funeral will take place from her late residence, 486 L st, between 10th & 11th sts, on Tue at 4 P M. [N Y & Calif papers please copy.]

Died: on Aug 1, after a long & painful illness, Mrs Catharine Norman, of Phil, in her 70th year. Her funeral will be observed on Monday at the residence of her son-in-law, Hon Thos B Florence, 614 7th st, South Washington. Interment on Aug 6, at 6 o'clock, in *Monument Cemetery*, North Broad st, Phil City.

Richmond, Aug 4. Wm P Bailey, of Balt, was run over & killed on the Petersburg railroad last night.

Trustee's sale of part of lot 1 in square 525, with a Brick Church, known as *Bouldin Church*; sale on Aug 26; by deed of trust made on Jul 28, 1862, recorded in Liber J A S, No 220, folio 343. –M V B Bogan, trustee -Green & Williams, aucts

Orphans Court of Wash Co, D C. Letters of administration on the personal estate of Edwin C Morgan, late of Wash, D C, deceased. –W Y Fendall, adm

TUE AUG 6, 1867
Obit-died: on Jul 10, 1867, in her 77th year, Catharine, relict of the late Reynold Grimes, of Barbadoes, & daughter of the late Wm Lindsay & Ann Calvert, of Va. She was for 40 years a consistent member of the Methodist Episcopal Church, & a truly devoted mother. Her children, most of whom were permitted to be present & witness her calm & peaceful departure, seemed to be, next to her God, the chief objects of her affection. Due to infirmity of age, she was, for several years subjected to much bodily affliction, which she bore without a murmur. She is now at rest. [Alexandria Gaz please copy.]

Tuscarora Academy, Pa, 50 miles west of Harrisburg, opens its 32nd year Sep 4. -J H Shumaker, A M, Academia, Juniata Co, Pa.

The following is the recommendation for mercy in the case of Mrs Surratt, prepared by Hon John A Bingham & signed by a majority of the court-martial which tried & convicted her: The undersigned, members of the military commission detailed to try Mary E Surratt & others for the conspiracy & the murder of Abraham Lincoln, Pres of the U S, etc, respectfully pray that the Pres, in consideration of the sex & age of said Mary E Surratt, if he can, upon all the facts in the case, find it consistent with his sense of duty to the country, to commute the sentence of death which the court have been constrained to pronounce to imprisonment in the penitentiary for life. Respectfully submitted: D Hunter, Maj Gen, Pres; Aug Kautz, Brig & Brvt Maj Gen; R S Foster, Brig & Brvt Maj Gen; Jas A Ekin, Brvt Brig Gen; Chas H Tompkins, Brvt Col & Acting Quartermaster. [Aug 7th newspaper: The Pres says the official record was presented to him by Gen Holt, & it was signed in his presence; that at that time no recommendation for commutation of sentence of Mrs Surratt was attached to the papers.]

An announcement was made yesterday of the sudden death of Col Camp, whose long residence in Wash had endeared him to many of our citizens. He entered the army in 1847; subsequently resigned, & was reappointed in 1857; in 1864 or 1865 he was assigned to duty at City Point, supplying the various armies in Va; more recently he has had the supervision of important depots on the frontier, & returned to this city about a month since. His death was sudden.
+
Died: on Aug 4, in Wash City, Brvt Lt Col Elisha E Camp, Assist Quartermaster U S Army. His funeral will take place at the Church of the Epiphany, on Aug 7, at 4 o'clock.
[Aug 8th newspaper: The remains of Col Camp were taken to the ***Congressional Burying Ground***; pall-bearers were: Brig Gen Pelouze, Brvt Brig Gen Perry, Brvt Brig Gen N Michler, Brvt Maj Gen Chard, Col Potter, Col Taylor, Lt Col Crilly, & Col M Luddington.]

King Otho, of Greece, whose death has been announced, was the 2nd son of Louis I, King of Bavaria. In 1832 the people of Greece offered him the throne, which he accepted, but he did not assume full control of the goverment until 1835, & in the succeeding year he married the Princess Frederica Amelia, of Oldenberg.

Chancery sale of improved real estate on L st, between 9th & 10th sts, by decree of the Supreme Court of D C, passed in chancery, No 711, docket 8, McDuell vs McDuell: public auction on Aug 17, next, on the premises, part of square 369, being the s e corner of lot 4: with a 2 story frame dwlg house, with attic & a small back bldg. -Robt McDuell, trustee -J T Coldwell & Co, aucts

Supreme Court of D C, Equity No 983, Docket 8. C W Sonnenschmidt et ux vs Jos Fugitt et al. On the motion of the cmplnts, by Mr Isaac L Johnson, their solicitor, ordered that the dfndnts Israel & Harriet McJilton cause their appearance on or before the first rule day occurring 40 days after this day. –R J Meigs, clerk

Fenwick & Stewart, Wholesale & Retail dealers in sash, doors, blinds, mouldings, brackets, etc. Ofc, west side of 7th st, at Canal Bridge, Wash, D C.

Orphans Court of Wash Co, D C, Aug 3, 1867. In the case of Harriott M Sullivan & John B Blake, excs of John T Sullivan, deceased, the executors & Court have appointed Sep 3 next, for the final settlement of the personal estate of the said deceased, of the assets in hand. -Jas R O'Beirne, Reg/o wills

WED AUG 7, 1867
Lynchburg Republican of Tuesday. On Sunday the Orange & Alexandria train ran over Ambrose Mitchell, who was lying on the track, & completely severed his right leg midway between the knee & ankle. When found he was completely dead, & it is supposed he was first killed then placed on the track. His right temple had a small wound, possibly from a pistol ball, known as a slug. Mr Mitchell was employed on the Va & Tenn railroad, at Forrest depot, & was on his way home, near Buford's depot, in Amherst. He was about 45 years of age, a worthy & deserving man, & leaves a family consisting of a wife & 5 or 6 children.

Orphans Court-Judge Purcell. 1-The will of Chas Keenan, deceased, of Wash City, D C, was admitted to probate, & letters of administration, W A, were granted to John F Callan; bond $12,000. 2-Eliz Ann Rhodes was appointed as guardian to the orphans of Jas Rhodes, deceased; bond $2,000. 3-Wm Chambers was appointed guardian to the orphans of Jas McDonald, of Wash, D C, deceased; bond $7,000. 4-Jos Redfern was qualified as adm to the personal estate of Saml Redfern, of Wash, D C, deceased; bond $140,000. 5-The first & final account of the adm of Edw H Fuller, deceased, was passed & approved. 6-The adm of the estate of Thos McGran, deceased, appeared before the court, declining to receive certain monies of the said estate, & desiring to be discharged from further duty as adm to said McGran. 7-Evelina P Morgan was appointed guardian to the orphans of Edwin Morgan, deceased; bond $6,500.

Equity Court-Aug 6, 1867. 1-Aaron S Gorham vs Truman Brush et al; order of publication. 2-Jas P Wollard vs John D Ellis et al; order appointing John D Ellis guardian ad litem. 3-Monica A Butler vs Mary Chiseltine, rule to show cause why injunction should not issue. 4-Henry Johnson vs Jos Nock et al, & Thos S Clayton vs same; orders setting Sep 3 for hearing motions for injunction; the order to serve as injunction until hearing. 5-In re estate of Susan Ford, an order was made appointing Robt C Fox trustee.

Levy Court-Aug 5, 1867. Communication received from Mrs Mary E Stanloup, praying abatement of a tax assessed against her property in the county; which was referred to the assessors. 2-The bill of the <u>Evening Star</u> for printing the valedictory speech of N Sargent, late president of the court, was presented, & referred to the Cmte on Claims. 3-The bills of W H Calhoun, Wm Smith, G H Plant, & B D Carpenter were presented & ordered to be paid.

Orphans Court of Wash Co, D C. Letters of administration on the personal estate of Saml Redfern, late of Wash City, D C, deceased. –Jos Redfern, W Wilson, adms

Fred'k College, Fred'k City, Md, will elect a Professor of Mathematics, Natural Philosophy, etc; applications must be sent to J S Bonsall, Principal, directed Winchester, Va, until Aug 17, afterwards to Fred'k City, Md. By order of the Board, Saml Tyler, Pres

Dr E O Donhoff lives on Jefferson st, between Brook & 1st st, & he & his lady spent a good deal of time in their garden. While the Dr was away for the day, Mrs Donhoff was bit twice by the bees, & later found a corpse in her garden. Her husband returned from the country, bringing her flowers, & soon heard the sad news. The deceased was subject to apoplexy, having had an attack a few years ago, & it was more probable that she was frightened into a fit of apoplexy by the sting of the bees. She was a lady beloved by all who knew her; an affectionate wife & mother. –Louisville Democrat, Aug 4.

The train that left Cincinnati for Chicago, on Friday, struck a broken rail near Royal Centre, & the sleeping cars were thrown from the track. A child was jolted through a window & killed, & Miss Kate Lee, of Cincinnati, severely injured.

Mrd: at the British Legation, in Berne, Switzerland, Jul 15, by Rev Edw Dillon, Horace Rumbold, Sec to her Majesty's Legation, to Caroline Barney, daughter of Hon Geo Harrington, American Minister near the Swiss Confederation.

Died: on Aug 6, after a lingering illness, Mrs Mary Ann White, aged 52 years. Her funeral will take place from the residence of her son-in-law, Jas C Dulin, Ga ave, near 10th st, on Aug 8 at 4 o'clock P M.

Died: on Aug 2, near Oxford, Talbot Co, Md, Thomas Corcoran Matthews, infant son of Chas M & Emily C Matthews, of Gtwn, D C, aged 5 months & 21 days.

Died: on Aug 6, Jas Fullalove, in his 80th year, a native of Lincolnshire, England, but for the last 50 years a resident of Gtwn, D C. His funeral will be on Thursday afternoon, at 5 o'clock, from the residence of his son-in-law, John M Stake, 54 Bridge st, Gtwn. [Express please copy.]

Harrisburg, Aug 6. Ex-Govn'r David R Porter died at his residence in this city this afternoon after a brief illness: he was in his 79th year; a man of large & vigorous mind, which remained unclouded until the hour of his death.

Balt, Aug 6. Mrs Jefferson Davis arrived in this city today on the steamer from Charleston, & proceed tomorrow to join her husband in Canada.

Charleston, Aug 6. Benj Thompson, a wealthy planter, of Beaufort, S C, recently placed in the insane asylum at Columbia, committed suicide by hanging yesterday. His insanity arose from depression caused by the present condition of the country.

Alnwick Seminary, for Young Ladies. The duties were suspended for a time, owing to the unsettled condition of the country. The school will be resumed on Sep 2. For particulars address M A Tyson & sisters, Laurel, Md.

THU AUG 8, 1867

Oldest Inhabitants monthly meeting was held yesterday, City Hall, Col Williams, vice pres, in the chair, & John F Callan, sec pro tem. Dr Jas Hall & Mr Brough were selected members. J C Brent submitted to the society an india ink sketch of the Old Capitol, made by the late Thos Underwood, of Phil, engineer in 1815, representing it as it was after the burning by the British troops; & Stell's tavern, on First st east, Elliott's school-house, as in 1805 & 1806; also, the old Bank of Wash, next to the Columbia Enigne-House, on N J, in the same years. Description of the same was contributed by Mr John Underwood, now of Dublin, Ind, & for many years a resident of Wash. Gardner, the photographer, will make copies of it for the benefit of the members.

Gustavius Dore is scarcely 30 years old, but he has made designs for over 50,000 wood engravings, which have been published.

Henry Gerhe, of Cincinnati, put his head out of the car window for a breath of fresh air near that city, Sunday, when the train was passing over a bridge the timbers of which struck his head, severing it instantly from his body.

A passenger train on the Connecticut River railroad, Monday, ran into a carriage near Springfield, Mass, containing Mrs Alex'r Chapin & Mrs Nathan Dunbar. Mrs Chapin will probably die from her injuries; Mrs Dunbar, though carried some distance by the locomotive, was not severely hurt.

Trial of John H Surratt, Aug 7, 1867. The jurymen are provided with food from their homes, the Gov't supplies ceasing from the moment the case is given to them. What the result will be no one can now tell; but it is generally believed that Surratt will either be acquitted or they will fail to agree. [Note: John H Surratt died on Apr 21, 1916, in Balt, Md.]

Ida Virginia Jones, age 4 years, daughter of Mr Jas H Jones, living on Church st, near Queen, was accidentally shot & killed by her brother, age 6 years, on Sat last. The gun was an old one that had been lying around for a length of time, without a hammer, not loaded. It is said by some that the boy struck the cone with a hammer, & by others that he fell & struck the cone against some hard substance, which caused the explosion. Both parents were home at the time. –Norfolk Day Book, 5th

J Rubel, a merchant in Milwaukee, hanged himself on Wed, on account of reverses in business.

Nashville, Aug 7. 1-At Clarkesville, on Sat, Frank McGuire was shot dead by Young, the bar-keeper that recently killed Gueretta. 2-On Sunday, the mate of the steamer J S Graham, was shot & killed in a difficulty with a young man in Clarkesville,

The reason assigned for Mr Tennyson's abandonment of his beautiful residence at Farrington, Isle of Wight, & his retreat to Hashmere, in Surrey, is, that he was tormented by the obtrusive attentions of the lion hunters, who hung onto his palings, peeped through his gates, & fairly crammed Freshwater Church on Sunday, in hope of seeing how a poet laureate said his prayers.

Died: on Aug 7, after a protracted illness, Col Jos Peck, [late a clerk in the 6th Auditor's Ofc,] in his 58th year. His funeral is on Fri at 4 o'clock, from his late residence, 379 E st.

Died: on Aug 7, in Wash City, in her 81st year, Mrs Margaret Smith. Her funeral is on Aug 9 at 4 o'clock, from the residence of her daughter, Mrs S V Walker, 431, corner of 14th & I sts.

Died: on Aug 6, at Brooklyn, L I, Harry, aged 1 year, 4 months & 24 days; & on Aug 7 Lillie, aged 4 months, children of Thos J & Charlotte M Fisher.

Ten handsome & desirable villa sites at auction on the **Heights of Oak Lawn**, the residence of Thos P Morgan; on Aug 15, on the road leading from 20th st, between the residences of John Little & Thos P Morgan, being the north portion of **Oak Lawn**, the residence of Thos P Morgan. -Cooper & Latimer, aucts

Dept of the Interior, U S Patent Ofc, Wash, Aug 5, 1867. Ptn of Charlotte B Thompson, admx of John H Thomspson, deceased, Jas M Thompson, & Hoses Q Thompson, of Holderness, N H, praying for the extension of a patent granted to the said Messrs Thompson Nov 15, 1853, for an improvement in Machine for Trimming Soles of Boots & Shoes, for seven years from the expiration of said patent, which takes place on Nov 15, 1867. -T C Theaker, Com'r of Patents

A Paris letter says Gen McClellan, who has been living very quietly for more than a year in Switzerland, has taken his passage home for November.

FRI AUG 9, 1867
Harrisburg, Pa, Aug 8. The funeral of Ex-Govn'r Porter was attended by a large concourse of persons; business was suspended, & depts were closed. The remains were deposited in **Mount Kalma Cemetery**. He leaves a widow, 4 sons, & 1 daughter.

$50 will be paid by the Mechanics' Lodge, No 18, I O O F, for the recovery of the body of P G T Fenton Evans, who is supposed to have drowned on Monday last between Giesboro & 6th st wharf. –J Dod Robinson, H G Divine, C C Thomas, Cmte +

The body of Mr T Fenton Evans was found; he is between 35 or 40 years old; a stout man with dark whiskers mixed with grey, goatee, hair on the head thin, with a pocket book containing a small sum of money, a double-cased silver watch & chain, a finger-ring, an Odd Fellows' breastpin, pinknife, dirk knife, & a pocket comb

We regret to announce the death of Col Jos Peck, an old & highly respected citizen of Wash, & for many years known as an extensive meat dealer in our market, & who with Mr Walker, as the firm of Walker & Peck, at one time were the heaviest butchers in Wash City. Col Peck was born in Gtwn; & at the one time a prominent member of the organization of the Pres' Mounted Guard, he was honored by the company by being elected captain. He commanded the company until its dissolution. He was appointed justice of the peace, & for the last 2 years has been a clerk of the 6th Auditor's Ofc. His funeral will take place this afternoon.

Fire Dept changes: Saml Dawes had been appointed hostler of No 2 engine, vice Phillip Estel, dismissed. Augustus Stitz appointed supernumerary of no 2 engine, vice Moulder, dismissed. The following changes have been made in the force of No 3 engine: E B Gatton, [hostler,] appointed fireman; Michl Kane, hostler; Conrad Kaufman, extraman; Noble Bassett, supernumerary, vice John Smoot, John Reynolds, & John Read; Frank Fay & John Gidney appointed supernumeraries, vice Jos A Smith, dismissed.

The Hannah More Academy, a School for Girls, near Reisterstown, 15 miles from Balt, Md, will begin Sep 18, 1867. –Rev Arthur J Rich, M D, Reistertown, Md.

N Y, Aug 8. The bark **Marco Palo**, from Bremen, has arrived. Three deaths occurred on board during the trip. On Aug 5 she fell in with a raft, on which was Capt Ginn, of the bark **Oak Ridge**, from Phil for Boston, which foundered in the hurricane of Aug 2. Capt Ginn was the only person saved. The crew consisted of 9 persons in all: Jas R Ginn was mate, & Albert H Ginn was seaman. The others were newly shipped & their names are unknown.

Chancery sale of valuable real estate at auction; Equity No 976. Johanna E Rupert & John Rupert, cmplnts vs Bernard Geier & Louisa Thomas, dfndnts. By decree of this Court I will sell, on Aug 22 next, on the premises, lot 11 in square 673, with improvements, which are, on part of Lot 22, a large 3 story brick house, with 13 rooms; the lot has a front of 70 feet on M st, & 136 feet deep; on lot 23 is a large 2 story frame house; lot fronts 137 feet 3 inches on North Capitol st, with a depth of 70 feet; making both pieces of property very valuable. –Bernard Geier, exc & trustee -Green & Williams, aucts

Trial of John H Surratt, Aug 8, 1867. Judge Fisher returned to the court-room at 6 o'clock this evening, &, as the jury was not yet prepared to report, he returned to his home in Gtwn, saying that he would not be back until tomorrow morning, at 10 o'clock. He gave the officers permission to go home, & the crowd, which had been in attendance all day, immediately separated & took their departure.

On Monday an engine, on its way from Connellsville to Pittsburg, exploded near Layton's station, & the conductor, Patrick Kelly was killed; & Saml Page, fireman, was killed. Mr John Carr, division foreman, was seriously hurt; the engineer, Mr Ludwick, was hurt badly in the side, & had his right leg broken; D Odinel, fireman, was hurt.

SAT AUG 10, 1867

Clara Louise Kellogg, the opera singer, purchased her old homestead at Hartford, Conn, last week, & after her return from Europe, this fall, it is said, will retire from the stage to private life there.

Jordan Potter, of Wiscasset, Maine, recently drove a nail into his own head, while partially insane, & died from the results in a few days after.

Trial of John H Surratt, Aug 9, 1867. At half-past 10 o'clock, the Surratt jury has not reported. It is now 59 days [including Sundays] since the first juror, Mr Todd, was sworn. The prisoner was visited this morning by his brother, Isaac Surratt. Mr Birth, one of the jurors, has been very sick all day, but he is somewhat better this evening. At 8:45 P M the crowd was ordered from the court-room; the Marshal closed the doors.

Green & Williams, aucts, on Tue, sold lots 63 thru 65, in subdivision of lots 1 thru 6 & lot 17, in sq 620, to John Rupert, at 20 cents per foot. Lot 66, in same subdivision to Nelson Adams, at 20 cents per foot. Lots 6 & 7, 68 thru 71, in same subdivision, to John Rupert, at 14 cents per foot, & lots 72 & 73 to John Rupert, at 19 cents per foot. Part of lot 22 in square 620, with a 3 story brick house, to John Rupert, for $5,000. Part of lot 23, in square 620, with a frame house to John Rupert, for $2,150. A 2 story frame house on 20th st west, between L & M sts, to Saml English, at $575.

Died: on Aug 9, Thos Fenton Evans, in his 43rd year. His funeral will be from his late residence, 4th, near Fred'k st, Gtwn, Sunday, tomorrow, at 4 o'clock P M. [Aug 12th newspaper: the funeral of T F Evans, who was accidentally drowned by falling from the steamer **Hi Livingston**, on Aug 3, took place yesterday from his residence in Gtwn. The Grand Lodge of I O O F, together with Mechanics' Lodge of Gtwn, accompanied by Heald's Band, escorted the remains to **Oak Hill Cemetery**, where the body was interred.]

Stanmore School for girls, Sandy Spring, Montg Co, Md: will commence on Oct 1. -C H Millen, principal. Mary P Coffin, Ellen Farquhar. References: Philip R Fendall, Wash, D C; Benj Hallowell & Richd S Kirk, Sandy Spring, Md.

Rock Hill, or *Kalorama*. This beautiful seat was orginally founded by Augustus H Scott, a lawyer of distinction & great wealth, who came here from Cambridge, on the eastern Shore, Md, & built an elegant home shortly after the capital was here located. There was a blood relationship as well as a warm friendship between Washington & this Scott family, & the former is known to have contributed his advice in the selection of *Rock Hill*, as *Kalorama* was originally named by its proprietor. The *Rock Hill Mansion*, which burnt a year or two ago during its occupation as a smallpox hospital, now stands with blackened & tumbling walls; the corner stone was laid about 1798; Washington regretted not being able to attend. Washington & his family often visited *Rock Hill Mansion*; Maj Wm Bushrod Scott, of the Marine Corps, & who, in the latter part of his life was for 12 years navy agent in Wash City, was a son of the proprietor of *Rock Hill*. Maj Scott's family still resides in Wash City. At the death of the *Rock Hill* proprietor, which ocurred more than half a century ago, the executors of the estate, sold the property for $16,000 to Joel Barlow, the famous poet & politician, who gave it the name of *Kalorama*. Joel Barlow was born in Conn in 1755, educated at Dartmouth & Yale Colleges, graduating at the latter in 1778; he studied law; then went into theology for 6 weeks, & thence into the army as a chaplain; at the close of the war he settled in the law at Hartford; in 1788 he went to England. Washington appointed him Consul to Algiers; he returned to this country & took up residence in Wash in 1805; in 1811 he was sent by Madison, Minister to France. He embarked in his Russian campaign, to a consultation at Wilna, & died on his way, in a Jewish cottage, whither he was borne in his sick condition, at Zarowitch, near Cracow, in Poland, in Dec, 1812. The brick tomb at *Kalorama* is still in a fine state of preservation. From the marble slabs inserted in the walls of the structure we copied: "Sacred to the repose of the mediatation of the living." Joel Barlow, patriot, poet, and philosopher, lies buried at Zarnaw, in Poland, where he died 26th December, 1812, aged 57 years. Ruth Baldwin Barlow, his wife, died 29th May, 1818, aged 62 years. Abraham Baldwin, her brother, died a Senator in Congress from Georgia, 4th March, 1807, aged 52 years. His memory needs no marble; his county is his monument; her constitution his greatest work. On the other slab are the following inscriptions pertaining to the family, who came to Kalorama as successors of the Barlow family: George Bomford, Colonel of the U S Ordnance Corps, died 25 March, 1848, aged 64. Clara, relict of Colonel Bomford, died 5th of December, 1855, aged 71 years. Henry Baldwin, whose epitaph is on this slab was a native of New Haven, & a graduate of Yale College; emigrated to Pa, & was a conspicuous lawyer & a member of Congress before going upon the bench. He died in Phil, as also Col Bomford, & all the above named members of the family, it is believed. Col Bomford resided many years at *Kalorama*; some years before his death, which occurred at Boston, in 1848, Col Bomford exchanged *Kalorama* for some property in Phil, & took up his residence in that city, though the family tomb of the Barlow, the Baldwin, & Bomford families seems to have been retained. Col Bomford invented the well-known bomb-cannon used in the war of 1812, named the Columbiad, which was slightly changed by Gen Paixhan, & called the Paixhan gun. Mr Fletcher exchanged property with Col Bomford, & with his family resided at *Kalorama* some years when the rebellion came. The place was leased early in the war to the Govn't at $5,000 per year, for a small-pox hospital. Johnny Graham, a kind old man, but so paralyzed to be unable hardly to give us his name, seems to have the care of the grounds for the owner, as his father before him. At the western side of the *Kalorama* seat, on the bank of Rock Creek, is the flouring establishment owned by John Quincey Adams when Pres, & which many years ago was purchased by its present enterprising proprietor, Mr Evan Lyons. Mr Lyons has a fine rural residence in the grove on the terraced declivity, with some 40 acres of fine land. It was on this territory that Madame Mopang, the stubbed, smart, nondescript French woman, cultivated her garden & poultry, & carried her vegetable & chickens-shikens-to market on her ancient jackass. Within the *Kalorama* tomb are deposited the *ashes of Cmdor Stephen Decatur, who fell mortally wounded in a duel, by the hand of Cmdor Jas Barron, in 1820. Cmdor Decatur, the prince of the American navy, was born at Sinnepuxent, Eastern Shore, Md, in 1779, the son of a cmdor of Rhode Island, whose honored name he bore. Cmdor Barron, son of the distinguished father, was born at Hampton, Va, in 1768. Commencing service as lt the same year as did Cmdor Decatur, in 1798, the date of the organization of the present navy, he had won a high place as an ofcr, being regarded as one of the best disciplinarians in the service, when, in 1807, the unfortunate affair of the **Cheseapeake** threw a shadow over his life. On Jun 22, 1807, the frig **Chesapeake** of 38 guns, bearing the broad pennant of Cmdor Barron, got under way from Hampton Roads, bound to the Mediterranean. On the same day the English ship **Leopard**, 50 guns, left the same anchorage, a few miles ahead. In the afternoon of that day the **Leopard**, hailing the **Chesapeake**, sent a despatch to Cmdor Barron, signed by Vice Admiral Berkely, ordering the search of the **Chesapeake** for deserters. The **Leopard**, ready for action, had taken the American ship in utter surprise, as she had proceeded to sea with her decks literally piled with cables, stores, & even cabin furniture. The guns were loaded, but rammers, wads, matches, gun-locks, & powder-horns were all wanting. The crew was raw, her force inferior, & she was utterly unable to engage the **Leopard**, the amazement being that a man-of-war should have ever gone to sea in such condition, though it should be stated that, according to the customs of the navy, the equipment for sea had been confided to Capt Gordon, who was the ofcr in immediate command, & of high standing. Cmdor Barron declined to allow the search, & the **Leopard** immediately opened, & continued fire till Cmdor Barron, finding himself helpless, ordered his colors struck. The ship received 21 shot, & had 3 killed & 18 wounded, Cmdor Barron being among the latter. Four men, claimed as English deserters, were taken out of her. They succeeded in firing one gun only on the **Chesapeake**, that by the use of a coal brought from the galley just as the colors were hauled down. Cmdor Barron was court-martialed for the affair, & suspended from duty for 5 years, without pay or emoluments, Cmdor Decatur being a member of the court that rendered the sentence. Barron was absent from the country during the war of 1812, & on his return, long after the sentence had expired, sought to be reinstated in duty. Decatur was exceedingly averse to his wishes, & hence arose the duel. They met at Bladensburg, Mar 22, 1820. Capt Wm Bainbridge was the second of Decatur, & Capt Jesse O Elliot of Barron. They fought with pistols at 8 paces. Capts Roger & Porter were among the spectators. Before the fire Barron said to Decatur, that "he hoped on meeting in another world, they would be better friends than in this;" to which Decatur replied, "I have never been your enemy sir." They fired & both fell to the ground, their heads were within 10 feet of each other. Decatur revived after a while, & he & Barron had a parley as they lay on the ground. [Decatur, over & over, in his correspondence with Barron, disclaimed all personal animosity.] He was brought to Wash City in a dying condition, & survived but a few hours, dying in the course of the night, at his residence, corner of H & 16½ sts, a spacious mansion, still known as the **Cmdor Decatur House**. He left no children. His death fell with overwhelming sorrow upon his wife, who betook herself to an almost entire seclusion from the world, becoming a most devout convert to the Catholic faith, & devoting her entire widowed life of some 40 years to the severest self denials & pious austerities. For many years she resided in a humble house near the college gate, on Gtwn Heights, & was ever to be daily found in the old Trinity Church, near her house, on her knees at her devotions till 12 o'clock, & this to the end of her life. In her last years she lived in a small & humble dwlg near the convent, & in pious converse & devotion with the sisters. She was very poor, being compelled in her extremity to part with even the magnificent sword & gold medal of her husband, presented him by Congress for his illustrious achievements in the Mediterranean. Her remains now slumber in the old **Catholic cemetery**, where so many of the best early citizens of the District have their last repose. Since writing this, we have been informed that the *remains of Decatur were transferred from the **Kalorama** vault, & after resting there nearly half a century, & are deposited by the side of those of his father, in Phil. The Barlows, Baldwins, & Bomford families were evidently allied to each other, & we believe such to be the case between them & the Decatur family.

MON AUG 12, 1867
Marshal D S Gooding has gone to his home in Chicago, where he expects to remain until October.

Fire in Gtwn-$13,000 worth of property destroyed for want of a fire alarm telegraph. Yesterday fire was discovered in a frame bldg occupied by C Myers as a wheelwright shop, on Prospect st, near High; the steam fire engine Henry Addison promptly responded. The principal sufferers were Henry Kengla, loss $5,000; Jas Ridgway, $3,000; R Pettit, $1,500; C Myers, $2,000; A Hess, [lot of meat] $500; Isaac Barrett, $180; John Reily, $300. The fire was undoubtedly the work of an incendiary.

Mr John Colburn, who died at his residence at 13th & N Y ave, on Aug 9, was connected with the business enterprizes of half a century ago in Wash City. He came to this city from the State of Vt, in 1814, at age 18 years, & was known & respected here as an intellgent & honorable business man & Christian gentleman. He was at one time the proprietor of the Mansion House hotel, but for some 40 years had been in the mercantile business; was on confidential intimacy with Pres Monroe; & a member of the Foundry Church. His funeral took place at the Foundry Church yesterday & his remains were deposited in the **Congressional Burying Ground**. Mr Coburn, at his decease, was 71 years of age. He leaves a wife & several sons & daughters to mourn their loss.

Mr J W Fitch, the Wash correspondent of the Boston Post, died at his residence in Gtwn, D C, on Sat, after an illness of 8 weeks, from typhoid fever. Although young, he has been connected with several prominent journals of the country. His funeral took place yesterday. [Aug 15th newspaper: Mr J Walton Fitch was born in Newton, Sussex Co, N J, Mar 1, 1844, & died in the city of Gtwn, D C, Aug 10, 1867; he was home instructed by his parents & private tutors, & entered the study of law in Milwaukie, Wisc, to which city his parents had removed, but his delicate health prevented him from completing his studies, & he entered upon his editorial career before he was 21, a local editor of the Milwaukie Daily News.]

Mr Chas Dickens is certainly coming to this country, his agent having left England to arrange the preliminaries.

Berry Amos, a well known sporting man, was shot & mortally wounded in Richmond, on Sat, by a man named Moses Levy.

London, Aug 11. Ira Aldridge, the celebrated African tragedian, is dead. He died while he was on a professional tour in Poland. [Aug 14th newspaper: Aldridge, whose real name is said to have been Hewlet, was born in a village called *Bellair*, near Balt, Md, around 1816, & was apprenticed to a ship carpenter, learning his trade in the same yard with Molyneux, the notorious negro pugilist & prize-fighter. From association with the German population, which is very large on the Western Shore of Md, he learned to speak the German language familiarly. He became the personal attendant of Edmund Kean in the U S & accompanied him to England. He was described as having been a full-blooded negro, with crinkly wool, flat nose, thick lips, & skin of the blackest hue. –N Y World]

Equity Court. Margaret Fitzgerald vs Margaret S Fitgerald, et al. R H Laskey is appointed guardian, *ad litem*, in this case.

Orphans Court, Aug 10, 1867. 1-The De Vaughan will case was again under consideration. The witnesses for the legatees & the validity of the will were examined. Messrs Hughes, Denver & Peck appear for creators, & Michl Thompson for legatees. The case was further considered until next Tuesday. 2-The argument in the Fearson will case, on an application for the court to appoint a receiver for the estate until the case is decided in the Supreme Court was continued today. The argument will be concluded next Sat. 3-Letters testamentary were granted on the estate of Andreas Fischer, deceased, to his widow, Margaret Fischer. The will of Andreas Fischer was admitted to probate. 4-Letters of administration were granted to Mary Essex & John F W Essex on the estate of Jas F Essex, deceased; bond $4,000. 5-The inventory of the personal estate of Philip Wetzel was approved & passed; also, that of F M Melline.

Died: on Aug 11, suddenly, John M Ford, in his 66th year. His friends & members of the Association of Oldest Inhabitants are invited to attend his funeral from his late residence, 24 Va ave, between 11th & 12th sts, on Tuesday, at 4 o'clock P M.

Hughes Ferguson, one of the oldest citizens of Louisville, died on Saturday.

Geo W Shields, surgeon in the U S army, died of yellow fever at New Orleans on Saturday.

Balt, Aug 11. The laying of the corner stone of the new **Catholic monastery**, under the auspices of the order of the **Passionists**, took place this afternoon, in the presence of from three to five thousand persons. The ceremonies were performed by Rev Dr Foley, administrator of the diocese, in the absence of Archbishop Spalding, who is now in Germany. The edifice, when completed, will cost about $50,000, & is the 4th monastery erected by this society since 1850.

Chicago, Aug 11. Col R A Gilmore, postmaster of this city, went out in the lake in a new boat, on Friday, & has not been seen since. It is supposed that he has drowned. The boat was found on the beach below the city last night. [Aug 15th newspaper: Mrs Gilmore was told that her husband would probably not return. Fragments of the boat in which he had gone out in, was discovered stranded on the shore near the Ill Central Round-house. Gen Gilmore, whose 34th birthday occurred last spring, was born in N Y; his father came to this city about 1850; the son did not come until 1854; he was married to a daughter of Judge Robt S Wilson, by whom he had 4 children, all of whom live to mourn his loss. Mourned by his family, regretted by his friends, he has left behind him a stainless reputation. –Chicago Tribune of Monday.]

Henley J Murray, a clerk in the post ofc at Boston, has been held for trial, in $5,000 bail, charged with stealing money from letters.

L Passano & Sons, Importers & Dealers in Notions, Fancy Goods, Hosiery, Trimmings, & Small Wares. 268 W Balt st, Balt, Md. [Ad]

Dr Montgomery Johns, Ph D, Boarding & Day School for Boys, near Hyattsville, PG Co, Md, will open on Sep 11. Apply at the store of Mr Fitzgerald, F st, near 8th st, or to the Principal at Postofc, Hyattsville, PG Co, Md.

Dr C W Sonnenschmidt, Homeopathic Physician & Surgeon: ofc 445 Mass ave, between 6th & 7th sts, Wash.

Sale of Real estate within a mile of **Greenwood Depot**, on the Va Centrail Railroad, Albemarle Co, under the provision of the will of Michl Wallace, deceased: public auction on Sep 11 next, of about 1,000 acres, with a dwlg house containing 7 rooms, with an ofc in the yard, & all necessary out-houses. Wm L Wallace resides on the land, & will show the farm. –Wm L Wallace, Robt B Prentis, adms b n c t a

Orphans Court of Wash Co, D C. Letters of administration on the personal estate of Jas F Essex, sr, late of Wash Co, D C, deceased. –Mary Essex, John T W Essex, adms

TUE AUG 13, 1867

Executive Mansion, Wash, D C, Aug 12, 1867. Sir: By virtue of the power & authority vested in me as Pres, by the Constitution & laws of the U S, you are hereby suspended from office as Sec of War, & will cease to exercise any & all functions pertaining to the same. You will at once transfer to Gen Ulysses S Grant, who has this day been authorized & empowered to act as Sec of War ad interim all records, books, papers, & other public property now in your custody & charge. Very respectfully yours, Andrew Johnson. To Hon Edwin M Stanton, Wash, D C

Francis Joseph, of Austria says, since the execution of Maximillan, that he will never sign another death-warrant.

Hon O A Lochkane, a prominent Georgia politician, has bought the Atlanta Opera House for $14,500.

Obit-died: Jul 6, aged 18 years, Gertrude H, youngest daughter of the late Wm & Emily Dalton. Consumption had early marked her for a victim & neither the love of sisters or the devotion of brothers, removed from her brow the seal that had been stamped upon it.

Jas S Harvey, an old citizen, died on Sat last, at his residence in the 2nd Ward. Mr Harvey was in his 74th year, & for many years engaged in the coal trade. He had not enjoyed good health for some time past; had acquired a handsome fortune, was a respected member of the Catholic Church, & a generous patron of St Aloysius Church; the senior member of the firm of Harvey, Clark, & Given. His decline was as peaceful as his days had been prosperous.
+
Died: on Aug 11, Jas S Harvey, in his 73rd year, a native of PG Co, Md, & for several years a resident of Gtwn, & for the last 40 years resided in Wash City. His funeral will at at St Aloysius Church this Thu morning, at 9 o'clock. [Balt Gaz & Catholic Mirror & Freeman's Journal, N Y, please copy.]

Died: on Aug 12, Catherine J Geiger, aged 42 years, 2 months & 4 days. Her funeral will be from the residence of J J Geiger, 350 4th st, this evening at 4 o'clock.

Fortress Monroe, Aug 12. C W Butz, Pres of the Colorado Gold Mining Co, suddenly disappeared from Norfolk a few days ago, when about being arrested by Gen Schofield, on the charge of swindling soldiers.

Dept of the Interior, U S Patent Ofc, Wash, Aug 7, 1867. Ptn of Henry Waterman, of Hudson, N Y, praying for the extension of a patent granted to him Nov 15, 1853, & reissued Jul 9, 1867, for an improvement in Safety Valves for Locomotive Engines, for seven years from the expiration of said patent, which takes place on Nov 15, 1867. -T C Theaker, Com'r of Patents

Lawrence Dalton, who has for a number of years been a dealer in fancy birds & dogs in Thames st, N Y, on Thu committed suicide, by cutting his throat from ear to ear. The death of his wife, which occurred a week ago, is said to have led to the act.

Orphans Court of Wash Co, D C. Letters testamentary on the personal estate of Geo W Young, late of Wash, D C, deceased. –Henrietta E Young, excx

WED AUG 14, 1867
The Metropolitan Railroad Co have just received per steamer one of the new cars, which it is intended to place upon their road in place of those drawn by 2 horses now used. The car is light, & neatly painted & decorated, & was built by John G Stephenson, of N Y. The car is built after the style of those of N Y, & needs no conductor. The general impression is that these one-horse arrangements will prove a success, as they will prove a great pecuniary saving to the company.

Died: on Aug 12, in his 30th year, Wm Henry Thompson, youngest son of Wm Thompson, of Wash City. His funeral is tomorrow afternoon, from Grace Church, [Island,] at 4 o'clock.

Orphans Court-Judge Purcell. 1-The will of Jas F Essex, deceased, of Gtwn, was filed & proven. 2-Benj Crier was appointed guardian to the orphans of Chas & Sallie Wood; bond $300. 3-The contested will of the late Saml De Vaughan occupied the court during a greater part of the sitting-the legatees being represented by M Thompson, & the contestants by Judge Hughes & Moore. A number of witnesses were examined, & finally it was agreed that Dr A McDonald Davis be appointed collector; bond $40,000.

Com'r of Patents; examiners: Primary Examiners:
[old examiners:]

T R Peale	J M Blanchard	T J Barnett
Wm B Taylor	N Crawford	Edw Bebb
B F James	T C Connolly	
C G Page	T J Fales	

Primary Examiners-new: Messrs A Schoepp, J M Thacher, Norris Peters, D S Stewart, & L Deane have been promoted from 1st Assists to Chief Examiners, & Geo W Gregory from 2nd Assist to Chief Examiner, thus completeing the list of primary examiners.

[Old First Assistants:]

G A Natile	N Theaker	T A Cook
A G Wilkinson	C M Parks	H T Munson
T C Folger	Wm Read	C Everett

Messrs A P Thayer, C L Coombs, G A Nolen, A L Hayes, C Mygatt, J C Tasker, Dudley Carle, T N Bovee, E Spear, & M C Mitchell have been promoted from 2nd to 1st Assists; & J S Grinnell from Clerk to 1st Assist, thus completing the list of 1st Assistants.

London, Aug 13. Conflict between two steamers of the American squadron in the Chinese waters & the pirates of the Island of Formosa; the U S authorities having received neither satisfaction or apology for the murder of the crew of the American bark **Rover**, the men-of-war **Hartford & Wyoming** were ordered to the scene of the outrage on the Island of Formosa. Lt Slidell Mackenzie, one of the landing party, was shot, & died of his wounds.

Trustee's sale of valuable property in Market Space between 8th & 9th sts, by severals deeds of trust to me from Thos Connolly, of John, dated Jul 21, 1843, Dec 16, 1843, & Mar 31, 1844, I will sell, at public auction, on Sep 5, part of lot 3 in square 498. The amount due under the 3 deeds of trust is $3,733.86, with interest from Feb 17, 1861. -Henry Naylor, trustee -Green & Williams, aucts

THU AUG 15, 1867
John Ehret, who was struck in the head with a lager-beer glass during a fracas at the 7th St Park last Friday, died on Wed at Providence Hospital. Mansback was held on preliminary examination in the sum of $500 for his appearance before the Criminal Court, but since the death of Ehret has not been seen in Wash City.

Died: on Aug 11, at the residence of her grandfather, Wm F Berry, in PG Co, Md, Edith, youngest daughter of Henry L & Anna E Taylor, aged 11 months. [Upper Marlboro papers please copy.]

Died: on Aug 13, at *Ingleside*, near Wash, D C, Mrs Mary Walbridge, relict of Chester Walbridge, after a long & painful illness, in her 73rd year. Her funeral will take place at her late residence, *Ingleside*, on Aug 16 at 4 o'clock P M. [Aug 23rd newspaper: Obit of Mrs Mary Walbridge. Doubtless she & her beloved husband are now before the throne of God. May their children prepare to follow them.]

The farm of Jas M Mason, near Winchester, Va, containing 94 acres, had been sold for $170 per acre.

On Tuesday Edw Jones, superintendent of the shooting-gallery in Barnum's Museum, N Y, was instantly shot dead by a young man whose name was unknown, & who fired a rifle at a target while Jones was in front of it. It is supposed he did not see Jones. He escaped from the Museum during the confusion that ensued.

U S Marshal's sale: on Sep 3, all Jennings Piggott's right, title, claim & interest in & to lot 16 in square 1,095, in Wash City, seized & levied upon as his property, & will be sold to satisfy execution 2,512 in favor of Silas H Swetland.
-D S Gooding, U S Marshal D C

U S Marshal's sale of superior gold lever watch & fancy gold chain, on Aug 24, seized & levied upon as the property of Chas Hertzberg, garnishee of Chas E Capehart, & will be sold to satisfy execution in favor of Jos Purcell.
–D S Gooding, U S Marshal D C

Dept of the Interior, U S Patent Ofc, Wash, Aug 9, 1867. Ptn of Robt Sinclair, jr, & Richd F Maynard, of Balt, Md, praying for extension of a patent granted them Nov 15, 1853, for improvement in Feed Rollers of Straw Cutters, for 7 years from the expiration of said patent, which takes place Nov 15, 1867.
-T C Theaker, Com'r of Patents

FRI AUG 16, 1867
Michl Riley was accidentally shot by a companion on Wed as they were returning from a hunting expedition. His right arm was badly lacerated, but not of a serious character.

A lad named J F McKenney, one of the carriers of the Republican, was bitten by a dog yesterday while delivering papers. His side was terribly torn, & it will be several weeks before he could recover.

Mrd: on Aug 14, at the house of the bride's father, Wash, D C, by Rev Mr Brown of the Foundry Church, John B Scott, of Md, to Miss Sarah E Broughton, of Va.

Died: on Aug 9, after a short illness, at Wmsburgh, Va, in her 59th year, Miss Rebecca Lowndes Ewell, daughter of the late Dr Thos Ewell & his wife, Eliz Stoddert, & sister of Gen Richd S Ewell, & of Prof Benj M Ewell. She was a humble Christian & a great loss to her relatives.

Died: on Aug 15, after a lingering illness, Mrs Ruth Anna Harvey, in her 70th year. Her funeral will take place at 12 o'clock M, on Aug 16, from Mrs Hannah Dyer's residence, 428 Carroll Pl, Capitol Hill.

Newark [N J] Journal: Newmarket, Middlesex Co, was on Monday night last, the scene of another horrible affair, which promises to result in the death of an old man named John Harris, aged 74 years. He was attacked while in his bed by his son-in-law, Wm Roantree, & after escaping to the yard he was again caught & stabbed, the blade entering the right side, & penetrating the right lung. Roantree then rushed upon the old man's wife, knocked her down with the butt end of a six-shooter. During the struggle the assassin received a gash in his head; he went to a bed inside to his wife & daughters, where he now remains. Mr Coriell, whose wife was murdered by Bridget Durgan was called to see the wounded man. Hannah Roantree, wife of the perpetrator, said a difference had existed since Christmas of 1865, about the old folks living in the house with them. Roantree was found nearby & taken to New Brunswick & put in the county jail. He is an Englishman by birth, about 40 years of age. He had served during the war as a private in the 11th N J volunteers; he had been wounded in the head.

Indianapolis, Aug 15. McMinnaroy, the murderer of Mr Johns, telegraph operator at Gosport, last spring, has been convicted, & sentenced to the State prison for life.

Omaha, Neb, Aug 14. Hard-fought battle between the Indians & the whites near *Fort Phil Kearney* on Aug 2: ox train of 30 wagons, guarded by 50 citizens & as many soldiers, under the command of Maj Powell & Lt Jennes, left the fort to gather fuel. Within 5 miles of the fort, a band of savages, at least 250, rode up & made an attack. Lt Jennes & others were killed. Maj Smith, with 2 companies of U S regulars & 2 howitzers, came to the rescue, when the red men retreated, leaving 5 dead bodies on the field. Maj Powell reports the total loss of the savages at 60 killed outright, & many wounded.

N Y, Aug 15. Wm H Knapp, one of the oldest telegraphers in the country, & until recently manager of the ofc at Newark, N J, died in Florida, on Aug 4, of congestion of the brain. Mr Knapp settled in Florida last year.

Jas Watson, one of the editors of the Hagerstown Mail, died suddenly on Wed, from disease of the heart.

A the Cathedral yesterday with all pomp & ceremony of a marriage mass, Capt Bernard G Cooper, of the Royal English navy, was wedded to Mrs Bessie Perine, daughter of the late Judge Z Collins Lee, of Balt. The vast Cathedral was crowded, & Revs Oliver Jenkins, Thos Foley, & others officiated. The happy pair left for a lengthened tour through Northern & Eastern States, prior to their departure for Europe.

Willis Casey, 26 years of age, son of Saml K Casey, of Joliet, formerly warden of the Ill penitentiary, was shot & instantly killed at Gardner, Ill, on Tues, while on a hunting excursion with a party of friends. He was pulling his gun from a buggy, when the contents were discharged, taking effect in his brain.

David Kurtz, Chief of Police at Lafayette, Ind, died on Sat from too much morphine, taken as a remedy for diarrhoea.

Kaloramo Family School, Staunton, Va-next session will commence on Oct 1st, & close the following June. Apply to Mrs Hanson or Miss Sheffey, Staunton, Va.

Montgomery Hall for sale-the subscriber offers for private sale the desirable estate on which he now resides: tract contains 300 acres; estate was formerly the residence of John H Peyton; with a spacious mansion-house & other bldgs erected by him for the accommodation of his large family. Communicate with the subscriber, or Hon Alex H H Stewart, or Hon John B Baldwin, Staunton, Va. –Wm J Shumate

Dept of the Interior, U S Patent Ofc, Wash, Aug 10, 1867. Ptn of Laura S White, admx of the estate of Jonathan White, deceased, of Antrim, N H, praying for the extension of a patent granted to him Nov 15, 185_, for an improvement in Uniting Shovel Blades to Handle Straps for seven years from the expiration of said patent, which takes place on Nov 15, 1867.

Orphans Court of Wash Co, D C. Letters testamentary on the personal estate of Andreas Fischer, late of Wash City, D C, deceased.

SAT AUG 17, 1867
The three year old daughter of L L Ellis, of Troy, died yesterday. A week ago she swallowed a nickel penny; symptoms were all those of virulent poison.
–Albany Argus

Promotions in Treasury Dept since Aug 1. Sec's Ofc-N A West, from 3rd to 4th class; J W Hubbard, from 1st to 2nd class; Lepold Helmle, from 2nd to 3rd class; Howard C Burr, from 2nd to 3rd class. Fourth Auditor's Ofc: F C Rau, from 1st to 2nd class; Wm Mertz, from 2nd to 3rd class. First Comptroller's Ofc: T C Dickinson, from 1st to 2nd sts. Statistical Bureau: D D T Leach, from 2nd to 3rd class. Internal Revenue Ofc: Alex'r Johnson, from 1st to 2nd class. Treasurer's Ofc: J G Davis, A Zollar, G Schermerhorn, A J De Moll, A K Quaiffe, Danl Byrne, from 2nd to 3rd class; J R Morhous, 2nd to 3rd class.

Mrs Bella Z Spencer, a young & gifted authoress, died Aug 1 in Tascaloosa, Ala, whither she had accompanied her husband, who is a register of bankruptcy there. Mrs Spencer was a native of London, England, but came to this country in early infancy, & was married to Gen Geo E Spencer in 1862. Her work "Tried and True" was publised in 1866.

Mr Hugh Gelston, of Balt, proprietor of the Central Hotel, 6th & Pa ave, which burned down in Feb last, is having erected on the same ground a fine pressed-brick bldg, 5 stories high; under the superintendence of Mr Edw Wools, architect & builder of this city. The cost will be about $28,000.

The Sec of the Treasury intends to send to Alaska, as special agent of that Dept, Capt Wm S Dodge, of Ill, lately of the army, & more recently in the civil service of the Gov't, who is instructed to attend to the interests of the revenue in that Territory. We also learn that Capt Dodge will accompany Gen Rousseau & the Russian Com'r, who leave for Alaska by next week's steamer from N Y.

Boston, Aug 16. Hon Edwin M Stanton arrived here this morning. He came by the Bristol line, & Superintendent Fulsom placed a special car at his disposal for the conveyance of himself & family from Bristol.

Died: on Aug 15, at Arlington, Va, Mary V Syphax, wife of Chas Syphax, in her 32nd year. She died in the full triumph of Christian truth. Before her death, she called her husband with the children to her bedside, & earnestly besought him to make the Lord his choice, & to train them up in the fear of the Lord, & live up to His glory. Her funeral is on Aug 17 at 2 o'clock, from her late residence on H st, between 15th & 16th sts.

Died yesterday, at Newcastle, Dela, James Lewis Edwards, in his 8th year, son of Dr Lewis A Edwards, surgeon of the U S army.

N Y, Aug 15. The steamer **Hammonia** has arrived from Southampton having on board the remains of Gen Wright, late Minister to Berlin. Mrs Wright & 2 children accompany the body.

House for rent: 326 H st, between 15th st & Vt ave; contains 12 rooms, gas, water, etc. Apply to Mrs S S Kall, 21st & Boundary sts, Kalorama Heights.

Household & kitchen furniture at auction, Aug 21, at the residence of the late C Keenan, 519 I st, between 6th & 7th sts, all the furniture & effects.
-Green & Williams, aucts

Valuable hotel property in Port Tobacco, Md, for sale: owned by us, known as **Brawner House**. Public sale before the Court-house on Sep 17 next. Attached to the property is a lot of about 2 acres. –Alex'r H Robertson, Saml Hanson

Orphans Court of Wash Co, D C, Aug 13, 1867. In the case of Moses Kelly, adm of Susan K Ingle, deceased, the administrator & Court have appointed Sep 7 next, for the final settlement of the personal estate of the said deceased, of the assets in hand.
-Jas R O'Beirne, Reg/o wills

Orphans Court of Wash Co, D C, Aug 13, 1867. In the case of Moses Kelly, adm of Jos Ingle, deceased, the administrator & Court have appointed Sep 7 next, for the final settlement of the personal estate of the said deceased, of the assets in hand.
-Jas R O'Beirne, Reg/o wills

MON AUG 19, 1867
A new post ofc is established at **Suitsville**, PG Co, Md, & Geo T Suit appointed postmaster. It is located 5 miles east of Bladensburg, & 6 miles west of **Oak Grove**.

Longwood, belonging to the estate of the late Col Jos F Harvey, lying on Pope's Creek & the Potomac, near Washington's birthplace, & containing 1,566 acres, has just been sold to Senator Nye for the sum of $16,000. This farm contains much valuable timber, & it is said the price paid is exceedingly low, considering the advantages of the estate.

Mr Berthemy, the French Minister, says the N Y Times' correspondent, is engaged to marry a Washington widow, & will retire from diplomatic services next spring. Mr De Ferriotte, his first Sec of Legation, has also formed an engagement of a similar character with another Washington lady.

Died: on Aug 17, Mary A Murphy, consort of J W Murphy, aged 35 years. Her funeral is this afternoon at 3 o'clock, from her late residence, Md ave, between 3rd & 4th sts east.

Died: on Aug 13, at the residence of his father, in Suisun City, Calif, Brvt Lt Col Wesley Owens, captain of the 5th U S cavalry.

Orphans Court-Judge Purcell, Aug 17, 1867. 1-The last will & testament of Jas Fullalove, deceased, was filed, proved, & admitted to probate. The property of the devisor is equally divided among the children of the deceased. 2-Mary Essex & John T W Essex were appointed as excs of the will of the late Jas F Essex, & gave bond of $4,000. 3-The first & final amount of the administrator of the estate of Alex'r H Derrick, deceased, was presented & passed. 4-The second account of the guardian of the orphan child of Hanson Dorsey, deceased, was presented & allowed. 5-The third & final account of the guardian of the orphan child of Jos Ingle, deceased, was presented & passed. 6-The Court was engaged during the remainder of the session in listening to the testimony in the contested will of the late Saml De Vaughan. The contestants in this case claim that there is no will before the Court, the testator having expressed a desire previous to his death, & while on his death-bed, for a lawyer to come & draw up a new one. Several interlineations occur in the instrument, in one of which the counsel for the defense claim that the original intent of the testator is changed-a circle being drawn around the works "and improvements," which diverts it from the place where originally placed, & transfers it from lot 22 to lot 20 in a certain square of ground. It was contended, on the other hand, that the circle in question was but a flourish of the pen, & did not alter the intent of the testator at all, & that it did not defraud any one interested in its provisions.

Phil, Aug 18. Wm Brophy, residing a few miles north of the city, shot his sister-in-law today, inflicting a mortal wound. The cause has not been ascertained. Brophy is a prominent politician here. [Name of the deceased was not given.]

Geo W L Bickley, the orginator of the order of the Knights of the Golden Circle, died at Balt, a few days since, aged 52. He was a native of Va, a graduate of the London Medical Univ, & a man of considerable learning. He was confined during the war, as a political prisoner, in the Ohio Penitentiary, **Fort Lafayette**, & **Fort Warren**, & was in prison altogether about 3 years.

Orphans Court of Wash Co, D C. Letters of administration on personal estate of Jas F Essex, late of Wash, D C, deceased. –Mary Essex, John T W Essex, adms, c t a

Jas Simmons who poisoned his father's entire family at Cincinnati, 13 years ago, causing the death of two of his sons, & who was sentenced to be hung, but afterwards was sent to the penitentiary for life, has been pardoned by Govn'r Cox. His father was a wealthy steamboat captain, & the son, it is alleged, administered the poison to get at his money bags.

TUE AUG 20, 1867
Boarding & Day School for Young Ladies, 411 13th st, Wash, D C will be resumed Sep 9. For circulars apply to the principal. Miss M J Harrover

For sale, the beautiful residence on the Heights of Gtwn, D C, formerly occupied by Gen Grant & known as *Lee's Hill*. Apply for terms to R B Scott, 312 Madison ave, Balt, Md.

Enfield Chase, a plantation situated near Collington, PG Co, Md, is offered at private sale, either entire or in part; tract contains 600 acres. Apply to the subscriber, residing on the premises, or to Danl Clarke, Atty-at-Law, Plant's Bldg, 15th & N Y ave, Wash City. -Nicholas H Shipley, Collingswood P O.

Dept of the Interior, U S Patent Ofc, Wash, Aug 9, 1867. Ptn of Wm B Bates, adm of the estate of Geo Wellman, deceased, of Mansfield, Mass, praying for the extension of a patent granted to said Geo Wellman Dec 6, 1853, & reissued Jul 30, 1867, for an improvement in Stripping Top Flats for Carding machines, for seven years from the expiration of said patent, which takes place on Dec 6, 1867.
-T C Theaker, Com'r of Patents

Dept of the Interior, U S Patent Ofc, Wash, Aug 1, 1867. Ptn of Geo W Livermore, of Cambridge, Mass, praying for the extension of a patent granted to him Mar 21, 1854, for an improvement in Machinery for making Barrels, for 7 years from the expiration of said patent, which takes place on Mar 21, [No year given.]
-T C Theaker, Com'r of Patents

WED AUG 21, 1867
Orphans Court-Judge Purcell, Aug 20, 1867. 1-The will of the late Jas S Harvey was filed & fully proven. After bequeathing $25 each to the pastors of St Patrick's & St Mary's, & $50 each to the Jesuit fathers & Dominican fathers for saying masses for his soul, he makes a bequest of $1,000 to St Vincent's Female Asylum, $1,000 to St Joseph's Male Asylum, $500 to St Ann's Infant Asylum, $1,000 to St Aloysius Free School, $800 to St Patrick's Free School, $1,000 to the poor of Washington, to be distributed by St Vincent de Paul's Conference. After making bequests ranging from $2,000 to $200 to his nephews & other relatives & friends, he bequeaths the remainder to his son, Arsemus J Harvey, who, with Henry A Clarke, he nominates executors. A codicil is attached to the will in which he gives $1,000 to St Patrick's Church for the erection of a new church. Letters testamentary were issued to A J Harvey, who qualified by giving bond in $50,000, Mr Clarke renouncing. 2-An exemplified copy of the will of the late Gilbert Cameron, from Greenock, Scotland, was filed & admitted to probate. He bequeathed his estate to Mary Mitchell, his wife, whom he nominates as executrix. 3-Margaret Ann Collison was appointed guardian to the orphans of Levin Dukes; bond $1,000. 4-Letters of administration were issued to W F Finn on the estate of the late Mary Finn; bond $1,500. 5-The first account of the guardian to Jefferson Rives; second to do to J C Rives, jr, & second do to Blair Rives, orphans of John C Rives, were approved & passed.
6-Mr J V Johnson closed his argument for the contestants of the will of the late Mary Ann Fearson, & Judge Purcell stated that he would give his decision on Tuesday next. The contestants are R L McPherson, of Gtwn; S T McPherson, of Balt; John Shaw, Henrietta Taylor, & Mary Ann Taylor, of PG Co, Md.

John H Reagan, Postmaster General under the rebel Gov't, writes to a friend in this city that he has received his pardon from the President, & will devote himself to securing early reconstruction, & restoring peace & harmony to the country.

Naval Orders. Passed Assist Surgeon W H Jones, detached from Navy Yard, Wash, & placed on waiting orders. Acting Master G W D Patterson ordered to the ship **Shawmut**. The resignation of Mate N B Walker, of the ship **Alleghany**, has been accepted. Masters A H Lewis & Henry J Wynd have been honorably discharged, to date from Aug 13, 1867.

Died: on Aug 11, at New Orleans, of sunstroke, in his 29th year, Jas R Y Fendall. A native of Wash City, but emigrated in 1860 to the State of Louisiana. His mind was strong; his heart affectionate; distinguished among the brave for gallantry of a soldier.

Died: on Aug 20, in Brooklyn, N Y, of congestion of the brain, Johnny, only son of John Russell & Rose Young, aged 2 years & 3 weeks. Interment at **Mt Olivet Cemetery**, Wash, D C.

Died: on Aug 18, at Galveston, Texas, of yellow fever, Mary Frances, wife of Col Wm S Abert, U S A.

Geo W Godfrey, late a clerk in the Herald ofc, was found dead yesterday, in his room, at the Tontine Hotel, N Y. Two bottles of laudanum were found nearby. One empty.
A verdict of suicide by poisoning was rendered. A few days ago he disappeared, taking with him checks & bills amounting to $1,000, the property of Mr Jas Gordon Bennett.

Dover, N H, Aug 20. Yesterday a party started in a boat for an island in Bow Lake, in Stafford, N H, to pick berries. The boat was capsized, & the following drowned: Mrs Jeremiah Davis & daughter, two daughters of Mrs John Day, a daughter of Mr Alfred Pendar, & a daughter of Mr M Gray. The bodies have been recovered.

Hon Wm B Campbell, late member of Congress for Nashville Dist, died at his residence, in Lebanon, on Monday, of disease of the heart. He was a native of Tenn; distinguished himself in the Mexican war, as colonel of a Tenn regt, at Cerro Gordo & at Monterey. -N Y Tribune

The wife of Jesse Carter, of Mobile, Ala, was recently killed by her son, who mistook her for a robber.

Mrs Donihu, of Glenville, N Y, while visiting Maison's grain elevator in Schenectady, on Monday, had her dress caught in a swift revolving shaft, & died a few moments after being extricated.

Mrs Adela E Aimar, while sitting in her pew at St Patrick's Church, in Charleston, on Sunday, suddenly fell forward, & died in a few moments; a case of apoplexy.

Guardians sale of val bldg lots on 8th st west, between K & L sts, & n e corner of 5th & L sts, at auction, on May 21, 1867, by order of the Orphans Court of D C; sale of part of lot 10 in sq 402. Sale of lot 10 in sq 514, unimproved. -Virginia Hollingsworth, Guardian of Margaretta B Doughty -Cooper & Latimer, aucts

Trustee's sale of valuable improved property on 4½ st, between H & I sts, by deed of trust from John Crowley & wife & Thos Coleman & wife to the subscriber, dated Mar 28, 1866, recorded in Liber R M H folios 491, of the land records of Wash Co, D C; public auction on Sep 13 next: lots 32, & 35 thru 37, in square 498, in Wash City, with two 4 story brick dwlg houses, supplied with gas & water, one large brick bldg used as a bottling establishment, one large brick stable, & all bldgs on the premises. –A Thos Bradley, trustee -Cooper & Latimer, aucts

THU AUG 22, 1867
Jacob Tripler, or, as he is better known, "Old Jake Tripler," the oldest fireman in the country, & one of the "institutions" of Phil, is now on a visit to Wash City & vicinity. He will be the guest of the Gtwn firemen, & will be present at a banquet given in his honor by Mr Rodier, of Analostan Island.

Sgt Jos Walling, of the police of the 4th Ward, was taken with a fit & fell to the pavement. He was carried into V Harbaugh's drug store, 7th & G sts, where proper restoratives were given him. He was then removed to his residence, & is now fast recovering.

Died: on Aug 20, at the residence of her grandmother, in Wash Co, Mary Estelle, youngest daughter of Jacob H & Fannie G Harleston, aged 9 months & 21 days. Her funeral will be from 335 10th st, Aug 22 at 4 P M, to proceed to Rock Creek Episcopal Church for interment.

Income of the Royal Family of England. Besides about a dozen palaces, Queen Victoria has a direct annual income of $1,870,000; Prince of Wales, $500,000; Princess of Wales, $50,000; Duke of Edinburgh, $75,000; Princess Royal of Prussia, $40,000; Princess of Hesse, $30,000; Princess Helena, $30,00; Duchess of Cambridge, $30,000; her oldest daughter, $15,000; her second daughter, $25,000; Duke of Cambridge, $60,000. Besides this, a man, named Neeld, passing over all his own relations, bequeathed to the Queen $1,750,000, which she accepted. Prince Albert, who was remarkably saving, left the Queen all his accumulations, estimated at $5,000,000.

Chas H Benson, a merchant from Uniontown, Fayette Co, Pa, came to Pittsburgh a few days since, & while under the influence of liquor, drank some oil of vitrol, mistaking it for water, & died soon after. The deceased was a wealthy & influential citizen.

The following officers, being no longer needed, are honorably mustered out of service: Capt W B Armstrong, Assist Quartermaster U S volunteers; J J Belamater, [Brvt Lt Col,] Surgeon U S volunteers; Adam C Swartzwelder, & Wm R De Witt, Brvt Lt Colonels; M H Hogan, Brvt Col; R Fletcher, Brvt Col; C J Kipp, Brvt Lt Col; J W Applegate, Patrick Glennan, Assist Surgeons U S volunteers.

Chicago, Aug 21. Mr Beadles, his wife & sister, & child of the latter, were drowned in the Pecatonicy river, near Rockford, Sat. The lost child went into the river & got beyond its depth, when the others perished in their efforts to rescue it.

Phil, Aug 21. Ex-Pres Buchanan is lying serious ill in this city, having been brought from Cape May yesterday. Fears are entertained for his life. [Aug 24th newspaper: Ex-Pres Buchanan's health is improving. He will probably start for *Wheatland* today.]

Marie Russler, a French Canadian woman, died at Brampton, at the age of 114, having been born while Canada was still a French colony.

Dr J Mason Warren, a well known surgeon & physician of Boston, died on Tuesday.

C Court Flint, who some time ago committed the crime of forgery at Norfolk, Va, & fled to New Orleans, has been demanded by Govn'r Pierpoint, of Va, & will be given up.

Miss Clara Louise Kellogg sailed for Europe yesterday, under the protection of her mother, & with Mr Jennings, of the London Times, & his young bride, nee Miss Madeline Henriques.

A promising child of Thos Potter, of Phil, acompanied by its nurse, were pushed overboard by the crowd at a ferry-bridge in that city last Fri, & both were drowned.

Rev Mark P Ladd, a rep to the General Assembly from Worcester, committed suicide by hanging, at Richmond, Vermont, Saturday. He was in independent circumstances. The coroner's verdict was suicide from insanity.

A few days ago Pierce Butler died at one of his estates in Georgia. He was a native of Phil; his family being rich, he was enabled to obtain a liberal education; he graduated with honors, studied law, & was admitted to the bar of Phil. In 1834 Mr Butler was married to Miss Fanny Kemble, the well-known actress & authoress, who had arrived in the U S from England about 2 years previous, & who retired definitely from the stage after this event. The marriage life was short & unhappy. Their tastes & temperments differed widely, & in 1849 the lady applied for a divorce. Mr Butler resisted the application, but finally a divorce from bed & board was granted. Mrs Butler took up residence with the Sedgwick family, at Lenox, Mass, & resumed her maiden name, Kemble. –N Y Herald

Col Ely S Parker, of Gen Grant's staff, who, with Gen Alfred Sully, of Minn, has been engaged all summer on an Indian peace commission on the Upper Missouri, returned to the city on Sunday.

FRI AUG 23, 1867
Adm's sale of the Coopering Establishment of the late Jas F Essex; by order of the Orphans Court of D C.; public auction on Aug 26, in front of the premises, on High st, near Water st, all the stock of tools. –Mary Essex, John T W Essex, adms -Thos Dowling, auct

Yesterday Patrick Shea purchased lot 14 in square 563, in Wash City, corner of N J ave & H st, with a 2 story frame house thereon, for $2,500.

Julius Fimacom, white, & Bernard Smith, colored, both about 14, were charged with setting fire to the house of Rev J V Lewis. They had broken into the house & robbed it of sundry articles, & set it on fire. Conrad Miller, for receiving stolen goods, was commited to jail in default of $500 bail.

Mrd: on Aug 20, at the Church of the Epiphany, by Rev Dr Hall, G Crawford Neilson, U S Navy, to Julia, daughter of Benj T Reilly, of Wash City.

Died: on Aug 22, Maurice Brady, son of Jas T & Cornelia J Clark, aged 3 months & 29 days. His funeral will be from 565 12th st, near Smithsonian Institute, on Friday at 3 o'clock.

Died: on Aug 17, at Laurel Hill, N C, Miss Catharine McLaurin, daughter of John McLaurin, deceased, aged 19 years. [Canada West papers please copy.]

St Louis, Aug 22. John McCarty, who murdered Ruth Langford in Balt on Jul 4, was arrested here night before last, & will be held until an ofcr arrives to take him to Md.

$10 reward for return of 3 volumes of Shakespeare's Works; one volume No 2 Nath'l Portrait Gallery of Eminent Americans, stolen from my parlor on Aug 21. Deliver the book to me, John R Murray, 26 4½ st, Wash.

SAT AUG 24, 1867
Richmond, Va, Aug 23. 1-Chas Stuart was shot & killed night before last by Rev Robt Gray, in Pulaski Co. Gray was in a house barricaded to resist a mob of negroes who had gathered around it, & shot Stuart outside by mistake. 2-The Carbon Hills coal mines were sold at auction today for $20,000 to John T Daly, of N Y.

Phil, Aug 23. John Birely, oldest ship-bldr in the U S, died this morning, aged 75 years.

Died: on Aug 23, at Langley, Fairfax Co, Va, Mosley Sorrel, youngest son of Wm W & Aminta Mackall.

The bodies of Miss Catherine Brimmer, of Gtwn, & Miss Georgianna Gray & Miss Margaret Barrett, of Wash, who were drowned by the upsetting of the stage-coach, on the Wash & Rockville line, on Thursday, near Tennallytown, were recovered yesterday & brought to the city. There is a small gully stream that crosses the road & runs through Mr Richd Williams' place, called Falls Run; ordinarily but 6 inches of water; on Wed the stream had risen, & Geo Fulton, the driver, halted, but seeing 2 horse ambulances cross over, he thought he would venture. The force of the current upset the stage. A gentleman, Christian Keefer, of Rockville, was also drowned. Fulton succeeded in getting out, just in time to save himself. Miss Gray extricated herself from the coach, but the current was so strong that she was almost instantly submerged. The bodies of the other ladies were found in the coach.

Railroad accident on the Annapolis railroad yesterday near Isaac's Gate, 1½ miles from Millersville; train was run off the tracks. Engineer, Richd Sewall, Gilbert Coleman, the fireman, & his son, a lad of about 12 years, were instantly killed. Capt Hammond, the conductor, was badly injured. Mrs Ellen Henderson, a lady passenger from Balt, had her right ankle broken.

Died: on Aug 16, at the residence of Miss Hannah Dwyer, on Capitol Hill, Mrs Ruth Anna P Harvey, in her 71st year. She was the wife of Thos Harvey, & daughter of the late Hon Edmund Key, of Md. She was noted for her Christian piety.

Died: on Aug 23, at the residence of N W Hilbren, 571 8th st, Patrick Reynolds, Sgt U S Marine corps, aged 48 years, & for many years orderly to the commandant. His funeral will take place on Aug 25 at 3 o'clock.

Died: on Aug 22, in Wash City, Wm P Fitzgerald. His funeral will be from the residence of his brother-in-law, Dr W Evans, 537½ H st, this afternoon, at 4 o'clock.

Died: on Aug 22, Margaret Barrett, aged 28 years. Her funeral will take place from her late residence, 230 G st, at 2 P M tomorrow, Sunday, Aug 25. [Herald]

Hotel in Gtwn, D C, for rent on lease. Messrs Walker & Deslonde, lessees, having failed to comply with the terms of their lease, I have repossessed myself of the property known as the Union Hotel, Gtwn, D C, & offer the same for rent or lease on reasonable terms. -Riley A Shinn, Gtwn, D C

In Chancery in the Circuit Court for Somerset Co, Md. John Romain vs Thos S Peers & wife, Jas Richmond & wife, Jos P Schooley & Abraham Price. The object of this suit is to procure a decree for the sale of certain mortgaged premises to pay the mortgage debt. On Jul 24, 1866, Thos S Peers & wife & Jas Richmond & wife, then residents of Somerset Co, Md, executed to John Romain a mortgage on certain land in said county, before that time sold by said Romain to said Peers & Richmond, to secure the sum of $10,000, due said Romain on a bill obligatory of same date with said mortgage with interest from Jul 12, 1866, payable annually from said date; that said bill obligatory provided for 5 years stay on the principal debt, if the interest should be kept punctually paid, & that in default of the payment of the interest punctually the whole principal debt should become due & demandable & that by a covenant in said mortgage said Peers & Richmond covenanted that they & their heirs & assigns would pay the principal debt & interest according to the terms of the said obligation, & that if default should be made in the punctual payment of the annual interest as it fell due, that the whole principal debt should become due & demandable; that said Peers & wife & Richmond & wife have removed from the State of Md & are believed to reside in N Y; that they have conveyed all their interest or equity of redemption to Jos P Schooley & Abraham Price; that Jos P Schooley resides in the State of Pa & Abraham P Schooley resides in Somerset Co aforesaid; that the annual interest fell due on Jul 12 last, & has not been paid, whereby the whole principal debt, with interest accrued, is due & demandable, & prays for a decree for the sale of the mortgaged premises for the payment of the mortgage debt. Absent dfndnts to appear in this court, either in person or by solicitor, on or before Jan 1 next. –Levin Woodford, clerk

MON AUG 26, 1867
Orphans Court-Judge Purcell, Aug 24, 1867. 1-Letters of administration on the estate of Eliz A Beall were issued to H Virginia Beall; bond $15,000. On the estate of John H Ford, to Wm T Ford; bond $2,000. 2-The case of the disputed account of Henry Seitz, guardian of Pauline Seitz, was argued by Mr Laskey for the ward, & Mr Schmidt for the guardian. 3-The will of the late Eliz Thompson was filed for probate & partially proven. She leaves her household furniture, goods & chattels, to her granddaughter, Dorcas Netter, & the balance of her estate to her friend, Benj McCoy, who is to keep the house for the sole & separate use of the granddaughter; & in case of her death, & she shall leave no issue, then it is to be descend to her grandson Geo Washington Netter. The granddaughter is directed to provide a home, in her house, for Dorcas Hambleton, her grandmother. Benj McCoy is nominated executor.

The school-house & lot belonging to the estate of the late Wm R Abbott, on West st, Gtwn, is offered for sale.

Mrs Buel will reopen her school on Sep 23, in the house lately occupied by Senator Sumner.

Mr & Mrs Wm C Fargo celebrated their golden wedding at Syracuse, N Y, on Wed.

Victims of stage disaster. The funeral of Miss Margaret Barrett, who drowned on Thu last, took place yesterday from her late residence 330 G st, & the body was taken from the house to St Matthew's Church, Rev Dr White officiating. Her remains were taken to **Mount Olivet Cemetery** for interment. The funeral of Miss Eliz Bremmar, of Gtwn, took place on Friday at Grace Church, Gtwn, Rev Dr Brown officiating. Her remains were interred in the **Presbyterian Burying ground**. The funeral of Miss Georgiana N Gray took place on Sat, from the residence of her mother, 367 N Y ave, & was largely attended.

Died: on Aug 25, Mrs Ellen J McClosky, relict of the late Richd McClosky. Her funeral will take place from the M St Methodist Church, at 3 o'clock on Aug 27.

Died: on Aug 11, at New Iberia, La, of yellow fever, Dr Thos Mattingly, son of the late Edw Mattingly, of Wash City.
+
Died: on Aug 5, at New Iberia, La, of yellow fever, Sidney, eldest daughter of Dr Thos Mattingly, formerly of Wash City.

Died: on Aug 24, at Mount Albans near Gtwn, D C, Col W Bevershout Thompson, aged 61 years. His funeral will take place at 3:30 P M, this afternoon, from St Albans Church, near Gtwn. [Balt Gaz, Richmond, Va, & Raleigh, N C, papers please copy.]

Died: on Sunday, Miss Teresa Hill, in her *7_th year of her age, a native of St Mary's Co, Md, & for 40 years an exemplary member of St Patrick's Church, in Wash City.
Her funeral is this afternoon, from St Patrick's Church, at 4 o'clock. [*There is a space next to the 7 with no number.]

Saratoga, Aug 25. J Theodore Jones, deputy jailor of Hudson City, N J, was shot & killed at the Union Hotel this morning by Wm J Kertley. Jones was intoxicated & went into the boot-room & started an altercation with Kertley. Kertley came from Balt, & is keeping a billiard room under the Leland Opera House. Kertley was committed to custody by the Coroner.

Vicksburg Daily Times of Aug 12. On Tuesday a gay party was at the residence of Mrs A L Hebron, the respected widow of the late Col John Hebron, near Bovina, in this county. Within the brief space of time since those glad young spirits parted Wednesday, 7 have died; 12 are ill. Those who have already perished: Miss Rebecca Hebron, Miss Ellen Tribble, Mr Jas Billingslea, Wm Tribble, Hal Wilkins, Thornton *Sthreshly, & Allen Auter. Those now ill: Miss Mollie Downing, of this city, Miss Victoria Bachelor, & Miss Viola Brabston, of the Bovina neighborhood, & Messrs Jos & Alex Johnson, [brothers,] Granville Hicks, Messrs Andrew & Henry Boiles, [brothers,] A C Brooks, Capt J M Bachelor, Henry Brabston, & Wm Hunter. All the parties had similar symptoms of cholera. The medical gentlemen in attendance concur that the guests were poisoned. We learn that 5 servants have died from the same cause. [*Copied as written.]

A few nights since Mrs Keller was shot & killed standing in the door of her house, about 9 miles from Galena, Ill. Her husband, going to the door was also fired at, but not injured. A man named PeterZower, a suitor for the hand of Julia, daughter of the murdered lady, is suspected of the crime, he having been twice rejected, & having sworn vengeance against the family in consequence.

Southern Home School for Young Ladies, est'd in 1842, at 197 & 199 North Chas st, Balt, Md. Mr & Mrs Wilson M Cary, Mrs General John Pegram, Principals, assisted by a full corps of able instructors. Duties resumed Sep 2.

Orphans Court of Wash Co, D C. Letters of administration on the personal estate of Eliz A Beall, late of Wash Co, D C, deceased. –H Virginia Beall, admx

TUE AUG 27, 1867
Postmaster Wilson, at New Albany, Ind, has fallen heir to $1,000,000 in England.

The **Sisters of Charity** of Providence Hospital, at 2nd & D st, Capitol Hill, desire us to state that they receive from the Gov't $1,000 per month for the support of 60 non-resident paupers, more or less, & but for this support would never have been able to keep up the Hospital. The bldgs cost $60,000, & the Gov't gave $30,000, while by subscription $10,000 more were added to this amount, leaving still a large amount of debt. The residents of Wash who cannot pay are supported free, & there is always a good number in the Hospital, while none are ever refused admission. The Sisters now desire funds to pay off the debt on the bldgs, & to raise means for the support of the poor residents of Wash, principally for the former purpose.

Yesterday Mr Wm Crowley & Jos Manders were standing at one of the stalls in Centre Market, & a pistol in the hands of Manders accidentally exploded, & the ball took effect in the right breast of Crowley. He died in a few moments. The parties were cousins, & warm personal friends. Crowley was in his 20th year, & resided with his father, on F st, between 10th & 11th sts. They were both hucksters, doing business at Centre Market. Manders was overwhelmed with grief at the unfortunate occurrence. The Justice dismissed Manders from custody.

St Vincent's School, corner 10th & G sts, under the charge of the **Sisters of Charity**, will open on Sep 2. For further particulars apply to the Sisters.

Supreme Court of D C, No 168 Equity-Docket 7. Fendall Marbury, adm of Wm Lyles, deceased, vs John Douglass. On motion of the cmplnt, by Messrs Fendall & Fendall, his solicitors, it is ordered that the dfndnts, Thos J Fisher & Wm H Smith, cause their appearance on or before the first rule day occurring 40 days after this Aug 26, 1867; otherwise the caue will be proceeded with as in case of default. –R J Meigs, clerk

On Aug 18, at Darlington district, S C, Mr Peter McIver, who lives in the Leavensworth neighborhood, had been for some time past troubled with rogues depredating among his poultry. On the night in question, Mrs McIver, for some reason or other, unknown to the family, went out into the yard; Mr McIlver had his son, almost of age, take a gun & go out into the yard; he returned & told his father he shot some person down. That person was his mother, who died in about 3 hours.

Jeremiah Day, D C, LL D, formerly the president of Yale College, died in New Haven, Conn, on Aug 22, in his 94th year. He was born in New Preston, Conn, Aug 3, 1773, educated at Yale College, where he graduated with high honor in 1795. His 48 years service at Yale added greatly to the reputation & influence of that institution.

WED AUG 28, 1867
Mrs John F Coyle, Miss Annie Coyle, & Mr Frank D Coyle, arrived at N Y on Monday by the steamer **Ville De Paris**.

The beautiful residence of M W Galt, on H st, near 14th, is rapidly approaching completion under the direction of Messrs Baldwin Bros, the contractors; it is probably the best bldg that has been erected in Wash this season.

Newark, Aug 27. Hon Ira C Whitehead, formerly a Judge of the Supreme Court of N J, died at his residence, in Morristown, in his 70th year. [No death date given-current item.]

Orphans Court-Judge Purcell, Aug 27, 1867. 1-The will of the late Teresa Hill was filed. After making provision for her interment at **Mount Olivet Cemetery**, $100 is bequeathed to St Vincent's Female Orphan Asylum of Wash; $100 to Francis Patrick Kendrick, of Balt; $100 to Francis Adams, of PG Co, Md; & the balance of her estate she leaves to Mrs C V Callan, her executrix. The will is dated Apr 14, 1862, & to it is a codicil dated Nov 6, 1865, revoking the bequests to St Vincent's Orphan Asylum, to F P Kendrick & Francis Adams. 2-The last will of the late Adam Gaddis was filed & fully proven. After making provision for the payment of his debts, he bequeaths all his personal & real estate to his wife during her life, & at her death to his children. Letters of administration, with the will annexed, were issued to Julia Ann Gaddis; bond $12,000. 3-The will of the late Henry Carrick was filed, partly proven, & admitted to probate, as regards personality. He bequeathes his house & lot on 6½ st, between D & E, to his wife during her widowhood, & if she should marry, the property is to be sold, & one-half of the proceeds shall be paid to her, & the balance be equally divided between his living brothers & sisters. In case she does not again marry, she may dispose of it as she chooses. All his personal estate is left to his wife, & his interest in the real estate of Henry Carrick, his father, he bequeathes to his brother, Jas P Carrick. Wm Edelen, of PG Co, Md, is nominated executor. 4-The will of the late Patrick Reynolds [orderly to commandant of the Marine Corps] was filed, fully proven, & letters testamentary issued to Thos Hutchingson, the executor named; bond $2,000. After the payment of his debts he bequeathes $200 to Mrs Mary Heilburn, & to Thos Hutchingson lots 11 thru 15 in square 974. 5-Letters of administration on the estate of the late E Bird were issued to Martha W Bird & W T Doniphan; bond $1,500. 6-The third general & second individual account of Emma Gibbs, guardian to the orphans of John H Gibbs, deceased; second general & fourth individual accounts of Bernard Geir, & Johanna E Ruppert, guardians to the orphans of Chas Thoma, deceased; & the second account of Wm Crux, guardian to Jas M Minor, deceased, were approved & passed.

A cable despatch announced the death of Alfred Armand Louis Marie Velpeau, the distinguished French surgeon. He was born at Breche, dept of Indre et Loire, May 18, 1795, & was brought up to assist his father, who was a farrier. He was enabled, by a benevolent neighbor, to study in the hospital of Tours. [No death date given-current item.]

U S Marshal's sale of valuable real estate on the corner of K st & N Y ave, by 12 writs of fieri facias issued from the Clerk's ofc of the Supreme Court of D C: sale on Sep 16 next, the following property of Geo Seitz: part of lot 1 in square 343;; with improvements; will be sold to satisfy executions Nos 2,308, John W Clampet, surviving partner of Wm H Clampet; 2,383, Yates & Selby; 2,409, J B Dodson; 2,582, Kavanaugh & Jameson; 2,613, Evan Lyons; 2,707, Evan Lyons; 2,780, Geo M Oyster; 2,968, Zimmerman & Van Camp; 3,764, Wall, Stephens & Co; 3,279, Jos R Spaney; 3,575, Herman Kaffel, all against Geo Seitz. –D S Gooding, U S Marshal, D C

Orphans Court of Wash Co, D C. Letters of administration, c t a, on personal estate of Adam Gaddis, sr, late of Wash, D C, deceased. –Julia Ann Gaddis, admx, c t a

Orphans Court of Wash Co, D C. Letters testamentary on the personal estate of Patrick Reynolds, late of the U S Marine Corps, deceased. –Thos Hutchingson, exc

The number of presidents of the **Chesapeake & Ohio Canal**, from it organization to the present time, are as follows:

1-Chas Fenton Mercer, Loudon Co, Va
2-John H Eaton, of Tenn
3-Geo C Washington, of D C
4-Francis Thomas, of Fred'k Co, Md
5-Michl C Sprigg, Allegany Co, Md
6-Wm Gibbs McNeill, of NY
7-Jas M Cole, of Fred'k Co, Md
8-Saml Sprigg, of PG Co, Md
9-Wm Grason, Queen Anne's Co, Md
10-Saml Hambleton, of Talbot Co, Md
11-Wm P Maulsby, of Fred'k Co, Md
12-L J Bringle, of Fred'k Co, Md
13-Jas Fitzpatrick, Allegany Co, Md
14-Alfred Spates, of Allegany Co, Md
15-Jacob Snivley, of Wash Co, Md

The canal was finished to Cumberland in 1850. The canal is divided into 6 divisions:
Gtwn division: 22 miles
Harper's Ferry div: 42 miles
Antietam div: 23 miles
Wmsport div: 22 miles
Hancock div: 27 miles
Cumberland div: 49 miles
A total of 185 miles.

Dissolution of copartnership under the firm of Wall, Stephens & Co, by mutual consent, T A Stephens withdrawing from the concern.
–W Wall, T A Stephens, B Robinson

Jos F Hodgson, the present official intendant of the Wash Asylum, having tendered his resignation to the Mayor, to take effect Sep 1st, Mayor Wallach has appointed Saml E Douglass, to the position.

Died: on Aug 25, at Galveston, Texas, of yellow fever, Col W S Abert, U S A, son of the late Col J J Abert, chief of Topographical Engineers.

Supreme Court of D C-811 Equity. Mary A Miller et al vs Miriane M Ellin et al. Sale made & reported by John B Turton, trustee in this cause, be ratifed & confirmed. -E Carusi, solicitor -R J Meigs, clerk [No details given on the sale.]

St Louis, Aug 27. Capt Arms, who had a fight with a large body of Indians on the Republican river, a few days ago, arrived at **Fort Hayes** yesterday. He reports losing 3 men killed, 35 wounded, & a loss of 40 horses. The indians' loss is reported at about 150.

THU AUG 29, 1867
Mr Chas F Wood is busily completeing the fine residence of Mr A S Solomons, of the firm of Philp & Solomons; house is the second on **Franklin Row**, on K st, between 12th & 13th sts, & was formerly one of the original row. The old bldg has been completely remodeled, & enlarged by the addition of another story & a large back bldg. The handsome press-brick front was erected by Mr John J McCollom, well known as a master bricklayer of Wash City.

Accidents: yesterday Allie Lincoln, about 11, son of John Lincoln, residing at 651 7th st, between D & E sts, Island, fell out of the 2nd story window, striking the pavement; internal injuries are feared. Albert Howard, about 12, residing in Gtwn, was accidentally run over by one the street cars yesterday; his feet were very badly injured; he was removed to his home. Wm C Browning, a bricklayer, employed on the bldg now being erected on 22nd st, near H, fell yesterday from the scaffold to the ground, 16 feet, & fractured his left shoulder; he was removed to his residence. On Tuesday, Christopher Hoffman, employed at Abner's weiss beer brewery, was injured in the arm by an accidental shot from a pistol in the hands of Wm Hess. The weapon exploded while being carelessly handled. Mr Laner, the Chief Engineer of the Gtwn Fire Dept, was seriously wounded yesterday, cutting his foot open with an adze while giving instructions to a workman, employed under him, at the Wash & Gtwn bridge.

Jas Hilton, charged with stealing a horse from O E Duffy, a farmer, near Bladensburg, was arrested on Tuesday by Lt Johnson, of the 2nd Precinct. Hilton was turned over to the authorities of Montg Co, & the horse turned over to its owner.

Explosion at the Bennington Powder Manufactory Co, in the village of Bennington, Vt, on Tuesday, instantly killed 3 men, Abraham Moon, Edw Cunningham, & Wm Downs.

Ramble about Alexandria. **Christ Church** & the church yard is most interesting in its memories. Fairfax parish was formed in 1863, though a small Episcopal church appears to have been built some years earlier. The vestry-book began in 1763; two churches within its limits-one near Little Falls Church, known by the same name; the other called Lower Church. It is believed that there was another church in the town, or very near it, before the establishment of Christ Church, which was not completed, till 1773, 31 years after Alexandia was founded. The vestry repaired the 2 original churches in 1765, at a cost of more than 32,000 pounds of tobacco. Mr Jas Wren drew a plan, which was adopted by the vestry. Mr Jas Parsons contracted to build "the Church at Alexandria," & was to have 600 pounds to do it, & 3 years to complete the contract. Mr Jas Wren built the Falls Church for 599 pounds & 15 shillings. Pohick Church, in Truro Parish, some 7 miles from Mount Vernon, was rebuilt; Washington was very prominent as a vestryman in the erection; Rev Lee Massey was rector of Pohick Church at this period. The pew which Washington purchased [for 36 pounds 10 shillings,] in the Alexandria Church in 1773 became the place in which he & his family were constant worshippers from the time that Pohick Church fell into disuse. The silver plate, with Geo Washington upon it, is still to be seen on the pew, as it was in the lifetime of the illustrious patriot. The plate was purloined during the war, but has since been recovered. The ancient bible belonging to the pulpit, presented by Washington, was removed, & has not been found. We did not find the name of Washington as vestryman of Christ Church till 1785. Vestry chosen for Fairfax parish, 28th March, 1785, with votes for each: John West, 340; Chas Alexander, 309; Wm Paine, 304; John Dalton, 281; Geo Washington, 274; Chas Broadwater, 260; Geo Johnston, 254; Townsend Dade, 252; Richd Sandford, 247; Wm Adams, 244; John Posey, 222; Danl French, 221. In Truro [Pohick] parish Washington was chosen vestryman the same year, receiving 259 votes; Geo Mason, 282; & Edw Paine, 277. The first rector was Rev Townsend Dade, whose father, Townsend Dade, was a planter near Alexandria. He was ordained by the Bishop of London in 1765. He was not a model clergyman; he neglected his congregation; Mr Dade eventually resigned. The deed of the Rectory & Parsonage to the vestry was made by Rev Townsend Dade, Jun 27, 1778, says the record. Rev Spence Grayson was a candidate for the parish, but they fixed upon Rev Mr West, from Md, who served about 2 years, resigning in 1779. Rev David Griffith was the next in succession; born in N Y C, in 1741; educated to the medical profession, receiving his degree in London, returned home & settled in his profession in the interior of his native province, in 1763; relinquished this profession & going to London, was ordained in that city by Bishop Terrick, in 1770, & was afterwards a missionary for a brief period, in Gloucester Co, N J; in Dec 1771, was elected rector of Shelburne parish, Loudoun Co, Va; in 1776 he was chaplain of the 3rd Va regt-for 4 years; in 1780 he took charge of Fairfax parish, till his death in 1789. He died in Phil, at the house of Bishop White, his bosom friend, while attending as delegate the Genr'l Triennial Convention, on the first day of which Convention he had formally resigned his election as bishop. When he died, he left 8 children, the oldest being but 16 years of age. His wife, Hannah Colville, of N Y C, whon he married in 1766, died at Alexandria in 1811. There was one daughter surviving a few years ago. Dr Griffith was well remembered by Mr Custis, of Arlington, who described him as tall, large, compact, & muscular, in person; gentle & courteous, but firm in manners & spirit. Rev Bryan Fairfax was the successor of Dr Griffith, in 1790; age 63 years. He died in 1802, at his place, called **Mount Eagle**, not far from Hunting Creek Bridge; he left 2 sons, Fernando & Thomas, by his first marriage, the latter of whom succeeded to the empty title. Mrs Chas Catlett was his daughter by a second marriage. Rev Thos Davis was chosen successor of Lord Fairfax, & was their minister from 1792 till 1806. He died on the Eastern Shore, Md. While the church was vacant, 1806, after Mr Davis left, the vestry invited Rev Mr McGraff, a Scotch Presbyterian minister, the principal of Wash Academy in Alexandria to officiate for them. Rev Mr Gibson, of Md, successor of Mr Davis, entered on his duties in 1806; his style of preaching culminated in an open quarrel between parish & pastor. He resigned in 1809. The friends of Mr Gibson, being voted down, withdrew & established St Paul's Church in 1810, Mr Gibson became its rector; resigning in Sep, 1811, & returning to Md, & was later dismissed for intemperance. He reformed & turned Methodist, & became a minister in that sect. In 1810, Rev Mr Barcley, who came to Md from the West Indies, became the minister of Christ Church, Bishop Claggett, of Md, certifying to his character. In the spring of 1811 his wife, whom he had deserted in the West Indies, appeared in Alexandria, where he had married again. He resigned & fled to parts unknown. In the fall of this year Wm Meade, then 21, succeeded as rector; graduated in 1809 at Princeton; ordained in 1811, at Wmsburg; when called to Alexandria he was working on a small farm, & assisting Rev Mr Balmaine in that parish. During Mr Meade's ministry, less than 2 years, the church was aroused, greatly enlarged, & the congregation multiplied, John Randolph & Jas Milnor being of the number. [Mr Milnor, abandoned law & politics, became an Episcopal clergyman, the celebrated Dr Milnor, of St George's Church, N Y C.] Mr Meade, afterwards Dr Meade, was succeeded in 1813, by Rev Oliver Norris, who for some 12 years, to the day of his death, was a most faithful pastor. He died in 1825. Bishop Meade preached his funeral sermon. He was of a Quaker family, being a convert to the Church which he adorned & blessed with his ministry. At this time Rev Wm H Wilmer, of Md, came to Alexandria as rector of St Paul's Church; the two ministers, both from Md, were kindred in spirit with Bishop Meade, contributing very largely to the recuscitation of the spiritual life in the Episcopal Church of Va. Mr Wilmer left St Paul's Church the same year in which Mr Norris died, to assume the presidency of Wm & Mary's College. Mr Wilmer was elected rector of St John's Church, in Wash, when that church was built in 1816, but he did not accept. He died in 1827. Dr Reuel Keith, professor in the Theological Seminary, then located in Alexandria, consented to act as pastor, & filled the place, with some interruptions, till Rev Geo Griswold, son of Bishop Griswold, became pastor in 1828. He resigned at the end of the year from ill health; was succeeded by Rev J P McGuire, who resigned at the end of the first year from weakness of eyesight. Rev Mr Mann succeeded, continuing 3 years & resigning in 1833, to accept an agency from The Theological Seminary. [Dr Keith, a native of Vt, graduated at Middleburg College in 1814, the Alexandria Seminary, established in 1823, was under his entire control in its first years, his mind, from great labor, became unstrung in 1842, & his brother took him to his early home in Vt, where he died insane the same year, at age 51 years; an able & good man.] Rev Chas B Dana, a native of Mass, succeeded Mr

Mann in 1833; he is now a rector of a church in Memphis. During the war Rev Mr Fugitt officiated for a time; after him-Rev John A Bowman, hospital chaplain in Alexandria, occupied the pulpit; succeeded by Rev Robt McMurdy, also a hospital chaplain, who left in 1866, to become the editor of the Freemason Journal in N Y C. For the last year Rev A M Randolph has served as the rector with great acceptance, but leaves in Oct to assume the rectorship of Emanuel Church, Balt, to which he had been called. We trust the vestry will be successful in their choice of a successor.

The President has appointed Mr Frank Sherman postmaster at Chicago.

Fort Hayes, Kansas, Aug 26. Three hundred cavalry, under the command of Maj Elliott, of the 7th U S infty, & Maj Moore, of the 18th Kansas, left here today on a expedition to chastise the Indians who attacked Maj Arms several days ago on the Saline. The health of the troops is excellent.

Galveston, Aug 28. The following removals for disloyalty have been ordered: S Crosby, com'r of the land ofc; W L Roberts, comptroller; M H Royston, treasurer; Wm Walton, atty gen; in whose places, Jos Spence, M C Hamilton, John T Allen, & Wm Alexander were appointed.

A cable despatch this morning announces the death of Prof Michl Faraday, the celebrated English physicist; born on Sep 22, 1791, in the parish of Newington, Surrey. The great scientific achievements of Mr Faraday began in 1820, with the discovery of the chlorides of carbon; in 1821 he discovered the mutual rotation of a magnetic pole & an electric current; in 1823, the condensation of the gasses.

John Coburn, who recently died, [Aug 9, 1867,] was one of our oldest residents. The ancestry of John Coburn was of the old Plymouth stock; his grandfather Capt Danl Coburn, was a capt in one of the first companies enrolled in the War of Independence, & died at 96. John was born at Charlton, Mass, on Sep 25, 1796; at age 4 years his father's family emigrated into Vt. Mr Coburn was one of the earliest masons in the District of Columbia, & long served as a worthy craftsman in New Jerusalem Lodge. Fifteen years since, under the influence of deep feeling, & during the revival of religion at the Foundry, under Rev Dr Jesse T Peck, he sought & found peace in his Redeemer, & was thereafter a consistent follower of Christ. He died as he had lived, & his large family have the sympathies of all. –J L

Dr Barnas Sears, agent of the trustees of the Peabody educational fund for the South, will, it is said, take up his residence in Staunton, Va.

Dept of the Interior, U S Patent Ofc, Wash, Aug 21, 1867. Ptn of Chas J Woolson, of Cleveland, Ohio, praying for the extension of a patent granted to him Dec 4, 1860, for an improvement in Design for Steve Plate, for seven years from the expiration of said patent, which takes place on Dec 4, 1867. -T C Theaker, Com'r of Patents

FRI AUG 30, 1867
There is now in course of erection by Messrs John O Evans & A Teemyer, contractors, a magnificent residence, owned by Dr N Horwitz, chief of the Medical Bureau of the Navy Dept, situated on the north side of K st, next to the corner of 13th st, fronting on Franklin Square, & is being built in accordance with plans prepared by Mr Henry R Searle, architect. The cellar extends under the entire bldg, & has a concrete floor, thoroughly grouted with hydraulic cement; the foundation walls are of granite, 18 inches thick; the bldg fronts 25 feet by a depth of 50 feet.

Albert Howard, son of Jas Howard, residing on Cherry st, Gtwn, who had his foot terribly lacerated by being run over by a street car on Wed, was yesterday removed from his home to Providence Hospital, at the suggestion of the attending physician. It will be necessary to amputate the foot, mortification having already set in.

A young German, Jos Zumbush, committed suicide in Cincinnati on Wed. He was in love with a young lady working in a store on Vine st & she refused his attentions. He went to the store & plunged a dagger into his heart, & fell to the floor a corpse.

Wm A Bradley, whose memory is identified with the history of Washington City, died on Aug 28, from an attack of diarrhoea on Monday, & sunk under it on Wed. He came here as a small boy, shortly after the removal of the seat of gov't to Wash City, & has ever since resided here. He held many prominent positions in our community. He had reached his 74th year. Some weeks ago he went into the mountains of Pa to reinvigorate his waning strength. His remains have been brought to Washington City, which his home.

John Mitchell, a laborer, residing on F st, employed upon the Metropolitan railroad, near Point of Rocks, was seriously injured on Wed by the premature explosion while blasting a tunnel. The injuries received may prove fatal.

Phil, Aug 29. Geo W Winnemore was executed today for the murder of Mrs Magilton. Part of his speech: it is an innocent man's life you are taking; one who had nothing to do with this crime, in word or deed. How terrible it is to hang a man for this, although death has no terrors for me. It is a mere change of breath.

Last Friday week, Mrs Wm H Brown, a widow lady, of Fairfield, Conn, 60 years of age, started from the White Mountain House, with a female companion & guide, to make the ascent of **Mount Washington**. Later in the afternoon it was discovered that Mrs Brown was missing. Search was made for her all night. Next morning, to the joy & surprise of all, she made her appearance at the foot of the railway. She was hungry & exhausted, & her clothing was torn & damp. She said she kept with the guide & companion for some time & suddenly found she was alone. I could not see anyone. She continued walking through the night. She is the widow of a late well-known ship-builder of N Y C, & is apparently none the worse for passing a night alone & unprotected among the mountains. –Boston Journal

Women's Rights. N Y, Aug 29. Susan B Anthony & Eliz Cady Stanton left last evening for Kansas, to advocate female suffrage until the election.

The following officers have been detailed as members of a general court-martial, to meet at *Fort Leavenworth*, Kansas, Sep 15, for the purpose of trying Brvt Maj Gen G A Custer, 7th cavalry, & others: Brvt Maj Gen W Hoffman, colonel 3rd infty; Brvt Maj Gen G W Davidson, lt colonel 10th cavalry; Brvt Maj Gen B W Grierson, colonel 10th cavalry; Brvt Brig Gen P Morison, retired list; Brvt Brig Gen M R Morgan, commissary subsistence; Brvt Brig Gen F D Callendar, ordinance dept; Brvt Lt Col T C English, 5th infty; Brvt Maj Henry Asbury, 3rd infty; & Brvt Maj J C Syford, ordnance dept; Capt Robt Chandler, 3rd infty, judge advocate. Gen Custer is charged with leaving his post, & being absent therefrom without permission.

The wife of Hon Benj Wood was found dead in her bed on Sat at her residence near Manhasset, L I. Disease of the heart is supposed cause.

U S Marshal's sale on Sep 18, of Walter Lenox's right, title, claim, & interest in the west half of lot 2 in square 347, in Wash City, D C, with improvements, & will be sold to satisfy execution in favor of John H & Albert W Kirkwood, No 1,016 S C. -W H Lamon, late U S Marshal, D C

SAT AUG 31, 1867
The funeral of Wm A Bradley will take place from his late residence, 336 N Y ave, on Sep 1, at 3:30 o'clock P M. [Sep 1st newspaper: The remains of Mr Wm A Bradley were placed in the public vault at *Glenwood Cemetery*. The pall-bearers were W W Corcoran, Dr J B Blake, Dr J C Hall, Mayor Wallach, Hugh Caperton, Fitzhugh Coyle, Thos Blagden, & J B North. The funeral cortege was very long, there being over 60 carriages in the line.]

New car arrangement. Mr L W Emmart, the Superintendant of the F st railroad, was engaged yesterday in receiving, at the Balt railroad depot, & sending to the stables of the company, five of the new one-horse cars to be used on the road. They are fine specimens of the workmanship of the manufacturer, Mr John Stephenson, of N Y,

J C Pickett, in his 75th year, was badly bitten by a dog yesterday at 3rd & C sts. It is not known whether the dog was afflicted with hydrophobia. Mr Pickett was passing along the pavement in a quiet manner when attacked by the dog.

Two boys, Chas G Dutrow & Michl Holland, residing in Gtwn, were badly injured by the explosion of a shot gun in the hands of another lad, Thos Trunnell, on Thursday. Trunnel was examined before Justice Buckey, but the evidence did not show the shooting was accidental, he concluded to hold him until the injuries received by the boys could be better ascertained. Yesterday Justice Buckey was satisfied that the shooting was accidental.

The two story brick dwlgs on the north side of La ave, near 6th st, formerly belonging to the late John P Ingle, & now owned by Owen Thorn, were withdrawn, the bid being only $6,900, & under the limit.

The charge of rape preferred against Dr W G McCreary by Miss Ellen Seip, was dismissed yesterday by Maj Richards, before whom the examination was held.

The Consolidated Business College, 7th & D sts, over the Bank of the Republc, will be resumed Sep 3. Address Henry N Copp, A M, Principal & Proprietor.

Mr & Mrs York will be at their school house, 14th & N Y ave, to meet those who may wish to see them, from 4 to 6 P M, on Sep 4th thru the 6th.

Dept of the Interior, U S Patent Ofc, Wash, Aug 24, 1867. Ptn of Jos Goedmark, of Brooklyn, N Y, praying for the extension of a patent granted to him Nov 22, 1853, for an improvement in Facing Ends of Percussion Caps, for seven years from the expiration of said patent, which takes place on Nov 22, 1867.
-T C Theaker, Com'r of Patents

MON SEP 2, 1867
Ex-Govn'r Thos Brown died at Tallahassee, Fla, Aug 24th, in his 82nd year of his age.

J S Kirby, late telegrapher & agent of the Union Pacific railroad at Topeka, Kansas, committed suicide at Americus, Kansas, last Thursday. It is reported that he was a defaulter to the company in the sum of $5,000.

Mr Edwin Green, an old & highly respected citizen of Washington, died very suddenly at his residence, 12th & K sts, [*Franklin Row,*] yesterday. He had been on a pleasure trip with his family to Cape May, & was returning on Friday, when, while in the cars, he was attacked by a diarrhoea, [similar to that to which the late Mr Bradley fell a victim.] He was very sick the remainder of the trip, & was brought to his home, where, after lingering until yesterday, he breathed his last. For many years he was an extensive manufacturer & dealer in furniture; some years ago he retired from active business.

Wm McCathran died at his residence, on the Navy Yard, on Sat. He was the principal of the Wallach school-house, & for years past has been known to our citizens as one of the best of our public school instructors. He was a brother of Donald McCathran, Alderman from the 6th Ward. The disease of Mr McCathran was consumption.

Partnership Notice. Having this day taken into partnership with me Mr L L Nicholson, of Wash City, the name & style of the firm here after will be McNeir & Nichols. –Wm McNeir, Real Estate Agent, 495 7th st.

Orphans Court-Judge Purcell, Aug 31, 1867. 1-The Seitz case, in which the ward, Pauline Seitz, disputes the correctness of the account of her guardian, Henry Seitz, was brought up before the Court, & witnesses of the ward examined. The examination of the witnesses for Mr Seitz, the guardian, was postponed until next Saturday. 2-Thos McFadden & Thos J Murray were appointed to appraise the goods & real estate of Eliz Beall, deceased. H Virginia Beall was duly appointed guardian to the children of Horatio & Eliz Beall, deceased. 3-Benj M McCoy was duly admitted as executor of Eliz Thompson, deceased; bond $300. 4-Richd Fullalove was admitted as executor of Jas Fullalove, late of Gtwn, now deceased; bond $5,000.

Mrd: on Aug 29, at the Church of the Ascension, by Rev Dr Pinckney, Jas M Moore, U S A, to Rosa B Bowlwell. [Aug 4th newspaper: Mrd: on Aug 29, at the Church of the Ascension, by Rev Dr Pinckney, Jas M Moore, U S A, to Rosa B Boutwell.]

Died: on Aug 30, suddenly, Julia A, beloved wife of Thos W Miller. Her funeral is this afternoon, from the residence of her husband, 451 N st, between 12th & 13th, at 3:30 P M.

Died: on Aug 31, Clara, youngest daughter of Geo W & Mary F Steen, aged 12 months & 21 days.

Saml Kirk & Sons, established 1817, 192 Balt st, Balt, Md. Manufacture of silverware, tea & dinner sets, spoons & forks.

Wm S Mitchell & Co will remove to 9th & Pa ave, Sep 2, & will show a complete stock of carpeting & house-furnishing dry goods, which they offer at the lowest market prices.

TUE SEP 3, 1867
Ads. 1-John S Hollingshead, notary public & com'r of deeds, pays particular attention to the preparation of legal papers. 2-John C Parker, 453 7th st, calls attention to his stock of school-books. 3-Francis Lamb, 237 Pa ave, near 13th, offers for sale an elegant assortment of mirrors & picture frames. 4-100,000 peach trees are offered for sale by John Perkins, at Morristown, N J.

The laying of the corner-stone of the German Lutheran Chapel & School-house, to be erected at 4th & High sts, Gtwn, took place yesterday; appropriate anthem was sung by German Saengerbund, of Wash, followed by prayer by Rev Saml D Finckel, who also delivered the address in German & English.

Dr W J C Duhamel has been reappointed physician to the jail by Warden Huestis. It will be remembered that when Mr Huestis entered upon his duties one of the first acts of his official career was to suspend Dr Duhamel.

Mrd: On Aug 26, at Newport, R I, by Rev J P White, Mr Peter Vermeren, of Wash, D C, to Madame V N Hermanny, of N J.

Wm W Nicholson, a native of Gtwn, was arrested in this city on Sat by Detectives Clarvoe & McDevitt, on the charge of having stolen a horse & buggy from M Bradbury, of Phil, & which property he afterwards sold. Yesterday Nicholson was delivered to Detective Levy, on a requisition from the Govn'r of Pa.

The funeral of the late Wm McCathran took place yesterday; Rev Geo V Leech, of the M E Church, officiated. The **Congressional Cemetery** was selected as the place of burial. The following gentleman were pall-bearers: Messrs Wm H Bowen, S A H Marks, jr, Saml Turner, Henry S Simmons, Geo Hunt, & Saml Cross. The deceased leaves a wife & child to mourn his loss.

Died: on Sep 1, after a brief illness, Edwin Green, in his 56th year. His funeral will take place from his late residence, 12th & K sts, this evening at 3 o'clock P M.

Died: on Sep 1, Mary Louisa Korff, in her 21st year. Her funeral will be on Wed at 3 o'clock P M, from 358 7th st, between I & Mass ave.

Richmond, Sep 2. Suicide. John Cady, a soldier of the 11th U S infty, cut his throat at headquarters this morning. He was from Newark, N J.

Newburyport Correspondence Boston Post, Aug 17. Triple funeral on Aug 29 will long be remembered in the pretty village of Gtwn, & of the disaster at Pentucket pond, by which 3 of a party lost their lives & 2 narrowly escaped. A party of 4 left the home of Rev Chas Beecher on Tuesday for a sail on the pond. Alarm was soon given that the party was in the pond. The citizens quickly rallied, but three of the party had disappeared. They were the two daughters, the youngest children of Rev Chas Beecher, Esther Lyman, aged 15, & Edith Harriet, aged 13 years. Albert Beecher, aged 20 years, was the youngest son of Rev Edw Beecher, of Galesburg, Ill, & with an older brother had arrived in Gtwn only the previous evening. These three sank at once. Eugene Beecher, an older brother of Albert, was rescued just as he was disappearing in an unconscious condition. Lockwook Coffin, the 5th of the party, clung to the boat. The bodies of Mr & the Misses Beecher were not recovered for nearly 3 hours. The family in different sections, were notified, & there were present today, Rev H W Beecher, of North Brookfield, Mass; Mrs Harriet Beecher Stowe, of Hartford, Conn; Mrs John Hooker, of same city; Mrs Dr Lyman Beecher, Prof Wm Smyth, of Bowdoin College, & Prof E C Smyth & wife of Andover. The church where Mr Beecher officiates was opened for the funeral; the coffins were placed one at either side of the pulpit, & the other directly in front of it. A triple funeral never occurred in the town before.

Elegant household & kitchen furniture at auction on Sep 12, at the residence of Count Wydenbruck, the Austrian Minister, corner of K & 12th sts.
– Cooper & Latimer, aucts

Excellent household & kitchen furniture at auction on Sep 9, at the residence of Rev N P Tillinghast, 59 First st. -Thos Dowling, auct

Orphans Court of Wash Co, D C, Aug 31, 1867. In the case of Chester M Colt, adm of Chester A Colt, deceased, the administrator & Court have appointed Sep 21 next, for the final settlement of the personal estate of the said deceased, of the assets in hand. -Jas R O'Beirne, Reg/o wills

For sale: a young stallion from the best trotting stock, Diamond. Address me at Darnestown, Montg Co, Md, John L Du Fief.

War Dept Claims Commission, Wash, D C, Aug 31, 1867. List of claims received for the month of Aug, 1867:
Claim of Michl Golder, for compensation for services as deputy provost marshal.
Hudson Town Co, for rent of hotel at Macon, Mo.
Claim of schnr **H S Lanfair**, for services rendered U S.
N T Herrick, for flour delivered to Commissary Dept at St Louis.
Wm Hendly, for moneys taken for use of U S Gov't.
Wm E Gere, for ice furnished U S, at Helena, Texas.
Mrs Eliza Patrick, for cotton seized by the U S at Baton Rouge, La.
A J Duncan, for property taken by U S troops.
Moses B Jacobs, for cattle taken by U S authorities.
T Q Jasper, for coal boats furnished U S army.
Oliver Bell, for extra-duty pay in 9th Missouri Vols.
R Sinclair & Co, for articles furnished U S, in 4th district, Md.
-De Witt Clinton, Brvt Lt Col, Recorder

Dept of the Interior, U S Patent Ofc, Wash, Aug 27, 1867. Ptn of Erastus T Brissell, of Indianapolis, Ind, praying for the extension of a patent granted to him Nov 29, 1853, for an improvement in Combined India Rubber & Steel Springs, for 7 years from expiration of said patent, which takes place on Nov 29, 1867. -T C Theaker, Com'r of Patents

WED SEP 4, 1867
Jennings Estate in England-London Times. The enormous property, estimated at from two to seven millions sterling, including estates in 11 counties in England, & money in all the old banks in London, is still in vigorous dispute. It was left by an enormous miser, Wm Jennings, who is described in the Annual register of 1798, as the riches Commoner in England. He was born in 1701, & died at his seat, **Acton Hall**, one of the most beautiful edifices in Great Britain. So mean were the habits of this old man, that he lived in the underground story of his great house, permitting, for the space of nearly 30 years, the approach of no woman. He died unmarried & childless, & left no will. The Baroness Howe, daughter of the celebrated Admiral Lord Howe, took possession of the old man's property, through a claim of intermarriage between a member of the Jennings family with that of the Cursons. Administration was not granted for 18 years, a significant fact. Wm Jennings was the godson of King Wm III, & served as page to the monarch. In connection also with his family at this period were Sarah Jennings, afterwards Duchess of Marlborough; Frances Jennings, [her sister,] Marchioness of Tyrconnell, wife of

Richd Talbot, the Lord Deputy of Ireland for King Jas II; &, little as it is supposed, Miss Hills, afterwards the famous rival & successor of the Duchess in the affections & favor of Queen Anne-Mrs Masham; in reality the creator of the fortunes of Harley, Earl of Oxford. Mrs Masham was a cousin of the Duchess of Marlborough, & was introduced at court by her. Frances, the Marchionness of Tyrconnell, was, in the days of her distress, the celebrated "White Milliner" appearing in the domestic history of Geo I, & commemorated in a modern comedy. Soame Jenys, the philosopher, & Constantine Jennings, [there are 11 different ways of spelling the name,] the possessor of 3 fortunes, who, notwithstanding, died in poverty in 1813, is known as "Dog Jennings" on account of his purchase of Alcibiades' Dog, were also of his family. He is supposed to have paid 2,000 guineas for the dog. The attraction of the great property lying open to the heirship of some persons undiscovered yet, if at all discoverable, draws claimants not only from the U S, but, to my familiar knowledge, from Cape of Good Hope, India, & Austrailia. I omit Ireland & Canada, which countries have sent to England claimants in profusion, with the proper proportion of lawyers & pedigree fanciers. Such is a story of wealth. Hargrave Jennings, London, Aug 17.

<u>Orphans Court</u>-Judge Purcell, Sep 3, 1867. 1-Christina V N Callan was duly admitted an excx of Teresa Hill, late of Wash, now deceased; bonds $4,000. The late will & testament of Teresa Hill, deceased, was duly admitted to probate & fully proven. 2-The last will & testament of Wm A Bradley, deceased, was fully proven. In it he bequeaths all of his real or personal estate to his son, Wm A Bradley, jr, & his cousin, A Thos Bradley; first to set apart the house in which he lived, together with all the household goods, to his wife; & out of the net income derived from his said estate of every sort, to pay to his wife one equal third part annualy or quarterly, as she may prefer. He next directed his trustees to divide all of his estate immediately after his death into four equal parts, which, if they cannot agree upon, they must call in a third uninterested party to aid them; one of the parts to go to his son, Wm A Bradley, jr; one part to the children of his son, now or hereafter born in lawful wedlock; one part to his daughter, Jeannete H Lenton; & one part to his daughter, Sidney T Edelin, whose portion shall embrace the property owned by him in N Y; & if either of his daughters should die without issue, their portions shall go to the children of his son, Wm A Bradley, jr, now & hereafter born. 3-The last will & testatment of Mrs Anna P Harvey, deceased, was filed & partially proven. She directed that the sum of $573.50 to be equally divided between Catherine Harvey & Ruth Benson, & all other money to Anna R McGregor, & some minor things which belonged to deceased; also, the sum of $500, which was the amount of the deceased's title in the bequest of her father, [Edw Key,] in his last will & testament; & to her husband's grand-daughter all of her bedchamber furniture. 4-Henry J McLaughlin was appoitned guardian to the orphans of Geo W Keating, deceased; bonds $2,000. 5-Truxton D Beall was admitted as administrator of the estate of Geo Beall, deceased; bonds $4,000.

Ex-Senator J A McDougall, of Calif, died at Albany, N Y on Sept 3; born in Albany Co, N Y not quite 50 years ago; received his education of the Grammar School in Albany.

Mr Robt Boswell, residing in Alexandria, & employed as pilot on board the ferry-boat **Winnisimmit**, arrived her yesterday with the boat, & since that time has not been seen, nor has anything been heard from him. He was last seen walking in the direction of the boat, having been to Sheckles' restaurant, near by.

Poughkeepsie, Sep 3. John D Jackson, who attempted to kill his father, Jos H Jackson, in this city a short time since, escaped from a lunatic asylum on Sat. The people here are much excited about it, as it is known he is determined to shoot down his father at sight. [Sep 13th newspaper: John T Jackson, the lunatic, was arrested at Ellenville, Ulster Co, on Sat. He stopped at the residence of Hon Geo T Pierce, but suspecting that he was watched, took to the mountains, where he was taken.]

Died: on Aug 15, in Huntsville, Ala, Ellen, wife of Geo A Gordon, & daughter of Geo F Beirne.

Died: on Sep 2, at Fairfax Court House, Va, at the residence of his grandparents, Charles Ford, infant son of Jos C & Antonia F Willard, aged 4 months & 20 days.

Washington High School for Boys, in the Union League Bldg, 9th, between D & E sts; commences on Sep 9, 1867. –Rev R B Williamson, A M, Principal, 444 6th st.

Chancery sale of valuable real estate at auction; No 276 Equity. Johanna E Rupert & John Rupert, cmplnts, vs Barnard & Louisa Thoma, dfndnts. Sale on Sep 17, lots numbered 22 & 24, in square 620, with the improvements, which are, on part of lot 22 a large 3 story brick house, containing 13 rooms; on lot 24 there are 3 two story frame house, fronting on Pierce st, or a 60 foot alley, making the above desirable property. –Bernard Geier, exc & trustee -Green & Williams, aucts

In the Circuit Court of Roanoke, last week, the suit of Utz's excs vs Booth was decided. This was an action of debt on 4 bonds for $18,000, given for the deferred payment of the puchase money of a fine estate near Bonsack's depot. The purchase was made in Oct, 1864. $10,000 was paid down in Confederate money. The excs claimed the deferred payments in specie or its equivalent. The dfndnt contended that the contract was a Confederate money contract, & that he should be allowed to scale it according to the rates on the day of purchase. The jury returned a verdict for the plntfs for about $11,000, having agreed to scale the debt. –Lynchburg News

THU SEP 5, 1867
The statue of Edw Everett, cast in bronze in Berlin, after the model made by W W Story, & to be placed in the Public Garden in Boston, is to be delivered early in October.

It has been ascertained from the ofc of Register of Deeds, Liber R M H, No 28, folio 44, that 3 acres & 20 perches of land, with the bldgs thereon, being the same that is now called Howard Univ, was purchased Dec 20, 1866, in the name of Gen Geo W Balloch, Disbursing Ofcr of Freedman's Bureau, who paid $12,000 for the same, out of the retained bounty fund [of which he was trustee] belonging to certain colored soldiers from Va & N C. The above bldgs have been enlarged & repaired out of the same fund, making the whole sum taken from this fund $25,000, more or less. By the 41st article of Revised Army Regulations, par 994, this act is made "felony & embezzlement."

Judge Lemuel D Evans, of Texas, was appointed, by the President, collector of internal revenue for the 4th district of his State. Col Minor, of Ohio, was yesterday appointed collector of the customs at Galveston, vice Kent, deceased.

Great match yesterday between the National Base-ball Club of Wash City, & the Unions of Lansingburg, N Y. The Nationals won by a score of 31 to 28.

Association of House Carpenters held a meeting on Tuesday. The following gentlemen were elected ofcrs for the enusing 6 months: president, Jas H Reed; vice-pres, O B Greenwell; rec sec, B L Nevins; financial sec, Chas M O'Bold; treas, John W Lansdale; sgt-at-arms, B F Snelling; also, elected as standing cmte, Messrs O B Greenwell, J E Davis, J Kersey, & B L Nevins.

Geo C Whiting, long & extensively known in Wash City as a valuable civil ofcr of the Gov't, & a prominent member of the Masonic fraternity, recently took a trip to Cape May, but returned on Monday, apparently better, but grew suddenly worse yesterday, Sep 4, when he breathed his last, at his residence on I st, between 20th & 21st st. He was born in Fauquier, Va, Dec 29, 1816, removed to Wash City in 1838; in 1855 he was appointed by Pres Pierce Com'r of Pensions. His funeral will take place from his late residence, & his remains will be buried in **Oak Hill Cemetery**.
+
Died: on Sep 4, Geo C Whiting, in his 51st year. His funeral will take place from his late residence, 202 I st, on Sep 6, at 3 o'clock P M.

Died: on Aug 27, at Manomet House, South Plymouth, Mass, Mary Gano, daughter of Frank R & Sarah E Benedict, of Gtwn, D C, aged 1 year, 11 months & 10 days.

Mr David Wiber, who for a long time past has occupied the assist foreman's position in the press room of the Gov't Printing Ofc, died on Tuesday, after an illness of two months, of consumption. He was a native of Wash, & a young man of such correct habits as to make every acquaintance a friend. He was a member of Central Lodge & Mount Nebo Encampment of Odd Fellows, who will attend his funeral tomorrow afternoon.

$50 reward for large black pocket-book lost on Sep 4. Return to the subscriber for the above reward. –Geo W Linville, 2nd & Indiana ave.

Chas Austin, about 24, unmarried, engaged as a sailor on the schnr **Hazleton**, of Taunton, now lying at the wharf of the Cumberland Coal Co, fell overboard on Tuesday night, while attempting to reach his vessel. The body has not been recovered. [Sep 7th newspaper: the body of John Osborn, a sailor on the schnr **Hazleton**, from Taunton, Mass, was recovered yesterday, & after an inquest, the remains were conveyed to the Methodist burial ground for interment. He came to his death by accidental drowning.]

Va Land Ofc: I do make known that it appears by a certificate of the escheator of the town of Staunton, Aug 23, 1867, received into the Land Ofc on Aug 26, that by an inquest held on Jul 5, 1867, two certain adjoining tracts of land, in the n w part of Staunton, Augusta Co, containing about 8½ acres, of which Martin Weigan died seized, have been found escheated to this Commonwealth.
–Hawes R Sutton, Reg Va Land Ofc

Chancery sale of forty-one one-acre lots, near Tennallytown, by decree of the Supreme Court of D C, Chancery No 795, wherein Jane C Dyer et al are cmplnts, & Giles F Dyer et al are dfdnts. Public auction Sep 20 next, on the premises, lots one to forty-one, [both inclusive] of the subdivision of the tract of land belonging to the estate of Giles Dyer, deceased. –Wm F Mattingly, trustee -Cooper & Latimer, aucts

Valuable improved & unimproved property on the Island at auction on Sep 11; part of the real estate of the late Henry M Morfit, deceased, viz: lot 2 in square 501, with a large 3 story brick house & brick stable; on south P st, near 4½ st. Lot 9 in square 598, fronting on First st west & Canal st; also lot 8 in square 603, at the corner of Second & Q st; also lot 2 in square 611, fronting on V, between First & Second sts.
-Green & Williams, aucts

U S Marshal's sale on Sept 24: dfndnt's right, title, claim, & interest to lot 5 in square 107, in Wash City, with improvements, the property of Louise E Averlhe, to be sold to satisfy execution 3,209 in favor of J H Hassell.
–D S Gooding, U S Marshal, D C

Supreme Court of D C, 429 Equity-docket 7. Catharine Dyer vs E C Dyer et al. Wm L Dunlop, trustee, reported that on Jul 25, 1867, he had sold lot 7 in square 315, to Anton Heitmuller, assignee of Catherine Smith, for the sum of $1,426.20, & Heitmuller has complied with the terms of the sale. –R J Meigs, clerk

Dept of the Interior, U S Patent Ofc, Wash, Aug 30, 1867. Ptn of Jas Watt, of Charlestown, Mass, praying for the extension of a patent granted to him Dec 6, 1853, for an improvement in Valve arrangement for Steam Hamers, for 7 years from the expiration of said patent, which takes place on Dec 6, 1867.
-T C Theaker, Com'r of Patents

FRI SEP 6, 1867
The Pres appointed Hon Thos N Stillwell, of Indiana, ex-member of Congress from that State, Minister Resident to the Republic of Venezeula, in place of Jas Wilson, deceased. Also, L W Scott, of Tenn, counsul at Matamoras; & Oliver B Bradford, of Pa, temporary consul at Brunai, Borneo.

Mrd: Sep 3, at the residence of Thos J S Perry, by Rev B Peyton Brown, Chas C Burr, of Hartford, Conn, to Jane, dght of the late Gassaway Perry, of Rockville, Md.

Died: on Aug 26, at Missaquague, Long Island, Marcia Augusta, wife of Jas Crutchett, of Wash City. A descendant of the original settlers of Long Island, through whom the Dutch Gov't surrendered Manhattan Island to the English.

Helmus' Restaurant, 509 7th st, near D, [rear of Tharp's Cigar Store.] None but the best wines & liquors supplied. –Wm Helmus, proprietor

Toronto, Sep 4. Col Wood, chief detective of the Wash, D C, force, assisted by the local dectective ofcrs, arrested in this city last evening Chas Ulrick & Adrian Harvey, who escaped recently from the Brooklyn jail, where they were awaiting trial for forgery & counterfeiting U S national currency of $500 & $100 denominations. Ulrick is a first-class engraver.

N Y, Sep 5. Despatch to the Herald, dated Key West today, states that the steamer **George Cromwell**, from New Orleans for N Y, with cotton, etc, was lost off Indian Key on Sep 3. She broke her shaft in her stern bearings, leaving her stem open & causing her to sink. Her passengers, 33 in all, were saved. Her master hopes to save the vessel by the aid of a steam pump.

The ill-fated miniature yacht **John T Ford** sailed from Balt under command of Capt Chas W Gould, with John Shaney as mate, & Capt Riddle & an English boy named Murphy, as the crew. Capt Riddle left the vessel on the coast of Maine, when she put into Halifax, a sailor named Armstrong was shipped in his place. Capt Gould was, for 9 years previous to 1860, employed by the Balt & Ohio railroad as an engineer; he then went to New Orleans & filled the same position on the Jackson & Miss railroad. When the war broke out he joined the Southern forces under Gen Beauregard, & commanded a blockade-runner, plying between Charleston & Nassau; he was captured on his 4th voyage, & his vessel was carried into Boston, where she was sold, & he was imprisoned at *Fort Warren* for nearly a year. As soon as he was released he returned to his family in Balt. John Shaney, his mate, was of this city, & had been the proprietor of a restaurant the past few years. He was son of Mr Jos Shaney, a well-known fisherman. The boy Murphy only shipped here as a means of getting to his home in England. Armstrong, the only survivor, was known as a thorough sailor. [The little craft was lost in the British Channel with all hands on board, except one, was reported by Cable.]

Antietam National Cemetery to be dedicated on Sep 17, 1867.

Chancery sale of valuable real estate on G st, near 14th & Md ave; by decree of the Supreme Court of D C, in Equity No 837, wherein White & Joyce are cmplnts, & Jos Johnson et al are dfndnts: public auction on Sep 30 next, lot 5 & part of lot 4 in square 1,050, with improvements. –Wm J Miller, trustee -Green & Williams, aucts

Lasell Female Seminary, at Auburndale, Mass: full term begins Sep 26. Address Chas W Cushing.

Supreme Court, D C, Equity No 836. Wm B Todd et al vs Julia Hallinan et al. Ordered that sale reported by the trustee in this cause be ratified. –R J Meigs, clerk [No details regarding the sale.]

SAT SEP 7, 1867
Police Com'rs: Private Saml W Taylor promoted to sgt, vice John T Sheid, dismissed. Wm L Dulaney reappointed an additional private for 90 days, to do duty in the Centre Market. Application of John Snow, for restaruant license, was rejected; same for John McPherson. Application of Ferguson & Sullivan for transfer of the restaurant license of the late John D Hammack to themselves was rejected. Application of Saml H Wright for license to keep an ordinary in Wash Co, beyond the Wash limits, was rejected. The application of R A Cronin for a transfer of Jacob Aigler's restaurant license to himself was rejected. In the case of Private John W Hanes, charged with conduct unbecoming an ofcr, the complaint was dismissed. In the case of Private Theodore Huysman, charged with conduct unbecoming an ofcr, the Board imposed a fine of $5. In the case of Sgt John T Sheid, charged with conduct unbecoming an ofcr, the Board ordered that he be dismissed the force. Elias Oliver was appointed a private, vice Saml W Taylor, promoted. Justice Jas Cull was appointed a police magistrate, at an annual salary of $800; Dr Erastus Chapin was appointed police magistrate, at an annual salary of $800.
+
Mr Taylor is a Washingtonian, born & bred; is a son of Mr Taylor, the old & highly respected messenger of the Gen Post-ofc, & has been in the police force ever since its organization. Sgt Sheid was found guilty of improper conduct, & charged with a brutal assault upon a female-the cause of his dismissal. Hitherto he had borne the reputation of an efficient ofcr.

Equity Court, Judge Wylie, Sep 5, 1867. 1-Robertson vs Robertson: decree of divorce from the bonds of marriage. 2-Wimpenny vs Spalding et al: order appointing J H Bradley, jr, guardian *ad litem*. Dorsey vs Keller: same order as above. 3-Bond et al vs Marshall: order appointing J H Bradley, jr, guardian *ad litera*.

Mr W W Corcoran has been suddenly called to depart for Europe on account of the sudden aggravation of the illness under which his daughter, Mrs Eustis, has for some time suffered. He left Wash City yesterday.

Obsequies of the late Geo C Whiting, late Grand Master of the Masonic Order of D C, & Past Grand of the I O O F, took place yesterday at 3 o'clock, from his residence, on I st, near 20th. A massive silver plate on the top of the lid of the coffin bore the inscription: George C Whiting. Born December 29th, 1816. Died September 4th, 1867. The services were conducted by Rev Dr Hall, of the Church of the Epiphany. The pall-bearers were: Hon C E Mix, Acting Com'r of Indian Affairs; Hon Jos H Barrett, Com'r of Pensions; P G M Fred D Stuart & PG Jas Chedal, of the Odd Fellows; Sir Knights W M Ireland, Past Grand Cmder of Phil, & P B Brown, of the Knights Templar; Josiah Essex & H O Hood, of the Royal Arch Masons; C Ingle, of the Consistroy; John J Beall, of the Lodge of Perfection; & P G Masters W M Ellis & J E F Holmead, Grand Lodge of Masons. The procession proceeded from 20th st along Pa ave to **Oak Hill Cemetery**, Gtwn. The coffin was placed in a box & taken into the chapel, where it will remain until the tomb is prepared for its reception.

Visit to Annapolis: located on the south branch of the Severn river; its name was given in 1708 in honor of Queen Anne, the then reigning monarch of England. The trip by rail takes 2¼ hours. Most of the private bldgs are plain; the streets are mostly short. The first noteworthy object is the new Episcopal Church, perched on a gentle eminence about 200 yards from the famous State House. The historic bldg, the State House, gave us a feeling of awe. The Senate Chamber is where the Father of his Country resigned his army commission; the restoring to the hands of Congress by the great Washington, on Dec 23, 1783, of the authority by which he had delivered the American people from foreign domination & tyranny. In a side room we were shown a full-length portrait, taken from life, of Wm Pitt, [Lord Chatham,] the friend of America in the British Parliament in the Revolutionary period. On the second floor are the rooms of the Govn'r, the Adj Gen of the State, the Supreme Court, & the Document Room. Ascending to the platform, near the top of the cupola, the visitor gets a fine view of the city spread out beneath him, & of its charming environs. He sees the Govn'r House, St John's College, & the bldgs & vessels connected with the Naval School. The Governor's House is in the vicinity of the Naval School & the water's edge. Its main bldg was erected by Edmund Jennings, & sold by him to Mr Eden, one of the early colonial governors. It has recently been transferred to the Nat'l Gov't for the use of the naval post cmder, who is now Admiral Porter. St John's College encompasses 4 acres of grassy park, with a pair of professors' residences. The nucleus of this venerable seat of learning was <u>King William's School</u>, established in 1696, which in 1795 was converted into the college. It was used as a barracks in the Revolutionary war by a French army, & occupied by a body of American troops in the war of 1812. Jas C Welling is now the principal of this college. The Naval School was established in 1845, while Mr Polk was President & Mr Bancroft Sec of the Navy; the professors here number 87, including assistants. The Harbor: moored to the shore is **old Ironsides**, or frigate **Constitution**, dear to the American heart.

Died: on Sep 6, Mr John V Wilson, late of Phil, aged 53 years. His funeral is on Sunday at 4 o'clock, from his late residence, 82 Second st, Gtwn. [Phil papers please copy.]

A Catholic church for the <u>colored population</u> at 1st & I st; the school house at that place being remodelled for that purpose. Fr Wiget, the pastor in charge of St Aloysius, has been obliged to take this action, as the number of colored attendants has increased so largely that there is no accommodation for them at St Aloysius. A new school bldg will be erected at once to supply the wants of the pupils.

Rochester Express, Wed. At a picnic at Lake Side, Wayne Co, yesterday, on the shore of Lake Ontario, a party of 13 men & women, boys & girls, went out for a ride on the lake. The boat was too full of its human freight, upset, & all but five were drowned. They were: Frank Almond, of Macedon; Patrick Duffy, Frank Pullman, Frank Smith, Miss Sarah Pye, Miss Adela Crandall, Miss Patience Diver, & Miss Hattie Turner.

Horrible murder just disclosed at Boonton, Morris Co, N J. A young man, Kean Carroll, aged 21, was found nearly dead in the street Sat. Before he died he stated he had been stabbed by John Dempsey. Dempsey, about 40, a resident of Boontown, was arrested.

Orphans Court of Wash Co, D C. Letters testamentary on the personal estate of Teresa Hill, late of Wash City, D C, deceased. –C V N Callan, excx

MON SEP 9, 1867
Orphans Court-Judge Purcell, Sep 7, 1867. 1-The will of the late Edwin Green was fully proven. He bequeaths to his nephew, Stephen A Green, of Alexandria, Danl McFarlan & Wm F Mattingly, in trust, certain real estate, for the sole use & benefit of his two daughters, Mary C & Julia Isabel Green, apart from their husbands, should they marry. The residue is bequeathed to his wife, Sarah, & after her death to be divided equally among the children. To his sister he gives an annuity of $200. 2-The will of John Reed, deceased, was filed, & partially proven. He directs that all his effects be sold, [except his wearing apparel, which he bequeaths to his son, John Jas Reed, of Jefferson Co, Va,] & his just debts be paid, with $50 to his friend, Gibson Brown, & the remainder to his son above named & his cousin, Susan Moore, to be equaly divided; & appointes Gibson Brown his exc. 3-Letters of administration were issued to H H Voss, on the estate of Lucy A Voss; bond $500. 4-Chas Smith was appointed guardian to the orphans of Chas Henry Rodier, deceased; bond $800.

Louisville, Sep 8. Govn'r John L Helm died today at his residence, near Elizabethtown. His funeral will take place on Tuesday, just one week from the day of his inauguration. All the powers & duties appertaining to the ofc must be exercised by Lt Govn'r Stevenson. An election for Govn'r is to be held on the first Monday of August next.

Ads. 1-T Lucas, corner of K & 22nd st, has two good work horses for sale. 2-Mrs Gen Wheeler's Seminary for Young Ladies will open in Gtwn on Sep 16.

Orphans Court of Wash Co, D C. Letters of administration on the personal estate of Lucy A Voss, late of Wash City, D C, deceased. –H H Voss, adm

Louisville, Sep 9. Abram Myers, the Conservative candidate for Mayor of Nashville, fell accidentally last evening from the 2nd story of a bldg, fracturing his skull, & died soon after. He was on a business visit to this city.

TUE SEP 10, 1867
Wash Corp, Sep 9, 1867. Cmte of Police-bills passed: ptn of D A Hall to erect an iron railing in square 533; allow Casper Offenstein to erect back building for blacksmith shop; certain privileges to Dr Jos T Howard. Bill for the relief of David Reardon, refunds $20 for a fine erroeously imposed-passed. Bill for the relief of Wm Owner, refunds $51 for erroneous assessment-passed.

L L Hayden will reopen his music classes Sep 16.

Last night, John Thompson, keeper of the draw at the Long bridge, was knocked off the bridge by a passing train. The alarm was given, & searching began. The dead body of Mr Thompson was found in the river. During the search Ofcr Evans, of the police force, was knocked into the river, & came near being drowned before assistance arrived.

Died: on Aug 11, in Mobile, Alfred F Irwin, aged 61 years; a native of PG Co, Md, & a resident of Mobile for the last 33 years.

The Pres has appointed Mr Frank Denver, of Nevada, com'r for the construction of the railroad line from the Missouri river to the Pacific ocean, vice Johnson. Mr Napoleon B Buford appointed com'r to examine the 10th section of Union Pacific railroad, vice Blair.

Reorganization of the Patent Ofc-yesterday. Appointment of the following second assistant examiners: J P Simpson, Dr J R Hayes, Wm Bates, E N Callan, Prof Henry Ernice, C W Fitch, Wm Burke, G A Sturgess, Chas Keller, J P Taylor, H L Jones, D C Lawrence, & T Mercer.

Fortress Monroe, Sep 9. The British brig **Cuba**, Capt Mackell, from Matanzas to Boston with molasses, has been totally wrecked near Hatteras light. The captain was badly injured. Only 2 seamen were saved. Lost were: Chas Cain, mate; Wm Williams, 2nd mate; Geo Smith, steward; M Macaulty & John A Lanagan, seamen; & a boy named Frederick.

Miss Jeannie O Abbot will resumed the duties of her School on Sep 9: 10 West st, Gtwn.

Havana, Sep 5. Cmder Roe, of the gunboat **Tacony**, by request of the Austrian cmder, claimed the body of the Emperor, & his request has been listened to. All generals condemned to death at Queretaro, including Castillo, have been pardoned. Gen O'Horan, on the 18th, was sentenced by court-martial to be shot on Wed. The sentence was carried out on the Plazuela de Mexcoaloo, against the remonstrances of the American Minister. O'Horan left letters to vindicate his memory. The Society of the **Sisters of Charity** has been abolished & another under patronage of the Republic established.

Deaths from yellow fever. 1-Alex'r Duhammel Renshaw, an engineer in the revenue service, & stationed at New Orleans, died of yellow fever at that place on Sep 2. He was a nephew of Dr Duhammel, of this city, & in his 20th year. He received his appointment as acting assist engineer in the navy in 1863, when about 16 years of age. When the steamer **Reliance** was captured in the Rappahannock he was taken prisoner by the Confederates, & kept in confinement for nearly a year. After his release he served with great credit during the remainder of the war. 2-Chas Eilson, inspector in the custom-house at Galveston, Texas, died of yellow fever in that city about the last of August.

Trustee's sale of valuable property in Anne Arundel Co, Md, near the city of Balt: in execution of a decree of the Circuit Court for Anne Arundel Co, in Equity, passed in a cause wherein Beverly W Cromwell & others were cmplnts, & Eliz B Cromwell & others were dfndnts; public sale on Oct 9, of 455 acres of land, about 5 miles from Balt. Lot 1 contains 162 acres, & is the home-place, lies on the south side of the Sweetzer Bridge road, & adjoins the lands of Jos M Brian & Thos Pumphrey; improvements consist of a large new frame dwlg house containing 10 rooms, stables, & out bldgs. Lot 2 adjoins lot 1 & contains 32 acres. Lot 3 adjoins lot 2 & contains 101 acres, with 2 frame dwlgs in good repair. Lot 4 does not adjoin the others, & contains 160 acres. The trustee will offer for sale all the interest which the said Randolph S Cromwell owned in the Sweetzer's Bridge Co, & property which was conveyed to him by deed from Saml S Linthicum & wife, dated Mar 14, 1865, recorded in Liber N H G, No 13, folios 150, of the Land Records of A A Co. Inquire of Mr Beverly W Cromwell, living on lot 3; or Wm H Dorsey, residing in the neighborhood; or the trustee Frank H Stockett, Annapolis.

Supreme Court of D C, 1,037 Equity, Dock 8. Eliza A Cox vs David B Cox. On motion of the plntf, by M Thompson, her solicitor, it is ordered that the dfndnt appear herein on or before rule day occurring 40 days after this day; otherwise the cause will be proceeded with as in case of default. –R J Meigs, clerk

Supreme Court of D C, 738 Equity, Dock 5. Eliz Brent vs Chas E Brent et al. Order that the sale reported by J Caroll Brent, trustee, be ratified, except the sales reported to have been made to Thos Coyle, which are not confirmed. –R J Meigs, clerk

WED SEP 11, 1867

Havana, Sep 8. 1-Francis Francoe, a citizen of New Orleans, died on the 14th instant, & received Masonic honors. 2-M Mayna, the Prussian Minister in Mexico, keeps in seclusion at San Luis. He is supposed to be insane, & is heedless of the orders from Prussia to leave the country. 3-Santa Anna continues a prisoner in San Juan D'Ulloa. It is believed he will not be shot.

Orphans Court-Judge Purcell, Sep 10, 1867. 1-Sarah Green was appointed guardian to the orphan of the late Edw Green, & gave bond in the sum of $8,000. 2-Letters of administration on the personal estate of the late Wm A Bradley, sr, were issued to Wm A Bradley, jr, & A Thos Bradley; bond $10,000. 3-Letters of administration on the personal estate of the late Edwin Green were issued to Sarah Green; bond $30,000. 4-Ann Brady was appointed admx of the late Thos Brady; bond $2,000. 5-The last will of John Reed, deceased, was fully proven & admitted to probate. 6-Jilson Brown was appointed administrator of the late John Reed; bond $1,000. 7-The argument in the disputed will case of the late Saml De Vaughan was continued on behalf of the devisees by Col M Thompson.

Savannah, Sep 10. Jos S Carruthers, the defaulting teller of the Central Railroad Bank, shipped on board the schnr **William Gregory**, as mate, for Havana. She was overhauled by a pilot boat 2 miles out at sea, & brought back in a leaky condition with 5 feet of water in the hold. Carruthers says he allowed a friend to overdraw his accounts, & had not a dollar himself.

Trustee's sale, by decree passed by the Supreme Court of D C, in Chancery, No 812, wherein Wm A Ward et al are cmplnts & Henry A Clark et al are dfndnts: public auction on Sep 25, of part of lot D of E B Todd's subdivision of lot 1 in square 352, situated on Md ave, between 10th & 11th sts, improved with a 4 story brick dwlg. –Wm F Mattingly, trustee -Green & Williams, aucts

Orphans Court of Wash Co, D C. Letters of administration on the personal estate of Thos Brady, late of Wash City, D C, deceased. Ann [her mark x] Brady, admx

Orphans Court of Wash Co, D C. Letters of administration on the personal estate of Edwin Green, late of Wash City, D C, deceased. –Sarah Green, admx, c t a

Dept of the Interior, U S Patent Ofc, Wash, ptn of Wm Wisdom, of Brooklyn, N Y, praying for the extension of a patent granted to him Dec 20, 1853, for an improvement in Cleansing Hair & Feathers from Insects, etc, for seven years from the expiration of said patent, which takes place on Dec 20, 1867. -T C Theaker, Com'r of Patents

Died: on Sep 9, suddenly, Mr Francis Hutchins, in his 67th year. His funeral is this afternoon, from his late residence, on 12th st, between M & N sts. [No time given.]

Died: on Sep 9, William Joseph, son of J W & M A Earp, of lockjaw, aged 12 years & 15 days. His funeral will be from his late residence, 495 11th st, 10 A M, Sep 11.

THU SEP 12, 1867
Wendell Phillips is in favor of Thad Stevens for President.

Galveston, Sep 11. Deaths from yellow fever: Rev J P Parham, Pres of the Howard Association of Corpus Christi, died Aug 20. Saml Adams, assist surgeon U S army, died on Sep 9. The fever has appeared at La Grange, Breham, & other interior towns.

Oak Hill Cemetery-enlargement of the grounds. The Board of Dirs of *Oak Hill Cemetery* are about concluding arrangements to purchase from Mr Chas Dodge, for the sum of $10,000, the 7 acres of ground owned by him & adjoining the Cemetery grounds on the east side. By this addition the Cemetery grounds will be extended as far east as Rock st, Gtwn, & there will be two entrances, one on the east side of the new addition, & the present gate at the south end of the original grounds. The house of the superintendent is to be raised one story, & otherwise enlarged & renovated.

The death of Lt A H McCormick has been announced as having occurred on board the steamer **Mahasset**, at New Orleans. This is not Lt A H McCormick, of Wash City, who is is known, by a letter received from him dated Aug 6, is alive & hearty on the school-ship **Macedonian**, then lying-to in the English channel.

Mrd: on Sep 2, at Ottawa, Kansas, by Rev Mr Satchwell, Edw E Fuller, of N Y, to Lena M, daughter of Maj P P Elder, president of the Bank of Ottawa.

Alexandria Museum: this ancient dilapidated institution, holding in its custody many historical relics of great value, was founded in 1812, & owes its origin to Timothy Mountford, who, on St John's Day in that year, proposed to his breatheren of the Alexandria Lodge the importance of such an institution; he was elected manager by the lodge, & continued as such till the day of his death. Since his decease it has fallen into neglect & desolation. The museum occupies 2 large rooms in the upper story of the market-house, over the Mayor's ofc. Mr Edw M Davis, of the police, procured us access. Alexandria Washington Lodge No 22: Washington was founder of this Lodge. In 1788 it passed under the jurisdiction of the Grand Lodge of Va. In the museum is a Turkish saddle, presented to Jefferson, & by him presented to the museum; an old oil portrait of Lord Fairfax, & one by West, of Wm Penn; an original letter of Washington, dated Mt Vernon, 12th Nov, 1799, in which he accepts an invitation to attend the assemblies at Alexandria the ensuing winter, but in which he adds, "Alas! Our dancing days are over." The letter is addressed to Jonathan Swift, Geo D Neill, Wm Newton, Robt Yard, Chas Alexander, Jas H Hooe, managers. Also: a flag borne by the 11th Va, Morgan's Rifle Regt; flag of Gen Lafayette; flag borne by Washington's body guard, bearing "Conquer or die" as its motto; also, a flag carried at the battle of Trenton; a white silk banner borne by the Alexandria Blues in 1781, at Yorktown, with "Emulation, Firm in Defence" for its motto; flag of the Richmond Rifle Rangers, with "Nevo Me Impune Lacessit" as its motto; & the bier on which the remains of the Father of his Country was borne to the tomb, & the national flag used on the occasion. The sword of the battle of Hastings, found, in 1078, on the spot where the battle of Hastings took place in 1066. It was deposited in the Tower of London, & given by the governor of that Tower to Dr Francis De Nalangen in 1780, & brought by his son, Dr Chas De Nalangen, to this country, & presented to this musuem in 1812. Bust of Paul Jones, bequeathed to Mr Mountford for the museum by the will of Bushrod Washington; it was taken in Paris, by Houdon, a short time before Jones' death. Washington's clock, which stopped at the moment of his death, five & one-fourth minutes past five o'clock. It is a small mantle timepiece, in a plain mahogany case, with "Geo Melhurst, London, printed upon its face. Relic of the Wash City: a piece of the coffin of Benj Young, who was an original proprietor of the land on which this city is located. "He died Feb 8, 1754, aged 57, & was buried in his own garden. On laying out a new street his remains were unvoidably removed from the spot where they had been deposited 75 years previous, Jul 18, 1829. Presented by Mr Wm Ward. The remains of the barometer & thermometer, many years the companions of Lord Nelson, given by Sr Richd Keats, of his Britannic Majesty's ship **Superb**, 74 guns, to John Jarvis, treasurer of the garrison of Gibraltar & consul of the U S, & by the latter given to Mr Mountford in 1806. Instruments for mensuration & surveying, mahogany triangles, etc, "made by Thos Jefferson, late Pres of the U S." Presented by Wm Small, Jul 8, 1812. Masonic relics: the leather chair first used in the Lodge by Washington; his bootstrap or garter won at Braddock's defeat; his farm spurs; pocket knife presented by his mother 56 years before his death; button worn by Washington at his first inauguration; right hand glove worn by him while in mourning for his mother; a brace of pistols, studded with brilliants, presented to Washington by Lous XVI, through the hands of Lafayette; the mantle in which Washington received baptism, & his grand masonic robes. *Christ Church grave-yard* & the forgotten graves. The fence was erected in 1830, the original enclosure having been built in 1783; no interments in the grounds for some quarter of a century, the latest being that of Chas Bennet, a benefactor of the city, over whose remains rises the massive obelisk, raised to his memory by the Common Council of the Corp in 1841. Inscription upon a small headstone: "Here lies the body of Mr Isaac Pierce. Born in Boston. Son of Mr Isaac Pierce, Distiller, who departed this life March 26, 1771. Aged 24 years. Another slate headstone: Thie monument is sacred to the memory of the once loved and esteemed Cat Geo Mumford, late of New Haven, in the colony of Conn. He departed this transitory life at Georgetown, Jul 7, 1773, in the 28th year of his age. An elaborate carved sandstone memorial not in its place, but leaning against the walls of the church: Erected to the memory of Eleanor, the second wife of Mr Daniel Wren, who departed this life in the year 1798, aged thirty-two years. Rev, chap xiv, verse 13. Blessed are the dead which die in the Lord, from henceforth. Yes, saith the Spirit, that they may rest from their labors; and their works do follow them. This stone was placed over her by Order of her disconsolate Husband, who was left with two Children to lament her Loss-John William Renwick, her son, being only three years old when his Mother departed this Life, and Dinah Eleanor Wren, their Daughter, Aged only seven Days. [Some scamp has chiseled the figure 9, so that the casual observer will read this as his 9th wife, & this had repeatedly been given publicity.] In another place there are two sandstone slabs: Her Lieth the Body of Robert Muir, son of Hugh Muir, merchant, of Dumfries, who departed this life Dec 21, 1786, aged about thirty-eight years. Her Lieth the body of John Muir, late merchant of Alexandria, oldest son of Hugh Muir, of Dumfries, in Scotland, who departed this Life March 29th, 1791, in the 60th year of his age. The grave of an eminent actress: a grey stone sarcophagus in which rest the ashes of one most gifted & unsullied female characters that shed delight upon the stage of her day-Miss Anne Brunton, for that was her maiden name, the daughter of a respectable manager & actor of Bath, England, was born in 1769. She appeared at Bath, for the first time, at her father's' benefit, as Euphrasia, the Grecian daughter. Brunton was the aged father. So was it with Kemble & his daughter, [Fanny Kemble,] & Cooper & his daughter, [Mrs Robt Tyler,] in a later generation. In 1792 Miss Brunton marred Robt Merry, a gentleman of literary attainments, & at the wish of her husband's family, retired reluctantly from the profession she loved. In 1796 he was willing for his wife to make an engagement with him. Mrs Merry made her first appearance in America, as Julia, at Phil, on Dec 5, 1796. Merry died at Balt in 1798, & in 1803 his wife was married to Wignell, who died suddenly 7 weeks after the marriage, in Phil. Three years after the death of Wignell his wife was married to Warren. It was an exceedingly happy marriage. When near his wife's confinement, in 1808, he was compelled to go with his company in their Southern tour, he yielded & let her accompany him on the journey. They had barely arrived at Alexandria when she was seized in travail, & died with epileptic fits. Her epitaph: Mrs Anne Warren, died in her 39th year. Dunlap, History of the Stage, says the year 1808 was remarkable in theatrical history, by the death of Mrs Anne Warren, in the 38th year of her life. Beneath this stone are deposited the remains of Mrs Anne Warren, daughter of John Brunton, [Eng,] and wife of William Warren, one of the managers of the Phil & Balt theatres. In her were combined the affectionate wife, the tender mother, and the sincere friend. She died at Alexandria on the 28th of June, 1808, aged thirty-ninth years. Twenty-four years later her husband died at Balt, in a cloud of misfortunes, when Jefferson, his brother, a third of century his bosom friend, as well as his brother-in-law by reason of a second marriage, saw Warrens' fortunes decline the year before he died, he was so distressed that he left the stage, & died at Harrisburg in 1832. Warren's second wife surived him, & the Falstaff House, named in honor of her husband's great character, is well remembered. Cooper lived some 15 years long, having been born in London in 1776. His daughter, retiring from the stage, became the wife of Robt Tyler during the Presidency of his father. Cooper was made Military Storekeeper in 1841; then Inspector of Customs, first at Phil, & then at N Y, till his death at his home in Bristol, Pa. Mrs Tyler watched tenderly over him in his last days. He was tall, erect, handsome, & solidly built. The first play performed in Washington was Venice Preserved, in 1800. Mrs Merry, Wignell, Warren, & Cooper were all in the cast. Cooper was a pedestrian & in 1802 walked from Phil to Balt, 104 miles, in less time than a friend could ride there without change of horses.

Orphans Court of Wash Co, D C. Letters testamentary on the personal estate of John Reed, late of Wash Co, D C, deceased. –Jilson [x his mark] Brown, exc

Appointed 1st class clerks in the Patent Ofc: C K Sherwood, C H Griggs, Jas M Chadsey, M T E Chandler, Robt Whittlesey, & Rev W B Evans.

Public sale of **Broad Creek Farm**, in PG Co, Md, by decree of the Circuit Court for said county, in Equity, passed in a cause, upon ptn & proceedings, to divide the real estate of Townly Munroe, late of said county, deceased; sale on Sep 19, all the real estate upon which Townly Munroe now resides, containing 40 acres, known as **Broad Creek Farm**, with commodious dwlg, & other necessary outbldgs. Mr Townly Munroe, who resides upon the premises, will show the property.
–C C Magruder, jr, trustee

Dept of the Interior, U S Patent Ofc, Wash, Sep 5, 1867. Ptn of Melvin Jincks, of Dansville, N Y, praying for the extension of a patent granted to him Dec 13, 1853, for an improvement in Turnkeys, for seven years from the expiration of said patent, which takes place on Dec 13, 1867. -T C Theaker, Com'r of Patents

FRI SEP 13, 1867
The ptn of Gen Fitz John Porter for a re-opening of the proceedings of the court-martial in his case had been referred by the Pres to the War Dept.

Yesterday afternoon, the delightful grounds of **Glenwood Cemetery**, were the scene of a most uncommon ceremony for such a locality. Miss McDaniel, residing not far from the Cemetery, unfortunate in the loss of an excellent mother, to whom she was exceedingly attached, but happy in a lover from the far & sunny South, had selected the spot where slumber her mother's ashes, & perchance hovers her mother's spirit, for the nuptial ceremonies. The throng of friends & the curious was very large. The nuptial party formed & walked in procession from the gateway to the grave. The bride, a modest & graceful girl, was attired in half-mourning for her mother, with black silk skirt & bodice, trimmed in black. Her bridegroom, Mr Dawson, of Ga, was an unusually fine-looking person, & altogether it was a fine-appearing bridal pair. It was certainly a very extraordinary idea, & yet there is something very touching & beautiful after all. The ceremonies were very pleasantly performed by Rev Mr Buck, rector of Rock Creek Church.

Yesterday Cornelius Matthews was run over & seriously injured by a market wagon, driven by a colored man. The boy had one of his ribs broken, sustaining severe injuries about his body. He was taken to his home & properly cared for.

Mrd: on Sep 12, at the Church of the Ascension, by Rev Dr Pinckney, Paul F Beardsley, of Richmond, Va, to C Alice, daughter of Alex H Young, of Wash City. No cards.

Dept of the Interior, U S Patent Ofc, Wash, Sep 6, 1867. Ptn of Lucian B Flanders, of Phil, Pa, praying for the extension of a patent granted to him Dec 6, 1853, for an improvement in Replacing Cars upon Railroad Tracks, for 7 years from the expiration of said patent, which takes place on Dec 6, 1867.
-T C Theaker, Com'r of Patents

Died: on Sep 8, at Dry Tortugas, of yellow fever, Dr Jos Sim Smith, U S A, late of Wash City.

Dept of the Interior, U S Patent Ofc, Wash, Sep 7, 1867. Ptn of Mathew Stewart, of Phil, Pa, praying for the extension of a patent granted to him Jan 3, 1854, for an improvement in Floor Plates of Malt K_ns, for seven years from the expiration of said patent, which takes place on Jan 3, 1868. -T C Theaker, Com'r of Patents

Dept of the Interior, U S Patent Ofc, Wash, Sep 6, 1867. Ptn of Jos Nock, of Phil, Pa, praying for the extension of a patent granted to him Dec 3, 1852, for an improvement in Hinge for Inkstand & Covers, for seven years from the expiration of said patent, which takes place on Dec 13, 1867. -T C Theaker, Com'r of Patents

Phil, Pa, Sep 12. The coroner's inquest in the case of Anne E Richards, aged 4 years, who died suddenly about a month since, has returned a verdict that she came to her death from strychnine, administered in a peach by Rachel & Mary Jones, two elderly maidens living in the neighborhood, in revenge for the child calling them old maids. The accused were committed to prison for trial.

Augusta, Ga, Sep 12. Jas Gregg, president of the Graniteville cotton factory, died this morning.

N Y, Sep 12. Caleb Van Lise, postmaster at Lyassett, Long Island, has been arrested for embezzling valuable letters. He was held in $5,000 bail.

SAT SEP 14, 1867
Lorenzo M Johnson, of Texas, has been appointed consular clerk in the State Dept. John S Fiske, of N Y, has been appointed consul at Leith.

On Thursday a cutting affair occurred at a drinking saloon at 2nd & Pa ave, which resulted in a soldier of the 12th infty, Geo Williams, being fatally cut by another soldier. Williams died last night. Eldridge & a brother soldier, McClelland, who was in the row, were committed to jail to await trial.

Rev N P Tillinghast, former rector of St John's Episcopal Church, Gtwn, has accepted a call to one of the Episcopal churches in Phil.

Mr John Hopkins, of Balt, who has a fortune of twenty millions, is imitating the good example of Mr Peabody. He has already founded & endowed a hospital & an educational institute, & is planning several other generous schemes.

Mrd: on Sep 12, at St Aloysius Church, by Rev Fr Stonestreet, S G Matlock to Miss Eleanor Bevier, both of Wash City. [Balt Sun & N Y Herald copy.]

Died: on Sep 13, Lucy, beloved wife of Wm H Marriott. Her funeral will take place from her late residence, 237 9th st, on Sunday, at 10 o'clock.

Excellent Household & kitchen furniture at auction on Sep 26, at the residence of Senor Luis Molina, Minister from Nicaragua & Honduras. -Cooper & Latimer, aucts

MON SEP 16, 1867

On Friday Mr John J Bogus sold for Mr Richd Petit his elegant mansion, on the corner of Second & Market sts, to Mr Saml F Savage, the well-known hardware dealer of Wash, for the sum of $25,000. This is one of the most elegant residences in Gtwn; the lot fronts 80 feet on Second st by 150 feet deep on Market st.

Mr Robt H Sherman, formerly Deputy State Engineer of N Y, died at Utica, on Sat, from injuries received the night before, while getting off from a railorad car.

Wm Johnston, the noted counterfeiter, was on Thu last sentenced at Pittsburgh, Pa, to pay a fine of $2,000, & undergo imprisonment of 7 years in the penitentiary.

Gen Frank Wheaton, commandant at New Orleans, was violently attacked with yellow fever on Friday night.

Gen Ramsey, the commandant of the **Arsenal**, has in contemplation to at once commence the erection of an additional magazine bldg, to be located near the two already in use, which are situated on the magazine grounds east of the ***Congressional Cemetery***. There is not sufficient accommodation for the deposit of ammunition & ordnance stores.

Geo Fayatte Washington, a citizen of Fred'k Co, Va, died last week, aged 78 years. He was born at ***Mount Vernon***, & was a son of Col Geo A Washington, & a ward of Gen Geo Washington. He was for many years one of the wardens of the Episcopal Church at Winchester, & was universally esteemed among his fellow citizens.

Mrd: on Sep 12, at the residence of Z D Gilman, by Rev Dr Sunderland, assisted by Rev Dr Gurley, Mr Wm Brooks Gurley to Miss Helen Parris Gilman, all of Wash City.

Died: on Sep 12, at the residence of her brother-in-law, A B Young, Sophia Pollock Yates, aged 73 years, daughter of the late Adolphus B Yates, of N Y C, & stepdaughter of the late John Marston, of said city. Her funeral will take place this morning at 11 o'clock from the residence of A B Young, 504 15th st west.

Clarence F Buhler is to be the poet at the Antietam dedication.

Abner Marks, charged with robbing the Adams Express Co, in Tenn, about a year ago, of $31,000, was arrested in Richmond on Saturday.

Pvt Geo Williams, of Co D U S infty, who was stabbed by Wm Eldridge & John D McLelland, members of Co B, same regt, at Rutherford's saloon, on Captiol Hill, on Thu last, died on Sat, at the Russell Barracks' Hospital. His remains were buried yesterday at the **Soldiers' Burial Ground** at **Arlington Heights**, with the usual military honors. The parties implicated are now confined in jail awaiting a final hearing before Justice Tucker.

Orphans Court-Judge Purcell, Sep 14, 1867. 1-Terrence Drury was appointed guardian to the orphans of Louisa M Drury, deceased; bond $6,000. 2-Letters of administration on the personal estate of the late Henry Cook were issued to Johanna Cook, who gave bond in the sum of $800. 3-Letters of administration on the personal estate of Jonathan Nichols, deceased, were issued to Henry C Brown; bond $1,000.

Galveston, Texas, Sep 15. Gen Griffin died at 11 o'clock this morning.

Orphans Court of Wash Co, D C. Letters of administration on the personal estate of Jonathan Nichols, late of Wash Co, D C, deceased. –Henry C Brown, adm

Orphans Court of Wash Co, D C, Sep 14, 1867. In the case of Francis Lamb, adm of Eliza Lamb, deceased, the administrator & Court have appointed Oct 12th next, for the final settlement of the personal estate of the said deceased, of the assets in hand. -Jas R O'Beirne, Reg/o wills

Orphans Court of Wash Co, D C, Sep 14, 1867. In the case of Richd W & Richd M Williams, excx of John M Williams, deceased, the executors & Court have appointed Oct 8 next, for the final settlement of the personal estate of the said deceased, of the assets in hand. -Jas R O'Beirne, Reg/o wills

TUE SEP 17, 1867
On Thursday evening, near the end of the tragedy of "The Apostate," where Pescara receives his death stab, Mr Edwin Booth was accidentally & quite severely wounded in several places in the right hand be a dagger used by Mr Vandenhoff. Dr C Johnston considered it advisable for him to suspend his engagement for a few days.

Jas N Fitzpatrick, son of the late John C Fitzpatrick, of the Secretary's ofc of the U S Senate, had his arm broken in two places on Sat, playing base-ball with the Active Club. He was reaching to get the ball, another player, who was running to base, trod upon his arm, & thus caused the fracture.

N Y, Sep 16. Theresa Wrerman was murdered today at Yonkers by Fred'k Schrafhouser, who subsequently committed suicide. Cause, disappointed affection.

Mr Frank A Baird appointed a first class clerk at the executive Mansion. He has been in the army for several years, & for the past year has been detailed as clerk at the Pres' House. He has now received his discharge, & being a faithful clerk, has been retained in his position.

Boston, Sep 16. The dwlg-house of Jarvis Keene, at East Abington, was burned last night. Mr Keene's two daughters, his only children, 19 & 21 years, were burned to death. Mr Keene is in New Orleans, & his wife & daughters were alone in the house. [Sep 20th newspaper: Mrs Keene, the mother of the two young ladies who were burned to death, has become insane on account of the sad calamity.]

Cooper & Latimer, aucts, who have in charge the sale of the *Oak Lawn* property, [lately owned by Mr Thos P Morgan,] sold, a day or two ago, to Mr Max Lansburgh, 48,316 feet of ground, being lots 6 & 7 of the original property. These lots were sold at the recent sale for seven cents per foot, & have been purchased by Mr Lansburgh at an advance upon that figure-how much, has not been divulged.

Belle Haven Institute, Alexandria, Va: the 9th session of this institution began on Sep 16, with experienced professors & teachers in each dept. –Miss E B Garber, Alexandria, Va

WED SEP 18, 1867
The forger Matthews, alias Depeyster, alias Livingston, who obtained $75,000 from the bank of Moses Taylor & Co, of N Y, last July, by forging the name of Cornelius Vanderbilt, was brought to N Y on Sat, from Chicago. In his possession were $10,000 in greenbacks, a portion of the forged checks.

A cannon exploded on board the steamer **Deutschland**, while in the Narrows, inward bound from Bremen, on Sat, killing Fred'k W Hammer, a German, aged 25; Wm Gege, a German, aged 17; Fred'k Matheke, a native of Russian Poland. All three had friends on board; the first a wife, the second a mother, & the other distant relatives. The wounded were borne to the hospital of the **Sisters of Charity**, in Hoboken. –N Y Tribune, 17th

The first locomotive used in America was the "John Bull," in 1833, between Albany & Schenectady. Her copper fixings were made by Peter Smith, of Albany. The "John Bull" is still alive, & is kept as a curiosity at the Albany Iron Works, near Troy.

Died: on Sep 15, near Gtwn, D C, Chas Gratiot Talcott, in his 34th year. [Richmond papers please copy.]

Brick storehouse-wholesale & retail grocery store, formerly occupied by the late H B Jenkins, at auction on Sep 24, situated on part of lot 10 in square 904, at 568 7th st, between G & I sts, Navy Yard. -Cooper & Latimer, aucts

THU SEP 19, 1867

Base-ball affairs: Yesterday the following gentlemen, who in part compose the Pastime Club of Richmond, arrived in the city: Messrs A G Babcock, J E Davidson, E E Taylor, Chas Gentry, W F Edwards, W Walsh, A Tomlinson, A T Aburtney, J R Macmurdo, E M Ezekiel, W Blout, F Patterson Redford, E Edwards, Geo Mountcastle, W B Keddick, & S Sprigg Campbell. They were met at the depot by a cmte of the National Club, who, after escorting them around Wash City, attended them to the Willard Hotel, where they were quartered.

The boat **Katie Wise** was purchased on Tuesday by John B Davidson, of the Potomac Towboat Co, for the sum of $7,500.

On Tuesday laborers began to demolish the late residence of Hudson Taylor. There are few residents of Wash that will not regret the destruction of this property. A year hence, on this lot, will be a magnificent structure; an edifice is to be dedicated to the use of a Christian association.

Died: on Aug 13, at **Fort Chadbourne**, Texas, of typhoid fever, Brvt Maj Michl J Kelly, capt 4th U S cavalry.

London Times. We have lately to lament the loss of Titian's "Peter Martyr," with several other master-pieces of the Venetian school. These pictures constituted the main attraction of the fine old Gothic church of San Giovannie Paolo, in Venice. They had been temporarily laid in the chapel dedicated to the Virgin of the Rosary, to allow of some repairs in other parts of the church. Fire broke out on the 15th ult & Titian's picture was utterly destroyed. One of the greatest painting of Gian Bellini, several Tintorettos, with wooden carvings & bronzes of the highest value, perished with it. On the 15th the Festivity of the Assumption was celebrated at the church, & oil lamps, & even, it is said, wax tapers were left burning at the altar after closing time. Titian's "Peter Martyr" ranked as the third of the world's pictures, a rival to Raphael's "Transfiguration," & Domenichino's "Last Communion," both in the Vatican.

The wife of Hon Henry Wilson, who has recently submitted to a painful surgical operation in the removal of a cancer, is now doing well, & hopes of her recovery are entertained.

In Posey Co, Indiana, four brothers named Bridenomer, attempted to unload a shell on Sunday. It exploded, killing one of the brothers, took the leg off another, an arm from the third, & the other was seriously injured.

Fortress Monroe, Sep 18. Reuben Clarke, who was indicted for murdering a man named McCarty, the bugler of the 5th U S artl, in May last, was discharged today by the county court sitting at Hampton, the jury rendering a verdict of not guilty.

Yesterday a soldier, Chas Dumas, of Co F, 44th U S infty, now stationed at Reynold's Barracks, in the White Lot, on 17th st, was stabbed in the breast by Jos W N Zimmer, & died at the post hospital, about 2 hours later. Zimmer was living with a woman who was not his wife, & Dumas was also acquainted with her. The woman was Lillie Jackson. Zimmer was held yesterday, & locked up to await the verdict of the Coroner's inquest. [Sep 20th newspaper: Jury returned a verdict yesterday that Chas Dumas came to his death by wounds inflicted, maliciously & murderously, by a weapon in the hands of Jos W N Zimmer. The prisoner was committed to jail to await his trial.]

Mr J B Munson, well known to the most of our older citizens, died at his residence, near Fall's Church, Va, yesterday, at the advanced age of 62. He was the owner of the property known as **Munson's Hill**, rendered historic during the late war, it having at the commencement of the war been fortified by the Rebs & used by them as a point of observation. In early bellum days the dome of the Capitol was used as a post from which to make observations of the doings of the "Johnnies" on **Munson's Hill**.

Balt, Sep 8. Edwin Booth is recovering from his stab wound. He has made another application for the remains of his brother, pleading very earnestly that his mother being very aged, craves the dead body so as to inter it before she dies, near that of his distinguished father, who is buried near this city. The request has been denied.

Memphis, Sep 18. Gen Yell, a prominent lawyer of Arkansas, is dead. [No death date given-current item.]

About a week ago Mr Fred B Sheppard, a well known citizen of Mobile, was shot by Capt Morris Schaff, commanding the Mount Vernon Arsenal, near that city, from the effects of which Mr Sheppard soon after died.

The late Catholic Bishop Timon, of Buffalo, left a will disposing of $10,000 in personal, & $1,000,000 in real property. The whole goes to the Church.

A duel took place in the "Shades," near Connersville, Ind, on Thu, between Hon J W Carmichael, formerly of the State Senate, & Jas W Mayo, a lawyer in Indianapolis. Duelling pistols once belonging to Hon Thos F Marshall, of Ky, were the weapons used. Carmichael received a flesh wound; Mayo received the discharge in the region of his heart, & was taken from the garden by his friends & a surgeon. The affair originated from Carmichael accusing Mayo with cheating at the gaming table.

Dept of the Interior, U S Patent Ofc, Wash, Sep 13, 1867. Ptn of R P Walker, of N Y, N Y, praying for the extension of a patent granted him Dec 20, 1853, for an improvement in Machine for Hulling & Scouring Coffee, for seven years from the expiration of said patent, which takes place on Dec 20, 1867.
-T C Theaker, Com'r of Patents

Chancery sale of valuable improved corner lots & other property in Gtwn, D C, by decree of the Supreme Court of D C, of Aug 2, 1867, & another passed Sep 5, 1867, in the cause of John Batemen & others vs Jane E Bateman & others: public auction on Oct 11, of lot 30, of old Gtwn, at Prospect & Fred'k sts, with 2 story brick dwlg-house. Lots 70 & 71 in Beatty & Hawkins' addition to Gtwn, with frame bldg, at First & Fred'k sts. Also, lot 71, in Threlkeld's additon to Gtwn at the n e corner of First & Fayette sts, with a 2 story brick dwlg house & large brick stable. Lot 13 in Gtwn, fronting on Bridge st, with two 3 story Brick Warehouses, adjoining the property of E M Linthicum. –R R Crawford, C Ingle, trustees -Thos Dowling, auct

Orphans Court-Judge Purcell, Sep 17, 1867. 1-The second & final account of Jane E Bateman, guardian to Jos Bateman, orphan of Joshua Bateman, deceased, was allowed. 2-The appraisement of the estate of Saml De Vaughan, was returned to the court. The amount is a trifle over $28,000. 3-Ordered that Jane E Bateman, guardian of Joseph, Sarah A, & A E Bateman, be allowed the sum of $250 per annum for board. 3-John Lang, adm of E R Lang, deceased, was ordered to settle accounts, returnable Sat, the 20th. 4-The inventory of the personal estate of Henry Cook, deceased, was returned to the court by the administrator, Johanna Cook. 5-Mary J Killmon, guardian to the orphans of John T Killmon, deceased, was ordered to appear on Tuesday next, & show cause why she should not settle the second & final account as guardian. 6-Thos McFadden & Thos J Murray were authorized to appraise the goods of Jonathan Nichols, late of Wash Co, D C.

FRI SEP 20, 1867
Hon Fred'k W A Bruce, Envoy Extraordinary & Minister Plenipotentiary from Great Britain to the U S, died on Sep 19, very suddenly, in Boston. He was the son, we believe, of the late Lord Elgin, who was well known from 1792 to 1814 as a diplomatist. His second brother, Earl Elgin, was here on a special mission to further the negotiation of the reciprocity treaty, & was Govn'r General of Canada, & afterwards Govn't Gen of India. Sir Fred'k Wm Adolphus Bruce, K C B, was born on Apr 14, 1814, being brother of the late, & uncle of the present Earl of Elgin & Kincardine, as also of Gen Bruce, who accompanied the Prince of Wales [as governor] when on a visit to this country. Messrs Barrington & Howard, of the British Legation, started to Boston yesterday to take charge of the remains, which were then in charge of Senator Sumner, chairman of the Senate Cmte on Foreign Relations. For the present Mr Francis Clare Ford, Sec of Legation, will represent his Gov't here.

Ads. 1-Wm H Stanford, merchant tailor, 488 Pa ave, has just received a new stock of gentleman's dress goods. 2-John A Baker, 88 & 89 La ave, has for sale an extensive assortment of agricultural implements, & all kinds of grass seed, guano, etc.

Patents issued to Washingtonians this week. 1-J M March, of Wash, for baggage label. 2-Chas Memmert, of Gtwn, D C, for a wardrobe trunk. 3-Jno Buckley, assignor to Thos J Logan, of Wash, D C, patent for a milk & oyster can.

Base-ball: National's vs Irvingtons of N J: yesterday on the Nathionals' grounds, & resulted in a victory for the Nationals by, a score of 33 to 22. Mr M E Urell was the umpire for the game. [Sep 21st newspaper: The National Club, of Washington City, left yesterday on a visit to Balt. They played a game with the Maryland Club, of that city, yesterday, which resulted in a score of 35 to 8 in favor of the Nationals. Today they play a match game with the Pastime Club, of Balt. Phil, Sep 20. The match game of base ball between the Irvingtons, of N J, & the Quaker City, of Phil, resulted in a victory for the latter by a score of 27 to 14.] [Sep 26th newspaper: Match game played at Phil yesterday between the Jefferson Base Ball Club, of this city, & the Athletic Club, of Phil: Athletic 50; Jefferson-14.] [Oct 1st newspaper: There will be a match-game of base-ball played this afternoon, on the Nationals' new grounds, between a nine composed of clerks from the First Nat'l Bank of Wash City & an organization from other banks, known as the Bankers' Nine. Mr H C Studley is captain of the First Nationals' nine.] [Oct 9th newspaper: Base-ball. The Nationals beat the Picked Nine: 44 to 12. Umpire: P Haskins, Union Club, of Wash. Scorers: Messrs H T Munson & Jas T Potts.] [Oct 11th newspaper: Numerous cases of a new disease, called "base-ball on the brain," have recently been developed in this community; but the case we now mention is the most serious that has as yet transpired. There is a gentleman in this city who has become so infatuated with the game of base ball that he insists on running the home machine on the base-ball system. His children being quite numerous, are divided off into nines. At the table they are assigned to their respective positions & the servant ordered to take the first base. His wife, whose word none dare dispute, is styled the umpire, & himself the batsman, his duty being to flog the children. When the youngest child cries he designates this a "foul bawl," & orders the servant to stop it.]

Thos Dowling, auct, yesterday, sold part of lot 1 on Bridge st, between Wash & Congress sts, with improvements, to Calvin Payne, for $3,800. He also sold lot 10, with a frame dwlg, between Green & Montgomery sts, to Mrs Alice Moran, for $1,400.

Harps are used in London churches. [In the "Mscl items."]

Health of Army ofcrs in New Orleans. New Orleans, Sep 18, 1867. Gen U S Grant, Commanding Armies of the U S. Gen Wheaton, Lt Col Wool, Maj Leslie Smith, 1st infty; Col McGonigle, A Q M, Lt Abbott, 6th cavalry; Surgeon Clemans, Assist Surgeon *Kpefer, Acting Assist Surgeons Auerbauck & Deal are in favorable condition. Lt Collman, 1st infty, & Boyle, 39th infty, condition not known. Capt Spangler, 6th cavalry, & Lt Rosander, 9th cavalry, died yesterday. –J A Mower, Brvt Maj Gen. Gen J K Barnes, Surgeon Gen U S A: Surgeon Clemans' condition is very favorable. -T A McParlin, Brvt Brig Gen, Surgeon. Capt Spangler, whose death is announced, is widely known as having served for a long time as Chief Quartermaster of the cavalry corps of the Army of the Potomac. [*Copied as written.]

Died: on Sep 18, Jas L Edwards, in his 82nd year. His funeral is tomorrow at 11 o'clock, from his late residence, 157 F st, near 19th.

Died: on Sep 19, Margaret, infant daughter of Wm H C & Emily Z Bayly, in her 2nd year. Her funeral will take place from the residence of her parents, E st, between 20th & 21st sts, Friday, Sep 20, at 4 o'clock. "Suffer little children to come unto Me."

Houston Telegraph, Sep 11. Among those attacked yesterday with the yellow fever we observe Rev Mr Reed, Mr J R Hand, & Capt Foster. Among the convalescents we observe Mr Kaumheimer, of the Board of Registration.

Yellow fever ravages at Galveston: on Sep 10th, the death from the fever were 33. Among the personals, we notice the death of a child of the late Dr Gantt; Maj Potter's wife is reported dying; & it is feared at this hour she is deceased. Maj Potter is slowing convalescing. Mr Cheney, of the Quartermaster's Dept, was taken down with fever on Monday. Mr Cheney, after attending on Col Howell, of the U S army, & then on the entire family of Maj Potter, has been forced to surrender to the tyrant. Mr Willden, of the Bulletin, is doing as well as could be expected. Mr Kenzel, of the German Union, is gradually gaining strength. Dr Toney, is in a favorable way. Dr Adams, assist surgeon U S army, died on Monday. Mr Shropshire, at the head of the house of Shropshire & Co, was taken down on Sat; also Mr Swisher, of Hewitt & Swisher. Dr Alexander is doing well as could be expected; he was taken on Sunday. Col Lawther is recovering. Dr Welch is gradually improving. Maj Williams is doing well. Lt Garretson, the gentlemanly post quartermaster, is improving. Mr C A Macmurphy, a brother-in-law of Lt Sherman, & brother of Mr G L Macmurphy, of Thompkins & Macmurphy died & was buried on Monday.

U S Marshal's sale Sep 24, at the store of Wm H & Thos P Stabler, 91 La ave, between 9th & 10th sts, sundry items from their store, seized & levied upon as the good & chattels of the said Stablers, to be sold to satisfy execution 3,891, in favor of Rittenhouse, Fowler & Co. –David S Gooding, U S Marshal, D C
-Wm L Wall & Co, aucts

SAT SEP 21, 1867
Geo Waters, of Gtwn, warns persons not to give credit to any one on his account.

John McHugh, capt of the canal boat **Molly Mack**, was drowned on Wed last, while the boat was at Eight Mile Level, on its way to Gtwn. At last accounts his body had not been found, although every effort has been made to find it.

The colored servant girl, Adelia Johnson, in the employ of Mr John Walters, on E st, died yesterday. She was terribly burned on Thu by the explosion of a can of kersene oil. Several physicians in attendance could do nothing to check the interior effects.

Mrd: on Sep 12, at Zion Church, N Y, by Rt Rev Bishop Southgate, Dr Sam B Fisher, of Fauquier Co, Va, & Miss Ancella Boag, of Charleston, S C, daughter of the late Wm Boag, of Cheshire, England.

Old Citizens: 1-Col Jas L Edwards, an old & highly respected resident of the First Ward, died on Thursday, at the advanced age of 82 years. 2-Dr R H Speake, a physician, well known & highly appreciated in this community, died at his residence, in Wash City, yesterday, at the age of 64 years. 3-Mr Richd Wimsatt, a well known resident of the Seventh Ward, died suddenly yesterday, at his residence, at the age of 69. He was sitting in his doorway on Thursday evening, engaged in conversation, when suddenly he was attacked with violent retchings, which continued for some time, rendering him speechless from exhaustion. He continued to grow worse until 11 o'clock yesterday morning, when death ensued. Mr Wimsatt was a native of St Mary's Co, Md, & came to Washington about 50 years ago. For many years he was engaged in business on the Island, & was distinguished for his innate love of honesty & fair dealing.

+

Died: on Sep 20, suddenly, of paralysis, Richd Wimsatt, in his 70th year. His funeral will be on Sep 22, Sunday, at 2 o'clock, from St Dominick's Church, corner 6th & F sts, Island. The friends & acquaintances of the family, & the Association of Oldest Inhabitants are respectfully invited.

Inquest was held on the body of Bun Bell, who was shot by Chas Wallace on Wed. Wallace was committed to jail to answer to the charge of murder.

Jas Sedwith, night clerk & watchman at Willard's Hotel for a number of years, was detected in the act of robbing the cigar case of Mr Rouse, which is in the front corridor of the bldg, on Thursday night. Mr Rouse has missed a large number of fine cigars, & could not account for their loss. A watch was placed in the hotel, & Sedwith was detected in the act. On examining his apts several hundred dollars' worth of tobacco, cigars, etc, were found. The accused was committed, in default of $300, for his appearance before court to answer the charge.

Elsworth, Kansas, Sep 20. 1-The camp of Thos Parker, railroad contractor, 46 miles above **Fort Hayes**, was attacked by Indians yesterday at noon. Forty men were in the camp at the time. Parker & five of his men were killed, & five mortally wounded. Parker's body was pierced by 14 bullet, lance, & arrow wounds. Eight Indians were killed. 2-Two brothers, named Farrell, were arrested at **Fort Harker** today, charged with the murder of Frank Johnson, which occurred a few days ago.

Mrs Randall, wife of Postmaster Gen Randall, is expected to arrive in N Y by the next steamer, from Scotland.

Died: on Sep 20, of consumption, Dr R H Speake, in his 64th year. His funeral is this morning at 10 o'clock, from his late residence, 324 G st, between 12th & 13th sts.

Supreme Court of D C, 840-Equity. Adams & Coltman vs Smith et al. Statement of the account in the hands of trustee on Sep 24, at my ofc, at 10 A M.
–Walter S Cox, auditor

Below we publish the order of Brvt Maj Gen Griffin, who has himself since fallen a victim to the pestilence at Galveston, announcing to his command in Texas the death of Brvt Lt Col Wm S Abert, major 7th cavalry, U S A. This young ofcr was born in Wash City on Feb 1, 1836, & the youngest son of the late Col J J Abert, who was an ofcr of the army for 55 years, & 31 of those years chief of the Corps of Topographical Engineers. He entered the army from civil life in Jun, 1855. At the commencement of the war, in 1861, he was under the command of Col Dimmick, at **Fortress Monroe**. After the close of the war, desiring & deserving rest, he obeyed his orders to Northwestern Texas, whither his wife & 2 children accompanied him. He had been complimented by two brevets, first of lt colonel, & next of brig general of volunteers.

Obsequies of Senor Manuel Carvallo took place on Aug 27, at 11 A M, at the Church Saint Jacques Sur Candenburg, in memory of his Excellency, who died at Compeigne on Jul 25 last. The son & son-in-law of the deceased were the mourners. Senor Erasmiz, Envoy Extraordinary & Minister Plenipotentiary of Chili to London, came in the name of his Gov't. They royal house was represented by Gen Bormann, aide de camp to the King, & an ofcr of ordinance; that of the Court of Flanders by Col Burnell, aide de camp of his Royal Highness.

Supreme Court of D C, 786-Equity. Cassandra V Johnston vs Dora M Johnston, et al. Statement of the trustee's account & distribution of fund received by dfndnts, Anthony & Mary Wagoner, etc; on Wed next, at 10:30 A M. –Walter S Cox, auditor

Supreme Court of D C, 1,471-Equity. Potomac Ins Co of Gtwn vs Chas H Van Patten. The above cause is referred to me to inquire into the debts due from the fund, & their priorities, & to state the trustee account on Sep 26, at 10 A M.
–Walter S Cox, auditor

Pres Lincoln's coach is offered for sale in N Y.

Gen Reuben Davis & wife arrived at Staunton, Va, on Monday.

MON SEP 23, 1867
Julis Finnieum, about 17, was seriously wounded yesterday by Michl Shea while carelessly handling a loaded pistol, the ball lodging in his right knee. On Sat, Abraham Curtis, a colored man, engaged in tearing down the walls of the Hudson Taylor property, while sitting in the window of the bldg in the second story, was seriously injured by the falling of a lot of brick. It has been found that his spinal column is broken.

Mr Tennyson is about to publish a volume of new songs, with music by Mr Arthur S Sullivan.

John B Gough has on his estate, at West Boylston, Mass, over 2,000 of the feathered tribe, turkeys, hens, ducks, pigeons, & geese.

The cornerstone of St Matthew's Church, in Wash City, was laid on Sep 21, 1838, by the Most Rev Archbishop Eccleston. The church was erected under the direction of a bldg cmte, composed of Thos Carbery, John Queen, Ignatius Mudd, & Jos Harbaugh. The bldg progressed slowly, & was not dedicated until Sep 21, 1840. That ceremony was performed by Archbishop Eccleston, on which occasion Dr Moriarty, of Phil, preached. The day was delightful. Rev Jno P Donelan was appointed first pastor, & remained as such until Sep, 1846, when he was transferred to St Vincent's Church, Balt. A pontifical mass was celebrated by Bishop Fenwick, of Boston, & sermon pronounced by Very Rev Dr Power of N Y. The Bishop of N Y, Rt Rev Dr Du Bois, was present in the sanctaury. Rev Jas B Donelan succeed his brother John P Donelan, & continued in office until Dec, 1855, when he resigned, & became assist pastor to Rev John Byrne. Dr Byrne remained pastor until Oct 30, 1853. Rev Mr Waldron became assist pastor in Jul, 1857. Rev Dr White was appointed pastor in Nov, 1857, & Rev John McNally his assistant in Oct, 1859. Rev McNally having been appointed pastor of St Stephen's Church, now in course of erection in the First Ward, Rev Desiderius De Wolf is the present assist of Dr White, at St Matthew's. Within the last 18 months a fine school-house has been erected within St Matthew's parish for the colored Catholics, in which schools are held & divine service regularly performed on Sundays & holidays. Rev F Barotti is pastor of this colored congregation. Thus 3 parishes have been organized out of the original parish of St Matthew's.

Ads. 1-Mr Mades, 10th & E sts, is agent for a fine, cheap Calif wine. 2-Rev Chas H Nourse will open his classical & mathematical academy on Sep 2.

Died: on Sep 21, Mrs Josephine F, widow of Theo J Turnburke. Her funeral is this morning at 10 o'clock, from St Dominick's Church.

Died: on Sep 21, Mrs Sarah Gallagher, the beloved wife of Thos Gallagher, in her 68th year. Her funeral will be this afternoon, Sep 23, at 3 o'clock, from the residence of her son-in-law, John Wise, First st west, between G & H sts north.

Died: on Sep 16, in Medea, Pa, in his 41st year, Theodoric Lee, formerly of the U S navy, & eldest son of the late Lt John Hite Lee, U S N.

The widow of Richd Hildreth, the historian, died of cholera in Naples last month.

Gen Tom Thumb is at Weedsport, Cayuga Co, N Y. His wife is at Rochester.

Cmder G W Young, of the U S steamer **Suwanee**, died off Manzanilla, about the *_ instant. He was buried at Mansanilla. [*The number is illegible.]

Robt E Pecker, a native of Concord, N H, but for the past 20 years a merchant in Boston, died Thursday of consumption, in Boston, in his 61st year.

Mrs Maria C Bell, widow of the late Major Bell, who was voted a handsome sword, with a golden scabbard, by Congress, for his gallant services during the war of 1812, died at Portsmouth, Va, on Thursday.

TUE SEP 24, 1867
The trustees of the Brookeville Academy have purchased of W Veirs Bouie trustees, the *Riggs farm*, most eligibily located a half a mile from the village of Brookeville, Md, to which the academy is to be removed. It is the intention of the trustees immediately to add & improve the present bldg, & to lay off & beautify the grounds upon the plan of schools of similar grade in England, so as to make this old & time honored institution one of the most desirable & attractive seminaries of learning in the Southern States.

Hon Stoddard B Colby, Register of the Treasury, died at Haverhill, N H, on Sat last, of typhoid diarrhoea, after an illness of some 5 weeks. He was a native of Vt, born in Feb, 1816; graduated at Dartmouth College in 1836, with distinguished honor, & had received the honorary degree of LL D just before his decease. He was a kind & considerate husband, a gentle & dutiful son, a forbearing parent, & a warm true friend. –I F R Washington, Sep 23

St Louis, Sep 20. An Omaha special says that John W Smith has just returned from *Fort Phil Kearney*, & that he charges Judge Kinney, special Indian agent at *Fort Kearney*, with gross injustice & fraud in his dealings with the Iowa Indians, compelling them to remain in the Sioux country against their will, for the purpose of securing trade; that the annuities of $25,000 promised 3 years ago were never paid, & the claims that the goods sold at Kinney's store to the Indians were furnished by the Govn't for free distribution.
+
Letter from Chas E Mix, Acting Com'r, to Hon J F Kinney, U S Special Indian Com'r, Wash, D C. Sir: I am in receipt of your letter of Sep 21, enclosing a slip taken from the newspapers, headed "Serious charge against an Indian agent." I have to say that you are not at present, nor have you ever been, a special Indian agent. The goods furnished by you for the Indians were not goods that had been purchased by the Gov't. Also, that no goods have been purchased for the Crow Indians, the tribes referred to, by the Govn't the present season; nor have any goods been sent to *Fort Phil Kearney* by this dept. This dept has no knowedge of any funds having been placed in your hands, or in the hands of com'rs for the purchase of goods or presents for the Indians. –Chas E Mix, Acting Com'r

Many of our old citizens will regret to learn of the death of Michl Walsh, formerly a resident of Wash, but for some years past a successful merchant of Ill & the West. The town of Walshville, Ill, was founded by him.

Jas Powles, an Englishman, aged 67, living in Portage Co, Ohio, died on Tuesday from poison, mysteriously administered in his food.

Dept of the Interior, U S Patent Ofc, Wash, Sep 19, 1867. Ptn of L Otto P Meyer, of Newtown, Conn, praying for the extension of a patent granted to him Dec 20, 1853, for an improvement in Processes of Vulcanizing Caoutchouc Compounds, for seven years from the expiration of said patent, which takes place on Dec 20, 1867.
-T C Theaker, Com'r of Patents

WED SEP 25, 1867
Equity Court-Judge Wylie. 1-Suit for alimony. Julia A Joslyn vs John C Joslyn. Ptn in this case sets forth alleged marriage, subsequent neglect & desertion, & recites charges of infidelity against the dfndnt. The answer admits the alleged marriage, but denies the desertion, & charges desertion on the part of the cmplnt. It also denies the allegation of infidelity. Claims a prior divorce in Henrico Co, Ohio, & claims that the cmplnt is not the wife of the dfndnt by reason thereof. Is also denies the jurisdiction of a court of equity to grant the relief prayed for by the cmplnts. The counsel base their claim for alimony on the following grounds: That it is the duty of the husband to support the wife; that alimony is not confined to the divorce law; that a court of equity has jurisdiction to grant alimony & costs of suit, even to grant counsel fees; that after a suit of divorce so granted the wife can bring suit for alimony as an independent right; that although the Ohio divorce is set up by the dfndnt, yet this court can look into the proceedings & examine as to the jurisdiction of the Ohio court; & that the courts of D C have ample jurisdiction, & the Ohio court has not; therefore the alimony is prayed. [Sep 26th newspaper: In the case of Joslyn vs Joslyn, for alimony yesterday, the Court ordered that the dfndnt pay the cmplnt or her solicitor for her maintenance, monthly, the sum of $50, pending this suit, to commence from Oct 1, 1867, until the further order of the Court.]

Orphans Court-Judge Purcell, Sep 24, 1867. 1-The last will of Robt Johnson, deceased, of Gtwn, was fully proven & admitted to probate. Isaac Davenport & Collins Cursor are excs of the will. Isaac Davenport, however, declines to be one of the executors. 2-The second & final account of Harriet M Sullivan & John B Blake, excs of the estate of John S Sullivan, deceased, was received & passed. 3-The case of Read vs Brown, exc of Richd Bustead, was further argued by Gen Terry for petitioner, & M Thompson, for respondent.

On Sat Mr Geo P Hamlin, keeper of a restaurant on Pa ave, near 7th st, was brought before Justice Morsell, to answer to the charge of passing a counterfeit $5 Treasury note on Geo Carpenter, colored, who is in the employ of Davis & Gaither, agents for Grover & Baker's sewing machines. It appears that Mr Hamlin had purchased a sewing machine, & had paid Carpenter for the same on its delivery with this counterfeit note.

Dr Blackburn excluded from amnesty. It was decided he was not entitled to such benefit, because the foul crime with which he is charged had rendered him amenable to a criminal prosecution; & during the war he was an agent of the rebel Gov't in a foreign country. He was notorious during the war for his effort to introduce the small pox into the Northern States by means of infected clothing.

Wash, Sep 19, 1867. The effect of the Pres' last proclamation of <u>amnesty</u> was to release a very large number of persons, it is not so well understood that very few prominent officials of the late Confederacy find themselves embraced by its provisions. I have taken some pains to ascertain the names of those thus released, & am able to specify those most prominent. First among those non pardoned are Hon Thos S Bocock, of Va, who served in the lower House of Congress from 1847 to 1861; chosen a member of the Confederate House of Reps at Richmond, & made Speaker for 2 terms. Next we have Hon Wm A Graham, former U S Sec of the Navy, & rebel Senator from N C; Robt W Barnwell, of S C, U S Senator a few years since, holding a similar position in the rebel Congress; Hon Jas Chesnut, U S Senator from S C, when the war broke out; then a member of the Confederate Senate, an aid to Pres Davis, & afterwards a brig gen; Henry A Wise, of Va, a brigadier in the rebel service; Edw Sparrow, Confederate Senator from La; Hon Robt W Johnson, of Ark, a member of the U S & Confederate Congress; Hon Humphrey Marshall, ditto; Roger A Pryor, of Va, former U S member of Congress, & a brigadier in the rebel service; Herschel V Johnson, of Ga, who ran on the ticket with Douglas for Vice Pres, & served in the rebel Senate; Martin J Crawford, of Ga, a member of the U S & of the rebel Congress; Chas L Scott, M C from Calif, & Major in the 4th Alabama Confederate regt; Geo P Kane, of Balt, who was imprisoned, & subsequently went South; & Mr D L Yulee, former U S Senator from Fla, but who appears to have held no military or civil position in the rebel service; he was imprisoned along with a number of prominent confederates at **Fort Pulaski** for some 6 months, &, thanks to an old family quarrel with his brother-in-law, Judge Holt, was about the last batch to be released; he had the satisfaction of seeing his comrades depart day after day, & his own dungeon door carefully shut, & of knowing all the while that the blow came from his own familiar friend. Members of the U S & rebel Congress excluded by the former proclamation of amnesty, have received special pardons. Among these are Hon Jas L Orr, of S C; Hon Jas L Pugh, of Ala; Hon J L M Curry, of Ala, now a Baptist clergyman; Hon John A Gilmer, of N C; Hon Wm Porcher Miles, of S C; Wm W Boyce, do; Hon D C DeGarnett, of Va; Hon Thos L Clingman, of N C; Hon C M Conrad, of La, Sec of War to Mr Fillmore; R W Walker, of Ala; Thos S Gholson, of Va; Hon Geo W Jones, of Tenn. Quite a number are dead. Hammond, of S C, senator at the time of secession died during the war at his home; Judge Hemphill, Senator from Texas, died in 1860-61; Hon Sydenham Moore, member of Congress from Ala, died of wounds received in the battles about Richmond; Henry C Burnett, U S Rep from Ky, & Confederate Senator, died since the war; Barksdale, member of Congress from Miss, fell mortally wounded in a charge of his brigade at Gettysburg; Ruffin, member of Congress from N C, fell in battle, as did Branch, from the same State, both brigadiers, I believe; M R H Garnett, one of the ablest & most conspicuous of the secession leaders, died during the war at his home, in Essex Co, Va. Embraced by the recent proclamation of amnesty is Hon Wm B Stokes, of Tenn, a member of the 36th Congress, who went into the rebellion & proposed to raise troops, now a Radical member of the late, &, I believe, also a member elect of the present House of Reps. The great mass of those restored to rights by the recent proclamation are those persons who left their homes inside the Union lines in Missouri, Md, & Ky, to join the rebel army, or otherwise aid the Confederacy.

These survivors number between thirty & forty thousand persons. These were specially excepted by Mr Johnson's first proclamation, in May, 1865. I come to those who are now still excluded from amnesty. Jefferson Davis, Miss, Pres; Alex H Stephens, Ga, Vice Pres; Robt Toombs, Ga, Sec of State from Feb 1861 to Jul, 1861; R M T Hunter, Va, Sec of State from Jul 1861, to Feb, 1862; Judah P Benjamin, of La, Sec of State from Feb 1862 to Apr, 1865; Jas L Sedden, of Va, Sec of War, 1862-63; John C Breckinridge, of Ky, Sec of War, 1864-65; S R Mallory, of Fla, Sec of the Navy, 1861 to 1865; Thos Bragg, of N C, Atty Gen, 1861-62. Some of Mr Davis' Cabinet have been specially pardoned: Hon John H Reagan, of Texas, Confederate Postmaster Gen all through the war, taken with Mr Davis when captured & imprisoned a long time in *Fort Warren*; Thos H Watts, of Ala, Atty Gen, 1862; Geo Davis, of N C, Atty Gen, 1863-64; Geo A Trenholm, of S C, Sec of the Treasury from 1864 to the close of the war, imprisoned in *Fort Pulaski*; to this number may be added Geo W Randolph, of Va, relative, we believe, to John Randolph & Thos Jefferson, who was Sec of War in 1862, & then resigned, went to Europe for his health, but came home since the war in the last stage of consumption, & died in April last. The following comprise a pretty full list of those who were "agents" of the Confederate Gov't in foreign States & countries. I take first the diplomatic & commercial agents. John Slidell, La, com'r at Paris.
Jas M Mason, Va, at London. N Dudley Mann, Va, at Brussels
L Q C Lamar, Miss, to Russia, & a colonel in Confederate States army.
John T Pickett, Ky, to Mexico in 1861; served afterwards on staff of Gen Breckinridge. Wm Preston, Ky, brig gen in Confederate States army; & sent as com'r to Maximilian. Emile La Sere, La, agent in Mexico.
Geo Eustis, La, Sec Legation to Slidell at Paris.
Jas E Macfarland, Va, Sec of Legation to Mason at London.
Henry Hotze, Ala, editor of Index, & commercial agent at London.
Chas J Helm, Ky, agent at Havana.
Walker Fearn, Ala, Sec of Legation to L Q C Lamar.
Edw De Leon, S C, employed as a writer in Paris.
Three of this class have been pardoned: P Rost, of La, one of the first 3 Confederate agents sent abroad; Bishop Lynch, of Charleston, com'r at Rome, & J A Quintero, special agent in Northern Mexico. Wm L Yancey, of Ala, conspicuous Southern leader, who figured as com'r in England, returned home & died in the South during the war. Among the miscellaneous agents excluded from the amnesty are: Hon Jacob Thompson, of Miss, com'r & agent in Canada. C C Clay, of Ala, com'r & agent in Canada. Gen E G Lee, of Va, com'r & agent in Canada. Beverly Tucker, of Va, commercial agent at Halifax, N S. Capt M F Maury, of Va; Capt Bullock, of Ga; ___ Ferguson, ___ Huse, & others were despatched to England for the purchase of supplies & clothing. J P Holcombe, of Va, agent in Canada, & Walker, commercial agent at Bermuda, have been pardoned. Heylign, agent at Nassau, is dead. Geo N Sanders, by many supposed to be a rebel agent, never held any position, whether civil or military, under the Confederate Gov't.
Military leaders still unpardoned:
Robt E Lee, Va, general
Jos E Johnston, Va, gen

G T Beauregard, La, gen
Saml Cooper, N Y, gen
Braxon Bragg, N C, gen
Jas E Longstreet, Ga, lt gen
Wm J Hardee, Ga, lt gen
John B Hood, Ky, lt gen
John C Pemberton, Pa, lt gen
E Kirby Smith, Fla, lt gen
Theophilus Holmes, N C, lt gen
Albert S Johnston, general, fell at Shiloh; & Stonewell Jackson, lt gen, died from wounds at Chancellorsville. Leonidas Polk, lt gen, fell in the Georgia campaign of 1864. A P Hill, lt gen, was killed near Petersburg, in Apr, 1865.
Among the major generals not pardoned we find John B Magruder, Va; Geo E Picket, Va; Jubal Early, Va; Sterling Price, Mo, Eugene McLaws, Ga; Howell Cobb, Ga; Mansfield Lovell, D C; Huger, S C; Gustavus W Smith, Ky; T C Hindman, Ark; Dick Taylor, La; Wade Hampton, S C; N B Forrest, Tenn; Cheatham, Tenn; S B Buckner, Ky; Field, Ky; Gordon, Ga; Wm Mahone, Va; Elzy, Md; & about 15 or 20 others.
Naval ofcrs: Admirals Semmes & Buchanan are not covered by the amnesty. Admiral Forrest has died since the war.
Among the list of Governors of States who are left out of the amnesty, we find Gov Wm Smith, Va; J G Harris, Tenn; Clarke, Miss; Moore, La; Lubbock, Texas; Rector, Ark; Jos E Brown, Ga; M L Bonham, S C; Magrath, S C; F W Pickens, S C, Acting Gov Alston, of Fla, & a few others.
Govn'r Letcher of Va; Govn'r S B Vance, of N C, & T H Watts, of Ala, have received special pardons. Govn'r Allen, of La, died in Mexico.
Nearly all the civil & military leaders noted above, since the war have rigidly abstained from any connection whatever with politics, whether State or Federal. Alex'r H Stephens, Gen Wise, & Gen Hampton making some addresses on one side, & we discover Gen Longstreet & Gen Jeff Thompson writing letters in favor of a union with the Radicals, & Gov Brown, of Ga, who seized **Fort Pulaski**, is, we believe, stumping that State for the Radical ticket. Lee is president of Wash College, Va; Joe Johnston & Beauregard are in charge of railroads; Cooper is in retirement in Va; Bragg is in N C; Hardee, Kirby Smith, Wood, Pickett, Magruder, Price, Buckner, Gordon, & others, are probably at their homes; Forrest is in commercial business & planting; Dick Taylor, do; Gustavus Smith has charge of extensive ironworks at Chattanooga; Brooke & Curtis Lee are professors at Lexington; Hampton is planting; Wise, Pryor, Bobock & Mosby are at the law. Among civilians we find Reagan farming in Texas; R M T Hunter farming in Essex Co, Va; J A Seddon & Gov Wm Smith similarly engaged; Memminger, Trenholm, Clay, Mallory, & Geo Davis at their homes in strict seclusion. Lamar, Watts, Conrad, & Clay are also practicing law. Breckinridge, Early, Slidell, Benjamin, Mason, Jacob Thompson, & others are in Canada or Europe. Jefferson Davis is in Canada, but is under bonds to answer at the Nov term of the U S Ciruit Court in Richmond. Besides those in exile the following Confederate officials have been imprisoned: Jefferson Davis & C C Clay at **Fortress Monroe**; Alex H Stephens & J H Reagan at

Fort Warren; Jas A Seddon, R M T Hunter, John A Campbell, Trenholm, Clark, Yulee, Alston, Magrath, & others, at *Fort Pulaski*; Mallory at *Fort Lafayette*; Preston Johnson, Lubbock, Burton Harrison, & others at various places. None of the prominent military men were imprisoned, being protected by their paroles. The effort to write up a feeling & have Gen Lee arrested was defeated, probably by the interposition of Gen Grant. Dr Gwin, on his return from Mexico, was imprisoned for a long time at *Fort Jackson*, but he had not been in the Confederate service, whatever may have been his sympathies, & the proceeding was apparently without justification.

The President has issued a pardon to Stephen R Mallory, of Fla, Sec of the Navy of the late Southern Confederacy. He was the only member of Mr Davis' cabinet who surrendered, & elected to throw himself upon the mercy of the U S Gov't. It is also said that the President will shortly pardon Alex'r H Stephens, late Vice Pres of the Confederacy, upon the recommendation of persons of influence & distinguished position.

Chattanooga, Sep 24. Col John H James, late quartermaster U S army, & afterwards quartermaster of the State of Tenn, died this morning, of liver & bowl complaint, at the Lookout Mountain House, of which he was proprietor.

Dr A Eaton, a half-brother of Pres Lincoln, dropped dead at Mumfordsville, Ky, a few days ago, while mixing medicine for a patient.

Col Wm P Maulsby, late a member of the Democratic Convention of Md, was taken to the insane asylum week before last. The cause of his insanity is attributed to the death of his wife. [Oct 2nd newspaper: Letters have been received stating that this report is utterly without foundation, & a pure fabrication, intended to injure the prospects of the election of Col Maulsby to the bench of the Circuit Court, comprising Montg & Fred'k counties, in which he is a tower of strength to the Conservative party.]

The partnership existing between Geo G Cornwell, Douglass Cornwell, & Gilbert Cornwell, trading under the name of G G Cornwell & Sons, was dissolved by mutual consent on Sep 23, 1867, Geo G Cornwell withdrawing from the concern. Geo G Cornwell will take charge of the wholesale dept of the American Tea Co at store 213 Pa ave, opposite Willard's Hotel.

Executor's sale of Iron Safe, Sep 28, at the store of Mr Jacob Schufley, 271 Pa ave, between 10th & 11th. I shall sell for cash, 1 large Herring Safe, in fine order, belonging to the estate of the late Jas Skirving. –John T Given, exc
-Cooper & Latimer, aucts

Cincinnati Commercial says: The venerable mother of Gen Garfield, age 70, on Fri night, drove a burglar from her house, in Huron, Portage Co, at the muzzle of a revolver.

THU SEP 26, 1867

Wm A Linton, an old citzen of Wash, died at his residence, on C st, between 1st & 2nd sts, on Tuesday. He was born in Dumfires, Va, in 1791; educated at the college of Wm & Mary, Va, studied the legal profession in his native village, & removed to Wash City in 1835, where he has resided ever since. He was rendered quite deaf when about 25 years of age, which incapacitated him from the practice of his profession. He was 76 years old.
+
Died: on Sep 24, Wm A Linton, in his 77th year. His funeral will take place from his late residence, 445 C st, this afternoon, at 3 o'clock P M. [Sep 27th newspaper: Mr Linton is survived by his orphan children, relatives, & friends.]

Died: on Sep 24, of pneumonia, Matthew, youngest child of Matthew F & Lydia M Pleasants. His funeral will be from the residence of his parents, 272 F st, on Sep 26, at 11 o'clock A M.

Accident-Mrs Margaret Ann Kennedy, residing on L st, near 19th st, while attempting, yesterday, to lift a vessel from the stove containing boiling water, was accidentally upset, scalding her feet severely.

Six cases of murder are on the jail docket for trial at the next term of the Criminal Court, viz: J H Surratt, Henry Johnson, Jos W N Zimmer, Chas Wallace, Wm Eldridge, & John D McClelland.

Key West, Sep 25. O'Laughlin, one of the Lincoln conspirators, died of yellow fever on Sep 23. All of the conspirators have been very attentive to the sick at the Dry Tortugas.

For sale: ***Normanstone***, known as the ***Barnard property***, on the Heights of Gtwn, containing about 23 acres of land, highly improved. The delightful rural mansion & fine well of water, gives attraction to this place. –Wm L Dunlop, atty, Gay st, Gtwn. Also, 3 lots of ground at the s w corner of Congress & West sts, Gtwn, fronting 77 feet on West st.

Wigton for sale; situated on the Potomac river, 2 miles from Alexandria, Va, containing 457 acres; the dwlg house, kitchen, & servants houses of brick; with good stable, corn-house, & other farm bldgs. Price very low; apply to C F M Johnston, or Johnston & Lloyd, Real Estate Agents, Alexandria, Va.

N Y Herald says: Gen Ord has just appointed J T Montgomery justice of the peace for the Davis Bend precinct, in Warren Co. Montgomery was the former slave of Mr Davis, & his confidential business manager, & discharged his duties with fidelity & rectitude. Like all who were faithful as slaves, Montgomery now possesses the confidence & respect of the white people.

Wm H Bartlett, associate justice of the Supreme Court of N H, died at Concord on Monday of consumption; aged 40 years.

Valuable improved property on the Navy Yard at auction, Oct 3, in front of the premises, the well known Grocery Stand, formerly occupied by L A Dellwig, & lately by the late J H B Jenkins as a wholesale & retail grocery store, 588 7th st, between G & I sts; improvements-a fine Brick Store Room. Title perfect. -Cooper & Latimer, aucts

Supreme Court of D C, at Law, no 4,024. Henry S Davis vs Wm H Winder & Wm E Spaulding. The writ in this case against Wm H Winder having been returned "not found," on Jul 25, 1867, it is ordered, on Sep 4, 1867, on motion of the atty for the plntf, that said dfndnt cause his appearance on or before the first rule day occurring 40 days after this date. –R J Meigs, clerk

Tuscora Female Seminary, 8 miles west of Mifflin Station, Pa railroad, announces that Prof Carl F Colbe, having returned from Europe, has resumed his duties as teacher of Music, French, & German-15 years experience in teaching. Miss R Annie French, connected with this School, whilst under the administration of Dr Agnew, & afterwards engaged in the Seminary at Selin's Grove, is now the principal teacher here. The present session opened Sep 4. –J Walker Patterson, A B principal, Academia, Juniati Co, Pa.

FRI SEP 27, 1867
New cars on the F st railroad. The twenty cars of the new style designed for a single horse commenced running yesterday. These cars will seat about 12 persons. They are of the omnibus pattern, passengers entering from the rear, & the fare will be deposited in a box in the front part of the car.

At St Aloysius Church, on Wed morning, John T Burch was united to Miss Mary Heffell. The nuptial mass was said & the marriage ceremonies performed by Rev B F Wiget, S J, president of Gonzaga College.

Died: on Sep 26, Mrs Sarah Bogan, wife of Benj L Bogan, aged 66 years & 5 months. Her funeral will be on Sat at 10 o'clock A M, at the residence of Dr Van Bogan, near Fairfax Station, Va. [Shenandoah & Rockingham, Va, papers please copy.]

Havana, Sep 25. Death of Capt Gen of Cuba. Gen Manzano died in the morning of typhoid fever. The body was embalmed, & is lying in state. Senor Balmazada has been sworn in as Provisional Capt General of the Island. The whole city is in mourning. The funeral will be Sep 27th. The remains will be sent to Spain on Sep 30th.

Memphis, Sep 19. A negro, named John Etheling, has been arrested here, upon his own confession of being the murderer of Dr Ramsey, of the Raleigh road, a short time since.

On Monday last, Mattie A Lee, daughter of Mr F J & Mrs E H Conrad, died at the residence of her parents, on Main, near 15th st, from the effects of opium administered by mistake for ipecac. The child was sick of croup, & under the care of Dr Waring. He prescribed 6 grains of ipecac & 20 grains of calomel, to be made into 6 powders. The clerk at the store of Mr R W Powers mistook ipecac for opium, & it cost the little sufferer her life. It is said the prescription was written indistinctly, & hard to decipher. Mattie was in the 4th year of her age.

R G Horton, editor of the N Y Day Book, died last Sunday, aged 40, of congestion of the lungs.

Bryan Casbrook, notorious a year ago in connection with a gift enterprise in Chicago, killed his two children at Denver City, a few days ago, & took poison himself, but his life was saved.

Ten years ago a Sister of Charity, with 3 companions of her order, went to Rochester, N Y, & opened a public hospital in a stone stable. Little by little she went on collecting money by extensive travel & inexhaustible patience. In 1864 a stately edifice was erected, & was filled with patients before it was finished. During the war, over 1,000 persons were accommodated, the most of whom were soldiers. A farm of 150 acres supplies milk, butter & vegetables. The lady who founded this insitution is the president, with 2 other Sisters & 2 gentlemen on the Board of Managers. It is called St Mary's Retreat, & no sufferer is rejected. A Protestant clergyman, in speaking of the history of the institution, says: "I would gladly name the originator & conductor of this truly Catholic hospital, but I should only grieve her modest nature.

Fatal case of yellow fever at Mobile on Sep 17. Major Tracey, Com'r of the Freedmen's Bureau, died on that day.

SAT SEP 28, 1867
The one horse railway cars have been initiated on the F st road, in Wash City. Lest our people might imagine that they are less roomy & comfortable than the fine two-horse cars on the same road, we would say that a trial of them dissipates such an erroneous idea. Certainly from $30,000 to $40,000 annually can be saved to the company by the new system.

A fine assortment of new goods for gentlemen's wear will be found at the store of Saml W Owen, near Willard's. [Ad]

Died: on Sep 26, Prof Jas Ferguson, Assist Astronomer U S Naval Observatory. His funeral will be on Sep 28 from his late residence, I & 20th sts, at 4 P M.

Died: on Sep 18, at the residence of Mr Edw Smoot, in Chas Co, Md, of congestive fever, after a few days illness, Mrs Mary Vaughan, in her 72nd year. She was a native of Wash City, & daughter of Robt Brown, deceased, a soldier of the Revolutionary war, from the State of Delaware. She was a very active & useful woman & enjoyed during her life almost uninterrupted health. Requiescent in pace.

Sons of Liberty-Election of Ofcrs, of the George Washington Camp: Past Chief, John W Thompson; Worthy Chief, Jos Hartley; Assist Chief, Alonzo D Shaw; Sgt at Arms, Jas Burns; Escorter, Wm D Hineline; Rep to the Grand Camp, Jas Edwards.

The purchase of square 623, lying between St Aloysius Church & the Gov't Printing Ofc, by Messrs Alex R Shepherd & Moses Kelly, insures the immediate improvement of this part of our city. The square has been sub-divided into over 100 bldg lots, & already some 20 three-story brick residences are under contract. It is contemplated to build the new Gonzaga College on grounds near St Aloysius Church. North Capitol st is opened & graded through to the road running to **Glenwood Cemetery**, & as soon as the depot of the Balt & Ohio railroad is removed from this street, it will be one of the very pleasantest & best thoroughfares in the city. Messrs Kilbourn & Latta, 7th & F sts, are agents for these lots. **Meridian Hill** is now being lithographed, & bldg lots will be offered for sale on terms similar to the above, in a few days, by Messrs Hall & Elvans.

Knights of Pythias-election of ofcrs-Webster Lodge, No 7: Worthy Chancellor, Harry V Cole; Vice Chancellor, A Forrest Altemus; Recording Scribe, W Miller Clarke; Financial Scribe, Philip Peyser; Banker, Jacob Peyser; Guide, Richd Goodheart; Inner Steward, H M Locke; Outer Steward, Wm H H Bradley.

Hon Wm H Bartlett, one of the Judges of the Supreme Court of this State, died at his residence in this city, Sep 24. He had been in feeble health for a long time, his disease being consumption, but was confined to the house only a few days. He was a native of Salisbury & a graduate of Dartmouth College; appointed Judge in Feb, 1861. He was about 40 years of age. He leaves a wife, the daughter of the late Abel Baker, but no children. -N H Patriot

Mrs Mary Arnod, probably the oldest woman in the U S, died at her residence in Douglas st, Brooklyn, on Sep 25, at the advanced age of 110 years. Mrs Arnod was born in Charleston, S C, in 1738, & moved to Long Island in 1791, where she dwelt until her death. She was the mother of 8 children, five of whom are still living, the eldest being 70, & the youngest 55 years of age.

Phil, Sep 27. Dr M V Gorman, Nat Keenly, & Miss Caroline Heron were arrested last night, charged with manufacturing counterfeit bank notes. It was ascertained that Gorman had a contract to supply $100,000 in First Nat'l Bank notes to this city next week. The parties have had a hearing before the U S Com'r today.

Louisville [Ky] Journal of Sep 24. Dr L P Blackburn, of Miss, a celebrated physician, & somewhat prominently identified with the late Confederate war, arrived at the Willard Hotel yesterday on his return from Toronto, Canada, where he has been living in exile for the past 3 or 4 years. He is en route to New Orleans, in which city he established a great reputation, in the good old days of peace, as a master of that deadly malady, yellow fever. His family, who have been residing in Louisville for the past 6 months, will continue to make this city their home.

St Louis, Sep 27. Gen Marcy, while returning from a tour of inspection in New Mexico, was attacked by Indians near Pawee Forks. Lt Williams, of the 5th infty, lost a leg, & one man was killed & 3 wounded. Maj Rodney Smith, with an escort of 40 men, was also attacked, but no damage done.

Norristown, Sep 27. Maj Gen Hancock visited his mother & his birth-place today.

Robt Bonnar, it is said, returns an income of $200,000.

Mr Robt Buchanan is writing a life of Audubon, from materials furnished by his widow.

John C Breckenridge, tired of the hubbub of the Paris Exposition, has gone to Switzerland.

Geo Drew, of West Concord, N H, 75 years old, died suddenly in his bed, Monday night.

A Golden wedding took place on Monday, at Rochester, on the occasion of the 50th anniversary of the marriage of Mr & Mrs Jos Hettig.

Miss Nellie Marshall, daughter of Gen Humphrey Marshall, of Ky, is ruralizing on **Beechland**, her father's splendid farm in Henry Co, engaged on a war novel.

Mr Pierre Soule was in New Orleans last week.

Ishmail Pacha, the present ruler of Egypt, is about 39 years of age, with a mild expression of countenance, a yellowish carroty beard, unually dyed, & an inordinate passion for amassing money. With a monoply of cotton & sugar in Egypt, he has contrived to render himself, perhaps, the rishest individual, privately, in Europe or Africa.

Col Chas B Lebbs, a well known & prominent lawyer of Loudoun Co, Va, died at Charlottesville on Thursday.

Lt Rossander, of the 6th cavalry, died at New Orleans with yellow fever on Wednesday.

Mr Alex T Stewart was recently the recipient of a public reception at Lisburn, Ireland.

Lt Wing, of the 4th U S cavalry, died at New Orleans on Thursday, of yellow fever. The other army ofcrs at that place are doing well.

Mrs Fanny Kemble arrived at Boston on Wed, by the steamer **Joan**, & left for Phil to see her children. Her husband, Pierce Butler, died a short time since in Georgia.

The fine residence of Dr Wood, surgeon U S navy, on I st, between 17th & 18th sts, was recently sold for $25,000 to Gen David Hunter, U S army. Part of lot 21, in old Gtwn, beginning at the n e corner of lot 22, fronting on the south side of Prospect st, with a depth of 120 feet, improved by a frame dwlg, was purchased by Mrs Maria Brown, for $1,850.

Near Rock Island, Ill, recently, Mrs Campbell Barthell was bitten by a rattlesnake in a field of watermelons. The whiskey cure was tried immediately, but failed to counteract the poison, & she died 6 days after being bitten.

Isaac Reynolds & Wm Quillins, both without legs & accomplishing locomotion with their arms, had a one mile race at Cincinnati a few days since, for a purse of $1,000. Reynolds weighs 105 & Quillins 120 pounds. The race was won by Reynolds in 11 minutes & 15 seconds.

Miss Ione Burke, a well known actress attached to Wallack's Theatre, N Y, was taken seriously ill on Thursday.

Dissolution of the partnership under the firm of Campbell & Godfrey, this day, by mutual consent. The business will be continued at the old stand by Mr Chas G Godfrey, sole proprietor. –C W Campbell, Chas G Godfrey

MON SEP 30, 1867
Orphans Court-Judge Purcell, Sep 28, 1867. 1-The first & final account of Chas Walter, guardian to Fred'k & Catharine Roemle, orphans of Danl Roemle, deceased, was approved & passed. 2-Messrs Brent & Phillips, representing the estate of the late Chas Carroll, of Balt, deceased, petition the court for the appointment of an administrator for the personal estate of said Carroll. This is done in view of the fact that there is now pending in the Supreme Court of D C a chancery suit in which the reps of said Carroll claim $500. 3-Dr Flodoardo Howard was qualified as administrator of the estate of Susan R Dorsey, deceased; bond $400. Sureties, Saml A Peugh & Flodoardo W Howard.

Judge Wilson, of the Superior Court of Chicago, has rendered a decision adverse to the widow of Stephen A Douglas, who claim dower in real estate worth $100,000, in the southern part of Chicago.

The Sec of the Treasury has received notification from the excs of Capt Ralph S Fretz, late of San Francisco, Calif, that said testator has bequeathed to the U S the sum of $20,000, in trust to be applied only towards canceling the national debt. The excs express the hope that this legacy may be but the forerunner of numerous similar exhibitions of patriotism to be made by other men.

The corner-stone of St Ann's Church [Catholic] was laid yesterday. Rev Fr Maguire, Pres of Gtwn College, officiated. The church is located near Tennallytown.

Yellow fever at Greenpoint, Long Island, Kings Co: Jacob Kaller died Sep 28 in a tenement house in Commercial st; on Sat last Lewis Smith died at his residence in Union ave; Thos Harvey, a youth, died on Wed last. He resided in Dupont st. All the victims were formerly employed in the glass factory of N S & O C Bailey, where they were inoculated with the fever, the epidemic having reached the factory from an Italian bark which hauled alongside the place. The factory will be disinfected. An unnecessary panic prevails in Greenpoint. –N Y, 28th

N Y, Sep 29. Gen Scott's will, just probated, bequeaths all his property to his daughter, the wife of Col Scott, his Pulaski sword to the West Point Academy, & his sword worn in Mexico to his grand-son Winfield Scott Hoyt.

Mrd: on Sep 28, by Rev D Evans Reese, Mr Richd W Claxton, of Wash City, to Mrs Eliz Davis, of Fredericksburg, Va.

Died: on Sep 28, Eliz N, wife of John W Wetherall, aged 28 years. Her funeral will take place from the residence of Mrs King, 512 12th st, between Pa ave & E st, today at 3 P M.

Died: on Sep 29, Mr Jas Miller, in his 56th year. His funeral will be from his late residence, 233 D st, between 3rd & 4½ sts, this afternoon, at half past 2 o'clock. It has pleased God to take from his family a loving husband & kind father. He was a good neighbor, & was respected by all who knew him. [Richmond papers please copy.]

N Y, Sep 29. A cable telegram announces the death of Prof Chas King, in Italy. He was president of the Columbia College in this city.

N Y World, 27th. Izzy Lazarus, the noted English pugilist died in this city yesterday, at his house, the Eagle Shades, 223 Centre st. He was a short man, but very fat, his weight a few months ago being over 300 pounds. He has been ill since last winter, but his disease lately showed an increased intensity, & kept him abed most of the time. He leaves a wife & 4 children, three sons & a daughter. The unfortunate Harry Lazarus was his eldest son. John keeps a hotel in Phil; Izzy jr, is at home with his parents; the daughter is very happily & respectably married. The remains of the late Israel Lazarus will be interred in **Greenwood Cemetery** on Sunday; the funeral is in the afternoon.

Gen Sterling Price is dangerously ill in St Louis.

Geo Francis Train has rented his hotel at Omaha for $10,500 a year.

W E A Mackintosh, jr partner in the house of Duncan, Sherman & Co, of N Y, died on Sep 22 in Scotland, whither he had gone to recruit his health.

The Lexington [Va] Hotel has been sold to Col C T O'Ferrall, of Staunton, & Wm W Major, of Rockbridge Co, for the sum of $48,000, possession to be given on Oct 1 next.

John T Mitchell, successor to Harper & Mitchell, 312 Pa ave, between 9th & 10th sts: all the novelties of the season in Dress Goods, Shawls, & Cloaks.

Trustee's sale of valuable real estate, by decree of the Circuit Court for PG Co, Md, in Equity, wherein Paulina A Berry & others are cmplnts & Alonzo Berry & Rachel W Berry excs of John E Berry, sr & others are dfndnts: public sale on the premises, at the residence of the late John E Berry, sr. On Oct 3: the tract in PG Co, of which the late John E Berry, sr, died seized & possessed called **Independence**, containing 500 acres of land, more or less, adjoining the lands of the late Albert B Berry, Jno E Berry, jr, & others. This estate was the residence of the late John E Berry, sr, & improved by a new frame dwlg, & necessary out-bldgs. –Alonzo Berry, Danl Clarke, trustees

A navel suit is before the Supreme Court in *Buffala: Nicholas Hyman asked for $2,000 damages from a woman named Ellen Burk, who wilfully cut off two long curls from the head of his daughter, Anna, aged 12 years. *Copied as written.

In St Louis, on Tuesday, Dr Hodgens performed the operation of lithotomy upon a patient, Jacob Wilhelm, who had gone to that city from Iowa for the purpose. The man was put under the influence of chloroform, & died from its effects when the operation was nearly completed. The coroner's jury exonerated the Doctor.

Dept of the Interior, U S Patent Ofc, Wash, Sep 13, 1867. Ptn of Wm H Sweet, adm of the estate of Henry L Sweet, deceased, of Foxborough, Mass, praying for the extension of a patent granted to said Henry L Sweet, Dec 20, 1853, for an improvement in Guides for Sewing on Binding, for seven years from the expiration of said patent, which takes place on Dec 20, 1867. -T C Theaker, Com'r of Patents

TUE OCT 1, 1867
The appointment of Register of the Treasury, vacated by the death of Hon S B Colby, has been tendered to Gen N L Jeffries, who won a high reputation during the war. Beginning as a captain in the service, he rose gradualy, by his own intrinsic merits, to rank of col & brvt brig gen, & was for a long time the assist provost marshal general of Wash City.

The Davenport [Iowa] Gaz says that Hon Wm H Seward has bought a large tract of land in Hamilton Co, near Webster city.

The Pres appointed the following as Gov't directors of the Union Pacific railroad: Jesse L Williams, of Ind; Timothy J Carter, of Ill; Jas S Rollins, of Mo, & Geo Ashmun, of Mass.

It will be seen by a telegram that Gen John A Logan favors the election of negroes to Congress, & is not opposed to having a negro for President.

Yellow fever in the South: Gen Wheaton was better on Wed, but not out of danger. Col Beck, with the Chief Commissary, is getting along well. Maj Williamson, Chief of Police, was taken down on Wed. Lt L A Arnold, son of Gen Arnold, of the old army, died yesterday of yellow fever at the Jackson Barracks; been there about 3 months. Nine soldiers died at the same place in the last 12 hours. Lt Col Wood, commanding ofcr of the post, just returned from Hotel Dieu, fully recovered from a severe attack, & Dr Clements, chief surgeon, is recovering.
–New Orleans papers to Sep 26th.

Yellow fever in Texas. At Millican the mortality is seventy per cent. At Houston, on Sep 20th, among the 12 deaths by fever, were Dr R Haynes, Mrs Dreyfus, Mrs Mary Turner, & L J Warner, chief clerk of Freedman's Bureau.

Gov Wm A Owens, of Florida, is dead.

Gen David Hunter has purchased for $25,000 the residence in this city built by Senator Gwinn, of Louisiana.

Rev Edw Dunbar, a Baptist minister, was arrested at Minneapolis, Miss, on Friday, on a charge of bigamy, & committed in default of $2,000 bonds.

Mrs Barrett, in Peekskill, N Y, gave her 3 children poison recently, under the supposition that it was medicine for worms, the drug clerk who filled her prescription having made a mistake. The prompt services of a physician alone saved the lives of the children.

On Sat N B Northrup, aged 74 years, died at his residence on Capitol Hill. He was well known in Wash City by his connection with what was known as the Guardian Society, & heretofore of a home for indigent females, located on the Island. Permission was obtained from Congress to occupy the ground on which he was engaged in erecting bldgs at the time of his death. He had been in ill health for some months, but was not thought to be seriously ill until Thu. On Sat he walked about a little, & during the afternoon he fell & almost immediately expired. Milstead, of the police, was notified, & supposing he was a pauper, he was buried at the expense of the Corp. On examining his effect, it was found he had left considerable money, in Gov't bonds, in the hands of one of his friends.

Mrs Henreitta Steritzing, a German woman, aged 65 years, was instantly killed at Hartford, Conn, on Sunday, while walking along the track.

New Milford, Conn, Sep 30. John J Conkling, cashier of the First Nat'l Bank, absconded. There is a defalcation of $50,000, caused by stock speculation.

Boston, Sep 30. Archibald Foster, the Brazilian-Consul, died suddenly last evening of heart disease.

Mr H R Colson, of Fairfax Co, was accidentally shot in the foot yesterday while passing through the grounds of the Smithsonian Institute. The pistol which he had in his pocket fell out while he was fastening his shoe strings, which caused it to explode. He was taken to his home in a carriage, & the wound properly dressed.

Yesterday Sgt-at-Arms Brown, of the Senate, appointed a colored man from Nashville as a member of the Capitol police. [No name given.]

Mrd: on Sep 26, at Martinsburg, West Va, by Rev Lewis F Wilson, Jas Lawson Norris, of Wash, D C, to Annie Virginia, daughter of the late Col Israel Robinson, of Berkeley Co, West Va.

Died: on Sep 10, in Hamburg, Germany, John Frederic William, infant son of John F & Rosa Wippermann, aged 15 months.

Died: on Sep 30, at the residence of Evan Lyons, on Rock Creek, near Gtwn, D C, Mrs Louisa E Lyons, in her 65th year. Her funeral is on Tues at 4 o'clock.

Died: on Sep 30, Wm J Toomey, of Clonmel, County Clare, Ireland, aged 42 years. His funeral is on Tues at 4 o'clock P M, from his late residence, No *__ Mass ave, between 3rd & 4th sts. Members of the Journeymen Bookbinders' Society & friends are requested to attend. *Copied as written.

WED OCT 2, 1867
Died: on Oct 1, Mrs Eliz McNeir, in her 72nd year, widow of the late Major Geo McNeir. Her funeral will be at 3 o'clock P M, on Thursday, from the residence of her son-in-law, Jourdan W Maury, 351 K st, between 12th & 13th sts. [Calif & Annapolis, Md, papers please copy.]

Patents issued to Washingtonians this past week. 1-To Alex'r & Victoria A Osborn, for book cover protector; may be adjusted to books of various sizes. 2-To Maurice Joyce, for boat-lowering & detaching apparatus.

New carpets for the Senate & Reps' Hall will be installed today by Mr John Alexander, upholsterer, who has the contract for laying the carpets.

Equity Court-Judge Wylie, Oct 1. 1-Stewart vs Stewart: decree appointing John F Ennis receiver. 2-Dorsey vs Keiler et al: decree appointing Wm F Mattingly trustee. 3-Thompson vs Arnold et al. Order appointing Ebenezer P Cross guardian *ad litum* of Lucy Connelly, Lillie D Ray, infant dfndnts. Answer of infant dfndnts by guardian *ad litum*. Order of publication. 4-Stott vs Williams: decree appointing Asbury Lloyd trustee, etc. 5-Smith vs Smith: decree of divorce ordered.

Orphans Court-Judge Purcell, Oct 1. 1-Hon B B French was appointed by the court administrator of the personal estate of N B Northrup, deceased, he giving a bond of $5,000. 2-Messrs A & B Edwards were appointed administrators on the personal estate of Col Jas L Edwards, deceased; bond $40,000. The adminstrators are the sons of the deceased. 3-The last will & testament of Dr J Rufus H Speake, deceased, was filed & fully proven. The deceased willed all his property to his wife & daughters, & named his wife, Georgiana F Speake, as the excx of his will. 4-The final account of J C Berry, adm of Franics H Cloud, was passed. 5-The third account of Richd P Jackson, guardian to the orphan children of Thos S Jones, deceased, was received & passed. 6-The final account of Harriet R & Jas H Richards, adms of Wm Richards, deceased, was received & passed. 7-The Fearson case is not yet concluded.

Louisville, Oct 1. Jos M Dawson, a noted comedian, died here last night. [Oct 8th newspaper: Mr Dawson was a native of Cumberland, England.]

The magnificent oyster house of T M Harvey was opened yesterday & attracted a large number of persons.

The death of M'me Sophie Despau, nee Carriere, at Biloxi, at the advanced age of 110 years, has added another feature of interest to what the U S Supreme Court has decided to be the most remarkable suit ever brought to trial in this country. M'me Despau was born in 1757, when Louisiana was held by France, of an old provincial family, & her name will be remembered in connection with that of her sister, Zulime Carriere. It was while under M'me Despau's care that Zulime, when 13 years of age, 1796, & celebrated for her beauty, married Des Grange, a French nobleman, who soon after subsided into a barkeeper or sirup maker. Some years after Des Grange proved to have been already married, & about the same time an attachment sprung up between her & Danl Clark, the Congressman, the land speculator, & foremost business man of his time. The attachment resulted in a marriage, according to M'me Sophie Despau & another sister, & according to all, in the birth of Mrs Myra Clark Garnes. M'me Despau, in her evidence in the Gaines case, testified that she was present when the marriage ceremony was performed in Phil, present with a third sister, & it was upon their evidence that the alleged ceremony rested, for the priest who officiated subsequently went to Ireland, the church was burned down, & the records destroyed. What added still more to the complication of the case, was that Zulime Carriere Des Grange Clark was subsequently united to Dr Gardette, & this during the lifetime of Clark. As Mrs Gaines' legitimacy depended upon the validity of Clark's marriage, the strain of the case turned upon the evidence of M'me Despau.

To test her veracity the evidence of some 35 to 40 witnesses were taken, who had known her while residing in this city, in Biloxi, Havana, Florida, & Spanish America. But the answers were in her favor, & in the interpretation given of the bewildering facts of this case by the last decision of the Supreme Court, her statements were taken as correct; & an estate now valued at $15,000,000 was adjudicated to her niece, Mrs Gaines; adjudicated 50 years after the making of the will, 30 after the commencement of the suit, & 6 appeals of the Supreme Court, & when the original suit had been divided into 500 separate actions against subsequent possessors of Clark's estate. Madame Despau, though living for more than a century, & though involved three-fourths of that period in the troubles of her sister, did not after all live to see the termination of the suit, & save $15,000 worth of the contested estate yielded by Mr Slidell during the recent war, none of the contested property has yet been recovered by its life-long claimant. -New Orleans, Sep 26.

A diabolical attempt was made recently to poison the family of Sohn Schenck, residing at New Haven. Some fiend bored holes in cabbages growing in the garden of Mr Schenck, & filled with holes with arsenic. The arsenic was discovered in time.

Wm H Ketchum, a well known stock broker of N Y, fell dead while eating his supper at a hotel, in Phil, Thursday night.

Rev Dr John M Krebs, for 35 years pastor of the old Rutgers st congregation, N Y, died on Monday. He was president of the Board of Foreign Missions, & a director of Princeton Seminary.

Yellow fever at New Orleans, reports to Friday, Sep 27. Gen Wheaton passed a bad night Wed. A son of Col Caldey, of Gen Mower's staff, was buried yesterday. Gen Mower, being in attendance at the funeral, was not at headquarters. 2nd Lt W Wing, of the 4th cavalry, died Wed at St James Hotel. Capt Beyer, recently placed in command of the company of Capt Spangler, deceased, was taken down yesterday. Mrs Spangler died Wed. Dr Schwartzwelder, chief medical ofcr of the Freedmen's Bureau, is sick. The chief of police, Maj Williamson, was more comfortable yesterday. Acting collector of internal revenue, Maj Wolfley, is down with fever, but not in dangerous condition. John T Timberlake, cashier in the custom-house, & R D Bovard, bonded clerk, were taken with fever Wed. Maj Wm M Robinson, of the Republican, who returned from Mexico Sat, was prostrated by yellow fever before noon on Sunday. His attack was quite severe, but he has now nearly recovered. The wife of Col Geo C Lee, assist adjutant general at the military headquarters, has yielded to the influences which produced the yellow fever, & is now under the most careful treatment for that disease. Col C M Bradford, a lawyer, & who during the war commanded a regt of La troops at Pensacola & on the Va Peninsula, is dead. Mayor Heath is unwell, but not, it is said, with yellow fever. M'me Blondelet, the charming actress of the Opera, is not dead, as reported. Mr Fernando, the baritone, did not die of yellow fever, but of a cold taken while hunting in the wood back of Bay St Louis.

The funeral of Gen Sterling Price, late a Gen in the Confederate army, took place on Monday at St Louis. Sterling Price was a native of Va, removed to Missouri, & represented the Third Dist of that State in Congress during the first 2 years of Pres Polk's administration. He held a colonel's commission in the U S army during the Mexican war, commanding the 2nd regt of Missouri volunteers, & on Jul 20, 1847, was promoted to the rank of Brig Gen of the U S volunteers. He was elected Govn'r of Missouri in 1853, held the position until 1857. Throughout the whole war he was one of the most active of the rebel generals, & one of the last to lose confidence in the final success of the Confederate arms.

Orphans Court of Wash Co, D C. Letters of administration on the personal estate of Nehemial B Northrop, late of Wash, D C, deceased. –B B French, adm

Orphans Court of Wash Co, D C. Letters of administration on the personal estate of Jas L Edwards, late of Wash, D C, deceased. –Lewis A Edwards, John L Edwards, adms

Supreme Court of D C, Oct 1, 1867. No 711-Equity Docket 8. McDuell vs McDuell. Ordered that the sale made by Robt McDuell, trustee, reported on Sep 26, 1867, be ratified & confirmed. –R J Meigs, clerk

THU OCT 3, 1867
Pigeon shooting match between Chas F Williams of Wash, & Gideon Yates, of Gtwn, for $50, at Fletcher's field, near Kalorama, umpire-Mr T P Stacey. Mr Williams killed 10 birds & Mr Yates killed only 9.

Ex-Senator Hunter, of Va, has been pardoned by the Pres.

Mrs Betsy Pettengill Eastman, of Salisbury, supposed to have been the oldest person in N H, died there on Monday, in her 105th year.

The daughter of Geo W Riggs, Miss Cecilia Riggs, was united in marriage yesterday to Henry Howard, attache of the British legation. On account of the recent death of Sir Fred'k Bruce, the British Minister, the wedding was entirely private, & the service was performed by Rev Fr Lynch, at St Cecelia's Chapel, which is on the grounds of Mr Riggs, adjoining his country seat. There were present the members of the family of the bride & a few members of the diplomatic corps.
+
Mrd: on Oct 2, at *Green Hill*, PG Co, Md, Henry Howard, of the British Legation, to Cecelia, daughter of Geo W Riggs, of Wash.

Died: on Sep 28, suddenly, at *Montrose*, Montg Co, Md, Mary Prout, infant daughter of Dr Jas & Sarah J Davidson, aged 16 months.

In the Equity Court Tues Judge Wylie made a decree divorcing Lottie H Smith from the bonds of matrimony with Jas C Smith, with permission to resume her maiden name of Lottie H Sheldon.

Oldest Inhabitants' Association regular meeting was held yesterday; Gen T P Andrews, retired general paymaster general of the army was present. Col J M Williams, vice pres, presided, & in the absence of Dr J McD Davis, the sec, J Carroll Brent, acting in his place. Dr J B Blake submitted a report; Messrs S Masi & J D Clark were nominated, & the ballot resulted in the election of Mr Masi as a marshal; & upon the motion of Mr Clark, his election was declared unanimous. Mr John F Callan, on behalf of the treasurer submitted a report. The following were nominated & elected members: Rear Admiral L M Goldsborough, Col Chas K Gardiner, Capt Benj M Dove, U S N; Dr Geo M Dove, A L McIntire, Wm H Nalley, Jas S Magee, John Fletcher, Geo M Davis, R Arnold, Jacob Colclaizer, & Jas H Boes. Mr John F Callan read a very interesting memoir of the late Fr Matthews, who was for nearly 50 years the pastor of St Patrick's Church. Fr Matthews was born in Md in 1780; educated in France; assumed the duties of pastor of St Patrick's Church on Jul 31, 1804; purchased the site of the present church out of his own funds; as his means allowed, he purchased early the whole of the square bounded by F & G sts, & 9th & 10th sts; built the brick bldg on F st, which was subsequently presented to Gtwn College, with the understanding that it should be used for instruction in the higher branches. He introduced the **Sisters of Charity** in Wash City, & established the Academy of the Visitation, in order to give the young ladies an opportunity of learning the branches usually taught in high schools. Mr Callan spoke of the burning of Washington by Gen Ross, & the great good which Fr Mathews accomplished in preventing the destruction of a number of bldgs. Fr Mathews died on May 1, 1854.

Yellow fever report to Sat at New Orleans. Jude W W Handlin is prostrated with fever-his condition shows the most favorable symptons. J B Carter, formerly superintendent of our public schools, Prof P M Williams, & Capt W B Barrett, late of the U S army, are recovering from the fever & doing well. The wife of Gen Hartsuff is sick with the fever. The General himself suffered a severe attack from the black vomit in 1853; but his wife, it seems, has not been before exposed to the fever. Street Com'r Baker, is down with the fever; his whole family is sick. R D Bovan, chief clerk for the collector of internal revenue, is at his post. Mr J G Taylor, the bonded clerk, will be out in a day or two. Mr Thos Shehan, entry clerk in the Custom-house, is convalescent. Maj Wolfley is reported easy, but no one is permitted to see him yet. Col J P Boyd was attacked by yellow fever on Thursday, but his condition is said to be excellent. Dr T Y Aby is prostrated by the prevailing sickness, but he is in good hands. Mr Condon, of the Picayune, & Mr Punch, of the Crescent, are prostrated with yellow fever. Mr J W Fairfax, of the Times, & Mr Robinson, of the Republican, are improving. Mayor Heath is again at his post, though still sick with a severe cold. Gov Flanders is again at his bureau in good health.

Mrd: on Sep 26, in N Y C, by Rev Dr Haughton, Dr John C Riley, of Wash, D C, to Louisa, daughter of the late Edmund Gibson.

The first use of a locomotive in America was on the Delaware & Hudson Canal Company's railroad, in Luzerne Co, Pa; one of the engines purchased in England by Horatio Allen arrived in N Y in 1829, & of this machine Appleton's Encyclopoedia, to which, & to "Mitchell's United States," published in 1835, we are mainly indebted for these facts, thus says: One of the engines built by Geo Stephenson at his works at Newcastle-upon-Tyne arrived in N Y in the spring of 1829, & was to be seen for some time in the yard of E Dunscomb, in Water st, its wheels raised about the ground, & kept running for the gratification of those interested. Another engine, built by Foster, Rastwick & Co arrived soon after, & was put on the road in the latter part of the summer of 1829.

A life size statue of the late Bishop Brownell, of Conn, cast at Munich, Germany, at a cost of $35,000, is to be placed on Cedar Hill, Hartford, Conn.

Col Amos Beckwith, Chief Quartermaster at New Orleans, has recovered from the late attack of yellow fever.

Two years ago Hugh Crawford Pollok, about 20 years old, suddenly disappeared from his home in Scotland, & it later became known that he came to this country with 500 pounds in his pocket. He sported about until his money ran short, & then enlisted in the 5th U S cavalry as a private solider. In the meantime his father died some 4 months ago, leaving Hugh heir to a baronetcy & a snug income of L5,000 per annum, or about $25,000 in gold. The young baronet was duly sought for, & it was found he was stationed at Cape Verde, Texas, discharging the duties of a farrier. Col Wm S Hillyer, of N Y, became interested in the case, induced Sir Fred'k Bruce to procure the discharge of Pollok, which was promptly acceded to by Gen Grant. The young Sir Hugh Crawford Pollok has therefore been telegraphed for, & has given up the occupation of shoer & curer of horses to enter upon a Scotch baronetcy & L5,000 a year. Such is life. -Cor N Y Herald

The Alexandria Gaz says: Information received of the death, from yellow fever, at New Orleans, of Brothers Urban & Savinian, prominent members of the Order of Christian Brothers. Both these brothers were well known in the Catholic communities of this neighborhood. Brother Savinian was, until very recently, sub-director of the Rock Hill College, at Ellicott City, Md.

Positive sale of valuable farm, on Oct 15; contains 134 acres, lying $1/4^{th}$ mile above Cabin John Bridge; 2 dwlg houses on the farm, one new & elegantly situated; my residence adjoins the above, which belongs to John C Devin. –Wm Reading, agent -Thos Dowling, auct

Lt Gov Bross & daughter, of Illinois, have gone to Europe.

Mr & Mrs Edwin M Stanton are at the country home of Judge Pierrepont, on the Hudson river.

Miss Avonia Jones, who returned from England some weeks ago, intending to star in Chas Reade's dramatization of "Griffith Gaunt," through this country, has been compelled to resign all her engagements on account of ill health. Her physicians have ordered her to Cuba. [Oct 7th newspaper: Avonia Jones died in this city yesterday at her residence, 2 Bond st; her disease was consumption; her death was sudden & unexpected. She was born in Richmond, Va, the daughter of the Count Joannes & Mrs Matilda Jones, his wife. Her remains will be taken to Mount Auburn, near Boston, for interment. –N Y Tribune]
[Oct 8th newspaper: Avonia Jones was the widow of G V Brooke, the tragedian, who was lost at sea nearly 2 years ago, & the daughter of Mrs Melinda Jones. Miss Jones had recently visited her mother & sister at Cambridgeport, Mass, but suddenly was prostrated by disease. At the time of her death Mrs Avonia Jones Brooke was between 29 & 30 years of age. Her funeral took place on Sat, at No 2 Bond st; religious services were conducted by Rev Dr Cook, of St Bartholomew's Church. Among those present were Mr & Mrs Barney Williams, Miss Matilda Heron, Mr J Gilbert,of Wallack's; Mr Baker, stage manager of the N Y Theatre; Mr E L Davenport, Mr Frank Rivers-her agent, Mr Jno Savage, author of the play in which she first appeared. The remains were taken to Cambridgeport last evening, where funeral services are to be held, the interment to be in Mount Auburn. Miss Jones was tall & robust in frame, with piercing black eyes & agreeable features, her voice powerful & distinct.]

FRI OCT 4, 1867
Upon the death of Mr Lincoln an effort was made to appropriate for his wife & family the sum that he would have received from the U S had he lived to finish his second term of office, to wit: $100,000; but it resulted in appropriating but $25,000, the amount of one year's salary as Pres. Of this sum, $3,000 was required to discharge standing obligations, leaving about $22,000, which, with the house & lot in Springfield, Ill, owned by Mr Lincoln previous to his election to the Presidency in 1860, was all the property which fell to Mrs Lincoln. Her present income, she states, is but $1,700 a year, of which $300 comes from the rent of her old house in Springfield. It appears from this that Mr Lincoln not only saved no money while he occupied the White House, but really lived beyond his income, which, in connection with the natural reluctance of his widow to return to the simple style of living to which she had been used to before her residence in Wash, has compelled her to part with some of his personal effects at the present time.
+
Chicago, Sep 1, 1867. Mr Brady: A notice in a N Y paper having attracted my attention, that you sold articles of value on commission prompts me to write you. The articles I am sending you to dispose of were gifts of dear friends, which only urgent necessity compels me to part with, & I am especially anxious that they shall not be sacrificed. The circumstances are peculiar & painfully embarrassing,

therefore I hope you will endeavor to realize as much as possible from them. Hoping soon to hear from you, I remain, very respectfully, yours, Mrs A Lincoln.
+
Articles sent to Mr Brady, Sep 1, 1867, Commission broker, 609 Broadway, N Y:
1 black centre camels' hair shawl, long-cost $1,500
1 white centre camels' hair shawl, long-cost $1,200
1 white centre camels' hair shawl, square-cost $400
1 black centre camels' hair shawl, square-cost $350
1 red centre camel's hair shawl, square-cost $100
2 small shawls, square-cost $50
white paisley shawl, long-cost $75
white paisley shawl, square-cost $50
3 superfine point black lace shawls-cost $1,500, $500, $300
2 superfine point black lace shawls-cost $50, $40
1 white point lace shawl, long-cost $2,000
1 white point lace dress, unmade-cost $4,000
1 white point lace flounce-cost $150
1 white point lace parasol cover-cost $250
1 white point lace handkerchief-cost $80
1 Russian sable cape-cost $1,500
1 Russian sable boa-cost $1,200
Also many other articles, including diamonds, rings, etc.

New Orleans Times, Sunday. Yesterday, a young man, Harry Rolande, a member of the Home Hook & Ladder Co, was mortally wounded during a fight between whites & blacks. He was shot through the head.

Mrd: on Oct 1, at the residence of the bride's father, R M Bartholow to Jennie, daughter of Chas Stott, both of Wash, D C.

Died: on Sep 30, at Balt, Md, Mrs Margaret R Harrison, widow of Robt H Harrison, late of Laurel, Md. Her funeral will be this evening, at 5 o'clock P M, from the Balt Depot.

Robt Wallace, a Pittsburgh hotel proprietor, fell from a third story window on Sunday, & was instantly killed.

Geo Cookman, a merchant of Phil, & president of the Christian Association, died suddenly on Tuesday night.

Wm H Hess, living 12 miles from Pittsburgh, was gored to death by a bull on Sat. The enraged bull tossed Mr Hess into the air several times. Mr Hess was about 60 years old.

Mrs Frank Hall, about 50 years old, residing about 4 miles north of Morris, in Grundy Co, Ill, was found by her son dead in her room on Monday. Suspicion rests on her husband, who is known to have threatened her. He has been arrested.

The Pres has appointed Chas W Shannon assist paymaster in the navy.

Wm H Dillon, Wm Nalley, & Danl McKenzie, who are sailors on the U S steamer **Penobscot**, which has recently arrived here from the East India squadron, were found to be deserters. They were captured yesterday & taken to the Navy Yard.

Equity Court-Judge Wylie. Barbary Wail vs Jonn Wail: petition for divorce from the bonds of matrimony. Decree granting the prayer of the petitioner.

On Tues last, in accordance with orders received at the Wash Arsenal by Gen Ramsey, the commandant of the post, from the War Dept, the bodies of John Wilkes Booth, Mary E Surratt, Lewis Payne, Geo A Atzerodt, David E Herold, & Henry Wirz were exumed from their places of burial in the old penitentiary grounds, & removed & deposited in another locality. This was rendered necessary in consequence of the projected improvements of the arsenal grounds, & was conducted with the greatest secrecy, the bodies being reinterred in a trench dug in warehouse No 1, near the north wall.

During the war the residence of David L Yulee, at Fernandina, Fla, was sold by the Gov't for non payment of taxes. About a year ago a certificate for redemption was granted to Mr Yulee, & the money paid [$1,700] returned to the purchaser. Since then the family have not been able to obtain possession, until a few days ago, when Mrs Yulee moved into it. The same night a mob assailed it, breaking windows & doing other damage.

New Orleans papers of Sunday-yellow fever at that place: Mrs Gen Hartsuff is much better; Dr Wm Cleary is dead. Also died: Anthony M Karbaum, Wm Schelling, Wm Pehi, & Chas G Sachow. Recovered: Lionel Brooks, Harvey W Perkins, Theodore Hastings, Edw D Munn, Benj Collins, Wm Myers, Dennis J Corkey, & Wm Deugan. At present under treatment: Geo McCosh, Wm O'Connor, John Walsh, Francis Flynn, Geo H Taylor, E O Wood, John B Hills, Henry Zell, Thos Lanning, Chas W Lang, David Weichmann, Andrew Reynolds, & Wm Turner. Mr Geo C Richardson, sub assist com'r of the Freedmen's Bureau, died yesterday of yellow fever & was buried last evening. He was a native of Lowell, Mass, age 27 years, & his father resides in Cambridge, near Boston. Mr Richardson came to this city from Washington about 3 weeks ago, to discharge the duties of his office. Eight Catholic priests, Frs Seelers, Jacobs, Meredity, Neidhart, of St Alphonsus Church; Frs Ryan & Smith, of St Joseph Church; Fr Coppens, of the Carrollton Church; also, the assist priest of St Augustine's Church, of this city, are prostrated with the yellow fever. Lay Brothers Gerard & Lawrence, of the Redemptorist order connected with St Alphonsus Church, died on Friday.

SAT OCT 5, 1867

Telegraphic despatches announce the demise of Hon Thos E Noell, Rep in Congress from the 3rd Dist of Missouri. He had been for some time in a precarious state of health, & the result had not been unexpected by his numerous friends at home. [Death date not given-current item.]

R M T Hunter, who has been pardoned by the President, says in his petition that he proposes to direct himself to the pursuit of private life; that he submits loyally to the authorities of the U S, & recognizes the power of the General Gov't to establish its policy in the South.

The court-martial of Assist Engineer Geo F Sawyer, U S Navy, for disrespect to & abuse of the President, was commenced at the Portsmouth NavyYard on Oct 2. Thirteen naval ofcrs constitute the court-martial. Messrs Butler, Cragin, & Hackett appear for the defence. [Oct 23rd newspaper: The accused was found guilty of the charge & sentenced by the court to be suspended from rank & duty for the period of one year, & to be placed upon half of "waiting orders" pay during that time, & to be publicly reprimanded by the honorable Sec of the Navy.
–Geo Welles, Sec of the Navy]

The Pres yesterday appointed John C Cox, a Justice of the Peace in & for the District of Columbia.

N Y, Oct 4. Elias Howe, jr, the sewing-machine inventor, died last night in Brooklyn. [Oct 11th newspaper: Elias Howe, jr, the inventor of the sewing machine, was a native of Spencer, Mass, & was born in 1819; commenced learning the trade of a machinist in 1836; 10 years later completed his model of the first sewing machine, & secured his patent, which was dated Sep 10, 1846. After making 4 machines, but finding no immediate sale for them, the high cost, which was then about $300, discouraging purchasers, he went to England. There he sold one of his machines for L250, & made an agreement with the purchaser to have other machines made & sold, on each of which the inventor was to receive L3. This contract, however, through the unfair dealing of the English agent, brought Mr Howe no profit, & he was utimately compelled to pawn his clothing & his model for the means to return to America. Here he found his invention appropriated, by several manufacturers, who had improved upon it, & after long litigation, obtained an acknowledgment of his rights. Since then he received a royalty upon all machines made in the country, amounting in all, it is estimated, to $2,000,000.
During the war he enlisted in the 17th Conn regt as a private soldier, refusing to accept a commission, for which he did not feel himself qualified. He served for some months, & at one time, when the men were suffering for their money, he advanced the Gov't the money to pay his regt.]

Died: on Sep 30, at Cheswick Plase, Henrico, Va, of a congestive chill, Annie Guion Moseley, daughter of Rev John W & M D Moseley, aged 2 years & 11 months.

The Bishop of Valence has just sent to the Pope the armchair in which Pius VI expired, & which had been deposited in the cathedral of that city, by order of the Directory, in 1799. Pius VI died while on his way to Paris.

Hon Thos A Jenckes, the author of the bankrupt bill, is one of the first applicants under it for relief from its indebtedness.

Hon Chas J Saxe, son of Judge Saxe, of Vt, & brother of John G Saxe, the poet, died at his residence in Troy on Tuesday, aged 59 years.

Alex'r H Bailey, of Rome, has been nominated for Congress by the Republicans to fill the vacancy occasioned by the election of Roscoe Conkling to the Senate.

The N Y World says that Mrs Lincoln, accompanied by her son Tad, & a female friend, appeared on Broadway on Thursday. Mrs Lincoln was modestly attired & did not attract any attention.

Gen Jos E Johnston has resigned the presidency of the Ala & Tenn River railroad, from Selma to Dalton, & his place has been filled by election of Franklin H Deland, of N Y.

Supreme Court of D C, Equity 856. All parties interested & creditors of Thos Hollinan, deceased, are to appear & be heard on Oct 11, at 12 M.
–Walter S Cox, auditor

Supreme Court of D C, 778 Equity, Docket 8. Henry C McLeod, Mary W McLeod, et al, vs Eugene M McLeod. The trustee reported that he sold the 2 story brick house, with lot attached, fronting 22 feet 8 inches on Jefferson st, to Francis McLean for the sum of $1,075, & the purchaser had complied with the terms of sale.
–R J Meigs, clerk

Nashville Banner Sep 15, at Jackson: last Wed a corporal in charge of a squad of militia stopped on the street Maj Thos H Hartmus, a member of Gen Bates' staff during the war, & demanded to know whether he had a pistol. Maj Hartmus replied he had, took his weapon from his pocket & handed it to the corporal, & in a quiet tone noted he had surrendered his pistol under protest. Without warning, almost before Maj Hartmus had ceased speaking, the militiaman shot him through the breast. At last accounts Maj Hartmus wound was considered mortal, with hardly a possibility that he could survive many hours. The name of the perpetrator was not given, & it is not known if he had been arrested.

Dept of the Interior, U S Patent Ofc, Wash, Oct 1, 1867. Ptn of Hezekiah B Smith, of Smithville, N J, praying for the extension of a patent granted to him Jan 10, 1854, for an improvement in Mortising Machine, for 7 years from the expiration of said patent, which takes place on Jan 10, 1868. -T C Theaker, Com'r of Patents

Dept of the Interior, U S Patent Ofc, Wash, Sep 30, 1867. Ptn of Jos Nason, of N Y, N Y, praying for the extension of a patent granted him Jan 3, 1854, for an improvement in Arrangement for Cutting Screws in Lathes, for 7 years from the expiration of said patent, which takes place on Jan 3, 1868.
-T C Theaker, Com'r of Patents

MON OCT 7, 1867
Orphans Court-Judge Purcell, Oct 5, 1867. 1-Georgianna F Speake was granted letters of administration upon the personal estate of Mr Rufus H Speake. 2-The first & final account of Richd H Taylor & John H Yeatman, excs of Harrison Taylor, deceased, was admitted by the court. 3-Thos J Murray & Thos McFadden, who were appointed by the Court to appraise the goods & chattels of the late N B Northrup, returned their appraisement at $2,500. 4-A petition was received from Jas W White for letters of administration on the personal estate of Wm J Tooney. The petition was ordered to be filed. 5-Messrs Hughes, Denver & Peck, attys for the contestants, prayed an appeal from the decision of the Court, which directed the will of the late Saml Devaughn to be admitted to probate. The appeal was filed. The Court has not yet rendered any decision in regard to the appeal. 6-Ptn of Anna E West, guardian to the orphans of John P West, for sale of real estate, filed Jun 25, was ordered not to be recorded. 7-The will of the late Robt Johnson was exhibited, fully proven, & admitted to record. 8-In the matter of the ptn of Anna E West, an order of ratification of sales was issued.

On Sat the house of Mrs Kennedy, at 15th & Boundary sts, was entered into by 2 burglars; she ran to the house of Ofcr Nutting, a few yards distant, & told him what was going on. He proceeded to the house & arrested one of the robbers, who made a desperate assault with a billy upon the ofcr. Mr Nutting used his baton, knocked the fellow down, & took him to the Guard-house. He gave his name as Jacob Voss, & said his brother was his associate burglar.

Decree of divorce was granted on Fri by Judge Wylie to Laura Ann Patch, from the bonds of marriage with Jos Patch, the dfndnt for the present having the custody of the children until further orders of the Court, & petitioner to pay $25 per month for their support.

The old family residence of the Chichesters, in Fairfax Co, Va, known as **Mount Wellington**, was destroyed by fire on Sep 30. The estate is now the property of Mrs F D Lemoine, & is one of the oldest & best known in Va. The fire is supposed to have originated from a spark falling on the roof, the weather being dry, & a high wind prevailing at the time. The premises destroyed were occupied by the families of Dr Jas C Hill & Maj Ennis, sons-in-law of Mrs Lemoine; but, in conseqquence of the absence of all grown members of the family at Accotink, nothing was saved except the clothes upon their backs. Some outhouses were saved & afforded temporary shelter to the family.

Lucy Spurgeon, a colored woman, was on Sat committed to jail by Justice Cull on the charge of murder, it being alleged that on Aug 31, with her own hands, strangled to death her new-born child.

Phil, Oct 6. Chas Porter, one of the oldest actors in America, died yesterday, aged 70 years. He had been over 50 years on the stage.

B W Greene, who murdered his wife at Hartford, Conn, several years ago, & was acquitted on the ground of insanity, died at the private hospital of Dr Buell, in Litchfield, on Fri. He was about 64 years of age, & leaves an estate of nearly $200,000.

[Nov 25th newspaper: Rev Wm H Green, was convicted of the murder of his wife, by poisoning her. He first became conspicuous in the western part of N Y, in the fall of 1861, as the "Rev Geo W Long"; after 2 weeks acquaintance he married in one of the neighboring towns, & took his wife home with him; he went to Dunkirk, Ohio; exits Rev Mr Long; enter at Utica, "Rev Wm H Green", a preacher, political speaker, & temperance orator; On Dec 20th last, Green married Mrs Searles, in Guilford, Chenango Co, N Y, & in March moved to West Cornwall, Conn, where he made his debut as a refugee from Texas; on May 6th, Mrs Green died with convulsions. In a month the Reverend left for Utica, where only 5 weeks later he married an Irish chambermaid employed at a hotel. The body of his wife was disinterred, strychnia was found in her stomach & liver. Green was convicted & sentenced to suffer the extreme penalty of the law. –Providence Herald.[

Mr Greeley thinks <u>female suffrage</u> would lead to quarrels in families.

Chancery sale on Oct 29th of the Lichau House, situated on part of lot 13 in square 490, with bldgs & improvements thereon. Chancery sale of personal property at the Lichau House, [La ave, near 6th st west,] by decree of the Supreme Court of D C; in Equity No 901, wherein Chas G Ball is cmplnt & Henry Lichau et al are dfndnts; sale on Oct 30th of excellent furniture & kitchen ware. -E Carusi, A Thos Bradley, Wm John Miller, Thos E Lloyd, Asbury Lloyd, trustees -Cooper & Latimer, aucts

Dept of the Interior, U S Patent Ofc, Wash, Oct 2, 1867. Ptn of Wm Wright, of N Y, N Y, praying for the extension of a patent granted him Jan 3, 1854, for an improvement in Operating Cut-off Valves of Steam Engines, for seven years from the expiration of said patent, which takes place on Jan 3, 1868. -T C Theaker, Com'r of Patents

Supreme Court of D C, equity No 1,055. Jas D G Knowles vs Geo A Davis. On motion of the plntf by Mr Chas M Matthews, his atty, it is ordered that the dfndnt cause his appearance to be entered on or before the first rule day occurring 40 days after this day, otherwise the cause will be proceed with as in case of default.
–R J Meigs, clerk

Orphans Court of Wash Co, D C. Letters testamentary on the personal estate of Rufus H Speake, late of Wash City, D C, deceased. –G F Speake, excx

TUE OCT 8, 1867

The bridge over *Tiber creek*, on H st, east of the Gov't Printing Ofc, will be opened for travel this morning. Councilman Wm H Nalley deserves the thanks of the community for the energy displayed by him in endeavoring to have this bridge got in readiness at such an early date.

Mobile Tribune of Sep 28-triple execution of negroes. Yesterday the majesty of the law was vindicated in the case of three negroes, Chas Robinson, Jim Richardson, & Tish or Ulysses Grant, who were convicted at the June term of the city court of outraging the persons of Mrs Fred'k Peters & her young daughter, at Dog river, in March last. They walked side by side & preceded Capt Granger & Col Dimon; mounted the scaffold with firmness, & continued to sing.

Wm York AtLee died at New Orleans of yellow fever. He was a son of Saml York AtLee, Librarian of the Treasury Dept. [No death date given-current item.]

Court in Equity-Judge Wylie. Dodson vs Dodson. Application for divorce. The testimony in this case corroborating the charges contained in the petition against the dfndnt, the court granted a decree of divorce of vinculo matrimonii.

Mrd: on Oct 7, at the Church of the Epiphany, by Rev Chas H Hall, D D, Mr Hugh Nisbet, of Phil, to Catharine, daughter of the late Wm Eaton Crossfield, of Wash City.

Died: on Sep 6, at San Francisco, Calif, Mrs Maria L Folger, aged 48, widow of Jas S Folger, formerly of Hartford, Conn. [Hartford, Conn & N Y papers please copy.]

N Y, Oct 7. Peter Lorillard, an old & well known & wealthy citizen, long prominent in the tobacco trade, died at Saratoga yesterday, at a good old age.

Miss Rose Etynge is getting the reputation of being the best dressed lady on the stage.

Antietam Cemetery: the contract for erecting a monument in the memory of the Union soldiers buried there was awarded to Mr J G Ballerson, of Hartford, Conn, who has also the contract for the monument for the *Gettysburg Cemetery*. The entire cost of the structure will be $30,000. –Balt Sun

Adm's sale of lumber, iron bedsteads, mattreses, old nails, blankets, comforts, frame of bldg, window sashes, etc, at auction, on Oct 11, at 2nd & Va ave, by order of the Orphans Court of D C., the personal effects of the late Nehemiah B Northrup, deceased. -B B French, adm -Green & Williams, aucts

Emily Jordan, the actress, was divorced recently from her husband, Geo Jordan, & married a couple weeks ago to Chas Ransom, a well known public man in N Y.

Chancery sale of valuable improved & unimproved property in Wash City, by decree of the Supreme Court of D C, passed on Mar 20, 1867, in Equity No 701: Jane E Strother vs Jas Nicholson: public auction on Oct 24, of part of lot 5 in square 196, on M st. Also, part of lot 6 in square 196, with a 2 story frame dwlg.
–Wm D Cassin, trustee -W L Wall & Co, aucts

For rent-the house & premises now occupied by Mrs Dr Houston, 38 Missouri ave, between 4½ & 6th sts. Possession given on Oct 15. –M W Beveridge, Odd Fellows' Hall, 7th st, Wash.

WED OCT 9, 1867
Yesterday was selected by the ladies of Grace Church parish, Montg Co, Md, to hold their Grand Tournament to raise funds to erect a rectory for the minister in charge. The day will include the tournament, the crowning of the Queen of Love & Beauty & her attendant maiden, the dinner, & finally, the dance. Ofcrs selected for the tourney were: Marshals: Wm Canby, Humphrey Perry, & J F Peirce.
Heralds: Smith Thompson & J C Estep. Judges: Francis P Flair, jr, G M Watkins, R W Burch, B T Swart, Dr Josiah Harding, Jasper M Jackson, Alfred Ray, R T Wilson, Saml B Anderson, & Washington Bowie.
The following knights entered for the contest:
Knight of Ingomar: L L Nicholson
Knight of Glenross: Thos Cissell
Knight of Stonewall: Saml Cashell
Knight of Before Last: Jas Gibbs
Knight of The Fair Sex: Guy H Thompson
Knight of Brown Lance: Boyle Stubbs
Knight of Spring Hill: E W Owen
Knight of Walnut Grove: Dr F Mannaker
Knight of Liberty: Hopkins Anderson
Knight of Prince George's: J F Smith
Knight of Potomac: Theo Mosher
Knight of Black Plume: Jas W Walsh
Knight of the "Dead Duck": S S Belt
Knight of Lone Star: H Jones
Knight of Fallen Chief: John Jones
Knight of Arlington: Richd Ray
Knight of The Ridge: B Magruder
Knight of Oak Grove: Dr Sol Waters
Knight of Ashland: Henry Bowie
Knight of Woodlawn: B Palmer
Knight of The Vale: Theo Lay
Orator of the Day: Gen John Tyler, of Va.
Queen of Love & Beauty: Miss Coie Palmer, of Brookville, Md;
1st Maid, Miss Lauran Robinson, of Brookville, 2nd Maid, Miss Rose Sands, of Wash; 3rd Maid, Miss Kate Wylie, of Montgomery.

Capt Wm Harvey has purchased of T M Harvey, the property known as **Piney Point**, on the Potomac river, about 10 miles from the mouth of the river, for the sum of $10,000 cash. Capt Mitchell has had a lease on the property for several years past, & it is his intention to immediately have the bldg renovated, & repaired, & a number of additional cottages erected, so that it will be a first class watering place by next season.

Orphans Court-Judge Purcell, Oct 8, 1867. 1-The Court granted an appeal from the recent decision in the Devaughn will case. The appeal was prayed by the attys for the caveators. 2-The final account of Richd W & Richd M Williams, excs of John W Williams, deceased, was received & passed. 3-The sworn account of Jas Green, guardian of John Mayer, orphan child of Patrick Mayer, deceased, was received. 4-The will of the late John W Pegg was filed & partially proven. He directs that this executor pay Mrs Ann Bond a just amount for her kindness during his illness; lot 2, square 880, to his cousin, Jos W Pegg; part of lot 6 in square 449, to his uncle, Ransdell Pegg, during his natural life; afterwards to revert to G F Gulick, to whom he also bequeaths ten shares of stock of the Eastern Bldg Association, as also all that is due him by his partner, which he is to hold in trust for the benefit of his cousin, Eliz C Greenwell; & names B D Greenwell executor.

Died: on Oct 8, Wm Thumlert, in his 82nd year, leaving an aged companion & affectionate children to mourn their loss. His funeral will take place on Thu at 2 o'clock P M, from the M st Methodist Church. [Balt Sun please copy.]

Some days since, the arrival from New Orleans of a Federal ofcr at Marion, Smythe Co, suffering from an attack of yellow fever was announced. We learn that the patient died on Thursday last after a week's illness. The name of the deceased was Cliffard Stickney, 1st lt in the 20th U S infty, & when attacked with the disease, was on his way to Albany, N Y, to be married. –Lynchburg News, Monday

The bridge across the Eastern Branch of the Potomac, at the termination of Mass ave, known as Benning's Bridge, has been thoroughly repaired in a strong & substantial manner. The work had been done by order of Gen N Michler, & under his direction. Maj Lubey, one of his assistants, having the immediate supervision of the bldg.

Yellow fever at New Orleans: Col Simpson, acting paymaster, is sick with fever. The wife of Gen Hartsuff, now in her 5th day's sickness, passed the last 2 nights badly. Maj Wolfrey, of the internal revenue dept, is worse. Rev Dr J B Smith is dead. Col N W Daniels, a native of Syracuse, N Y, who adopted Louisiana as his home, & was delegate elect to the consitutional convention from the parish of Jefferson, died yesterday of yellow fever, after a short illness. New Orleans Republican, Wed

Trustee's sale of valuable estate on the line of the Balt & Wash Railroad; by decree of the Circuit Court of PG Co, [Md] in Equity, dated Dec 10, 1866, wherein Walter H S Taylor was cmplnt, & Wm H Minnix & Henrietta his wife, were respondents: public sale at **Muirkirk Furnace**, about 3 miles from Laurel, Md, on Oct 22, that valuable estate now in the occupancy of Wm H Minnix, adjoining the Furnace property, containing 350 acres; with dwlg & all necessary out-bldgs.
–Edw W Belt, Geo C Merrick, trustees

The Douglas Estate. Chief Justice Wilson, of the Superior Court of Chicago, has just decided an important case, on which it is understood that large amounts were incidentally depending, though the sum directly in dispute was but about $40,000. The parties were Schuchardt & Gebhardt, of this city, against Adele Williams, late Douglas, [widow of the Hon Stephen A Douglas,] her present husband, & others; & this was the ground of dispute: In 1858, [when making his famous canvass against Abraham Lincoln for U S Senator,] Mr Douglas borrowed $13,000 in cash from Jas T Soutter, banker of this city, & gave as security for the loan a mortgage on certain valuable out-lots in Chicago. This mortgage was executed by Mr Douglas & his wife, & [as was supposed] duly acknowledged by the letter before H Kreissmann, notary public, who attested the fact, but failed to set forth in his notarial certificate that Mrs Douglas was personally known to him. That she actually was so known, & that her relinquishment of dower was voluntary & perfect, was not disputed; but it was held that the failure of the notary to set forth that fact in his certificate had invalidated her relinquishments, & authorized her to claim dower as though no such deed had been given. It was held that a law of Ill expressly required the certificate to state the fact in question, & that three several decisions of the courts of Ill had affirmed that position. The case was argued for the plntfs [assignees of Soutter] by Geo Shea, of our city bar, whose position is indorsed by the Chief Justice in his opinion as "the true view of the question," & he concludes: "I am bound to decide that the demurrer here is not sufficient; in other words, that by her acknowledgment as set forth & admitted, she [Mrs Douglas] did in fact convey her right of dower. The demurrer to the bill must be overruled." Before the case was argued, the plntf's counsel offered to pay the dfndnts $10,000 if they would waive their demurrer. They declined the offer, went to trial, & got nothing. –N Y Tribune

Orphans Court of Wash Co, D C, Oct 8, 1867. In the case of Emma Smoot, admx of Dr Saml C Smoot, deceased, the administratrix & Court have appointed Nov 2 next, for the final settlement of the personal estate of the said deceased, of the assets in hand. -Jas R O'Beirne, Reg/o wills

Dept of the Interior, U S Patent Ofc, Wash, Oct 3, 1867. Ptn of Edw A Tuttle, of Brooklyn, N Y, praying for the extension of a patent granted to him Jan 3, 1854, for an improvement in Hot Air Registers, for 7 years from the expiration of said patent, which takes place on Jan 3, 1868. -T C Theaker, Com'r of Patents

Dept of the Interior, U S Patent Ofc, Wash, Oct 3, 1867. Ptn of John Donlevy, of N Y, N Y, praying for the extension of a patent granted to him Jan 3, 1854, for an improvement in Method of Forming Plates for Polychromatic Printing, for 7 years from the expiration of said patent, which takes place on Jan 3, 1868.
-T C Theaker, Com'r of Patents

THU OCT 10, 1867
Danl B McOrn, of Cheraw, S C, a merchant there, & Mayor of the place during the rebellion, was run over & instantly killed by a coach in N Y on Wed night. He had bought goods to the extent of $10,000 during the day.

The corner stone of the monument to be erected in the *Soldiers' National Cemetery*, near Hampton, Va, was laid on Thursday, in the presence of a large audience of people.

Central Bldg Association meeting held Tuesday; the following were elected ofcrs for the ensuing year: Asbury Lloyd, pres; Jas Towles, vice pres; Jas Fraser, treasurer; Wm W Moore, Sec; directors-A J Falls, E C Eckloff, Wm H Johnson, Silas H Moore, Wm H Nalley, Chas P Wannall, John R Major, Jas J Campbell, & Bushrod Robinson.

We regret to announce the death, from typhoid fever, of Mr John Y Bryant, jr, of Wash City; he was a native of Wash, & a graduate of Columbian College. His funeral will take place from the residence of Mr A D Harmon, on Friday, at 11 o'clock.
+
Died: on Oct 9, at the residence of A D Harmon, 516 L st, John Y Bryant, jr, aged 26 years, son of John Y & Anna J Bryant, formerly of Wash City. His funeral is on Oct 11th, at 11 o'clock. [Evening Express please copy.] [Oct 12th newspaper:The remains of Mr Bryant were deposited in the *Congressional Cemetery*.]

Cable despatches yesterday announced the death of M Achille Fould, the distinguished French statesman, whose decease occurred in Paris, night before last. M Fould, who was the son of a wealthy Jewish banker, was born in 1800; having perfected a collegiate education, at the Lycee Charlemagne, by traveling in Italy & in the East, he entered his father's business pursuits in 1842; was 4 times Minister of Finance under Louis Napoleon; he had received many foreign decorations, & had been a Cmder of the Legion of Honor since Dec 8, 1852. [Oct 30th newspaper: Paris, Oct 15, 1867: the remains of Mr Fould were committed to the grave with great splendor, the funeral cortege moving from the magnificent private hotel of the deceased, in Faubourg St Honore, to the old French Protestant Church of the Oratoire, near the Louvre, & thence again by the Boulevards to the *Eastern Cemetery* of Paris, or as it is usually called, *Pere la Chaise*.]

Geo Augustus Sala is in the London Court of Bankruptcy; his debts amount to L2,659, & he replied to the usual questions, that he had no property of any description. His largest debts are to a life insurance company & 2 newspapers, to which he is a contributor.

Mrd: on Sep 18, at St Aloysius Church, by Rev L Rocoffort, S J, Chas J Hitselberger to Miss Lizzie M Bunyan, both of Balt Md. [Balt & Richmond papers please copy.]

Died: on Oct 9, Annie Lee, youngest daughter of Robt & Eliz G Israel, aged 3 years & 4 months. Her funeral will be this afternoon at 4 o'clock, from the residence of her parents, corner of 7th & I sts.

Ralph S Fritz, of San Francisco, bequeathed $20,000 to help pay the national debt.

Mr Jas Piper, of Barre, Mass, died on Thursday last, at the patrirachal age of 104. He was the oldest Free Mason in the State.

Chancery sale of real estate, by decree of the Supreme Court of D C, passed Oct 7, 1867, in Equity 920, wherein Margaret A Eckels & her husband Lewis G Eckels, are cmplnts, & Catharine Barrett et al, are dfndnts: public auction, on Nov 4 next, of lots 2, 15, & 16, in square 836; lot 4 in square 837, in Wash City, D C. –M Thompson, R S Davis, trustees -Green & Williams, aucts

Eaton Stone, the veteran bare-back rider, has fitted up his farm at Passaic, N J, as a wintering place for the circus profession, where they may practice their horses & keep their own muscles in condition.

Marshal's sale on Oct 29 next, of all dfndnt's right, title, claim, & interest in lot 11 in square 401, with improvements thereon, in Wash City, seized & levied upon as the property of Jas B Smith, & will be sold to satisfy execution 3,309, in favor of Geo Keith. -D S Gooding, U S Marshal, D C

FRI OCT 11, 1867
Appointments by the Pres: R H Somerville, of Ala, appointed to be Register of the Land Ofc at Ala. John J Godfrey, appointed to be Collector of Customs, at St Mary's, Ga.

Frank Ewing, of Ala, has been sentenced to 90 days imprisonment in the Dry Tortugas, for speaking disrespectfully of Congress, & condemnning the registration system as a humbug.

Yesterday Dr Skillman, of the Ordnance Dept, was united in the holy bonds of wedlock to Miss Alice, daughter of D W Middleton, the Clerk of the U S Supreme Court. The ceremony was performed at 12½ o'clock, by Rev Thos Addison, Trinity Church, assisted by Rev Osborn Ingle. The bride was attended by 5 bridesmaids: Miss Julia Middleton, [sister;] Miss Maury, of Wash City; Miss Peacham, of Phil; Miss Hyde, of Balt; & Miss Perry, of Wash City. The groom was waited on by Dr Young, Messrs Horace & D W Middleton, jr, [brothers of the bride,] & 2 gentlemen of N Y. The happy party, after 3 hours spent in receiving the congratulations of the large & brilliant assembly, took the Northern train for their bridal tour.
+
Mrd: on Oct 9, by Rev Thos G Addison, assisted by Rev Julian E Ingle, Enos A Skillman, of New Brunswick, N J, to Alice, daughter of D W Middleton, of Wash.

Died: on Oct 7, at Richmond, Va, after a lingering illness, Wm A Baker, aged 5 years & 4 months, only child of W R & Charlotte Baker.

Cincinnati, Oct 10. Danl Hertzler, a wealthy citizen of Springfield, Ohio, was murdered this morning by burglars, who entered his house for the purpose of robbing him. The murderers escaped, taking away with them Mr Hertzler's horse & buggy.

Yesterday Mr Welch tendered his resignation as Mayor of Gtwn. Various stories have been raised in consequence of an investigation now going on as to an alleged deficit in the accounts of Mr Welch while Tax Collector of Gtwn. Mr Welch is a highly respected citizen of Gtwn, & his many friends assert that the investigation will entirely free him from any charges.

Equity Court-Judge Wylie. *In re* estate of Wm Holmead. An order approving the order of the Orphan's Court authorizing the sale of the real estate of infant heirs.

Patents issued to Washingtonians: to Foster Henshaw, for a filter. To J M Curran & J C Baxter, for a metallic hame-tug. These gentlemen claim a hame-tug having its body formed of a single strap of metal with the eye, having a hinged or detachable piece, & its rear end formed for attaching the buckle. To J E Beardsley, A F Boyle, E M Lewis, & M S Clancy, for an apparatus for recording votes. This invention takes the votes, counts them, & prints the voters' names-it is said to be an ingenious contrivance.

The Union Hotel, of Gtwn, which has been recently remodeled & renovated by the owner, Mr R A Shinn, has by him been rented to Mr John O'Leary, a well known saloon proprietor of this city. Mr O'Leary proposes to open the Union on the European plan.

It is stated that Mr R B Mohun, of the firm of Blanchard & Mohun, has purchased from Mr Franck Taylor the bookstore which for years he has been proprietor of, on Pa ave, between 4½ & 6th sts. The price paid by Mr Mohun was $6,000.

The oldest wooden house in the U S is in Dorchester, soon to be a part of Boston. It was built in 1633, & is called the **Minot House**, from the name of the first owner. The house was occupied by Gen Washington & his body-guard for a season, during the Revolution. The house is 2 stories high, & the outside has by no means a bad look; its frame is of oak, either Irish or white, & the beams are as sound as ever, & likewise the whole frame, with the exception of the sills, is in a good state of preservation. During the early years of Dorchester the Indians were very troublesome. The Neponset tribe made their headquarters in the village now of that name, & the chief's name was Chicatawbut, hence the name of the street on which the house stands. Mr Minot, being absent one day, an Indian came & tried to get admittance, but the heroine wife refused to admit him, knowing that it could be for no good intent, & taking down her husband's loaded gun, she fired it at him, wounding him severely, & then, in a moment, threw a pailful of boiling water into his bosom. He fled to the woods &, as tradition says. Was found dead the next morning nearby, having died of his wounds. The woman was honored for her bravery by the inhabitants of the place, by the presentation of a gold wristlet, with her name upon it, & the word, "Who slew the Naraganset Indian." The house is now occupied by a family who pay $80 annual rent.

Death has been unusually busy of late among the scientific men of Paris. Three celebrated physicians, Velpeau, Royer, & Chartroule, have died within the past month. The last death, which took place a few days since, was that of Dr Chartroule, of the Academy of Medicine, who devoted his talents to diseases of the lungs. He was age 56 years, when an attack of paralysis terminated fatally. [No death dates given-current item.]

Hon Chas Greeley Loring, a distinguished Mass lawyer, died at his summer residence, near Boston, on Tuesday, in his 74th year. He was born in Boston, May 2, 1794, & completed his education at Harvard College, where he graduated in 1812; studied law under Hon Chas Jackson & Hon Saml Hubbard. He was a sincere & devoted Christian.

N Y Freeman's Journal. Robt A Bakewell, well known in St Louis as a very sound lawyer & a good Catholic, tells of what God has done for one of his children, his eldest child, 11 years old last Feb, whom they call Cissey at home. She has suffered for some time with pain in her right leg, & took to her bed for 4 weeks, or laid on the sofa, with the hip disease which attacked her first cousin in early childhood, & the poor child was a cripple from age 10 years. The leading surgeons found the leg diseased and the leg affected was already longer than the other limb. The child suffered from pain day & night. Mr Bakewell writes: On Sep 17, my wife paid a visit to some of the devout ladies of the congregation of the Sacred Heart, at this place. She was told that steps were now being taken to commence proceedings at Rome, for an examination of the virtues, etc, of Madam Barrat, the foundress of the order, who died some time since in the odor of sanctity; that 14 miracles had already been worked by her relics, & a sister gave my wife a relic, which she advised to her to apply. I may state that the maternal grandmother of my child had been educated at the Sacred Heart in Paris, & was especially loved by the vernerable lady of whom I speak. My wife applied the relic on her return home and our child fell asleep, as did my wife. Neither had a good sleep for a long time. I was reading in my room the next morning, when my wife came in, pale, with an expression that startled me. She could not speak at first, & burst into tears. At last I understood her to say, Cissey is cured by a miracle. I did not believe a word of it. My wife left me indisgust; my airs of superior wisdom having no effect upon her, so far as I could see. In about 20 minutes I went downstairs, sat upon the child's bed & the little girl merely said, Papa, I am cured. When I came home in the evening, my wife & all the children, including Cissey, had gone to the Sacred Heart convent, [on foot & by street cars,] a distance of 3/4^{ths} of a mile, to return thanks. They soon returned in the best of health & spirits. Cissey made her first communion a year ago last Easter, & plays football with her brothers in the garden. Dr Gregory examined her and pronounced her completely cured. Myself, my wife, my child, her grandparents, uncles & aunts, the servants, the instrument man, & the doctors are all prepared, if called upon, to corroborate them, & will, if required, do so upon oath; each one as to the fact or facts within his or her personal knowledge of the case. Yours, very truly & affectionately, R A Bakewell.

The gold reduction & assay works of John N Wyckoff, at Greenpoint, Long Island, were burned on Sunday night. Loss, $30,000. Partially insured. Milo F Barber, superintending chemist, had a narrow escape with his life.

Yellow fever reports from New Orleans to Wed state that Gen Wheaton was out of danger. Gen Hartsuff was somewhat well. His wife is recovering.

Mrs Emily Jordan, the actress, so well know to theatre-goers, is married. Chas Ransom, a wealthy New Yorker, is the happy man.

The stable of John Overton, near Burkeville, Va, was fired by an incendiary on Tuesday night last. Several very valuable horses perished in the flames. Suspicion resting upon a negro, a bloodhound belonging to Mr Overton was put on the trail, & the guilty party was ferreted out.

San Francisco, Oct 7. John R Ridge died at Grass Valley on Oct 5. He was a prominent Calif politician, poet, & journalist. His father was chief of the Cherokee Nation.

SAT OCT 12, 1867
The non-commissioned ofcrs of Co G, 4th regt of U S cavalry, pay tribute to the late Brvt Maj Michl J Kelly, late company cmder, who died on Aug 13, 1867. He was a gentleman & a soldier in every sense of the word. He died far away from relatives & home; but here, in the wilderness, the compartively untrodden soil of the Texas frontier enshrouds his body, & the winds murmur a mourningful requiem over his grave. –Arthur F Marsh, Acting 1st Sgt, Co G, 4th U S Cavalry

Mr Chas C Stone died in New Orleans of yellow fever; he was a graduate of Gtwn [D C] College, & for several years a resident of Md. He was a nephew of the late Roman Catholic Archbishop Fitzpatrick, of Boston. His only surviving sister is a nun. [No death date given-current item.]

Mrd: on Oct 10, at the residence of the bride's father, in Wash City, by Rev John Vaughan Lewis, Gen J P Hawkins, U S A, to Jane Bethune, daughter of Gen H K Craig, U S A.

Died: on Oct 10, Susan Dant, widow of the late Wm Dant, aged 72 years. Her funeral will be on Oct 13, at 2:30 P M, from her late residence, 452 D st, between 2nd & 3rd sts.

Died: on Sep 8, of yellow fever, at Dry Tortugas, Dr Jos Sim Smith, U S A, in his 30th year.

Died: on Sep 18, of yellow fever, at Dry Tortugas, Henry Price, only son of Lizzie P & the late Dr J S Smith, U S A, aged 3 years, 6 months & 12 days.

When Gen Washington began to look over this territory in earnest as the possible site of the national capital, he found that the portion now west of 7th st extending to Gtwn nearly all included in a plantation owned by David Burns. This estate had descended to him from his Scottish ancestors through several generations, & he was living in the rustic cottage built by his father, & with a large number of slaves was cultivating his farm in quiet seclusion. The old cottage, still standing on Mansion Square, in good preservation, cannot be less than 125 years old. Washington found Burns fully set against the project of the capital. He had a great force of servants, whom he would not sell, & he could not think of leaving the old farm, sacred to the memory of ancestral memories. A story from Burns family said that when Washington found nothing else would do, he visited Mr Burns & told him he had been authorized to select the location of the national capital; I have selected your farm as a portion of it, & the Gov't will take it at all events. I trust you will, under these circumstances, enter into an amicable arrangement. Burns henceforth entered cordially into the wishes of Washington, & earnestly persuaded other owners to do likewise. The landholders were to cede their farms to the Gov't & when laid off into a city they were to have every other lot. For all land used for public bldgs, squares, & walks, they were to receive L25 per acre; nothing was allowed for streets & alleys. The land of David Burns was conveyed by deed, dated Jun 29, 1791, & signed by him & his wife to the commissioners, Thos Beall & John Mackall Gantt, in trust, to be laid out as part of the Federal City. This deed is the first of record among the land records of Wash City. David Burns had 2 children, a son & a daughter. The son had deceased while a student in the law ofc of Luther Martin, some years before the Gov't came here, in 1800, & at that time the daughter had finished her school days, & at the age of 18 years, with her widowed mother, an inmate of the old cottage, was known as the beautiful heiress. Her name was Marcia. Among the intimate friends of the family was Luther Martin, the great Md lawyer; it was in his family, at Balt, that Marcia Burns, during her school days, enjoyed, with his daughters, the advantages of the best school in that city, & polished society. Among her suitors was a lawyer, age 30 years, handsome, polished in manners, a native of Columbia Co, N Y, & a graduate of Columbia College, who came into Congress in 1801, & whose suit against the numerous & distinguished rivals, patronized by Aaron Burr, then Vice Pres of the U S, was successful in making Gen John P Van Ness, the happy possessor of the young heiress & her large fortune. That Aaron Burr acted a part in the contest is not a mere tradition. <u>The Van Ness family</u>: The father, Judge Peter Van Ness, resided in Vt at one period of his married life, & one of his sons, if no more-was born in that State. He subsequently founded **Lindenwald**, the magnificent seat, with its four or five hundred acres, which, after the founder's death, was sold by the son, Wm P, to Van Buren. It was Judge Wm P Van Ness who acted as second to Burr in the lamented duel with Hamilton. Judge Wm P Van Ness was a scholar, & as well as an able District Judge of N Y, his political papers from his hand, were under the signature of Aristides. He was the friend of Irving, & it was in his family, at **Lindenwald**, that was written the most of Knickerbocker's History of New York. It was here he found the original Ichabod Crane, the credulous Yankee schoolmaster, whose adventures in the Legend of Sleepy Hollow are familiar to all. His name was Jesse Merwin, & his school was near the lodge gate of **Lindenwald**.

The wife of Judge Van Ness was a sister of the great Edw Livingston, & their children were Col Eugene Van Ness, Paymaster, U S A, who died at Balt during the war; Edw Livingston Van Ness, living in England; Chas W, living in N Y, & Matilda E, deceased a few years ago. By a second wife there was one child, Christina, married to Mr D'Aubey, & living in N Y. The older brother of Gen Van Ness, Cornelius P, or, as he was generally known, Govn'r Van Ness, was born in Vt in 1781, bred to the law. After the death of his brother, Gen John P Van Ness, he was for some years a resident of this city, settling the estate. He died suddenly in Phil in 1852, while on his way from this city to N Y. His remains were deposited in the Van Ness mausoleum in this city. His children were as follows: Cornelia, wife of Judge Jas J Rosevelt, N Y; Marcia, wife of the late Sir Wm Gore Ousley, at one period British Minister to Brazil, now residing in London; Cornelius P Van Ness, jr, an early resident of Texas, & Minister to France prior to its admittance into the Union, killed by a accidental shot from his own gun on a hunting excursion; Gen Jas Van Ness, late Mayor of San Francisco. Those in this family were all alive when Gen Van Ness died in 1846. Gen Van Ness had one sister, Gertrude, who married into the Hoffman family, of N Y. The only child, Catherine, married Gen Henry G Philip, who resided on the old Van Ness estate at **Claverack**, near Hudson, N Y. Their children were John Van Ness, a naval ofcr, who died at Key West, of yellow fever, during the war; Wm, a lawyer in this city, & M Hoffman, who succeeds his father at **Claverack**, which has been in the family from the time of its founder, the grandfather of Gen John P Van Ness, with whom we now return from this long geneological digression. We give him the military title, although he was not a military ofcr till some 2 years after his marriage, when Jefferson appointed him major of the District militia & subsequently brigadier general in the same service. Mr Van Ness & Miss Burns were united in marriage Sunday morning, May 9, 1802, the day on which the bride was 20 years of age, the nuptial ceremonies taking place in the parlor of the old cottage; it is believed that Rev Walter Addison married them. There was at the time no Episcopal church in Gtwn. Before the marriage Mr Van Ness had begun the erection of the large brick house still standing, with its old fashioned hip roof, at 12th & D sts, south of the avenue. They lived in a house near the Kirkwood House, & where Walter Jones afterwards for some years resided during the summer, moving into the new house in the autumn of 1802. Mrs Burns lived with them much of the time, & they all went to the old cottage during the time of the fruit every year. This continued after the mother died, Mrs Van Ness always insisting upon being in her old home a portion of each year, till they moved into the mansion, about 1817. The corner stone of the Van Ness Mansion was laid Jul 4, 1816, the same season in which St John's Church was built, both edifices being designed by Latrobe, the architect of the Capitol. The mansion is 70 by 42 feet on the ground; modeled after the Presidential Mansion. Beneath the basement was a solid stone cavern that Baker's gang had it that the conspirators had originally planned to have old Abe immured. On such insane pretexts, Mr & Mrs Green were seized after the assassination, & for 46 days closely incarcerated in the old Capitol, & then released. Mr Green was always known as a Union man, quiet & retired, & did not know even the name of Booth. While the family was incarcerated the military had possession of the mansion, & the soldiers did their work of plunder very thoroughly. The mansion was built, seemingly, without regard to cost. Every part of it was finished in the most solid & durable manner. The elegant stuccoed brick stable was burnt in 1861. There was an old stone warehouse on the s e corner designed by Gen Van Ness to anticipate the mercantile business which, in his mistaken ideas, was speedily to give activity to the southern terminus of 7th st. The entire expense of the improvements cannot have been less than $75,000; the cost of the mansion alone was more than $60,000. Mrs Van Ness lived some 15 years after they became occupants of the new mansion. They had but one child, Ann Elbertina, who, inheriting much of her mother's loveliness & excellence, was in her 19th year, in 1822, married to Arthur Middleton, of the distinguished S C family of Revolutionary fame. The wedding took place in the drawing room. The nuptial rites were performed by Rev Wm Hawley, of St John's Church. The following inscription, copied from above the door of the mausoleum erected in her memory, records the sad story: Sacred to the memory of Ann Ebertina Middleton, wife of Arthur Middleton, of South Carolina, and daughter of General John P and Marcia Van Ness. She was born 12th June, 1803; died 22nd November, 1823. Her infant daughter, Marcia Hellen, within this monument, is placed beside her. The spot on which the monument stands is the old family burying ground of the Burns family. Mausoleum Square, as it was called after the monument was built, was given to Mr Middleton before his wife died, though not deeded to him till 1833, 10 years after her death, & one year after the decease of Mrs Van Ness. Mr Middleton was abroad with Govn'r Van Ness as secretary during the nine years he was Minister to Spain, & about 1842 was married a second time. His wife was the daughter of an Italian, Gen Bertevoglio, from which union there were 3 children, two of which, & the mother also, it is believed, survive. Mr Middleton died some years ago at Rome, which was his residence, & where the family still reside. Their agent is now selling their interest in Mausoleum Square, lots to the amount of some $70,000 having been already sold, & more than that amount still remaining to be sold. The children having become of age, demand the sale & division. The mausoleum was erected immediately after the death of Mrs Middleton, whose remains were at first buried on the spot where the monument stands. The remains of David Burns & wife were buried on the farm of Mr Wightt, a brother of Mrs Burns, near Rock Creek Church. Within the mausoleum are the remains of Mrs Middleton & child, Mrs Van Ness, Gen Van Ness, Govn'r Van Ness Mrs Resin Orme, & Mr Montgomery, who was for a time consul to Porto Rico, & a friend of the Van Ness family. The memorial was designed by Geo Hadfield, an exact copy of the beautiful Temple of Vesta at Rome. The material is sand-stone, & was wrought by Mr Birth, whose establishment was near the old lower bridge leading to Gtwn. The death of Mrs Van Ness. After the death of her only child, Mrs Van Ness was more than ever devoted to works of benevolence, especially to the care of orphans. A large meeting of the citizens of Washington was held at the Western Town House, on the evening of her death, called to order by John H Houston & John N Moulder, Jas Gooch sec. Her death was characterized as a public misfortune, extending its influence throughout all the ramifications of society. The following cmte was appointed to furnish a place, with appropriate inscription, for the coffin: John Wells, jr, John H Houston, G W Dashiell, H C Williams, John Williams S Parker, Wm Gordon, Gideon Pearce, F C

Shelton, W Randolph Spalding, G Cozens, & Wm Hunter. The inscription upon the plate:
The Citizens of Washington,
In Testimony of Their Veneration for
Departed Worth,
Dedicate This Plate to the Memory of
Marcia Van Ness,
The Excellent Consort of J P Van Ness. If piety, charity, high principle, and exalted worth could have averted the shafts of fate, she would still have remained among us a bright example of every virtue. The hand of death has removed her to a purer and happier state of existence, and while we lament her loss, let us endeavor to emulate her virtues. Upon a small place below the one above was the following record:
Born 9th May, 1782
Married 9th May, 1802
Died 9th Sept, 1832
The body was placed by the side of her daughter, & the following was inscribed on the exterior of the monument, by the side of the epitaph already copied of the daughter:
Sacred to the memory of Marcia Van Ness, daughter of David Burns, and wife of General John P Van Ness.
Born 9th May, 1782.
Married 9th May, 1802.
Died 9th Sept, 1832.
She whom the Poor deplore, the good revered,
The wise admired, the vicious feared,
In whom sense, sweetness, and accomplishment,
New charms to dignity and virtue lent,
Is gone! But shall we doubt the Almighty's love!
Is not all Earth below, all Heaven above?
And thou, her Partner, sunk in grief thy own,
Be hushed, since bursts from everyheart a groan!
Though struck down thus by thunder of the skies,
When sympathy like this supports, arise!
The cholera was at this time raging with death & terror in it sweep through our city.
The Jas Burns farm house. A younger brother, James, occupied a portion of David Burns' plantation. His farm house stood on the spot now occupied by the E st Baptist church. One of the first bldgs erected on Mausoluem Square was the schoolhouse of Johnny McCloud, the Scotchman, famous in the early schoolmaster annals of Wash City. Above his schoolhouse, in large letters were inscribed:"Order is Heaven's first law."
On that spot now stands the most charming residence of Mr M W Galt. Jas Burns, his wife, nee Orme, & their children, 4 sons & 2 daughters, are nearly all buried in

the grounds containing the monument-one child only surviving. The Burns spring, afterwards called St Patrick's spring, was a delicious fountain belonging to this farmhouse in the olden time; here the Burns children played. It was smoothed down & is now the site of St Patrick's Church. The excavation of the cellar for the Masonic Hall has unearthed the old spring. The servants which descended to Mrs Van Ness from her father were all retained in the family, & at her death become the property of her husband, though with a provision, verbal, if not written, that at his death they were all who survived to have their freedom, as they in fact did. Uncle Simon was the chief butler & master over all the servants & everything about the Van Ness Mansion for many years. After Gen Van Ness died, he was chief butler at the Austrian Minister's, where he died. His funeral was large; Dr Pyne preached a funeral sermon. His remains were buried by the side of the mausoleum. From the time of the death of Mrs Van Ness, in 1832, till his own death, in 1846, his household was presided over by his niece, Miss Matilda E Van Ness, & Miss Ann G Wright, [sister Gertrude,] ladies of great accomplishments, the former of whom died a few years ago, & the latter is still living. He gave a dinner every Friday, & his hospitalities were large & generous. At the time of his wife's death he was Mayor of Wash City. The Wash City Asylum bldg was erected on a lot given by Mrs Van Ness, adjoining the lot on which the remains of her daughter had been enshrined. She constantly, to the day of her death, made contributions to the institution. & in her last days she gave directions that a legacy left her by an old friend, the relict of Govn'r Blount, of N C, should go to the asylum. Mrs Madison was the first directress of the society, & Mrs Van Ness succeeding her, continued to fill the position to the end of her life. She laid the cornerstone of the new asylum bldg. Mrs Van Ness, in her last sickness, conveyed all her real estate to trustees, [Stephen Decatur, Thos Swan, & another,] to be by them conveyed to her husband, who died intestate, Mar 7, 1846. Richd Smith, as trustee of the heirs of Gen Van Ness, with the assent of his heirs, who signed the conveyance, dated 25th April, 1840, sold Mansion Square to Mr Thos Green, the present owner. The heirs were Govn'r Cornelius P Van Ness, Col Eugene Van Ness, Chas W Van Ness, Matilda E Van Ness, Edw Van Ness, M H Hoffman, Gertrude Hoffman, the last mentioned being the grandmother of the Philip children

The trial of Dr Thos J Gardner, indicted with Dr J E Turner, in Binghamton, for setting fire to the N Y State Inebriate Asylum, in 1864, was concluded with a verdict of not guilty.

The trial of Dr Thos J Gardner, indicted with Dr J E Turner, in Binghamton, for setting fire to the N Y State Inebriate Asylum, in 1864, was concluded with a verdict of not guilty.

MON OCT 14, 1867
The Pres, upon the recommendation of Gov Pierrepoint & Atty Gen Stanbery, pardoned Saml Barron, of Va, ex-cmdor of the confederate navy.

A duel was fought near Augusta, Ga, on Sat, between Col H P Farrow, of Atlanta, & Maj O'Connor, of Rome. After an interchange of shots the affair was settled. The difficulty grew out of a newspaper article.

Wm W Parker, whose trial has been progressing at Wilmington, Dela, for the last 2 days, has been convicted of murder in the first degree. He killed his own children in 1863. The evidence was circumstantial.

Orphans Court-Judge Purcell, Oct 12, 1867. 1-The will of Stoddard R Colby, [former Register of the Treasury,] late of Wash, D C, deceased, was filed, & partially proven, & admitted to probate & record. After providing for the payment of his just debts, the deceased bequeathed the residue of his estate, being all personal property, & consisting of principally of U S stock, to his wife, Ellen C Colby, & son, Jabez P Colby, as joint trustees in trust for the exclusive benefit & support of said wife, & two minor children, Ellen Rebecca Colby & Frank Moore Colby; & orders & directs that no bond be required of said trustees to secure the discharge of their duties; & advises, but does not order, that said trustees procure a suitable homestead for the use & occupation of his wife & children to be purchased out of the trust fund. 2-Chauncey Smith was appointed guardian to the orphans of Prosley W Guthrie, late of the U S army, deceased; bond $500. 3-The will of Arnold Somerville was filed & fully proven. 4-The will of Basil Fletcher, of Wash City, D C, deceased, was filed & partially proven. The deceased constitutes & appoints as his executor Thos Dulaney. 5-Geo A Bohrer was appointed guardian to Wm H Bohrer, orphan of Alex'r A Bohrer, deceased; bond $8,000. 6-The first account of Louisa Libbey, admx of Jos Libbey, deceased; the first & final account of the administrator of Eliza Lamb, deceased; the third account of the guardian of the orphans of John Robinson, deceased; the guardian's account of the personal estate of Eliza Lamb, deceased; the third account of the executor of Danl W Hall, deceased; & the second supplementary account of the excs of David English deceased, were approved & passed.

Equity Court-Judge Wylie. 1-Brown vs Brown: order appointing L S Williams guardian ad litem, & of reference to Auditor. 2-*In Re*. Petition of Julia Ann Forrest, guardian, etc. Decree confirming the order of the Orphans Court. 3-Pierce vs Hall. Bill dismissed.

Died: on Oct 12, Mr John P Miller, in his 65th year. His funeral will take place from his residence, corner of Delaware ave & M st north, this evening at half-past two o'clock. It has pleased God to take from his family a loving husand & kind father. He was a good neighbor, & respected by all who knew him.

Died: on Sunday, Oct 13, Miss S L Manning.

Died: on Oct 2, at Hartford, Conn, after a lingering illness, Harriet A, wife of Richd R Crawford, of Gtwn, D C, & daughter of the late Wm H Jones, of New Haven, Conn.

Inventory of the estate of Abraham Lincoln, late Pres of the U S, so far as the same has come to my knowledge. -David Davis, adm
In registered bonds bearing 6%, payable in coin: $57,000.00
In temporary loan bearing 6%, in currency: $2,781.04
In Treasury warrants, issued to him for salary, & not paid:
No 554: $1,981.67   No 990: $1,976.22
No 826: $1,981.67   No 1,217: $1,981.67
Draft of Nat'l Bank of Springfield: $183.00
Balance of salary received from the Treasurer of the U S: $847.83
Claims against Robt Irwin, of Springfield, which Mr Condell paid: $9,044.41
Balance in hands of Riggs, banker of Wash: $1,373.53
Balance in hands of First Nat'l Bank, Wash: $381.66
Total: $79,482.20
The sum if all invested in U S securities, bearing interest.
Also, the following:
N B Judd's note, dated Sep 1, 1859, bearing 10% interest, for $3,000.00
Thos J Turner, [Freeport] Jul, 1858, due Nov 1, 1858; interest 10%: $400.00
A & J Hains, [Pekin] two notes for $200 each, one due Oct 15, 1858, the other Jan 1, 1859: $400.00
With the following credits:
Feb 15, 1859, $50; May 2, 1859, $50.00; Jul 14, 1859, $100; Sep 12, 1859, $50; Aug 13, 1860, $50.00
M B Church, [Springfield,] Nov 5, 1864, at 5 months, given at Washington
Jas H & J S McDaniel, [Sangamon Co,] Apr 23, 1863, one day, 10% interest: $250.00
Golden Patterson, [Vermilion Co,] Apr 25, 1859, due one year after date: $60.00
Milton Davis, [Vermilion Co,] Nov 7, 1857, due Dec 25, 1857, 10%, with credit of $30.00, Mar 28, 1859: $50.00
John P Mercer, [Shelbyville,] May 25, 1852: $7.69
Real estate in Illinois.
Mr Lincoln's homestead in Springfield, Ill, on lot 5 & part of lot 7, in Block 10, E Iles' addition to Springfied. Lot 3, in Block 19, Town of Lincoln, Logan Co, Ill.
Real estate in Iowa: Crawford Co, Iowa: 120 acres east half, n e & n w, n e section 18, township 84, range 39.
Tama Co: 40 acres, description not recollected. Certificate of entry in hands of C H Moore, of Clinton, De Witt Co, Ill. –David Davis, adm, etc
The following is a transcript of the oath filed by Judge Davis upon taking out letters of administration:
State of Ill. Sangamon Co: David Davis, being duly sworn, deposes & says that Abraham Lincoln, late of Sangamon Co, Ill, is dead, & that he died on or about Apr 14, A D, 1865, intestate, as it is said, & that his estate will probably amount to the sum of $85,000; that said Abraham Lincoln left at the time of his decease, Mary Lincoln, his widow, & Robt T Lincoln & Thos Lincoln, his children.
–David Davis-Subscribed & sworn before me this 14th day of June, A D, 1865.
–N W Matheny, clerk

The above figures speak for themselves. To be added to them, however, is the $25,000 appropriated by the last Congress on account of Mr Lincoln's salary, making altogether the total value of the personal estate to be about $110,000, to say nothing of the real estate described in the schedule above. So that the statement that Mr Lincoln saved nothing & left nothing from his salary, & that Mrs Lincoln has no resources but what remains from the appropriations of Congress, $22,000, & the rents of the homestead, returning altogether but $1,700 per year, cannot possibly be true. That Mr Lincoln did not leave his family wealthy is very evident; but no one, in view of the above inventory, will say that they are in the deplorable condition of "want" & "destitution," in regard to which the public has with so much astonishment just been informed. We say this much, not for the purpose of preventing "personal contributions" from being made to Mrs Lincoln, if she desires them, much less to deter Congress from making a further appropriation for her support, which we should be glad to have it do; but simply in order that the people of the nation may not suppose that Mrs Lincoln is in anything like destitute circumstances. Her income may not be sufficient to meet all her wants & necessities, but it is certainly large enough to maintain her at least as comfortably as she lived before going to Washington.

Maj Geo B Simpson, paymaster U S army, had returned but recently from an extended tour of duty in Texas & gave us an interesting report on the condition of the country & the progress of the epidemic. Little did we think at the time that we should be called so soon to record his death; but the ways of Providence are inscrutable. Maj Simpson was a faithful ofcr, & had won the respect & esteem of all who knew him in this dept. Peace to his ashes. New Orleans Times, Oct 5. [Oct 16th newspaper: Died: on Oct 4, at New Orleans, of the prevailing epidemic, Maj Geo B Simpson, paymaster U S army. He was a faithful public ofcr, a dutiful son, & a husband whose tender devotion to his wife amounted almost to religion, such was Maj Geo B Simpson.]

Hon David L Seymour, of Troy, N Y, delegate at large to the State Constitutional Convention, died at Lansboro, Mass, on Friday, aged about 65 years.

The body of Wm Ryan, the missing fireman employed aboard the steamer **Dean Richmond**, was found on Sunday. An inquest was held over the remains, & the jury, it is understood, rendered a verdict holding the ofcrs of the steamer **Vanderbilt** guilty of culpable negligence, which, they aver, caused the collision between the steamers.

Phil, Oct 13. John Rudd, of the navy, a cmdor on the retired list since 1861, died here yesterday. He entered the service at age 14, & has been in it over 50 years. He was a native of Va.

TUE OCT 15, 1867
Died: on Oct 14, Jos H Crider, in his 30th year. His funeral will be from Mrs Sutton's, 461 E st, between 5th & 6th sts, this afternoon, at 4 o'clock.

Died: on Oct 10, Sarah Pamelia Conway, eldest daughter of the late Dr Wm D Conway. [Balt, Cincinnati, & Lawrence, Kansas papers please copy.]

Died: on Oct 13, Miss Sallie L Manning. Her funeral will take place at St Matthew's Church, on Wed, at 9 o'clock. [Oct 17th newspaper: A requiem mass was read by Rev Dr White; the deceased was a prominent member of St Matthew's congregation, as well as a leading member of the various female Catholic societies of Wash City. The church was crowded with friends & acquaintances of the deceased. Miss Manning was interred in *Mount Olivet Cemetery*.]

Rev T B McFalls has resigned his pastorate of the Assembly's Presbyterian Church because of failing health. He designs visiting Texas in the hope that a milder climate will recuperate him. The congregation seem unwilling to accept the resignation, but propose to allow him a leave of absence. [Oct 16th newspaper: The leave of absence cannot be accepted-Rev McFalls has been appointed a chaplain in the regular army, & assigned to duty at *Fort Chadburne*, Texas. The appointment has been accepted by Mr McFalls, in the hope that a change of climate will restore his health.]

Ex-Pres Franklin Pierce was serenaded in Concord, N H, on Wed night, by the Democrats who were rejoicing over the election returns.

Mrs Martha Webster died in Brooklyn on Saturday from the effects of an overdose of morphine, which had been inadvertently prepared by a druggist's assistant in a store on Third ave, in that city. The clerk was arrested & held to await the result of the coroner's investigation.

Supreme Court of D C, at Law, No 2,499. Alex'r R Shepherd, plntf, vs Solon Mudgett et al, dfndnts. On the motions of the plntf, by Brent & Phillips, his attys, it is ordered that the dfndnt, Solon Mudgett, cause his appearance to be entered herein, on or before the first rule day occurring 40 days after this date; otherwise the cause will be proceeded with as in case of default.

Public auction on Oct 23, 1867, on the premises, at Bladensburgh, Md, that valuable property known as the Branch Hotel, being, from family considerations, about to relinquish public business & remove to another State, offers for sale, said Hotel, Fittings-up, Outhouses, & a large Garden Lot, containing 3 acres, more or less. Apply on the premises to D Howell.

Nashville, Oct 14. 1-Wm & Henry Crockett, of Williamson Co, have been brought here, charged with the murder of Jos Drakel, colored, & shooting at his wife. The negroes were employed by the Crocketts in making a crop. Their bail is $5,000 for their appearance tomorrow. They are confident of acquittal. 2-Joe Wharton was convicted today, in the Criminal Court, of an attempt to commit rape some years ago, & sentenced to the penitentiary for 10 years.

Orphans Court of Wash Co, D C, Oct 12, 1867. In the case of Susan L Hall, admx of Edw Hall, the administratrix & Court have appointed Nov 5 next, for the final settlement of the personal estate of the said deceased, of the assets in hand.
-Jas R O'Beirne, Reg/o wills

Canton, Ohio, Oct 14. On Sunday, in the German Reformed Church, Ferdinand Hoffman, recently discharged from the penitentiary, approached a young woman, Caroline Jast, who was some time since divorced from him, & demanded a kiss, & while she was in the act of complying, he drew a large butcher knife & plunged it into her person several times, inflicting fatal wounds. The desperado fled, but was soon arrested. [Oct 24th newspaper: Mrs Hoffman died of her wounds last Sat, & the next night Hoffman hanged himself in his cell.]

WED OCT 16, 1867
The square on which the Church of the Ascension stands was part of the estate which descended to Mrs Van Ness from her father, David Burns, whose plantation formed a large portion of the site of Wash City. When the daughter, & only child, Ann Elbertina Van Ness, who had been married to Arthur Middleton less than a year, suddenly died, in 1832, the afflicted parents erected a Memorial temple in the ancient family burial ground of the Burns' family to her memory. Soon after this period Mrs Van Ness & her husband, Gen John P Van Ness, determined to consecrate to the purposes of an Episcopal church the lot adjoining the mausoleum grounds on the one side, & the lot on the other side for a Protestant Orphan Asylum. The remainder of the square was verbally given by Mrs Van Ness to Mr Middleton. The Asylum bldg was commenced in 1827, completed & occupied in 1829. The church lot was conveyed for its purpose by deed dated Jan 15, 1827. The corner lot at the junction of H & 9th sts, with the unconveyed remainder of the square, was conveyed to Arthur Middleton by Gen John P Van Ness, by deed dated Apr 9, 1833. The Middleton heirs claim that the church has a title to only so much of the 125 feet running easterly from the centre of the mausoleum as lies outside the east wall of the mausoleum grounds. It is to recover some 550 square feet in all, that Mr Jas Towles, the agent of the heirs, Mrs Middleton & two children, residing in Italy, has instituted an action, & called the parish into court. The counsel for the plntfs is Wm F Mattingly; for dfndnts, Walter Cox. The church bldg was erected in 1845. A petition signed by owners of property in that neighborhood, headed by Jos F Brown, pray the removal of the mausoleum & the remains from that square to a more appropriate place, was on Monday last, presented to the Board of Aldermen. The reasons for the removal is that the enclosure is disagreeable & unsightly; that it discourages improvements, & that such removal would be in accordance with the precedent established in the case of the vault, the removal of which was ordered some time ago from the St Patrick's Church grounds. This monument has not been cared for since the death of Gen Van Ness, in 1846. At one time the vault, entered by the small windows in the rear, was converted into a den for graceless boys to carry on gambling operations, the coffins being used as tables. During the war the mausoleum was much cut & disfigured by the soldiers. It is well known that when the Protestant Orphan Asylum Society had last year completed their new & spacious edifice, which is now occupied

for the State Dept, on 14th st, then sold the bldg which they had occupied adjoining the mausoleum grounds since it completion in 1829, to the <u>Sisters of the Holy Cross</u>, in charge of St Joseph's Male Orphan Asylum, in Oct, 1866, for $25,000. In our visit to the place, in connection with the preparation of this article, we found 64 little orphans there in the care of Sister Alphonsa, of ages ranging from five to ten, clean, bright, & happy to look upon, as in fact is ever the case with the little ones that a good Providence guides into the care of blessed, self sacrificing women, such as preside in this institution.

Winnie Butler, colored, aged 107 years, died on Monday at a house on Madison st, between M & N & 6th & 7th sts. Her death was not unexpected, as, from extreme old age, she had been in a declining state of health for several months past. The deceased was interred at the expense of the Corporation.

Maj Mathew Selden Ward, editor of the Panola [Miss] Star, died in Memphis, Tenn, a few days ago, of typhoid fever. Maj Ward was a native of Rochbridge Co, Va, but raised in Indianapolis, Ind, were he left many relatives & friends.

The trial of Dr Sebring, for the murder of his wife, just closed at Elkhart, Ind. In 1864 Mrs Sebring was slightly injured by a fall from a horse. Confined to bed, she soon manifested symptoms of poisoning, & ultimately died under her husband's treatment. Chemical analysis of her stomach revealed large quantities of arsenic. The husband had left the place in company with Minerva Winebenner, a woman who assisted in the care of his wife during her sickness. They settled in Lawrence, Ind, & remained there until the Doctor was recognized & arrested. The defence on the trial claimed Mrs Sebring had been in the habit of taking arsenic; that she might have died from the effects of the fall; or that arsenic might have been given by the woman Winebenner; the jury acquitted the prisoner.

<u>Equity Court</u>-Judge Wylie. Carr vs Carr. Case where alimony had been allowed. Rule to show cause why attachment for contempt should not issue in default of payment of allotment. The answer of the dfndnt was, in effect, inability to pay the said alimony, & the rule was discharged on the promise of the dfndnt's mother to pay the money.

Mrd: at the Church of the Ascension, by Rev Dr Pinkney, John C Moore, of Richmond, Va, to Miss Almira E Gordon, of Wash, D C. No cards. [Richmond papers please copy.] [No marriage date given-current item.]

Yesterday, Chas Miller, a young man, was feared fatally injured by being kicked in the head by a horse, attached to a wagon which was standing in front of the Centre Market. Miller was conveyed to his father's residence, in the 7th Ward, in a very critical condition, his skull being badly fractured.

Castine, Me, Oct 14. A Castine fishing vessel wrecked off the coast of New Brunswick. Capt Sylvester & a crew of 17 were drowned. Nine of the men leave families.

Orphans Court-Judge Purcell, Oct 15, 1867. 1-An exemplified copy of the last will & testament of Teresa Hoffman, deceased, was received from a probate court in Delaware, & filed in this court. 2-Letters testamentary were granted to Anna P Stockton, on the estate of Francis B Stockton, deceased. 3-The last will & testament of Basil Fletcher was admitted to probate & record, & letters testamentary issued to Thos Dulany; bond $1,000. 4-The will of Arnold Somerville was admitted to probate & record, & letters testamentary issued to Wm Bates; bond $500. 5-Letters testamentary were issued to Catherine Johnson on the estate of Robt Johnson, deceased; bond $400. 6-Harriet J Pickett was appointed guardian to Geo Randolph Pickett, orphan of John A Pickett, deceased; bond $3,000. 7-The first account of Benj F Bellinger, guardian to Chas Bellinger, his son, & heir at law of Jos Libbey, deceased; & the first & final account of the executor of Geo H Edmonds, deceased, were approved & passed.

Fashionable Wedding. Miss Carrie Farnham, daughter of the late Robt Farnham, of Wash City, was yesterday united in marriage to Mr Chas Curtis, formerly of Conn, now of Wash City, in the Church of the Epiphany, which was thronged by the youth, the grace, & the beauty of Washington. The bridal party was very fashionable, & the marriage ceremonies were performed by the rector, Dr Hall, in his usual happy manner. The bridal party went North, on a bridal tour yesterday afternoon.

Mr Geo Dubant, the present proprietor, having completed fine improvements, reopened his restaurant at 6th & Pa ave, Oct 15. It originally established & kept by Snow, a mulatto man, who made a large amount of money in the business. It was sold out to Messrs Benter & Peter M Dubant; Benter sold out his interest to Mr Peter M Dubant, & he became sole proprietor. Finally he retired, & relinquished his business to his brother, Geo Dubant. [The <u>oldest restaurant</u> in Washington.]

Chancery sale, by decree of the Supreme Court of D C, in the cause of J P Von Essen vs Waring et al, No 815 Equity: auction on Nov 6, of the brick dwlg & ground attached on Congress st, Gtwn, fronting 40 feet on Congress, & running back, of that width, 121 feet & 6 inches. –Walter S Cox, trustee -Thos Dowling, auct

Burrell D Munson, of Williston, Vt, an old man of 78, has completed an 8 day clock which will keep a record of the seconds, minutes, hours, days, weeks, months, & years, to the close of the century. It is 8 feet high, occupied 3 years in construction, & is valued at $500. Mr Munson made all the castings & mouldings himself.

N Y, Oct 14. Dr Sillian Ives died here yesterday. He was at the head of the Catholic Protectory Asylum at Westchester, N Y. He was a convert from Protestanism, having formerly been Episcopal Bishop of North Carolina.

Hartford, Conn, Oct 14. A brutal murder occurred at Colchester late on Sat night. Several Irishmen, under the influence of liquor, killed John Kilday. His head was pounded to a perfect jelly with stone & clubs. Danl Sullivan, the supposed murderer, escaped.

THU OCT 17, 1867
The President, we understand, appointed Jas W Hancock, of Texas, collector of customs for the district of St Luria, Texas, vice Chas Taylor, deceased. Mr Hancock is an old resident of Texas, & served faithfully in the Union army during the rebellion.

Despatch to the Boston Herald says that 2nd Assist Geo F Sawyer, U S navy, who has been on trial at Portsmouth before a court martial, has been found guilty of disrespect to his superior ofcr, in declaring that the President ought to be impeached, &, by order of Sec Welles, has been suspended from duty for one year on half pay.

Thos Dowling, auct, sold at private sale the property of Wm H Wheatley, fronting 60 feet on Washington st, by a depth of 120 feet, improved by a large 2 story frame dwlg, to Maj Chas Dodge, for $9,000. A vacant lot fronting 40 feet on First st, by a depth of 90 feet, belonging to R H Trunnel was sold to Wm L Dyer, for $1,000 cash. Also sold, on Tuesday, the farm of Mr John C Devin, containing 134 acres, on Conduit road, $1/4^{th}$ miles above Cabin John's bridge, with a dwlg, barns, & other bldgs, to Gustavus White, for $29 per acre.

A despatch from Springfield says: The Coroner's investigation into the killing of John L Brooks, in the riot at Westfield on Sat, keeps the excitement in that town at fever heat. [Oct 21st newspaper: Springfield, Mass, Oct 29. The coroner's jury in the case of John T Brooks, of Westfield, who was killed by Deputy Constable Chapin, in the recent riot in that town, have returned a verdict justifying the ofcrs, who fired upon the mob in self-defence.]

Mr Wm Towers, a resident of the 7th Ward, & for many years a grocer in the 1st Ward, died quite suddenly on Tuesday, while being conveyed to his residence. He had been ill for some weeks past, & had ventured out on the avenue, when he was again taken sick. The occasion of his death is supposed to have been disease of the heart.

Mrd: on Oct 15, at St Paul's Church, Balt, by Rev Dr Hall, of Wash, Mr Nathl B Fugitt, of Wash City, to Miss Bettie, daughter of Robt Dade, of Balt. No cards.

Vicksburg, Miss, Oct 16. Owing to the prevalence of the yellow fever here Gen Ord has removed his headquarters to Holly Springs. The yellow fever, however, is abating.

Milwaukee, Oct 15. The small propellar **Waukazoo**, on the eastern shore, was lost in a storm at the mouth of the Kalamazoo river on Sat. The passengers & crew were rescued, except two children of Rev John Cathcom, who were lost.

The habeas corpus case of Eliz Turner, colored, aged 14 years, before Chief Justice Chase, [in chambers,] was this morning disposed of, she being discharged from the custody of Philemon T Hambleton, of St Michael's, Talbot Co, to whom the Orphans Court of that county had apprenticed her on Nov 3, 1864, & given over to the care & guardianship of her mother, Eliz Mincky, [formerly Turner,] whose husband, Chas Henry Mincky, through counsel, Messrs Henry Stockbridge, O F Bump, & N M Pusey filed the petition for the writ, which was made returnable on Tuesday.

Orphans Court of Wash Co, D C, Oct 15, 1867. In the case of Jos Mountz, exc of John Mountz, deceased, the executor & Court have appointed Nov 12 next, for the final settlement of the personal estate of the said deceased, of the assets in hand. -Jas R O'Beirne, Reg/o wills

FRI OCT 18, 1867
Dr Warren Stone, the celebrated physician of New Orleans, his wife, daughter, & son, are at Willard's.

We have received intelligence of the death, from yellow fever, of R J Jenkins, a young man well known in Wash City. His death occurred on Sep 28, at Vermillon parish, La. Mr Jenkins was the eldest son of Thos Jenkins, who resides in Wash Co, near the Navy Yard bridge.

Michl Phelan has invented a combination of dining table & billard table. After dinner the top of the table is removed as well as the cloth, & by turning a lever screw at one end of the bed of the billard table, which then appears, is raised to a proper level.

On Nov 1st a change of proprietors will take place on the Evening Star of Wash City, Mr W D Wallach having sold his interest to Messrs C B Baker, Crosby S Noyes, Alex R Shepherd, & Geo Adams, [correspondent of the World.] Mr Kaufman, a clerk in the Treasury Dept, & former editor of a paper in the West, is mentioned in connection with that of Mr Noyes in the editorial dept of the Star. Mr Baker will attend to the business interest of the new firm.

Mrd: on Oct 17, at the Seaton House, in Wash City, by Rev John Trimble, Mr Albert G Conway to Miss Sue B Roberts, all of Orange Co, Va. [Orange & Culpeper papers please copy.]

Mrd: on Oct 9, at St Luke's Church, Bladensburg, Md, by Rev John Collins McCabe, D D, Wm H May, of Cecil Co, to Anna M W, daughter of the late Henry C Mackall, of *Wilna*, near Elkton, Md.

Mrd: on Oct 15, in Alexandria, Va, by Rev Mr Morton, at the residence of the bride's father, Mr P B Hove to Miss M H Daingerfield, daughter of John B Daingerfield. [Richmond papers please copy.] [Oct 19th newspaper: Mrd: on Oct 15, at Alexandria, Va, Philip B Hooe to Miss Mary H, daughter of John B Daingerfield.]

Mrd: on Oct 15, at the Church of the Epiphany, by Rev Dr Hall, Wright Curtiss, of Bridgeport, Conn, to Carrie, daughter of the late Robt Farnham, of Wash City.

Mrd: on Oct 15, at Portsmouth, N H, Hon Chas A Page, U S Consul at Zurich, Switzerland, to Grace, only daughter of the late Saml E Coues, for many years Chief Examiner in the Patent Ofc, Wash. No cards.

Died: on Oct 17, Miss Frances Elvans, in her 53rd year. Her funeral will take place from the residence of her nephew, John R Elvans, 515 M st, this afternoon at 3 o'clock.

Died: on Oct 9, suddenly, in N Y, of heart disease, Walter F Clarke, in his 15th year, only son of Geo & Margaret Clarke, late of Balt.

Balt, Oct 17. Last night as a militia negro regt were parading near Franklin & Howard sts, 12 or 15 shots were fired in the streets. Chas A Ellermeyer, white, aged 18, was instantly killed. Great excitement prevailed. A large force of police were soon there. All quiet now. [Oct 22nd newspaper: The funeral of Chas A Ellermeyer took place yesterday, from the residence of his father, 14 Ensor st. The remains were followed to **Baltimore Cemetery** by several thousand persons. The services were by Rev Mr Barnes, of the Monument St Methodist Episcopal Church.
–Balt Sun, Monday]

Jerome Park, N Y, opened on Tuesday; a rider, Martin Cassidy, age about 25 years, was killed. He leaves a wife & children. The horse he was riding, Negrita, fell headlong, threw the rider, & fell upon him crushing his skull.

Dissolution of the partnership, of Holland & Kelly, this day by mutual consent. Franklin G Holland will still continue the Painting Business at the old stand, 371 D st, between 8th & 9th sts. –Franklin G Holland, Wm Kelly, Wash, D C, Oct 17, 1867.

Dept of the Interior, U S Patent Ofc, Wash, Oct 14, 1867. Ptn of Chas R Harvey, of N Y, N Y, praying for the extension of a patent granted to him Jan 24, 1854, for an improvement in Air-Heating Furnaces, for seven years from the expiration of said patent, which takes place on Jan 24, 1868. -T C Theaker, Com'r of Patents

The daughter of Hon Wm Dennison was married at Columbus, Ohio, on Wed, to Gen W Forsythe, of Maj Gen Sheridan's staff. Gen Sheridan & ex-sec Stanton were present.

New Orleans, Oct 17. Gen Hartsuff is lying here dangerously ill of cholera morbus. Fever interments for 24 hours ending at 6 o'clock this morning were 31.

The copartnership of Calvert & Doran will be dissolved this day by mutual consent. Mr G W Calvert will continue the Business & sign in liquidation for the old firm. -Geo W Calvert, T W Doran, Wash, Oct 16, 1867.

Trustees sale of valuable distillery near Gtwn, in Wash Co, D C; by decree of the Supreme Court of D C, in Chancery, passed on Oct 12, 1867; John Van Riswick, plntf, & Edw Lynch & others, dfndnts: auction on Nov 19, on the premises, the **Foundry property**, formerly belonging to Gen John Mason, & conveyed to John S Berry by Wm Selden, trustee, by deed dated Feb 23, 1856, recorded in Liber J A S No 111, folios 200 et seq, of the land records of Wash Co, D C; the said Foundry property is situated between the Chesapeake & Ohio canal & the Potomac river, except the section which was conveyed by John S Berry, Allen Dodge, & John P Berry to Horatio E Berry, by deed dated on or about Jun 14, 1858, recorded in Liber J A S No 161, folios 104, et seq, & also the easternmost portion thereof sold & conveyed by said John S Berry, Allen Dodge & John P Perry to John Cochran, by deed dated on or about Mar 3, 1860, recorded in Liber J A S, No 203 folios 35, et seq, one of the said land records, together with the improvements, including a perpetual right of way for man, beast, & vehicle through the premises so conveyed to Horatio E Barry on the north & south side of the stone boring mills situated thereon, & also a perpetual right of way for the water pipes appurtenant to the residence of said real estate & the right of ingress, egress, & regress for all purposes incident to the use of said water pipes, & also a perpetual right of way over the wagon-road between said canal & river, & leading from Gtwn to the Foundry or Columbia mills. Stream called Mill Branch runs through the premises. –Richd H Laskey, Jno D McPherson, trustees. -Green & Williams, aucts

SAT OCT 19, 1867
The steamship **Persia**, from Liverpool, reached N Y on Thu, having among her passengers Most Rev Archbishop Spalding. Very Rev Dr Thos Foley, administrator of the diocese, & Rev J A Gibbons, left Balt on the same day, & will escort the Archbishop to his home, in that city, reaching there today. The formal reception of the Archbishop will take place at the Cathedral on Sunday at 11 A M.

Mr Richd B Mohun has associated with him in the book-selling & stationery business, 402 Pa ave, Mr Orson H Bestor.

Chas D Liebermann, son of Dr Liebermann, of Wash City, has purchased of John T Burch his book & stationery store, 509 9th st, under Seaton Hall.

Died: on Oct 8, at **Barnaby Manor**, Mrs Eleanor Hawkins Callis, widow of the late Henry Addison Callis, aged 73 years.

Falling of a gravel bank in the First Ward yesterday, while a force of laborers in the employ of Mr John E Ashbaugh, street contractor, were engaged in cutting out the sand bank on 16th st, between Rhode Island ave & P at, it fell or caved in. Hugh Adams, white, was found lying upon his face, his skull crushed & his body horribly mangled. His body was conveyed to his late residence on 25th st, between I & K sts. Adams was an Irishman, about 30 years of age, unmarried. Jacob Johnson, colored, was mortally wounded & not expected to recover. He was about 35 years old & unmarried. Jas Taylor was slightly bruised & placed in an ambulance & conveyed to the Freedman's Hospital. Taylor is about 35 years of age & unmarried.

The **Meridian Hill** property was formerly a large suburban domain, of near 130 acres, & was formerly the **Porter estate**. Its front is Boundary st, extending from the west line of the Columbia College property to the line of 18th st west. Its rear is the Gtwn Ridge road.
+
Great sale of **Meridian Hill** lots to commence at R M Hall's Real Estate Exchange, 71 Louisiana ave, Wed morning, Oct 23, 1867. An ofc will also be opened on the Grounds during the continuance of sales, from 9 A M to 5 P M. Carriage on hand to take persons to the Grounds. 120 acres subdivided into 500 lots, offered on five years time, one-fifth cash. Prices low, fine streets, see our plat! This high & splendid land, long the favored spot for the President's House. Perfect Title. Before five years it will double in value.

On Thu Messrs Green & Williams sold at auction the property known to most of our citizens as **Columbia Gardens**, at the corner of 12th & Ohio ave. The purchaser was W S Huntington, for the sum of $10,050.

Died: on Oct 18, in Gtwn, D C, after a lingering illness, Philip Harry, civil engineer, a native of Bodmin, Cornwall, England, but for the last 30 years a resident of the U S. His funeral will take place from his late residence, 84 Prospect st, Gtwn, D C, on Oct 20 at 3 o'clock.

Died: on Oct 18, Eva Frances, daughter of Geo E & Eveline S Baker. Her funeral will take place on Sunday at 3 P M, at 371 13th st, above L.

Thos Dowling, auct, sold at public auction, on Thursday, the Union Soap & Candle Works on the new cut road, with a lot of 210 feet front by 110 feet deep, together with the machinery & stock therein, to Richd Petit, for $3,400.

St Louis, Oct 18. Wm Murphy, who had been confined in the Missouri penitentiary for the last 2 years, having been sentenced by a military commission for boat burning on the Mississippi river during the war, was brought before the U S Circuit Court on Wed, & the case argued on an application for discharge. Judge Miller decided the case today, discharging the prisoner, on the ground of the unconstitutionality of the tribunal by which Murphy was tried & sentenced.

For sale or rent: 310 acres of choice lands, located in Maury Co, 4 miles south of Columbia, on Bigbyville pike, belonging to Miss Nacissa P Saunders, in the State of Tenn. There are several comfortable houses on the place. Apply to Anderson, Johnson & Smith, Agents, Nashville, Tenn.

Boston, Mass, Oct 18. Mrs Caroline Ware, house-keeper in a family residing on Boyleston st, was last evening burned to death, & a German girl named *Watts, employed in the same house, was also fearfully burned, & it is feared her injuries will prove fatal. The catastrophe occurred from the ignition of a can of benzine with which the two women were cleaning furniture. [Oct 23rd newspaper: Boston Post of Oct 19: yesterday, in the residence of Mr Wm Munroe, 106 Boyleston st, while Mr Munroe & his family were away for a few days, his house-keeper, Mrs Caroline Ware & a German domestic named Miss Waltz, were fatally burned in a fire caused by the ignition of a can of benzine. Mrs Ware was dead when found; Miss *Waltz died that night. *German girl's name-2 spellings: Watts/Waltz.]

House for sale: residence o Maj Chas Dodge, on Montgomery st, Gtwn Heights. The House is brick, & contains all the modern conveniences; now occupied by Hon O Browning, Sec of Interior. Terms easy. –Robt F Dodge, Geo Fred McLellan, Wm B Reed. -Dodge, McLellan & Co, 448 15th st, over Metropolitan Nat'l Bank.

MON OCT 21, 1867
Orphans Court-Judge Purcell, Oct 19, 1867. 1-An inventory of appraisers of the personal estate of the late Jas L Edwards, amounting to $43,735, was reported, sworn to, & filed. 2-The first & final accounts of the excs of the late will of the late Cornelia Wittemore, the guardian to Mary Wittemore; & the guardian to Eleanore Ailer, daughter of the late Geo Ailer, were filed & approved. 3-A copy of the first accounts of John A Smith, adm of the will annexed of the late Francis S Key, was filed & recorded in lieu of the original papers lost or mislaid. 4-The will of the late Wm Thumlert was filed, & partially proven. He leaves his estate to his widow, whom he nominates as his executor. 5-Letters of admiistration on the estateof the late W M Stuart was issued to Jas E Stuart; bond $1,000. 6-Letters testamentary were issued to Jabez P Colby, on the estate of the late Stoddard P Colby; bond $15,000.

$200,000 was stolen from the house of Gen Clinton Fiske, at St Louis, on Friday.

Mrd: on Oct 16, at Abingdon, Va, by Rev Mr Wharton, of the Episcopal Church, at the residence of the bride's mother, Wm M Taliaferro, of the Abingdon bar, to Miss Sue H Michel, youngest daughter of the late Harvey Michel, of Wash City.

The Wash Schuetzen Verein were out in large numbers yesterday headed by Weber's brass band, attending the funeral of their late member Mr Bacher. The funeral cortege moved to **Prospect Hill Cemetery**, where the body was interred.

Boiler explosion in N Y, on Friday, at the pier of the Inman line of steamers, No 45 North river. Christopher Gerry, engineer, killed; Owen Kelly, fireman on steamer **City of Baltimore**, killed; Wm Keer, blacksmith, scalded; Thos Loftus, laborer, dangerously injured internally; Thos Kane, blacksmith, severely injured; Alex'r Deyburgh, storage inspector, slightly injured. Missing: Nicholas Gerry, assist engineer, & son of Christopher Gerry, was blacking his boots at the rear of the boiler when the explosion took place & has not been seen since. The cause of the explosion is supposed to be the sudden ejection of cold water upon the over-heated surface of the boiler.

Chas Dickens sails for this country on next Satruday.

The undersigned, as agents of the owners, will offer at public sale, at the farm of the late Mr Jas Waring, known as **Heart's Delight**, near Suitsville in PG Co, Md, on Oct 30th, 25 valuable work horses; 7 yoke of oxen & 3 steers; 3 bulls, one a fine young Devon; 12 fine milch cows & 2 heifers; about 80 sheep, 50 pen hogs, & 30 shoats; extensive farming utensils & wagons & carts, etc. –Richd W W Bowie, Jas Mackubin

Chancery sale of desirable bldg lots on M st north, near 14th st, by decree of the Supreme Court of D C, cause No 495, docket 7: *Barrand et al vs Ransone et al: public auction on Nov 30, on the premises, lot 14 in square 214, in Wash City, D C, fronting 67 feet on M st north, between Vt ave & 15th st west, running back 145 feet, to be sub-divided into 3 bldg lots, 22 feet 4 inches front each. –W Y Fendall, trustee -J T Coldwell & Co, aucts
+
Extensive sale of valuable property, belonging to the estate of the late Gen Lawson, by decree of the Supreme Court of D C, in chancery cause No 495, docket 7: *Barnard et al vs Ransone et al: public auction on the premises: lots 20 thru 28 in square 169; lot 21 has a brick stable & coach house upon it; lot 27 is improved by a large brick double house, with back bldgs. All the above are now under rent to the Gov't, & used as part of the Quartermaster General's Dept; but possession has been promised not later than Jan 1, 1869. –W Y Fendall, trustee -J T Coldwell & Co, aucts [*Note: Both records are chancery No 495, docket 7; the name Barrand is on the first record & the name Barnard is on the second record.]

On Sat Detective McDevitt & ofcrs Roth & Hill arrested John Garner, Michl J McCormick, & Edw Oston, on the charge of setting fire to the hay shed of Mr Bligh. They were locked up to await a hearing of their case.

Earl Russell is seriously ill in Ireland. His Lordship has had a fit & had to be carried home, &, though better, remains in a precarious condition.

A German woman named Schilling, aged 60 years, was run over on Friday by a train of cars on the Union railroad, passing through Troy, N Y, & died within a few moments.

Memphis, Oct 20. Rev Chas A Davis, of the Cumberland Presbyterian Church, died this afternoon of yellow fever.

For sale: the late residence of Mr R S Cox on Gtwn Heights; the grounds contain 5 acres, commanding a splendid view of the cities & river. Will be sold on accommodating terms. –R W Downman, No 2 Intelligencer Bldg

TUE OCT 22, 1867
Ads. 1-Mrs M J Fowle, Paris milliner, 324 Pa ave. 2-W G Metzerott & Co call attention to the superiority of the Steinway pianos.

M de Rothschild has refused to lend to the King of Bavaria the sum of four millions of florins, which the latter was desirous of borrowing on his civil list, for the construction of an opera house & a new street.

Lynchburg News: Mr Jas T Williams, of this city, has sold his interest [7-16] in the Hot Springs, in Bath Co, to Mr Saml C Tardy, of Richmond, for $56,000 cash. This is one of the largest, [if not the largest,] sale of real estate made in Va since the close of the war.

Supreme Court of D C commenced its regular fall term yesterday; on the court being opened, Mr Kennedy remarked that the court having several terms since made a rule admitting the graduates of Columbian College Law School without the usual examination, he would move the admission of the graduates of last term, & they were thereupon admitted. The graduates are:

H _ Barry	E M Gibson	Henry R Rolard
H D Beam	Edwin M Hall	Chas N Richards
C H Buxton	H C Harmon	Chas Potter
Chas L Catlin	G B Holden	Thos S Samon
Fred Chase	W A Hunt	Winfield S Strawn
A P Childs	R G Kirkpatrick	Albert N Seip
H V Cole	J G Kimball	W _ Spencer
C Eaton Crucy	Yong Lanktree	Frank A Spencer
A W Clinton	H K Leaver	Wm F Scott
J W Corey	Gayler T Mason	A K Tingle
T E Davis	C G McLeran	M Tromble
W H Day	J B McCullis	W _ Todd
W Sumner Dodge	M S McCullogh	E Tompkins
W H Doolittle	J M Mason	J B Warfield
Benj Eglin	J F Myers	Woodbury Wheeler
Edgar T Ensign	N B Mulliker	W L Wilson
H R French	S A Moulthrop	J N Whitney
E E Forsyth	J L Murphy	Jos Woodruff
G F Graham	J McClary Perkins	

A cmte will examine the qualifications of Mr Judson T Bull as a member of the bar.

Died: on Oct 20, Mrs Julia A Brenner, wife of Peter Brenner, in her 70th year. Her funeral will take place from the Church of the Immaculate Conception at 11 o'clock this morning.

It is announced that Miss Clara Louise Kellogg has been engaged in Lirique, in Paris, for the winter.

Henry C Lane, of Wash City, was united in marriage to Mrs C A Lamb, last evening, at the Calvary Baptist Church. The nuptial ceremonies were performed by the pastor of the church, Rev Dr Howlett, in a pleasant manner. There was a large & radiant throng to witness the interesting scene.

Rosewood parlor furniture, piano-forte, household & kitchen furniture at auction on Oct 29, at the residence of Gen Tompkins, 332 K st, between 13th & 14th sts. -Cooper & Latimer, aucts

Supreme Court of D C, 711 Equity. McDuel vs McDuel. The above cause is referred to me to state the account of the trustee, on Oct 26, 1867.
–Walter S Cox, auditor

WED OCT 23, 1867

Orphans Court-Judge Purcell, Oct 22, 1867. 1-The will of the late Philip Harry, of Gtwn, was filed for probate. He bequeathed to his daughter Kate, wife of A H Clements, his gold snuff-box, mounted with 112 diamonds, & various other articles of jewelry, silverware, family portraits, piano, etc; to his son Charles, his gold watch, box of mathematical drawing instruments, & shot gun; to his niece, Maria Harry, his Malachite mantel clock; to Dr R K Stone, his sketch of a scene at **Burnt Mills**; also, any other couple of sketches of scenery he may select; to his brother, John Deacon Harry, of Woolwich, England, his pistols. The balance of his property, real & personal, he bequeaths to his children, Kate, Jas Philip Harry, & Chas Harry, & his niece, Maria Harry. He nominates W H Dougal, to whom he bequeaths his book of old & rare etchings & engravings. 2-The will of Alfred P Hewett was also filed for probate. He bequeaths to Mrs Barbara Wall all his real estate on Union st, between L & M, during her life, & after her death it shall be sold to pay a note held by his brother, & surplus paid over to his son, Chas A Hunt. He nominates Mrs Wall as excx. 3-The will of the late Wm Thumlert was fully proven. 4-Sarah Johnson was appointed guardian to the orphans of John Williams, deceased; bond $500. 5-The first accounts of Adelaide J Brown, as guardian to the orphans of W V H Brown; third & supplmental account of R G Lumkin, exc of Thos Lumkin; first & final of Chas Rousseau, adm of Ruppert; of S E Arnold, adm of Geo Poole; of Catherine Morgan, admx of Bernard Morgan; & second account of Jesse B Wilson, guardian to the orphans of Saml Conner, were approved & passed. 6-The will of the late Sallie L Manning was filed & partially proven. After providing for the payment of her just debts, etc, she bequeaths to her sister, Catharine A Roach, all her household furniture, as also the house 453 13th st, the latter subject to legacies of $1,400 each to her three sisters & brother, the same amount to Wm N Roach, in trust for her nephew, W M Greenwell, & in case of his death to go to the children of her deceased sister, Fanny Colt. To W N Roach is bequeathed lots 1, 2, 17, & 18, in Square 280, corner of 12th & N sts, in trust for the benefit of her brother & sisters & their children, with the right to sell the same if he thinks best, when he may retain $1,000 & divide the balance. Lot 3, square 552, she bequeaths to her nephew, Jos E, & niece, Sallie B Roach.

John E Risley, who has just been appointed Deputy Com'r of Internal Revenue, is a lawyer of N Y C, & of the firm of Coe & Risley. He resided in Indiana until 1863, when he removed to N Y, where he has since been engaged in his profession.

Jacob Bogan, of the firm of Bogan & Wylie, received the following despatch on Monday, announcing the sad news of his brother's death. Mount Vernon, Ill, Oct 21. Jos Bogan is dead; killed accidentally while hunting; will be buried tomorrow. –G H Varnell The deceased was but 23 years of age, unmarried. He is the next youngest son of Mr Benj L Bogan, formerly of Wash City, but now residing in Md, & has of late years about equally divided his time between his father's residence & his brother-in-law's. Last year he spent with his father, & left early last spring for Illinois, where, as above stated, he was killed. [Oct 26 newspaper: Suspicion that Jos Bogan was murdered; examination of his body revealed a stab in the side from a large knife, the wound having been inflicted by a left-handed person.]

Yesterday, Thos Dowling, auct, sold part of lot 72, fronting 26 feet on Fred'k st, between 1st & 2nd sts, running back 96 feet, to Wm Daw, for $17 per front foot.

Balt American, Tues. Another shooting affair in Balt: Elisha Brady, a well known ward politician, was shot & killed by John Bowers, stepson of John Waltenmeyer, 518 Penn ave, over a hickory pole which had been erected by the Democrats of the 20th Ward. Bowers had been struck with a billy by a young man named Horatio Tuttle, whereupon he fired his pistol, killing Brady almost instantly. The body of Brady was taken charge by his friends, & removed to the residence of his mother, 153 Hoffman st. He was about 27 years of age, & leaves a widow, who resides on Pierce st.

Paris, Oct 8, 1867. M Achille Fould died suddenly on Sat of apoplexy, at his villa at Tarbes. This is a real loss, both to the emperor & the country.

New Orleans, Oct 22-Ofc of the Picayune. Telegraphic despatch from San Antonio, Texas: Geo Wilkins Kendall, senior associate, died at his residence, Post Oak Springs, near Boerne, yesterday, caused by congestive chills. Mr Kendall was about 60 years of age; he leaves a wife & 4 children. –A M Holbrook [Oct 26th newspaper: Geo Wilkins Kendall was born in Amherst, now Mount Vernon, N H, about 1810; he left this city in 1835 & went to New Orleans, where he commenced the publication of the Picayune, in partnership with L A Resancon. Tall, robust, swarthy, was "George:" his hair the color of a raven's wing; his eyes large, blank, & piercing as an eagle."]

Mrd: on Oct 22, at the parsonage of the Foundry Church, by Rev Peyton Brown, Mr Norval W King to Emuella F, daughter of Wm L Jones, both of Wash City. [Dayton, Ohio papers please copy.]

Mrd: on Oct 22, at the Church of the Ascension, by Rev Dr Pinckney, Thos H Upperman, of Leavenworth, Kansas, to Rachel, eldest daughter of J B Dodson, of Wash City.

Died: on Oct 21, Mrs Ellen Miller, in her 73rd year. Her funeral will take place from her late residence, 11th st east, between E & G sts south, on Oct 23 at 2 P M.

Died: on Oct 22, at the residence of R A Janvier, Mary Riddell, formerly of New Castle, Delaware.

Died: on Sep 27, 1867, at New Orleans, of yellow fever, E C Collier, formerly of Wash, D C. Poem followed by L A Anderman, Wash, Oct, 1867. A line from the poem: Fell far from home & youthful friends, Where rolls the Mississippi's tide, etc

Petersburg Express states that on Tuesday last Miss Mary Davis, residing in that place, aged about 25 years, died from excessive corpulency. She had been confined to her bed for nearly 9 months, utterly helpless, & suffered much during the summer weather. Her appetite was good to the last, & she died of an excessive accumulation of flesh.

Supreme Court of D C, Equity 573. Geo W Utermehle vs Adolph F Lippard et al. Above cause is referred to me to ascertain the amount of the indebtedness of the dfndnt Lippard, under the deed of trust, if any, & also on cmplnt's judgment, up to this date. Meeting at my ofc on Oct 28. –Walter S Cox, auditor

Orphans Court of Wash Co, D C, Oct 22, 1867. In the case of Henrietta W Andrews, admx of Christopher Andrews, deceased, the administratrix & Court have appointed Nov 30th next, for the final settlement of the personal estate of the said deceased, of the assets in hand. -Jas R O'Beirne, Reg/o wills

THU OCT 24, 1867
Maj Gen Geo H Steuart died in this city yesterday, in his 77th year. Previous to the late war, he for some 20 years commanded the First Light Division of Md Militia, & in his younger days represented the city in the State Legislature. He was also at one time a member of the City Council. During the late war with Great Britain the deceased was one of the brave men who defended the city of Balt when attacked by Gen Ross. –Balt Sun

Mr Henry W Slicer, jr, a member of the firm of Cooper & Slicer, ship-builders, of Balt, died on Sunday.

On Tues the spoke & carriage bent stuff manufactory of W M Gorris & Co, & the machine tool manufactory of A M Badger & Co, on Hill st, Buffalo, N Y, were destroyed by fire.

The sale of the lots on **Meridian Hill** yesterday was a wonderful success, the amount of sales reaching near $24,000. The following lots were sold: lots 1 & 2 in block 6, on Crescent st, to J F Callan, at 12 cents per square foot; lots 29 & 31 in block 6 on Meridian ave, to M P Callan, at 12 cents per square foot; lots 3 & 4 in block 8, on Prospect & Boundary sts, to Moses Kelley, at 16 cents per square foot; lot 5 in block 3, fronting on Prospect & Boundary sts, to J W Nairn, at 16 cents per square foot; lots 3 & 4 in block 6, on Crescent st, to Jos F Brown, at 14 cents per square foot; lot 9 in block 3, on Prospect & Boundary sts, to Geo H Plant, at 16 cents per square foot; lots 1, 2, & 3 in block 7, on Prospect st, to Col D L Eaton, at 17 cents per square foot; lot 4 in block 1, on Columbia ave, to C H Bliss, at 17 cents per square foot; lot 11 in block 6, corner of Central ave & Crescent sts, to A G Hall, at 13 cents per square foot; lots 1, 2, & 3 in block 5, fronting on Crescent st, to Col W L Jackson, at 16 cents per square foot; lot 6 in block 18, on Columbia st, to W A Steidham, at 11 cents per square foot; lot 7 in block 18, fronting on Columbia st, to J E Darnell, at 11 cents per square foot; lot 4 in block 5, fronting on Crescent & Prospect sts, to R T Bryan, at 16 cents per square foot; lot 1 in block 3, fronting on Boundary st, to Jas W Joyce, at 18 cents per square foot. [Oct 25th newspaper: sales of **Meridian Hill** lots yesterday: lot 5 in block 1, to C B Pearson, 12 cents per square foot; lot 6 in block 1, to G W Buchee, at 12 cents per square foot; lot 7 in block 1, to Dr H B Noble, at 12 cents per foot; lots 1, 2, 3, 2, & 27, in block 4, to C S Bunday, at 10 cents per foot; lot 10 in block 5, to Noah L Jeffries, Register of the Treasury, at 16 cents per square foot; lots 11 & 12 in block 5, to Maj G M Head, at 16 cents per foot; lot 5 in block 18, to Wm F Stidham, at 11 cents per foot; lots 4 & 5 in block 7, to J T Stevens, at 17 cents per square foot.]

Yesterday, as Mr Willett was about to start with his son, Dr John E Willett, to take an airing in his buggy, an accident occurred at Va ave, between 3rd & 4½ sts, when Mr Willett, in the act of getting into his buggy, his foot slipped, & at the same time his horse started, & one of his legs became entangled in the wheels. His son, the doctor, being an embecile in mind, & the horse unmanageable, he lost all control over him, & one leg became terribly lacerated, so that from the loss of blood & consequence exhaustion, he died in about half an hour after the injury. The deceased was a native of Montg Co, Md, about 60 years of age, & greatly esteemed by those who knew him. His son, Dr Willett, was a few years ago, one of the most popular & promising of the rising physicians of Wash City, but, from some inscrutable dispensation, became suddenly insane, & for some time was an inmate of the Insane Asylum of the District. His fond & devoted parent was in the act of giving him an airing, with the view of improving his health, when this melancholy accident deprived him of life. Dr Jas R Reilly was prompt in attendance, but the nature of Mr Willett's injuries was such as to defy the efforts of medical skill.

Died: on Oct 22, Albert Pinckney, infant son of Robt M & Rebecca Johnson, aged 3 months.

Died: on Oct 2, at his residence, Parish of St Landry, La, Mr Benedick Simms, a native of Md, aged 47 years.

Mobile, Oct 23. Col Chas Headley, brother of Gen Headley, U S marshal for Alabama, died this morning of yellow fever.

Mr Andrew Rock, draw-keeper at the northern end of the Long Bridge, met with a serious accident on Tues. He was ascending from a lower to an upper abutment of the bridge, when he lost his hold, & in falling struck his chin against a plank. He was insensible for some time, & yesterday his condition was considered critical. [Oct 26th newspaper: Wm J Rock died of his injuries yesterday at his residence on 6th st. He leaves behind an interesting family, a wife & 5 children, to mourn his loss. His funeral will take place under the auspices of the Masonic fraternity, of which he was a member.]

Burlington, Vt, Oct 23. Chas Walcott, jr, of Burlington, fell from the cars on the Vt Central railroad yesterday, & was killed.

Phil, Oct 23. Wm Furman, alias Balt Billy, died tonight from the effects of a stab inflicted by Wm Hagan last night, during a fracas growing out of a dispute about a prize fight. Hagan is in custody.

FRI OCT 25, 1867
Pittsburg, Pa, Oct 24. Thos G Thomas committed suicide yesterday by taking arsenic, while laboring under a temporary fit of insanity.

Board of Police-Thu. Following were re-appointed additional privates for 90 days:

F J Meyer	Wm H Muldorn	Frank Porter
Edw O'Connor	Wm Reed	Edw Gunson
Geo W Wise	Wm J Smith	Wm Wilson
Chas F Segourney	Saml W Sloan	

David L Watson, to duty at the U S Treasury Extension.
F L Payne to do duty on Pa ave, between 9th & 11th sts.
Pvt J W Davis was ordered to be reprimanded for conduct unbecoming an ofcr.
Pvt Jas O Wallingsford was fined $10 for gross neglect of duty.
Pvt S A Bailey was dismissed the force for intoxication & conduct unbecoming an ofcr.
The application of Jas Steel, of Gtwn, for tavern license was approved, & the following applications for the same privilege were rejected: John Mooney, Mich Reynolds, & John Moran, all of Gtwn.

Mrd: on Oct 24, at St Aloysius Church, by Rev Fr Lynch, S J, J Hartley Soule to Miss Helen M Bayliss, daughter of Buckner Bayliss, of Wash City.

Mrd: on Oct 23, at the residence of the bride's father in Cumberland, Md, Mr J S Craigen, of Wash City, to Miss Annie M Minkie, of Cumberland.

Mrd: on Oct 23, by Rev Dr McCabe, C D Liebermann, of Wash, D C, to Miss J A Ferrall, of PG Co, Md.

Mrd: on the 15th ult, at Salem, Ohio, in the Methodist Episcopal Church, H N Adams to Miss America Cornwell, of that place. The bride was for some time a clerk in the treasury Dept in Wash City, in which vocation as in the social walks, her fine qualities of head & heart won her troops of friends, who will read this announcement with all good invocations upon the event.

Died: on Oct 16, in La Fayette, Indiana, Henry M Nourse, son of the late Col M Nourse, in the 43rd year of his age.

On Tuesday last the popular & efficient chief clerk of the Appointment Bureau of the Treasury Dept, C Eaton Creecy, was married to Miss Sallie Fenwick, of Wash City. The attendants were Lt E W Creecy, U S Army, Mr Fenwick, of Wash; Mr Wm Lackey, of Va, & Miss Brooks, of Wash Co, Md. The ceremony was performed by Rev Mr Lynch, in the presence of a numerous company of distinguished guests, including the Sec & Assist Sec of the Treasury & nearly all bureau ofcrs of the Dept.

SAT OCT 26, 1867
The President has yet to sign the pardon of Gen Marmaduke, but he has been recommended for pardon by the Atty General.

The impreachment testimony regarding Pres Johnson is being printed at the Govn't Printing Ofc, at the rate of 10 or 12 pages a day.

Died: on Oct 16, in Portsmouth, Va, Eliz, wife of Solomon Wilkins, aged 56 years, & in the same place on Oct 22nd, Solomon Wilkins, aged 61 years, the parents of Benj F Wilkins, of Wash City.

Cmdor Vanderbilt's income is $4,000 a day.

For sale: two valuable farms in PG Co, Md: the undersigned, as attys for the owners, will offer at public sale, on Nov 9, ***Paint Branch Switch Farm*** & ***Waverly***, the estate of the late Alex'r Keech. ***Paint Branch Switch Farm*** contains 205 acres, adjoining the Agricultural College of Md; with a nearly new house, containing 7 rooms & a kitchen, a large barn, & corn-house. ***Waverly Farm*** contains about 250 acres, about 3/4^{ths} mile of the above mentioned place, with a new handsome residence; numerous out bldgs, about a mile from ***Scragg's Station*** & ***College Station.*** Mill & schoolhouse adjoin the place. Title perfect. Apply to Dr Thos A R Keech, Bladensburg, who will show the property, or to C S Keech, Atty at Law, Upper Marlboro, Md. –Wm S Keech, Atty at Law, Towsontown, Md, Attys for the owners.

The trial of John H Surratt, indicted for the murder of the late Pres Lincoln, was called in June last, & the Dist Atty challenged the array of the panel of criminal jurors, the Court decided that the law had not been carried into effect, & they were discharged. In compliance with the act of Congress providing for the selection of jurors, etc, F A Boswell, City Register; N Callan, Clerk of the Levy Court, & Wm Laird, Clerk of Gtwn, met at the ofc of R J Meigs, Clerk of the Supreme Court of the District, on Thursday, & drew from the jury-box the following persons to serve as jurors at the ensuing term of the Circuit Court, to commence on the first Tuesday in Nov. [County refers to Washington County.]

J C Lewis, county
Fred'k Stomberger, 8th Ward
Patrick NcNulty, 4th Ward
Richd Cruit, jr, Gtwn
Benj F Moxley, sr, Gtwn
Jos S Tucker, 6th Ward
John F McElderry, Gtwn
Wm Chase, 1st Ward
E M Chapin, 4th Ward
David Jackson, Gtwn
Jacob G Smoot, Gtwn
Jas Piling county

Jas J Barrett, Gtwn
W B Lacey, county
Wm Linkins, 1st ward
Z Williams, county
Ambrose Bradley, 7th Ward
Geo Hutchinson, 6th Ward
John Douglas, county
Thos Proby, Gtwn
Wm Wetzel, county
Chas H Anderson, 4th Ward
Edw Browning, 6th Ward
Nelson Isdell, 6th Ward

Chancery sale of valuable lot in Gtwn, D C; by decrees of the Supreme Court of D C, dated Aug 3 & Sep 5, 1867, in the cause of John Bateman & others vs Jane E Bateman & others, public auction, on the premises, on Nov 16 next, subdivision of lot 30, of old Gtwn, at the n e corner of Prospect & Fred'k sts, with the 2 story brick dwlg house thereon, now in the occupancy of Mrs Gen Wheeler. –R R Crawford, C Ingle, trustees -Thos Dowling, auct

MON OCT 28, 1867
On Friday the remains of a laboring man, Richd Alvord, were brought to his home, on Va ave, between 2nd & 3rd sts, & Mrs Alvord reported to Lt Gessford that her husband had been murdered. Mr Alvord was in the employ of the Western Md railroad near Union Bridge, & on Wed last he was paid off, & with 2 others left his boarding-house that night. On Thu his body was found in the woods with the head crushed in. The Md authorities will take measures to arrest the perpetrators.

Orphans Court-Judge Purcell, Oct 26, 1867. 1-Wm H Dougall gave bonds in the sum of $10,000, & was appointed executor of the personal estate of Philip Harry, late of Wash Co. He gave bonds in the sum of $40,000, & was appointed guardian of the orphans of the late Philip Harry. In the will of Philip Harry, which was proven & admitted, there was a bequest to his daughter, Mrs Alex'r Clements, of a gold snuff-box, mounted with 112 diamonds. 2-The will of the late Sallie L Manning was fully proven & admitted to record.

Maj J C Elston, father-in-law of Senator Lane & Gen Low Wallace, died in Crawfordsville, Indiana, on Wed. He was an early settler there, having taken up his residence in Indiana before the admission of that State to the Union.

Died: on Oct 27, Dr Horace P Middleton, eldest son of D W Middleton, Clerk of the Supreme Court of the U S. [Oct 29th newspaper: Dr Horace P Middleton has been sick for some time past, & his death was not unexpected. He was a gentleman of much promise, & his decease will be deeply regretted by his many friends in Wash City. His funeral will take place this afternoon, at 2½ o'clock P M, from the residence of his father, D W Middleton, 568 N J ave, Captiol Hill.]

Died: on Oct 23, at Clemmont, Md, the residence of her sister, after a long & painful illness, Mrs Rebecca Freeman, relict of the late Ezeckiel Freeman, of Balt.

Obit-Gone Home: Harry Hahn Wolf, 2nd child & eldest son of Simon & Caroline Wolf, born in new Phil, Ohio, Oct 11, 1861; died Oct 26, 1867.

Cincinnati, Oct 27. The passenger train on the Little Miami railroad coming to this city met with a serious accident last night at Xenia, within 150 yards of the depot. The freight train had just arrived, & the switch was left open, & the passenger train ran into the caboose of the freight train. One man in the passenger car, Geo Boss, of Xenia, was disabled & caught in the wreck, where he burned to death. His cries were heard in the flames, but rescue was impossible. John R Hampton, passenger, had a leg broken.

Albany, Oct 26. Wolcott J Humphrey, Senator from the 13th Dist, was arrested by police ofcr Kelley, of this city, at Warsaw, Wyoming Co, & brought before Police Justice Cole today, upon a warrant charging him with bribery & corruption in ofc, issued upon an affidavit made by Hugh B Willson. The warrant charges that he did feloniously accept $500 to influence his action on a bill then pending before the Railroad Cmte of the Senate in relation to the Manhatan Railway Co, to construct certain tunnels & railways in N Y C.

Household & kitchen furniture at auction on Oct 30, at the residence of Mrs Morley, 337 Pa ave, south side, between 6th & 7th sts. -Cooper & Latimer, aucts

Orphans Court of Wash Co, D C. Letters of administration on the personal estate of Wm J Toomy, late of Wash City, D C, deceased. –Jas W White, adm

Orphans Court of Wash Co, D C. Letters testamentary on the personal estate of Phillip Harry, late of Wash Co, D C, deceased. –Wm H Dougal, exc

TUE OCT 29, 1865
Hon John H Hubbard, of Conn, has purchased the house that was to have been occupied by Senator Sumner this winter.

Assaults: 1-Robt Scott, an inmate of the jail, was charged with assaulting, with intent to kill, Alex'r Adams, a fellow prisoner. Both of the parties are colored. 2-Alfred M Seipe, arrested for an assault with intent to kill Dr W G McCreary, was held for a hearing.

Died: on Oct 28, Virginia, 3rd daughter of Ann M, & the late John L Anderson. Her funeral will be from the residence of her mother, 378 13th st, between N Y ave & I sts, on Oct 30, at 2 o'clock P M.

Lt Newton Whitten, V R C, for the last two years on duty in the Freedman's Bureau in this city, has been assigned to Burkesville, Nottaway Co, Va, as sub-assist commissioner.

Wanted: two Professors at Washington College, Kent Co, Md. –P Wroth, Pres of the Board of Visitors of Washington College.

Dept of the Interior, U S Patent Ofc, Wash, Oct 24, 1867. Ptn of Aaron Palmer, of Brockport, N Y, & Stephen G Williams, of Janesville, Wisc, praying for the extension of a patent granted to them Jan 24, 1851, for an improvement in Grain Harvesters, for seven years from the expiration of said patent, which takes place on Jan 24, 1868. -T C Theaker, Com'r of Patents

Saco, Me, Oct 28. O C Adams, mail agent between Boston & Portland, was shot at last night in one of our principal streets by a ruffian, who then attacked him with the butt end of the pistol. The would be murderer is unknown.

Mrs Helen Smith, who lives in Oxford Place, Boston, was seized by a man while walking in Harrison ave, on Sunday night, who blindfolded her & then cut her throat, inflicting a probably fatal wound. The woman thinks it was her husband, whom she had not been living with for some time.

Charleston Courier, Oct 22. We learn that there is a prospect of the early release of Lt J C Braine, of the late Confederate navy, who has been, since the close of the war, & is now, a prisoner at **Fort Delaware**. He had never had a trial, & it is understood that he will be released upon parole, & when his case is called a ***nol pros*** will be moved by the Dist Atty of the district in which he may be indicted. All that is necessary now to effect his restoration to liberty is the amount which will be required to pay the expenses of a process to satisfy the forms of the law.

A correspondent at **Fort Dodge,** Kansas, gives details of the killing by Indians of John H Felch & Jas Young. These men were working at a wood camp, & having killed a buffalo near by, started with a team to secure the meat. When but a short distance from camp twenty Indians swept down upon them, & after a short fight, killed & scalped both. The Indians also stole fifty mules, & drove them across the Arkansas river.

Lafayette Hotel, on the European Plan, 595 Broadway, opposite Metropolitan Hotel, N Y. -Chas F Prescott -Henry S Marsh-formerly of Metropolitan Hotel. [Ad]

WED OCT 30, 1867
Sales of real estate belonging to Hon John Wentworth were made in Chicago last week to the amount of $400,000.

Meridian Hill sales: lot 7 in block 5, on Prospect & Crescent sts, to E T Peters, managing editor Chronicle, at 16 cents per square foot; lot 9 in block 5, on same sts, to Dr Wm A Brown, at 16 cents per square foot; lot 14 in block 18, on Columbia ave, to Geo A Dummer, at 14 cents per foot; lots 4 & 5 in block 8, on Morris st, to T N Wotz, superintendent Smithsonian Institute, at 11 cents per square foot; lot 13 in block 7, on Columbia ave, to L W Kimball, at 14 cents per square foot; lot 19 in block 8, on same ave, to B M'Lellan, at 10 cents per square foot; lots 5 & 6 in block 4, to F J Newland, at 10 cents per square foot; lot 5 & part of lot 6 in block 3, to Col W L Wall, at 16 cents per foot; the whole of block 21, to A L Sturtevant, Solicitor of Treasury Ofc, at 7 cents per square foot.

Annapolis Gaz. On Sat last the steam launch **Albemarle**, belonging to Admiral David D Porter, Superintendent of the U S Naval Academy, exploded in the Severn river, opposite the academy, & about 20 yards from the monitor **Tonawanda**. The launch was being put to an experimental test by Chief Engineer Hoyt, of the academy, who was a gentleman of superior qualifications & of great scientific research. The entire crew consisted of Chief Engineer Hoyt, Wm Clark, engineer, John Shay, coxswain; a colored man, fireman, & 2 sailor boys. Engineers Hoyt & Clark were swimming about, but before the sailors got near enough to them they both sank to rise no more. Their bodies were afterwards caught. Mr Shay & the colored man were both found in the launch. The colored man was so badly scalded it was hard to tell whether he was white or black. Admiral Porter was about stepping on board, but not being well, concluded not to go. He was standing on the wharf of the Academy, looking at the vessel, when the explosion occurred.

Appointments by the Postmaster General: E E Kelly was yesterday appointed chief clerk, & Wm J Lee assist, on the postal car between Wash City & Weldon.

Died: on Oct 15, near New Orleans, La, of the yellow fever, Gen Danl J Kelley, of the late volunteer service. R I V.

Supreme Court yesterday: 1-W E Carr appeared in court on an attachment of contempt issued on the petition of Mrs Eliz Carr. The petition was read, & charges the said W E Carr with destroying a certain letter which was of mportance in connection with a suit which Mrs Carr had entered for a divorce. The statement of Mr Ashford, the examiner in the divorce case, was read, which corroborated the statement made in the petition. Hearing is set for today.

New Orleans, Oct 29. There were 11 deaths from yellow fever today; among them Lt Geo Lee, who has been acting as assist adjutant general of the 5th District.

For sale: another lot of fine Northern Horses. –J B Olcott & Son, Livery & Sale Stables, 471 & 473 8th st, between D & E sts.

Orphans Court-Judge Purcell. 1-The first & final account of Mary Sioussa, excx of John Sioussa, deceased, was filed & approved. 2-The will of Frances Elvans, deceased, was filed & partially proved. The testator devised her property, personal estate, as follows: To Rachel Virginia Reeder, of Waynesboro, Augusta Co, Va, $500; to Mary Ann King, of the same place, $300; to Geo W Gellespy, of Balt, Md, $50; & to Ella A Thompson, $25. To balance of her property, consisting of real estate, described as lot 25, 26, & 27, in square 236, she orders to be sold & the proceeds to be divided between her 3 sisters, Mary Larlius, Grace Ramsey, & Catharine Reeder, & her niece, Georgianna Elvans. John R Elvans is appointed executor.

Thoroughfare Mills for sale-Dec 5, 1867, by decree of Circuit Court of Prince Wm Co, pronounced at the Oct term, 1867, in suit of Horner et al, vs Chapman, the undersigned commissioners of sale, will offer at Manassas station, that splendid Mill Bldg & Water Power; also the Saw Mill Bldg & Walter Power, known as the ***Throughfrare Mills***, lately the property of John Chapman, deceased. At the same time will be offered for sale 2 tracts of land, about 300 acres each, one adjoining the described Mills, partly in Fauquier & partly in Prince Wm Co, said land being also the property of the late John Chapman, each with a small dwlg house. Apply to John S Chapman, 68 Prince st, Alexandria, Va. –John S Chapman, Rice W Payne, Eppa Hunton, J B Brooke, Com'rs, Prince Wm Co, Va.

Fauquier land for sale, on Nov 25, by decree of the Circuit Court of Fauquier Co, Va, pronounced at its Sept term, 1867, in the consolidated suits of Horner vs Chapman, & Glasscock vs Chapman, the com'rs of sale will offer, at Warrenton, about 400 acres of splendid land, it being a portion of the tract of the late Dr Chapman. The tract has one small dwlg house. Apply to John S Chapman, 68 Prince st, Alexandria, Va. -John S Chapman, John S Mosby, Com'rs, Fauquier Co, Va.

Orphans Court of Wash Co, D C. Letters testamentary on the personal estate of Wm Thumlert, late of Wash Co, D C, deceased. –Esther Thumlert, excx

THU OCT 31, 1867
Died: on Oct 29, Luther A McCord, of disease of the heart, aged 33 years. His funeral will take place today at 3 o'clock P M, from the residence of his brother-in-law, David Pool, 499 Mass ave.

Died: on Oct 9, on board the U S steamer **De Soto**, off Vera Cruz, Mexico, aged 23 years, Arthur Gale Steele, Engineer U S navy.

Fine Chinchilla, Castor, Beaver, & Irish Frieze Overcoats for sale. Odeon Hall, 446 Pa ave. –Philip Wallach

U S Marshal's sale on Nov 18, all Henry C Steers' right, title, claim, & interest in & to lots 46 & 47 in square 545, in Wash, D C, with all & singular improvements; will be sold to satisfy Judicial No 11, May Term, 1861, in favor of Watts & Lavender. –Wm Shelden, late U S Marshal, D C

Somerville, N J, Oct 30. In the case of Jacob Von Arsdale, indicted for the murder of Jasper B Baird, on Jun 29 last, the jury, after an absence of 3 hours, rendered a verdict of guilty in the first degree.

FRI NOV 1, 1867
Died: on Oct 29, in Lynchburg, Va, Rev T O Sears, late pastor of the Catholic Church at that place. [Nov 2nd newspaper: Rev Fr Sears died after a lingering illness of nearly 4 months; for 8 years, up to about 18 months since, he was the pastor of the Catholic Church in this city; he was a native, we believe, of Wash City. He had not attained his 40th year. His funeral will take place from the Catholic Church, at 1 o'clock this afternoon, & the remains will be taken thence to ***Spring Hill Cemetery***, where they will be interred. Among the officiating priests will be Fr McGraw, of Wash City, Fr Heydencamp, of Wytheville; Fr Kane, of Winchester; Fr Ferran, of this city, & others. -Lynchburg Republican, 31st]

Looking-glasses: fine assortment of Parlor & other Mirrors, in gold & walnut frames. Old work regilt. Engaged for the past 26 years in the above business.
–Francis Lamb, 237 Pa ave, near 13th st, Wash.

Army orders. 1st Lt P M Skinner, 18th infty, resigned; 1st Lt L M De Motte, 28th infty, resigned; Brvt Col A G Salisbury, additional paymaster, honorably discharged & mustered out.

Boston, Oct 31. The flags are flying at half-mast on the State House, & other public places in memory of ex-Govn'r Andrew. He was on the eve of leaving for Washington when stricken with death. His funeral will take place tomorrow. [Nov 2nd newspaper: Ex-Govn'r John Albion Andrew, of Mass, died of apoplexy on Oct 30; born in Windham, Me, May 31, 1818, he had reached his 50th year; graduated at Bowdoin College, Me, in 1837. The remains of ex-Govn'r Andrew will be conveyed to Mount Auburn, Dunham, Mass. –Boston Journal] [Nov 4th newspaper: Funeral of ex-Govn'r Andrew: Rev Jas Freeman Clarke, the pastor of the Arlington st Church, intimate friend of the deceased, read from the Scripture; Rev D Garnet pronounced a benediction. The pall bearers were Geo Tyler Bigelow, Chief Justice of the Supreme Court; Otis Norcross, Mayor of Boston; Henry Wilson, U S Senator; Jas M Slocum, Speaker of the House of Reps; ex-Govn'r Levi Lincoln, ex-Govn'r Geo S Emory Washburne, ex-Govn'r Henry J Gardiner, ex-Govn'r N P Banks, ex-Lt Govn'r Joel Hayden, & Rev Thus Hue, Pres of the Howard University.]

Toronto, C W, Oct 31. Chas Ulrich & Adrian Harcq, the escaped counterfeiters from the Brooklyn jail, were committed yesterday for extradition. Ofcrs of the U S secret service will leave with them in charge tonight.

SAT NOV 2, 1867

Meridian Hill: we are informed that the agent of Mrs Gen Gaines is negotiating for the purchase of site for the magnificent mansion she intends erecting in this city.

Col D J Reilly, whose death near New Orleans, of yellow fever, was announced Wed, was a gallant ofcr in the late war, & was badly wounded in the mouth at the battle of Port Republic, Va, & lay sick for a considerable time at the Providence Hospital in Wash City. He was an intelligent, as well as gallant soldier. He was a native of Waterford, Ireland, & about 36 or 37 years of age. He served in the French army; in the Irish brigade, & Italy; & in the beginning of the war, he [with Capt Keogh, Coppinger, O Keefe, & other Irish ofcrs, then in Italy] came to this country at the instance of Archbishop Hughes, & took service in the Union army, where they all displayed much bravery.

Mrd: on Oct 29, at the residence of the bride's mother, Washington, by Rev Dr Pinckney, D D, John H Coale, U S A, to Emilie Carter, daughter of the late Geo H Jones.

Mrd: on Oct 30, at the residence of the bride's father, by Rev Fr Lynch, Henry M Zimmerman to Miss Fannie Simons, all of Wash. No cards.

Died: on Oct 31, after a long & painful illness, Mrs E M Smith, a native of Portsmouth, England, in her 62nd year. Her funeral will be from her son-in-law's, L Vessey, 313 L st north, tomorrow, Sunday, at half past 2 o'clock P M.

Died: on Nov 1, Mary, infant daughter of Hampton B & Mary Denman. Her funeral will take place from the residence of Mrs Geo W Young, 435 6th st, today at 3 o'clock.

Frederick W Alexander, Real Estate Broker & Claim Agent, 493 12th st. [Ad]

Dept of the Interior, U S Patent Ofc, Wash, Oct 26, 1867. Ptn of Geo E Burt, of Harvard, Mass, praying for extension of a patent granted to him Feb 7, 1854, for an improvement in Machines for Cleaning & Assorting Bristles, for seven years from the expiration of said patent, which takes place on Feb 7, 1868.
-T C Theaker, Com'r of Patents

Sale of valuable real estate in Wash City, D C, by deed of trust from Wm B B Cross to the subscriber, dated Apr 9, 1860, recorded in Liber J A S No 192, folios 452 etc; public auction on Dec 3, on the premises, lot 6 in square 218, on I st, east of 15th st west, being improved by a handsome brick dwlg erected in the last 8 or 9 years.
–Robt Ould, trustee -W L Wall & Co, aucts

U S Marshal's sale on Nov 11, in Wash City, a parcel of land in square 455, being parts of lots 11 & 13 in said square, described in a deed of conveyance from E G Emack & wife to Henry Rockaway, recorded in Liber N C Towle, No 5, folios 82, & by said Rockaway leased to Edw Rauschor for the term of 10 years commencing Mar 1, 1864, by deed recorded in Liber N C T, 57, folio 453, which title was by sundry assignments transferred to dfndnt. Seized & levied upon as the property of Jos Bla_tler & wife & will be sold to satisfy execution No 3,069, in favor of Henry Knoll. –D S Gooding, Marshal, D C

Wanted: an operator for the Singer Sewing Machine. Enquire at Lansburgh & Bro.

MON NOV 4, 1867

Real Estate. Mr John J Bogue, real estate agent, has sold at private sale the handsome & desirable residence of the late Col Wm Noyes, corner of West & Montgomery sts, Gtwn, for $11,900. Messrs Green & Williams, aucts, have sold part of lot 12 in square 490, with improvements, to John M Young, for $15,000. This property has for many years been known as Towers' Printing Ofc. The 3 story brick bldg, 60 High st, Gtwn, has been disposed of by F A Carroll to Mr H T Baker for $6,000.

Indianapolis, Ind, Nov 1. 1-John Patterson & a man named *Hatchell, in jail at Franklin, Ind, -Patterson accused of the murder of David Lyons, at Greenwood, Ind, & *Hatchill as an accomplice of Patterson, & of murder in Ky, were forcibly taken from the jail last night by a mob, & conveyed to Schofield's woods, near town, & hung. At the first attempt to hang *Hatchett the rope broke, but another was procured & the hanging completed. [*Note: names copied as written: Hatchell/Hatchill/Hatchett.] 2-Milton White, the murderer of Happas, at Anderson, Ind, in June last, was executed today. [Nov 6th newspaper: Patterson, accused of the murder of D Lyons; & an accomplice, Hatchell, were lynched by a party of 100 men, who arrived on horseback, broke open the doors of the jail, & took the prisoners to Schofield's woods, where they were hung. -Indianapolis Herald, Sat]

Pittsburgh, Nov 1. At a meeting of the Republican cmte of Alleghany Co yesterday, a resolution was adopted, nominating Gen Grant for the Presidency.

Montreal, Nov 1. Dr Oliver Wendell Holmes, of Harvard Univ, arrived here today to take steps to secure a copywright for his works.

On Sat, Chas Green, aged 9 years, son of Thos Green, residing on C st, near 1st st, was almost instantly killed near the depot of the Wash & Gtwn street railroad, on N J ave. Green got up on the hind part of a car backing out on the main track, & he fell off, striking his head & crushing his skull in a horrible manner. He was taken home & Dr Munder attended him, but the case was hopeless. The little sufferer lived but a few moments.

Salem, Mass, Nov 1. Francis Peabody & Capt Jeremiah Page both died here last night. The latter was President of the Salem Mechanics' Ins Co.

Orphans Court-Judge Purcell, Nov 2, 1867. 1-The general & individual accounts of the guardians of the orphan of Saml C Smoot, deceased; the first & final account of the administrator, with will annexed, of Eleanor R Lang; the first of the administrator of Jas Little; the first of the guardian to the orphan of Jas M Minor, & the second account of the guardian to the orphan of Geo Burns, & accounts of income, were filed & approved. 2-Jas F Meline was appointed guardian of the orphan of F M Meline; bond $2,000. 3-The last will of the late Frances Elvans was fully proven & admitted to probate, & letters testamentary issued to John R Elvans; bond $9,000. 4-The last will of the late Eliza Wilkins, bequeathing her estate to her children, & nominating S P Robertson & Saml Cassidy as executors, was filed for probate.

Mrd: on Oct 16, at *Society Hill*, St Mary's Co, Md, by Rev Fr Boone, Wm J Hickey, of this District, to Miss Alice L Edelen, eldest daughter of Dr Wm J Edelen.

Mrd: on Oct 31, by Rev Alfred Ames, Capt Augustus De Vivier Tassin, U S A, to Mary, daughter of Chas Tilley, of Wash, D C. No cards.

Died: on Nov 3, after a severe illness, George, son of Edw E & Lillie W Gilbert, aged 6 years & 3 months. His funeral will take place on Nov 5, at 11 o'clock A M, at the residence of his father, on D st, between 2nd & 3rd sts.

Gen Tom Thumb, his little wife, & Cmdor Nutt & Miss Nannie Warren, will commence a series of their pleasant receptions today & this evening at Metzerott Hall.

The funeral of Mr Geo Strom, who died on Friday last from the effects of injuries received while at work on the Insane Asylum grounds, on Thu, took place yesterday, & was attended by the Knights of Pythias & several other benevolent organizations, of which the deceased was a worthy member.

The new jail is to be on the public reservation, fronting on N J & Va avenue, just south of the Carroll estate.

1844 Andrew J Joyce & Co. Carriage Manufacturers, 477 & 479 14th st, Wash. Particular attention given to repairing.

Adm's sale: on Nov 7, all the personal estate of Wm J Toomey, deceased, excepting two bonds of the U S. At Green & Williams, aucts, 7th & D sts. -Jas W White, adm

TUE NOV 5, 1867
Died: on Nov 4, Brvt Lt Col Jas E Harrison, Capt 5th cavalry, aged 38 years. His funeral will take place from 89 Pa ave, at 3 o'clock on Nov 6.

Miss Clara Louise Kellogg, the American prima donna, made her first appearance in Europe, at her Majesty's Theatre, on Thu last, as "Margaret," in the opera Faust. The house was completely filled. The Prince of Wales was present & occupied the royal box.

Meridian Hill sales: lot 8 in block 5, to John Meigs, at 16 cents per foot; lot 3 in block 8, to Webster Elmes, at 11 cents per foot; lot 6 in block 8, to Mrs H McDermott, at 12 cents per foot; lots 17 thru 19 in block 9, to John Collins, at 7 cents per foot; lots 22 & 23 in block 9, to E W Down, at 7 cents per foot; lot 12 in block 13, to Mrs E M Zane, at 6 cents per foot; lot 10 in block 18, to Maj F H Moore, at 11 cents per foot; lot 2 in block 17, to Miss Lizzie Tucker, at 9 cents per sq foot.

Died: yesterday, Louise Blanche, infant daughter of Rev T B & Mrs Lou E McFalls, aged 6 months. Her funeral will be on Wed at 10 o'clock A M, from 397 E st, between 9th & 10th sts.

Insure your property at home. Nat'l Union Fire Ins Co of Wash, ofc 71 La ave, first door east of 7th st. Capital: $1,000,000. Chartered by Congress. Ofcrs: Chas Knap, pres; Geo W Riggs, vice-pres; Noble D Larner, sec. Directors: Chas Knap, Geo W Riggs, Thos Berry, Geo S Gideon, Marshall Brown, R Wallach, D Dodd, Wm Dixon, H D Cooke.

Orphans Court of Wash Co, D C. Mrs Eliz Kraft, guardian to the children of Peter Kraft, deceased, reported this day that she sold, as guardian, according to the order of said court May 2, 1867, east part of lot 2 in square 553, on O st, for $255.30; Jul 11, 1867, east part of lot 3 in square 553, for $168.70; also, Jul 11, 1867, the west part of lot 2 in square 553, for $115.05, & the expense thereof being $74.70; the purchasers have complied with the terms of sale. –Wm F Purcell, Judge of the Orphans Court. -Jas R O'Beirne, Reg/o wills

WED NOV 6, 1867
Mrd: on Jul 9, 1867, at the parish of St John's Church, S H Morison, of Jersey City, N J, to Miss Clara C Martin, of Wash City.

Died: on Tuesday, John Wightman, in his 32nd year, late a clerk in the Bureau of Provisions & Clothing. His funeral will take place on Thursday afternoon, at 2 o'clock, from the residence of his mother-in-law, Mrs Fletcher, 502 K st, between 4th & 5th sts.

Partnership under the name of R T Heiston & Co is dissolved this day by mutual consent. Successors are Hieston & Barrett. –R T Heiston, H F Payne, Gtwn, D C.
+
The Wood & Coal business will be cont'd by R T Hieston, Jas J Barrett, Gtwn, D C.

Orphans Court-Judge Purcell, Nov 5, 1867. Geo L Sheriff was appointed guardian to the orphans of the late John T Killmon; bond $2,000.

Rt Hon Wm Parsons, Earl of Rosse, [Lord Rosse] Astronomer, died. Lord Rosse was born Jun 17, 1800; in 1841 he succeeded to his father's title, & was elected one of the representative peers for Ireland, a life ofc. He resided chiefly at Birr Castle, Ireland, where he first set up his telescope. [Death date not given-current item.]

Phil, Nov 4. Dr Wilson Jewell, a prominent physician of this city, died suddenly today. He was connected with the Board of Health for many years.

U S Marshal's Ofc: Public sale on Nov 15, for cash, all Thos Coyle's interest in & to the sandbank on the farm lately owned by John A Smith, bordering on 7th st turnpike & Boundary st, in said District, containing 2 acres, being a lease for said 2 acres from said Smith & running 2 years from Jan 1, 1867. Seized & levied upon as the property of Thos Coyle, & will be sold to satisfy execution No 2,994, in favor of David Brady, & No 3,681, in favor of John F Bridget, both against Thos Coyle. –D S Gooding, U S Marshal, D C

Dept of the Interior, U S Patent Ofc, Wash, Oct 29. 1967. Ptn of Jas McCarty, of Reading, Pa, praying for extension of a patent granted him Jan 31, 1854, for an improvement in Rollers for Scarfing the Edges of Skelps for Lap-welded Tubes, for 7 years from the expiration of said patent, which takes place on Jan 31, 1868. -T C Theaker, Com'r of Patents

Dept of the Interior, U S Patent Ofc, Wash, Oct 30, 1867. Ptn of Wm Burnett, of San Francisco, Calif, & John Absterdam, of N Y, N Y, praying for the extension of a patent granted to them on Feb 28, 1854, for an improvement in the use of Fusible Disks in Steam Boilers, for seven years from the expiration of said patent, which takes place on Feb 28, 1868. -T C Theaker, Com'r of Patents

Norristown, Pa, Nov 5. The boiler in the cotton & woollen mill of J & G Lee, at Conshohocan, exploded this morning, killing Engineer McCarthy.

New Orleans, Nov 4. A general order from Gen Mower rescinds the order of Sat, removing Sheriff Hayes. Gen Grant disapproved of the appointment of Bullitt as Hayes' successor.

Carriages: large assortment of my own make, at reduced rates. A lot of second hand Carriages cheap. –Robt H Graham, Repository, 374 D st, between 8th & 9th sts. Shop: 477 8th st, near D st.

THU NOV 7, 1867
Col Wm H Philip purchased a 3 story, attic, & basement, pressed brick front house & lot on Jackson Place, opposite Lafayette Square, for $22,500 cash. Mrs Mary E Hill purchased lot 30 in square 236, on U st, between 13th & 14th sts, for $600. Mrs J P O Barnside purchased a cottage-house & lot on 14th st, between R & S sts, for $4,700. Mrs Annie Thompson purchased lot 133 in square 623, for $1,400.

Association of the Oldest Inhabitants meeting was held yesterday; vice-pres Col Peter G Washington, in the chair. Mr R W Clarke presented the old capstome, made by Coade, of London, in 1793, which ornamented the arch to the side entrace of the Old Capitol, on A st. The following gentlemen were elected members of the association: Seth Wyatt, John Lacomte, sr, Jas Lynch, A W Denham, W H Godey, Geo Thomas, & Jas Pilling. On motion of Mr Brent, Mr John Underwood, of Dublin, Ill, a former citizen of Wash, was elected an honorary member. Col J S Williams read an interesting printed account of the Masonic ceremonies at the laying of the corner stone of the Capitol in Sep, 1793, which, together with the brigade order book of the brigade of the District, in 1814, were presented by him to the association. Mr Nicholas Callan presented to the association a file of the Washington Expositor for 1808. Mr J Brent offered & read an interesting historical papers from John Underwood, giving, also, a pleasant account of the old hunting & fishing grounds about Washington over half a century ago, accompanied by a sketch of the Potomac from near the mouth of the Tiber, made in May, 1815. Also, a book called "A Short Introduction to Latin Grammar," printed in Balt in 1800. Dr Blake gave notice that at the next meeing he would read a biographical sketch of the life of the late Wm Jones.

The following county ofcrs were elected in Montg Co, Md, on Tuesday last, by over fifteen hundred majority: for State Senate, Dr Nicholas Brewer; for the House of Delegates, Saml Riggs, of R, Nicholas D Offutt, Thos Y Conley; for Clerk of the Circuit Court, E Barrett Prettyman; for State Atty, Geo Peter, for Sheriff, Jas H Clagett; for Reg of Wills, Robt W Carter; for Judges of the Orphans Court, Wm Thompson, of R, Hazel B Casbell, Dr Abraham H Sommers; for County Com'rs, Thos J Holland, Wm Reid, Benj C Gott, John L DuFief, Thos Rawlings; for Surveyor, Wm Grady.

Died: on Nov 5, Mary Ella, daughter of Maria & the late J Fred'k Speiser, aged 15 years & 4 months. Her funeral will be from the residence of her mother, 529 11th st, Navy Yard, near Ga ave, this afternoon at 4 o'clock.

The funeral of Col Jas E Harrison, Capt 5th U S cavalry, took place yesterday; the body was laid out in full uniform, encased in a handsome walnut coffin, with glass face, silver handles, & a silver plate with the inscription: Lieutenant Colonel James E Harrison, U S A, born April 17, 1829. Died November 4, 1867. The services were conducted by Rev Dr Hall, of the Epiphany Church. The following gentlemen acted as pall-bearers: Col Geo W Wallace, Col Taylor, A A G, Maj Mason, Gen Robt Williams, A A G, Gen E A Carr, & Gen L H Pellouze. The remains were interred in the ***Congressional Cemetery***.

Copartnership. Wm Sibrey & Chas Callahan have this day entered into copartnership, under the firm of Sibrey & Callahan, for the purpose of conducting the business of Plain & Ornamental Plastering & Mastic Work in all its various branches. They respectfully solicit the partonage of their friends & the public.
–Wash, D C, Nov 1, 1867

Singleton A Mercer, for 20 years Pres of the Farmer's & Mechanics' Bank, of Phil, died at Paris, on Oct 14, in his 57th year.

Burrell H Leeke, who was a practicing lawyer at Cassville, Ga, for several years previous to the war, & who had been residing at Cedar Keys, Fla, since, was killed at the latter place on Oct 15. He became involved in a difficulty with Dr Hodge, a practicing physician there, with whom he had been previously friendly, & in an altercation which took place, Dr Hodge kicked him in the stomach, from which he died in 3 hours. Dr Hodge being the only physician in the vicinity, attended him after the injury, & did all in his power to relieve him. He was with him when he died. Mr Leeke leaves a large family.

FRI NOV 8, 1867
I offer for sale the well known Farm called **Barnaby Manor**, the residence of the late Mrs E A Callis, in PG Co, Md. Also, a Farm for sale near Good Hope, D C. -Anthony Addison, Cole brook, PG Co, Md

Board of Metropolitan Police meeting yesterday: the resignation of R J McCallan, of the 8th Precinct, was accepted to take effect from date. Hamlet Dixon was appointed additional private to do duty at Wisewell barracks. John S Daily was appointed additional private to do duty at the depot of the Wash & Gtwn railroad, on N J ave. Henry C Jones was recommissioned as additional private to do duty at Metropolitan Hall. E G Townsend was recommissioned as additional private to do duty at Kendal Green & Campbell barracks. Jas E Beall was transferred from 2nd Precinct to the county & mounted. W H Orton appointed private on the force, vice S A Baily, dismissed. Pvt Jas E Arnold, of the 8th Precinct, to be mounted. Applications for Gtwn licenses were rejected as follows: Dennis O'Donovan, Johanna Brown, John Pilla, Hillery Hutchens, & Michl Lynch. Application for Wash licenses were also rejected: Chas Essig, Bernard Henze, Thos Green, Furguson & Sullivan.

Mrd: on Nov 6, at the Fourth Presbyterian Church, by Rev J C Smith, D D, Mr Z W Cromwell to Miss Belle Dunbar, both of Washington. No cards.

The Jail. Warden Heustis recommends the discharge of about 50 of his boarders from incarceration, as he has too many for comfort at the jail. The parties so recommended have been confined for several months for minor offences only.

SAT NOV 9, 1867
The corner-stone of St Paul's Episcopal Church, to be erected on 23rd st, between K & Pa ave, was laid yesterday; ceremonies commenced by the rector of the church, Rev A Jackson; Rev J V Lewis, of St John's parish, laid the corner-stone. The contractors for the stonework is Mr John Popkins, & for the carpenter's work, Mr Wm Chapin. The cost of the bldg will be about $10,000.

Rev Fr Hitzelberger, of St Aloysius Church, is lying very ill at the residence of a friend in Petersburg, Va.

We learned yesterday, officially, that Jas A Seddon, late Sec of War of the Confederacy, has been pardoned by the President. This act of clemency was extended upon the recommendations of Horace Greeley, Henry Ward Beecher, Hon Wm E Dodge, [late a Republican member of Congress,] Gen Burnside, & the following gentlemen of N Y C: Mayor Hoffman, John J Cisco, [sub treasurer,] H Van Dyke, Augustus Schell, & A A Love.

Susan Brockenburg, a colored girl, was committed to jail for robbing her step-father, Henry Giles, of $133. Susan refunded $68, & accounted for the remainder in new clothing & shoes.

Household & kitchen furniture at auction Nov 15, at the residence of the late Philip Harry, 84 Prospect st, between Market & Fred'k sts. Painting of "Noah's Sacrifice" by Leonarda da Vinci. Folios of Engravings; studies from Nature-painted in oil; & other valuable Oil Paintings & Drawings. –Wm H Dougall, exc -Thos Dowling, auct

Supreme Court of D C, Equity 274. Oliver & Marcellus Donn vs Orlando H Donn, John Y Donn, Geo S Donn, Alphonso T Donn, Mary Ann Donn, Oscar Martin, Saml A Raney, Theodosia J Raney, Louisa J Simpson, Thaddeus K Preuss, Erasmus J Middleton, & Richd J Clark. The above cause is referred to me to ascertain the liens upon the property mentioned in this cause, & their privities, if any, & whether the property is susceptible of divisons, or a sale will be necessary for the interests of the parties concerned. Parties to appear on Nov 12 at 10 o'clock. –Walter S Cox, auct

MON NOV 11, 1867
Phil, Nov 10. John Culp, implicated in the murder of Wm Riddle in this city in May last, was captured yesterday at North East, in Md. He made no opposition to coming to the State without the formality of a requisition, & has been committed for trial.

Orphans Court-Judge Purcell, Nov 9, 1867. 1-The second general & second individual accounts of R G Polley, guardian to the orphans of Thos McGuire, deceased, were approved & passed. 2-F A Jones & Geo E Johnson were appointed appraisers of the estate of Chas B Reynolds. 3-H C Noyes was appointed to appraise the goods & chattels of Peter W Magruder, late of Wash Co.

Ads. 1-Thos Russell & Co, successors to E C Dyer & Co, 256 Pa ave, have just received a large supply of the popular "Little Belt" cigars. 2-D H Stearns, 51 La ave, will sell at auction this morning, a lot of fine butter. 3-Wm Ballantyne will, in a few days, remove his store to 519 7th st, in the Intelligencer bldg, where he will be enabled to display to a better advantage his fine assortment of books & stationery.

Appointments: Sec McCulloch appointed Jas T Worthington, of Cincinnati, a revenue agent, with special instructions & authorizations. Postmaster Gen has appointed H Ray Myers an assist special agent of the Post Ofc Dept, at the pay of $1,600 per annum & $2 per diem, to take effect from Nov 5, 1867.

Special despatch from Oswego, N Y, announced the death, in that city, yesterday, of Mrs Elsie B Nye, consort of Hon Jas W Nye, Senator from Nebraska. She had been in failing health for some months past; but the illness which terminated her life was sudden & of short duration, she having been completely well until within 48 hours of her death. She died at the residence of Mr Page, a near relative, & her husband & daughter were at her side in her last illness. She was a native of N Y State, & at the time of her death in about her 53rd year. –Chronicle, 10th

Mr John Russ appointed drawkeeper at the north draw of the Long Bridge, vice Mr Andrew J Rock, who died lately from injuries received while working at the bridge.

The partnership under the name of J D Edmond & Co, has been dissolved by mutual consent. J E Kendall will settle up the business. –J D Edmond, Jas E Kendall, Nov 1. J D Edmond is retiring. A partnership has been formed to carry on the Hardware business, at the old stand, 513 7th st, under the name of J W Kennedy & Co. -John E Kendall, J W Kennedy

Capt David Hinkley, of Livermore, Maine, died on Friday, aged 102 years. He voted for Washington for President, & remembered Gen Arnold's expedition up the Kennebec river.

A despatch from Detroit states that on Saturday four lives were lost by the upsetting of a boat at Grand Haven. Those drowned are Silas F Cobb, J H Marcy, A Fletcher, & a child. They were strangers, going North.

Col W H McCaudle, the editor of the Vicksburg Times, was on Friday placed in confinement by order of Gen Ord. The charge is not known, though a special to the Crescent says it was for personal denunciation.

Leonidas Moses, a mail carrier in Arkansas, was assassinated recently by some unknown person while riding along a lonely road. His body was not found until 8 days after the murder, & all this time his mule stood guard over the corpse. The faithful animal had to go a mile & a half for water, but invariably returned & resumed its singular vigil.

Valuable country residence on 7th st at auction, on Nov 18, the beautiful country seat of H H McPherson, containing 6½ acres, with a fancy-built cottage, frame house in good repair, containing some 17 rooms, new stable, cow & carriage house, gardener's house, with 3 rooms, & greenhouse, etc. -Green & Williams, aucts

Miss Blanche Roberts, a young lady residing at Painesville, Ohio, while on her way to church with another young lady, was accosted by a young man named Sharp, who had formerly been in the employ of Mr Roberts, father of the young lady, & without a word, deliberately shot her with a revolver, striking her in the groin, inflicting a dangerous wound. He then fired at her 3 times, the balls passing through her clothing.

Pianoforte, chamber furniture, oil paintings, household & kitchen furniture, carriages, wagons & carts, etc, at auction on: Nov 18, on the premises of H H McPherson, [known as Dr Page's Place,] just above the junction of the 7th st cars. -Green & Williams, aucts

Leavenworth, Kansas, Nov 10. Susan B Anthony, Lucy Stone, Mrs Eliz Cady Stanton, & several prominent ladies of Kansas, members of the Female Suffrage Cmte, feeling encouraged at the very flattering votes given in favor of female suffrage in this State, have projected a campaign in the Eastern & Western States. Geo Francis Train telegraphed he will also be present & speak.

Died: on Nov 9, at her residence, in Wash City, Emily Pomeroy, beloved wife of N L Dodge, in her 56th year. Her funeral will take place on Tuesday, 12 M, at 249 I st.

Died: on Oct 22, at New Orleans, of yellow fever, Arthur Fronson Williams, aged 40 years, formerly of Wash City, & a son of the late Ezra Williams, of the Treasury Dept. He was struck with the disease immediately after having devotedly & successfully nursed a friend.

Died: on Sunday, Jessie May, aged 3 years & 3 months, youngest daughter of Jas T & Hannah F Blakeney. Her funeral is today at 2 o'clock, from the residence of her grandparents, 647 L st north. [Balt Sun please copy.]

The residence of John F McQuinn is offered for sale on moderate terms; good dwlg & 20 acres of land; near Fairfax Seminary, within 5 miles of Wash. Inquire on the premises.

TUE NOV 12, 1867
Dr Macgowan has failed in his efforts to introduce the telegraph into China.

Mr Josiah Trowbridge, residing about 6 miles from Wash City, was thrown out of his carriage yesterday, near 8th & I sts, & was badly bruised & cut. He was taken to his residence.

The Fourth Presbyterian Church, [Rev Dr Smith's] on 9th st, was on Wed last, the scene of one of those unusually interesting occasions-a marriage. The church was crowded by the many friends of Z W Cromwell, [of the firm of Chas Stott & Co, druggists,] & of his beautiful bride, Miss Belle K Dunbar, who are both members of the church. The bridal couple were attended by R F Baker & Miss B Goodrich. The organist played the wedding march, & the service was performed by the pastor, Dr Smith. The happy couple left that evening for Phil, & will spend their honeymoon in that city & Carlisle.

Mayor Wallach received yesterday, the resignation of Mr Jos H Bradley, sr, Corporation Atty. Jos H Bradley, jr, was appointed Corporation Atty by the Mayor, & was confirmed Nov 8, 1867.

C B Caswell, a clerk in the Freedmen's Bureau, died on Sunday very suddenly, & will be buried today from his late residence, 32 9th st, at 12 o'clock. He was about 60 years of age, & a gentleman very highly esteemed by all who enjoyed his acquaintance.

Supreme Court of D C, Equity No 701-Docket 8. Jane E Strother vs Jas Nicholson. Ordered that sales report by Wm D Cassin, trustee, for the sale of the real estate of Francis M Strother, be ratified & confirmed. Amount of sales reported: $1,854.12. –R J Meigs, clerk

Supreme Court of D C, Equity No 739. Jas S Wilson vs Wm H Wilson & others. R P Jackson, trustee in the above cause, reported he made sale of part of lot 54, in Beall's addition to Gtwn, to Jas B Vanderwerken, for $1,620, who assigned his purchase to Andrew Fray, & the terms of sale have been complied with. The trustee also sold part of lot 113, in Beatty & Hawkins' addition to Gtwn, to Benj F Moxley, for $2,600, & the purchaser has complied with the terms of sale. –R J Meigs, clerk

Richmond, Nov 11. Gen Schofield today ordered a court-martial on Nov 18 in the case of Col Rose, the conductor of the elections here, who is formally charged by citizens with conduct unbecoming an ofcr & a gentleman, drunkenness, etc, on election day.

The *Foundry property*, formerly belonging to Gen John Mason, was sold to Edwin B Cadley for $26,050 yesterday, Green & Williams aucts.

Equity Court-Judge Wylie.
Ward vs Clark et al. Order ratifying trustee's sale, & reference to order.
Smoot et al, vs Tenley et al. Decree ratifying trustee's sale.
Mack vs Wagner. Order continuing cause to Nov 18 instant.
Gittings et al vs Cross et al. Order appointing B B Cross guardian *ad litem*.
Brown vs Brown et al. Decree trustee to sell.
Tell vs Dowling. Decree confirming trustee's sale.
McLeod vs McLeod. Final ratification of trustee's sale.
Terret vs Terret. Order ratifying trustee's sale, & referring to Auditor.
Alexander et al vs Bouldin et al. Order for cmplnt to bring in certain books.
E A Cox vs D B Cox. Decree of divorce a *vinculo matrimonii*.
Strother vs Nicholson. Order ratifying trustee's sale *nisi*.
Miller vs Miller. Order directing trustee to redeem from tax sale.
Ruppert vs Geier et al. Order confirming trustee's sale *nisi*.
Brown vs Beak et al. Order confirming trustee's sale, & reference to Auditor.
Wilson vs Wilson et al. Order confirming trustee's sale, & reference to Auditor.
Stewart vs Eccleston et al. Order to report on receiver's acts, etc.
Weber vs Weber. Order appointing E Lockwood guardian *ad litem* to infant.

Toronto, Canada, Nov 11. The consecration of Bishop Walsh took place yesterday.

Supreme Court of D C, Equity No 804. Brown vs Brown & others. R P Jackson, trustee, reported that he sold part of lot 29 in Beatty & Hawkins' amended addition to Gtwn, to Thos A Newman, for $630; also, part of lot 21, in old Gtwn, to Thos A Brown, for $1,850, & each purchaser had complied with the terms of sale.
–R J Meigs, clerk

Dept of the Interior, U S Patent Ofc, Wash, Nov 6, 1867. Ptn of Saml G Levis, of Kellyville, Pa, praying for extension of a patent granted to him Feb 14, 1854, & reissued Oct 22, 1867, for an improvement in Making Thick Paper, for 7 years from the expiration of said patent, which takes place on Feb 14, 1867.
-T C Theaker, Com'r of Patents

Circuit Court-Chief Justice Cartter; jurors called yesterday:

Fred'k Stromberger	Wm Chase	Zadok Williams
Wm Hickey, jr	Erastus M Chapin	John Douglass
J E Young	David Jackson	Thos Proby
Richd Cruit	Jas Pilling	Chas H Anderson
B F Moxley	Jas G Berrett	Nelson Isadell
Jos S Tucker	W B Lacy	
John T McKelden	Wm Jenkins	

The search for the missing body of Edw Devlin, the soldier supposed to have been murdered by his comrades, is still going on. Cannon were fired yesterday & today over the water to endeavor, if possible, to raise the corpse.

Victor Becker, Piano Tuner & Repairer, established in 1855. Orders received at Dempsey & O'Toole's Engravers, 326 Pa ave; F C Riechenbach's Piano Store, 498 11st st. References: J P Caulfield, Miss Juliana May, Academies of the Visitation in Gtwn & Wash; & Wm Knabe & Co.

WED NOV 13, 1867
Dr Pope, at the earnest solicitation of many friends, will, during the season, resume in part his out-door practice, which the pressure of his ofc consultations has, for the last 2 years, compelled him generally to resign. Ofc consultations are held during the morning, close at noon; resume at 3 P M & cease at nightfall.

Trustee's sale of fine farm near Wash, D C; by decrees of the Circuit Court for PG Co, [Md] in Equity, wherein Henry C Kirkwood & others are cmplnts, & Mary Jane Kirkwood & others are respondents; public sale on the premises, Dec 6, of all the real estate of the late Dr Wallace Kirkwood, situated in said county, containing about 136½ acres, of which 100 acres are cleared, the rest in wood; lives between the farms of Geo W Riggs, [lately that of the late Mrs Diggs,] & Robt Clark; about 2½ miles n w of Bladensburg, near the Dist of Columbia line. Improvements consist of a good frame dwlg, containing 7 rooms; stable, corn-house, & other our-houses. Apply to Shelby C Clark, Atty, Upper Marlboro, or to Wm R Woodward, Atty, City Hall, Wash, D C. -Mary Jane Kirkwood, Wm R Woodward, trustees

Supreme Court of D C, in Equity. Sarah C Kobb, ptn, vs John G Kobb, dfndnt. It is ordered that the dfndnt appear on or before the first rule day occurring 40 days after this day; otherwise the cause will be proceeded with as in case of default.
–R J Meigs, clerk

Mr Job Angus leased the property corner of G & 11th st, formerly occupied by Harvey, & intends improving the bldgs, converting it into dwlgs.

Leavenworth, Kansas, Nov 12. The proprietor of the Planter's House, Platte City, Mo, named Jenkins, was shot & killed by a negro man this morning, who had been discharged from his service for misconduct. $500 reward has been offered for his apprehension.

Orphans Court of Wash Co, D C, Nov 12, 1867. In the case of Jos Redfern, adm of Louis Vivans, deceased, the administrator & Court have appointed Dec 7 next, for the final settlement of the personal estate of the said deceased, of the assets in hand.
-Jas R O'Beirne, Reg/o wills

Mrd: on Nov 12, in PG Co, Md, by Rev Fr Lenneghan, John A Hamilton, of Wash, D C, to Maggie, daughter of Col Jas Edelin, U S Marine Corps. [Express & Balt Sun please copy.]

Died: on Nov 11, Miss Susanna Hughes, daughter of the late Jeremiah Hughes, formerly of Annapolis, Md. Her funeral will be from the residence of her brother, 111 Wash st, Gtwn, at 3½ o'clock, this evening.

Died: on Nov 12, at Phil, Mr Christopher Haeberle, until recently a resident of this District. He leaves a widow & 10 children, none of them as yet provided for. A large circle of both American & German friends mourn his untimely departure from this world.

Orphans Court-Judge Purcell, Nov 12, 1867. 1-The last will of Owen Black, deceased, was filed for probate. 2-The testator bequeathes all his personal & real property to his wife, Theresa Black, & appoints Horatio Browning his executor. 3-First & final account of the adm of Henry Felson & Eliz Jane Felson. First account of Harriet A Lee, guardian to Henry Felson, orphan of Henry & Eliz Felson, deceased; & fifth & final account of Jos Mountz, exc of John Mountz, deceased. First & final account of Sarah L Parkhurst, admx of Wm G Parkhurst. First individual account of Sarah L Parkhurst, guardian to Madelina Parkhurst, orphan of Wm G Parkhurst. All approved & passed.

Supreme Court of D C, Equity No 679. Patrick White, adm, etc, vs Maria McGuire et al. The trustee, Jas Maguire, reported the sale in the above entitlee cause to the court, the said sale is, on this 11th day of Nov, 1867, confirmed. [No other information.]

THU NOV 14, 1867

Thos Dowling, auct, sold, at private sale, lot 20, fronting 20 feet on High st, opposite 4th st, running back 130 feet, improved by a small dwlg, belonging to Mr Noble Hurdle, to Mr Jas H Payne, for $1,000. Messrs Coldwell & Co, aucts, sold a small house & lot on 3rd st, between Va ave & D st, to Michl Leahy, for $825.

Equity Court-Judge Wylie. 1-Gericks vs Gericks: divorce a vinculo matrimonii. 2-Lee vs Rapley et al: appointing Geo F Appleby, guardian *ad litem*.

Henry Warner, U S marine corps, attached to the U S ship **St Cloud**, now at the Norfolk navy yard, was arrested in Norfolk on Monday night, charged with murdering a comrade, Alex'r Carter. Warner hails from this city; is between 30 & 35 years of age, tall & slender, with light complexion & hair. He enlisted Jul 29 last in the marine corps. He says his people all live here. Carter was a Scotchman, with dark complexion, black hair, side whiskers, about 40. He came to Wash in Jul, 1866, from Chicago. Warner claims self-defence; he has been held to answer for the crime before the grand jury, which meets on the 4th Wed in Feb next.

F M Peterson, a druggist of Chicago, attended a dance there, & on returning to his residence found his wife & some lady companions sitting up. He poured out a glassful of rasberry wine for each of them, & in a few minutes after drinking his potion was a corpse. He had recently failed in business, & it is supposed he drugged his wine before drinking it, & thus committed suicide.

Americans in Paris: John M Varnum, Horatio King, Henry F King, Mrs Schliecker, H B Titus, W Harper, Edw Green, Mrs Claude D Blanchard, & C Conrad Blanchard, of Wash City.

Miss Jennie Olds, a young lady of Onalaska, Wisc, has been abducted by a party of 20 Indians who had been encamping in the neighborhood. Parties are in pursuit.

The oldest person known in the U S is Mrs Flora Stuart, a colored woman residing in Londonderry, N H. She was born in Boston in 1750, 117 years ago, & has now living 2 sons & a daughter. Her parents were slaves, belonging to the Simpson family, of Windham, N H.

San Francisco, Nov 13. Dr W J Knox, of San Jose, died in this city today. He was Senator from Santa Clara Co, a Democrat.

N Y, Nov 13. Mary Husband, a native of Spain, attempted to commit suicide by shooting herself through the head. Her recovery is considered impossible.

Nashville, Nov 13. Maj Jas Nork, formerly a rich slaveholder, & a resident of this city, but more recently of Bowling Green, Ky, committed suicide by cutting his throat with a razor. [No death date given-current item.]

A horrible murder at Chattanooga: a few weeks ago the jewelry store of Henry Deutch, in that city, was robbed of a number of watches. Andy Williams & Jos Johnson, 2 negro boys, were convicted of the theft, & sent to jail for 20 days. While confined, Andy Williams sent word to the jeweller that if he would accompany him to a cornfield 5 miles from Chattanooga, the watches could be recovered, as they had been buried there. The jeweller was very busy, & sent his brother, Adolph Deutch, who agreed to go with the negro without a guard. Several days later Deutch was found murdered in the cornfield. He had been struck over the head with a fatal bludgeon. The murderer is being pursued.

Miss Ellen J Vans, a maiden lady about 40 years of age, a teacher of elocution in N Y, was accidentally poisoned at 209 East 26th st, N Y C, on Thu. While in her room, Miss Eliz M Taylor, living in the house, was startled by hearing Miss Vans cry, "Eliz, Eliz, come quickly, I have swallowed cyanite of potassium by mistake for tincture of rhubarb.: Miss Taylor sent for the physicians, but arrived after Miss Vans had expired. The deceased was a lady of unusual intelligence, a native of Boston, where her mother & other relations live.

Brookville, Pa, Nov 13. Mrs Lena Miller, a German woman, who poisoned her husband last winter, was hanged in the jail-yard here today. She made a full confession.

Horses, cows, hogs, shoats, wagons, ox & horse carts, ploughs, harrow, etc, at auction, on Nov 25, on the farm of Zadoc Williams, over the Navy Yard Bridge, opposite the Insane Asylum. -Green & Williams, aucts

Supreme Court of D C. The Board of Public Works of Va, vs John A English, Jas W English, Cave W English, Zeph English, Ann M Adams, Peter Lucas, Sallie W Gray, Mary Berry, Ann E Lucas, Dullabella Lucas, Fielding Lucas, Walter Lucas, Mary S Kalonback, Fielder Long, Eliz Maddan, John A Holtzman, Wm B Holtzman, Robt B McCormick, Eliz J Berry, Sarah C Drayer, Susan E Freas, Mary V Withers, Louisa Withers, Achsah Withers, Thos Withers, Mary Withers, Naomie Withers, Margaret Kennerly, Roberta Kendrick, Jennette Mosly, John B Withers, Atta Gulick, Geo W Samson, et al. The object of this suit is, in part, to subject certain real estate in Wash, & owned by John Withers, deceased, to sale, for payment of his indebtedness to the cmplnts. On motion of cmplnts, by W S Cox, their solicitor, it is ordered that the dfndnts cause their appearance to be entered herein on or before the first rule day occurring 40 days after this date; otherwise the cause will be proceeded with as in case of default.

Supreme Court of D C, Equity 341, Docket 7. Matilda Grammer vs Todd & Probasco. Ordered that the sale made to Summerville & Leitch of the south 25 feet front, by depth of lot 15, & the north half of lot 16, in square 258, in Wash City, for $4,531, be ratified & confirmed. –R J Meigs, clerk

FRI NOV 15, 1867

Fraud on the Pension Ofc. The Com'r of Pensions has been informed that Wm Breeden & John W Dunn have been arrested at Santa Fe, New Mexico, upon a charge of perjury & forgery. A forged power of atty was presented by one of those parties, upon which $500, due a pensioner, was paid by the pension agent at Santa Fe. They have been held to bail in the sum of $3,000 each for trial at the next term of the U S Court at Santa Fe. On Nov 11 Juliana Hoega, a pensioner, was committed at Phil, in default of bail, for trial at the next term of the U S Dist Court. This pensioner is charged with perjury, in swearing that she was a widow, & receiving upwards of $300, when, at the time, she was a married woman, & not entitled to pension after a second marriage.

Thos Dowling, auct, Gtwn, sold at public auction, on Wed, lot 28, fronting 60 feet on Prospect st, between Frederick & Market sts, running back 138 feet, 6 inches, improved by a large two story frame dwlg, belonging to the estate of the late Phillip Harry, to Mr A H Clements, for $5,200. Green & Williams, aucts, sold at auction, yesterday, the brick dwlg & lot on south F st, between 8th & 9th sts west, being lots 10 & 11 in square 413, improved by a well built substantially built two story house, to John B Abell, for $3,000.

Patents for Washingtonians during the past week. 1-E B Olmsted, for a machine for making paper bags & envelopes. 2-Kellis Horde, for a toy in which fine mechanism is seen. 3-Geo H Heron, for a method of preparing fish for food.

Wesley Chapel, on Nov 11, was the scene of an interesting marriage ceremony, performed by Rev Dr Ames, the happy parties being Mr Robt J Walker, of Boston, & Miss Susie V Flenner, of Wash City. The proceedings were both solemn & impressive. The newly married pair left in the noon trian on a bridal tour to the North.

Mr John Graham, formerly foreman of the press room of the Gov't Printing Ofc under Mr Dufrees, died of consumption at his residence, in First st, on Wed, after a protracted illness. He was about 45 years of age, & a native of Phil. He was esteemed by all who knew him; of strict integrity & a genial friend.
+
Died: on Nov 13, Mr John Graham, formerly of Phil, aged 45 years. His funeral will be from his late residence on First st west, between G & H sts, today, at 2 o'clock P M. [Nov 16th newspaper: The Columbia Typographical Union, of which the deceased was a member, attended the funeral in full numbers, accompanied by Heald's Band. The remains were interred in ***Glenwood Cemetery***.]

Mrd: on Nov 12, in San Francisco, Calif, by Rev E R Lathrop, Hon Chas N Harris, of Nevada, to Miss Clementine, daughter of Jas S Magee, of Wash City, D C.

Mrd: on Nov 11, at the residence of the bride's father, by Rev A A E Taylor, Mr V E Ramsburg to Miss Anna G Ross, both of Gtwn, D C.

Equity Court-Judge Wylie, Nov 14, 1867. 1-Chesseldine vs Chesseldine: appointing guardian *ad litem*. 2-Ruppert vs Geier & Tooma: reference to Auditor to report. 3-Boechkie vs Dickson: injunction. 4-Scrivener vs Powell: appointing A Lloyd trustee to sell.

Supreme Court of D C, 976 Equity. Johanna E Rupert & John Rupert, cmplnts, vs Bernard Geier & Louisa Thoma, dfndnts. It is ordered by the Court that the sales made & reported by Bernard Geier, trustee for the sale of the real estate of Chas Thoma, deceased, be ratified & confirmed. –R J Meigs, clerk [No other details.]

The heirs of Anneke Jans, who claim the Trinity Church property, in N Y, met in convention at Poughkeepsie on Wed. There were 200 men & women present.

Rodney M Whipple, real estate agent in Chicago, charged with connection with forgeries against the Gov't perpetrated by Quartermaster Kills, at Nashville, Tenn, has surrendered himself to the authorities, & been put under $10,000 bonds.

Balt, Nov 14. About noon today, as E A Pollard, the historian of "Lee & his Lts," was passing in front of the Maltby House, he was approached by a son & nephew of Henry A Wise, named John & Douglass, each of whom fired at Pollard, one of the balls pasing through the right arm of Pollard, he having his wife on the left hand at the time. Pollard drew his pistol, but was unable to raise it on account of his wound, & the ball struck the pavement. The assailants came here this morning from Richmond to obtain satisfaction from Pollard for a letter recently published by the latter in reply to a letter of Henry A Wise on his [E A Pollard's] history of the war, & had previously declared their intention to shoot him on sight. They are both in custody to await examination.
+
Balt, Nov 11. This afternoon John & Douglas Wise were arraigned before a magistrate, & were bailed in the sum of $3,000 each, to appear before the grand jury on Sat next. Pollard's wound is severe, the bone being shattered, but is not necessarily dangerous. He is now doing well. [Nov 16th newspaper: It appears that Mr John S Wise, a son, some 20 years of age, of Gen Wise, left Richmond on Wed for this city, with his cousin, Capt Geo Douglass Wise, for the alleged purpose of chastising Mr E A Pollard. Dr J Pembroke Thorn & St Geo W Teackle were the bondsmen for John & Douglas Wise.]

SAT NOV 16, 1867
Henry C Gooding, late of Wash City, has located in the practice of his profession at Evansville, Ind, his native State. He was for the past 2 years a member of the District bar, & enjoyed a fine practice, perhaps the most lucrative of any criminal lawyer in Washington, & very successful in the issue of most of his cases.

Yesterday, at the Mayor's Office, City Hall, Mr Jacob D Hutton was awarded the sewer contract at the following prices: main sewer, $4.13 per foot; laterals, $3; man-holes, $65 each; traps, $1.50 each; drops, $45.

A T Stewart brought home from France a $7,000 carpet for his house.

The Prince of Wales was 27 years old last Saturday.

Horrible accident. Last evening, as Mrs Talty, wife of John Talty, who keeps a grocery store at Ohio ave & 14th st, was taking a lighted coal oil lamp from the pendent in the store, it slipped out of her hand, & falling upon the floor broke into fragments, the light igniting the coal oil, which spread into a flame, & communicated to Mrs Talty's dress. In an instant her clothing was on fire; & her husband, who was in an adjoining room, startled by the cry of fire, rushed into the store, & endeavored to tear the clothing off, & in doing this had his hands terribly burned. Mrs Talty fell upon the floor & died in a few moments. Mrs Talty was about 32 years of age.

Phil, Nov 14. Gen Lyle, sheriff elect, broke his leg two weeks since, by being thrown from a carriage. He is not believed to be in danger.

N Y, Nov 15. This evening the boiler of a donkey engine on the steamer **Matanzas** exploded killing Henry McGee, quartermaster. Another of the crew is missing, & he is supposed to have been blown overboard.

Supreme Court of D C, Equity 925. Alice E Caynor et al vs Edw A Manyett et al. Ordered that the sales made by R R Crawford, trustee, for the sale of the real estate of Anthony Manyett, deceased, be ratified. The amount of the sale is $1,684.

Chicago, Nov 15. The case of J Buchanan Cross, the notorious forger, which has been on trial in the Recorder's Court for some days, was concluded today by the jury bringing in a verdict of guilty. He was sentenced to 6 years imprisonment in the penitentiary.

MON NOV 18, 1867
Geo Wilkins Kendall, of the New Orleans Picayune, left an estate worth half a million dollars.

Chas P Freeland commited suicide in one of the cells of the prison. Yesterday he was observed walking on the avenue, acting in a strange manner. Ofcr Wallingsford arrested him & took him to Police Headquarters, where they were unable to elicit information from him other than he was a clerk in the Internal Revenue Ofc & spoke of Mr Harlan, of 363 K st. Mr Harlan had lived there, but had moved. Mr Julius H Mott, of the same ofc, knew Mr Freeland. He said he is simply a victim of imtemperance, & aside from that habit, is one of the finest young men in the city. He was given some supper & lodging in one of the cells, with John Stewart, who had "tramped" from Balt yesterday. Freeland soon after cut his throat with a common penknife & died in 5 minures. He was a native of N Y C, where his family now reside. Thus rum has claimed another victim.

Hon David Davis, administrator of the estate of the late Abraham Lincoln, made a final settlement of the estate at Springfield, Ill, last Thursday. After paying all the debts there remained $110,294.62, which, divided among the widow & heirs, gives $36,765.30 to Mrs Lincoln, & the same amount to each son. Robt T Lincoln received his share, & also that of the minor heir, Thos [Tad.] The amount due Mrs Lincoln, less about $4,000 heretofore drawn by her, is subject to her order.

The funeral of Mrs Belinda Talty, the wife of John Talty, who was burned to death on Friday last, took place yesterday at 3 o'clock P M, from St Matthew's Church. The funeral services were conducted by Rev Fr De Wolf, the assistant pastor of the Church. Her remains were conveyed to **Mount Olivet Cemetery** for interment.

On Sat at Binghamton, N Y, a freight engine exploded, instantly killing the engineer, Edw Caton, & the fireman, Wm Rose, both of Syracuse.

In St Paul, Thursday, at a large party at the residence of Gen H H Sibley, a large kerosene lamp exploded, severely burning several parties. Gen Sibley was injured in one arm; his daughter, Gussie, was burned on the breast & arms, & a servant girl will die from the injuries she received. None of the guests were seriously hurt.
+
St Paul, Minn, Nov 17. Gen Sibley's residence, kerosene lamp exploded: Maggie Murphy, a servant girl, died of her injuries; Miss Gussie Sibley will lose one of her arms. [Nov 23rd newspaper: Augusta, [Gussie] was badly burned; her sister, Sallie, was not hurt; Mrs Sibley was badly burned on both hands; Miss Mary Steele, niece of Gen Sibley, thought the house was on fire; John Murphy, the hired man, finished extinguishing the flames. The funeral of Maggie Murphy took place yesterday at St Mary's Church.]

Orphans Court-Judge Purcell, Nov 16, 1867. 1-Last will & testament of Owen Black admitted to probate, & letters testamentary issued to Horatio Browning. Bond in sum of $1,000, with Saml Cross & Wm Morgan as sureties. 2-*In re*, Eleanor Miller's will. Caveat filed in open court of Sarah B Hutton & her husband to the paper writing propounded as the last will, etc, of Eleanor Miller, deceased. The caveators proceed to allege that a certain paper writing, bearing date 21st day of Oct, 1867, is not the last will & testament, & ought not to be admitted to probate for the following reasons, to wit: That the said Eleanor Miller was not, at the time she signed or made her mark to said paper, of sound & deposing mind, memory, & understanding to know the difference between real & personal estate; & that the said paper, if admitted to probate in its present form, would give all her real or personal property to her daughter, Eleanor Miller, during her life, etc; & further, that the said Eleanor Miller never did will or desire that her daughter should have all her real & personal property for life, & that the said Eleanor Miller signed or made her mark to the said paper through mistake; & lastly, that, in fact, the said writing is not her last will & testament. Witnesses were examined as to the facts in the case. M Thompson, solicitor for the caveator. The decision in the matter was reserved.

A small English Terrier, having on a silver collar marked J H S, escaped from the jail on Friday. As the initials suggest, the dog belongs to John H Surratt, & is very highly prized by him as the companion of many months of solitude. If found return to Warden Heustis.

Mrd: on Nov 11, by Rev Dr McFalls, at the residence of the bride's parents, J S Luff, of Calif, to Mrs E A Cox, of Wash City.

Mrd: on Nov 5, at the house of Rev Wm Howe, in Cambridgeport, Mass, by the bride's father, Maj Henry C Dane, of Wash, D C, to Miss Angie A Parker, daughter of Rev J W Parker, D D, of Cambridge, Mass.

Died: on Nov 16, Mrs Catharine Mohun, consort of the late Philip Mohun, aged 87 years. Her funeral will take place from her late residence, on 3rd st west, between F & G sts, on Oct 18, at 9:30 o'clock A M.

Died: on Nov 16, Miss Maris Miller, daughter of the late Maj Thos R Miller, of Caroline Co, Va. Her funeral will take place from her late residence, 422 N Y ave, on Oct 19 at 11 o'clock.

Died: on Nov 17, Helen Willett, only child of Edw E & Lillie Gilbert, aged 10 months & 22 days. Her funeral will take place on Nov 19 at 2 P M, from the residence of her father, 449 D st, between 2nd & 3rd sts.

The President has pardoned Maj G B Crittenden, late of the rebel army, a son of the late Senator Crittenden, of Ky.

Orphans Court of Wash Co, D C. Letters testamentary on the personal estate of Stoddard B Colby, late of Wash City, D C, deceased. –Jabez P Colby, adm

St Louis, Nov 17. Seymour Voulliere, a prominent criminal lawyer of this city, formerly circuit atty, was shot last night by M Ruth, a clerk in the post-ofc. The affair grew out of an unpleasant relation between Voulliere & his wife, resulting in a divorce to her last week; Ruth being her most important witness. Last night Ruth was accompanying the divorced wife to the theatre, & when returning home they met Voulliere, who fired at Ruth, but missed. Ruth returned the fire hitting Voulliere in the right breast, inflicting a dangerous wound. He now lies in critical condition. Ruth surrendered himself.

TUE NOV 19, 1867
Worcester, Mass, Nov 18. Shepherd, the wife murderer, was captured in Canterbury, Conn, this morning. He was observed coming out of a barn, where he had slept, & was soon taken without any resistance. The ofcrs are expected to reach this city this afternoon with their prisoner.

Died: on Nov 13, in her 24th year, Jane R or B, wife of Henry D Foster, U S N, & daughter of Robt & Martha A Clarke. Her funeral will be today from the residence of her parents, 462 K st, between 8th & 9th sts, at 2 o'clock P M.

Died: on Nov 14, in Montg Co, Md, in her 55th year, Mrs Verlinda Green, wife of Edw Green, & eldest daughter of the late Jas Darne, of Loudoun Co, Va. Thus death has removed from us a devoted wife & indulgent mother, a faithful sister & kind neighbor. [Rockville papers copy.]

Trustee's sale of property & wharf in Gtwn, D C; by deed of trust to the subscriber, from Wm L Dawson, dated Apr 26, 1866, recorded in Liber R M H, No 13, folio 122; sale on Nov 28, all that parcel of ground & premises fronting about 127 feet on the north side of Water st, & binding on Fred'k st about 130 feet running back from Water st to the canal, & improved with a large 3 story brick warehouse. The wharf property is in front of said premises. –John L Kidwell, trustee -Thos Dowling, auct

Rochester, N Y, Nov 18. Ex-Major Gen Gould was stricken with apoplexy & died this morning.

New Orleans, Nov 18. W H Riley, manager of the St Charles Theatre, died suddenly of a chill on Sat evening. He had arrived but a few days before from Indianapolis. He was buried on Sunday eveing with Masonic honors.

Orphans Court of Wash Co, D C, Nov 16, 1867. In the case of Wm R Woodward, Wm L Dunlop, & John Marbury, jr, excs of Wm Reden, deceased, the executors & Court have appointed Dec 10th next, for the final settlement of the personal estate of the said deceased, of the assets in hand. -Jas R O'Beirne, Reg/o wills

WED NOV 20, 1867
Green & Williams, aucts, have sold the country seat of H H McPherson, containing about 6½ acres, with a cottage frame house, out-house, green-house, hot-beds, etc, the property being about half a mile above Park Hotel, on 7th st, to Mr John Widmeyer, for $16,000.

Orphans Court-Judge Purcell, Nov 19, 1867. 1-In the case of Mary Drury, admx of Woodford Stone, deceased, the exception of W P Tisdale to answer of Mary Drury, filed on Nov 12, was set for Thu week. 2-In the matter of the ptn of Julia Ann Forrest, for sale of orphans' real estate, was set before the court, but not acted upon. 3-Martha Ann Truxell gave bond in $1,000, & was appointed guardian to the orphans of F I Truxell. 4-Thos McFadden & Thos J Murray were authorized to appraise the goods & chattels of the late Owen Black. 5-The fourth account of the personal estate of the late Andrew Coyle was received. 6-An inventory of the personal estate of Wm Thumbert was returned by the executor. 7-In the estate of Woodford Drury the answer of Mary Ann Drury was filed.

Phil, Nov 19. Margaret Ward, alias Wilmington Mag, was found dead at 7th & St Mary's sts this morning. She is supposed to have been murdered. A man named Campbell has been arrested upon suspicion of having killed her.

Tragedy in Cleveland, Ohio, on Nov 18. Mrs J H Gregory, wife of the photograph artist, [& their little girl Ida,] found her husband in his gallery with his throat cut, & dead, & Isabella Roy, aged 19, who had been in his employ for some time, lying a corpse, with an empty revolver by her side. Mr Gregory cut his throat outside the door after he shot & killed Isabella Roy. He wrote a letter stating that troubles with his wife, whom he charged with giving false testimony against him, had led him to commit the awful crime. He requested that a Mr Pugh select a burying place for his remains in **Woodland Cemetery**; that the body of "this girl" might be buried with him; that his wife, Willie, & Ida Belle, might have burying lots next to his. The letter had no signature. A year ago a fierce family quarrel eniminated in Gregory's arrest, at the instance of his wife, on the charge of abusing her.

The wife of Hon Wm B Reed died in Phil on Friday last.

Equity Court-Judge Wylie. Young vs Goodwick: appointing Wm P Lasalle guardian *ad item*.

Wm Burchard has leased the restaurant over Wall & Co's clothing store, & has fitted it up in the most recherche manner, & is now prepared to entertain his patrons with the delicacies of the season, served in a style that will please the taste of the most fastidious epicure.

Mohawk, N Y, under date of Nov 15: Mr Robt H Pomeroy, last cashier of the bank in this place, took poison today & died in a few minutes. He was removed from the position of cashier when a deficit was found in cash & bonds. He left a letter which affirms his innocence.

Worcester, Mass, Nov 19. Geo A Ransome, who has been under arrest for complicity in procuring an abortion upon Mrs Cynthia A Newton, causing her death, was discharged by the police court today, there not being sufficient evidence to warrant his further detention.

Chicago, Nov 18. Col Alfred Clark Hills, for more than a year past connected with the editorial dept of the Chicago Tribune, died in this city yesterday. He formerly practiced law in N Y for a short time, & was once local editor of the N Y Evening Post.

Chancery sale of valuable property on 12th st, near Mass ave, by decree of the Supreme Court of D C, in Chancery, passed Nov 14, 1867, in the cause of Scrivener et al vs Powell et al, No 969 Equity: public auction, on Nov 30, of lot 17 in square 283, with a frame dwlg house. –Asbury Lloyd, trustee -Wm L Wall & Co, aucts

Orphans Court of Wash Co, D C, Nov 19, 1867. In the case of Geo Clendenin, exc of Emma Boscow, deceased, the executor & Court have appointed Dec 17 next, for the final settlement of the personal estate of the said deceased, of the assets in hand. -Jas R O'Beirne, Reg/o wills

Orphans Court of Wash Co, D C, Nov 19, 1867. In the case of John D McPherson, adm of Chas F Robertson, deceased, the administrator & Court have appointed Dec 17 next, for the final settlement of the personal estate of the said deceased, of the assets in hand. -Jas R O'Beirne, Reg/o wills

Dept of the Interior, U S Patent Ofc, Wash, Nov 15, 1867. On the ptn of Jas Pitts, of Clinton, Mass, praying for the extension of a patent granted to him Feb 28, 1854, for an improvement in Cotton Picker Cylinders, for seven years from the expiration of said patent, which takes place on Feb 28, 1868. -T C Theaker, Com'r of Patents

THU NOV 21, 1867
Gen Stevens, an ex-Confederate ofcr, & latterly the superintendent & chief engineer of the Vera Cruz & Mexican railway, is reported to have died on Nov 12.

New Haven, Nov 20. Fitz Greene Halleck died at Guilford last night, aged 80. The news of the death of Fitz Greene Halleck, one of America's earliest poets, will be received with deep sensation by men of genius & of literary taste throughout the world. [Nov 23rd newspaper: Mr Halleck was born in Guilford, Conn, in 1795; his mother was an Elliott, & a descendant of John Elliot, "the apostle to the Indians." Mr Halleck came to N Y in 1818; entered the mercantile house of Jacob Barker, employed there for many years; afterwards was in the service of John Jacob Astor, by whom he was nominated one of the trustees of the Astor Library. Since 1849, Mr Halleck has lived in his native place, retired from business.]

Circuit Court-Chief Justice Cartter. Philip Platt vs Henry Knox. Action for money had & received to recover $274. Davis for plntf, Grammer for dfndnt. Verdict for plntf.

Mrd: on Nov 19, at the residence of J V Grant, by Rev Danl E Reese, D D, Mr Benj F Bean, of Wash City, to Martha, youngest daughter of the late Robt Harrison, of Catlettsburg, Ky.

Died: on Nov 20, Mrs E Donnelly, in her 73rd year. Her funeral will take place at 3:30 P M, on Oct 21, at the residence of her son-in-law, John J Bogue, 51 1st st, Gtwn, D C.

Died: on Nov 19, in Richmond, Va, of apoplexy, at the residence of Col Arther Anderson, Miss Ann Gertrude Wight. Her friends are invited to attend her funeral at the Chapel of **Oak Hill Cemetery**, Gtwn, D C, on Thu, Nov 21, at 3 o'clock P M.

Jurors for the Dec Term of the Criminal Court:
Grand Jury:

Wm Emerson	Chas O'Hare	Chas Trunnel
Reuben Daw	Richd J Saffill	John H Newman
John Fowler	Richd G Dove	Thos Irwin
B P Nichols	Geo McClelland	John B Davidson
W H Brawner	Wm Beattie	Jenkin Thomas
Henry Koch	P H Donegan	Saml H Ellis
Jos Chick	Henderson Fowler	
F M Jarboe	Geo F Coningham	

Petit Jury:

J P Klengle	Chris F Eckloff	J J McCollum
Lewis H Scrivener	E E White	Ed S Holmes
Louis P Rodier	H B Walker	Edmund Handley
Herman Gasch	W H Chase	John E Cox
H C Hepburn	E R Brown	N C McKnew
Saml V Hurdle	Christian T Vollard	Thos Summerville
A Kiesicker	J Carter	W H Brereton
W H Marlow	Z C Robbins	Peter A Cassiday
Chirs F Eckloff	Wm Kickham	
E E White	Tazewell B Amoss	

Fred Benedict was committed to jail yesterday, on the charge of stealing a gold watch from the store of Mr Branninger, 287 Pa ave, on Tuesday.

Henry T Fant has sold his farm of 261 acres, on the railroad, between Warrenton & the Junction, for $12,000, to Capt Robt Minor.

Patents to Washingtonians during the past week:
1-For a journal box for cars, to G H Clemens, assignor to himself & Henry A Chadwick. 2-A System for cooling air & other substances, to Danl E Somes. For this the inventor claims a system of atomizing liquids by means of a fan-blower. 3-An elastic packing for the joints of doors, lids, & the like, to Danl E Somes. 4-For a paper file, to Wm Fallon, who claims a combination of a folding extension-back to file binders, with flap in front & India-rubber strap, with reinforces on each end & clasps for the same. 5-For a mode of attaching ferrules to handles, to Asa L Carrier, of Wash, who claims a ferrule which is easily constructed & applied to tool handles, umbrellas, & canes.

Scott Holderman, formerly a member of the 6th Kansas regt, was hung at Lawrence, Kansas, on Friday. He was convicted of the murder of a soldier, about 2 years ago in Linn Co. He was 24 years of age, & made a dying confession to the effect that he had, during the last few years, murdered 16 men, mostly rebels.

Moses J Moses, head book-keeper of the N Y Co Bank for 18 years, committed suicide in N Y C on Monday. He was 70 years of age, & no cause is as yet assigned for the act.

Gen Sickles was mustered out of service as a major general of volunteers, the order was issued in May, 1866, instead of 1867, so that Gen Sickles, & the other volunteer ofcrs recently mustered out & yet to be dispensed with, have been retained in service for 18 months after the order for their discharge.

Hon Reverdy Johnson, who has been deprived of sight in one of his eyes for the last 30 years, can see out of his remaining eye as well as he ever could. Rumors that he was becoming blind, is an entire mistake.

By order of the Sec of War, Col Edgar M Gregory, 91st Pa volunteers, [brvt major general, U S volunteers,] is hereby mustered out & honorably discharged the service of the U S, to date Nov 30, 1867, on account of his services being no longer required.

A T Leving, of Buffalo, who arrived in N Y about 2 weeks since, has not been seen or heard of since Nov 9, when he left his hotel with $35,000 in his pocket. It is feared he has been foully dealt with.

The bronze statue of Edw Everett, cast at Munich, from a model by Wm W Story, was placed on its pedestal, in the Public Garden, at Boston, on Monday. The statue is 9 feet in height, & stands on a pedestal designed by Henry Greenough, & executed by Edw F Meany. It represents Mr Everett in the attitude of speaking, with his right arm lifted. The ungracious pantaloons & frock coat detract necessarily from the general effect; but to have presented Mr Everett in any other costume would have been objectionable.

Hon F Stone, member of Congress from the 5th Congressional Dist of Md, is detained at home by severe domestic affliction, his wife having died a few days since.

N Y, Nov 29. 1-The steamer **Arizona**, from Panama, has arrived. Australian advices state that cannibals of Fejee had murdered & eaten Rev T Baker, Wesleyan missionary, & 6 Christian natives. A British war vessel has gone there to punish the murderers. 2-The American residents of Melbourne gave a complimentary dinner to Mr Latham, the American Consul, who has just arrived. 3-The ship **Arizona** brings $187,840 in specie.

Dept of the Interior, U S Patent Ofc, Wash, Nov 18, 1867. Ptn of Geo W Coats & Jas Russell, of Springfield, Mass, praying for the extension of a patent granted to them Aug 1, 1854, for an improvement in Machines for Sticking Card Teeth, for seven years from the expiration of said patent, which takes place on Aug 1, 1863. -T C Theaker, Com'r of Patents

Headquarters Fifth Military Dist, New Orleans, Nov 20, 1867. Special Orders, No 181. [Extract] The present incumbents being impediments to reconstruction, under the law of Congress, the following removals & appointments of civil ofcrs in La are hereby ordered: Paul E Heard, Judge 4th Dist Court, parish of Orleans, is removed, & J P Boyd appointed in his place; Rich C Bond, clerk 4th Dist Court, parish of Orleans, is removed, & Wm L Randall, appointed in his place; Wm Waelper, clerk 6th Dist Court, parish of Orleans, is removed, & H C Caulkins appointed in his place; Paul W Collins, 3rd justice of the peace, parish of Orleans, is removed, & Eugene Stas appointed in his place; D C Byrly, clerk 3rd Dist Court, parish of Orleans, is removed, & John D Carter appointed in his place; Thos Askew, State tax collector 4th Dist, is removed, & John L Davies appointed in his place. -By command of Brvt Maj Gen Jos A Mower. -Nathl Burbank, A A A G

U S Marshal's sale: on Nov 27, one sausage stuffer, one sausage cutter, one lard press, & 2 iron caldrons, seized & levied upon as the goods & chattels of John Desel, & will be sold to satisfy execution No 3,523, in favor of John Bowers.
–D S Gooding, U S Marshal, D C, per Thos Dowling, auct.

Supreme Court of D C, Equity 834. John Bateman et al vs Jane E Bateman et al. Ordered that the sales made by C Ingle & R R Crawford, trustees for the sale of the real estate of Joshua Batemen, deceased, be ratified & confirmed. The report states the amount of sales to be $16,100. –R J Meigs, clerk

Supreme Court of D C, Equity 804. Augustus Brown, vs Wm Beak, Sarah Beak, Annie Brown, Addison Brown, Thos Brown, John Brown, John Brown, Washington Brown, Victorine Brown, Kate Brown, John Fowler, Caroline Fowler, Jefferson Robertson, & Matilda Robertson. The above cause is referred to me to state the trustee's account & the proper distribution. All parties interested to appear before me on Nov 26. -Walter S Cox, auditor

FRI NOV 22, 1867
Col J S Haldeman, of Harrisburg, Pa, formerly U S Minister to Sweden, fell down a hatch 3 days ago, & broke both legs.

Thos Dowling, auct, Gtwn, sold the frame house & lot on Jefferson st, 300 feet from Water st, to Mr A Kenchel, for $1,325. They also sold lot 23 in Old Gtwn, fronting 60 feet on Prospect st, between Market & Fred'k sts, by a depth of 79 feet, to W O Sanger, for $1,600 cash. Green & Williams, aucts, sold lot 21 in square 390, improved by a good frame house, containing 4 rooms, on G st between 9th & 10th sts, Island, to John Myers, for $2,300.

Capt John O'Brien, an old resident of the 7th Ward, died suddenly yesterday, after an illness of only a few hours. He had been in feeble health for sometime, but his friends had no apprehension of such a speedy dissolution. Capt O'Brien was about 55 years of age, & enjoyed a large acquaintance & popularity in this community.

The iron-clad **New Ironsides**, burned & sunk at Phil last winter, has been sold to Col Norton, of N Y, for $50,000. He is now engaged in raising her hull.

Yesterday John R Montcastle, of Richmond, who was stopping at the boarding house of Mr Michl Murphy, on N Y ave, between 6th & 7th sts, jumped out of the 3rd story window, & fell upon the pavement, a distance of 30 feet, sustaining serious internal injuries, besides being bruised about the face & head by the fall. He was sent to Providence Hospital, in charge of Lt Noonan. Mr Montcastle was in a fit of delirium tremens when he commited the act.

Board of Police. The following reappointments of special ofcrs were made yesterday for 90 days: Jesse W Kitchen, duty in Gtwn, D C; Jonathan M Clarvoe, [not the detective,] to do duty on 9th & 10th sts, from L to M st; W E Dubant, to duty at the Treasury extension; Henry M Dubant, duty at the Treasury extension; Henry M Lowry, duty at the ofc of the Nat'l Safe Deposit Co, 15th st & N Y ave. John S Waugh appointed a private, vice R J McClellan, resigned. Pvt Geo H Thompson, for neglect of duty & insubordination, was ordered to be reprimanded & pay a fine of $20. The Board refused to reconsider their action in refusing to grant a license to sell liquor to the following parties: Michl Lynch, Gtwn; Dennis O'Donovan, Gtwn; Ferguson & Sullivan. They also rejected the applications of the following parties: Johanna Brown, Gtwn; Burnhard Shearar, Tennallyton; Philip Weber, Mrs E Baumann, Jos Barrett, Jas Maher, Mary Jane Carr, Catherine Morgan, Dennis Byrone, John Flynn, Mary McKenny, Arnold Holston, Thos White, Wm Sweeny, Wm Carey, M McCarthy, Jas Cole, August Horsch, John Davison, John Roney, Jas M Jackson, Adolph Gotts, Michl Kelly, Jas Lawnes, Philip Selzer, Hugh Fitzsimons, Catherine Becker, Wm McCarthy, Wm Kennedy, Henry Oentrick, Harmon Smith, Wm Shearar, C C Willard, G Godfrey, John Talty.

Wash Nat'l Monument Ofc, Nov 21, 1867. The secretary announced the death of Mr Wm Dougherty, late superintendent of the Monument; which occurred on Nov 6, at Memphis, Tenn. Sincere expressions of sympathy of this society to his family.

A large & fashionable audience was present yesterday afternoon, at the Church of the Epiphany, to witness the nuptials of Baron Henry Van Henri, 2nd secretary of the Belgian Legation, to Miss Camilla Webb, an accomplished & beautiful lady of Wash City. The groomsmen were Mr Maurice Delfosso, the Belgium Minister, & M Cantagalli, sec of the Italian Legation. The bridesmaids were Miss Mary Webb, sister of the bride, & Miss S A Anderson, of Wash City. The happy couple left for N Y last evening, & will sail from thence to Belgium, where they will remain until spring. + [Nov 23rd newspaper:]
Mrd: on Nov 18, at St Aloysius Church, by Rev Chas Stonestreet, & on Nov 21, at the Church of the Epiphany, by Rev C H Hall, Baron Henri Von Havre, Sec of the Belgian Legation & Camilia H, daughter of the late J W Webb, of Wash City.

Died: yesterday, Mrs Nellie Vickers, widow of the late Sgt Thos Vickers, aged 70 years. Her funeral will take place from Grace Church, Island, at 2 P M tomorrow, Saturday.

Died: on Nov 21, of typhoid fever, Edmund G, only child of Edmund G & S A Wheeler, aged 19 months & 6 days. His funeral will take place at the residence of his parents, 127 E st, between 6th & 7th sts. [No time given.]

Died: on Nov 21, George Jasper, son of John B & Mary A Conway, aged 2 years & 11 months. His funeral will take place from his parents residence, 456 2nd st, near St Peter's Church, Capitol Hill, this evening at 3 o'clock P M.

Cincinnati, Nov 21. Shocking railroad accident on the Cincinnati, Hamilton, & Dayton railroad this morning. The train due at 6 o'clock was detained at Lockland by the frieght train coming South. While waiting to take the side track, another freight train following ran into the rear of the car of the express train before the signal-man could get the flag out. Four ladies & one man were burned to death, & nearly all the train was burned to ashes. Three of the ladies killed were sisters, named Morgan. They had tickets from Detroit for Louisville. The other woman lived at Detroit. The man was named Jackson, & was from Boston. Others were injured. [Nov 23rd newspaper: the names of the killed are Harriet, Eliz, Sarah, & Rebecca Morgan, of New Orleans, & Chas Jackson, of Boston. Mr Jackson lost his life in endeavoring to save the ladies. The remains of the Misses Morgan & Mr Chas Jackson have been removed to Spring Grove vault, there to await the orders of their relatives.] [Nov 25th newspaper: wounded: Richd Carr, Toledo; John Weller, Wapakoneta; Chas Shires, Wapakoneta; David Brown, Boston, Mass; Christopher Hoffman; E Goscroft, Dayton; C W Cowden, Van Wert, & Mrs C H Culbertson, of Troy; C Haynes, 428 George st; Mrs Jones, colored, N Y; Peter Colter, N J; Miss Wunder, Cincinnati-she was returning from a party at Hamilton. Messrs Bell Brown, Hoffman, & Carr were taken to St Luke's Hospital for treatment. Also injured: Miss Lizzie Ewing, Miss Belle Wunder, Miss Tillie Wunder, Eugene Zimerman, Del Martin, Chas Heintz, all of Cincinnati. The young ladies above mentioned were all returning, in company with others, from the party at Hamilton. Mr Brewer, the engineer of the train, was badly burned in attempting to rescue the sisters Morgan. Mr Allison escaped with slight bruises. Letters in the sisters' trunks revealed that they were of a wealthy family of New Orleans, their given names being Harriet, Rebecca, Sarah, & Elizabeth. They left home in New Orleans in June last, & spent the summer & fall at St Catharine's Wells & Toronto, Canada West. When killed they were on their way home. A letter from Chas Harrod, Magazine & Natchez sts, New Orleans, was signed as their affectionate brother; also a letter from his wife, Clara M Harrod, signing herself as their affectionate sister, from which is inferred that Mr Harrod is their brother-in-law. The gentleman killed was Mr Chas Jackson, of Boston, who was not scratched but roasted alive. Mr Erwin House, of this city, was unhurt; Mr Jas Gale, of Boston, was thrown through the front window & entirely uninjured. Conductor Sliter was at the station, & sent for surgeons.]

San Francisco, Nov 21. Mrs Cunningham, of the Burdell Cunningham notoriety, is the plaintiff before the Dist Court in a divorce suit.

Notice. I forewarn all persons from trusting my wife on my account, as I will pay no debts which may be contracted by her from this date. —Conrad Knatz, Nov 22, 1867.

SAT NOV 23, 1867
Green & Williams, aucts, sold a brick house with lot whereon it is situated, fronting on 8th st west, between O & P sts north, to Craven Ashford, for $1,900.

Ads 1-A family horse is for sale by Thos Taggart. 2-Large stock of furniture may be found at the store of John Q Wilson, 9th & D sts.

A colored woman, Adeline Harris, was shot by Wm Carter, a colored man, about midnight on Thu, in a frame shanty on C st, between 4½ & 6th sts, & died almost instantly. After examination, it was found she was shot by Jas Henry Carter, colored, Abraham Hill was an accessory. The murderer is still at large.

Circuit Court-Chief Justice Cartter. 1-Deeley vs Shannahan was submitted to the jury, without argument. The jury returned a verdict that Joanna Deeley was not competent to execute the deed at the time of the signing. Mr Merrick moved for a new trial.

We regret to announce the death, in this city, of Col J Howard Skinker, of Stafford Co, Va, a true man, a cultivated gentleman, & a sincere friend. A the outbreak of the late rebellion he contributed largely of his picuniary means, in the shape of beeves, horses, mules, & subsistence. At the headquarters of the Provost Marshal General of the Army of the Potomac Col Skinker rendered invaluable services, which were appreciated & acknowledged by Gen Patrick, & many others. He leaves his sisters, who remain at the denuded homestead, bereft of their brother, & the means of support.

Mrd: on Nov 18, at St Aloysius Church, by Rev Chas Stonestreet, & on Nov 21, at the Church of the Epiphany, by Rev C H Hall, Baron Henri Von Havre, Sec of the Belgian Legation & Camilia H, daughter of the late J W Webb, of Wash City.

Died: on Nov 23, Miss Lucy Roy Miller, daughter of the late Maj Thos R Miller, of Port Royal, Caroline Co, Va. Her friends & those of her brother, Dr Thos Miller, are invited to attend her funeral from her late residence, 424 N Y ave, this afternoon, at 2 o'clock P M.

Died: on Nov 21, at the Boston Navy Yard, in her 25th year, Eliz M McCawley, daughter of Jas & Eliz M Colgate, & wife of Maj Chas G McCawley, of the Marine Corps. Her remains will be interred at *Mount Auburn Cemetery*. [Nov 25th newspaper: Mrs McCawley was known in this, the city of her birth, as Lizzie Colegate.]

Equity Court-Judge Wylie. 1-Ragan vs Ragan; appointing T L Murray guardian *ad litem*. 2-Wm F Mattingly to sue dfndnt's undivided moiety.

Michl Sullivan, a young man, residing at Auburn, N Y, on last Thursday, visited Miss Georgia Stearns, a young lady of that place, who rejected his addresses. While she was playing the piano he drew a seven-shooter, & sent a bullet through her neck, inflicting a severe but not fatal wound. The assassin is in jail.

Supreme Court of D C, Equity 939. Jas S Wilson, Leotine Wilson, vs Mary H Wilson, Jane R Matthews, Wm H Wilson, Thos J Anderson, & Romana Anderson. Statement of the account of the trustee & distribution of proceeds of sale; Nov 26, at my ofc, at 10 o'clock. –Walter S Cox, auditor

U S Marshal's sale: at the auction store of John B Wheeler & Co, on La ave, between 6th & 7th sts, Wash City, mscl furniture-the goods & chattels of Moses Switzer, & will be sold to satisfy attachment in favor of Henry S Martin. –D S Gooding, U S Marshal, D C

MON NOV 25, 1867

Cooper & Latimer, aucts, have sold part of lot 8 in square 323, with a brick tenement, 323 D st & Pa ave, between 11th & 12th sts, to Fred'k Koones, for $4,300.

The funeral of Christopher Friess yesterday was attended by Oriental Lodge I O O F, accompanied by Heald's Band. The remains were interred in **Prospect Cemetery**.

Impeachment: Under the Constitution of the U S, the House of Reps has the sole power of impeachment, while the Senate has the sole power of trial.

A Catholic man was lately married to a Protestant lady in St Aloysius, with the necessary dispensation of the Most Rev Archbishop; the intention of these parties to appear afterwards before a Protestant minister, there to be married again, not being known either to us when they were married here, or to the Archbishop when he gave the dispensation to the man to marry a Protestant. By the order of the Most Rev Archbishop, regret is hereby publicly expressed for what occurred at that late marriage, the Archbishop having disapproved of the same, & required this public announcement, lest it should pass into a precedent, & that all Catholics may understand such marriages are contrary to the discipline of the Church. Thus far, the order of the Most Rev Archbishop. We may only add, reminding the people, that according to the laws of the Church, any of the faithful who presume to get married out of the Church, by the very act incur excommunication.

Died: on Nov 23, in Wash City, after a lingering illness, Henry M B McPherson, aged 32 years, son of the late Dr Wm McPherson, of Chas Co, Md. His funeral will be from the residence of Mrs Parish, 416 E st, between 8th & 9th sts, at 2 o'clock. [Funeral date not given-could be today.]

Court of Equity, Nov 22, 1867. Brown vs Beckett et al, involving the status of colored connubial relations. The cmplnt, as rep of creditors of Clement Beckett, applies to set aside a deed for the use of Mary Beckett, who was alleged to be the wife of said Clement, for the purpose of selling such property under an execution against Clement. It appears that the land in question was originally purchased in the name of Beckett, but Mary Beckett improved it out of her own earnings, & also paid off an incumbrance of $1,500, for which Clement deeded her the lots. She has spent some $4,000 of her own earnings as a washerwoman on the lots. The Judge says, "Still we are bound to decide that however worthless the husband may be, all the earnings & savings of the wife are his, & are therefor liable for his debts; & if she has even paid off incumbrances upon the property to an amount exceeding its value that will not save her, but the deed which proposes to secure it for her use must be set aside as fraudulent as against creditors, whose claims were in existence at the date of its execution. He holds that these principles do not apply to this case, because Mary Beckett was not in law the wife of Clement; the evidence shows that when they came together in 1836, they were slaves, & to the code of slavery the relation of husband & wife was a stranger. After they were emancipated they continued to live together Both parties, in sworn answers, deny that they were ever married subsequently to the acquisition of their freedom. Consent, not cohabitation, makes marriage. The injustice threatened to be done to this poor woman & her children by seizures on the fruits of labor, economy, & thrift, & applying them a second time to the payment of the debts of a thriftless & trifling drone, whom she has fed, clothed, & sheltered, because he was the father of her children, may fortunately be averted without the violation of any of the statblished rules of law. The bill should be dismissed with costs.

Mrd:on Nov 12, at the Calvary Church, by Geo F Seymour, D D, Chas M Bergen, of Brooklyn, N Y, to Susie A Fletcher, step-daughter of Henry Parry, of N Y.

Orphans Court-Judge Purcell, Nov 23, 1867. 1-Letters of adm on the estate of Jas Sutton were issued to Wm Nixon; bond $1,400. 2-The first account of Danl McFarlan, guardian to Ida Moore Baldwin, orphan of H Clay Baldwin, was approved & passed. 3-The caveat recently filed by Sarah B & Geo Hatton against the probate of the will of the late Eleanor Miller came up. Certain testimony touching the testamentary capacity of the testatrix, offered by the counsel for the caveators, was objected to by the counsel for the propounders of the will, on which a lengthy discussion on legal propositions occurred at the close of which a plenary proceeding was ordered by the Court & the Reg of Wills was directed to take all the testimony in writing. This case involves a large amount of real estate in this District, bequeathed by the late Mrs Miller to one of her daughters. Mr R Leech, counsel for the propounders of the will, & Mr M Thompson for the caveators.

Died: on Nov 19, in N Y, Ellen Pearson, only daughter of John & Anna M Farley. Her remains were deposited in the family vault at Brentwood near Wash on Nov 23.

Albert Barlett, from Cumberland, a boatman on the canal boat **Cygnet**, fell in the canal in Gtwn, on Friday last, & was drowned. At the time he was intoxicated; he had no means. His body was turned over to Sanitary Ofcr Sebastian for interment. Bartlett was a single man, aged 27 years.

Dept of the Interior, U S Patent Ofc, Wash, Nov 20, 1867. Ptn of John B Holmes, of N Y, N Y, praying for the extension of a patent granted to him Feb 21, 1854, for an improvement in Derricks, for seven years from the expiration of said patent, which takes place on Feb 21, 1868. -T C Theaker, Com'r of Patents

Dept of the Interior, U S Patent Ofc, Wash, Nov 20, 1867. Ptn of Sidney S Turner, of Westboro, Mass, praying for the extension of a patent granted to him Mar 25, 1856, & again reissued May 16, 1865, for an improvement in Sewing Machines, praying for the extension of a patent granted to him Aug 22, 1868.
-T C Theaker, Com'r of Patents

Orphans Court of Wash Co, D C. Letters of administration on the personal estate of Jas Sutton, late of U S army, deceased. —Wm Nixon, adm

TUE NOV 26, 1867
The Cincinnati Commercial says, P B Stanbery, son of Atty Gen Stanbery, was married, on Wed, to one of the belles of Pomeroy, Ohio. The happy pair left on the steamer **Success** for Wash City, on Thursday. [Neither the marriage date nor the bride's name was given.]

Impeachment evidence: testimony of Gen U S Grant & Gen Wm S Hillyer
Jul 18, 1867: Gen Ulysses S Grant was sworn & examined. Jul 18, 1867: Wm S Hillyer was sworn & examined.

Dept of the Interior, U S Patent Ofc, Wash, Nov 21, 1867. Ptn of Lotto P Meyer, of Newtown, Conn, praying for extension of a patent granted to him Feb 28, 1854, for an improvement in Vulcanizing India Rubber & other Gums, for 7 years from the expiration of said patent, which takes place on Feb 28, 1868.
-T C Theaker, Com'r of Patents

Dr J W Bulkley has removed from 324 G st, corner of 8th st, to 313 F st, corner of 11th st, opposite Sear's Drug Store.

WED NOV 27, 1867
Impeachment. As the Intelligencer has over & over again tabooed the idea of impeachment, either as to just causes or to the supposition that it could obtain among partisans having common sense, we have now to recede from that position in so far as a majority of the House Cmte on the Judiciary are concerned.

Promotion yesterday in the Internal Revenue Dept: Col John Dowling, a well know gentleman of Wash City, went up higher, from 1st to 2nd class clerkship.

Mr Josiah Melvin, a well known printer of Wash City, died yesterday at his residence, near 10th & O sts. His funeral will take place tomorrow, & will be attended by the Odd Fellows & Sons of Temperance, of both of which he was a member.

Board of Police & the Liquor-sellers. The Board reconsidered & rejected the applications of the following persons for licenses: John Rooney, Edw Vought, W A H Mack, Thos Biggins, Louis Rothschild, Harman Smith. The applications of the following were rejected: Darby Coen, Matthew De Atley, John Pfulger, John Shannahan, J T Martin, & Michl Shay.

Impeachment: testimony of Hon E M Stanton, May, 1867.

Yesterday Patrick Fitzgerald, laborer, while at work in a sewer being built in 19th st, suddenly fell from the platform, in a spasm, & breathed his last. His body was taken to his residence on 23rd st, between L & M sts, where his family reside.

Orphans Court-Judge Purcell, Nov 26, 1867. 1-The ptn of Martha An Truxell, guardian for sale of real estate, filed. Wm F Mattingly solicitor for petitioner. Decree for sale in same case filed. 2-The last wills & testaments of Lucy A Miller & Maria Miller were filed & partically proven.

On Sunday, near Long Bridge, Amsey Spriggs, colored, a laborer, was found murdered. The murderer is unknown.

Yesterday, Mr Stuart, gunner of the Washington Navy Yard, was superintending the placing in position of a large cannon, the derrick with which it was being raised fell. Mr Stuart was caught under it, & it is feared he is fatally injured. He was conveyed to his residence, where medical assistance was obtained. [Dec 11th newspaper: Gunner Stewart is rapidly recovering from his bruises, & expects soon to be able to attend to his duties.]

Mrd: on Nov 26, by Rev Fr McCarthy, Walter B Williams to Clara V Gittings, all of Wash. No cards.

Mrd: on Nov 26, at the parsonage, by Rev Fr Jamison, J G Kengla to Hellen R Yeabower, all of Gtwn. No cards. [Leesburg, Va, & Cumberland, Md, papers please copy.]

Died: on Nov 24, at Phil, Mrs E E McLaren, wife of Surgeon A N McLaren, U S A, & daughter of the late Maj D S Townsend, Paymaster U S A.

Gen Fitzhugh Lee will be married to Miss Bolling, of Petersburg, tonight.

Phil, Nov 26. The funeral of Chief Engineer Lyle will take place on Thursday, & is to be attended by the Fire Dept in a body, with delegations from other cities.

Ex-Govn'r Isham G Harris, who left Nashville on the approach of the Federal forces in 1862, returned there on Sunday. He went directly to the Govn'r, who received him kindly, & allowed him to depart to his home in Henry Co, on giving his parole of honor to appear at the Federal court in March next, to answer an indictment for treason which is pending against him. He left England on Nov 6.

Supreme Court of D C, Equity 895, Docket 8. Wm H Wood et al vs Geo W Wood et al. On motion of the cmplnts, by M Thompson, their solicitor, it is ordered that the real estate of Mary Wood, deceased, as made by the com'rs be reported to this Court, ratified & confirmed. –R J Meigs, clerk

Orphans Court of Wash Co, D C. Letters of administration on the personal estate of Frances M Kean, late of Charleston, S C, deceased. –Richd Kelly, adm

Orphans Court of Wash Co, D C, Nov 26, 1867. In the case of John D McPherson, exc of John T Cochran, deceased, the executor & Court have appointed Dec 21 next, for the final settlement of the personal estate of the said deceased, of the assets in hand. -Jas R O'Beirne, Reg/o wills

Orphans Court of Wash Co, D C, Nov 26, 1867. In the case of Chas G Page, adm of Jerry L Page, deceased, the administrator & Court have appointed Dec 21 next, for the final settlement of the personal estate of the said deceased, of the assets in hand. -Jas R O'Beirne, Reg/o wills

Chancery sale of valuable real estate on La ave, near 6th st, known as the *Lichau House*; by decree of the Supreme Court of D C, in Equity 901; wherein Chas G Ball is cmplnt & Henry Lichau et al are dfndnts: public auction, on Dec 19, part of lot 13 in square 490, together with bldgs & improvements thereon. –Eugene Carusi, A Thos Bradley, Wm J Miller, Thos E Lloyd, Asbury Lloyd, trustees
-Cooper & Latimer, aucts

THU NOV 28, 1867
Impeachment Case-Jul 2, 1867: 1-Jas Speed, of Louisville, Ky, sworn & examined.

U S Marshal's sale: on Dec 5, part of lot 2 in square 289, fronting on F st, between 12th & 13th sts, formerly occupied by dfndnts as an ice cream saloon, in Wash City, seized & levied upon as the property of Wm H Singston & W C Crocker, No 3,870, in favor of C Collier, & No 3,871, in favor of same, vs F P Crocker, & C W Crocker, & No 3,872, W H Lewis vs C W Crocker & Wm Crocker.
–D S Gooding, U S Marshal, D C

Mrd: on Nov 27, at St John's Church, Wash, by Rev Mr Lewis, Jas R Hall, of Balt to Alice C, daughter of the late John Hopkins, of Gtwn, D C.

FRI NOV 29, 1867
Saratoga, Nov 28. Ex-Chancellor Walworth died here today, aged 79 years.

Impeachment Case: May 20, 1867: Hon Henry Stanbery sworn & examined. John C Braine was an ofcr of the Confederate navy during the war; he with several other men, took passage on the ship **Chesapeake**, a passenger vessel, at N Y, for Portland, Maine. They passed themselves off as a party of recruits for the U S army, & paid their passage money. After getting to sea, during the night, they rose upon the ofcrs & crew, & captured the vessel, killing one of the crew in the melee. Braine is known to have been a Confederate ofcr; but there seems no legal certainty that he was before or at the time of this exploit. Braine has been in jail more than a year, having been indicted at Brooklyn for piracy & murder on the high sea. At the next term of the court Braine will be tried on the indictment.

The funeral of the late Josiah Melvin took place yesterday from the M st Methodist Church; services conducted by Rev Mr Tudor; the church was crowded with the friends of the deceased. The remains were escorted to **Glenwood Cemetery** by Columbia Lodge No 10, the Grand Lodge I O O F, of which Mr Melvin was past Grand Master, & Columbia Typographical Union, of the District.

Yesterday, in Hudson Co, in the town of South Bergen, the explosion of a can of nitro-glycerine caused the killing of: John Hicks, blacksmith-he leaves a wife & 7 children; two brothers, Miller, carpenters, both residents of Bergen; Thos Burns, foreman of blasting; Ned Foster, a boy, employed to carry drills to be sharpened. Thos Burns went into the blacksmith shop for the purpose of drying a can of glycerine which had become damp; he took a poker, & after heating it red hot, thrust it down into the can. Instantly a most terrific explosion occurred. Mr Burns was intoxicated at the time.

Cumberland Alleganian. Obit-died: on Nov 10, 1867, at Cumberland, Allegany Co, Md, Estelle F Perry, beloved wife of Capt Roger Perry, U S Navy, & daughter of B Ogle Tayloe, of Wash, D C, in her 35th year. In these days of substitution & evasion she dared to be a mother to her own children & the mistress of her household. Husband & children grieve not alone. She was a noble wife, a faithful mother, a valuable friend, a true Christian.

SAT NOV 30, 1867
Messrs Wall & Co, on Wed, sold a 2 story brick house & lot on 2nd st, between F & Va ave, to John Walsh, for $2,155. Thos Dowling, auct, sold, at private sale, lot 128, fronting 97 feet on Wash st, between Dunbarton & Beall sts, Gtwn, by a dept of 60 fet, improved by a 2 story brick dwlg house, to J H Phillips, for $5,600, cash.

Mrs Gen Gaines has arrive in New Orleans to prosecute her claims for the estate of her father, Danl Clark.

Hon Walter Preston, a distinguished lawyer, died at Abingdon, Va, a few days since. He was one of the most brilliant men of Va. His eloquence at times was worthy of the finest orators the State has ever produced, from Henry down, & was electric in its influence on the people.

Dickens takes a 10 mile walk into the country regularly every day. His sustained & vigorous stride usually tires out adventurous companion who seek to keep pace with him. He visited the school ship in Boston harbor on Saturday.

Mr Frank Rawles, of Oakalona, Miss, received a despatch last week from Memphis, requesting him to come immediately & settle a debt of $2,700. He procured the money & started from his house to the depot. He had not gone a dozen yards, when he was shot down & robbed. He died almost instantly. No clue as to who the assassin could be.

Mrd: on Nov 27, at the residence of the bride's father, in PG Co, Md, by Rev W M D Ryan, Jas W McKee to A C Josephine, daughter of T B Robey.

Mrd: on Nov 27, by Rev Fr Early, S J, O C Green, of Rosedale, D C, to Miss Sarah H, daughter of the late Alfred Price, of Kent Island, Md.

Mrd: on Nov 27, by Rev A D Gillette, Wm Chambers, of Wash City, to Mary A Higdon, of Alexandria, Va.

N Y, Nov 29. Admiral John Drake Sloat died at his residence on Staten Island, yesterday, aged 87 years. He will be buried on Sunday. Admiral Sloat entered the navy on Feb 12, 1800, & received his commission as rear admiral on Jul 25, 1866. He has had 17 years & 6 months sea service, besides 20 years & 3 months on shore duty. He returned home from his last cruise in Dec, 1852.

Died: on Nov 29, Charles E, infant son of Henry & Eugenia E Woodard, aged 10 months.

MON DEC 2, 1867
Three iron-clads-the ironclads **Tennessee, Nashville, & Osage**, were sold at auction at New Orleans a few days since for $21,000. The **Nashville** lises sunk near the bank. The **Tennessee & Nashville** were celebrated Confederate rams, the former, almost unaided & alone, commanded by Admiral Buchanan, having encountered & fought the immense Federal fleet of iron & wooden ships commanded by Admiral Farragut in Mobile. Divested of her formidable armament, the **Tennessee**, once the pride of the nation, lies a helpless mass of wood & iron. The **Tennessee**, we think, was built at Selmy, & cost about $1,500,000, in what was termed in those days "new issue." The **Nashville** was built at some point on the Alabama river, & cost about $1,000,000. She participated in no naval engagement, but was present during the attack on Spanish Fort & Blakely, just before the evacuation of Mobile.

Died: suddenly, at the Burnett House, in Cincinnati, Ohio, Jos Gales Dorsey, in his 28th year, son of E J Dorsey, of Wash City, D C. [No death date given-current item.]

Died: on Nov 20, in Wash City, in her 66th year, Mrs Harriet J Chase, widow of the late Col Cyrus Chase, of Boston, Mass. The funeral services will be at the house of Dr Hatch, 270 F st, today at 2 o'clock. Interment will take place in Salem, Mass.

Died: on Nov 30, Wm Donoho, in his 29th year. His funeral will be from his late residence, on L st, between 19th & 20th sts, this afternoon, at 3 o'clock.

For sale: the National Intelligencer, bound in volumes, from 1801 to 1862. Inquire of Jos F Kelley, Real estate Agent, Ofc 363 8th st, near I st.

TUE DEC 3, 1867
Mark Grayson, a Kansas pedestrian, walked 100 miles, this week, at the Leavenworth fair grounds, in 23 hours & 6 minutes. He is a young man of 23, & weighs 135 pounds.

Railroad accident on Tuesday last on the Mobile & Great Northern railroad, with Costello's circus & menagerie on board, ran off the track near Martin's Mills. Six cars were precipitated down a 40 foot embankment. A lion, three bears, two tigers, a hyena, & hippotamus were turned loose. One of the bears getting hold of a beautiful American deer made short work of her. The animals were secured with great difficulty. Lewis Burrows, attached to the circus dept, was killed, & 4 others were severely wounded.

Despatch from Montreal, Canada, Nov 25, says Mrs Howell, Mr Davis mother-in-law, died there that morning, at the residence of John Lovell. The deceased lady was a native of Georgia, & about 65 years of age.

Leopold O'Donnell, Marshal & ex-Minister of Spain, & at one time Govn'r of Cuba, died on Nov 5; he was of Irish extraction; born about 1809, & entered the Spanish army at an early age.

Mrd: on Nov 30, by Rev C C Meador, Wm J Lee, of Va, to Miss Jennie E Sinnott, of Richmond, Va.

Died: on Dec 2, Henry Edmund Clark, aged 40 years. His funeral will be from the residence of his father, John D Clark, 403 H st, at 8:30 A M, Wednesday morning, Dec 4. His funeral service will take place at St Patrick's Church, at 9 A M.

Trustee's sale of valuable real estate, by deed of trust executed to me, to secure a certain debt therein mentioned by Saml Owen, dated Jul 30, 1864, recorded in Liber N C T, No 42, folios 148 to 152, of the land records for Wash Co, D C: for sale, at the premises, on Dec 26, part of lot 3 in square 225, in Wash City, with a substantial 5 story brick house, fitted up for a hotel. –Geo W Riggs, trustee
-Cooper & Latimer, aucts

Cincinnati, Dec 2. 1-The family of C W Cook, of McMinnville, Tenn, was poisoned a few days since by the mistaken use of arsenic for soda in making the bread. Four of the family, including Mr Cook, have died. 2-The negro who committed the outrage on Mrs Baker, of Princeton, Indiana, was caught the same night, & made a full confession of the crime. He was then seized by a mob & stabbed, shot, & beaten until he was dead.

Orphans Court of Wash Co, D C, Nov 30, 1867. In the case of John B Hutchinson, exc of Jacob Loewenthal, deceased, the executor & Court have appointed Dec 28 next, for the final settlement of the personal estate of the said deceased, of the assets in hand. -Jas R O'Beirne, Reg/o wills

Dept of the Interior, U S Patent Ofc, Wash, Nov 27, 1867. Ptn of A M Sawyer, of Athol, Mass, praying for the extension of a patent granted to him Mar 7, 1854, for an improvement in Machines for Splitting Rattans, for seven years from the expiration of said patent, which takes place on Mar 7, 1868. -T C Theaker, Com'r of Patents

WED DEC 4, 1867
Mrd: on Nov 20, at St James Church, Lancaster, by Rev J S Membert, D D, Robt Acheson Gray, of Stafford Co, Va, to Adelaide Gettys, daughter of the late Wm Hayman, of Gtwn, D C. No cards.

Died: on Dec 2, Mr Francis Lowndes, in his 84th year. His funeral will take place this afternoon at 2 o'clock, from his late residence, 116 Prospect st, Gtwn.

Mr Dickens declines an offer of $2,000 a night to read in Chicago.

Saml McLean offers for sale the property he at present occupies in the town Alexandria, corner of Cameron & St Asaph sts; handsome modern built 3 story dwlg, with back bldg, & all necessary out-houses; with a 2 story brick ofc on the premises. Apply on the premises.

Supreme Court of D C, Equity 953. Bassett et al vs Thorn et al. Ordered that the sale made by Eugene Carusi, trustee, be ratified & confirmed. –R J Meigs, clerk [No other details.]

Supreme Court of D C, Equity 1,112, Docket 8. John A Ruff vs G J Musser et al. It is ordered that the dfndnt, Ebenezer Scott, if living, or if dead, that his heirs cause his or their appearance to be entered herein on or before the first rule day occurring forty days after this day; otherwise the case will be proceeded with as in case of default. –R J Meigs, clerk, Dec 4, 1867

Dept of the Interior, U S Patent Ofc, Wash, Nov 29, 1867. Ptn of Warren Gale, of Peekskill, N Y, praying for the extension of a patent granted to him Mar 7, 1854, for an improvement in the gauge of Straw-Cutters, for seven years from the expiration of said patent, which takes place on Mar 7, 1868. -T C Theaker, Com'r of Patents

THU DEC 5, 1867

Equity Court-Judge Wylie. 1-John A Goodrich & Wm Goodrich vs Mary Goodrich. Ordered that Henry H Young, trustee in said cause, show cause on or before Dec 10, 1867, why an attachment should not issue against him for failing to pay said John A Goodrich the sum awarded & due him in said cause.
2-Cryer vs Cryer, divorce a *vinculo matrimonii*.

Orphans Court of Wash Co, D C, Dec 3, 1867. In the case of A Thomas Bradley, adm c t a, of Wm M Walker, deceased, the administrator, c t a, & Court, have appointed Dec 28 next, for the final settlement of the personal estate of the said deceased, of the assets in hand. -Jas R O'Beirne, Reg/o wills

Orphans Court of Wash Co, D C. Letters of administration on the personal estate of Emily Pomeroy Dodge, late of Wash City, D C, deceased. –N S Dodge, adm

Oldest Inhabitants' Association meeting yesterday: Mr J Thomas to confer with Mr Carusi in reference to the invitation extended the association to be present at the reopening of his saloon. The following gentlemen were proposed & elected members: Gen Geo D Ramsay, Nathl P Causin, Thos Plumsill, & John Clements, of Gtwn. Dr Blake read a memoir of the late Dr Wm Jones, who was born near Rockville, Montg Co, Md, on Apr 12, 1790, & educated at the Rockville Academy, under the charge of Dr John Breckinridge, & was, during the late war with Great Britain, appointed assistant surgeon in the U S army. Subsequently he resigned a permanent appointment in order to practice as a private physician. He was appointed Postmaster of Washington under Jackson's, Tyler's, & Buchanan's administrations, in all a period of nearly 17 years. Mr John F Callan offered the resolution that the next meeting be held at Willard's Hotel, Jan 1, 1868, for the purpose of paying our respects in a body to the Pres of the U S. John F Callan, J Thomas, & E J Middleton were appointed on the cmte.

Died: on Dec 4, at his residence, 463 9th st, Joseph Lyons, aged 63 years. His funeral will take place on Dec 6 at 11 A M, from his late residence.

The famous horse Loadstone, bred by John Harper, of Ky, & purchased 2 years ago by M H Sanford, of N Y, for $7,500, died on Saturday last. Loadstone was a remarkable horse.

Orphans Court of Wash Co, D C. Letters of administration on the personal estate of Henry Becker, late of Wash, D C, deceased. –Chas Walter, adm

Geo T Rice, one of our most prominent citizens, & for several years president of the Worcester & Nashua railroad, & president of Worcester Gas Co, died on Thanksgiving Day, at Worcester, Mass.

Our exchanges announce the death of R A Alexander, of Ky; foremost in every agricultural enterprise; his stables were stocked with the most valuable English & Arabian horses, & English & European cattle. [No death date given-current item.]

Despatch from Boston dated Monday says: Mr Chas Dickens' first appearance in America as a reader was the great event here this evening. Tremont Temple, one of the largest halls in the city was filled in every available part by perhaps one of the most appreciative, fashionable, & brilliant audiences ever assembled in New England. He read his "Christmas Carol," which occupied about one hour & a half. The reading of the "Trial," from Pickwick, convulsed the audience with laughter throughout its entirety.

FRI DEC 6, 1867
Wm F Given purchased lot 17 in square 283, with a 2 story frame house, on 12th st, between L & Mass ave, on Saturday, for $2,800.

Patent to a Washingtonian: to Mr J Bell Alexander for a device for attaching burners to lamps.

Jas F Haliday, an old & much respected citizen of Wash City, died at his residence, 391 N Y ave, yesterday. For some time past he has been in bad health, & he was finally carried off by that insidious disease, consumption. Mr Haliday died at the advanced age of 60 years; was a native of Wash City, by profession a printer; was for a long time foreman in the printing establishment of Gen Peter Force, after which he was for several years foreman at the ofc of the Congressional Globe; was representative in the Councils of Wash City, & in 1856-58 was elected Collector of Taxes; since 1860 he had been engaged in the real estate business, & was a member & director of the Washington Library. His funeral will take place at 2 o'clock today from his late residence.
+
Died: on Dec 5, Mr Jas F Haliday, aged 60 years. His funeral is this afternoon, at 2 o'clock, from his late residence, 391 N Y ave, between 12th & 13th sts.

Terrible hurricane has devasted the West Indies; the U S steamer **De Soto**, & the steamer **Monongahela**, are both lost. The **De Soto** was commanded by Cmdor Chas S Boggs, of N Y. The **Monongahela** was commanded by Cmdor Simon B Bissell, [whose family reside in Gtwn.] Private information from Havana, via N Y, states that a large portion of the ofcrs & crew were saved.

On Wed David S Gooding, of Indiana, & U S Marshal for D C, was, on motion of Atty Gen Stanbery, admitted to practice as an atty & counsellor of the U S Supreme Court.

Orphans Court of Wash Co, D C. Letters of administration on the personal estate of Emily Pomeroy Dodge, late of Wash City, D C, deceased. –N S Dodge, adm

Board of Metropolitan Police. The following applications for liquor licenses were reconsidered & rejected: Alvis Miller, Jas Cole, Ferguson & Sullivan, Dennis Byrne, M McCarthy, John Thomas, Benj Cooley, Chas G Godfrey, Jas Lawns, & Timothy McCormick. Applications rejected: Jos Gerhardt, F Wetzel, & Francis Butler. Pvt Geo H Thompson was dismissed to force on being found guilty of drunkenness & disorderly conduct. Pvt John H Mastin, for intoxication & conduct unbecoming an ofcr, was fined $25 & ordered to be severely reprimanded. Pvt Robt French, for neglect of duty & conduct unbecoming an ofcr, was fined $30 & ordered to be severely reprimanded. Pvt Wm H Fuss, for conduct unbecoming an ofcr, was fined $25 & ordered to be severely reprimanded.

Orphans Court of Wash Co, D C, Dec 3, 1867. In the case of A Thomas Bradley, adm c t a, of Wm M Walker, deceased, the administrator, c t a, & Court, have appointed Dec 28 next, for the final settlement of the personal estate of the said deceased, of the assets in hand. -Jas R O'Beirne, Reg/o wills

Orphans Court of Wash Co, D C, Dec 3, 1867. In the case of A Thomas Bradley, adm c t a, of Wm M Walker, deceased, the administrator, c t a, & Court, have appointed Dec 28 next, for the final settlement of the personal estate of the said deceased, of the assets in hand. -Jas R O'Beirne, Reg/o wills

Equity Court-Judge Wylie. 1-Wilson vs Wilson. Bill for divorce & alimony. Mr Swann, for dfndnt, asked that testimony be taken before an examiner as to the amount of income of the dfndnt. Granted. 2-Wallach vs West. Order appointing Eugene Carusi guardian *ad litem*. 3-M L Larner vs A J Larner. Appointing G M Appleby guardian for minor children. 4-*In Re*. Estate of Francis I Truxell. Decree confirming Orphans Court proceedings. 5-Weber vs Weber. Order for sale. Appointing M Thompson trustee.

Mrd: on Dec 3, at **Mount Pleasant**, by Rev B Peyton Brown, Mr Robt Ricketts to Miss Eliza A Little.

Died: on Dec 5, Mrs Biddy, relict of the late David M Wilson, aged 67 years. Her funeral will take place from the residence of her son-in-law, J McMakin, 340 N Y ave, on Sat, Dec 7, at 2 o'clock P M.

Died: on Dec 4, in Wash City, John Julian Sanborn, formerly of Charlestown, Va, aged 70 years. His funeral will be this afternoon at 2½ P M, at 490 I st, near 7th st.

Chancery sale of real estate, by decree of the Supreme Court of D C, passed on Dec 5, 1867, in a cause in Chancery, No 1,092, in which Eliza A Weber is cmplnt & Mary A Weber et al are dfndnts: public auction, on Dec 22, of the south half of lot 17 in square 163, measuring 12 feet 6 inches on 18th st west, by a depth of 110 feet, with a brick house & bakery thereon; fronts on 18th st. –M Thompson, trustee -Green & Williams, aucts

Chancery sale of real property, by decree of the Supreme Court, dated Dec 4, 1867, in Equity, No 743, in which Julia V Ragan is cmplnt, & Thos Ragan et al are dfndnts: public auction, on Dec 20 next, of lots 25 & 26 in square 265, with 2 frame houses thereon; lot 29 in square 265; lot 20 in square 265, being subdivision of lot 7, in square 265, with frame house thereon; lot 17 in square 265, with frame house thereon; lot 28 in square 265, as made & certified by W Forsyth, Surveyor, on Jan 5, 186_, recorded in Liber W F, folio 163. –Julia V Ragan, guardian
-Green & Williams, aucts

Nominations made by the President on Wed to the Senate: Hon Edmund Cooper, of Tenn, to be Assist Sec of the Treasury; Gen Noah L Jeffries, of Md, to be Register of the Treasury; J Warren Bell, late of Tenn, to be collector of customs at Brownsville, Texas; E T Wood, to be collector of internal revenue for the 3rd district of N Y, vice T C Callicott, suspended; Jacob Carmany, assessor for the 10th dist of Pa; Gen John E Mulford, collector for the 3rd dist of Va; John S Walton, treasurer of the branch mint at New Orleans, vice Wm R Whittaker, suspended; Wm J Clark, surveyor of the customs at Saybrook, Conn, vice G Blague, deceased; Edwin J Klopfer, John C Cox, & John H Goddard, justices of the peace for the Dist of Columbia.

SAT DEC 7, 1867
Thos Dowling, auct, sold at auction part of the lot fronting 17 feet on Jefferson st, between Canal & Water sts, Gtwn, having a depth of 105 feet, with the improvements thereon, to Fred'k Pascoe, for $405.

N Y, Dec 5. John C Braine, alleged Chesapeake pirate, now confined in Kings Co penitentiary, Atty Gen Stanbery has refused to interfere, he having some time ago been appealed to for his opinion as to whether the prisoner could be included in the terms granted to rebels at surrender. The Atty Gen suggests that he be tried, when the jury may determine with reference to his connection with the Confederate service. Braine's trial, consequently, will be proceeded with.

Mrd: on Dec 4, by Rev Oliver Cox, Mr Geo Hopkins, of Wash City, to Mrs L F Moore, formerly of Shenandoah Co, Va.

Sale of real estate, by decree of the Circuit Court of Wythe Co, Va, entered at its Oct Term, 1867, in the case of Cyrus Schweigart vs Jesse Schweigart & others, in Chancery: public auction, on Feb 10, of a tract of land in said county, 8 miles east from its Court House, on a macadamized road, containing 220 acres; improvements tolerable. The title is believed to be unquestionable.
–J H Fulton, Cyrus Schweigart, com'rs

Supreme Court of D C, Equity 962. John Van Riswick vs Edw Lynch et al. The trustees reported that they sold the real estate & promises mentioned in the proceedings in said cause to Edw B Cadley, at the sum of $26,050, & Cadley has complied with the terms of sale. -R J Meigs, clerk

MON DEC 9, 1867
Real Estate: Cooper & Latimer, aucts, sold part of lot 16 in square 321, on 11th st, between E & F st, improved by a 3 story brick front dwlg, with back bldg, to Ferdinand Butler, for $9,000. Also, part of lot 4 in square 499, improved by 2 frame dwlgs, to Capt P Young, for $4,800. Messrs Wall & Co, aucts, sold part of lot 22 in square 252, fronting 25 feet & 9 inches on 13th st, between G & H sts, having a depth of 104 feet, improved by a 2 story & basement brick house, to R R Aymer, for $8,000.

Mrs Louise Morris Eustis, the wife of Hon Geo Eustis, of Louisiana, & only daughter of our esteemed fellow-citizen W W Corcoran, died on Wed last, in Cannes, France. She was well known & greatly admired as one of the belles of Washington a few years ago. Her marriage with Mr Eustis, an elegant & dashing Representative from Louisiana, was an event long remembered in this district. Since her marriage she has resided principally abroad. Some time ago she was smitten with consumption, from which she slowly declined. Her grief-stricken father had been already summoned, & was present at the time of her death. Mrs Eustis was the grand-daughter of Cmdor Morris, U S Navy, & extensively connected in Wash City. She leaves 3 young children.

Richd T McLain, of Wash City, formerly engaged in the Interior Dept, has been appointed Chief Clerk of the Agricultural Dept, in place of J W Stokes, resigned.

Col B B G Twyman, Consul of Mexico under Buchanan, & formerly editor of several newspapers in Ky, committed suicide at the St Charles Hotel, at Cairo, Ill, on Friday, by taking a solution of arsenic. Despondency, produced by pecuniary misfortunes, caused the act.

Orphans Court-Judge Purcell, Dec 7, 1867. 1-The will of Saml De Vaughan was admitted to probate. 2-The will of J Hopkins Smith was admitted to probate. 3-Letters testamentary were granted to Susan Brayfield as executrix of the will of Saml De Vaughan; bond $50,000; sureties M Thompson, W H Nalley, & Mary R Bradford. 4-Susan Boteler was appointed guardian of the orphan children of Wm Boteler; bond $2,000. 5-First & final account of Jos Redfern, administrator of Louis Vivans, filed. 6-Wm H Devaugn gave bond in the sum of $10,000 as the administrator of John Devaughn. H F Zimmerman & G E Kirk securities.

Columbia Typographical Society meeting on Sat; election of ofcrs: Pres, Chas I Canfield; vice-pres, F M Detweiler; rec sec, E MacMurray; financial sec, A T Cavis; treasurer, Michl Caton; marshal, Danl Harbaugh. Since the last meeting the society has lost 3 members: Messrs John Graham, Josiah Melvin, & Jas F Haliday.

Mrd: on Dec 2, in Wash City, by Rev M L Olds, of Christ Church, A S Bryan to Miss Fannie, daughter of R H Keeling, of Richmond, Va.

Mrd: on Dec 4, in Mexico, Missouri, Mr Walter Evans, 2nd son of the late Augustus H Evans, of St Louis, to Miss Amanda C Brooks, 2nd daughter of Rev John T Brooks, of the former place. No cards.

Died: on Dec 4, at Cannes, Alpes Maratime, France, Louise Morris Eustis, wife of Hon Geo Eustis, of Lousiana, & daughter of W W Corcoran, Wash, D C. [New Orleans papers please copy.]

Died: on Dec 7, Mrs Catharine R Blackfan, wife of Jos H Blackfan. Her funeral will be this day at 3 P M, from the house, 364 Mass ave, between 11th & 12th sts, after which the remains will be removed to Trenton, N J.

Valuable bldgs lots on 2nd st, between D & E sts, at auction; in the matter of the petition of Jas McSherry, guardian of Helen N McSherry, Mary C McSherry, & Jas C McSherry, minor heirs of Thos Carbery, deceased. Public auction on Dec 20, of lot 6 in square 570, divided into two bldg lots, each fronting 17 feet 6 inches on Second st, running back by that width 167 feet & 6 inches to an alley.
–Jas McSherry, guardian -Jos F Kelly, auct

Chancery sale of valuable unimproved property in Gtwn; by decree of the Supreme Court of D C, dated Mar 14, 1865, wherein E M Linthicum & Co were cmplnts, & the widow & heirs-at-law of Richd Jones dfndnts, the same being Equity 249, Docket No 7; public auction on Dec 23, on the premises, lots 18 & 19, in Peters' Square of said town, fronting 48 feet on the Chesapeake & Ohio Canal, between Congress & High sts, by a depth of 133 feet to an alley. –J Carter Marbury, trustee -Thos Dowling, auct

Orphans Court of Wash Co, D C. Letters of administration, c t a, on the personal estate of Saml De Vaughan, late of Wash Co, D C, deceased.
–Susan Brayfield, admx c t a

Orphans Court of Wash Co, D C, Dec 7, 1867. In the case of Patrick Fleming, adm of John Fleming, deceased, the administrator & Court have appointed Dec 31st next, for the final settlement of the personal estate of the said deceased, of the assets in hand. -Jas R O'Beirne, Reg/o wills

Burlington, Vt, Dec 8. Victor Wright, president of the State Agricultural Society, & a prominent citizen of Middleburg, was thrown from his wagon & instantly killed on Friday.

TUE DEC 10, 1867
The funeral of the late Thos E Pyles, a well known citizen of Wash, will take place from the East Wash M E Church this afternoon, at 2 o'clock. The Independent Order of Odd Fellows, [Harmony Lodge & Magenenu Encampment,] Knights of Pythias, & Rechabites, to which organizations he belonged, will attend.

Telegraphic despatches from St Louis announce the death of Edw Wm Johnston, veteran editor & correspondent; connected at one time or another with most of the leading newspapers of the country. Over the signature of Il Segretario he attained a high reputation as a correspondent. He has died ripe in years, & his loss will be regretted by thousands who knew him well in life.
+
St Louis, Dec 9. Edw Wm Johnston died on Dec 9 of a long illness. He was a brother of Gen Jos E Johnston.

Equity Court-Judge Wylie. 1-Myers et al vs Berry et al. Order *pro confesso* against G M Berry & Emma Berry. 2-Gibson vs Garden. Order for rule to show cause why an attachment should not issue.

Mrd: on Dec 8, at Bradley, Prince Wm Co, Va, by Rev J E Nourse, Levi Hixson to Rachel; & Wm S Hixson to Martha Virginia, daughters of Saml Wolverton.

Died: on Dec 6, at Gilford, Balt Co, after a painful illness, Dr Edw Gill, in his _0th year. [Possibly 80th year.]

The undersigned will sell at private sale the Farm known as the **Woodyard Mill** property, situated 6 miles from Upper Marlboro, in PG Co, Md, containing 188 acres; with a commodious dwlg, containing 12 rooms, with all necessary out-bldgs; upon the farm is a 2 story Brick Mill. Address Mrs Ann Marshall, Robeystown, Md, or to Mr Robt Marshall, living near **Fort Meigs** Wash, D C, or to Wm H Marshall, Box 102 Shelbyville, Ky. –Wm H Marshall, Ann Marshall

Orphans Court of Wash Co, D C. Letters of administration on the personal estate of John De Vaughan, late of Alexandria, deceased. –Wm H De Vaughn, adm

WED DEC 11, 1867
Mr Benedict Swain, a former member of the City Councils, & well known & much respected citizen of the Navy Yard, died on Monday, after a long illness of consumption. He was a prominent member of the Masonic & Odd Fellows fraternity, & they will attend his funeral, from his residence, this afternoon.

Geo McCauley was charged with stealing overcoats from the halls of a number of dwlg houses in this city. McCauley was committed to jail for court.

Fire near Laurel. Sunday the country residence of Mr Francis Mohun, of Wash City, was burned. The furniture of the house was totally destroyed, & the overseer of the place, Mr Owen, who was asleep in the house, barely escaped with his life, losing all his wearing apparel & all of his money. The house was valued at $6,000, & was partially insured [$1,500] in the Mutual Ins Co of Montg Co, Md.

Died: on Dec 1, of paralysis, at Crawfordsville, Ga, Mrs C P Culver, eldest daughter of the late Wm M Morrison, of Wash City.

Shocking incident on Friday last at the Bright Hope coal pits, in Chesterfield Co. The unfortunate victim, Mr John Weatherman, was standing on a platform about 600 feet below the surface, his duty being to unhitch the empty descending car, & to place in the iron cage the one just loaded. An emply car descended rapidly, & Weatherman did not hear the warning, & was struck with full force, knocking him 300 feet lower to the bottom of the shaft, killing him instantly. At the same time a messenger was on his way to the pits to tell him of the sudden death of his wife, who resides in Manchester. -Richmond Despatch, Dec 9.

Orphans Court-Judge Purcell, Dec 10, 1867. 1-The last will of the late Maria Miller was filed, proved, & admitted to probate. The entire personal & real estate of the deceased is bequeathed to her two sisters, during their lifetime. The sum of $400 is bequeathed to Mary Washington. Thos Miller is named executor. 2-The last will of the late Lucy R Miller was filed, proved, & admitted to probate. The testator bequeaths her real & personal estate to her sisters, Harriet & Maria, & to their survivors. Thos J Miller is named as executor. 3-The last will of the late Jas F Haliday was filed, proved, & admitted to probate. After providing for the payment of his just debts as soon as practicable, the testator bequeaths to his sister, Harriet E Marsh, All his household goods, furniture, & personal apparel, except his silver & certain other articles. To his sisters, Annie M Lowry & Harriet E Marsh, to be equally divided between them, he bequeaths all his silverware & other articles presented to him by the late John C Rives; to his nephew, Jas Haliday Lowry, his gold watch; to his sister-in-law, Mary Ann Cox, $500; to his brother, Henry H Haliday, the undivided one-third part of all the rest of his estate. For his sister, Harriet E Marsh, he gives to Wm Morgan & Wm H Ward, in trust, one entire undivided third of his estate. For his sister, Annie M Lowry, he bequeaths to the same trustees one other undivided third of his estate. A codicil assigns to his sister, Martha Isabella Cockrell, of Mississippi, the sum of $1,000. A second codicil declares that the former disposition of his personal estate shall not be disturbed, & that no portion thereof shall be disposed of for the payment of his debts, but directs that a certain lot in Square A, & if necessary, certain unimproved property, shall be sold by his executors for the payment of the same. A third codicil revokes the appointment of Wm H Ward as one of the executors, & names in his place his brother Henry A Haliday & his sister Harriet E Marsh as executor & executrix in his place. 4-Letters of administration issued to Jennie M Sherburne, admx on the personal estate of Edw W Sherburne; bond $2,000. E B Olmstead, Chas E Ramus, sureties. 5-First & final account of the excs of Wm Redin, deceased, approved & passed. 6-First & final account of Alex'r McDonald Davis, collector of the personal estate of Saml De Vaughn, approved & passed. 7-Busteed blank check. Gen Terry arguged this case this morning in regard to the jurisdiction of this court in regard to the blank check which was issued Helen R Reed. Petitioner wants an order of the Court to the executor to make him account to her for the $500 alleged to be the intention of said Busteed to give before he died. Thompson, as solicitor for executor, resisted the motion on the ground that it was not a blank check, but a **carte** blank.

Criminal Court-Judge Olin. Conrad Miller, indicted for receiving stolen goods, was acquitted. Frank Kelly, indicted for larceny; *nolle prosequi*. Jeremiah Miller, larceny; found guilty. Jas T Price, petit larceny; found guilty. Catharine McDougal, petit larceny; *nolle prosequi*. Albert H Sipes, assault & battery; found guilty. Nicholas Manning; assault & battery; found guilty. Geo W Burch, alias Mortimer, assault & battery with intent to kill.

Patents to Washingtonians during the past week. 1-To Wm F Brown & J Nottingham Smith, for a hay raker & loader. 2-To Edw A Elsworth/Edsworth, for a nut lock & washer. 3-To Jos Bell Alexander, for a lamp.

Orphans Court of Wash Co, D C, Dec 10, 1867. In the case of Wm King, Geo W Beall, & Jenkin Thomas, excs of Peter Von Essen, deceased, the executors & Court have appointed Jan 7th next, for the final settlement of the personal estate of the said deceased, of the assets in hand.   -Jas R O'Beirne, Reg/o wills

Dept of the Interior, U S Patent Ofc, Wash, Dec 5, 1867. Ptn of Chauncey D Woodruff, of Toledo, Ohio, praying for the extension of a patent granted to him Mar 7, 1854, for an improvement in Suspending Eaves' Troughs, for seven years from the expiration of said patent, which takes place on Mar 7, 1868.
-T C Theaker, Com'r of Patents

Dept of the Interior, U S Patent Ofc, Wash, Dec 6, 1867. Ptn of Jas H Sweet, of Pittsburgh, Pa, praying for the extension of a patent granted to him Mar 14, 1854, for an improvement in Hanging of the Griping Jaw of Spike Machines, for 7 years from the expiration of said patent, which takes place on Mar 14, 1868.
-T C Theaker, Com'r of Patents

THU DEC 12, 1867
Richmond, Dec 11. The locomotive of the passenger train hence for Petersburg exploded at the half-way house this afternoon, killed Richd Norris, engineer, & a colored fireman.

N Y, Dec 11. Fatal recontre this evening in front of the Fifth Ave Hotel between Kelly, of Kelly & Leon's Minstrels, & Sam M Sharpley, of the Theatre Comique. It was over an old grudge. Sharpley shot Kelly first, slightly wounding him in the head. Kelly returned the fire, instantly killing Sharpley. [Dec 13th newspaper: Thos Sharpely, brother of Saml M Sharpley, was killed. Thos Sharpley has but a short time been a resident of this city, formerly lived in Phil, engaged in business as a broker; age 31 years, & leaves a wife & 2 children.

Died: on Dec 6, at Geneva, N Y, aged 26 years & 19 days, Jeannie Smith, wife of Franklin E Town, lt 11th U S I.

Died: on Dec 11, at his residence, near Beltsville, Md, Jos R Thompson, in his 65th year, a native of Annapolis, Md, but for the last 40 years a resident of Wash City. Time of funeral will be announced in the evening papers.

Died on Dec 11, William Henry, only son of William & Margaret Kennedy, aged 1 year & 2 months. His funeral will take place from the residence of his parents, 525 11th st, at 3 P M, Dec 12.

The President yesterday nominated to the Senate the following persons:
Wm D Fouts, to be Assessor of Internal Revenue for the Second Dist of Indiana.
Wm J Chandler, Collector of Internal Revenue for the Fifth Dist of Missouri.
John F Flint, Consul at La Union.
Edw A Wright, Consul at San Salvador.
J C Mathe, Consul at Tonsonati, San Salvador.
Gideon H Hollister, of Conn, Minister Resident & Consul General at Hayti.

Household & kitchen furniture at auction on: Dec 16, at the residence of Richd Morgan, on Md ave, between 9th & 10th sts. Also 2 horses, carriage, buggy, etc, -family leaving the city. -W L Wall & Co, aucts

Adms sale of brewery horses, wagons, bar fixtures, household & kitchen furniture at auction at 487 10th st, between D & E Sts, by order of the Orphans Court of D C., the personal effects of Henry Becker, deceased. –Chas Walter, adm -Nagle & Co, aucts

Supreme Court of D C, Equity No 1,115. David L Morrison, cmplnt, vs Wm Harris et al, dfndnts. On the motion of the cmplnt by M Thompson, his solicitor, it is ordered by the court that the dfndnts, Wm Harris & Mary his wife, Ella Javins, Chas Javins & Isabella his wife, Wm Javins, J Randolph Javins, Thos Javins & Emily his wife; Jas Monroe & Amanda his wife; Arthur Jenkins, Michl Lynch & Cornelia his wife; Gilbert Simpson & Laura his wife; Thos Simpson & Marion his wife; Wm Jenkins, Emma Jenkins, Norman Jenkins, Thos Javins, Fanny Walker, Wm Walker, Florence Walker, Chas Javins, Geo Javins, Henry Harrington & Sarah his wife; Edw Rig_y & Gertrude his wife; Frances Walker, & Jane E Walker cause their appearance on or before the first rule day occurring 40 days after this date, Dec 12; otherwise the cause will be proceeded with as in case of default. -R J Meigs, clerk

FRI DEC 13, 1867
On Wednesday next the feast of the Expectation of the <u>Blessed Virgin</u>, one of the festivals of the Catholic Church, preparatory to Christmas, the 50th anniversary of the ordination of Rev Fr Young, will be celebrated at St Dominick's Church, South Washington. Rev Fr Rooney will deliver a lecture on the Celebacy of the Priesthood. Rev Fr Young is a native of lower Md, & is now in his 74th year of his age; in excellent health. He was ordained at Bardstown, Ky. He was the founder of the first Catholic Church in Cincinnati.

Edw Wm Johnston died yesterday at his house on Dayton st, at age 68 years, after a protracted & painful illness. He died in full communion with the Roman Catholic Church. Mr Johnston was a native of Va; his father was an ofcr in the Light Horse Cavalry, commanded by Gen Henry Lee, of Revolutioanry celebrity. He was a brother of that able Confederate soldier, Gen Jos E Johnston, who will be here to attend the funeral of one between whom & himself there existed the tenderest relations of fraternal confidence & love. From his father, who was a man of remarkable culture & taste for letters, Mr Johnston imbibed those tastes for literary pursuits which occupied all his years. His funeral will take place upon the arrival of his brother, Gen Johnston. -St Louis Republican, Dec 10.

Bayard Taylor is seriously ill at Rome.

Equity Court. 1-Rupert vs Geier et al. Order ratifying trustee's sales & authorizing trustee to pay taxes. 2-Morrison vs Harris et al. Order of publication against non-resident dfndnts.

Criminal Court-Judge Olin. 1-Moses Ross acquitted of stealing a watch. 2-Pink Jackson, guilty of larceny; sentenced to 3 months in the county jail. 3-John Bell & Barney Clinkall, assault & battery upon Maj Murphy in Fighting Alley, No I, on the Island. Verdict, John Bell guilty, & capias to hear judgment; Barney Clinkall, **nolle pros**. 4-Jas Austin, charged with stealing one mule the value of $75, the property of Jas Seldon, near **Fort Slocum**; he sold the mule. 5-John Fox, alias Taylor; larceny: guilty. 6-Robt Jenkins; larceny; guilty. 7-Wm Caton; larceny. Sentenced to county jail for 30 days.

Mrd: on Dec 11, by Rev Mr Kimball, Maj Franck E Taylor, U S A, to Anna Mary, daughter of Cornelius Wendell, of Wash City.

Mrd: on Dec 11, in Wash City, at the residence of Cmdor Powell, by Rev Mr Addison, rector of Trinity Church, Mr S B Logan, of Winchester, Va, to Jeanette B, eldest daughter of Alfred B Thruston, deceased, & grand-daughter of the late Col Chas Magill, of Winchester.

Mrd: on Dec 12, by Rev C C Meadore, Mr Edw H Dougherty to Miss Emily Cooper, 4th daughter of Mr Wm Cooper, all of Wash City.

Died: on Dec 11, at his residence, near Beltsville, Md, Jos R Thompson, in his 65th year, a native of Annapolis, Md, but for the last 40 years a resident of Wash City. His funeral will take place from the residence of R O Polkinhorn, 411 E st, between 9th & 10th sts, at 2 o'clock this P M.

On Monday last, at 107 Atlantic st, Brooklyn, Mrs Catharine Fall, about 40, & her daughter, Miss Jennie Fall, were found dead in their apartment. After post mortem examinations, it was determined that the mother gave her daughter strychnine, & then took some herself.

St Louis, Dec 12. A man named Pepya, living near Alton, Ill, was murdered on Sunday, with his wife & 2 children. The weapon used was an axe. A mulatto, Jos Marshall, was arrested here today, supposed to be the murderer.

Dept of the Interior, U S Patent Ofc, Wash, Dec 7, 1867. Ptn of Ellsworth D S Goodyear, of North Haven, Conn, praying for the extension of a patent granted to him Mar 28, 1854, for an improvement in Processes for Treating India Rubber, for 7 years from expiration of said patent, which takes place on Mar 28, 1868.
-T C Theaker, Com'r of Patents

SAT DEC 14, 1867
Hon Thos C Theaker, Com'r of Patents, has tendered his resignation, to take effect Jan 15 next.

Thos Dowling, auct, sold the house & ground, 20 feet front, on which it stands, in lot 4, fronting 40 feet on High st, between First & Dunbarton sts, by a depth of 130 feet, to W R Hurdle, of $3,900. Part of lot 85 was sold, having a front of 20 feet on First st, between High & Dunbarton sts, by a depth of 150 feet, improved by a small frame dwlg house, to J B Welles, for $900.

The boiler of a railroad engine exploded on Monday, at Glover's Gap, about 40 miles this side of Wheeling, killing the Conductor-Delany, residing in Wheeling, & the engineer, Hobbs, living in Skyesville, Md. The engineer's body was picked up in all directions, except one foot, which has not been found.

The Senate confirmed the following nominations yesterday:
Capt Theodore P Greene, to be commodor in the navy, on the active list.
Cmdor Egbert Thompson, to be captain.
Lt Cmder Francis H Baker, to be commander.
Lt Cmder Austin Pendergrast, to be commander.
Assist Surgeon A A Hochlin, to be surgeon; & Wm S Bowen, of Rhode Island; Adam Frank, of Pa; & Alfred Griffith, of Md, to be assist surgeons in the navy.
1st Lt Wm J Squires, to be captain in the Marine Corps.
Israel H Washburne, to be 1st lt in the Marine Corps.
Wm J Chandler, to be collector of internal revenue for the 5th Dist of Missouri.

On Nov 23, Chief Justice Slough, of the U S District Court, held Eben Everett to bail in the sum of $3,000, & Abram Ortez in the sum of $2,000, to answer, with Wm Breeden & John W Dunn, to the charge of conspiring to defraud a pensioner out of $530, or more. Abram Ortez, the magistrate, now admits that the power of atty on which Wm Breeden drew the pension is false, the pensioner never having been before him to swear thereto, & the witnesses to the signature of the claimant state that the paper was not explained to him before their signatures were affixed. Their trial will take place at Santa Fe, New Mexico, during the ensuing term of the U S Court.

Aug 1, 1867: the major generals, according to rank, are: Halleck, Mead, Sheridan, Thomas, Hancock Brig generals: McDowell, Cooke, Pope, Hooker, Schofield, Howard, Terry, Ord, Canby, Rousseau. Besides these there are brig generals as follows: Rawlins, chief of staff; Thomas, Adj Gen; Holt, Judge Advocate; Meigs, Quartermaster Gen; Eaton, Commissary Gen; Barnes, Surgeon Gen; Brice, Paymaster Gen; Humphreys, Chief Engineer; & Dyer, Chief of Ordnance. Col R B Marcy is ranking Inspector Gen, & Col A J Myer, Chief Signal Ofcr.

Equity Court-Judge Wylie. 1-Edmonston vs Cammack et al. Order appointing Jos H Bradley, jr, guardian ad litem. 2-Pepper et al vs Seaton et al. Order appointing cmte to assign guardian.

Criminal Court-Judge Olin. Elenora Booth, larceny, *nolle pros*. Francis Burke, grand larceny, verdict guilty. Jas Richards, grand larceny, guilty-sentenced to 1 year in the Albany Penitentiary. Jas Richards, larceny, *nolle pros*. Jonathan Waters, grand larceny, guilty. Conrad Miller, larceny, verdict guilty.

Board of Managers of the Industrial Home School, on Wed, appointed the following cmtes: Household: Mrs A K Browne, Mrs J S Brown, Mrs A J Dietrick. Education: Mrs Z Richards, Mrs R M Bigelow, Mrs M A Blackford, Mrs D M Kelsey, Mrs Carter. Home: Mrs C M Hart. Clothing: Mrs J R Wilson, Mrs E A Richardson. Ways & Means: Mrs A H Gangewer, Mrs R M Bigelow, Mrs D M Kelsey. Mr J C Harkness declined to serve as treasurer, on account of ill health.

Whereabouts of Ex-Confederate Generals. Maj Gen J G Walker, of Walker's old division, is at Versailles, Woodford Co, Ky: cultivating a farm of some 100 acres. Gen M Jeff Thompson, now in New Orleans, will return North. Gen Hindman is president of the Iron Mountain railroad, in Mo. Gen Marmaduke is engaged in the commission & forwarding business in St Louis. Gen Forrest is at his home in Memphis. Gen Magruder is at present in Balt. Gen Longstreet has been in N Y. Gen Wigfall is in London, engaged in active paying pursuits. So is Mr Benjamin, who is practising law. Gen E Kirby Smith is at the head of an institution of learning in Ky, which is under the control of Episcopalians. Gen Buckner is the president of the Commercial Ins Co of New Orleans. Gen Bragg is at the head of the city waterworks of New Orleans. Gen Fagan is practicing his profession [law] in Little Rock. Gen Hawthorn is in the Brazilian army, with the rank of colonel. Gen John Johnston has resigned his position as president of a railroad company, & is at present travelling in the North & East. Gen Beauregard is still president of the New Orleans & Jackson railroad, headquarters in New Orleans. Gen Dick Taylor is making money with his canal contract in New Orleans. Generals Wirt & Dan Adams are also engaged in business in New Orleans. So are 15 other major & brigadier Confederate generals, including Maury, Wheeler, etc. Gen Shelby is in or near St Louis

Mrs Margaret A Johnston died in St Louis on Monday, a few hours after the demise of her husband, Edw Wm Johnston, a brother of Gen Jos E Johnston.

A cable despatch announces the death of the inventor of the famous needle gun. Herr Von Dreyse, of whom very little is known beyond that fact that he gave to Europe one of the most effective of modern weapons of warfare, & was born in Sommerda, a small town near Erfurt, in Saxony. He died at age 79 years, & was, a few months ago, represented to be vigorous in mind & body.
[No death date given-current item.]

MON DEC 16, 1867
Died: in Norristown, Pa, Mrs Catharine P McKnight, widow of the late Capt John McKnight, of Alexandria, in her 88th year. Her remains will be taken to Alexandria. Her funeral will be from the Second Presbyterian Church in that city, at 11 o'clock A M, Oct 17. [No death date given-current item.]

Obit-died: on Dec 12, after a brief illness, at Chelsea, PG Co, Md, Wm J Berry, aged about 54 years. He died at the family homestead, which was his birthplace, & the spot where he had passed the whole of an earnest, useful, & irreproachable life. As the head of a family he was all that a kind indulgent, loving husband & father could be, & truly merited, as he possessed the unbounded love & respect of his cherished wife & children. He was a devout & humble follower of the Saviour. -Z

Thos Lee, a well known citizen of Boston, died on Sat, aged 88 years. Hon Thos M Wield, another prominent citizen, died suddenly on Friday night.

Detroit, Mich, Dec 15. Hon Geo Martin, Chief Justice of this State, died today in this city.

The New Orleans Crescent of Dec 3: the funeral of the four Morgan sisters, killed by a railroad accident near Cincinnati, was one of the largest & saddest ever witnessed in this city. The remains were enclosed in four coffins, & conveyed to the cemetery in four hearses, followed by a very long line of carriages. The spectacle of four hearses moving to one family tomb together was probably never before witnessed in this city.

Supreme Court of D C. Thos W Stewart vs Chas Eccleston et al-1053. The report of the Receiver to be heard on Dec 21. –Walter S Cox, auditor

Orphans Court of Wash Co, D C, Dec 14, 1867. In the case of Geo R Schenig, exc of Eliza J Schenig, deceased, the executor & Court have appointed Jan 14 next, for the final settlement of the personal estate of the said deceased, of the assets in hand. -Jas R O'Beirne, Reg/o wills

Criminal Court-Judge Olin. Francis Burke, guilty of stealing a coat: fined $20.

TUE DEC 17, 1867
A S Cox, a resident of Washington for 12 years past, beloved by all who knew him, died last evening a victim of consumption. For several months he was a patient sufferer. Among the bereaved mourners present was Hon S S Cox, so well & favorably known.

By the will of the late Robt A Alexander, the famous breeder, all his Ky & Scottish property goes to his brother, John Alexander. The extensive Illinois estate is to be divided between the two sisters, Mrs Jas L Walter, of Chicago, & Mrs Deeds, of London. Some devises are made to other relatives.

Mrd: on Dec 10, by Rev Mr Olds, Roger C Glascock, of Fauquier Co, Va, to Neta, daughter of the late Dr John M Roberts, of Wash City.

Died: on Monday, of typhoid fever, after a short but painful illness, Harriett Jane, daughter of Jas R & Virginia E Clayton, in her 15th year. Her funeral will be from the residence of her parents, 219 Vt ave, on Dec 18 at 2 o'clock.

Died: on Dec 16, in his 26th year, Dr Stanly Brown, in the communion of the Catholic Church. His funeral service is on Tuesday, at 3 o'clock, at his late residence, 310 F st.

WED DEC 18, 1867
The President today sent to the Senate the following nominations: Oliver B Bradford, of Pa, to be Consul at Bruno, Borneo. Edwin Higgins, of Mich, Sec for Utah Territory.
Owen Thorn, Geo H Plant, & C M Nichols, to be members of the Levy Court.

Mrd: on Dec 10, at Christ Church, N Y, by Rev F C Ewer, Wm T Forbes, of Phil, to Hattie M, youngest daughter of Chas Gordon, of Wash, D C. No cards.

Died: on Dec 16, Mr A S Cox, in his 37th year. His funeral will take place from his late residence, 349 10th st, between L & M sts, on Dec 19, at 11 o'clock A M.

Cmdor Bissell has officially notified the Navy Dept of the loss of the steamer **Monongahela**. She was lifted by the waves over the warehouses in the town of Frederickstadt, St Croix, during the late terrible earthquake, & landed in the streets.

Mrs Hannah Boone & her 4 children, the oldest aged 13, were found in their room, at 29 Amity st, N Y, on Sunday, suffering from the effects of laudanum, which had been administered by Mrs Boone herself, on account of her distressing poverty. They were taken to Bellevue Hospital, where they are recovering. [Dec 21st newspaper: Mrs Boone denies that she gave them laudanum, but says that they were nearly suffocated by gas.]

N Y, Dec 17, 1867. Hon G Welles, Sec of the Navy. We arrived last night from St Thomas, with the remains of Admiral Palmer & Capt Burroughs. The Admiral died on Dec 7, of yellow fever.
+
Rear Admiral Jas S Palmer was born in N J, on Oct 13, 1810; appointed midshipman in the U S navy on Jan 1, 1825; has had 19 years & 7 months sea service, & 4 years & 10 months shore duty; promoted to the rank of Admiral on Jul 25, 1866, for distinguished services during the rebellion, which were principally performed in the West Gulf squadron, under Admiral Farragut, & was appointed cmder of the North Atlantic squadron Dec 4, 1865. His term of service there had just terminated, & he would have been ordered home in a short time. Capt John A Burroughs, of the Marine Corps, was born in Pa, on May 2, 1837; entered the corps as 2nd lt on Jun 5, 1861; was promoted to a captain on Sep 1, 1864, & died on board the ship **Susquehanna**, at St Thomas, W I, of yellow fever, on Nov 28, 1867.

The marriage of Dr Warren Stone, jr, of New Orleans, with Miss Charlotte Cooly, was celebrated by a reception in the Crescent City yesterday. The new votaries of Hymen's altar have the sincere good wishes of a host of friends.

Orphans Court-Judge Purcell. 1-Jas Crutchett gave bond in the sum of $5,000 as administrator of the personal estate of JasHenry Crutchett, deceased. Christopher Mades & Fred P Stanton, sureties. 2-The will of Francis Lowndes was admitted to probate. The testratrix names Richd P Jackson as executor. 3-Geo W Mitchell gave bond in the sum of $5,000 as guardian of the orphan children of Martha Ann Mitchell, deceased. C F Perrie & Susan Brayfield, sureties. 4-First account of Simon Fennel, adm of Lawrence Conroy, [sometimes called Frank Hall,] deceased, filed. 5-First & final account of Geo Clendenin, exc of Emma Bascon, deceased, filed. 6-Henry H Haliday & Harriet Marsh gave bonds in the sum of $10,000 as execs of the will of Jas F Haliday. O W Marsh, C Buckingham, A F Cunningham, M K Walsh, & M R Coombs, sureties.

Orphans Court of Wash Co, D C. Letters testamentary on personal estate of Jas F Haliday, late of Wash City, D C, deceased. –Henry H Haliday, Harriet Marsh, excs

Dept of the Interior, U S Patent Ofc, Wash, Dec 6, 1867. Ptn of Henry B Myer, of Cleveland, Ohio, praying for the extension of a patent granted to him May 3, 1859, & again reissued Oct 8, 1861, for an improvement in Converting Railroad Car Seats into Beds or Lounges, for seven years from the expiration of said patent, which takes place on Sep 19, 1868. -T C Theaker, Com'r of Patents

Established in 1852, the most complete Piano & Music establishment in the U S. Agent for three best Parlor Organ factories. –John F Ellis, 306 Pa ave, New Iron Front.

THU DEC 19, 1867
Edw M Cleveland, son of P M Cleveland, of Hartford, Conn, has been appointed by Cmder Henry Wilson, of the U S steamship **Saco**, as his clerk. She is to sail the last of this week on a year's cruise for the Gulf of Mexico, West Indies, & the northern part of South America. This ship is one of the finest of that class in the service.

Buffalo, Dec 18. The N Y express train from Cleveland, on the Lake shore Road, met with a serious accident; the two rear passenger cars were thrown over an embankment 20 feet high. Killed: J M Strong, of Buffalo; Mary Freeman, residence unknown; J P Hayward, agent of the road at the State line. Injured: J C Cribb, of Salem, Pa; & Grant Hurley, of Correy, Pa. Stephen Steuart, president of Oil Creek road, is missing. [Dec 20th newspaper: In addition to those already reported as killed, the following have also been mentioned: Jasper Fuller & wife, Spartansburg, Pa; Mr Grover, residence unknown; W H Ross, North Bend, Pa; E B Forbitsh, Buffalo; Mrs W Freeman, Norwich, Pa; Mrs Hubbard, St Catharine's, C W; Frank Walker, Buffalo. Additional wounded: Henry Jackson, Ill; S T Howard, N Y C; Jas Walsh, Brooklyn, N Y; W C Patterson, Old Creek; Mrs Fisher, Minnesota, insensible; Chas P Wood, Buffalo; A E Fisher, Owatona, Minn.] [Dec 21st newspaper: The accident was occasioned by the breaking of a wheel. No fault is to be attached to the ofcrs of the road. The daughter of Mrs Cleadicar, of Titusville, cannot possibly recover. Mr C W Patterson, of Oil Creek, is thought to be dying. In addition to previous lists of the killed, the following bodies have been recognized: Stephen Stewart, pres of the Oil Creek road; S F Thompson, Worcester, Mass; A H Spier, Northeast N Y; & Hiram W Martin, residence unknown. Mr A S Fisher, of Minn, one of the injured by the Lake Shore accident, died at Angola on Dec 19. Mrs Fisher is not expected to live. Mrs Cheydeynes & daughter, of Titusville, are not dead as reported, although they are very low. Mr CE Kent & wife, of Tonawanda, N Y, left Jamestown on the train to which the accident occurred, & their bodies are supposed to be among the charred remains.] [Dec 23rd newspaper: As nearly as can be ascertained, the next to the last car of the train was thrown from the track on striking a frog at the switch just this side of Angola station, & was dragged over the ties nearly to the bridge before the car behind it became unseated from the rails. Mr Hayward, agent of the road at State Line, met death outright. At the houses of Mr Josiah Southwick & Mr Frank E Griffith the injured were receiving the best medical attention from Dr Wetmore, of this city; Dr Hoyer, of Tonawanda; & Dr Curtis, of Angola. On one bed lay the two Misses Sayles, of Corfu; one seriously injured, the other not so seriously injured. In the kitchen lay the broken body of Mrs Chedyne's daughter, who was having convulsions, & thought to be sinking fast. In an adjoining room, on the floor, lay Mr W C Pattison, of Oil Creek, his left thigh fractured, badly cut, & quite delirious. Here also lay Mrs Mary Moore, of Brooklyn, with a fractured jaw; Mr A E Fisher, of Minnesota, injured internally. In a house on the opposite side of the creek we found Mrs Thompson, of Worcester, Mass, badly bruised, feet burned, & a little delirious. She was asking for her brother, S E Thompson, who had been killed. Forty-four bodies were recovered from the wreck & deposited in the bldg formerly used as the Soldier's Rest, on Exchange st, opposite the Central Depot. The bodies were placed in pine coffins. The body of young

Frank Walker had been washed & dressed. The corpse of P P Harvey, a large man, had terrible cuts in the face. Next were the remains of Mr E B Forbush, of this city, badley bruised. Jos Fuller, of Spartansburg, Pa, had a hole in the centre of his forehead. Close by was the corpse of his wife Mrs Eunice Fuller, who had the left side of her head literally smashed out of all resemblance to a countenance. Husband, wife, father & mother, they died together. Mrs Clara Freeman, of Norwich, Dela, her body was cut, but her expression was natural. Next lay the body of Norman Wohls, with a gash in his head. Next lies S E Thompson, of Worcester, Mass, a handsome man, with black side-whiskers. The remains of A H Spear & J P Hayward, both of Northeast, Pa, completed the mourning list of the recognizable dead . Both were washed, dressed in grave-clothing, & placed in coffins. Three more bodies were recognized that evening: Stephen Stewart, of Oil Creek; W W Towner, of Erie, & J Alex'r Martin, of Erie. List of dead & injured as far as they can be ascertained: Dead: R B Graves, Brooklyn, N Y; A H Spier, Northeast, Pa; E B Forbush, Buffalo, Eunice Fuller, Spartansburg, Pa; Jaspar Fuller, Spartansburg, Pa; Mrs Wm Freeman, Norwich, Del; J P Hayward, Northeast, Pa; Jas Sheridan, residence unknown; Frank Walker, Buffalo, W W Towner, Erie, Pa; J A Martin, Erie; S E Thompson, Worcester, Mass; Mrs J H Strong, Buffalo; Miss Chedyne, Titusville, Pa; Stephen Stewart, Oil Creek, P; E P Harvey, Pottsdam, N Y; Jas Brown, Buffalo; Emma Teller, Utica; Miss Barthlomew, Angola; twenty-one could not be recognized. Seriously injured: Fred Robbins, Buffalo; S E Howard, N Y; Ira Babcock & wife, Syracuse; Mary Chedyne, Corfu; W C Patterson, Oil Creek; Maria Sayles, Corfu; A E Fisher, Minnesota; Mrs Christian Laing, Minneapolis; John C Cripps, Salem, Pa; Robt Stewart, Oneida; Robt Dixon, Buffalo; Mrs H M Gale, Buffalo; Lizzie Thompson, Worcester, Mass; R M Russell, Franklin, Tenn; Chas Wood, Buffalo; J C Whitney, Nashua, N H; Henry Jackson, Ill; A H Thomas, Rochester.] [Dec 30th newspaper: Buffalo, Dec 29. It is established that the rear car was not thrown from the track by a broken wheel, but by an axle of the Cleveland & Toledo coach, the rear coach being sprung, thus throwing the wheels an inch & a half out of their proper position. No compromise cars were attached to the train on which the accident occurred.]

Senate Cmte on the Judiciary, to whom was referred the credentials of Hon Philip F Thomas. John R Thomas, a son of the Senator elect from the State of Md, Philip F Thomas, admitted he was in the Confederate army, & that before going thither he was repeatedly earnestly invoked by his father not to do so. Furthermore, a coolness occurred between them in consequence of such conversations. The money given by Mr Thomas to his son was to buy him personal comforts, & not to aid in the rebellion. These statements were brought out in cmte, the father being privileged to propound questions to his son with reference to the case.

Wm Pardoe, a farmer of Mercer Co, Pa, aimed his rifle at a hog, but the cap snapping twice, he laid the gun in the hollow of his arm to prime it again. It discharged, & the ball passed through the head of his 11 year old, killing him instantly.

On Monday a tenement house, 596 Second ave, N Y, was burned down at an early hour. List of the dead: Mrs Margaret O'Meara, aged 50, suffocated; Bridget O'Meara, aged 19, daughter of above, suffocated; Ellen O'Meara, aged 17, sister of above, suffocated & burned; Mary O'Meara, aged 15, sister of above, suffocated. Bridget & Mary were found locked in each other's arms, the mother & other sister lying beside them. Ellen Murphy, aged 17; Mary Murphy, aged 15, & Thos Murphy, aged 13, all suffocated. Injured: Patrick Murphy, aged 45, jumped out of a window; Rosanna Murphy, aged 40, suffocated-both in critical condition. John O'Meara, body asphyxiated, husband of Mrs O'Meara, & father of the O'Meara girls deceased, is in a critical condition. Mrs Julia Kelly, aged 38, wife of Thos Kelly, badly injured about the spine by jumping from a 3rd story window. Mary Ann Corry, aged 13, daughter of Mrs Kelly by a former husband, is improving. Ellen Duffy, a young girl who boarded with the Murphy family, was badly burned about the face & hands by sliding down a clothes-line from the 4th & the 2nd floor. On reaching the 2nd floor she became exhausted & dropped to the sidewalk. The youngest son alone in the O'Meara family & his father, are alive, although the father is in critical condition. Of the Murphy family, which consisted of husband, wife, & 3 children, the latter are all dead, & the father & mother are not expected to live. [Dec 20th newspaper: The fire was originated by Max Miller, & censures the owners of the house. Miller was committed without bail.[

FRI DEC 20, 1867
Board of Police: The resignation of Justice E M Chapin, police magistrate of the 6th Precinct, 3rd Ward, was received & accepted, & Justice J T C Clark was appointed in his stead. Privates Chas A Kimall & F A A Evans, for intoxication, were dismissed the force.

Mrd: on Dec 18, by Rev Dr Samson, John G Culverwell to Mrs Mattie Scrivener, all of Wash City. No cards.

Mrd: on Dec 18, by Rev P F McCarty, at the residence of the bride's father, G L Ellsworth, of the Interior Dept, to Mary E Diggs.

Died: on Dec 18, of consumption, Rebecca Minitree, beloved wife of R M Johnson, aged 24 years. Her funeral will be Dec 20, at 2 o'clock, from 402 8th st west.

Died: on Dec 19, Catharine Alice Coolidge, daughter of the late Dr R H Coolidge, U S A. Her funeral will be on Sat next at 12 M from the Church of the Epiphany.

Buffalo, Dec 19. Jas Graham, formerly a ticket agent of this city, was convicted today in the Supreme Court of forgery, committed in 1866. He ante dated insurance tickets, to cover an accident which occurred on the previous day, upon which the Railway Passenger Ins Co, of Hartford, Conn, paid the estate of Thos C Hunt, who was killed on the Lake Shore road Nov 13, 1866. His sentence has not yet been passed.

Wash City: Organization of a Providence Society-meeting held last evening, Mayor Wallach presided, & Mr F A Boswell acted as sec. Ofcrs elected: Pres, Hon Peter Packer; vice president, Rev Dr C H Hall; sec, F A Boswell; treasurer, A R Sheperd; directors-J P Tustin, Wm Slowen, John L Pfaln, S A Peugh, John T Given, W H Nally, Geo Savage, Geo F Gulick, J C Dulin, Wm Dixon, S S Baker, C S Noyes.
Appointed to solicit subscriptions in the Depts: Col John A Graham, Register's Ofc Col Wm Hemphill Jones, 1st Comptroller's Ofc; C P Balckman, 2nd Auditor's Ofc J J McGrew, 6th Auditor's Ofc; Saml Hein, U S Coast Survey
J L Larman, Printing Bureau
For the Navy Dept: Jas C Dulfn, Mr Stickney, John T Hogg
War Dept: J T Roach, John Potts
Quartermaster Gen's Ofc: Z W Denham, Wm A Gordon, Col Jas A Tait
State Dept: Geo E Baker, R S Chilton, E J Pratt
Post Ofc Dept: Dr C F McDonald, A G Prevost, Gen J S Crocker
Interior Dept: T C Connell, H C Lauck
Land Ofc: Jos S Wilson
Wash Arsenal: F White
Navy Yard: J M Dalton, W M Hutchins, A B Norton
Paymaster Gen's Ofc: T Y Myers
Surgeon gen's Ofc: Dr C A Otis, Dr Buck
The following were appointed to canvass the wards of the city:

F Schneider	W B Todd	John W Mead
Geo T McGlue	J Y Davis	E Frederick
John B Turton	F A Lutz	Geo A Bohrer
Geo B Fillebrown	P M Dubant	T E Clark
Dr J H Thompson	S E Norman	R M Coombs
Saml B Niles	Jas J Campbell	Lemuel Gaddis
Geo F Schafer	Dennis Connell	A F Bully
J W Barker	Andrew Gleason	F Schoenboin
Z Richards	John Crowley	H M Knight
Geo H Plant	W F Mattingly	W C Bamberger
A Rutherford	Robt Ball	T E Lloyd
Wm Kilgour	W H Claggett	H P Hepburn
John T Given	Wm Schwing	H A Clark
Wm Wall	N Acker	Chas Hendley
Thos Phillips	J R Arrison	John Webster
Wilham Galt	W A Mulloy	Saml Pumphrey
W G Metzerott	Gen Chipman	John T Bailey
Chas Kloman	Geo A Bassett	Geo T Brown
S Aman	J J Johnson	

Phil, Dec 19. Wm B Schnider, Grand Tyler of the Grand Lodge of Pa, of the Masonic Order, died this morning. He possessed remarkable powers of memory, & the lapse of time seemed powerless to efface from his mind the image of any man he had once met.

Reminiscences. In Feb, 1865, the death of Mr Blanchard, of the old established firm of Blanchard & Mohun, leaving the latter named member of the firm alone in the establishment, has had the good fortune to secure the assistance of Mr Orson H Bestor, who had been, from a boy, in the store of Franck Taylor, having commenced his continuous service of 21 years there in 1844. In Oct last Franck Taylor retired from business, & Mr Bestor entered into partnership with Mr Mohun. The store was founded at 11th & Pa ave, in 1834, by Robt Farnham, who was suddenly cut down by a railroad casualty in the midst of a useful career, in 1857, the concern passing into the hands of Blanchard & Mohun the same year. Mr Farnham's old store, which in 1852 gave place to the present fine structure at 11th & Pa ave, is familiar in the memories of the older class of our people. There is a beautiful book, photographed by Gardner, of Washington. Allusion is made to Tani O'Shanter, Burns' masterpiece, illustrated by E H Miller, photographed by Gardner, of Washington, & published by W J Middleton, N Y. Wm Ballantyne is another of the old & successful book merchants of Wash City. He came here a young man in 1852 & commenced business at 498 7th st, between D & E, for nearly 16 years, till in Oct last he removed his establishment across the street, into the very large & handsome new store in the Intelligencer Bldg. He came here from N Y, from the publishing house of Carter & Bros, [which comprised 3 brothers.] Mohun & Bestor-The Franck Taylor Bookstore is another old establishment; the oldest inhabitants will remember when Peter Force, in the store under Brown's Hotel, & Pishey Thompson, near the Kirkwood, were the chief, if not the only book merchants of the city. It was from Pishey Thompson's store that Franck Taylor, then just entering upon his manhood, went down to the store near the Nat'l Hotel, then, in 1832, occupied as a bookstore by old Mr Cole, who had begun there in 1830, & purchasing the establishment, enter upon a business which he prosecuted for 35 years, achieving honorable distinction, as well as wealth in his career. On Oct 10 last, Mr Bestor, who as already stated, had been brought up in this store, & whose intelligence, taste, & judgment in his business, united with uprightness of character & personal courtesy, made him respected by everybody, entered into partnership with Mr Mohun, of the firm of Blanchard & Mohun, though entirely distinct from that firm, under the name of Mohun & Bestor, in the purchase of Franck Taylor's establishment, & the old fashioned style which Mr Taylor took pride in retaining to the last has given way to the modern ideas. The front windows, closed up for a whole generation with brick, as we write, are giving place to spacious show windows. In the past year, at 9th & D sts, there is an establishment which has passed from the hands of Burch & Brophy into the charge & ownership of C D Liebermann, an excellent young man, & a son of one of our most eminent physicians & surgeons. The specialty in this establishment is that of Catholic books, school books, & stationery. Mr J P Brophy is rendering assistance in the establishment. Another enterprising store has been recently opened by A H Barbour, 7th st, between H & I sts; a good stock of standard & miscellaneous books, & a full supply of stationery. In connection with his establishment Mr Barbour has a fine circulating library. Philp & Solomons, is not only not the last in its dignity, enterprise, & extent, but, in fact, if not superior, is fully equal to the best. This house was founded in 1858, in the place which they still occupy; in 1860 they enlarged the premises.

Phil, Dec 19. Wm B Schnider, Grand Tyler of the Grand Lodge of Pa, of the Masonic Order, died this morning. He possessed remarkable powers of memory, & the lapse of time seemed powerless to efface from his mind the image of any man he had once met.

Atlantic Cable. A meeting of the Atlantic Telegraph Co was held in London on Dec 2, at which Rt Hon J S Wortley, who presided, stated it had been proved that the deeper the cable is submerged the safer it is. They now have 2 cables across the Atlantic. Their receipts had been most satisfactory, amounting to about L1,000 a day. Mr Lawson, stated that the earnings of the first year were L792 a day, & for the second year L934 a day.

SAT DEC 21, 1867
Chas Dickens will give a reading in Hartford shortly. Price, $3,000.

A very old mulatto woman, Nancy Carter, reported to be upwards of 114 years of age, died in Alexandria on Thursday, in a house on Cameron st, between Patrick & Henry. She as well known to many of the old residents of the city, having lived there nearly all her life. She had outlived all her children, sixteen in number.

Mrd: on Dec 19, in Wash City, by Rev Mr Brown, of the Foundry Church, Mr Wm E Morcoe, of Wash City, to Miss Sarah A Busey, of Rockville, Md.

The Morrison Bookstore, corner of 4½ st & Pa ave, is widley known to the public men who have figured in the national capital in the last quarter of century as any business establishment in Wash. Wm M Morrison came from N Y, a young man, & established as a bookseller in Alexandria in 1823. In 1853 he removed to the national capital in a small store adjoining the old Brown's Hotel, which stood where now stands the Metropolitan Hotel. This store was nearly, if not exactly, on the spot now occupied by the store of M A Stevens. In 1840 he took up his location in the place which his successors still occupy, & prosecuted his business for 12 years longer, when in May, 1852, he associated with his son, Wm H Morrison, & his nephew O B Morrison, as partners, under the firm of Wm M Morrison & Co. In May, 1857, he retired from the business, relinquishing the establishment to the son & nephew, the latter of whom had grown up from a mere boy in the store. The firm assumed its present name of W M & O B Morrison. Wm M Morrison, after devoting his earlier yesrs of retirement with great enthusiasm in agricultural pursuits, died in Jan, 1863, leaving his family a well earned fortune. Another of the long established book merchants of the city is W D Shepherd, whose store is 7th & D sts; in 1857 he opened a very small room in the bldg which he now owns; in 1861 he secured an adjoining room & made a wider store; he associated with himself in the business his brother-in-law, J S Riley, who continued with him from 1861 to 1865, when retiring from the firm, Mr Riley went into business in Richmond, but has this season returned, & is now the head salesman in Mr Shepherd's establishment. Hunter's Antiquarian Bookstore started some 18 years ago, on a very small scale; he has leased a very large store on Pa ave, & will be moving into this spacious establishment. J W Kennedy & Co, hardware dealers, on 7th st, between D & E, have a complete assortment of skates; a full stock of builders & other hardware. I Alexander's, 240 Pa ave, near 13th, is one of the most reliable of our jewelry stores. Jas S Topham & Co, 500 7th st, may be regarded as the pioneer in trunk manufacturing in Washington. Kilbourn & Latta, 7th & G sts, suggests substantial holiday gifts, which may be enjoyed for generations; presents worth giving & receiving. De Wolfe, jeweller, on the Metropolitan Hotel Block, has greatly enlarged his establishment & stock; it extends from street to street-from the avenue to C. J W Boteler & Co, 300 Metzerott Hall, is an old established house furnishings establishment, & is worthy to visit from those who care to provide useful presents. Stephens & Co, 310 Pa ave, between 9th & 10th sts, are prepared to furnish neatly fitting suits of clothing for men & boys. Wm E Riley & Bro, 30 Central Stores, opposite the Centre Market, is ready to please shoppers with every description of dress goods. Bryan & Bro, 319 Pa ave, have laid in an ample supply of Christmas groceries. Webb & Beeridge, at Odd Fellows Hall, have a complete assortment of fancy china. Jas Y Davis, under the Metropolitan Hotel, the veritable Genin of Wash, can't be surpassed for excellence of materials & beauty of style of tiles of every description, soft hats & hard hats, stovepipes, jockeys, shiny hats & felt hats. Noah Walker & Co, Metropolitan Hotel Bldg, a branch of the world renowned Balt establishment, have on hand a complete stock of men's & boy's clothing. John W Wilson, 9th & D sts, offers a splendid assortment of cabinet furniture. M Taylor & Co, 42 Centre Market Space, preparing to move to a new establishment, offers their stock of staple & fancy dry goods, woollens, silks, cottons, linens, & dress goods, at reduced prices.

The Senate yesterday confirmed the following nominations: Edw Higgins, of Mich, to be Sec of Utah. C H Nichols & Geo H Plant to be members of the Levy Court.

Dept of the Interior, U S Patent Ofc, Wash, Dec 17, 1867. Ptn of Willis Humiston, of Troy, N Y, praying for extension of a patent granted him Apr 4, 1854, & reissued Mar 6, 1866, for an improvement in Candle Mould Apparatus, for 7 years from the expiration of said patent, which takes place on Apr 4, 1856.
-T C Theaker, Com'r of Patents

Patrick White, adm of John McGuire vs Maria M McGuire et al, Equity No 697. Notice to the creditors of the late John McGuire, deceased, I shall proceed to state the account of the trustee appointed, at my ofc, on Jan 4, at 12 o'clock M.
–W S Cox, auditor

Mrs Gen Sam Houston died of yellow fever at Independence, Texas, Dec 5.

By the breaking of the hawser on board the steamship **Ville de Paris**, at N Y, on Wed, one sailor was killed & 11 seriously injured. [No names were given.]

The Chicago Tribune suggests the name of Schuyler Colfax for Vice President on the ticket with Grant, under certain contingencies, & the Journal endorses the suggestion.

A despatch from Vicksburg announces the death, on Friday, of Gen Jasper A Maltby, of yellow fever, after 17 days illness. At the time of his death he was Mayor of Vicksburg, by the appointment of Gen Ord.

The proprietors of the <u>Staats Zeitung</u>, have purchased from Mr Ben Wood the property on Tryon Row, in N Y, for $220,000, & will erect a handsome bldg on the lot next year.

<u>Criminal Court</u>-Judge Fisher. 1-Aholiab Sawyer, who gave security to appear as a witness in the case of Henry Johnson, indicted for the murder of Smoot, was surrendered by his surety, & was ordered into commitment. 2-Lucinda Johnson, guilty of keeping a bawdy house. Capias to hear judgment. 3-Robt McGee, indicted for assault on C H Barnes, fined $5 by the Court. 4-Edw Edwards, assault & battery: guilty. 5-Zachariah Thomas, assault & battery: guilty. 6-Geo Coates, larceny: guilty. 7-Geo Humphreys, larceny: bench warrant issued. 8-Geo Dresher, assault & battery: ***nolle pros***. 9-Geo Coates, sentenced to one month in jail. 10-Henry West, alias Nicholas Carter, grand larceny. Sentenced to Albany Penitentiary for one year.

MON DEC 23, 1867
It is said that Mr T B Brown, Mr Heustis' predecessor as warden, has been before the grand jury, & there presented Mr Heustis on a charge of malfeasance in ofc, in that he has concerted with Johnson to induce the witnesses against him to leave the city. Mrs Aholiah Sawyer, one of principal witnesses, & in whose house the homicide occurred, states to Mr Brown that she had received a considerable sum of money from Mr Heustis to induce her to leave the District. Another of Mr Brown's charges before the grand jury is that Heustis, acting as the agent for Johnson, has offered to divide two farms, owned by the latter in Va, among the witnesses, provided they will also make it convenient to be absent when the case is called for trial. Another statement with regard to the above, & which charge also comes from Mr Brown, is that Johnson has given Mr Heustis the title deeds to some valuable real estate, upon consideration that he will get the witnesses out of the way, so that they will not be forthcoming when the case is called for trial. -Express

On Sat, a man named W S Skidmore, a mechanic employed on the Aqueduct bridge, at Gtwn, fell from the staging, & was seriously injured. He was taken to his boarding house & attended by Dr Peters, of that city, & is still in a critical condition. Mr Skidmore is a resident of Fredericksburg, Va.

Capt C F Smith's extensive stave & heading factory & saw mill, near Darnestown, Md, was destroyed by fire yesterday. The works were partialy insured.

Holiday goods: Our Holiday Directory. Burdette, 7th st, deals in carpeting & other dry goods. Odeon Hall Clothing Store, Wallach, clothing establishment, near the corner of 4½ & Pa ave. W D Wyville, 4½ & Pa ave, manufacturer of various articles in tin & iron. Shillington's Bookstore, book, periodical, & newspaper establishment in the lower part of Wash City. M'Dermott's Coach Factory, between 3rd & 4½ sts, Pa ave. Wm L Wall & Co, auctioneers: extensive catalogue; selection of books. Cooper & Latimer's Book auction: valuable miscellaneous private library selection. Perry & Bro, one of the oldest dry goods firms in the city; located at corner of 9th & Pa ave. Wm M Shuster & Bro, another old & reliable dry goods firm. Lansburg & Bro; store in the Intelligencer Bldg; extensive stock of dry goods of all kinds. Henning, clothing store, 7th & Md ave. Teel, fashionable tailor, on the avenue, between 9th & 10th sts. J J May & Co, dry goods.

Died: on Dec 21, in Wash, D C, of apoplexy, Robt B Fowler, in his 67th year. His funeral will be from his late residence, 268 Vt ave, on Monday afternoon, at 3 o'clock. [Balt papers please copy.]

Orphans Court-Judge Purcell, Dec 21, 1867. 1-*In re*. The estate of John Forrest, deceased. Amendment of decree for sale. J E Williams for petitioner. 2-Account of the personal estate of Adolph Eisenbeiss, deceased, filed. First & final account of Rosa Eisenbeiss, admx of Adolph Eisenbeiss, passed. 3-Final account of Alex'r Provost, exc of Wm H Winter, passed. 4-Susanna J Snyder gave bond in the sum of $500 as admx of the personal estate of J H Snyder. 5-The Court delivered a decision in the case of Helen C Read vs A K Browne, adm of R K Busteed. The Court said Miss Read had attended Busteed as a nurse, faithfully, in his last sickness. Busteed, before his death, gave her the paper with his signature thereon, &, by that act, had evidently intended to make her a preferred creditor. It was not a **donatio mortis causa**, but an order for money, in compensation for services rendered. These services were rendered at a time when he was utterly helpless, & it would not be an act of justice to deprive Miss Read of a fair equivalent for her services, & the consequent ill health resulting from such services. The Court has jurisdiction under the 13th section of the statute of 1798. Browne is an ofcr of this court, & the decree of the Court is that he pay over the money in his hands, drawn on the bank check, to Miss Read. Mr Thompson took an appeal from the decision of the Court.

Chancery sale of valuable lots on 7th st, between M & N sts: by decree of the Supreme Court of D C, in Equity No 1,080, wherein Geo C E Mitchel is cmplnt & Mary B Dayton et al dfndnts: sale on Jan 7 next, of 4 lots in square 424, being part of lot 11, & lots 12, 13, & 14. –John J Johnson, trustee -J B Wheeler & Co, aucts

Orphans Court of Wash Co, D C, Dec 21, 1867. In the case of Zachariah F Borland, adm of John Lange, deceased, the administrator & Court have appointed Jan 21 next, for the final settlement of the personal estate of the said deceased, of the assets in hand. -Jas R O'Beirne, Reg/o wills

Gen Francis Pierce, of N J, is at Willard's Hotel.

Criminal Court-Judge Fisher. 1-Henry West, for grand larceny; guilty; one year in the Albany penitentiary. 2-The following prisoners were discharged on their own recognizance in the sum of $50 for their appearance at court: Annie Dorsey, Wm Wesley, Britannia A Johnson, & Matilda Brown. Louis Wallis & Edmund B Rice were discharged finally. 3-Geo Coates, found guilty of petit larceny, was sentenced to one month in jail. 4-The following prisoners were found guilty, & were sentenced: Jos Duncan, assault & battery, one month in jail. W King, larceny of a horse from Mr Graham, in consideration of his having been sentenced already for 5 years, the Court only gave him 2 more years, to commence on the expiration of his previous sentence.

Circuit Court for Talbot Co, [Md] in Chancery, Nov Term, 1867. Wm Clash vs Wm Haskins. The object of this suit is to procure a decree for sale of certain mortagaed premises in said county, which were on Sep 1, 1866, mortgaged by the dfndnt, Wm Haskins, to the cmplnt Wm Clash. The bill of cmplnts states that on or about Sep 1, 1866, the said Wm Haskins conveyed certain real estate unto Wm Clash, by way of mortgage, to secure the sum of $2,600, with interest, from Mar 21, 1866, & payable by instalments as stated in said bill & mortgage filed as exhibit with said bill; that the first instalment became due on Jan 1, 1867, & the dfndnt paid on said day the sum of $500, part thereof leaving the balance of the said instalments due & unpaid; that the dfndnt resides out of the State of Md. Absent dfndnt to appear in this court, in person or by solicitor, on or before May 15th next. –J A Wicke
-John Baggs, clerk, Talbot Co.

TUE DEC 24, 1867
We failed to notice the bookstore of John C Parker, 458 7th st, near F, formerly occupied by Mr Chas H Anderson, & later by Messrs McConnell & Herbert. Mr Parker's store will compare favorably with any establishment in Wash City. Messrs W M Galt, at their immense flour & feed house, have a good supply of both apples & venison; corner of Indiana ave & 1st st. Bouquets & christmas trees, Mr Jno Saul, on 7th st, opposite the Patent Ofc; & beautiful dried flowers. Seymour, in Gtwn, has a full stock of beautiful furs of every grade, from the finest mink & sable to the common squirrel. A nice suit of clothes can be found at Col Sam Owen's, Pa ave, above Willard's. Our affiable young friend A Saks, 7th & D sts, is the proprietor of a gentleman's clothing emporium. His stock of gents' furnishing goods is large & varied. A nice present would be the brick house that Mr Dowman, 3 Intelligencer Bldg, advertises to sell for $8,500. A fine piano would be a very handsome present, & Messrs Dessau & Kaiser advertise that the instruments made at their manufactor in Wash City are of very fine tone & superior finish. Their display is at the store of W B Moses, 7th & La ave. Fine groceries can be found at Mr R J Ryan's, 9th st, between D & E sts. Messrs Z M P King & Son, Vt & 15th st, have a fine supply of elegant groceries. Grapes, citron, etc, at F C Weston & Co, 519 9th st. Z D Gilman, 350 Pa ave, has a rich variety of elegant articles. Wines, liquors & cigars, at Thos Russell & Co, Pa ave, between 12th & 13th sts. This house, under the direction of the late E C Dyer, achieved a fine reputation for fine Havana cigars. A good picture of one's self is always acceptable to our friends. Mr A Gardner has for years past given

satisfaction to all who come to him for photographs. The Market Store of Messrs Linkins & Sons, 387 20th st, between G & H is recommended to our readers. H F Zimmerman will continue the furniture business under the name of Zimerman & Van Camp, at 530 7th st. W R Snow & Co, 107 Water st, Gtwn, have on hand a very large lot of fuel. H N Barlow, 237 Pa ave, fine collection of oil paintings. M William, 336 Pa ave, large assortment of flowers & trimmings. Chamberlain & Robbins, 53 La ave, everything in the produce line can be obtained of this firm. J W Kennedy & Co, 513 7th st, presents such as skates, tool chests, sleighs, & builder's hardware. Geo Willner, 464 9th st, French & American paper hangings & upholstery goods. J M Young & Bro, 403 Pa ave, fashionable carriages & other vehicles. Brown & Bowen, 477 & 483 9th st, showroom of elegant chandeliers, brackets, etc; added to their branch of business as plumbers & gas fitters. C Gautier, 252 Pa ave, importer of wines & liquors; & cigars. Messrs Jno B Wheeler & Co, 61 La ave, between 6th & 7th sts, elegant goods, especially plated glass table-ware, which is a novelty in Wash City.

Last week the jury of condemnation proceeded to condemn the right of way for the use of the Washington & Point of Rocks railroad. They came to Barnesville, & passed over the route to Germantown, & thence to this place, doing nothing between Germantown & Gaithersburg, but condemn the right of way from the last named place to Rockville. The following is the result to this date: John H & Wm Reed, 5½ acres, $380; John W Darby, 12½ acres, $800; Wm Grant, 9 acres, $400; Mrs C R Nichols, 5¾ acres, $400; Sampson P Nichols & wife, one cent; [the depot between Barnesville & Germantown is located on their land;] John McAtee, $900; Richd Burdett, private contract; Horace Waters, 1¼ acres, $100; Jos Leaman, $300. The above constitutes the amount of damages between the places mentioned, embracing 8 miles. On arriving at Gaithersburg the jury began work again; Chas Saffe, private contract; F C Clopper give the right of way for 2 miles, upon condition that the company construct a switch at a point designated by him; Nathan Cook, 5 acres, $100; Lemuel Clements, 1¼ acres, $175; Thos R Suter, 3¾ acres, $1,700; heirs of Mrs Belmear, 7 acres, $600; Marchant Ricketts, 5 3/8 acres, $950; Philemon Griffith, 2 acres, $530; Chandler Keys, 3¾ acres, $1,500; Mrs Thos Garret, 2 acres, $126; Mrs Howard, [commonly called the *England farm*, adjoining this town,] 10½ acres, $4,900; the route at this point taking the entire bldg. The distance so far settled by the jury is 15 miles. The following is a list of the jury, just selected, to condemn land between Rockville & the District line: E L Hays, Jas B Claggett, A Pumphrey, Saml Briggs, W Huddleston, Wm R Beall, Wm Rice, O Z Muncaster, Jos Thompson, W E Pumphrey, Jas M Benton, Wm Councilman, Robt Spates, W H Magruder, Jas R Benson, Saml Thift, John Wilson, Jas W Campbell, Rufus H Bouie, & John H Higgins. On Monday they will renew their work by commencing on the land of R A Shekell.

The Hudson Taylor Book & Stationery Store, 334 Pa ave, will keep open till 12 o'clock, on Tuesday, & also the next day, Christmas, till 12 o'clock M. They will also deliver parcels at all places in the city & Gtwn, free of charge.

Hon C S Hamilton, of the 8th Congressional Dist of Ohio, was killed by the hands of his own son, whose insanity had hurried his departure from Washington. A father going home to his family to preserve & save one of his offspring, & thus to gladden the family hearth on an occasion of general festivity, is suddenly sent into eternity by the frantic hand of his child. [No other details-current item.]
+
Cincinnati, Ohio, Dec 23. Despatches from Maysville, Ohio, tell of the killing of Hon C S Hamilton at that place, yesterday, by his son, 18 years of age, who had lately become deranged. He was struck in the head with an axe. The son then inflicted a severe wound on his younger brother before he could be secured. He is now a hopeless, raving maniac. Mr Hamilton was a man of very considerable property, & leaves a wife & 6 children.

At Fair Haven, Ct, last Thu, the body of Miss Catharine E English was found in the well in the rear of the residence of her brother, Mr N S English, where she had been living. The lady had been suffering from aberration of mind.

Mr Jos Jefferson, the comedian, was married at Chicago, on Friday, to Miss Mary A Warren, a niece of Mayor Rice, of that place.

A fatal accident at the Fulton ferry, N Y, on Sunday. Mr John Kempston, clerk of the Superior Court, was run over & instantly killed by a cart which was coming off the ferry-boat. A coroner's jury censured the ferry company for negligence.

Jos & Josephine Brown, were arrested last week at Hartford, Conn, charged with murdering a child at Canaan, Columbia Co, N Y, & then firing the house, for the purpose of obtaining $5,000, for which the life of the child was insured, arrived at Albany on Sunday, under a requisition from Gov'n'r Fenton. The woman accuses Brown of the crime, & says he had effected an insurance for a like sum on her life, & that she believed he intended to destroy her also.

Mrd: on Dec 17, in Boston, Mass, by Rev A P Peabody, D D, Capt C D Hebb, U S Marine Corps, to Miss Minnie Gertrude, daughter of the late Wm Lambert.

Died: on Dec 20, at her residence, 91 Camden st, Balt, Md, in her 78th year of her age, Mrs Rebecca Butler, wife of Richd Butler; & on Dec 18, in his 2nd year, their grandson, Willie Mercer, & son of L H & F M Breed. [Annapolis & PG Co papers please copy.]

Boston, Dec 22. The express train from N Y for Boston ran into a freight train this morning near Natick. Jas McCurdy, a brakeman, had both legs broken, & died a few hours afterwards. Only four passengers, Messrs U S Wroe, S B Gilman, Hatch & Hopkins, were slightly injured.

Died: on Dec 22, at St Bernard, Fauquier Co, Va, Eliza Ariss, wife of B Frank Gallaher, & daughter of the late Richd Bernard Buckner, of Fauquier Co, Va, aged 34 years, 2 months & 20 days. [Va papers please copy.]

Reading, Pa, Dec 23. The locomotive Iowa, belonging to the Reading Railroad Co, exploded this morning, instantly killing the engineer, Albert Kline, & so mutilating the fireman that he survived but a half hour. Both of the men left families in this city. [No name given for the fireman.]

Criminal Court-Judge Fisher. 1-Bernard Smith convicted of grand larceny, sentenced to 18 months in the Albany penitentiary. He was also convicted of petty larceny, & sentenced to 1 day in the county jail. 2-Conrad Miller convicted of petty larceny, sentenced to 2 months in jail. 3-Frank Brown, larceny from Jas Lavender on Aug 8, 1867, pleaded guilty; 30 days in jail. 4-Anderson Scott, larceny. Recognizance forfeited. Anthon Coats security. 5-Anthony Bundy, assault & battery with intent to kill. Recognizance forfeited. 6-John Hangshuby, petit larceny. *Nolle pros.*

Trustee's sale, by deed of trust from Richd A Callan & Owen E Duffy to me, recorded in Liber F S No 2, folios 8, of the land records of PG Co, Md: public sale on Thursday next, the Farm whereon the said Duffy now resides, called part of Beall's [blank,] containing 21 acres, 3 roods, 8 perches. It adjoins the lands of Arundel Smith, Wm F Deakins, & others. –John McDermott, trustee

John P Von Essen vs Edw B Waring, Mary E Waring, Sally W Waring, Anna S Peck, Clement A Peck, Mary H Beall, & Wm W Corcoran. Equity No 815. Notice is given to the parties to this cause, to Benj Fawcett & Marion Fawcett his wife; to Peter Simpson & Christina Simpson his wife, to the heirs-at-law of the late Martha Clagett, deceased, & to the trustee appointed to sell the property mentioned in the proceedings, that, on Jan 7, next, at 12 o'clock M, at my ofc, 36 La ave, Wash, pursuant to the order of reference in said cause, I shall proceed to state the account of the said trustee, & the distribution of the fund in his hands. –C Ingle, special auditor

Dept of the Interior, U S Patent Ofc, Wash, Dec 19, 1867. Ptn of Marinda Starks, of Genoa, N Y, admx of the estate of Isaac Starks, deceased, & Lyman Perrigo, of Groton, N Y, praying for the extension of a patent granted them on Jun 13, 1854, for an improvement in Device for Holding Pieces in Spoke Machines, for seven years from the expiration of said patent, which takes place on Jun 13, 1868.
-T C Theaker, Com'r of Patents

WED DEC 25, 1867
The dedication of the Episcopal Church called the Church of the Incarnation, at N & 12th st, was held last evening. The Church cost $21,000 to erect. Rev Mr Lowry, rector, announced that there was still a debt of $8,000 on the bldg.

The marriage of Col Eli S Parker, of Gen Grant's staff, to Miss Minnie O Sackett, took place on Monday at the residence of Dr Hall, rector of the Church of the Epiphany.

Mrs Christina Barcley, aged 102 years, died last week in Mt Washington, Ky. She was born in Phil, & once dined with Gen Washington. On her 100th birthday she joined the young folks in dance.

Waco [Texas] Register: on Friday last the Bureau agent at Cotton Gin, Capt C E Culver, with private Stockler, started out on the road leading to Springfield. They came upon a Mr Stewart, near his house, with a gun. Capt Culver told Stewart it was against his orders to go armed, & ordered him to give it up. Stewart said he would not give up the gun, but put it back in the rack. Culver ordered the private to fire on Stewart, which he did. Stewart then fired. In the conflict Culver & the private were killed, Stewart was very dangerously wounded. A ball also struck Mrs Stewart in the head. During the conflict Stewart called on his son to attack with the ax or hatchet, which the boy did, inflicting a deep gash in the head of Culver. Capt Emerson, the commandant at this post, visited the scene on Sunday. He found the bodies of Culver & Stockler laid out in good coffins & proper clothing at the court house in Springfield, awaiting his call. The bodies of the deceased were brought to Waco, & on yesterday buried by the military. Rev R C Burleson officiated at the burial. Capt Culver did not belong to the regular army, but was detailed from private life.

Christmas, so called from the two Latin words, Christi & Missa, signifying the Mass, or offering of Christ, is the great festival of the ecclesiastic year.

The Christmas tree, in Germany, & the North of Europe, as also very extensively in America, is a splendor & delight in the eyes of all children. The custom was early introduced into this country by the German emigrants, but was hardly known to England till within the present century. The first forming of the Christmas tree in England is believed to have been done by a German in the household of Queen Caroline, wife of George IV, who saw few happy Christmas trees after her marriage in 1795. The custom did not become general there till Prince Albert came over from Germany to be the husband of Queen Victoria, & since then it has become almost universal in that country.

Orphans Court, Judge Purcell. 1-Francis J Jones gave bond in the sum of $1,000, as guardian of the orphan child of Carey Carter, late of Augusta, Ga, deceased. Sureties, J F Cain & E S Dow. 2-Ann McGrath gave bond in the sum of $1,200, as admx of the personal estate of John McGrath, deceased. Sureties, Timothy Dahey & Edw McGraw. 3-First & final account of Isaac Talks, guardian to Isaac S Hollidge, minor child of Thos Hollidge, filed. 4-M Antoinette Swain & Mary Virginia Swain gave bond in the sum of $500, as admx of Benedict Swain, deceased. C G Langley & Wm Talbert, sureties.

Mr Anton Leitner was absorbed by quicksand in Nebraska, & his body was not found for two days. Then it was found that he was only buried a foot, & could easily have been got out.

Equity Court-Judge Wylie. 1-In the case of Martha A Wilson vs Thos Wilson, an action for divorce, the application by the dfndnt for permission to have the custody of his son was refused until an answer should be filed in the cause. 2-*In re*, Estate of John Forrest; decree confirming decision of Orphans Court. 3-West et al vs Lucas: publication of non-residence. 4-Iardella vs Iardella: order referring claim of Dr Ford to auditor.

Criminal Court-Judge Olin. 1-Mary E Bowie, indicted for petty larceny, was found guilty & sentenced to 2 months in the county jail. 2-Geo A Perrie, indicted for vending lottery tickets, was put upon trial. The jury returned a verdict of guilty. 3-Francis Brumgard, found not guilty of larceny of goods, from Jas E Sherwood, in Gtwn, on May 12th last.

Mrd: on Dec 23, by Rev Chas H Hall, D D, Ely S Parker, U S army, to Minnie, daughter of the late Col Sackett, U S volunteers.

Died: on Dec 23, of heart disease, Azariah Cooley, aged 69. His funeral will be on Dec 26, at 10 o'clock, from the residence of his son-in-law, J M Towers, 343 21st st.

Bank robber in Haverhill, Mass, on Monday, shot Ofcr Burnham when he attempted to arrest him. No robbery was effected, & the thief made his escape.

St Louis, Dec 21. Hon Robt Smith, formerly a member of Congress from the Alton dist of Ill, died at his residence near Alton last week. He was a native of Peterboro, N H.

Dept of the Interior, U S Patent Ofc, Wash, Dec 19, 1867. Ptn of Horace Smith & D B Wesson, of Springfield, Mass, praying for the extension of a patent granted to them on Aug 8, 1854, for an improvement in Cartridges, for seven years from the expiration of said patent, which takes place on Aug 8, 1868. -T C Theaker, Com'r of Patents

Dept of the Interior, U S Patent Ofc, Wash, Dec 19, 1867. Ptn of Ambrose Nicholson, of Poland, N Y, praying for the extension of a patent granted to him Mar 21, 1854, for an improvement in Self-fastening Shutter Hinges, for seven years from the expiration of said patent, which takes place on Mar 21, 1868.
-T C Theaker, Com'r of Patents

FRI DEC 27, 1867
Jefferson Davis & family arrived at Havana on Dec 25th, en-route for New Orleans.

When the last steamer left England, the death of Cardinal Bofondi, prefect of the censorship, & spoken up as one of the most liberal members of the Sacred College, was momentarily expected. His death would make another Cardinal's hat vacant, leaving 19 at the Pope's disposal.

Criminal Court-Judge Olin. 1-Thos Myers, who plead guilty to the charge of grand larceny, was sentenced to 2 years in the Albany penitentiary. 2-Jas Smith & Peter McCabe, for horse stealing; penitentiary 3 years. 3-Jas Alatin, convicted of grand larceny, sentenced to 2 years in the Albany penitentiary. 4-Wm H King, 5 years in the Albany penitentiary for burglary. His sentence to take effect from the expiration of his previous sentence of 2 years for horse stealing.

On Wed night as 3 men, John Tongman, S McHenry, & David Ellwood, were passing along L st & Conn ave, they met a colored man & woman, & it is stated that Tongman unintentionally jostled the colored man, who instantly drew a revolver & fired at him, below the nipple. Tongman was taken into Mr Wm Luney's house, nearby, & Dr W J Craiggen was summoned. Yesterday morning, he was removed to Providence Hospital, where he died at 1 o'clock. Tongman was about 35 years of age, a stonecutter by trade, unmarried, & is said to have always been a quiet man. He boarded at the house of Mrs Davis, corner of 12th & F sts.

Dr W J C Duhamel, the physician to the jail, has been dismissed from this position by Warden Heustis, owing to personal differences. Heustis did not want a desperate character, prisoner Geo Williams, taken to the hospital for treatment of erysipelas, but to remain in his cell for treatment. He feared Williams would effect an escape if put in a hospital ward.

Mr Wm Lewis, a prominent citizen of New Haven died suddenly of apoplexy on Wed, aged 57 years.

Last Wed, in Arkansas, 40 miles below Memphis, Henry A Burgett was shot by his partner, J H Grider. The two quarreled about a cotton plantation which they had been operating together.

Among the killed by the railroad accident at Angola, was Chas Lobdell, associate editor of the La Crosse [Wisc] Democrat. He was on his way to Bridgeport, Conn, to spend the holidays with his relatives.

Patapsco Female Institute, near Balt, Md, in full operation, with complete corps of Teachers & Professors. Address the Principal, Robt H Archer, Ellicott's Mills, Md.

The Forrest divorce case is still in the courts at N Y. Judge Jones, of the Superior Court, on Tuesday, delivered a decision at the instance of Mr Forrest's former wife, the substance of which is that the alimony must be paid. The total amount now due is said to be about $100,000.

The remains of Gen Griffin, who died recently of yellow fever in Texas, arrived in N Y yesterday. They will be brought to this city. [Dec 30th newspaper: The remains of Maj Gen Chas Griffin & his son, both stricken down with yellow fever, at Galveston, Texas, arrived in N Y on Thu last, on the New Orleans steamer **Bienville**, & reached this city on Saturday morning, at 5½ o'clock, and were received at the depot by a guard of honor, composed of a detail of 30 men from the 12th U S infty, under command of Brvt Col August G Tassin, & Lts E H Parsons, & L A Nesmith. The metallic coffins, encased in zinc, were placed on a catafalque in the large hall of the depot, covered with American flags, & surrounded by a guard of the brave and gallant soldiers he once commanded. During the morning there was a large assemblage of persons in and about the depot present to pay their last tribute of respect to one who was beloved by all who knew him. By 11 o'clock the troops composing the escort, commenced to arrive, & were drawn up on N J ave, with the right resting on B st, under the orders of Brvt Brig Gen Buell, colonel 29th infty, commanding the escort in place of Col Wallace, cmder of the garrison of Washington, who was indisposed. Gen Porter, of Gen Grant's staff, & Brvt Gen Carroll, of the 21st infty, before the arrival of the troops, visited the depot with the undertaker, Mr Harvey, and placed on the coffin of the deceased Gen two beautiful crosses and a wreath of japonicas; also, a cross and wreath on the coffin of his son. Col Tassin also placed a beautiful japonica on the coffin of the General. About 11:30 the officiating minister, Rev J V Lewis, of St John's Church, and the pall bearers arrived, as also Gen Grant, Lt Gen Sherman, Gen Comstock, & Gen Badeau, of Gen Grant's staff, Gen Michler, & Col Snyder, capt 3rd infty, who came on in charge of the bodies & others. The procession included the troops with reversed arms, 12th infty, about 480 men, under command of Maj Nicodemus, accompanied by their fine band; 19th infty, about 250 men, under command of Maj Lawrence, headed by a drum corps, commanded by Maj Gardner; co K, 5th cavalry, about 60 men, under command of Brvt Col Mason, with the regimental band; carriage containing the officiating minister Rev J V Lewis; carriages containing the pall bearers, Gens Emory, Barr, Ricketts, Hunter, Hardee, Humphrey, Rawlings, and Augur; hearse with the remains of the Gen, over the top of which was thrown the national colors, the hearse being drawn by four white horses, followed by a smaller hearse, in which was the body of his son, being flanked by the sgts detailed to carry the coffins. Then came a horse attended by two of the 5th cavalry, the sword & boots of the deceased suspended from the pommel of the saddle. Then came a carriage were Gen Grant, Lt Gen Sherman, and Gen Comstock, followed by other carriages, which were officers of the army and friends of the deceased. The procession moved along Pa ave to Gtwn, along Bridge, up Washington st to ***Oak Hill Cemetery***, the troops forming in line outside and presenting arms as the funeral cortege passed into the cemetery. The remains were taken into the chapel, where Mrs Griffin, accompanied by Gen Porter, of Gen Grant's staff, with a few of the personal friends of the deceased, had assembled and after the service of the Episcopal Church had been read, were placed in the vault of the Carroll family. Upon the door of the compartment designed for the reception of Gen Griffin's remains is the inscription, "Major General Charles Griffin; died September 15, 1867, of yellow fever, at

Galveston, Texas. Honor the brave." The pavements along the route of the procession were crowded with spectators, and flags were at half mast in different parts of the city].

Died: on Dec 25, of dropsy, in Wash City, John H D Williams, aged 26 years. His funeral will take place on Dec 27, at 2 o'clock P M, from the E st Baptist Church.

Died: on Dec 25, Annie Virginia, aged 3 months & 4 days, only child of Henry & Annie E Douglas. Her funeral will be on Dec 27, at 11 o'clock A M, from 252 G st.

Memphis, Dec 26. A policeman, John Fenton, whilst attempting to arrest 3 drunken men on Main st yesterday, was mortally shot. In the melee, a German lad, Jas Schiller, was killed by a stray shot. The assassins have all been arrested & held for trial.

SAT DEC 28, 1867
Patent laws were unknown among the ancients, & in Europe have existed only during the last two centuries. Before the adoption of the Federal Constitution the several States, as sovereign powers, granted patents. On Apr 10, 1790, Congress passed an act entitled "An act for promoting the progress of the useufl arts." This was repealed, & an amended one passed, on Feb 21, 1793. The first 3 patents issued were: to Saml Hopkins, for making pot & pearl ashes, dated Jul 31, 1790. To Josiah S Samson, for making candles, dated Aug 6, 1790. To Oliver Evans, for making flour & meal, dated Dec 18, 1790.
The first of which a record exists was granted to Thos Bidwell for improving yellow color. The first Com'r appointed under the act of reorganization was Henry L Ellsworth, who applied himself for several years with great assiduity.
Superintendents:
Wm Thornton, of Tortola, W Ind, appointed 1802.
Thos P Jones, of Pa, appointed Apr 12, 1828.
John D Craig, of Pa, appointed Jan 1, 1830.
Jas C Pickett, of N C, appointed Jan 1, 1836.
Com'rs: Henry L Ellsworth, of Conn, appointed Jul 4, 1836.
Edmund Burke, of N H, appointed May 5, 1845.
Thos Ewbank, of N Y, appointed Sep 3, 1850.
Silas H Hodges, of Vt, appointed Nov 1, 1852.
Chas Mason, of Iowa, appointed Mar 24, 1853.
Jos Holt, of Ky, appointed Sep 10, 1857.
Wm D Bishop, of Conn, appointed May 23, 1859.
Philip F Thomas, of Md, appointed Feb 16, 1868.
D P Holloway, of Indiana, appointed Mar 28, 1861.
Thos C Theaker, of Ohio, appointed Aug 17,1865.

Mr John Conners, a well known Corporation paving contractor, died on Thursday, at his residence, on Mass ave, between 2nd & 3rd sts. His illness was of short duration.

The burial corps of the Quartermaster's Dept are now at work at **Point Lookout**, exhuming the bodies of the soldiers buried there. Yesterday 700 bodies were brought to this city on barges. They were taken to **Arlington Cemetery** for interment.

The funeral of the late Brvt Maj Gen Chas Griffin, U S army, till take place on Dec 28, at 12 P M. Burial will be in the **Gtwn Cemetery**. The pallbearers selected are: Maj Generals Emory, Hardie, Carr, Humphrey, Ricketts, Rawlins, Hunter, & Augur.

Criminal Court-Judge Olin. 1-Washington Meredith, assault & battery, guilty. Recognizance forfeited, & capias to hear judgment. 2-Augustus Jones, assault & battery, on Oct 3 last, on Wm H Pettit, in Gtwn; guilty, sentenced to jail for 25 days. 3-Robt Scott, assault & battery, guilty; sentenced to 2 months in county jail. 4-Chas Boyd, petit larceny, guilty. 5-Peter Sprow, assault & battery on Ofcr Yeatman, guilty; jail 3 months.

St Louis, Dec 25. 1-Santa Fe, New Mexico letter dated Dec 17: Chief Justice Slough was shot by Capt Rynerson, a member of the territorial Senate, last Sunday. The affair grew out of strictures pased upon Judge Slough by Capt Rynerson, during the session of the Senate. After Slough fell, shooting him again, inflicting a mortal wound from which he died 3 days after. Judge Slough was colonel of the 1st Colorado cavalry during the war, & at one time commanded at Alexandria, Va. 2-Jacob Schoff, an old citizen of Belleville, Ill, whose wife was recently divorced from him, fatally stabbed both her & himself yesterday. 3-Wm G Petties, one of the oldest citizens of St Louis, died yesterday.

Phil Enquirer: On Wed last the keeper of Romeo-the elephant, Mr W S Williams, went to see him, & ordered Romeo to perform sundry tricks, which he refused to do, & was whipped. Later in the day Mr Williams went into the cage to wash Romeo's face & tusks. The elephant threw out his massive trunk, & winding it about the unfortunate man, hurled him to the ground again & again, & thrust his broken tuck into the body of the victim. Mr Williams expired in about an hour; he belonged to London, Canada West, where he owned a farm; was about 40 years of age, married, but with no children. His wife was with him at Hatborough, Montg Co, 16 miles north of Phil. Mr Williams had been Romeo's keeper for about 5 years, for 10 years engaged otherwise, & until just one year to a day, before his death, again took charge of Romeo.

Springfield, Mass, Dec 27. Ezra C White, of Wmsburg, in a quarrel this morning, shot Mrs Maria L French through the head, inflicting a fatal wound. He is now in jail in default of $10,000 bail.

Orphans Court of Wash Co, D C. Letters of administration on the personal estate of John McGrath, late of Wash City, D C, deceased. –Ann [x-her mark] McGrath, admx

Boston, Dec 27. The cashier & receiving teller of the Shawmut Bank, Bryant F Henry, fell short about $50,000. Henry has been absent from the city for a week, his whereabouts are unknown. It is supposed he stepped across into Canada, or went to Europe by steamship. The bank has a capital of $750,000, with a surplus of $150,000, so that the defalcation will not affect the standing of the institution in the least. [Dec 30, 1867: It is ascertained that the cash of the defaulting teller, Henry, is short five to six thousand dollars, from omitting to credit deposits when received. The balance, $27,000 in compound interest notes, & $27,000 in bills, was stolen from a trunk in the bank vault the day that the defaulter disappeared.]

Died: on Dec 18, Mrs Harriet M Marshall, wife of Judge Marshall, of Frederick City, Md. For the last 20 years of her life she was in very delicate health. Those who knew her best loved her most. Her devotion as a mother & wife was unbounded.

Trustee's sale of valuable real estate, by decree of the Circuit Court of PG Co, Md, in Equity, passed in the case of Thos A L Mitchell vs Henry W Darnall & wife, I will expose to public sale, on Jan 2, on the premises, near the residence of Mr Richd N Darnall, about 2 miles from the village of Bladensburg, all that parcel of land number 4, which was allotted to the said Henry W Darnall by Commissioners appointed by the said court to divide the real estate of Francis L Darnall, deceased. It contains 58½ acres. -N C Stephen, trustee

MON DEC 30, 1867

Gen Granger has been relieved from command of the district of Arizona, & ordered to assume command of the military operations in Nevada. Gen Crittenden is named as his successor.

Miss Caroline M Richings, the well-known American prima donna, was married at Boston on Christmas Eve to Pierre Bernard, of N Y C. Mr Bernard is a member of the Richings; Opera Troupe.

The basement story of St Stephen's Catholic Church, in the First Ward, near the Circle, was dedicated yesterday with a solemn high mass celebrated with the pastor, Rev Fr McNally as celebrant; Rev Fr Cleary as deacon; & Rev Mr Lancaster as sub-deacon. Discourse was delivered by Rev F X Boyle, pastor of St Peter's Church. The basement is very comfortably furnished, & will be used until the main portion of the bldg is read for consecration.

The German Lutheran Church, High & 4th sts, Gtwn, was dedicated yesterday; services conducted by Rev Dr Finckel; Rev J G Butler, pastor of St Paul's Lutheran Church of this city, & Rev Mr Nelson, of the Baptist Church, Gtwn, assisted. An antique Bible, printed in 1730, was presented to the church by Mr Jas Gaezler.

Criminal Court-Judge Olin. 1-Ames Pratt, charged with keeping a disorderly house; guilty. 2-Margaret Dick, alias Mary Gibson, indicted for keeping a bawdy house: guilty. Capias to hear judgment. 3-Wm H Dover, petit larceny; fined $20.

Orphans Court-Judge Purcell, Dec 28, 1867. 1-The will of Edmund Walsh, devising all his estate to his wife, Ellen Walsh, to be used for the benefit of his children, was filed & partially proven. 2-Fourth individual account of Margaret Bayly, guardian to Geo J Bayley, orphan of Wm F Bayley, deceased, filed & passed. Same, as guardian of Mary E Bayley, orphan of Wm F Bayley, filed & passed. 3-John H Goddard gave bond in the sum of $2,000 as guardian of the orphans of Wm Flaherty; Peter Conlan & Theodore Sheckel sureties. 4-Ezekiel Cox gave bond in the sum of $4,000 as administrator of the estate of A S Cox; Wm P Partello & Henry Beard, sureties. 5-*In re*. Petition of Richd Vigle. Citation ordered & issued against Mrs Sarah Naylor & E Seymour, requiring them to show cause why they should not bring into court the body of John W Vigle, for the purpose of apprenticing him. J E Williams for petitioner. 6-In the case of the account of Mary E Lawson against the estate of Andrew Small, deceased, laid over until Tues next.

Boston, Dec 28. Letter received here from Rio, dated Nov 24, & published in the Traveller, of this city: This morning a Brazilian steamer has arrived from Montevideo, bringing the news of the loss of the English mail steamer **Santurn**, in a terrible gale off that place a week ago. She was iron-clad, & one of the finest looking steamers I ever saw. She left the harbor of Bahia while we were at anchor there. When she went down she had on board 400 persons, including the crew & passengers. Among the latter was the English Minister, who had just been relieved to enable him to make a short visit home. He, with the rest, was lost, only 14 out of the whole being saved.

Mobile, Ala, Dec 28. Dist Atty L V B Martin met Judge Busteed, of the U S Court, this morning in front of the custom-house, & said, "Judge, will you allow that indictment against me to take its course?" Judge Busteed replied,"Sir, the law must take its course." Martin then drew a revolver & fired 3 shots at Busteed, who fell, with a ball below the breast bone & another in the right leg. Martin had been indicted by the U S grand jury for revenue frauds & extortion. He is now in jail. Judge Busteed's wounds are not considered mortal.

Burlington, Vt, Dec 29. John Harrigan, an employe of the Vt Central railroad, was run over by the cars in the depot in this city, last night. He lived but a few hours.

Boston, Dec 29. Robt Preston, clerk of the Dorchester Mutual Fire Ins Co, is charged with appropriating $10,000, with which he has disappeared.

Wash Corp: 1-Cmte of Claims: Bill for the relief of the widow of the late Geo Dean was passed. Same cmte: bill for the relief of Wm Turner: passed. Same cmte: bill for the relief of Mary Reidy: passed.

Orphans Court of Wash Co, D C. Letters testamentary on the personal estate of Alex S Cox, late of Wash City, D C, deceased. –Ezekiel T Cox, exc

Headquarters of the Army, Adj Gen's Ofc, Wash, Dec 28, 1867. Genr'l Orders No 101. By direction of the Pres of the U S, the following orders are made:
I-Brvt Maj Gen E O C Ord will turn over the command of the 4th Military Dist to Brvt Maj Gen A C Gillem, & proceed to San Francisco, Calif, to take command of the Dept of Calif.
II-On being relieved by Brvt Maj Ord, Brvt Maj Gen Irvin McDowell will proceed to Vicksburg, Miss, & relieve Gen Gillem in command of the 4th Military Dist.
III-Brvt Maj Gen John Pope is hereby relieved of the command of the 3rd Military Dist, & will report, without delay, at the Headquarters of the Army for further orders, turning over his command to the next senior ofcr until the arrival of his successor.
IV-Maj Gen Geo G Mead is assigned to the command of the 3rd Military Dist, & will assume it without delay. The Dept of the East will be commanded by the senior ofcr now on duty in it, until a cmder is named by the Pres.
V-Brvt Maj Gen Water Swayne, colonel 45th U S infty, is hereby relieved from duty in the Bureau of Refugees, Freedmen, & Abandoned Lands, & will proceed to Nashville, Tenn, & assume command of his regt. By command of Gen Grant.
-E D Townsend, Assist Adj Gen

Sale, by deed of trust, dated Aug 10, 1866, executed to the undersigned as trustee by Emily F Wiley, recorded in Liber R M H No 18, folios 406; sale on Jan 22, on the premises, part of square 527, on 3rd & I st, with two good houses thereon. This property will be sold subject to the right of dower of the widow of the late C P Brown. -John Carroll Brent, trustee -Cooper & Latimer, aucts

Orphans Court of Wash Co, D C. Letters of administration on the personal estate of Benedict Swain, late of Wash City, D C, deceased. –M Antoinnette Swain, M Virginia Swain, admx

TUE DEC 31, 1867
Equity Court-Judge Wylie. 1-Coyle vs Coyle et al. Order appointing Annie McNeir Coyle guardian *ad litem*. 2-McCann vs Eckhardt et al. Order making Florian Hitz a party cmplnt. 3-Owen et al vs Henderson et al. Order appointing J L Johnson trustee to sell real estate.

John Nance was hanged for murder at Rutledge, Tenn, on Friday, in the presence of 3,000 people. The rope by which he was executed was too long, & he was slowly strangled to death. Jacob Huff was executed at Hamilton, the same State, the same day.

Botts & Poston, Attys-at-Law, Plants Bldg, corner of 15th st & N Y ave, Wash, D C. -Chas L Botts, Chas D Poston

Advertisements:
Fred'k W Alexander, Real Estate Broker & Claim Agent, 493 12th st, Wash, D C.

Wm W Boyce, [formerly of S C,] Atty-at-Law, 281 G st, Wash.

P Phillips, [formerly of Ala,] has resumed the practice of Law in Wash City: ofc-n w corner of La ave & 6th st. Residence: 273 Vt ave, between H & I sts.

T & C Ewing, Attys & Counsellors at Law, 460 7th st, between F & G sts, Wash, D C. Practice in the Supreme Court, the Court of Claims, & in the Depts.
–Thos Ewing, jr, Chas Ewing.

Hughes, Denver, & Peck. Attys & Counsellors-at-Law, 252 G st, Wash City.
-Jas Hughes, Indiana; Jas W Benver, Calif; Chas F Peck, Illinois

A G Haley, Atty-at-Law, Market Space, Wash, D C.

<u>Residences of the Chief Justice & Assoc Justices of the Supreme Court of the U S:</u>
Mr Chief Justice Chase, northwest corner of E & 6th sts.
Mr Justice Nelson, National Hotel.
Mr Justice Grier, No 6 north A st.
Mr Justice Clifford, National Hotel.
Mr Justice Swayne, No 232 F st.
Mr Justice Miller, National Hotel.
Mr Justice Field, No 232 F st.
<u>Ofcrs of the Court:</u>
D W Middleton, Clerk, 568 N J ave.
R C Parsons, Marshal, Willard's Hotel.
John Wm Wallace, Reporter, National Hotel.

Mr A H Davenport, the actor, announces that he is not dead. On Dec 15 the following despatch was sent from N Y to New Orleans: "Please send body of A H Davenport, deceased, by steamer, to his mother,__ st, N Y C." To which Mr Davenport replied: "I will try & bring my body myself-never better able to do so in my life. –A H Davenport."

A

Aarme, 245
Aaron, 13, 39
Abadie, 116
Abbey, 190
Abbot, 26, 173, 382, 383
Abbott, 150, 211, 257, 261, 359, 396
Abeel, 88
Abel, 226
Abell, 42, 106, 248, 250, 282, 286, 485
Abercrombie, 159, 243
Abercrombie Farm, 153
Abert, 354, 364, 399
Abjoison, 62
Abney, 44
Absterdam, 474
Aburtney, 393
Aby, 420
Academy of the Visitation, 287, 420
Acheson, 286
Acker, 105, 117, 250, 254, 527
Ackley, 30, 57, 115, 156, 201
Acton, 115
Acton Hall, 373
Adam, 43
Adams, 9, 44, 83, 86, 104, 109, 128, 135, 153, 156, 212, 237, 286, 291, 339, 341, 362, 365, 385, 397, 398, 451, 454, 463, 466, 484, 520
Adamson, 113, 287
Addison, 30, 53, 60, 69, 95, 222, 275, 278, 342, 434, 439, 453, 476, 518
Addiston, 14
Adger, 53
Adler, 57, 93, 329
Agnew, 408
Agnus, 91
Aigler, 79, 165, 379
Aiken, 3, 89, 213, 225, 226, 232
Aileinger, 176
Ailer, 58, 455
Aimar, 355
Alasko, 151
Alatin, 539
Alban, 115
Albert, 288
Alden, 107, 214, 294
Aldman, 53
Aldrich, 92, 104, 259
Aldridge, 343
Ale, 6
Alexander, 85, 95, 130, 156, 182, 189, 214, 251, 255, 365, 367, 385, 397, 416, 470, 480, 509, 516, 522, 530, 545
Alexandria Museum, 385
Alford, 22, 88
Allback, 60
Allderick, 133
Allen, 2, 17, 34, 48, 68, 72, 83, 95, 108, 120, 129, 132, 134, 155, 237, 271, 329, 367, 405, 421
Alley, 53
Allis, 112
Allison, 53, 89, 224, 497
Almond, 215, 381
Alnwick Seminary, 336
Alsen, 208
Alston, 252, 405, 406
Altemus, 410
Alver, 89
Alvord, 464
Aman, 527
Ambler, 104
Ambrose, 9
Amee, 58
Ames, 156, 208, 238, 472, 485
Amey, 20
Amici, 301
Ammen, 264
Ammon, 113
amnesty, 403
Amocer, 191
Amonet, 151
Amos, 343
Amoss, 493
Amsler, 200
Ancona, 109

Anderman, 460
Anderson, 6, 7, 22, 24, 40, 41, 56, 62, 80, 97, 118, 151, 203, 228, 234, 241, 285, 294, 430, 455, 464, 466, 481, 492, 496, 499, 533
Andress, 53
Andrew, 469
Andrews, 112, 130, 132, 159, 192, 309, 420, 460
Androit, 177
Angel, 17
Angerman, 100
Angus, 161, 482
Anthon, 329
Anthony, 40, 93, 282, 369, 479
Antietam Cemetery, 429
Antietam National Cemetery, 378
Antisell, 142, 143
Antonelli, 256
Appleby, 320, 483, 510
Applegate, 4, 356
Appler, 183
Appleton, 38, 194, 421
Apthrop, 73
Archansbault, 319
Archduchess Matilda, 277
Archer, 255, 539
Archibald, 19
Arey, 46
Arington, 261
Ariss, 536
Aristides, 438
Arits, 151
Arlington Cemetery, 542
Arlington Heights, 391
Armes, 287
Armington, 121
Armistead, 53
Armooer, 191
Armour, 282
Arms, 364, 367
Armstrong, 26, 102, 105, 109, 127, 143, 212, 356, 378
Army bulletin, 100

Army Bulletin, 56, 57, 63, 66, 69, 72, 94, 99, 102, 106, 109, 122, 123, 127, 133, 138, 144, 149, 155
Army Ofcrs, 107
Armyx, 280
Arnod, 410
Arnold, 5, 12, 41, 86, 99, 135, 239, 259, 330, 415, 420, 458, 476, 478
Arny, 108
Arrants, 62
Arrison, 527
Arsenal, 390
Asboth, 149
Asbury, 369
Ashbaugh, 454
Ashford, 156, 175, 308, 467, 498
Ashiwara, 316
Ashley, 3
Ashmead, 112, 312
Ashmore, 41
Ashmun, 415
Ashton, 99, 227, 231, 302
Askew, 495
Askley, 112
Aston, 59
Astor, 64, 492
Aswold, 39
At Lee, 212
Atchinson, 34
Athertons, 163
Atkins, 107, 114
Atkinson, 3, 5, 50, 182, 214, 270, 298
Atlantic Cable, 529
AtLee, 429
Atwood, 17, 109
Atzerodt, 55, 72, 260, 262, 263, 268, 270, 297, 309, 424
Atzerott, 7
Auchmuty, 94
Audenried, 116, 117
Audubon, 411
Auerbauck, 396
Auffert, 25
Augerman, 240
Augur, 2, 181, 242, 263, 267, 272, 540, 542

Augustine, 143, 282
Auldridge, 36
Aulgar, 179
Aulick, 214
Aunt Milly, 28
Austeile, 5
Austin, 135, 156, 377, 518
Auter, 360
Averill, 34, 311
Averlhe, 377
Avery, 3, 17, 50
Ayers, 70, 312
Aymer, 512
Ayres, 5, 87, 109

B

Bab, 7
Babbitt, 83
Babcock, 85, 137, 393, 525
Babeman, 312
Babey, 299
Baca, 88, 116
Bacar, 12
Bache, 74, 129
Bachelor, 360
Bacher, 455
Bachford, 57
Bachmeyer, 116
Bachus, 301
Bacon, 27, 55, 73, 92, 97, 115, 134, 214, 239, 251, 255, 277
Badeau, 540
Badeaux, 286
Baden, 54, 58, 64
Badgely, 143
Badger, 461
Baer, 5
Baggs, 533
Bagiola, 61
Bailey, 1, 104, 105, 143, 150, 182, 253, 255, 281, 285, 291, 332, 413, 426, 462, 527
Baily, 476
Bainbridge, 341
Bair, 191
Baird, 265, 392, 469

Baker, 24, 41, 61, 62, 92, 106, 115, 126, 140, 147, 175, 210, 214, 217, 223, 233, 262, 264, 270, 280, 310, 315, 395, 402, 410, 420, 422, 434, 439, 451, 454, 471, 479, 494, 507, 519, 527
Bakewell, 436
Balckman, 527
Baldwin, 57, 115, 214, 217, 251, 280, 295, 316, 340, 349, 362, 500
Ball, 2, 56, 79, 156, 171, 183, 249, 250, 255, 284, 286, 287, 428, 503, 527
Ballantyne, 172, 217, 250, 254, 477, 528
Ballenger, 239
Ballerson, 429
Balloch, 376
Balmain, 156
Balmaine, 366
Balmazada, 408
Balt Billy, 462
Baltimore, 227
Baltimore Cemetery, 452
Bamberger, 79, 527
Bancroft, 28, 70, 210, 257, 302, 380
Band, 103
Banders, 270
Baner, 193
Bangs, 270
Bankhead, 234
Banks, 73, 195, 469
Banman, 300
Bannerman, 299
Bapst, 309
Barber, 93, 121, 437
Barbour, 20, 206, 211, 217, 251, 255, 276, 528
Barclay, 8, 248
Barcley, 366, 537
Barden, 143
Bardwell, 135
Barg, 3, 5
barge **Col E E Kendricks**, 280
barge **Delhimes**, 330
barge **H F Tracy**, 75

bark **Marco Palo**, 338
bark **Maria Henry**, 8
bark **Martha & Susan**, 20
bark **Mary E Libby**, 73
bark **Oak Ridge**, 338
bark **Rover**, 347
Barker, 217, 243, 328, 492, 527
Barksdale, 403
Barlett, 501
Barlow, 105, 195, 340, 534
Barlowe, 312
Barnaby Manor, 453, 476
Barnaclo, 247
Barnard, 34, 112, 127, 190, 264, 456
Barnard property, 407
Barnes, 1, 5, 36, 134, 160, 164, 165, 216, 217, 222, 256, 281, 312, 327, 396, 452, 520, 531
Barnett, 346
Barney, 335
Barnhart, 102, 138, 203, 329
Barnhill, 164, 171
Barnitz, 302
Barnside, 474
Barnsley, 136
Barnum, 38, 170, 256, 301, 347
Barnwell, 89, 109, 403
Barotti, 400
Barr, 79, 153, 250, 255, 540
Barrand, 456
Barras, 154
Barrat, 436
Barrett, 8, 58, 64, 69, 92, 97, 106, 165, 183, 190, 194, 203, 243, 304, 331, 342, 358, 359, 380, 415, 420, 434, 464, 473, 475, 496
Barrineau, 57
Barrington, 41, 395
Barron, 225, 265, 341, 442
Barrow, 64, 65, 120
Barry, 22, 35, 42, 52, 60, 61, 79, 206, 207, 217, 238, 241, 246, 300, 453, 457
Barslow, 312
Barthell, 412
Barthlomew, 525

Barthlon, 102
Bartholomew, 127
Bartholow, 287, 423
Bartlett, 56, 61, 118, 133, 163, 164, 176, 311, 408, 410, 501
Barton, 8, 9, 12, 44, 76, 85
Bascon, 523
Base-ball, 396
base-ball on the brain, 396
Bassatt, 322
Basse, 156
Bassett, 51, 120, 201, 300, 338, 507, 527
Bastianelli, 287
Batchelder, 15, 25, 83, 150
Bateman, 46, 246, 395, 464, 495
Batemen, 246, 395, 495
Bates, 90, 127, 215, 217, 250, 254, 294, 303, 353, 382, 426, 449
Batham, 43
Bauer, 164
Baugert, 156
Baugham, 17
Baum, 11, 49, 189, 217, 248
Bauman, 156, 300
Baumann, 496
Baury, 46
Baxter, 138, 311, 435
Bayant, 182
Bayfield, 115, 293
Bayley, 44, 62, 544
Baylis, 135, 198
Bayliss, 90, 156, 462
Baylor, 23, 69
Bayly, 397, 544
Baynard, 67
Bayne, 53, 143, 278
Beabam, 118
Beach, 275
Beadle, 130
Beadlee, 332
Beadles, 356
Beahan, 198
Beak, 480, 495
Beake, 230
Beale, 60, 158

Beall, 6, 22, 29, 64, 83, 151, 329, 332, 359, 361, 371, 374, 380, 438, 476, 480, 516, 534, 536
Beals, 195
Beam, 246, 457
Bean, 40, 131, 492
Beard, 302, 544
Beardsley, 388, 435
Beasley, 223
Beattie, 493
Beatty, 78
Beaumont, 42, 50
Beauregard, 35, 264, 378, 405, 520
Beavers, 319
Bebb, 60, 346
Beck, 57, 415
Becker, 132, 481, 496, 508, 517
Beckett, 168, 500
Beckley, 145, 271
Beckshaffe, 123
Beckshaft, 97
Beckwith, 11, 162, 233, 421
Bedford, 117
Beebe, 42, 208, 311
Beech, 270
Beecher, 75, 100, 154, 372, 477
Beechland, 411
Beens, 182
Beeridge, 530
Behn, 220
Behren, 156
Beidler, 108
Beirne, 375
Belamater, 356
Belcher, 195
Belencour, 291
Beler, 240
Belknap, 259
Bell, 22, 54, 56, 65, 76, 144, 155, 162, 163, 165, 173, 234, 241, 267, 315, 323, 330, 373, 398, 401, 511, 518
Bell's Plains, 180
Bellair, 343
Belle Haven Institute, 392
Bellinger, 449
Bellini, 393

Belloe, 28
Belman, 151
Belmear, 534
Belmont, 320
Belt, 5, 43, 430, 431
Belvidere, 189
Belvoir, 321
Benavente, 43
Bencine, 120
Bender, 190, 224
Bends, 223
Bendy, 15
Benedick, 15
Benedict, 376, 493
Benet, 69
Benglass, 62
Benham, 127, 264, 302
Beninghaus, 282
Benjamin, 259, 404, 405, 520
Bennet, 386
Bennett, 26, 135, 142, 175, 179, 193, 261, 284, 287, 354
Benning, 144
Benning's Bridge, 431
Benoist, 57
Benson, 217, 236, 272, 355, 374, 534
Benter, 156, 449
Bentley, 98
Benton, 8, 52, 115, 534
Benver, 546
Benzinger, 32, 193
Berdan, 216
Berg, 216
Bergen, 102, 500
Berger, 287
Bergling, 40
Berkely, 341
Berkly, 239
Bernard, 543
Bernheimer, 88
Beron, 69
Berotti, 324
Berrett, 239, 481
Berry, 5, 36, 97, 109, 148, 182, 206, 215, 227, 238, 249, 250, 254, 255,

306, 347, 414, 417, 453, 473, 484, 514, 521
Bertevoglio, 440
Berthemy, 351
Bertram, 92
Bertroff, 159
Besse, 87
Best, 223, 294
Bestor, 79, 80, 147, 191, 217, 453, 528
Bethune, 437
Betts, 304
Betzwell, 40
Beuhler, 156
Bevan, 156
Beveridge, 70, 86, 217, 430
Beverly, 9
Bevershout, 360
Bevier, 390
Beyer, 418
Bickley, 352
Bickly, 10
Biddle, 169, 196
Biddy, 510
Bidlow, 12
Bidwell, 118, 541
Bier, 151
Bigelow, 469, 520
Biggins, 502
Biggs, 117, 134
Bigham, 5
Bigler, 34
Bill, 107
Billinger, 311
Billingslea, 360
Binckley, 227
Bingham, 24, 74, 83, 115, 116, 333
Binney, 41
Biraghe, 53
Biraghi, 143
Birch, 14, 217
Bird, 36, 281, 325, 362
Birely, 357
Birnie, 287
Birth, 239, 255, 269, 339, 440
Birtwirtle, 57

Bisbee, 11
Bisby, 87
Bishop, 62, 213, 214, 541
Bissell, 311, 317, 319, 320, 509, 522
Bivin, 239
Bla_tler, 471
Blachford, 304
Black, 3, 34, 112, 156, 183, 482, 488, 490
Blackburn, 319, 402, 411
Blackfan, 513
Blackford, 277, 520
Blackwell, 67, 70
Bladgen, 250
Blagden, 217, 249, 254, 369
Blague, 511
Blair, 92, 135, 193, 214, 382
Blake, 27, 39, 71, 80, 85, 128, 145, 147, 159, 270, 271, 272, 279, 284, 326, 334, 369, 402, 420, 475, 508
Blakely, 64
Blakeney, 479
Blanchard, 9, 15, 18, 39, 40, 62, 214, 217, 270, 295, 346, 435, 483, 528
Bland, 3
Blanton, 34
Blavens, 217
Bledscoe, 310
Bleecker, 259
Blessed Virgin, 517
Bligh, 53, 89, 456
Blinn, 260, 264, 314
Bliss, 87, 93, 143, 248, 302, 317, 461
Blissner, 5
Block, 143
Blodgett, 131
Blondelet, 418
Bloodgood, 74
Bloomfield, 104
Blosser, 164
Blount, 240, 287, 442
Blout, 393
Blue, 31
Blue Plains, 244
Blunt, 99, 127, 265
Boag, 397

Board of Police, 132, 221, 240, 265, 462, 496, 502, 526
Boarman, 75, 156, 274, 283
Boarman's Meadows, 274
Boarman's Rest, 274
boat **Cygnet**, 501
boat **Katie Wise**, 393
boat **Molly Mack**, 397
Boaz, 92
Bobock, 405
Bockius, 115
Bocock, 35, 281, 403
Bodell, 108
Bodisco, 225, 248, 258, 293, 326
Boechkie, 486
Boerman, 303
Boes, 420
Bofondi, 539
Bogan, 152, 217, 332, 408, 459
Boggs, 217, 286, 509
Bogue, 260, 471, 492
Bogus, 390
Bogy, 22, 109
Bohrer, 69, 191, 206, 250, 254, 255, 284, 443, 527
Boice, 123
Boiles, 360
Bolan, 50
Boleinius, 104
Bolingbroke, 28
Bolling, 41, 502
Boltwood, 183
Bombury, 70
Bomford, 156, 340
Bond, 379, 431, 495
Bones, 68
Bonford, 156
Bonham, 405
Bonnaffon, 123
Bonnar, 411
Bonnell, 56
Bonneral, 5
Bonsack, 375
Bonsall, 335
Booey, 120
Booker, 70, 257, 283

Boone, 472, 522
Booth, 7, 36, 55, 66, 72, 95, 113, 119, 223, 256, 257, 260, 262, 263, 267, 268, 270, 272, 273, 274, 283, 285, 290, 292, 297, 303, 304, 309, 317, 375, 391, 394, 424, 439, 520
Bordin, 8
Boreland, 80
Boreman, 116
Borhuler, 120
Borland, 532
Bormann, 399
Borney, 185
Bornport, 115
Borven, 131
Boscow, 492
Bosman, 250
Boss, 292, 465
Bosse, 216
Bosssieau, 151
Boston, 31
Boswell, 6, 18, 287, 375, 464, 527
Bosworth, 302
Boteler, 29, 84, 215, 217, 512, 530
Botts, 204, 205, 545
Boucher, 282, 309, 313, 314
Boughter, 85
Bouie, 271, 401, 534
Bouldin, 480
Bouldin Church, 332
Bourcey, 143
Boutwell, 371
Bovall, 238
Bovan, 420
Bovard, 418
Bovee, 346
Boves, 76
Bowdoin, 16
Bowen, 87, 102, 104, 143, 156, 162, 168, 315, 331, 372, 519, 534
Bower, 144
Bowerman, 144
Bowers, 138, 459, 495
Bowie, 15, 43, 94, 95, 282, 294, 430, 456, 538
Bowling, 307

Bowlwell, 371
Bowman, 102, 151, 175, 287, 367
Box, 7
Boyce, 4, 61, 97, 104, 403, 545
Boyd, 22, 44, 73, 128, 420, 495, 542
Boyden, 138
Boyer, 26
Boyland, 147
Boyle, 11, 53, 131, 143, 147, 165, 220, 269, 287, 324, 396, 435, 543
Boyne, 239
Boynton, 104
Bozzle, 71, 164
Brabston, 360
Braceland, 286
Bradbury, 372
Braddock, 386
Bradford, 92, 149, 152, 378, 418, 512, 522
Bradley, 10, 21, 37, 69, 80, 84, 86, 109, 110, 183, 215, 217, 227, 237, 242, 244, 248, 287, 300, 309, 326, 327, 328, 355, 368, 370, 374, 379, 384, 410, 428, 464, 479, 503, 508, 510, 520
Brady, 61, 135, 156, 283, 285, 384, 422, 459, 474
Bragassa, 286
Bragg, 50, 202, 252, 264, 404, 405, 520
Braine, 466, 504, 511
Brammell, 122
Branch, 151, 403
Brandt, 190, 323
Brandywine, 323
Brannan, 1, 30, 284
Branner, 3
Branninger, 493
Brasnahan, 156
Bratton, 121, 317
Brawner, 493
Brawner House, 351
Bray, 224
Brayfield, 512, 513, 523
Breaker, 60
Breck, 57

Breckenridge, 411
Breckinridge, 205, 404, 405, 508
Breed, 217, 254, 535
Breeden, 34, 485, 519
Breese, 62
Bremmar, 359
Bremmerman, 270
Breneman, 99, 122
Brennam, 49
Brennan, 49, 85, 291
Brenner, 286, 458
Brent, 5, 37, 43, 47, 67, 80, 94, 95, 147, 183, 190, 285, 336, 383, 412, 420, 446, 475, 545
Brentman, 315
Brereton, 156, 227, 493
Bresnahan, 177, 216
Brewer, 14, 165, 170, 178, 221, 475, 497
Brian, 383
Brice, 520
Brickett, 73
Brickley, 53
Bridenomer, 393
Bridge, 259, 265
Bridges, 138
Bridget, 146, 474
Bridgman, 115
brig **Carmen**, 18
brig **Cuba**, 382
brig **Edwin N Filler**, 280
brig **Jenny Morton**, 10
brig **Meg**, 10
brig **Ocean Belle**, 234
Briggs, 115, 534
Brigham, 83
Bright, 5, 58, 207, 327
Brill, 32
Brimmer, 358
Bringle, 363
Brink, 302
Brinsmade, 31
Brinthall, 328
Briscoe, 97, 121, 156, 207
Brissell, 373
Britt, 309

Britton, 85, 142, 189, 208, 217
Broa, 3
Broad Creek Farm, 388
Broadders, 53
Broadus, 145
Broadwater, 365
Brocchus, 311
Brockaway, 276
Brockenburg, 477
Brocten, 182
Brogden, 24, 303
Brook, 85, 243
Brooke, 83, 92, 94, 197, 253, 284, 405, 422, 468
Brooker, 18, 20, 167
Brookett, 267
Brooks, 2, 23, 46, 80, 105, 145, 252, 295, 312, 360, 390, 424, 450, 463, 513
Broom, 12
Broome, 203
Brophy, 352, 528
Bross, 421
Brough, 246, 336
Brougham, 79
Broughton, 348
Brow, 143
Browing, 251
Brown, 3, 5, 8, 14, 16, 17, 28, 41, 45, 53, 56, 58, 60, 65, 68, 78, 82, 83, 84, 86, 89, 92, 94, 95, 96, 117, 118, 122, 127, 132, 134, 137, 138, 140, 141, 144, 145, 147, 148, 153, 156, 167, 171, 174, 176, 179, 190, 192, 198, 213, 214, 215, 217, 228, 230, 237, 238, 249, 252, 254, 260, 270, 273, 281, 282, 287, 292, 293, 300, 309, 311, 318, 324, 348, 359, 368, 370, 378, 380, 381, 384, 388, 391, 402, 405, 410, 412, 416, 443, 447, 458, 460, 461, 467, 473, 476, 480, 481, 493, 495, 496, 497, 500, 510, 516, 520, 522, 525, 527, 528, 529, 531, 533, 534, 535, 536, 545
Browne, 4, 121, 132, 143, 190, 233, 286, 316, 520, 532

Brownell, 272, 421
Browning, 2, 4, 6, 29, 91, 101, 105, 215, 319, 364, 455, 464, 482, 488
Bruce, 44, 182, 395, 419, 421
Brumbaker, 226
Brumgard, 538
Bruner, 1, 78
Brunton, 387
Bruscup, 94
Brush, 334
Brutton, 312
Bryan, 167, 183, 214, 215, 251, 255, 461, 512, 530
Bryant, 10, 47, 77, 92, 125, 169, 197, 214, 311, 433
Buchanan, 27, 97, 204, 270, 356, 405, 411, 505, 508, 512
Buchannan, 324
Buchee, 461
Bucher, 238
Buchler, 62, 257
Buchley, 223
Buchly, 279
Buck, 5, 58, 388, 527
Buckalew, 220
Bucker, 137
Buckey, 14, 156, 217, 246, 310, 369
Buckingham, 523
Buckley, 74, 101, 159, 395
Buckly, 217
Buckner, 264, 405, 520, 536
Budd, 100, 179
Budington, 102
Buel, 43, 69, 359
Buell, 182, 428, 540
Buff, 270
Buffington, 104, 202
Buford, 264, 382
Bugbee, 24
Bugh, 115
Buhler, 390
Buistat, 257
Bulfinch, 234
Bulger, 86
Bulkley, 182, 238, 501
Bull, 457

555

Bullitt, 474
Bullman, 22
Bullock, 23, 163, 330, 404
Bully, 527
Bumgarden, 72
Bump, 451
Bunday, 461
Bundy, 76, 536
Bunker, 62
Buntoon, 85
Bunyan, 433
Burbank, 83, 115, 142, 495
Burch, 90, 97, 208, 221, 229, 236, 258, 408, 430, 453, 516, 528
Burchard, 491
Burche, 217, 306
Burchell, 214
Burd, 156
Burdett, 254, 534
Burdett's Neck, 289
Burdette, 217, 250, 532
Burgess, 9, 60, 216
Burgett, 539
Burk, 138, 414
Burke, 25, 279, 288, 291, 300, 331, 382, 412, 520, 521, 541
Burleson, 537
Burley, 5
Burman, 173
Burnell, 399
Burnet, 193, 317
Burnett, 4, 116, 202, 403, 474
Burnham, 121, 538
Burns, 137, 263, 410, 438, 439, 441, 447, 472, 504, 528
Burnside, 77, 96, 265, 477
Burnt Mills, 458
Burr, 55, 283, 284, 350, 378, 438
Burrall, 169
Burrers, 2
Burrill, 195
Burroughs, 5, 523
Burrowes, 72
Burrows, 506
Burt, 470
Burtis, 33, 133

Burton, 5, 8, 115, 134, 138, 286, 293, 406
Burwell, 67
Busey, 157, 529
Bush, 88, 92, 118, 133, 144, 182
Bustamente, 286
Bustead, 402
Bustee, 316, 324
Busteed, 4, 179, 190, 192, 229, 515, 532, 544
Bute, 189
Butler, 2, 105, 111, 128, 138, 142, 155, 230, 235, 241, 282, 306, 334, 356, 412, 425, 448, 510, 512, 535, 543
Butterfield, 74, 121, 133, 174, 320
Butts, 43
Butz, 345
Buxton, 246, 457
Byers, 109
Byrd, 109, 267
Byrly, 495
Byrne, 107, 156, 286, 350, 400, 510
Byrnes, 117, 149
Byron, 84
Byrone, 496
Byrum, 82

C

Cadell, 63, 324
Cadley, 480, 511
Cady, 40, 87, 95, 147, 170, 369, 372, 479
Cahill, 170
Cain, 4, 38, 156, 382, 537
Caire, 143
Cake, 169
Caldey, 418
Caldwell, 5, 85, 118, 154, 165, 280
Calhoun, 71, 74, 334
Callaghan, 58
Callahan, 209, 215, 475
Callan, 18, 20, 80, 92, 147, 156, 183, 255, 287, 334, 336, 362, 374, 381, 382, 420, 461, 464, 475, 508, 536
Callendar, 369

Callender, 190
Callicott, 511
Callis, 453, 476
Callowhill, 168
Calvert, 130, 295, 332, 453
Camalier, 286
Cameron, 20, 140, 149, 173, 280, 303, 314, 315, 317, 329, 353
Cammack, 183, 217, 520
Camp, 332, 333
Camp Barry, 257, 260
Camp Douglas, 182
Camp Nelson, 88
Campbell, 13, 68, 76, 97, 118, 120, 134, 170, 194, 217, 271, 315, 324, 329, 354, 393, 406, 412, 433, 491, 527, 534
Campion, 116
Canby, 79, 83, 106, 116, 264, 265, 430, 520
Candee, 83
Cane, 172
Canfield, 512
Cantagalli, 496
Cantwell, 38, 64, 318
Capehart, 347
Caperton, 206, 275, 282, 369
Capitol police, 416
Carbery, 400, 513
Carden, 165
Carew, 22, 294
Carey, 321, 496
Carico, 239
Carl, 17
Carland, 290
Carle, 346
Carleton, 231
Carlile, 322
Carlin, 59, 135, 210
Carlisle, 34, 238, 286, 326
Carlo, 6
Carlton, 65, 217, 282, 312
Carmany, 511
Carmichael, 394
Carnes, 42
Carney, 32

Carnochan, 61
Carpenter, 22, 53, 121, 131, 334, 402
Carr, 4, 263, 282, 339, 448, 467, 475, 496, 497, 542
Carrick, 362
Carrier, 493
Carriere, 417
Carrington, 10, 173, 222, 227, 238, 249, 251, 306, 307, 323, 328
Carrol, 4, 25, 128
Carroll, 3, 4, 44, 86, 89, 107, 129, 144, 147, 156, 173, 247, 285, 298, 300, 319, 381, 412, 471, 540
Carruthers, 384
Carter, 5, 6, 11, 28, 29, 53, 56, 89, 102, 104, 121, 127, 143, 153, 156, 188, 354, 415, 420, 475, 483, 493, 495, 498, 520, 528, 529, 531, 537
Carter Place, 153
Cartier, 133
Cartter, 120, 136, 139, 149, 153, 154, 308, 326, 328, 481, 492, 498
Cartwright, 79
Cartwrights, 318
Carusi, 10, 11, 19, 23, 50, 80, 90, 139, 167, 190, 224, 271, 272, 364, 428, 503, 507, 508, 510
Carvalho, 328
Carvallo, 43, 90, 399
Carvin, 86
Cary, 42, 361
Casbell, 475
Casbrook, 409
Case, 53, 112, 179, 199
Casey, 96, 156, 328, 349
Cashell, 430
Casparis, 165
Cassell, 229
Cassiday, 493
Cassidy, 178, 452, 472
Cassin, 24, 71, 164, 288, 430, 480
Castillo, 248, 383
Castle, 245
Castleman, 217
Caston, 175
Caswell, 37, 480

Cate, 287, 330
Cathcart, 123, 269
Cathcom, 451
Catholic cemetery, 342
Catholic Cemetery, 61
Catholic Miracle, 49
Catholic monastery, 344
Catlett, 366
Catlin, 246, 457
Caton, 236, 488, 512, 518
Caughy, 286
Caulfield, 481
Caulkins, 495
Causin, 508
Causten, 43
Cavanagh, 263
Cavanaugh, 36
Cavis, 512
Cavmody, 259
Cayen, 89
Cayner, 231
Caynor, 487
Caynot, 5
Cazenove, 156
Cedar Mount, 131
Chadsey, 388
Chadwick, 214, 493
Chalfant, 85
chalice, 247
Chalmers, 285
Chamberlain, 143, 221, 300, 303, 534
Chamberlaine, 4
Chambers, 52, 334, 505
Champlin, 56, 177
Chancellor, 156
Chandler, 81, 83, 102, 117, 126, 135, 156, 205, 313, 330, 369, 388, 517, 519
Chaney, 13
Chapin, 53, 79, 89, 91, 264, 279, 325, 336, 379, 450, 464, 476, 481, 526
Chaplin, 34
Chapman, 30, 134, 156, 214, 327, 331, 468
Chard, 333
Charles, 147

Charlotte Hall School, 121
Charr, 261
Chartroule, 436
Chas II, 321
Chase, 15, 34, 127, 139, 161, 320, 328, 457, 464, 481, 493, 506, 546
Chasmar, 57, 63
Chassing, 76
Chatain, 179, 221
Chatham, 380
Cheatham, 405
Chedal, 380
Chedyne, 525
Cheeshapteamuck, 175
Cheever, 83, 89
Cheney, 222, 397
Cherbonnier, 83
Chesapeake & Ohio Canal, 363
Cheshire, 230
Chesley, 53, 143
Chesnut, 403
Chesseldine, 486
Chester, 129, 270, 312
Chestney, 68, 241
Chetain, 34
Chewes, 304
Cheydeynes, 524
Chicatawbut, 435
Chichesters, 427
Chick, 493
Childs, 29, 246, 457
Chilton, 29, 34, 246, 287, 527
Chinn, 164
Chipman, 3, 4, 5, 56, 527
Chiseltine, 334
Chiswell, 271
Choate, 57, 85
Chorpenning, 8
Christ Church, 365
Christ Church grave-yard, 386
Christie, 163
Christmas, 537
Christmas Carol, 509
Christmas tree, 537
Christopher, 259, 302
Chubbuck, 92

Chur, 211
Church, 189, 215, 259, 444
Church of the Incarnation, 536
Churchill, 97, 138, 144
Chutkowski, 143
Ciampi, 174
Cilley, 102
Cinelar, 45
Circuit Court, 133, 136, 149, 153, 154, 161, 498
Cisco, 477
Cissell, 430
Cist, 103
Clabaugh, 69
Clagett, 81, 161, 210, 215, 244, 307, 314, 475, 536
Claggett, 366, 527, 534
Claiborne, 151
Clampet, 363
Clancey, 24
Clancy, 435
Clarence, 55
Clark, 4, 5, 15, 16, 18, 22, 25, 35, 37, 42, 57, 62, 63, 73, 82, 83, 85, 87, 93, 118, 127, 131, 135, 143, 156, 165, 178, 205, 212, 226, 232, 238, 240, 243, 249, 253, 270, 287, 292, 302, 315, 320, 345, 357, 384, 406, 417, 420, 467, 477, 480, 481, 504, 506, 511, 526, 527
Clarke, 7, 22, 29, 70, 76, 88, 156, 184, 214, 215, 216, 237, 247, 255, 271, 293, 298, 308, 325, 353, 393, 405, 410, 414, 452, 469, 475, 490
Clarkson, 79, 97, 175
Clarvoe, 223, 297, 298, 306, 372, 496
Clary, 83, 100
Clash, 533
Class, 133
Claubaugh, 275
Clausen, 223
Claverack, 439
Claxton, 413
Clay, 24, 88, 135, 163, 279, 404, 405
Clayton, 188, 238, 334, 522
Cleadicar, 524

Cleary, 71, 156, 287, 424, 543
Cleaveland, 142
Cleaver, 68, 76, 165, 166, 167, 169, 170, 184, 262, 296, 297, 317
Cleburne, 26
Cleever, 68
Cleghorn, 310
Cleman, 143
Clemans, 396
Clemens, 40, 493
Clements, 17, 97, 129, 221, 307, 415, 458, 464, 485, 508, 534
Clendenin, 492, 523
Clepner, 247
Clermont, 99
Cleveland, 524
Cliffburne, 318
Clifford, 239, 546
Clifton Factory, 189
Clingman, 403
Clinkall, 518
Clinton, 5, 143, 182, 234, 280, 329, 373, 457
Clopper, 534
Cloridge, 175
Cloud, 417
Clough, 40
Clover Hill, 151, 239
Clymer, 214
Cmdor Decatur House, 342
Coade, 475
Coale, 470
Coates, 531, 533
Coats, 494, 536
Cobb, 320, 405, 478
Coburn, 342, 367
Cocherell, 34
Cochran, 29, 177, 215, 453, 503
Cochrane, 53, 97
Cock, 284
Cockburn, 26
Cocke, 264
Cockrell, 515
Codwise, 284
Coe, 459
Coen, 502

Coffin, 116, 158, 339, 372
Cofrau, 34
Cogan, 11, 90, 171, 272
Coggshell, 41
Cohen, 28, 183, 217
Coit, 77, 172
Coker, 106
Colbank, 67
Colbe, 408
Colbert, 120
Colburn, 221, 342
Colby, 180, 328, 401, 414, 443, 455, 489
Colclaizer, 420
Colclazar, 182
Colclazer, 315
Colder, 73
Coldwell, 273, 333, 456, 483
Cole, 105, 151, 173, 176, 185, 191, 238, 240, 243, 246, 363, 410, 457, 465, 496, 510, 528
Colegate, 498
Coleman, 16, 31, 79, 128, 151, 214, 242, 260, 285, 286, 330, 355, 358
Colemen, 52
Coles, 135
Colfax, 138, 531
Colgate, 271, 498
Colineau, 156
College of Gtwn, 285
College Station, 463
Colley, 88, 188, 275
Collier, 285, 460, 503
Collins, 14, 22, 55, 62, 64, 76, 80, 83, 93, 108, 127, 132, 145, 174, 198, 239, 259, 275, 286, 291, 302, 424, 473, 495
Collinsworth, 309
Collison, 316, 353
Collman, 396
Colman, 167
Colored Cemetery, 269
colored convention, 10
colored population, 381
Colson, 416
Colt, 102, 217, 373, 459

Colter, 497
Coltman, 153, 308, 398
Colton, 78
Coltos, 156
Columbia Gardens, 454
Columbia Lying Hospital, 277
Columbus, 36, 40
Colville, 365
Colvocoressis, 30
Com'r of Pensions, 77
Combs, 156
Commger, 197
Commons, 62
Compton, 37
Comrie, 134
Comstock, 69, 540
Conant, 85
Condell, 444
Conden, 259
Condert, 88
Condon, 126, 128, 420
Condry, 195
Cone, 3
Cones, 87, 143
Coney, 12, 73
Confirmations & rejections, 108, 118, 129, 130, 134, 136, 140, 149
Confry, 151
Congdon, 118
Conger, 223, 273, 315
Congor, 116
Congressional Burial Ground, 287
Congressional Burial Grounds, 308
Congressional Burying Ground, 333, 342
Congressional Cemetery, 10, 47, 54, 81, 154, 178, 326, 372, 390, 433, 475
Coningham, 493
Conkling, 173, 416, 426
Conlan, 44, 544
Conley, 139, 475
Connel, 145
Connell, 527
Connelly, 76, 201, 417

Conner, 5, 22, 42, 161, 165, 241, 309, 458
Conners, 541
Connolly, 346, 347
Connor, 39, 85, 156, 286, 424, 443, 462
Conolly, 105
Conover, 26, 65, 133, 176, 184, 330
Conrad, 281, 403, 405, 409
Conrad's Tavern, 58
Conroy, 24, 245, 283, 523
Constable, 18, 83
Constine, 156
Conway, 446, 451, 497
Cook, 8, 15, 19, 60, 77, 129, 181, 202, 216, 221, 231, 236, 239, 287, 296, 346, 391, 395, 422, 507, 534
Cooke, 3, 4, 11, 109, 203, 214, 265, 269, 326, 328, 473, 520
Cooklan, 62
Cookman, 423
Cooley, 510, 538
Coolidge, 31, 526
Cooly, 523
Coombes, 165
Coombs, 96, 97, 156, 217, 278, 346, 523, 527
Coomes, 317
Coon, 130
Coone, 125
Cooper, 55, 82, 95, 130, 169, 192, 260, 269, 329, 349, 387, 405, 460, 511, 518, 532
Coorin, 2
Copeland, 67, 88
Copley, 17
Copp, 201, 370
Coppens, 424
Coppinger, 470
Corbett, 182
Corbin, 134
Corbit, 82
Corcoran, 13, 80, 117, 124, 144, 153, 155, 159, 206, 214, 270, 286, 369, 379, 512, 513, 536
Corder, 88

Cordero, 216
Cordobla, 88
Corey, 246, 457
Coriell, 83, 111, 231, 348
Corkery, 281, 286
Corkey, 424
Corley, 221
Cornell, 312
cornerstone of Christ Church, 305
Cornick, 275
Cornwallis, 321
Cornwell, 97, 406, 463
Corran, 4
Corry, 526
Corse, 132
Corson, 225
Coryell, 317
Cosby, 88
Cosgrove, 175, 317
Cosley, 151
Costello, 506
Coster, 71, 136
Costigan, 156
Cottingham, 285
Cottle, 166
Cottrell, 66
Couch, 51, 265
Couche, 143
Coues, 297, 452
Coughlin, 138
Couley, 194
Coulter, 221
Coulton, 13
Councilman, 534
Couper, 126
Courche, 53
Court in Equity, 71, 136, 139, 146, 154, 159, 164, 168, 429
Court of Equity, 60, 97, 131, 133, 144, 161, 190
Courtenay, 181
Courtney, 79
Cousin, 65
Covell, 222
Cowan, 109, 279, 310, 312
Cowardin, 286

Cowden, 497
Cowle, 11
Cowles, 259
Cox, 4, 12, 15, 21, 42, 45, 53, 71, 92, 133, 136, 151, 156, 179, 183, 217, 236, 244, 283, 291, 293, 313, 327, 331, 352, 383, 398, 425, 426, 447, 457, 480, 484, 489, 493, 511, 515, 522, 544
Coyle, 156, 188, 190, 215, 239, 253, 266, 273, 362, 369, 383, 474, 490, 545
Cozens, 441
Craft, 159, 210
Cragg, 109
Cragin, 425
Craig, 14, 118, 127, 437, 541
Craigen, 463
Craiggen, 539
Crain, 160, 189
Cramer, 108
Cranch, 147, 194
Crandall, 118, 200, 217, 251, 381
Crandell, 200
Crane, 15, 40, 44, 100, 107, 109, 134, 249, 254, 438
Crank, 115
Crapo, 62
Craven, 92, 196
Cravens, 259
Craway, 138
Crawford, 3, 55, 57, 64, 69, 92, 108, 210, 214, 231, 282, 313, 315, 346, 395, 403, 421, 443, 464, 487, 495
Creacy, 246
Creamer, 118
Creary, 138
Creecy, 463
Cresconi, 143
Cresswell, 303
Crew, 135
Cribb, 524
Crichton, 104
Crider, 445
Crier, 346
Crilly, 333

Criminal Court, 24, 25, 31, 33, 65, 67, 70, 71, 77, 80, 97, 100, 105, 107, 128, 133, 137, 144, 145, 147, 148, 156, 159, 161, 165, 173, 174, 179, 516, 518, 520, 521, 531, 533, 536, 538, 539, 542, 543
Cripps, 217, 525
Crise, 87
Crittenden, 323, 489, 543
Crocker, 503, 527
Crockett, 446
Crofton, 155
Crome, 39, 71, 216
Cromer, 138
Cromwell, 33, 57, 140, 156, 191, 383, 476, 479
Cronan, 324
Crone, 212
Cronin, 330, 379
Cropley, 30, 217, 329
Crosby, 57, 367
Cross, 22, 61, 83, 88, 104, 132, 139, 146, 151, 232, 233, 234, 308, 372, 417, 470, 480, 487, 488
Crossfield, 429
Crossley, 208
Crow, 70, 80
Crowe, 121
Crowl, 180
Crowley, 242, 355, 361, 527
Crown, 125
Crownrich, 286
Crucy, 457
Cruger, 286
Cruit, 188, 214, 464, 481
Crump, 204
Cruse, 172
Crutchett, 156, 292, 307, 378, 523
Cruttenden, 21, 25
Crux, 329, 362
Cryer, 326, 508
Cuddy, 24
Cudlip, 144
Cudlipp, 73
Culbert, 57, 77, 109
Culbertson, 135, 497

Cull, 379, 428
Cullom, 92
Cullum, 264
Culp, 477
Culpeper, 321
Culver, 9, 514, 537
Culverwell, 130, 526
Cuming, 27, 52
Cummings, 12, 31, 164, 239
Cummins, 201, 217
Cuniffe, 108
Cunningham, 36, 259, 286, 295, 364, 498, 523
Curack, 175
Curd, 4, 89
Curley, 18
Curran, 23, 263, 435
Curry, 121, 276, 403
Cursons, 373
Cursor, 402
Curtin, 96
Curtis, 50, 173, 182, 208, 235, 270, 399, 449, 524
Curtiss, 452
Curts, 178
Cushack, 240
Cushing, 115, 245, 285, 286, 379
Cushman, 77, 320
Custer, 60, 198, 255, 296, 314, 369
Custis, 34, 365
Cutler, 143
Cutter, 122
Cutts, 60, 99
Cuvilier, 156
Cuyler, 312
Cyler, 286
Cyrus W Field, 167

D

D'Aubey, 439
D'Bille, 320
da Vinci, 477
Dade, 365, 450
Daggett, 299
Dahey, 537
Dahlgren, 128

Daily, 97, 476
Daingerfield, 452
Dalamara, 143
Dale, 243
Daley, 239
Dalles, 34
Dalrymple, 165
Dalton, 327, 345, 346, 365, 527
Daly, 357
Dameron, 150
Damon, 76
Dana, 83, 122, 212, 366
Dane, 489
Danenhower, 214
Danforth, 11
Daniels, 10, 24, 202, 431
Dant, 22, 159, 437
Darbee, 108
Darby, 217, 258, 534
Darling, 99, 143, 177
Darnall, 543
Darne, 490
Darneille, 141
Darnell, 461
Darnes, 190
Darr, 297
Darrow, 241, 277
Darwart, 327
Dashiell, 440
Daugherty, 269
Daval, 259
Davenport, 64, 204, 223, 402, 422, 546
Davidge, 188, 215, 243, 293, 331
Davids, 4, 143
Davidson, 25, 69, 77, 245, 280, 369, 393, 419, 493
Davies, 140, 495
Davis, 1, 4, 5, 17, 19, 26, 32, 34, 38, 46, 63, 68, 73, 89, 104, 130, 136, 137, 143, 145, 149, 154, 156, 161, 178, 179, 181, 183, 187, 193, 196, 198, 204, 205, 207, 214, 215, 216, 220, 231, 235, 236, 246, 250, 251, 255, 259, 261, 266, 276, 293, 295, 302, 310, 312, 324, 331, 335, 346,

350, 354, 366, 376, 385, 399, 402, 403, 404, 405, 406, 407, 408, 413, 420, 428, 434, 444, 457, 460, 462, 488, 492, 506, 515, 527, 530, 538, 539
Davison, 229, 496
Daw, 459, 493
Dawes, 28, 134, 301, 338
Dawson, 15, 18, 217, 267, 272, 388, 417, 490
Day, 95, 151, 204, 246, 354, 362, 457
Dayton, 213, 532
De Atley, 502
de Bodisco, 209
De Bow, 122, 128
De Ferriotte, 351
de Fillippi, 143
De Ford, 95
De France, 161
De Frondat, 59
De Grers, 149
de Lamballe, 215
De Leon, 404
De Mariel, 159
De Moll, 350
De Motte, 469
De Nalangen, 386
de Puebla, 286
de Rothschild, 457
De Teschenberg, 36
De Vaughan, 293, 343, 346, 352, 384, 395, 512, 513, 514
De Vaughn, 331, 514, 515
De Voss, 157
De Witt, 234, 280, 356
De Wulf, 324
DeAhna, 8
Deakins, 536
Deal, 194, 396
Dean, 20, 226, 297, 544
Deane, 8, 310, 346
Dearborn, 132
Dearing, 53, 282
Death penalty, 88
DeBow, 86, 109
Decatur, 156, 341, 442

Deckerson, 4
Decuir, 151
Deeble, 229
Deeds, 522
Deeley, 498
Deely, 10
Deep Falls, 207
Defrees, 94
DeGarnett, 403
Deibstich, 156
Deitz, 236
DeKay, 203
DeKrafft, 278
Dekstadt, 177
DeL'French, 85
Delafield, 217
Deland, 426
Delaney, 156
Delany, 519
Delfosso, 496
Dellwig, 408
Demar, 14
Dement, 37
Demlin, 176
Demongeot, 161, 248
Demoss, 11
Dempsey, 275, 291, 381, 481
Denham, 61, 236, 475, 527
Denison, 216, 273
Denman, 470
Denning, 24
Dennis, 2, 11, 142, 168
Dennison, 16, 157, 259, 325, 452
Denslow, 182
Densmore, 146
Denson, 47
Dent, 252
Denty, 33
Denver, 214, 343, 382, 427, 546
Depeyster, 392
Dergan, 231
Dermott, 45
Derrick, 312, 352
Derring, 202
Des Grange, 417
Desel, 495

DeShon, 297
Deslandes, 38, 79
Deslonde, 358
Despau, 417
Despommier, 152
Dessan, 248
Dessane, 291
Dessau, 533
DeTilley, 307
Detrick, 121
Deturbe, 76
Detweiler, 512
Deugan, 424
Deutch, 484
DeVaughan, 287
Devaughn, 427, 431, 512
Devaugn, 512
Devers, 136, 173
Devin, 421, 450
Devinning, 116
Devlin, 481
Devling, 156
Dewdney, 40
Dewees, 157, 241, 322
Dewey, 5, 83
DeWitt, 2
Deyburgh, 456
Dick, 1, 543
Dickens, 20, 343, 456, 505, 507, 509, 529
Dickenson, 304
Dickerson, 129, 202
Dickey, 113, 166, 191, 295
Dickinson, 119, 134, 180, 265, 350
Dickson, 119, 217, 281, 285, 286, 292, 486
Dietrick, 520
Digges, 121
Diggs, 173, 270, 329, 481, 526
Digny, 44
Dikeman, 214
Dilks, 236
Dillingham, 302
Dillon, 143, 335, 424
Dimitry, 285, 331
Dimmick, 217, 399

Dimock, 320
Dimon, 429
Dinsmore, 72, 208
Dissoway, 191
Ditmer, 247
Dittrich, 78
Diven, 182
Diver, 381
Dives, 107
Divine, 338
Dix, 272
Dixon, 54, 102, 156, 174, 217, 282, 312, 473, 476, 525, 527
Dixson, 161
Dobbyn, 79
Dockery, 4, 89
Dodd, 265, 473
Dodge, 15, 156, 179, 198, 202, 246, 261, 263, 350, 385, 450, 453, 455, 457, 477, 479, 508, 509
Dodson, 217, 248, 363, 429, 460
Doherty, 170, 223
Doid, 142
Dolan, 1
<u>Dolbear Commercial College</u>, 151
Dole, 249, 250
Dolphy, 5
Domenichino, 393
Don, 316
Donahoe, 151, 266
Donald, 12
Donaldson, 29, 83, 215, 275
Donegan, 493
Donelan, 156, 400
Donhoff, 335
Donihu, 354
Doniphan, 362
Donlevy, 432
Donn, 317, 477
Donnelly, 14, 113, 119, 131, 492
Donoghan, 147
Donoho, 80, 117, 128, 506
Donohoe, 151
Donohoo, 190, 211
Donovan, 72, 73, 476, 496
Dooley, 171

Doolittle, 246, 457
Doran, 291, 453
Dore, 336
Doree, 242
Dorrance, 118
Dorsett, 147
Dorsey, 58, 60, 236, 239, 262, 325, 326, 352, 379, 383, 412, 417, 505, 533
Dorsheimer, 134
Doswell, 204
Doubleday, 162
Dougal, 458, 465
Dougall, 464, 477
Dougherty, 103, 157, 165, 213, 242, 496, 518
Doughty, 280, 288, 355
Douglas, 11, 87, 192, 225, 283, 285, 302, 403, 412, 464, 541
Douglas Estate, 432
Douglass, 73, 134, 149, 153, 154, 156, 159, 236, 298, 361, 364, 481
Dourman, 100
Dove, 24, 156, 420, 493
Dover, 543
Dow, 269, 537
Dowell, 281
Dowling, 82, 113, 131, 140, 188, 191, 210, 225, 232, 239, 246, 248, 261, 263, 267, 276, 284, 307, 395, 396, 450, 454, 480, 483, 485, 495, 501, 504, 511, 519
Dowman, 533
Down, 157, 473
Downey, 41, 134, 156
Downing, 46, 79, 274, 360
Downman, 457
Downs, 157, 225, 289, 364
Doyle, 1, 14, 143, 286
Drake, 173, 239
Drakel, 446
Dran, 121
Drane, 275
Draper, 215
Drayer, 484
Drennan, 100

Drennen, 318
Drennon, 141
Drescher, 328
Dresher, 531
Drew, 8, 53, 135, 199, 283, 411
Dreyer, 11
Dreyfus, 415
Driggs, 57, 133
Driscoll, 326
Driver, 31
Drohan, 313
Drudge, 105
Drury, 104, 132, 249, 252, 391, 490
Du Bois, 400
Du Bose, 104
Du Fief, 373
Dubant, 215, 449, 496, 527
Dubarry, 319
DuBarry, 301
Dubas, 143
Dubus, 5
Duckworth, 15
Duffy, 22, 112, 286, 364, 381, 526, 536
Dufief, 268, 304
DuFief, 475
Dufrees, 485
Dugan, 62
Duggan, 144
Duhamel, 371, 539
Duke, 34
Duke of Cambridge, 184
Duke of York, 184
Duker, 316
Dukes, 155, 304, 353
Dukes of Orleans, 184
Dulaney, 240, 281, 379, 443
Dulany, 281, 449
Dulin, 309, 335, 527
Dull, 22, 226
Dumas, 394
Dummel, 277
Dummer, 467
Dummerth, 88
Dumont, 122, 141
Dunbar, 183, 336, 415, 476, 479

Duncan, 48, 67, 100, 176, 373, 414, 533
Dunham, 65, 102, 184
Dunlap, 259, 304, 323, 387
Dunlop, 66, 293, 298, 377, 407, 490
Dunn, 92, 132, 217, 265, 277, 311, 485, 519
Dunscomb, 421
Dunton, 65
Dunweady, 127
Dur, 73
Duran, 24
Durance, 175
Durand, 13
Durant, 4, 139, 215, 240, 248
Durgan, 83, 111, 211, 348
Durham, 180
Durlop, 89
Durney, 286
Dutilley, 313
Dutrow, 369
Duvall, 6, 78, 141, 213, 232, 243, 271, 330
Dwight, 91
Dwyer, 54, 121, 358
Dye, 257, 258, 260
Dyer, 9, 23, 24, 35, 43, 66, 74, 75, 84, 97, 134, 154, 286, 288, 298, 306, 348, 377, 450, 477, 520, 533

E

Eabarke, 72
Eadie, 129
Eafer, 122
Eagan, 109, 125, 217
Eagle, 130
Ealer, 3
Eames, 13, 114, 126, 128, 301
Early, 236, 264, 281, 300, 405, 505
Earp, 385
Easby, 183, 249, 250
Eastern Cemetery, 433
Eastman, 9, 292, 419
Easton, 83
Eastwood, 15
Eater, 143

Eaton, 36, 115, 259, 363, 406, 461, 520
Ebaugh, 147
Ebbets, 123
Ebbitt House, 283
Ebel, 160
Eber, 10
Eberly, 217
Ebert, 2, 95
Ebertson, 82
Eccleston, 400, 480, 521
Eckells, 190
Eckels, 300, 434
Eckerson, 100
Eckhardt, 545
Eckington, 69
Eckloff, 167, 241, 274, 433, 493
Eddie, 91
Eddy, 77, 83
Edelen, 362, 472
Edelin, 274, 319, 374, 482
Eden, 380
Edes, 69, 87, 182
Edmond, 478
Edmonds, 449
Edmonson, 11, 103
Edmonston, 70, 71, 80, 93, 103, 217, 277, 520
Edson, 157
Edsworth, 516
Edwards, 93, 114, 119, 198, 206, 287, 351, 393, 396, 398, 410, 417, 419, 455, 531
Egan, 42, 50
Eggers, 10
Eggleston, 183
Eglin, 246, 457
Ehret, 347
Eichbaum, 9
Eichelberger, 109
Eichhorn, 217, 239
Eiler, 209
Eils, 331
Eilson, 383
Eisenbeiss, 532
Ekin, 83, 333

Elder, 172, 385
Eldred, 320
Eldridge, 212, 389, 391, 407
Elgin, 395
Eliot, 71, 217, 275
Elis, 18
Ellar, 80
Eller, 154
Ellermeyer, 452
Elley, 286
Ellin, 131, 144, 364
Elliot, 284, 286, 287, 341, 492
Elliott, 3, 63, 102, 109, 182, 217, 305, 336, 367
Ellis, 2, 62, 80, 98, 157, 172, 215, 221, 249, 273, 318, 334, 350, 380, 493, 523
Ellsworth, 526, 541
Ellwood, 539
Elmes, 473
Elmwood, 284
Elrod, 263
Elston, 465
Elsworth, 516
Elvans, 60, 177, 215, 249, 254, 410, 452, 468, 472
Elwell, 44
Elwood, 30
Ely, 85, 157, 357
Elzy, 405
Emack, 22, 471
Emerson, 493, 537
Emery, 215, 250, 254
Emig, 132
Emmart, 369
Emmerick, 182
Emmert, 140, 240
Emmett, 316
Emmitt, 316
Emmons, 308
Emory, 264, 540, 542
Emperor Maxmillian Ferdinand, 278
Empress Charlotte, 258
Emrich, 101, 103, 105, 114, 115, 164, 256
Enfield Chase, 353

Engard, 28
England farm, 534
Englehart, 91
English, 47, 157, 169, 179, 213, 258, 339, 369, 443, 484, 535
Ennam, 234
Ennis, 10, 142, 282, 417, 427
Ensign, 246, 457
Entwisle, 217
Equity Court, 20, 25, 62, 110, 334, 402, 417, 420, 424, 435, 443, 448, 480, 483, 486, 499, 508, 510, 520, 538, 545
Erasmiz, 399
Ermsley, 56
Ernice, 382
Erskine, 134, 314
Eslin, 16
Essex, 282, 329, 343, 344, 346, 352, 357, 380
Essig, 476
Estel, 338
Estep, 430
Etheling, 409
Etter, 130
Etynge, 429
Eustis, 379, 404, 512, 513
Evans, 10, 16, 43, 54, 76, 88, 105, 144, 170, 179, 182, 217, 243, 252, 265, 287, 338, 339, 358, 368, 376, 382, 388, 513, 526, 541
Evarts, 186
Evening Express, 242
Evening Star, 334
Everett, 71, 146, 346, 375, 494, 519
Everett's Theatre, 294
Eversfield, 15, 103
Everts, 282
Ewall, 83
Ewbank, 541
Ewell, 264, 348
Ewer, 522
Ewing, 4, 37, 149, 215, 294, 434, 497, 546
Exanters, 240
excommunication, 499

Executive Mansion, 1, 18, 27, 69, 317, 326, 345
Ex-Govn'r of Md, 146
Ezekiel, 393

F

Fagan, 103, 520
Fahenstock, 4, 182
Fahey, 188
Fahnstock, 89
Failing, 300
Fairchild, 36, 265
Fairfax, 213, 321, 366, 385, 420
Fairly, 138
Falconer, 110, 130, 157
Fales, 346
Faley, 117
Falkner, 34
Fall, 518
Fallon, 493
Falls, 433
Fant, 39, 271, 279, 493
Faraday, 367
Farenholt, 67, 100
Fargo, 359
Farley, 163, 500
Farmer, 103
Farnham, 214, 449, 452, 528
Farnsworth, 168
Farquhar, 287, 339
Farr, 65
Farragut, 188, 278, 505, 523
Farrar, 120, 287
Farrell, 61, 87, 109, 141, 157, 191, 253, 286, 398
Farrow, 12, 443
Fatio, 230, 235
Fauk, 53
Faulkes, 151
Faulkner, 174
Fause, 62
Fawcett, 244, 536
Faxon, 32, 136
Fay, 143, 188, 302, 338
Fearn, 404

Fearson, 52, 58, 67, 79, 80, 83, 106, 157, 184, 187, 190, 194, 203, 217, 243, 288, 293, 300, 304, 324, 327, 331, 343, 353, 417
Fechtig, 49
Fegan, 217
Feinour, 212
Felch, 466
Felf, 140
Felke, 22
Felker, 202
Fell, 49, 83
Fell's Point, 26
Felson, 157, 482
female suffrage, 428
Female Suffrage Cmte, 479
Fendall, 21, 31, 38, 136, 175, 180, 190, 265, 275, 327, 331, 332, 339, 354, 456
Fendell, 246
Fenn, 311
Fennel, 523
Fenton, 223, 535, 541
Fenwick, 55, 171, 215, 334, 400, 463
Fenwick Farm, 325
Ferguson, 135, 179, 257, 284, 344, 379, 404, 409, 496, 510
Fernandez, 143
Fernando, 418
Fernankez, 4
Ferrall, 463
Ferran, 469
Ferriere, 89, 143
Ferris, 1
Ferry, 79, 153
ferry-boat **Winnisimmit**, 375
Fessenden, 112
Fetherstone, 93
Fewell, 21
Field, 61, 115, 167, 188, 312, 314, 405, 546
Fielder, 27
Fields, 227
Fill, 320
Fillebrown, 139, 165, 527
Filley, 119

Fillmore, 268, 403
Fimacom, 357
Finch, 88
Finckel, 164, 182, 223, 371, 543
Finckle, 53
Findley, 239
Finekel, 308
Finkel, 257
Finley, 169, 282
Finn, 41, 353
Finnieum, 399
Finny, 151
Finster, 301
Firdley, 143
First Colored Baptist Church, 164
first use of a locomotive, 421
Fischer, 343, 350
Fish, 40, 42, 108, 233
Fishback, 182, 188
Fisher, 1, 5, 6, 8, 10, 14, 23, 63, 68, 74, 75, 106, 139, 145, 157, 173, 176, 178, 180, 184, 213, 227, 244, 249, 251, 276, 298, 319, 331, 337, 339, 361, 397, 524, 525
Fisk, 66, 134, 281
Fiske, 389, 455
Fitch, 193, 217, 343, 382
Fithian, 319
Fitshugh, 4
Fitz, 266
Fitzclarence, 184
Fitzgerald, 8, 24, 54, 71, 157, 192, 343, 344, 358, 502
Fitzherbert, 184
Fitzhugh, 25, 41, 502
Fitzpatrick, 245, 263, 272, 283, 291, 297, 300, 329, 363, 391, 437
Fitzsimmons, 28, 67, 71
Fitzsimons, 496
Fix, 8
Flaesch, 273
flagship **Franklin**, 278
Flaherty, 544
Flair, 430
Flander, 57
Flanders, 240, 389, 420

Flanegan, 151
Flanigan, 34, 118
Flank, 26
Flannagan, 157
Flannery, 251, 255
Fleetwood, 3
Fleetwood Estate, 211
Fleming, 13, 81, 127, 138, 251, 254, 513
Flemming, 18
Flenner, 485
Fletcher, 94, 137, 163, 217, 263, 287, 300, 356, 419, 420, 443, 449, 473, 478, 500
Fleury, 98
Fling, 157
Flinn, 254
Flint, 92, 287, 356, 517
Florence, 60, 326, 332
Florey, 3
Floyd, 270
Flyman, 73
Flynn, 237, 250, 253, 257, 258, 259, 266, 424, 496
Foard, 15
Fogarty, 1, 131
Fogler, 146
Foley, 3, 157, 190, 344, 349, 453
Folfree, 62
Folger, 208, 346, 429
Folkner, 270
Follansbee, 28
Fonda, 93, 198
Foot, 308
Foote, 161
Forbes, 15, 522
Forbett, 228
Forbitsh, 524
Forbush, 525
Force, 183, 217, 509, 528
Ford, 26, 75, 86, 135, 143, 145, 148, 157, 217, 233, 256, 290, 292, 295, 306, 318, 334, 343, 359, 375, 395, 538
Ford Dodge, 305

Ford's Theatre, 256, 260, 267, 290, 292, 295, 303
Forest, 38
Forman, 285
Formance, 57
Fornshall, 271
Forrest, 38, 92, 147, 157, 211, 216, 217, 275, 276, 282, 285, 303, 405, 443, 490, 532, 538, 539
Forrester, 150
Forsyth, 68, 246, 457, 511
Forsythe, 452
Fort Benton, 291
Fort Brown, 308
Fort Bunker Hill, 283
Fort Chadbourne, 393
Fort Chadburne, 446
Fort Clarke, 57
Fort Columbus, 74
Fort Delaware, 82, 127, 144, 155, 466
Fort Dodge, 115, 314, 466
Fort Fisher, 50, 195
Fort Gibson, 310
Fort Harker, 287, 314, 398
Fort Harrison, 129
Fort Hayes, 314, 364, 367, 398
Fort Hays, 233
Fort Hill, 71
Fort Kearney, 133, 181, 401
Fort Lafayette, 352, 406
Fort Laramie, 24, 149, 181, 198
Fort Larned, 314
Fort Leavenworth, 92, 118, 311, 369
Fort Madison, 135, 203
Fort Marshall, 329
Fort McHenry, 127
Fort Meigs, 514
Fort Monroe, 226, 259
Fort Phil Kearney, 24, 181, 313, 349, 401
Fort Pulaski, 403, 404, 405
Fort Riley, 314
Fort Scott, 92
Fort Sedgwick, 296, 314
Fort Slocum, 518
Fort Smith, 181, 234

Fort Stevens, 182
Fort Sully, 271
Fort Sumter, 198
Fort Union, 133
Fort Wallace, 277, 302, 314
Fort Warren, 127, 352, 378, 404, 406
Fort Washington, 127, 330
Fort Wayne, 23, 27, 94, 127, 242
Fort Whipple, 127, 130, 279
Forteney, 16
Fortress Monroe, 23, 142, 187, 193, 207, 226, 230, 269, 345, 382, 393, 399, 405
Foscue, 290
Foster, 17, 53, 71, 108, 115, 123, 134, 211, 264, 265, 299, 333, 397, 416, 421, 490, 504
Fould, 433, 459
Foundry Burial Ground, 269
Foundry cemetery, 268
Foundry M E Church, 146
Foundry property, 206, 453, 480
Fouts, 517
Fowle, 75, 117, 457
Fowler, 15, 115, 151, 168, 170, 215, 230, 239, 249, 250, 265, 268, 282, 397, 493, 495, 532
Fox, 6, 7, 8, 134, 193, 194, 209, 285, 334, 518
Foxcroft, 172
Foy, 115, 141, 296
Frafley, 62
Frail, 302
Frailey, 259
Frainas, 99
France, 258, 271
Francine, 129
Francis, 172, 329
Francoe, 384
Frank, 275, 519
Franklin, 25, 32, 62, 65, 76, 125
Franklin Row, 106, 364, 370
Fraser, 157, 239, 270, 433
Fray, 480
Frayser, 216
Frazer, 165

Frazier, 71, 88, 120, 140, 157, 235
Frear, 209
Freas, 484
Frechett, 317
Frederick, 135, 527
Freeland, 487
Freeman, 39, 134, 217, 269, 465, 524, 525
Freer, 41
Freidenwall, 157
French, 56, 160, 246, 264, 281, 365, 408, 417, 419, 429, 457, 510, 542
Frepell, 164
Fretz, 17, 413
Friel, 71
Friendship, 261
Fries, 105
Friess, 499
frig **Chesapeake**, 341
frigate **Constitution**, 380
Frisbie, 29
Frissell, 258
Fritz, 433
Frizzell, 243
Fronz, 302
Frost, 62
Frothingham, 65
Frugillo, 88
Fry, 40, 83, 101, 140, 322
Fugitt, 217, 333, 367, 450
Fuld, 263
Fullalove, 335, 352, 371
Fuller, 139, 197, 217, 301, 334, 385, 524, 525
Fullerton, 19, 137, 164, 166
Fulleylove, 10
Fulmer, 263
Fulsom, 280, 350
Fulton, 46, 48, 63, 358, 511
Fultz, 234
Funks, 308
Furey, 83
Furguson, 217, 303, 476
Furman, 24, 168, 182, 462
Fushgart, 305
Fuss, 510

Fyffe, 123

G

Gaddis, 79, 165, 312, 313, 362, 363, 527
Gadsby, 157, 170
Gaezler, 543
Gaffney, 277
Gaines, 15, 417, 470, 504
Gaither, 131, 402
Gale, 497, 507, 525
Gales, 69, 181, 276
Gallacher, 22
Gallagher, 53, 400
Gallaher, 186, 536
Gallant, 28, 239
Galt, 31, 40, 125, 214, 215, 239, 255, 266, 362, 441, 527, 533
Galvin, 293
Gampfel, 24
Gamtreaix, 53
Ganesvoort, 56
Gangewer, 520
Gangewher, 212
Gano, 376
Gansevoort, 127
Gantt, 397, 438
Garabaldi coat, 307
Garber, 392
Garden, 514
Gardette, 417
Gardiner, 186, 420, 469
Gardner, 92, 157, 191, 234, 299, 310, 336, 442, 528, 533, 540
Gardon, 14
Garey, 296
Garfield, 406
Garges, 329
Garland, 46
Garner, 4, 143, 161, 315, 456
Garnes, 417
Garnet, 212, 469
Garnett, 403
Garrenge, 209
Garret, 534
Garretson, 397

Garrett, 270, 281
Garrette, 208
Garrettson, 22
Garrigus, 134
Garrison, 26, 299
Garter, 4
Garvey, 53, 182
Gary, 181, 204
Gasch, 217, 493
Gaskill, 168, 182
Gaskins, 5
Gass, 241
Gassaway, 165, 246
Gasselin, 143
Gaston, 177
Gates, 151
Gatewood, 14
Gatton, 338
Gault, 174
Gautier, 248, 534
Gautreaux, 89
Gawlor, 148
Gay, 62
Gayle, 229
Gaylor, 324
Gaynor, 239, 248
Gear, 174
Geary, 32, 65, 110, 146, 177, 185
Gebhardt, 432
Gege, 392
Geib, 306
Geier, 338, 375, 480, 486, 518
Geiger, 345
Geir, 362
Geis, 240
Gellespy, 468
Gelston, 101, 350
Gelstrip, 53
Gentry, 88, 310, 393
George, 310, 319
George IV, 537
Gerard, 118, 123, 312
Gere, 373
Gereocke, 242
Gerhardt, 249, 510
Gerhe, 336

Gericks, 483
Germain, 240
German Lutheran Chapel, 371
German Lutheran Church, 543
Gerry, 222, 456
Gessford, 464
Gettings, 84
Getty, 149
Gettys, 507
Gettysburg Cemetery, 429
Gherardi, 28
Gholson, 403
Gibbons, 5, 7, 48, 73, 453
Gibbs, 87, 151, 161, 298, 362, 430
Giberson, 138
Gibson, 28, 54, 63, 83, 92, 97, 107,
 144, 157, 165, 211, 246, 258, 302,
 315, 366, 421, 457, 514, 543
Giddings, 239
Gideon, 99, 473
Gidney, 338
Giegoldt, 199
Giesboro Point, 215
Giesking, 217
Gifford, 134, 290, 303
Gilbaux, 3
Gilbert, 20, 96, 143, 236, 292, 422,
 472, 489
Gildenstrip, 89
Giles, 477
Gill, 514
Gillard, 251
Gillem, 29, 203, 265, 545
Gillespie, 294
Gillette, 29, 218, 505
Gilliam, 5, 53
Gillis, 3
Gillman, 123
Gillmore, 264, 265
Gilman, 131, 249, 250, 304, 390, 533,
 535
Gilmer, 403
Gilmore, 62, 92, 94, 138, 169, 171,
 212, 259, 268, 344
Gilroy, 83
Ginn, 338

Ginnochio, 93
Gitter, 24
Gittings, 165, 239, 250, 255, 480, 502
Given, 127, 183, 247, 251, 255, 345, 406, 509, 527
Gladding, 41
Gladmon, 157
Glasco, 6
Glascock, 522
Glass, 112, 200, 257
Glasscock, 468
Glatfelter, 4
Glazebrook, 327
Gleason, 8, 76, 527
Gleeson, 115, 180
Glen Mary, 32
Glenn, 107, 174, 280
Glennan, 356
Glenny, 134
Glenwood, 105
Glenwood Cemetery, 65, 146, 169, 255, 306, 369, 388, 410, 485, 504
Glick, 239
Glines, 313
Glisson, 30
Gloetzback, 33
Glover, 71
Gobright, 217, 225, 226, 232
Gockler, 84
Goddard, 39, 69, 128, 223, 511, 544
Godey, 217, 282, 322, 475
Godfrey, 306, 354, 412, 434, 496, 510
Godsy, 205
Godwin, 142
Goedmark, 370
Goff, 287
Gogelein, 73
Goheens, 157
Going, 240
Golden, 79, 266
Golden wedding, 411
Golder, 373
Goldin, 55, 84, 282
Golding, 288
Goldsborough, 420
Goldstein, 120

Goltz, 179
Gone, 221
Gonun, 168
Gonzaga College, 283, 309
Gonzales, 311
Gooch, 440
Good Hope, 177
Goodall, 215, 238
Goode, 151
Goodheart, 410
Gooding, 75, 146, 153, 188, 189, 225, 228, 241, 244, 246, 268, 272, 274, 327, 342, 397, 486, 509
Goodman, 286
Goodnow, 106
Goodrell, 134
Goodrich, 40, 273, 309, 479, 508
Goodrick, 25
Goodspeed, 134
Goodwick, 491
Goodwin, 120, 159, 259, 310
Goodyear, 53, 97, 519
Gordon, 39, 79, 80, 104, 112, 159, 161, 165, 183, 231, 375, 405, 440, 448, 522, 527
Gorham, 142, 334
Gorlinski, 287
Gorman, 36, 123, 410
Gorris, 461
Gorsuch, 160
Gorton, 4, 89
Goruile, 88
Goscroft, 497
Goshen, 2
Goss, 140
Goszler, 91, 93, 179, 246
Gott, 475
Gotts, 496
Gouch, 208
Gough, 189, 212, 399
Gough's Wharf, 189
Gould, 17, 378, 490
Gouldman, 23
Grace, 261
Grady, 48, 127, 475
Grafton, 60, 66, 97, 245

Graham, 5, 15, 61, 93, 157, 165, 182, 199, 212, 217, 246, 281, 282, 312, 337, 340, 403, 457, 474, 485, 512, 526, 527, 533
Grahame, 87
Gramm, 109, 197
Grammer, 484, 492
Grandey, 129
Granger, 61, 264, 429, 543
Grant, 1, 40, 41, 48, 50, 87, 122, 137, 195, 215, 242, 247, 252, 257, 264, 265, 313, 323, 345, 353, 357, 396, 406, 421, 429, 471, 474, 492, 501, 531, 534, 537, 540, 545
Grason, 363
Grass, 42
Grassland, 174
Gratz, 34
Graves, 525
graveyard, 146
Graw, 5
Gray, 83, 87, 143, 157, 192, 217, 239, 354, 357, 358, 359, 484, 507
Graybill, 216
Grayson, 13, 365, 506
Greasey, 240
Gredley, 134
Greeley, 89, 125, 132, 153, 204, 205, 428, 436, 477
Green, 1, 7, 21, 24, 39, 60, 61, 67, 71, 107, 109, 118, 151, 175, 213, 218, 230, 231, 299, 323, 328, 370, 372, 381, 384, 428, 431, 439, 442, 471, 476, 483, 490, 505
Green Hill, 419
Greenawalt, 268
Greenbrier White Sulphur Springs, 209
Greene, 36, 92, 149, 162, 320, 322, 428, 519
Greenes, 163
Greenleaf, 57, 63, 259
Greenmount Cemetery, 312
Greenough, 494
Greenway Court, 321
Greenwell, 376, 431, 459

Greenwood Cemetery, 270, 413
Greenwood Depot, 344
Greer, 287
Greeves, 24, 217
Gregerson, 280
Gregg, 79, 389
Gregory, 150, 181, 232, 346, 436, 491, 494
Greierson, 4
Grider, 64, 539
Gridley, 109, 181
Grier, 310, 546
Grierson, 369
Griffen, 103
Griffin, 5, 57, 187, 265, 282, 391, 399, 540, 542
Griffing, 33
Griffith, 22, 48, 365, 519, 524, 534
Griffiths, 46
Griggs, 388
Grigsby, 76
Grillo, 260
Grimes, 259, 332
Grinder, 146, 169, 218, 251
Grinnell, 32, 97, 346
Grinnet, 264
Griscom, 210
Griswold, 108, 121, 366
Gritten, 87
Grober, 280
Groese, 171, 172
Groetsch, 70
Groff, 111
Groome, 318
Gross, 42, 220, 276
Grosschell, 291
Grosse, 188
Groupe, 171
Grove, 143
Grover, 134, 135, 402, 524
Grow, 62
Grubb, 5
Grupe, 76
Gtwn Cemetery, 542
Gtwn College, 285
Gubitosi, 301

Gueretta, 337
Guerney, 76
Guernsey, 140
Guerwardi, 302
Guest, 26
Guigan, 92
Guild, 265
Guilford, 68
Guion, 425
Gulick, 174, 196, 215, 251, 431, 484, 527
Gullard, 239
gunboat **Ascutney**, 33
gunboat **Ashland**, 195
gunboat **Brave**, 48
gunboat **Cayuga**, 47
gunboat **Tacony**, 383
Gunn, 134
Gunnell, 62, 157
Gunnells, 231
Gunson, 462
Gunten, 37
Gunton, 157, 215
Guppy, 314
Gurley, 188, 190, 224, 247, 284, 328, 390
Guscetti, 46, 100, 141
Gustine, 134
Guthrie, 443
Guy, 36, 91, 142
Guyol, 151
Gwin, 406
Gwinn, 415
Gwynn, 300

H

Habadil, 83
Hackett, 151, 425
Hadden, 185
Hadfield, 440
Hadley, 98
Haeberle, 482
Hagan, 292, 462
Hagar, 182, 260
Hagart, 33
Hager, 79, 87, 165, 170
Hagerman, 28
Hagerty, 26, 291
Haggerty, 25
Haggis, 142
Hagle, 92
Hagner, 214
Haines, 239, 329
Hainey, 1
Hains, 444
Halcro, 67
Haldeman, 495
Hale, 85, 92, 95, 163, 277
Haley, 1, 546
Haliday, 79, 509, 512, 515, 523
Halinan, 126, 128
Hall, 5, 18, 34, 59, 83, 91, 94, 98, 116, 138, 157, 181, 203, 213, 218, 224, 231, 238, 241, 246, 249, 250, 261, 271, 283, 286, 288, 295, 296, 328, 336, 357, 369, 380, 382, 410, 424, 429, 443, 447, 449, 450, 452, 454, 457, 461, 475, 496, 498, 503, 527, 537, 538
Hallard, 63
Halleck, 66, 122, 149, 264, 265, 492, 520
Halley, 41
Hallinan, 126, 128, 237, 327, 379
Halloran, 126, 128, 294
Hallowell, 5, 115, 232, 339
Halpine, 54
Halsey, 83
Hambleton, 359, 363, 451
Hambright, 313
Hamil, 44
Hamilton, 5, 10, 16, 20, 22, 36, 73, 107, 136, 218, 314, 367, 438, 482, 535
Hamlin, 273, 326, 402
Hammack, 154, 164, 172, 178, 193, 225, 379
Hammer, 106, 392
Hammond, 108, 119, 285, 312, 358, 403
Hammtrack, 171
Hample, 320

Hampshire, 36
Hampton, 405, 465
Hancock, 52, 106, 181, 255, 264, 265, 411, 450, 520
Hand, 73, 397
Handley, 493
Handlin, 420
Handy, 240, 271, 275, 287
Hanes, 379
Haney, 36, 277
Hanford, 89
Hangshuby, 536
Hanker, 164
Hanley, 121
Hanna, 83, 328
Hannah More Academy, 338
Hannum, 116
Hansberger, 281
Hanscom, 34
Hansell, 312
Hanson, 88, 113, 157, 211, 218, 222, 349, 351
Hapler, 97
Happas, 471
Harbaugh, 98, 147, 249, 355, 400, 512
Harcq, 470
Hardee, 123, 302, 405, 540
Harden, 108
Hardie, 542
Hardin, 149
Harding, 10, 430
Hardy, 131, 146, 168, 211, 308
Harford, 181
Hargis, 35
Hargous, 89, 291
Harkenss, 318
Harkins, 157
Harkness, 157, 218, 270, 287, 319, 520
Harlan, 283, 487
Harle, 22
Harleston, 355
Harley, 91, 374
Harmon, 32, 67, 246, 320, 433, 457
Harper, 56, 96, 134, 151, 218, 414, 483, 508

Harps, 396
Harrelson, 267
Harrigan, 544
Harrington, 68, 102, 103, 335, 517
Harris, 19, 26, 28, 35, 37, 40, 41, 43, 44, 92, 109, 134, 144, 145, 157, 179, 189, 208, 256, 285, 301, 305, 328, 348, 405, 485, 498, 503, 517, 518
Harrison, 24, 74, 76, 79, 114, 140, 258, 272, 293, 296, 300, 303, 329, 406, 423, 472, 475, 492
Harrod, 497
Harron, 138
Harrover, 218, 250, 254, 352
Harry, 454, 458, 464, 465, 477, 485
Hart, 16, 30, 44, 74, 112, 147, 216, 271, 520
Hartley, 218, 410
Hartmus, 426
Hartsuff, 240, 250, 420, 424, 431, 437, 453
Harvey, 74, 90, 114, 157, 162, 218, 277, 283, 345, 348, 351, 353, 358, 374, 378, 413, 417, 430, 452, 482, 525, 540
Harwell, 62
Harwood, 127, 142
Haskins, 396, 533
Haslet, 93
Haslett, 212
Haslup, 68
Hassell, 377
Hassler, 113
Hastings, 99, 157, 199, 424
Hatch, 25, 228, 506, 535
Hatchell, 471
Hatchett, 471
Hatchill, 471
Hatfield, 319
Hathaway, 1, 14, 107
Hathorn, 118
Hatton, 142, 500
Hauck, 66
Haughton, 421
Haun, 109
Hauntman, 66

Hauptman, 225
Haven, 58
Havener, 270
Havenner, 177
Havens, 118
Haver, 236
Haw, 142, 214
Hawes, 3, 4, 253
Hawkins, 11, 297, 326, 327, 437, 453
Hawks, 49, 212
Hawlett, 31
Hawley, 40, 440
Hawthorn, 520
Haxall, 204
Hay, 3, 133, 157, 228, 302
Haycroft, 87
Hayden, 46, 58, 63, 145, 286, 382, 469
Hayes, 108, 130, 218, 239, 316, 329, 346, 382, 474
Hayman, 507
Haynes, 415, 497
Haynie, 119
Hays, 31, 142, 264, 534
Hayward, 188, 524, 525
Hazard, 92, 275
Hazel, 64, 126, 233
Hazeltine, 127
Hazelton, 212
Hazen, 4
Hazleton, 130
Hazlett, 15, 199
Hazzard, 265
Head, 116
Headley, 123, 165, 462
Headquarters of the Army, 545
Heald, 339, 485
Healing Springs, 243
Heap, 112, 127, 318
Heard, 495
Heart's Delight, 456
Heath, 134, 250, 418, 420
Heaton, 121
Hebb, 535
Hebron, 360
Heckel, 136

Hedick, 142
Hedrick, 40, 102, 142, 285
Heenaz, 35
Heffell, 408
Hefferman, 20
Heiberger, 218
Heights of Oak Lawn, 337
Heil, 128
Heilburn, 362
Heimer, 49
Hein, 527
Heine, 180
Heinson, 211
Heintz, 216, 497
Heiskell, 131
Heiss, 293
Heiston, 473
Heitman, 323
Heitmuller, 377
Hellen, 30, 31, 33, 37, 39, 93, 128, 145, 218, 271, 279, 440
Heller, 2, 13
Helm, 381, 404
Helmick, 218, 251, 254
Helmle, 350
Helmus, 277, 378
Helmuth, 240
Hemm, 277
Hemphill, 403
Hempstead, 211
Hemsler, 36
Hemsley, 36
Hendershott, 121
Henderson, 43, 358, 545
Hendley, 527
Hendly, 373
Hendricks, 92
Hendrickson, 115
Henley, 16
Hennan, 105
Hennessy, 291
Henning, 157, 218, 287, 294, 532
Henricks, 259, 324
Henriques, 178, 356
Henriquez, 227

Henry, 30, 32, 81, 95, 100, 112, 120, 145, 157, 238, 302, 543
Henshaw, 40, 435
Henze, 296, 476
Henzo, 240
Hepburn, 239, 251, 255, 313, 493, 527
Herbert, 157, 318, 533
Herberts, 153
Herman, 100, 103, 144, 145
Hermanny, 371
Hern Cliffs, 78
Herold, 7, 55, 260, 263, 268, 273, 283, 424
Heron, 156, 410, 422, 485
Herr, 225, 246
Herrick, 53, 89, 302, 373
Herridon, 54
Herriet, 178
Herring, 62
Herron, 162, 170, 250, 286
Herrons, 28
Hershberge, 203
Hershberger, 135
Hertmiller, 28
Hertzberg, 79, 347
Hertzler, 434
Herzberg, 165, 218
Hess, 226, 290, 342, 364, 423
Hettig, 411
Heustis, 476, 489, 531, 539
Hewett, 458
Hewitt, 12, 53, 65, 91, 143, 397
Hewlet, 343
Heydencamp, 469
Heylign, 404
Heyser, 49
Heyward, 91
Heywood, 212
Hickey, 19, 153, 180, 472, 481
Hickman, 36
Hicks, 92, 103, 106, 174, 221, 305, 360, 504
Hidden, 179
Hieston, 69, 329, 473
Higdon, 132, 505
Higginbotham, 87

Higgins, 157, 185, 227, 329, 522, 530, 534
Higginson, 311
Higinston, 132
Hilbren, 358
Hildebrand, 112
Hildreth, 400
Hill, 11, 25, 75, 79, 88, 92, 99, 104, 105, 132, 143, 144, 173, 176, 184, 192, 218, 255, 265, 279, 286, 323, 360, 362, 374, 381, 405, 427, 456, 474, 498
Hillary, 95
Hills, 2, 4, 87, 97, 374, 424, 491
Hillyer, 421, 501
Hilton, 79, 218, 221, 239, 364
Hinckle, 75
Hindman, 405, 520
Hineline, 410
Hines, 13, 115, 129, 147, 173, 179
Hinkle, 182
Hinkley, 478
Hinks, 291
Hinman, 118
Hirsch, 143
Hiscock, 238, 243
Hise, 192
Hitchcock, 134, 310
Hite, 181, 400
Hitselberger, 433
Hitz, 133, 139, 545
Hitzelberger, 476
Hitzelburger, 229
Hixley, 38
Hixon, 272
Hixson, 514
Hobart, 91, 260
Hobble, 53
Hobbs, 26, 161, 519
Hobson, 102, 151
Hochlin, 519
Hock, 143
Hockness, 270
Hodge, 83, 476
Hodgens, 414
Hodges, 83, 541

Hodgkin, 92
Hodgkinson, 131
Hodgson, 90, 161, 364
Hoega, 485
Hoffar, 285
Hoffman, 26, 28, 109, 157, 272, 364, 369, 439, 442, 447, 449, 477, 497
Hofmeister, 19
Hogan, 54, 104, 172, 356
Hogg, 79, 318, 527
Hogue, 118
Hoke, 116
Holabaird, 83
Holabird, 100
Holbrook, 31, 47
Holcombe, 404
Holden, 246, 457
Holderman, 493
Holgate, 108
Holladay, 41
Holland, 143, 220, 369, 452, 475
Holliday, 312
Hollidge, 537
Hollinan, 426
Hollingshead, 92, 94, 371
Hollingsworth, 119, 121, 152, 159, 182, 242, 280, 355
Hollister, 34, 517
Hollohan, 14, 313, 314
Holloran, 5, 231, 293, 297
Holloway, 60, 182, 238, 249, 541
Hollowell, 233
Hollywood Cemetery, 205
Holman, 4, 89, 332
Holmead, 108, 119, 270, 306, 380, 435
Holmes, 19, 82, 87, 118, 182, 405, 471, 493, 501
Holohan, 157, 297
Holoran, 296
Holston, 496
Holt, 52, 63, 142, 233, 333, 403, 520, 541
Holtkamp, 192
Holton, 97
Holtzman, 18, 484

Holywood Cemetery, 279
Homann, 281
Homer, 24, 285
Homiller, 40
Hommon, 18
Honore, 281
Hood, 35, 118, 134, 159, 237, 380, 405
Hooe, 218, 385, 452
Hooker, 134, 192, 265, 372, 520
Hooks, 272
Hooper, 18, 322
Hoover, 31, 39, 67, 164, 191, 332
Hopkins, 15, 24, 156, 176, 184, 189, 212, 213, 319, 389, 503, 511, 512, 535, 541
Hopper, 109
Horde, 485
Horn, 135
Hornby, 160
Horne, 8
Horner, 296, 304, 468
Hornig, 315
Horsch, 496
Horton, 33, 125, 184, 409
Horwitz, 368
Hosier, 11
Hosmer, 3, 4, 5
Hotze, 404
Houchey, 322
Houdon, 386
Hough, 73, 157, 244
Houghten, 314
Hougland, 35
House, 497
Houston, 57, 125, 430, 440, 530
Hove, 452
Howard, 4, 9, 85, 118, 143, 144, 151, 157, 159, 206, 208, 218, 246, 260, 262, 265, 277, 317, 364, 368, 382, 395, 412, 419, 520, 524, 525, 534
Howard Univ, 376
Howarth, 78
Howe, 8, 41, 42, 50, 85, 102, 250, 281, 373, 425, 489

Howell, 74, 157, 218, 220, 397, 446, 506
Howes, 259
Howke, 302
Howland, 20
Howle, 57, 83
Howlett, 77, 79, 105, 458
Hoyberger, 81
Hoye, 299
Hoyer, 524
Hoyes, 226
Hoyt, 35, 83, 92, 187, 202, 286, 413, 467
Hubbard, 8, 26, 41, 44, 80, 282, 286, 350, 436, 465, 524
Hubbell, 92
Huddleston, 534
Hudson, 88, 143, 156, 291
Hue, 469
Huestis, 311, 330, 371
Huff, 5, 545
Huger, 405
Hugh, 294
Hughes, 11, 64, 76, 136, 142, 144, 159, 179, 184, 191, 245, 253, 343, 346, 427, 470, 482, 546
Hugle, 240
Huilan, 120
Hulburd, 52, 101
hulk **Zephyr**, 121
Hull, 240
Humbert, 277
Hume, 218
Humes, 22, 287
Humiston, 530
Humphrey, 54, 121, 155, 465, 540, 542
Humphreys, 108, 196, 241, 264, 520, 531
Humphreyville, 239
Hunman, 76
Hunt, 5, 53, 57, 63, 83, 89, 96, 109, 139, 151, 170, 246, 247, 251, 255, 372, 457, 458, 526

Hunter, 41, 149, 157, 161, 223, 259, 298, 312, 333, 404, 405, 406, 412, 415, 419, 425, 441, 529, 540, 542
Huntington, 214, 328, 454
Hunton, 468
Huntoon, 108
Hurdesty, 87
Hurdi_ty, 280
Hurdle, 483, 493, 519
Hurlbut, 54
Hurley, 96, 108, 167, 311, 524
Hurrell, 74
Hursey, 105, 197
Husband, 483
Huse, 404
Husted, 140
Hutchens, 476
Hutchingson, 362, 363
Hutchins, 218, 384, 527
Hutchinson, 44, 121, 191, 464, 507
Hutton, 9, 114, 269, 328, 486, 488
Huyck, 36
Huysman, 379
Hyatt, 80, 167, 225
Hyde, 13, 14, 15, 60, 98, 218, 236, 259, 260, 292, 434
Hyman, 414
Hymel, 143

I

Iardella, 7, 174, 293, 538
Idlewild, 32
Ihre, 72
Ihrig, 101
Ihriz, 101, 104, 105
Impeachment, 499, 501, 504
Income of the Royal Family, 355
Independence, 414
Indolence, 180
Ingalls, 76, 83, 133
Ingle, 24, 93, 157, 237, 244, 282, 291, 351, 352, 370, 380, 395, 434, 464, 495, 536
Ingleside, 328, 347
Ingram, 223
Ireland, 218, 380

Irich, 115
iron clad **Monitor**, 234
iron-clad **New Ironsides**, 496
ironclads **Tennessee**, **Nashville**, & **Osage**, 505
Irving, 40, 146, 438
Irwin, 5, 30, 135, 143, 182, 382, 444, 493
Isaacs, 151
Isadell, 481
Isbell, 123
Isdell, 464
Isenstein, 112
Isherwood, 65, 176
Israel, 433
Ives, 131, 315, 449
Ivey, 145, 150, 263
Ivil, 6

J

Jackman, 204
Jackson, 1, 3, 9, 63, 79, 88, 122, 127, 151, 155, 168, 201, 206, 218, 230, 258, 260, 265, 266, 268, 270, 272, 297, 299, 317, 322, 328, 375, 394, 405, 406, 417, 430, 436, 461, 464, 476, 480, 481, 496, 497, 508, 518, 523, 524, 525
Jacobs, 13, 36, 40, 284, 309, 373, 424
Jacobson, 129, 246
Jacques, 104
James, 5, 42, 58, 88, 112, 119, 157, 242, 346, 406
Jameson, 363
Jamison, 85, 119, 502
Janes, 15
Jans, 486
Janvier, 460
Jaques, 259
Jaraman, 329
Jarboe, 36, 220, 493
Jarnagin, 100
Jarvis, 58, 108, 320, 386
Jaslyn, 118
Jasper, 373
Jast, 447

Javens, 89
Javins, 517
Jay, 208
JBowen, 164
Jefferies, 41
Jefferson, 149, 151, 385, 404, 439, 535
Jeffreys, 198
Jeffries, 56, 74, 76, 200, 229, 284, 414, 461, 511
Jenckes, 426
Jenkins, 2, 134, 141, 157, 222, 226, 240, 272, 297, 300, 349, 392, 408, 451, 481, 482, 517, 518
Jennes, 349
Jennings, 9, 28, 178, 227, 312, 356, 373, 380
Jenys, 374
Jernegon, 302
Jerome, 289
Jesuit fathers, 12
Jesup, 320
Jesus Mary Convent, 49
Jett, 5, 270
Jewell, 157, 218, 474
Jewett, 308
Jillard, 157, 239
Jincks, 388
Joannini, 103
Joes, 69
Johannsen, 105
John, 290
John Bull, 392
Johns, 13, 180, 187, 344, 348
Johnson, 4, 5, 8, 15, 25, 26, 28, 37, 39, 44, 45, 47, 52, 54, 62, 64, 71, 73, 76, 80, 89, 95, 96, 102, 129, 135, 147, 149, 151, 153, 155, 157, 173, 176, 177, 187, 189, 204, 214, 215, 234, 236, 243, 246, 252, 256, 262, 270, 272, 273, 275, 278, 281, 282, 285, 286, 293, 294, 299, 301, 302, 305, 308, 310, 312, 318, 326, 331, 333, 334, 345, 350, 353, 360, 364, 379, 382, 389, 397, 398, 402, 403, 404, 406, 407, 427, 433, 449, 454, 455,

458, 462, 463, 477, 484, 494, 526, 527, 531, 532, 533, 545
Johnston, 31, 34, 35, 48, 75, 83, 102, 139, 140, 218, 264, 310, 365, 390, 391, 399, 404, 405, 407, 426, 514, 518, 520
Johnstone, 286
Jolliffe, 3
Jones, 2, 5, 6, 10, 15, 16, 20, 21, 24, 39, 42, 45, 47, 49, 55, 61, 62, 65, 66, 80, 92, 97, 113, 118, 120, 122, 127, 130, 135, 136, 137, 140, 142, 143, 151, 157, 174, 197, 212, 234, 238, 239, 259, 270, 275, 284, 287, 293, 302, 304, 312, 313, 326, 328, 336, 347, 354, 360, 382, 386, 389, 403, 417, 422, 430, 439, 443, 460, 470, 475, 476, 477, 497, 508, 513, 527, 537, 539, 541, 542
Jordan, 54, 79, 99, 184, 224, 430, 437
Joseph, 38, 345
Joslyn, 402
Jourdan, 120, 329
Joyce, 27, 218, 249, 287, 379, 416, 461, 472
Juarez, 278
Judah, 75
Judd, 83, 122, 444
Judkiewicz, 122
Juenemann, 301
Julius, 86

K

k, 46, 246, 296
Kaffel, 363
Kahn, 152
Kaiser, 26, 191, 248, 533
Kaldenbach, 285
Kall, 351
Kaller, 413
Kalonback, 484
Kalorama, 340
Kamara, 45
Kandler, 240
Kane, 69, 76, 172, 338, 403, 456, 469
Karbaum, 424

Kauffman, 111
Kauffmann, 296
Kaufman, 156, 338, 451
Kauker, 267
Kaumheimer, 397
Kautz, 333
Kavanagh, 291
Kavanaugh, 302, 363
Kay, 247
Kealy, 280
Kean, 343, 503
Keanedy, 93
Keaney, 157
Kearney, 129
Kearns, 57, 118
Kearson, 121
Keasbey, 301
Keason, 283
Keating, 211, 306, 324, 374
Keats, 386
Keddick, 393
Keddy, 53
Keech, 463
Keefe, 44, 317, 470
Keefer, 358
Keel, 329
Keeler, 89, 330
Keeling, 65, 68, 129, 177, 512
Keely, 134, 165
Keen, 3, 96
Keenan, 40, 53, 175, 211, 334, 351
Keene, 23, 102, 134, 392
Keene tract, 259
Keeney, 22, 53
Keenly, 410
Keer, 456
Kege, 223
Kehoe, 53
Keickhoeffer, 214
Keiffer, 315
Keiler, 417
Keith, 366, 434
Keleher, 79, 165, 170
Kelleher, 144, 317
Keller, 109, 142, 242, 332, 360, 379, 382

Kelley, 24, 63, 73, 183, 220, 221, 238, 251, 304, 315, 461, 465, 467, 506
Kellian, 240
Kellogg, 66, 81, 105, 136, 209, 302, 339, 356, 458, 473
Kells, 122
Kelly, 116, 157, 218, 285, 291, 339, 351, 393, 410, 437, 452, 456, 467, 496, 503, 513, 516, 526
Kelsey, 92, 520
Kelso, 112
Kemble, 356, 387, 412
Kemper, 299
Kempff, 62
Kempston, 535
Kenchel, 495
Kendall, 183, 459, 478, 487
Kendell, 218
Kendrick, 362, 484
Kendrup, 103
Kengla, 342, 502
Kennarty, 5
Kennedy, 4, 29, 37, 73, 79, 93, 102, 113, 136, 138, 144, 162, 166, 218, 251, 407, 427, 457, 478, 496, 517, 530, 534
Kennel, 88
Kennerly, 484
Kenney, 15
Kennon, 173
Kenny, 173
Kenofsky, 234
Kensal Green Cemetery, 132
Kent, 185, 191, 256, 376, 524
Kenzel, 397
Keogh, 470
Kerichar, 27
Kernan, 73
Kerner, 151
Kerr, 177, 291
Kersey, 376
Kertley, 360
Ketcham, 194
Ketchum, 418
Kett, 21
Kettell, 34

Kettler, 105
Key, 35, 285, 358, 374, 455
Keyes, 134, 159, 264
Keys, 82, 534
Keyser, 134, 329
Keyworth, 136, 241, 244, 308
Kibbey, 14, 215
Kibby, 218
Kibly, 149
Kickham, 493
Kidd, 104, 138
Kidder, 296, 314
Kidwell, 79, 88, 131, 165, 218, 252, 254, 281, 300, 490
Kieckhoefer, 285
Kieffer, 76
Kiesecker, 292
Kiesicker, 493
Kiger, 54
Kilafoyle, 309
Kilbourn, 410, 530
Kilday, 450
Kilduff, 317
Kilgore, 34
Kilgour, 332, 527
Killmon, 327, 395, 473
Kills, 486
Kimall, 526
Kimball, 83, 124, 200, 292, 317, 457, 467, 518
Kimbell, 246
Kimmell, 218
Kincaid, 138
King, 12, 32, 34, 35, 53, 61, 63, 74, 77, 78, 97, 106, 110, 113, 118, 143, 147, 149, 157, 172, 184, 188, 210, 218, 227, 236, 244, 263, 264, 268, 290, 293, 294, 297, 310, 413, 460, 468, 483, 516, 533, 539
King George, 136
King William's School, 380
Kingman, 78, 157, 284
Kingsbury, 35, 102, 104, 107
Kingsley, 37
Kinney, 5, 22, 211, 313, 401
Kinsley, 37

Kipp, 127, 356
Kirby, 151, 279, 370
Kirgan, 35
Kirk, 83, 157, 339, 371, 512
Kirkham, 83
Kirkpatrick, 105, 246, 457
Kirkwood, 369, 481
Kitchen, 221, 496
Klaine, 182
Klaus, 8
Klein, 277
Klengle, 183, 493
Kley, 221
Kline, 536
Klink, 287
Kloman, 240, 270, 527
Klopfer, 157, 511
Klosterman, 123
Klotz, 165
Klous, 8
Knabe, 481
Knap, 473
Knapp, 116, 141, 182, 300, 349
Knatz, 498
Kneeland, 129
Knight, 66, 149, 177, 249, 328, 527
<u>Knights of Pythias</u>, 410
Knoll, 471
Knowles, 180, 428
Knowlton, 115
Knox, 101, 259, 483, 492
Kobb, 482
Koch, 218, 493
Koehe, 26
Kolb, 10
Kolquin, 105
Koones, 499
Koontz, 4, 319
Koppel, 145, 161
<u>Koran</u>, 95
Korff, 372
Kosciuszko Place, 55
Kotz, 315
Kountz, 285
Kpefer, 396
Kraft, 166, 169, 473

Krauser, 235
Kreachler, 86
Krebs, 418
Kreis, 5
Kreissmann, 432
Kroeger, 164, 171
Krouse, 215
Kruse, 87, 182
Kubank, 243
Kueffner, 104
Kuhl, 287
Kuhn, 138
Kurtz, 105, 108, 264, 349
Kyle, 4

L

La Belle, 307
La Blanc, 62
La Fontaine, 205
La Porte, 19
La Rue, 4
La Sere, 404
Lacaze, 5
Lacey, 118, 224, 464
Lachanine, 49
Lackey, 134, 463
Lacombe, 311
Lacomte, 475
Lacy, 151, 481
Ladd, 356
Laderson, 5
Lafayette, 385, 386
Lafayette Square, 267, 268
Lafitte, 165
Laforge, 161
Lahmer, 17
Laing, 525
Laird, 14, 464
Lake, 175
Lalouette, 147
Lamar, 404, 405
Lamb, 85, 143, 182, 251, 292, 371, 391, 443, 458, 469
Lambell, 157
Lambert, 297, 535
Lambrie, 265

Lamder, 99
Lamon, 157, 312, 369
Lanagan, 382
Lanas, 286
Lancaster, 4, 286, 543
Lanckton, 10
Land, 25, 170
Lander, 118
Landholt, 53
Landon, 75
Landon Female Seminary, 291
Landrum, 104
Lane, 12, 17, 88, 138, 218, 251, 266, 270, 458, 465
Laner, 364
Lang, 42, 395, 424, 472
Langdon, 41, 51, 120
Lange, 532
Langford, 17, 151, 357
Langhorne, 286
Langley, 36, 255, 327, 537
Langton, 115
Lankford, 135
Lanktree, 246, 457
Lanning, 424
Lansburg, 215, 532
Lansburgh, 218, 392, 471
Lansdale, 161, 376
Lapham, 62
Lapping, 17
Larabee, 142
Larker, 125
Larlius, 468
Larman, 157, 286, 527
Larned, 157, 269
Larner, 80, 473, 510
Larney, 314
Larose, 95
Larrison, 270
Lasalle, 491
Lasell Female Seminary, 379
Laselle, 168
Lash, 112
Laskey, 10, 75, 343, 359, 453
Laster, 2
Latham, 28, 176, 494

Lathrop, 116, 485
Lathrope, 214
Latimer, 55, 130, 532
Latrobe, 439
Latta, 410, 530
Laub, 282
Lauck, 287, 527
Lauffert, 83
launch **Albemarle**, 467
Laurance, 238
Laurie, 18, 53
Laurio, 143
Lautner, 13
Lavender, 469, 536
Lavier, 135
Law, 157
Lawler, 95
Lawlor, 69
Lawnard, 56
Lawnes, 496
Lawns, 510
Lawrence, 116, 121, 123, 130, 218, 382, 540
Lawrie, 229
Lawson, 88, 157, 223, 456, 529, 544
Lawther, 397
Lawton, 62
Lay, 430
Laylor, 108, 253
Layton, 151
Lazarus, 138, 413
Lazenby, 286
Le Compte, 287
Le Fevre, 112
Leach, 19, 36, 215, 221, 257, 309, 350
Leachman, 61
Leacock, 90, 238
Leadbetter, 264
Leahy, 483
Leaman, 534
Leaming, 118
Lear, 53
Leary, 122
Leaver, 246, 457
Lebbs, 411
LeConte, 271

Lederman, 166
Ledyard, 135
Lee, 8, 13, 39, 63, 66, 76, 77, 87, 103, 116, 145, 155, 179, 214, 227, 250, 262, 264, 265, 281, 285, 292, 295, 298, 311, 317, 319, 335, 349, 400, 404, 405, 406, 409, 418, 467, 468, 474, 482, 483, 486, 502, 506, 518, 521
Lee's Hill, 353
Leech, 116, 170, 372, 500
Leeke, 476
Leftwich, 43
Lehne, 160, 161
Leighton, 32
Leis, 80, 209
Leitch, 484
Leitner, 538
Lemantia, 152
Lemert, 118
Lemoine, 427
Lenman, 98, 214
Lenneghan, 482
Lenox, 40, 157, 369
Lenthall, 268, 269
Lenton, 374
Leon, 516
Leonard, 25, 52, 122
Lepreux, 269, 277
leprosy, 44
Lernail, 100
Lester, 240
Letcher, 405
Lettig, 23
Leutze, 66, 180, 259
Levine, 73
Leving, 494
Levis, 481
Levy, 343, 372
Lewin, 281
Lewis, 33, 47, 54, 60, 62, 68, 98, 107, 108, 157, 161, 165, 168, 177, 183, 216, 218, 238, 250, 266, 286, 354, 357, 435, 437, 464, 476, 503, 539, 540
Leydon, 18

Leyford, 102
Libbey, 218, 443, 449
Libby, 218
Lichau, 104, 428, 503
Lichau House, 503
Lichtenheim, 234
Lieberman, 177, 218, 236, 256
Liebermann, 453, 463, 528
Lilliendahl, 89
Lilly, 121, 267, 281, 282
Lincoln, 7, 20, 36, 50, 55, 96, 198, 204, 224, 227, 228, 229, 253, 256, 258, 262, 274, 285, 295, 296, 333, 364, 399, 406, 422, 426, 432, 444, 469, 488
Linden, 8
Lindenkohl, 246
Lindenwald, 438
Lindins, 157
Lindley, 138
Lindsay, 332
Lindsey, 71, 76, 135, 222, 235
Lindsley, 38, 142, 218, 238
Lingh, 56
Linkins, 231, 464, 534
Linthicum, 136, 137, 218, 307, 313, 383, 395, 513
Linton, 407
Linville, 376
Lippard, 460
Lippitt, 142
Lipscomb, 221
Liscum, 99
Lisdell, 230
Liszt, 38
Littelle, 135
Little, 23, 64, 112, 135, 157, 180, 218, 238, 239, 259, 337, 472, 510
Littlefield, 314
Littlehales, 126
Littleton, 288
Litzenberg, 318
Livermore, 279, 353
Livingston, 101, 129, 134, 170, 275, 392, 439
Livingstone, 124

Lloyd, 4, 40, 93, 105, 157, 221, 250, 254, 268, 285, 292, 304, 315, 407, 417, 428, 433, 486, 491, 503, 527
Loadstone, 508
Lobdell, 539
Lochkane, 345
Locke, 33, 410
Lockett, 151
Lockhart, 266
Lockman, 103
Lockroad, 127
Lockwood, 3, 53, 201, 480
Locust Grove, 325
Loeliger, 132, 157
Loewenthal, 507
Loftus, 456
Logan, 57, 60, 151, 259, 295, 319, 395, 415, 518
Loliger, 10
Lomas, 195
Lomax, 194
Long, 40, 53, 428, 484
Long Meadows, 159, 315
Long Old Fields, 289
Longnecker, 24
Longstreet, 405, 520
Longwood, 351
Look, 203
Loomis, 15, 60, 117, 208, 312
Lopez, 252
Lorch, 274
Lord, 44, 97, 239
Lord Rosse, 474
Lorillard, 186, 429
Loring, 436
Lory, 291
Lott, 5
Louden, 293
Loughborough, 174
Louis, 152
Lous XVI, 386
Lovaire, 45
Love, 477
Lovejoy, 25, 73, 322
Lovell, 78, 112, 264, 405, 506
Lovett, 12

Low, 3, 23, 134, 143
Lowe, 5, 40, 62, 78, 143, 218, 315
Lowell, 22
Lower, 130
Lowery, 218
Lowndes, 15, 348, 507, 523
Lowry, 134, 142, 496, 515, 536
Loyd, 62
Loyzance, 291
Lubbock, 405, 406
Lubey, 431
Lucas, 31, 189, 190, 484, 538
Luck, 113
Luckett, 286
Luckie, 151
Luddington, 333
Ludington, 83
Ludlow, 80, 280, 302
Ludwick, 339
Luff, 489
Lugenbeel, 270
Lull, 289
Lulley, 101
Lully, 101
Lumkin, 458
Lumpkin, 14, 240
Luney, 539
Lupton, 92
Lusich, 234
Luster, 7
Lutterill, 257
Lutz, 174, 183, 215, 527
Lyddan, 157
Lydecker, 108
Lyle, 487, 502
Lyles, 285, 286, 298, 361
Lyman, 191, 270, 372, 536
Lynch, 5, 22, 36, 52, 58, 67, 76, 90, 92, 132, 134, 138, 145, 230, 236, 250, 324, 404, 419, 453, 462, 463, 470, 475, 476, 496, 511, 517
Lynde, 102
Lyon, 23, 85, 264, 291, 325
Lyons, 204, 205, 208, 256, 341, 363, 416, 471, 508
Lyster, 47

M

M'Dermott, 532
M'Kiernan, 123
M'Lellan, 467
Maas, 5
Macaulay, 30
Macaulty, 382
Macdonald, 221, 224
Mace, 157, 209, 330
Macfarland, 404
Macgowan, 479
Machie, 136
Mack, 62, 480, 502
Mackall, 107, 158, 218, 282, 285, 286, 357, 438, 451
Mackay, 142
Mackel, 76, 171
Mackell, 382
Mackenheimer, 47, 294
Mackenzie, 6, 347
Mackintosh, 414
Mackubin, 456
MacLeod, 80
Macmurdo, 393
Macmurphy, 397
MacMurray, 512
Maddan, 484
Maddox, 3, 5, 257, 267, 288, 306
Mades, 218, 400, 523
Madison, 1, 41, 186, 340, 442
Maedel, 171
Mag, 491
Magee, 14, 57, 112, 155, 211, 212, 306, 420, 485
Mageveny, 267
Magill, 518
Magilton, 176, 194, 368
Magrath, 405, 406
Magraw, 51, 55, 58
Magruder, 1, 2, 4, 14, 15, 93, 184, 251, 264, 265, 306, 329, 388, 405, 430, 477, 520, 534
Maguire, 37, 74, 112, 135, 158, 251, 255, 413, 482
Magurder, 218
Mahan, 315
Maher, 134, 236, 496
Mahew, 309
Mahone, 405
Mahoney, 258
Mahony, 279
Maison, 354
Majia, 248, 278
Major, 157, 189, 323, 414, 433
Malcom, 85
Male, 142
Mallery, 151
Mallory, 285, 286, 404, 405, 406
Malone, 225
Maltby, 531
Manders, 361
Manderson, 329
Mangum, 159, 161, 260
Mann, 23, 145, 151, 366, 404
Mann gun, 23
Mannaker, 430
Manning, 145, 443, 446, 458, 464, 516
Manquette, 157
Mansback, 347
Mansfield, 64, 127, 206, 259, 264, 265
Manson, 295
Manyett, 487
Manzanet, 222
Manzano, 408
Maples, 4, 89, 143
Mapp, 281, 282
Marbury, 69, 137, 153, 158, 218, 219, 246, 298, 361, 490, 513
Marceron, 294
March, 395
Marcy, 57, 411, 478, 520
Marden, 36
Marders, 232
Mardis, 1
Mareau, 319
Maretzek, 66
Maria Carlotta, 278
Markell, 157
Markham, 142, 143
Markland, 143

Markle, 114
Markley, 123
Markriter, 218, 251, 255
Marks, 97, 218, 221, 300, 372, 391
Markwood, 6
Marlock, 324
Marlow, 493
Marmaduke, 463
Marony, 30
Marr, 133, 224, 228
Marriott, 132, 390
Marsh, 52, 134, 151, 437, 467, 515, 523
Marshal, 34
Marshall, 53, 87, 93, 133, 143, 175, 192, 255, 379, 394, 403, 411, 514, 519, 543
Marsteller, 286
Marston, 390
Martin, 3, 4, 16, 26, 36, 89, 91, 92, 103, 130, 143, 223, 282, 288, 315, 325, 327, 438, 473, 477, 497, 499, 502, 521, 524, 525, 544
Maryman, 64, 126, 158
Masham, 374
Masi, 59, 420
Mason, 5, 35, 71, 87, 93, 97, 105, 155, 219, 224, 236, 246, 270, 347, 365, 404, 405, 453, 457, 475, 480, 540, 541
Masoner, 31
Massey, 365
Massi, 298
Massie, 120
Massingill, 329
Masson, 273, 284
Masters, 2
Mastin, 510
Mathe, 517
Matheke, 392
Matheny, 444
Matherland, 311
Mathias, 4
Matingly, 158
Matlock, 239, 271, 272, 390
Mattaponi, 15

Matthew, 235
Matthews, 14, 32, 102, 138, 140, 158, 298, 303, 316, 335, 388, 392, 420, 428, 499
Matthison, 2
Mattingly, 7, 10, 60, 98, 160, 162, 183, 218, 241, 249, 287, 292, 298, 305, 311, 360, 377, 381, 384, 417, 447, 499, 502, 527
Mattison, 310
Mattoon, 236
Maull, 74
Maulsby, 363, 406
Mauphin, 87
Maupin, 120
Maury, 244, 308, 404, 416, 434, 520
Mavelas, 124
Maxcy, 158
Maximilian, 404
Maximillan, 345
Maximillian, 278
Maxwell, 63
May, 142, 189, 213, 238, 251, 451, 481, 532
May,, 219
Maydell, 247
Mayer, 83, 122, 431
Mayhew, 2
Mayna, 384
Maynadier, 69, 224
Maynard, 135, 348
Maynett, 231
Mayo, 394
Mazon, 63
McAlliser, 157
McAllister, 69, 304
McAnally, 68
McAnaly, 68
McArthur, 261
McAtee, 534
McAuly, 309
McAver, 220
McBlair, 170
McBride, 29, 116
McCabe, 162, 279, 312, 451, 463, 539
McCafferty, 82

590

McCahill, 285
McCalla, 223, 275
McCallan, 476
McCann, 74, 222, 545
McCarron, 82
McCarthy, 24, 70, 275, 474, 496, 502, 510
McCarty, 226, 277, 357, 393, 474, 526
McCastillo, 56
McCathran, 69, 92, 370, 372
McCaudle, 478
McCauley, 30, 81, 514
McCauly, 137
McCausland, 62
McCausley, 48
McCawley, 498
McCay, 281
McChesney, 85
McClary, 457
McClellan, 40, 144, 152, 199, 250, 259, 265, 337, 496
McClelland, 92, 389, 407, 493
McClerment, 144
McClermont, 273
McClernand, 312
McClosky, 360
McCloud, 241, 441
McClure, 83, 91, 105, 118, 203
McColgan, 180
McCollom, 364
McCollum, 165, 220, 493
McConihe, 223
McConnell, 55, 153, 274, 533
McCook, 107, 138
McCord, 468
McCormack, 25
McCormick, 14, 127, 135, 147, 191, 207, 385, 456, 484, 510
McCosh, 424
McCoy, 35, 92, 359, 371
McCraith, 4
McCrea, 103
McCreary, 370, 466
McCrellis, 246
McCristal, 239
McCrummill, 211

McCue, 64
McCullis, 457
McCulloch, 15, 74, 303, 315, 477
McCullough, 178, 246, 287, 318
McCurdy, 535
McCutchon, 166
McDaniel, 48, 178, 219, 388, 444
McDermot, 36
McDermott, 42, 62, 76, 120, 250, 473, 536
McDevitt, 223, 297, 298, 372, 456
McDonald, 5, 223, 334, 346, 527
McDonough, 272
McDougal, 516
McDougall, 83, 107, 375
McDowell, 100, 122, 264, 265, 520, 545
McDrennan, 76
McDuel, 458
McDuell, 175, 333, 419
McElderry, 464
McElrath, 34
McElwee, 65, 123
McFadden, 371, 395, 427, 490
McFalls, 446, 473, 489
McFarlan, 381, 500
McFarland, 34, 113, 204, 210, 214
McFerran, 83
McFullar, 3
McGarvey, 70, 93, 95
McGaughey, 53, 182
McGee, 487, 531
McGham, 183, 218
McGhan, 157
McGill, 218
McGinness, 69
McGinnis, 41, 61, 299
McGlue, 250, 254, 527
McGonigle, 396
McGowan, 15
McGraff, 366
McGran, 334
McGrann, 239, 250, 286, 287
McGrath, 44, 45, 83, 140, 160, 537, 542
McGraw, 469, 537

McGregor, 374
McGrew, 527
McGroaty, 41
McGruder, 151
McGuire, 11, 47, 102, 164, 215, 257, 337, 366, 477, 482, 530
McGunnegle, 259
McHenry, 99, 539
McHugh, 397
McIntire, 420
McIntosh, 277
McIntyre, 42, 84, 118, 121
McIver, 361
McJilton, 333
McKay, 282
McKean, 92, 135, 196
McKee, 52, 92, 143, 182, 197, 323, 505
McKeefe, 45
McKelden, 218, 287, 481
McKelvy, 134
McKenna, 29, 151
McKenney, 25, 147, 174, 348
McKenny, 128, 496
McKenzie, 140, 158, 424
McKibbin, 41
McKim, 35, 37, 43, 75, 100, 206, 215
McKimon, 8
McKinley, 221
McKinstry, 102
McKnew, 56, 255, 493
McKnight, 158, 521
McLain, 251, 512
McLane, 140, 308
McLaren, 91, 502
McLaughlin, 38, 90, 214, 374
McLaurin, 177, 357
McLaws, 405
McLean, 47, 52, 95, 227, 247, 255, 426, 507
McLellan, 214, 455
McLelland, 219, 391
McLennan, 202
McLeod, 99, 426, 480
McLeran, 246, 457
McLevel, 95

McMahon, 58, 67, 286, 319
McMakin, 510
McManagan, 113
McManus, 11, 90, 93, 272, 275
McMillan, 22, 278, 307
McMillen, 303, 307, 314, 317, 319
McMinaway, 187
McMinnaroy, 348
Mcmullen, 103
McMurdy, 367
McNalley, 85
McNally, 27, 96, 277, 324, 400, 543
McNamara, 293, 315
McNantz, 309
McNeil, 103, 243
McNeill, 211, 212, 266, 363
McNeir, 18, 20, 370, 416, 545
McNerhany, 3, 53, 207, 221, 241
McNier, 170
McNulty, 220
McOrn, 432
McParlin, 396
McPhail, 4
McPherson, 4, 5, 31, 243, 265, 304, 353, 379, 453, 478, 479, 490, 492, 499, 503
McQuade, 132
McQuillan, 239
McQuinn, 479
McRae, 98
McSherry, 513
McTavish, 44
McTyre, 151
McVeah, 312
McVeigh, 20, 231
McVey, 131
Mead, 73, 277, 520, 527, 545
Meade, 122, 231, 264, 265, 311, 366
Meador, 190, 506
Meadore, 518
Meagher, 291
Means, 40
Meany, 494
Mears, 115, 218
Meek, 191
Meeker, 259

Meeks, 234
Meem, 80
Meigs, 2, 136, 224, 237, 241, 242, 244, 248, 264, 265, 281, 283, 284, 298, 310, 318, 326, 464, 473, 520
Meintzer, 173
Meister, 173, 301
Meldon, 112
Melhurst, 386
Meline, 303, 327, 472
Melline, 343
Mellis, 309
Mellon, 162
Melrose tract, 29
Melville, 57
Melvin, 502, 504, 512
Membert, 507
Memmert, 395
Memminger, 405
Men of the Times in England, 184
Menefee, 211
Menger, 285, 286
men-of-war **Hartford & Wyoming**, 347
Mercer, 83, 89, 363, 382, 444, 476, 535
Meredith, 148, 204, 296, 542
Meredity, 424
Meridian Hill, 87, 410, 454, 461, 467, 470, 473
Merrick, 17, 63, 94, 219, 227, 244, 431, 498
Merrill, 99, 198, 259, 276, 284, 314
Merriman, 218
Merrit, 264
Merry, 387
Merryman, 87
Mertz, 350
Merwin, 147, 438
Merz, 52
Metler, 129
Metropolitan Gas-light Co, 60
Metzerott, 90, 176, 219, 273, 287, 457, 527
Metzgar, 24, 115
Meyer, 402, 462, 501

Meyers, 246
Mhoon, 281
Miazzo, 53
Michel, 455
Michie, 155
Michler, 333, 431, 540
Mickey, 135
Middleton, 9, 98, 157, 181, 215, 224, 225, 296, 324, 326, 328, 434, 440, 447, 465, 477, 508, 528, 546
Mids, 89
Mifford, 92
Milburn, 146, 287
Miles, 64, 157, 403
Millard, 262
Millen, 339
Miller, 23, 27, 31, 40, 41, 53, 67, 68, 83, 102, 108, 122, 123, 131, 135, 143, 151, 157, 159, 167, 171, 172, 178, 185, 187, 211, 218, 225, 237, 249, 259, 294, 306, 310, 318, 330, 357, 364, 371, 379, 413, 428, 443, 448, 454, 460, 480, 484, 488, 489, 498, 500, 502, 503, 504, 510, 515, 516, 520, 526, 528, 536, 546
Milligan, 120, 211
Milliken, 246
Millinger, 87
Millington, 310
Mills, 129, 183, 266, 268, 304
Millward, 41
Milne, 123
Milnor, 366
Milstead, 304, 415
Mincky, 451
Miner, 5, 134
Mingle, 47
Minitree, 526
Minkie, 463
Minnix, 431
Mino, 182
Minor, 5, 237, 362, 376, 472, 493
Minot House, 435
Miramon, 248, 278
Missile, 38
Mistrot, 152

Mitchel, 254, 532
Mitchell, 5, 9, 27, 53, 96, 102, 121, 158, 183, 208, 218, 238, 248, 250, 257, 259, 265, 280, 293, 317, 329, 334, 346, 353, 368, 371, 414, 421, 430, 523, 543
Mitchell's Cross Roads, 221
Mix, 13, 32, 194, 380, 401
Mizpah, 247
Mockabee, 21
Mohoney, 297
Mohun, 157, 218, 435, 453, 489, 514, 528
Mohwinkle, 205
Molan, 225
Molina, 118, 390
Molineux, 98
Molyneux, 343
Monck, 240
Moncure, 89, 235
Moneypennyy, 118
Monhouse, 5
monitor **Tonawanda**, 467
Monk, 102
Monkur, 9
Monroe, 16, 36, 155, 250, 318, 330, 342
Monson, 246
Montague, 87, 143
Montcastle, 496
Monteiro, 281
Monterey Springs, 260
Montgomery, 83, 179, 208, 407, 440
Montrose, 419
Monument Cemetery, 332
Moon, 364
Mooney, 462
Moonlight, 102
Moore, 30, 33, 35, 40, 52, 62, 77, 78, 82, 83, 87, 92, 112, 116, 118, 133, 151, 166, 176, 195, 230, 232, 249, 251, 312, 316, 346, 367, 371, 381, 403, 405, 433, 444, 448, 473, 500, 511, 524
Moorhead, 118
Mopang, 341

Moran, 95, 107, 219, 396, 462
Morcoe, 206, 529
More, 218
Morean, 40
Moreland, 70
Morey, 114
Morfit, 377
Morford, 92
Morgan, 2, 16, 21, 28, 63, 64, 79, 92, 155, 201, 218, 232, 272, 281, 311, 322, 325, 326, 327, 331, 332, 334, 337, 369, 385, 392, 458, 488, 496, 497, 515, 517, 521
Morhous, 350
Moriarity, 153
Moriarty, 228, 400
Morison, 369, 473
Morius, 149
Morley, 465
Morrell, 264
Morrice, 107
Morrill, 91
Morris, 3, 15, 22, 142, 143, 153, 176, 221, 228, 289, 512, 513
Morrison, 53, 218, 223, 239, 243, 250, 514, 517, 518, 529
Morrow, 3, 36, 144, 178
Morse, 4, 134, 243, 286
Morsell, 22, 64, 136, 153, 157, 194, 218, 255, 261, 402
Mortimer, 10, 208, 236, 516
Mortimore, 156
Morton, 91, 93, 135, 146, 452
Mosby, 224, 405, 468
Moseley, 425
Moses, 13, 158, 162, 164, 194, 218, 238, 247, 478, 494, 533
Mosher, 275, 282, 430
Mosley, 51
Mosly, 484
Motley, 228
Motley Hall, 207
Mott, 44, 212, 487
Moulder, 338, 440
Moulthrop, 246, 457
Moulton, 10

Mount Alto, 191
Mount Auburn Cemetery, 498
Mount Beverly, 223
Mount Eagle, 321, 366
Mount Kalma Cemetery, 337
Mount Olivet Cemetery, 37, 247, 252, 269, 359, 362, 446, 488
Mount Pleasant, 307, 510
Mount Pleasant farm, 142
Mount Vernon, 290, 321, 390
Mount Washington, 368
Mount Wellington, 427
Mountain House, 240
Mountcastle, 393
Mountford, 385
Mountz, 451, 482
Mower, 107, 396, 418, 474, 495
Mowison, 173
Moxley, 188, 218, 464, 480, 481
Moylan, 291
Mt Olivet Cemetery, 43, 325, 354
Mudd, 244, 296, 400
Mudgett, 446
Mueler, 261
Muhlinghaus, 101, 105, 139, 141, 167
Muir, 387
Muirkirk Furnace, 431
Muldorn, 462
Mulford, 511
Muligan, 59
Mullen, 138
Muller, 87, 124
Mullet, 177
Mullett, 86
Mulligan, 69, 100, 157
Mulliker, 457
Mullikin, 38
Mullin, 240
Mulliner, 33
Mullins, 301
Mulloy, 227, 244, 297, 527
Mumford, 386
Muncaster, 191, 534
Munce, 285, 286
Munday, 104
Munder, 471

Mundin, 224
Mundy, 282
Munger, 191
Munn, 424
Munro, 117, 194
Munroe, 93, 225, 388, 455
Munson, 15, 109, 121, 141, 346, 394, 396, 449
Munson's Hill, 394
Murdock, 218
Murphey, 68, 211
Murphy, 50, 62, 71, 87, 115, 120, 143, 246, 281, 282, 300, 311, 351, 378, 454, 457, 488, 496, 518, 526
Murray, 22, 23, 26, 46, 60, 75, 83, 85, 102, 107, 127, 171, 215, 286, 302, 312, 344, 357, 371, 395, 427, 490, 499
Murry, 218
Murtagh, 255
Murtenbaugh, 53
Murtersbaugh, 143
Muse, 302
Musser, 507
Mutchler, 115
Muzzy, 192
Myer, 520, 523
Myers, 20, 53, 83, 94, 157, 166, 204, 324, 328, 342, 382, 424, 457, 477, 495, 514, 527, 539
Mygatt, 346
Myrick, 281

N

Nabb, 22
Nachman, 296
Nagle, 28, 248, 307, 517
Naibel, 167
Nailer, 146
Nailor, 133, 139, 214, 237, 263
Nairn, 461
Naler, 13
Nalle, 235
Nalley, 147, 420, 424, 429, 433, 512
Nally, 527
Nance, 545

Napoleon, 433
Nash, 48, 92, 135, 158
Nason, 427
Nassau Hall, 286
Nat'l Cemeteries, 129
Natile, 346
National Base-ball, 376
National Cemetery, 152
National Intelligencer, 506
Naval Orders, 354
Navy Bulletin, 2, 9, 11, 13, 15, 19, 23, 26, 28, 30, 33, 38, 39, 45, 46, 48, 52, 55, 56, 57, 60, 62, 63, 66, 67, 69, 74, 76, 77, 78, 81, 84, 97, 100, 103, 109, 115, 121, 122, 123, 131, 132, 138, 141, 155, 163
Naylor, 104, 158, 183, 219, 295, 347, 544
NcNulty, 464
Neal, 53, 112, 286
Neary, 50, 71, 243
Neason, 102
Needham, 56
Neeld, 355
Neff, 103
Neidhart, 424
Neil, 302
Neill, 385
Neilson, 53, 357
Neiman, 47
Nelson, 34, 70, 83, 386, 543, 546
Nesbit, 228
Nesmith, 127, 149, 540
Netter, 359
Nettle, 13
Nevin, 112
Nevins, 376
New cars, 408
new jail, 472
Newberry, 89
Newbold, 63, 123
Newburg, 75
Newbury, 53
Newcomb, 57, 67
Newcomer, 281
Newland, 467

Newlin, 78
Newman, 14, 219, 239, 481, 493
Newrath, 79, 165
Newton, 17, 135, 209, 261, 264, 287, 385, 491
Nichols, 70, 83, 96, 120, 247, 259, 263, 295, 302, 370, 391, 395, 493, 522, 530, 534
Nicholson, 208, 259, 281, 370, 372, 430, 480, 538
Nickens, 319
Nickinson, 10
Nicodemus, 85, 540
Nigto, 102
Niles, 214, 527
Nipfia, 293
Nipfla, 293
Nisbet, 429
Nix, 52
Nixon, 97, 229, 300, 500, 501
Noble, 115, 208, 320, 461
Nock, 334, 389
Noell, 425
Noland, 6
Nolen, 346
Nolte, 77
Noon, 129
Noonan, 42, 54, 221, 496
Noonon, 39
Norcross, 469
Nork, 483
Norman, 332, 527
Normanstone, 407
Norment, 219
Normile, 285
Norris, 110, 125, 135, 216, 265, 326, 332, 366, 416, 516
North, 103, 369
Northern Neck of Va, 321
Northland, 168
Northrop, 286, 419
Northrup, 415, 417, 427, 429
Norton, 17, 66, 135, 257, 283, 496, 527
Norwood, 106

Nourse, 75, 100, 126, 130, 139, 145, 400, 463, 514
Nowland, 109, 222
Nowton, 161
Noyes, 101, 121, 130, 135, 214, 228, 287, 312, 330, 451, 471, 477, 527
Nugent, 24
Nulton, 200
Nunn, 192
Nuns, 88
Nutt, 472
Nutting, 427
Nutze, 287
Nutzy, 299
Nye, 18, 120, 351, 478

O

O'Bannon, 266
O'Bierne, 292
O'Bold, 376
O'Brien, 19, 23, 31, 73, 114, 150, 196, 280, 495
O'Connor, 158
O'Day, 5
O'Donnell, 506
O'Donohoe, 135
O'Dwyer, 158
O'Farrell, 143
O'Ferrall, 414
O'Hara, 252
O'Hare, 79, 165, 493
O'Horan, 383
O'Laughlin, 300, 407
O'Leary, 14, 211, 283, 435
O'Meara, 526
O'Neale, 158
O'Neil, 281
O'Neill, 286, 324
O'Shanter, 528
O'Toole, 481
Oak Grove, 351
Oak Hill Cemetery, 105, 121, 206, 224, 229, 275, 329, 339, 376, 380, 385, 492, 540
Oak Lawn, 337, 392
Oakland, 77

O'Beirne, 19, 66, 91, 161, 166, 223, 233, 235, 245, 260, 266, 268, 272, 276, 278, 285, 292, 299, 300, 301, 307, 312
Obold, 158
Ockert, 239
Odinel, 339
Oentrick, 496
Offenstein, 382
Offert, 298
Offutt, 14, 26, 113, 131, 282, 286, 475
Ogden, 315
Ogle, 504
Oglesby, 53, 59
Okers, 11
Olando, 234
Olcott, 89, 468
Old Bowery Theatre, 173
old Ironsides, 380
Oldcott, 9
Oldest Inhabitants, 5, 80, 147, 160, 162, 183, 275, 284, 336, 343, 398, 475, 508
Oldest Inhabitants Association, 160
Oldest Inhabitants' Association, 420
oldest person, 483
oldest restaurant, 449
oldest wooden house, 435
Oldham, 318
Olds, 59, 483, 512, 522
Olin, 2, 7, 22, 23, 26, 42, 59, 61, 71, 74, 93, 99, 110, 117, 139, 173, 186, 237, 240, 241, 242, 244, 248
Oline, 285
Oliver, 7, 92, 185, 244, 379
Olliver, 241
Olmstead, 216, 270, 515
Olmsted, 485
one horse railway, 409
Onions, 6
Only, 143
Oppenheim, 38, 79
Opry, 152
Oram, 127, 129
Ord, 264, 265, 407, 450, 478, 520, 531, 545

Ordway, 47
Orffutt, 258
Organ, 92
original settlers, 378
Orman, 53
Orme, 5, 215, 251, 295, 440, 441
Orphans Court, 13, 31, 39, 42, 45, 54, 58, 60, 64, 66, 75, 76, 83, 93, 95, 103, 107, 114, 117, 126, 128, 139, 144, 155, 164, 171, 179, 190, 211, 225, 327, 331, 334, 343, 346, 352, 353, 359, 362, 371, 374, 381, 384, 391, 402, 412, 427, 431, 443, 449, 455, 458, 464, 468, 472, 473, 477, 482, 488, 490, 500, 502, 512, 515, 523, 532
Orr, 403
Ortez, 519
Orton, 476
Osborn, 75, 151, 377, 416
Osborne, 48, 62, 118, 162, 281
Osbourne, 158
Osbury, 8, 80
Osman, 158, 200
Osmon, 135
Ostermayer, 101, 106, 126
Oston, 456
Oswill, 309
Otho, 333
Otis, 3, 54, 250, 312, 527
Ott, 178
Ottarson, 237
Otterback, 219
Otterburg, 312
Ottomeyer, 151
Ould, 470
Ousley, 439
Outten, 3
Overton, 437
Owen, 3, 4, 22, 32, 35, 85, 103, 108, 119, 206, 277, 292, 409, 430, 506, 514, 533, 545
Owenby, 124
Owens, 20, 32, 60, 151, 239, 283, 284, 319, 352, 415
Owing, 311
Owings, 257
Owner, 382
Oyster, 135, 363

P

Pabst, 79, 165
Pace, 234
Pacha, 411
Pack, 274
Packard, 43
Packer, 527
packet **Europe**, 326
Packman, 23
Paddock, 89
Padgett, 132
Padworth, 180
Page, 3, 27, 53, 78, 92, 105, 158, 174, 182, 194, 203, 253, 255, 289, 339, 346, 452, 472, 478, 479, 503
Pageot, 5
Paget, 168
Paine, 44, 72, 73, 76, 139, 267, 365
Paint Branch Switch Farm, 463
Painter, 70
Paixhan, 340
Paland, 152
Palen, 112
Palfrey, 265
Palley, 90
Palm, 92
Palmer, 11, 17, 118, 129, 153, 219, 241, 264, 270, 304, 430, 466, 523
Pannell, 320
Paolo, 393
Papal Guard, 72
Papal Zouaves, 281
Pape, 82
Papendic, 326
Paramour, 270
Pardoe, 525
Parepa, 24
Parham, 385
Parish, 323, 499
Parke, 212, 241, 264, 265
Parker, 8, 10, 13, 19, 35, 94, 118, 137, 158, 163, 173, 219, 250, 254, 271,

288, 293, 319, 357, 371, 398, 440, 443, 489, 533, 537, 538
Parkhurst, 172, 482
Parkman, 224
Parks, 56, 128, 144, 145, 236, 346
Parmer, 93
Parr, 234
Parris, 226, 390
Parrott, 110
Parry, 174, 500
Parsons, 3, 5, 12, 44, 61, 133, 208, 365, 474, 540, 546
Part of Calvert's Hope, 274
Partello, 304, 544
Partridge, 170, 317
Pascoe, 511
Passano, 344
Passionists, 344
Patch, 427
Patent laws, 541
Patis, 236
Patrick, 373, 498
Patten, 220, 253
Patterson, 1, 71, 94, 99, 107, 116, 120, 121, 123, 134, 151, 155, 158, 181, 199, 206, 219, 253, 285, 302, 354, 408, 444, 471, 524, 525
Pattison, 524
Patton, 22, 232
Paul, 5, 18, 259
Paulding, 18, 204
Paulick, 291
Paxton, 11, 25, 58
pay of army ofcrs, 125
pay of officers, 122
Payne, 7, 24, 55, 118, 159, 264, 265, 272, 281, 298, 396, 424, 462, 468, 473, 483
Peabody, 99, 185, 269, 389, 472, 535
Peace, 39
Peacham, 434
Peacock, 4, 5
Peak, 239
Peake, 62, 158
Peale, 346
Pean, 41

Pearce, 8, 53, 87, 143, 295, 440
Pearson, 115, 117, 131, 214, 251, 254, 279, 461, 500
Pease, 103
Peck, 97, 103, 123, 182, 191, 219, 222, 337, 338, 343, 367, 427, 536, 546
Pecker, 400
Pecor, 38
Pedon, 135, 202
Pedrick, 306
Peer, 211
Peers, 358
Pegg, 431
Pegram, 265, 361
Pehi, 424
Peirce, 430
Peirson, 323
Pelins, 84
Pell, 89
Pella, 158
Pellouze, 475
Pelouze, 333
Pemberton, 137, 405
Pendar, 354
Pendergast, 116
Pendergrast, 519
Pendleton, 234, 259
Penkey, 206
Penky, 107
Penn, 51, 168, 385
Pennington, 312
Pennock, 278
Penny, 320
Penodin, 143
Penrose, 56, 102
Pepper, 81, 93, 95, 103, 106, 221, 520
Pepya, 519
Pere la Chaise, 433
Perea, 56
Pereigoy, 239
Perine, 349
Perkins, 8, 100, 118, 246, 259, 314, 371, 424, 457
Perley, 9
Perrie, 538

Perrigo, 536
Perrin, 135
Perry, 83, 112, 144, 176, 211, 212, 219, 245, 249, 250, 319, 332, 333, 378, 430, 434, 504, 532
Pescara, 391
Peter, 158, 173, 475
Peters, 14, 36, 53, 94, 107, 116, 143, 147, 155, 158, 228, 346, 429, 467, 531
Peterson, 132, 233, 256, 483
PeterZower, 360
Petigru, 8
Petit, 390, 454
Petrikin, 155
Pettengill, 188, 419
Pettey, 319
Petties, 542
Pettit, 46, 257, 294, 342, 542
Peugh, 28, 158, 412, 527
Peyden, 202
Peyser, 410
Peyton, 55, 56, 142, 182, 209, 349
Pfaln, 527
Pfulger, 502
Phelan, 181, 219, 451
Phelps, 105, 129, 228, 316
Philip, 22, 60, 61, 158, 439, 442, 474
Philips, 161, 249
Phillippi, 138
Phillips, 11, 15, 53, 60, 108, 140, 151, 158, 166, 219, 220, 328, 385, 412, 446, 504, 527, 546
Philp, 219, 249, 528
Philps, 8
Pickarell, 47
Pickens, 151, 405
Pickering, 52, 62, 211
Picket, 405
Pickett, 2, 80, 147, 369, 404, 405, 449, 541
Picking, 76
Pickrel, 69
Pickrell, 219
<u>Pickwick</u>, 509

Pierce, 35, 42, 50, 60, 85, 104, 163, 182, 193, 211, 280, 328, 375, 386, 443, 446, 532
Pierpoint, 356
Pierpont, 244, 326
Pierrepoint, 442
Pierrepont, 227, 323, 422
Pierreport, 274
Piggott, 38, 347
Pike, 102
Piles, 306
Piling, 464
Pilla, 476
Pilling, 219, 238, 475, 481
Pillsbury, 135, 259
Pinckney, 10, 43, 241, 371, 388, 460, 462, 470
Piney Point, 430
Pinknay, 235
Pinkney, 79, 223, 230, 280, 448
Pinner, 9
Pinney, 134
Pino, 88
Piper, 434
Pitcher, 302
Pitmas, 120
Pitt, 263, 380
Pitts, 249, 492
Pius VI, 426
Pixley, 150
Pizzini, 180
Plander, 77, 100
Plant, 98, 214, 249, 250, 255, 334, 461, 522, 527, 530
Platt, 158, 492
Pleasanton, 149, 264
Pleasants, 5, 99, 407
Pleasonton, 61
Pleufger, 293
Plugge, 93
Plumer, 65
Plumper, 261
Plumsill, 508
Poe, 190
Poffenberger, 138
Poindexter, 87, 226

600

Point Lookout, 542
Poland, 286
Polk, 264, 380, 405, 419
Polkinhorn, 5, 219, 287, 518
Pollak, 219
Pollard, 242, 246, 271, 486
Polley, 477
Polleys, 112
Pollock, 99, 133, 161, 390
Pollok, 421
Pomeroy, 83, 115, 479, 491, 508, 509
Pomfrey, 182
Pond, 194
Pool, 468
Poole, 102, 309, 458
Poore, 282
Pope, 28, 72, 104, 109, 149, 162, 250, 264, 265, 426, 481, 520, 545
Popkins, 476
Poplar Springs, 318
Porcher, 403
Port Deposit, 51, 58, 134
Porter, 56, 83, 115, 150, 264, 335, 337, 341, 380, 388, 428, 462, 467, 540
Porter estate, 454
Posey, 211, 286, 365
Post, 116
Postelwait, 287
Posthoff, 5
Postlewait, 281
Postmaster, 2, 8, 13, 17, 22, 26, 29, 35, 41, 56, 110, 120, 162, 169, 170, 250, 270, 310, 330, 354, 361, 398, 404, 467, 477, 508
Postmasters, 92, 102, 104, 105, 108, 109, 110, 112, 116, 118, 120, 123, 129, 134, 135, 136, 140, 302, 311
Poston, 545
Potter, 63, 73, 83, 92, 115, 329, 333, 339, 356, 397, 457
Potter's Field, 91
Potts, 62, 78, 137, 215, 275, 302, 396, 527
Pourtales, 214

Powell, 53, 89, 99, 105, 152, 207, 281, 287, 294, 329, 349, 486, 491, 518
Power, 286, 400
Powers, 23, 261, 291, 409
Powles, 401
Poyner, 210
Prather, 13, 17, 158, 219
Pratt, 9, 21, 42, 51, 65, 93, 100, 102, 115, 118, 198, 231, 243, 289, 323, 527, 543
Preaux, 145
Prentice, 138
Prentis, 344
Presburg, 214
Presbury, 142
Presbyterian Burying ground, 359
Prescott, 467
Preston, 19, 185, 404, 504, 544
Preuss, 477
Prevost, 123, 245, 527
Prewith, 237
Price, 2, 44, 53, 266, 282, 303, 358, 405, 414, 419, 437, 505, 516
Prince, 176
Prince Albert, 355, 537
Prince of Wales, 355, 473, 487
Princess Frederica Amelia, 333
Princess of Wales, 355
Princeton College, 286
Prindle, 39, 148
Prior Park, 72
Probasco, 484
Proby, 464, 481
Proctor, 36
Prom, 54
propellar **Waukazoo**, 451
Prosise, 183, 220
Prospect Cemetery, 499
Prospect Hill Cemetery, 105, 106, 164, 455
Prout, 158, 419
Provine, 234
Provost, 219, 532
Provosty, 286
Prue, 294
Pryor, 403, 405

Puckett, 4, 89, 151
Pugh, 3, 85, 403, 491
Pulizzi, 106
Pullen, 151
Pullman, 381
Pulman, 5, 89
Pumphrey, 158, 263, 296, 297, 383, 527, 534
Punch, 420
Purcell, 11, 19, 28, 83, 167, 225, 232, 243, 253, 258, 266, 282, 288, 293, 300, 304, 316, 324, 347, 353, 473
Purcey, 78
Purdy, 215
Purnell, 196, 317
Pursell, 116, 126, 128
Pusey, 451
Putnam, 21
Putnan, 182
Pyatt, 109
Pye, 285, 381
Pyles, 267, 513
Pyne, 90, 442
Pywell, 317

Q

Quaiffe, 350
Quail, 41
Queen, 3, 53, 162, 211, 253, 283, 400
Queen Anne, 380
Queen Caroline, 537
Queen Victoria, 93, 136, 184, 355, 537
Quenby, 37
Quigley, 4
Quigly, 89
Quillins, 412
Quimby, 56
Quin, 130
Quinn, 58, 86
Quintero, 404
Quirk, 79, 110, 165
Quitman, 299

R

Racicot, 314
Racke, 17
Radcliff, 132
Radcliffe, 208, 331
Radford, 282
Ragan, 139, 153, 232, 499, 511
Rahme, 302
Rainals, 70, 103
Raines, 85
Rainey, 262, 296
Rains, 264
Ralston, 266
Ramsay, 69, 112, 508
Ramsburg, 2, 14, 255, 485
Ramsell, 283
Ramsey, 15, 390, 409, 424, 468
Ramus, 515
<u>Randall</u>, 2, 8, 17, 22, 26, 35, 56, 84, 86, 91, 145, 214, 219, 398, 495
Randolph, 34, 111, 118, 138, 148, 149, 366, 367, 404
Raney, 477
Rannay, 118
Ransom, 8, 73, 430, 437
Ransome, 491
Ranson, 83
Ransone, 456
Raphael, 393
Raphun, 4
Rapley, 219, 483
Rapp, 129
Rastwick, 421
Ratcliff property, 106
Rathbone, 301
Rathburn, 256
Rau, 350
Raub, 32, 58
Rauschor, 471
Rauterberg, 85
Raverdy, 89
Rawles, 505
Rawling, 116
Rawlings, 31, 137, 158, 475, 540
Rawlins, 247, 520, 542

Ray, 22, 111, 219, 238, 255, 265, 286, 417, 430
Raybold, 290, 295
Raymond, 30, 108, 304
Reach, 104
Read, 92, 312, 338, 346, 402, 532
Reade, 422
Reading, 158, 421
Reagan, 71, 105, 354, 404, 405
Reap, 116
Reardon, 315, 382
Rease, 269
Rebhun, 223
Reckless, 120
Rector, 405
Reddick, 289
Reddington, 104
Redemptorist order, 424
Reden, 490
Redfern, 40, 219, 309, 334, 335, 482, 512
Redfield, 278
Redford, 305, 393
Redgrave, 233
Redin, 66, 82, 148, 188, 297, 515
Redman, 331
Redmond, 40
Redstake, 251
Redstrake, 255
Reed, 36, 80, 129, 145, 219, 258, 269, 281, 288, 316, 324, 376, 381, 384, 388, 397, 455, 462, 491, 515, 534
Reeder, 468
Rees, 104
Reese, 26, 83, 221, 258, 302, 317, 413, 492
Reeside, 177, 317
Reeve, 68, 112, 129, 195, 317
Reeves, 76, 165, 166, 167, 270, 307, 311
Reid, 4, 57, 89, 105, 173, 475
Reidy, 544
Reill, 122
Reilly, 281, 357, 461, 470
Reily, 342
Reiter, 238

Remey, 259
Remick, 167
Reminiscences, 528
Remmonds, 163
Renear, 105
Renehan, 275
Renneker, 221
Reno, 265
Renshaw, 62, 383
Renwick, 386
Repplier, 286
Resancon, 459
Reside, 166
Resin, 440
Rexvost, 4
Reyburn, 245
Reynolds, 14, 75, 129, 223, 225, 239, 243, 264, 329, 338, 358, 362, 363, 412, 424, 462, 477
Rheem, 121
Rhett, 89, 264
Rhey, 155
Rhinehart, 232
Rhoberts, 247
Rhodes, 14, 143, 245, 258, 283, 284, 290, 327, 328, 334
Rice, 75, 134, 508, 533, 534, 535
Rich, 133, 158, 338
Richards, 30, 46, 47, 87, 101, 115, 127, 165, 183, 219, 246, 300, 306, 313, 317, 370, 389, 417, 457, 520, 527
Richardson, 3, 36, 52, 53, 56, 113, 118, 120, 135, 137, 219, 248, 330, 424, 429, 520
Richberg, 103
Richerson, 3
Richey, 171
Richings, 291, 543
Richmond, 56, 135, 358
Richter, 305
Rickers, 220
Rickets, 286
Ricketts, 103, 264, 287, 510, 534, 540, 542
Riddell, 460

Riddle, 3, 25, 137, 223, 227, 378, 477
Ridenour, 250, 254
Rider, 158
Ridgate, 34
Ridge, 437
Ridgeley, 3, 53
Ridgely, 115, 209, 253
Ridgway, 237, 324, 342
Riechenbach, 481
Riemer, 138
Rig_y, 517
Riggles, 108, 270
Riggs, 2, 158, 219, 251, 279, 419, 444, 473, 475, 481, 506
Riggs farm, 401
Rile, 133, 146
Riley, 57, 83, 146, 158, 219, 285, 348, 421, 490, 529, 530
Ringgold, 181
Riordan, 67, 300, 316
Ripley, 108
Risley, 99, 144, 459
Risque, 128
Ritchie, 216
Rittenhouse, 122, 206, 261, 397
River, 81
Rivers, 422
Riversdale, 130
Rives, 68, 116, 219, 231, 261, 304, 353, 515
Roach, 326, 458, 527
Roantree, 348
Robb, 134
Robbe, 211
Robbins, 72, 138, 249, 329, 493, 525, 534
Robe, 56
Roberts, 2, 45, 90, 104, 116, 126, 135, 138, 151, 158, 166, 183, 195, 200, 230, 319, 330, 367, 451, 478, 522
Robertson, 85, 151, 158, 242, 351, 379, 472, 492, 495
Robertson Co, 62
Robeson, 245
Robey, 505
Robinett, 60

Robinson, 1, 5, 14, 23, 31, 39, 44, 87, 92, 118, 123, 129, 133, 182, 219, 239, 267, 301, 320, 338, 363, 416, 418, 420, 429, 430, 433, 443
Roby, 124
Roch, 89
Rochat, 165, 252
Roche, 4, 194, 231
Rochefort, 98
Rochester, 83
Rock, 462, 478
Rock Hill, 340
Rock Hill College, 160, 275, 421
Rock Hill Mansion, 340
Rockaway, 471
Rockburn, 222
Rockett, 315
Rocks, 137
Rockwell, 323
Rocoffort, 433
Roden, 329
Rodgers, 30, 127, 133
Rodier, 42, 221, 355, 381, 493
Rodman, 23
Rodney, 9, 286
Roe, 57, 383
Roellinger, 100, 141
Roemle, 412
Roes, 78
Rogers, 11, 53, 57, 118, 141, 190, 233, 237, 258, 286, 308, 313
Rohrer, 267
Rolande, 423
Rolard, 457
Rolfe, 128
Roller, 246
Rollinger, 46
Rollins, 415
Romain, 358
Roman Catholics, 131
Roney, 496
Rood, 87
Rooney, 502, 517
Root, 17
Ropes, 124
Rosander, 396

Rosch, 281
Rose, 302, 480, 488
Rosecran, 265
Rosecrans, 122, 264, 326
Rosenthal, 219
Roser, 4
Rosette, 67, 178
Rosevelt, 439
Roso, 230
Ross, 1, 10, 24, 36, 54, 57, 80, 82, 90, 91, 105, 111, 118, 153, 219, 251, 254, 259, 286, 330, 420, 460, 485, 518, 524
Rossander, 411
Rost, 404
Roth, 456
Rothchild, 10
Rothschild, 502
Rouse, 38, 398
Rousseau, 78, 148, 159, 171, 199, 350, 458, 520
Routh, 299
Rowe, 115, 213
Rowland, 97, 115, 158
Rowley, 112
Rowzee, 289
Roy, 491
Royal, 233
Royel, 133
Royer, 216, 436
Roys, 85
Royston, 145, 367
Rozal, 93
Rozel, 95
Rubel, 337
Rucker, 13, 83
Rucks, 56
Rud, 17
Rudd, 10, 18, 319, 445
Ruddington, 87, 143
Rudolph, 285
Ruff, 155, 164, 165, 166, 193, 266, 309, 507
Ruffin, 403
Ruger, 92, 112, 202
Ruggle, 106
Ruggles, 238
Rumbold, 335
Rumley, 311
Runge, 62
Runyan, 118
Rupert, 177, 310, 338, 339, 375, 486, 518
Ruppert, 152, 219, 362, 458, 480, 486
Rush, 259
Russ, 330, 478
Russell, 2, 10, 17, 54, 72, 88, 91, 98, 117, 118, 119, 135, 161, 183, 188, 212, 306, 354, 456, 477, 494, 525, 533
Russler, 356
Ruth, 230, 331, 489
Rutherford, 67, 77, 79, 97, 114, 391, 527
Ruttle, 44
Ryan, 5, 15, 24, 61, 70, 73, 142, 287, 293, 424, 445, 505, 533
Ryder, 102
Rye, 70
Rynd, 116
Rynerson, 542
Ryon, 223

S

Sachow, 424
Sackett, 537, 538
Sadler, 227
Saengerbund, 371
Saffe, 534
Saffill, 493
Safford, 136
Sagar, 5
Sage, 92, 197
Sailor, 273
Saks, 533
Sala, 433
Sales, 29
Salisbury, 469
Sallade, 196
Salter, 5, 108
Salvo, 18
Samon, 457

Samson, 154, 243, 246, 281, 484, 526, 541
Samuels, 19, 95
Sanborn, 34, 510
Sanders, 5, 53, 143, 182, 404
Sanderson, 104, 118
Sandford, 193, 365
Sands, 81, 430
Sanford, 10, 154, 508
Sanger, 248, 289, 495
Sangston, 258
Sanner, 183
Santa Anna, 384
Santmyer, 312
Santos, 270
Sargeant, 235
Sargent, 334
Sarran, 151
Satchwell, 385
Satterlee, 83, 107
Saul, 40, 219, 287, 533
Saulsbury, 81
Saunders, 8, 135, 175, 199, 455
Savage, 41, 60, 266, 390, 422, 527
Saviers, 302
Saville, 207
Savinian, 421
Sawles, 273
Sawtelle, 83
Sawyer, 6, 62, 133, 212, 262, 425, 450, 507, 531
Saxe, 185, 426
Saxton, 123, 243, 250, 265
Sayles, 26, 88, 524, 525
Sayre, 5
Sayres, 34, 206
Scaggs, 67
Scala, 136, 190
Scales, 286
Scanlon, 211, 231
Scatterday, 118
Schafer, 210, 527
Schaff, 394
Schaffer, 293
Schaurte, 149
Scheffer, 18

Scheifley, 165
Schell, 204, 205, 477
Schelling, 424
Schenck, 56, 418
Schenig, 226, 521
Schermerhor, 93
Schermerhorn, 350
Schiller, 541
Schilling, 456
Schliecker, 483
Schmidt, 267, 281, 359
Schneider, 36, 255, 287, 527
Schnider, 527, 529
Schnieder, 254
schnr **Alert**, 110
schnr **Amytis**, 87
schnr **E M Dyer**, 10
schnr **Eagle**, 328
schnr **H S Lanfair**, 373
schnr **Hazleton**, 377
schnr **J S Havens**, 33
schnr **Julia Smith**, 234
schnr **Lydia Ann**, 151
schnr **Messenger**, 234
schnr **Sarah Jay**, 94
schnr **Shemsis**, 121
schnr **William Gregory**, 384
schnr **Willis Lincoln**, 170
Schober, 66
Schoef, 57
Schoeff, 67
Schoenboin, 527
Schoenemoun, 92
Schoepp, 346
Schoff, 542
Schofield, 41, 51, 122, 265, 345, 471, 480, 520
Schonborn, 133
School, 58
Schooley, 358, 359
Schrader, 116
Schrafhouser, 391
Schriven, 289
Schroag, 54
Schroeder, 9, 12
Schuchardt, 432

Schuetzen Verein, 455
Schufley, 406
Schultz, 312
Schurcardi, 291
Schutter, 160
Schuttler, 191
Schuyler, 302
Schwan, 149
Schwartz, 26
Schwartzwelder, 418
Schweigart, 511
Schwing, 527
Scofield, 265
Scotch Neck, 289
Scott, 30, 37, 67, 84, 88, 105, 129, 229, 246, 272, 287, 300, 303, 309, 318, 320, 324, 340, 348, 353, 378, 403, 413, 457, 466, 507, 536, 542
Scragg's Station, 463
Scrivener, 486, 491, 493, 526
Scruggs, 4
Seabright, 182
Seal, 118
Seaman, 115
Searle, 368
Searles, 428
Sears, 16, 212, 235, 253, 257, 367, 469
Seaton, 65, 118, 232, 319, 520
Seavers, 297
Sebastian, 36, 240, 265, 501
Sebree, 259
Sebring, 448
Sebury, 208
Sedden, 404
Seddon, 405, 406, 477
Sedgwick, 356
Sedwith, 398
Seelers, 424
Seely, 210
Seffert, 151
Segar, 3, 143
Segourney, 462
Segur, 143
Segura, 143
Seip, 246, 370, 457

Seipe, 466
Seith, 327
Seitz, 79, 87, 161, 165, 331, 359, 363, 371
Selby, 25, 309, 363
Selden, 151, 252, 453
Seldon, 518
Selee, 284
Seliott, 49
Sells, 3, 4
Selzer, 496
Semken, 219
Semmes, 22, 27, 55, 83, 93, 215, 239, 243, 286, 405
Senate nominations, 34
Serritt, 17
Sessford, 282
Seufferle, 250, 254
Sevame, 225
Severance, 9
Severns, 109
Severon, 187
Sewall, 213, 358
Seward, 1, 7, 124, 180, 224, 267, 415
Sexton, 252
Seyfert, 285
Seymore, 119
Seymour, 92, 203, 230, 445, 500, 533, 544
Shaaf property, 284
Shackelford, 323
Shafer, 42
Shaffer, 210
Shaffield, 193
Shakespeare, 221
Shakespeare's Works, 357
Shallcross, 34
Shanahan, 193, 211, 216
Shane, 110
Shanes, 12
Shaney, 378
Shankland, 287
Shanks, 133
Shannahan, 498, 502
Shannon, 53, 273, 424
Sharp, 33, 136, 478

Sharpley, 516
Shaw, 49, 219, 229, 259, 304, 330, 353, 410
Shawner, 39
Shay, 467, 502
Shea, 54, 132, 357, 399, 432
Sheads, 181
Shearar, 496
Sheckel, 544
Sheckels, 274
Sheckles, 375
Shedd, 214
Sheets, 4, 89
Sheffey, 349
Shehan, 420
Sheid, 379
Sheifly, 196
Shekell, 14, 191, 534
Shelby, 64, 255, 520
Shelden, 469
Shelding, 97
Sheldon, 127, 420
Shelton, 158, 441
Shepard, 195
Sheperd, 527
Shephard, 295
Shepherd, 76, 158, 166, 214, 215, 280, 410, 446, 451, 489, 529
Sheppard, 394
Sherburne, 131, 515
Sheridan, 58, 122, 149, 175, 195, 240, 250, 264, 265, 285, 286, 452, 520, 525
Sheridan's Point, 290
Sheriff, 239, 251, 255, 304, 473
Sherman, 6, 22, 50, 51, 63, 72, 122, 149, 156, 200, 201, 206, 243, 247, 264, 265, 303, 314, 319, 367, 390, 397, 414, 540
Shermer, 282, 329
Sherwood, 40, 294, 388, 538
Sherwood Forest, 25
Shields, 119, 344
Shilcutt, 192
Shilling, 236
Shillington, 532

Shinn, 249, 358, 435
ship **Alleghany**, 121, 354
ship **Arizona**, 494
ship **Ascutney**, 11
ship **Buckthorne**, 122
ship **Canandaigua**, 45, 52
ship **Chattanooga**, 52
ship **Chesapeake**, 504
ship **Connemaugh**, 19
ship **Constellation**, 46, 115
ship **Constitution**, 123
ship **Daffodil**, 122
ship **De Soto**, 60, 74
ship **Estrella**, 11, 122
ship **Franklin**, 57, 259
ship **Frolic**, 66
ship **Fulton**, 278
ship **Gettysburg**, 97
ship **Glasgow**, 122
ship **Huron**, 23
ship **Independence**, 279
ship **Ino**, 66
ship **Jamestown**, 63, 74, 78
ship **John Bright**, 86
ship **Lancaster**, 115
ship **Lenapee**, 97
ship **Leopard**, 341
ship **Macedonian**, 385
ship **Madawaska**, 57, 62
ship **Mahaska**, 74, 77
ship **Marblehead**, 23, 28
ship **Memphis**, 2, 13, 17, 19
ship **Miantonomah**, 57
ship **Michigan**, 45
ship **Minnesota**, 259
ship **Mohican**, 77
ship **Monongahela**, 15, 28, 30, 60, 67, 74, 81
ship **Moravian**, 73
ship **New Hampshire**, 67, 100
ship **Newbern**, 100
ship **Niagara**, 205
ship **Ocean Queen**, 185
ship **Ohio**, 100, 109
ship **Osceola**, 13, 30
ship **Patos**, 66

ship **Paul Jones**, 17, 48, 122
ship **Pawnee**, 9, 74
ship **Penobscot**, 13
ship **Peoria**, 9, 13, 131, 132, 138
ship **Pi_guin**, 57
ship **Potomac**, 45, 122, 123
ship **Quinnebaug**, 259
ship **Relief**, 9, 163
ship **Richmond**, 78, 97
ship **Sabine**, 57, 123
ship **Saginaw**, 62
ship **Santee**, 123
ship **Saranac**, 46, 77, 100
ship **Savannah**, 138
ship **Scotia**, 185
ship **Shawmut**, 354
ship **St Cloud**, 483
ship **St Louis**, 33
ship **Superb**, 386
ship **Susquehanna**, 26, 74, 523
ship **Suwanee**, 62, 63
ship **Swatara**, 109
ship **Tacony**, 57, 62, 74
ship **Tahoma**, 28
ship **Tallapoosa**, 11, 122, 131, 163
ship **Vandalia**, 123
ship **Vanderbilt**, 62
ship **Vermont**, 9, 19, 30, 74, 76
ship **Ville de Paris**, 301
ship **Wachusett**, 141
ship **Wyoming**, 63, 234
ship **Yantic**, 57, 63, 77
Shipley, 353
Shippen, 176, 257
Shires, 497
Shirley, 234
Shoemaker, 183, 206, 239
Shoomaker, 245
Short, 79, 215
Shorter, 2
Shortly, 175
Shreves, 219
Shrewsury, 93
Shropshire, 397
Shryock, 143
Shubrick, 91, 286

Shugrue, 131
Shul, 28
Shumaker, 332
Shuman, 206
Shumate, 349
Shunk, 114
Shurtz, 134
Shuster, 238, 249, 532
Shyne, 287
Sibley, 74, 81, 206, 488
Sibrey, 475
Sickles, 61, 494
Sicotte, 307
Sides, 152
Sidney, 23
Sieber, 133
Sigler, 34
Sigston, 137
Siler, 5
Silver Spring, 193
Silvey, 302
Simmes, 180
Simmington, 4
Simmons, 3, 33, 44, 66, 158, 219, 255, 352, 372
Simms, 11, 14, 75, 76, 113, 151, 219, 225, 238, 251, 275, 284, 286, 297, 307, 332, 462
Simonds, 120, 182
Simons, 159, 259, 470
Simpson, 3, 9, 86, 97, 133, 143, 144, 182, 219, 221, 260, 287, 328, 382, 431, 445, 477, 483, 517, 536
Sims, 282
Sinclair, 348, 373
Singleton, 55, 135
Singston, 503
Singzan, 291
Sinnott, 506
Sinon, 244
Sioussa, 252, 255, 276, 468
Sipes, 105, 196, 300, 516
Sir Walter Scott, 324
Sisson, 223
Sister Alphonsa, 448
Sister Mary F Thomas, 49

Sister Mary Vincent, 111
Sister of Charity, 409
Sisters of Charity, 324, 361, 383, 392, 420
Sisters of the Holy Cross, 448
Sisters of Visitation, 236
Sitgraves, 29
Skaggs, 139, 194
Skeen, 53
Skelley, 36
Skeritt, 302
Skidmore, 261, 263, 531
Skillman, 434
Skinker, 498
Skinner, 5, 178, 224, 469
Skippen, 292, 298
Skippon, 58
Skirving, 406
Slack, 134
Slade, 27
Slater, 158, 309
Slaughter, 323
Slaughter's Mountain, 323
Slevia, 140
Slicer, 460
Slidell, 324, 404, 405, 418
Slingluff, 116
Sliter, 497
Sloan, 17, 307, 462
Sloat, 505
Slocum, 51, 135, 154, 265, 469
sloop **R L Simonson**, 142
sloop **Union**, 234
Slough, 519, 542
Slowen, 527
Slusher, 119
Smackum, 128
Small, 150, 152, 155, 164, 165, 193, 266, 386, 544
Smalley, 141
Smallwood, 33, 182
Smeed, 262
Smidley, 293
Smith, 2, 4, 5, 12, 13, 15, 19, 23, 25, 26, 31, 32, 33, 40, 54, 60, 62, 64, 66, 68, 71, 76, 79, 82, 83, 85, 89, 91, 92, 99, 102, 104, 106, 108, 115, 116, 120, 126, 127, 129, 130, 132, 135, 140, 146, 149, 153, 158, 165, 166, 173, 182, 183, 184, 189, 190, 192, 209, 219, 220, 229, 231, 235, 236, 251, 254, 262, 264, 265, 272, 275, 278, 281, 282, 286, 287, 288, 294, 298, 299, 302, 312, 313, 314, 323, 325, 334, 337, 338, 349, 357, 361, 381, 382, 389, 392, 396, 398, 401, 405, 411, 413, 417, 420, 424, 426, 430, 431, 434, 437, 442, 443, 455, 462, 466, 470, 474, 476, 479, 496, 502, 512, 516, 520, 531, 536, 538, 539
Smithers, 104
Smithson, 136, 158
Smoet, 323
Smoot, 21, 182, 219, 262, 338, 410, 432, 464, 472, 480, 531
Smooth, 142
smothered to death, 95
Smyth, 372
Smythe, 312
Sneak, 263
Snelling, 376
Snively, 49
Snivley, 363
Snobel, 81
Snoud, 316
Snow, 134, 379, 449, 534
Snowden, 41, 173
Snyder, 39, 57, 72, 118, 158, 243, 250, 532, 540
Soban, 40
Society Hill, 472
Softly, 84
Sol, 100
Soldiers' Burial Ground, 391
Soldiers' National Cemetery, 433
Soles, 8
Sollenberger, 201
Solomon, 106
Solomons, 219, 364, 528
Solp, 328
Somborn, 79

Somers, 325
Somerville, 269, 434, 443, 449
Somes, 212, 493
Sommers, 178, 475
Sonnenschmidt, 85, 333, 344
Soper, 144, 285
Sorrel, 357
Souble, 73
Soule, 98, 142, 143, 411, 462
Southall, 115, 269
Southampton, 305
Southard, 43
Southgate, 397
Southwick, 524
Southworth, 219
Soutter, 432
Spalding, 54, 100, 164, 166, 168, 170, 198, 209, 214, 344, 379, 441, 453
Spalding's Dist, 306
Spaney, 363
Spangler, 290, 396, 418
Sparks, 88
Sparrell, 312
Sparrow, 403
Spates, 363, 534
Spaulding, 137, 408
Speake, 324, 398, 417, 427, 429
Speaks, 327
Spear, 76, 346, 525
Spears, 11
Spedden, 288
Speed, 503
Speiden, 86
Speight, 317
Speir, 306
Speiser, 475
Spence, 367
Spencer, 8, 83, 87, 246, 319, 350, 457
Spicer, 244
Spier, 524, 525
Spignul, 287
Spink, 118, 198
Spinner, 328
Spofford, 183
Sprague, 83, 221, 270
Sprigg, 363

Spriggs, 502
Spring Hill Cemetery, 469
Springman, 183
Sproeger, 48
Sproull, 125
Sprow, 542
Spryt, 324
Spurgeon, 428
Spurrier, 131
Squire, 4, 85
Squires, 96, 519
St Ann's Church, 413
St Anna's Hall, 328
St Clair, 6, 154, 310
St Marie, 72, 281, 317
St Matthew's Burying Ground, 269
St Matthew's Church, 400
St Paul's Episcopal Church, 476
St Peter's Burial grounds, 269
St Stanislaus Female Acadmy, 274
Staats Zeitung, 531
Stabler, 262, 397
Stables, 34
Stace, 32
Stacey, 419
Stack, 118, 286
Stacom, 291
Staffer, 13
Stake, 69, 166, 335
Stallings, 62
Stamps, 280
Stanbery, 134, 442, 501, 504, 509, 511
Stanborough, 92
Standeford, 118
Standford, 80
Stanford, 187, 395
Stanley, 264
Stanloup, 334
Stanmore School, 339
Stannard, 2, 92
Stant, 170
Stanton, 40, 67, 83, 136, 219, 247, 282, 345, 350, 369, 422, 452, 479, 502, 523
Stapleton, 148
Stark, 135, 199

Starks, 536
Starr, 11, 18, 20, 48, 81, 167
Starrow, 144
Stas, 495
Staub, 210
Stealley, 34
steamboat **Morning Light**, 143
steamboat **P E Belt**, 299
steamer **Arizona**, 204, 494
steamer **Bienville**, 540
steamer **Bremen**, 26
steamer **Calahaula**, 88
steamer **City of Baltimore**, 456
steamer **City of New York.**, 287
steamer **De Soto**, 468, 509
steamer **Dean Richmond**, 445
steamer **Deutschland**, 392
steamer **E C Knight**, 33
steamer **Elm City**, 208
steamer **Fancy Brandies**, 88
steamer **Florida**, 234
steamer **George Cromwell**, 378
steamer **George D Palmer**, 119
steamer **Guard**, 209
steamer **Hammonia**, 351
steamer **Hi Livingston**, 275, 339
steamer **Joan**, 412
steamer **Lansing**, 208
steamer **Laurel Hill**, 280
steamer **Mahasset**, 385
steamer **Matanzas**, 487
steamer **Mercury**, 117, 119
steamer **Mississippi**, 301
steamer **Monongahela**, 509, 522
steamer **Niagara**, 207
steamer **Nova Scotia**, 303
steamer **Otsego**, 234
steamer **Pembina**, 234
steamer **Penobscot**, 127, 424
steamer **Pereire**, 209, 258
steamer **Peruvian**, 278
steamer **Platte Valley**, 29
steamer **Princeton**, 186
steamer **Reliance**, 383
steamer **Sacramento**, 22
steamer **Santiago de Cuba**, 220

steamer **Santurn**, 544
steamer **Simta**, 234
steamer **St Laureate**, 72
steamer **Success**, 501
steamer **Susquehanna**, 234
steamer **Suwanee**, 400
steamer **Swatara**, 55, 74, 76
steamer **T L McGill**, 17
steamer **Thomas Collyer**, 319
steamer **Thompson**, 291
steamer **Tigress**, 87
steamer **Vanderbilt**, 445
steamer **Ville De Paris**, 362
steamer **W F Curtis**, 276
steamer **Wateree**, 204
steamer **Winooski**, 269
steamer **Wisconsin**, 220
steamship **Andalusia**, 103
steamship **Arizona**, 245
steamship **Australian**, 125
steamship **City of Bath**, 73
steamship **Persia**, 453
steamship **Saco**, 524
steamship **Ville de Paris**, 530
Stearns, 164, 477, 499
Stebbins, 102, 134
Steedman, 59, 140
Steel, 462
Steele, 4, 192, 468, 488
Steen, 371
Steers, 109, 469
Steidham, 461
Steile, 309
Steinberg, 2
Steinberger, 52
Steiner, 42
Steinway, 273
Steinway Pianos, 90
Stell, 336
Stemble, 45
Stephen, 6, 543
Stephens, 29, 82, 309, 363, 404, 405, 406, 530
Stephenson, 41, 51, 211, 346, 369, 421
Steritzing, 416

Stern, 179
Steuart, 21, 23, 460, 524
Stevens, 5, 8, 34, 98, 110, 116, 120, 132, 153, 214, 264, 319, 385, 461, 492, 529
Stevenson, 2, 53, 89, 102, 143, 381
Steward, 161
Stewart, 3, 5, 20, 35, 40, 89, 97, 104, 112, 115, 158, 172, 189, 219, 223, 240, 257, 275, 283, 298, 312, 317, 334, 346, 349, 389, 412, 417, 480, 487, 502, 521, 524, 525, 537
Sthreshly, 360
Stick, 325
Stickney, 219, 259, 431, 527
Stidham, 461
Stier, 38
Stiles, 144, 302
Stillwell, 378
Stilson, 22, 139
Stilwell, 26
Stimson, 135
Stinchcomb, 158
Stinemetz, 116, 135, 150, 152, 164, 165, 251, 271
Stinson, 4, 89
Stinzing, 220
Stitz, 338
Stockbridge, 77, 87, 153, 451
Stocke, 93
Stockett, 383
Stockler, 537
Stockton, 449
Stoddert, 348
Stokes, 151, 209, 403, 512
Stomberger, 309, 464
Stone, 53, 60, 63, 79, 102, 110, 134, 135, 138, 158, 164, 199, 203, 207, 219, 222, 225, 230, 256, 264, 269, 274, 287, 434, 437, 451, 458, 479, 490, 494, 523
Stoneburner, 182
Stonestreet, 180, 281, 390, 496, 498
Stonewall, 265
Stoops, 287
Storch, 240

Story, 375, 494
Stoske, 83
Stott, 417, 423, 479
Stottenmeyer, 12
Stoughton, 214, 251, 255
Stoutenburgh, 319
Stover, 1, 116
Stowe, 154, 372
Stowell, 26
Stowers, 82
Strand, 14
Stratton, 16
Straus, 235
Strauss, 10
Strawn, 246, 457
Strayer, 313
Streeks, 39, 77
Street, 123
Streeter, 92
Streets, 77
Striblen, 3
Stringfellow, 3, 20, 21, 45
Strobell, 266
Strogger, 105
Strom, 472
Stromberger, 481
Strong, 22, 52, 83, 110, 122, 142, 248, 265, 330, 524, 525
Strother, 430, 480
Strouse, 54
Strubblefield, 5
Stuart, 24, 265, 299, 357, 380, 455, 483, 502
Stubbs, 155, 236, 430
Studley, 396
Stump, 286
Sturdy, 4, 89, 182, 259
Sturgess, 382
Sturmsfels, 149
Sturtevant, 467
Sudbrook, 99
suffrage, 40
Suit, 351
Suiter, 191
Suitsville, 351

Sullivan, 4, 16, 44, 89, 98, 118, 120, 127, 135, 138, 163, 191, 201, 219, 259, 334, 379, 399, 402, 450, 476, 496, 499, 510
Sully, 357
Sumers, 158
Summers, 3, 61, 223
Summerville, 484, 493
Summy, 180, 255, 265, 270
Sumner, 359, 395, 457, 465
Sunderland, 105, 237, 253, 255, 390
Surbury, 31
Surgens, 302
Surratt, 36, 55, 72, 74, 75, 78, 81, 105, 126, 179, 224, 227, 244, 249, 250, 254, 256, 257, 258, 260, 262, 263, 267, 268, 270, 272, 273, 274, 276, 278, 281, 283, 285, 287, 290, 292, 295, 297, 298, 300, 301, 303, 306, 307, 309, 311, 313, 314, 317, 319, 320, 323, 333, 336, 339, 407, 424, 464, 489
Suter, 534
Sutherland, 83, 107, 115
Sutton, 119, 309, 377, 445, 500, 501
Swahan, 331
Swain, 79, 214, 514, 537, 545
Swallow, 273
Swan, 442
Swann, 5, 30, 42, 219, 288, 510
Swart, 79, 430
Swartz, 49, 134
Swartzwalder, 182
Swartzwelder, 356
Swayne, 545, 546
Sweeney, 6, 10, 294
Sweeny, 23, 140, 161, 253, 327, 496
Sweet, 46, 53, 100, 414, 516
Sweetzer, 383
Sweitzer, 33
Swetland, 347
Swett, 46
Swift, 28, 116, 118, 151, 385
Swindle, 36
Swisher, 181, 397
Switz, 123

Switzer, 499
Sydecker, 127
Syford, 369
Sylvester, 449
Syme, 143
Synder, 76
Syphax, 350
Szabo, 181

T

Tackett, 92
Taggart, 196, 498
Tait, 100, 256, 527
Talbert, 93, 304, 537
Talberts, 145
Talbot, 73, 176, 286, 374
Talburtt, 21, 286
Talcott, 392
Taliaferro, 87, 455
Talks, 537
Tally, 145
Talmadge, 311
Talty, 214, 487, 488, 496
Tamar's Outlet, 180
Tanner, 41
Tardy, 127, 457
Tarleston Hall, 321
Tarleton, 39
Tarr, 120
Tasker, 97, 346
Tassara, 108
Tassin, 472, 540
Tate, 47, 132, 318
Tatem, 138
Tattoo, 211
Tausig, 259
Tayloe, 25, 180, 214, 215, 504
Taylor, 5, 6, 9, 10, 30, 36, 40, 54, 56, 58, 73, 76, 92, 93, 94, 95, 106, 109, 120, 130, 138, 142, 151, 158, 165, 167, 171, 188, 197, 208, 219, 243, 249, 292, 296, 304, 308, 324, 333, 346, 347, 353, 379, 382, 392, 393, 399, 405, 420, 424, 427, 431, 435, 450, 454, 475, 484, 485, 518, 520, 528, 530, 534

Tazelwell, 320
Teackle, 486
Teel, 29, 532
Teemyer, 368
Tegethoff, 44
telegraph line, 181
Tell, 480
Teller, 525
Temocley, 211
Tempest, 75
Temple, 16
Tenley, 480
Tenney, 187, 208, 232, 249, 251
Tennyson, 337, 399
Terrall, 97
Terrell, 83
Terret, 480
Terrett, 7, 21, 158, 241
Terrick, 365
Terry, 265, 402, 515, 520
Tetter, 92
Teufel, 110
Thacher, 346
Tharp, 277, 378
Thatcher, 41, 302
Thayer, 346
The Way of the Cross, 132
Theaker, 3, 45, 235, 239, 243, 245, 289, 298, 310, 313, 317, 320, 323, 346, 519, 541
Thecker, 232
Theeman, 134
Theikuhl, 158
Thieman, 66, 138
Thierry, 291
Thift, 534
Thistle, 35
Thoma, 152, 310, 362, 375, 486
Thomas, 1, 50, 97, 112, 119, 122, 138, 151, 165, 175, 204, 205, 207, 221, 241, 243, 251, 254, 264, 265, 276, 329, 338, 363, 462, 475, 493, 508, 510, 516, 520, 525, 531, 541
Thompkins, 397
Thompson, 3, 6, 15, 22, 31, 34, 45, 58, 71, 81, 85, 101, 110, 114, 119, 130, 134, 136, 155, 158, 181, 191, 213, 219, 236, 238, 239, 241, 260, 277, 283, 300, 310, 311, 336, 337, 343, 346, 359, 360, 371, 382, 383, 384, 402, 404, 405, 410, 417, 430, 434, 468, 474, 475, 488, 496, 500, 503, 510, 512, 515, 517, 518, 519, 520, 524, 525, 527, 528, 532, 534
Thorn, 40, 191, 219, 221, 370, 486, 507, 522
Thornbohn, 77
Thornburgh, 35
Thornbury, 92, 120
Thornton, 9, 19, 52, 122, 142, 200, 263, 541
Thoroughfare Mills, 468
Thrall, 194
Three iron-clads, 505
Threlkeld's addition, 228
Thruston, 518
Thumb, 400, 472
Thumbert, 490
Thumlert, 431, 455, 458, 468
Thurmond, 151
Thweatt, 151
Thyson, 219, 239, 251
Tibbetts, 295
Tiber creek, 429
Tidball, 107, 144
Tidings, 46
Tilden, 85
Tileston, 53
Tilghman, 150, 158, 264
Tilley, 259, 472
Tillinghast, 372, 389
Tillotson, 199
Tilston, 219, 270, 316, 317, 318, 325, 331
Tiltson, 324
Timberlake, 418
Timon, 168, 326, 394
Tingle, 246, 457
Tinker, 319
Tinsley, 303
Tintorettos, 393
Tippett, 315

Tisdale, 490
Tisdell, 110
Titcomb, 280
Titian, 393
Titsworth, 91
Titus, 315, 483
to *Oak Hill Cemetery*, 286
Tobriner, 238
Toby, 73
Todd, 4, 7, 69, 126, 128, 129, 158, 215, 231, 237, 240, 246, 249, 250, 255, 284, 292, 327, 339, 379, 384, 457, 484, 527
Todd's subdivision, 293
Toffey, 263
Toledana, 3
Toliver, 1
Tolson, 299
Tomlinson, 180, 393
Tommy, 127
Tompkins, 77, 83, 246, 318, 333, 457, 458
Toner, 206, 211, 225, 285
Toney, 309, 397
Tongman, 539
Tongue, 89
Tooma, 486
Toombs, 313, 404
Toomey, 416, 472
Toomy, 465
Tooney, 427
Topham, 219, 251, 252, 530
Tophan, 251
Toppin, 302
Torbert, 315
Torney, 287
Torrans, 311
Torrey, 120
Totten, 3, 302, 312
Tottin, 91
Tourtelotte, 96
Tower, 104, 264
Towers, 136, 142, 176, 241, 244, 255, 326, 450, 471, 538
Towles, 219, 433, 447
Town, 107, 516

Towner, 525
Townsend, 104, 169, 212, 265, 476, 502, 545
Townshend, 31, 299
Tozcer, 312
Tracey, 86, 409
Tracy, 5, 123, 208
Train, 414, 479
Travers, 214, 238
Travis, 112
Treadwell, 9
Tree, 45, 85
Tremain, 61
Trenholm, 165, 404, 405, 406
Trent, 151
Trepler, 14
Tretler, 275
Trevelyan, 30
Tribble, 360
Tridy, 9, 12
Trimble, 3, 15, 54, 246, 451
Trinity Church Cemetery, 181
Tripler, 107, 355
Triplett, 306
Tripp, 311
Troll, 165
Tromble, 457
Trook, 58
Trott, 85, 166, 190
Trotter, 144
Trowbridge, 479
Trull, 118
Truman, 92
Trumbull, 286
Trumpbour, 138
Trunnel, 369, 450, 493
Trunnell, 133, 268, 369
Trussell, 59
Truxell, 490, 502, 510
Tryon, 13
Trzeciak, 121
Tuck, 4, 15
Tucker, 3, 4, 5, 13, 33, 36, 53, 89, 92, 94, 143, 183, 191, 234, 240, 309, 391, 404, 464, 473, 481
Tudor, 68, 504

Tudor Place, 173
Tufts, 134
tugboat **Fisher**, 331
Tuller, 140
Tulley, 79
Tunnell, 3
Tuohy, 286
Turly, 21
Turnbull, 102
Turnburke, 183, 400
Turner, 14, 25, 30, 45, 98, 111, 143, 234, 286, 372, 381, 415, 424, 442, 444, 451, 501, 544
Turpin, 101, 105, 151
Turton, 131, 144, 364, 527
Tuscarora Academy, 332
Tuscora Female Seminary, 408
Tustin, 80, 527
Tuttle, 34, 80, 186, 311, 432, 459
Tweedy, 269
Twinning, 155
Twyman, 512
Tyler, 19, 60, 66, 83, 94, 95, 104, 155, 186, 211, 260, 292, 296, 335, 387, 430, 508
Tyson, 336

U

U S Patent Ofc, 3, 15, 17, 39, 40, 45, 68, 80, 82, 98, 104, 106, 110, 119, 131, 136, 141, 145, 146, 150, 154, 167, 169, 172, 174, 177, 178, 179, 187, 203, 208, 216, 221, 228, 235, 239, 243, 245, 289, 298, 310, 313, 320, 323, 337, 345, 348, 349, 353, 367, 370, 373, 377, 384, 388, 389, 394, 402, 414, 426, 427, 428, 432, 452, 466, 470, 474, 481, 492, 494, 501, 507, 516, 519, 523, 530, 536, 538
Uber, 302
Ubhoff, 183
Uhl, 34
Uhlman, 293, 299
Ulle, 76
Ulrich, 119, 470
Ulrick, 378
Underhill, 13, 222
Underwood, 35, 147, 269, 336, 475
United States cemetery, 132
Updike, 26
Upfold, 245
Upperman, 79, 280, 460
Urah, 20
Urann, 122
Urban, 421
Urell, 396
Urguhart, 53, 143
Usrey, 5
Utermehle, 10, 19, 23, 28, 42, 58, 111, 139, 219, 460
Utz, 375

V

Vail, 175
Valentine, 140
Valley Forge, 321
Van Anterp, 149
Van Arden, 101
Van Arnum, 85
Van Bogan, 408
Van Buren, 438
Van Camp, 363, 534
Van Cleaf, 118
Van Demark, 198
Van Demosk, 93
Van Dieman's Land, 291
Van Dyke, 477
Van Hazen, 173
Van Henri, 496
Van Horn, 14, 100
Van Hovenburg, 60
Van Lear, 169
Van Lise, 389
Van Ness, 22, 60, 61, 91, 148, 206, 438, 441, 442, 447
Van Patten, 158, 399
Van Rensselaer, 90
Van Riswick, 219, 249, 254, 284, 326, 453, 511
Van Vliet, 83
Van Vranken, 113

Van Wert, 198, 302, 497
Van Wickle, 53, 89, 143
Van Wyck, 90, 158
Van Zandt, 278
Vanbibber, 158
Vance, 151, 153, 209, 405
Vandenhoff, 391
Vanderalice, 62
Vanderbilt, 62, 392, 463
Vanderhyden, 48
Vanderpoel, 29, 264
Vanderwerken, 480
Vandeventer, 9
Vans, 484
Vansant, 11, 107, 148
Varnell, 459
Varnum, 483
Varrals, 13
Vasquez, 275
Vaughan, 410
Vaughn, 92
Veazie, 81, 118
Vedder, 83
Veech, 261
Veirs, 401
Velpeau, 363, 436
Venable, 40
Venniegerholz, 5
Verdi, 267
Verdier, 120
Verill, 37
Vermeren, 371
Vermilye, 61
Verner, 291
Vernes, 181
Vernon, 79, 102, 165
Verplanck, 219
Verrill, 37
Vervalin, 171
Very, 9, 30
vessel **Magiecienne**, 8
Vessey, 470
Veter, 291
Vickens, 95
Vickers, 497
Viehmeyer, 305

Vigle, 544
Vincent, 94, 99
Vinson, 3, 53, 182, 188
Vinton, 83
Vivans, 482, 512
Voelekers, 19
Voigt, 240
Volany, 1
Volkman, 36
Vollard, 493
Von _asen, 191
Von Arsdale, 469
Von Dreyse, 521
Von Essen, 244, 449, 516, 536
Von Havre, 496, 498
Von Kamecke, 54
Von Schneidan, 289
Voss, 199, 296, 381, 382, 427
Vought, 328, 502
Voulliere, 489
vulcanized rubber, 97

W

Waddell, 312
Waddey, 286
Wade, 52
Wadsworth, 140, 177, 220
Waelper, 495
Waggenstein, 181
Wagner, 76, 83, 88, 480
Wagoner, 87, 399
Waifel, 246
Wail, 424
Wailes, 134, 149, 170
Wainwright, 68, 83, 107, 259
Wait, 330
Waite, 9, 30, 81
Wakefield, 35, 214
Walbridge, 328, 347
Walcott, 5, 462
Waldo, 317
Waldron, 400
Wales, 63, 102
Walker, 4, 5, 21, 22, 25, 27, 57, 67,
   77, 80, 82, 83, 93, 114, 121, 125,
   135, 138, 152, 169, 182, 189, 232,

247, 252, 253, 281, 282, 302, 305, 309, 312, 337, 338, 354, 358, 394, 403, 404, 485, 493, 508, 510, 517, 520, 524, 525, 530
Wall, 25, 56, 85, 188, 219, 220, 327, 363, 397, 430, 458, 467, 504, 527, 532
Wallace, 83, 121, 127, 216, 235, 344, 398, 407, 423, 465, 475, 540, 546
Wallach, 90, 148, 173, 178, 220, 227, 247, 259, 301, 364, 369, 451, 469, 473, 479, 510, 527, 532
Wallack, 185, 412, 422
Waller, 43
Walling, 355
Wallingsford, 82, 462, 487
Wallis, 533
Wallsmith, 26
Walpole, 133
Walsh, 1, 28, 86, 139, 145, 183, 281, 282, 287, 309, 393, 401, 424, 430, 480, 504, 523, 524, 544
Waltars, 302
Waltenmeyer, 459
Walter, 19, 32, 39, 110, 266, 282, 288, 307, 322, 412, 508, 517, 522
Walters, 77, 282, 285, 286, 397
Walton, 15, 181, 259, 343, 367, 511
Waltz, 455
Walworth, 503
Wambold, 236
Wannall, 433
War Dept Claims Commission, 3, 87, 142, 181, 234, 280, 329, 373
Ward, 6, 15, 36, 56, 62, 66, 68, 84, 86, 100, 112, 116, 123, 132, 154, 180, 184, 219, 220, 233, 240, 264, 285, 292, 296, 384, 386, 448, 480, 491, 515
Wardwell, 89
Ware, 455
Warfield, 319, 457
Waring, 67, 305, 307, 409, 449, 456, 536
Waring's Grove, 305
Warmbold, 257

Warner, 16, 41, 53, 81, 95, 97, 121, 415, 483
Warren, 41, 87, 130, 144, 264, 265, 356, 387, 472, 535
Warrington, 242
Warton, 97
Warwick, 17, 204
Wash Schutzen Corps, 240
Washburne, 137, 279, 469, 519
Washington, 59, 68, 76, 80, 95, 117, 127, 145, 147, 176, 224, 228, 268, 274, 275, 284, 286, 290, 321, 340, 351, 363, 365, 385, 390, 435, 438, 475, 478, 515
Washington College, 466
Washington High School, 375
Washington Seminary, 283
Washington Zouaves, 294
Wass, 140
Wassign, 208
Wassmer, 286
Waterman, 345
Waters, 69, 85, 147, 220, 255, 330, 397, 430, 520, 534
Waterson, 214
Watkins, 220, 430
Watner, 165
Watson, 23, 60, 67, 103, 158, 167, 183, 185, 286, 295, 322, 349, 462
Watt, 191, 216, 377
Watterson, 3
Wattles, 148
Watts, 4, 39, 404, 405, 455, 469
Waugh, 496
Waull, 81
Waverly, 174, 317, 320, 463
Way, 308
Wayland, 58
Wayne, 65, 286, 312
Wead, 112
Weale, 151
Weare, 100
Weart, 123
Weast, 286
Weatherman, 515
Weaver, 108, 171, 281, 307

619

Webb, 17, 37, 86, 92, 93, 112, 115, 120, 214, 238, 246, 318, 496, 498, 530
Weber, 59, 455, 480, 496, 510
Webster, 4, 18, 79, 89, 105, 163, 253, 255, 259, 446, 527
Weckerling, 151
Weeks, 201
Weichman, 72, 273, 274, 276, 278, 297, 298, 300, 303, 306, 309, 314, 317
Weichmann, 273, 424
Weigan, 377
Weigart, 181
Weightman, 275
Weill, 325
Weisbrod, 102
Weiser, 176
Weitzel, 108, 264, 265
Welch, 107, 111, 204, 219, 397, 435
Welcker, 31
Weldman, 134
Weller, 87, 223, 497
Welles, 1, 5, 12, 48, 278, 425, 450, 519, 523
Welleseley, 41
Welling, 380
Wellman, 353
Wells, 5, 18, 92, 118, 140, 167, 170, 193, 240, 247, 248, 314, 330, 440
Welsh, 14, 156, 160, 208, 302
Welsman, 165
Welthan, 58
Wemershkirch, 281
Wendell, 249, 518
Wentworth, 72, 467
Wentz, 190, 205
Werden, 325
Wesley, 533
Wesman, 45
Wesson, 538
West, 1, 63, 67, 97, 103, 123, 141, 220, 228, 259, 323, 350, 365, 385, 427, 510, 531, 533, 538
Westcott, 270

Western Holmead's Burial Grounds, 268
Westfall, 138, 314
Westmoreland, 288
Weston, 100, 533
Westwood, 303
Wetherall, 413
Wetmore, 4, 223, 319, 524
Wetzal, 316
Wetzel, 331, 343, 464, 510
Whalen, 58
Wharton, 115, 121, 158, 446, 455
Wheatland, 356
Wheatley, 69, 185, 219, 329, 450
Wheaton, 23, 390, 396, 415, 418, 437
Wheeler, 2, 4, 15, 62, 74, 84, 108, 121, 127, 219, 220, 223, 246, 306, 317, 325, 382, 457, 464, 497, 499, 520, 532, 534
Wheelock, 248
Whelan, 238, 274
Whipple, 264, 309, 486
Whitaker, 320
Whitall, 14, 19
White, 4, 28, 40, 67, 86, 89, 95, 98, 158, 167, 175, 188, 208, 211, 220, 255, 280, 286, 287, 324, 335, 349, 359, 365, 371, 379, 400, 427, 446, 450, 465, 471, 472, 482, 493, 496, 527, 530, 542
Whitebill, 11
Whitehead, 362
Whiteley, 139
Whitely, 69
Whitemore, 126
Whiting, 49, 224, 275, 376, 380
Whitley, 77
Whitman, 134, 256
Whitmarsh, 9
Whitmore, 158
Whitney, 135, 171, 246, 457, 525
Whittaker, 511
Whittemore, 62
Whitten, 116, 329, 466
Whittingham, 303
Whittlesey, 64, 75, 92, 115, 388

620

Whitty, 290
Wiber, 117, 376
Wicke, 533
Wickersham, 3
Wicomico Fields, 207
Widmeyer, 490
Wield, 521
Wiele, 144
Wiget, 241, 247, 381, 408
Wigfall, 91, 520
Wiggin, 73, 163
Wiggins, 108, 182, 323
Wight, 492
Wightman, 473
Wightt, 440
Wignell, 387
Wigton, 407
Wilburn, 196
Wilcox, 57, 265
Wilder, 168, 209, 246
Wildes, 62
Wildo, 17
Wiles, 151
Wiley, 65, 116, 123, 126, 545
Wilford, 25
Wilhelm, 414
Wilkerson, 309
Wilkes, 55, 58, 64, 280
Wilkeson, 85
Wilkins, 459
Wilkins,, 158, 182, 360, 463, 472
Wilkinson, 108, 112, 147, 174, 214, 234, 346
Will, 105
Willard, 134, 139, 214, 220, 375, 496
Willden, 397
Willet, 29, 40, 300
Willett, 127, 239, 260, 461, 489
William, 534
Williams, 5, 7, 12, 16, 18, 20, 24, 39, 47, 54, 55, 60, 61, 67, 80, 88, 95, 97, 99, 102, 108, 115, 118, 119, 123, 128, 132, 133, 135, 139, 158, 163, 173, 174, 185, 200, 201, 208, 220, 223, 234, 237, 238, 241, 244, 247, 251, 255, 256, 259, 266, 281, 285, 286, 289, 292, 295, 296, 297, 302, 309, 310, 312, 319, 326, 336, 358, 382, 389, 391, 397, 411, 415, 417, 419, 420, 422, 431, 432, 440, 443, 457, 458, 464, 466, 475, 479, 481, 484, 502, 532, 539, 541, 542, 544
Williamson, 88, 190, 375, 415, 418
Willis, 31, 32, 312
Willner, 171, 172, 534
Wills, 18
Willson, 220, 465
Willstorff, 260
Wilmer, 366
Wilna, 451
Wilner, 90
Wilson, 3, 4, 7, 9, 14, 17, 19, 21, 25, 44, 60, 77, 79, 89, 92, 94, 97, 102, 108, 118, 121, 133, 137, 153, 158, 183, 186, 189, 219, 227, 228, 233, 236, 238, 241, 246, 252, 255, 256, 264, 265, 269, 285, 286, 287, 294, 302, 344, 361, 381, 393, 412, 416, 430, 432, 457, 458, 462, 469, 480, 498, 499, 510, 520, 524, 527, 530, 534, 538
Wiltberger, 158, 213
Wimpenny, 379
Wimsatt, 398
Winda_, 60
Winder, 408
Windsor & Ford's subdivision, 193
Winebenner, 448
Winebrener, 66
Winehouse, 277
Winfield, 129, 246
Wing, 62, 412, 418
Wingard, 83
Wingate, 62, 122
Winn, 29, 31
Winnemore, 176, 194, 368
Winter, 532
Wippermann, 416
Wirle, 110
Wirt, 520
Wirz, 424
Wisdom, 384

Wise, 95, 214, 219, 259, 295, 302, 305, 400, 403, 405, 462, 486
Wiseman, 105
Wismer, 74
Wistar, 146
Wiswall, 188
Withenberry, 182
Withenburg, 143
Witherow, 220
Withers, 158, 484
Withrop, 16
Wittemore, 455
Wittenaur, 281
Witter, 118
Wm III, 373
Wohls, 525
Wolf, 36, 129, 135, 200, 400, 465, 488
Wolfe, 85, 530
Wolff, 303
Wolfley, 418, 420
Wolfrey, 431
Wollard, 334
Wolverton, 514
woman suffrage, 40
Women's Rights, 369
Wood, 4, 15, 62, 69, 71, 92, 93, 102, 119, 136, 141, 142, 151, 158, 159, 163, 169, 173, 190, 199, 226, 248, 259, 283, 300, 319, 346, 364, 369, 378, 405, 412, 415, 424, 503, 511, 524, 525, 531
Woodard, 505
Woodbridge, 52, 89
Woodburn, 121
Woodbury, 98, 134, 264, 457
Woodford, 359
Woodhull, 46, 77, 238
Woodland, 93
Woodland Cemetery, 491
Woodly, 189
Woodman, 309
Woodruff, 95, 114, 246, 457, 516
Woods, 95, 121, 220, 280, 312
Woodsides, 269
Woodson, 198

Woodward, 2, 3, 8, 13, 22, 79, 119, 164, 166, 212, 220, 481, 490
Woodyard Mill, 514
Wool, 396
Wooldroff, 277
Woolfold, 64
Woolley, 14, 19
Wools, 350
Woolson, 367
Woolverton, 144
Wooster, 31, 40
Works, 261, 310
Wortham, 109
Worthen, 130
Worthington, 219, 477
Wortley, 529
Wotz, 467
Wren, 365, 386
Wrerman, 391
Wright, 23, 44, 79, 80, 83, 85, 104, 112, 135, 136, 178, 204, 205, 210, 220, 256, 264, 271, 279, 351, 379, 428, 442, 513, 517
Wroe, 40, 322, 535
Wroth, 466
Wunder, 158, 497
Wurdeman, 220
Wurdemann, 77
Wyatt, 475
Wyckoff, 316, 317, 318, 325, 437
Wycoff, 324
Wydenbruck, 372
Wylie, 16, 18, 22, 43, 69, 127, 133, 139, 251, 254, 272, 379, 420, 427, 430, 459, 491
Wylly, 316, 318
Wynd, 354
Wyvill, 59, 219, 298
Wyville, 532

Y

yacht **Fleetwing**, 69
yacht **Henrietta**, 19
yacht **John T Ford**, 378
Yancey, 404
Yard, 385

Yarrington, 120
Yates, 153, 187, 188, 363, 390, 419
Yeabower, 158, 232, 233, 502
Yeakel, 143
Yeakle, 87
Yeatman, 108, 169, 427, 542
Yeaton, 123
Yeats, 187
Yell, 394
Yerby, 151
Yingling, 260
York, 370
Yost, 134
Young, 4, 5, 15, 48, 63, 93, 103, 117, 120, 135, 144, 147, 158, 190, 215, 220, 251, 275, 290, 304, 337, 346, 354, 386, 388, 390, 400, 434, 466, 470, 471, 481, 491, 508, 512, 517, 534
Yulee, 403, 406, 424

Z

Zahn, 129
Zailner, 265
Zane, 174, 473
Zeigler, 102
Zell, 231, 424
Zellar, 53
Zengen, 62
Zenzon, 302
Zephaniah Jones subdivision, 193
Zeringue, 143
Zeverly, 238
Ziegler, 4, 67
Zimerman, 497, 534
Zimmer, 394, 407
Zimmerman, 301, 363, 470, 512, 534
Zollar, 3, 350
Zulime, 417
Zumbush, 368
Zumstein, 143
Zwinglus, 277

Other Heritage Books by Joan M. Dixon:

National Intelligencer *Newspaper Abstracts
Special Edition: The Civil War Years
Volume 1: January 1, 1861–June 30, 1863*

National Intelligencer *Newspaper Abstracts
Special Edition: The Civil War Years
Volume 2: July 1, 1863–December 31, 1865*

National Intelligencer *Newspaper Abstracts
Jan. 1, 1869–Jan. 8, 1870*

National Intelligencer *Newspaper Abstracts
Volume 1866–Volume 1868*

National Intelligencer *Newspaper Abstracts
Volume 1840–Volume 1860*

National Intelligencer *Newspaper Abstracts, 1838–1839*

National Intelligencer *Newspaper Abstracts, 1836–1837*

National Intelligencer *Newspaper Abstracts, 1834–1835*

National Intelligencer *Newspaper Abstracts, 1832–1833*

National Intelligencer *Newspaper Abstracts, 1830–1831*

National Intelligencer *Newspaper Abstracts, 1827–1829*

National Intelligencer *Newspaper Abstracts, 1824–1826*

National Intelligencer *Newspaper Abstracts, 1821–1823*

National Intelligencer *Newspaper Abstracts, 1818–1820*

National Intelligencer *Newspaper Abstracts, 1814–1817*

National Intelligencer *Newspaper Abstracts, 1811–1813*

National Intelligencer *Newspaper Abstracts, 1806–1810*

National Intelligencer *Newspaper Abstracts, 1800–1805*

www.ingramcontent.com/pod-product-compliance
Lightning Source LLC
Chambersburg PA
CBHW071131300426
44113CB00009B/942